The Birth of American Law

Carolina Academic Press
Legal History Series
H. Jefferson Powell, Series Editor

❧

Louis D. Brandeis's MIT Lectures on Law (1892–1894)
Robert F. Cochran, Jr., editor

Law in War, War as Law
Brigadier General Joseph Holt and the Judge Advocate General's Department
in the Civil War and Early Reconstruction, 1861–1865
Joshua E. Kastenberg

Gentlemen of the Grand Jury
The Surviving Grand Jury Charges from Colonial, State,
and Lower Federal Courts Before 1801
Stanton D. Krauss, editor

A View of the Constitution of the United States of America
Second Edition
William Rawle with Foreword, Introduction,
and Notes by H. Jefferson Powell

Commentaries on the Constitution of the United States
Joseph Story with Introduction by
Ronald D. Rotunda and John E. Nowak

Our Chief Magistrate and His Powers
William Howard Taft with Foreword, Introduction,
and Notes by H. Jefferson Powell

The Fetha Nagast
The Law of the Kings
Abba Paulos Tzadua, translator, and Peter L. Strauss

The Birth of American Law
An Italian Philosopher and the American Revolution
John D. Bessler

The Birth of American Law

An Italian Philosopher and the American Revolution

John D. Bessler

ASSOCIATE PROFESSOR OF LAW
UNIVERSITY OF BALTIMORE SCHOOL OF LAW

CAROLINA ACADEMIC PRESS
Durham, North Carolina

Library of Congress Cataloging-in-Publication Data

Bessler, John D., author.
  The Birth of American law : an Italian philosopher and the American revolution /
John D. Bessler.
      pages cm. -- (Legal history series)
  Includes bibliographical references and index.
  ISBN 978-1-61163-604-8 (alk. paper)
  1. Law--United States--History. 2. Ria, Cesário da Béca. 3. Law--Philosophy. I.
Title.

  KF352.B47 2014
  349.7309'033--dc23

                        2014010877

Engraving of Cesare Beccaria courtesy of
Harvard Art Museums / Fogg Museum

Carolina Academic Press
700 Kent Street
Durham, North Carolina 27701
Telephone (919) 489-7486
Fax (919) 493-5668
www.cap-press.com

In memory of

U.S. Magistrate Judge
John M. "Jack" Mason
(1938–2002)

my former law partner
George O. Ludcke
(1952–2004)

a good friend
and a lawyer's lawyer
John P. Sheehy
(1955–2012)

and my late colleague
Prof. Barry E. Carter
(1942–2014)

Cesare Beccaria

The name of Beccaria has become familiar in Pennsylvania, his authority has become great, and his principles have spread among all classes of persons and impressed themselves deeply in the hearts of our citizens. You yourself must have noticed the influence of these precepts in other American states. The tyranny of prejudice and injustice has fallen, the voice of a philosopher has stilled the outcries of the masses, and although a bloody system may still survive in the laws of many of our states, nevertheless the beneficent spirit sown by Beccaria works secretly in behalf of the accused, moderating the rigor of the laws and tempering justice with compassion.

—William Bradford, Jr., James Madison's Princeton classmate and
Pennsylvania's Attorney General, from a 1786 letter to
Luigi Castiglioni, an Italian botanist who toured the
United States of America from 1785 to 1787

Contents

Acknowledgments   xi
Introduction   3

Chapter 1 · Cesare Beccaria: "The Celebrated Marquis"   25
   Pioneering Abolitionist   25
   The Italian Philosopher   28
   On Crimes and Punishments   36
   Pleasure vs. Pain: Deterrence and the Prevention of Crime   46
   Post-Publication Events   58
   A Postscript   71

Chapter 2 · The Runaway Bestseller: *On Crimes and Punishments*   75
   The Translation of Beccaria's Treatise   75
   The English Radical: John Wilkes   81
   The Promotion of Beccaria's Book   87
   Jeremy Bentham and the French Connection   95
   The French Philosophes and Americans in Paris   100
   The Worldly Jefferson   105
   Jefferson and Castiglioni: Tours of Italy and America   108
   Foreign and Cultural Exchanges   114
   The Beginnings of Penal Reform   120
   The Popularity of Beccaria's Treatise   124
   The Science of Legislation   132
   Beccaria's "Masterly Hand"   136
   The Dissemination of Beccaria's Ideas   142
   Reactions to Beccaria's Treatise   146

Chapter 3 · The Founding Fathers: The American Revolution   151
   George Washington   151
   Washington's Generals   156
   The Justices: James Wilson and John Jay   163
   The Attorneys General and the Poet   169
   John Adams and John Quincy Adams   173
   Thomas Jefferson: A Beccaria Admirer   182
   Jefferson's Italian Neighbor, Philip Mazzei   195
   Aaron Burr and John Witherspoon   202
   James Madison   205
   Hugh Henry Brackenridge   209
   The Pennsylvania Abolitionists: Benjamin Rush and Benjamin Franklin   211

Chapter 4 · American Penal Reform: Reshaping the Law   219
    Major European Influences: Montesquieu, Beccaria and Blackstone   219
    The Pennsylvania Experiment   226
    Reformers in Connecticut and New York   232
    A National Movement   240
    Early American Pamphlets and Printers   244
    State Constitutions and Declarations of Rights   245
    Vermont, South Carolina and New Hampshire   256
    Virginia, Kentucky and Beyond   261
    Edward Livingston and Other Abolitionists   263
    Beccaria's Role in Reform   270

Chapter 5 · Rethinking Bloody Codes: The Rise of the Penitentiary   273
    English and Early American Punishments   273
    The Club of Honest Whigs   276
    In Jefferson's America: Capital and Corporal Punishments   282
    "Sanguinary" Laws and Punishments   285
    Quakers and Puritans: Divergent Views   293
    A Call to Action   295
    Benjamin Banneker and the Scourge of Slavery   306
    Republican Architecture: Architects, Laws and Juries   311
    The Rise of the Penitentiary System   317
    Pamphlets and Prisons   321
    The Construction of Penitentiaries   325
    The Livingston Code   332
    The Promise of the Penitentiary System   340
    The Crockett-Madison Correspondence   344
    "The Spirit of the Age"   347

Chapter 6 · An Enduring Legacy: Toward a More Perfect Union   353
    The American Revolution: Tyranny to Liberty   353
    From Barbarism to Reason   360
    A New Paradigm of Proportionality   368
    Capital Punishment and Torture   375
    The Right to Bear Arms   390
    Infamy, Cruelty, Dueling and Suicide   393
    Education, Pardons, Extradition Treaties and Debtors   399
    The English Common Law   404
    The Codification of American Law   412
    Beccaria's Lasting Legacy   421

Conclusion   431
Notes   457
Bibliography   569
Index   579

Acknowledgments

This book builds upon my prior scholarship on the Italian philosopher Cesare Beccaria. I have long advocated the abolition of capital punishment, and Cesare Beccaria (1738–1794)—of a noble family from Milan, but now a little-known figure except among criminologists—was the first Enlightenment thinker to make a comprehensive case for abolishing executions. In 1764, Beccaria's slender Italian treatise, *Dei delitti e delle pene*, a product of the Italian Enlightenment and the rationalistic sentiment it inspired in Milan's coffeehouses and salons, first appeared in print. In it, Beccaria—using his native language—opposed capital punishment and torture. Beccaria's book specifically emphasized the tyrannical nature of unnecessary punishments, and argued for proportion between crimes and punishments. Written at a time of rampant state brutality and when intellectuals on both sides of the Atlantic were hungry for new ideas, the Italian treatise was translated into English three years later as *On Crimes and Punishments*. Though Beccaria lived in southern Europe in a locale once governed by Roman law and customs and then by Lombard laws, *Dei delitti e delle pene* would transform English and American law and the world writ large, with Beccaria essentially founding the field of criminology. A number of countries abolished torture in the decades after the appearance of Beccaria's book, and Anglo-American lawyers and jurists, including America's Founding Fathers, especially admired Beccaria's treatise, which was quickly translated into an array of other languages.

Many of America's founders, including Benjamin Franklin and Thomas Jefferson, took an abiding interest in the Italian Enlightenment and the products of it. Although America's senior statesman, as scholar Antonio Pace notes in *Benjamin Franklin and Italy*, "never set foot on Italian soil," Dr. Franklin—the famed American inventor—favored law reform and corresponded with Italian scientists with strong connections to Beccaria's social circle. Franklin also exchanged letters with Gaetano Filangieri (1752–1788), an Italian penal reformer whose own great work, *La Scienza della legislazione*, appeared in the 1780s. Thomas Jefferson likewise carefully studied Beccaria's writings before drafting a bill to curtail executions and better proportion crimes and punishments in Virginia, his home state. Fulfilling a long-held desire, Jefferson—the Virginia plantation owner turned diplomat—actually did travel to the Duchy of Milan and the surrounding Italian countryside in April 1787 shortly before the U.S. Constitution was framed in Philadelphia. As described in George Green Shackelford's richly detailed book, *Thomas Jefferson's Travels in Europe, 1784–1789*, Jefferson—a lover of art, music and architecture—endured rough, mountainous roads as he made his way into the region by mule and two-horse carriage, spending two days and three nights in Milan, the capital of what was then known as Lombardy. Both Franklin and Jefferson, as well as other prominent American revolutionaries such as John Adams and James Madison, carefully considered Beccaria's ideas—ideas that ultimately shaped American laws and penal codes.

Sadly, Beccaria's substantial influence on early American law and social thought has long been neglected, and today, most Americans—even most lawyers—know little if anything about Beccaria and his ideas. I was particularly struck by one conversation I had in 2012 with a successful Minneapolis lawyer I know who said he'd never even *heard* of Beccaria before. And that instance is hardly an aberration. In polling roughly a hundred of my Georgetown and University of Baltimore law students, I got much the same reaction, mostly blank stares. In fact, only one student showed any recognition at all when I brought up Beccaria's name. Even that first-year law student, I noticed, only tentatively raised his hand, perhaps worried I'd use the Socratic method and call on him to recount details of Beccaria's life he likely didn't remember anymore. While Sir William Blackstone and Jeremy Bentham are penal reformers that law students and even some undergraduates are likely to encounter in their studies, the name of Beccaria—very familiar to American revolutionaries in 1776, the year of America's birth—is now largely forgotten, relegated to the discard pile of history. That circumstance, I decided, badly needed to be remedied, hence the book you are now holding in your hands—or at least reading on your iPad, Nook, or Kindle as an e-book.

I began my research on Cesare Beccaria as a visiting professor at The George Washington University Law School in Washington, D.C. I initially published some of my findings in a 2009 article in the *Northwestern Journal of Law and Social Policy* titled "Revisiting Beccaria's Vision: The Enlightenment, America's Death Penalty, and the Abolition Movement." I later compiled additional research on Beccaria in my recent book, *Cruel and Unusual: The American Death Penalty and the Founders' Eighth Amendment*, then did further investigation of Beccaria's impact on the American Revolution in preparing for lectures I gave in Norway and Spain in 2012 and 2013. This book, *The Birth of American Law*, contains a wealth of new material on Beccaria's life and his enormous influence on early American society and its legal culture, but I am forever grateful to prior editors and fellow scholars who, in years past, provided helpful comments on my earlier work. The writings of Yale Law School professor Akhil Amar, who I've gotten to know through our mutual interests in the U.S. Constitution's Eighth Amendment and my daughter's education at Yale University, have—in my thinking about the Constitution—been enormously helpful, as has the scholarship of law professor Sandy Levinson at the University of Texas-Austin.

I am particularly thankful to my colleagues at the University of Baltimore School of Law and the Georgetown University Law Center for supporting my scholarly agenda, as well as faculty members at the University of Maryland School of Law who reviewed portions of my book manuscript. One of my colleagues, Tim Sellers, is an expert on the Enlightenment, and I have benefitted enormously from his scholarship, as well as from the comments or writings of José Anderson, James Maxeiner, and constitutional law scholars Garrett Epps, Mike Meyerson, C.J. Peters, Elizabeth Samuels and Max Stearns. Summer grants from The George Washington University Law School and the University of Baltimore School of Law made my research—and thus this book—possible, so I also want to thank the deans and faculty members, among them Ron Weich, Phil Closius, Michael Higginbotham and Fred Lawrence, who approved the grant applications. I am grateful, too, for the exemplary work of my University of Baltimore research assistants, Jordan Halle and Yosef Kuperman, as well as that of my executive assistant, Rose McMunn. The encouragement of friends like Terry Anker, Sandra Babcock, Tom Banchoff, Bruce Beddow, Michael Handberg, Rob Hendrickson, Owen Herrnstadt, Dave Jensen, Robin Maher, John Symington and Mark Taticchi also made the writing easier.

A small cadre of lawyers and scholars continue to take an abiding interest in Cesare Beccaria's work, and to them I am likewise indebted. I would especially like to thank Brian Saccenti, Michel Porret, Elisabeth Salvi and Pascal Bastien. Brian Saccenti, a Maryland public defender, brought to my attention one of Maryland's founders, Charles Carroll of Carrollton, who—like so many American founders—displayed considerable admiration for Beccaria's treatise. Brian, who teaches an Appellate Advocacy Clinic at the University of Maryland and who works in Baltimore in the Appellate Division of the Office of the Public Defender, also provided me with details surrounding the adoption and history of the "sanguinary Laws" clause of Maryland's Declaration of Rights of 1776. Pascal Bastien, a history professor at the Université du Québec, Montréal, invited me to speak at a major, world-class conference in Geneva, Switzerland, on Beccaria and his legacy. That invitation prompted me to redouble my efforts to trace Beccaria's influence on American law, which led to the drafting of a new book manuscript as I prepared for that conference. After the symposium, Pascal also graciously agreed to translate my findings into French. Professors Michel Porret and Elisabeth Salvi, of the Université de Genève, are the much-respected Beccaria scholars who organized that 2013 conference, which focused on Beccaria's global reception and heritage. Michel and Elisabeth have long studied Beccaria's influence in Europe and have become experts in what one source describes as "Beccaria studies." It is my hope that this book will be a welcome addition to that scholarship.

I have others to thank as well. At the international conference in Geneva, Donald Fyson—an historian at the Université Laval Québec who has studied Beccaria's reception north of the U.S.-Canadian border, in Québec—ably served as a translator for me, allowing me to gather much-needed additional information on Beccaria from the Francophone presenters. Emmanuelle de Champs—an expert on Beccaria and Jeremy Bentham at the Université Paris—was also tremendously helpful and good-natured about my lack of French, as were the many other multi-lingual conference participants and attendees, among them Vincent Sizaire, a French magistrate affiliated with the Université Paris-Ouest; Lilith Malagoli, an Italian law student; Dario Ippolito of the Università Roma; Serena Luzzi of the Università degli studi di Trento; Elio Tavilla, a professor of the history of medieval and modern law at the Università di Modena e Reggio Emilia; and Laure Zhang, another Université de Genève academic who has studied Beccaria's influence in China. I was especially grateful to find an entire display at the Université de Genève's library devoted to Beccaria's legacy, replete with well-labeled reproductions of various editions and translations of *On Crimes and Punishments*. The oral explanations of the exhibit provided by our two principal hosts, Michel Porret and Elisabeth Salvi, gave me a much better understanding of aspects of Beccaria's life and legacy and also opened up new avenues of inquiry for me. For the hospitality I received in February 2013 at the Université de Genève, including from its professors, students, and dedicated library staff, I am extremely grateful. *Merci beaucoup!*

In addition, I would like to extend my gratitude to Dr. Lill Scherdin and Per Ystehede at the University of Oslo, as well as a host of U.S. librarians and other individuals and scholars who assisted me in tracking down relevant information. On one of my first forays into a rare book room, Elizabeth Frengel, a research librarian at Yale's world-renowned Beinecke Rare Book & Manuscript Library, skillfully assisted me as I retrieved a 1770 copy of *On Crimes and Punishments*—a copy likely owned at one time by John Trumbull, the American painter who palled around in Paris with Thomas Jefferson, or his cousin, another John Trumbull, who studied law with John Adams. Michael Lotstein—an archivist at Yale University Library—also graciously answered one of my many follow-up queries regarding Beccaria's writings. The library staff at the Georgetown University Law Center was equally helpful in directing me to important rare books. Erin Kidwell, the Curator of Legal History for Georgetown's extensive collection of rare books, as well as her colleague Hannah Miller, were particularly gracious. My sincere appreciation also goes to Scott Pagel, the Associate Dean for Information Services at The George Washington University Law School, who provided capable assistance at that school's rare book room.

I would also like to single out and thank the following academics, archivists, librarians, curators and others for providing helpful responses to my questions: Jim Acker, Barbara Austen, Betsy Boyle, Jodi Boyle, Doug Brown, Jane Calvert, Steve Charnovitz, Margaret Chisholm, Joanne Colvin, Constance Cooper, Bill Copeley, Bill Creech, Jane Cupit, Dick Dieter, Jim Gerencser, Roy Goodman, Sarah Hartwell, James Heller, Rachel Jirka, Tracey Kry, Valerie-Ann Lutz, Patty Lynn, Linda Oppenheim, Alison Paul, Mary Person, John Pollack, Frances Pollard, Bob Pool, Kimberly Reynolds, Ed Richi, Susan Riggs, Bijal Shah, Nancy Shawcross, Lee Shepard, Jonathan Siegel, Julie Silverbrook, Steve Smith, Sabrina Sondhi, Gabriel Swift, Linda Tesar, Will Tress and Mike Widener. Lilith Malagoli—the Italian law student I met in Geneva who has studied, in her native Europe, the Napoleonic Code promulgated in the wake of the French Revolution—was especially kind in providing content and translations from afar. Andrea Bartoli and his son Pietro—both Italian speakers—also aided me in my quest to better understand early American connections to the Italian Enlightenment, in addition to giving me the correct pronunciation of Cesare Beccaria's name. Andrea—now the Dean of the School of Diplomacy and International Relations at Seton Hall University—received his Ph.D. from the University of Milan and has long been involved with the Community of Sant'Egidio, an organization that opposes capital punishment. Pietro's translations of some of Beccaria's letters and the Italian portions of Thomas Jefferson's commonplace book were especially helpful. *Grazie mille!*

I would also like to thank the following institutions and organizations for their invaluable assistance: the American Antiquarian Society, the American Philosophical Society, the Boston Public Library, Brown University Library, the Charleston Library Society, the College of Charleston, the Connecticut Historical Society, the Constitutional Sources Project, the Dartmouth College Library, the Delaware Historical Society, the Georgia Historical Society, the Harvard Law School Library, the Harvard College Library, the Harvard University Archives, the Historical Society of Pennsylvania, the Kentucky Historical Society, the Library of Congress, the Maryland Historical Society, the Massachusetts Historical Society, the National Archives, the National Death Penalty Archive at the University of Albany, the New Hampshire Historical Society, the New Jersey Historical Society, the New York Public Library, the New York Society Library, the North Carolina State Archives, Princeton University Library, the Ohio Historical Society, the Rhode Island Historical Society, Rutgers University Libraries, the Society of the Cincinnati, the South Carolina Historical Society, University of Pennsylvania Libraries, the Vermont Historical Society, the Virginia Historical Society, the Waidner-Spahr Library and the Archives and Special Collections at Dickinson College, the William & Mary Law Library, Yale University Library, the Arthur W. Diamond Law Library at Columbia Law School, and the Lillian Goldman Law Library at Yale Law School. The Washington, D.C.-based Death Penalty Information Center, a non-profit funded by individual donors and organizations such as the Roderick MacArthur Foundation, the Open Society Foundation and the William and Mary Greve Foundation, also regularly produces high-quality reports that were helpful to me.

Beccaria's influence on American law—the subject of this book—is not minor or inconsequential. On the contrary, Beccaria's writings shaped the very fabric of the American Revolution, as well as the Founding Fathers' views on happiness and tyranny, and crime and punishment in particular, in fundamental ways. Although America's founders naturally looked to English laws and traditions as they crafted early state constitutions, bills of rights, and the U.S. Constitution itself, their abiding admiration for Italian thought and Beccaria's treatise shaped those legal documents and the founders' understanding of them. On January 24, 1783, in the *Journals of the Continental Congress*, "Beccaria's works" were specifically referenced in "a list of books" on "Politics" that were deemed "proper for the use of Congress"—a list prepared by a committee made up of American founders James Madison, Hugh Williamson and Thomas Mifflin. Madison took the lead in drafting the U.S. Bill of Rights; Williamson, a Pennsylvania native who studied at the College of Philadelphia and in Europe, was a physician now best known for representing North Carolina at the Constitutional Convention; and Mifflin—a Philadelphia merchant and politician—became the first governor of Pennsylvania. Beccaria's writings influenced America's founders almost a decade before the signing of the Declaration of Independence, and that impact would be felt for many decades thereafter. While a wide array of offenses, including witchcraft, adultery and sodomy, resulted in executions in colonial times, the death penalty's use—including for the crime of murder itself—was openly questioned and debated after the 1760s publication and translation of Beccaria's book.

The influential nature of *On Crimes and Punishments* in early America is evident in the many changes in American law that took place in the wake of its printing. As American states moved from traditional common-law crimes to statutory penal codes, the number of capital crimes appreciably declined in number. And during the late colonial and post-1776 period, America's Founding Fathers—both famous and, in some cases, now little remembered—regularly consulted Beccaria's treatise as those changes in the law were taking place. The only Roman Catholic signer of the Declaration of Independence, Charles Carroll of Carrollton, was, for example, an admirer of Beccaria's treatise. A Maryland planter and an early advocate of independence, Carroll was—as fate would have it—also the last surviving signatory of America's founding document, dying at the age of 95 in 1832. By the time he died, America's penal system—thanks in part to Beccaria's treatise—had been transformed from torturous dungeons and horrid, disease-ridden local jails to a series of state prisons designed by leading thinkers and architects. By the 1830s, when the Frenchmen Alexis de Tocqueville and Gustave de Beaumont came to America to visit its prisons and to study its new-fangled laws and penal practices, penitentiaries dotted the American landscape and Americans had a much different conception of justice than the one they inherited from England. This American story deserves to be told, and Beccaria's crucial role in it should, once again, become part of the broader American consciousness.

Writing a book takes years, and bringing it into the world requires the assistance of many people. I want to express my gratitude at the outset to Duke law professor H. Jefferson Powell, the Carolina Academic Press Legal History Series editor, for recommending this book for publication; publisher Keith Sipe and Senior Law Acquisitions Editor Jefferson Moors for taking on this project; and production designer Grace Pledger and the rest of the Carolina Academic Press staff for their efforts. Last, but certainly not least, I want to thank my wife Amy and my daughter Abigail for their understanding and devotion. Beccaria wrote a lot about torture and capital punishment, but he also knew how to enjoy life and wrote about everything from republics and imagination to style, scents and happiness. My wife, Amy Klobuchar, the senior U.S. Senator from Minnesota, has done a tremendous job serving our country and the people of Minnesota, and every day—through her work—she makes Minnesotans, like me, proud. She and Abigail, the loves and lights of my life, have given me the generous gifts of joy and laughter, and for that, I am eternally grateful. With Amy doing her work in the Senate and Abigail now off studying at Yale, I could not be prouder of all their accomplishments. Through their wit, humor, and stories, they daily energize me and provide me with much-needed respite from the solitary labors of my writing life. Abigail's first column for the *Yale Daily News* — a beautifully written piece titled "The Obstacles Are the Path" — made me laugh aloud and reminded me just how lucky I am; her first magazine profile, about an 84-year-old Italian-American who still volunteers at a senior center every day, literally moved me to tears. Amy and I celebrated our twentieth wedding anniversary in 2013, the same year Abigail turned eighteen, and I look forward to all the many fun-filled years that are still to come.

The American Declaration of Independence — a document inspired in part by Beccaria's writings — famously speaks of "the pursuit of Happiness." In *Seven Pleasures: Essays on Ordinary Happiness*, the essayist Willard Spiegelman writes of reading, walking, looking, dancing, listening, swimming and writing. Over the past two decades, I have immensely enjoyed doing all of those things with Amy and Abigail. And those simple pleasures of life, to which I would add bicycling and traveling, as well as cooking and (at least occasionally, when time permits) eating home-cooked meals together, have meant the world to me. Though Abigail is now off at college, leaving Amy and I as "empty nesters," I eagerly await our next weekend adventure together to Lanesboro, Minnesota, for another hilarious play at the Commonweal Theatre, or to Tofte or Grand Marais, Minnesota, for yet another beautiful hike along the rocky, rugged terrain of Lake Superior's North Shore.

The Birth of American Law

Introduction

The 1764 publication of a little treatise, *Dei delitti e delle pene*, helped inspire the American Revolution and sparked a worldwide movement to abolish capital punishment—a movement that, some 250 years later, continues to this day in the United States of America and elsewhere.[1] That book, written by the Italian philosopher Cesare Beccaria, vocally opposed torture and capital punishment, quickly drawing the ire of some but also the rapt attention of Europeans and Americans alike. The treatise was translated into English in 1767 as *On Crimes and Punishments*, and—through multiple editions and translations—has been influencing Anglo-American law ever since.[2] In the American colonies, writes Pulitzer Prize-winning historian Bernard Bailyn, the writings of Beccaria—as well as social critics like Voltaire, Rousseau and Montesquieu—"were quoted everywhere."[3] "One of the best-known works of the Enlightenment," notes another scholar, "was Cesare Beccaria's *On Crimes and Punishments*."[4] Beccaria was hailed in the Revolutionary War era as "wise" and "immortal," and copies of his book were sold in the American colonies and owned by early U.S. Presidents. "It was part of the wave of Enlightenment thought that helped mold ideas in the colonies and contributed to the Revolutionary War, the Declaration of Independence, and the U.S. Constitution," historian Rebecca Stefoff explains of Beccaria's much-heralded treatise.[5]

Beccaria's influence in continental Europe and on Anglo-American law was sizeable—and that influence was felt almost immediately.[6] In *Catherine the Great: Portrait of a Woman*, Pulitzer Prize-winning biographer Robert K. Massie recounts that Russian monarch Catherine II was inspired to reform Russia's penal system by both Montesquieu and Beccaria. The Russian empress, he writes, laboriously drafted in French (with her secretary then translating her work into Russian and other languages) what she called her *Nakaz*, formally published on July 30, 1767, as *Instruction of Her Imperial Majesty Catherine the Second for the Commission Charged with Preparing a Project of a New Code of Laws*. Of its 526 articles, Massie explains, 294 were adapted or taken from Montesquieu's *The Spirit of Laws*, published in 1748; another 108 articles were drawn from Beccaria's treatise, which made its first appearance in the Tuscan port city of Livorno, also known as Leghorn, on April 12, 1764.[7] In Virginia, Thomas Jefferson—tasked with a revisal of Virginia's criminal laws—also drew particular inspiration from *On Crimes and Punishments* as he drafted legislation in the 1770s. "Drawing on the legal writings of the Italian philosophe Cesare Beccaria," scholar Darren Staloff emphasizes of the resulting bill to proportion crimes and punishments, Jefferson sought, in his legislative proposal, to eliminate the death penalty for almost all crimes. "Liberal and humane," Staloff explains of the draft legislation, "Jefferson's revision of the laws of Virginia was, like his constitutional schemes, a model of enlightened political activism."[8]

The substantial impact of Beccaria's book was felt close to Beccaria's home in Milan as well as far away, in places as diverse as England, France, Russia and America. "Beccaria's ideas," one criminology textbook records, "took hold especially in France; many of them were incorporated in the French Code of 1791, which ranked crimes on a scale and affixed a penalty to each." In the debate on the adoption of that French penal code, Robe-spierre—who later changed his mind, calling for the execution of Louis XVI—argued vigorously for the abolition of capital punishment.[9] The 1791 French code, adopted during the French Revolution by the Constituent Assembly and reducing the number of capital crimes from 119 to 32, sought to treat all similarly situated offenders equally regardless of their status. The guillotine—first employed in March 1792—was itself intended to cause the instantaneous death of offenders, a method of execution developed by a French doctor that was believed to be a less painful, and more humane way to kill the condemned than prior methods such as disembowelment and drawing and quartering.[10] In the U.S., Pennsylvania founder James Wilson, a leading legal scholar of the time, likewise specifically credited Beccaria with influencing his thinking on the deterrent function of punishment.[11] Beccaria's book, history shows, also fueled significant anti-death penalty sentiment worldwide. As University of Minnesota law professor Michael Tonry emphasizes: "Inspired by Beccaria, the death penalty for murder was abolished by the rulers of Tuscany and Austria in 1786 and 1787 and, under the empresses Elizabeth and Catherine II, also came close to being abandoned in Russia."[12]

Translated into French, English, Spanish, German and an array of other languages, Beccaria's *On Crimes and Punishments* first drew accolades and sustained praise in France and Great Britain, America's mother country. Voltaire and the French *philosophes* were mesmerized by Beccaria's rationality and humanity, and leading English jurists and lawyers, including Sir William Blackstone and Jeremy Bentham, were also greatly influenced by Beccaria's reform-minded treatise. Blackstone's popular treatise, *Commentaries on the Laws of England*, explicitly referred to Beccaria,[13] with the fourth volume of that treatise, published in 1769, calling Beccaria "an ingenious writer."[14] Bentham—the well-known English social reformer—read *On Crimes and Punishments* around the time he was admitted to the bar in 1769, writing of Beccaria: "Oh, my master, first evangelist of Reason ... you who have made so many useful excursions into the path of utility, what is there left for us to do?"[15] "When Beccaria came, he was received by the intelligent as an Angel from heaven would be by the faithful," Bentham wrote in *A Fragment on Government*, an April 1776 essay in which Bentham also quoted Montesquieu, Beccaria's intellectual predecessor. "In England," two scholars note, "Bentham and his follower, Sir Samuel Romilly, developed and applied Beccaria's ideas to the reform of the English criminal law."[16] Bentham himself called Beccaria "the father of Censorial Jurisprudence," adding that Montesquieu's *Spirit of the Laws* (1748) "was a work of the mixed kind," part expository and part censorial. "Before Montesquieu," Bentham recorded in 1776 in critiquing existing laws and Blackstone's *Commentaries*, "all was unmixed barbarism."[17] *A Treatise on the Police of the Metropolis*, published in London in the late eighteenth century, explicitly lauded Beccaria as an "able writer," an "elegant writer," and "[t]hat acute Reasoner."[18]

In the 1760s, intellectuals and reformers in Italian states were paying close attention to events in the British colonies in North America, with an Italian translation of William and Edmund Burke's *An Account of the European Settlements in America* appearing in Venice in 1763.[19] Across the Atlantic, meanwhile, many of America's Founding Fathers—among them, John Adams, John Hancock, Thomas Jefferson, Thomas Paine and James Wilson—were paying considerable attention to European writers, being especially inspired by Montesquieu's ideas and Beccaria's essay on the criminal law.[20] After reviewing 15,000 sources written between 1760 and 1805, including newspapers, pamphlets and books, two academics, Donald Lutz and Charles Hyneman, found that Sir William Blackstone, John Locke, David Hume and Beccaria were among the European writers most frequently cited by America's founders. Of the thirty-six most cited authors, Beccaria comes in at number seven. At Benjamin Franklin's house, for example, Dr. Benjamin

Rush—a Philadelphia patriot who got his medical degree in Europe and who served as a Continental Congress delegate—specifically invoked Beccaria's name during a reading he gave in March 1787 about public punishments.[21] "The Duke of Tuscany, soon after the publication of the Marquis of Beccaria's excellent treatise upon this subject," Rush emphasized, "abolished death as a punishment for murder."[22]

A prominent physician and later a professor at the College of Philadelphia, Dr. Rush had close friendships with a who's who of American revolutionaries, everyone from Thomas Paine and Thomas Jefferson to James Madison and John Adams. In fact, Dr. Rush himself suggested the title *Common Sense* for Thomas Paine's famous book. A deeply religious man, Dr. Rush looked to Beccaria's writings as he advocated for the total abolition of executions. As one legal scholar has written: "Rush challenged the widely held view that the executioner was God's servant, labeling it sacrilegious for public officials to claim that they shared with God the right to punish by death. Rush urged incarceration, with the possibility of rehabilitation, in lieu of executions."[23] Dr. Rush, who privately engaged Thomas Jefferson in correspondence on the question of his Christian faith, was especially close with Benjamin Franklin, America's elder scientist and statesman who shared an abiding passion for penal reform. Regrettably, Dr. Rush—the father of America's anti-death penalty movement who, through an actor, made a cameo appearance in HBO's TV miniseries *John Adams*—is today remembered only a little more by Americans than his Italian counterpart, Cesare Beccaria. Criminologists and legal historians still study Beccaria's and Dr. Rush's writings, but to the broader American public, Beccaria and Rush have become obscure, largely unknown figures.[24]

But that state of affairs was not always the case. Beccaria and Dr. Rush, side by side with Jefferson and Madison, were once central actors in the drama of the Enlightenment, the American Revolution and the law reforms that they inspired. Because Beccaria's treatise was immensely popular in the 1770s, the decade in which the American Revolution began, it played a key role in shaping America's entire founding era. Biographer Catherine Drinker Bowen writes of how John Adams had "written to London" for Beccaria's book and consulted it in 1770 as part of his law practice, including in his defense of British soldiers accused of murder following the Boston Massacre.[25] Beccaria's treatise also led men such as Dr. Rush to vocally oppose executions and to gain national prominence of their own by advocating for penal reform—an effort stirred by Beccaria's treatise that ultimately led to the passage of new laws and the building of state penitentiaries. Beccaria's influence, from a political standpoint, reached to the highest echelons of American society. The evidence reveals that George Washington—the hero of the American Revolution and America's first President—was himself a reader.

In 1774, the Continental Congress—as a body—itself invoked the stirring words of the "celebrated Marquis Beccaria" in a letter to the inhabitants of Quebec, with signers of America's Declaration of Independence deeply moved by *On Crimes and Punishments*. Richard Henry Lee—the Virginia politician who, in 1776, moved the Continental Congress to declare America's independence from Great Britain—was part of the congressional committee, along with Massachusetts native Thomas Cushing and Pennsylvania lawyer John Dickinson, that drafted that "Address to the Inhabitants of the Province of Quebec." Known as the "Penman of the Revolution" for his *Letters from a Farmer in Pennsylvania*, Dickinson—like Adams—had been keenly affected by Beccaria's prose.[26] By the time the American people, in 1788, ratified the U.S. Constitution—what Yale law professor Akhil Amar calls "one of the most important texts in world history"—Beccaria's fame had only grown to more spectacular heights.[27] Inspired by what they read in the Italian philosopher's book, yet tailoring Beccaria's ideas to their own peculiar time and circumstances, America's founders—and, ultimately, Americans themselves—charted a bold new course

in the history of mankind. While women and minorities, especially slaves, were left behind in 1787 by Constitutional Convention delegates in Philadelphia, Beccaria's ideas—
reflected in Jefferson's Declaration of Independence and provisions of the U.S. Bill of
Rights—would end up shaping American law for decades to come.

Beccaria's treatise was particularly influential in the realm of the criminal law. Especially after the publication of Beccaria's book, England's "Bloody Code," which made
scores of crimes, even minor ones, punishable by death, came to be seen by America's
founders as cruel and barbaric. Viewed as a vestige of a monarchical system, the English
approach—then dominated by hangings and outdated common-law traditions—came
under attack as too "bloodthirsty" in nature. Accordingly, strenuous efforts were made to
change American laws to jettison, at least in large part, England's Bloody Code and its harsh
treatment of offenders. Such efforts were made by larger-than-life personalities such as
Benjamin Rush and Thomas Jefferson, but also by lesser-known men such as the Rev.
Henry Holcombe (1762–1824), a Baptist minister and a member of the South Carolina
State Convention that met in Charleston in 1788 to approve the U.S. Constitution. Holcombe, a biographer writes, "was practically the father of the Georgia penitentiary system." As that biographer, William Northen, writes: "Shocked by the execution of a man
named Rice for the comparatively small crime of stealing a gun, he was the first to urge
in the State a milder system of punishment. This he did in a memorial to the Legislature
in September, 1802; following up this effort with great zeal and pertinacity." "The result,"
his biographer notes, "was that the penitentiary system was adopted instead of the bloody
code of earlier days."[28] In short, the morality and efficacy of harsh corporal punishments,
even non-lethal ones such as whipping and ear cropping, was heavily scrutinized in the
founding era as Americans—first on a state-by-state basis, and then at the national level—
reflected on their own criminal justice practices and reconsidered the relationship between crime and punishment.[29]

Cesare Beccaria—the rationalistic yet passionate advocate for penal reform—was an
economist whose works were read alongside those of Adam Smith, author of *The Wealth
of Nations* (1776).[30] "Beccaria," writes one scholar, pointing out that the Italian empiri-
cist also wrote *A Discourse on Public Economy and Commerce* (1769) in which he advocated for public education, "seems to have *felt* the cruelty of criminal repression the way
Adam Smith believed we feel the pain of our 'brother on the rack.'"[31] "The reforms advocated by the utilitarian economist Cesare Beccaria," author Steven Pinker cogently explains in *The Better Angels of Our Nature: Why Violence Has Declined*, "led to the abolition
of cruel punishments," with reforms of the Enlightenment "designed to reorient criminal
justice away from the raw impulse to make a bad person suffer and toward the practical
goal of deterrence."[32] The American public's view of *cruelty*—a concept explicitly referenced in the U.S. Constitution's Eighth Amendment—was thus transformed by Beccaria's pen. Moved by Beccaria's treatise, James Madison and one of his closest college
friends, William Bradford, Jr., an eminent Pennsylvania lawyer and jurist who became
the second Attorney General of the United States, both made strenuous efforts to curtail
executions in their respective states, Virginia and Pennsylvania. Indeed, even before those
legislative efforts in the 1780s and 1790s, Thomas Jefferson—the principal drafter of the
Declaration of Independence—had demonstrated that he was especially intrigued by
Beccaria's ideas, copying twenty-six passages from Beccaria's treatise into his commonplace book. In the 1770s, Jefferson cited Beccaria's treatise multiple times in his draft legislation to reform Virginia's penal laws, a bill carried by Madison in the 1780s but defeated,
much to his chagrin, in Virginia's legislature by a single vote.[33]

Beccaria's writings, appearing in the decade before Americans declared their independence from Great Britain, resonated with American revolutionaries on multiple lev-

els. "A lightning strike is needed to stop a fierce lion who is provoked by a gunshot," Beccaria wrote in *On Crimes and Punishments*, words penned roughly a dozen years before real gunshots broke out at Lexington and Concord, Massachusetts, in the spring of 1775. "But as souls become softened by society," Beccaria had added in his book, using the mathematics terminology he preferred, "sensitivity grows" and "as it does so, the severity of punishments ought to diminish, if the relation between the object and the sensation is to remain constant."[34] Just as Independence Hall and the Liberty Bell in Philadelphia came to be seen as iconic American symbols, colonial Americans viewed *On Crimes and Punishments* as a clarion call for independence and freedom and, at the same time, for a moderation of punishments. An indictment of the tyrannical practices long used by monarchs, Beccaria's book spoke of justice and happiness, ideas that appealed to the men who ultimately fought the British Empire in the Revolutionary War and who heard Philadelphia's bells ring on July 8, 1776, to mark the Declaration of Independence's first public reading.[35] The 1774 letter to the inhabitants of Quebec—signed by Henry Middleton, a South Carolina plantation owner—began "We, the Delegates of the Colonies." Quoting Beccaria, it then recounted how "royal authority" had been "so audaciously and cruelly abuse[d]."[36]

While Beccaria, in *On Crimes and Punishments*, wrote of men's happiness and the right to life, the Declaration of Independence—the product of Thomas Jefferson's pen and the craftsmanship of a congressional committee familiar with ancient Roman republics and Enlightenment thinkers—echoed Beccarian sentiments, unequivocally proclaiming that "Life, Liberty and the pursuit of Happiness" are "unalienable Rights."[37] Not only did Beccaria's words inspire countless American revolutionaries, but during and after the Revolutionary War those words strongly influenced and stirred to action the nation's lawmakers. As Robert Cottrol—a George Washington University Law School professor—has written in the *Stanford Law Review* of Beccaria's impact on American revolutionaries: "Beccaria's views had a significant influence on late eighteenth century American criminological thought. James Madison expressed disapproval of the death penalty. Thomas Jefferson and Benjamin Franklin favored limiting the death penalty to murder and treason."[38] In *On Crimes and Punishments*, in his own distinctive style, Beccaria himself had written of then-existing laws as "the residue of the most barbarous centuries," saying that it is "only after they have experienced thousands of miscarriages in matters essential to life and liberty, and have grown weary of suffering the most extreme ills," that "men set themselves to right the evils that beset them."[39] As the Founding Fathers sought to forge a new society built on civility and republican ideals, those words—indeed, Beccaria's whole treatise—captured the imagination of the American people and its leaders.

The American war for independence, in fact, was just the beginning of the love affair with Beccaria's treatise. As early Americans struggled to establish law and order in the aftermath of the Revolutionary War, Beccaria's treatise continued to captivate them even as they dealt with periodic crises such as Shays' Rebellion (1788–1787) in central and western Massachusetts, the Whiskey Rebellion (1791–1794) in western Pennsylvania, and Fries's Rebellion (1799–1800), a tax revolt among Pennsylvania Dutch farmers. During the ratification process for the U.S. Constitution, which began immediately after delegates to the Constitutional Convention met in Philadelphia in 1787, America's founders continued to bandy about Beccaria's name. While some openly praised Beccaria's writings during the tumultuous 1787–1788 ratification process for the U.S. Constitution, others—using Greek and Roman pseudonyms to shield their identities, allowing them to speak freely but without fear in that time of enormous social upheaval—embraced Beccaria's ideas more behind the scenes.[40] Just as real battles had been fought at places like Bunker Hill, Quebec and Yorktown during the Revolutionary War, the post-war period witnessed a fierce battle of ideas between those favoring tradition and those embracing innovative ways of thinking.

The state-by-state ratification debates over the U.S. Constitution were one place in which this battle of ideas took place. For example, according to Francis Childs' notes of the New York ratification debates, on June 21, 1788, delegate John Williams—a London-trained physician who immigrated in 1773 to what, through war, became America—rose to address the chair. Williams professed that it was now time "to investigate and decide upon a Constitution, in which, not only the present members of the community are deeply interested, but upon which the happiness or misery of generations yet unborn is in a great measure suspended." "In forming a constitution for a free country, like this," Williams urged his colleagues, "the greatest care should be taken to define its powers, and guard against an abuse of authority." It was in that context that another delegate, businessman Melancton Smith, quoted Beccaria's "forcible words" that had been included in the address of the Continental Congress to the people of Quebec: "In every human society, there is an effort continually tending to confer on one part of the height of power and happiness, and to reduce the other to the extreme of weakness and misery. The intent of good laws is to oppose this effort, and to diffuse their influence universally and equally."[41]

In June 1788, at New York's ratification convention, the delegates included the likes of Alexander Hamilton, John Jay and Robert R. Livingston. In that context, Melancton Smith had strategically used Beccaria's words to frame the high-stakes debate—a debate that, in many ways, closely resembles America's current, highly contentious political debate over tax rates, income inequality, and the corrosive role of money in politics. In speaking of how the burden of taxation "will bear upon the different classes," Smith argued that "the number of representatives should be so large, as that while it embraces men of the first class, it should admit those of the middling class of life." Noting that "the influence of the great will generally enable them to succeed in elections," he worried that "[a] substantial yeoman of sense and discernment, will hardly ever be chosen." In arguing for more representatives for the American people, Smith warned: "From these remarks it appears that the government will fall into the hands of the few and the great. This will be a government of oppression." "It has been the principal care of free governments to guard against the encroachments of the great," Smith argued before pulling out his quote from Beccaria—the same words invoked with such passion by the Continental Congress itself in 1774, the year before the Revolutionary War broke out.

While Melancton Smith—a proponent of equality—did not want to exclude any class of citizens from the honor of public service, he argued that middle class participation in government was critical to the success of representative democracy. After quoting Beccaria's candid assessment that every society tends to confer "the height of power" on a few while reducing others to "weakness and misery," Smith—a member of the anti-slavery New York Manumission Society along with Alexander Hamilton, John Jay and Robert R. Livingston—reiterated the importance of the "middling class." A "sufficient number of the middling class," he said at New York's ratification convention, was necessary to "controul" greed and "hereditary nobility." "A representative body, composed principally of respectable yeomanry is the best possible security to liberty," Smith observed, adding: "When the interest of this part of the community is pursued, the public good is pursued; because the body of every nation consists of this class." Saying that "[a] system of corruption is known to be the system of government in Europe," Smith took the position that a "great danger" of "corruption" would result from a small number of representatives. In *On Crimes and Punishments*, long before twenty-first century talk of "class warfare," Beccaria himself had advised that the laws should "favour individual men more than classes of men."[42]

Less than a year before Smith's 1788 speech, "Brutus"—in addressing New Yorkers on October 18, 1787, on whether "the thirteen United States should be reduced to one great republic"—had similarly looked in the ratification period to "the opinion of the greatest and wisest men who have ever thought or wrote on the science of government." Invoking his favorite European writers, Brutus—whose identity is still a matter of speculation—stated matter-of-factly: "Among the many illustrious authorities which might be produced to this point, I shall content myself with quoting only two. The one is the Baron de Montesquieu, *Spirit of Laws*." "Of the same opinion," Brutus emphasized, "is the Marquis Beccarari [sic]."[43] For the Founding Fathers, a *monarchical* or "sanguinary" system was anti-republican and meant unduly harsh laws that made frequent use of executions; a *republic*, meanwhile, came to be associated with milder, more humane punishments.[44] But reaching a consensus on exactly what that meant—on where to draw the line between *sanguinary* and *non-sanguinary* actions—was a different matter entirely. While Beccaria's treatise set forth general principles, they were not self-executing, forcing American lawmakers to confront issues for themselves. In 1776, in his draft constitution for the Commonwealth of Virginia, Jefferson himself proposed one line: that the state's general assembly "have no power to pass any law inflicting death for any crime, excepting murder, and those offenses in the military service for which they shall think punishment by death absolutely necessary"; "all capital punishments in other cases are hereby abolished," Jefferson's draft constitution read.[45]

When the Continental Congress and the First Congress debated the country's first federal criminal laws, "Beccaria's name"—to quote one scholar—had already become "a household word."[46] Those federal deliberative bodies, however, only had responsibility for the young nation's national defense and an otherwise circumscribed scope of authority in the criminal-law arena. In particular, the national government of the United States of America, as the country became known, could only legislate on topics impacting federal interests, such as articles of war for the military, or occurring in U.S. territories that had not yet achieved statehood. The states themselves retained the bulk of responsibility for legislating on crimes and punishments. And at a time when maintaining order was paramount, the leaders of the new republic, sometimes averse to trying new ways of doing things, often fell back on old habits and relied on summary proceedings to adjudicate guilt or innocence. For example, the Northwest Ordinance of 1787 created the Northwest Territory, but that July 1787 law delegated to the newly appointed governor and judges the power to "adopt and publish" such laws "as may be necessary and best suited to the circumstances." When territorial governor Arthur St. Clair and territorial judges Samuel Holden Parsons and James Mitchell Varnum published "A Law respecting Crimes and Punishments" in September 1787, it made treason, murder and lethal arson punishable by death; provided that manslaughter "shall be punished as at the common law hath heretofore been used and accustomed"; and provided for prison terms, forfeiture of property or fines, whipping, and the use of the pillory for crimes such as non-lethal arson and burglary.[47]

Early American penal laws were a mix of harsh and milder sanctions. "An Act for the Punishment of Certain Crimes Against the United States," passed by the First Congress in 1790, laid out the code of laws to govern the nation in a more typical fashion, without Congress delegating responsibility to others, as it had in the Northwest Ordinance. That 1790 crimes act, signed by Frederick Augustus Muhlenberg as Speaker of the U.S. House of Representatives and by John Adams as U.S. Vice-President and President of the Senate, was approved by President George Washington on April 30, 1790, over a year after the establishment of the new federal government.[48] Although the 1790 federal statute made multiple crimes capital offenses, Congress's list of capital crimes was much shorter than that contained in England's ferocious Bloody Code. At that time, most American states had yet to ameliorate the severity of British penal laws, and the U.S. government itself was seen as having relatively limited authority, with states and individual localities handling the vast majority of criminal prosecutions.

The U.S. Constitution, as proposed and ratified, did confer certain powers on the federal government, leading, for example, to the creation of the District of Columbia, over which Congress had the express power to legislate. Among Congress's enumerated powers in Article 1, section 8: "To exercise exclusive Legislation in all Cases whatsoever, over such District (not exceeding ten Miles square) as may, by Cession of particular States, and the Acceptance of Congress, become the Seat of the Government of the United States, and to exercise like Authority over all Places purchased by the Consent of the Legislature of the State in which the Same shall be, for the Erection of Forts, Magazines, Arsenals, dock-Yards, and other needful Buildings." Although Beccaria's treatise, by the late 1780s, had already inspired some criminal-law reforms at the state level, George Mason—speaking at Virginia's ratification convention, and worried about what the future would hold—expressed the view that "there were few clauses in the Constitution so dangerous as that which gave Congress exclusive power of legislation within ten miles square." The nation's capital, Mason feared, "may, like the custom of the superstitious days of our ancestors, become the sanctuary of the blackest crimes." "Now, sir," Mason argued, "if an attempt should be made to establish tyranny over the people, here are ten miles square where the greatest offender may meet protection."[49]

Cesare Beccaria—a family man who didn't like to travel—never physically visited the United States of America. His intellect and perceptive writings, though, were partly responsible for revolutionary attitudes and law reform efforts, especially since his ideas were so often adopted or adapted by American civic leaders and the American polity. After Beccaria and his European and American disciples spoke out against the cruelty of then-existing punishments, U.S. political leaders began to do away with barbarous practices and what were then known as "sanguinary" laws—a movement that began in earnest in the last quarter of the eighteenth century. In place of "sanguinary" punishments—a synonym for "bloody" or "cruel" ones—America's founders chose to use fewer executions and more life sentences. In place of death sentences and executions, which had come to be seen as being imposed and carried out too frequently, hard labor and solitary confinement within prisons—thought to be a cure for idleness and criminality—grew in popularity and became viable alternatives to the punishment of death and lesser corporal punishments. In *Solitude in Imprisonment* (1776), the English penal reformer Jonas Hanway specifically wrote of the "solitary imprisonment of *malefactors*" with "proper profitable labour, and a spare diet." Hanway emphasized that "[t]he number of Malefactors" is "too great for the Gallows" and that "*solitude in imprisonment*" is "the most humane and effectual means of bringing malefactors who have forfeited their lives, or are subject to transportation, to a right sense of their condition." The American penitentiary system—largely a Quaker, religious-based innovation and the intellectual successor of English workhouses and bridewells—was thus born close in time to the U.S. Constitution's ratification.[50]

The Founding Fathers and the generations of Americans who came after them appropriated substantial sums of money to build America's first penitentiaries, and men like James Madison and Thomas Jefferson saw in those new institutions the potential to eliminate unnecessary acts of cruelty—including executions—as regards the treatment of offenders. Americans also gradually moved away from once popular, non-lethal corporal punishments, such as flogging and the pillory, as attitudes about criminals and criminality changed, though slaves—especially in the South, where penal codes facially treated blacks more severely than whites—were still regularly brutalized. Many slaves were executed in the wake of slave rebellions in places such as Virginia, and slave owners and overseers, exercising absolute authority, unmercifully whipped slaves—sometimes to death. Jefferson himself owned more than 600 slaves during his lifetime, and Jefferson knew that young Monticello slaves—boys, in some cases, not yet even teenagers—were subjected to the lash to boost productivity at his own nail factory. Although John and Samuel Adams, along with Alexander Hamilton and Thomas Paine, did not own slaves, many of America's Founding Fathers—from Maryland's Samuel Chase to Massachusetts' John Hancock, and from New York's John Jay, to Virginia's George Washington and James Madison, to South Carolina's Charles Cotesworth Pinckney and Edward Rutledge—were, at least at one time, slaveholders.[51]

The contradiction of America's founders fighting for liberty and equality while continuing to enslave blacks and subjugate women, denying the right to vote to both groups, would not begin to be resolved on a countrywide basis, for the health and betterment of the nation, until long after the Founding Fathers' deaths. A hard-fought women's suffrage movement proved necessary to give women the rights and privileges of citizenship, while it took the Civil War—and Abraham Lincoln's leadership—to start the country down the path, still being traveled today, towards racial equality. Abigail Adams was unable to convince her husband John and his legislative colleagues to "Remember the Ladies," and the institution of slavery, with all its barbarity, proved to be a stubborn opponent, especially in the South. When President Thomas Jefferson, in 1801, wrote to Thomas Mann Randolph—the husband of Jefferson's daughter Martha and someone quite familiar with the goings on at Jefferson's Monticello nail factory—Jefferson only made this request of his son-in-law: "I forgot to ask the favor of you to speak to Lilly as to the treatment of the nailers. [I]t would destroy their value in my estimation to degrade them in their own eyes by the whip. [T]his therefore must not be resorted to but in extremities. [A]s they will be again under my government, I would chuse they should retain the stimulus of character." Gabriel Lilly—the slave overseer to whom Jefferson referred, and the man Jefferson put in charge of the nailery in his absence—was known for whipping slaves "for truancy." Lilly—a man so feared and despised that one hired slave tried to poison him—once viciously whipped a very sick James Hemings, the 17-year-old son of Critta Hemings, for missing a couple days of work at Jefferson's nailery. James Oldham, a white carpenter at Monticello, reported of Hemings that Lilly "whipped him three times in one day, and the boy was really not able to raise his hand to his head."[52]

The story of Beccaria's meteoric rise in America—a country sill struggling with issues of gender and racial equality—is a fascinating one. As Beccaria's treatise became a bestseller on multiple continents, the European Enlightenment—of which Beccaria was a major part—simultaneously spread to America as fast as ships could then travel. People of means, promoting trade and commerce, regularly traveled between Europe and North America in the period before the U.S. Constitution was ratified in 1788, and those seeking educational opportunities in Europe also made the weeks' long ocean voyage. Both before and after the appearance of Beccaria's treatise, a thriving transatlantic book trade not only existed but grew rapidly in the eighteenth century. As historian James Raven notes in *London Booksellers and American Customers*: "Against formidable obstacles of cost, risk, and time, the transatlantic book trade hugely increased during the second half of the eighteenth century." "This expansion," he writes, "was partly a result of the limited and unbalanced development of colonial printing, but partly also a result of the strength of the cultural and social bonds of empire." The American colonies did not manufacture printing presses until the 1760s, but despite the monopolistic trade practices of British merchants, early American printers such as Benjamin Franklin and Mathew Carey—wanting to produce American content—took on such formidable challenges and beat the odds. A native of Ireland, Carey—who extensively promoted Beccaria's ideas in America—had met Dr. Franklin and the Marquis de Lafayette, one of George Washington's Revolutionary War generals, on a trip to Paris in 1779. Lafayette—the wealthy Frenchman who loved America and fought for its independence—would himself advocate for penal reform and loan Carey, a Jesuit-educated, Irish Catholic, the start-up money he needed for his printing business to spread republican ideas.[53]

In the eighteenth century, a number of Americans battled the high seas and the seasickness that so often accompanied it, making the treacherous voyage to Europe to be educated in the most prestigious schools of England, France and Scotland, where respected universities had long thrived. Europeans likewise came to America, whether to escape religious persecution, find economic opportunities, or simply to tour the newly formed country forged through the Revolutionary War—a war that ended in 1783 with the Treaty of Paris. Count Luigi Castiglioni—an Italian botanist from a Milanese noble family with close ties to Cesare Beccaria's social circle—was, as fate would have it, one of those travelers. Castiglioni, in planning his trip to America in the mid-1780s, first made contact with Benjamin Franklin in 1784 in Passy, on Paris' Right Bank, before sailing from England to America the next year. Taking note of the American Revolution, what he called "one of the most memorable events of this century," Castiglioni—in his *Viaggio*, a later published travelogue—emphasized that he "was moved by curiosity to see the political birth of a Republic composed of diverse nationalities, scattered over vast provinces far removed from one another, and varied in climate and products." That travelogue, originally published in Milan in 1790 by Giuseppe Marelli, was fully titled, in Italian, *Viaggio negli Stati Uniti dell'America Settentrionale fatto negli anni 1785, 1786, e 1787*. "On April 13, 1785," the first chapter of Castiglioni's travelogue begins, "I went aboard the 250-ton American vessel *Neptune*, which was to sail from Deal for Boston in Massachusetts." That ship would land in Boston thirty-four days later, bringing yet another European—and one well acquainted with Beccaria's ideas—to American soil.

The close interaction of European and American elites—along with the widespread distribution of *On Crimes and Punishments* and the publication of American newspapers and magazines that serialized or cited it—made Beccaria's book a hot topic of conversation and debate. When Count Luigi Castiglioni, a nephew and later brother-in-law of Beccaria's elder Italian mentor Pietro Verri, came to America, he met notables such as George Washington, Benjamin Franklin and Dr. Benjamin Rush, among many others. In those encounters, it is hard to imagine Cesare Beccaria's name—and Beccaria's ideas—not coming up. Indeed, in his *Viaggio*, Castiglioni himself took special note of America's early history as regards punishment, recounting how in Salem, Massachusetts, "the horrors of the Inquisition were revived in North America" when colonists had fallen "into the most superstitious ignorance" and "many poor old women were condemned to the fire as witches." Most notably, perhaps, Castiglioni—in making his way to all thirteen American states, including to such places of higher learning as Yale and Harvard College—met with many of the men most responsible for American penal reform. This cross-cultural exchange brought American ideas back to Europe and simultaneously further facilitated the growth of Beccaria's fame. After meeting in the State of Georgia with Nathanael Greene—one of George Washington's most trusted Revolutionary War major-generals and an officer nicknamed "The Fighting Quaker" who kept Blackstone and Beccaria's treatises at his house—Castiglioni commented: "I went to see him at his new home, and in talking with him I found him very well informed about the history of the wars of Italy and much more so about that of his native country and its political situation."[54]

Luigi Castiglioni's observations on American life, penned decades before Alexis de Tocqueville came to the United States and wrote *Democracy in America*, provide a revealing glimpse into America's now distant past. Though most of Castiglioni's notes were about trees and plants and then-prevailing U.S. social customs, Castiglioni—the Italian noble and globe-trotting botanist—also recorded a few choice observations about American law and how America's penal laws had already been transformed through legislative reform. According to Antonio Pace, the translator of Castiglioni's Italian-language travelogue, an appendix attached to an earlier draft of Castiglioni's book suggests that "Castiglioni met in person and associated more or less intimately with such notables as John Adams, Samuel Adams, John Hancock, Robert Morris, Charles Thomson, Nathanael Greene, Henry Knox, and Benjamin Lincoln." In fact, Count Castiglioni's impressions of various American revolutionaries, recorded in his *Viaggio*, reflect his unusual access—aided by Benjamin Franklin's good offices—to such men. On John Adams: "Mr. Adams is 40 to 50 years old, short and corpulent; and his kindly but simple face gives no indication of the range of his knowledge." On Benjamin Franklin, whose portrait Castiglioni acquired for an Italian friend: "He is about 70 years of age, and his face is even-featured, venerable, and sincere. His manners are simple. He is likeable and courteous, but at the same time a skillful and wise statesman."

Castiglioni's trip to the United States was part of an eighteenth-century tradition that involved "Grand Tours," whether of Italian states or the American wilderness. "It was about 1750," according to one Italian-American history, "that it became fashionable for well-to-do American families to send their sons to Italy after they completed their studies in England." As that history notes: "[T]he first American to start the custom was the young Quaker, Francis Rawle, who went over in 1748, but 'the great impetus to Italian travel' occurred in 1760, when Chief Justice Allen provided his 21-year-old son, John, with a letter of credit. Then he sailed for Leghorn with his cousin, Colonel Joseph Shippen, and a letter of introduction to Sir Horace Mann, the English representative at Florence." William Allen (1704–1780), the Chief Justice of the Province of Pennsylvania, also sponsored the painter Benjamin West's 1760 trip to Italy. In his *Viaggio*, Castiglioni—making the trip the opposite way—described the knowledge of one of America's most prominent patriots, Patrick Henry, who reviled torture, as extending "not only to politics and government but also to literature and the sciences." Castiglioni further characterized James Madison as having "likable manners and unaffected modesty." As for Henry Knox, a Continental Army officer and later the first U.S. Secretary of War, Castiglioni made this evocative observation: "In the course of the war, in which he lost the fingers of his left hand, he commanded the artillery, and was so skillful at directing the artillerymen that by the end of the war the French themselves were amazed at their readiness and activity." Castiglioni likewise reported that, at war's end, Knox—a man quite familiar with Beccaria's treatise—"said laughingly" to other Revolutionary War officers, one of whom, like Knox, had been a bookseller, "Now we can return home and reopen our shops."[55]

In fact, American bookstores and libraries regularly stocked or lent out Beccaria's treatise—a book that infiltrated the American consciousness before America's founders signed the Declaration of Independence and the U.S. Constitution. In a 1786 letter to Luigi Castiglioni that remains little known to this day, buried as it is in an endnote in tiny font to Antonio Pace's translation of Castiglioni's *Viaggio*, William Bradford, Jr. specifically lavished praise upon Cesare Beccaria, whom Bradford believed to be Castiglioni's uncle. As Bradford—one of James Madison's closest friends, then serving as Pennsylvania's attorney general—wrote to Castiglioni, the naturalist with a zest for walking and wanderlust: "The name of Beccaria has become familiar in Pennsylvania, his authority has become great, and his principles have spread among all classes of persons and impressed themselves deeply in the hearts of our citizens. You yourself must have noticed the influence of these precepts in other American states."[56] In particular, Beccaria's opposition to tyrannical treatment and his anti-death penalty advocacy made an enormous impact on American leaders, especially as regards penal reform and the treatment of non-homicide offenders. After waging a protracted war against King George III, scholar Jill Lepore explains in *The Story of America*, "adopting Beccaria's recommendations came to seem, in a fundamental sense, American, as if the United States had a special role to play, as a republic, in the abolition of capital punishment."[57]

Among other locales, Castiglioni's lengthy trip to America included a tour of Thomas Jefferson's plantation. Jefferson, a fellow Beccaria admirer, was in Europe during Castiglioni's trip, with Jefferson arriving in France in 1784 as one of three U.S. treaty commissioners, the other two being John Adams and Benjamin Franklin. But Castiglioni—made to feel at ease visiting Jefferson's Virginia home, Monticello, even in Jefferson's absence—had already, by then, met Jefferson at Benjamin Franklin's residence in France. After Jefferson's arrival in Europe, Dr. Franklin had retired from his diplomatic post in 1785 and returned to the United States, with Jefferson presenting his diplomatic credentials to Louis XVI on May 17, 1785, at the court of Versailles.[58] That same year—1785—also saw the publication of the Frenchman Abbé de Mably's *Remarks Concerning the Government and Laws of the United States of America*, in which de Mably, after reading American constitutions, commented that "[w]hilst almost every European nation remains plunged in ignorance respecting the constitutive principles of society ... your thirteen republics have, in the same moment, discovered the real dignity of man, and proceeded to draw from the sources of the most enlightened philosophy those humane principles on which they mean to build their forms of government."[59] In a sketch written in 1787, Castiglioni wrote this of America's future President and the man who, with the Declaration of Independence, set those changes in motion: "Mr. Jefferson is a man of about 50 years of age, lean, of a serious and modest appearance. His uncommon talents are not readily visible at first encounter, but as one talks with him about the various subjects in which he believes himself to be informed, he very quickly gives evident proof of his judgment and application."[60]

The publication of *On Crimes and Punishments* altered Jefferson's worldview and, like no other book, shaped the landscape of penology itself.[61] In *Fifty Key Thinkers in Criminology*, the editors of that text emphasize: "Beccaria's influence has been wide ranging since *On Crimes and Punishments* was first published." In fact, Beccaria's treatise has been described as "probably the most influential essay ever written on the subject."[62] After Beccaria's death in Milan in 1794, an obituary and remembrance later published in London specifically noted that *On Crimes and Punishments* had "raised its author to the pinnacle of fame" and that "few books ever produced so memorable a revolution in the human mind, in government, and in courts of justice."[63] Not only did Beccaria's then-novel, largely utilitarian views shape European and American penal codes, but Beccaria's treatise influenced thought on a whole range of subjects, including Americans' views of the right to bear arms, a right set forth in the U.S. Constitution's Second Amendment. As Saul Cornell writes in *A Well Regulated Militia*: "An admirer of the Italian Enlightenment theorist Cesare Beccaria, Jefferson endorsed Beccaria's observation that laws prohibiting individuals from carrying firearms only worked to the benefit of criminals." Beccaria's Romanesque, pro-republican views, urging equality of treatment yet supportive of penal labor, even shaped—at least indirectly—the drafting of the U.S. Constitution's Thirteenth Amendment, which abolished slavery except as a punishment for crime.[64]

On Crimes and Punishments, first published in 1764, is now approximately 250 years old. As Americans continue to debate the proper interpretation of the U.S. Constitution, it thus seems a fitting time to reexamine Beccaria's influence on America's founders and framers. Both "originalists" and "living constitutionalists," it turns out, have tried to capture Beccaria's legacy for their own policy or jurisprudential purposes. For example, in *Payne v. Tennessee*, a 1991 U.S. Supreme Court case, Chief Justice William Rehnquist—an advocate for curtailing habeas corpus rights—wrote the majority opinion, overruling prior cases from 1987 and 1989 and finding that the Constitution's Eighth Amendment did not prohibit sentencing juries from considering victim impact evidence. "The principles which have guided criminal sentencing—as opposed to criminal liability—have varied with the times," Rehnquist wrote, quoting Beccaria after making this observation: "The book of Exodus prescribes the Lex talionis, 'An eye for an eye, a tooth for a tooth.' Exodus 21:22–23. In England and on the continent of Europe, as recently as the 18th century, crimes which would be regarded as quite minor today were capital offenses." As Chief Justice Rehnquist spun Beccaria's 1764 text: "Writing in the 18th century, the Italian criminologist Cesare Beccaria advocated the idea that 'the punishment should fit the crime.'" By contrast, in *Furman v. Georgia*, the landmark case that temporarily put a halt to American executions, Justice Thurgood Marshall—in a concurring opinion—cited Beccaria for the proposition that "[p]unishment as retribution has been condemned by scholars for centuries." As a lawyer, Marshall—who saw executions as *per se* violations of the Eighth Amendment's Cruel and Unusual Punishments Clause—had represented men charged with capital offenses. When it comes to Beccaria's writings, a fair amount—it must be said—apparently lies in the eyes of the beholder.[65]

Though examining Beccaria's ideas—and their reception in eighteenth-century America—cannot answer the question of how *living* U.S. judges should interpret the Constitution, what history reveals with remarkable clarity is that Beccaria's ideas played a pivotal role in America's founding era and in shaping Anglo-American law. A 2011 biography of Cesare Beccaria, written by a London solicitor, John Hostettler, sums it up nicely, noting that Beccaria's treatise "had a crucial impact on the Constitution of the United States of America, its Bill of Rights and eventually the English criminal justice system."[66] For example, in London, a lawyer, Basil Montagu, authored *The Opinions of Different Authors on the Punishment of Death*, and, in the summer of 1808, in conjunction with Quaker philanthropist William Allen, Richard Phillips and others, formed a society for "the diffusion of knowledge upon the punishment of death." As one biographical sketch notes, Montagu's "efforts for the abolition of hanging for forgery and other crimes without violence, in conjunction with those of Sir Samuel Romilly, Mr. Wilberforce, and others, were at length rewarded by complete success." Montagu was Romilly's friend and a disciple of the utilitarian philosopher Jeremy Bentham, himself a Beccaria admirer.[67]

Indeed, to fully understand the American Revolution and the impulses that led to it, one must carefully study Enlightenment principles and Beccaria and Montesquieu in particular because those writers provided inspiration for that revolution. In *Struggle for American Independence*, historian Sydney George Fisher—writing of the founders' intellectual influences—explains of America's Declaration of Independence: "By understanding the writings of Burlamaqui, Locke and Beccaria, which the colonists were studying so intently, we know the origin of the Declaration and need not flounder in the dark, as so many have done, wondering where it came from, or how it was that Jefferson could have invented it." While Montesquieu's gift to American revolutionaries was to inspire separation of powers, Beccaria's major contribution—other than fomenting sentiment against British tyranny—was to ameliorate harsh criminal sanctions in the new republic. The Declaration of Independence, informed by a Beccarian spirit that carried Thomas Jefferson, a slaveholder, into the terrain of equality and human rights, created the United States of America out of thick, revolutionary air. In turn, the U.S. Constitution and its Bill of Rights—

those written bulwarks of liberty and justice for all—laid the groundwork for American government, enterprise, and the Rule of Law.

Abraham Lincoln—the Great Emancipator who watches over the U.S. Capitol from his perch at the Lincoln Memorial in Washington, D.C.—was himself exposed to Beccaria's ideas at an early age through Sir William Blackstone's *Commentaries on the Laws of England*. Just as the abolitionist Frederick Douglass viewed the rights to life, liberty and the pursuit of happiness as "the basis of all social and political right," President Lincoln viewed the Declaration of Independence—which proclaims those universal rights as "self-evident" truths—as America's premier foundational document. At his 1863 Gettysburg Address, President Lincoln highlighted the Declaration of Independence's primacy, declaring: "Four score and seven years ago our fathers brought forth on this continent, a new nation, conceived in Liberty, and dedicated to the proposition that all men are created equal." In an 1861 speech at Philadelphia's Independence Hall, President-elect Lincoln also forcefully declared: "I have never had a feeling politically that did not spring from the sentiments embodied in the Declaration of Independence."[68]

In rejecting British ideology and fighting for political independence, America's founders expressed their own steadfast belief in natural law principles and the idea of God-given rights. As intellectual ammunition, they did not just talk and search and rummage amongst themselves; instead, they thrived on reading Enlightenment authors, regardless of place of birth. Jean-Jacques Burlamaqui (1694–1748)—now a little-known figure—was a Swiss natural law and political theorist who had a major influence on America's founders; John Locke (1632–1704)—much better known today—was an English physician and philosopher whose writings influenced Voltaire and Rousseau as well as early American political leaders; and Beccaria—through his pioneering writings, with further inspiration closer to home from figures such as Thomas Paine—would, collectively, help stir Americans to agitation and action. "Beccaria," the historian Sydney George Fisher wrote, cataloging the Italian philosopher's now underappreciated American influence, "stated most beautifully and clearly the essential principles of liberty." As Fisher explained of Beccaria: "His foundation doctrine, that 'every act of authority of one man over another for which there is not absolute necessity is tyrannical,' made a most profound impression in America. He laid down also the principle that 'in every human society there is an effort continually tending to confer on one part the highest power and happiness, and to reduce the other to the extreme of weakness and misery.'" Those principles, Fisher notes of the complex historical events that led to the Revolutionary War, helped inspire America's "checks and balances" and became "the life-long guide of many Americans" and "a constituent part of the minds of Jefferson and Hamilton."[69]

Ultimately, early American political leaders—wanting to cast off tyranny but still the product of eighteenth-century upbringings and traditions—were unwilling to totally outlaw executions. They found Beccaria's ideas about proportionality extremely appealing, but those ideas—propounded in an era of slavery and brutal corporal punishments—had yet to be tested in practice. And because of the lack of developed prison facilities in the 1770s, pursuing reform along the specific lines Beccaria proposed was not so easy for either European or American lawmakers. In the United States, where the Revolutionary War raged into the 1780s, making reform especially difficult, there was not even yet sufficient infrastructure—in terms of secure prisons—to try to fully implement, or experiment with, those ideas. Accustomed to rigid English sentencing practices, with colonial lawyers trained within England's custom-bound, common-law tradition, early American lawmakers struggled mightily with how—and if—to put Beccaria's ideas into practice. For many, abandoning executions altogether, especially for the crimes of treason and murder, was seen as a step too far. The customary English punishment for many offenses was to be hanged, and the notion of abolishing the gallows entirely seemed too imprudent for a majority of eighteenth-century American legislators. Instead, they decided to keep death penalty laws on the books, at least for certain classes of offenders. But even in the late eighteenth century, some Americans—inspired by Beccaria and his many disciples—were willing to rid society of executions, or at least consider the prospect that more experience and evidence might be gathered to warrant that step. In spite of this major societal disagreement, pitting abolitionists against retentionists, a consensus was reached in many places that less serious offenders—thieves, for example—should not suffer the state's ultimate sanction.[70]

The Birth of American Law—the product of much archival and online research, made possible through the digitization of early English and American sources—describes this all-too-human contest of wills. It shows how American laws were influenced by *On Crimes and Punishments* and by the feisty debate over the state of the law it inspired. Provisions of the U.S. Bill of Rights were copied from English law, in some cases nearly verbatim, with its conservative, common-law tradition. But Beccaria's treatise—written in continental Europe and in a civil law locale—nonetheless materially informed the Founding Fathers' attitudes and views of such provisions. For instance, the U.S. Constitution's Eighth Amendment—based on language in the English Bill of Rights of 1689 and its American counterpart, the Virginia Declaration of Rights of 1776—does not say what particular punishments qualify as "cruel and unusual." Beccaria's ideas, though, clearly shaped the founders' understanding of cruelty. Likewise, early American state constitutions barring "cruel," "unusual" or "sanguinary" punishments do not say what specifically qualifies as such; instead, America's founding era provisions variously bar such penalties only in general terms, without making a laundry list of what conduct is barred under them. If there is uncertainty today as to what the Founding Fathers meant by those terms, and there certainly is, it seems equally clear that there was also disagreement over the meaning of such legal provisions even at the time of their eighteenth-century enactments.[71]

This book—a study of Cesare Beccaria's legacy—traces the rise of Beccaria's influence in what became, in 1776, the United States of America, a country the travel-wary Beccaria never had the chance to see for himself. The Italian Enlightenment produced an array of prominent scientists, philosophers, and writers, and *On Crimes and Punishments* was one post-Renaissance text that attracted special attention. Beccaria's treatise—an eighteenth-century bestseller read, debated and discussed by lawyers and non-lawyers alike[72]—was regularly found on bookshelves and in libraries on both sides of the Atlantic as the Enlightenment caught fire.[73] The subject of considerable English and American commentary,[74] Beccaria's book was—the evidence shows—frequently offered for sale by leading English and American booksellers, with Beccaria's ideas becoming deeply embedded in the American mind.[75] By the time the U.S. Constitution and the U.S. Bill of Rights were ratified in, respectively, the late 1780s and early 1790s, Beccaria had become a familiar name, with his fame extending across the coming decades as even more English subjects and American citizens read his treatise.

Beccaria's ideas shaped Anglo-American thoughts on both governmental policies and government itself. In discussing "human nature" in *A Defence of the Constitutions of Government of the United States of America* (1787–1788), John Adams first invoked Montesquieu for the proposition that "every man invested with power is apt to abuse it," pushing on "till he comes to something that limits him." Adams also cited Montesquieu for the idea that "[t]o prevent the abuse of power, it is necessary, that, by the very disposition of things, power should be a check to power." But Adams then specifically cited Beccaria and quoted from *On Crimes and Punishments*, recording in Italian: "*Ogni uomo si fa centro di tutte le combinazioni del globo.*" The translation of that sentence, part of a larger work that also discussed the abuse of capital punishment by ancient republics: "Every man makes himself the center of his whole world."[76] In *Thoughts on the Punishment of Death for Forgery*, published in London in 1830, the British jurist and barrister Basil Montagu—the prominent social reformer—continued, like so many Americans of his day, to advocate for law reform, referring to Beccaria multiple times in that new title.[77] By the 1830s, in fact, America's anti-death penalty movement—with Beccaria providing much of the inspiration at the grassroots level—had gathered considerable momentum. Another source, published in 1837 and titled *The Punishment of Death*, quotes Beccaria on the title page and also makes multiple references to him, including one to "the enlightened Beccaria."[78] Such references and encomiums—such enthusiastic praise—typifies the respect accorded Beccaria and his treatise many decades ago.[79]

The Birth of American Law lays bare the choices the Founding Fathers made as regards U.S. law and penal reform in particular. Sources that both pre-date and post-date the adoption of the U.S. Constitution and the subsequent ratification of the U.S. Bill of Rights in 1791, show how Beccaria's ideas infiltrated U.S. society, took root and shaped lawmakers' choices. The book specifically demonstrates how the Italian philosopher's writings impacted America's political climate, its social and legal culture, and the debate over America's earliest laws. One principle Beccaria set forth in *On Crimes and Punishments*—that the *certainty* of punishment is more important than its *severity*—was especially popular with a number of America's founders.[80] Thus, *On Crimes and Punishments* not only shaped criminal justice reform in Europe, Beccaria's place of residence, but it played a major role in the United States as its political leaders—expressing their heart-felt sentiments in early American constitutions and statutes—sought to strip punishments of their "sanguinary" or "cruel" hue.[81] A review of early U.S. writings reveals just how significantly Beccaria's ideas on infamy, and topics as diverse as happiness, dueling, the right to trial by jury, gun ownership, and the deterrence of crime, shaped American laws.[82] This book, both on a macro and a micro level, seeks to contextualize that impact while also showing how Beccaria's ideas on education and crime prevention affected American political debate for generations after their appearance.

To set the stage, the book begins by telling Beccaria's personal story. The book then goes on to describe the reception and legacy of Beccaria's writings, first in Europe and then in the United States. Chapter 1 thus presents a sketch of Cesare Beccaria's life in what later became a unified Italy, and of the book, *On Crimes and Punishments*, that brought him so much fame. That treatise was first published anonymously for fear of persecution, though after royal figures in Europe praised it and Beccaria's authorship became clear, Beccaria's identity was revealed and he was hailed as an enlightened reformer. Chapter 2 then recounts how *On Crimes and Punishments* first came to America and how, in the fertile soil of the pre-Revolutionary War period, it gained an audience and popularity there. "Beccaria, the Italian reformer of the eighteenth century," one writer explained in 1912, "was the first one to arouse public sentiment against the judicial cruelties of the times, while his contemporary, John Howard, the English reformer, was the first to suggest that prisons (which up to that time had been used merely as places of detention for the accused awaiting trial, and the condemned awaiting execution) might be utilized for purposes of punishment, and also for reformation."[83] The fact that John Adams looked to both Montesquieu and Beccaria in mounting his defense of the U.S. legal system in the 1780s shows just how important—indeed, indispensable—Enlightenment writers were to America's founders.

Just as Montesquieu's writings—as one scholar notes—"had a profound influence on Cesare Beccaria,"[84] Beccaria's treatise made a lasting impression on a whole host of Enlightenment thinkers. The long arm of Beccaria's reach included America's most influential founders and framers, men such as George Washington, John Adams, Thomas Jefferson and James Madison, as well as Europeans like Jeremy Bentham (1748–1832) and John Howard (1726–1790) whose writings were well known in America. "Most influential of all," Steven Pinker writes of the Age of Reason and Enlightenment humanism, "was the Milanese economist and social scientist Cesare Beccaria, whose 1764 bestseller *On Crimes and Punishments* influenced every major political thinker in the literate world, including Voltaire, Denis Diderot, Thomas Jefferson, and John Adams." "Beccaria," Pinker notes, "began from first principles, namely that the goal of a system of justice is to attain 'the greatest happiness of the greatest number' (a phrase later adopted by Jeremy Bentham as the motto of utilitarianism)."[85] Bentham himself called Beccaria "the father of Censorial Jurisprudence"—"the first thinker," as Beccaria scholar Richard Bellamy puts it, "to attempt a critical or 'censorial', as opposed to a merely expository, account of the law."[86] The French *philosophes* Denis Diderot (1713–1784) and Jean-Antoine Nicolas de Caritat de Condorcet (1743–1794) likewise greatly admired Beccaria's work, as did John Howard, the English sheriff who visited prisons across England, Scotland and Wales, exposing the horrendous conditions within gaols and campaigning for change. In the climate of the Enlightenment, Beccaria, like his disciples Howard and Bentham, gathered many accolades from early American political leaders.[87]

In later chapters, *The Birth of American Law* discusses in greater detail how Beccaria's treatise specifically influenced America's founding generation throughout the original thirteen British colonies and, later, the newly formed country, the United States. In particular, Chapter 3 highlights the influence Beccaria's treatise had on the foremost military, social, religious and political leaders who lived during America's founding era. For example, in Pennsylvania, Beccaria's writings inspired men such as Dr. Benjamin Rush and James Wilson, both signers of the Declaration of Independence. Both men would go on to play prominent roles—along with William Bradford, Jr.—in advocating for American penal reform. In Massachusetts, John Adams—who drafted the world's oldest continuously operating constitution, the Massachusetts Constitution of 1780 that bars "cruel or unusual punishments"—not only owned Beccaria's treatise but prominently utilized it in his work as a lawyer. And in Virginia, Thomas Jefferson—who, following Adams' presidency, became the third U.S. president—also closely studied Beccaria's treatise in the 1770s and repeatedly consulted it while preparing what Virginia's founders considered a long-overdue revisal of Virginia's antiquated penal laws.[88]

The Birth of American Law describes how the uncertainty and chaos of the colonial period and the Revolutionary War gave way, due in part to Beccaria's ideas, to what jurists today would refer to as the Rule of Law. Though law reform played out differently in their respective locales, both English and American social reformers were almost magnetically drawn to Beccaria's work, which advocated precise, easily understood legal codes and the milder punishment of offenders. In place of runaway judicial discretion, frequent executions and the shameful abuses of notorious jurists like Lord Chief Justice George Jeffreys of the King's Bench, Enlightenment thinkers sought a more rational and predictable style of justice. Whereas British penal reformer Samuel Romilly did not succeed in repealing English laws punishing small thefts with death until 1808, some American politicians—as highlighted in the chapters that follow—successfully pushed for the abolition of death sentences for such crimes much earlier.[89] Romilly, who met Beccaria's French translator, André Morellet, as well as John Adams and Thomas Jefferson at a dinner on April 15, 1786, at the London home of the British radical Thomas Brand Hollis, was—like Jefferson—fascinated by Beccaria's ideas. Taken with what he had read in *On Crimes and Punishments*, Romilly repeatedly invoked Beccaria and noted the "cruelty" of death sentences for crimes other than murder.[90]

The last half of the eighteenth century was, to be sure, a time of great social and political upheaval, with both the American and French Revolutions transpiring in that period. The Founding Fathers, bitterly resentful of British tyranny and oppression, were inspired to fight for their independence by Thomas Paine's *Common Sense* but also by Enlightenment writers such as Montesquieu and Beccaria. The Continental Congress threw caution aside in issuing its Declaration of Independence on July 4, 1776, with America's founders pledging their lives, their fortunes, and their sacred honor to the cause of self-determination. Prior to the onset of the Revolutionary War, America's founders—faced with the Stamp Act and the Intolerable Acts—grappled with how to handle what they saw as the abuse of their rights as Englishmen, then decided to break away from their mother country, leaving big divisions within the society as British loyalists saw their neighbors become full-fledged Americans. America's founders also showed antipathy and distaste for Great Britain's Parliament and the British monarchy's oppressive "Bloody Code," which made scores of crimes—even relatively minor ones—punishable by death. For example, shooting a rabbit, disturbing a fishpond or killing or maiming cattle could result in a death sentence. In commenting on a commodore's letter to the secretary of the Navy in 1816, Richard Rush—Dr. Benjamin Rush's son and then the Attorney General of the United States—was still lamenting four decades after independence that the U.S. government had, at least in certain respects, "copied, closely enough, the bloody code of England."

Inspired by the writings of Montesquieu, Beccaria and others, early Americans sought to forge a new approach to law and to the relationship of members of society to it. Highly suspicious of concentrated power, they set up the U.S. Constitution's much-heralded system of checks and balances. They also grappled with whether English common-law principles should be adopted, altered or discarded in American society, and through their constitutions and statutes, they took a much more enlightened approach to the criminal law than that taken by England's tyrannical monarchy. "Americans launched a polemic attack upon English criminal codes," law professor Steven Wilf writes in *Law's Imagined Republic: Popular Politics and Criminal Justice in Revolutionary America*. "Criticism of the Bloody Code became commonplace in American writings of the 1780s and 1790s," he notes. As Wilf explains, "It was found everywhere: newspapers, periodicals, letters, charges to grand juries, and political pamphlets."[91] Ultimately, Americans chose to retain a common-law system, but they rejected those portions of the English common-law that did not suit their purposes or that, to them, seemed antiquated.[92] Americans also adopted *written* constitutions and penal codes in moving away from an overdependence and reliance on custom and discretion, an approach subject to the vagaries and whims of individual decision makers. While Chapter 4 of *The Birth of American Law* discusses the specific reforms Beccaria's book inspired, Chapter 5 highlights the rise of America's penitentiary system—a system in which hard labor and life sentences, along with solitary confinement, came to be seen as viable and indispensable alternatives to "cruel" and "sanguinary" death sentences.

Following the book's review of Beccaria's influence on American civic leaders and the creation of the penitentiary system, Chapter 6 then describes Beccaria's broader impact on American law—and the legacy *On Crimes and Punishments* left behind for future generations to consider. Beccaria's writings played an influential role at both the state and federal levels, and this final chapter of *The Birth of American Law* discusses Beccaria's material contributions across the spectrum to American debate and political and legal discourse. In particular, Chapter 6 discusses how Beccaria's views shaped the founders' understanding of the Declaration of Independence, the U.S. Constitution's First, Second and Fifth Amendments[93] and the Eighth Amendment bar against "cruel and unusual punishments." The latter proscription, derived from its similarly worded English and Virginia predecessors, is found in many state constitutions, albeit in different textual variants.[94] As Pulitzer Prize-winning historian Gordon Wood emphasizes: "Many of the Revolutionary state constitutions of 1776 evoked the enlightened thinking of the Italian reformer Cesare Beccaria and promised to end punishments that were 'cruel and unusual' and to make them 'less sanguinary, and in general more proportionate to the crimes.'" While state-law provisions differ slightly, variously prohibiting "cruel," "cruel or unusual," "cruel and unusual," or "sanguinary" punishments, the aversion to inhumane treatment of criminals—an aversion spawned in large part by Beccaria's treatise—is readily apparent.[95]

The Birth of American Law concludes by putting Beccaria's legacy—including his continuing influence on American law—in context. A Scottish Enlightenment painter, Allan Ramsay, once dismissed Beccaria's treatise, *Dei delitti e delle pene*, by placing it into "the category of Utopias," books that display, he claimed, "the wit, the humanity and the goodness of their authors, but which never have had nor ever will have any influence on human affairs."[96] But *On Crimes and Punishments*—a book that inspired a whole generation of revolutionaries—was destined to reframe and forever reshape Anglo-American law. And it did so in multiple ways, in both the Founding Fathers' time and beyond. Beccaria's treatise led to serious reevaluation of past practices and to consideration of alternatives to death sentences, and it also led to the curtailment of American executions, particularly for non-homicide offenses.[97] Over time, *mandatory* death penalty statutes—the norm in America's founding era, and that *required* the execution of delineated convicted felons—came to be seen as too rigid and morally unacceptable. In their place, such statutes—on a state-by-state basis—were replaced in the U.S. by discretionary sentencing schemes, with Americans engaging in other significant law reform over time. As eighteenth-century novels, through their use of detail, humanized people of all backgrounds, races and creeds, even criminals, or what Heidelberg University fellow Anthony Santoro calls "the other," *On Crimes and Punishments*—Beccaria's work of non-fiction—became a go-to source for readers thinking about human rights issues.[98]

People across the globe, as Christof Heyns, a South African law professor and human rights scholar, has documented, have long struggled for basic human rights. Though wars have often impeded their realization, the American Revolution was a time of particular struggle, with the quest for peace and recognition of the inalienable "rights of man" proceeding amidst horrific bloodshed. If the War of 1812 (1812–1815) hindered American criminal-law reform, such reform came to a screeching halt with the onset of the Civil War (1861–1865). That latter war shook America to its core, took hundreds of thousands of lives, and—to a large extent—made Beccaria's writings seem less relevant. With innocents dying on a regular basis on the battlefield, the fate of criminals and convicted killers took a back seat. The changes in American law that the Civil War brought about—the so-called Reconstruction Amendments—did, however, rekindle the promise of the Declaration of Independence. And those constitutional amendments thus echoed back to what Beccaria had written about more than a century before, that is, equality of treatment and the notion of the perpetual enslavement of offenders. The Thirteenth Amendment, approved in 1865, abolished slavery and involuntary servitude "except as a punishment for crime"; and the Fourteenth Amendment, ratified in 1868, guaranteed "equal protection of the laws," a protection that fundamentally altered U.S. law by—among other things—making the U.S. Bill of Rights applicable to the states. Long before those Reconstruction Amendments, *On Crimes and Punishments* had magnified the Founding Fathers' own awareness of the dangers of inquisitorial practices and shaped a consensus against torture. Beccaria's support for "perpetual slavery"—life imprisonment in today's terms—had itself led America's founders to consider the viability of that option, especially as Beccaria's ideas on proportionality began to be flushed out by other Enlightenment writers more focused on the design and maintenance of prison facilities.

Many of Beccaria's ideas were, plainly, inspired by other thinkers such as Montesquieu and Francis Hutcheson[99] and later refined by other writers. But it is equally clear that Beccaria's writings—however indebted to others' earlier prose—fundamentally reshaped Anglo-American practices and America's socio-legal landscape.[100] The British philosopher Jeremy Bentham—who, in 1776, in *A Fragment on Government*, had effusively praised Beccaria[101]—would go on to promote an innovative prison design, befriend Aaron Burr and other American revolutionaries, and write to President James Madison in 1811 to offer to draft a comprehensive U.S. legal code.[102] Bentham's prison design—known as the Panopticon—envisioned a circular penitentiary allowing prison guards at the center to constantly monitor the prisoners in their cells.[103] Madison decided not to engage the services of Bentham, a foreigner, to draft and codify U.S. laws, but Americans—receptive to innovation—nevertheless built a number of penitentiaries in the years after the signing of the U.S. Constitution, coming up with their own designs in the wake of the publication of the writings of Beccaria and his reform-minded disciples. Indeed, in thinking about penal reform issues, leading American social reformers—among them, William Bradford, Jr. and Dr. Benjamin Rush of Philadelphia—routinely looked to Beccaria for guidance. William Eden's *Principles of Penal Law* (1771) and William Howard's *The State of the Prisons in England and Wales* (1777) both cited Beccaria's treatise multiple times, as did other eighteenth-century writers, as was then extremely common.[104]

Since *On Crimes and Punishments* was published two and half centuries ago, it is especially fitting now to look back—and to simultaneously look ahead—at what Beccaria's ideas have meant, and may still mean, for American law. In particular, *The Birth of American Law* seeks to answer a series of questions: How did Beccaria's views alter America's social and legal landscape, especially as regards penal reform and how lawmakers viewed their societal role? What impact did Beccaria's ideas have on America's founders? Have American courts properly read and interpreted constitutional provisions, including the Eighth Amendment's prohibition against "cruel and unusual punishments," in a manner consistent with the founders' understanding? And after the Fourteenth Amendment's ratification, and in light of the general wording of the Cruel and Unusual Punishments Clause, is that even the right question at this juncture? America's founders, as well as Beccaria himself, died well before the Civil War and the subsequent ratification of the Fourteenth Amendment, forcing a full-throated exploration of that question. Because Beccaria's treatise played such an important role in the origins of American law, a reassessment of the scope of that influence seems particularly warranted. This is especially so since a number of the U.S. Supreme Court's decisions—in the Eighth Amendment context in particular—are decided by 5 to 4 votes.[105]

Exploring the origins of American law can sometimes lead to more questions than answers, especially when one treads into the treacherous territory of constitutional interpretation—a terrain that pits "originalists" against "living constitutionalists" and that has spawned such terminology as "textualists" and "strict constructionists." Beccaria's book forthrightly spoke of "equal punishments," and the Declaration of Independence, drafted by Jefferson when slavery was still prevalent, spoke of "all men" being "created equal."[106] Yet, the guarantee of "equal protection of the laws" was not added to the Constitution, via the Fourteenth Amendment, until long after America's founders had all passed away. Jefferson and Madison—the men most responsible for the Declaration of Independence and the U.S. Bill of Rights—both owned slaves, as did George Washington, the country's first commander-in-chief, so equal treatment under the law never came anywhere close to fruition in the founding period.[107] Given that American law has evolved in fundamental ways since America's founding and Beccaria's time, what should the history of the origins of American law actually tell us? And how, if at all, should such history guide us, the living? More specifically, what does the proliferation of American penitentiaries—a development started, but not finished, in the Founding Fathers' time—mean for America's death penalty and the future of penal reform? And how, if at all, should Americans in the twenty-first century take into consideration Beccaria's ideas and principles?

Chapter 1

Cesare Beccaria: "The Celebrated Marquis"

Pioneering Abolitionist

The death penalty's use throughout human history, to persecute religious minorities or to kill political dissidents or criminals, is well documented. "During the first three centuries of the Christian era," writes Davison Douglas, a William and Mary law professor, "the question of the death penalty was quite real for Christians as they were frequent victims of Roman executions, particularly during the reigns of Emperors Decius and Diocletian in the third and fourth centuries." But early Christians—even after coming to power—also used state-sanctioned killing, examining the issue through the lens of the Old Testament and various biblical passages. "When Emperor Constantine converted to Christianity during the early fourth century and established Christianity as the official religion of the Roman Empire," Douglas explains, "Christian views on capital punishment took on greater significance." While Constantine issued decrees against heretics and pagans and non-sanctioned views on religion were punishable by death, early legal codes solidified the death penalty's use for a wide array of offenses. The fifth-century Theodosian Code had 120 provisions mandating death, and the sixth century's Justinian Code—to use Douglas' words—"went even further," with Emperor Justinian using the death penalty "to crush religious dissenters." "Three centuries later," Douglas notes, "Emperor Leo V is estimated to have killed over 100,000 Paulician heretics."

A few early Christians, rulers and dissenters opposed executions.[1] As far back as the mid-1600s, for example, some radical English dissidents—the equality- and tolerance-seeking Levellers and, later, the Quakers—had suggested the death penalty's abolition or curtailment. But the Italian philosopher Cesare Beccaria—who provided, in one historian's words, "a systemic argument in favor of abolition"—is widely credited as the first Enlightenment thinker to call for the death penalty's abolition.[2] "The late eighteenth century," legal historian Lawrence Friedman writes, "was a period in which intellectuals began to rethink the premises on which criminal law rested." In that respect, Beccaria—like his French predecessor, Montesquieu—was a pioneer. As Friedman writes: "Great reformers—men like Cesare Beccaria, whose *Treatise on Crime and Punishment* was written in Italy in 1764—suggested that at least some of the premises were wrong and argued for a more enlightened criminal law."[3] In his treatise, Beccaria asserted: "the purpose of punishment is not that of tormenting or afflicting any sentient creature, nor of undoing a crime already committed." "Can the wailings of a wretch," he asked rhetorically, "undo what has been done and turn back the clock?" As Beccaria emphasized: "The purpose, therefore, is nothing other than to prevent the offender from doing fresh harm to his fellows and to deter others from doing likewise. Therefore, punishments and the means adopted for inflicting them should, consistent with proportionality, be so selected as to make the most efficacious and lasting impression on the minds of men with the least torment to the body of the condemned."[4] This kind of thinking sparked a wholesale reevaluation of the efficacy of bodily punishments, including the death penalty.

Prior to the publication of Beccaria's book, various ancient legal codes—from the Code of Hammurabi to the Code of Draco, and from Rome's Twelve Tables to the Justinian Code—had made a wide array of offenses, both serious and small, punishable by death.[5] While modern-day Italy, a death penalty-free country, now lights up the Roman Coliseum every time another state or country abolishes capital punishment, at one time under Roman law scores of offenses were punishable by death. Among the numerous crimes that warranted death under Roman law were treason, homicide, theft, sacrilege, arson, counterfeiting, perjury, sodomy, libel and rape. Unchaste vestal virgins were buried alive and murderers, traitors and false witnesses were thrown off the Tarpeian Rock, a popular execution site, in ancient Rome. And on such occasions, the intentional infliction of pain had been very much on the punishment agenda and on the minds of emperors and monarchs. Among others, Roman methods of execution ranged from decapitation to burning to crucifixion, the latter punishment often inflicted on slaves.[6] The ancient Greek lawgiver Solon (c. 658–560 B.C.) had once curtailed the severity of Draco's Grecian laws, which made even minor offenses punishable by death. But Solon's code—which still punished murder and treason with death—was temporal in nature and did not survive.[7] Once Beccaria's *Dei delitti e delle pene* appeared in Tuscany, a place that had seen its own share of executions, it thus quickly generated debate and controversy, sparking self-reflection and penal reform across the globe as it was translated into twenty-two languages.[8]

The English-speaking world, with its pre-existing, common-law tradition of affording criminals jury trials and habeas corpus rights, was no exception. Great Britain, which got the English translation of Beccaria's treatise, *An Essay on Crimes and Punishments*, in 1767, was slower to act in initiating large-scale criminal law reform, though reforms would eventually come. In contrast, Americans—long under the boot of England's oppressive monarchy, and ready to free themselves of tyranny and taxation without representation—were highly receptive to Beccaria's principles from the outset. In *A Defence of the Constitutions*, John Adams—who broke with British loyalists to side with those favoring American independence—compared "the laws of Draco" with those of "Solon, of an ancient royal family," and spoke of "arbitrary sentences of death." Noting that Draco had once been appointed as "a lawgiver," Adams emphasized that Draco's approach was "that of inflicting capital punishments in all offences" and that "the laws of Draco were written in blood"—a state of affairs, Adams remarked, "which struck the imagination and touched the heart, and therefore, soon rendered this system unpopular." "Solon's reputation for wisdom and integrity was universal," Adams wrote.

John Adams—no stranger to thinking about the criminal law and to looking for ideas on how to prevent crime—was part of the receptive American audience for Beccaria's treatise. "We cannot presume," Adams had observed elsewhere in *A Defence of the Constitutions*, "that a man is good or bad, merely because his father was one or the other; and we should always inform ourselves first, whether the virtues and talents are inherited, before we yield our confidence." After recounting the story of a "young woman" who "was lately convicted at Paris of a trifling theft, barely within the law which decreed a capital punishment," Adams noted that she had refused a pardon and insisted on being hanged because her grandfather, father and brother "were all hanged for stealing." In wrestling with the nature of crime and the propensity of offenders to be shaped by their upbringings, Adams mused: "An hereditary passion for the halter is a strong instance, to be sure, and cannot be very common; but something like it too often descends, in certain breeds, from generation to generation."[9] The whole concept of *corruption of blood*, in fact, served to strip offenders' would-be heirs of inheritance and property rights. The idea was that a person's blood was tainted through the commission of a crime. Under the medieval English law of "deodand," when an animal or inanimate object caused the death of someone, that animal or object was, itself, actually automatically forfeited to the Crown. Convicted felons—under a process known as *attainder*—forfeited chattels to the Crown and their land reverted to the local lord, with a felon's heirs losing any right to their ancestor's property under the doctrine of corruption of blood.[10]

Beccaria's more rational ideas took time to filter out to the wider world, but not too long, as *On Crimes and Punishments* was quickly translated and reprinted in multiple locales. The first Italian edition, consisting of 104 numbered pages, appeared in opera librettist Marco Coltellini's Livorno printing office in July 1764 and was published anonymously. The father of a famous soprano, Coltellini—as one source reports—had acquired that printing shop "in 1763, probably with English funds, and which between 1770 and 1779 was to publish the third edition of the *Encyclopédie*."[11] That Leghorn edition of Beccaria's treatise was edited by Giuseppe Aubert, described in one book as "the printer and man of letters" who "directed Marco Coltellini's printing shop until 1770." A second "pirated" Italian edition, produced by Andrea Bonducci, was released in Florence a few months later; and a third Italian edition was, once more, printed in Coltellini's Livorno printing office.[12] Some of the later editions published by the Coltellini press were produced under the direction of Tommaso Masi, though without the author's name and using a false imprint.[13] In a place where the Inquisition and censorship went hand in hand, publishing could be a risky and dangerous endeavor, making anonymous authorship an attractive option. In the sixteenth century, a court of the Inquisition had been established in Milan, Parma, Tuscany, Venice, and other Italian states, with an inquisitor sent from Rome and death sentences handed out by that body. Even if offenders were not executed, they faced severe consequences, including torture and corporal punishments, for any writings that ran afoul of ecclesiastical tastes.[14]

As word of Beccaria's treatise spread beyond Italian states, the excitement over it grew and the book got reprinted elsewhere, too. A French translation, prepared by André Morellet in 1765, was titled *Traité des délits et des peines*; a Swedish translation was published in 1770; and German translations appeared in Hamburg as early as 1766 and a year later in Ulm, with still another German translation appearing in 1778.[15] The latter translation, printed in Breslau and translated from the Italian, was titled *Des Herren Marquis von Beccaria unsterbliches Werk von Verbrechen und Strafen*.[16] Morellet—who radically reorganized the book for his French translation, transposing entire paragraphs and sentences within paragraphs—was a French *philosophe* who lived in Paris and was a contributor to the famed Enlightenment era *Encyclopédie*.[17] Thomas Jefferson would later meet Morellet in the summer of 1785 at the Château de La Roche-Guyon in Normandy, and after giving Morellet a copy of his *Notes on the State of Virginia*, Morellet pleaded with Jefferson to let him translate it.[18] Although Morellet and Beccaria exchanged letters near the end of 1765, Morellet completed his translation of *Dei delitti e delle pene* without consulting Beccaria in advance. When Morellet's translation of Beccaria's book was printed it falsely mentioned Lausanne—rather than Paris—as the place of publication. Morellet's "reorganized French version" of Beccaria's treatise, it has been noted, was frequently the source of other foreign translations of the treatise.

The celebrated Voltaire, meanwhile, prepared his own complimentary commentary on Beccaria's treatise, offering up to the public as early as September 1766 his *Commentaire sur le Traité des Délits et des Peines*. "Voltaire's decision to write a commentary on this work," explains Nicholas Cronk, the general editor of the *Complete Works of Voltaire*, "was motivated in part by his genuine engagement with the issues of political justice which it raised—and in part too by a desire to seize the moment and to exploit, and even share some part of, Beccaria's success." "Very quickly," Cronk writes, "publishers with an eye on the market began producing combined editions, in which Voltaire's commentary follows Beccaria's text—no matter that Voltaire's 'commentary' is not really a commentary at all—and it was in this form that Voltaire's text became known to the English reading public." That commentary, as another scholar explains, warmly congratulated the young Milanese philosopher on his literary achievement. The commentary, signed *par un avocate de province* ("by a provincial lawyer"), may have been researched—and perhaps even written in part— by Voltaire's younger friend, the lawyer Charles-Gabriel Frédéric Christin. While its first English translation, produced in 1767, says the commentary is "attributed" to Voltaire, after 1778 the translations simply say the commentary is "by" Voltaire. One English translator addressed the authorship issue this way: "With regard to the Commentary, attributed to Monsieur de Voltaire, my only authority for supposing it to be his, is the voice of the public, which indeed is the only authority we have for most of his works. Let those who are acquainted with the peculiarity of his manner judge for themselves."[19]

The Italian Philosopher

Born in Milan in 1738, Cesare Beccaria was the eldest son of an aristocratic family in Lombardy, then part of the Habsburgs' Austrian Empire. In 1740, the Austrian monarch, Maria Theresa, succeeded her father, Holy Roman Emperor Charles VI (1685–1740), the same year that Frederick II ascended to the throne in Prussia.[20] The daughter of Charles VI, Maria Theresa—who reigned from 1740 to 1780—was immediately forced to defend her throne in the War of Austrian Succession (1740–1748), in which her empire fought France, Spain, Prussia and other German states. As rulers, Maria Theresa and her son Joseph II—the Holy Roman Emperor from 1765 to 1790 and who, following his mother's death, reigned over the Habsburg dominions from 1780 to 1790—began a series of penal reforms. Inspired in part by Beccaria's writings, some of those reforms—initiated in an era rife with vicious bodily punishments—related to the treatment of criminals and criminal suspects. When Maria Theresa came to power, those accused of crimes were commonly tortured to extract confessions, a practice then widespread in continental Europe. But in 1776, in the post-*On Crimes and Punishments* era, she abolished torture in lands she controlled. In 1762, Voltaire—the French writer and social activist—had railed against the breaking on the wheel of Jean Calas, a French Protestant wrongfully convicted of murdering his son and then tortured and brutally put to death. It was only after the publication of Beccaria's treatise—a book written shortly after the Calas execution that had so captivated Europe—that Maria Theresa took the initiative and abolished torture.[21]

A Roman Catholic and a voracious reader of philosophy,[22] Beccaria went to a Jesuit school in Parma before attending the University of Pavia from 1754 to 1758.[23] In the latter year, Beccaria received his law degree, the product of a traditional—and rather stifling and conservative—educational experience. Because Italy had not yet been unified, it was a German tribe, the Lombards, which gave Beccaria's native region, Lombardy, its name.[24] The Governor-General of Lombardy, Count Karl Joseph Firmian (1716–1782), was from a prominent family in Salzburg and was posted as a minister to Milan by Maria Theresa. There, he regularly interacted with locals as well as artists and musicians such as Wolfgang Amadeus Mozart, who first performed there in 1770. Count Firmian was a patron of the arts, understood multiple languages, and his library contained some 40,000 books. Mozart performed several times at the count's home, with one commentator, Charles Burney, calling the cultured and reform-minded Count Firmian, the Austrian minister plenipotentiary, "a sort of King of Milan."[25] As one encyclopedia describes this period of rule: "In Lombardy the administration of Maria Theresa and of her minister Count Firmian was a period of returning happiness for that fine country, after the vicissitudes of the preceding wars and the previous long misrule of the Spanish governors."[26] Beccaria, a Milan native, "lived in the region of Italy with the greatest ties with France and Britain," notes one text, with Beccaria—as that source explains—"much influenced by the Encyclopedists," who in turn later quoted Beccaria "with noisy praise, to the world."[27]

When Beccaria's *Dei delitti e delle pene* was first published in 1764, a review of the laws in the Habsburgs' territory was already underway. A codification of the civil law had been ordered in 1753, with a draft of the so-called *Codex Theresianus* and a draft penal code, *Nemesis Theresiana*, presented to Empress Maria Theresa in 1766. "The draft penal code," notes historian Franz A. J. Szabo, "was considerably more progressive than the old code of Charles VI, but it retained provisions for such cruel forms of capital punishment as being burned alive or drawn and quartered, and it sanctioned the judicial torture of suspects in capital crimes." In places such as England, France and Spain, drawing and quartering and burning at the stake were also still in use. In that European milieu, the Vienna-born diplomat, Prince Wenzel Anton von Kauntiz-Rietberg, a trusted confidante of Maria Theresa, suggested revisions to the draft codex. In response, the empress—who personally reviewed all capital cases to see if clemency was warranted—ordered that changes be made. A reexamination of the laws ensued, a battle that ended in a stalemate in Maria Theresa's time between hard-line conservatives and reformers, thus spilling over into Joseph II's reign.[28] Joseph II (1741–1790)—whose sister, Marie Antoinette, was famously guillotined in France in 1793—ruled for a decade following his mother's death and saw himself as a reformer.[29] As one source puts it: "Joseph II was a zealous reformer, having imbibed, like Frederick the Great, the principles of philosophy which prevailed in that age."[30]

As a young man, Beccaria had devoured Montesquieu's *Persian Letters*, Rousseau's *The Social Contract*, and many other books by French, English and Scottish Enlightenment writers.[31] In *The Spirit of Laws*, first published anonymously in 1748 under the supervision of Jacob Vernet in Geneva as *De l'esprit des lois*, Montesquieu had surveyed the criminal-law practices of nations. Though he did not recommend abandoning executions altogether, Montesquieu had advocated for less severe criminal codes. In his book, which the Anglo-Irish writer and scholar Thomas Nugent had translated into English in 1750, with successive reprints in 1751, 1752, 1756 and 1758, Montesquieu thus presented the case for criminal law reform, contending that certain crimes, then punishable by torturous deaths, should no longer be punished in that fashion.[32] "It certainly comes as no surprise, therefore," explains University of Tennessee political scientist David Carrithers, "that Cesare Beccaria was very substantially influenced by *The Spirit of Laws* in formulating his own views on legal procedures and on punishment and that, in tribute to his mentor, he referred to 'the immortal Montesquieu' in the preface to his *On Crimes and Punishments*."[33] Montesquieu, Beccaria said, deserved "the secret thanks of the unknown and peace-loving disciples of reason."[34]

Beccaria came of age when human rights—and fiction and sentimentality—were coming of age, too. In the last half of the eighteenth century, historian Lynn Hunt notes in *Inventing Human Rights*, novels and newspapers proliferated, with readers becoming more sensitive to acts of cruelty as they empathized with the characters in popular novels and stories. For example, Rousseau's best-selling novel, *Julie, or the New Héloïse* (1761), recalled the well-known story of a twelfth-century Catholic cleric, Peter Abelard, who seduced his pupil, Héloïse, then was castrated and separated forever from his lover. The new Héloïse fell in love with a penniless tutor but ultimately gave in to her authoritarian father's demand that she instead marry an older Russian soldier. No less than one hundred and fifteen editions of the French version of Rousseau's novel were published between 1761 and 1800, with ten English editions also appearing in that time period.[35] In 1792, James Madison himself wrote to his father, James Madison, Sr., to recommend "two or three books" for his sister Fanny. Among the books that Madison recommended for his younger sister were two translations of *Les Aventures de Télémaque, fils d'Ulysses*, a political novel that advocated economic reform, limited monarchy and a separation of church and state. The author of *Télémaque*, the educator and theologian François de Salignac de La Mothe Fénelon, was a proponent of education for women, explaining Madison's brotherly recommendation.

Much later, Cesare Beccaria's own grandson, Alessandro Manzoni, would carry on the tradition of writing fiction, penning a novel in the 1820s titled *The Betrothed* that—as one source puts it—"constituted a kind of bible for Italian nationalists." As that source, edited by Lynn Hunt and others, notes: "Manzoni, the grandson of the Italian Enlightenment hero Cesare Beccaria, set his novel in the seventeenth century, when Spain controlled Italy's destiny, but his readers understood that he intended to attack the Austrians who controlled northern Italy in his own day. By writing this book (the first historical novel in Italian literature) in the Tuscan dialect, Manzoni achieved two aims: he helped create a standard national language and popularized Italian history for a people long divided by different dialects and competing rulers."[36] The Duchy of Milan had been controlled by Louis XII of France in the early sixteenth century, but later in that century, in 1521, Emperor Charles V of Spain took control of Milan for the Spanish Empire. Milan had remained one of the crown jewels of the Spanish Empire until 1706 when the Austrian Habsburgs occupied the city. Cesare Beccaria's own family had originally come from Pavia, of which—as one source puts it—"the Beccaria family held the government for a short time in the fourteenth century."

As a member of an aristocratic family in the then Austrian-dominated region of Lombardy, the Jesuit-educated Beccaria had important social connections. Among his close friends and confidantes as he wrote *On Crimes and Punishments* were two Milanese counts, Alessandro and Pietro Verri, the latter of whom had served in an Italian regiment in Saxony in the war between Austria and Prussia. Alessandro Verri (1741–1816), who held the position of "protector of prisoners," was born in Milan, the son of Count Gabriele Verri, a magistrate and future president of Milan's senate. Count Firmian—the governor of Lombardy—was Alessandro's friend and patron. Later in life, Alessandro would produce an Italian version of *The Iliad*, that ancient Homeric epic, and write works such as *Roman Nights*, which was translated into English. Like Beccaria, Alessandro studied law and, in his public position, was tasked with visiting prisons, inspecting conditions in them, reporting any abuses, giving aid, and recommending pardons. Because of his friendship with Alessandro, one source notes, Beccaria was exposed to "demonic" brutality and "witnessed a penal system ridden with corruption and dependent on the idiosyncratic discretion of individual judges."

In 1761, joined by Beccaria and other like-minded friends, Alessandro and his older brother Pietro formed the *Società dei Pugni*, or Society of Fists, a social club in Milan known for its lively, pugilistic discussions that inspired its name. Shortly thereafter, in 1762, Beccaria wrote a pamphlet that translates as the *Bad State of the Milanese Currency*, a subject Pietro Verri had urged Beccaria to take up in light of the poor state of affairs that had existed since Spanish rule. In 1764, the two Verri brothers also started the periodical *Il Caffé*, which translates as *The Coffeehouse*, a publication published until 1766. That periodical—modeled after *The Spectator*, an English periodical published earlier in the century by the English essayist and statesman Joseph Addison and his childhood friend, the Dublin-born Richard Steele, a Whig member of the House of Commons—got its name because its contributors sometimes met at a Milanese coffeehouse in addition to their regular meetings at Pietro Verri's home. "In this pugnacious intellectual environment," an encyclopedia of Italian literary studies notes, Alessandro "found the opportunity to enhance his social and political awareness by reading the works of thinkers such as Voltaire, Montesquieu, Jean-Jacques Rousseau, Etienne Condillac, John Locke, David Hume, Giambattisa Vico, and other writers." The group formed by the Verri brothers, and joined by Beccaria, was at the very center of the Italian Enlightenment, an intellectual awakening that America's Founding Fathers would later imbibe.

Count Pietro Verri (1728–1797), thirteen years older than his brother Alessandro, was ten years older than Beccaria and became his mentor. A political economist, writer and social reformer, Pietro was a civil servant in Milan, where one of his younger brothers, Carlo Verri (1743–1823), an Italian politician, also lived. A member of the Council of Economy instituted by Maria Theresa for the Duchy of Milan, Pietro was later made a knight of St. Stephen and became a leading member of Milan's "Patriotic Society," formed by Maria Theresa in 1776 to promote agriculture, arts and manufacturing. Under the tutelage of Pietro, Beccaria studied Enlightenment authors and became enthralled by Montesquieu and other writers.[37] Pietro himself suggested that Beccaria take up the subject of crime and punishment, and Pietro—a more experienced writer—edited the manuscript for *On Crimes and Punishments* and helped facilitate its publication in Italy and France.[38] In a letter, Pietro Verri later described how Beccaria's book came together. "[T]he bulk of the ideas it contains," he wrote, "are the result of daily conversations between Beccaria, Alessandro, Lambertenghi, and myself." Another friend of the Verris, Count Luigi Lambertenghi was a mathematician and physicist. As Pietro explained of their daily discussions and Beccaria's writing process:

> Beccaria began to write some ideas down on some loose sheets of paper, and we encouraged him with enthusiasm and prodded him such that he wrote a great mass of ideas. After meals we would take walks and discuss the errors of criminal jurisprudence, we would debate and argue, and that evening he would write. But writing for him is so laborious, and costs him such effort, that after an hour he cannot take it any longer and has to stop. Piled up high as the material was, I wrote it down, some order was given to it, and a book was made.

From the start, Pietro Verri was enormously impressed by Beccaria, writing in a letter in April 1762: "Among the gifted young men who are forming a distinguished company at my home I will name a certain Marquis Beccaria, of good family ... whose vivid imagination together with his careful study of the human heart make of him an exceptionally remarkable man." Not surprising then, the first Italian edition of Beccaria's book was published by Giuseppe Aubert of Leghorn, now known as Livorno, with whom Pietro Verri had a personal connection. In 1763, just a year before Beccaria's book first appeared in Italian, Aubert had published Pietro's own work, *Meditazioni sulla felicità*, which translates as *Meditations on Happiness*. That "treatise on ethics"—as the *Encyclopedia of Italian Literary Studies* explains—"follows the lines of Locke, Helvétius, and especially Rousseau" and "was immediately considered a manifesto of the Milanese Enlightenment." Holding a variety of posts in the Austrian administration, Pietro Verri, the military veteran who married Maria Castiglioni (1753–1781), would go to become the vice-president of the Chamber of Counts in 1772, and then, in 1780, its president.[39]

In Beccaria's time, major European cities were peppered with social clubs and coffeehouses. "Before and during the eighteenth century," historian Nancy Koehn writes, "coffeehouses flourished in Italy, England, Austria, and France and were popular forums for political and literary debate." "In Italy's leading cities," she notes, "men and women crowded into simple, low-ceilinged rooms for companionship, news, and gossip."[40] After getting his law degree, Beccaria had first joined one prestigious social academy, the *Accademia dei Trasformati* (Academy of the Transformed), run by a wealthy count, Giuseppe Maria Imbonati. One of the many European salons and literary societies of the 1700s, that group included poets and Beccaria's friend Pietro Verri, who later broke away, starting what became known as the *Accademia dei Pugni* (Academy of Fists).[41]

The latter, more informal *accademia* or society was modeled after the activities of the French *philosophes*, public intellectuals who applied reason to the study of various social issues and who were distrustful of organized religion.[42] In the capital city of Milan, one source emphasizes, "Beccaria found himself one of a small group of friends, who discussed among themselves the dominant questions of the day" and "planned to form a colony, based upon French philosophy, 'in distant America.'" While Beccaria, a shy young man, was perfectly comfortable in Milan, the travel plans and schemes of his friends were hardly far-fetched. In the 1760s, Italian immigration to America was already underway. For example, in 1763, Andrew Turnbull, an English physician, encouraged 1,500 Italians to come to British East Florida to work at his plantation. For Italian nobles, as Luigi Castiglioni's trip to America later made clear, a trip to the New World was certainly a realistic possibility.

And colonial and early Americans—always interested in trade—took a keen interest themselves in events abroad, whether in England or France or with respect to bustling Italian ports. For example, George Washington corresponded with the Anglican clergyman Andrew Burnaby (1734–1812) in the 1760s while Burnaby was in Leghorn. Burnaby had visited America, including two trips to Mount Vernon, and later wrote *Travels through the Middle Settlements in North-America* (1775), published in London. While in Philadelphia in 1760, Burnaby had written to Washington that "Philadelphia is beyond my Expectation" and that "I am lost in Admiration of that Great Man Mr Penn, who by his Wisdom and vast foresight, has been able to Accomplish such things." After corresponding with Washington in 1761 while back in London, Burnaby later served as a chaplain in Leghorn and wrote to Washington from there, too. In a December 1763 letter, Burnaby described Leghorn as "a Small, neat, pretty fortified city" of "about 40,000 Inhabitants, which consist of all Nations under the Sun." In another letter, written in April 1765, Burnaby told Washington that ships only seldomly left Leghorn's port that were bound for America, but that Burnaby hoped Washington might one day make "a trip to Leghorn, where we would shew You a new World" with "many beauties and much Welcome." "At present," Burnaby wrote, "we are making great preparations here for the arrival of the Arch-Duke and Duchess." In his 1775 travelogue, Burnaby would try to heal the British-American rift and bring Americans and the British together again, writing at one point: "Let every Englishman and American, but for a moment or two, substitute themselves in each other's place, and, I think, a mode of reconciliation will soon take effect.—Every American will then perceive the reasonableness of acknowledging the supremacy of the British legislature; and every Englishman, perhaps, the hardship of being taxed where there is no representation, or assent."[43]

While no evidence could be found that the travel-averse Beccaria, who felt very much at home in his native Milan, ever planned to travel to America, he certainly owed much to foreign influences. To the French translator of *On Crimes and Punishments*, Beccaria later openly confessed: "I owe everything to French authors; they have revealed to me human feelings that eight years of a fanatical education had suffocated." Among the "glorious names" Beccaria said he idolized: French naturalist Georges-Louis Leclerc, Comte de Buffon, whom Thomas Jefferson later presented with a copy of his *Notes on the State of Virginia*; French mathematician Jean-Baptiste le Rond d'Alembert, co-editor with Denis Diderot of the *Encyclopédie*; Diderot, the French philosopher and art critic who had studied law before becoming a writer; Claude Adrien Helvétius, the Frenchman who published *De l'esprit*, translated as *Essays on the Mind*, in the late 1750s; and David Hume, a Scottish philosopher who wrote *A Treatise of Human Nature* and spent time in Paris in the 1760s.[44] The writings of the French *philosophes*, in turn, frequently mention Beccaria, with his name, for example, coming up repeatedly in late 1766 in various letters. Among those in which Beccaria's name is found from September to December 1766: one from André Morellet to David Hume; one from Voltaire to Etienne Noël Damilaville; one from Jean François Marmontel to Voltaire; one from André Morellet to Voltaire; one from Voltaire to Jean le Rond d'Alembert; and one from Paul-Henri Thiry, baron d'Holbach, to Voltaire.[45]

Before joining the Academy of Fists and rising to fame, Beccaria had a life-changing event, a bitter disagreement with his parents that would radically alter his worldview. In 1760, while in his early twenties, Beccaria fell in love with sixteen-year-old Teresa di Blasco, the daughter of an army officer, Domenico di Blasco, from a noble family of Sicilian-Spanish origin. The Marchese Gian Beccaria Bonesana — Cesare Beccaria's father — believed, however, that Teresa's family was not sufficiently wealthy for his son, making Teresa a poor match.[46] Consequently, Beccaria's father, also known as Giovanni Saverio Beccaria, vehemently disapproved of the object of his son's affection. This prompted a determined Cesare Beccaria — who ultimately married his chosen bride against his father's wishes — to take up his pen and write a bitterly worded letter to his father in a futile attempt to gain his father's blessing. "Please be assured that only death can destroy my resolution, and the idea of death doesn't frighten me," the strong-willed Beccaria wrote to his father, adding: "I swear before God that I will not change my decision. I ask you in the name of Jesus Christ to stop putting obstacles to this marriage and to stop doing violence to my will and my conscience." It took time after the marriage took place — and the advice and intervention of Beccaria's friend and fellow noble, Count Pietro Verri — before Beccaria and his father would reconcile.[47]

This was no ordinary family squabble. Unable to convince his headstrong son to abandon the relationship, Beccaria's father prevailed upon magistrates to put his son under restraint "in order that he might the more leisurely reflect on his condition." After Cesare was placed under house arrest, Teresa's own father took things into his own hands, attempting to counteract Beccaria's father's maneuver by appealing to Empress Maria Theresa and emphasizing his own nobility. Teresa's father stressed the dowry he was prepared to provide, as well as Cesare Beccaria's own affection for his daughter. After three months of confinement at his family's house, Cesare Beccaria was finally set free in February 1761, whereupon he promptly married Teresa against his family's wishes. The newlywed's first child, Giulia, was born in 1762, named after the heroine in Jean-Jacques Rousseau's novel *La Nouvelle Héloïse*. Only after some time had passed would Beccaria's father and mother, variously identified as Maria Beccaria, Maria Visconti de Saliceto, or Donna Maria Visconti da Rho, reconcile with their son Cesare and their new daughter-in-law, Teresa.[48] University of Chicago professor Bernard Harcourt notes that "[t]here is debate over Beccaria's proper title of nobility and, thus, his name." As Harcourt explains: "He is often referred to as the 'Marquis of Beccaria,' including in the *Encyclopædia Universalis* and the *Larousse*; however, recent research suggests that the title of nobility that his grandfather obtained in 1711 was for Gualdrasco and Villareggio."[49]

The Academy of Fists, which Beccaria joined after the painful episode with his father, held reformist views that did not find favor elsewhere.[50] The small group, which included Pietro Verri, Pietro's brother Alessandro, and other men, mostly in their twenties, dedicated itself to contributing to the public good.[51] In particular, the men sought to win over the Austrian rulers of Lombardy to a program of reform.[52] Alessandro Verri, one of the most prolific contributors to *Il Caffé*, contributed thirty-two articles on different subjects, including on the need for law reform. Because Alessandro worked as a prison inspector, he was able to share valuable insights with Beccaria as Beccaria worked on his manuscript for *On Crimes and Punishments*. According to an Italian studies encyclopedia, Alessandro "shared the same perspectives of Cesare Beccaria's enormously influential *Dei delitti e delle pene* (On Crimes and Punishments, 1764), which in turn owes much in concept and structure" to the work of the Verri brothers. Though the Academy of Fists was short-lived, the ideas Beccaria and the Verri brothers produced as a result of their association with it were substantial and still endure, continuing to shape penal reform and the world's death penalty debate.[53]

It was in 1761, in the midst of his familial turmoil, that Beccaria bonded with Pietro and Alessandro Verri, the two intellectuals who would so profoundly shape his literary career.[54] The members of the Academy of Fists, ranging from poets to economists, wrote on an array of topics, everything from political and economic theories to cultural, literary and scientific matters. Every ten days the group published *Il Caffè*, the inaugural edition of which was aimed at accomplishing "what good we can for our country" through the distribution of "useful knowledge."[55] According to one historian, Maria Theresa's Austrian minister of foreign affairs, a prince of the Holy Roman Empire often referred to simply as Kaunitz, "was not only familiar with the outpourings of the *Il Caffè* group, but often much influenced by their thought." As that historian, Franz A. J. Szabo, writes of the *Il Caffè*'s contributors: "Many of its most prominent members found service in the Austrian administration of Milan, or were granted academic engagements thanks to Kaunitz." "These included," Szabo notes, "the leading political economists of their day, Pietro Verri and Alfonso Longo, the historian and economist, Gianrinaldo Carli, the influential social reformer and philosopher, Cesare Beccaria, the outstanding poet, Giuseppe Parini, and above all, the mathematician and encyclopedic *philosophe*, Paolo Frisi, whose erudition Kaunitz especially prized."[56]

Paolo Frisi (1728–1784)—Cesare Beccaria's friend, a math professor at the Scuola Palatine in Milan, and a philosopher and astronomer interested in Newtonian theory, hydraulics, electricity and light—had direct contact with America's senior statesman, Benjamin Franklin, a contact that Frisi was more than willing to share. For example, in 1784, Frisi wrote Benjamin Franklin, who he had met in London, to introduce Dr. Franklin to the Milan noble Luigi Castiglioni, the botanist then planning his extended tour of North America. Writing from his French home in Passy later that year, Franklin wrote back to Frisi: "I received with great Pleasure the Line you were pleased to write to me by the Chevalier Castiglioni, and am oblig'd to you for making me acquainted with a Gentleman so intelligent and so amiable." "If in his American Travels I can be of any Service to him," Franklin wrote, "he may command me, on his own Account as well as in respect to your Recommendation." "With great Esteem," Franklin signed off, "I have the honour to be, Sir, Your most obedient and most humble Servant."[57] In his later published *Viaggio*, Castiglioni—the well-connected fellow scientist with a passion for plants—referred to himself as "Patrician of Milan, Knight in the Order of St. Stephen, P[ope] and M[artyr], Member of the American Philosophical Society of Philadelphia and of the Patriotic Society of Milan."[58] The Patriotic Society of Milan had been created in 1776 by Maria Theresa of Austria to encourage industry, agriculture and the arts in Lombardy. At Castiglioni's suggestion both Benjamin Franklin and Benjamin Rush were added "by acclamation" as foreign members of that organization in 1786, a decade later.[59]

In Milan, a city of 120,000 inhabitants, Paolo Frisi was among the prominent local men that the Austrian administration consulted in their efforts to reform that locality, as were Pietro and Alessandro Verri and Cesare Beccaria. Indeed, Beccaria would later become a civil servant, living out his life in that commercial center. "There is no city in Italy where foreigners are better received than at Milan," one traveler noted of the city, explaining that "[t]here are many great and rich families at Milan" and that "[a]ll the nobility speak French." "The Marquis Beccaria," that traveler wrote in his memoirs, "was a man of great genius, and of perfect urbanity of manners."[60] Social connections between

Milanese and French intellectuals ran deep, with Frisi himself sending a copy of Beccaria's book to Jean le Rond d'Alembert, the French mathematician, physicist, philosopher, music theorist, and *Encyclopédie* co-editor. After receiving it, d'Alembert thanked Frisi. In his letter, d'Alembert—the Parisian intellectual—noted that after reading Beccaria's book he had passed it around to "several good *philosophes* here and they all returned the same judgment as I," that is, that despite its small size, "it was enough to assure its author an immortal reputation."[61] In Lombardy itself, Count Firmian, also known as Carlo di Firmian, actually coordinated the effort to make reform a reality. Firmian led efforts to overhaul the financial system and, in 1768, transferred book censorship from the Inquisition—and the Milanese senate—to an imperial commission.[62] Frisi's younger acquaintance, Luigi Castiglioni, was born in Milan in 1756, and had studied botany with Giovanni Scopoli, a teacher at Beccaria's alma mater, the University of Pavia. Castiglioni would travel throughout France and England in 1784 before making his way to America in 1785.[63]

Beccaria's own writings for *Il Caffè* were diverse. After falling in love with Teresa di Blasco, Beccaria published his first pamphlet, a study of currency problems in Milan, in 1762. In all, Beccaria wrote seven articles for *Il Caffè* on topics ranging from the trivial and whimsical—the statistical probabilities of winning a card game and an "Essay on Odors"; to the literary—a "Fragment on Style"; to the serious—an essay on smuggling.[64] Edited by Pietro and Alessandro Verri, *Il Caffè* has aptly been described as "one of the most influential journals of the Italian Enlightenment."[65] As David Young, a translator of *On Crimes and Punishments*, once noted: "The Habsburgs had held Lombardy since 1707, but did not begin the process of reform until the end of the War of the Austrian Succession in 1748. The initial impetus in Lombardy, as elsewhere, was the need to improve the administration of finances and the economy in order to reduce the massive deficit created by the cost of war." The *Il Caffè* contributors, including Beccaria, who also gained considerable renown as an economist, would substantially contribute to those reform efforts.[66] As one commentator explains: "During the Italian Enlightenment of the late eighteenth century, economists—from Ferdinando Galiani and Antonio Genovesi in Naples to Pietro Verri and Cesare Beccaria in Milan, Andrea Tron in Venice and Carlo Salerni in Otranto—were systematically exploring and codifying the mechanisms of economic development."[67]

One product of the Academy of Fists was the publication of Beccaria's landmark treatise, *Dei delitti e delle pene*, at first published anonymously in 1764 due to fear of persecution and ecclesiastical censorship.[68] In fact, the Roman Inquisition banned it on pain of death in February 1766, placing it on the Index of Forbidden Books, with Beccaria's treatise remaining on the list of condemned works until the 1960s.[69] Early French translations of Beccaria's treatise, published in 1766, actually listed the place of publication as "PHILADELPHIE," an idealized fictional utopia as the true places of production were Paris, France and Yverdon, Switzerland.[70] Cesare Beccaria—the author of *Dei delitti e delle pene*—was thus initially not even identified by name as its creator, such were the fears of the Inquisition at that time. But Beccaria's anonymity did not last long. Once Milan's more progressive-leaning authorities expressed no animosity toward the book's content, and in fact welcomed the treatise, Beccaria's identity was revealed. At first, rumors circulated and swirled about that the elder Pietro Verri had written *On Crimes and Punishments*. These rumors were only fueled by the fact that Verri had, in 1763, published *Meditations on Happiness* with the same publisher. But to his credit, Verri quickly denied authorship and came to Beccaria's defense. "I suggested the topic to him," Verri acknowledged, but freely admitted that the book itself "is by the Marquis Beccaria."[71] As a result, it was Beccaria's name—not Verri's—that would become so well known, and so celebrated, throughout Europe and in colonial America.

Beccaria, who initially feared persecution, had legitimate reasons to be fearful. "While writing my book," Beccaria later told his French translator, the Abbé André Morellet, "I had before my eyes the examples of Galileo, Machiavelli, and Giannone," all of whom faced dire consequences for their views.[72] Galileo, found to have committed heresy, had been forced to confess to "vain ambition, pure ignorance, and inadvertence" in advancing Copernicanism and had been threatened with torture before being imprisoned in Rome.[73] Machiavelli, the author of *Il Principe*, later translated into English as *The Prince*, had been tortured and confined.[74] And Giannone, who commented on the Vatican in his *History of Naples*, was imprisoned in the citadel of Turin for twenty years.[75] In his own book, Beccaria dealt with the always controversial subject of crimes and punishments and did so in a novel and philosophical manner, advocating jury trials,[76] speedy trials,[77] and condemning traditional state practices, torture and executions, as antiquated and unnecessary. In a letter, Beccaria confessed to Morellet, his French translator, that having "heard the clanging chains of superstition and the howls of fanaticism suffocating the faint moans of truth," he felt "compelled to be obscure and to envelop the light of truth in a pious mist" because he "wanted to be a defender of humanity without being its martyr."[78]

On Crimes and Punishments

On Crimes and Punishments covered a wide array of topics, though its major focus is—as its title suggests—the criminal law. In the 1775 translation printed in London and owned by John Adams, the "Preface of the Translator" begins: "Penal laws, so considerable a part of every system of legislation, and of so great importance to the happiness, peace, and security of every member of society, are still so imperfect, and are attended with so many unnecessary circumstances of cruelty in all nations, that an attempt to reduce them to the standard of reason must be interesting to all mankind." "It may however be objected," that translator wrote, catering to a largely English audience, "that a treatise of this kind is useless in England, where, from the excellence of our laws and government, no examples of cruelty or oppression are to be found." "But," the preface continued, acknowledging that English law was less than perfect, "it must also be allowed, that much is still wanting to perfect our system of legislation: the confinement of debtors, the filth and horror of our prisons, the cruelty of jailors, and the extortion of the petty officers of justice, to all which may be added the melancholy reflection, that the number of criminals put to death in England is much greater than in any other part of Europe, are considerations which will sufficiently answer every objection." "I say, with my author," the anonymous translator concluded, "that if I can be instrumental in rescuing a single victim from the hands of tyranny or ignorance, his transports will sufficiently console me for the contempt of all mankind."[79]

It was at the age of twenty-six, on what is now Italian soil, that Beccaria—the eldest son of his noble family—first saw his short treatise, *Dei delitti e delle pene*, in print. That book, initially appearing in Italian, was translated into English by its unknown and unidentified translator three years later as—according to its full title—*An Essay on Crimes and Punishments, Translated from the Italian; with a Commentary Attributed to Mons. De Voltaire, Translated from the French*.[80] In it, Beccaria—inspired by Montesquieu and others and using a mathematician's lingo—argued that "there must be proportion between crimes and punishments." Keeping company with respected mathematicians such as Paolo

Frisi, Beccaria believed that crimes are "distributed across a scale that moves imperceptibly by diminishing degrees from the highest to the lowest" and that "[i]f geometry were applicable to the infinite and obscure combinations of human actions, there would be a corresponding scale of punishments, descending from the most severe to the mildest." "If the same punishment is prescribed for two crimes and injure society in different degrees," Beccaria wrote, "then men will face no stronger deterrent from committing the greater crime if they find it in their advantage to do so."[81] Because of his attempt to apply "the geometric spirit" to the study of the criminal law, Beccaria's friends—aware of his efforts to approach the law as a scientist might—even nicknamed him "Newtoncino," or little Newton.[82]

This notion—of proportioning punishments to crimes—was then still seen as a relatively novel proposition, as least as conceived of, and formulated, by Beccaria. As the author of an 1856 book titled *Dealings with the Dead* later pointed out: "The Marquis of Beccaria, in his treatise ... seems to have awakened legislators from a trance, in 1764, by propounding the simple inquiry—*Ought not punishments to be proportioned to crimes, and how shall that proportion be established?* A matter, so apparently simple, seems not to have been thought of before."[83] The concept of proportionality, however, was hardly unknown to English law—and actually dated back many centuries. In fact, the Magna Carta, issued in Latin in 1215 and requiring King John to proclaim certain liberties, contained strong echoes of that concept. "A freeman," one provision read, "shall not be amerced for a slight offence, except in accordance with the degree of the offence; and for a grave offence he shall be amerced in accordance with the gravity of the offence, yet saving always his 'contenement.'" "[T]o save a man's 'contenement,'" historian William McKechnie explains, "was to leave him sufficient for the sustenance of himself and those dependent on him." "Earls and barons," another provision of the Magna Carta, or Great Charter, provided, "shall not be amerced except through their peers, and only in accordance with the degree of the offence."[84] Centuries later, the English Bill of Rights of 1689 also explicitly provided, "That excessive bail ought not to be required, nor excessive fines imposed, nor cruel and unusual punishments inflicted."[85]

It was thus Beccaria's distinctive *approach* to the concept of proportionality that made such a lasting mark in the 1760s in Great Britain and its colonies. While early English legal instruments spoke of tailoring punishments to fit the crime and avoiding "excessive" or "cruel" sanctions, Beccaria's forceful advocacy against the death penalty drew widespread public attention because of its novelty. In their book *Proportionality Principles in American Law*, scholars Tom Sullivan and Richard Frase note of Beccaria's approach: "The eighteenth-century philosopher Cesare Beccaria argued in favor of criminal penalties that are proportional to the seriousness of the offense, as measured by the harm done to society." "Beccaria," they note, "argued that punishment must be not only proportionate to the crime but also 'necessary, the least possible in the circumstances.'" Jeremy Bentham—the famous utilitarian—would say much the same thing, arguing that punishment should be used as sparingly as possible and that a penalty should not be used if "the same end may be obtained by means more mild." While retributive theory considers the harm caused by a crime and deems it just to punish the offender in proportion to that harm, the utilitarian approach—which also requires proportionality—diverges substantially from a purely retributive approach. As Sullivan and Frase explain: "retributive theory disregards the crime-control benefits, as well as the collateral consequences of imposing punishment; proportionate sanctions are deemed inherently valuable." Two such collateral consequences: the deleterious and stigmatizing effect of an execution on the offender's immediate family, and the de-humanizing and brutalizing effect of executions on the larger society.[86]

When Beccaria penned his *Dei delitti e delle pene* manuscript, he wanted to transform penal codes littered with draconian punishments. His treatise—as translated into English—thus railed against "cruelty," "cruel punishments," "useless cruelty," "barbarous and useless torments," "cruel imbecility" and "those cruel formalities of justice." His "Introduction" further lamented "barbarous torments" and "useless severity," then argued—citing Montesquieu—that "[e]very punishment, which does not arise from absolute necessity ... is tyrannical." "[T]here ought to be a fixed proportion between crimes and punishments," Beccaria implored, asking—and then answering—a series of questions for his readers: "Is the punishment of death really *useful*, or necessary for the safety or good order of society? Are tortures and torments consistent with *justice*, or do they answer the end proposed by the laws? Are the same punishments equally useful at all times?" "Crimes," Beccaria advised in one of the core principles he developed, "are more effectually prevented by the *certainty*, than the *severity* of punishment."[87] "The swifter and closer to the crime a punishment is, the juster and more useful it will be," he wrote. Beccaria emphasized "promptness of punishment" because "the smaller the lapse of time between the misdeed and the punishment, the stronger and more lasting the association in the human mind between the two ideas *crime* and *punishment*." "In proportion as punishments become more cruel," Beccaria added, "the minds of men, as a fluid rises to the same height with that which surrounds it, grow hardened and insensible."

On Crimes and Punishments—the product of an author with a noble pedigree and a conservative education—called for stricter enforcement of the law, but also milder, more humane punishments. "One of the most effective brakes on crime," Beccaria wrote, "is not the harshness of its punishment, but the unerringness of punishment." As Beccaria emphasized: "This calls for vigilance in the magistrates, and that kind of unswerving judicial severity which, to be useful to the cause of virtue, must be accompanied by a lenient code of laws." "The certainty of even a mild punishment," Beccaria argued, leery of harsh codes that were not always enforced, "will make a bigger impression than the fear of a more awful one which is united to a hope of not being punished at all." Taking notice of acts of clemency and judges who did not always adhere to the letter of the law in the course of their duties, Beccaria observed: "For, even the smallest harms, when they are certain, always frighten human souls, whereas hope, that heavenly gift which often displaces every other sentiment, holds at bay the idea of large harms, especially when it is reinforced by frequent examples of the impunity accorded by weak and corrupt judges." As Beccaria explained: "The harsher the punishment and the worse the evil he faces, the more anxious the criminal is to avoid it, and it makes him commit other crimes to escape the punishment of the first." "The times and places in which the penalties have been fiercest," Beccaria reasoned, "have been those of the bloodiest and most inhuman actions." That was the case, Beccaria wrote, "[b]ecause the same brutal spirit which guided the hand of the lawgiver, also moved the parricide's and the assassin's."

In his treatise, Beccaria then conjured up two hypothetical nations as part of an extended argument that "harsh punishments" had "disastrous consequences." As Beccaria urged his readers: "Imagine two states, in which the scales of punishment are proportionate to the crimes and that in one the worst punishment is perpetual slavery, and that in the other it is breaking on the wheel. I maintain that there would be as much fear of the worst punishment in the first as in the second." In identifying two specific "disastrous consequences" flowing from "harsh punishments," Beccaria wrote: "One is that it is not easy to sustain the necessary proportion between crime and punishment because, despite all the efforts of cruelty to devise all manner of punishments, they still cannot go beyond the limits of endurance of the human organism and feeling." "Once this point has been reached," Beccaria emphasized, "no correspondingly greater punishments necessary to prevent the more damaging and atrocious crimes can be found." Another consequence, Beccaria wrote, "is that the harshness of punishments gives rise to impunity." "Men's capacity for good and evil," Beccaria noted in that era of torturous punishments and public executions, "is confined within certain bounds, and a spectacle which is too awful for humanity cannot be more than a temporary upset, and can never become a fixed system of the sort proper to the law." "If the laws are truly cruel," Beccaria explained, "they must either be changed or they will occasion a fatal impunity."[88]

In *On Crimes and Punishments*, Beccaria — the father of the world's anti-death penalty movement[89] — pointedly questioned whether executions were really necessary for the security or good order of society? "By what right," he pondered, "can men presume to slaughter their fellows?" "It seems absurd to me," Beccaria wrote, "that the laws, which are the expression of the public will, and which execrate and punish homicide, should themselves commit one, and that to deter citizens from murder they should order a public murder." The frontispiece to the third edition of *Dei delitti e delle pene*, published in 1765, illustrated one of the most important objectives of Beccaria's treatise: to replace executions with incarceration and hard labor. A copperplate engraving based on a sketch Beccaria provided, the frontispiece depicts an idealized figure, Justice, shunning an executioner who is carrying a sword and axe in his right hand and who is trying to hand Justice a cluster of severed heads with his outstretched left hand. Justice's gaze is instead transfixed on a pile of prisoner's shackles and worker's tools — the instruments symbolizing imprisonment and prison labor.[90] It was hard labor — whether performed by convicts on the streets of Philadelphia or within the confines of prisons — that would later emerge in America as a viable alternative to harsh corporal punishments and executions.[91]

Beccaria's book condemned the barbarity of state-sanctioned executions, viewing them as violative of natural law. "[S]overeignty and the laws," Beccaria wrote, "are nothing but the sum of the smallest portions of the personal liberty of each individual; they represent the general will, which is the aggregate of particular wills." "Who has ever willingly given other men the authority to kill him?" he asked rhetorically, adding that "the death penalty is not a *right*, but the war of a nation against a citizen."[92] In a chapter devoted specifically to the death penalty, Beccaria wrote, "[t]his futile excess of punishments, which have never made men better, has impelled me to consider whether the death penalty is really useful and just in a well-organized state." "The death penalty," Beccaria argued, "is not useful because of the example of cruelty that it gives to men." "If one were to raise the objection that in almost all ages and almost all nations the death penalty has been prescribed for some crimes," Beccaria continued, "I would reply that this objection amounts to nothing in the face of the truth — against which there is no legal remedy — and that the history of mankind gives us the impression of a vast sea of errors, in which a few confused truths float about with large and distant gaps between them." If monarchs left "the ancient laws in place," Beccaria said, "it is because of the infinite difficulty in stripping the venerated rust of many centuries from so many errors."

Viewing life itself as "a natural right,"[93] as did other Enlightenment writers such as John Locke, the son of a country lawyer,[94] Beccaria vehemently called for the death penalty's abolition. In doing so, Beccaria radically departed from the conventional wisdom of earlier European thinkers, a number of whom were natural law theorists. The Italian St. Thomas Aquinas (1225–1274), educated at the University of Naples, had written of "[t]he precepts of natural law" in the Middle Ages, but had said that rulers — though not private persons — had the right to kill criminals. Other philosophers such as Thomas Hobbes, Hugo Grotius, Samuel von Pufendorf, John Locke, Francis Hutcheson, Jean Jacques Burlamaqui and Emmerich de Vattel, had all made their own intellectual contributions to the subject of natural law, albeit in an era when the death penalty was a widely accepted, often unquestioned practice.[95] For example, the English philosopher and physician John Locke (1632–1704), born in a cottage about twelve miles from Bristol, had identified "life, liberty, and estate" as natural rights, though he did not advocate the abolition of capital punishment. On the contrary, Locke had asserted that a criminal could "forfeit" his life and liberty—an idea that the Due Process Clause of the U.S. Constitution's Fifth Amendment alludes to in procedural terms, providing, as it does, that no person shall "be deprived of life, liberty, or property, without due process of law." "The power of making laws of life and death is indeed a mark of sovereignty," Locke wrote, emphasizing that government magistrates could pronounce death sentences; that "[p]olitical power" included "a right of making laws with penalties of death"; and that the Biblical passage "Whoso sheddeth man's blood, by man shall his blood be shed" was "that great law of nature."

John Locke posited that man once lived in a state of nature to which he might return, and that in that state of nature, man was governed by natural law and possessed certain natural rights. Those rights, Locke believed, included the rights to conscience, happiness, liberty, life and property. As Locke—the Father of Classical Liberalism—wrote of his views on rights and punishment:

> Man being born, as has been proved, with a title to perfect freedom, and uncontrolled enjoyment of all the rights and privileges of the law of nature, equally with any other man, or number of men in the world, hath by nature a power, not only to preserve his property, that is, his life, liberty, and estate, against the injuries and attempts of other men; but to judge of and punish the breaches of that law in others, as he is persuaded the offence deserves, even with death itself, in crimes where the heinousness of the fact, in his opinion, requires it.[96]

"Even as late as 1648," one historian writes of John Locke's time, "Puritan zeal for orthodox belief caused an ordinance to be passed which made anyone liable to the death penalty 'who denied the Trinity, Christ's Divinity, the inspiration of the scriptures, or a future state,' and set prison penalties for other heresies."[97]

Locke's writings—as well as the writings of other natural law theorists—would later influence a host of American founders, including Benjamin Franklin and James Madison, the latter of whom studied Locke's *Essay Concerning Human Understanding* (1690) as a young man. In *Poor Richard Improved* (1748), Benjamin Franklin specifically took note of the death in 1704 of "the famous John Locke," described by Franklin as "the Newton of the *Microcosm*." "*Man is rightly called* a little world," Franklin wrote, "*because he is a* Microcosm." Locke's death was noted in the same section of *Poor Richard Improved* in which Franklin described Pennsylvania's William Penn as "the great founder of this Province; who prudently and benevolently sought success to himself by no other means, than securing the *liberty*, and endeavoring the *happiness* of his people"; and in which Franklin wrote of the 1618 beheading of "sir Walter Rawleigh ... to the eternal shame of the attorney general, who first prosecuted him, and of the king, who ratify'd the sentence." Sir Walter Raleigh (c. 1554–1618)—a soldier, poet, historian, scientist and adventurer who was knighted by England's Queen Elizabeth I (1533–1603)—was given a patent to colonize North America in 1584; envisioned permanent settlements on American soil, naming one of its regions "Virginia" after his royal patron, sometimes called "The Virgin Queen"; popularized the use of tobacco in English high society; was imprisoned in the Tower of London for thirteen years after being sentenced to death for plotting to dethrone Queen Elizabeth's successor, James I (1566–1625), a sentence that was later suspended; led an expedition to search for gold mines and the fabled city of El Dorado; and, after an unauthorized siege of a Spanish fort, had his death sentence reinstated by James I. Raleigh was executed on October 29, 1618, with his last words—as the executioner hesitated to raise the axe—"What dost thou fear? Strike, man, strike!"[98]

John Locke's influence on America's founders was pervasive. John Adams paraphrased Locke's *Essay on Toleration* in the late 1760s on more than one occasion, and Thomas Jefferson recommended Locke's books along with Montesquieu's *Spirit of Laws*. Jefferson himself once described Sir Francis Bacon, John Locke and Sir Isaac Newton as "the three greatest men that have ever lived, without any exception." Those men, Jefferson told the American painter John Trumbull, had "laid the foundations of those superstructures which have been raised in the Physical & Moral sciences." The source of American patriots' views on natural rights, explains one source, "were the ideas and writings of the leading thinkers of the European Enlightenment: Voltaire, Rousseau, Beccaria, Grotius, Pufendorf, Burlamaqui, Vattel, and Locke."[99] With Locke's *Two Treatises of Government* (1689), published shortly after England's Glorious Revolution of 1688, arguing that the primary purpose of government is to protect citizen's natural rights, Locke has aptly been described as "one of the most important philosophers to influence the thinking of America's founders."[100]

In comparison to John Locke, the Scottish philosopher Francis Hutcheson (1694–1746)—another influential Enlightenment thinker read by Beccaria—believed that "*Unalienable Rights* are *essential Limitations* in all Governments." In his frequently reprinted *Inquiry into the Original of Our Ideas of Beauty and Virtue* (1725), Hutcheson wrote of the difference between "*Unalienable*" and "*alienable*" rights, concluding that the "*Right of private Judgment*, or of our *inward Sentiments*, is *unalienable*." Hutcheson also concluded that "our *Right of serving* GOD, in the manner which we think acceptable, is not *alienable*," and that in "[t]he same way," "a direct Right over our Lives or Limbs is not alienable to any Person; so that he might at Pleasure put us to Death, or maim us." In his book, Hutcheson—whose writings exerted a tremendous influence on Beccaria's thinking—repeatedly referred to the "cruel," "evil," "inhuman," "malicious," "treacherous" and "unjust" actions of mankind.[101] "Beccaria," writes one scholar, noting Hutcheson's popularity in Lombardy, "was inspired by the ideas of the founder of the Scottish Enlightenment, the Glaswegian philosopher Francis Hutcheson, and by Hutcheson's pupil Hume (whose 'profound metaphysics' he praised generously)." As that scholar, criminologist Piers Beirne, writes: "When Beccaria introduced *Dei delitti* with the enigmatic sentence 'Mankind owes a debt of gratitude to the philosopher who, from the despised obscurity of his study, had the courage to cast the first and long fruitless seeds of useful truths among the multitude!' he was undoubtedly referring to Hutcheson, who had explicitly termed himself 'an obscure Philosopher.'" Beirne specifically emphasizes: "[i]t is almost certain that Beccaria had read Hutcheson's *Inquiry into the Original of our Ideas of Beauty and Virtue*, probably in a French translation of 1749."[102]

Hutcheson and Beccaria, the two European philosophers, did not agree on everything—and one thing they disagreed on was the death penalty's propriety. In fact, in a later work, *A System of Moral Philosophy*, printed in 1755 after his death, Hutcheson made clear that he did not oppose the death penalty for all crimes. In that book, written before Beccaria picked up his pen, Hutcheson emphasized—in line with such thinkers as St. Thomas Aquinas—that, "when 'tis necessary for the publick safety," magistrates had the right "to take away the lives of criminals." Having served as a Professor of Philosophy at the University of Glasgow, Hutcheson argued as follows in a section of his posthumously published book on the rights arising from injuries to others: "The publick, or mankind as a system, have even a further right of inflicting such further evils as are necessary to deter others from the like attempts." As Hutcheson explained: "This last right the person who was in danger of immediate wrong should not execute alone, but in conjunction with others who have no private cause of resentment. Such horrid attempts, such as those of murder, assassination, poisoning, robbery, or piracy, shew so desperate a wickedness, that scarce any sufficient security can be obtained to society against the repetition of the like crimes, but the deaths of the criminals."

But in his posthumously published book, Hutcheson—as Beccaria must have seen—was clearly struggling with the legitimacy of the death penalty's application in particular situations and with just how brutal state-sanctioned executions should be made to be. "[A]s to those who are bankrupt through their own vices, as they are often far worse criminals than thieves, and do greater wrongs," Hutcheson wrote, "a capital punishment, if it could do any good, would be no more cruel in the one case than the other." "To condemn them to perpetual slavery," Hutcheson immediately clarified, though, "would have a better effect; in contributing a little to repair the wrongs they had done, and to deter others by the example." In considering the manner in which executions should be carried out, Hutcheson argued: "It may justly be questioned however, whether in increasing of punishments on account of horrid crimes, there be not a certain pitch of suffering beyond which nothing severer should be inflicted." As Hutcheson opined: "If death is the penalty of any deliberate murder or robbery, one's indignation would move him to inflict something worse upon the more horridly cruel murderers, and to torture such as had tortured others; or to use tortures where the gentler kinds of death inflicted seem scarce sufficient to deter men from the crime." "But on the other hand," Hutcheson emphasized, "horrid spectacles of torture, especially if they are frequently presented, may have a very bad effect upon the minds of spectators."[103]

Unlike Locke, Hutcheson and other natural law theorists, Beccaria took the right-to-life concept a step further than European philosophers had taken it before. "[I]f I can demonstrate that the death penalty is neither useful nor necessary," the idealistic Beccaria proclaimed in words that would later stir figures such as Dr. Benjamin Rush to action, "I will have won the cause of humanity."[104] For Beccaria, who recognized that crimes differed in magnitude, there were two classes of crime: "the first consists of serious crimes beginning with murder and including all the worst villainies; the second consists of minor crimes." "This distinction," Beccaria wrote, aware that crimes could be either violent or non-violent, "has its foundation in human nature," though Beccaria, drawing heavily on the metaphors used in Hutcheson's *System of Moral Philosophy*, did not favor executions for either class of crime. "The safety of one's own life is a natural right," Beccaria asserted, contrasting "the protection of property" as "a social right."[105] As for the right to life, which found expression in the rights clause of Thomas Jefferson's elegantly phrased Declaration of Independence, America's founders similarly believed in natural and universal rights and a system of laws determined by God and nature. The Declaration of Independence itself begins by invoking "the Laws of Nature," "Nature's God," and "the powers of the earth," and ends—in its concluding paragraph—by "appealing to the Supreme Judge of the world for the rectitude of our intentions." "And for the support of this Declaration, with a firm reliance on the protection of divine Providence," the founders proclaimed, "we mutually pledge to each other our Lives, our Fortunes and our sacred Honor."[106]

For Beccaria, executions—the ultimate exercise of state power—brutalized societies. "If the passions or the necessities of war have taught us how to shed human blood," he believed, "the laws, which moderate the conduct of men, should not augment that cruel example, which is all the more baleful when a legal killing is applied with deliberation and formality."[107] To persuade skeptical readers, Beccaria posed a series of questions: "Can the cries of an unfortunate wretch rescue from time, which never reverses its course, deeds already perpetrated?" "When reading history, who does not shudder with horror at the barbaric and useless tortures that have been cold-bloodedly invented and practiced by men who considered themselves wise?" "What must men think when they see wise magistrates and solemn ministers of justice, who with tranquil indifference have a criminal dragged with slow precision to his death, and as a poor wretch writhes in his last agonies while awaiting the fatal blow, the judge goes on with cold insensitivity—and perhaps even with secret satisfaction at his own authority—to savour the comforts and pleasures of life?"[108] In England, the "Bloody Code"—the pejorative label traditionally applied to England's criminal laws during the period from 1688 to 1815, and a set of laws once justified and defended by figures such as Philip Yorke (1690–1764), 1st Earl of Hardwicke—made the death penalty a central feature of the English penal code. A barrister who became Lord Chancellor, Yorke viewed executions as necessary because of the wickedness of the age. "The heart of the Bloody Code," as one historian explains, "was its extensive provision for capital punishment."[109]

In the 1775 English-language edition of Beccaria's book, John Adams would have read these words—Beccaria's framing of the issue he saw for society—in chapter XXVIII: "whether the punishment of *death* be really just or useful in a well governed state?" "What right, I ask," Beccaria wrote, "have men to cut the throats of their fellow-creatures?" These questions were the very same questions that would later be actively debated on American college campuses in the 1780s and 1790s. "[I]f I can further demonstrate that it is neither necessary nor useful," Beccaria wrote of capital punishment in his singular style, "I shall have gained the cause of humanity."[110] This radical new idea—that the death penalty was neither necessary nor useful—was one specifically picked up on by William Bradford, Jr. in his *Enquiry How Far the Punishment of Death Is Necessary in Pennsylvania*. Written in 1792, when it was presented to Pennsylvania lawmakers, and published in 1793, Bradford's essay invoked both Beccaria and Montesquieu and emphasized that every punishment "*which is not absolutely necessary*" to prevent crimes "*is a cruel and tyrannical act.*"[111]

Dr. Benjamin Rush, Bradford's Pennsylvania friend, also expressed similar views, believing that "[t]he punishment of death has been proved to be contrary to the order and happiness of society." As Dr. Rush wrote: "Every man possesses an absolute power over his own liberty and property, but not over his own life. When he becomes a member of political society, he commits the disposal of his liberty and property to his fellow citizens; but as he has no right to dispose of his life, he cannot commit the power over it to any body of men." "To take away life, therefore, for any crime," Dr. Rush wrote, "is a violation of the first political compact." Suicide—it had long been asserted by the founders' intellectual predecessors—was a sinful and wrongful act. In his *Summa Theologiae*, written in the thirteenth century, St. Thomas Aquinas, for example, had proclaimed that suicide is "totally wrong" and a "mortal sin." "God alone," Aquinas wrote in response to his self-formulated question *Is Suicide Permissible?*, "has authority over life and death." After John Quincy Adams wrote in 1785 to his cousin William Cranch about Elizabeth Duncan's suicide, with Duncan—the depressed woman—drowning herself in the Merrimack River, the following notation was made on the letter: "JQA Nov 15th. 1785 Haverhill Death of Mrs. Duncan (felo de se)." The Latin *felo de se* translates as "a felon against herself."[112]

Beccaria—residing in a region that knew all too well the tragic consequences of war—did carve out a narrow exception to his otherwise absolutist stance against capital punishment. In *On Crimes and Punishments*, Beccaria thus expressed the belief that it might be necessary to execute someone who might "endanger the security of the nation" or "produce a dangerous revolution in the established form of government." In effect, Beccaria worried about total lawlessness and conceived of a circumstance—then a very realistic possibility—where a rival vying for a monarch's throne might, even if imprisoned, jeopardize the monarch's reign. "But even in this case," Beccaria candidly clarified, "it can only be necessary when a nation is on the verge of recovering or losing its liberty; or in times of absolute anarchy, when the disorders themselves hold the place of laws." Thus, for all intensive purposes, Beccaria — living in a monarchical society — viewed death sentences as only being necessary in times of lawlessness, nation building, or where an offender, though confined in prison, might risk the very collapse of the government. The only other possible justification for capital punishment — that it might deter crime — was one Beccaria would reject elsewhere in his treatise as not being supported by the evidence.

The mid-eighteenth century saw a deluge of military conflicts. The War of Austrian Succession (1740–1748) involved most of the powers in Europe over the question of whether Maria Theresa — a woman — could secede to the throne of the House of Habsburg, and that war spawned King George's War (1744–1748) in North America, the third of the four French and Indian Wars. That war took place in the British provinces of Massachusetts Bay, New Hampshire, New York and Nova Scotia, and heavy losses were sustained in the fighting. But "in a reign of tranquility" or a state "well fortified from enemies without," John Adams' copy of Beccaria's treatise read in its London-printed ink, "there can be no necessity for taking away the life of a subject." "The death of a criminal is a terrible but momentary spectacle," Beccaria concluded, "and therefore a less efficacious method of deterring others, than the continued example of a man deprived of his liberty, condemned, as a beast of burthen, to repair, by his labour, the injury he has done to society." "The punishment of death," Beccaria reasoned, "is pernicious to society, from the example of barbarity it affords." "Is it not absurd," Beccaria asked, "that the laws, which detest and punish homicide, should, in order to prevent murder, publicly commit murder themselves?"[113] In short, Beccaria saw state-sanctioned killings in peacetime as just as morally reprehensible as killings carried out by criminals.

On Crimes and Punishments also spoke out against torture — a concept long associated with the intentional infliction of pain.[114] In chapter XVI, titled "Of Torture," Beccaria — worried about false confessions and inflicting "cruelty" on innocents — condemned the practice in no uncertain terms. "The torture of a criminal, during the course of his trial," John Adams' copy of Beccaria's treatise read, "is a cruelty consecrated by custom in most nations." "It is used," Beccaria wrote, "with an intent either to make him confess his crime, or explain some contradictions, into which he had been led during his examination; or discover his accomplices; or for some kind of metaphysical and incomprehensible purgation of infamy; or, finally, in order to discover other crimes, of which he is not accused, but of which he may be guilty."[115] For example, in a chapter titled "Crimes difficult to prove," Beccaria wrote that "adultery and sodomy" are "hard crimes to prove," but that in such cases, "the cold and iniquitous teaching of some learned men who presume to offer norms and rules to the judiciary, torture exercises its cruel prerogatives on the body of the accused, the witnesses and even the whole family of the unfortunate." "I do not mean to belittle the just revulsion which these crimes deserve," Beccaria wrote in the 1760s — a time much different than our own and in which homosexual acts were treated as criminal offenses. "But," he added, "having pointed out their sources, I think I am allowed to draw a general conclusion, which is that one cannot say that a punishment for a crime is exactly just (meaning necessary) until the law has instituted the best possible means in a given nation's circumstances for preventing such a crime."[116] In short, Beccaria equated the *necessity* of punishment with *justice* itself.

In *On Crimes and Punishments*, Beccaria specifically argued that torture is unlikely to produce truthful testimony and violates the principle that innocent people not be punished.[117] "No man," Beccaria wrote, "can be considered *guilty* before the judge has reached a verdict, nor can society deprive him of public protection until it has been established that he has violated the pacts that granted him such protection."[118] According to a more recent English-language translation of Beccaria's treatise, Beccaria expressed himself in this way in offering his critique of torture as then permitted by the civil law:

> [A]dultery and sodomy, which are crimes difficult to prove, are ones that, according to accepted principles, admit of the tyrannical presumptions of *quasi-proofs* and *semi-proofs* (as if a man could be *semi-innocent* or *semi-guilty*, which is to say, *semi-punishable* and *semi-acquittable*), in which torture exercises its cruel power over the person of the accused, over the witnesses, and even over the entire family of the poor wretch, as is taught with cold iniquity by some doctors of law who offer themselves to judges as substitutes for norms and laws.

"Verdicts and proofs of guilt," Beccaria wrote in another chapter of his treatise, "should be public, so that opinion, which is perhaps the only cement holding society together, may impose a restraint on force and passions, and so that the people may say, 'we are not slaves, and we are protected'—a sentiment that inspires courage and is worth as much as a tax to a sovereign who knows his own true interests."[119]

In the Anglo-American tradition, the protection of the innocent—and the judiciary's requirement that proof of guilt be shown beyond a reasonable doubt, as with the custom that jury verdicts in criminal cases be unanimous—has a long and storied heritage. Benjamin Franklin himself, in a letter he wrote to Benjamin Vaughan in 1785, expressed the view that "it is better 100 guilty Persons should escape than that one innocent Person should suffer." That "Maxim," Dr. Franklin wrote, echoing similar sentiments from European figures such as Blackstone and Voltaire, "has been long and generally approved."[120] In the United States, the requirement that the guilt of criminal defendants be proven "beyond a reasonable doubt" emerged in the eighteenth century. That formulation and well-settled legal protection is now considered so fundamental that—in one scholar's words—the U.S. Supreme Court "has read it into our constitutional law, even though the phrase 'reasonable doubt' appears nowhere in the Constitution."[121]

Beccaria especially decried the use of torture to punish infamy, writing in *On Crimes and Punishments* that "a man judged infamous by the law" should not suffer "the dislocation of his bones." "Torture itself," Beccaria emphasized, "causes real infamy to its victims." Beccaria worried particularly about "the risk of torturing an innocent person," and called efforts "*to purge a man from infamy*" a "ridiculous motive for torture." "Ought such an abuse to be tolerated in the eighteenth century?" Beccaria asked. Saying "infamy is a stain," Beccaria concluded that "torture renders the victim infamous, and therefore cannot take infamy away." "A person accused, imprisoned, tried, and acquitted," Beccaria wrote, "ought not to be branded with any degree of infamy." Beccaria's argument was straightforward. "A man on the rack, in the convulsions of torture," he wrote, "has it as little in his power to declare the truth, as in former times, to prevent without fraud the effects of fire or boiling water." "It would be superfluous," Beccaria wrote, "to confirm these reflections by examples of innocent persons, who, from the agony of torture, have confessed themselves guilty: innumerable instances may be found in all nations, and in every age." After noting that torture had been abolished in Sweden, Beccaria emphasized: "torture has not been thought necessary in the laws of armies." "By inflicting infamous punishments, for crimes that are not reputed so," Beccaria added, "we destroy that idea where it may be useful."

In his separate chapter on torture, Beccaria wrote about a "strange consequence" of the brutal practice: "[T]he innocent individual is placed in a worse condition than the guilty; for if both are tortured, every outcome is stacked against him, because either he confesses to a crime and is convicted or he is declared innocent and has suffered an undeserved punishment." As Beccaria, describing torture as "a cruelty," observed in *On Crimes and Punishments*: "[T]he impression of pain may increase to such a degree that, filling the entire sensory capacity, it leaves the torture victim no liberty but to choose the shortest route to relieve his pain momentarily." "Under these circumstances," Beccaria concluded, "the statements made by the accused are as inevitable as the impressions made by fire and water."[122] In Medieval judicial ordeals, the precursors to what modern Americans know as waterboarding, the accused was subjected to some harsh test, whether it be holding a hot iron or being cast into water, with a finding of guilt or innocence riding on the outcome. Thomas Jefferson himself, in 1809, lamented "how many human lives" conflicts over religion had "cost the Christian world!" Jefferson regretted the "oceans of blood" that had been spilt, referring to the "regions of the earth" that had been "desolated by wars & persecutions, in which human ingenuity has been exhausted in inventing new tortures for their brethren."[123]

Pleasure vs. Pain:
Deterrence and the Prevention of Crime

In the Enlightenment, the concepts of *pain* and *pleasure* were much discussed, including by philosophers such as Beccaria and John Locke. "That we call *Good*," Locke wrote, is that "which *is apt to cause or increase Pleasure, or diminish Pain in us.*" In *An Essay Concerning Human Understanding* (1690), Locke had written: "the highest perfection of intellectual nature lies in a careful and constant pursuit of true and solid happiness." "The stronger ties we have to an unalterable pursuit of happiness in general, which is our greatest good," Locke wrote in a passage about the foundation of liberty, "the more are we free from any necessary determination of our will to any particular action." In *The Reasonableness of Christianity*, Locke also argued that "Mankind" must be allowed "to pursue their happiness," with Locke viewing the pursuit of happiness as "the chief end" of mankind. Among the authors that Jefferson had read before 1776 in formulating the language of the Declaration of Independence were Locke and Beccaria, as well as William Blackstone, Jean-Jacques Burlamaqui, Thomas Hobbes, Francis Hutcheson and David Hume.[124] "The art of life," Thomas Jefferson would say, "is the art of avoiding pain; and he is the best pilot who steers clearest of the rocks and shoals with which it is beset."[125]

While torture was a common feature of criminal procedure in continental Europe, English writers such as Blackstone had extolled what one writer described as "the superiority of England's torture-free procedure."[126] In Roman canonical law, all capital crimes had to be proven by a defendant's confession or through two reliable eyewitnesses. Because serious crimes often lacked more than one witness, torture was frequently used to extract confessions from criminal suspects. Only if the suspect withstood judicial torture was the subject acquitted and released from custody. Torture, however, was prohibited by the English common law, and the English Privy Council was stripped of the right to issue torture warrants in 1640 — though torturous practices persisted in parts of Europe for many decades to come. For example, in France, Robert-François Damiens — a domestic servant — was publicly executed in 1757 after attempting to assassinate King Louis XV. Damiens was first tortured with red-hot pinchers and had his hand burnt with sulphur. After molten wax and lead, as well as boiling oil, were poured into his open wounds, he was then harnessed to horses and drawn and quartered, the traditional form of execution for regicides. It was also ordered that Damiens' limbs and body be "consumed by fire" and "reduced to ashes." His execution was the last drawing and quartering in France, but torturous means of execution took place elsewhere, too. In England, the last burning at the stake—of a woman, Mary Bayley—took place in 1784 just three years before the framers gathered in Philadelphia to draft the U.S. Constitution, while the last burning at the stake in Spain took place in 1781.[127]

The severity of judicial torture depended somewhat on the locale. In his *Laws and Customs of Scotland in Matters Criminal* (1678), Sir George Mackenzie insisted that torture was "warranted by our uncontroverted Law," though he wrote that "Torture is seldom used with us" and reported that the Privy Council's use of torture was "tender" in application. "Torture," Mackenzie wrote, "is intended for bringing the Verity to Light." An anonymous pamphlet about the Scottish Inquisition, published in Edinburgh in 1689, also described the brutal techniques of Charles II's ministers in enforcing religious and political conformity. That pamphlet noted attempts by officials to obtain information "all by Torture with their engines of Cruelty, the Boots, fired Matches betwixt the Fingers, and Thumbkins, and after torturing hanged several, tho' thereby they could extort nothing." Only after the Anglo-Scottish Union of 1707, notes scholar Clare Jackson, was "judicial torture" said to be "entirely proscribed by the British parliament of Queen Anne in 1708." "[A]mong those Enlightenment commentators who subsequently celebrated its statutory abolition," Jackson notes, "was Baron David Hume, for whom judicial torture remained 'a vestige of barbarity.'"[128]

By the time Beccaria wrote his treatise, Americans such as Benjamin Franklin had—due in part to English traditions, as well as personal proclivities—already come to see acts of torture as cruel and inhumane. Writing in 1729, Dr. Franklin had decried innocent men being "dragg'd into noisome Dungeons, tortured with cruel Irons, and even unmercifully *starv'd* to Death." And such views would continue to be expressed by American founders after the publication of Beccaria's treatise, with Jefferson showing his own disdain for torture, too. In a draft constitution for the Commonwealth of Virginia, Jefferson wrote in 1776 that "[t]he General assembly shall have no power … to prescribe torture in any case whatever." In his *Notes on the State of Virginia*, first published in Paris in 1784 and translated by André Morellet, the same man who translated Beccaria's *Dei delitti e delle pene* into French, Jefferson compared the torture of slaves under Roman law with Virginia's practice of not resorting to slaves for evidence. One of Jefferson's Virginia colleagues, Edmund Pendleton, himself emphasized that "the most respectable writers," including Montesquieu and Locke, "properly discard from their system, all the severity of cruel punishments, such as tortures, inquisitions, and the like."[129]

To be sure, Beccaria believed violent crimes, including murder, should be punished severely. But he simultaneously believed that the *prevention* of crime—and not the intentional *infliction* of pain—was the purpose of punishment. Expressing his preference for life imprisonment over capital punishment, Beccaria wrote: "To those who would say that permanent penal servitude is as painful as death, and therefore, equally cruel, I shall reply that, adding up all of the unhappy moments of slavery, it may very well be even more so, but these moments are drawn out over an entire lifetime, while death exerts the whole of its force in a single moment." In other words, while the impact of a death sentence was concentrated in a single moment, the consequences of a life sentence were spread out over the rest of an offender's natural life. "And this," Beccaria wrote, "is the advantage of penal servitude, which frightens those who witness it more than those who suffer it, for the former consider the entire sum of unhappy moments, while the latter are distracted from future unhappiness by the unhappiness of the present moment." "The purpose of punishment," Beccaria added, attempting to gauge the necessity of a punishment against its usefulness as a deterrent, "is none other than to prevent the criminal from doing fresh harm to fellow citizens and to deter others from doing the same." "Therefore," Beccaria emphasized, "punishments and the method of inflicting them must be chosen such that, in keeping with proportionality, they will make the most efficacious and lasting impression on the minds of men with the least torment to the body of the condemned."

For Beccaria, "perpetual penal servitude"—or life imprisonment, in today's parlance—was, in his judgment, the best, and most just and efficacious way to deter others.[130] Echoing Montesquieu, Beccaria emphasized—in a maxim that Americans would recite for decades to come[131]—that "every act of authority of one man over another that does not derive from absolute necessity is tyrannical." "For a punishment to be just," Beccaria wrote, trying to turn the act of punishment from a purely physical one into a psychologically orientated endeavor, "it must have only that degree of intensity that suffices to deter men from crime." "Now, there is no one who, upon reflection, would choose the total and permanent loss of his own liberty, no matter how advantageous a crime might be," Beccaria argued, writing that, "therefore, the intensity of perpetual penal servitude, substituted for the death penalty, has all that is necessary to deter even the most determined mind." "Indeed," Beccaria wrote of enslavement, "I would say that it has even more: a great many men look upon death with a calm and steady gaze, some out of fanaticism, some out of vanity (which almost always accompanies man beyond the grave), and some out of a final and desperate attempt either to live no longer or to escape from poverty." "But neither fanaticism nor vanity," Beccaria added, "survives in fetters or chains, under the cudgel and the yoke, or in an iron cage; and the desperate man finds that his woes are just beginning rather than ending."

In his book, Beccaria—like so many of America's founders—paid considerable homage to Montesquieu, calling him a "great" and "immortal" man. "As the great Montesquieu says," Beccaria wrote, in a theme that Americans would magnetically latch on to and repeat again and again, "every punishment that does not derive from absolute necessity is tyrannical." But while praising Montesquieu effusively, Beccaria—as he had done with Francis Hutcheson—parted ways with his French predecessor in some important respects, including on the particulars of the death penalty's use. While Beccaria saw no need for executions, Montesquieu's *Spirit of the Laws* favored executions for homicide—and even for the crime of theft.[132] Though Montesquieu had traveled widely, he was still a product of his times—a reality made clear by writings of the Scottish jurist and historian James Mackintosh. In Mackintosh's *Vindiciæ Gallicæ*, subtitled "Defense of the French Revolution and Its English Admirers, against the Accusations of the Right Hon. Edmund Burke," Mackintosh wrote in 1791: "The same Montesquieu, who at Paris reasoned as a philosopher of the eighteenth, was compelled to decide at Bourdeaux as a magistrate of the fourteenth century. The apostles of toleration and the ministers of the Inquisition were contemporaries. The torture continued to be practised in the age of Beccaria."[133]

Like Beccaria, Montesquieu—a forceful advocate for governmental separation of powers—was a favorite writer among America's founders and framers. At least in terms of the sheer number of references in speeches and writings, Montesquieu appears to have been even more popular and regularly invoked than Beccaria himself. Montesquieu's name, in fact, frequently appears in state ratification debates over the U.S. Constitution. In *The Federalist No. 47*, published on January 3, 1788, no less a figure than James Madison invoked Montesquieu repeatedly, writing: "The accumulation of all powers legislative, executive and judiciary in the same hands, whether of one, a few or many, and whether hereditary, self appointed, or elective, may justly be pronounced the very definition of tyranny." In that *Federalist Paper*, Madison—writing under the ancient Roman name "Publius" and addressing "the People of the State of New York"—referred to Montesquieu by name five separate times.[134]

In more traditionalist European quarters, executions—even after Beccaria's treatise was published—continued to be seen by most monarchs, judges and citizens as a necessary component of the criminal justice system. For example, when English barrister Martin Madan published his 1785 book, *Thoughts on Executive Justice*, he—like many others of his time—continued to see "severity" in the treatment of criminals as the best way forward. Exerting severity "by making examples of the guilty," Madan concluded, would help prevent crimes.[135] By contrast, Beccaria took a longer and much different view, seeing milder punishments, education and forced labor as the best means to prevent crimes and punish offenses such as theft.[136] And Beccaria's treatise—despite some hostility from figures such as Madan—made significant inroads in changing attitudes as readers, already squeamish about draconian punishments, responded to it. "Education," notes writer Frank McLynn in *Crime and Punishment in Eighteenth-Century England*, "was the key to a process of transcending the legacy of biology, of replacing instinct with intellect, unreason with reason." Even in England's tradition-bound legal culture, where executions had occurred at places such as Tyburn for centuries, Beccaria's ideas gained traction. As McLynn writes of eighteenth-century England: "The influence of Enlightenment criminologists like Beccaria was particularly strong here. By the 1790s the overwhelming intellectual response to the Bloody Code was that it was untenable: not only did it manifestly not work; it was also arbitrary, unfair, cruel, and inhumane."[137]

On Crimes and Punishments not only held up perpetual imprisonment as a viable alternative to executions, but it articulated a sensible rationale for that position. "It is not the terrible but fleeting spectacle of a criminal's death that is the most powerful brake on crimes," Beccaria reasoned, "but the long and arduous example of a man deprived of his liberty, who, having become a beast of burden, repays the society he has offended through his toils." "It is not the intensity of the punishment that has the greatest effect on the human mind," Beccaria wrote, "but its extension, for our sensibility is more easily and firmly affected by small but repeated impressions than by a strong but fleeting action." Seeing executions as ineffective and counterproductive, Beccaria observed: "With the death penalty, every example given to the nation requires a crime; with permanent penal servitude, a single crime provides many and lasting examples." In other words, Beccaria saw life sentences as far and away the most effective way to curtail crime; executions, he believed on the other hand, were sending the wrong message—and a corrosive one—to members of society. Anglo-American lawmakers themselves would later come to see public executions as "brutalizing" spectacles that often only prompted pickpocketing and crime, sometimes in the very shadow of the gallows. From the 1830s to the 1930s, American public executions gradually disappeared, replaced by executions within prisons or enclosures adjoining prisons. Connecticut, Massachusetts, New Hampshire, New Jersey, New York and Pennsylvania all passed laws in the 1830s prohibiting public executions, while England's Capital Punishment Within Prisons Bill gained passage in 1868.

In *On Crimes and Punishments*, Beccaria forcefully expressed the idea that a criminal's death could be justifiable only when a regime faced a dangerous threat of lawlessness or if the death penalty could be shown to deter others from committing crimes. "The death of a citizen," Beccaria wrote, "cannot be deemed necessary, except on two grounds." "The first," he opined, making his stance clear, "is when he retains such connections and such power that he endangers the security of the nation even when deprived of his liberty, that is, when his very existence can provoke a dangerous revolution in the established form of government." In that extremely limited circumstance, where the very collapse of a regime might be precipitated, Beccaria felt an execution could be justified. In the 1760s and 1770s, such a circumstance—the possibility of a government falling—was certainly a realistic possibility, with the War of Austrian Succession demonstrating the lust for power and control. The lands of southern Europe and the Italian states had changed hands over the preceding centuries, with monarchs coming and going, and the American colonies themselves experienced the pangs of war and revolution. The British colonization of North America led to violent clashes with Native Americans, and the colonists also became embroiled in the series of wars between France and Great Britain for control of North America. "But," Beccaria asserted in his treatise, "when the calm rule of law prevails, under a form of government that has the support of the nation, which is well-fortified both externally and internally by both force and opinion (which is perhaps more efficacious than force itself), and in which the power to rule is vested only in the true sovereign and wealth can buy only pleasures not authority, I do not see any need to destroy a citizen, unless his death were the only real way to deter others from committing crimes." Bottom line: Beccaria viewed executions as a last resort, to be used only if society was falling apart or if the government was at serious risk of being overthrown.

On the issue of deterrence, the death penalty's other possible justification, Beccaria made abundantly clear in *On Crimes and Punishments* that he saw no need for executions. The "second reason for believing that the death penalty could be just and necessary," Beccaria emphasized, was deterrence, though Beccaria found no evidence whatsoever that executions were necessary or effective in carrying out that stated objective. In that regard, Beccaria wrote that "centuries of experience" had taught him "the ultimate punishment has never deterred men determined to harm society."[138] Many murders had occurred in Europe in the preceding centuries and decades, and Beccaria may have sensed or contemplated what the hard-and-fast statistics surrounding such Enlightenment era homicides later revealed when compiled by modern historians: that most were committed by men, and that men in their twenties, the most likely to kill, often behaved badly even in the face of severe consequences.[139] In spite of death penalty laws, Beccaria recognized, murders and other crimes continued to take place—and no amount of death sentences and executions had been able to stop or arrest such criminal activity. Cold-blooded killings and crimes of passion had not stopped, no matter how harsh punishments or how brutal execution methods had become. In those days, there were no sophisticated statistical and regression analyzes, but Beccaria relied on his intellect, and what anecdotal evidence he had before him, to reach his conclusions. In drafting his manuscript, he thoughtfully reasoned that violent crime had remained a stubborn fact of life despite the centuries-old use of executions. Executions, then, were not the answer to solving the problem of violent crime.

After *On Crimes and Punishments* appeared in print, whether executions were necessary to deter crime would remain a central feature—as it is today—of the death penalty debate. For example, in his 1793 essay, *An Enquiry How Far the Punishment of Death Is Necessary in Pennsylvania*, William Bradford tabulated what crime statistics he could find pertaining to the efficacy—or lack thereof—of death penalty laws. If statistics were available to bolster his case that executions were unnecessary, Bradford was quick to cite them. At one point, Bradford—showing in part how he had come to his own views—wrote that "[t]he celebrated Beccaria is of opinion, that no government has a right to punish its subjects unless it has previously taken care to instruct them in the knowledge of the laws and the duties of public and private life." At another juncture, Bradford lamented: "sanguinary punishments, contrived in despotic and barbarous ages, have been continued when the progress of freedom, science, and morals renders them unnecessary and mischievous." In Bradford's 73-page report with extensive notes, Beccaria's name appears five times, and on the title page one finds the following quotation from Montesquieu: "If we enquire into the cause of all human corruptions, we shall find that they proceed from the impunity of crimes, and not from the moderation of punishments."[140]

In the years that followed the publication of *On Crimes and Punishments*, Beccaria would repeat his anti-death penalty views. In a government report he co-authored in 1792, just a year after the ratification of the U.S. Bill of Rights, Beccaria also added one more reason — the irrevocability of capital punishment — to support his abolitionist stance.[141] That report, written by Beccaria and two of his colleagues, Francesco Gallarati Scotti and Paolo Risi, articulated the minority position of a committee charged with drafting a new penal code for Austrian Lombardy. The minority report favored "perpetual enslavement" and "forced labour" for the most serious crimes, finding that "the death penalty should not be prescribed except in the case of absolute necessity." "[I]n the peaceful circumstances of our society, and with the regular administration of justice," Beccaria and his co-authors noted, "we could not think of any case of absolute necessity other than the situation in which the accused, in plotting the subversion of the state, was capable, either through his external or internal relationships, of disturbing and endangering society even while imprisoned and closely watched." Citing the Austrian and Tuscan codes they had received as models, Beccaria and his two co-authors felt compelled "to expose candidly and succinctly" their anti-death penalty views. "[W]e believe that the death penalty is not suitable," they wrote, "because it is not just, since it is not necessary"; "because it is less efficacious than perpetual punishment equipped with a good deal of continuous publicity"; and "because it cannot be undone."[142]

In *On Crimes and Punishments*, Beccaria — in the 1760s — also covered other important ground, including the method by which criminal suspects ought to be judged, the use of lesser corporal punishments and fines, and how the law should treat suicide. "The law according to which every man should be tried by his peers is a very useful one," Beccaria wrote in one chapter, "because, when a citizen's freedom and fortune are at stake, the sentiments inspired by inequality should be silenced." And "loss of freedom being a punishment," Beccaria offered in another chapter, "a man should suffer it no longer than necessary before being sentenced." "Remand in custody," Beccaria emphasized of what Americans would call *pre-trial detention* in today's terminology, "is the simple safe-keeping of a citizen until he may be judged guilty, and since this custody is intrinsically of the nature of a punishment, it should last the minimum possible time and should be as lacking in severity as can be arranged." "The minimum time," he said, "should be calculated taking into account both the length of time needed for the trial and the right of those who have been held the longest to be tried first." On the subject of suicide, Beccaria called laws punishing suicide "useless and unjust." As Beccaria wrote: "for even if it is a sin which God will punish, because only He can punish after death, it is not a crime before men, since the punishment, instead of falling on the malefactor, falls on his family." "Suicide," Beccaria emphasized, "is a crime which seems not to allow of being punished strictly speaking, since such a thing can only be visited either on the innocent or on a cold and insensible corpse."

In yet another chapter of his treatise, on the "Public peace," Beccaria pondered aloud as to the propriety of corporal punishments, especially taking into account his conception of tyranny and the inequality of wealth in Italian society. As Beccaria asked in *On Crimes and Punishments*: "Are torture and corporal punishment *just* and do they serve the *purpose* for which the laws were set up?" While Beccaria vehemently opposed torture and capital punishments, he did not see the injustice of non-lethal corporal punishments — at least for certain offenses. As Beccaria wrote without specifying which specific corporal punishments he had in mind: "Some crimes are assaults on persons, others are offences against goods. The former should always be punished with corporal punishment: the rich and the powerful should not be able to put a price on assaults on the weak and the poor; otherwise wealth, which is the reward of industry under the protection of the laws, feeds tyranny." "Thefts without violence," Beccaria argued in contrast, "should be punished with fines." Explaining that theft was often "the crime of poverty and desperation," Beccaria concluded: "the most fitting punishment shall be the only sort of slavery which can be called just, namely the temporary enslavement of the labour and person of the criminal to society, so that he may redress his unjust despotism against the social contract by a period of complete personal subjection." "But when violence is added to theft," Beccaria wrote, distinguishing between violent and non-violent offenses, "then the punishment ought to be likewise a mixture of corporal punishment and penal servitude." Disturbers of the public peace, Beccaria advised his readers, "must be ejected from society" and "banished."[143]

It was the exile or *transportation* of criminals to American and Australian penal colonies that would ultimately, in part, be responsible for populating those locales. Offenders had been sentenced to penal servitude and transported to Virginia plantations under a statute put in place by Queen Elizabeth in 1597, and transportation became a popular sentencing option in England. Between 1718 and 1776, roughly 50,000 British convicts were exiled to the American colonies to perform forced labor, a phenomenon that drew the ire of colonists. As Benjamin Franklin's *Pennsylvania Gazette* editorialized in 1751: "When we see our papers filled continually with accounts of the most audacious robberies, the most cruel murders, and infinite other villainies perpetrated by convicts transported from Europe, what melancholy, what terrible reflections it must occasion!" "What will become our posterity! These are some of thy favours, Britain!" the newspaper railed, the paper's ink continuing in a rant: "Thou art called our Mother Country; but what good mother ever sent thieves and villains to accompany her children; to corrupt them with their infectious vices, and murder the rest?" Benjamin Franklin, using his sharp wit, even suggested that Pennsylvanians, in exchange for English convicts, send rattlesnakes to be distributed throughout London and its sprawling St. James's Park, with Franklin saying that the snakes should be placed "in the gardens of the Prime Ministers, the Lords of Trade and Members of Parliament; for to them we are most particularly obliged."[144]

On the issue of corporal punishment, John Adams—in May 1776—himself contemplated such penalties as he wrestled with his own thoughts on the American social compact about to be formed—and who, exactly, would have the right to vote. To Massachusetts lawyer James Sullivan, who had written two letters that had been placed in Adams' hands by "[o]ur worthy Friend, Mr. Gerry," a reference to Massachusetts merchant Elbridge Gerry, Adams wrote: "Your Idea, that those Laws, which affect the Lives and personal Liberty of all, or which inflict corporal Punishments, affect those, who are not qualified to vote, as well as those who are, is just. But, So they do Women, as well as Men, Children as well as Adults." In writing about his own eighteenth-century-centric conception of the social compact, Adams told Sullivan:

> It is certain in Theory, that the only moral Foundation of Government is the Consent of the People. But to what an Extent Shall We carry this Principle? Shall We Say, that every Individual of the Community, old and young, male and female, as well as rich and poor, must consent, expressly to every Act of Legislation? No, you will Say. This is impossible. How then does the Right arise in the Majority to govern the Minority, against their Will? Whence arises the Right of the Men to govern Women, without their Consent? Whence the Right of the old to bind the Young, without theirs.
>
> But let us first Suppose, that the whole Community of every Age, Rank, Sex, and Condition, has a Right to vote. This Community, is assembled—a Motion is made and carried by a Majority of one Voice. The Minority will not agree to this. Whence arises the Right of the Majority to govern, and the Obligation of the Minority to obey? from Necessity, you will Say, because there can be no other Rule. But why exclude Women? You will Say, because their Delicacy renders them unfit for Practice and Experience, in the great Business of Life, and the hardy

Enterprizes of War, as well as the arduous Cares of State. Besides, their attention is So much engaged with the necessary Nurture of their Children, that Nature has made them fittest for domestic Cares. And Children have not Judgment or Will of their own. True. But will not these Reasons apply to others? Is it not equally true, that Men in general in every Society, who are wholly destitute of Property, are also too little acquainted with public Affairs to form a Right Judgment, and too dependent upon other Men to have a Will of their own? If this is a Fact, if you give to every Man, who has no Property, a Vote, will you not make a fine encouraging Provision for Corruption by your fundamental Law? Such is the Frailty of the human Heart, that very few Men, who have no Property, have any Judgment of their own. They talk and vote as they are directed by Some Man of Property, who has attached their Minds to his Interest.

Referring to the English political thinker James Harrington (1611–1677), whose seventeenth-century utopia *The Commonwealth of Oceana* (1656) Adams was fond of quoting, Adams' letter to James Sullivan continued:

Harrington has Shewn that Power always follows Property. This I believe to be as infallible a Maxim, in Politicks, as, that Action and Reaction are equal, is in Mechanicks. Nay I believe We may advance one Step farther and affirm that the Ballance of Power in a Society, accompanies the Ballance of Property in Land. The only possible Way then of preserving the Ballance of Power on the side of equal Liberty and public Virtue, is to make the Acquisition of Land easy to every Member of Society: to make a Division of the Land into Small Quantities, So that the Multitude may be possessed of landed Estates. If the Multitude is possessed of the Ballance of real Estate, the Multitude will have the Ballance of Power, and in that Case the Multitude will take Care of the Liberty, Virtue, and Interest of the Multitude in all Acts of Government.

In rejecting Sullivan's assertion that men without property — in Sullivan's words, "every person out of wardship" — should have the right to vote, Adams concluded his letter:

Depend upon it, sir, it is dangerous to open So fruitfull a Source of Controversy and Altercation, as would be opened by attempting to alter the Qualifications of Voters. There will be no End of it. New Claims will arise. Women will demand a Vote. Lads from 12 to 21 will think their Rights not enough attended to, and every Man, who has not a Farthing, will demand an equal Voice with any other in all Acts of State. It tends to confound and destroy all Distinctions, and prostate all Ranks, to one common Levell.

Sullivan had suggested a two-tiered voting system, that would take relative wealth into account, a suggestion Adams also rejected as impractical.[145]

In addition to discussing corporal punishments, the concept of exile, and his own ideas on the ideal shape of republicanism, Beccaria's treatise addressed other more philosophical subjects, too, including the very origins of punishment and the justification for law. "If we open our history books," Beccaria wrote in his introduction, "we shall see that the laws, for all that they are or should be contracts amongst free men, have rarely been anything but the tools of the passions of a few men or the offspring of a fleeting and haphazard necessity." "They have not been dictated," Beccaria wrote, "by a cool observer of human nature, who has brought the actions of many men under a single gaze and has evaluated them from the point of view of whether or not they conduce to *the greatest happiness shared among the greater number*."[146] Beccaria's conception of law, as he articulated it, thus differed markedly from Machiavelli's *realpolitik* and the ancient writers who wrote about English common law. For example, the English jurist Henry de Bracton — the author of *The Laws and Customs of England*—wrote in the thirteenth century about "What law is and what custom." "We must see what law is," Bracton wrote from an entirely different perspective. "Law," Bracton recorded, "is a general command, the decision of judicious men, the restraint of offences knowingly or unwittingly committed, the general agreement of the *res publica*." According to Bracton: "Justice proceeds from God, assuming that justice lies in the Creator, and thus *jus* and *lex* are synonymous. And though law (*lex*) may in the broadest sense be said to be everything that is read (*legitur*) its special meaning is a just sanction, ordering virtue and prohibiting its opposite." On the topic of English traditions, Bracton opined thus: "Custom, in truth, in regions where it is approved by the practice of those who use it, is sometimes observed as and takes the place of *lex*. For the authority of custom and long use is not slight."[147]

In Beccaria's view, executions were unjust and were—in an ideal world, one prosperous and free of tyranny and injustice—to be excised from the law. "Laws," Beccaria noted in the first chapter of his treatise, describing his preferred version of a social compact, "are the terms under which independent and isolated men come together in a society." "Wearied by living in an unending state of war and by a freedom rendered useless by the uncertainty of retaining it," he wrote, "they sacrifice a part of that freedom in order to enjoy what remains in security and calm." After invoking Montesquieu, that guiding hand for so many Enlightenment thinkers, for the proposition that punishments not derived from "absolute necessity" are "tyrannous," Beccaria described "the necessity of defending the repository of the public well-being from the usurpations of individuals" as "the foundation of the sovereign's right to punish crimes." Beccaria also made specific reference to the "social contract"—a concept wrestled with by philosophers such as Thomas Hobbes, John Locke and Jean-Jacques Rousseau. The social contract "compelled men to give up a part of their freedom," Beccaria wrote, adding that "pleasure and pain are the motive forces of all sentient beings" and that "justice" is "the restraint necessary to hold particular interests together, without which they would collapse into the old state of unsociability." "Any punishment that goes beyond the need to preserve this bond," Beccaria wrote, "is unjust by its very nature." "Justice," Beccaria argued, promoting the concept of *common utility* as the foundation of human justice, "is simply a way whereby humans conceive of things, a way which influences beyond measure the happiness of all."

Instead of following old customs, Beccaria favored codified, well-publicized laws—non-arbitrarily applied—that would be followed to the tee. "Where the laws are clear and precise," he explained, "the judge's task is merely to discover the facts." As Beccaria wrote in his own particular and sometimes long-winded style:

> When a fixed code of laws, which must be followed to the letter, leaves the judge no role other than that of enquiring into citizens' actions and judging whether they conform or not to the written law, and when the standards of just and unjust, which ought to guide the actions of the ignorant citizen as much as those of the philosopher, are not a matter of debate but of fact, then the subjects are not exposed to the petty tyrannies of the many individuals enforcing the law, tyrannies which are the crueller the smaller the distance between him who inflicts and him who suffers.

"Nothing is more dangerous than the popular saw that we ought to consult the spirit of the law," Beccaria argued, noting that every person—and hence every judge—"has his own point of view." "It is for this reason," Beccaria explained, "that we see the same court punish the same crime differently at different times, because it consults not the constant and fixed voice of the law, but the erring instability of interpretations."

Beccaria devoted a whole chapter of his treatise to the interpretation of the laws. As Beccaria, in *On Crimes and Punishments*, wrote on that subject and the obscurity of the laws, seeking a way to remedy the problem: "it is the greatest of evils if the laws be written in a language which is not understood by the people and which makes them dependent upon a few individuals because they cannot judge for themselves what will become of their freedom or their life and limbs." "The more people understand the sacred code of the laws and get used to handling it, the fewer will be the crimes," Beccaria added, advocating an informed citizenry and elsewhere making reference to the "Creator," "the Almighty," "His Omnipotence," and "God." With chapter four of Beccaria's treatise devoted exclusively to the interpretation of the laws, one translator of *On Crimes and Punishments* puts it this way of that chapter: "The entire chapter is a reaction against the unbridled judicial discretion characteristic of Beccaria's day." As that translator, David Young, notes: "With the blend of Roman law, local custom, royal decrees, judicial commentaries, and court precedent which constituted the legal systems in most of Europe, judges had all but total authority to decide what laws would be applied and to whom." Beccaria himself strongly favored precisely worded codes over vaguely understood or unpublished or ill-defined customs as the basis for punishment, sentiments that would spill over into American legal culture.

In *On Crimes and Punishments*, Beccaria also had much to say on the subject of honor and duels between nobles. "Private duels, whose origin lay in the very anarchy of the laws," Beccaria wrote, "arose from this need for others' esteem." In diagnosing what drove respectable men to duel and why laws making dueling a capital offense had failed to eliminate the practice, Beccaria editorialized: "Attempts to put a stop to this custom by decrees of death against those who engage in duels have been in vain, for it is founded on something which some men fear more than death." Rooted in medieval codes of chivalry, duels in Europe—whether fought with swords or pistols—had a long history, especially among military officers and gentlemen. "Deprived of the esteem of others," Beccaria noted, "the man of honour sees himself doomed to become either a merely solitary being, which would be an insupportable condition for a sociable man, or the butt of insults and slander, whose combined effect would be greater than the danger of punishment."

In the Middle Ages and early modern Europe, men—and occasionally women—squared away in these affairs of honor, often assisted by *seconds*, who facilitated the duels. In Italy, a famous duel had been fought in 1552 by two young women, Isabella de Carazzi and Diambra de Pettinella, over the affections of Fabio de Zeresola, a much sought-after bachelor in sixteenth-century Naples; and duels in Britain, Ireland, France, Russia and Spain were well known, too. The Irish *Code Duello*—a set of twenty-five rules respecting "the practice of duelling and points of honor settled at the Clonmel summer assizes, 1777, by gentlemen delegates of Tipperary, Galway, Sligo, Mayo and Roscommon, and prescribed for general adoption throughout Ireland"—itself became generally accepted in England, continental Europe and North America as a code for duels, though themselves, as a matter of law, illegal. In 1762, before the publication of Beccaria's treatise, the Englishman John Wilkes—a member of Parliament—fought a particularly high-profile duel with Lord Talbot, and the following year, in Hyde Park, Wilkes also dueled another man, Samuel Martin, over Martin's use of the phrase "cowardly scoundrel." In February and March of 1764 alone, England saw four prominent duels.[148]

Libels and slanders—even petty slights taken the wrong way—were the cause of many duels, and this was also true in colonial and early America. In 1777, Button Gwinnett—a signer of the Declaration of Independence—actually died as the result of wounds suffered in a Georgia duel caused by a feud with another man, Lachlan McIntosh. "Why is it," Beccaria pondered in his own native city of Milan, "that ordinary people for the most part do not duel as noblemen do?" "It is not just that they are unarmed," Beccaria explained, "but because the need for others' esteem is less common among the humble classes than it is among those who, being exalted, regard each other with greater circumspection and jealousy." Beccaria's prescription, drawn from the writings of other commentators: "It is not useless to repeat what others have written, which is that the best way to prevent this crime is to punish the aggressor, that is, the person whose action caused the duel, and to absolve him who, through no fault of his own, was compelled to defend what the current laws do not guarantee, his good name." While defamation suits have replaced duels in modern American life, eighteenth-century elites saw monetary compensation as insufficient. "Personal injuries which damage honour, that is, the proper esteem that a citizen can rightly expect from others," Beccaria wrote in *On Crimes and Punishments*, "ought to be punished with public disgrace."

As for the punishment of debtors, a subject that would engage Americans in the years to come, Beccaria believed it important "to distinguish between the fraudulent bankrupt and the innocent bankrupt." "The former," he wrote, "ought to be punished with the same penalties which attach to the counterfeiter, because counterfeiting a metal coin, which is a token of the obligations citizens owe to each other, is no greater crime than counterfeiting the obligations themselves." "But the innocent bankrupt," Beccaria pointed out, "is one who, after thorough investigation before his judges, has shown that he was stripped of his goods either by the wrongdoing of others, by the misfortune of others, or by circumstances beyond human control." As to that category of debtor, Beccaria raised the following question: "On what barbarous grounds should he be thrown into prison, deprived of the sole, blighted good which is freedom, to suffer the miseries of the guilty, and, with the desperation of oppressed righteousness, perhaps go so far as to repent of his own innocence in which he lived peacefully under the protection of the laws, which it was beyond his power not to break?" "Men's most superficial feelings," Beccaria wrote, "lead them to prefer cruel laws." "Nevertheless," Beccaria advised, "when they are subjected to them themselves, it is in each man's interest that they be moderate, because the fear of being injured is greater than the desire to injure." "The distinctions between serious and mild offences," he wrote, "should be fixed by blind and impartial laws, not by the dangerous and arbitrary discretion of judges."

In *On Crimes and Punishments*, Beccaria also set forth his views on a whole host of other issues, ranging from the propriety of extradition treaties, to smuggling and bounties, to accomplices and attempted crimes, to asylums, rewards, pardons and the prevention of crime. For example, Beccaria wrote that "as to whether extradition is useful I would not dare say until there are laws better suited to human needs, and more lenient punishments that put an end to dependence on fickleness and mere opinion." "Nevertheless," he added, "the belief that there is no scrap of ground on which real crimes are tolerated would be an extremely effective way of preventing them." "Although the laws do not punish intentions," Beccaria wrote elsewhere, "surely an action which shows a clear intent to commit a crime deserves to be punished, albeit less harshly than the actual execution of the crime would be." On pardons, Beccaria offered this advice: "As punishments become milder, clemency and pardons become less necessary." "To show men that crimes can be pardoned, and that punishment is not their inevitable consequence," Beccaria wrote of clemency, the traditional prerogative of the throne, "encourages the illusion of impunity and induces the belief that, since there are pardons, those sentences which are not pardoned are violent acts of force rather than the products of justice."

In his chapter on "How to prevent crimes," Beccaria emphasized the betterment of society, beginning as follows: "It is better to prevent crimes than to punish them. This is the principal goal of all good legislation, which is the art of guiding men to their greatest happiness, or the least unhappiness possible, taking into account all the blessings and evils of life." As Beccaria argued in *On Crimes and Punishments*: "Make sure that men fear the laws and only the laws. Fear of the law is salutary; but man's fear of his fellows is fatal and productive of crimes." "Slavish men," Beccaria wrote in an era still dominated by indentured servants and the slave trade, "are more debauched, more sybaritic and crueller than free men. The latter ponder the sciences and the interests of the nation, they envisage and aspire to great things; but the former are content with the present moment and seek amid the din of depravity a distraction from the emptiness of their everyday lives." With abject poverty rampant in Europe and economic and human development high on his agenda, Beccaria took a forward-looking approach. "Do you want to prevent crimes?" Beccaria queried. "Then make sure that the laws are clear and simple and that the whole strength of the nation is concentrated on defending them, and that no part of it is used to destroy them." "Then see to it that enlightenment and freedom go hand in hand." "Finally," Beccaria added, "the surest but hardest way to prevent crime is to improve education."

In a chapter on "False ideas of utility," Beccaria further lamented "the false ideas of utility held by some lawgivers." "The laws which forbid men to bear arms are of this sort," Beccaria wrote, saying that such laws "only disarm those who are neither inclined nor determined to commit crimes." As Beccaria editorialized: "Can it be supposed that those who have the courage to violate the most sacred laws of humanity and the most important in the civil code will respect the lesser and more arbitrary laws, which are easier and less risky to break, and which, if enforced, would take away the personal freedom—so dear to man and to the enlightened lawgiver—and subject the innocent man to all the annoyances which the guilty deserve?" "These laws," Beccaria added, "make the victims of attack worse off and improve the position of the assailant. They do not reduce the murder rate but increase it, because an unarmed man can be attacked with more confidence than an armed man."[149] In his commonplace book, Thomas Jefferson—picking up on Beccaria's assertions on gun ownership—copied by hand at great length from Beccaria's treatise. Among other things, Jefferson's copied Beccaria's assertion that "[l]aws that forbid the carrying of arms ... disarm only those who are neither inclined nor determined to commit crimes."[150]

In summing up all that he had written, Beccaria—in his conclusion and taking a much different approach than the English common law—said "it is possible to draw a very useful general axiom, though it little conforms to custom." That axiom: "*In order that punishment should not be an act of violence perpetrated by one or many upon a private citizen, it is essential that it should be public, speedy, necessary, the minimum possible in the given circumstances, proportionate to the crime, and determined by the law.*"[151] In other words, Beccaria—through his treatise—was attempting to change, not conform to, custom. He believed that the law could be made more just through the death penalty's abolition, and saw customary practices such as torture and executions as impediments to the idealized world he saw might be possible. The English Bloody Code was the antithesis of the model of criminal justice Beccaria had in mind, and as Americans grew more and more dissatisfied with British rule in the 1760s and 1770s, they naturally gravitated into Beccaria's orbit. The major themes of Beccaria's treatise—public and speedy justice, the proportionality of crime and punishment, and the assessment by lawmakers of the necessity of particular punishments—would dramatically play out in America in the decades following the publication of Beccaria's book.

Upon reading Beccaria's treatise, American colonists and early American lawmakers latched onto and took many of Beccaria's ideas to heart. For one thing, they began moving away from discretion-dependent, common-law crimes and started promulgating more detailed, statutory criminal codes to take their place. Early Americans often expressed hostility toward various aspects of the English common law, something Justice Hugo Black, of the U.S. Supreme Court, later noted by employing a comparison to escaping bondage. Writing in 1958, Justice Black emphasized: "Those who formed the Constitution struck out anew free of previous shackles in an effort to obtain a better order of government more congenial to human liberty and welfare. It cannot be seriously claimed that they intended to adopt the common law wholesale." As Black wrote of America's framers' ambivalent and conflicted attitudes toward the English common law: "They accepted those portions of it which were adapted to this country and conformed to the ideals of its citizens and rejected the remainder." "In truth," Black added, "there was widespread hostility to the common law in general and profound opposition to its adoption into our jurisdiction from the commencement of the Revolutionary War until long after the Constitution was ratified." In the U.S. Constitution's Sixth Amendment, early Americans also specifically provided that the accused "be informed of the nature and cause of the accusation," with the U.S. Supreme Court, in 1812, holding that federal courts had no power to adopt common law crimes and that their authority flowed only from the U.S. Constitution and Congress.[152]

Post-Publication Events

From a publishing standpoint, *On Crimes and Punishments* was a huge success, though reactions to the book's substance varied widely depending on the reader. "Published anonymously in Livorno for fear of repercussions," scholar Bernard Harcourt notes, "it was panned in the *Parisian Gazette littéraire de l'Europe* as a simple restatement of Rousseau's *Social Contract* and attacked in Italy as the work of a 'socialista.'" But the little treatise quickly attracted the attention of a small group of French *philosophes* known as the *Encyclopédistes*. Those Frenchmen opposed a 1716 French law that provided for the death penalty for all categories of desertion, regardless of extenuating circumstances, in times of war and peace. In 1765, a lengthy, anonymous article titled "Transfuge" — later attributed to the Marquis de Jean-François Saint-Lambert — appeared in the *Encyclopédie* that was highly critical of the 1716 law. A letter written by Voltaire in 1766 contained similar ideas, stating in part: "One uselessly kills a number of fine men who could have been useful, without having the slightest impact on desertion."

Shortly after the original anonymous publication of Beccaria's treatise in Livorno, André Morellet, an abbé of the Sorbonne, completed his French translation of it. Morellet reportedly translated Beccaria's Italian treatise after it was brought to the attention of the *philosophes* by French statesman Guillaume-Chrétien de Lamoignon de Malesherbes. At a dinner party, Malesherbes discussed *Dei delitti e delle pene*, asking Morellet to try to translate it. Among those at the dinner: economist Anne-Robert-Jacques Turgot, then the *intendant* of Limoges, and Jean le Rond d'Alembert, co-editor with Denis Diderot of the *Encyclopédie*. "With amazing rapidity," scholar Matthew Pauley recounts of *On Crimes and Punishments*, "the book became the toast of salons and courts from Paris to Vienna."[153] Between February and September of 1766, Morellet's French translation of Beccaria's treatise went through seven printings of 1,000 copies each.[154] By 1766, Voltaire's *Commentaire sur le livre des délits et des peines* was also available in print, and Beccaria — praised as "a teacher of laws in Italy" — was said to have "opened the eyes of many of the lawyers of Europe who had been brought up in absurd and inhuman usages."[155]

In the introduction to his 1963 translation of Beccaria's treatise, the late classics professor Henry Paolucci writes of the aftermath of the publication of *On Crimes and Punishments*, saying it was "as if an exposed nerve had been touched, all Europe was stirred to excitement." Morellet's French translation, *Traité des délits et des peines*, was publicly released in December 1765, and in a letter to Beccaria dated January 3, 1766, Morellet sent Beccaria regards from Diderot and d'Alembert; Helvétius and Buffon; Paul-Henri Thiry, baron d'Holbach; and David Hume, then living in Paris. All of these men, Morellet wrote, had read and enjoyed the new translation. Morellet also told Beccaria that a copy of the book had been delivered to Rousseau, with Morellet—who acquired much fame through his translation—inviting Beccaria to come to Paris. There, Rousseau had befriended Diderot and d'Alembert in the bohemian cafés of Paris, with Rousseau making contributions to Diderot and d'Alembert's famous *Encyclopédie*, edited from 1746 to 1758. A Genevan philosopher whose writings were avidly read by John Adams and Thomas Jefferson, and whose books later inspired the French Revolution, Rousseau published his *Discourse on the Origin and Basis of Inequality Among Men* in 1754, with Rousseau's *The Social Contract* (1762)—which generated enormous interest after its publication—asserting that "Man is born free, and everywhere he is in chains." In no time at all, as Paolucci emphasized in his introduction to his translation of *On Crimes and Punishments*, "Beccaria became a world celebrity." As icing on the cake, Voltaire, the famous French writer, praised Beccaria's book as *le code de l'humanité* and took the time to write his long commentary on it.[156] By the end of the eighteenth century approximately sixty editions of *On Crimes and Punishments* had been published.[157]

Voltaire's 1766 commentary on Beccaria's treatise, frequently reprinted with later editions of *On Crimes and Punishments*, helped to fuel its success. Voltaire had corresponded with Beccaria about his earlier work on monetary reform, and James Macdonald, a young Scotsman returning from Italy, delivered to Voltaire an Italian edition of *On Crimes and Punishments*.[158] "I was engrossed by a reading of *On Crimes and Punishments*," Voltaire's passionate commentary begins. "It was tyranny in particular," Voltaire declared, "that first decreed the death penalty for those who differed with the established Church on some dogmas." "It is clear," Voltaire added, "that twenty robust thieves, sentenced to labour on some public works for all of their lives, serve the state through their suffering, and that their deaths will only benefit the public executioner, who is paid to kill people in public." Although Voltaire wanted to meet Beccaria, the two men—according to a number of accounts—never met face to face, though an allusion to a meeting between the men in Ferney, the French town along the Swiss border where Voltaire lived for many years, is found in one 1791 English source. "The compassionate author of *On Crimes and Punishments*," Voltaire explained in his commentary to Beccaria's treatise, "is more than justified to complain that punishment is too often excessive in relation to the crime, and that sometimes it is even detrimental to the state it was intended to benefit." Reciting the adage that "a hanged man is good for nothing," Voltaire urged his readers to "read and reread the work of this lover of humanity."[159]

Other commentaries on Beccaria's book, such as Muyart de Vouglans' *Réfutation des principes hasardés dans le Traité des délits et des peines*, published in Lausanne, also followed by 1767—the same year Joseph Michel Antoine Servan (1737–1807) published his *Discours sur l'administration criminelle* in Yverdon. The prominent French jurist Pierre-François Murat de Vouglans—as it is sometimes spelled in translation—attacked Beccaria's ideas, making the odd argument that "the person likely to experience" torture "must be regarded as more than half convicted of the crime, so that the danger of confusing the innocent with the guilty is not so much to be feared." This illogical argument, as one commentator later wrote, provided an opening for Voltaire's scathing sarcasm, with Voltaire—skewer in hand—writing that "half proofs are admitted, which is a palpable absurdity for we know that there are no half-truths." "But at Toulouse," Voltaire needled, alluding to the well-publicized case of Jean Calas, "they allow quarter and eighths of proof." Calas, a dealer in woolen goods, had suffered mightily due to his despondent son, Marc-Antoine, who hanged himself on the night of October 13, 1761. After Jean Calas' family tried to conceal the suicide in light of a French law requiring that any suicide victim's corpse be dragged through the streets, the parliament of Toulouse— voting eighteen to thirteen—decreed on March 9, 1762, that Jean Calas be broken on the wheel and that his son Pierre be banished in perpetuity.[160] Servan's views, in contrast to those of Pierre-François Murat de Vouglans, were much closer to Beccaria's, though not identical. A member of Parlement of Grenoble, Servan—inspired by Beccaria, as he wrote Morellet in 1767—attacked torture and prevailing customs. Criticizing detention pending trial, Servan called—as Beccaria had—for major criminal justice reforms.[161]

After its 1764 publication, Beccaria's book garnered enough accolades that he became a sought-after personality. No doubt flattered by all the attention his book had received, Beccaria eventually decided to accept the invitation of Turgot, one of the French *Encyclopédistes*, and Malesherbes, d'Alembert and others.[162] Though young Cesare loathed the idea of leaving his wife and was not at ease in the limelight, Pietro and Alessandro Verri persuaded him to go to Paris. Scarcely thirty miles outside of Milan, however, Beccaria— eager to meet his Parisian admirers yet already missing his wife Teresa—expressed his misgivings and apprehensions. "I am continually oscillating between joy and hypochondria," he wrote. Worried that his friends would mock his quick onset of homesickness if he turned around, Beccaria continued on, arriving in the City of Light on October 18, 1766, accompanied by Alessandro, the Verri brother closer in age to young Cesare. There, Beccaria's French admirers greeted them warmly and with much hospitality. "No sooner had Beccaria arrived at Paris than Baron d'Holbach invited him to his suppers, where Helvetius, Rousseau and all who called themselves followers of the philosophy of humanity met and by their discussions prepared the social revolution," Carlo Calisse explains in *A History of Italian Law*.[163]

While in Paris, Beccaria—then only twenty-eight—met with French intellectuals, including Jean-Charles Philibert Trudaine de Montigny and the Marquis de Chastellux, and attended the salons of Suzanne Churchod Necker and Marie Thérèse Rodet Geoffrin. The people he met—and the Frenchmen interested in his book—had substantial ties to the English-speaking world, with word traveling fast about Beccaria's little treatise. For example, François Jean de Beauvior, Marquis de Chastellux, wrote to Jeremy Bentham in 1778 and referenced "Mr. *Beccaria*." Likewise, the Earl of Shelburne had met André Morellet—the translator of *On Crimes and Punishments*—at the house of Madame Trudaine, with the relationship between the Earl and Morellet developing into a friendship. As one source reports: "They agreed to correspond, and in the following year Morellet visited Bowood, where in the company of Franklin and Garrick, and Barré and Priestley, he seems to have found almost the equivalent of the brilliant society he had left on the other side of the Channel." Morellet had been confined to the Bastille from April to August of 1760, and upon his release had dedicated himself to law reform. The Earl of Shelburne— much influenced by Morellet's work—would himself make Beccaria's acquaintance in the early 1770s in Milan. For his own part, Morellet distributed copies of his translation of Beccaria's book, *Des délits et des peines*, to Englishmen such as David Garrick, a playwright and pupil and friend of Dr. Samuel Johnson.[164]

The cultural institutions associated with the Enlightenment—reading clubs, coffeehouses, political societies, and salons—flourished in both French and Italian society, though French and Italian intellectuals had their differences. "Special conditions in Italy helped to stamp enlightened ideas coming from that area with a particular form," one encyclopedia notes. "The power of the pope," that source emphasizes, "reached widely and penetrated deeply into the political fabric of Italian states." "D'Holbach and the others," Enlightenment historian Jonathan Israel writes of the Paris trip by Cesare and Alessandro, "went out of their way to welcome and encourage them." But after spending a few weeks in France, a taciturn Beccaria—missing his wife and still feeling ill at ease—became anxious, quarreled with Alessandro, and cut his trip short. "Remember that I love you tenderly, that I prefer my dear wife, my children, my family, my friends in Milan, and you chiefly, to the whole of Paris," a lovesick Beccaria had written to his wife Teresa from Paris just a day after his arrival there. In another letter, written just a week later, Beccaria spoke in much the same vein. As Cesare wrote to Teresa: "Nothing distracts me; nothing can make me forget that you are away from me. If I had the means necessary to get you to come here, I would do so; but it is impossible; the expense is very great. I shall therefore return to Milan." While Cesare returned to his native city in December 1766, the more adventurous Alessandro traveled on to London, back to Paris, then to Rome.

While Alessandro became—in Jonathan Israel's words—"[d]isgusted by the Parisian *encyclopédistes'* irreligion," his now estranged friend, Cesare Beccaria, once back in Milan, retreated into relative isolation, though his name and his ideas remained anything but obscure. One printer in Naples requested the King's permission to reprint *On Crimes and Punishments* "in order that the money of purchasers might remain in the kingdom," and the Economic Society of Berne awarded the treatise author—then still not publicized— a gold medal. "While of only pamphlet proportions," lawyer Richard Sipe wrote in the *Indiana Law Journal* in the 1940s, "Beccaria's treatise is certainly the most brilliant single contribution to criminal law reform that has ever appeared." Whereas Alessandro Verri, after his travels, fell in love in Rome and stayed there, Beccaria—still interested in reform—went on to accept an appointment as a professor of political economy at the Palatine School in Milan and, later, one in the Habsburg administration working as a member of the Supreme Economic Council of Milan. Having been unfairly accused of sedition and impiety following the publication of his book, Beccaria largely retreated from the public limelight, lecturing and preparing government reports on everything from corn stores and coinage reform to demographics and weights and measures, proposing a metric system in 1780 based on astronomical properties.[165]

After reading Beccaria's treatise, some European monarchs also expressed their particular affection for Beccaria's enlightened approach. In Russia, Catherine II—much impressed by Beccaria's intellect, albeit from afar—even asked Beccaria to come to personally assist in the reform of her country's criminal laws. "Every sentence," says one writer of Catherine II's draft penal code, "is directly inspired by Beccaria's *Dei delitti e delle pene*, or by Montesquieu's *L'Esprit des Lois*."[166] In a September 6, 1777 letter to Voltaire, Prussian monarch Frederick II—singled out by Beccaria in his treatise as "one of the wisest monarchs of Europe" because of the abolition of torture in lands he controlled—also returned Beccaria's compliment. In his letter, Frederick II lauded Beccaria by writing: "Beccaria has left nothing to glean after him; we need only to follow what he has so wisely indicated."[167] Frederick II—as one source explains—"was one of the best-educated and most cultured monarchs in the eighteenth century. He was well versed in Enlightenment thought and even invited Voltaire to live at his court for several years." "For a time," that source notes, "Frederick seemed quite willing to follow the philosophes' suggestions for reform. He established a single code of laws for his territories that eliminated the use of torture except in treason and murder cases."[168]

In another letter to Marquis de Condorcet, written on October 14, 1785, Frederick II put it this way: "I come to the articles of laws, so well explained by Beccaria, and on which you have likewise written. I am entirely of your opinion that judges ought not to be hasty in pronouncing sentence, and that to save the guilty is better than to murder the innocent." Frederick II expressed the view that "there are cases in which the atrocity of the crime demands rigour in the chastisement," but he wrote of "perpetual imprisonment" and emphasized in his letter: "I have done every thing in my power to reform the laws, and obviate the abuses of courts of justice." In an earlier letter to de Condorcet, dated June 29, 1785, Frederick II had written: "With respect to your opinion on the punishment of death, I am glad it is the same with that of the marquis Beccaria. In most countries, culprits are only punished with death for atrocious crimes." In his letter, Frederick II then qualified his position, writing: "A son who kills his father, a poisoner, and other flagrant offenders, require exemplary punishment; that fear may detain the depraved, who might otherwise be capable of similar guilt."[169] A first-rate scientist and an advocate of women's suffrage and racial equality, Condorcet — who spoke against Louis XVI's execution — corresponded with Benjamin Franklin and wrote pamphlets read with interest by John Adams, Thomas Jefferson and James Madison. In 1774, in an early statement of American belief in the equality of white and black children, Benjamin Franklin wrote to the Marquis de Condorcet that black children were "not deficient in natural understanding, but they have not the Advantage of Education."[170]

Beccaria's treatise was read throughout Europe, especially among the cultured elite. Shortly after its publication, Kaunitz—the Austrian diplomat so trusted by Maria Theresa—decided to write to Philipp von Cobenzl, a minister in Belgium. Kaunitz stated that "humanity" opposed judicial torture and that the existence of torture showed "how little legislators have appreciated the value of men." According to Kaunitz's biographer, Franz Szabo, *On Crimes and Punishments* "made a great impression upon Kaunitz." As Szabo writes: "When Beccaria, who was a native of the Duchy of Milan, was invited by Empress Catherine II of Russia to come to St. Petersburg to assist in the legal reforms she was then undertaking, Kaunitz made every effort to keep him in Milan." "In April 1767," Szabo writes of Kaunitz's efforts in that respect, "he wrote to his governor, Firmian, that on the strength of the *Essay*, it would be disastrous to lose such an educated, perspicacious and independent thinker." Kaunitz, who earned praise from Voltaire for supporting Beccaria's efforts, thus endorsed Firmian's suggestion that Beccaria be offered a teaching position in Milan. Beccaria, for his part, would praise Count Firmian as "an angel deputed by a superior Providence" to return Lombardy "to the glory of letters." Firmian took the young Milanese philosopher under his protection, and "dissipated" — to use Beccaria's words — "the clouds which had thickened round his head" after Beccaria's treatise, the subject of censorship, came under attack from establishment figures.[171] In 1769 Beccaria received his chair in political economy, and when a commission recommended that Beccaria receive an annual salary of 2,000 Lire, Kaunitz intervened with Empress Maria Theresa to up that salary to 3,000 Lire.[172]

The profound effect of Beccaria's treatise on European elites is made clear by other writings of its members. "It was in the spirit of Beccaria's *Essay*," Franz Szabo writes, "that Kaunitz submitted a memorandum" to Maria Theresa on February 20, 1769, "only two days after the *Nemesis* had been accepted." Kaunitz emphasized that the draft penal code still referenced witchcraft and other superstitions, which he felt were "laughable" in "enlightened times," and he also opposed judicial torture, taking particular exception to the code's graphic illustration of torture methods. University of Vienna professors Karl Anton Martin and Joseph von Sonnenfels joined Kaunitz in that critique, leading Empress Maria Theresa to order an investigation into whether torture should be retained, restricted, or eliminated. Some members of the Council of State favored its retention, but Joseph II staked out his position in August 1775, saying the abolition of torture would be "a just and harmless measure, but a necessary one." After Kaunitz endorsed that view, Maria

Theresa then issued a decree on January 2, 1776, abolishing torture in Austria, Bohemia, Galicia and the Banat. That very day, Kaunitz was also ordered to negotiate with the provincial administrations of the Austrian Netherlands and the Duchy of Milan to extend that reform to those provinces. "Though Kaunitz implemented these instructions immediately," Szabo writes, "local conservative resistance" delayed the extension of the reform to those locales until after Maria Theresa's death.[173]

In an era often bereft of personal liberties such as freedom of speech and freedom of religion, Beccaria walked a thin line. Right from its publication, *On Crimes and Punishments*—as Beccaria no doubt expected—generated enormous controversy and decidedly mixed reviews.[174] The Venetian Inquisition blocked importation of the book into Venetian territory in August 1764, and an Italian monk, Ferdinando Facchinei, anonymously published a harsh rebuke of it in 1765. The Roman Inquisition banned the book in February 1766, and in 1777, a Spanish translation of the book was likewise forbidden in Spain.[175] Despite references to God and man's relationship to God in *On Crimes and Punishments*,[176] one critic called Beccaria "an enemy of Christianity, a wicked man and a poor philosopher" as well as "a declared enemy of the Supreme Being."[177] When the Roman Inquisition put *On Crimes and Punishments* on the Index of Prohibited Books on February 3, 1766, Beccaria was worried enough that he asked his publisher to remove his name and any other identifying information from the cover of a new edition to be released. Reluctantly, the publisher complied, so when, in March 1766, the new edition was released, it was—as one Beccaria scholar notes—"printed without Beccaria's name and with a falsified place of publication."[178] Despite the papacy's ban on Beccaria's treatise, Count Firmian supported Beccaria, and it was through his good offices, and as part of educational reform, that Beccaria secured the university position.[179] Ironically, in the 1500s, a different Beccaria—one Gioacchino Beccaria da Pavia—had served as an inquisitor in Pavia and Milan, with one woman burned as a witch in 1519 in front of the Basilica di Sant'Eustorgio in Milan.[180]

Beccaria's critics pulled no punches, though the Verri brothers—when the heavy-handed criticism arrived—had immediately come to Beccaria's defense. In *Notes and Observations on the Book Entitled 'On Crimes and Punishments,'* Ferdinando Facchinei—the monk—dismissed Beccaria's book, saying it had not proved "that the death penalty and torture are useless." "It is absolutely certain," Facchinei asserted, "that on this earth there never has been a perfect society created by the express will and choice of free men, as our author imagines, and I challenge the socialists and anyone else to find me a single example in all the histories and annals of the world of societies created in that way." At that time, such criticism, bordering on outright mockery, was not far-fetched. In 1780, to his friend Edmund Jenings, a Marylander who relocated to Europe after being educated at Eton, Cambridge and the Middle Temple, John Adams wrote of the Massachusetts constitution ultimately adopted that year. In writing of the people's efforts to frame a constitution in his own state, Adams emphasized, "it is the first Example, that has happened in the Progress of human Society: of a People, deliberating so long so patiently, so cautiously, in the formation of a Government. The Result I now send you is still to be laid before the whole Body of the People in their Town Meetings, that every Man may have an opportunity to express his Mind, and suggest his amendments." "No Government," Adams wrote in his letter, "was ever made so perfectly upon the Principle of the Peoples Right and Equality. It is Locke, Sydney, Rousseau and Mably reduced to Practice in the First Instance." Even Rousseau—the author of *The Social Contract*, and one of the writers on John Adams' list—accepted the death penalty's legitimacy, though the trail-blazing Beccaria, a Rousseau reader and a writer who freely borrowed ideas, referring himself to the "general will," was determined to show the death penalty's inefficacy.

In his full-throated critique, Ferdinando Facchinei accused the still-anonymous author of *On Crimes and Punishments* of wanting to be the "Rousseau of the Italians." This
scathing review prompted a lengthy written response, also anonymously published, from
Pietro and Alessandro Verri. To a printer in Switzerland, the Verri brothers wrote: "A
monk in Venice vomited libelous accusations of heresy, sedition, impiety, and so on."
That anonymously published response, drafted as if it had come from the author of *On
Crimes and Punishments*, painted the reviewer as out of touch, saying "[m]y accuser
scarcely knows the temperament of today's sovereigns." In a note "To the Reader" that
accompanied later editions of *On Crimes and Punishments*, Beccaria adopted that response as his own and emphasized that he had given "public affirmation of my religion
and of my obedience to my sovereign in the reply to the *Notes and Observations*."[181] In other
words, Beccaria—while ultimately excommunicated from the church for his views—
believed in God and had respect for authority. There was at that time a growing confrontation between Pope Clement XIII's Roman Catholic Church and the Enlightenment,
with works by Voltaire, Rousseau, Beccaria and others banned by the church in the
1760s.[182]

Beccaria's book, in fact, would spark controversy—as well as praise—for decades to
come, with Beccaria's readers usually anything but indifferent. Writing in the late 1760s,
the Scottish painter and political essayist Allan Ramsay, an active member of the Select Society of Edinburgh, was critical of Beccaria's treatise. Supportive of a strong royal executive
to further commerce and generate societal and individual wealth, Ramsay took particular
issue with Beccaria's approach in a letter to the French *philosophe* Denis Diderot. Calling
the social contract theory on which Beccaria's book rested a "metaphysical idea which was
never the source of any real transaction, whether in England or elsewhere," Ramsay argued:
"those who propose, in governments of a certain nature, to suppress torture, the wheel,
impalement, the rack ... tend to deprive themselves of the best means of security, and
would abandon the administration of the state to the discretion of the first armed rebels who
like better to command than obey." One of Beccaria's biggest critics was the Prussian philosopher Immanuel Kant, an ardent death penalty advocate. Kant—who believed all murderers should be executed—said Beccaria's anti-death penalty arguments amounted to
"sophistry."[183]

On the other hand, Voltaire, as his commentary made clear, genuinely adored Beccaria's book, and drew on his own considerable fame—gained as an advocate in France,
including in securing a posthumous exoneration and compensation for the Calas family
after Toulouse's brutal execution of Jean Calas—to promote it.[184] In Milan, the reform-
minded Count Carlo Firmian, the plenipotentiary of Empress Maria Theresa who took
Beccaria under his wings, also stepped up and defended Beccaria against charges of subversion and sacrilege.[185] In the end, Beccaria's book not only garnered the attention of
Russian, Prussian and other monarchs,[186] but it led to serious calls for criminal law reform
and the death penalty's curtailment elsewhere in Europe and in America.[187] Beccaria's
treatise, historian Lorraine Daston notes, "took the French intellectual world by storm, and
enjoyed greater success in France than in Beccaria's native Italy."[188] Although Empress
Catherine II had invited Beccaria to assist in the reform of Russia's penal code, an offer
Beccaria considered for a time, he ultimately turned down the once-in-a-lifetime opportunity, opting to stay in his native Milan so he could be close to his family and friends.

In his own lifetime, Beccaria witnessed only modest success—dying alone in his
house in 1794 in the midst of the bloody French Revolution (1789–1799). Beccaria's
death came just a few years after the now-notorious French physician, Dr. Joseph-Ignace
Guillotin, proposed the use of the beheading machine with which he became so closely
associated.[189] Dr. Guillotin—the founder of the French Academy of Medicine and an

opponent of capital punishment—had himself read Beccaria's treatise and was inspired by it. Dr. Guillotin and other French revolutionaries envisioned the bladed, beheading machine as what one source describes "as an intermediary step" toward the eradication of capital punishment "that would," in the meantime, "make execution more equitable across social classes." Dr. Guillotin, who first perfected his device on cattle and sheep, was upset by botched executions he had seen, and thus sought a method of execution that was swift and—in comparison to prior means of execution, such as breaking on the wheel and grisly public beheadings via an executioner's axe—as free of unnecessary pain as possible. A member of a royal French commission with Benjamin Franklin that investigated mesmerism in 1784, the palliation-minded Dr. Guillotin—who had once resolved to move to America—had put forward his beheading proposal in December 1789, with France's National Assembly authorizing the use of his machine in March 1792.[190]

Though Beccaria himself lived to see only limited success in terms of penal reform, his ideas made an enormous impact and would continue to do so over time. A book written by William Falconer and published in London in 1781 referred to Beccaria's "goodness of heart," calling the Italian philosopher "the justly-celebrated Marquis Beccaria, who is himself a striking and living instance, how much the knowledge of legislation, and of the true interests of mankind, are promoted by an acquaintance with the arts and sciences." "By 1792," another book explains, "Dr. Guillotin had succeeded in establishing a single mode of execution, common for all citizens." Some of the delegates to France's National Convention, including Robespierre, that text notes, had also adopted Beccaria's anti-death penalty views, though Robespierre—it points out—later "made an exception in the case of the king and eventually, it appears, in the case of most other people." In the early 1790s, during the French Revolution's infamous Reign of Terror led by Robespierre, approximately 17,000 executions of presumed enemies of the state took place. But speeches like those of French philosopher and politician Nicholas de Condorcet, delivered on December 3, 1792, show that Beccaria's ideas had filtered out into the wider world. In contemplating the fate of Louis XVI, Condorcet stated that "[t]he question here, without doubt, is whether society has the right to sentence a man to death; whether such a penalty may be so necessary as ever to render it just." Using words that paralleled Beccaria's as he spoke of his "obligation to express an opinion" on that subject, Condorcet stated: "I believe a capital sentence to be unjust whenever it is applied to a guilty man who can be imprisoned without danger to society." As Condorcet said: "I believe that, with the exception of this case alone, which should not occur under a truly free constitution once it is well established, the absolute suppression of the capital penalty is one of the most efficacious means for the perfection of the human species, by destroying that penchant to ferocity which has too long been a dishonor to man."[191]

The streets of Paris were drenched with blood during the French Revolution, a revolution that followed America's Revolutionary War in which the English Bloody Code had hung over U.S. leaders' heads like the Sword of Damocles. But Beccaria's ideas—even after the Italian philosopher's death in distant Milan—were highly influential not only in the 1760s and 1770s, but far beyond, proving very durable over the long haul. Indeed, over time, the translation of Beccaria's book by enterprising French, English and other intellectuals breathed much life into Beccaria's vision. Once read and translated, Beccaria's writings moved powerful monarchs and their royal underlings but also scores of open-minded European and American military, social and religious leaders of different political persuasions.[192] "In fact, in a curious twist," notes historian David Rothman in *The Oxford History of the Prison*, "the new Americans"—the ones who had just declared their independence from Great Britain—had "embraced the ideas of such Enlightenment thinkers as Cesare Beccaria" in a very distant land; in criticizing England's harsh, execution-fraught laws, Rothman notes, Americans—who experienced much lawlessness and violence during the Revolutionary War—"blamed the codes themselves for the persistence of crime."[193]

In Europe, Beccaria's writings did have some concrete, if ephemeral, successes. "Like Thomas More and Machiavelli," one historian notes, "Beccaria believed that necessity should be the criterion by which punishments should be imposed"—and the reforms he advocated "bore most fruit in the central European monarchies of Prussia and Austria." In 1786, persuaded by Beccaria's ideas, Grand Duke Leopold of Tuscany adopted a Tuscan penal code that totally eliminated the death penalty.[194] And in 1787, Holy Roman Emperor Joseph II, Leopold's brother, followed suit, abolishing Austria's death penalty save for crimes of revolt against the state.[195] The preamble to Grand Duke Leopold's 1786 edict asserts that the death penalty had not been inflicted in Tuscany since 1772, that is, for fourteen years, and even before the death penalty was abolished in Austria in 1787, Emperor Joseph II had made clear in 1781 that a death sentence could only be imposed with his special mandate. Just as Frederick II of Prussia took steps to stamp out torture in his dominion, penal reform—a hot topic in the late eighteenth century—would also wash up on America's shores, with Americans paying close attention to the developments in Europe.[196]

The rapidity with which Beccaria's treatise made an impact is crystal clear in the case of North America. Even before 1776, when the United States of America was formed, the Continental Congress collectively praised Beccaria *by name*. The delegates of the Continental Congress, then assembled at Philadelphia, had consulted one another "concerning the best methods to obtain redress of our afflicting grievances," as they put it in an open letter drafted in 1774 and addressed to the inhabitants of the Province of Quebec. That letter, seeking Canadian support for their cause, is thought to be the work of Pennsylvania (and later Delaware) lawyer John Dickinson, and was later widely reprinted, including in Philadelphia; New London, Connecticut; and Annapolis, Maryland. In his diary entry for October 4, 1774, John Adam himself recalled—in terms of its circulation among American revolutionaries—that "[t]his Evening General Lee came to my Lodgings and shewed me an Address from the C. [Congress] to the People of Canada which he had." Taking note of how English officials had "so audaciously and cruelly" abused "royal authority" and "dared to violate the most sacred compacts and obligations," the letter of the Continental Congress quoted Beccaria in an effort to educate their "Friends and fellow-subjects" in Quebec on the "form of government" that "you are now undoubtedly entitled to."

As the Continental Congress's October 1774 open letter read, reciting Beccaria's stirring prose in language that would preview the promulgation of the Declaration of Independence less than two years later: "'In every human society,' says the celebrated Marquis *Beccaria*, 'there is an *effort, continually tending* to confer on one part the heighth of power and happiness, and to reduce the other to the extreme of weakness and misery. The intent of good laws is to *oppose this effort*, and to diffuse their influence *universally* and *equally*.'"[197] Noah Webster (1758–1843)—the Yale-educated lexicographer—labeled that process "the equalizing genius of the laws," with James Madison—worried about the direction of the American Revolution—advising Jefferson in the late 1780s: "In all the Governments which were considered as beacons to republican patriots and lawgivers the rights of persons were subjected to those of property. The poor were sacrificed to the rich."[198] The Declaration of Independence's equality principle is thus attributable, in part, to Beccaria's treatise, the very one the Continental Congress itself invoked less than two years earlier as congressmen wrestled with how best to appeal to the Canadian people.

The letter to the inhabitants of Quebec was, like other actions of political bodies, developed in committee, the product of the times, and informed by a host of views. In mid-July 1774, for example, a committee for the province of Pennsylvania had met and been appointed to "prepare and bring in a draught of instructions" after considering the grievances of the colonies and the colonists' constitutional rights. That committee completed a draft a couple of days later, and an essay was prepared to accompany those instructions—an essay prepared by John Dickinson, the successful attorney who served as a Revolutionary War militia officer. The instructions, taking note of the "dissensions between Great-Britain and her colonies on this continent," stated that, "commencing about ten years ago," those dissensions had been continually increasing. In fact, the instructions noted the brewing dispute had "grown to such an excess as to involve the later in deep distress and danger" and "have excited the good people of this province to take into their serious consideration the present situation of public affairs." Though the colonists pledged their loyalty and allegiance to George III, the instructions invoked the names of Enlightenment writers such as Blackstone, Burlamaqui, Grotius, Locke, Montesquieu and Pufendorf. For example, one of Burlamaqui's works—stating that "liberty and independence" is "a right naturally belonging to man"—was cited for the following proposition: "Nature has made us all of the same species, all equal, all free and independent of each other; and was willing that those, on whom she has bestowed the same faculties, should have all the same rights." The "desire of happiness, and of society," are two of the "certain laws" of "nature" of the "all wise Creator of man," Dickinson would explain in his essay.

The instructions hastily prepared in Pennsylvania in 1774 laid out the stark choices facing colonists. The "power claimed by *Great-Britain*, and the late attempts to exercise it over these colonies," the instructions ominously asserted, "present to our view two events, one of which must *inevitably* take place, if she shall continue to insist on her pretensions." "Either," the instructions read, "the colonists will sink from the rank of freemen into the class of slaves, overwhelmed with all the miseries and vices, prov'd by the history of mankind to be inseparably annexed to that deplorable condition: Or, if they have sense and virtue enough to exert themselves in striving to avoid this perdition, they must be involved in an opposition dreadful even in contemplation." Translation: a revolutionary war would be commenced. "*Honour, justice*, and *humanity*," the instructions continued, "call upon us to hold, and to transmit to our posterity, that liberty, which we received from our ancestors." English radicals, Irish republicans and the liberty-seeking American colonists were all deeply dissatisfied with the English monarchy, with Jeremy Black's *George III: America's Last King*, reporting these lines of verse from an imprisoned Irishman, no doubt reflective of many Americans' views at the time: *May we but live to see the day / The crown from George's head shall fall, / The people's voice will then bear sway / We'll humble tyrants one and all.*[199]

Saying it was "our duty" to "leave liberty" to "our children," the 1774 instructions forcefully proclaimed:

> No infamy, iniquity, or cruelty, can exceed our own, if we, born and educated in a country of freedom, entitled to its blessings, and knowing their value, pusillanimously deserting the post assigned us by divine Providence, surrender succeeding generations to a condition of wretchedness, from which no human efforts, in all probability, will be sufficient to extricate them; the experience of all states mournfully demonstrating to us, that when arbitrary power has been established over them, even the wisest and bravest nations, that ever flourished, have, in a few years, degenerated into abject and wretched vassals.

"Despotism, unchecked and unbounded by any laws," the instructions read, citing Montesquieu, had preyed upon liberty to such a degree that the colonists had come to this conclusion: "To us therefore it appears, at this alarming period, our duty to God, to our country, to ourselves, and to our posterity, to exert our utmost ability, in promoting and establishing harmony between *Great Britain* and these colonies, ON A CONSTITUTIONAL FOUNDATION." "For attaining this great and desirable end," the instructions read, "we request you to appoint a proper number of persons to attend a congress of deputies from the several colonies, appointed, or to be appointed, by the representatives of the people of the colonies respectively in assembly, or convention."

From the time of Parliament's notorious Stamp Act of 1765, which generated intense anger among American colonists, the colonists felt their grievances were not being addressed. Some colonists began calling themselves Sons of Liberty, and the colonists' rage, fueled by oppressive taxes and the British occupation of Boston, led to the Boston Tea Party in 1773. The work of John Dickinson—appointed along with Joseph Read and Charles Thomson to be "a committee to write to the neighboring colonies, and communicate to them the resolves and instructions"—would itself find a receptive audience through its publication. Indeed, it was resolved on July 21, 1774, that "the whole work"—which set forth the colonists' grievances—"ought to be published, as highly deserving the perusal and serious consideration of every friend of liberty within these colonies." The colonists' hope: "to attain some degree of certainty concerning our lives, liberties and properties." In August 1774, *An Essay on the Constitutional Power of Great-Britain over the Colonies in America*, written by Dickinson, was thus published and sold in Philadelphia by William and Thomas Bradford "at the *London Coffee-House*." The essay—distributed at the Philadelphia coffee-house said to be "the pulsating heart of excitement, enterprise, and patriotism" of the city—was reportedly "written in such haste, under so great indisposition, and amidst such a confusion of public affairs," that a disclaimer at the beginning of the essay noted that "it is hoped, its inaccuracies will be looked upon with indulgence." As the disclaimer read: "If longer time could have been bestowed upon its correction it would have been at least shorter, if not more exact. The first appointment of a committee to form a draught of instructions, was made on the fourth of last month."

In that much-read essay, to which notes were added after the vote to publish it, a resolution was reprinted thanking John Dickinson for the "great assistance" the Pennsylvania committee had received from him. In response, Dickinson graciously acknowledged the compliment, stating: "I heartily thank this respectable Assembly for the honour they have conferred upon me, but want words to express the sense I feel of their kindness. The mere accidents of meeting with particular books, and conversing with particular men, led me into the train of sentiments, which the committee are pleased to think just." One of those books: *On Crimes and Punishments*. In the essay itself, Dickinson wrote of the oppressive use of power and a "cruel" monarch—George III—who had set up a "COUNCIL OF BLOOD." "What would the liberties of the people of *England* have been at this time," Dickinson queried, "if precedents could have made laws inconsistent with the constitution?" "Precedents tending to make men unhappy," he wrote as a reader of Beccaria's treatise, "can with propriety of character be quoted only by those beings, to whom the misery of men is a delight." "A Parliamentary power of internal legislation over these colonies," Dickinson wrote on behalf of Pennsylvania colonists, "appears therefore to us, equally contradictory to humanity and the constitution, and illegal." It is a "maxim of law," Dickinson wrote, that "a bad usage ought to be abolished," with Dickinson—asserting that colonists claimed only the rights of Englishmen—quoting another source for the following proposition: "If the usage had been immemorial and uniform, and ten thousand instances could have been produced, it would not have been sufficient; because the practice must likewise be agreeable to the *principles of the law*, in order to be good." England's attempt to extinguish the rights of freedom-loving colonists, Dickinson contended, "is offensive to reason, humanity, and the constitution of that state."

Dickinson thus spoke passionately of the colonists' rights, including their right to pursue happiness. As Dickinson wrote:

> The happiness of the people is the end, and, if the term is allowable, we would call it the body of the constitution. Freedom is the spirit or soul. As the soul, speaking of nature, has a right to prevent or relieve, if it can, any mischief to the body of the individual, and to keep it in the best health; so the soul, speaking of the constitution, has a right to prevent, or relieve, any mischief to the body of the society, and to keep that in the best health.

Expressing concern about the deprivation of the right to trial by jury and emphasizing the right to habeas corpus and to "life," "liberty" and "property," Dickinson wrote: "For these ten years past we have been incessantly attacked. Hard is our fate, when, to escape the character of rebels, we must be degraded into that of slaves: as if there was no medium, between the two extremes of anarchy and despotism, where innocence and freedom could find response and safety." "Why should we be exhibited to mankind, as a people adjudged by parliament unworthy of freedom?" Dickinson pondered, calling the very thought alone "insupportable." As Dickinson reasoned in contrasting the geographic-dependent rights of American colonists versus Englishmen: "Even those unhappy persons, who have had the misfortune of being born under the yoke of bondage, imposed by the cruel laws, if they may be called laws, of the land, where they received their birth, no sooner breathe the air of *England*, though they touch her shore only by accident, than they instantly become freemen." "Strange contradiction," Dickinson wrote of the situation in which "[t]he *same* kingdom at the *same* time" was both "the *asylum* and the *bane* of liberty."

That Dickinson's essay was inspired in part by Beccaria's treatise is clear. One of the footnotes added to Dickinson's essay referenced Beccaria not once, but twice. That note appears in the context of a sentence from the essay commenting on the fact that American colonists were divided "into many provinces" and were "incapable of union, except against a common danger." "The genius of a *Beccaria*, suggested to him the condition of a large empire verging into servitude," Dickinson wrote in the context of his essay about the colonists' grievances against the British Empire. As Dickinson's note explained of Beccaria's views: "An overgrown republic (says he, and such a limited monarchy as that of *Great-Britain* with such an extent of dominions, may well be called 'an overgrown republic,') can *only* be saved from despotism, *by subdividing it into a number of confederate republics*." "But how is this practicable?" Dickinson's note continued, writing of a "despotic dictator" and the experience of the Romans. "If he be an ambitious man, his reward will be immortal glory; if a philosopher, the blessings of his fellow citizens will sufficiently console him for the loss of authority," Dickinson explained. "What was argument in *Italy*," Dickinson wrote of Beccaria's words, "is reality to *Great-Britain*, with this additional circumstances in her favor, that she must always continue if she wisely conducts her affairs, though less than *all*, yet greater than *any*."

After taking note of Beccaria's plan for subdividing a large empire into confederate republics, Dickinson—who invoked "the masterly hand of a Beccaria" in a latter portion of his note—wrote that the "advantages" of what he was writing about "are worthy the closest attention of every *Briton*." As Dickinson—hoping to avoid violence and reconcile the interests of Great Britain and the colonists—wrote in his note of the advantages Beccaria's plan offered:

To a man, who has considered them with that attention, perhaps it will not appear too bold to aver, that, if an archangel had planned the connexion between Great-Britain and her colonies, he could not have fixed it on a more lasting and beneficial foundation, unless he could have changed human nature. A mighty naval power at the head of the whole—that power, a parent state, with all the endearing sentiments attending the relationship—that never could disoblige, but with design—the dependant states much more apt to have feuds among themselves—she the umpire and controuler—those states producing every article necessary to her greatness—their interest, that she should continue free and flourishing—their ability to throw a considerable weight into the scale, should her government get UNDULY POISED—she and all those states PROTESTANT— are some of the circumstances, that delineated by the masterly hand of a *Beccaria*, would exhibit a plan, vindicating the ways of heaven, and demonstrating, that humanity and policy are nearly related.

Dickinson further emphasized that "[a]n *Alexander*, a *Caesar*, a *Charles*, a *Lewis*, and others have fought through fields of blood for universal empire." But Dickinson—who expressed the view that Great Britain had "glory and prosperity without measure"—noted that "wise ministers" of Great Britain, that "most astonishing" and "well founded power the world ever saw," preferred "a pepper corn" when it came to recognizing colonists' rights. Having spoken earlier of Great Britain's taxation policies, Dickinson—writing of the way "the colonies have been treated" and at another point referencing Great Britain's Glorious Revolution of 1688—feared that "[a]t last a civil war may be worked up."[200]

In America's Declaration of Independence, drafted principally by Thomas Jefferson, another avid reader of Beccaria, the Continental Congress would formally "dissolve the political bands" between Great Britain and America. In its very first sentence, the members of the Continental Congress would recite, "among the powers of the earth," the people's right to "the separate and equal station to which the Laws of Nature and of Nature's God entitle them." "We hold these truths to be self-evident," the Declaration of Independence famously reads, "that all men are created equal, that they are endowed by their Creator with certain unalienable Rights, that among these are Life, Liberty and the pursuit of Happiness." Proclaiming that "Governments are instituted among Men, deriving their just powers from the consent of the governed," the Declaration of Independence boldly announced: "That whenever any Form of Government becomes destructive of those ends, it is the Right of the People to alter or to abolish it, and to institute new Government, laying its foundation on such principles and organizing its powers in such form, as to them shall seem most likely to effect their Safety and Happiness." While the well-read Jefferson, before drafting that document, had been influenced by scores of Enlightenment authors, including John Locke, Beccaria's moving words had clearly made an impression on the Continental Congress and, it seems, on Jefferson himself.

With the American Revolution inspired in part by the writings of Beccaria and Montesquieu, as well as by Thomas Paine's home-grown *Common Sense*, the Declaration of Independence—the salvo that severed all political ties with Britain's monarchy—railed against "absolute Despotism" and the "absolute Tyranny over these States." In discarding "their former Systems of Government," the thirteen "united States of America"—as the Declaration of Independence proclaimed—took it upon themselves to rid themselves of the British monarchy. The members of the Continental Congress, in indictment-like fashion, set forth in the Declaration the "long train of abuses" and the "repeated injuries and usurpations" of "the present King of Great Britain." "To prove this," the Declaration read, "let Facts be submitted to a candid world." Among King George III's transgressions: "He has refused his Assent to Laws, the most wholesome and necessary for the public good." "He has obstructed the Administration of Justice, by refusing his Assent to Laws for establishing Judiciary powers." "He has constrained our fellow Citizens taken Captive on the high Seas to bear Arms against their Country, to become the executioners of their friends and Brethren, or to fall themselves by their Hands." "A Prince whose character is thus marked by every act which may define a Tyrant," the Declaration of Independence proclaimed, "is unfit to be the ruler of a free people." After issuing that scathing indictment, the founders made their collective, life-threatening pledge. "[W]e mutually pledge to each other our Lives, our Fortunes and our sacred Honor," the fifty-six signatories to the Declaration of Independence collectively asserted.[201]

A Postscript

Beccaria's rift with the Verri brothers, precipitated during Beccaria's visit to Paris, reportedly came about, at least in part, from Beccaria's unwillingness to acknowledge the contributions made by the Verri brothers to *Dei delitti e delle pene*.[202] Although Pietro Verri had facilitated the reconciliation of Beccaria and his father after Beccaria's marriage to Teresa di Blasco in 1761, Beccaria and the Verri brothers had a tense—often uncomfortable—relationship after the 1766 trip to Paris. While Beccaria became known throughout the world for *On Crimes and Punishments*, the Verri brothers—still influential in their own country, though now rather obscure figures—pursued their own literary pursuits. Pietro published essays such as *Meditations on Political Economy* (1771), *Discourse on Nature of Pleasure and Pain* (1773), *Observations on Torture* (1777) and *Discourse on Happiness* (1781), while Alessandro—who had moved to Rome—translated the works of Shakespeare into Italian and published novels such as *The Adventures of Sappho* (1780). In their earlier, more congenial days, when the members of the Academy of Fists were still meeting, Pietro and Alessandro had protected Beccaria, then still in his twenties. Their defense of Beccaria's treatise, published as *Reply to a Document entitled Notes and Observations on the Book of Crimes and Punishments*, was reprinted in a translation of Beccaria's treatise as late as 2008.[203]

Still, even after the Parisian debacle that caused the strain in their once tight relationship, Beccaria and the Verri family had substantial contacts with one another over the years. As the men grew older together, Beccaria's daughter Giulia—a beautiful young woman, by all accounts—had a scandalous affair with Giovanni Verri, the playboy brother of Pietro and Alessandro Verri. Cesare Beccaria sought to halt the affair with his nineteen-year-old daughter, a love that was forbidden in that society. As writer Dianne Hales explains of the "feckless" Giovanni Verri in her meditation on the Italian language, *La Bella Lingua*: "In addition to his reputation as a womanizer, the younger Verri was a Knight of the Cross of Malta and held a quasi-military, quasi-religious rank that forbade marriage at pain of loss of both prestige and income." Hastily, Pietro Verri—as one source puts it—"arranged Giulia's marriage to the obscure Count Pietro Manzoni, twenty-six years her senior, as if that could stop the affair." Three years later, in 1785, Giulia Beccaria "gave birth to Alessandro, whom her husband acknowledged although he was (presumably) Giovanni Verri's son." Don Pietro Manzoni, Hales writes, was "a forty-six-year-old widower, count, and religious conservative." "After seven years in a steadily worsening relationship," *The Cambridge History of Italian Literature* notes of the mismatched couple's eventual separation, "Giulia went to live with Carlo Imbonati, a rich merchant banker, and Alessandro was farmed out to various religious boarding schools." Giulia's paramour, Carlo Imbonati, had never met Giulia's son Alessandro, but Carlo invited him to Paris in 1805. The wealthy businessman, however, died before Alessandro Manzoni's arrival in the City of Light, "making Giulia his heiress and laying the foundations of her son's future financial well-being."[204]

In Paris, Giulia Beccaria—Cesare Beccaria's daughter and Alessandro Manzoni's mother—became a high society hostess and forged a tight bond with Alessandro, the son she had barely gotten to know before he had been whisked off to boarding schools starting at age five. As the Manzoni family's biographer notes: Giulia's "maiden name of Beccaria, which was known to everyone in cultured and worldly circles," resulted in Giulia meeting "a cordial and lavish reception wherever she went" because "[e]veryone remembered her father and his famous book." Giulia, meanwhile, took a keen interest in America, even playing a tangential role—though the details are sketchy—in what would become Carlo Botta's *History of the War of Independence of the United States of America.* That book laid out the story of American independence in two volumes, and—among other things—reprinted a 1774 letter from the Continental Congress to the people of Great Britain. In that September 5, 1774 missive, the Americans asserted that "we consider ourselves, and do insist, that we are and ought to be as free as our fellow subjects in Britain"; that "no power on earth has a right to take our property from us without our consent"; and that "the legislature of Great-Britain" was not authorized to "establish a religion, fraught with sanguinary and impious tenets, or to erect an arbitrary form of government in any quarter of the globe."

In 1806, the Italian historian Carlo Botta (1776–1837) had visited the Paris home of Giulia Beccaria Manzoni, where she lived with her son Alessandro Manzoni, the cosmopolitan poet and novelist who married a Swiss bride. As Botta himself wrote in an 1835 letter to George Washington Greene, a relative of General Nathanael Greene:

> About 1806 Madame Beccaria was in Paris…. At that time I frequented her house along with many others who enjoyed conversing with a beautiful, virtuous and intelligent woman. One evening the topic of conversation was: which modern theme could be an adequate subject for a heroic poem. After some discussion, finally all agreed that only one modern example could be of use to mankind, and that was the American effort which carried the United States to independence. Returning home that evening, crossing the square then called Revolution Square, and now Concord Square—I mulled thus: *If that event can be a convenient subject for a poem, why not for a history?* It seemed to me that it could be so; and so, feeling naturally attracted to history, and having already determined in my soul to write any history, I then resolved to write the history of American independence. I searched in all corners to collect material; then I wrote, and so was born my history of America.

"The popular *History of the War of Independence of the United States of America,*" notes another source, "was published in Turin in 1809"; "had ten editions in the United States in twenty years (the famous Otis's translation)"; and was "conceived during conversations and discussions with Milanese political theorists in the salon of Giulia Beccaria."[205]

Giulia Beccaria—in an historical footnote—actually crossed paths in Paris with Maria Cosway, the woman Thomas Jefferson, by all accounts, fell deeply in love with in Paris. Cosway, the English artist and musician, had met Giulia Beccaria in Paris during the Peace of Amiens, when Maria painted "a lively oil sketch" of Giulia, probably in 1802–1803.[206] Alessandro Manzoni, who lived in Paris until 1810, would, for his part, gain notoriety for writing his popular novel, *The Betrothed,* as well as *History of the Column of Infamy.*[207] The Column of Infamy refers to a pillar erected on the spot where two men were executed after being tortured with a hot iron, deprived of their right hands, and being broken on the wheel for being suspected of spreading the plague, all on the basis of false confessions.[208] Manzoni had received a conservative Catholic education at a series of boarding schools, but came to admire the *philosophes* after returning in 1801 to Milan, where he also acquired republican beliefs as he read the poetry and writings of Giuseppe Parini and Vittorio Alfieri—men who had been critical of aristocracy and condemned tyranny. As a writer himself, Manzoni went on to write a tragedy in which a soldier was unjustly executed for treason.[209] In Jefferson's famous 1786 letter to Maria Cosway, Jefferson wrote a "dialogue" between "my Head" and "my Heart"—a letter in which Jefferson wrote of America that "there is not a country on earth where there is greater tranquillity, where the law's are milder, or better obeyed." Americans, he wrote, were busily building canals, roads and schools and "abolishing sanguinary punishments." "If our country, when pressed with wrongs at the point of the bayonet, had been governed by its heads instead of its hearts," Jefferson mused, "where should we have been now? Hanging on a gallows as high as Hamans."[210]

In terms of his own personal life, Cesare Beccaria—of a Roman Catholic family, and reportedly "extremely" shy and rather "modest, but tenacious of his opinions"—had three siblings and married twice. As one source puts it: "With his two brothers, Francesco and Annibale, and his sister, Maddalena, he was brought up in the family house on Via Brera. Like all of the aristocratic families in Italy at that time, the Beccarias were Roman Catholics, and Cesare was separated from his family at the early age of 8 and sent to the Jesuit College ... where he received his first 8 years of education."[211] As another source, recording Cesare's two marriages and the children that resulted from them, notes of his family life: "The wife of his youth, Teresa Blasco, gave him two daughters, Giulia and Maria; she died in 1774 and he promptly married Anna, Contessina Barnaba Barbò, by whom he had his only son Giulio."[212] Teresa, aged 29, died after a long illness on March 14, 1774, and Beccaria's marriage to Anna—the daughter of Count Barnaba Barbò—occurred just four months later. Shortly before he had been appointed a magistrate, and would go on to serve on various commissions of inquiry, including one that examined the reform of Lombardy's civil and criminal jurisprudence.[213] Cesare Beccaria, who—as a biography of the Manzoni family puts it—"had become enormously fat" as the years went by—saw his grandson Alessandro just once. Alessandro—Cesare's grandson—later recalled his grandfather "rising heavily from an armchair to get him a chocolate."[214]

On November 28, 1794, Cesare Beccaria suddenly died, reportedly of apoplexy or a stroke, and at the time in apparent obscurity despite all the fame that had come his way starting in the 1760s. "Beccaria's later years were troubled by family disputes and litigation on property and problems of health," one source notes.[215] According to an edition of *The Encyclopaedia Britannica* published in 1854, Beccaria's death "was unnoticed by his country, and his tomb remained without a name or epitaph."[216] In the years before his death, Beccaria had—for the most part—retreated into private life. On one traveller's journey in 1784 and 1785, the traveler's journal reported this of a visit to Milan: "[o]f the literati of this place I have only made acquaintance with a few." As the traveler's journal continued: "To the marquis Beccaria, the celebrated author of the book Dé delitti e dell pene, I was indeed very desirous of finding access, but no favourable opportunity happened, and importunity is not my practice. He is at present a member of the magistracy, lives quite retired, and works no longer for the public."[217] In contrast, a biographical dictionary published shortly thereafter, around the turn of the century after Beccaria's death in 1794, gave this report: "The marquis Beccaria was a great lover of men of letters, a kind patron to those who were entering the career of literature, and a cordial friend."[218]

Only later would his native Milan give Beccaria true honors, with a piazza named after him and monuments erected in his honor. The Lombard sculptor and Milan native Pompeo Marchesi sculpted a marble monument in 1838 depicting Cesare Beccaria that is in Milan's Palazzo di Brera—a museum that also contains a marble statue of Count Pietro

Verri. And most fitting, another monument in Milan's Piazza Beccaria—a bronze statue that is a replica of a damaged marble sculpture by Giuseppe Grandi (1843–1894)—stands on the same site as that formerly occupied by the hangman's house. Grandi's sculpture was unveiled in 1871, decades after Beccaria's death in the city most famous today for its opera house, Leonardo da Vinci's Renaissance painting, *The Last Supper*, and the Duomo of Milan. At the March 19, 1871 inauguration of the statue, Pasquale Stanislao Mancini opened his speech with these words: "The grateful Nation raises a Monument to Cesare Beccaria, to the first who dared to ask lawmakers and peoples to abolish bloody torture, in forceful and heeded words." In a March 4, 1865 letter sent in appreciation for being nominated to be a part of the commission to erect the Milan monument in Beccaria's honor, the French writer Victor Hugo—the author of his own abolitionist work, *The Last Day of a Condemned Man* (1829)—wrote these words of congratulations and appreciation: "Setting up a statue to Beccaria is equivalent to abolishing the scaffold. If, once set up, the scaffold came up from the ground, the statue would go back into it."[219]

As for Cesare Beccaria's literary legacy, *On Crimes and Punishments*—both before and after its author's death—continued to sell copies and to make an impact locally, in the broader European community, and across the Atlantic. The Grand Duke of Tuscany, Pietro Leopold (or Leopold II as he became known in 1790 after succeeding his brother, Joseph II), ordered the burning of instruments of torture, and was apparently pleased with the results, reporting in 1789 that "mild laws together with a careful vigilance" had reduced common crimes and almost eliminated "the most atrocious" ones.[220] A French report devoted to houses of correction specifically invoked the "immortal work of Beccaria,"[221] and European and American intellectuals, including Jeremy Bentham and Dr. Benjamin Rush, cited the Tuscan example in their own anti-death penalty advocacy.[222] In that way, what had started as an Italian example would be replicated in multiple jurisdictions in the years to come. In fact, Beccaria's celebrity, cultivated through his words and multiple editions and translations of his treatise, would only blossom over time.

So famous did Cesare Beccaria become that the death of his son Giulio Bonesana Beccaria (1774–1856)—who compiled editions of his father's work in Milan in 1821—was reported in the press decades after his father's death.[223] Giulio—a coin collector who, in the nineteenth century, renovated the house, now at 6 Via Brera, where his father once lived—had assembled his father's autographed manuscript, consisting of a small leather volume, a manuscript now in the possession of the Biblioteca Ambrosiana in Milan. Near the entrance to the door where Cesare Beccaria and his family once lived is a simple inscription reading: "In this house Cesare Beccaria was born in 1738 and died on November 28, 1794."[224] Though most young people no longer read Cesare Beccaria's treatise as they did centuries ago, *On Crimes and Punishments* is still considered one of the most influential books of the past three centuries on those subjects.[225] Its impact on Anglo-American law would prove so substantial that, truth be told, it is almost impossible to fully measure.

Chapter 2

The Runaway Bestseller: *On Crimes and Punishments*

The Translation of Beccaria's Treatise

English translations of *Dei delitti e delle pene* made Beccaria's essay readily accessible to English and American readers.[1] The first Italian-to-English translation of Beccaria's book—accompanied by Voltaire's commentary—was "Printed for J. ALMON, opposite *Burlington-House, Piccadilly*," in London in 1767.[2] The "Preface of the Translator" states that "[t]he author is the *Marquis* Beccaria, of *Milan*."[3] John Almon, of London, was a bookseller, journalist and printer who, from 1775 to 1784, published *Remembrancer*, a journal to—as an editor of Benjamin Franklin's writings described it—"more accurately present the American perspective of events to a British readership." The first edition of that journal reprinted an abridged version of John Adams' "Novanglus" letters, written in late 1774 and early 1775; Virginia's Declaration of Rights (1776) appeared in a later issue; and the Liverpool-born Almon, even earlier, had printed proceedings of the Continental Congress. Writing as "Novanglus," meaning *New Englander*, Adams wrote of "Cæsare in Rome," "tyranny," "freeman," "[t]he love of liberty," and "revolution." Arguing that "death is better than slavery," Adams, in his letters, referenced a whole host of Enlightenment writers, including Grotius, Pufendorf, Locke and Sidney. In 1777, John Almon—once tried and convicted in the Court of King's Bench and fined by Lord Mansfield for selling a magazine containing content offensive to the king—himself issued a supplementary volume to *The Remembrancer* titled *A Collection of Interesting, Authentic Papers, Relative to the Dispute between Great Britain and America; shewing the Causes and Progress of that Misunderstanding, from 1764 to 1775.*[4]

John Almon was, for years, a man interested in what was happening in North America. In 1770, Almon published *Observations on the Several Acts of Parliament*, a pamphlet by Boston merchants outraged by George III's "many Grievous and unreasonable restrictions upon Trade." In addition, "J. ALMON in Piccadilly" is listed, along with a Mr. Dilly, as one of the sellers in 1774 of an eight-page pamphlet titled *A Clear Idea of the Genuine and Uncorrupted British Constitution in an Address to the Inhabitants of the Province of Quebec from the Forty-nine Delegates in the Continental Congress in Philadelphia.* That pamphlet, which reprinted the Beccaria-quoting congressional address to Quebec's inhabitants, included the following "ADVERTISEMENT" after the title page: "The Generality of the People of *England* are extremely ignorant of the Fundamental Principles of the *British* Constitution: They have as much need of Instruction as the poor Papists, who are the Inhabitants of *Quebec*; and, to answer this Purpose, the present Extract is printed." In a June 1777 letter to Benjamin Franklin, *Common Sense* author Thomas Paine—whose "Crisis" series was published from 1776 to 1783, with the first "Crisis" famously recording "[t]hese are the times that try men's souls"—even suggested, "I think Almon might venture to publish the Second Number" of "a Little Production of mine (the Crisis)."⁵

Prior to the Revolutionary War, John Almon, the eminent bookseller, had direct contact with America's Benjamin Franklin. On November 7, 1774, Franklin—economizing his words—wrote to Almon: "Dr. Franklin presents his Compliments to Mr. Almon, and sends him a M. S. which he has perus'd and thinks well written so as probably to be acceptable to the Publick at this time. If Mr. Almon should be of the same Opinion, it is at his Service." That letter led to the December 5, 1774 publication in London of *An Appeal to Justice and Interests of the People of Great Britain, in the Present Disputes with America.* That pamphlet, published by Almon, who told Franklin on December 6 that "it is probable that it will be reprinted," as it was the following month, was attributed to Arthur Lee, Richard Henry Lee's brother. With Almon anticipating a reprinting and believing that Dr. Franklin—Arthur Lee's friend—had "a considerable share in the composition," Almon's letter to Franklin of December 6 read in part: "Should be glad therefore of notice of any errors (per penny post, or otherwise)."⁶

During the American Revolution itself, John Almon printed a number of books whose emphasis was on liberty and which, more specifically, referenced Beccaria's treatise. One of his titles, *Take Your Choice!*, was written by the English reformer John Cartwright (1740–1824) under the pen name "A Fellow Citizen," with the title page of that 1776 book starkly laying out the choices facing English subjects. "Representation and Respect" and "Annual Parliaments and Liberty" were put in one column, while "Imposition and Contempt" and "Long Parliaments and Slavery" were put in another. Dedicated "To The Commons of Great-Britain," the political essay, which quoted Beccaria, discussed "those Rights and Privileges" which "Ancestors thought worth preserving." In the introduction to *Take Your Choice!*, Cartwright raised the following questions, among many others: "Are not our sanguinary statutes, by which we year by year spill rivers of blood, a reproach to the political knowledge, to the humanity, to the religion of our island? And are not our prisons and our treatment of prisoners shocking and foolish?" Though Cartwright wrote of the "excellence" and "truly *glorious*" nature of "our common law," he emphasized: "Departing from former precedents and decisions which are any way defective, in order to come nearer and nearer to the perfection of human reason, its determinations continue to vary and to refine, as experience and wisdom dictates. When the perfection of reason, on any point, is once attained; then, and not till then, is our law *unalterable*." "'It may be alledged,' says Beccaria, 'that the interest of commercial should be secured,'" Cartwright wrote, quoting the Italian philosopher, "'but commerce and property are not the end of the social compact, but the means of obtaining that end.'"

Before quoting Beccaria again, Cartwright added: "Every man is free; and therefore he ought to vote." "If a wealthy person is to be indulged with more votes than one, 'tis evident that, in exact proportion as this practice shall prevail, the value of every poor man's vote will be diminished." In the book published by John Almon, Cartwright concluded, lifting a lengthy passage from *On Crimes and Punishments*:

> The pernicious consequences of partial and unjust laws are finely represented by the Marquis Beccaria in the person of a robber or assassin, whom he supposes to reason with himself thus: "What are these laws, that I am bound to respect, which make so great a difference between me and the rich man? He refuses me the farthing I ask of him, and excuses himself, by bidding me have recourses to labour, with which I am unacquainted. Who made these laws? The rich and the great, who never deigned to visit the miserable hut of the poor; who have never yet seen him dividing a piece of mouldy bread, amidst the cries of his famished

children and the tears of his wife. Let us break those ties, fatal to the greatest part of mankind, and only useful to a few indolent tyrants. Let us attack injustice at its source. I will return to my natural state of independence. I shall live free and happy on the fruits of my courage and industry."[7]

Another title published by John Almon in 1776 also referred to "the Marchese Beccaria" and "his most excellent book of humanity."[8]

John Almon's printing operation, sympathetic to the American cause, was one that attracted America's founders' attention. Writing from Passy in 1779 to Thomas Digges, a descendent of a prominent Maryland family and a pro-American expatriate in London, Benjamin Franklin — with an eye to history — even made a special request that Almon's publications be collected. As Franklin wrote to Digges: "Be so good as to procure from Mr. Almon the remembrancers Debates in Parliament since the American Disputes and all Such other Pamphlets as may be of use to an Historian, who proposes to write the late revolution." The historian, William Gordon, after receiving the requested materials from Digges, later wrote *The History of the Rise, Progress, and Establishment, of the Independence of the United States of America* (1788). In his own letter of March 3, 1780, Digges — writing from London — advised John Adams to get a subscription to Almon's *London Courant*, a morning newspaper. Almon himself printed materials pertaining to the Massachusetts Constitution of 1780 in his *London Courant* and in *The Remembrancer* for 1780.[9]

Shortly thereafter, in 1781, John Almon retired, leaving his business to John Debrett, the London-born son of a French cook who had apprenticed with him. In *The Ghosts of Piccadilly*, a book recording the eventual demise of John Almon's bookshop, the author lamented that Almon's shop "was gone, succeeded by Debrett, who had been in partnership with him." "A 'Letter to Edmund Burke' in 1782," that book's author, historian George Street, wrote, "refers pleasantly to 'that common sink of filth and fiction, the shop of Almon and Debrett in Piccadilly.'" In his book, George Street went on to reminisce about all the "political antagonisms" that had occurred at shops like "Almon's, a great Whig firm."[10] Charles Dilly (1739–1807), the other salesman of *A Clear Idea of the Genuine and Uncorrupted British Constitution* being simultaneously promoted by John Almon, was a bookseller who ran a publishing house with his brother Edward. "Their house," one source reports, "was a meeting place for literary men in London." *A Catalogue of Books Printed for, and Sold by Charles Dilly, in London*, later published in 1787, included John Adams' *Defence of the Constitutions of Government of the United States*, Benjamin Franklin's *Philosophical and Miscellaneous Papers*, *Locke's Works*, and Dr. Samuel Johnson's *Dictionary*.[11]

Along with John Almon's release of Beccaria's *On Crimes and Punishments* in London in 1767, another English edition of Beccaria's treatise, printed by John Exshaw in Dublin, also appeared in 1767,[12] while still another — printed for "F. Newbery" in London and labeled "THE SECOND EDITION" — came out in 1769.[13] In between, in 1768, in an advertisement for "J. ALMON, opposite Burlington-House, in Piccadilly," Beccaria's book was listed among titles that would be published "[i]n a few days." The title in which that ad appears: *A Sentimental Dialogue Between Two Souls, in the Palpable Bodies of an English Lady of Quality and an Irish Gentleman*, written by John Hall-Stevenson under the pseudonym "Tristram Shandy." Both Irish and English republicans — as well as legal commentators in places like England, Scotland and Ireland — clearly enjoyed reading Beccaria's treatise and, as the years went by, its success fed even more publicity.[14] John Exshaw — the Irishman — came from a prominent family of booksellers, and he did multiple printings of Beccaria's treatise, including a "FIFTH EDITION" — printed in Dublin at "No. 86, DAME-STREET" — in 1777.[15]

Francis Newbery—whose business in London was located at the Corner of St. Paul's Church-Yard—was either John Newbery's son or nephew. The son, Francis Newbery, had taken over part of the family's printing business in 1767 after the death of his father, John Newbery. A long-time printer who gained notoriety by profitably publishing children's books in the 1740s, John Newbery counted among his close friends the famed lexicographer Dr. Samuel Johnson. John Newbery—who published books by Dr. Johnson and other prominent figures—is the same person for whom the prestigious Newbery Medal is now named. "The works of John Newbery," the author of *Learning to Read and Write in Colonial America* notes, "made their way across the seas to American bookstores and American children, at least in the major seaports."

John Newbery's son Francis had begun studying at Oxford's Trinity College in June 1762, then enrolled at Cambridge in 1766, but returned to London in the latter part of 1767 on account of his father's severe illness. After his father's death, Francis took over part of the family's business. The other Francis Newbery, John Newbery's nephew, also worked in John Newbery's book business and continued in the printing trade after his uncle John's death. "It was not until after John Newbery's death in 1767," one historian writes, "that Francis Newbery, his nephew, who had been previously issuing books from Paternoster Row, went to 20 Ludgate Street—the corner of St. Paul's Churchyard—where the business was continued by his widow."[16] The English language translations of *On Crimes and Punishments* produced by both John Exshaw and Francis Newbery once again listed "[t]he author" as "the *Marquis* Beccaria of *Milan*."[17]

As Beccaria's treatise became better known in English-speaking countries, more and more people wanted to read it. Yet another English-language edition, no doubt spurred by demand, was printed for Robert Urie in Glasgow in 1770.[18] And in an era when American colonists often studied in England or Scotland,[19] "F. Newbery"—apparently getting good sales—also brought out a third edition of Beccaria's book that year in London.[20] London and Glasgow were places where intellectuals gathered and both cities had major universities, with the University of Glasgow founded in the fifteenth century.[21] Municipalities like Edinburgh, London and Glasgow were hubs of culture where Enlightenment texts got printed, and Beccaria's treatise was much sought after in those locales, with colonial-era Americans—attracted by the vibrant intellectual climate in Europe—often studying in such places to advance their careers.

For example, a wealthy Boston merchant, James Bowdoin II (1726–1790), paid for his only son, James Bowdoin III (1752–1811), better known as "Jemmy," to study law at Oxford—and, later, to travel throughout Europe—after his graduation from Harvard in 1771. On a trip to Italy with Ward Nicholas Boylston, described by one historian as "an affluent young dandy who had not bothered to attend college," Jemmy and his friend reportedly "visited sumptuously decorated cathedrals, storied natural wonders, and eye-opening archaeological excavations, and they marveled at the wealth and style of the aristocratic and commercial society of Naples and Rome." When Jemmy finally returned to Massachusetts in December 1775 after reading about the Battle of Lexington, the Revolutionary War was already in full swing, with the Italian philosopher, Cesare Beccaria, having spurred on the colonists through his treatise. James Bowdoin II would later serve as the second governor of Massachusetts from 1785 to 1787, and his son, James Bowdoin III, became an American minister to France and Spain during the Napoleonic era.[22]

In the late eighteenth-century, the Scottish Enlightenment, in particular, was brimming with intellectual curiosity about thinkers focused on everything from medicine, botany and mathematics to politics and political philosophy. And Scotland itself was attracting a number of Americans who came to study and imbibe its cultural and intellectual offerings. For instance, Dr. Benjamin Rush—who made abolishing the death penalty a life-long cause—studied medicine at the University of Edinburgh from 1766 to 1768.[23] It was likely in that time period—or, at most, shortly thereafter—when Dr. Rush first encountered Beccaria's *On Crimes and Punishments*. "One of the university's character-istic features," writes historian Jürgen Martschukat of Dr. Rush's time there, "was its con-cern with the interaction between mind and body, in the context of the Scottish Enlightenment and its philosophers such as Francis Hutcheson or Adam Smith."[24] "Eighteenth-century Glasgow," author Richard Sher writes of that city's intellectual life, "was also home to Robert Urie, who published English-language editions of works by Voltaire, Rousseau, and many classical authors"; Glasgow, he notes, "nurtured a thriving trade in the publishing and reprinting of evangelical sermons and other religious books."[25]

In the English-speaking world—America, England, Scotland and Ireland—*On Crimes and Punishments* became an instant hit. The second edition of *The Annual Register, or a View of the History, Politics, and Literature, for the Year 1767*, published in London in 1772, extracted extended portions of Beccaria's treatise. It also gave this report of the widely acknowledged success of Beccaria's essay on the criminal law: "The merit of the essay before us is so generally known and allowed, that it may seem unnecessary to inform our readers, that it has gained the attention of all ranks of people in almost every part of Eu-rope; and that few books on any subject have ever been more generally read, or more universally applauded." Not only did Beccaria's treatise get cited in multiple editions of Sir William Blackstone's *Commentaries on the Laws of England* beginning in the year 1769, but Beccaria's ideas were also invoked and discussed in multiple editions of William Eden's *Principles of Penal Law*, first published in 1771 and reprinted in places like Dublin in 1772. In Cambridge, Massachusetts, Beccaria's "*del Delitti et delle Pene*" also appeared in Harvard College's 1773 library catalog, the Latin-titled *Catalogus Librorum*, along with "Black-stone (Judge) all his Works," "Burlamaqui on Natural Law," "Condillac's Origin of Human Knowledge," "Locke, Esq. (John)—all his Works," "Montesquieu-Oeuvres de," and "Syd-ney (Algernon) on Government."[26]

Continental Europeans of that time were, simultaneously, continuing to publicize Bec-caria's treatise in their own works. An English translation of Voltaire's *The Man of Forty Crowns*, published in 1768 in London, referenced Beccaria, then emphasized, in a bit of sarcasm, that "those who made the laws were not geometricians." And when Giacinto Dragonetti's *A Treatise on Virtues and Rewards* was published in London in 1769, the pref-ace—which followed the translator's dedication of March 20, 1769 to Lord Viscount Chewton—editorialized: "Jacinto Dragonetti is the author of the following treatise, first published at Naples, and received with an applause little inferior to that which had celebrated the name of Beccaria." In 1770, the two-volume Italian language title, *Il Vero Dispotismo*, about despotism, also referenced the author of *On Crimes and Punishments*. That London-published work was written by Count Giuseppe Gorani, born into a noble but impoverished Milanese family in the 1740s. Gorani's book referred to "*Signor March-ese* Beccaria" and the "*celebre Marchese Beccaria*" and his work seeking the death penalty's abolition. A soldier, writer and ambassador, Gorani had taken part in the Seven Years War, been taken prisoner, then studied law in Prussia, becoming interested in the reforms of Frederick II. A friend of Cesare Beccaria, Pietro Verri, Voltaire and other enlighten-ment figures, Gorani was a member of the *Il Caffé* group of Italian thinkers but ultimately fell out of favor with Lombard authorities, relocating to Geneva after being banished.[27]

In *Considerations on Criminal Law*, published in Dublin in 1772, its author, Henry Dagge, gave this telling report on Beccaria's success and literary achievement: "Several Authors of great abilities, who have wrote on the subject of Criminal Laws, agree that the Penal Codes of most nations are very defective; particularly with regard to capital punishments. Among others, the Marquis of *Beccaria*, seems to have considered this subject with great attention." The "celebrated" and "benevolent Marquis Beccaria" also got play in lesser-known titles such as *Free Thoughts on Seduction, Adultery, and Divorce*, written by "Civilian" and published in London in 1771.[28] Beccaria's treatise did so well that, in 1769, London publishers James Dodsley and John Murray printed another Beccaria-authored text, *Discourse on Public Oeconomy and Commerce*. In that book, published in London in 1769, Beccaria wrote of Italy's "antient republican spirit" and of "Liberty and industry." In his reprinted lecture, delivered shortly after his academic appointment in Milan, Beccaria noted the while his native city had often been ravaged by war, "we have seen it raised to a happy and flourishing condition, by laws equally simple and comprehensive; laws which have removed the destructive influence of arbitrary power."[29]

By 1775, the year America's Revolutionary War broke out, Beccaria's name was being quoted everywhere. *The Patriots of North-America* (1775), a long-form poem published in New York, began: *Men plac'd, by Chance, or sov'reign Fate, / in Life's low, unambitious State; / Whilst undeprav'd, all amply share, / Wise, bounteous Nature's, equal Care.* The poem later contained these two lines: *Midst Power despotic, Monkish Cells, / Thy Beccaria peaceful dwells.* That same year, American diplomat Dr. Arthur Lee (1740–1792)—after detailing a number of "American grievances"—also quoted Beccaria in *A Speech Intended to Have Been Delivered in the House of Commons, in Support of the Petition from the General Congress at Philadelphia*. As Dr. Lee observed: "Under so shameful a violation of Parliamentary Faith, what confidence, what respect can you desire from America? What other bond of Government will be left you, but fear? And let me ask in the words of the sagacious Beccaria, 'What ought we to think of that Government which has no other means of managing the subject, but fear?'"[30]

With so much interest in *On Crimes and Punishments*, a fourth edition of Beccaria's treatise, translated from the Italian, and again with commentary attributed to Voltaire, was printed in 1775 for "F. Newbery" at "the Corner of St. Paul's Church-Yard" in London.[31] St. Paul's Churchyard—where locals knew Francis Newbery's premises well—was a place where English booksellers congregated and sold their offerings.[32] For example, in an advertisement published in another "F. Newbery" title published in 1775—*A Modern System of Natural History*, a multi-volume treatise written by the Rev. Samuel Ward—a "new Edition" of Beccaria's "Essay on Crimes and Punishments" is listed for sale for five shillings. The advertisement in that book—a title that gave descriptions of animals, vegetables and minerals—noted elsewhere in a "General Address" of "rational entertainment" and "the tender feelings of humanity" allowing readers "to exercise every passion by which the man is distinguished from the brute."[33] In another advertisement in a different "F. Newbery" title published in 1777—*The Life of Mr. Richard Savage*—Beccaria's treatise is also listed for sale "*at the Corner of* St. Paul's Churchyard" for five shillings.[34]

The 1775 version of *On Crimes and Punishments* owned by John Adams, the second President of the United States, had been printed in London and then found its way into his hands, with that book now residing in the Boston Public Library Rare Book Collection.[35] While John Adams had been dispatched to France by the Continental Congress in 1778 and had returned to France as a Minister Plenipotentiary to negotiate a peace treaty with the British, John and Abigail Adams first arrived in London in the mid-1780s after Adams became a diplomat. The 1775 copy of Beccaria's book that Adams acquired, therefore, likely was exported from London and purchased elsewhere.[36] The use by John Adams of Beccaria's book at an even earlier time, following the Boston Massacre trial, makes crystal clear that Adams had closely studied the ideas in Beccaria's treatise long before the 1775 edition of Beccaria's treatise rolled off the presses. "After John Newbery's death," one history reports of the family that printed the English-language edition of Beccaria's treatise, "Francis Newbery the nephew, seems to have set up his share of the Newbery business in the house at the corner of St. Paul's Churchyard, while Francis Newbery the son, carried on his share in the house No. 65 St. Paul's Churchyard."[37]

The English Radical: John Wilkes

By 1775, British radicals, like American colonists, had, for more than a decade, been exasperated by the tyranny of George III's administration. In 1762, the same year that Voltaire took up the cause of Jean Calas, one such English radical, John Wilkes (1726–1797), an MP, started editing his own newspaper, *The North Briton*. "The wit and severity of the latter instantly gave it a very extensive circulation," the London printer John Almon later reported of the paper, which Wilkes created in response to, and as a parody of, *The Briton*, a pro-government newspaper run by Tobias Smollett. Issue "No. 45" of *The North Briton*, published on April 23, 1763, became the most famous edition, with Wilkes, using "The North Briton" as a pseudonym, issuing—as Almon put—"this celebrated paper, the forty-fifth Number." "THE NORTH BRITON makes his appeal to the good sense, and to the candour of the English nation," No. 45 began. "The NORTH BRITON," it continued, "desires to be understood, as having pledged himself a firm and intrepid assertor of the rights of his fellow-subjects, and of the liberties of WHIGS and ENGLISHMEN."

In *The North Briton*, which Americans such as Benjamin Franklin were almost immediately familiar, Wilkes anonymously satirized and took aim at George III's administration. Quoting Cicero and attacking "THE *King's Speech*" before Parliament in favor of a negotiated peace treaty with France as "the *Speech of the Minister*," No. 45 of *The North Briton* lambasted the actions of the government and, in particular, its "*Scottish* prime minister of *England*," John Stuart, the Earl of Bute. Wilkes—whose newspaper published allegations of an affair between Lord Bute and the king's mother—expressed the view that too many concessions were made to France in the 1763 peace treaty, signed in Paris, ending the Seven Years War, a war that consumed Europe's great powers, claiming hundreds of thousands of lives. No. 44 of *The North Briton* had taken note of Lord Bute's resignation on April 8, 1763, with "The North Briton"—in No. 45—making this inflammatory assertion: "The *Stuart* line has ever been intoxicated with the slavish doctrines of the *absolute, independent, unlimited* power of the crown." "Some of that line," Wilkes wrote, "were so weakly advised, as to endeavour to reduce them into practice: but the *English* nation was too spirited to suffer the least encroachment on the ancient liberties of this kingdom." Recalling a 1603 speech of James I to the English Parliament in which James I proclaimed "*I am a* SERVANT" and that his "*principal honour*" was "*to be the* GREAT SERVANT *of the commonwealth*," Wilkes emphasized in No. 45: "The *prerogative* of the crown is to exert the constitutional powers entrusted to it in a way, not of blind favour and partiality, but of wisdom and judgment. This is the spirit of our constitution." "Freedom *is the English subject's* Prerogative," No. 45 concluded, quoting "the fine words of DRYDEN," said to be "engraven on our hearts."

John Wilkes—a libertine, and one of the most colorful figures in English history— had become a member of Parliament in 1757, a colonel in the militia, and had an ambition to become either an ambassador to Constantinople or the governor of Quebec, showing an interest in the latter post, reportedly, so that he could show the French "the advantages of the mild rule of laws, over that of lawless power and despotism." In 1760, George III had, at age 22, inherited the British throne, and quickly sought to consolidate his power, installing his friend and mentor, the unpopular Lord Bute, in positions of power. William Pitt—a popular prime minister who had urged a continuation of the war against France until its total defeat—resigned his post in October 1761, with Lord Bute—his successor—later burned in effigy in the cider-producing regions of the West Country and Herefordshire after a higher excise tax on cider was imposed to cover war-related debts. Pitt had effectively organized a successful war effort against France in the French and Indian War, ultimately helping to secure Canada, as well as Louisiana, for Britain. The same month that Pitt resigned, Wilkes became acquainted with John Almon, the future printer of the English translation of Beccaria's treatise and, much later, Wilkes' own biographer.

John Stuart, the 3rd Earl of Bute, had been appointed by the newly installed monarch, George III, to the post of Secretary of State for the Northern Department in spite of a lack of experience. "The king's insistence on appointing Bute as Secretary of State," one historian notes, "created tensions within the Cabinet, only increased by difficulties over Spain as the Seven Years War continued." A member of Parliament, Wilkes was taken into custody in April 1763 for his suspected role in the publication of *The North Briton* by virtue of a warrant from his majesty's secretary of state, whereupon a habeas corpus proceeding was commenced to procure his release. The "General Warrant" instructed the king's messengers to seek out and arrest the "Authors, Printers & Publishers of a seditious and treasonable paper," to wit, "the North Briton Number 45." In all, forty-nine men were arrested in three days, Wilkes last among them. In effect, George III—who later, in a royal message, called *North Briton* No. 45 "that most seditious and dangerous libel"—had decided to chill speech and discontent by going after his political opponents through a high-stakes criminal prosecution.

By then, George Grenville—the Chancellor of the Exchequer and a man who Lord Bute had appointed Northern Secretary and First Lord of the Admiralty—had become prime minister, so it was Grenville's ministry that had Wilkes arrested for seditious libel and put in the Tower of London as part of the concerted effort to quash opposition to George III and his policies. "It was Grenville," Ann Lyon writes in her *Constitutional History of the United Kingdom*, "who sowed the wind in the form of the Stamp Act of 1765 that was to reap the whirlwind of the American Revolution." The sustained efforts of Wilkes and his many supporters, followed closely by Americans in the lead up to the Revolutionary War, eventually caused the English courts to declare general warrants illegal (1769), with Englishmen also winning the right to publish parliamentary debates in newspapers (1771). Released from the Tower of London in May 1763, Wilkes—never one to back down—quickly got himself into even more trouble after hiring journeymen to help him reprint, in volume form, *The North Briton*, and *An Essay on Woman*, a satire on Alexander Pope's 1730s *Essay on Man* and a parody that was not intended for public consumption.

The lascivious *Essay on Woman*, written years before by Wilkes or his friend Thomas Potter (1718–1759), perhaps both, put—in one commentator's words—"obscene and blasphemous remarks" into the mouth of William Warburton (1698–1779), the Bishop of Gloucester, a literary executor who had reissued Pope's *Essay on Man* with notes. Wilkes had issued strict instructions that only twelve copies of *An Essay on Woman* were to be printed and that no copies should leave Wilkes' house at 13 Great George Street, the place of their printing. But one of his journeymen surreptitiously stole a copy of *Essay on Woman*, then turned it over to the government, allowing Wilkes to be charged with libeling Bishop Warburton. The *Essay on Woman* made crude allusions to the chastity of the bishop's wife, leading the House of Lords to accuse Wilkes of publishing an obscene and blasphemous libel that violated the rights of Bishop Warburton, one of its members. The accusation was made by Lord Sandwich, who scandalously read these lines of verse, stolen by the printer, to the House itself:

> Awake, my Fanny, leave all meaner things,
> This morn shall prove what rapture swiving brings.
> Let us (since life can little more supply
> Than just a few good Fucks and then we die)
> Expatiate free o'er that lov'd scene of Man;
> A mighty Maze! for mighty Pricks to scan.

Wilkes' troubles only intensified after the British politician Samuel Martin, in mid-November, challenged him to a duel. A former Secretary of the Treasury vilified in No. 40 of *The North Briton*, Martin rose in the House of Commons and called the anonymous author of the paper a "cowardly rascal, a villain, and a scoundrel." The very next day, Martin and Wilkes fought a duel with pistols in Hyde Park, and Wilkes was shot in the abdomen. After being wounded in the 1763 duel with Martin, one of George III and Lord Bute's supporters, Wilkes—recognizing that the Parliament was likely to expel him—secretly fled to France on Christmas Eve in 1763 before facing trial or being expelled. In failing to appear for his sentencing despite being summoned, Wilkes would officially become an outlaw in 1764 after being tried and convicted in absentia before Lord Mansfield for publishing libels in *The North Briton* and the *Essay on Woman*. In Paris, his daughter Polly's place of residence, Wilkes—safe from English authorities, unlike John Williams, another printer of the *North Briton* who was pilloried in February 1765 at New Palace Yard—quickly fell in love with an eighteen-year-old Italian beauty, Gertude Corradini, with whom he commenced an affair. In the City of Light, Wilkes also reconnected with the *philosophe* Paul-Henri Thiry d'Holbach, then known as Baron d'Holback, his long-time friend from his days at the University of Leiden. "His association with some of the leading French *philosophes* and their families," writes historian John Sainsbury of Wilkes' time in Paris, exposed him to "progressive ideas" even as the *philosophes* offered him and his daughter Polly hospitality.

Before leaving England to convalesce in France, however, Wilkes spoke candidly—and with great force—in the Court of Common Pleas in the context of his habeas corpus proceeding. "I feel myself happy to be at last brought before a court, and before judges, whose characteristic is the love of liberty," Wilkes said. Wilkes railed against "ministers of arbitrary principles," further observing that "the liberty of an English subject is not to be sported away with impunity, in this cruel and despotic manner." "As an outlaw," Ann Lyon writes of Wilkes' precarious position upon his leaving England, "he was subject to perpetual imprisonment if he set foot again on English soil, and was in any case liable to be tried for seditious libel, with heavy penalties if he was found guilty." The "warrant of commitment" previously issued against him, "in his majesty's name," labeled Wilkes "the author and publisher of a most infamous and seditious libel, intitled the North Briton, number 45, tending to inflame the minds and alienate the affections of the people from his majesty, and excite them to traiterous insurrections against the government." In his courtroom speech, Wilkes—asserting privileges as a member of Parliament as part of his legal defense—emphasized "[t]he particular cruelties of my treatment, worse than if I had been a Scottish rebel," and asked for "justice" and "redress." In the Tower of London, Wilkes had been held in *close confinement*, meaning the warders had been ordered to keep a constant watch on him, were told to permit no person to have access to the room in which he was confined, and even monitored communications he wrote to his daughter and servants on the only two occasions he was given access to pen, ink and paper.

Only years later did Wilkes, suffering financial difficulties and fearing imprisonment for debt in France, decide the time and the political climate were right in his native England to make a political comeback. Leaving Paris for Calais on November 22, 1767, Wilkes crossed the English Channel on December 3, then returned briefly to London. But after consulting his friends, he left again, this time for The Hague. Determined to wait in Flanders until the eve of the impending dissolution of the British Parliament, Wilkes—wanting vindication and to regain his position in English society—hoped to secure a seat in the new Parliament, with the added benefit of obtaining a privilege from arrest against his creditors. Going back to London in early February 1768, Wilkes promptly announced his candidacy for election to the House of Commons from the City of London. He also sought a pardon from George III, sending a letter by footman to the gate of Buckingham Palace.

At first ignored by authorities worried about fomenting further public discontent, Wilkes was neither pardoned nor arrested, allowing him to openly advertise his candidacy and to move about the city. Campaigning on "two important questions of public liberty, respecting General Warrants and Seizure of Papers," Wilkes—a late entrant in the field—appeared at a banquet held in his honor by "a great number of the nobility and livery" at the King's Arms Tavern in Cornhill. After losing the election, Wilkes, undeterred, attributed his defeat to his late entry and, to the delight of the crowd, announced his intention of contesting the County of Middlesex, the election for which would begin five days later. "Ministerial influence, assisted by private malice," he proclaimed, "has been exerted in the most arbitrary and unconstitutional manner, and by means of the basest chicanery and oppression."

Avoiding arrest during the election by pledging to "present" himself to the Court of King's Bench at "the beginning of the ensuing term" on the libel charges against him, Wilkes, yet to be punished, and his supporters—known as Wilkites—went to work. Backing their populist hero, Wilkites—wearing blue cockades adorned with "Wilkes" and "45"—sometimes resorted to intimidation, or engaged in mob activities such as breaking windows of the coaches and houses of the English aristocracy. The election of the two Knights of the Shire for the County of Middlesex took place in late March 1768, with Horace Bleackley's *Life of John Wilkes* reporting that, soon after 6:00 a.m. on the morning of the election, "a stream of hired coaches, decked with blue favours—nearly 250 in all—was making its way along the Acton road, conveying hundreds of excited Wilkites towards Brentford"—and the polls. "Register, register, register" had become the candidate's motto, with Wilkites running the eighteenth-century equivalent of a modern-day, get-out-the-vote grassroots campaign, albeit with particularly nasty and unsavory tactics. With authorities declining to announce the election results until the next morning, silk, anti-Wilkite banners appeared at Hyde Park Corner reading "No Blasphemer" and "No French Renegade." But during the heated campaign and election season, Wilkites—not limiting themselves to peaceful expression as they traveled in carriages marked "No. 45"—beat up or insulted supporters of the establishment candidates. At Lord Bute's stately residence, every pane of glass was broken.

Ultimately, Wilkes won the hard-fought election, receiving 1,292 votes, the most of any candidate. Viewed as a victory for the working classes, "No. 45" appeared in area doors, candles were lit, and coaches were not allowed to pass roadways unless adorned with "blue favours," leading even noblemen to decorate their coaches in that manner and to cheer, if only half-heartedly, "Wilkes and Liberty." The Austrian ambassador, in the mob's hands, was even dragged from his coach and had "45" chalked onto the soles of his shoes. As Benjamin Franklin wrote to his son William from London in April 1768, explaining what had transpired: "The scenes have been horrible. London was illuminated two nights running at the command of the mob for the success of Wilkes in the Middlesex election." As Franklin explained, giving these details: "The mob, (spirited up by numbers of different ballads sung or roared in every street) requiring gentlemen and ladies of all ranks as they passed in their carriages to shout for Wilkes and liberty, marking the same words on all their coaches with chalk, and No. 45 on every door; which extends a vast way along the roads into the country."

Still, the House of Commons had not yet seated Wilkes, with Wilkes—honoring his pledge to show up at the Court of King's Bench at the first day of the Easter term—appearing before Lord Mansfield on April 20th. As Franklin put it in his letter to his son, referring to Wilkes: "The ferment is not yet over, for he has promised to surrender himself to the Court next Wednesday, and another tumult is then expected; and what the upshot will be no one can yet foresee." "In a speech to the judge," Horace Bleackley's biography notes, "he pleaded that there was not a word of disrespect towards the king in 'No. 45,' and that having privately printed only twelve copies of the 'Essay on Woman' for his personal friends, he could not be deemed guilty of publishing the poem." "Neither of the two verdicts could have been found against me," Wilkes contended, "if the records had not been materially altered without my consent." Ostensibly, because the Attorney General had neglected to compel Wilkes' appearance before the court via a writ of *capias ut legatum*, Lord Mansfield declared that the newly elected Wilkes was not, in fact, legally before the court. Therefore, Wilkes—still a free man—was not immediately sent to prison for his previously adjudicated offenses. "The Court of King's Bench," Benjamin Franklin editorialized around that time, "postponed giving sentence against Wilkes on his outlawry till the next term, intimidated as some say by his popularity, and willing to get rid of the affair for a time till it should be seen what the parliament would conclude as to his membership." Only after time passed did the Attorney General—wary of Wilkes' growing political power—sign the necessary paperwork to bring Wilkes back before the court, to facilitate his detention, and to allow Wilkes to formally challenge the "outlawry" finding. Even the Lord Chief Justice of the King's Bench, Lord Mansfield, while denying Wilkes' bail, thus sending Wilkes to prison, sensed the danger and volatile community sentiment, judiciously offering: "God forbid that the defendant should not be allowed the benefit of every advantage he is entitled to by law."

At a time when some Londoners still expected Wilkes to be released and to take his seat in Parliament in May, a large crowd gathered outside the House of Commons and shouted "Wilkes and Liberty!" A much larger crowd also gathered in St. George's Fields at King's Bench Prison, the site of Wilkes' confinement. Fearful an effort might be made to free Wilkes, authorities took extra precautions to guard the King's Bench Prison. Wilkites did, in fact, hold regular demonstrations on behalf of their idol, disturbances broke out, and when May came, rumors swirled about surrounding Wilkes' future, raising pressing, new questions about whether Wilkes, though in prison, would be allowed to take his seat in Parliament. Naturally, this caused even larger crowds to gather in front of the king's prison, further exacerbating the risk of a full-on riot. Scottish troops were ordered to the scene to protect the prison, but after the mob outside it learned that Wilkes would not be released, its members began throwing rocks at the soldiers.

Magistrates read the Riot Act, with historian Merrill Jensen, in *The Founding of a Nation: A History of the American Revolution*, describing what happened next on May 10, 1768, drawing a parallel to the still-to-come Boston Massacre: "The soldiers fired, killed five or six, and wounded several more, some of them women. In the course of the brawl soldiers chased into a private home and killed a young man, William Allen, who apparently had nothing to do with the rioting." In Benjamin Franklin's words, written in a letter to Joseph Galloway on May 14, 1768, this is what happened outside the prison where Wilkes was confined: "Great mobs of his adherents have assembled before the prison, the guards have fired on them: it is said five or six are killed and fifteen or sixteen wounded, and some circumstances have attended this military execution, such as its being done by the

Scotch regiment, and pursuing a lad and killing him at his father's house &c. &c." From a historical standpoint, Jensen writes, the Massacre of St. George's Fields "was to be followed less than two years later by a 'massacre' in Boston, Massachusetts, and the example of the first massacre was not lost on the participants in the second."[38]

Wilkes, long a target of government persecution, never gave up on his quest for high office, the Massacre of St. George's Fields only serving, from his perspective, to confirm that he, not any British minister, was the one fighting for liberty and against tyranny and oppression. In early June, amidst fresh protests by the Wilkites, the judges of the King's Bench—who had themselves received threats—unanimously decided that the outlawry finding against Wilkes was null and void and should be reversed. The rationale, a rather technical one: outlawry could not be found because the words "of the County of Middlesex" had been omitted from the sheriff's writ. Despite the high hopes of Wilkites, when Wilkes appeared before the King's Bench ten day's later, Judge Joseph Yates, to whom the responsibility for sentencing fell, did not let Wilkes off scot-free. Instead, he fined Wilkes £1000 and sentenced him to twenty-two months in prison for seditious libel for republishing *North Briton* "No. 45" and for publishing "The Essay on Woman." At George III's insistence, Wilkes—though getting himself elected and reelected as a city alderman while in prison—was not allowed to take his seat in the House of Commons. After a debate that lasted until three o'clock in the morning, with Wilkes brought from the prison to attend the marathon session, the House of Commons—despite raucous protests—voted to expel Wilkes.

Once transported back to prison, Wilkes only fought harder. He prepared a handbill to the "Gentlemen, Clergy, and Freeholders of the County of Middlesex," in which he contended that English citizens had the right "of naming their own representatives." As Wilkes contended: "If ministers can once usurp the power of declaring who *shall not* be your representative, the next step is very easy, and will follow speedily. It is that of telling you whom you *shall* send to Parliament, and then the boasted Constitution of England will be entirely torn up by the roots." On February 16, 1769, finding that argument appealing, Middlesex residents, "by the unanimous voice of above two thousand of the most respectable freeholders," again chose Wilkes to represent them in Parliament. The very next day, however, the House of Commons, on the motion of Lord Strange, had its own vote, deciding that Wilkes could not sit in Parliament because he had previously been expelled, including for his publication of *North Briton* No. 45. After Wilkes won yet another election on March 16th, again unanimously, it was—predictably—declared void, with the Middlesex electorate still just as determined to seat Wilkes as George III and Parliament were to deny him the honor. When Wilkes later won still another vote, this time by a margin of 1,143 to 296, with voters waving flags reading "Magna-Carta" and "Bill of Rights," the House of Commons did more than simply declare Wilkes' election a nullity. Instead, that body went a step further, deciding to seat his losing opponent, Colonel Henry Lawes Luttrell, the man the English ministry had persuaded to run and who reportedly was a "fearless bull of a man" and a "notorious rake." After a rancorous debate, Parliament reconfirmed its controversial decision on May 8th, and the following day—as Merrill Jensen notes—"when George III drove to Westminster to close the session he drove through a storm of shouted insults."[39]

With a long history of having to live in fear, Wilkes, like Beccaria, saw himself as a law and penal reformer. He was an advocate for freedom of the press and he made the first motion in the House of Commons to extend the franchise to all adult males, a suggested reform that, in his time, failed to pass. In 1769, while Wilkes was still in prison, Wilkites started a fundraising arm for Wilkes' benefit known as the Society of Supporters of the Bill of Rights, a reference to the English Bill of Rights of 1689 that, among other things, prohibited "cruel and unusual punishments." "Wilkes's every move," notes his biographer, "was followed in the American press, and his victories over government celebrated in the colonies." As that biographer, Arthur Cash, notes of Wilkes, who secretly sent money to America during the war: "He corresponded with Samuel Adams, John Hancock, and other of the founding fathers and was among the foremost supporters of American causes through essays, petitions, and speeches in Parliament."

In mid-April 1769, the American patriot Joseph Warren wrote directly to John Wilkes, telling him that Wilkes' expulsion from Parliament had "filled America with Grief." "Our eyes are at present fixed on the county of Middlesex," one man, Thomas Young, wrote from Boston as the tug of war between Middlesex electors and Parliament was still going on, and fellow Bostonian John Adams, as informed from a tavern in London, was himself elected in 1773 as a member of the new Society of Supporters of the Bill of Rights. In *The Founding of a Nation*, historian Merrill Jensen sums up the impact Wilkes made on American life as follows: "Wilkes had been toasted occasionally in America during 1766, but by the end of 1768, 'Wilkes and Liberty' was the toast from one end of the colonies to the other, and '45' was almost a sacred number."

Burnishing a reputation for himself as a friend of the common man, Wilkes was later, in 1771, elected one of the sheriffs for London and Middlesex, becoming the honorific Lord Mayor of London in 1774 and the Chamberlain of the City of London in 1779. In 1772, Wilkes and a colleague—just a few short years after the publication of Beccaria's treatise—specifically recommended the "revision of those laws which inflict capital punishment for many inferior crimes." "It was our care, while we paid due obedience to the laws now in force," they said, "to alleviate their harshness by lenity and tenderness to every unhappy object." In a collection of *The North Briton*, published in 1769 under the pseudonym "A Friend to Civil and Religious Liberty," one finds a specific reference in the appendix to "the great friend of man, the *Marquis Beccaria*." George III called the steadfast supporter of the American Revolution "that devil Wilkes," while Voltaire, the French *philosophe*, told Wilkes directly, "You set me in flames with your courage, and you charm me with your wit."[40]

The Promotion of Beccaria's Book

Over the coming years and decades, Beccaria's treatise—the subject of considerable, if not constant, attention—would continue to be printed in English and sold in large quantities.[41] In 1778, English-language editions of *On Crimes and Punishments* were printed in Edinburgh for Alexander Donaldson and by "Bell & Murray, for W. Gordon and W. Creech."[42] Donaldson, who sold his books at his shops in Edinburgh and London, also offered for sale works by Locke, Shakespeare, Rousseau, Montesquieu and Voltaire, the latter of whom continued writing about Beccaria in French, his native language, in works such as *Prix de la justice et de l'humanité* (1778). In one advertisement, "Books printed by ALEXANDER DONALDSON, at No. 48, in St. Paul's Church-Yard, the corner next Cheapside, London," were said to be "neatly bound in calf and lettered:—they are, in general, from thirty to fifty per cent cheaper than the usual London prices."[43] The firm of Bell & Murray, based in Edinburgh, would also become the publisher of *Essays on the Principles of Morality and Natural Religion* by Lord Kames, a central figure in the Scottish Enlightenment and a well-known advocate and judge. At the Court of Session in Edinburgh in 1777, Kames and other Scottish judges ruled that Jamaica's slave laws were unjust and should not be enforced by a Scottish court, thus freeing an escaped black slave,

Joseph Knight.[44] The Bell & Murray firm was owned by John Murray (1737–1793), a London bookseller and the son of an Edinburgh legal writer (the equivalent of an English solicitor), and John Bell (1735–1806), Murray's London co-publisher. Bell has been described as "a prolific figure in the London printing and book trade during the late eighteenth and early nineteenth centuries."[45] James Donaldson—the son and heir of Alexander Donaldson, the famous Scottish bookseller and preeminent reprinter of the age—published still another edition of Beccaria's treatise in Edinburgh in 1788.[46]

American newspapers and magazines, which proliferated in the 1780s and helped set the American agenda, also promoted Beccaria's ideas. "During 1786," historian Lyon Richardson notes, "five magazines were established in the United States: two in Connecticut, and one in each of the states of Massachusetts, Pennsylvania, and New Jersey." Although *The American Musical Magazine* (1786–87), published in New Haven, Connecticut, had no reason to mention Beccaria, other more politically oriented publications did reprint Beccaria's ideas. The 1786 American magazine start-ups were *The New-Haven Gazette, and the Connecticut Magazine* (1786–89), published by Yale graduate Josiah Meigs and his business partner, Eleutheros Dana; *The Worcester Magazine* (1786–88), published by Isaiah Thomas; and two monthlies, *The New-Jersey Magazine, and Monthly Advertiser* and *The Columbian Magazine, or Monthly Miscellany*. Meigs, later a tutor at Yale and a member of the bar, counted as Yale classmates Noah Webster and Joel Barlow as well as jurist Zephaniah Swift and Oliver Wolcott, the man who succeeded Alexander Hamilton as Secretary of the Treasury. In his magazine, Meigs reprinted materials focused on penal reform, including Benjamin Franklin's "Speech of Miss Polly Baker." Meigs also published an extract of Montesquieu's *Persian Letters* and works by Dr. Benjamin Rush, and mocked Connecticut's "Blue Laws," chronicling—as historian Lyon Richardson points out—"such records as the punishments of whipping for stealing, and of fines for kissing, and of public shame for illicit relations between the sexes." Meigs also chose to reprint *On Crimes and Punishments*, serializing Beccaria's treatise—first in his newspaper, then concluding in his magazine—from February to August 1786.[47]

The following year, 1787, also saw the creation of two other U.S. magazines: *The American Magazine*, edited by Noah Webster; and *The American Museum*, edited by Mathew Carey, a firm supporter of penal reform.[48] Carey's own writing career—initiated at age seventeen when he wrote a 1777 newspaper article against dueling—began well before he started his American magazine. Carey's first pamphlet, *The Urgent Necessity of an Immediate Repeal of the Whole Penal Code against the Roman Catholics*, was published in Ireland in 1779. In Paris, the Catholic, reform-minded Carey—who had left his native country for fear of prosecution—worked for Benjamin Franklin, a fellow printer, but later returned to Ireland at the end of 1780. After a libel case was filed against Carey, however, he fled that country once more, leaving on September 7, 1784, on the ship *America*, which sailed to Philadelphia.

Arriving in heady, post-Revolutionary War America, Carey started a newspaper, the *Pennsylvania Evening Herald*, then launched *The American Museum* in January 1787. *The American Museum*—which enjoyed a nice run—was published until 1792, covering important topics of the day. Dr. Benjamin Rush was among the contributors that Carey, a supporter of Thomas Jefferson, regularly published. For example, *The American Museum* published an article by Dr. Rush in the January 1787 issue that proposed a national university.[49] *The American Museum*, as well as other early American pamphlets and magazines, contain a number of writings about capital punishment or that mention Beccaria. One writer, taking note of Dr. Rush's abolitionist views, characterized Dr. Rush in 1788 as someone who expected "that within a century hence, all mankind will be of the same opinion, with him." Dr. Rush, that writer editorialized, "wishes that his performance may live so long, to testify … there was at least one man in the year 1788, who was as enlightened and humane as they will be."[50]

By that time, efforts to further disseminate Beccaria's ideas in America had already been made. On January 5, 1787, under the heading "To the Patrons of Fine Arts," an advertisement was published in Philadelphia pertaining to the prospective publication of an American edition of Beccaria's book. That advertisement began: "The following PROPOSALS, are laid before those Ladies and Gentlemen, who choose to promote Science in America, for Printing by Subscription BECCARIA on Crimes & Punishments." The advertisement then contained the following "conditions": "I. The American Edition of Beccaria on Crimes and Punishments, to be printed on good Paper and new Types: the Book will be neatly bound and lettered in a handsome Pocket Volume." "II. The Price to Subscribers will be *One Dollar*, Those who subscribe for SIX Copies will be allowed a SEVENTH Gratis. No money expected until the delivery of the Book." The advertisement concluded: "When one Hundred Encouragers are pleased to approve of these Conditions, by the favour of subscribing their Names, the Work will be immediately carried into Execution, and finished with proper Expedition—Subscribers Names are gratefully received by ROBERT SMITH, the Publisher, at the South-East Corner of Market and Third Streets, by *William Woodhouse*, *Thomas Dobson*, and *Francis Bailey*."[51]

The men mentioned in the advertisement were prominent Philadelphia citizens. Philadelphia printer Robert Smith, a former employee of John Dunlap, was the first person to publicly print the U.S. Constitution, publishing it on September 18, 1787 as a broadsheet. The broadsheet, inserted into the regularly scheduled installment of *The Evening Chronicle*, was printed under the heading "PLAN of the *New Federal Government*." *The Evening Chronicle*, a semi-weekly Federalist newspaper printed on Front Street next door to "the Coffee-House," was published in Philadelphia by Robert Smith and later, in partnership, with James Prange. It was not until September 19, 1787, that several other Philadelphia newspapers, including Dunlap's, printed the text of the newly proposed constitution. When Robert Smith started publishing *The Evening Chronicle*, he had reached out to the broader community, sending a letter to Charles Biddle, the Vice-President of Pennsylvania's Supreme Executive Council, in which he wrote: "I beg leave to request you will be pleased to inform the honorable the Supreme Executive Council, that I have lately established a Newspaper in this City, 'The Evening Chronicle,' which I hope will meet the approbation of the Public." "The patronage of the Council by an Encouragement equally with other Papers," Smith added, "will more immediately tend to give it a general Circulation."[52]

The printer Robert Smith is not to be confused with another man of the same name. Robert Smith (1722–1777)—the architect—was a leading Philadelphia citizen who designed the Walnut Street Prison. Originally built in 1774–1775 on the south side of Walnut Street, between Fifth and Sixth Streets, architect Robert Smith—born in Scotland—had played the leading role in building that structure. Smith, the architect-builder, also designed Princeton University's Nassau Hall and its president's house. "The Walnut Street Prison," notes one writer, "was available just in time to become infamous for the inhumane housing of American prisoners captured at the battles of the Brandywine and Germantown, who died in large numbers from starvation, maltreatment, and want of medical care during the winter of 1777–1778." Only after the Revolutionary War was the notorious Pennsylvania jail converted into a penitentiary. "The penitentiary," explains Blake McKelvey in *American Prisons: A History of Good Intentions*, "was one of the byproducts of the intellectual and humanitarian movements of the eighteenth century that contributed so generously to the founding of the American nation." With the building of two new prisons in Pennsylvania, the Walnut Street Prison—originally designed for use by the City and County of Philadelphia, but converted in 1790 to a state penitentiary—was ultimately demolished in 1835.[53]

The other men involved with soliciting subscribers for a new American edition of Beccaria's treatise were also respected community members. The 1785 "Muster Roll" of the Fifth Company, Second Battalion of the Philadelphia Militia, commanded by Lieutenant Colonel James Read, lists among its members Robert Smith, William Woodhouse and Thomas Dobson.[54] Thomas Dobson, another printer, was involved—along with such notables as Mathew Carey—in handling the publication of Dr. Benjamin Rush's thoughts on the yellow fever epidemic in Philadelphia in the 1790s. That epidemic ravaged the city from 1793 to 1798 and lingered on even after that time period. Dr. Rush's book, *An Account of the Bilious remitting Yellow Fever, as It Appeared in the City of Philadelphia, in the Year 1793*, was printed in 1794 by Dobson at the "Stone-House" on "South Second-Street." In that book, Dr. Rush wrote that "[m]any people were seized with the disorder in consequence of their exertions on the night of the 7th of September, in extinguishing the fire which consumed Mr Dobson's printing-office, and even the less violent exercise of working the fire engines for the purpose of laying the dust in the streets, added frequently to the number of the sick."[55] In 1793, Thomas Dobson also published William Bradford's *An Enquiry into How Far the Punishment of Death Is Necessary in Pennsylvania*, a title that referenced and extensively relied upon Beccaria's writings.[56]

William Woodhouse, a Philadelphia bookbinder, bookseller and stationer from 1765 until his death in 1795, had—in 1782—established the only pencil manufactory in the United States. He printed everything from Bibles to political tracts such as James Burgh's *Political Disquisitions; or, An Enquiry into Public Errors, Defects, and Abuses* in association with Robert Bell. Bell, another prominent Philadelphia publisher, had published an octavo edition of Beccaria's treatise in 1778. Burgh's book, published and sold by Woodhouse and Bell in 1775, also cited Beccaria more than once. In that book, which appeared in Philadelphia in the same year that the Revolutionary War started, Burgh wrote that Beccaria "holds capital punishment wholly unnecessary, excepting only where the life of the offender is clearly incompatible with the safety of the state." Burgh's book also emphasized that Beccaria "thinks death an absurd punishment for duelling, because they that will fight, shew that they do not fear death." In a diary entry dated August 11, 1781, Robert Morris—known as the American Revolution's financier—recorded his own direct association with William Woodhouse. On that date, Morris noted that he "Issued Warrant in favour of Wm. Woodhouse for £6. Specie for 1 Ream large Paper."[57]

Francis Bailey, the final individual listed in the subscription offer, was related to a local clerk of courts who—as a history of American printing notes—"came from a dynasty of printers and papermakers." Bailey, that source reports, "is now recognized as one of this country's first type founders." In addition to printing an edition of the New Testament around 1788 as well as many other titles, he was—as that history of printing emphasizes—"the publisher of a maverick newspaper, the *Freeman's Journal*, and an official printer for Congress and the Commonwealth of Pennsylvania." As Bailey's exploits are reported in *An Extensive Republic: Print, Culture, and Society in the New Nation, 1790–1840*: "With printing offices in both Philadelphia and Lancaster, Francis Bailey was deeply involved in the area's book trade, counting as associates and customers most of the local bookmen and many prestigious civic leaders and institutions. Business associates extended from Boston south to Charleston, South Carolina." "One indication of Francis Bailey's centrality in the trade," notes another source, "is the fact that he was one of three witnesses to the codicil of Benjamin Franklin's will, drawn up by Franklin on June 23, 1789."[58]

In the English-speaking world, Beccaria's name was, by the late eighteenth century, almost as famous as any and rolled off the tips of reformers' tongues. For example, in

The Monthly Review—printed in London for "R. Griffiths" and sold by "T. Becket" in Pall Mall—there is a review of a 1791 publication published by John Almon's successor, John Debrett, titled *Inquiry into the Legality of Capital Punishments*. That publication raised the following questions: "Does the Sovereign possess any power which has not been delegated to him by society? Does society, as an aggregate body, possess any right which had not previously appertained to the individuals who compose it? Did individuals ever possess the right of abridging the duration of their own lives?" The review then noted: "Many of the ideas, that occur in the discussion of these points, will be found in Beccaria's celebrated Essay on Crimes and Punishments."[59]

Likewise, a new Boston publishing firm, Hall & Nancrede, a partnership between Thomas Hall and Harvard's French instructor and pamphleteer Joseph Nancrede, opened its doors in 1795, reportedly using "a quotation in Italian from Beccaria" in making "its bow to the Boston public."[60] In 1796, in a demonstration that English-speaking lawyers and law students often strove to read *On Crimes and Punishments* in French or even in the original Italian, one finds in one title, *The Correspondent*, a reprinted letter "*From a Young Gentleman, intended to be articled to an Attorney, to his Father*." That letter reads in part: "I can write and converse in French, with fluency and a moderate share of correctness, and have read in that language M. le president Montesquieu's Spirit of Laws; and the translation of Beccaria's Essay on Crimes and Punishments."[61]

And as time elapsed, Beccaria's *On Crimes and Punishments*—a must-read for lawyers, but which also appealed to the public at large—continued to be printed and advertised for sale. For example, in 1809, an American edition of Beccaria's treatise with Voltaire's commentary was brought out by William Farrand of Boston's Farrand & Mallory; in 1809, the prominent New York City publisher Stephen Gould also released another edition of Beccaria's treatise. "At the time of the Revolution," explains M. H. Hoeflich, the author of *Legal Publishing in Antebellum America*, "the number of lawyers practicing in the United States was relatively small. This meant that the market for specialized law texts was also small, because only lawyers—and the occasional library—were likely to purchase such texts." During the new nation's first decades, Hoeflich emphasizes, the books that tended to be available for purchase were imported or of local use, with Beccaria's treatise being a notable exception. "Even such fundamental works as Sir William Blackstone's *Commentaries on the Laws of England*," he notes, "were first offered by subscription, a technique designed to reduce the financial risk to the publisher and bookseller." The appeal of *On Crimes and Punishments*, though, Hoeflich writes, "was universal to all reform-minded citizens," leading to the multiple editions of Beccaria's treatise that appeared in early America.[62]

In *A Collection of Cases Decided by the General Court of Virginia, Chiefly Relating to the Penal Laws of the Commonwealth Commencing in the Year 1789, and Ending in 1814*, "Beccaria on Crimes" was advertised for sale in Philadelphia for $1.00. In another advertisement, published in 1823, one seller of law books, W. R. H. Treadway, let it be known that he "imports from London twice a year." Through that advertisement, in *Reports of Judicial Decisions in the Constitutional Court, of the State of South-Carolina*, Treadway promoted a "Second American Edition" of *On Crimes and Punishments*. The case reporter published by Treadway in Charleston, South Carolina listed his publishing house as "No. 42, Broad-Street, Sign of Lord Coke." Stephen Gould, a bookseller and frequent printer of law books, including, naturally, Beccaria's treatise, is known to have commissioned other printers to print law books for him, to have co-published titles with Treadway, and to have had a sign with Lord Edward Coke's bust portrait on it. An 1820 title, *Digest of the Laws of Actions and Trials at Nisi Prius*, was specifically listed as being published by "Gould & Treadway" in South Carolina. "In choosing an image of the great lawyer Edward Coke as his trade sign," M. H. Hoeflich explains, "Gould followed a bookselling tradition of adopting images that represented the shop's specialty." "[O]ne of Gould's bookselling contemporaries in New York, Naphtali Judah, who specialized in revolutionary political works," Hoeflich notes, "chose the head of Thomas Paine as his insignia." An early American Jew, Naphtali Judah (1774–1855) held anti-slavery views, had a small interest in a paper mill, and was—as one source describes him—"a stationer-cum-publisher." His business partner, Benjamin Gomez (1769–1828), was the country's first Jewish publisher, printing such works as Montesquieu's *The Spirit of Laws*.[63]

Beccaria's reach thus extended from New England into the American South, where slavery was more prevalent and punishments tended to be especially severe. For instance, the literary societies at the University of North Carolina, including its "Debating Society" formed in June 1795, had close familiarity with Beccaria's treatise. The list of the first fifteen books ever purchased by those literary societies included Beccaria's *On Crimes and Punishments*, confirming its societal prominence. Such books no doubt came in handy as North Carolina students debated important public policy questions of the day. On multiple occasions, North Carolina students vigorously debated whether dueling is ever justifiable, a topic squarely addressed in Beccaria's treatise. On the question of the propriety of dueling, students were divided, twice concluding in the affirmative and once in the negative. North Carolina students also debated other significant questions of the time, including "Shall Corporal Punishment be Introduced Into the University?" On that question, voting in their own self-interest, they concluded with a resounding no.[64] In any event, the variety of topics addressed in Beccaria's treatise provided intellectual ammunition to students and political leaders alike as they thought about the criminal law.

By the beginning of the nineteenth century, Beccaria's name had been invoked by countless writers and in the British Parliament, with one "Lordship" concluding a speech "with some apposite quotations from Beccaria's excellent Treatise on Crimes and Punishments."[65] *On Crimes and Punishments*—as one historian put it—would remain, in fact, "the most influential tract on penal policy well into the second half of the nineteenth century."[66] An 1812 biographical dictionary of the world's "most eminent persons" notes that "few works were read with more avidity, or more directly tended to introduce a humane and wise system in the criminal law."[67] And the evidence, drawn from early Anglo-American sources, bears out such claims, which may at first blush seem hyperbolic to a twenty-first century reader unfamiliar with the intensity with which Beccaria's writings were initially received. For example, in 1782, the London publisher "J. Debrett"—listed as "successor to Mr. Almon" in Piccadilly—and "C. Dilly," the person for whom the book was printed, issued a new title by Manasseh Dawes of London's Inner Temple. The title of that book, which was dedicated to the Right Honorable the Earl of Huntington, shows all by itself just how prominent Beccaria's name had become. The title chosen: *An Essay on Crimes and Punishments, with a view of, and commentary upon Beccaria, Rousseau, Voltaire, Montesquieu, Fielding, and Blackstone.* In his commentary, Dawes noted Beccaria's anti-death penalty position; repeatedly discussed Beccaria's ideas; and wrote that, while Beccaria "may be civilly right" about his views on capital punishment, "revelation goes further, and absolutely points out death as a punishment for murder." Despite their clear philosophical disagreements, Dawes—who had carefully read *On Crimes and Punishments*—wrote of "[t]he humane Beccaria" and certainly could not ignore the Italian writer's treatise.[68]

The sheer number of references to Beccaria in early America and Europe are staggering. In a utopian memoir, titled *Memoirs of the Year Two Thousand Five Hundred* and translated into English and published in Dublin in the early 1770s, the French writer Louis-Sébastien Mercier imagined a time when suffering would be eliminated. He foresaw a time when there would be no dungeon, rack or wheel, and in which humans would not intentionally inflict pain. He also pictured himself in the "King's Library" in Paris which, centuries later, contained only a small number of books. The librarian had burned all of the "frivolous," "useless," "dangerous," and "bad" books, and had kept only those volumes that, "by their merit," had "obtained the approbation of our age." The small number of books remaining in the King's Library included Greek authors such as Homer, Sophocles, Plato and Plutarch; the Latin authors Virgil, Pliny and Titus Livy; French writers such as Descartes and Montaigne; and "[t]he celebrated Treatise of Crimes and Punishments." In another of his books, *Fragments of Politics and History*, Mercier wrote that penal reformers like Montesquieu and Beccaria "have flattered us with the hope of a humane and regular legislation." "They have," he emphasized, "rejected those laws of blood, those processes invented by tigers." "Thanks to these writers," he added, "it has been recognized that those whom the laws have to govern are sensible beings, and that man (for such was his earliest duty) is obliged to be tender of the life of his fellow-creature: crimes may be repressed without the destruction of the guilty."[69]

Throughout the eighteenth century, educated men reveled in discussing political philosophy and the public good, and Beccaria's writings squarely fit into those genres. The commonplace book of Massachusetts lawyer Josiah Quincy Jr. (1744–1775), for example, makes reference to Beccaria's "Essay on Crimes + Punishments,"[70] and an entry in a 1769 edition of *The Gentleman's Magazine* further noted the publication of Beccaria's newly issued book on public economy and commerce. The latter source had this to say: "This discourse is translated from the Italian, written by the Marquis Beccaria, author of the celebrated Essay on Crimes and Punishments; and was pronounced by him on his being advanced last year to the new professorship instituted at Milan."[71] In Robert Gray's *Letters during the Course of a Tour Through Germany, Switzerland and Italy, in the Years M.DCC.XCI, and M.DCC.XCII, with Reflections on the Manners, Literature, and Religion of Those Countries*, Gray wrote this in his book, published in London in 1794: "In agreement with what Beccaria has advanced upon this subject, it may be observed, that whatever natural or civil right man may be supposed to possess over the life of man, must result from the consideration of strict necessity—which necessity has been supposed not to exist in some cases where death is decreed even by the laws of our country; the severity of which hath, therefore, been mitigated in execution of them."

Citing Beccaria's treatise, George Dyer's 1793 title, *The Complaints of the Poor People of England*, in a chapter titled "*Disproportion between Crimes and Punishments*," likewise begins with these words: "Next to what I have already observed, I complain of the GREAT DISPROPORTION between crimes and punishments. This is the evil that has been so well marked out by a writer, worthy of the esteem of all mankind; an evil which particularly affects the poor." Libraries in both smaller towns and big cities—whether in Europe or America—frequently owned Beccaria' treatise, with *On Crimes and Punishments* listed in a 1797 catalogue of books belonging to the Carlisle Library Company in Carlisle, Pennsylvania. At the sedition trial of the English-born Unitarian minister, Rev. Thomas Fyshe Palmer, before the Circuit Court of Justiciary held in Perth, Beccaria was even described as among "the greatest constitutional writers," put in the same category as Hugo Grotius and Samuel von Pufendorf. On October 15, 1816, writing from Milan to a "Mr. Murray," the famed Lord Byron (1788–1824)—the English Romantic poet who spent considerable time in Italy—himself reported to his correspondent an "anecdote" involving Beccaria, who, Byron reported, "published such admirable things about the punishment of death."[72]

And in terms of Anglo-American printing presses, more editions of Beccaria's treatise were yet to come. In 1819, Philip Nicklin at No. 175 Chesnut Street in Philadelphia, also released a new Italian-to-English translation of Beccaria's *On Crimes and Punishments* prepared by Edward D. Ingraham, a member of the Philadelphia Bar. That 1819 edition, which reprinted a French-to-English translation of Voltaire's commentary, was described as a "Second American Edition" and was snapped up by libraries such as the New York State Library and the U.S. State Department library.[73] While library catalogues in the 1820s continued to reflect the ready availability of Beccaria's treatise in institutional settings,[74] individuals — as their writings show — themselves continued to read and rely upon that treatise. In 1834, Thomas Upham — the Professor of Mental and Moral Philosophy at Bowdoin College — specifically titled a section of his work "*Remarks of Beccaria on mildness of punishments*." Saying "the science of legislation involves the doctrine of Crimes and Punishments," Upham quoted Beccaria's treatise for multiple propositions. Among them: "Crimes are more effectually prevented by the *certainty*, than the *severity* of punishment."[75]

Other writers were just as eager to discuss Beccaria's treatise. In *The Christian Disciple*, published monthly by Joseph Buckingham in Boston, one anonymous author, said to be "a foreigner, who has for some years been a resident in a neighbouring state, and who is venerated both for age and learning," wrote this in May 1817 under the heading "Capital Punishments":

> The public attention seems lately to have been turned to the question of the right of society to inflict capital punishment. This question was much agitated in Europe in the latter part of the last century. The Marquis *Beccaria*, in his elegant treatise on crimes and punishments, and *Voltaire*, in an essay on the same subject, discussed it with much ingenuity; and urged the policy, and developed the numerous advantages of its abolition. How honourable would it be to *America*, if this great desideratum could be effected in this country.

The article then repeated many of Beccaria's own arguments, with the anonymous author stating, for example, that "it is a matter of experience, that in the proportion that punishments are more severe, and more frequently inflicted, crimes are usually more common."[76]

As the decades went by, precious copies of Beccaria's book, as with other valued Enlightenment texts, were sentimentally bequeathed or transferred from one generation to the next, as is made clear by multiple notations in a 1769 London edition of Beccaria's *On Crimes and Punishments* printed for "F. Newbery" at the corner of St. Paul's Churchyard. That book, now held at the Virginia Historical Society in Richmond, Virginia, has marks of ownership for Adam Hunter (1739–1798), Lucas P. Thompson (1797–1866), John Strother Pendleton (1802–1868), and Archibald Gerald Robertson (1889–1985). The book bears the armorial bookplate of Adam Hunter, along with an inscription: "The property of Lucas P. Thompson, purchased of Jo. S. Pendleton, Mar. 9, 1821."[77] Adam Hunter was the brother of James Hunter, the largest slaveholder in Stafford County, Virginia, and Adam worked as a merchant in Fredericksburg, Virginia.[78] Lucas Thompson, a member of the Virginia House of Delegates from 1826 to 1830, was a judge of the General Court of Virginia from 1831 to 1851, the Special Court of Appeals from 1855 to 1857, and a circuit court judge from 1851 to 1866.[79] John Strother Pendleton, a Virginia lawyer admitted to the bar in 1824, was a member of the Virginia legislature for many years in the 1830s. He also served as a diplomat in Chile and Argentina and as a U.S. Congressman from 1845 to 1849.[80] Archibald Gerald Robertson — the final citizen-owner listed in the book — was a graduate of the University of Virginia who married in 1923 and lived in Richmond, explaining the book's present location.[81] Another copy of Beccaria's treatise, one of sixteen editions now held in the rare book room of George Washington University's law school, indicates that it was obtained in exchange for a copy of *Plutarch's Lives*.[82]

Jeremy Bentham and the French Connection

In the eighteenth century, many Europeans and Americans—it should come as no surprise—studied and spoke more than one language. This made Beccaria's treatise accessible in either Italian or, say, in French, at least for Americans and English subjects familiar with such languages. With the exception of the first Italians with access to Beccaria's treatise, the French—led by Voltaire and others—were the quickest to recognize the importance of Beccaria's book, leading to its almost immediate translation. Historian Bernard Harcourt notes that André Morellet's translation of Beccaria's treatise "was made public at the end of December 1765," and that Voltaire's commentary "was printed regularly as a preface to Morellet's translation in all subsequent French editions, propelling Beccaria's tract to fame." Morellet, born at Lyons in 1727, had been educated in a seminary and at the Sorbonne, then served as a tutor to a young nobleman at a college and on a tour of Italy. He did some writing in Rome in 1758, then returned to Paris, where he read philosophy and got confined for a time to the Bastille for a satirical piece of writing. Spending time in prison, no doubt, had made Morellet particularly receptive to the idea of translating Beccaria's book. It was after Morellet had done his translation of Beccaria's treatise that he visited England, where, on his 1772 trip, he made the acquaintance of Benjamin Franklin, among many others.

The French and English translations of Beccaria's book would heavily influence the work of other reformers. For example, Jeremy Bentham, who published a pamphlet, *A View of the Hard-Labour Bill*, in 1778, was immediately attracted to Beccaria's ideas. Bentham, in fact, cited Beccaria's work in his own subsequently published treatise, *The Rationale of Punishment,* and in other writings.[83] The French historian and philosopher Michel Foucault—best known for *Discipline and Punish: The Birth of the Prison*—notes that the French translation of Beccaria's treatise, *Traité des délits et des peines*, was published in 1766 and that Voltaire's *Commentaire sur le Traité des délits et des peines* was published in Paris, also in 1766. Foucault's masterwork, *Discipline and Punish*, published in the 1970s but recalling the brutality of France's past, begins by graphically describing the torturous public execution in 1757 of Robert-François Damiens, a French domestic servant who attempted to assassinate King Louis XV. Foucault—who cites Beccaria's book in the very first chapter, indicating its importance—then goes on to describe the development of prisons, the institutions designed to confine inmates in the wake of the publication of Beccaria's treatise.[84]

In *The Rationale of Punishment*, written roughly a decade after Beccaria burst into the limelight but not published until the 1820s, Jeremy Bentham—the son of a wealthy London solicitor—devoted two chapters to the death penalty. "Although in this book, written around 1775, he did not oppose capital punishment categorically," writes the late American death penalty scholar Hugo Adam Bedau, "by the end of his life, in 1832, he did, and his arguments then were essentially the same as his early objections." *The Rationale of Punishment*—like so many leading books of decades past—references Beccaria's writings multiple times. "Establish a proportion between crimes and punishments," wrote Bentham, wrestling with where to set societal responses to crime, "has been said by Montesquieu, Beccaria, and many others." "The maxim," Bentham editorialized, "is, without doubt, a good one, but whilst it is thus confined to general terms, it must be confessed it is more oracular than instructive." "Nothing," Bentham offered, "has been accomplished till wherein this proportion consists has been explained, and the rules have been laid down by which it may be determined that a certain measure of punishment ought to be applied to a certain crime." Bedau—the Tufts University scholar who long studied America's death penalty and the U.S. Constitution's Cruel and Unusual Punishments Clause—

emphasized that Beccaria himself saw the death penalty as a "cruel" punishment that "gives to men the example of cruelty." "Ever since Beccaria wrote those words," Bedau noted, "abolitionists have echoed them and have never tired of explaining why the death penalty is a cruel punishment and why it therefore ought to be abolished."[85]

Bentham's *Rationale of Punishment* gives a sense of the era, with Bentham—in recounting execution methods—noting how corporal punishments were then common. "The most obvious method of inflicting this species of punishment, and which has been most commonly used," Bentham wrote, "consists in exposing the body to blows or stripes." "When these are inflicted with a flexible instrument," Bentham explained, "the operation is called whipping." "Another species of punishment formerly practised in this country, but now rarely used," Bentham pointed out, "consisted in subjecting the patient to frequent immersions in water, called ducking." "The individual," as he described it, "was fastened to a chair or stool, called the ducking-stool, and plunged repeatedly." That punishment—ruled impermissible by the Pennsylvania Supreme Court in 1825—was once used to punish women convicted of "scolding."[86]

In *Rationale of Punishment*, Bentham—who studied law at Lincoln's Inn and Oxford, writing prolifically on penal reform—also gave his readers a vivid impression of what corporal punishments were like in Beccaria's neck of the woods. "In Italy, and particularly in Naples," Bentham observed, "there is a method, not uncommon, of punishing pickpockets, called the *Strappado*." That method, Bentham said, involved raising an offender "by his arms, by means of an engine like a crane, to a certain height, and then letting him fall, but suddenly stopping his descent before he reaches the ground." The effect: "The momentum which his body has acquired in the descent, is thus made to bear upon his arms, and the consequence generally is, that they are dislocated at the shoulder."[87] In the eighteenth century, Romans used different means of punishment and torture, one of which was the *corda*, a machine consisting of a scaffold with a crossbar and a series of pulleys and ropes. After a sentence was imposed, the offender's arms were tied behind his back with the rope connected to a pulley. The offender was then hoisted up to a height of up to ten meters, then dropped, whether roughly or gently depending on the severity of the offense. "Three *tratti di corda* or jerks of the rope was the standard penalty for violations of public order," one scholar notes.[88]

In his book, Bentham divided capital punishment into two distinct categories: *simple* and *afflictive*. "I call it simple," he wrote, "when, if any bodily pain be produced, no greater degree of it is produced than what is necessary to produce death." "I call it *afflictive*," he explained by way of comparison, "when any degree of pain is produced more than what is necessary for that purpose." "It was the opinion of Beccaria," Bentham wrote, citing and specifically quoting from *Des Délits et des Peines*, "that the impression made by any particular punishment was in proportion to its duration, and not to its intensity." "Notwithstanding such respectable authority," Bentham then wrote in *Rationale of Punishment*, "I am apt to think the contrary is the case." Bentham felt that death was "regarded by most men as the greatest of all evils" and that men "are willing to submit to any other suffering whatever in order to avoid it."

"Death, considered as a punishment," Bentham argued, "is almost universally reckoned too severe, and men plead, as a measure of mercy, for the substitution of any other punishment in lieu of it." "It is not without reason," Bentham conceded, "that with respect to the higher class of offenders, M. Beccaria considers a punishment of the laborious kind, moderate we must suppose in its degree, will make a stronger impression than the most excruciating kind of death that can be devised." "It appears however to me," Bentham wrote elsewhere in his book, "that the contemplation of perpetual imprisonment, accompanied with hard labour and occasional solitary confinement, would produce a deeper impression on the minds of persons in whom it is more eminently desirable that that impression should be produced, than even death itself." The "prodigal use made by legislators of the punishment of death," Bentham advised, was the result of "erroneous judgments." Heinous murderers, he believed, would not necessarily respond to the prospect of death at the hands of the state in the same way. It showed "a total want of judgment and reflection," Bentham contended of the death penalty, "to apply it to a degraded and wretched class of men, who do not set the same value upon life" as virtuous men.

In *Rationale of Punishment*, published after Beccaria's work had become well-known, Bentham freely acknowledged that people had started questioning the morality of capital punishment, at least for less serious offenders. "This punishment," he wrote, "is far from being popular: and it becomes less and less so every day in proportion as mankind become more enlightened, and their manners more softened." "There is, however," Bentham clarified, "one case in which it does seem to be popular, and that in a very high degree; I mean the case of murder." As Bentham explained of the public's fondness for executing murderers, often justified by the *lex talionis* doctrine: "The attachment seems to be grounded partly on the fondness for analogy, partly on the principle of vengeance, and partly perhaps by the fear which the character of the criminal is apt to inspire." "Blood it is said will have blood," Bentham reported, emphasizing: "the imagination is flattered with the notion of the similarity of the suffering, produced by the punishment, with that inflicted by the criminal." In the reign of England's Richard I, an order had been issued in 1190 by the crusading king, known as "Richard the Lionheart," that very much reflected that approach. "Whoever shall slay a man on ship board, he shall be bound to the dead man and thrown into the sea," read one part of the order. "If he shall slay him on land he shall be bound to the dead man and buried in the earth," read another.

"In other cases," Bentham noted in *Rationale of Punishment*, "the punishment of death is unpopular"—an "unpopularity" that led victims of crime and witnesses not to cooperate with the prosecution of offenders "for fear of bringing them to the scaffold." "In fine," Bentham concluded, giving his own opinion, "I can see but one case in which it can be necessary, and that only occasionally: in the case alleged for this purpose by M. Beccaria, the case of rebellion or other offence against government of a rebellious tendency, when, by destroying the chief you may destroy the faction, where discontent has spread itself widely through a community, it may happen that imprisonment will not answer the purpose of safe custody." The fear: "The keepers may be won over to the insurgent party, or if not won over, they may be overpowered." "If," Bentham concluded, "it be determined to preserve the punishment of death, in consideration of the effects it produces *in terrorum*, it ought to be confined to offences which, in the highest degree, shock the public feeling—for murders, accompanied with circumstances of aggravation, and particularly when their effect may be the destruction of numbers."[89]

In a letter to the Rev. John Forster, written in 1778, Bentham himself described at length how he had rather circuitously come to be engaged in law reform. "A few years ago you may remember," Bentham wrote to his friend, "I used to talk with you about a project I had formed of trying to penetrate into the interior parts of South America." Bentham had hoped to use his knowledge of botany, chemistry and the natural sciences, however limited, "to be of service to mankind by exploring the productions of those fertile and untrodden regions." Because of a "weakness" of his "constitution," and "partly" due to "the instruction I gather'd from Helvetius," though, Bentham emphasized that he had "gradually" been "weaned" from that idea. "From him," Bentham said of Helvétius, "I got a standard to measure the relative importance of the several pursuits a man might be engaged in: and the result of it was that the way of all others in which a man might be of most service to his fellow creatures was by making improvement in the science which

I had been engaged to study by profession." For Bentham, that profession was law. "From him," Bentham emphasized of Helvétius, "I learnt to look upon the tendency of any institution or pursuit to promote the happiness of society as the sole test and measure of its merit," and to "regard the principle of utility as an oracle which if properly consulted would afford the only true solution that could be given to every question of right and wrong." "Much about the same time," Bentham added, "M. Beccaria's book of crimes and punishments, and the Empress of Russia's instructions for a Code of Laws, gave me fresh incentives and afforded me further lights."

In explaining to Rev. Forster what he had been doing around that time, Bentham told his "good old friend" this: "I was working hard, though in a manner underground, and without producing any apparent fruits: for I was working deep. I was engaged in a set of speculations which insensibly led me into the formation of a plan for (a general reform in Jurisprudence) determining upon fixed principles (what ought to be the Law) the best Laws under every head of Jurisprudence." "I have now settled my leading principles," Bentham reported to Forster, adding: "I have advanced some way in the execution of my design: and see I think with tolerable clearness through the whole of it: the completion of it will be the business of my life." "For about a year and a half," Bentham noted, "I have been employ'd principally in writing a Theory of Punishment which I hope to (be able to) send to the press in the course of two or three months." In his letter, Bentham also praised "Mr Howard's Book on Prisons," with Bentham calling the noted English penal reformer John Howard "that intelligent and indefatigable friend to the distressed" who took "extraordinary tours" all over England and continental Europe for "the purpose of inspecting the state of the prisons, in order to suggest improvements in that branch of the police." "I had not the least personal acquaintance with him," Bentham added of Howard, "but he paid me a visit t'other day of his own accord, on occasion of the *View of the Hard-labour Bill* and told me he was just going to set out on another tour to compleat his plan."

Writing in 1778 in the midst of the Revolutionary War "To the Revd. Mr Forster at the Empress's Palace Petersburg," Bentham specifically described his personal involvement in English legislative reform. "About 6 weeks ago," Bentham told Forster, "a draught of a Bill fell into my hands, for changing the punishment of Transportation into Hard-labour, to be performed in Houses which it proposes to establish for that purpose throughout England." "The Bill," Bentham reported in discussing William Eden's involvement, "I understood to be the composition of Mr. Eden, Author of the *Principles of Penal Law*, Under Secretary of State under Lord Suffolk, a Lord of Trade, and who within these few days is gone out one of the 3 Commissioners to America." "Having no time to lose," Bentham wrote, aware that the bill would soon be coming before Parliament, "I put together a few thoughts on the subject which in the compass of little more than three weeks I made up in to a Pamphlet intitled *A View of the Hard-labour Bill*." "It has been out about a fortnight," Bentham explained at a time that concrete penal reform efforts as well as attempts to reconcile America and Great Britain were being pursued.

In his letter to Rev. Forster, Bentham further noted that he had learned from the *Leyden Gazette* of January 21, 1774, that "the Government of Moscow gave public invitations at that time to Jurists to study a list of questions there exhibited from *Beccaria*, relative to the subject of criminal Jurisprudence." "I thought myself within an ace t'other day of being of his party to America," Bentham added of William Eden's work as a commissioner after recounting communications with "Mr. Eden" and Sir William Blackstone and talking about the favorable reception of his own *Fragment on Government* and *A View of the Hard-labour Bill*. "Governor Johnstone, who is another of the Commissioners," Bentham noted of George Johnstone, a former governor of West Florida, "I had heard was very fond of the *Fragment*, and used to carry it about with him in his pocket."[90]

Trained in the law, the penal reformer William Eden, wanting to bring Americans back into the fold of the British Empire, was highly receptive to making substantial concessions to the American colonies, the loss of which had—in one historian's words—"caused the British penal system," then heavily reliant on sentences of transportation, "to go into meltdown." Eden's mentor was William Blackstone, whose lectures Eden had heard as an Oxford undergraduate, but Eden had also closely studied the continental writings of Beccaria, Pufendorf and Montesquieu and wanted to reform England's outdated system, supporting the idea of penitentiaries and long-term incarceration for felons. Part of a peace mission led by Frederick Howard, the Earl of Carlisle, to try to put a stop to America's War of Independence, Eden's trip to America—which he helped organize—proved a dismal failure, however. "The so-called Carlisle Commission," writes historian Joseph Morton, "reached Philadelphia in early June 1778 and received a chilly reception." "Congress," Morton explains, "declared that negotiations could begin only after all British troops and naval forces were withdrawn and after Britain formally recognized the independence of the United States of America." Eden—who had interests in America—showed a particularly keen awareness of the consequences of Great Britain's loss, with Eden writing in correspondence: "It is impossible to see what I can see of this Magnificent Country and not to go nearly mad at the long Train of Misconducts and Mistakes by which we have lost it."[91]

Although Jeremy Bentham never got the chance to be part of, or to assist, the Carlisle Commission's group of British negotiators that traveled to Philadelphia, during his life he had considerable contact with Americans, most notably, perhaps, the former U.S. Vice President Aaron Burr. Indeed, Bentham spent the bulk of his adult life engaged in—and lobbying for—criminal law reform across the globe, including in distant America. Bentham's views, like most people's, would continually evolve, even as he produced one piece of writing after another. After publishing *A View of the Hard-Labour Bill* in 1778, in which he questioned the use of capital punishment for certain offenders, Bentham published *Introduction to the Principles of Morals and Legislation* in 1789. The latter book cited Beccaria's treatise in chapter XIV, titled "Of the Proportion Between Punishments and Offences," and in chapter XVII, headed "Of the Limits of the Penal Branch of Jurisprudence." In that book, Bentham invokes both Montesquieu and Beccaria, noting of *On Crimes and Punishments*: "The Marquis Beccaria's book, the first of any account that is uniformly censorial, concludes as it sets out, with penal jurisprudence."[92] In 1791, Bentham also published *The Panopticon, or the Inspection House*, in which he set forth a unique, circular prison design that would allow watchmen to observe all the inmates of an institution without the inmates being able to tell whether or not they were being watched. After publishing *Manual of Political Economy* in 1793, he published *Poor Laws and Pauper Management* in 1797, with other works coming out in the decades that followed. *Introductory Views of the Rationale of Evidence* was printed in 1812, and another of his titles, *The Rationale of Judicial Evidence*, came out in 1827. The latter title was edited in London by a young John Stuart Mill (1806–1873), the thinker who, with Bentham himself, founded the philosophy of utilitarianism. In John Stuart Mill's own book, *On Liberty* (1859), Mill lamented that Socrates had been "put to death by his countrymen."[93]

Like early American offerings, Jeremy Bentham's writings helped to further popularize Beccaria's ideas, with Bentham endeavoring to put those theoretical ideas into practice. "Bentham," one source notes, "did more than any other writer of his time to rationalize the theory of punishments by consideration of their various kinds and effects, their true objects, and the conditions of their efficacy." "Much of what came to light in Bentham's lifetime," that source records, "was edited by his friends, and some of it appeared first in French under the supervision of Dumont." The Genevan political writer Étienne Dumont, who met Bentham in 1779, worked extensively with him, with Bentham entrusting Dumont with manuscripts Bentham had written. While Beccaria's 1764 treatise provided what one criminology textbook calls "a 'tipping point' of public opinion on justice," Bentham was an experimentalist as well as a penal theorist who successfully lobbied for an English penitentiary to be built.[94] In 1811, Dumont — Bentham's editor and translator — himself emphasized of the Italian writer he, too, greatly admired: "Beccaria first examined the efficacy of punishments by considering their effect upon the human heart."[95] "After Montesquieu and Beccaria, we may leave in peace a whole library of books, more or less valuable, but which are not distinguished by any great character of originality," Dumont once emphasized in an advertisement for Bentham's work.[96]

The French Philosophes and Americans in Paris

During America's revolution, Americans looked to Europe for loans and financing — and in the lead up to the Revolutionary War, they looked to Europe for ideas, too. Both France and Italy produced a number of Enlightenment writers, and their books proved to be extremely popular among Americans. Along with Holland and its wealthy businessmen, France — led by King Louis XVI — loaned substantial sums of money to the Continental Congress, so European assistance was — in more ways than one — on the minds of America's political leaders. The Marquis de Lafayette — who fought alongside George Washington and other American revolutionaries — loaned $200,000 of his own money to fund the cause, becoming a French hero of the Revolutionary War. France, anxious to aid the American rebels and weaken its rival, Great Britain, thus not only provided manpower at a critical juncture, but it gave Congress grants and loans of million of *livres*, the French currency at the time. It is little wonder, then, that when France's National Assembly later debated the fate of Louis XVI and, on a divided vote, decided to execute him in the midst of the French Revolution, many Americans felt angry or — at the very least — highly ambivalent about his execution. Thomas Paine vocally opposed the guillotining of Louis XVI — the man Dr. Benjamin Rush called "the best king in Europe" — and John Adams told his wife Abigail that he had no heart for "king-killing." "Mankind," Adams told one correspondent, "will in time discover that unbridled majorities are as tyrannical and cruel as unlimited despots."[97]

In France itself, the French *philosophes* were tremendous admirers of Beccaria's treatise, and American diplomats such as John Adams, Benjamin Franklin, Thomas Jefferson and William Short had personal contact with such figures and engaged in the Parisian intellectual and social scene. William Short — who graduated from the College of William and Mary in 1779, and in whom Jefferson took a special interest — had met the Marquis de Lafayette in Virginia in 1777. Once back in France, Lafayette and others hosted gatherings for U.S. diplomats, with American and French citizens mingling freely and exchanging ideas. Thomas Jefferson and William Short, who served as Jefferson's secretary in Paris and, later, as *chargé d'affaires* at the American Legation during the French Revolution's opening years, were frequent guests at Lafayette's townhouse at the Rue de Bourbon on the Seine's left bank. While Jefferson became acquainted with Lafayette during the American Revolution, the two became close friends in 1785 after Jefferson's arrival in France. As Dr. Franklin's successor as Minister to the Court of Louis XVI, Jefferson — who arrived in Paris with his daughter Martha in August 1784 before the French Revolution — was himself forever grateful for France's Revolutionary War assistance. The "exertions of France for us," Jefferson said, "have not only made real impression on the leaders of the people, but are deeply felt by the people themselves." In Paris, the wealthy socialite,

Comtesse Adrienne Cathérine de Noailles de Tessé, Lafayette's aunt, also hosted lively social functions, and the Americans stationed there became enmeshed in Parisian life. After William Short, then twenty-five years old, arrived in France in November 1784, he worked side by side with Jefferson, then living in a house not far from the Comédie Italienne. It was in Paris that the renowned painter John Trumbull—the son of Connecticut governor Jonathan Trumbull—introduced Jefferson to Richard and Maria Cosway. Though Maria, a child prodigy who grew up in Italy and became a talented artist and musician, was married to Richard, a prominent English portrait painter, Jefferson promptly fell in love with her.

John Trumbull (1756–1842), the gifted American painter who, like other artists, did a European tour, had been introduced to Thomas Jefferson in England in the spring of 1786 by John Adams. Trumbull had served as an aide-de-camp to General Washington during the Revolutionary War, with Washington affectionately calling Trumbull's father, "Brother Jonathan." John Trumbull—who then traveled to Paris in August 1786, accepting Jefferson's invitation to stay in the Hôtel Langeac—had a cousin, another John Trumbull (1750–1831), who wrote poetry, graduated from Yale in 1767, studied law with John Adams from 1773 to 1774, and became a leader of a group of intellectuals called the "Wits of Connecticut" before serving in the Connecticut legislature and becoming a judge of the Connecticut Superior Court and the Supreme Court of Errors.[98] "An influential element in the life of Connecticut after the Revolution," notes one author, George Clark, in *A History of Connecticut*, "was the group of nine men known as the 'Hartford Wits.'" Originally nicknamed Wicked Wits and also known as the Connecticut Wits, the Hartford Wits were bound together by geography, faith, and their support of Federalist policies. "The 'Wits,'" Clark explains, "were a band of young graduates of Yale, who, while connected with the college as students for the master's degree or tutors, formed a school for the cultivation of letters, and did much to liberalize the scholastic curriculum of Yale."

The members of the Hartford Wits, which promoted poetry and the arts, were John Trumbull, Timothy Dwight, Joel Barlow and David Humphreys. "Its associates," Clark notes, "were Theodore Dwight, Richard Alsop and the three physicians, Elihu Smith, Mason Cogswell and Lemuel Hopkins."[99] "To Beccaria's *On Crimes and Punishments*," writes Kenneth Ball in *A Great Society: The Social and Political Thought of Joel Barlow*, "the idea of Barlow's humanitarianism and liberalism.... has been traced." "The influence of Beccaria," Ball explains, taking note of efforts to abolish the death penalty, "is permanent in Barlow," with one book, *Roots of Democracy: American Thought and Culture, 1760–1800*, emphasizing that Americans blamed British criminal codes for crime and that "[a] wonderful confluence existed between Beccaria's work and Americans' perceptions of their own colonial experience." One of the Hartford Wits' most notable contributions, the twelve-part "American Antiquities," was published between 1786 and 1787 in Connecticut and—as one source puts it—"offered Americans a picture of their own chaotic times by means of extended passages from a putative ancient epic, *The Anarchiad*, which the authors claimed had recently been excavated in the Ohio Territory."[100] Eighteenth-century Americans were creating their own history, and Beccaria's treatise was helping to shape it.

John Trumbull, the lawyer-poet, whose father was a trustee of Yale College, wrote an epic poem, *M'Fingal*, at the request of various congressmen as an aid in the struggle for independence. First published in 1782 in Connecticut, the poem—set in Massachusetts in 1775, and later said to be written by "a warm friend of American Independence" and "a friend of republican government, and rational liberty"—sought to "ridicule the claims of the British Parliament." The first canto of the poem, set at "The Town-Meeting, A.M.," opens with these lines—*When Yankies, skill'd in martial rule, / First put the British troops to school*—then said "*Stephen's Chapel*," a reference to the place where the British Parliament once met, *Took slav'ry for the Bill of Rights; / Trembled at whigs and deem'd them foes, / And stopp'd at loyalty her nose*. In the second canto, Trumbull also penned these lines: *I see afar the sack of cities, / The gallows strung with Whig-Committees*. And these: *What pill'ries glad the Tories' eyes / With Patriot-ears for sacrifice! / What whipping-posts your chosen race / Admit successive in embrace*. Lines in "Canto III" similarly read:

> All punishments the world can render,
> Serve only to provoke th' offender;
> The will's confirm'd by treatment horrid,
> As hides grow harder when they're curried;
> No man e'er felt the halter draw,
> With good opinion of the law;
> Or held, in method orthodox,
> His love of justice in the stocks;
> Or fail'd to lose by sheriff's shears
> At once his loyalty and ears.

A later published version of poem, printed in Boston in 1799, included an advertisement for an American edition of "Beccaria on Crimes and Punishments," offered for sale for 75 cents at Ebenezer Larkin's Boston bookstore.[101]

Even today, Beccaria's influence among Connecticut natives is still apparent. Yale's Beinecke Rare Book & Manuscript Library—in New Haven, Connecticut—contains multiple copies of Beccaria's treatise, including a 1770 edition of *On Crimes of Punishments* bearing a "J. Trumbull" signature. That signature was most likely made more than two centuries ago by jurist John Trumbull or the painter John Trumbull, now best known for his famous painting, *Signing of the Declaration of Independence*, that hangs in the rotunda of the U.S. Capitol. The signature "C. Gore" also appears on that 1770 edition of Beccaria's treatise, likely a reference to Christopher Gore (1758–1827), a prominent Massachusetts lawyer. Gore, a devout Christian, built a successful law practice in Boston and served in the Massachusetts legislature before being appointed the U.S. District Attorney for Massachusetts. After serving in the latter role from 1789 to 1796, Gore was appointed by President Washington in April 1796 to serve on a commission with Maryland's William Pinckney and Connecticut's John Trumbull under the fourth article of "Jay's Treaty." A much sought-after painter, Trumbull had served as John Jay's secretary during the negotiation of that treaty, and Trumbull—who befriended Lafayette—had later witnessed the outbreak of the French Revolution in Paris. In his role as a commissioner, Gore traveled to London and also spent several months in Paris. With letters of introduction from John Jay, Gore was—as his biographer notes—"at once admitted to the highest circles" of European society. A Federalist, Gore later became the governor of Massachusetts and a U.S. Senator. A graduate of Harvard, starting his studies there at the tender age of thirteen and finishing them in 1776, Gore became close friends in college with Trumbull and Rufus King, the latter of whom was later a U.S. Senator from New York and the U.S. Minister to Great Britain.

As a lawyer, Christopher Gore had once defended Rachel Wall, a twenty-nine-year-old woman executed for highway robbery in 1789—the last woman to be hanged in Massachusetts. Wall had a long rap sheet even before being sentenced to death for attempting to steal a bonnet and assaulting a woman in the process. Wall had previously pled guilty, in 1785, to stealing goods from Perez Morton, one of Boston's top lawyers, and had—on that occasion—been fined and sentenced to have fifteen lashes laid on her bare back. She had also previously pled guilty to housebreaking and theft and been fined and sentenced to be publicly whipped and to sit on the gallows for one hour with a noose around her neck. As historian Alan Rogers describes Wall's execution, conducted at the same time as two other offenders: "On October 10, 1789, four days before President George Washington made a triumphant visit to Boston, William Smith, William Denoffee, and Rachel Wall were hanged on Boston Common. The woodcut illustration appearing on the broadside reporting Wall's *Last Words* shows a portable gallows, a house like structure on wheels with a cross beam on top on which hangs three bodies." Six years later the Massachusetts legislature would make highway robbery committed by an unarmed person a non-capital crime.[102]

The painter John Trumbull—as history shows—had good reason to be interested in Beccaria's treatise. The son of Jonathan Trumbull (1710–1785), the Connecticut colonial governor who sided with the American cause and went on to serve as Connecticut's first governor, John Trumbull—his father's youngest son—had graduated from Harvard in 1773 and become an officer in the Revolutionary War and a prominent painter. He had gone to London in 1780 to study his craft under the American painter Benjamin West, known for his portraits of George III, but was imprisoned there in retaliation for the hanging of a British major, John André. André, who had recruited General Benedict Arnold as a spy, had himself been adjudged a spy after Benedict Arnold's treasonous conduct. In the anger and paranoia that developed in England following André's execution, Trumbull—originally granted permission to travel to London from the British secretary of state—was imprisoned as a rebel spy. Trumbull was held at Tothill Field Prison until Edmund Burke secured his release on the condition that Trumbull leave the country within thirty days. Later, in Paris, Trumbull painted a miniature portrait of Jefferson that Trumbull would eventually copy in his much-larger work depicting the signing of the Declaration of Independence.[103]

It was in France, through André Morellet's French translation of *Dei delitti e delle pene*, as well as Voltaire's much-read commentary on it, that Beccaria's treatise really first skyrocketed to fame.[104] As in the United States, there was in France a sense that old ways of thinking should give way to new ideas. The Marquis de Lafayette—the Frenchman who fought for America's independence under George Washington's command—was certainly of that opinion and his views bear striking Beccarian features. He called for the death penalty's abolition in France and would famously observe: "I shall demand the abolition of the penalty of death, until you show me the infallibility of human testimony." "At all periods," Lafayette said in a speech delivered decades after the American Revolution began, "has the abolition of capital punishment been advocated by the most eminent statesmen." "The Senate of the United States is at present occupied with the consideration of this question, which has been proposed by Edward Livingston," he observed on that occasion. "I confess, gentlemen," he added, "that ever since the period of our political tempests I have felt an invincible horror of the punishment of death."[105] Both Lafayette and André Morellet, the French *philosophe* also frequently referred to as Abbé Morellet, had meaningful relationships with Thomas Jefferson, who was in France from 1784 to 1789 on his American diplomatic mission.[106]

The French Enlightenment itself stirred up considerable discussion of penal reform and the need to do away with *sanguinary* punishments—a term regularly associated with death sentences. In 1759, before Beccaria even began writing *On Crimes and Punishments*, Voltaire wrote *An Essay on Universal History*, later translated into English. In that book—a second edition of which was published in 1759—Voltaire noted that, "in the time of Charlemaign," the kings' ministers and underlings "hardly ever condemned a person to suffer death, or corporal punishment: for if we except Saxony, where Charlemaign made sanguinary laws, almost all offences in the rest of his empire were attoned for by money." "Rebellion alone," Voltaire wrote, "was punished with death, and the kings in this case reserved to themselves the power of giving judgment." The brutal execution of Robert-François Damiens in 1757 for the attempted murder of Louis XV, however, had awakened French interest in penal reform, with Voltaire's interest only intensified by his reading of Beccaria's book. Americans in Paris and England, where Beccaria's book influenced William Eden and a host of other thinkers, had direct contact with prominent European penal reformers, thus building the momentum for reform. Morellet not only knew Jefferson, but Morellet had met Benjamin Franklin—an early advocate of reform—in April 1772. As Jean Paul de Lagrave writes in *Voltaire's Man in America*: "Morellet, made famous by his translation of Beccaria's *Treatise on Crime and Punishment*, had engaged in numerous exchanges with Franklin, particularly at the home of William Fitzmaurice, Earl of Shelburne."[107]

In short, the American diplomats in Europe had substantial interaction with Enlightenment figures who had their own exposure, and intense reactions, to Beccaria's treatise. Morellet, who had impressed Dr. Franklin at an English house party by performing a trick, famously ended up translating Jefferson's *Notes on the State of Virginia*, though Jefferson disliked Morellet's translation. As a Jefferson biographer puts it, "a certain coolness developed in their relationship" after Jefferson gave Morellet "a seven-page list of seventy errors." But at one time, their relationship was anything but icy, with Jefferson paying weekly visits to Morellet's apartment, which had a splendid view of the Tuileries Gardens.[108] Jefferson, in fact, collaborated with Lafayette—the Frenchman so revered by Americans—in drafting a declaration of rights that Lafayette introduced in France's National Assembly.[109] Lafayette's children—one of whom was named George Washington in honor of his American hero—sang American songs for guests, and Lafayette gave this explanation for why, in his study, a large blank placard hung beneath a framed copy of the American Declaration of Independence: "It is there so that the Declaration of French Rights may be written on it."[110] Lafayette, who included the right to life in his drafts of the French Declaration of the Rights of Man and of the Citizen, was influenced by Beccaria's treatise to see the injustice of executions.[111] That declaration—inspired by natural law theorists and the writings of Rousseau, Montesquieu and other Enlightenment figures—was ultimately approved by France's National Assembly on August 26, 1789.[112] As law professor William Schabas explains of Beccaria's influence in *The Abolition of the Death Penalty in International Law*, Beccaria's treatise convinced Lafayette "of the uselessness and inhumanity of capital punishment" even as it "led to ephemeral measures abolishing the death penalty in Austria and Tuscany."[113]

The ideas of Beccaria, Bentham and like-minded writers would play a central role in shaping the French Declaration of the Rights of Man and of the Citizen. Article VIII of that Declaration, which Lafayette was involved in preparing as a leader of a group of liberal French nobles seeking a constitutional monarchy, reads: "In order for punishment not to be … an act of violence of one or of many against a private citizen, it must be essentially public, prompt, necessary, the least possible in the given circumstances, proportionate to the crimes, dictated by the laws." That language, highly reflective of language one finds in the *denouement* of *On Crimes and Punishments*, plainly shows Beccaria's imprint. "It was in large measure due to Beccaria, and to Voltaire's promulgation of the principles contained in *On Crimes*," writes David Williams in *The Enlightenment*, "that torture ceased to be an official part of due process in France, and that by 1788 the death sentence was becoming relatively rare." The French Declaration, Beccaria's English biographer, John Hostettler, also notes, "was largely the work of the Marquis de Lafayette after consulting with Thomas Jefferson in Paris where he was then American Minister to France." For his part, Jefferson—as America's minister—would write George Washington that France "has been awakened by our revolution, they feel their strength, they are enlightened."[114] Once back in America, Jefferson—along with Washington himself—would work with the Frenchman Pierre L'Enfant on the layout and design of Washington, D.C.

after a 10-mile square piece of land was set aside for the new federal district. Trained as a painter before coming to America in 1777, L'Enfant—commissioned by Major General Lafayette to paint George Washington's portrait—had served as Lafayette's and Washington's military engineer during the Revolutionary War.[115]

The Worldly Jefferson

Although Thomas Jefferson lived out most of his life in his beloved Virginia, he had a long-standing interest in France and Italy. He also had a passion for the languages of their inhabitants. Jefferson's library at Monticello contained more than one hundred volumes in Italian, with titles in his library touching on Italy such as *Guide pour le voyage d'Italie en poste*, Carlo Bianconi's *Nuova guida di Milano*, and Joseph Addison's *Remarks on Several Parts of Italy*.[116] Even Jefferson's crush on Maria Cosway had an Italian flair. Cosway, born in Italy to expatriate English parents, had grown up in Florence and had studied in Rome, where she studied art at the atelier of Pompeo Batoni, a famous painter. After her father died in 1781, she had moved to London and had accepted a marriage proposal from Richard Cosway, the court painter to the Prince of Wales. Maria herself became a successful artist, in which capacity she later befriended Giulia Beccaria, Cesare Beccaria's daughter and the child of the philosopher Jefferson so steadfastly admired.[117] "Mrs. Maria Hadfield Cosway," writes historian George Green Shackelford, "seems to have been the lady in whom Jefferson had the greatest romantic interest after Martha Jefferson's death in 1783." John Trumbull recorded that "Mr. Jefferson joined our party almost daily," and Jefferson—who escorted Mrs. Cosway about Paris to view its art and to sample its music— ended up giving Maria a miniature portrait of himself painted by Trumbull.[118]

Jefferson's love of all things European—from fine wine to books to good food—is clear. When Luigi Castiglioni, the Italian, visited Monticello in Jefferson's absence with one of Jefferson's neighbors, Colonel Nicholas Lewis, Castiglioni made special note of Jefferson's extensive library. As Castiglioni wrote: "what renders Monticello most noteworthy is a copious library of the best and rarest English, French, Italian, Greek, and Latin books that Mr. Jefferson gathered, not indeed as a matter of luxury, but for his own edification, since he understands the languages."[119] By the time Jefferson sold his library at Monticello to the federal government to reconstitute the Library of Congress after the British burned it in 1814, Jefferson's collection consisted of 6,487 books. Aside from English, the languages represented in Jefferson's extensive library included French, German, Greek, Latin, Russian and Spanish titles.[120] The fact that Beccaria's writings were held in the Library of Congress shows, all by itself, the significance of those writings to American political life. "Although Jefferson was in many ways a most practical man, looking to the utility of things," writes George Green Shackelford, "he was interested in the study of foreign languages more for their own sake and as a diversion than for practical use." Obviously, Jefferson's French and Italian came in very handy while he was posted as a diplomat in Europe.

Jefferson's interest in foreign languages was more than a passing fancy. As Shackelford writes of Jefferson's studies: "He had studied Latin, Classical Greek, and Italian in Virginia, and John Paradise had taught him a little Modern Greek."[121] John Paradise (1743–1795), born in Greece while his father was British consul there, spent part of his childhood in Padua, studied at Oxford on the family's return home, and became a respected scholar and linguist, speaking French, Italian, Greek and Turkish. In London, in 1769, Paradise had married Lucy Ludwell, of a prominent Virginia family, and the couple gave lavish parties, hosting American and European diplomats and personalities, including John Adams, Thomas Jefferson, Count Paolo Andreani, and the Italian poet Vittorio Alfieri. Thomas Jefferson became a close friend of the family, and Paradise—sympathetic to America's cause—took an oath of allegiance to the United States in Paris in 1780, doing so in the presence of Benjamin Franklin, then the U.S. minister to France. In the fall of 1787, the same season in which the Constitutional Convention was doing its work in Philadelphia, Paradise and his wife sailed for Virginia. There, they made a series of visits to Virginians, including a three-day visit to George and Martha Washington at Mount Vernon. George Washington's diary for December 30, 1787, reports: "Mr. Paradise and his Lady, lately from England but now of Williamsburgh, came in on a visit." Washington's entry for January 2, 1788, then records: "Colo. Humphreys and myself accompanied Mr. Paradise and his lady to Alexandria. Dined with Mr. Charles Lee and returned in the Evening—leavg. Mr. and Mrs. Paradise there."[122]

Beccaria's writings, of course, were not the only ones from Europe that exerted an influence on early American leaders. For example, the Swiss and English political theorist Jean-Louis de Lolme, a Genevan forced into exile in England in 1768, wrote a book, *Constitution de L'Angleterre* (1771), later translated as *The Constitution of England* (1775) in what became the first of many subsequent English editions. Thomas Jefferson recommended that others read that book; George Washington and James Madison were familiar with it; Alexander Hamilton's *Federalist No. 70* alludes to it; and John Adams praised the book as "the best defence of the political balance of three powers that ever was written." *The Constitution of England*—which described how the English constitution made possible English liberty—itself referenced *On Crimes and Punishments*, with de Lolme, like Beccaria, among the top ten authors cited by America's founding fathers in their writings and speeches. By 1784, *The Constitution of England*—which one commentator notes "treated the English constitution as a piece of machinery in which king, lords, and commons, each armed with an independent veto, served as balancing weights—had passed through four editions.[123]

It is hard to underestimate the significance of Enlightenment writers such as de Lolme to American intellectuals. In a chapter discussing "the criminal Judicature in England," the much-quoted de Lolme—writing about the rights of English subjects—wrote of how an English justice of the peace would examine criminal suspects, then either bring charges or set the person "at liberty." If charged, de Lolme emphasized, "the party accused must give bail for his appearance to answer the charge; unless in capital cases, for then he must, for safer custody, be really committed to prison, in order to take his trial at the next Sessions." At every session, de Lolme pointed out, the sheriff would appoint a grand jury whose function was "to examine the evidence that has been given in support of every charge." If twelve grand jurors "do not concur in the opinion that an accusation is well grounded," de Lolme noted, "the party is immediately discharged; if, on the contrary, twelve of the grand Jury find the proofs sufficient, the prisoner is said to be indicted, and is detained in order to go through the remaining proceedings." When it came time to ratify the U.S. Bill of Rights, Americans were sure to approve a grand jury protection and a prohibition against "excessive bail."[124]

After further discussing how English criminal defendants, once indicted, could invoke a right to trial by a twelve-man jury, de Lolme distinguished the English system from continental Europe's "Civil Law" system. "[U]nlike to the rules of the Civil Law," de Lolme wrote, "the witnesses deliver their evidence in the presence of the prisoner: the latter may put questions to them; he may also produce witnesses in his behalf, and have them examined upon oath." After taking specific note of the defendant's rights "to Trial by Jury" and "to have a Counsel to assist him," de Lolme added: "To all these precautions taken by the law for the safety of the Subject, one circumstance must be added, which indeed would alone justify the partiality of the English Lawyers to their laws in preference to the Civil Law, — I mean the absolute rejection they have made of torture." "Without repeating here what has been said on this subject by the admirable Author of the Treatise on *Crimes and Punishments*," de Lolme wrote, "I shall observe only, that the torture, in itself so horrible an expedient, would, more especially in a free State, be attended with the most fatal consequences." "Even the convicted criminal must be spared," de Lolme recorded in his book.[125]

Thomas Jefferson's letters also show that, in addition to Beccaria and de Lolme, he was familiar with the writings of Montaigne, who wrote on a wide range of subjects, including cruelty. "I think it is Montaigne who has said," Jefferson recollected in 1794 in a letter to Edmund Randolph, "that ignorance is the softest pillow on which a man can rest his head."[126] Michel Eyquem de Montaigne (1533–1592) — a prominent government official, nobleman and winegrower from southwestern France — had witnessed the lynching of a local official as a teenager and came of age at a time when executions were commonplace. In Montaigne's time, Catholics and Protestants quarreled and fought bitterly, with bloodshed and loss of life often the end result. When a new lieutenant-general, Blaise Monluc, was sent to "pacify" a violent, troubled region of France, he carried out his duties by hanging Protestants in large numbers. As Montaigne's biographer, Sarah Bakewell, writes of that time: "so many executions took place in the area that the supply of gallows equipment ran low."[127] The brutal execution of Jean Calas in Toulouse in 1762 — an event that especially galvanized Enlightenment fervor — would later make clear, yet again, the staying power of violent, religious intolerance in French society. Only after Voltaire published two essays inspired by the case, *Histoire d'Elisabeth Canning et de Jean Calas* and *Traité sur la tolerance*, did French officials reexamine the case and determine — three years after Calas's breaking on the wheel — that an injustice had been done.[128]

Montaigne himself developed an unwavering aversion to cruelty, writing an essay on the subject. "I mortally hate cruelty," he wrote, "both by nature and judgment, as the very extreme of all vices: nay, with so much tenderness that I cannot see a chicken's neck pulled off without trouble, and cannot without impatience endure the cry of a hare in my dog's teeth, though the chase be a violent pleasure." "For my part, even in justice itself," Montaigne wrote, speaking at a time when breaking on the wheel and many other cruelties were still in use, "all that exceeds a simple death appears to me pure cruelty." After referencing a Roman execution, Montaigne emphasized: "Those natures that are sanguinary towards beasts discover a natural proneness to cruelty. After they had accustomed themselves at Rome to spectacles of the slaughter of animals, they proceeded to those of the slaughter of men, of gladiators." "Nature has herself, I fear," Montaigne mused, "imprinted in man a kind of instinct to inhumanity; nobody takes pleasure in seeing beasts play with and caress one another, but every one is delighted with seeing them dismember, and tear one another to pieces." "Even the executions of the law, however reasonable they may be," Montaigne offered, "I cannot witness with a steady gaze." As for occasions when Montaigne was called upon to sentence criminals, he confessed: "I have tended to fall short of justice." Among the admirers of Montaigne's essays: Jean-Jacques Rousseau and Denis Diderot, the French philosopher who rose to fame for his *Encyclopédie*.[129]

As for Italian itself, the worldly Jefferson made substantial efforts to learn the language. He bought Baretti's *Italian-English Dictionary* on February 4, 1764, the same year *On Crimes and Punishments* first appeared, and he also played a key role in having an Italian, Charles Bellini, appointed in 1779 as the first professor of modern languages at the College of William and Mary.[130] James Madison and Thomas Jefferson were also close friends with an Italian émigré, Philip Mazzei, whose Virginia estate was next to Jefferson's Monticello. When Mazzei, a physician turned businessman, came to Virginia to grow vines, Mazzei brought his Florentine school friend, then going by the name of "Carlo" Bellini, with him. Bellini and Mazzei became close friends of Jefferson and Madison, among others. As America's minister to France, Jefferson corresponded with Bellini, sending him a letter from Paris in 1785, writing in part of his European experience: "The truth of Voltaire's observation, offers itself perpetually, that every man here must be either the hammer or the anvil."[131] At Madison's request, Mazzei and Madison actually corresponded entirely in Italian, no doubt so Madison could practice and improve his written Italian.[132] Dr. Benjamin Rush, as well as John Adams and his oldest son, John Quincy Adams, likewise studied Italian, Beccaria's native tongue.[133] Just as Voltaire had read Beccaria in Italian, it is clear that some of America's Founding Fathers did, too.[134]

Jefferson and Castiglioni:
Tours of Italy and America

In the spring of 1787, Thomas Jefferson toured northern Italy, sampling local wines and visiting the cities of Turin, Vercelli, Milan, Pavia, Tortuna and Genoa. Anxious to bring a superior variety of rice back to America, Jefferson—though told the Government of Turin made exporting rice punishable by death—even took a calculated risk and smuggled out some rice to send to rice-producing regions in the United States. In the Italian towns he visited, Jefferson—fulfilling a desire to see the luscious, mountainous landscapes and glories of Italy—was warmly greeted by local officials and prominent residents. Jefferson's visit to Italy in 1787, part of a longer trip that also included stops in France, lasted just a little more than three weeks, meaning Jefferson did not have time for everything. But Jefferson—who mixed business with pleasure—had a splendid trip through France and Italy, as he latter wrote in a letter to John Banister, Jr. in June 1787. "I went as far as Turin, Milan, Genoa, and never passed three months and a half more delightfully," Jefferson wrote. Writing from Paris in July 1787, Jefferson also told John Adams: "While passing thro' the towns of Turin, Milan and Genoa, I satisfied myself of the practicability of introducing our whale oil for their consumption and I suppose it would be equally so in the other great cities of that country."

In Milan, the bustling city that had played such a key role in the Italian Enlightenment, Jefferson met Milanese nobleman Francis dal Verme. Although Alessandro Verri had moved to Rome by that time, only returning to Milan for two brief stays in 1789 and 1794, Alessandro's older brother Pietro was in Milan when Jefferson visited. The Conte Francesco dal Verme (1758–1832), as he was also known, belonged to a wealthy family of Milan and Verona and was friends with the Austrian ambassador in London. He also had an uncle, Giacomo d'Aquino, Principe di Caramanico, who served as Neapolitan ambassador to London, and was an acquaintance of John Adams and Benjamin Franklin. "Among a great many houses painted al fresco," Jefferson noted of his two days in Milan, from April 21 to 22, 1787, "the Casa Roma and Casa Candiani by Appiani, and Casa Belgioiosa by Martin are superior." The Italian botanist Luigi Castiglioni, meanwhile, was just preparing for his return to Europe from his own tour of America where he had walked Philadelphia's streets and seen Jefferson's Monticello, among many other remarkable sites.[135]

Count dal Verme—Jefferson's Milan tour guide—had himself visited the United States in 1783–1784, bearing letters of introduction from John Adams, Henry Laurens and Benjamin Franklin. Franklin, for example, penned a letter to Robert R. Livingston from Passy on April 27, 1783, that began as follows: "The Count Del Verme, an Italian Nobleman of great Distinction, does me the honour to be the Bearer of this. I have not the satisfaction to be personally acquainted with this Gentleman, but am much sollicited by some of my particular Friends, to whom his Merits & Character are known, to afford him this Introduction to you." "He is, I understand," Franklin wrote, "a great Traveller, and his view in going to America is merely to see the Country, & its great Men: — I pray you will shew him every Civility, & afford him that Counsel which as a Stranger he may stand in need of." John Adams, writing on April 28, 1783, to John Hancock, also provided a letter of introduction for dal Verme, with Adams writing of the Italian count: "He will be happy in an Opportunity to see so illustrious an American as the Governor of Massachusetts, for which Reason I take the Liberty to introduce him to your Excellency."

In a letter dated July 8, 1783, to George Washington, Elias Boudinot — a New Jersey lawyer then serving as the president of the Continental Congress, and later appointed by President Washington as Director of the United States Mint — also provided his own letter of introduction, writing as follows: "This will be handed to your Excellency by the Count Del Vermé, a nobleman of Milan in Italy — By Means of his Cousin Prince Caraminici an Ambassador at the Court of London, he was recommended by the Duke of Portland to Dr Franklin Mr Laurens & Mr Adams, who have warmly addressed this illustrious Traveller to the Notice of Congress." "Permit me Sir," Boudinot wrote Washington, "to request your kind attention to the Count on his visit at Head Quarters — His design is to make a Tour through the united States, and to see the principle Men of each State." Washington, in turn, recommended "the Count del Vermé," "an Italian Nobleman of Family & distinction," to various American politicians, including Jonathan Trumbull, Sr., in August 1783, writing, "This Gentleman comes warmly recommended by our Ministers at the Court of Versailles and from the Acquaintance I have had the pleasure to make with him does honor to his high birth & Education." In an expression of his fondness for the man, Washington continued recommending the Italian count to other Americans in September 1783 as the count made his way across America.[136]

On his own trip to North America, Luigi Castiglioni gathered notes for what would become his *Viaggio* and a botanical appendix titled "Observations on the Most Useful Plants of the United States." In the course of his U.S. travels, which ended on May 16, 1787, when he departed from America on a Spanish ship, he also recorded notes about Americans' everyday lives — everything from the food they ate to their social customs. In the Commonwealth of Massachusetts, his first stop: "The fare of the Bostonians is frugal, and the tables covered with few, but substantial foods, as in England. Meats, butter, and vegetables are excellent, as are fish, among which salmon and mackerel are the most esteemed." "Salted cod," Castiglioni added, "is not only eaten boiled but also, garnished with fresh butter, and hard-boiled eggs, is eaten on the Sabbath all year around, and many taste no other food on that day, although it is hard to digest and as a consequence causes headaches." Castiglioni also wrote of eating "fat" and "delicious" pigeons, further recording that squirrels "are quite common in all parts of Massachusetts," and that they "are plump and tasty," with "their hides" sold "at a very low price."

In New York, Castiglioni commented on everything from the food to the prison facilities he saw to the treatment of slaves. "During the night," he noted in one passage, "thousands of frogs could be heard croaking in the bogs and among them could be easily made out the one particular to America called bullfrog, which, sometimes reaching half a foot in width, surpasses in size all other species, and with its cry imitates very closely the bellowing of an ox." "The French used to prepare a rather delicate dish with them, finding them very juicy and tasty," Castiglioni noted, adding that "the Americans, who have, like the English, a general repugnance for this food, have no use at all for them." The "drinking water," he observed, "is brought every morning from a spring some distance away" and "is sold in barrels as in Leghorn." "There are, it is true, cisterns in the city, the water of which serves for domestic uses, but there are in it often a quantity of insects that produce a revolting tickle in the throat and even stomach pains to those that drink it," Castiglioni pointed out after examining New York City water under a microscope.

As regards important New York buildings, Castiglioni wrote of Anglican, Presbyterian, Congregationalist, Calvinist, Lutheran and Quaker churches; a Jewish synagogue; and "[t]the statehouse, where the Congress of the United States and the New York Assembly meet." "In the Hall of Congress," he noted, "there are the portraits of Louis XVI, King of France, and of his Queen Consort sent by the King to the United States as a gift." "The poorhouse, the penitentiary, and the prison," Castiglioni wrote of New York City, "are situated in a large irregular square in the northern part of the city and deserve some consideration, as do also the hospital and the college." On the topic of "negroes" and "slaves," Castiglioni's *Viaggio* observed that a slave plot in the past had been uncovered that resulted in its leaders being condemned to death and that "a law was passed which is still in effect to imprison all negroes found on the streets at night unless they are with their master or sent on an errand by him." In a paragraph noting that John Jay and New York Governor George Clinton had joined a society to promote the liberation of slaves, Castiglioni added: "Surely it is a matter of surprise and pity for a European to read about the sale of slaves here in the newspapers, and all the more so if these notices are compared with those put out for the sale of horses, from which they differ not a bit."

On his way from New York to Georgia, Castiglioni—traveling on horseback and by carriage—also paid a visit to George Washington at Mount Vernon, a visit described in his later published *Viaggio*. "I left Alexandria on the morning of the 25th of December," Castiglioni wrote, noting that he "reached Mount Vernon, the delightful retreat of the immortal American Cincinnatus." On that Christmas Day in 1785, Castiglioni arrived at Washington's house with Colonel Burgess Ball, the husband of one of Washington's nieces, and William Hunter, a Scottish businessman. Hunter lived in Alexandria and belonged to the same Masonic lodge as Washington himself. "General Washington," Castiglioni recorded of his visit, "is about 57 years old, tall, of a sturdy physique and majestic and pleasant mien, and although toughened by military service, he does not give the appearance of being of advanced age." "This famous man who opened and brought to a happy conclusion the American war," Castiglioni remarked, "seemed produced by nature to free America from European subjection and to create an epoch in the history of human revolutions." "I spent four days there," Castiglioni noted of his visit to Mount Vernon, saying he had been "favored by the General with the greatest hospitality, as he is accustomed to do with strangers, who come in great numbers to admire such a famous personage." "Applying himself to agriculture and presiding over a large number of negroes who under his direction are scarcely aware of being slaves," Castiglioni noted of Washington, "he put his fields in tiptop condition, sticking to the best products, without multiplying wine and silk, which require an excessively expensive cultivation in a country short of farmers."

On December 13, 1785, Tench Tilghman—an officer in the Continental Army who served as an aide de camp to General Washington—had written his own letter of introduction for Count Castiglioni. Writing from Baltimore, Tilghman's letter began: "I do myself the honor to introduce to you Count Castiglioni knight of the Order of St Stephen, an Italian Nobleman, who, in pursuit of Botanical Knowledge, has thought it worth his while to visit this, hitherto, almost unexplored Continent. The recommendations he brings from Europe, not only ascertain his Rank, but, what you will esteem of more consequence, they speak in the most favorable manner of the amiableness of his private Character." "The Count having other introductory letters from your Friends to the North-ward," Tilghman continued, "rendered this, in fact, unnecessary," with Tilghman simply noting that "I could not however refuse his request of adding mine to the number." Be-fore Castiglioni noted his departure from Mount Vernon on December 29, he wrote of his wishes for General Washington in his *Viaggio*: "Heaven grant that, by living for many years, he may long serve as an example of virtue and industry for his fellow citizens, as he served as an example to Europe in the victories that consecrated his name to an eter-nal fame."[137]

In Georgia, Castiglioni caught a glimpse—or at least heard about—the operation of that state's criminal justice system. As Castiglioni reported: "A famous horse thief, who stole various horses during the war, went to Wilkes County in Georgia in the spring of 1786, where he was recognized by one of the inhabitants and put in prison. When exam-ined by the judges, he was absolved as guilty only of crimes anterior to the peace treaty, in which it is stipulated that all offenses perpetrated by the Whigs and Tories during the war must be pardoned." In his *Viaggio*, Castiglioni described what happened next: "He was released in accordance with the verdict, and then a number of those people under the leadership of Colonel C_____ (well known in America for his turbulent character) seized him again and took him outside of the city of Golphintown to hang him. Upon reaching the place where they intended to carry out this horrid function, they were stopped in their plan by the lack of rope, and they sent a man on horseback to the nearby city to get some." "Meanwhile," Castiglioni noted, "the wretch tried to escape by flight, but he was very quickly caught by some of the party, who struck him several times in the head with sabers, and he was again put in chains." The end result, as described by Castiglioni: "The news having meanwhile spread about in the city, Mr. Pendleton, attorney general for the state, who happened to be at that time with the judges in that city, moved by such an illegal and barbaric behavior, went to the spot, and arguing for the life of the poor fellow they wanted to sacrifice, with great difficulty succeeded finally in persuading them to reconsign the man to prison, where he died the following morning from the wounds received." "It will seem strange," Castiglioni lamented, "that such an assault should remain unpunished in a country which has just published Constitutions most favorable to personal security; but that confirms all the more the defect of the present system which, by limiting too much the executive power, renders it incapable of controlling an already vicious multitude."

In South Carolina, Castiglioni encountered people concerned about smallpox and had his own battles with ticks as he navigated wooded areas. "If one does not remove it," he wrote of the tick, "it buries itself in the skin head and all, and as it sucks blood it swells enormously, taking on then a gleaming ashen color." "Two of these insects," Castiglioni reported, "fastened themselves onto one of my arms, and not noticing it until the fol-lowing day since their sucking doesn't hurt, I had great difficulty in pulling them off, and they left my skin red and sore for several days." In a section on the "Present Condition of South Carolina," Castiglioni also described plantation owners who "often vent their ill temper on the poor negroes, who, to the shame of mankind, are scarcely reputed to be human beings, and for the slightest failing are exposed to the lash of a slave driver, when the master himself does not take the barbaric pleasure of tormenting them." As Castiglioni wrote of South Carolina masters in his *Viaggio*: "It is true that some treat their slaves with moderation, but one finds too many of them completely unjust and inhuman. One of them said that he had calculated that, if a negro lived for five years, he repaid amply the money spent to buy him, and consequently he forced his slaves to work at night by the light of pine torches until, exhausted by labor, they were taken by fever and died with-out any attention." As Castiglioni continued: "I myself happened to hear an owner, who, to justify his vicious behavior toward negroes, declared without blushing that they were a kind of animal closer to monkeys than to man. Those who raise rice and indigo, who are poor, treat their few slaves (if it is possible) with greater cruelty, often letting them go almost completely naked." Such brutality, as recently depicted in the movie adaptation of Solomon Northup's *Twelve Years a Slave*, would continue well past the founding era, with racial violence and oppression in the South leading to scores of lynchings and the passage of Jim Crow laws.[138]

In Virginia, Castiglioni paid a particularly satisfying visit to John Banister (1734–1788), a lawyer educated in London's Middle Temple with whom Jefferson corresponded. Banister—who once bought a horse from George Washington—was listed as a shareholder in Philip Mazzei's 1774 plan for an agricultural company, was a member of the Virginia Convention in 1776, and served in the Virginia House of Burgesses before becoming a member of the Continental Congress from 1778 to 1779. During the Revolutionary War, he was a major and lieutenant colonel under General Washington, with Washington writing Banister a lengthy letter in 1778 from Valley Forge. As a respected political figure, Banister corresponded with prominent figures such as Jefferson and Washington and was a framer and signer of the Articles of Confederation. In a letter written to Banister's son, John Banister, Jr., from Paris in 1785, Jefferson recommended Rome as offering "the best seminary for the education of youth in Europe" but insisted that, for Americans, studying in America—one's own country—offered distinct advantages. Studying in Europe, Jefferson warned, might lead to "a fondness for European luxury" and a fascination with "the privileges of the European aristocrats," with Jefferson praising, by contrast, "the lovely equality which the poor enjoys with the rich" in American life. John Banister's grandfather, another John Banister (1650–1692), had studied at Oxford, left for Virginia in 1678, and became the first English botanist, and a very prominent one, in the New World. As Castiglioni himself wrote in his *Viaggio*, taking note of the connection to the world of the study of plants: "One mile from Petersburg there is the home of Colonel Banister, who owns a vast plantation. He is a grandson of the celebrated John Banister who, as Professor of Botany and Librarian at Oxford University, abandoned his occupations in England and came to settle in this part of Virginia, where he collected and described a quantity of rare plants with great care and discrimination."[139]

In the section on Virginia life, Castiglioni's *Viaggio* also noted the abuse of slaves, copying an article he had read in the *American Museum* that included the following passage: "The poor negro slaves alone work hard, and fare still harder. It is astonishing and unaccountable to conceive what an amazing degree of fatigue these poor but happy wretches undergo, and can support." The *American Museum* piece emphasized that "hard" and "severe labour" of the slaves would begin at "day-break" and continue in the field "until dusk," whereupon the slaves "repair to the tobacco houses, where each has his task in stripping allotted him, which employs him for some hours." A slave's work day was interrupted only by a lunch of "homminy and salt, and, if his master be a man of humanity, he has a little fat, skimmed milk, rusty bacon, or salt herring, to relish his homminy, or hoe-cake, which kind masters allow their slaves twice a week." "If it be found, next morning, that he has neglected, slighted, or not performed his labour," the article relayed, "he is tied up, and received a number of lashes on his bare back, most severely inflicted, at the discretion of those unfeeling sons of barbarity, the overseers, who are permitted to exercise an unlimited dominion over them." "In submission to injury and insults," the article continued, "they are likewise obliged to be entirely passive, nor dare any of them resist, or even defend himself against the whites, if they should attack him without the smallest provocation; for the law directs a negro's arm to be struck off, who raises it against a white person, should it be only in his own defence."

In Pennsylvania, Castiglioni—always on the lookout for trees and other plants—noted the presence of "white and black walnut, Canadian ivy, western briar, American sumac, poison ivy, and the laurels sassafras and benzoin." In Philadelphia proper, Castiglioni observed that "[o]ne can consider this city, both for beauty and size, the metropolis of the United States." "The streets of Philadelphia," he emphasized, "are very regular, and all intersect at right angles." Castiglioni also described Quaker practices and views and how the Quakers had dealt with the outbreak of the Revolutionary War. "[T]hey have," Castiglioni wrote of the Quakers, "given up the custom of doffing their hats in greeting, substituting for it the handshake; and speaking to one another, they always use the title 'Friend,' calling their sect the Society of Friends." As Castiglioni wrote of the Revolutionary War's impact on the Quaker sect: "Since the Quakers consider war the most horrible of evils, they always refused to bear arms, and if a few praised this opinion of theirs, the majority despised it as if coming from their lack of patriotism, fear, or cowardice. The younger Quakers were unwilling to put up with this accusation, and quite a few of them abandoned the Society in order to take up arms." On an excursion outside of Philadelphia, Castiglioni—who reported leaving Philadelphia on July 20, 1786—was joined by Giuseppe Mussi, an Italian transplant described by Castiglioni as "a fellow Milanese of ours, a young man of pleasant manners, who has been established there for some years as a merchant."[140]

By the time of Castiglioni's visit, substantial artistic, commercial, scientific and cultural bonds existed between Philadelphians, Italians and new European immigrants. Benjamin Franklin took an interest in Italian agriculture, literature and science, expressing a fondness for foods such as macaroni and polenta, and his own newspaper, *The Pennsylvania Gazette*, advertised a concert by the Italian John Palma in 1757. Tickets, the notice advised, could only be purchased at William Bradford's London Coffee House, a popular Philadelphia tavern and merchants' exchange. Another Italian musician, John Gualdo, sold brandy, beer and rum in the 1760s at his Walnut Street store, also putting on concerts, offering music lessons, and selling clavichords, flutes, guitars, mandolins, spinets and violins. *The Pennsylvania Gazette* also ran advertisements for an Italian surgeon, Joseph Batacchi, as early as 1765, and, in 1774, for the opening of a new, Italian-owned dance, music and language academy offering French and Italian lessons. Yet another ad, published in 1772 in the *Pennsylvania Packet and the General Advertiser*, promoted the business of "Anthony Vitalli, Sausage Maker, Late from Italy," near "the house of Edward Shippen, Esq."

Edward Shippen (1729–1806), a prominent Philadelphia lawyer who had spent time in both England and France, studying law in London's Middle Temple, became the Chief Justice of the Pennsylvania Supreme Court after Chief Justice Thomas McKean became Pennsylvania's governor in 1799; in January 1776, Shippen—noting the growing revolutionary sentiment—had written to his brother-in-law, Jasper Yeates, of how Thomas Paine's book, *Common Sense*, "in favor of a total separation from England, seems to gain ground with the common people." In Richard Juliani's *Building Little Italy*, Giuseppe Mussi—Castiglioni's own Pennsylvania traveling companion—is described as having first come to Philadelphia around 1784 and having become a U.S. citizen two years later. At his death in 1832, Mussi—who had no immediate heirs—left his substantial estate, built up from his activities as a merchant and landowner—to his nephews and nieces in Milan.[141]

Jefferson's trip to Italy was just as memorable as Castiglioni's American trip, though the sights and sounds—and the food and personalities—were far different. Having left Paris on February 28, 1787, just a few months before Castiglioni finished his North American tour, Jefferson journeyed south as part of a 1,200-mile journey that took him along the French and Italian Riviera. Traveling as a private citizen from Virginia with one small trunk and a *valet de place* named Petitjean he hired at Dijon, Jefferson eventually crossed the Agogna River before entering Milan, choosing to stay at the Albergo Reale. "The Conte Francesco dal Verme," historian George Green Shackelford writes, "proved to be a hospitable friend, directing him to whatever merited most attention in the Lombard capital during a visit of three nights and two days." An acquaintance of Benjamin Franklin and John Adams, the Conte Francesco dal Verme would later be the recipient of a gift of books from Jefferson, including Jefferson's *Notes on the State of Virginia*. For his travels, Jefferson not only had letters of introduction to Italian scholars prepared by prominent men such as his Virginia neighbor, the Italian Philip Mazzei, but Jefferson was given entrée by men the likes of Gaudenzio Clerici, a gentleman from Milan who had a friendship with David Ramsay, a South Carolina botanist. Later, Jefferson would ask William Short to procure marble for him at Genoa for use with Monticello's fireplaces and to buy at Naples a pasta mold for making macaroni and spaghetti. "Probably carrying Jefferson's guidebooks for Turin, Milan, and Genoa, as well as Addison's *Travels in Italy*," George Green Shackelford writes in his biography of William Short, Short would set out on his own grand tour of Italy in 1788, a tour that included visits to several Italian counts in Milan.

Jefferson—always intellectually curious and anxious to see as much as he could—had a busy agenda on his southern European trip, though his hurried visit left little time to sightsee. As Shackelford notes in *Thomas Jefferson's Travels in Europe*: "Jefferson's visit to Milan was so brief that he could not accept, as William Short did eighteen months later, the invitation of Conte Luigi di Castiglioni to inspect his villa, about a dozen miles from the city on the way to the Italian lakes." Jefferson, however, took note of the Casa Candiani and the Casa Belgiojoso—two Milanese town houses—on his trip, and he stayed at Pavia's best hotel, the Albergo Croce Bianco, hiring a local guide to show him the botanical gardens, the city, and the university where Beccaria had studied years earlier. It was from 1786 to 1789 that William Short—the 1779 graduate of the College of William and Mary—served as Jefferson's private secretary in Paris. From Short's account, Jefferson most certainly would have enjoyed seeing Castiglioni's villa and spending time with its occupants. Castiglioni and his in-laws, Short reported, were "zealous" botanists "as much attached to American plants & trees as ... to Americans, themselves." As nephews of the Verri brothers, Luigi and Alfonso Castiglioni—brothers themselves—studied Linnaeus and sought to make their own stamp, in Italy, on the field of botany.[142] This was a time of vibrant and lively exchange of ideas, and Beccaria's ideas—as part of the Italian Enlightenment—were then very much in vogue. As one history points out, "Beccaria was admired by many of the British Dissenters and American radicals primarily for his views on criminal justice reform."[143]

Foreign and Cultural Exchanges

America's Founding Fathers and their Italian-speaking counterparts, in fact, regularly communicated by letters and in person. John Rutledge Jr., Thomas Lee Shippen and William Short—Jefferson's protégé—all traveled in Italy in 1788, just a short time after Jefferson made the trip. "Armed with Jefferson's letters of introduction," historian George Green Shackelford writes of their Italian tour, "Rutledge and Short found several Italian counts to shepherd them through the gaieties of Milan." On July 13, 1788, Jefferson—then in Paris—had written to the Italian count Francis dal Verme and others to assist the American travelers. "The readiness with which you were so kind as to shew me what was most worth seeing in Milan and it's neighborhood when I had the honour of seeing you there, encourages me to address to you two of my young countrymen who will pass thro' Milan in a tour they are taking," Jefferson wrote dal Verme. "The one," Jefferson noted, "is Mr. Rutledge, son of Governor Rutledge of South Carolina, the other Mr. Shippen of

Philadelphia nephew of Mr. Lee late President of Congress." Richard Henry Lee, Thomas Lee Shippen's uncle, had written in 1784 to his nephew, Thomas Lee Shippen: "Julius Cæsar showed his ambition as much when he preferred being the first man in a small village to the second in Rome, as when he grasped the imperial purple." Jefferson also penned a letter of introduction to Gaudenzio Clerici of Milan, with whom Jefferson had corresponded in 1787.[144]

Writing to Jefferson from Milan on October 28, 1788, Short reported back that Rutledge's "acquaintance with Castiglioni … have rendered Milan so agreable [sic] to him, that I do not think he was disposed to quit it." Short also thanked Jefferson for his letter to "Count Dal Verme," who—Short wrote—had extended "civilities" and "cordial offers of them." "He is at present in the country," Short told Jefferson, "but desires I wd not fail to return you his thanks for your remembrance." His letter to Jefferson, Short's professional and father-like mentor, then noted: "Count Castiglioni also, who out of gratitude for his treatment in America, seems attached to all Americans, desires I will recall him to our remembrance & assures me of his respect & friendship for you." Short and Rutledge—the latter a recently admitted member of the Charleston, South Carolina bar—spent time with Count Castiglioni and Castiglioni's brother, also "a zealous botanist," and dined at their estate about nine miles from Milan. "Notwithstanding the family is ancient, noble, rich & surrounded with a numerous train of servants," Short wrote to Jefferson, "they live in the simplicity of manner & harmony of a good American family." "We went yesterday to see a dairy where Parmesan cheese is made," Short commented, saying that, on one outing after examining a plant species, Count Castiglioni's brother "insisted on my taking some of the seed for you." "I did it to please him," Short wrote, "but suppose it may be easily got from the King's garden at Paris."

On their extended trip to Italy, the starry-eyed Americans would make many new friends and acquaintances. "After Shippen sailed from Genoa," Shackelford notes, "Short and Rutledge made between October 1788 and April 1789 a leisurely tour of Italian places Jefferson never visited: Vicenza, Venice, Rome, Naples, and Florence." Thanks to Jefferson's letter of introduction to Cardinal de Bernis, the French Ambassador to the Holy See, Short and Rutledge—who got a two-day tour of the Vatican led by an architectural tutor—were especially hospitably treated in Rome, with Short telling Jefferson that "on the whole" he had "received infinite satisfaction" from his visit there. After visiting monuments of antiquity, attending a papal Christmas mass, and experiencing the charms of Rome's high society, Rutledge exclaimed: "Everything seems like enchantment. Wherever I go, I seem to be on fairy ground." Short also declared that he was "stunned" by Rome's Pantheon, reporting he felt "the effect of the sublime." During their trip to Italy, a book about Count Francesco dal Verme notes, "Dal Verme and Castiglioni took them in hand and introduced them to every luminary, from the renowned Marquis Beccaria to the Countess Amelia Litta, whose Friday evening receptions attracted all of the first women of Milan." In Florence, Short and Rutledge stayed with Philip Mazzei's friends, Adamo and Giovanni Fabbroni. Though they did not avail themselves of the opportunity, the Fabbronis even offered to present them to Grand Duke Leopold in Pisa.[145]

John Rutledge Jr. (1766–1819)—a South Carolina Federalist; the son of that state's first governor John Rutledge, later the second Chief Justice of the U.S. Supreme Court; and the nephew of Edward Rutledge, the youngest signer of the Declaration of Independence—had met up with Short in Milan and then traveled with him through Italy and France. Giovanni Fabbroni (1752–1822), a Florentine scholar, would himself exchange letters with Jefferson on a wide array of topics. For his part, William Short (1759–1849)— even before his trip—formed a bond with Madame Castiglioni that resulted in a series of letters written in 1788–1789. Before journeying to various Italian cities, Short had made the acquaintance of Madame Castiglioni in Paris, and Madame Castiglioni was—in the words of two scholars—"a sympathetic listener to his confidences." In a letter written to Short from Milan on August 22, 1788, Madame Castiglioni wrote of "*poor in Love Mr. Short*."[146] "Before Jefferson returned to America in 1789," explains historian George Green Shackelford, "Short had commenced a love affair with Charlotte Alexandrine, the beautiful young Duchesse de La Rochefoucauld, whom everyone called Rosalie."[147]

The same year that Beccaria's treatise first appeared in Italy, another set of Americans had also traveled through various Italian cities and locales. In 1764, Samuel Powel and Dr. John Morgan of Philadelphia—founder of America's first medical school—visited a series of Italian towns after Morgan finished his European medical studies. Dr. Morgan was a friend of Benjamin Franklin and Dr. Benjamin Rush, with Morgan earning his doctorate degree from the University of Edinburgh in 1763. Powel—his traveling companion—was a fellow townsman. After crossing thru the south of France, Dr. Morgan and Powel—who spent about eight months together on their journey—went to Genoa, Leghorn, Pisa, Florence, Rome and Naples, then through Loreto, Bologna, Ferrara, Padua, Venice, Vicenza, Verona, Mantua, Parma, Placentia, Milan and Turin. In Turin, as part of their 1760s grand tour, they called on the famed scientist and electrician, Giambatista Beccaria (1716–1781), the same man Ezra Stiles also encouraged his friend Henry Marchant—a Rhode Island lawyer who signed the Articles of Confederation—to visit. On their European trip, Dr. Morgan and Samuel Powel also met the Duke of York, had a private audience with the Pope, visited the General Hospital of Milan, and paid a visit to Voltaire in Geneva. In October 1775, the Continental Congress appointed Dr. Morgan as the Director-General to the Military Hospitals and Physician-in-Chief to the American Army. As another doctor noted of that appointment, concluding that "no more fitting appointment of Chief Medical Officer could have been made": "The success which had attended the medical department of the College of Philadelphia under his guidance was of itself a first-class endorsement."[148] It was Dr. Benjamin Rush—Dr. Morgan's friend—who went on to play such an important role in disseminating Cesare Beccaria's ideas in America.

During that era, prominent Americans regularly corresponded with—and consulted—Italian thinkers, further strengthening the growing bonds between the two societies. Benjamin Franklin, for instance, regularly corresponded with Giambatista Beccaria—the Italian priest and famous electrician who shared Franklin's passion for scientific inquiry.[149] Father Beccaria, as he was known, publicized Franklin's ideas in Italy, and Franklin, in turn, was partially responsible for having Father Beccaria's book, *Concerning Artificial and Natural Electricity*, translated into English.[150] Franklin's *Experiments and Observations on Electricity*, published in London in 1769, makes multiple references to "*Pere Beccaria*," also referred to as "the Rev. Father BECCARIA" and "that most ingenious electrician father *Beccaria*." Joseph Priestley's book, *The History and Present State of Electricity with Original Experiments*, also published in 1769, likewise refers to "*Signior*" Beccaria—the prominent scientist—more than a dozen times.[151] In addition, Priestley's *Experiments and Observations on Different Kinds of Air* and *Observations on Respiration and the Use of the Blood*, published in the 1770s, respectfully references Father Beccaria's own experimentation.[152] Because they were both Italians, Father Beccaria, the scientist, and Cesare Beccaria, the political philosopher, were sometimes, by Englishmen and Americans, actually confused with one another.[153]

Benjamin Franklin had begun his own study of languages in 1733, and had taken up Italian after acquiring a mastery of French. In 1762, shortly before Cesare Beccaria's treatise was published, Franklin expressed his admiration for the Italian language in a letter to his friend Giambatista Beccaria, the Scalopian cleric and a Professor of Physics at the

University of Turin. In a letter dated July 13, 1762, Franklin wrote: "In honour of your musical language, I have borrowed from it the name of this instrument, calling it the Armonica." In 1767, Alessandro Verri—who met Franklin in England during a three-month stay there the prior year—described Franklin's armonica to his brother Pietro in great detail. As Alessandro wrote to his brother: "I have been to see the Newton of electricity, the famous Franklin. He is a man of over fifty years of age. You know that by pressing and sliding a moistened finger over the edge of a glass a sound is produced. He has made the instrument on this principle." As Alessandro's letter to his brother continued: "He has strung on a spindle, or common axis, as many glass bells as correspond to the pegs of a harpsichord, proportionally graduated. The spindle turns by means of the left foot, with a wheel, as the knife grinder does. At the same time one touches with the fingers, as one does a harpsichord, the bells which spin like wheels, after having first wet them slightly with a sponge. A melody comes out which goes to the heart."

In his 1762 letter to Father Beccaria, Franklin told his correspondent that he had "once promised myself the pleasure of seeing you at Turin," but emphasized that "is not now likely to happen" as Franklin was "just about returning to my native country, America." "Among the most striking attestations of Franklin's contact with Italian," writes Antonio Pace in *Benjamin Franklin and Italy*, "are several documents in that language penned by his own hand." "One," Pace notes, "is a note to the Turinese jurist Gioanni de Bernardi dissuading him from going to America to exercise his profession." Bernardi was excited by "the fame of the glorious union of the thirteen colonies of America" and "the wise legislation with which they have assured for themselves that happy liberty which their valor had procured them." Sparked by that knowledge, he had written to Franklin in 1779 of his "desire to see with my own eyes that nascent republic and to offer her my services in the capacity of jurisprudent."

As Gioanni de Bernardi, penning his letter in Italian, wrote to Franklin from Turin on March 20, 1779:

> The reputation acquired throughout Europe by the glorious thirteen American colonies, their success and wise legislation, have aroused in me a desire to see this new republic with my own eyes and offer it my services as a jurist. The best way I can think to accomplish this is to turn to you. I realized that you know nothing about my qualifications, but I trust in your acumen and your kindness. Should you give me some encouragement, I shall send you my credentials. I am a twenty-four-year-old lawyer and citizen of Milan, currently living in Turin.

Franklin's reply, dated April 1st, was in French, with Franklin writing as follows: "Thank the Gentleman for his Good will and Offers of Service to America in qualité of Jurisconsulte but that our Laws and Language being different from those he is acquainted with, I can neither advise nor encourage him to go thither—."

In Italy itself, Giuseppe Saverio Poli—at the University of Naples—promoted Dr. Franklin's ideas, too, penning a treatise on *The Formation of Thunder, Lightning, and of Various Other Meteors Explained According to the Ideas of Mr. Franklin*. In 1767, Alessandro Verri—on his trip to London—happily reported to his brother Pietro of his visit with Dr. Franklin: "I asked Franklin whether he knew Father Beccaria of Turin. He knows him and is in correspondence with him."[154] Naples itself was a hotbed of intellectual activity, with the Italian political philosopher and economist Antonio Genovesi (1712–1769)—a teacher of the Italian penal reformer Gaetano Filangieri—hailing from that city. One of the first holders of a chair in political economy in Europe, Genovesi published a two-volume text on that subject between 1765 and 1767. "The word *philosopher*," Genovesi once specified, "incorporates the idea of a great and magnificent person, knowledgeable of both divine and human affairs, and an indifferent observer of worldly matters, which he utilizes to the extent to which they are useful to life; priest and interpreter of the laws of the world, friend of God and of men, reparative of the rights of humanity."[155]

Philip Mazzei—who came to love Virginia—also traveled in high-level American circles, interacting and corresponding with many Founding Fathers, and serving as a go-between as regards Italian and American political leaders. In a letter to Philip Mazzei written from Philadelphia in 1775, Benjamin Franklin praised "the fine Language of your Country" and wrote that "[i]t was with great Pleasure I learnt from Mr. Jefferson, that you were settled in America." "I am myself much pleas'd," Franklin noted in his letter to Mazzei, "that you have sent a Translation of our Declaration to the Grand Duke; because having a high Esteem for the Character of that Prince, and of the whole Imperial Family, from the Accounts given me of them by my Friend Dr. Ingenhauss and yourself, I should be happy to find that we stood well in the Opinion of that Court." Jan Ingenhousz (1730–1799), a Dutch physiologist, biologist and chemist who met Franklin in London, was best known for inoculating Habsburg family members in Vienna against smallpox in 1768, and was later named the personal physician to the Austrian Empress Maria Theresa. Ingenhousz—or IngenHousz, as his name often appears—showed that light was necessary for photosynthesis, and he conducted his own research on electricity and heat conduction. Ingenhousz himself spent considerable time in Italy, where he inoculated the Grand Duke of Tuscany, and he corresponded with Dr. Franklin on scientific matters and also met Dr. Guillotin in Paris.[156]

The Mazzei-translated Declaration of the Causes and Necessity of Taking up Arms, the Second Continental Congress's explanation for why Americans were fighting the British, was prepared by Thomas Jefferson—the future U.S. President—and Colonel John Dickinson, who wrote *Letters from a Pennsylvania Farmer*. "Mr. Fromond of Milan, with whom I had the Pleasure of being acquainted in London," Franklin added in his letter to Mazzei, "spoke to me of a Plant much used in Italy, and which he thought would be useful to us in America." "I received from the same M. Fromond Four Copies of a Translation of some of my Pieces," Franklin concluded, telling Mazzei: "I beg your Acceptance of one of them, and of my best Wishes for your Health and Prosperity."[157] The Lombard scientist Giovanni Francesco Fromond, of Milan, was known for his particular skill in polishing prisms and had met Franklin in London during a trip there in the 1772–1773 time period. In Mazzei's own memoir, *My Life and Wanderings*, Mazzei references "the peculiarities of the plant called *Ravizzoni* in Lombardy, the seeds of which M. Fromond sent to Franklin from Milan."[158]

A number of Americans, in fact, visited Italian states in the colonial period, further strengthening cross-cultural ties and connections even beyond those that occurred by mail. "A year after Beccaria had published his book," historian Alexander DeConde writes, "Henry Benbridge, a Philadelphian of twenty-one, arrived in Rome to study art, the second American painter of note to do so." Benbridge would stay in Italy until October of 1769. The first painter to study in Italy—Quaker Benjamin West—was "a young ingenious" artist from Philadelphia who knew Benbridge. Benbridge, who got to know Benjamin Franklin during a later visit to London, was himself a well-connected member of the American Philosophical Society, an organization founded by Benjamin Franklin in 1743. West, who visited Italy from 1760 to 1763, specifically went to improve his artistic craft, traveling to Leghorn on a ship carrying flour, sugar and wheat with John Allen and his cousin Joseph Shippen (1732–1810). The 21-year-old John Allen—who spent a few months in Italy building trade relationships in 1760—was the son of William Allen, the Chief Justice of Pennsylvania. All of these young men would admire Italy's artistic masterpieces, with Allen and Shippen setting sail from Philadelphia for Livorno with their cargo. Richard Izard—a South Carolinian—also visited Italy in 1774 to gain a better appreciation for its art and music.[159]

In a 1940 article on Italians and Italian travelers in eighteenth-century Pennsylvania, its author, Howard Marraro, also notes that Count Paolo Andreani—a physicist and naturalist—came to America in 1790 and presented to President George Washington a copy of Vittorio Alfieri's "Ode to America's Independence." The Italian poet and dramatist Vittorio Alfieri (1749–1803) had traveled throughout Europe, wrote his ode to American liberty from 1781 to 1783, and had—as is clear from his writings and poetry—a palpable hatred for tyrants. For his part, Count Andreani had attracted widespread attention in 1784 for being the first Italian to ascend a hot-air balloon in his garden in Milan. In September 1783, King Louis XVI, Marie Antoinette, and a crowd of spectators had—in France—watched in awe as two French brothers, Jacques and Joseph Montgolfier, coaxed a duck, a rooster and a sheep into a 41-foot paper-and-fabric balloon in the garden at Versailles, with the balloon—fueled by a wood fire inside the balloon's basket—then lifting off and landing safely in a nearby forest two miles away. Two months later, the Montgolfier brothers loaded a soldier and a scientist into another balloon, decorated in blue and gold, and they drifted over Paris for 25 minutes to the astonishment of Parisians. "Philip Mazzei, the life-long friend of Jefferson, introduced Andreani to James Madison," Marraro notes, pointing out that Andreani was elected a member of the American Philosophical Society in 1792. With so many personal relationships between Americans and Italians, including ones made in America itself as Italians visited or emigrated, it is hardly surprising that Italian ideas on republicanism and crime and punishment filtered into American society.[160]

Italians were obsessed with liberty and America's independence as much as Americans were enthralled by the Italian Enlightenment itself. And even if Americans—many of whom had direct contact with Italian speakers—did not always agree with everything the humane Beccaria wrote, they took his ideas very seriously. As part of the Italian-American interchange of ideas and culture, Italians—more than intrigued by what had happened in North America—came to America to see for themselves what freedom meant. For example, Lorenzo Da Ponte (1749–1838), who had lived as a priest in Venice until being banished in 1779 by that city's Council of Ten for immoral behavior, emigrated to America to start a new life after working for years in the European cities of Vienna and London. A one-time bookseller who had printed Beccaria's *Dei delitti e delle pene* for Lackington, Allen, & Co., Da Ponte set sail for Philadelphia in 1805 after selling, in April of the prior year, 2,000 of his "Superb & extremely valuable" books—"Consisting," as the auction catalogue put it, "of almost every Author in the Italian Language." Mozart's gifted librettist, Da Ponte—who penned the words to *The Marriage of Figaro* (1786), *Don Giovanni* (1787) and *Così fan tutte* (1790)—sold soap and spices in Elizabethtown, New Jersey, and operated a general merchandise store in Philadelphia before becoming a Professor of Italian at New York's Columbia University. In New York, Da Ponte befriended Clement Moore, the author of *'Twas the Night Before Christmas*, and augmented his salary by selling Italian books. In 1825, attacking W. H. Prescott's October 1824 essay on "Italian Narrative Poetry" in *The North American Review*, Da Ponte penned these words in Italian: *Roba vecchia Beccaria! roba vecchia Filangieri! roba vecchi Alfieri!*

The Marriage of Figaro—originally a play by the French playwright Pierre-Augustin Caron de Beaumarchais, first produced in Paris in April 1784 before being adapted into an opera by Mozart and Da Ponte—depicts clever and virtuous servants in juxtaposition to venal aristocrats and shows up in a letter written by Abigail Adams. Beaumarchais—best known in English-speaking countries for his plays *The Barber of Seville* and *The Marriage of Figaro*, and who published Voltaire's writings and once faced the prospect of being executed over a dispute with a powerful judge—was himself an early French supporter of America's War of Independence, overseeing the delivery of munitions to the American rebels before France even officially sided with the Americans. "The cause of

America is in many respects the cause of humanity," Beaumarchais once observed. After American diplomat Silas Deane, a delegate to the Continental Congress, was sent on a mission to Paris in 1776 to secure aid from the French, Beaumarchais—the Frenchman—had helped to secure that aid. "To him … more than to any other person," a paper titled *Beaumarchais, The Merchant*, read before the New York Historical Society, explains, "belongs the credit of making Louis XVI comprehend the political importance of aiding the Colonies in their struggle with Great Britain; he planned and executed the ingenious scheme by which the aid was to be extended; he sent the first munitions of war and supplies which the Colonists received from abroad and he sent them too, at a time when, humanly speaking, it was reasonably certain that without such aid from some quarter, the Colonists must have succumbed."[161]

A number of early Americans—in addition to their abiding interest in Italian art, music and culture—also studied French or were conversant, to one degree or another, in that language. Benjamin Franklin studied French as well as Italian and Spanish; James Madison studied French under his tutor Donald Robertson and at the College of New Jersey and later recommended that Congress acquire French-language books; Thomas Jefferson studied French and acquired a number of French titles for his library; and in the summer of 1767, Dr. Benjamin Rush—a product of the Enlightenment—studied French with a tutor. And the list—which includes early U.S. Presidents and their families—goes on. In 1778, John Adams and John Quincy Adams studied French aboard the American frigate *Boston* with the assistance of a French army surgeon. James Monroe and his wife Elizabeth, who spent considerable time in France when Monroe served as America's Minister to France, also spoke French fluently.[162] This fluency in French also gave these early Americans the ability, if they so chose, to access André Morellet's French translation of Beccaria's book, *Traité des délits et des peines*. Morellet's aim—as Aaron Thomas, a translator of Beccaria's book, puts it—"was to turn *On Crimes and Punishments*, which in the original Italian possessed the immediacy of a political pamphlet, into a systematic juridical treatise, as the very title of the French edition suggests."[163]

Not every American founder had a working knowledge of French. Indeed, "few of the Founding Fathers spoke French or could read it fluently," asserts Thomas Schaeper, author of *France and America in the Revolutionary Era*. But, it must be said, the ones that made an effort to learn French—or that actually did speak or master it, at least in some fashion—were some of America's most influential figures. Indeed, despite the lack of French fluency among a broad swath of American society, Schaeper acknowledges that "the works of several French writers were well-known in America, and beginning in 1768 several Frenchmen were granted membership in the American Philosophical Society." "Though Montesquieu's political ideas were popular in America," he argues, downplaying the critical importance of the French and Italian Enlightenments on American thought, "the colonists derived most of their philosophical and political ideas from English and Scottish writers."[164] The treatises of Montesquieu and Beccaria, however, were clearly among the many French and Italian Enlightenment texts that so many of America's framers had great familiarity with, even if—in some cases—they read about the ideas in those books only in English translations.

The Beginnings of Penal Reform

The thirst for penal reform—both in Europe and in America—was often the product of specific cases and societal injustices. In colonial and early America, harsh corporal punishments and executions—as in Europe—were a fact of life, with such punishments regularly seen by the public or read about in the newspapers. The pillory and the stocks were used in broad daylight in the public square, just as executions were often publicly conducted at midday so large numbers of people could see them. For example, on July 7, 1737, Andrew Bradford's *American Weekly Mercury* ran the following item almost forty years before America declared its independence: "On Saturday last, just before Twelve, *Henry Wilemon*, a Nailer, and *Catharine Smith*, alias *Connor*, were Executed here, for *Burglary*." "One *Isaac Bradford*," the paper reported, "receiv'd Sentence of Death at the same Time for a Robbery, and was to have been executed with them, but he was Repriev'd, and did the Office of the Executioner. *A very hard Choice.*" At that time, convicts—in exchange for a reprieve—were often pressed into service as executioners, a job that was not easy to fill. "The same Day," the Philadelphia paper noted without fanfare, "one *Joseph Beven* was executed at *Chester*." Previously convicted of crimes in 1736 and sentenced to hang in Philadelphia alongside two men, Catharine Smith—who went to the gallows in 1737, leaving "a young Child behind her"—had avoided execution in the prior year only because she had been pregnant and had been granted a reprieve by the governor in light of her condition.[165]

In the following decades, English and American newspapers, broadsides and books continued covering the minute details of executions and the offenders' lives, even as societal attitudes towards criminals radically changed as the ideas of the Enlightenment made their way to America. "John Adams seems to have had doubts about capital punishment as early as 1768," one book records, noting that Adams successfully defended Samuel Quinn on a capital rape charge then recorded Quinn's praise of him in his diary. As Adams described his role and Quinn's gratitude: "I was appointed, and the Man was acquitted, but remanded in order to be tryed on another Indictment for an assault with Intention to ravish. When he had returned to Prison, he broke out of his own Accord— God bless Mr. Adams. God bless his Soul I am not to be hanged, and I dont care what else they do to me."

Sometimes, Anglo-American authorities—in particularly graphic assertions of state power—carried out more than one execution at the same time, as with the 1790 double execution in Oxford, England, of murderers Charles Shury and John Castle. In 1830, the *Register and North Carolina Gazette*—describing another double execution, this one in Raleigh, North Carolina—specifically reported on the hanging of a white convicted murderer, Elijah Kimbrough, and a burglar, "negro Carey." After the two men were hanged in public, the newspaper gave the basic details, but then editorialized about what had occurred. "We feel it our duty to state the humiliating fact, that a large proportion of the crowd assembled on this occasion were females," the newspaper relayed, further observing: "We cannot close this account, already sufficiently long, without a few additional remarks naturally suggested by the disparity of the offences for which these unfortunate men suffered."[166] In early America, the death penalty—as historian Thomas Foster points out—was "meted out disproportionately on the basis of race: of six men executed for rape in eighteenth-century Massachusetts, four were black, one was Native American, and one was Irish."[167]

As was frequently the case with execution coverage, the Raleigh newspaper story from 1830 was anything but brief, often vacillating between reportage of facts and editorial comment. Kimbrough—the North Carolina paper wrote—was convicted of the crime of murder, "the greatest which can be committed." That murder, the paper said, was committed "under circumstances almost unparalleled for their barbarity and atrocity." "Perhaps his was a case," the paper offered, "in which the law justly awarded death as the proper punishment." "But in the case of Carey, admitting the full extent of his guilt," the paper asked, "what was his crime?" As the newspaper wrote of Carey's offense: "He broke into a kitchen or out-house where no person slept, and robbed it of articles, worth perhaps five dollars!" "And yet the criminal law of this State," the paper emphasized, "so blends all distinctions of guilt, as to inflict the same punishment on him as upon Kimbrough who was convicted of the murder of his step-father." "Now we presume all will agree," the Raleigh newspaper wrote, "that to prevent the perpetration of crimes, it is necessary to punish offenders; but few will be found, we think, to coincide in opinion with Draco, who gave as a reason for his sanguinary course, that small crimes deserved death, and he could find no severer punishment for the greatest." "We lay it down as a general proposition," the paper continued, echoing Beccaria's advice, at least in part, "that all punishments (except perhaps in a very few cases) ought to be moderate and corrective, not cruel and exterminating—they ought to be merciful not rigorous, proportionate to the crime not excessive, and should tend to the reformation of the delinquent, not to his destruction." "We hope that the our Legislature will, at no distant day," the paper concluded, "take measures for the establishment of a Penitentiary, and experience will prove here, as it has done elsewhere, that the certainty of punishment, more effectually deters from the perpetration of crime, than the severity of it."[168]

Colonial and early American times, in must be recalled, presented unique law enforcement challenges. In an era when new identities could be easily assumed and in which convicted felons, at least before the Revolutionary War, were regularly transported from England to America, Americans—in lieu of executions—often resorted to branding criminals. Convicts who were not executed were branded with letters: *A* for adulterer; *B* for burglar; *M* for someone committing manslaughter; *T* for thief, and so on and so forth. In addition, other demeaning or harsh corporal punishments—the stocks or even the public threat of execution—were often employed. For example, in the October 22, 1785 edition of the *Massachusetts Centinel*, that Boston paper—under the heading of "Springfield, October 4"—lists the following item:

> *Priscilla Wharfield* of Westfield, for adultery with a negro man, while her husband was in the army, to set one hour on the gallows with a rope about her neck, be severely whipped 20 stripes in the way from the gallows to the goal [jail], and forever after wear a capital A two inches long and proportionable bigness, cut out in cloth of a contrary colour to her cloaths sowed upon her outer garment on her back in open view, and pay costs.

Branding criminals—whether on the hand or forehead—allowed members of the general public to identify potential threats to their personal safety or property. Sometimes, as an item in the *American Weekly Mercury* again made clear, convicted felons might escape the gallows if they agreed to perform the stigmatized role of executioner—a job shunned by members of the community at large. For instance, on January 18, 1762, it was reported that two New York criminals had been reprieved until the following month because "the sheriff cannot find any person to act as a hangman."[169]

Benjamin Franklin first showed an identifiable interest in the operation and inequity of colonial America's penal codes in 1747, the year he wrote *The Speech of Miss Polly Baker*, what one scholar, Marcello Maestro, calls "a semi-facetious piece" that is "often described as one of Franklin's hoaxes because many readers were led to believe that it was the account of a real event." Published anonymously in London in the April 15, 1747 edition of *The General Advertiser*, "The Speech of Miss Polly Baker"—as it was titled—was purportedly made "before a Court of Judicature" in Connecticut where she was supposedly "prosecuted the Fifth Time, for having a Bastard Child." In her speech to "the Honourable Bench" and "your Honours," the "poor unhappy Woman" with "no Money" and no lawyer asked for a remission of her fine, noting: "This is the Fifth Time, Gentlemen, that I have been dragg'd before your Court on the same Account; twice I have paid heavy Fines, and twice have been brought to Publick Punishment, for want of Money to pay those Fines." In that era, the birth of a "bastard" child carried legal consequences with it. As a 1777 English title, *The Laws Respecting Women*, reported: "A charge of having a bastard child is cognizable by the court of general quarter sessions of the peace." In a section of that book titled "*Punishment for having bastard Children*," that book noted: "It is left to the discretion of the justices what degree of punishment shall be inflicted on the mother and reputed father of a bastard child."[170]

A master humorist, Dr. Franklin used sarcasm to question the legitimacy of laws allowing unwed mothers to be prosecuted. "This," Polly Baker's speech continued, "may have been agreeable to the Laws, and I don't dispute it; but since Laws are sometimes unreasonable in themselves, therefore repealed, and others bear too hard on the Subject in particular Circumstances," "I take the Liberty to say, That I think this Law, by which I am punished, is both unreasonable in itself, and particularly severe with regard to me." "I have brought Five fine Children into the World," she addressed the jurists in Franklin's imagined colloquy, asking: "Can it be a Crime (in the Nature of Things I mean) to add to the Number of the King's Subjects, in a new Country that really wants People?" "I should think it a Praise-worthy, rather than a punishable Action," her speech continued. "What Need is there," she asked, speaking of "my Misfortunes with Stripes and Infamy," "of your additional Fines and Whipping?" Citing "the Duty of the first and great Command of Nature, and of Nature's God, *Encrease and Multiply*," Miss Polly Baker — referring to her birthing experiences and that "Duty, from the steady Performance of which, nothing has been able to deter me" — concluded her appeal: "for its Sake, I have hazarded the Loss of the Publick Esteem, and have frequently endured Publick Disgrace and Punishment; and therefore ought, in my humble Opinion, instead of a Whipping, to have a Statue erected to my Memory."[171]

As historian Marcello Maestro points out in his 1975 article, "Benjamin Franklin and the Penal Laws," *The Speech of Miss Polly Baker* received considerable attention. Franklin's witty piece was reprinted by a number of London newspapers within a month of its initial appearance and on July 20th it appeared in *The Boston Weekly Post-Boy*, making a jump across the Atlantic. Shortly thereafter, the piece was also published in *The New York Gazette* and *The New York Weekly Journal*. "The 'Speech,'" Maestro notes, "soon became known also in France where several writers — among them Voltaire, Diderot, and Morellet — found its contents helpful and made use of it in their fight for a more enlightened society." Franklin later wrote another much-read piece — this time based on a real event, the brutal massacre of Indian families in Lancaster County, Pennsylvania, in December 1763. In that piece, Franklin lamented: "poor defenceless Creatures were immediately fired upon, stabbed and hatcheted to Death!" In *A Narrative of the Late Massacres*, Franklin — emphasizing how "Men, Women and little Children" were "inhumanly murdered" in "cold Blood" — railed against "those cruel Men" and "[t]he barbarous Men who committed the atrocious Fact, in Defiance of Government, of all Laws human and divine, and to the eternal Disgrace of their Country and Colour." "Do we come to America to learn and practise the Manners of *Barbarians*?" Franklin asked rhetorically. "[E]ven the *cruel Turks*," Franklin noted, "never kill Prisoners in cold Blood."[172]

The brutal execution of Jean Calas, in Toulouse, France, also inspired men such as Franklin, Voltaire and Beccaria to take up and press the cause of criminal justice reform. Calas, a Protestant merchant, was living in a mostly Roman Catholic country with Catholicism as the state religion. In 1761, one of Calas' sons had tragically been found dead in the family's house, and rumors swirled about that Calas had killed his son because he intended to convert to Catholicism. After the family first claimed that their dead son, Marc-Antoine, had been killed by a murderer, they reversed course and declared that he had committed suicide, then considered a serious crime necessitating the defilement of the dead body. Although evidence pointed to a suicide, the family had reflexively concealed that fact to avoid their son's naked body being dragged through the streets and exhibited in a gibbet, the accepted penalty of the day. When authorities in Toulouse, without any credible evidence, decided that Jean Calas had murdered his son, Calas was tortured in an effort to pry a confession from him. But Calas maintained his innocence even as his limbs were pulled out of his sockets; thirty pints of water were poured down his throat; and all his limbs were systematically broken with an iron bar. Ultimately, Calas—the subject of judicial torture in a civil law country—was executed by breaking on the wheel in 1762. Not until 1765, largely through Voltaire's advocacy, was Calas posthumously exonerated of all charges. "The judicial murder of Calas, at Toulouse," it has been noted, caused a "European sensation." One of the French "Encyclopedists," that source explains, wrote to a member of a Milan literary society to say this after the brutal execution: "Now is the time to rise against religious intolerance and the exaggerated severity of Penal Legislation." It was at the height of what became known as the "Calas affair" that Beccaria, of Milan, joined the public debate by advocating the abolition of torture and capital punishment.[173]

Voltaire's advocacy and writing—as well as the Calas affair itself—captivated America's political leaders, as did Beccaria's treatise. On September 30, 1764, Benjamin Franklin, then in Philadelphia, wrote to Henry Bouquet, a British officer in the French and Indian War, also known as the Seven Years' War (1756–1763). "I have lately receiv'd a Number of new Pamphlets from England and France, among which is a Piece of Voltaire's on the Subject of Religious Toleration," Franklin wrote. "I will give you a Passage of it," Franklin wrote, "which being read here at a Time when we are torn to Pieces by Factions religious and civil, shows us that while we sit for our Picture to that able Painter, tis no small Advantage to us, that he views us at a favourable Distance." After quoting a passage from the pamphlet about Philadelphia and tolerance, Franklin continued: "The Occasion of his Writing this *Traité sur la Tolérance*, was what he calls 'le *Meurtre* de Jean Calas, *commis* dans Toulouse *avec le glaire [glaive] de la Justice*, le 9me Mars 1762?'" "There is in it," Franklin noted of Voltaire's essay, "abundance of good Sense and sound Reasoning, mix'd with some of those Pleasantries that mark the Author as strongly as if he had affix'd his Name." Writing to Samuel Cooper from London on April 14, 1770, Dr. Franklin also mentioned the Calas case. "Mr. Beaumont, a famous Advocate of Paris, the Defender of the Family of Calas," Franklin noted in that letter, "wrote the *Reflexions d'un Etranger desinteressé*, which I send you." "Since Franklin had a good reading knowledge of Italian," Marcello Maestro speculates of Franklin's familiarity with *On Crimes and Punishments*, "it may well be that he was able to acquaint himself with Beccaria's views from the original edition of the book."[174]

The Popularity of Beccaria's Treatise

Because of the general public interest in penal reform, Beccaria's book—in English, Italian, French and other languages—was soon in libraries[175] and the shops of booksellers throughout Europe and the United States.[176] For example, Harvard's well-stocked library in Cambridge, Massachusetts, is known to have contained a copy of Beccaria's treatise before the Revolutionary War broke out. The undergraduate library at Harvard in 1773 contained Beccaria's *Dei delitti e delle pene* as well as works by Montesquieu,

Blackstone, Vattel, Pufendorf, and Burlamaqui.[177] In 1800, a student orator at New Hampshire's Dartmouth College also took up the question "Ought the punishment of Death to be abolished?" And records reflect that at Williams College in Berkshire County, Massachusetts, the Adelphic Union Library owned a copy of Beccaria's treatise as shown in its 1812 catalogue.[178] In one book, *A Well-Regulated Militia*, Saul Cornell writes that "slightly more than a third of all libraries in the period 1777–90 contained a copy of the essay by Beccaria favored by Jefferson."[179]

Not surprisingly, therefore, library catalogs from antebellum America are replete with references to Beccaria's treatise.[180] For instance, an early American catalogue of books belonging to the Charleston Library Society lists two editions of Beccaria's treatise, one published in London in 1769 and another published in London in 1785.[181] "By 1778," historian Aaron Palmer writes of what was then known as the Charles Town Library Society, "the law collection included John Taylor, *Elements of the Civil Law*; Montesquieu, *Persian Letters*; Jacques Burlamaqui, *Principles of Natural Law*; Blackstone's *Commentaries*; and Beccaria, *On Crimes and Punishments*." Although the "gentlemen's library" had only 128 members by 1750, its membership included prominent men such as Henry Laurens and Charles Pinckney.[182] "During the years when Laurens was an active member," another source notes, "the society ordered copies of the works of Vattel, Montesquieu, Pufendorf, Burlamaqui, Sidney, and Beccaria, along with books dealing with the fall of Rome and the political history of Britain."[183] The Charleston Library Society, formed in 1748 after Benjamin Franklin founded the Library Company of Philadelphia in 1731, was the third oldest subscription library in the country. The Company of the Redwood library at Newport, Rhode Island, was formed in 1747, with the New York Society library not formed until 1754.

In Boston, the bookseller Benjamin Guild (1749–1792) is also known to have stocked Beccaria's treatise. As one source notes: "Benjamin Guild of the Boston Bookstore offered a general stock of books among which are listed Beccaria *On Crimes and Punishments* and Voltaire's *General History* in French." *On Crimes and Punishments* is thus listed in the *New Select Catalogue of Benjamin Guild's Circulating Library, Containing Principally Novels, Voyages, Travels, Poetry, Periodical Publications, and Books of Entertainment at the Boston Book-Store, No. 59, Cornhill* (1789). Guild, a tutor at Harvard College starting in 1776, was said in a letter to John Adams to have "acquitted himself with Capacity and Honours" in that role and to have gone abroad "to enlarge his Knowledge of the World, to extend his Connections and make useful Observations of which he is very capable." Guild—whose name appears in correspondence between John Quincy Adams and John Adams, and whose "copy write" services are referenced in a 1790 letter from Mary Smith Cranch to Abigail Adams—spent time in both France and the Netherlands, and in 1784 married Elizabeth Quincy (1757–1825), a daughter of Colonel Josiah Quincy. Before that marriage, John Thaxter—writing from Amsterdam—informed Abigail Adams via a July 1781 letter that "Mr. Guild has this moment come in to see me," with Thaxter adding: "I never in my life saw a Man more matrimonially mad, and more impatient to get home."[184] Notably, an early nineteenth-century Boston Atheneum library catalogue, from Guild's native city, lists a "Lond. 1770" edition of *On Crimes and Punishments* on "Shelf 466," while a Yale College catalogue, dated 1808, reflects a 1786 edition of Beccaria's treatise in that collection.[185]

And Beccaria's treatise did not just sit on shelves; it was put to use. As historian A. London Fell writes: "in an anonymous essay of 1783, addressed to the people of South Carolina in connection with the formation of its constitution, the author frequently cites and quotes a variety of writers such as Beccaria, Montesquieu, Blackstone, Puffendorf, Virgil, and Cicero."[186] Today, not surprisingly, the libraries of major universities, such as Harvard and Yale, still contain multiple copies of Beccaria's treatise—and not just in

English.[187] One broadside, created in 1787 by publisher Robert Smith Jr., actually came out the same year that America's founders met in Philadelphia to draft the U.S. Constitution. Addressed "To the public" and "Friends and countrymen," that broadside touted "the benefits of a well-regulated news-paper," noting that "[a] number of gentlemen, impressed with this idea, have determined to give their assistance to publish a news-paper in this city, under the title of *The evening chronicle, or, the Philadelphia advertiser*." On the verso, or opposite side of the sheet, it read: "Philadelphia, January 5th, 1787. To the patron of fine arts." Also included was the proposal for printing by subscription Beccaria's *On Crimes and Punishments*.[188]

Eighteenth and nineteenth century auctions, conducted after the death of prominent figures, also show the popularity of *On Crimes and Punishments*.[189] A catalogue of "the Late Right Honourable Denis Daly," published in Dublin in 1792, lists a 1767 Dublin edition of Beccaria's treatise in a list of books to be auctioned in that city. A catalogue of the library of "Richard Wright, M.D.," published in Scotland Yard, also lists a 1764 edition of Beccaria's treatise to be sold at auction in 1787. Similarly, *A Catalogue of the Greater Portion of the Library of the Late Edmond Malone, Esq.*, published in London in 1818, lists a 1766 edition of *Dei delitti e delle pene* and a 1767 Dublin edition of Beccaria's "Essay on Crimes and Punishments" to be sold by "Mr. Sotheby." In still another London catalogue, printed in 1829, the catalogue lists a 1780 edition of *Dei delitti e delle pene*, "*fine paper, blue morocco, borders of gold*," to be sold at auction among other books.[190] The growing popularity of Beccaria's treatise over time in the U.S. can be further glimpsed from an auction that took place in Philadelphia on September 9, 1830. That auction, of the stock of either a law bookseller or publisher, offered for sale forty-five copies of Beccaria's writings.[191]

By the time Americans declared their independence from Great Britain, the European Enlightenment—including on the issue of penal reform—was well underway, with reformist ideas advancing alongside, indeed as part of, the American Revolution itself. "[T]he European Enlightenment, or *Illuminismo*, as the Italians call it," notes historian Antonio Pace, was "that cheerful moment in the history of western civilization characterized by a dominant faith in the power of man's rational faculty to plumb the physical and moral universe and, through the diffusion of knowledge, to achieve a sort of terrestrial paradise." Milan—the capital of Lombardy—was one of the Enlightenment's epicenters and, in Pace's words, was "actively involved in the social and intellectual ferment of the time." Following the publication of Beccaria's treatise in 1764, everyone from European monarchs to French *philosophes* took notice, as did educated Americans thousands of miles away from the locale where Beccaria himself had first scrawled out his ideas. Milan itself was benefiting at that time from a vigorous, multi-cultural exchange of ideas. "Although the province of Lombardy was an appanage of the House of Austria," Pace explains, "liberality and reform were the order of the day, and under the generous rule of Maria Theresa and Joseph II, and the even more progressive and pro-Italian direction of the minister plenipotentiary Count Karl Joseph von Firmian, Milan was abreast of what was going on in the rest of Europe beyond the Alps."[192]

In America, the prominent European-educated Philadelphia physician, Benjamin Rush, and a leading Pennsylvania lawyer, William Bradford, Jr., were among Beccaria's sturdiest admirers. An early convert to abolition, Dr. Rush expressed admiration for Beccaria's ideas before the adoption of the U.S. Constitution as he sought to abolish capital punishment in America. As historian David Brion Davis, an expert on America's anti-death penalty movement, once wrote: "Benjamin Rush, whose studies in pathology had convinced him that crime resulted from a disease of the moral sense, gave an address in 1787 advocating the total abolition of the death penalty. Borrowing from Beccaria's *Essay*, Rush answered critics in 1792 with his *Considerations on the Injustice and Impolity of Punish-*

ing Murder by Death." "Joined by William Bradford, the attorney general of Pennsylvania," Davis emphasized in one article, "Rush was instrumental in achieving a compromise between total abolition and regulation of executions."

In 1794, Pennsylvania — at the urging of Quakers and other civic leaders — passed a novel law dividing murder into degrees, putting in place what Davis aptly called "a unique system for diminishing the number of cases to which the death penalty might be applied and setting an example to be followed by other states during the next half century."[193] Destined to become the nation's top lawyer, Bradford had attended Princeton — then known as the College of New Jersey — with James Madison. There, the two young men became close friends, referring to each other as "Jemmy" and "Billey" in their letters to one another. Bradford — like Dr. Rush — looked to Beccaria for guidance, with Madison himself playing a crucial role in the formulation of the U.S. Bill of Rights. In a February 1793 letter to her "dear Child" Abigail Adams Smith, Abigail Adams herself wrote of "the Nature and disposition of the humane Heart," warned of "a Government not properly balanced," and the need to "establish a good Government upon a solid Basis." "[T]he 17 Cent[u]ry," Abigail added in discussing "the French Arms over the Prussians & Austerians" in her letter, "is staind with their crimes & cruelties."[194]

William Bradford — as reflected in the 1792 legislative report he wrote — even had contact with Luigi Castiglioni, the Italian nobleman he believed to be Cesare Beccaria's nephew. As noted by Bradford in his later published report, *An Enquiry How Far the Punishment of Death Is Necessary in Pennsylvania* (1793), Beccaria's nephew — or at least someone believed to be Beccaria's relative — had traveled to America and communicated directly with Bradford on criminal law issues. "I understood from the nephew of Marquis Beccaria, while he was in America," Bradford wrote, without identifying the nephew by name, that "beneficial effects" had resulted from distinguishing between criminals "armed with dangerous and mortal weapons" and those without any "violent intentions."[195] The Italian traveler, the evidence suggests, was almost certainly Luigi Castiglioni, the botanist from Milan who may not have been Beccaria's nephew but who — to gain better entrée to American elites — naturally would have basked in the ascribed familial association with Beccaria in any event. Castiglioni traveled throughout North America from 1785 to 1787, and later recorded his extensive observations about American life decades before Alexis de Tocqueville, the more famed traveler, wrote *Democracy in America.*[196]

Luigi Castiglioni (1757–1832) planned his overseas trip the old-fashioned way, getting a sought-after letter of introduction from Benjamin Franklin, who then provided entrée to other prominent men. "Yesterday morning I went to Mr. Franklin's in Passy, to whom I presented your letter, and who received me with all the cordiality imaginable," Castiglioni reported by letter in 1784 to the Lombard astronomer and mathematician Paolo Frisi, who had provided Castiglioni with an initial letter of introduction to the eminent Dr. Franklin. Before Frisi died in November of that year, Castiglioni also penned a letter in October 1784 thanking Frisi, his learned colleague, for putting him in touch with so many notable people in Paris, including "Mr. Franklin," a man "worth knowing for his affability and character no less than for his fame," Castiglioni reported. Franklin and others had "showered their attentions upon me," Castiglioni wrote, noting how Franklin "favored me with letters for London and more distant regions."

Franklin himself thanked Frisi for making the introduction, with Franklin describing Castiglioni — one of many Italian scientists Franklin respected — as "a gentleman so intelligent and so amiable."[197] And as it turned out, Castiglioni, of Milan, had an ambitious itinerary, visiting all thirteen American states between 1785 and 1787, effectively using the introduction to Benjamin Franklin he procured through his association with Frisi, the noted Milan engineer and mathematician. Frisi — who had studied Franklin's ideas on electricity and how to protect buildings from lightning—would once write of how "America, which had hitherto been unable to defend herself against European artillery, taught Europe how to defend herself against fire from the sky." The direct beneficiary of Dr. Franklin's kindness, Castiglioni would write to Frisi to tell him of how Franklin had received him "with all the cordiality imaginable."

In his Italian travelogue, *Viaggio negli Stati Uniti dell'America Settentrionale fatto negli anni 1785, 1786, e 1787*, Castiglioni mainly took note of the types of flora and fauna in various American locales. "The most common trees are elm, spruce, hemlock, sugar maple, Pennsylvania maple, and beech," Castiglioni recorded of his time in the territory of Vermont. In recording his observations of Philadelphia, he further noted that some of its streets were named "after American trees, such as Chestnut, Walnut, and Spruce." In terms of American law, Castiglioni's *Viaggio* also recorded a few choice tidbits about how penal reforms were unfolding in America, including in Philadelphia, following the publication of *On Crimes and Punishments*. Castiglioni's overseas trip was by no means unique in that era, especially among the privileged class. "Many other educated Italians," Valentine Belfiglio emphasizes in his article on Italian culture in eighteenth-century Philadelphia, "visited Philadelphia during the eighteenth century as part of their American tours."[198] But Castiglioni—because of his special access to high-level government officials—did have a unique perspective, with the Italian botanist making special note on his trip of the history and influence of Pennsylvania's Quakers, or "the Society of Friends."[199] At that time, the inhabitants of continental Europe, including Castiglioni, had a fascination with Quakers, with Voltaire devoting four published letters to the Quakers in his *Letters Concerning the English Nation*.[200]

In the late seventeenth century, Pennsylvanians—under the leadership of the province's founder William Penn—had adopted in 1682 what became popularly known as the "Great Law," which severely restricted the availability of death sentences as a punishment for crime. Born in 1644 in London, William Penn had attended the University of Oxford and became a violence-loathing, peace-loving Quaker. He had traveled to Ireland in 1666 to take care of his father's property in the county of Cork, but was, in an era rife with religious intolerance, imprisoned by local officials because of his religious convictions. To pay off a debt owed to his father, the English Crown ultimately gave William Penn a grant of territory in North America in 1681, with Penn and several of his friends sailing for America in 1682 to make a new life for themselves. Along with urging religious freedom, Penn and his fellow Quakers—both in England and America—also actively promoted penal reform and sought to make punishments less horrific in nature. In the place of executions, the Quakers urged incarceration and silent introspection for the purpose of reforming offenders. "As they argued," writes one criminologist, "solitary cells would allow for penitence on the part of the offender." "To reflect this humanitarian outlook," that criminologist notes, "prisons were called penitentiaries."[201] This Quaker perspective made an impact on America's founders, who—even if not of the Quaker sect—became circumspect about rushing to judgment and resorting to harsh punishments. John Adams thought "[p]enitence must precede pardon"; Thomas Jefferson wrote that "[t]he sword of the law should never fall but on those whose guilt is so apparent as to be pronounced by their friends as well as foes"; and Thomas Paine opined in 1795 that "[a]n avidity to punish is always dangerous to liberty" for "[i]t leads men to misinterpret and to misapply even the best of laws."[202]

Luigi Castiglioni, who sailed to America more than a century after William Penn made the voyage,[203] was a respected botanist and the nephew of Beccaria's close associates, Pietro and Alessandro Verri.[204] As historian Antonio Pace writes: "Luigi's mother was a member of the large and influential Verri clan and sister of those two sparks of the Milanese Enlightenment, Pietro and Alessandro." In April 1785, Castiglioni—after spending time elsewhere in Europe—sailed into the English Channel aboard a ship bound for America, later recording his observations about the New World and all the discoveries he made there. In terms of his background, Castiglioni—about whom relatively little is known—appears to have studied with Giovanni Scopoli before his travels. Scopoli was a Professor of Chemistry and Botany at the University of Pavia, where Beccaria attended and studied law. Despite whatever language difficulties might have been present, Castiglioni—as the Rev. Dr. Jeremy Belknap put it—"speaks English well." Recommended to Benjamin Franklin in 1784 by Sir Joseph Banks, the president of the Royal Society of London, as a "well informed young man," Castiglioni was introduced to the Rev. Jeremy Belknap as "a perfect master of Botany"; described in 1785 as "a true disciple of Linnaeus" by Dr. Aaron Dexter of Boston; and had contact with George Washington, Benjamin Franklin, Benjamin Rush and Yale College president Ezra Stiles, among many other prominent Americans.[205]

An American clergyman who wrote a three-volume text, *The History of New-Hampshire*, Dr. Jeremy Belknap had heard about Castiglioni from Manasseh Culter in 1785. Culter had written Belknap of "the Count Castiglioni, an Italian gentleman from Milan, who is on his tour through the United States, principally with a view of examining their natural productions." In his own history of New Hampshire, Belknap had written of how the Quakers—four of whom were executed in Boston—were previously targeted by "a succession of sanguinary laws," "of which imprisonment, whipping, cutting off the ears, boring the tongue with an hot iron, and banishment on pain of death, were the terrible sanctions." Belknap had also written of how men had "lived to see the folly and incompetency of such sanguinary laws," calling specific punishments—whether inflicted by Indians or Europeans—"*cruel*" acts. As Belknap wrote of Indian tribes in his New Hampshire history: "We are struck with horror, when we hear of their binding the victim to the stake, biting off his nails, tearing out his hair by the roots, pulling out his tongue, boring out his eyes, sticking his skin full of lighted pitch-wood, half roasting him at the fire, then making him run for their diversion, till he faints and dies under the blows which they give him on every part of his body." "But is it not as dreadful," Belknap reasoned, "to read of an unhappy wretch, sewed up in a sack full of serpents and thrown into the sea, or broiled in a red hot iron chair; or mangled by lions and tigers, after having spent his strength to combat them for the diversion of the spectators in an amphitheatre? and yet these were punishments among the Romans in the politest ages of the empire." "If civilized nations, and those who profess the most merciful religion that ever blessed the world, have practiced these cruelties," Belknap added, "what could be expected of men who were strangers to every degree of refinement either civil or mental?"[206]

The diary entries of prominent Americans, however brief, give a flavor for Castiglioni's free-ranging U.S. tour, providing a glimpse of those with whom he mingled and dined. The Rev. Thomas Smith wrote this entry for July 29, 1785, a reference to Gov. John Hancock and Castiglioni: "The governor and lady here; an Italian Count also."[207] George Washington's diary for 1785 contains these entries, showing that Castiglioni spent Christmas at Mount Vernon: "Sunday, December 25—Count Castiglioni came here to dinner. December 29—Count Castiglioni went away after breakfast on his tour to the southward."[208] The diary entry of Ezra Stiles also contains this entry for August 29, 1786: "This day I was visited by the ingenious young Count Castaglioni an Italian Nobleman from Milan, on his Travels thro' the United States. He was educated in the University of Pavia 20 Miles from Milan: & has travelled from Georgia to beyond Boston, & up North River into Vermont."[209] And Noah Webster's diary contains these entries for December 23, 1785, and March 12, 1787, respectively: "Read Lectures to a larger audience. Introduced to the Count Castiglioni, an Italian Nobleman, who attends the Lect." "Dine at Mr. Logan's at Germantown. [H]e has a good estate, but not an esteemable man. Count Castiglioni & Mr. Vaughn dine there."[210]

Castiglioni, the Italian who may or may not have been related to Cesare Beccaria's family in some fashion,[211] was described this way by John Vaughan, the librarian and corresponding secretary of the American Philosophical Society: "Count Castiglioni is of a family of very ancient nobility, being a knight of one of the highest orders of Europe. Is of great influence in his country as Nephew to the Gov. of Milan, is devoted to science & related to Father Becharia."[212] Cesare Beccaria and the distinguished Italian scientist called "Father Beccaria," were not related as far as is known, at least not in any close or identifiable manner. Father Beccaria's principal work was his treatise *Dell' Elettricismo Naturale ed Artificiale* (1753), translated into English in 1776. Whatever Castiglioni's actual familial relationships, that Castiglioni spent four days at Mount Vernon and got a tour of Monticello shows that the young botanist had important social connections.[213] In his *Viaggio*, his published travelogue, Castiglioni specifically notes that, during his travels in Virginia, he paid a special visit to the Charlottesville area, writing as follows: "[O]n the morning of the 20th of May I climbed to the top of one of the Southwest Mountains, where stands the villa of Monticello belonging to His Excellency Mr. Thomas Jefferson, at present Ambassador of the United States in Paris."[214]

Tellingly, upon his return to Europe, Castiglioni also made the acquaintance of William Short, Thomas Jefferson's private secretary in Paris. Records of the American Philosophical Society indicate that Short, while in Europe, met Luigi Castiglioni and the Marchioness Paola Castiglioni-Litta (1751–1846), the latter of whom opened a famous salon in Milan.[215] At that time, salons were breeding grounds for intellectual curiosity and advancement. As one source reports of Cesare Beccaria himself: "Beccaria knew practically nothing about crime and punishment until he was selected by the intellectual salon to devote time to the topic." Only with the assignment given to him by Pietro Verri in the Milanese salon, that source relays, was Beccaria—with the assistance of Pietro and Pietro's brother Alessandro—able to get "the help and the suggestions he needed" to write *On Crimes and Punishments.* Castiglioni—along with a handful of other respected men from abroad, including the much-revered penal reformer John Howard—was ultimately named as a "Foreign Member" of the American Academy of Arts and Sciences, an organization once led by John Adams; whose corresponding secretary was John Quincy Adams; and whose American membership included Alexander Hamilton, Thomas Jefferson, Oliver Ellsworth, John Jay, Benjamin Rush, John Trumbull, Noah Webster and others.[216]

While working his way across America, Castiglioni systematically befriended a wide range of people, even attending meetings of the prestigious American Philosophical Society, the country's first scholarly association. Indeed, on July 21, 1786, Castiglioni was voted into its august membership. This honor was simultaneously bestowed upon more than thirty others, including distinguished European writers and doctors such as London's physician-editor Benjamin Vaughan, a friend of Benjamin Franklin. The minutes of the American Philosophical Society show that Castiglioni attended meetings on December 15, 1786, and March 2, 1787. In his travels in Pennsylvania, where he spent time with both Franklin and Dr. Rush, Castiglioni was, predictably, accompanied at times by his friend Giuseppe Mussi, the Philadelphia merchant who once called Milan home. The American Philosophical Society, into which Castiglioni was inducted, was composed of America's most highly influential scientists and professionals, with its list of officers for 1770–1771 including Franklin as president and Dr. Rush as curator. Notably, both Benjamin Franklin and Benjamin Rush—likely at Castiglioni's instance—were in turn elected in 1786, in a reciprocal fashion, to the Italian Società Patriottica. That society, instituted by Empress Maria Theresa, was based in Castiglioni's native city of Milan.[217] "Castiglioni himself," one historian notes, "became a member of the Società in 1789, and president in 1792."[218]

One political leader Castiglioni met on his travels — William Bradford, Jr. — was especially influential in shaping American penal reform. In his 1793 essay, *An Enquiry How Far the Punishment of Death Is Necessary in Pennsylvania*,[219] Bradford not only advocated for the death penalty's abolition for all crimes except murder, but he said of Pennsylvania that "as soon as the principles of Beccaria were disseminated, they found a soil that was prepared to receive them."[220] Indeed, even before the appearance of Beccaria's book, some public sentiment disfavored executions, with Francis Bernard — the British governor of the Massachusetts Bay colony — acknowledging the "popular prejudices against capital punishments in this country" in a 1761 speech to Massachusetts legislators. Excerpts from Bradford's essay — which gave voice to some of the concerns — were reprinted in *The New-York Magazine* in 1793, with Bradford asserting that any punishment that is not absolutely necessary constitutes "a cruel and tyrannical act."[221] Most revealing, perhaps, as regards Bradford's mindset, however, is a letter that Bradford wrote to Castiglioni before Bradford penned his *Enquiry*. In his 1786 letter to Luigi Castiglioni, accompanied by a recent English translation of *On Crimes and Punishments*, Cesare Beccaria's famous book, Bradford wrote that the new American edition is "a new proof of the veneration that my fellow citizens entertain for the sentiments *of your relative*."

Written from Philadelphia on August 10, 1786, during the summer in which Castiglioni was there, Bradford's letter to Castiglioni began: "I have the honor to present you with an American copy of the famous book on *Crimes and Punishments* that will be delivered to you by the bearer of this letter." After noting how his fellow countrymen venerated Beccaria's opinions, Bradford's lengthy letter — focused on Beccaria's treatise — continued:

> I should like it to be known by the author of this book, so well received in the Old World, that his efforts to extend the domain of humanity have been crowned in the New World with the happiest success. Long before the recent Revolution this book was common among lettered persons of Pennsylvania, who admired its principles without daring to hope that they could be adopted in legislation, since we copied the laws of England, to whose laws we were subject. However, as soon as we were free of political bonds, this humanitarian system, long admired in secret, was publicly adopted and incorporated by the Constitution of the State, which, spurred by the influence of this benign spirit, ordered the legislative bodies to render penalties less bloody and, in general, more proportionate to the crimes. The necessity of establishing our political existence and the concerns that multiply about a nascent republic kept the legislative bodies from undertaking this beneficial reform, but under the pressure of public opinion that it be no longer deferred, those august tribunals have turned their hand to this important task. A plan has already been drafted and approved, and it has been published in order to see the reaction of the citizens; and all that remains is for the coming session of the General Assembly to give it legal force. Then, when this change in our penal laws has taken place, the lash, branding, mutilation, and death will be replaced by strenuous and continuous labor for variable periods of time, and instead of one hundred sixty capital crimes in the country from which we have recently separated, there will be only four in Pennsylvania. Then a happy new era will begin, and I dare hope that, instructed by experience, Pennsylvania will persevere in these ideas until that point of perfection is approached at which *every punishment will be public, immediate, and mandatory, the smallest possible in the given instance, proportionate to the crime, and determined by the laws*.

In 1786, the Pennsylvania legislature passed "An Act Amending the Penal Laws of This State," substituting "hard labor, publicly and disgracefully imposed" as the punishment for crimes formerly made capital in nature. Bradford specifically credited *On Crimes and Punishments* with altering public attitudes about American penal codes. As Bradford wrote to Castiglioni in his August 1786 letter:

> One must attribute mainly to this excellent book the honor of this revolution in our penal code. The name of Beccaria has become familiar in Pennsylvania, his authority has become great, and his principles have spread among all classes of persons and impressed themselves deeply in the hearts of our citizens. You yourself must have noticed the influence of these precepts in the other American states. The tyranny of prejudice and injustice has fallen, the voice of a philosopher has stilled the outcries of the masses, and although a bloody system may still survive in the laws of many of our states, nevertheless the beneficent spirit sown by Beccaria works secretly in behalf of the accused, moderating the rigor of the laws and tempering justice with compassion.

"I am," Bradford signed off, "Respectfully yours."[222]

The Science of Legislation

On Crimes and Punishments was not the only Italian treatise America's Founding Fathers read and admired. Gaetano Filangieri's multi-volume treatise, *La Scienza della Legislazione*, which translates as *The Science of Legislation*, was also nearly as influential as Beccaria's *On Crimes and Punishments*.[223] An Italian nobleman who studied law, Filangieri dreamed of living in America. Writing to Benjamin Franklin on December 2, 1782, Filangieri explained: "Philadelphia has attracted my gaze ever since I was a child. I have so gotten used to consider it the only country in which I can be happy that my imagination cannot rid itself of this idea." "Perhaps my works of legislation," Filangieri told Franklin, "could persuade you to invite me to contribute to the great code of laws that is being prepared in the United Provinces of America, the laws of which must decide not only their fate, but also that of this new hemisphere?" "What more reasonable motive could I give to justify my departure?" Filangieri asked, further explaining to Franklin: "I could also, in principle, ask my court permission to leave for a while, to not exacerbate it with a permanent dimension; but, once in America, who could take me back to Europe! Could I, from the exile of virtue, from the fatherland of heroes, from the cities of brothers, desire a return to a country which is corrupted by vice and degraded to serfdom?" "Could ever my soul, accustomed to the delight of an emerging liberty," Filangieri mused, "adapt again to the spectacle of an omnipotent despotic authority in the hands of a single man?"[224] With European locales still ruled by despotic monarchs, some blatantly tyrannical and others more enlightened, many Europeans—Filangieri included—saw America's republic, and its experiment with democratic principles, as an enlightened refuge.

Filangieri, whose original plan contemplated a massive, seven-volume treatise, was dissatisfied with then-existing works on the law, saying, for example, that "some, like Montesquieu, have dealt with what has been done rather than what needs to be done" and that "no one has yet made of this vast subject a clear and orderly science, uniting means with rules and theory with practice." In *The Science of Legislation*, which Alexander Hamilton got a translation of in 1793 from Edinburgh bookseller Samuel Paterson, Filangieri made a special appeal to Americans. "Free citizens of independent America," he wrote, condemning the death penalty being decreed for military deserters, "you are too virtuous and too enlightened not to know that by winning the right to govern yourselves, you have contracted in the eyes of the universe the sacred duty of being wiser, more moderate, and happier than all other peoples." "Why, in forming the great Code that is expected of you," Filangieri wrote, "should you not remember that you are, in the great Continent which you inhabit, the only depository of liberty and the most dire example for despotism and tyranny?" "Do you not realize," Filangieri emphasized, "that such a law would offer to the vile partisans of despotism a means of calumniating liberty …?" "You will have to account before the court of the human race," Filangieri urged, "for all the sophisms that your errors may produce against freedom."[225]

Throughout Europe—and among reform-minded Americans like Benjamin Franklin—Filangieri's treatise was a godsend. As Antonio Pace writes in *Benjamin Franklin and Italy*: "*The Science of Legislation* won immediate and universal acclaim from the moment the first two books appeared in 1780." "He was," Pace writes of Filangieri, "received with special warmth by the French *philosophes*, for they recognized in Filangieri an intellectual brother whose ideas, although inspired in large part by Montesquieu and the Encyclopedists, were tempered in an exciting way by the Italian philosophic tradition of Gravina, Vico, Genovesi, Galiani, and Cesare Beccaria." The Piedmont jurist, Francesco Dalmazzo Vasco, described Filangieri's contribution this way: "Beccaria went directly and brilliantly to the point and sowed the seeds of the useful truths which aroused the interest of the enlightened men of Europe in the establishment of a just and peaceful society, while Filangieri was the first man who had enough courage, patience and intelligence to write out a complete plan of criminal legislation." Like Beccaria, Filangieri called for clear and precise laws, a just proportion between crimes and punishments, and the abolition of torture. To Benjamin Franklin himself, Filangieri—who sought to eliminate the death penalty for all crimes except treason and murder—wrote of trying to participate in some way in advising American lawmakers.[226]

A portion of *The Science of Legislation* dealt specifically with the criminal law, and Filangieri—who served as a courtier to King Ferdinando IV of Naples from 1777 to 1783—wrote of "sparing the guilty" and the law's purpose as being to prevent crimes. "[T]he legislator," he advised, "ought not to go beyond the severity in punishment which is necessary to repress the vicious intentions which result in crime."[227] According to Filangieri, "[t]here are five classes of rights, and, consequently, five kinds of penalties." "There are," he wrote, "capital punishments, infamous punishments, fines, incarceration, and deprivation of municipal privileges." In examining "the general principles which should direct their application," Filangieri explained, "we can the more easily develop the real theory of the relation and proportion of punishment or penalties with crime." While Montesquieu and Beccaria had already pioneered the concept of proportionality, Filangieri had his own thoughts on how the proportionality principle should be put into practice. "Although Filangieri did not subscribe to Beccaria's outright stand against capital punishment," explains historian Marcello Maestro, "he nevertheless made it clear that he wanted the application of the death penalty reduced to a minimum; and in accordance with the principle of a right proportion between crimes and punishments he asked that it be reserved only for those guilty of treason or deliberate murder."

In his *Italian Journey*, the German writer and poet Johann Wolfgang von Goethe, who got to know Filangieri personally, made clear that Filangieri was particularly fond of talking about Montesquieu and Beccaria. As Goethe recorded on March 5, 1787:

During the last few days I have made the acquaintance of a remarkable man, the Cavaliere Filangieri, who is well known for his work *Science of Legislation*. He is one of those noble-hearted young men to whom the happiness and freedom of mankind is a goal they never lose sight of. His manners are those of a gentleman and a man of the world, but they are tempered by a delicate moral sense which pervades his whole personality and radiates charmingly from his speech and behavior. He is devoted to his King and the present monarchy, even though he does not approve of everything that is going on. He is also oppressed by his fears of Joseph II. The thought of a despot, even as a phantom possibility, is horrible to noble minds. He told me quite frankly what Naples might expect from this man. He likes to talk about Montesquieu, Beccaria and his own writings — all in the same spirit of good will and of a sincere youthful desire to do good. He must still be in his thirties.[228]

Benjamin Franklin first obtained copies of the first two volumes of Filangieri's comprehensive work from Luigi Pio, the *chargé d'affaires* of the Kingdom of Naples in Paris. Luigi Pio was a close friend of Filangieri, and wrote to him in 1781 of his dealings with Franklin, just a year after the first two volumes of Filangieri's treatise, *The Science of Legislation*, appeared. In his letter of September 11, 1781, Pio wrote: "Mr. Franklin, to whom I am bound by feelings of friendship, expressed the desire of reading your work, of which I had talked to him. I am glad I was able to satisfy him." "To show his gratitude," Pio wrote of Franklin, "the American philosopher gave me a large quarto edition of his essays on scientific experiments and I have been reading them with great enjoyment." Pio's letter to Filangieri continued: "Mr. Franklin reads Italian rather slowly, but he understands it perfectly well. He told me that he derives much pleasure from your theories which — these are his words — are presented with the utmost clarity and precision. He asked me to tell you that he is anxiously waiting for the volumes dealing with criminal legislation because they will be of special interest to his nation, still needing to be enlightened on this subject." A few days after sending this letter, Pio wrote to Filangieri again, telling him that Dr. Franklin had given him some of his own writings, asking Pio to send them to Filangieri as a gift. After this shipment reached Naples after a long delay, Filangieri thanked Franklin for the "precious gift." In his August 24, 1782 letter, Filangieri told Franklin that he had almost finished the criminal law portions of his work, adding that it would consist of two components: one concerning procedure, and one dealing with penal codes. On December 2, 1782, Filangieri again wrote Franklin to tell him that the criminal law portion of his work had gone to the presses. "Filangieri's two volumes on criminal law," Marcello Maestro reports, "were published in the summer and fall of 1783."

In spite of Filangieri's desire to emigrate to America, Dr. Franklin dissuaded Filangieri from leaving Italy in 1783. The following year, however, Franklin encouraged Filangieri, albeit unsuccessfully, to try to be nominated as a representative of the Bourbon government to the new republic. "With regard to your Project of removing to America," Franklin had advised in 1783, "tho' I am sure that a Person of your Knowledge, just Sentiments, and useful Talents would be a valuable Acquisition for our Country I cannot encourage you to undertake hastily such a Voyage; because for a Man to expatriate himself is a serious Business, and should be well considered, especially where the Distance is so great, and the Expence of removing thither with a Family, and of returning if the Country should not suit you, will be so heavy." While Filangieri's letters to Dr. Franklin were written in Italian, Franklin's letters to Filangieri were in English. Though he occasionally wrote letters in Italian to Italian correspondents with less proficiency in English, Franklin mostly preferred writing in English, his native tongue, and receiving letters in Italian, as he told his fellow scientist and friend Giambattista Beccaria: "I am pleased to hear that you read English, although you do not write it. I am in the same case with Italian. Hence we can correspond, if this pleases you, more easily if each of us writes his own language."

Filangieri's multi-volume treatise, published from 1780 to 1783 and later translated into English in 1792 and 1806, sparked further American debate about capital punishment. Filangieri—an adherent of natural law—believed that "man in the state of nature has the right to life" and "cannot renounce this right," though he argued "he can lose it as a result of crime." "Filangieri does not advocate the abolition of Capital Punishment," one English barrister recorded in 1865 in editing the anti-death penalty writings of another European, University of Heidelberg professor Karl J. A. Mittermaier, "but limits the infliction of death to a few crimes, viz., murder with intent after cold-blooded deliberation (a sangue freddo), treason, and high treason." In that particular source, Cesare Beccaria's *Dei delitti e delle pene* was called a "celebrated and influential work" that had "wide circulation," with "thirty Italian editions" and "four editions of the English translation" published from 1767 to 1778. "Filangieri differs from Beccaria with regard to the punishment of death, and opposes his reasoning without mentioning his name," that compilation of Professor Mittermaier's writings reports, though it emphasizes in a footnote that the 1792 and 1806 English-language translations—the latter by Sir Robert Clayton—did not translate the criminal law portions of Filangieri's work. "Those who remember what draconic severity prevailed in our Criminal Code at the time when this translation was published," the English barrister, John Macrae Moir, recalled in his 1865 book, *Capital Punishment*, of the 1806 translation, "will agree with us in thinking that Sir R. Clayton was mistaken, both in his Yankeelike praise of the English Government, and in his exaggerated laudation of English law."

Born in Naples in 1752, Filangieri died there in 1788 at the age of thirty-six, but not before cementing a pen-pal friendship via correspondence with Benjamin Franklin, who first read Filangieri's treatise when it appeared in Paris. In 1782 Filangieri had sent Franklin the first volumes of his work and Franklin asked to receive multiple copies of his later writings. Having been ill for nearly three months, Franklin wrote Filangieri from Passy on January 11, 1783, after receiving two letters from him. "The two first Volumes of your excellent Work, which were put into my hands by M. Pio," Franklin wrote, "I perus'd with great pleasure." Franklin further noted: "They are also much esteem'd by some very judicious Persons to whom I have lent them. I should have been glad of another Copy for one of those Friends, who is very desirous of procuring it, but I suppose those you mention to have sent to M. Pio did not arrive." "I was glad to learn, that you were proceeding to consider the criminal Laws," Franklin added, explaining: "None have more need of Reformation. They are every where in so great Disorder, and so much Injustice is committed in the Execution of them, that I have been sometimes inclin'd to imagine, less would exist in the World if there were no such Laws, and the Punishment of Injuries were left to private Resentment." "I am glad therefore," Franklin concluded, "that you have not suffered yourself to be discouraged by any objections or Apprehensions, and that we may soon expect the Satisfaction of seeing the two Volumes on that Subject which you have now under the Press."

Not only did Franklin publicize Filangieri's multi-volume treatise in American circles, but Franklin sent him French translations of American state constitutions as well as a copy of the U.S. Constitution, which would be translated into Italian.[229] "Believing it may [be] a Matter of some Curiosity to you, to know what is doing in this Part of the World respecting Legislation," Franklin wrote to Filangieri from Philadelphia on October 14, 1787, "I send you inclos'd a Copy of the new federal Constitution propos'd by a Convention of the States." "We are now so remote from each other," Franklin noted, "that it is difficult to keep up a regular Correspondence between us, and it is long since I had the Pleasure of hearing from you."[230] In that letter, Franklin asked for nine copies of book three of Filangieri's treatise dealing with the criminal law and eight copies of Filangieri's other books dealing with subjects such as education, religion and property.[231] Unfortunately, Franklin's letter—arriving in Italy in July 1788, and sent to his fellow soulmate interested in penal reform—arrived too late for Filangieri to read it. In a letter written on September 27, 1788, that did not reach Franklin until early 1789, Filangieri's wife reported her spouse's death. As her letter advised: "The Chevalier Gaetano Filangieri, my husband and my friend, is no more. He died on the 21st of July, in the flower of his age, the victim of a cruel disease, and with him my happiness is gone."[232]

In *The Politics of Enlightenment*, a book about Filangieri's work, another author, Vincenzo Ferrone, emphasizes "how strongly contemporaries felt there was a connection between Filangieri's work and the American experience." The 1807 Leghorn edition of the *Scienza della Legislazione*, Ferrone notes, was dedicated to Thomas Jefferson, while a preceding edition, issued in 1799, was dedicated to George Washington.[233] Still, as between Beccaria's treatise and Filangieri's treatise, *On Crimes and Punishments*—if William Bradford's 1786 letter is any indication—must be considered the most important of the two texts. Beccaria's treatise came first, while Filangieri's followed. Also, unlike *The Science of Legislation*, *On Crimes and Punishments* was published before the Revolutionary War and the drafting of the Declaration of Independence. While Filangieri's Italian treatise appeared before the U.S. Constitution and the Bill of Rights were drafted, the criminal law portions of Filangieri's treatise were not translated into English by then, making them less accessible. Dr. Franklin, with his felicity for foreign languages, had read them in Italian, but Filangieri's ideas on the criminal law were not nearly as widely distributed in America by 1787 as Beccaria's treatise. In the book on Professor Mittermaier's scholarly writings, one finds the same perspective: "Although of these two Italian writers Filangieri had more learning and depth, Beccaria's treatise made a greater impression on his contemporaries, and had more influence on legislation." The publication of *On Crimes and Punishments*, that source recounts, led to Tuscany's abolition of capital punishment and inspired anti-death penalty advocates throughout the world to set limits on capital punishment.[234]

Beccaria's "Masterly Hand"

The Founding Fathers themselves were avid readers of Beccaria's treatise, described by one source as "a canonical text among the radicals of the late eighteenth century."[235] In 1774, John Dickinson—the successful lawyer and politician from Philadelphia, and one of Pennsylvania's delegates to the First Continental Congress—had, most notably, referred to "[t]he genius of a Beccaria" and "the masterly hand of a Beccaria."[236] Likewise, the Charleston Library Society ordered Beccaria's treatise in 1771 and its library—as reflected in its records—also owned later editions.[237] In Massachusetts, John Hancock's library, consisting of approximately 150 books, also contained "Beccaria on Crimes,"[238] though Hancock's library was much smaller than Jefferson's. If anything, the fact that Beccaria's book was among Hancock's smaller library only serves to confirm its significance. In 1793, Hancock himself urged Massachusetts lawmakers to end capital punishment for burglary. "Degrees of guilt," he contended along Beccarian lines, "demand degrees of Punishment in order to maintain the equity of the Government."[239]

Even before Charleston's library society snapped up a copy of Beccaria's treatise, the Library Company of Philadelphia had ordered a copy. In a letter to Charles Thomson and Thomas Mifflin, written from London on January 27, 1769, Benjamin Franklin noted: "Enclos'd is Bill of Lading and Invoice of the Books you order'd, which I wish safe to hand." The minutes of the Library Company of Philadelphia contain an invoice from William Strahan (1715–1785), a Scottish printer and publisher and a friend of Benjamin Franklin, of the books he shipped for Franklin. Among the books: Giuseppe M. A. Baretti's *An Account of the Manners and Customs of Italy: with Observations on the Mistakes of Some Travellers* (London, 1768); Cesare Beccaria's *An Essay on Crimes and Punishments, Translated from the Italian; with a Commentary attributed to Mons. de Voltaire, Translated from the French* (London, 1767); Samuel Sharp's *Letters from Italy; Describing the Customs and Manners of that Country* (3d ed., London, n.d.); *A View of the Customs, Manners, Drama, etc. of Italy … as They Are Described … by Mr. Baretti* (London, 1768); and Laurence Sterne's *A Sentimental Journey through France and Italy* (London, 1768). Charles Thomson (1729–1824), the Scots-Irishman who became a Sons of Liberty patriot leader in Philadelphia during the Revolutionary War, was married to the sister of Benjamin Harrison, a signer of the Declaration of Independence. Thomson also went on to serve as the secretary of the Continental Congress throughout its existence (1774–1789); to design, with William Barton, the Great Seal of the United States reading "E Pluribus Unum"; and to translate the Bible from Greek. While Thomson became known as "The Sam Adams of Philadelphia," Thomas Mifflin was—at the time of Benjamin Franklin's 1769 letter— then a merchant, having returned from a trip to Europe in 1765. The Library Company of Philadelphia, started by Benjamin Franklin in 1731, still has multiple copies of Beccaria's book in its collection. That collection lists 1767, 1777, 1778, 1780, 1793, 1795 and 1809 editions of Beccaria's treatise as well as the 1766 commentary of Voltaire.[240] Commonplace in both France and England, Beccaria's book has been hailed as "[a]mong the most popular law books in leading colonial domestic libraries."[241]

After the Continental Congress, in 1776, formed the United States of America, forged through the efforts of its leaders and the sacrifice and bloodshed of the Revolutionary War, Beccaria's influence only grew stronger. "Beccaria's treatise," historian David Brion Davis writes, "aroused the enthusiasm of reformers in Europe and America and strongly influenced Catherine II of Russia and Grand Duke Leopold of Tuscany."[242] In the *Edict of the Grand Duke of Tuscany, for the Reform of Criminal Law*, published in England as a pamphlet in 1789, the English-language editor noted that "he is fully persuaded that there are many things in it which are well deserving of *notice* and *imitation*; and that whenever a revisal of our own penal laws shall take place, many useful hints may be derived from this code for their *improvement*." The edict, issued "by the Grace of God" by Peter Leopold, "Prince Royal of Hungary and Bohemia, Archduke of Austria, Grand Duke of Tuscany," labeled existing criminal laws "too severe, in consequence of their having been founded on maxims established either at the unhappy crisis of the Roman empire, or during the troubles of anarchy." The edict abolished "*the pains of death*, together with the different tortures and punishments, which were immoderate, and disproportioned to the transgressions." "And as those who are guilty of the crimes formerly deemed capital … should continue to live, to atone by some good actions for the bad ones they have committed," the edict read, "we order that public labour during the term of their natural life, as the greatest punishment for the men, be substituted for the pain of death, which we abolish."[243]

Neither language nor geography limited the reach of *On Crimes and Punishments*. One English source, from 1787, noted that "many learned and pious men in Europe, like Sir Henry Spelmen, have questioned the propriety and lawfulness of inflicting capital punishment for theft." "The system of satisfactions proposed by Sir Thomas More, and the

Marquis de Beccaria, at the distance of more than two centuries," that source emphasized, "were much nearer an obedience to the infallible law of God, than the sanguinary statutes of any of the Christian Kingdoms are at this day."[244] In another source, one finds reference to an October 31, 1787 letter from Jeremiah Smith—later a Congressman, governor and chief justice of New Hampshire. In that letter to William Plumer, later a governor and U.S. Senator, Smith recounts his studies in the library of the brother of James Otis. After graduating from Rutgers College in 1780, Smith reported: "I spent a year after I left college undetermined which way to shape my course. At length I resolved on the study of the law; and having the offer of my board and a good library to serve as private instructor in a gentleman's family at Barnstable (that of Brigadier Otis, brother of James Otis), I embraced it, and spent a year there, reading under the direction of Mr. Bourne." As Smith's letter specifically recounted: "I perused the books usually read on the Law of Nature and of Nations, and Montesquieu, Beccaria, and Blackstone's *Commentaries*, with some degree of attention; constantly attending the courts, and seeing what practice was to be seen."[245] James Otis—a lawyer in colonial Massachusetts—was an early American patriot who spoke out forcefully against oppressive British policies toward the colonists. His *Rights of the British Colonies Asserted and Proved*, in which he wrote of the "civil rights of the British colonies" and the "grand pillars of liberty," was published in 1763.[246] In *A Vindication of the British Colonies*, reprinted in London in 1769 for the freedom-loving "J. Almon," the ideas of Boston's James Otis on liberty and civil rights reached an even wider audience.[247]

By 1789, forty-eight American libraries and booksellers in different cities are known to have had copies of Beccaria's treatise.[248] And *On Crimes and Punishments*, notes Henry May in *The Enlightenment in America*, was "read increasingly through the 1790s."[249] When Thomas Jefferson advised a prospective law student in 1790, for example, he put together a reading list of forty volumes for the young man. "Of these," writer Emiliana Noether emphasizes, "it is only Beccaria and Blackstone which are listed without title." "Jefferson clearly assumed that anyone who professed an interest in law would already know the name of Beccaria," Noether states, adding: "James Wilson, Associate Justice of the Supreme Court of the United States, in his 1790 lectures on law to students in Philadelphia repeatedly quoted Beccaria on the need for reformation."[250] New York Society Library circulation records also show that, from 1790–1791, Beccaria's treatise was checked out by Anthony Bleecker, a New Yorker who served as a major in the Continental Army in 1775 and later became a merchant and real estate auctioneer; Rev. Dr. William Linn, a New York City preacher and theologian who graduated from Princeton in 1772; and Marinus Oudenarde, a member of the New York Society Library from 1790 to 1792.[251]

It was a distaste for British rule—and the bitter aftertaste that rule left—that drove Americans into Beccaria's camp, with Beccaria's writings fueling further outrage at their mistreatment by the English monarchy and the British Parliament. "A reading of the Enlightenment tract of Cesare Beccaria," David Rothman wrote in *The Discovery of the Asylum*, "verified for Americans in the 1790's the line between barbaric laws and deviant behavior." "The young republic," Rothman notes of Americans' embrace of Beccaria's themes, "quickly took this message to heart, for it fit well with its own history and revolutionary ideals." As Rothman explained in his book: "Americans fully appreciated that the laws could be a tool of the passions of a handful of men. Did this not explain almost every piece of British colonial legislation after 1763?" "They believed," Rothman wrote of American revolutionaries, "that they had also witnessed the self-defeating quality of cruel punishments. Had not colonial juries often let a prisoner go free rather than condemn him to the gallows for a petty theft? In this way, criminals had escaped all discipline, and the community had allowed, even encouraged, them to persist in their ways."[252] So popular did Beccaria's treatise become that, in the nineteenth century, in the world of lawyers at least, it acquired its own citation or abbreviation: "Bec. Cr."[253] Like Sir Edward Coke and Sir William Blackstone, both known for their English law commentaries, Beccaria's treatise had joined the pantheon of classic texts and become a must-read.[254]

Commentators, however, were not of one mind, especially when it came to the centuries-old institution of state-sanctioned executions. For example, the Prussian philosopher Immanuel Kant, a fierce death penalty proponent who emphasized retribution, or so-called "just deserts," disliked Beccaria's treatise and had no difficulty saying so.[255] In *The Philosophy of Law*, published in the 1790s, Kant attacked Beccaria's "sophistry" and his "compassionate sentimentality." Kant believed that sexual crimes should be punished with castration, and he called for the death penalty for murderers, contending that "no substitute" for capital punishment "will satisfy justice." In *The Philosophy of Law*, Kant referred to "the Principle of Equality" and "the Right of Retaliation (*jus talionis*)," writing that "whoever has committed Murder, must *die*." "There is no *Likeness* or proportion between Life, however painful, and Death; and therefore there is no Equality between the crime of Murder and the retaliation of it but what is judicially accomplished by the execution of the Criminal," Kant contended. Calling for the criminal to receive "the desert of his deeds," Kant wrote: "The Equalization of Punishment with Crime is therefore only possible by the cognition of the Judge extending even to the penalty of Death." The death penalty, certainly, remained on the books in many locales. It was retained, among many other places, in the Penal Code of Bavaria, drafted by Paul Johann Anselm Ritter von Feuerbach (1775–1833) and published in 1813.[256]

But, in general, *On Crimes and Punishments* garnered high praise — or at least respect — throughout the Enlightenment.[257] When booksellers, local libraries and lawyers acquired law books, as was the case in 1804 with Connecticut attorney Seth Beers, Beccaria's treatise was thus likely to be among the purchases.[258] "*On Crimes and Punishments*," notes one history, "was widely catalogued by American booksellers in the 1780s," a reality that clearly did not change as Americans entered the nineteenth century.[259] And more often than not, Beccaria was painted in a positive light among Anglo-American lawyers. For example, in *A Letter of a Remonstrance to Sir Robert Gifford, Knight, His Majesty's Attorney General*, published in 1820, one finds the following statement: "For all the wise and useful purposes of legislation, I recommend you to study Beccaria. His is worth all your law books."[260] Indeed, it has been noted that, by the early nineteenth century, "it was Beccaria's philosophy rather than Kant's that would come to dominate the field of penal justice." "By the 1830s," that source emphasizes, "the American penitentiary had become world famous, attracting visitors such as Alexis de Tocqueville, Gustave Auguste de Beaumont, Harriet Martineau, and Charles Dickens."[261]

Charles Dickens (1812–1870) actually wrote a series of letters to *The Daily News* in 1846 on "the effect of Capital Punishment on the commission of crime," making this observation: "Out of one hundred and sixty-seven persons under sentence of Death in England, questioned at different times, in the course of years, by an English clergyman in the performance of his duty, there were only three who had not been spectators of executions." "[A]n execution," Dickens wrote in one of his letters, "is well known to be an utterly useless, barbarous, and brutalising sight," with "the sympathy of all beholders, who have any sympathy at all," "certain to be always with the criminal, and never with the law."[262] Dickens — the famous author of *A Christmas Carol*, *A Tale of Two Cities* and *Bleak House* who also wrote a travelogue, *Pictures from Italy*, after spending a year in Genoa — traveled to the United States in the early 1840s to do his own tour of the place. One of the spots he most wanted to visit: the Eastern State Penitentiary in Philadelphia. Dickens got a full tour, but concluded that while the "motives" of reformers were "humane," the penitentiary experiment—in particular, its system of prison discipline, with prisoners passing their sentences in nearly uninterrupted solitude—was "cruel and wrong." At the penitentiary, prisoners were locked in their cells at all times, ate alone, and were required to wear masks or hoods on the rare occasion when they were permitted outside their cells. Dickens assessment: "I hold this slow and daily tampering with the mysteries of the brain to be immeasurably worse than any torture of the body." Dickens wrote of the Eastern State Penitentiary as "a living tomb."[263]

In the antebellum era, those studying law in the New World were certainly encouraged or required to read Beccaria's treatise. In an 1833 edition of *The City-Hall Reporter, and New-York Law Magazine*, published monthly by John Lomas, it was noted that "[t]he names of Pastoret and Beccaria, and Bentham and Burgh, are familiar to every reader conversant with criminal law, or studied in its primitive principles." Noting that those writers' "scholastic lore" and "their developed researches" had "long been a topic of deserved admiration," that "Short-hand and General Law Reporter" emphasized: "Sanguinary laws—cruel edicts— and revoltingly tyrannical mandates, highly calculated to render the human mind the residence not only of *resentment*, but of *pardonable revenge*, led them to denounce, and endeavour to explode the systems of other periods, and, in judging of their tendency to the advancement of their opinions, to effect a revision of the penal statutes which then existed." Likewise, in David Hoffman's *A Course of Legal Study*, published in Baltimore, Maryland, in the first half of the nineteenth century, the author of *Dei delitti e delle pene* is called "the amiable and eloquent champion of the rights of humanity."

After Beccaria's "fine talents and enlarged philanthropy" are discussed in a section devoted to Beccaria's treatise, David Hoffman's book took note of the American lawyer Edward Livingston's attempt to carry on Beccaria's legacy by advocating the abandonment of executions. Livingston—the 47th Mayor of New York City, serving from 1801 to 1803—had been a member of the U.S. House of Representatives from New York and became a Congressman and U.S. senator from Louisiana. Later, Livingston—following in Jefferson's shoes—was tapped to be the United States Minister to France. In the early 1820s, Livingston had single-handedly drafted a revised penal code for Louisiana. Following his reading of works like *On Crimes and Punishments*, he became an evangelist for ridding society of capital punishment—an effort that bore some fruit in America, but which did not entirely succeed. Louisiana, the place for which Livingston had designed his draft code, rejected it, though other states made some modifications to their then-existing laws in the wake of its issuance. "Still," Hoffman wrote in his book for aspiring lawyers, "we have not gone the whole length of Beccaria; and have need the exertions of the benevolent and powerful legislator for the state of Louisiana, against this relic of pagan barbarity,—the ultimum supplicium." "Mr. Livingston's argument," Hoffman emphasized, "demonstrates the cruelty, impolicy, and evils consequent upon the infliction of death, unless where the public and private peace imperiously require it."[264]

David Hoffman, a Baltimore-born lawyer, teacher and historian, was a prominent member of the Maryland bar. He taught at the University of Maryland, and his *Course of Legal Study* was published in 1817, the same year Harvard Law School was founded. In a review published in the *North American Review*, Joseph Story, the renowned American jurist who himself later taught at Harvard as a professor, called Hoffman's book "by far the most perfect system for the study of the law which has ever been offered to the public." Hoffman's *Course of Legal Study*, Story asserted, should be recommended to "all lawyers, as a model for the direction of the students who may be committed to their care." Hoffman's section on "The Law of Crimes and Punishments" opened with the following quotation from Beccaria himself: "It was necessity which forced men to give up a part of their liberty. It is certain then, that every individual would choose to put into the publick stock the smallest portion possible; as much only as was sufficient to engage others to defend it. The aggregate of these, the smallest portions possible, forms the right of punishing; all that extends beyond this is abuse, not justice." Hoffman explicitly recommended that aspiring lawyers read, among other things, Beccaria's *On Crimes and Punishments* and writings by Jeremy Bentham and William Eden, two other penal reformers.

Of Beccaria's treatise, Hoffman said this: "This excellent little work is from the pen of Cæsar Bonesana, marquis of Beccaria. He was a man of pre-eminent talents, and no doubt of equal virtue; though his enemies, hostile to his liberal and philanthropick doctrines, have accused him of venality in the discharge of his official duties, and have compared him, both as to talents and corruption, to Bacon." Francis Bacon—an English statesman—served as both Attorney General and Lord Chancellor of England. "Beccaria," Hoffman emphasized, "was much esteemed by the learned of his country, whose protection he needed and received, when persecuted on account of the principles contained in his 'Essay on Crimes and Punishments.'" Hoffman added: "When we reflect on the genius of the government and religion under which the marquis lived, we cannot but additionally estimate the enterprise and boldness of the man who ventured to disseminate such wholesome truths." "Happily for this land," Hoffman wrote of America, "we need no advocate for humanity, liberty, philanthropy; they are indigenous growths of our soil, which need but little culture, and which, under any circumstances, can never, we hope, be entirely eradicated." Hoffman also offered glowing praise for Bentham's writings in his *Course of Legal Study*.[265]

Even among non-lawyers, Beccaria's book—because of its accessible style—proved to be a popular title. For example, in his 1791, 107-page pamphlet advocating universal public education, Robert Coram—a Wilmington, Delaware librarian, schoolteacher, newspaper editor, and Revolutionary War veteran—drew heavily upon Beccaria's treatise.[266] A midshipman in the Revolutionary War, Coram—having secured a letter of recommendation from Benjamin Franklin in 1779 while in Passy—sailed on two missions aboard the *Bonhomme Richard* for Captain John Paul Jones, earning praise for his bravery and gallantry. The famed naval commander, John Paul Jones, had met Benjamin Franklin in Paris in 1777, and had used the French translation of Franklin's *nom de plume*, "Poor Richard," to name the *Bonhomme Richard*.[267] A British man-of-war had captured Coram aboard a different ship, the *South Carolina*, making him especially sympathetic to the plight of prisoners. He and fellow prisoners of war were held in New York City in horrendous conditions, locked beneath the decks of disease-ridden prison ships until their release, under the armistice, in 1783. Coram's pamphlet on public education, which he sent to George Washington, was the product of countless hours of thought and reading at the library he oversaw for the city. After joining the Wilmington Library Company and offering to serve as its custodian, Coram, on May 26, 1790, transported its entire library—approximately eight hundred volumes—to his home. Among those in the city's collection: Blackstone and Beccaria. In 1791, the self-educated Coram—an active member of the Republican Party—would himself be elected to help rewrite Delaware's state constitution, with that state's 1792 constitution providing "for establishing schools and promoting arts and sciences."[268] American military treatises—produced for use by sailors and soldiers—also regularly referenced Beccaria's writings.[269]

The Dissemination of Beccaria's Ideas

In both England and America, Beccaria—like few other Enlightenment figures—had a tremendous impact on his readers. Just as Bentham and Blackstone, both educated at Oxford, had discussed Beccaria's ideas in their writings, early American legal commentators, including Nathan Dane, William Rawle and Joseph Story, cited Beccaria's writings in their own treatises. Massachusetts lawyer Nathan Dane wrote a digest of American law; William Rawle, of Pennsylvania, wrote *A View of the Constitution of the United States*; and Joseph Story wrote *Commentaries on the Constitution*, a treatise published in 1833.[270] And these men were highly connected and well respected—indeed, at the top of their profession—in the field of law. For example, in an 1804 letter to James Madison that also references Edward Livingston, Thomas Jefferson refers to Joseph Story's "oration"— *An Oration, Pronounced at Salem, on the Fourth Day of July, 1804, in Commemoration of Our National Independence*. In that speech, Story had defended the Jefferson Administration's policies, including its acquisition of Louisiana. Likewise, William Rawle (1759–1836) was a leading Philadelphia lawyer and U.S. Attorney for the District of Pennsylvania. Appointed by George Washington to serve in the latter position, Rawle—educated in London at the Middle Temple—corresponded with Alexander Hamilton and Thomas Jefferson.[271]

Beccaria's treatise, because of its contents and the moral stakes it raised, caused a great stir, with Americans all abuzz in talking about it. The American patriot and lawyer James Otis is most famous, perhaps, for the revolutionary slogan commonly attributed to him: "taxation without representation is tyranny!" When his sister, the historian Mercy Otis Warren, penned her three-volume history of the American Revolution, it is thus not surprising that she should turn to the tyranny-loathing Beccaria. In her history, she included a passage from Beccaria's treatise, paraphrasing Beccaria's quotation as follows: "We must consult the human heart, says the marquis Beccaria, for the foundation of the rights of both sovereign and people."[272] In a January 1775 letter, Mercy Otis Warren also asked John Adams these questions: "A man may be greatly criminal towards the society in which he lives; but how far, Sir, do you think it justifiable for any individual to hold him up as the object of public derision? Is it consistent with the benevolent spirit of christianity to vilify the delinquent, when we only wish to ward off the fatal consequences of his crimes?"[273] As the Italian historian Marcello Maestro wrote in the *Journal of the History of Ideas*, "Beccaria became quickly one of the most famous European writers." "An attitude of greater respect for human life had undoubtedly emerged," Maestro wrote of America's founding era, explaining how Beccaria "was certainly responsible in great measure for this attitude and for the substantial reduction in the number of executions throughout the nation."[274]

Even America's Declaration of Independence—that foundational document of American liberty—has strains or echoes of Beccaria's ideas. Beccaria had railed against cruelty and tyrannical punishments, including torture and capital punishment, and— as translated—had written of "the greatest happiness for the greatest number."[275] His words, which received many accolades, sent waves and ripples throughout continental Europe and through the minds of members of Anglo-American society.[276] In a commonplace book dated 1781 to 1785, Jeremy Bentham—who had seen the phrase "the greatest happiness of the greatest number" in Joseph Priestley's *An Essay on the First Principles of Government* (1768)—also indicated that he may well have gotten that utilitarian idea from Beccaria, with Bentham writing: "Priestly was the first (unless it was Beccaria) who taught my lips to pronounce this sacred truth: That the greatest happiness of the greatest number is the foundation of morals and legislation."[277] "The year 1769 was to me a most interesting year," Bentham wrote in his memoirs, recalling that he read Montesquieu, Beccaria and other Enlightenment authors that "set me on the principle of utility."[278] Thomas Jefferson — who had discovered Beccaria at around the same time — later drafted the Declaration of Independence, which not only served as an indictment of King George III and the "absolute Tyranny" and "Cruelty" of his reign, but also proclaimed the "unalienable Rights" to "Life, Liberty and the pursuit of Happiness." In its declaration, the Continental Congress had lambasted George III, listing among the grievances the following: "He has plundered our seas, ravaged our Coasts, burnt our towns, and destroyed the lives of our people. He is at this time transporting large Armies of foreign Mercenaries to compleat the works of death, desolation and tyranny, already begun with circumstances of Cruelty and perfidy scarcely paralleled in the most barbarous ages, and totally unworthy of the Head of a civilized nation."[279]

Beccaria's name, in fact, was routinely invoked in eighteenth-century writings and speeches,[280] cited by political leaders and college students alike. For example, at Yale's 1788 commencement day exercises, *On Crimes and Punishments* — as in other college debates — became a popular source for those debating the death penalty.[281] After a debate over "whether capital punishment was in any case lawful," Jeremiah Mason — one of the graduates and debate participants, facing off against a classmate identified as "the Rev. Dr. Chapin" in Mason's autobiography — recorded in his diary: "I held the negative. I stole most of my arguments from the treatise of the Marquis Beccaria, then little known in this country. It was new, and consequently well received by the audience; indeed, its novelty excited considerable notice." "I was flattered and much gratified by being told that my performance was the best of the day," Mason wrote in his diary, adding later in his memoirs: "In the course of a long and active life I recollect no occasion when I have experienced such elevation of feelings." As a college student, Mason had habitually attended "the law trials in New Haven," which inspired him to become a lawyer, a profession in which he developed friendships with such notables as Joseph Story and Daniel Webster. Though Beccaria's arguments were well received, Mason's impression as a student that they were little known was not accurate. "Had the student realized that just two years earlier a local newspaper had serialized Beccaria's essay," writes historian Louis Masur of young Jeremiah, "he might have been less zealous in his plagiarism."

"In the 1780s," Masur notes, "most catalogues of books for sale in America included an edition of Beccaria's essay, and periodicals such as the *New-Haven Gazette and Connecticut Magazine* serialized Beccaria for their readers."[282] In 1784, the Yale senior class had already debated whether capital punishment was "too severe & rigorous in the United States for the present Stage of Society."[283] And following such debates, at least some of the college students and debate participants went on to distinguished careers in law and politics and to defend those facing capital charges. Jeremiah Mason (1768–1848), admitted to the bar in 1791, became attorney general of New Hampshire from 1802 to 1805 and served as a U.S. Senator from New Hampshire from 1813 to 1817. Writing in her own diary in 1843, Mary Elizabeth Mason — Jeremiah Mason's daughter — wrote this about her father's intersection with capital punishment: "In speaking of the effect of capital punishment, he said that he went to Norwich to a hanging, when he was about ten years old, which frightened him so that he did not go to bed for years without thinking of it. Since that time he had defended half-a-dozen criminals, and saved them all from that punishment; he said he preferred being on that side to the other, but it was disagreeable business, and one that he had always been pressed into."[284]

In retrospect, it should not be surprising that a European philosopher such as Beccaria should gain such popularity in distant America. After Italian, French, and English editions of *On Crimes and Punishments* were released in Europe, translations of Beccaria's treatise inevitably made their way to America. And Beccaria's treatise spoke to American concerns at a time when the English Parliament and King George III were at odds — to put it mildly — with American colonists. While a select group of Founding Fathers knew French or Italian, English-language editions of Beccaria's essay — also serialized in the *Worcester Gazette* in 1786, making Beccaria's treatise more accessible to the general public — were advertised in American newspapers as early as 1771.[285] In Charlestown, South Carolina, David Bruce — a printer who, at his own expense, published a reprint of Thomas Paine's widely popular *Common Sense* — released his own edition of *On Crimes and Punishments* in 1777.[286] A Scotsman, Bruce sold the new books at his shop on Church Street.[287] Bruce's printing business also published a newspaper, the *South-Carolina Weekly Gazette*.[288] The transatlantic book trade brought many new ideas to America, and even though Beccaria had written his landmark treatise in his 20s, Beccaria's thoughts — like those of other Enlightenment thinkers — were among those that made their mark in American circles. The library of South Carolina College, a university founded in 1801, is known — as just another example — to have kept a copy of Beccaria's treatise.[289]

Texts in those days were liberally copied, and printers made their money where they could. In eighteenth-century America, where Beccaria's treatise — as evidenced by William Bradford's letter to Luigi Castiglioni — was much in demand, frequent reprintings of it were the only way to keep up with that demand. In 1778, in Philadelphia, Robert Bell — Scottish by birth and trained as a bookbinder in Glasgow[290] — printed and sold an edition of Beccaria's book next door to St. Paul's Church on Third Street.[291] That same year, Bell published *Miscellanies by M. de. Voltaire* and David Hume's autobiography, titled *The Life of David Hume, Esq.; the Philosopher and Historian, Written by Himself.* It would be — as one scholar puts it — "the first work of Hume's to be separately published in North America." Benjamin Franklin, no stranger to autobiography, himself corresponded with the Edinburgh-born David Hume (1711–1776) in 1760 and 1762 and in the early 1770s before Hume's death.

In a particularly poignant letter dated May 10, 1762, Hume wrote to Dr. Franklin from Edinburgh: "I am very sorry, that you intend soon to leave our Hemisphere. America has sent us many good things, Gold, Silver, Sugar, Tobacco, Indigo &c.: But you are the first Philosopher, and indeed the first Great Man of Letters for whom we are beholden to her: it is our own Fault, that we have not kept him." "We are all very unwilling to think of your settling in America, and that there is some Chance for our never seeing you again," Hume lamented in his letter. For his part, Franklin — in a reply from London — told Hume: "I nevertheless regret extreamly the leaving a Country in which I have receiv'd so much Friendship, and Friends whose Conversation has been so agreable and so improving to me; and that I am henceforth to reside at so great a distance from them is no small Mortification." In a 1772 letter, after seeing Franklin again a decade later in Edinburgh, with Franklin visiting and actually lodging with him, Hume forthrightly expressed his hope, which didn't come to fruition in his lifetime, that an American edition of his works might be printed. As Hume, expressing the desire for his ideas to "have recourse to America for Justice," wrote Franklin in February of that year: "You told me, I think, that your Countrymen in that part of the World intended to do me the Honour of giving an Edition of my Writings; and you promised that you should recommend to them to follow this last Edition, which is in the Press. I now use the Freedom of reminding you of it."[292]

In Hume's essay, "Of the Liberty of the Press," Hume would preview themes later repeated by Beccaria himself. In his *Essays, Moral, Political and Literary* (1742), Hume began his essay on the freedom of the press: "Nothing is more apt to surprise a foreigner, than the extreme liberty, which we enjoy in this country, of communicating whatever we please to the public, and of openly censuring every measure, entered into by the king or his ministers." After taking notice of "a remark of Tacitus with regard to the Romans under the emperors" about "slavery" and "liberty," Hume wrote of "the Roman government under the emperors as a mixture of despotism and liberty, where the despotism prevailed." Hume saw "the English government as a mixture of the same kind, but where the liberty predominates," then made this observation:

> No action must be deemed a crime but what the law has plainly determined to be such: No crime must be imputed to a man but from a legal proof before his judges; and even these judges must be his fellow-subjects, who are obliged, by their own interest, to have a watchful eye over the encroachments and violence of the ministers. From these causes it proceeds, that there is as much liberty, and even, perhaps, licentiousness in Britain, as there were formerly slavery and tyranny in Rome.

Worried about "arbitrary power" and "giving to the court very large discretionary powers to punish whatever displease them," Hume spoke of the British people as "the lovers of liberty."[293]

In the anonymous work titled *A Philosophical and Religious Dialogue in the Shades, Between Mr. Hume and Dr. Dodd* (1778), the following remarks attributed to the Scottish philosopher David Hume are recorded in a "dialogue" with the Rev. Dr. William Dodd (1729–1777), a popular English Anglican clergyman—nicknamed the "Macaroni Parson"—who was publicly executed for forgery at Tyburn: "Your idea, Doctor, of mitigating the rigor of penal laws was worthy of a philosop[h]ical sage. Some reformation of that kind is still wanted in the polished countries of Europe: but till such a reformation is effected, I am of opinion that the established laws ought to be impartially executed." A footnote in the "dialogue" specifically referenced Dodd's sermon on the subject of penal reform and mentioned "'The Essay on Crimes and Punishments', written by that profound and amiable philosopher the Marquis Beccaria." Despite petitions seeking Dodd's pardon, one with 23,000 signatures, George III declined to issue one. In Dodd's *Thoughts in Prison*, Dodd penned the following lines of verse: *Wise and enlighten'd. Should not equal laws / Their punishments proportionate to crimes*. An advertisement in Robert Bell's *The Life of David Hume*, released two years after Hume's death, included this advertisement: "The following New Publications, in Literature, Are just arrived from London by the way of Egg-Harbour, and are now for Sale at Bell's Book Store, in Third-street, Philadelphia": "Montesquieu's Spirit of Laws" and "Beccaria on Crimes."[294]

In 1771, Bell had become one of the first booksellers to publish a law treatise on American soil when he printed Blackstone's *Commentaries on the Laws of England*[295]—a treatise that itself made reference to, and thus helped further publicize, Beccaria's ideas.[296] The 840 subscribers that supported Bell's printing of Blackstone's treatise at the Union Library, with Bell able to sell 1,587 copies of the pirated edition of Blackstone's treatise, included Edmund Pendleton and St. George Tucker, the prominent Virginia lawyers. In January 1776, Bell—more famously—had printed the first edition of Thomas Paine's runaway bestseller, *Common Sense*. A friend of Thomas Paine, Dr. Benjamin Rush himself had disliked Paine's working title, "Plain Truth," and suggested the now-immortal title for Paine's runaway bestseller. With Enlightenment writers like Montesquieu and Beccaria providing the spark, *Common Sense* ignited public sentiment in favor of American independence and set the relationship between Americans and those loyal to the Crown aflame.[297]

To satisfy the public's growing appetite for Beccaria's treatise after the ratification of the U.S. Bill of Rights in 1791, other publishers also got into the act. In 1793, William Young—another entrepreneur—thus printed a new and corrected edition of Beccaria's treatise in Philadelphia on Second Street at the corner of Chestnut Street.[298] Young, an immigrant from Glasgow, had moved to Philadelphia and, with the help of family and friends, devoted himself—in one historian's words—"to bringing the Scottish Enlightenment," of which David Hume had been a prominent part, to his new country.[299] Other editions of *On Crimes and Punishments* also would be printed in America in the following decades, saturating the American market in a way that few books did in that era.[300] Reading Beccaria's book—as Thomas Jefferson recommended aspiring lawyers do—had become, in effect, a rite of passage, a regular practice, certainly, among American intellectuals, law students and legal practitioners.[301] As Marcello Maestro wrote of Jefferson's own personal affection for the Italian philosopher's treatise: "Among the early admirers of Beccaria in America was also the first citizen of Virginia, Thomas Jefferson. In his *Commonplace Book* we find no less than twenty-six extracts from Beccaria's *Essay on Crimes and Punishments*, all long passages in the original Italian, transcribed around 1775 in Jefferson's own handwriting."[302] The passages relating to Beccaria's treatise occupy eighteen pages in Jefferson's commonplace book.[303]

Reactions to Beccaria's Treatise

The Enlightenment figure François-Marie Arouet, better known by his pseudonym, Voltaire, was—through his force of personality—responsible for much of the attention *On Crimes and Punishments* initially received. After reading Beccaria's book, Voltaire—an immensely popular writer among the Founding Fathers—called Beccaria "a brother" and "a beneficent genius whose excellent book has educated Europe." Voltaire had successfully campaigned in the early 1760s to exonerate Jean Calas, the wrongfully condemned man; had written on the subject of the death penalty and the need for criminal law reform; and had direct contact with America's Founding Fathers, including Benjamin Franklin and Dr. Benjamin Rush.[304] Voltaire's commentary, which regularly accompanied the treatise's text,[305] further publicized Beccaria's ideas as Voltaire was then a well-known figure.[306] Voltaire's much-read *Treatise on Tolerance* was published in 1763, but the prolific Voltaire had been publishing letters and essays for decades. His dogged efforts to exonerate Jean Calas—begun almost immediately after Calas had been broken on the wheel—were aided by a number of allies, including a banker, a lawyer, a minister, and other advocates.[307] In the 1775 edition of Beccaria's treatise that John Adams later gave to his son Thomas, Voltaire begins his commentary by noting that he had "read, with infinite satisfaction, the little book on Crimes and Punishments." "Where charity is wanting," Voltaire wrote, "the law is always cruel." "The sword of justice is in our hands," Voltaire wrote, "but we ought rather to blunt than to sharpen its edge."

Calling Beccaria a "humane" and "judicious author," Voltaire added his own heart-felt sentiments, writing: "It hath long since been observed, that a man after he is hanged is good for nothing, and that punishments invented for the good of society, ought to be useful to society. It is evident, that a score of stout robbers, condemned for life to some publick work, would serve the state in their punishment, and that hanging them is a benefit to nobody but the executioner."[308] Taking specific note of a French jurist and England's notoriously execution-happy Lord Chief Justice George Jeffreys (1648–1689), James II's brutal agent and a scandalously corrupt fixture of the King's Bench and the Old Bai-

me judges who were passionately fond of spilling
or his extraordinary wit and publicly critical of
nmentary: "Nature never intended such men for
n countries where a trifling domestic theft, or
Voltaire editorialized, "is not the disproportioned
ire added: "If, on the contrary, the punishment
o are guilty of a breach of trust be condemned
ot hesitate to bring the offender to justice, and
mmentary on the section of Beccaria's treatise
nankind may read with attention the work of
s, Voltaire specifically referred to "sanguinary"
a severe punishment."[310]

eatise — picking up on Voltaire's lead — then
ngs or orations.[311] That was certainly the case
r "To the Inhabitants of the Province of Que-
ental Congress, wherein John Dickinson had
nembered as an opponent of American inde-

in 1776 due to his desire to reconcile with Great Britain, Dickinson is, ironically, also considered—in one historian's words—"the 'Penman of the Revolution' because
of his clear, well-argued, and very influential writings of the revolutionary period." Urging a republican form of government while also, in his open letter, discussing "the Fab-
rick of the British Constitution" and the people's "Right" to govern themselves, Dickinson—
though hoping to avoid war and violence—no doubt felt tremendous kinship with his
Italian and French counterparts, Beccaria and Montesquieu, when he wrote these words:

> "In every human Society," says the celebrated Marquis Beccaria, following the steps
> of the immortal Montesquieu in impressing sentiments of Humanity, "there is an
> Effort continually tending to confer on one Part the height of Power and Happiness,
> and to reduce the other to the extreme of Weakness & Misery. The intent of good
> Laws, is to oppose this Effort, and to diffuse their Influence, universally, & equally."[312]

"Few men," Dr. Benjamin Rush would later write, "wrote, spoke and acted more for their
country from the years 1764 to the establishment of the federal government than Mr.
Dickinson."[313]

With American colonists exasperated with the British Parliament, John Dickinson's
use of the quotation from Beccaria's treatise was meant to encapsulate, or sum up, frustrations with British rule. "These few Lines," Dickinson himself emphasized, "have intensely collected into a small Compass, the (Principles) Causes of almost all Civil Discords.
Rulers stimulated by the pernicious 'Effort,' and Subjects, animated by the just 'Intent of
opposing good Laws against it,' have that vast Variety of Dissensions, that fill the Histories of so many Nations.'" The Continental Congress itself went on to approve Dickinson's
letter containing the reference to Beccaria and that letter was signed in Philadelphia by Henry
Middleton (1717–1784), a South Carolina plantation owner and the President of the Continental Congress following Peyton Randolph's departure due to illness. Printed in English and French by order of the Continental Congress, a German edition of the letter,
which Pennsylvania's delegates took responsibility for, was also printed, with the address
to Quebec residents then widely reprinted in American cities and towns. For example,
the letter was reprinted in *Plain Truth*, a political essay opposing independence written
by British loyalist James Chalmers under the pseudonym "Candidus" and printed in
Philadelphia in 1776. Chalmers sought to refute the arguments in favor of independence
that had been advanced by Thomas Paine in *Common Sense*.

The letter to the inhabitants of Quebec was also translated into French to be distributed among Canadians. But it was in America that Beccaria's words had the most impact, with Beccaria's "forcible words" in that letter later quoted by Melancton Smith in New York's 1788 convention on the adoption of the federal constitution. Indeed, Beccaria's words about "happiness" and "[t]he intent of good laws"—words that stuck to early Americans like glue—were also quoted by others in the founding era, including in the U.S. Congress and the British House of Commons.[314] For example, Beccaria's name shows up in 1776 in *Remarks upon the Late Resolutions of the House of Commons, respecting the Proposed Change of the Poor Laws*, written by Henry Zouch, a Justice of the Peace, and published in Leeds. In 1785, the address of Congress to the inhabitants of the province of Quebec also shows up in Noah Webster's *A Grammatical Institute of the English Language*, thereby exposing American schoolchildren to Beccaria's quotation.[315]

As might be expected, the final version of John Dickinson's letter to the inhabitants of Quebec—the product of a congressional drafting committee made up of Dickinson, Thomas Cushing and Richard Henry Lee—also caught the attention of English readers. For instance, in the December 1776 edition of London's *Town and Country Magazine*, in an article titled "The Rise and Progress of the present unhappy War in America," the writer noted that, in the letter to the inhabitants of Quebec, Congress had quoted Beccaria and Montesquieu.[316] Issued near in time to the British Parliament's Quebec Act of 1774, which set governance rules for the people of that province, the letter "To the Inhabitants of the Province of Quebec"—translated into French by Fleury Mesplet, a French printer in Philadelphia—represented an attempt by Americans to convince their Canadian neighbors of their right to democratic governance. The invocation of Beccaria's words by the Continental Congress in its 1774 letter to Quebec residents, with the adoption of the Declaration of Independence still two years away, highlights what a powerful spell Beccaria's treatise had cast among the founders themselves. Lead bullets would prove to be the ammunition to defeat the British Empire, but Beccaria's ideas—along with those of other Enlightenment writers such as Montesquieu and Paine—would provide the intellectual firepower to convince Americans to make the costly sacrifice of human lives, of blood and treasure.

Even those opposing American independence, such as New York lawyer Peter van Schaack, looked to Beccaria for guidance. In an August 14, 1778, letter to fellow New Yorker John Jay, van Schaack began: "I owe it to the friendship which formerly subsisted between us, to explain myself on a very serious subject, before I quit this country, perhaps forever." "Let me entreat you," he wrote, "to recur to first principles; your government, professed to be formed upon them, is too young to excuse inattention to them. Read with the same temper *you used*, Locke, Montesquieu and Beccaria, upon the rights of individuals, and the duties of those in power, and compare them with the *present practice*, and I fancy *you* will think that Great Britain has not alone trampled upon the rights of mankind." After annotating Beccaria's book, among others, in the winter of 1775–1776, van Schaack quoted Beccaria in "Observations on the Banishing Act of the Senate and Assembly of the State of New-York, 1778," as follows: "'Though punishments be productive of good,' (says the excellent Marquis Beccaria, whom I quote because his authority has the approbation of the Congress,) 'they are not on that account more just; to be just, they must be *necessary*.'"[317] Though van Schaack ended up leaving America for Great Britain in 1778, Beccaria's treatise, plainly, had become an authoritative book for British loyalists and American revolutionaries alike. The common take-away, it seems, was that to be just, punishments had to be necessary. If a punishment was necessary, it was just; if a punishment was unnecessary, it was classified as tyrannical.

As law reform efforts got underway in the newly formed United States of America, citations to Beccaria's work—as was the case in England, too—only became more ubiquitous. This, in turn, influenced still more forward-thinking citizens to demand rights or to call for the abolition or curtailment of death sentences.[318] In the anonymously authored *Rudiments of Law and Government, Deduced from the Law of Nature*, published in Charleston, South Carolina, in 1783, Beccaria's treatise is—in the year the Revolutionary War ended—cited multiple times. In a section on "Personal Safety," the author observed: "Both humanity and policy dictate that the members of society should be protected in life, limb, organ and feature." "Nothing but indispensible necessity in self-defence," the author wrote in that section, "can warrant the effusion of another's blood." "To deduce the propriety of capital punishments from the power of individuals," it was urged, "is to argue from the abuse for the right." In another section titled "Of the Administration of Justice," the anonymous author expressed the view that "advantage will accrue to the community" from the use of "exile," awards of damages to individuals, and from "servitude and even hard labor in public service for a term or for life." "[B]ut none from death," the author argued.[319] The French utilitarian philosopher Claude Adrien Helvétius (1715–1771), whose own work had so influenced Beccaria, even cited Beccaria in his own writing, including in Helvétius's posthumously published work, *A Treatise on Man, His Intellectual Faculties and His Education* (1777), translated from French into English.[320]

"A. F.," a student at London's Inner Temple, also cited Beccaria for a whole array of propositions in an 1804 book. That book, in a manner reflective of the age and the then-existing terminology of crimes recognized by law, had this long-winded title: *The Criminal Recorder; or, Biographical Sketches of Notorious Public Characters; Including Murderers, Traitors, Pirates, Mutineers, Incendiaries, Defrauders, Rioters, Sharpers, Highwaymen, Footpads, Pickpockets, Swindlers, Housebreakers, Coiners, Receivers, Extortioners, and Other Noted Persons Who Have Suffered the Sentence of the Law for Criminal Offenses.*[321] Though the law had once made the bulk of such crimes punishable by death, the social changes brought about in large part by Beccaria's treatise would change all that as fewer and fewer crimes became death-eligible offenses. On the hundredth anniversary of the publication of Beccaria's treatise, a British magazine was still urging its subscribers to read "[t]he Marquis of Beccaria's work on crimes and punishments."[322] "The opponents of capital punishment still use the arguments presented with such eloquence by Beccaria," Marcello Maestro notes of Beccaria's long-lasting influence, though he accurately notes that "his name is rarely mentioned now," a casualty—no doubt—of the passage of time.[323]

Chapter 3

The Founding Fathers:
The American Revolution

George Washington

Many of America's Founding Fathers—including early U.S. Presidents—owned copies of Beccaria's treatise or were familiar with it.[1] The first President of the United States, George Washington, bought a copy of Beccaria's treatise,[2] likely in 1769.[3] *On Crimes and Punishments* thus appears in a "Catalogue of Books for Master Custis" prepared by George Washington in 1769.[4] John Parke Custis was George Washington's step-son, and was six years old at the date of his mother Martha's second marriage to George Washington in 1759. On May 30, 1768, a year before that "Catalogue of Books" was prepared, George Washington referred to Master Custis, then a teenager, as "my son in Law & ward" in a letter seeking a new tutor for him. "He is a boy of good genius, about 14 years of age, untainted in his morals & of innocent manners," Washington wrote of his son-in-law in 1768.[5] That same year, Washington's neighbor, George Mason, the man later responsible for drafting Virginia's Declaration of Rights, wrote from his own plantation at Gunston Hall, commenting on April 9, 1768: "I wish it was in my power to advise anything that wou'd be agreeable to you & Mrs. Washington with Regard to Master Custis." Mason noted that a "Mr. Campbell" was "a good Classic Scholar, as well as a good Mathematician, & very capable of teaching."[6] George Washington, in looking out for his step-son, clearly wanted the best education for him, and a good education at that time meant reading Beccaria's treatise.

Though George Washington bought the book for his step-son, it seems readily apparent that the future commander-in-chief read it too. In the midst of the Revolutionary War, in 1778, then-General Washington told the Continental Congress that he wanted an exploration of an "intermediate" punishment between death and the infliction of lashes. In his letter to the Continental Congress dated August 31, 1778, Washington spoke of "[t]he frequent condemnations to capital punishments, for want of some intermediate" punishment between the penalty of death and "a Hundred lashes (the next highest under our present military articles)." In that era, soldiers guilty of offenses were often either executed or whipped, commonly with thirty-nine lashes on their bare backs, though sometimes with many more. In the eighteenth century, both British and American military justice could be incredibly severe, with Martin Griffin's history, *Catholics and the American Revolution*, giving this report: "On May 16th, 1778, Patrick Mullen of the Roman Catholic Volunteers tried by Court Martial for desertion and attempting to cross the River Schuylkill in order to join the Rebel army is found guilty of Desertion and sentenced to received one thousand lashes in the usual manner."[7]

Because of the lack of intermediate punishment, Washington wrote in his 1778 letter, "the necessity of frequent pardons" had been the "consequence," causing Washington—as he reported to Congress—"to lay the matter before a Board of Officers for them to consider, whether some mode might not be devised of equal or greater efficacy for preventing crimes and punishing Delinquents when they had happened, less shocking to humanity and more advantageous to the States, than that of Capital execution."[8] From this letter alone, it seems apparent that Washington himself had absorbed—and was sympathetic to—the ideas in Beccaria's treatise. In seeking more graduated punishments and critiquing the need for frequent pardons, Washington—as he fought for America's independence—was largely parroting what Beccaria had written. In his own September 1775 address "*To the Inhabitants of* CANADA," Washington wrote of "[t]he hand of tyranny," how arms had been taken up "in defence of our liberty," and of "the freeborn sons of *America*, animated by the genuine principles of liberty and love of their Country." "The cause of *America* and of liberty," Washington emphasized, "is the cause of every virtuous *American* citizen, whatever may be his religion or his descent."[9]

A former British officer, Washington's military training taught him that executions were necessary for discipline and to keep order—a sentiment reflected in eighteenth-century military law and shared by fellow Revolutionary War commanders. For instance, the 19th Article of the Articles of War authorized the death penalty for those "convicted of holding correspondence with, or giving intelligence to the enemy, either directly or indirectly." Individuals punished for spying give some flavor for the times. On July 19, 1777, for example, Major General Israel Putnam wrote to General Washington to express the following viewpoint: "I think, the Speedy Execution of Spie's is agreable to the laws of Nature & nations & absolutely necessary to the preservation of the Army & without Such power in the Army, it must be incompetent for its own Safety." Putnam's letter came four days after the capture of Edmund Palmer, a New Yorker taken prisoner near Peekskill after breaking into a house and attacking its occupants. "Should be glad of your Excellency's Advice & direction in the premises," Putnam added, seeking Washington's views. After Palmer was tried and convicted of spying and sentenced to death in late July by a court-martial at Peekskill, New York, he was hanged at Cortlandtown's "Gallows Hill" on August 1, 1777.

Likewise, on September 14, 1778, it was reported in General Orders that at a court martial held in January 1778 by order of General Putnam, "Matthias Colbhart of Rye in the State of New-York was tried for holding a Correspondence with the Enemy of the United States, living as a Spy among the Continental Troops and inlisting and persuading them to desert to the British Army." Colbhart was "found guilty of the whole Charge alledg'd against him" and "therefore sentenced to be punished with Death—by hanging him by the Neck until he is dead." In the General Orders of September 14, 1778, which issued from Headquarters, Colbhart's fate was summarized as follows: "Which Sentence was approved of by Major General Putnam. His Excellency the Commander in Chief orders him to be executed tomorrow morning nine o'clock on Gallows Hill."[10] In early America, public places—be it Boston Common, a town square, or on a gallows hill—were regularly designated as places of execution and were well known to the public at large.[11]

Part of the appeal of Beccaria's book—and why it became so famous so fast—is that it came at the right time, with colonial Americans, already ambivalent about executions, viewing the English Bloody Code with contempt. In a biographical sketch of Cesare Beccaria, University of Minnesota sociologist Elio Monachesi wrote in 1956 of how eighteenth-century criminal law "was, in general, repressive, uncertain and barbaric." As Monachesi explained: "Its administration permitted and encouraged incredibly arbitrary and abusive practices. The agents of the criminal law, prosecutors and judges, were allowed tremendous latitude in dealing with persons accused and convicted of crimes, and corruption was rampant throughout continental Europe." "This," Monachesi adds, "was the status of the criminal law and it is against this backdrop of abuses, vagaries, cruelties and irrationalities that we must place Beccaria's treatise in order to appreciate its human and revolutionary character."

Noting that Beccaria had borrowed many of his ideas from Montesquieu and Rousseau's social contract theory, Monachesi contextualized the success of *On Crimes and Punishments* this way: "The acclaim it received was not because its contents were exclusively original, as a matter of fact, many of the reforms Beccaria advocated had been proposed by others, but rather because it constituted the first successful attempt to present a consistent and logically constructed penological system — a system to be substituted for the confusing, uncertain, abusive and inhuman practices inherent in the criminal law and penal system of his world." As Monachesi continued: "The book, easily read, and exceptionally lacking in the usual trappings of pedantry was most opportune and formulated in a convincing fashion the hopes and desires of a great many vigorous and outspoken reformers of his day." "Beccaria's slim but potent book," he concluded, "was a success primarily because it advocated changes deemed desirable and supported by public opinion."[12]

Thus, when criminals or spies were executed under then-mandatory death penalty laws, American revolutionaries — split on the propriety of executions, especially depending on the type of offense at issue — often experienced pangs of sorrow, regret or remorse. Major John André — the young British Army officer hanged as a spy in 1780 for conspiring with Benedict Arnold in a British plot to seize the fort at West Point, New York — was tried by a senior board of Continental Army officers, with General Nathanael Greene serving as the presiding officer. A handsome, five-foot-nine soldier with dark hair, André — a talented and well-liked artist whose sketch of Benedict Arnold's wife, Peggy Shippen, is owned by the Yale University Art Gallery — was part of the British force that occupied Philadelphia during the winter of 1777–1778. The year 1777 — known as "the year of the hangman" because the sevens resembled gallows — saw at least a dozen Tory spies and recruiters executed, with British loyalists, in turn, welcoming the arrival of English forces. The dashing, London-born André — then a captain — had Huguenot ancestors and was once described as "the handsomest man I ever laid eyes on." "During the winter of 1777–78, in Philadelphia," one biographical sketch reports, "André was the life and soul of the numerous festivities by which the brilliant British staff-officers endeavored to propitiate the loyalty of Philadelphia society." Another history describes his many gifts and talents this way: "He spoke a cultured English, plus French, Italian, and German. He played the flute and sang. He danced superbly. He wrote and recited poetry. And he showed exceptional talent as an artist, drawing sketches of street scenes and portraits of his friends."

Educated in Geneva, Switzerland, where his father had been a native before relocating to London, André had, on the strength of his own confession, been adjudged a spy and been sentenced to death "according to the laws and usages of nations." Afterwards, the Prussian-born Baron von Steuben, a Major General of the Continental Army and one of the officers who sat in judgment, said this, sympathetically, after the verdict: "It is not possible to save him, and yet we would gladly save him." Although Major André, as an officer and a gentleman, appealed to General Washington to allow him to be executed by firing squad, he was hanged as a spy, at age 29, in Tappan, New York on October 2, 1780. Writing to Lieutenant Colonel John Laurens a few days after the execution, Alexander Hamilton himself reported of the fate of André: "Never perhaps did any man suffer death with more justice, or deserve it less." Hamilton had visited André several times during his confinement, and spoke of André as "a man of the world" who had, as a cultured Englishman, simply wanted a more befitting mode of execution. As Hamilton wrote to Laurens: "When his sentence was announced to him, he remarked, that since it was his lot to die there was still a choice in the mode which would make a material difference to his feelings, and he would be happy, if possible, to be indulged with a professional death." Hamilton further reported that, when asked if he had any final statement to make, André had answered: "nothing, but to request you will witness to the world, that I die like a brave man."[13]

Although General Washington did not grant André his request to be shot instead of being hanged, Washington — in the conduct of the war — did frequently set certain limits with his own subordinates on the severity or type of punishments to be inflicted.[14] As Richard Brookhiser writes in *What Would the Founders Do?*: "When Colonel Henry Lee, a brash cavalry officer, proposed beheading deserters, Washington advised him that that particular form of execution was too drastic." "Examples however severe," Washington advised, "ought not to be attended with an appearance of inhumanity otherwise they give disgust and may excite resentment rather than terror."[15] That notion — that executions could be counterproductive — was one shared by Beccaria himself. Ultimately, Beccaria's ideas would shape Washington's views on military justice, and lead him to call for milder punishments and the curtailment in the frequency of executions. "I always hear of capital executions with concern, and regret that there should occur so many instances in which they are necessary," Washington wrote during the Revolutionary War. That war saw multiple executions on both sides, with Nathan Hale — a graduate of Yale College who became a Continental Army soldier — but one of them. Hale undertook a spying mission in New York City but was captured by the British and hanged. Nathan Hale's last words: "I only regret that I have but one life to give for my country."[16]

Multiple letters written to and by General Washington show his compassionate side. For example, in August 1777, Major General John Sullivan wrote to Washington respecting John Murphy and Daniel Brown. Those men, Sullivan noted, "are under Sentence of Death." "When your Excell[enc]y," Sullivan reported, "was pleased to permit me to pardon one at the Gallows I made out one for John Murphey, a Servant of Major Stewart Who had Ever Sustained a Good Character & did not belong to the Army." In planning to carry out Daniel Brown's execution, Sullivan arranged for the whole Division to see it, ordering "the Major who was the Field officer of the Day" that Brown be executed first but that Murphy's pardon be kept secret until the very last moment before being revealed. A few minutes before Brown was about to be executed, though, another soldier rode from the place designated for the execution and — as Sullivan put it — "[i]nformed me that Brown" was "Certainly Innocent" and that Brown's character not only was "without Blemish but Remarkable for Sobriety & faithfulness." The soldier on horseback reported that Brown's "penitent behaviour at the Gallows" and "his Solemn protestations of Innocence Convinced Every officer present that there was Some Mistake in the Sentence."

Sullivan's lengthy letter to General Washington, dated August 7, 1777, made an immediate impression on America's commander-in-chief. "At the Special request of all the Field officers of the Division," Sullivan had specifically urged Washington to grant clemency "toward the unhappy prisoners." "[I]f Severity must be used," Sullivan added, "much fitter objects may present themselves." That letter from Washington's subordinate quickly bore fruit, with General Washington writing back from headquarters "near German Town" on August 10, 1777. As Washington's letter advised of his change of heart toward the two prisoners at issue: "From the Representation made to me respecting Brown and Murphy, I then thought it became necessary to execute one of them by way of Example, but as you are of Opinion that the necessity is in some degree removed, and from late discoveries, that there is a possibility of their not being guilty, you have my free consent to pardon them both, as it is my most sincere wish, that whenever we are guilty of an Error in matters of this Nature, it may be on the Side of Mercy and forgiveness." Washington also showed receptivity to alternatives to executions in other instances, too. In April 1778, Washington wrote to express his preference for "detention and confinement" over "capital punishment" for a soldier; and on February 1780, Washington signed a clemency order, remitting a death sentence "on account of the frequency of capital punishments."[17]

So focused was George Washington on curtailing executions and bringing about law reform that he penned another lengthy letter, in February 1781, to Samuel Huntington, then President of the Continental Congress. As Washington wrote in the midst of the Revolutionary War:

> I have on different occasions done myself the honor to represent to Congress the inconveniences arising from the want of a proper gradation of punishments in our military code; but, as no determination has been communicated to me, I conclude a multiplicity of business may have diverted their attention from the matter. As I am convinced a great part of the vices of our discipline springs from this source, I take the liberty again to mention the subject. The highest corporal punishment we are allowed to give is a hundred lashes; between that and death there is no medium. As instances daily occur of offences for which the former is altogether inadequate, courts-martial, in order to preserve some proportion between the crime and the punishment, are obliged to pronounce sentence of death. Capital sentences on this account become more frequent in our service, than in any other; so frequent as to render their execution in most cases inexpedient; and it happens from this, that the greater offences often escape punishment, while the less are commonly punished; which cannot but operate as an encouragement to the commission of the former.
>
> The inconveniences of this defect are obvious. Congress are sensible of the necessity of punishment in an army, of the justice and policy of a due proportion between the crime and the penalties, and, of course, of the necessity of proper degrees in the latter. I shall therefore content myself with observing, that it appears to me indispensable that there should be an extension of the present corporal punishment, and that it would be useful to authorize courts-martial to sentence delinquents to labor on public works; perhaps even for some crimes, particularly desertion, to transfer them from the land to the sea service, where they have less opportunity to indulge their inconstancy. A variety in punishment is of utility, as well as a proportion. The number of lashes may either be indefinite, left to the discretion of the court, or limited to a larger number. In this case I would recommend five hundred.
>
> There is one evil, however, which I shall particularize, resulting from the imperfection of our regulations in this respect. It is the increase of arbitrary punishments. Officers, finding discipline cannot be maintained by a regular course of proceeding, are tempted to use their own discretion, which sometimes occasions excesses; to correct which, the interests of discipline will not permit much rigor. Prompt and arbitrary punishments are not to be avoided in an army; but the necessity for them will be more or less, in proportion as the military laws have more or less vigor.[18]

While Washington's early military career, especially in the mid-eighteenth century, shows an eagerness and proclivity toward the use of executions to deter desertions and other crimes, Washington's later writings on the subject are, on balance, more measured. In the 1750s, Washington—as the British commander of the Virginia Regiment—urged hangings and floggings to "terrify" deserters, explaining in one communication in 1757: "I have a Gallows near 40 feet high erected (which has terrified the rest exceedingly)." "I am determined, if I can be justified in the proceeding, to hang two or three on it, as an example to others," Washington wrote. In justifying the hanging of Ignatious Edwards and William Smith "just before the companies marched for their respective posts," Washington—in discussing those two men singled out for execution—did apologize to British colonial administrator Robert Dinwiddie for hanging the men instead of shooting them. But in doing so, Washington offered a then-common military justification for his actions, emphasizing that "[i]t conveyed much more terror to others; and it was for example sake, we did it." Adam Stephen—a Scottish-born physician and military officer who immigrated to North America and served under Washington in Virginia's colonial militia during the French and Indian War and, later, in the Revolutionary War—gives some indication of just how brutal lashings could be for deserters who were not, ultimately, executed. Reporting from Fort Cumberland, Dr. Stephen wrote that "we catched two in the very act of desertion and have whaled them till they pissed themselves and the spectators shed tears for them."[19]

After Beccaria's treatise appeared, the tone of Washington's orders and correspondence changed. As Washington wrote to the Continental Congress on January 29, 1778: "Capital crimes in the army are frequent, particularly in the instance of desertion; actually to inflict capital punishment upon every deserter or other heinous offender, would incur the imputation of cruelty, and by the familiarity of the example, destroy its efficacy; on the other hand to give only a hundred lashes to such criminals is a burlesque on their crimes rather than a serious correction, and affords encouragement to obstinacy and imitation."[20] As he fought the Revolutionary War, Washington thus sought a middle ground: not too many executions, while reserving the state's right to use them. In his native Virginia, by contrast, slaves were, with little fanfare, commonly hanged—and sometimes even had their bodies displayed for all the public to see. From 1706 to 1784, 555 slaves were sentenced to be hanged, and from 1785 to 1865, at least 628 slaves were sent to the gallows. For example, following a slave rebellion in 1800, twenty-six slaves were hanged for their role in the rebellion, though Thomas Jefferson warned then-Virginia governor James Monroe: "Where to stay the hand of the executioner is an important question." In his letter, sent from Monticello, Jefferson wrote that "there is a strong sentiment that there has been hanging enough," with Jefferson adding: "The other states & the world at large will forever condemn us if we indulge in a principle of revenge, or go one step beyond absolute necessity." From 1706 to 1809, it is estimated that, in Virginia, at least 25 slaves had their bodies or heads displayed after an execution, and that at least seven slaves had their bodies quartered before being displayed.[21]

Washington's Generals

George Washington's views on executions were not the only ones influenced by Beccaria's treatise. Henry Knox—a Revolutionary War general and George Washington's first Secretary of War—had familiarity with Beccaria's treatise, too. In 1771, at age twenty-one, Knox opened a fashionable bookstore in Boston called the London Book Store, stocking it with titles of progressive thinkers that included Beccaria, Hume, Voltaire and Frederick II, the Prussian king known as Frederick the Great.[22] Those who fought in the Revolutionary War, explains one historian, "found intellectual challenges and political inspiration in the trunks of leather-bound books that arrived seasonally from Europe." "When the continent's philosophical fashions landed in America," that historian, Stephen John Hartnett, notes, "they were devoured by those who longed for the imprimatur of the Old World's high style and aristocratic elegance." "For example," Hartnett writes, "the famous

Italian philosopher, Cesare Beccaria, was received during the Revolutionary era as more than just another reformer; he was a star, a celebrity, a cause to be debated and honored; he was, as James Madison lamented many years later, 'in the zenith of his fame as a Philosophical Legislator.'"[23]

The early American articles of war permitted capital punishment, but America's first military leaders still debated the efficacy of executions.[24] The Marquis de Lafayette—the French aristocrat who served as a major-general in the Continental Army under General Washington—was especially influenced by Beccaria's treatise. In Charles Spear's *Essays on the Punishment of Death*, Lafayette—the military man who worked closely with Thomas Jefferson in France when Jefferson served as America's minister there—is quoted on the title page as follows: "I shall ask for the abolition of the Penalty of Death until I have the infallibility of human judgment demonstrated to me. The Punishment of Death has always inspired me with feelings of horror since the execrable use made of it during the former Revolution."[25] "The Marquis of Beccaria," another high-level military man, General Charles Lee, wrote at one point, seeking guidance from the Italian thinker, "is of opinion, that a community ought to punish with death such criminals only whose existence is absolutely pernicious to the community; if his reasoning is just, a criminal king is almost the only criminal on whom death ought to be inflicted, as his existence, (if not always absolutely destructive,) is undoubtedly highly dangerous to society."[26] In other words, an American debate was taking place—even in the conservative atmosphere of the military—as to whether executions were really necessary.

During the Revolutionary War, the propriety of "retaliation"—a code word for executions—was itself a frequent topic of discussion. Though George Washington railed against "Inhuman Treatment" as "a flagrant violation of that Faith which ought to be held sacred by all civilized nations," Washington—in the midst of war—also expressed the view that should "the claims of humanity" be disregarded, "Justice and Policy will require recourse to be had to the Law of retaliation, however abhorrent and disagreeable to our natures in cases of Torture and Capital Punishments." For example, one hanging—of Joshua Huddy, a militia artillery captain—took place in New Jersey on April 12, 1782 at the direction of William Franklin, Benjamin Franklin's loyalist son. Huddy had been hanged by British loyalists in retaliation for the murder of one Philip White and the "Cruel murders of our Brethren." After the Huddy execution, George Washington inquired of his subordinates: "Is retaliation justifiable and expedient?" For his part, Washington initially believed that "this instance of Barbarity ... calls loudly for Retaliation." When it was decided to retaliate and select, by lot, a British officer of equal rank for execution, however, a heated controversy arose. The young British officer selected to die, Captain Charles Asgill, was just seventeen years old and the only son of Sir Charles Asgill, the wealthy, one-time Lord Mayor of London. The idea of sacrificing a teenage officer on the altar of retaliation stuck many Americans as repugnant and barbaric.

Henry Knox and Alexander Hamilton, General Washington's aide-de-camp, exchanged passionate letters about the Asgill controversy. Hamilton expressed the view that the proceedings against Asgill "if persisted in will be derogatory to the national character." "A sacrifice of this sort," Hamilton wrote, "is entirely repugnant to the genius of the age we live in and is without example in modern history nor can it fail to be considered in Europe as wanton and unnecessary." As Hamilton emphasized: "so solemn and deliberate a sacrifice of the innocent for the guilty must be condemned on the present received notions of humanity, and encourage an opinion that we are in a certain degree of barbarism." "My sentiments on frequent executions at this or any other period," Knox replied, "are very similar to yours." "I am persuaded that after reflexions will convince dispassionate and enlightened minds that executions have been too frequent, under the color of the Laws of the different states and they hereafter will be recited to sully the purity of our cause." At one point, James Madison, weighing in on the affair, told Edmund Randolph that, with regard to "selecting" an "innocent" officer, George Washington "seems to *lean to the side of compassion* but *asks the direction of Congress.*"

Ultimately, in the fall of 1782, Congress—at Washington's urging—decided to release Captain Asgill, avoiding the sight of a young man being executed in his prime. Washington said that, under the circumstances, "humanity dictates a fear for the unfortunate offering and inclines me to say that I most devoutly wish his life may be saved."[27] On November 13, 1782, Washington himself wrote to Asgill to give him the good news, with Washington telling Asgill it was his "singular pleasure" to transmit the Act of Congress "by which you are released from the disagreeable circumstances in which you have so long been." Washington's letter, which enclosed a passport for Asgill's use, then closed as follows: "I cannot take leave of you Sir without assuring you, that in whatever light my agency in this unpleasing affair may be viewed, I was never influenced thro' the whole of it by sanguinary motives; but by what I conceived a sense of my duty, which loudly called upon me to take measures however disagreable, to prevent a repetition of those enermities which have been the subject of discussion—And that this important end is likely to be answered without the effusion of the Blood of an innocent person is not a greater relief to you than it is to Sir Yr most obt and hble servt."[28] On October 7, 1782, Washington had written to his Secretary of War, Benjamin Lincoln, about "the case of Captain Asgill" that was then before Congress for its consideration. In that letter, Washington made his personal views on the matter crystal clear. "Was I to give my private Opinion respecting Asgill," Washington wrote, "I should pronounce in favor of his being released from his Duress and that he should be permitted to go to his Friends in Europe."[29]

During the Revolutionary War itself, the treatment of prisoners of war—both of American servicemen and British soldiers—was a subject that occupied much time and attention of America's founders. Elias Boudinot (1740–1821), the wealthy, Philadelphia-born politician who relocated to New Jersey and whose daughter Susan married Madison's friend William Bradford in 1784, served as an aide-de-camp to General William Livingston during the Revolutionary War. George Washington also tapped Boudinot, a lawyer elected to the Continental Congress in 1778, to serve as commissary general of prisoners. In the latter role, the deeply religious Boudinot—who founded the American Bible Society in 1816—worked closely with Quakers to feed and clothe the prisoners. As Boudinot, then a congressman, said on the subject of slavery before the First Congress in 1790: "Many of the Quakers I have long lived in the habits of friendship with, and can testify to the respectability of their characters and the regularity of their lives." Noting that he had "the honor of serving the United States at the commencement of the war as Commissary General of prisoners," Boudinot reported that when Congress was unable to afford supplies for prisoners, many Quakers "exercised such humanity towards them as did honor to human nature."[30]

In 1775, during the war's early hostilities, one particular incident attracted special interest from the get-go: the British capture of Vermont revolutionary Ethan Allen and some of his Green Mountain Boys as they ventured into Canada to try to capture Montreal. Allen and his men were imprisoned on ships, then taken to Ireland and England before being brought back to North America. In Ethan Allen's *Narrative of the Capture of Ticonderoga, and of His Captivity and Treatment by the British*, written by Allen himself and originally published in 1779, Allen wrote of his "long and barbarous captivity" and "the cruel and relentless disposition and the behaviour of the enemy, towards the prisoners in their power." And Ethan Allen's treatment was, certainly, not unusual or isolated in nature. The British — as one source puts it — "imprisoned between 24,850 and 32,000 Americans in and around Manhattan alone during the war." As that source reports: "Between 9,150 and 10,000 were held in the city's prisons, churches, and warehouses. Some 11,000 died in the abominable prison ships."[31]

After Ethan Allen fell into enemy hands, Thomas Jefferson drafted a declaration in January 1776 on the subject of the British mistreatment of Allen. "When necessity compelled us to take arms against Great Britain in defence of our just rights," the draft declaration began, "we thought it a circumstance of comfort that our enemy was brave and civilized." As the draft continued: "It is the happiness of modern times that the evils of necessary war are softened by refinement of manners and sentiment, and that an enemy is an object of vengeance, in arms, & in the field only. It is with pain we hear that Mr. Allen and others taken with him while fighting bravely in their country's cause, are sent to Britain in *irons*, to be *punished* for pretended treasons; treasons created by one of those very laws whose obligation we deny, and mean to contest by the sword." "To those who, bearing your arms, have fallen into our hands," Jefferson's draft declaration read, "we have afforded every comfort for which captivity and misfortune called." "Should you think proper in these days to revive antient barbarism, and again disgrace our nature with the practice of human sacrifice," Jefferson warned, "the fortune of war has put into our power subjects for multiplied retaliation." As Jefferson explained in his draft:

> To them, to you, and to the world we declare they shall not be wretched, unless their imprudence or your example shall oblige us to make them so; but we declare also that their lives shall teach our enemies to respect the rights of nations. We have ordered Brigadier General Prescot to be bound in irons, and confined in close jail, there to experience corresponding miseries with those which shall be inflicted on Mr. Allen. His life shall answer for that of Allen, and the lives of as many others as for those of the brave men captivated with him. We deplore the event which shall oblige us to shed blood for blood, and shall resort to retaliation but as the means of stopping the progress of butchery. It is a duty we owe to those engaged in the cause of their country, to assure them that if any unlucky circumstance, baffling the efforts of their bravery, shall put them in the power of their enemies, we will use the pledges in our hands to warrant their lives from sacrifice.[32]

In 1780, as American and British forces were fighting a war and an international public relations battle, John Adams himself decried British misconduct. As Adams wrote: "The English are degenerating in the Conduct of the American War into greater and greater Degrees of Cruelty and Barbarism. But there is a kind of Consulation in Seeing that they pursue the Same Maxims towards other nations, which they pursued, first towards Us." "When all Nations shall see that they have become Tyrants towards them," Adams emphasized in a letter to the Dutch lawyer Jean Luzac, one of the most influential European newspaper editors of the day, "they will at length believe that they have been Tyrants in America."[33]

Nathanael Greene — another of Washington's generals — loved books, and like Adams and Jefferson, he too had an easy familiarity with Beccaria's treatise. In *The Life of Nathanael Greene*, his biographer, George Washington Greene, recounts how Nathanael Greene's library included "Locke's Essay" and "the four beautiful quartos of Blackstone from the Oxford press." "Beccaria's golden treatise, the first application of a humane philosopher to the theory of crimes and punishments," was there, too, his biographer reported. In another telling anecdote, Greene received a letter in 1776 from John Clark, Jr., whom Greene's biographer characterizes as "a spirited young Pennsylvanian, Major in McCallister's battalion, who won so upon Greene's good opinion that he afterwards took him into his family as an aid." Clark, a young lawyer "fond of fun and frolick" who distinguished himself at the Battle of New York, became General Nathanael Greene's aide-de-camp and an American spy. Writing from "Mr. Lawrence's, at Rockland, on the 8th of November, in a delicate, lady's hand," Clark reported that he had "ordered a fisherman to catch a few pike; hope to have the pleasure of presenting you with a mess very soon." "Pray tell Major Blodget there is a fine pond to employ his angling in, and that I think an exercise of this kind will be conducive to his health." In the postscript, Clark added: "Pray don't forget to send for Beccaria on 'Crimes and Punishments' for me, and furnish me with Sterne's 'Sentimental Journal.' I'll take care of it, and return it safe."[34]

General Greene's own grandson, historian George Washington Greene (1811–1883), used Beccaria's name and ideas in his own writings. George Washington Greene studied at Brown University, then spent two decades in Europe, including a stint as the United States consul in Rome from 1837 to 1845. He published French and Italian textbooks, wrote histories of the American Revolution and his grandfather, and corresponded with the likes of Henry Wadsworth Longfellow, once sending him an 1870 speech he had given in the Rhode Island House of Representatives in favor of making imprisonment for debt illegal. That speech—as with other of George Washington Greene's writings—referenced Beccaria's *Tratto dei Delitti e delle Pene* (1764). In his *History and Geography of the Middle Ages for Colleges and Schools* (1857), Greene wrote of "LEGISLATION OF THE BARBARIANS." In writing of "the ancient usages of Germany," he remarked: "Among nations long accustomed to a life of violence and devastation, and whose daily occupation is war, the punishment of murder is left to the relations of the murdered man, unless they choose to accept a pecuniary compensation (*wehrgeld*), which is fixed by law according to the rank or dignity of the victim." "Capital punishment," Greene added of the one-time German custom, "is reserved for cowardice and treason, often even for theft, which is held to be the most dangerous of all perfidy among a wandering people, who have no other safeguard for their property but mutual confidence."

Writing in 1875 in the preface to one of his histories, *The German Element in the War of American Independence*, George Washington Greene noted that "[i]n the first decade of the present century one of the most attractive saloons of Paris was the saloon of a lady whom, out of reverence for the memory of her father, Italians loved to call Madame Beccaria, although she was already the mother of Alessandro Manzoni." In his history, Greene then recounted how his fellow historian Carlo Botta, "a young Canavese" who had suffered "persecution in his own Italy," had attended Madame Beccaria's literary gathering one evening. "Following up the train of thought which the evening's conservation had awakened," Greene wrote of how Botta had decided to write his history of American independence by mulling over the prior discussion at Madame Beccaria's home as he walked in Paris "through that square so deeply stained with the blood of the victims of the Reign of Terror." "The very next morning," Greene wrote of Botta's 1806 epiphany in that square, "he began his studies, and in 1809 gave his great classic to the world." Carlo Botta's Italian-language writings reference both Beccaria and Filangieri, the dynamic duo of Italian penal reformers, and Botta's *History of the War of Independence of the United States of America*, published in Paris in 1809, became a classic.[35]

Charles Lee—a former British officer and another of Washington's Revolutionary War generals—was, like Nathanael Greene, especially taken with Beccaria's book. The youngest son of John Lee, a British infantry colonel, Charles Lee was born in the early 1730s, received a commission in the army at age eleven, studied Greek and Latin, and acquired a working knowledge of French. "In later years, in the course of his rambles about Europe," it has been noted, "he became more or less proficient in Spanish, Italian, and German." After his father's death, Charles Lee received a commission as a lieutenant and was ordered to America in 1754 under the command of its lieutenant colonel Thomas Gage. According to one of Lee's biographers, "his sympathetic appreciation of Beccaria's great treatise on 'Crime and Punishment' was much to his credit; as a schoolboy in Switzerland he had learned republican theories under good teachers; and there is no reason for doubting his sincerity in hating and despising the despotism which then prevailed almost everywhere on the continent of Europe." According to that biographer's sketch of Lee: "He was a radical free-thinker of the unripe, acrid sort, like his contemporaries, John Wilkes and Thomas Paine." On June 17, 1775, the Second Continental Congress appointed Lee—well-connected with George Washington, Thomas Mifflin and other revolutionaries—to the rank of second major-general in the Continental Army. In immediately resigning his British commission, he wrote to Lord William Barrington, the British secretary of war, to complain of English measures "so absolutely subversive of the rights and liberties of every individual subject, so destructive to the whole empire at large, and ultimately so ruinous to his Majesty's own person, dignity, and family, that I think myself obliged in conscience, as a citizen, Englishman, and soldier of a free state, to exert my utmost to defeat them."[36]

In "A Political Essay," published along with General Lee's memoirs, Lee—the American revolutionary—praised *On Crimes and Punishments* as an "incomparable treatise." In Lee's essay, he envisioned a future society—premised on Beccaria's ideas—in which "capital punishments should be confined to delinquent kings alone; that all other delinquents, let their crimes be what they will, should be sent into exile; their estates, money, and goods confiscated to the use of the community."[37] Under English law, *transportation*—a punishment once used by English judges to send convicts to the American colonies—had long before emerged as a popular alternative to death sentences. Although seventeenth-century English judges viewed transportation across the seas as a discretionary sentencing power, the British Parliament codified the practice's legitimacy in the Transportation Act of 1718. Tens of thousands of felons ultimately avoided execution on the condition that they be exiled as indentured servants. As Lee summarized his main, Beccaria-inspired propositions before coming to the conclusion that, in America, exile should take the place of death sentences: "first admitting Beccaria's position to be just, *that a community ought not to punish with death any criminal whose existence is not absolutely pernicious, or highly dangerous to the community*; and further admitting *that a criminal king is the only criminal whose existence can be pernicious or highly dangerous*." By the time Lee penned those words, it is clear that Beccaria's ideas had filtered far beyond English radicals and the French *philosophes*, working their way into the minds of America's battle-hardened military commanders.

Indeed, the writings of Charles Lee reveal the shifting views of the time. In "A Sketch of a Plan for the Formation of a Military Colony," Lee—the ex-British soldier who had aspired to be the Continental Army's commander in chief—wrote of his plans for organizing and structuring a large military community. "With respect to criminal matters," he wrote, "I would adopt Beccaria's scheme; its excellencies have been demonstrated in the Tuscan dominions."[38] Lee, like other Americans, was very aware of the fact that in 1786, persuaded by Beccaria's ideas, Grand Duke Peter Leopold of Tuscany had abolished capital punishment. Similarly, Lee and others also knew that Russia's Empress Elizabeth of Moscovy—another Beccaria admirer—had adopted anti-death penalty views.[39] As Lee himself characterized the Tuscan and Russian experiences with Beccaria's approach:

> When the present Grand Duke acceded to the ducal throne, he found Tuscany the most abandoned people of all Italy, filled with robbers and assassins. Every where, for a series of years previous to the government of this excellent prince, were seen gallows, wheels and tortures of every kind; and the robberies and mur-

ders were not at all less frequent. He had read and admired the Marquis of Beccaria, and determined to try the effects of his plan. He put a stop to all capital punishments, even for the greatest crimes; and the consequences have convinced the world of its wholesomeness. The galleys, slavery for a certain term of years, or for life, in proportion to the crime, have accomplished what an army of hangmen, with their hooks, wheels and gibbets, could not. In short, Tuscany, from being a theatre of the greatest crimes and villainies of every species, is become the safest and best ordered State of Europe.

It is a known fact, that since the adoption of this plan, there have been but two murders committed: one by a little boy of eleven years old, in a stroke of passion; and the other, not by a native Italian subject, but by an Irish officer. But if we had not this example, and that of the Empress Elizabeth, (who adopted the same plan, which had the same good effect) before our eyes, the inculcating an idea in a military people that death is the most terrible of all punishments, is certainty the most absurd of solecisms. Nothing great can be expected from a community which is taught to consider it as such.[40]

"I am therefore absolutely and totally against capital punishments, at least in our military community," Lee concluded. In their place, Lee suggested the following:

Let the loss of liberty, and ignomy, be inculcated as the extreme of all punishments: common culprits therefore are, in proportion to the degree of their delinquency, to be condemned to slavery, for a longer or shorter term of years; to public works, such as repairing high ways, and public building, with some ignominious distinction of habit, denoting their condition. As to those who have been guilty of crimes of a very deep dye, such as wanton murder, perjury, and the like, let them be mutilated, their ears cut off, their faces stamped with the marks of infamy, and whipped out of the State.[41]

According to *The Papers of James Madison*, General Charles Lee also "had a large share in drafting" the address "To the Inhabitants of the Province of Quebec," which quoted Beccaria.[42]

Military men in the late eighteenth and early nineteenth centuries were certainly familiar with Beccarian principles. For example, in John M'Arthur's *Principles and Practice of Naval and Military Courts-Martial*, there are multiple references to Beccaria's ideas. "[T]he rule laid by Beccaria, and other writers on criminal law, ought to be attended to," M'Arthur wrote of Beccaria's proportionality principle. "The philosophic Beccaria, in his Essay on Crimes and Punishments," M'Arthur added in another passage of his treatise, "has remarked that it is an essential point, in all legislations, to determine exactly the degrees of credibility which ought to be given to witnesses, and the proofs necessary to confirm a crime." In commenting on treason and Montesquieu's view that laws that condemn a man to death should require at least two witnesses, M'Arthur further noted: "Beccaria, with his usual humanity, delivers a similar opinion."[43] In the U.S. Constitution itself, America's founders specifically provided that "[n]o Person shall be convicted of Treason unless on the Testimony of two Witnesses to the same overt Act, or on Confession in open Court." As historian Armstrong Starkey sums up in *War in the Age of Enlightenment, 1700–1789*: "Beccaria sought to ameliorate the cruelty of the age, and in doing so left an indelible mark on the subject of criminal justice."[44]

Alexander Hamilton, while not adhering to Beccaria's position on the need to abolish capital punishment, nevertheless pushed for penal reform after the Revolutionary War's conclusion. In a December 1799 letter to James McHenry, Hamilton expressed the view that "[a] complete revision of the Articles of War is desireable, as they require amendment in many particulars." And Hamilton's letter reflects the changing public sentiment. As Hamilton wrote:

> The proper mode of treating the crime of desertion has been in most countries an embarrassing subject. In ours it is particularly so. The punishment of death except in time of War is contrary to the popular habits of thinking. Whipping is found ineffectual. I have a hope that confinement and labour would prove more effectual. Believing this punishment to be within the discretion of Courts Martial, I encourage its adoption.

"It is not however my idea to abolish Death," Hamilton offered, saying that penalty "in some aggravated cases, would be proper even in time of peace and in time of war ought invariably to ensure." "I incline even to the opinion that the power of pardoning ought to be taken away in this case," Hamilton added, "certainly in every instance of desertion or an attempt to desert to enemies or Traitors."[45]

A general order issued in 1800, dealing with the court martial of a private in the 2nd Regiment of Artillerists and Engineers, showed the evolution in Hamilton's thinking on how to handle offenders. After being found guilty of "repeated desertion," the man—alias Parker Hosmer—had been sentenced to pay the expenses attending his apprehension, to "receive ninety-nine lashes upon his naked back, at three different times, with two days, thirty-three lashes at each time; have one half of his head shaved, and one eye-brow; and be publicly drummed out of the garrison with a halter round his neck, and rendered incapable ever again to serve in the army of the United States." The general order noted that "major general Hamilton confirms the sentence and orders its execution," but also contained this remark: "Whether whipping and a discharge from the service, even in the most disgraceful manner, is the mode of punishment best calculated to prevent the crime of desertion, is a question which demands the consideration of future Courts Martial." The general order further read:

> Hardened in infamy, and lost to shame, the discharged deserter waits only the moment when the disgraceful marks of his punishment shall disappear, to reinlist himself in some other corps, again to receive a bounty, and defraud the United States. Against offenders of this description what guard can be placed, or what punishment can be inflicted, sufficient to prevent a crime so ruinous to an army a desertion. Major general Hamilton is strongly inclined to believe, that hard labour for the term which remains to them to serve, and confinement in such manner as to clog all attempts if not bar all hope of escape, gives the fairest prospects of success. Should this opinion be adopted, Fort Independence, in the harbour of Boston, Ellis Island, in the harbour of New-York, and Fort Mifflin in the Delaware, are designated as places of safe confinement.[46]

The Justices: James Wilson and John Jay

George Washington's presidential appointments—among them, his judicial nominees—also included Beccaria admirers and advocates of penal reform. James Wilson, appointed to serve on the newly formed U.S. Supreme Court, frequently cited Beccaria's treatise,[47] and spoke of Beccaria in his law lectures.[48] Educated in Scotland, Wilson—an active participant in Philadelphia's 1787 Constitutional Convention—became the University of Pennsylvania's first law professor in 1790. "The Marquis of Beccaria," Wilson said in one lecture, "thinks himself authorized to assert, that crimes are to be measured only by the injury done to society." In that lecture, in a section titled "Of the Nature of Crimes; and the Necessity and Proportion of Punishments," Wilson featured Beccaria, with Wilson stating in the early 1790s: "The theory of criminal law has not, till lately, been a subject of much attention or investigation. The Marquis of Beccaria led the way. His performance derives much importance from the sentiments and principles, which it contains: it derives, perhaps, more from those, which its appearance has excited in others. It induced several of the most celebrated literati in Europe to think upon the subject."[49]

In a grand jury charge in the U.S. Circuit Court for the District of Virginia in 1791, Wilson also repeated many of Beccaria's themes and specifically referred to "the eloquent and benevolent *Beccaria*."[50] "Gentlemen of the Grand Jury," he began, sounding a Beccarian tone in these opening sentences of his charge: "To prevent crimes is the noblest end and aim of criminal jurisprudence." "There are, in punishments, three qualities, which render them the fit preventives of crimes. The first is their moderation. The second is their speediness. The third is their certainty." Saying "[t]he impunity of an offender encourages him to repeat his offences," Wilson urged "moderate and mild" punishments, concluding that such punishments would help hold criminals accountable for their actions. As Wilson advised as he rode the circuit: "Let the punishment be proportioned—let it be analogous—to the crime. Let the reformation as well as the punishment of offenders be kept constantly and steadily in view: and, while the dignity of the nation is vindicated, let reparation be made to those, who have received injury." "Let the law diffuse peace and happiness," Wilson added, "and innocence will walk in their train."

In his lengthy grand jury charge, Wilson took particular aim at capital punishment. "It is the opinion of some writers, highly respected for their good sense, as well as for their humanity, that capital punishments are, in no case necessary," Wilson recounted in one section of his charge, adding: "It is an opinion, which I am certainly well warranted in offering—that nothing but the most absolute necessity can authorize them." "Another opinion I am equally warranted in offering," Wilson spoke of executions, is "that they should not be aggravated by any sufferings, except those which are inseparably attached to a violent death." As Wilson argued: "It was worthy only of a tyrant—and of a tyrant it was truly characteristick—to give standing instructions to his executioners, that they should protract the expiring moments of the tortured criminal; and should manage the butchering business with such studied and slow barbarity, as that his powers of painful sensation should continue to the very last—*ut mori se sentiat*." After describing Sir Edward Coke's prior imposition of a sentence of hanging, disembowelment, decapitation and drawing and quartering at the 1606 trial of the Gunpowder Plot conspirators, Wilson offered these words to grand jurors: "I relieve your feelings by a custom which was observed among the Jews. They gave wine mingled with myrrh to a criminal at the time of his execution, in order to produce a stupor, and deaden the sensibility of the pain." The conspirators in the Gunpowder Plot, a failed assassination attempt that involved a plan to blow up the House of Lords during the opening of Parliament, led to the plotters' violent deaths at the hands of the state.[51]

Wilson—as a U.S. Supreme Court Justice—also paraphrased Beccaria's words in another grand jury charge in 1793 in Boston, Massachusetts.[52] Noting that England's Bloody Code, in Blackstone's time, made "no fewer than one hundred and sixty actions" punishable by death, Wilson spoke of the opportunity that Americans now had to shape their own laws, adding that "sanguinary laws" are "a political distemper of the most inveterate and the most dangerous kind."[53] In Wilson's own state, Pennsylvania's constitution of 1776 provided that "[t]he penal laws as heretofore used shall be reformed by the legislature of this state, as soon as may be, and punishments made in some cases less sanguinary, and in general more proportionate to the crimes."[54]

The writings and law lectures of James Wilson, in fact, contain a large number of references to Beccaria's ideas. A product of the Enlightenment and a frequent speaker at the Constitutional Convention in Philadelphia, Wilson expressed the view, for example, that "the happiness of the society is the *first* law of every government." "[A]ll power," he said, "is derived from the people—that their happiness is the end of government."[55] A perusal of Wilson's writings, edited by Robert McCloskey, reveal a near obsession with the Italian philosopher. The following excerpts from Wilson's writings show Wilson's plain admiration for Beccaria ideas:

> "'An overgrown republick,' says the Marquis of Beccaria, in the exquisite performance, with which he has enriched the treasures of legislation—'an overgrown republick can be saved from despotism, only by subdividing it into a number of confederate republicks.'"
>
> "These reflections naturally lead us to one illustrious source of the propriety of a jury to decide on matters of evidence. 'It is much easier,' says the Marquis of Beccaria, 'to feel the moral certainty of proofs, than to define it exactly. For this reason I think it an excellent law, which established assistants to the principal Judge, and those chosen by lot: For that ignorance which judges by its feelings is little subject to errour.'"
>
> "Would you prevent crimes? says the Marquis of Beccaria: let the laws be clear and simple: let the entire force of the nation be united in their defence: let them, and them only, be feared. The fear of the laws is salutary: but the fear of man is a fruitful and a fatal source of crimes. Happy the nation, in which pardons will be considered as dangerous!"
>
> "All trials, says Beccaria, should be publick; that opinion, which is the best, or, perhaps, the only cement of society, may curb the authority of the powerful, and the passions of the judge; and that the people, inspired with courage, may say, 'We are not slaves; we are protected by the laws.'"
>
> "On the other hand—I now speak from Beccaria—a man of enlightened understanding, appointed guardian of the laws, is the greatest blessing that a sovereign can bestow on a nation. Such a man is accustomed to behold truth, and not to fear it: unacquainted with the greatest part of those imaginary and insatiable necessities, which so often put virtue to the proof, and accustomed to contemplate mankind from the most elevated point of view, he considers the nation as his family, and his fellow citizens as brothers."
>
> "There was a time, says Beccaria, when the crimes of the subjects were the inheritance of the prince. At such a time probably it was, that the judge himself became the prosecutor. In several of the feudal nations, this was, indeed, the case. The gross impropriety of this regulation appears at the first view. The prosecutor is a party: without the last necessity, the prosecutor ought not to be both a party and a judge."
>
> "'In extreme political liberty,' says the Marquis of Beccaria, 'and in absolute despotism, all ideas of honour disappear, or are confounded with others. In the first case, reputation becomes useless from the despotism of the laws; and, in the second, the despotism of one man, annulling all civil existence, reduces the rest to a precarious temporary personality. Honour, then, is one of the fundamental principles of those monarchies, which are a limited despotism; and in these, like revolutions in despotick states, it is a momentary return to a state of nature and original equality.'"

"The Marquis of Beccaria goes farther: he thinks himself authorized to assert, that crimes are to be measured only by the injury done to society. They err, therefore, says he, who imagine that a crime is greater or less according to the intention of the person by whom it is committed; for this will depend on the actual impression of objects on the senses, and on the previous disposition of the mind; and both of these will vary in different persons, and even in the same person at different times, according to the succession of ideas, passions, and circumstances.... That crimes are to be estimated by the injury done to society, adds he, is one of those palpable truths, which, though evident to the meanest capacity, yet, by a combination of circumstances, are known only to a few thinking men, in every nation and in every age."

"If, indeed, it is an errour, as the Marquis of Beccaria alleges it to be, to think a crime greater or less according to the intention of him by whom it is committed, it is, in the common law, an errour of the most inveterate kind; it is an errour which the experience of ages has not been able to correct."

"'It is not only,' says the Marquis of Beccaria, 'the common interest of mankind that crimes should not be committed; but it is their interest also that crimes of every kind should be less frequent, in proportion to the mischief which they produce in society. The means, therefore, which the legislature use to prevent crimes, should be more powerful in proportion as they are destructive of the publick safety and happiness. Therefore there ought to be a fixed proportion between punishments and crimes.' 'A scale of crimes,' adds he, 'may be formed, of which the first degree should consist of such as tend immediately to the dissolution of society; and the last, of the smallest possible injustice done to a private member of society.'"

"In many countries, his confession is considered as absolutely indispensable to the condemnation of the criminal. The Marquis of Beccaria conjectures that this rule has been taken from the mysterious tribunal of penitence, in which the confession of sins is a necessary part of the sacrament: thus, says he, have men abused the unerring light of revelation."

"In the case of oaths, says Beccaria, which are administered to a criminal to make him speak the truth, when the contrary is his greatest interest, there is a palpable contradiction between the laws and the natural sentiments of mankind. Can a man think himself obliged to contribute to his own destruction? Why should he be reduced to the terrible alternative of doing this, or of offending against God? For the law, which, in such a case, requires an oath, leaves him only the choice of being a bad Christian, or of being a martyr. Such laws, continues he, are useless as well as unnatural: they are like a dike opposed directly to the course of the torrent: it is either immediately overwhelmed, or, by a whirlpool which itself forms, it is gradually undermined and destroyed."

"It may, however, be urged, on the principles of Beccaria, that to the conduct of which he has been convicted, he was probably drawn by a motive of interest; and that, if no such motive exists in the present instance, the inference from the past to the present is without foundation."

"'How happy would mankind be,' says the eloquent and benevolent Beccaria, 'if laws were now to be first formed!' The United States enjoy this singular happiness. Their laws are now first formed. They are formed by the legitimate representatives of free citizens and free states. Among those citizens and those states they now begin to be diffused."

In the preface to James Wilson's papers, Bird Wilson—James Wilson's son, another lawyer—also quoted Beccaria, perhaps as an homage to his father's fondness for the Italian thinker. "'The laws,' says the celebrated Beccaria,' Bird wrote, "'are always several ages behind the actual improvement of the nation which they govern.'" "If this observation is true, and I believe it to be true, with regard to law in general," Bird added, "its truth is of peculiar importance, with regard to criminal law in particular." "For on the excellence of the criminal law," Bird emphasized, "the liberty and happiness of the citizens chiefly depend."[56] James Wilson, during his own life, had called English law "defective to a degree both gross and cruel"; called for proportionate punishments that would be "moderate and mild"; and cited Sabacos (716–702 B.C.), an Ethiopian king who ruled Egypt and replaced capital punishment with life sentences to be carried out "in the publick works." James Wilson—who clearly had spent much time with *On Crimes and Punishments* in his hands—felt that if capital punishment were to be imposed for any crime, premeditated murder fit the bill. But his own son Bird—in an act of conscience—later resigned his Pennsylvania judgeship because of his personal opposition to the death penalty. As a judge of the Court of Common Pleas, Bird had condemned a man to die, then left the legal profession to pursue a calling as a minister and theologian. When a friend and his niece were at his bedside near the end of his life, Bird was heard to say: "He was launched into eternity unprepared; but O God! impute it not to me!"[57]

Another Washington appointee, John Jay—the first chief justice of the U.S. Supreme Court—also favored penal reform. In the midst of the Revolutionary War, Jay had to adjudicate criminal cases and, in that role, had to decide between severe punishments and mercy. On May 3, 1777, Jay had been elected chief justice of the New York State Supreme Court of Judicature, a position in which—as he told his wife Sarah—he found "trying criminals" "the most disagreeable part of my Duty." "Punishment," he wrote in that violent-ridden, wartime setting, "must of course become certain & Mercy dormant—a harsh System repugnant to my Feelings, but nevertheless necessary." "In such Circumstances," Jay wrote of frequent robberies and the woods affording criminals "Shelter & the Tories Food," "Lenity would be Cruelty, & Severity is found on the Side of Humanity."[58] As New York's governor, though, Jay spoke in favor of fewer capital crimes and the legislature responded, "expunging" from the criminal code—as Jay's son William put it—"many of the sanguinary features which it had borrowed from the jurisprudence of the mother country." In particular, the number of capital crimes was curtailed and a provision was made for the erection of two prisons, one of which, in Greenwich Village, was opened to receive prisoners in November 1797.[59]

Jay's views on crime and punishment are apparent from his days as a judge. In a grand jury charge Jay gave in New York, Connecticut, Massachusetts and New Hampshire in 1790, Jay spoke, in particular, of the purpose of punishment. "The end of punishment," Jay said, "is not to expiate for offences, but by the terror of example to deter men from the commission of them." "To render these examples useful," Jay instructed, "policy as well as morality requires not only that punishment be proportionate to guilt, but that all proceedings against persons accused or suspected, should be accompanied by the reflection *that they may be innocent.*" "We are happy that the genius of our laws is mild," Jay emphasized to the grand jurors. "Warm, partial, and precipitate prosecutions, and cruel and abominable executions, such as racks, embowelling, drawing, quartering, burning and the like," he added, "are no less impolitic than inhuman; they infuse into the public mind disgust at the barbarous severity of government, and fill it with pity and partiality for the sufferers."[60] Traditionally, executions and harsh corporal punishments were—as historian Robert Sullivan writes—"filled with pomp and circumstance." As Sullivan explains: "Floggings, the amputation of an ear or a hand, placing a convict in the stockade—these were all ceremonial affairs designed to affirm the power of the state and even its glory."[61]

Jay himself had much personal experience with the way in which punishments were meted out. Before authoring some of *The Federalist Papers* and becoming the country's first Chief Justice, Jay lamented to his wife on August 3, 1778, during the midst of the Revolutionary War, that his stay at the family farm at Fishkill "will probably be short, as the number of persons charged with capital offenses now in confinement requires that courts for their trial be speedily held." As Jay emphasized in his letter to his wife in very Beccarian terms: "Delays in punishing crimes encourage the commission of crime. The more certain and speedy the punishment, the fewer will be the objects."[62] Although Jay believed executions were a Biblical command in cases of murder, he opposed capital punishment for lesser crimes and argued that proper "establishments for confining, employing and reforming criminals" were "indispensable." As New York's governor, Jay thus took a keen and personal interest in the construction of the state's first penitentiary.[63] As one history of America's corrections system explains: "In 1794, the Philadelphia Society for Alleviating the Miseries of Public Prisons had launched into an extensive campaign of correspondence with other states. Possibly as a direct result of the society's contact with Governor John Jay of New York, Jay sent a team to study the reforms at the Walnut Street Jail—namely, General Philip Schuyler, a Revolutionary War hero, and Thomas Eddy, a Quaker financier."[64]

In their lifetimes, the Founding Fathers began to witness—and in some cases directly plan—the construction of state penitentiaries throughout America. After Jeremy Bentham's first plan for a Panopticon-style prison was submitted to the British Parliament in 1790, New York prison reformer Thomas Eddy—a big Beccaria admirer—oversaw the construction in 1797 of the Newgate Prison along the Hudson River.[65] "The eloquent Beccaria," Eddy wrote in 1801, "roused the attention of civilized Europe, and, by his answerable appeal to reason and humanity, produced those successive efforts to meliorate the systems of penal laws, which constitute the greatest glory of the present age." Eddy's visit to Philadelphia's Walnut Street Prison, then already in operation, inspired Eddy's own project in New York. "Though restrained for a time," Eddy wrote of Pennsylvania, which had seen the adoption and repeal of William Penn's milder laws, "the spirit of reform revived with the revolution; and, strengthened by the discussions of the general principles of freedom, and the writings of Beccaria and others, at length produced that system of punishment for crimes, which reflects so much honour on that State." Eddy not only quoted Beccaria more than once, but he did so specifically on the issue of deterrence—an issue Beccaria had written about with passion.[66]

In a letter to Thomas Jefferson dated February 9, 1802, Thomas Eddy—recapping earlier penal reform efforts—emphasized that "[t]he Sanguinary Penal Laws of Europe, wch. were continued in their full extent in the United States, very soon claimed the attention of a people attached to principles of Freedom, Moderation & Justice." "The Province of Pennsylvania under the Administration of the virtuous Penn," Eddy wrote, had "early, but in vain, attempted the Establishment of a Code of Laws by which each crime received a punishment in proportion to its degree of enormity—Soon after the Revolution, encouraged by the spirit of Freedom to investigate a subject which they held of the first importance to Civil society, they framed a System of Penal Laws which reflects lasting credit on that State." "This State," Eddy then wrote of New York, "became enamoured with the alteration & Establishment made in Pennsylvania, and in 1796 adopted similar Laws." "The Prison in New York," Eddy noted, "serves to receive the Convicts of the whole State," with Eddy writing that he felt it his "duty" as a prison inspector to "spread principles tending to promote the general good of Mankind, wch. perhaps when more known may be the means of bringing forward similar establishments." "I was induced to publish a Pamphlet giving an account of this benevolent institution," Eddy told Jefferson, appealing to Jefferson's humanity as he forwarded a copy of that pamphlet along with the salutation "RESPECTED FRIEND." As Eddy wrote to Jefferson: "Perfectly satisfied that thou are attached to a reform, founded on the pure principles of Christianity, I am induced, without the pleasure of being personally known, to take the liberty of presenting thee with the account I have just published, and of wch. I crave thy kind acceptance."[67]

In colonial America, criminal sentences—as Jefferson and Eddy knew—could be incredibly severe, extending to death and a whole series of lesser, non-lethal corporal punishments. In seventeenth-century colonial New York, humiliating punishments such as whipping and the stocks, while perhaps somewhat rare in practice, were part and parcel of the criminal justice system and its administration.[68] In fact, one law provided that "[e]very Towne shall at their charge provide a paire of Stockes for offenders" and that "Prisons and Pilloryes are likewise to be provided in these Towns where the Severall Courts of Sessions are to be holden."[69] As Herbert Johnson, John Jay's biographer, has written of early American punishments: "In regard to lesser crimes, sentences were also remarkable for their severity." In November 1768, Johnson notes, Jay's friend, Robert R. Livingston, Jr., specifically pointed to "the pitiable plight of a young woman given a temporary stay of execution from a death sentence so that she might give birth to an unfortunate child that would be left motherless by her execution a few days after its birth."[70] In the eighteenth century, ear cropping was still a fact of life while the punishment of pregnant women—both in the U.S. and abroad— was, by custom, often temporarily deferred in consideration of their pregnancies.[71]

After the publication of *On Crimes and Punishments*, New Yorkers were drawn to the cause of penal reform as never before. As Edwin Burrows and Mike Wallace write in *Gotham: A History of New York City to 1898*, "Beccaria became a pillar of enlightened opinion" in the 1770s and 1780s. After Beccaria's ideas influenced the popular English penal reformer John Howard, the authors of *Gotham* note, "Howard and Beccaria in turn fired the imagination of Thomas Eddy." A Quaker philanthropist originally from Philadelphia, Eddy had settled in New York after the Revolutionary War and became a successful insurance broker. Eddy specifically acknowledged the influence of Montesquieu, Howard and Beccaria. "In the mid-1790s," Burrows and Wallace recount, "Eddy marshaled politically influential acquaintances—Philip Schuyler and George Clinton, among others—to reform the state's antiquated criminal code." Eddy called that code a relic of "barbarous usages" and "monarchical principles" that was not suited to "a new country, simple manners, and a popular form of government." "Eddy's reform," the authors of *Gotham* explain, "bore fruit in 1796 when the state legislature abolished corporal punishment and trimmed the number of capital offenses from sixteen to three (treason, murder, theft from a church)." "Persons convicted of less crimes like burglary and arson," they emphasize, "were sentenced to hard labor in Newgate Prison, the state's first penitentiary, which stood on the Hudson River shore at the foot of Amos (now 16th) Street in Greenwich Village." Eddy—the industrious and hands-on social reformer—became the warden of that institution when it opened in November 1797.[72]

The Attorneys General and the Poet

The first United States Attorney General was Edmund Randolph (1753–1813). Born in Williamsburg, Virginia, and a College of William and Mary graduate, Randolph had read law with his father John Randolph and his uncle Peyton Randolph. After being admitted to the bar in 1774, Edmund Randolph supported the cause of the American Revolution, as did his uncle Peyton Randolph, twice president of the Continental Congress. It was Peyton Randolph who once told Thomas Jefferson that *A Summary View of the Rights of British America* (1774) had almost gotten Jefferson, its author, on an early kill list. "I was informed afterwards by Peyton Randolph," Jefferson recorded of the conversation, that his *Summary View* had "procured me the honor of having my name inserted in a long list of proscriptions enrolled in a bill of attainder commenced in one of the houses of parliament" but that was "suppressed in embryo by the hasty step of events which warned them to be a little cautious." In 1785, Edmund Randolph—who later petitioned Governor Beverley Randolph to oppose an execution—wrote that Virginia's executive had "at last" been "persuaded of their power to make the Beccarian experiment on the condemned." After serving as Virginia's first attorney general, becoming Virginia's governor, and playing a major role at Philadelphia's 1787 Constitutional Convention, Edmund Randolph was tapped by George Washington to serve as the country's first Attorney General of the United States—a position he served in until 1794, when he replaced Thomas Jefferson as Secretary of State.

In 1794, President Washington appointed William Bradford, Jr., the respected Pennsylvania lawyer and a conservative Federalist, as the country's second Attorney General. Another lawyer highly sympathetic to penal reform, Bradford had graduated from the College of New Jersey in 1772, and in his time there had befriended an array of future revolutionaries. Those men included Hugh Henry Brackenridge, Aaron Burr, Philip Freneau and—most notably—James Madison.[73] Bradford, once described as one of Philadelphia's "Enlightenment literati," previously served on Pennsylvania's Supreme Court. An open admirer of Beccaria's treatise, Bradford had been approached, shortly before his presidential appointment, by Pennsylvania's governor, Thomas Mifflin, to help curtail executions in the state. Mifflin—the President of the Continental Congress from 1783 to 1784—served as Pennsylvania's governor from 1790 to 1799.[74]

The poet Philip Freneau (1752–1832), Madison's friend who wrote anti-British poetry during the Revolutionary War, gave his poems titles such as "The Rising Glory of America," "To the Memory of the Brave Americans," and "The Republican Genius of Europe." The latter poem, published in *The Jersey Chronicle* in 1795, contained these verses celebrating the American and French Revolutions:

> In western worlds the flame began:
>   From thence to France it flew—
> Through Europe, now, it takes its way,
> Beams an insufferable day,
>   And lays all tyrants low.
>
> Genius of France! pursue the chace
>   Till Reason's laws restore
> Man to be Man, in every clime;—
> That Being, active, great, sublime
>   Debas'd in dust no more.

Freneau, of Huguenot descent and the grandson of a New York wine importer, also authored essays for *The Freeman's Journal*, a Philadelphia newspaper he edited from 1781 to 1784. In the November 28, 1781 issue of that paper, its editor declared "that native, wanton and inherent cruelty is nowhere so conspicuous as in the inhabitants of Britain," with "[t]housands of unfortunate wretches" annually "hurried out of the world for trifling thefts and other pretty crimes." Freneau wrote continuously about liberty, and after being held captive on a ship, his poem, "The British Prison Ship," included these lines, a swipe at Benedict Arnold and his ilk: *Traitors, lost to every sense of shame, / Unjust supporters of a tyrant's claim.* In the post-war period, in 1809, Freneau also dedicated a poem to "Mr. Jefferson" as Jefferson approached his retirement from the presidency. Among its lines, printed in Trenton, New Jersey's *True American*: *That* INDEPENDENCE *we had sworn to gain,* / *By you asserted (nor* DECLARED *in vain)* / *We seized, triumphant, from a tyrant's throne,* / *And Britain tottered when the work was done.*[75]

Before the ratification of the U.S. Bill of Rights in 1791, Bradford—like so many of his contemporaries—would come, as James Wilson had, to sing Beccaria's praises. Not only did Bradford lavish praise on Beccaria's treatise in his 1786 letter to the Italian botanist Luigi Castiglioni, but he invoked Beccaria's name both before and after the ratification of the U.S. Bill of Rights in other writings. For example, in 1790, Colonel Timothy Pickering—destined to become George Washington's Secretary of State in 1795—sought William Bradford's advice. In a letter to Colonel Pickering dated February 7, 1790, Bradford specifically brought up Beccaria's name, writing:

> Agreeably to your request, I have considered the article in the proposed plan of government, which enables the party accused before a court of oyer and terminer to remove the proceedings into the Supreme Court. I must take the liberty of saying that I do not readily perceive the necessity of this clause. If it is apprehended that the Justices of that Court will be incompetent to the task assigned them, the power of trying capital offences ought not to be given to them. If otherwise, there can be no reason in preventing them from exercising it. It is the opinion of Beccaria, and all enlightened philosophers on this subject, that punishment should follow the crime as quickly as possible; but the clause in question proceeds on a different principle, and its natural operation is to postpone the punishment till the remembrance and detestation of the crime is weakened or lost.[76]

Beccaria's fingerprints are also found all over Bradford's 1793 *Enquiry How Far the Punishment of Death Is Necessary in Pennsylvania*. In his essay, excerpted in *The New-York Magazine* in 1793, Bradford viewed any punishment that is not absolutely necessary as a "cruel and tyrannical act." Bradford had been asked by Pennsylvania Governor Thomas Mifflin to advise the state legislature on the issue of capital punishment, and in response Bradford had exhaustively researched the issue and then took up his pen to air—and declare—his views.[77] In his legislative report, Bradford—a frequent correspondent of his Princeton classmate James Madison—borrowed many of Beccaria's ideas.[78] Cribbing from Beccaria's treatise had become extremely common in those days, and Bradford—while giving attribution—was no exception as he looked to one of his favorite books, *On Crimes and Punishments*, for guidance. In a much more recent book, *The Hanging of Susanna Cox*, an historical account of a Pennsylvania woman executed in 1809 in Reading, Pennsylvania, the authors point out: "Bradford's popular essay to the legislature, 'An Inquiry How Far the Punishment of Death Is Necessary in Pennsylvania,' was modeled on Beccaria's work and was influential in limiting the implementation of the death penalty in Pennsylvania."[79] Though Bradford did not go quite as far as Beccaria, with Bradford hesitant to conclude in the early 1790s that the death penalty should be abolished for premeditated murderers, he sought the abolition of capital punishment for all other offenders.[80]

In his legislative report, which was transmitted to Pennsylvania's governor on December 3, 1792, before being reprinted in 1793 in the *Journal of the Senate of the Commonwealth of Pennsylvania*, Bradford put Beccaria front and center. Indeed, Bradford's report—which relied on several arguments made in *On Crimes and Punishments*—opened by acknowledging that "Montesquieu and Beccaria led the way" in settling the general principles "upon which penal laws ought to be founded."[81] Using a metaphor Luigi Castiglioni, the botanist, might have embraced, Bradford—the primary author of Pennsylvania's 1786 reform bill—argued that "the severity of our criminal law is an exotic plant and not the native growth of Pennsylvania." "It has been endured, but, I believe, has never been a favorite," Bradford said. "The religious opinions of many of our citizens," Bradford wrote, "were in opposition to it: and, as soon as the principles of Beccaria were disseminated, they found a soil that was prepared to receive them." Thomas Mifflin himself came from a family of Quakers, though he had been expelled from the Society of Friends because of his involvement with the military. Early in the Revolutionary War, Mifflin — a Philadelphia merchant — had left his position as a delegate to the Continental Congress to serve in the Continental Army.[82] Bradford's report, which specifically refers to "[t]he celebrated Beccaria," was highly influential when it first appeared in 1792 and 1793, getting reprinted as time went on, including on June 20, 1799 by Mathew Carey, the publisher of the *American Museum* magazine.[83]

Bradford's 1793 essay — heavily influenced by Beccaria's general approach — articulated three principles said to have attained "the force of axioms": first, that the prevention of crimes is "*the sole end of punishment*"; second, that every punishment "*which is not absolutely necessary for that purpose is a cruel and tyrannical act*"; and third, that every penalty "*should be proportioned to the offence.*" "These principles," Bradford explained, "serve to protect the rights of humanity," "to prevent the abuses of government," and "are so important that they deserve a place among the *fundamental* laws of every free country." In his essay, Bradford further emphasized: "sanguinary punishments, contrived in despotic and barbarous ages, have been continued when the progress of freedom, science, and morals renders them unnecessary and mischievous." In fact, Bradford specifically cited state constitutional provisions declaring that punishments should be "proportioned" to crimes; that "sanguinary punishments" ought to be avoided; and that "cruel punishments" should not be inflicted. "But," Bradford queried in discussing these provisions with their variable, non-uniform language, "does not this involve the same principle, and implicitly prohibit every penalty which is not evidently necessary?" "One would think, that, in a nation jealous of its liberty," Bradford concluded, "that the infliction of death" would "seldom be prescribed where its necessity was doubtful." In other words, regardless of the actual language of the state-law provisions, the key issue — indeed, the only issue — was whether the punishment was absolutely necessary.

Beccaria's treatise — as it turned out — made a major impact, including on Bradford's way of thinking. In his essay, Bradford argued that the death penalty was not necessary for "the Crime Against Nature." "[T]o punish this crime with death," Bradford contended, "would be a useless severity." In that document, Bradford also opposed executions for counterfeiting, rape, arson and other non-homicide offenses. For arsonists, Bradford wrote that solitude and hard labor would be "as efficacious" as death. For anyone who believed a prison sentence would be too lenient for non-homicide offenders, Bradford suggested a visit to "the penitentiary house lately erected as part of the gaol of Philadelphia," a reference to the newly remodeled Walnut Street Prison. As Bradford wrote: "When he looks into the narrow cells prepared for the more atrocious offenders — When he realizes what it is to subsist on coarse fare — to languish in the solitude of a prison — to wear out his tedious days and long nights in feverish anxiety — to be cut off from his family — from his friends — he will no longer think the punishment inadequate to the offence." Just a year after Bradford wrote those words, Pennsylvania — in 1794 — became the first state to divide murder into degrees, curtailing death sentences by making only first-degree murderers punishable by death.[84] "[I]t was largely through his efforts," a legal history of Pennsylvania recounts of Bradford's role, "that the Act of April 22, 1794, abolishing the death penalty in all cases except murder in the first degree, was passed."[85]

Having been inspired by Beccaria's treatise, Bradford — as acknowledged by many of his fellow citizens — thus made a major contribution to American penal reform. For example, Richard Rush, one of Dr. Benjamin Rush's sons and a prominent figure in his own right, had high praise for William Bradford's service to the country, writing as follows:

> William Bradford was among the most gifted men Pennsylvania has produced, an honor and an ornament to the State. He was a profound lawyer—more than this, his mind by its enlargement was able to use the vantage ground of jurisprudence and survey its broadest principles, as the noblest of human sciences practically applicable to mankind—amongst the testimonials of so expanded an understanding, was his treatise on 'Capital Punishment' a work written at the request of Governor Mifflin, and intended for the use of the Legislature of Pennsylvania, in the nature of a report, when that subject was first under consideration in that body. He had before that time been Attorney General of Pennsylvania—To abilities of the first order as a lawyer he added true accomplishments of a scholar and an orator, the zeal of a patriot and the virtues of a man and a gentleman.[86]

After graduating from the College of New Jersey in 1797, the youngest in a class of thirty-three students, Richard Rush himself would become a respected lawyer and go on to serve his country in varying capacities. After being admitted to the Philadelphia Bar in 1800, Rush—a Republican—practiced law, then attracted President James Madison's attention through his opposition of a renewal of the charter of the First Bank of the United States. After Madison appointed Richard Rush to the position of Comptroller of the Treasury in 1811, President Madison tapped Rush in 1814 to replace William Pinkney as Attorney General of the United States. William Pinkney (1764–1822), the 7th United States Attorney General, made the following argument in asserting that states had the right to tax the National Bank: "It is an authority inherent in, and incident to, all sovereignty.... It is no more a distinct exercise of sovereign power than that of inflicting capital punishments." But during Richard Rush's tenure as Attorney General, Richard Rush was more circumspect about the state's power to take life and engaged in an effort to codify U.S. laws. As one source notes, "Rush made his first important contribution to the new nation; he superintended the publication of *The Laws of the United States from 1789 to 1815* (1815), the first codification of the laws of the United States." Rush continued serving as Attorney General during James Monroe's administration until President Monroe appointed him as Secretary of State. Monroe later appointed Rush to the post of Minister Plenipotentiary to the Court of St. James to replace John Quincy Adams, a position Rush served in until 1825.[87]

John Adams and John Quincy Adams

The second U.S. President, John Adams, also read *On Crimes and Punishments* and invoked its ideas long before America declared its independence from Great Britain.[88] In the late 1760s, Adams—as a lawyer—had represented John Hancock, who had been charged with unlawfully aiding and assisting in unloading a sloop, *Liberty*, at Boston that was carrying "one hundred and twenty seven Pipes" of wine from Madeira. The charge: that Hancock, with intent to defraud his Majesty George III, had assisted Nathaniel Barnard, the ship's master, in unloading the ship while knowing that the duties on the wine had not yet been paid. The Crown's information sought treble damages for the value of the goods, asking Boston's Court of Vice Admiralty for an assessment of "Nine Thousand Pounds Sterling Money of Great Britain." In that context, Adams—as reflected in a draft of his argument, though he did not specifically reference *On Crimes and Punish-*

ments in that instance—apparently looked to Beccaria's ideas for guidance. "The Degree of severity in any Poenal Law," he wrote, "is to be determined only by the Proportion between the Crime and the Punishment."[89]

Though the timing of his first exposure to Beccaria is unclear, Adams had great familiarity with, and real affection for, Beccaria's treatise. In March 1770, as counsel for the defense in the trial of the British soldiers charged with murder in the aftermath of the Boston Massacre, Adams forcefully quoted Beccaria's words at the very beginning of his argument.[90] *"May it please your Honors, and you, Gentlemen of the Jury,"* he began. "I am for the prisoners at the bar," he opened after that customary salutation, "and shall apologize for it only in the words of the Marquis Beccaria, 'If I can but be the instrument of preserving one life, his blessing and tears of transport, shall be a sufficient consolation to me, for the contempt of all mankind.'" "As the prisoners stand before you for their lives," Adams continued, "it may be proper, to recollect with what temper the law requires we should proceed to this trial." Adams then emphasized that "the spirit of the law upon such occasions, is conformable to humanity, to common sense and feeling; that it is all benignity and candor." Josiah Quincy, Jr., another lawyer for the defense, also quoted a passage from Beccaria's treatise on the topics of "credibility" and "justification."[91] At the Boston Massacre trial, the stakes—life versus death—could not have been higher, with Adams pleading justifiable homicide and relying on Beccaria's words to help make his case. In the Supreme Court chamber in Boston, four judges—headed by the Chief Justice of the Province—presided over the case. The judges, as Adams described them, wore "immense judicial wigs" and were "arrayed in their ... rich robes of scarlet English broadcloth."[92]

That Adams chose to quote Beccaria at the very outset of his argument—and that Quincy, his co-counsel, also looked to Beccaria for guidance—shows the high esteem with which lawyers held Beccaria's treatise. It also demonstrates that Beccaria was already—even in 1770—a well-known enough figure that lawyers felt comfortable quoting his words and ideas in open court. Indeed, Josiah Quincy, Jr.—Adams' co-counsel—also invoked Beccaria's name in another context, in making observations on the Boston Port Act of 1774. That Act of Parliament, promulgated in the wake of the Boston Tea Party, was one of the measures variously called the Intolerable Acts, the Punitive Acts, or the Coercive Acts. In discussing the notion of standing armies and civil society, Quincy quoted these much-repeated words from Beccaria's treatise: "in every society, there is an effort constantly tending to confer on one part the height of power, and to reduce the other to the extreme of weakness and misery." Right before quoting that passage from Beccaria's treatise, Josiah Quincy, Jr. wrote in the very same paragraph: "The proper object of society and civil institutions is the advancement of 'the greatest happiness of the greatest number.' The people (as a body, but never interested to injure themselves and uniformly desirous of the general welfare) have ever made this collective felicity the object of their wishes and pursuit." Josiah Quincy, Jr., in making his observations, also concluded: "'The greatest happiness of the greatest number' being the object and bond of society, the establishment of truth and justice ought to be the basis of civil policy and jurisprudence." "But this capital establishment," Quincy opined, expressing his aversion to standing armies, "can never be attained in a state where there exists a power superior to the civil magistrate, and sufficient to control the authority of the laws."[93]

John Adams' and Josiah Quincy, Jr.'s invocation of Beccaria's name at the Boston Massacre trial shows just how popular Enlightenment ideas had become in revolutionary America. "The wear and tear on his Grotius, Puffendorf, Beccaria, Ogilvie," a Boston Public Library bulletin notes of the books of John Adams, "show that he read them over and over."[94] In fact, John Quincy Adams—who, like his father, was a bibliophile—later recalled "the electrical effect produced upon the jury" by Beccaria's words at the high-stakes Boston Massacre murder trial.[95] John Adams, who, in 1780, is known to have bought a copy of Beccaria's writings in the original Italian while in Paris, drafted the Massachusetts Constitution of 1780—calling for "a government of laws and not of men"—after returning from his first diplomatic mission to France.[96] And even before that, Adams was consulting Beccaria's treatise outside his use of the Italian philosopher in the court-room. In a June 28, 1770, diary entry, John Adams—noting Beccaria's words, the ones he employed in the courtroom—also referenced *On Crimes and Punishments* in this way: "If, by supporting the Rights of Mankind, and of Invincible Truth, I shall contribute to save from the Agonies of Death one unfortunate Victim of Tyranny, or of Ignorance, equally fatal; his Blessings and Tears of Transport, will be a sufficient Consolation to me, for the Contempt of all Mankind."[97] In another instance, Adams also referenced Becca-ria, writing of the Greek historian Polybius: "Polybius ... is more charitable in his repre-sentation of human nature than Hobbes, Mandeville, Rochefoucauld, Machiavel, Beccaria, Rousseau, De Lolme, or even than our friend Dr. Price."[98]

In 1788, in his *Defence of the Constitutions of Government of the United States*, John Adams cited Beccaria yet again, this time on the same page in which he made reference to Junius, Rochefoucauld, de Lolme, Hobbes, Rousseau, and "Dr. Price and Dr. Priest-ley." From Junius, Adams transcribed the following line: "Laws are intended not to trust to what men will do, but to guard against what they may do." From Beccaria, the next entry, Adams copied these words: "*Ogni uomo si fa centro di tutte le combinazioni del globo.*" Taken from chapter 2 of the Italian version of Beccaria's treatise, they translate as follows: "Every man makes himself the center of his whole world."[99] Joseph Priestley—an English theologian, chemist and political theorist who came to America in 1794 after a mob burned down his home and church—himself cited Beccaria's ideas in his own writings. In his *Lectures on History and General Policy*, Dr. Priestley footnoted *On Crimes and Punishments* after discussing the reasonableness of providing compensation to an in-nocent man who has been charged with a crime or whose joints have been dislocated. "Beccaria," Priestley also noted in his book, speaking of "the greatest abuses of religion," reported that more than a hundred thousand witches had been "condemned to die by Christian tribunals." "False principles of religion," Priestley emphasized elsewhere, also citing Beccaria's treatise, "have encouraged men to commit the most horrid crimes." Priest-ley's scientific and political writings had a major impact on Thomas Jefferson, with Priest-ley—who made many American friends by supporting the American Revolution—dedicating one of his many books, *General History of the Christian Church*, to Jefferson himself.[100]

The regularity with which Beccaria's treatise was consulted shows just how much Bec-caria's reformist ideas impacted the American psyche. And John Adams' appointment of judges who were leading proponents of penal reform also shows that Adams—despite his willingness to use executions—was open to new ideas. For example, on February 18, 1801, President John Adams nominated George Keith Taylor, an outspoken Virginia penal re-former, for a seat on the U.S. Circuit Court for the Fourth Circuit. Taylor played an instrumental role in reforming Virginia's penal laws in 1796, and—unlike protracted nomination fights today—was confirmed by the U.S. Senate just two days after Adams nominated him.[101] Like-wise, in 1801, Adams selected Jeremiah Smith, of New Hampshire, to be a judge of the United States Circuit Court. Judge Smith's grand jury charges often reflected a Beccarian spirit. For example, one reads as follows: "Laws should be mild; where punishments are mild, shame follows the finger of the law, but where they are severe, there is a sympathy excited for the offender, and he is viewed as a martyr to arbitrary power. Experience has abundantly proved, that mild laws are more efficacious than severe ones, and that rigor-ous punishments tend rather to produce, than to prevent crimes." "Every unnecessary re-straint is tyrannical and unjustifiable," Judge Smith instructed, "for every member of the state is of right entitled to the highest possible degree of liberty which is consistent with the safety and well-being of the whole." "The certainty of punishment is more efficacious to prevent crimes, than the severity of it," Smith emphasized.

Judge Smith's other grand jury charges likewise reflect a focus on preventing crime, a major emphasis of Beccaria's treatise. In an 1807 grand jury charge, Judge Smith instructed: "A society which has no other method of promoting virtue, but by punishing offences when committed, will have a great many punishments to inflict. The gallows will be crowded with victims, and the executioner's axe constantly wet with blood. The great object of government, in all their institutions, should be to prevent the commission of crimes." In another grand jury charge, given in 1809 before he retired from the bench, Judge Smith put it this way:

> There have been many thefts committed under the gallows, during the time of a public execution. A code of penal laws, however excellent, is by no means a power adapted to extirpate the depravity which pervades a great portion of mankind. It corrects the distemper, but does not eradicate it. This can only be accomplished by the Christian religion, which is a part of the common law of this state, and by far the noblest part. Its excellency and utility are expressly recognized in our constitution.

"It is surely better," Smith said, "to reform mankind, by giving them good dispositions, than to punish them for having bad; to make them good citizens, and useful members of society, rather than shut them up in prisons, or take away their lives." Smith, a Congressman during George Washington's time as America's president, also served as New Hampshire's governor and as the chief justice of New Hampshire's highest court.[102]

As a lawyer, John Adams handled capital cases, including in close proximity to the release of the first English translation of Beccaria's treatise. For example, in September 1768, Adams represented a man, Samuel Quinn, accused of rape—then a capital offense—and obtained an acquittal. After his acquittal, a thankful Quinn remarked, "God bless Mr. Adams. God bless his Soul, I am not to be hanged."[103] Adams, during a trip he took to Plymouth on January 28, 1770, recalled that courtroom victory, paraphrasing a familiar quotation from Beccaria as he remembered the 1768 trial. "I have received such Blessings and enjoyed such Tears of Transport," Adams wrote, adding, "there is no greater Pleasure, or Consolation!"[104] As President, John Adams—the lawyer who had worked in the trenches defending clients and outcasts—also sometimes pardoned capital offenders.[105]

In fact, throughout his life, Adams remained fascinated by Beccaria's words. On July 7, 1780, while in Paris, Adams recorded that he paid "Mr. Borzachini"—a reference to Marcel Borzacchini, a professor of the Italian and English languages in Paris—for "2 Italian Grammars and 11 Lessons." The very next day, Adams recorded that he bought an Italian dictionary and a version of "Dellitti e Pene" associated with one "Molini."[106] John Adams bought a copy of Giuseppe Baretti's dictionary of the English and Italian languages, autographing it "John Adams, July 1780," and on the cover page of a 1766 "Edizione" of *Dei delitti e delle pene*, published after Beccaria's book was placed on the *Index Librorum Prohibitorum*, one finds the following language: "*Chez Molini Libraire, Quai des Augustins.*" This was an edition published by Giovan Claudio Molini (1724–1812), a bookseller in Paris who—as one source puts it—"produced one more virtually identical 'French' version" of Beccaria's treatise "called the sixth (*edizione sesta di nuovo corretta e accresciuta*), bearing the indication of *Harlem* and *A Paris*." Jean Claude Molini, as he was also known, was Giuseppe Molini's uncle and had his own extensive network of contacts in Italy, once reprinting, without authorization, the poetry of Vittorio Alfieri's works, to the Italian poet's "great fury."

In Florence, the younger Giuseppe Molini (1772–1856)—a prominent Italian publisher and bookseller—ran a library, had a printing office, and oversaw an English Reading Room, with his shop on Via Archibusieri selling English books and paper, pens and pencils. The Florentine Dr. Giuseppe Molini—as one source put it—"'is a bookseller and an intelligent man succeeded to his father's business after having taken a Drs degree at Pisa'"; he was, that source adds, "a partner in the London house of the same name," "one of the most extensive and best informed booksellers in Florence," formerly Librarian to the Grand Duke of Tuscany, and "speaks English well." The "London branch" of the Molini operation was "in King William Street off the Strand," reportedly "the main source in Britain for Italian books." "Sig. Molini," one traveler's guide noted, "undertakes to send to London any quantity of books which British Travellers may purchase of him. He has, in Paternoster Row, a Relation, Mr. Frederick Molini, to whom his books are consigned; and who delivers them to their purchasers, on receiving the amount of freight, duty, and insurance."

Thomas Jefferson himself was a customer of Jean Claude Molini's Left Bank bookshop, with *The Road to Monticello: The Life and Mind of Thomas Jefferson* noting of Jefferson's patronage while he resided at the Hôtel d'Orléans: "The first bookseller he patronized was Jean Claude Molini, whose shop was on the Rue Mignon. Specializing in Italian books, Molini imported much of his stock from Italy, but he also published some reprints of classic works of Italian literature, including Tasso's *Aminta* and Guarini's *Il Pastor Fido*." Upon his arrival in Paris, Jefferson—on one occasion alone—spent fifty-eight francs on books at Molini's bookshop. "Throughout his time in Paris," writer Kevin Hayes emphasizes of Jefferson in *The Road to Monticello*, "he would frequently return to the Rue Mignon to acquire additional books from Molini, Italian and otherwise." Benjamin Franklin himself had long known Jean Claude Molini, as is clear from a 1768 letter that Franklin sent to Jean Chappe d'Auteroche (1728–1769), a French astronomer and traveler. In that letter, Franklin wrote the Abbé d'Auteroche:

> I sent you sometime since, directed to the Care of M. Molini, a Bookseller near the Quây des Augustins a Tooth that I mention'd to you when I had the pleasure of meeting with you at the Marquis de Courtanvaux's. It was found near the River Ohio in America, about 200 Leagues below Fort du Quesne, at what is called the Great Licking Place, where the Earth has a Saltish Taste that is agreeable to the Buffaloes and Deer, who come there at certain Seasons in great Numbers to lick the same.

For Jefferson, acquiring Italian-language books was certainly not something new. "His surviving copy of *La Storia di Tom Jones*, Pietro Chiari's translation of the Henry Fielding novel," Hayes notes, "contains Jefferson's ownership inscription on the title page. The inscription is dated 1761." In Virginia, Jefferson spoke Italian with the Italian émigré Philip Mazzei and his Italian laborers, earning Mazzei's admiration. "Jefferson," Mazzei reported, "understood the Tuscan language very well, but he had never heard it spoken. Nevertheless, he could converse with my men in Italian, and they were so pleased by the fact that he could understand them that I was touched." In Paris, Jefferson's memorandum book indicates he bought "tickets to Italian comedy," an indication he attended the then new Théâtre des Italiens. That venue, built in 1782 on the site of the Hotel de Choiseul, did theater productions after it opened in 1783 and was later converted into an Italian opera house.[107]

In thinking about how best to structure government, deal with criminality and protect against abuses of power, John Adams—like Jefferson—read scores of books, and not just in English. In addition to *On Crimes and Punishments*, his library contained

Montesquieu's *Spirit of the Laws*, Gaetano Filangieri's *La scienza della legislazione*, Voltaire's *Traité sur la tolerance*, and a number of histories of Italian republics. For example, Adams owned Francesco Guicciardini's *The History of Italy* and Giovanni Battista Felice Gasparo Nani's *The History of the Affairs of Europe in this Present Age, but More Particularly of the Republick of Venice*. "Among the numerous autographs" in Adams' extensive collection of books, a catalogue of them notes, "are those of James Otis, Elbridge Gerry, T. Brand Hollis, Dr. Benjamin Rush," the latter of whom addressed an autographed copy of his *Medical Inquiries and Observations* to John Adams. In that book, Dr. Rush wrote about crime and punishment, and—addressing "VENERABLE SAGES and FELLOW CITIZENS in the REPUBLIC OF LETTERS"—said that "monarchs and rulers of the world" had it within their power "to extirpate war, slavery, and capital punishments, from the list of human evils." Adams also owned Dr. Gamaliel Bradford's *State Prisons and the Penitentiary System* (1821), Charles Glidden Haines' *Report on the Penitentiary System in the United States* (1822) and Josiah Quincy's *Remarks on Some of the Provisions of the Laws of Massachusetts, Affecting Poverty, Vice, and Crime* (1822). Before the end of the Revolutionary War itself, Adams had, in fact, played a major role in drafting the Massachusetts Constitution of 1780—a constitution that prohibited "cruel or unusual punishments."[108]

For John Adams, as for Madison's friend William Bradford, the necessity of the punishment at issue seemed to be the central and all-important inquiry. Under that logic, any punishment that was not necessary could not be justified and, thus, should not be inflicted. In *The Prince*, the Italian historian and diplomat Niccolò Machiavelli (1469–1527) had articulated "the methods and rules for a prince as regards his subjects and friends." The son of a lawyer, Machiavelli—in Rome—had witnessed the actions of Pope Alexander VI (1431–1503) and his son Cesare Borgia (1475–1507) in ruling, making alliances, and accumulating power. In his posthumously published book, first printed in 1532, Machiavelli had offered this advice: "A man who wishes to make a profession of goodness in everything must necessarily come to grief among so many who are not good. Therefore it is necessary for a prince, who wishes to maintain himself, to learn how not to be good, and to use it and not use it according to the necessity of the case." In a chapter titled "OF CRUELTY AND CLEMENCY, AND WHETHER IT IS BETTER TO BE LOVED OR FEARED," Machiavelli added: "I say that every prince must desire to be considered merciful and not cruel. He must, however, take care not to misuse this mercifulness." Noting that "Cesare Borgia was considered cruel," but that "his cruelty had settled the Romagna, united it, and brought it peace and confidence," Machiavelli contended: "A prince, therefore, must not mind incurring the charge of cruelty for the purpose of keeping his subjects united and confident; for, with a very few examples, he will be more merciful than those who, from excess of tenderness, allow disorders to arise, from whence spring murders and rapine; for these as a rule injure the whole community, while the executions carried out by the prince injure only one individual."[109]

America's Founding Fathers were well versed in Machiavelli's writings before their exposure to Beccaria's treatise. As a young man, James Madison—like many of his contemporaries—read classic works by Virgil, Horace, Justinian, Lucretius, Plato, Plutarch and Thucydides, and his commonplace book for the period from 1759 to 1772 also makes reference to Machiavelli. In that commonplace book, Madison excerpted the following maxims from the memoirs of Cardinal de Retz (1614–1679): "Whatever is necessary ought not to be hazardous." "One of the greatest misfortunes which the despotic Power of the Ministers of the last Age has brought upon the State, is the Custom wch. their private (but mistaken) Interest has introduced, ever to support the superiour against the Inferiour. That Maxim is one of Machiavel's, whom most of his readers do not understand, and whom others take to be a great Politician for no other reason but for having ever been Wicked." In a 1782 letter from Robert R. Livingston, Benjamin Franklin was also requested to buy

"Machiavels-political Works," with James Madison—in his 1783 list of books for the use of Congress—further recommending the purchase of "Machiavelli's works."

Not only was Thomas Jefferson familiar with Machiavelli's writings, but John Adams kept a 1775 edition of Machiavelli's writings in his library—a library that, like others of the age, contained a number of books on Italian history. In a May 1787 letter to Richard Cranch, Abigail Adams herself—after sending along a review of her husband's *Defence of the Constitutions* from the April 1787 edition of *Critical Review*—noted that "mr Adams" was then "considering the I[t]alian Republicks through the middle age," what Abigail called "a work of no small labour" and an "expensive" project in terms of the number of "Books." A little more than a year before the start of the Constitutional Convention in Philadelphia, Adams had also been thinking about Beccaria's treatise. On July 20, 1786, while in London, John Adams recorded in his diary the following Beccaria quotation from chapter 2 of his own English translation of *On Crimes and Punishments*: "Every Act of Authority, of one Man over another for which there is not an absolute Necessity, is tyrannical."[110] Adams then wrote out the following words in Italian: *Le Pene the oltre passano la necessita di conservare il deposito della Salute pubblica, sono ingiuste di for natura.* The translation: "All punishments that go beyond the requirements of public safety are by their very nature unjust." Again, the overriding idea—one expressed again and again in America's founding era—was that executions, per Beccaria and his predecessor, Montesquieu, should only be used if absolutely necessary.

In recording that portion of his diary entry in Italian, John Adams was quoting from his own copy of the Italian text of Beccaria's treatise—a book published in 1780 that he had acquired in July 1780 and presumably read as he took Italian lessons from the language instructor Marcel Borzacchini in Paris. That same year, as well as in 1782, it is also known that Beccaria's treatise was cited in patriotic speeches in Boston, the same city that had, in 1773, seen the Sons of Liberty destroy a large shipment of tea—a shipment of 342 chests containing 92,586 pounds of tea—sent by the East India Company. In his July 20, 1786 diary entry, Adams further editorialized: "The Sovereign Power is constituted, to defend Individuals against the Tyranny of others. Crimes are acts of Tyranny of one or more on another or more. A Murderer, a Thief, a Robber, a Burglar, is a Tyrant."[111] In yet another diary entry, written in England in 1787, Adams—then serving as a diplomat for his country—still seemed to be reflecting on the proper proportion between crimes and punishments, trying to work out his own ideas on paper. Writing in July of that year after traveling and being unable to find "a single Bed to be had" in a town because "the Court of Assize" was being held there for the week, Adams had time to jot down his thoughts on the concept of proportionality. In particular, Adams reflected on a shepherd in a shepherd's cottage watching over a flock of sheep "owned by some Lord, or Duke." "If poverty, hunger and want should tempt him to slay the poorest Lamb of the flock," Adams recorded, speaking of the shepherd, "the penal Laws of this Land of freedom would take his Life, from thence I presume the old proverb took its rise, one had as goods be hanged for a Sheep as a Lamb, and if the Lord or Duke was murderd the poor man would no more forfeit his life, than for the Sheep or Lamb, yet surely the crime is very different."[112]

By 1793, John Adams appears to have rejected Machiavelli's approach in favor of a milder approach. In sending what he forthrightly described as a "Love Letter" to his wife, Adams—writing from Philadelphia—recorded in his letter of February 3, 1793: "I hope the Boston Rejoicings were at the success of the Arms of France, and not intended as Approbation of all the Jacobinical Councils. I am enough in the Spirit of the Times to be glad the Prussians and Austrians have not Succeeded, but not to exult in the Prison or Tryal of that King to whom though I am personally under no Obligation, my Country is under the greatest." Louis XVI had been arrested in August 1792, was tried and convicted by

France's National Convention, and—though news traveled much slower than it does today—had already, by the time of Adams' letter, been executed on January 21, 1793. The French queen, Marie Antoinette, would also be guillotined at the Place de la Révolution later that year, on October 16th. "The accursed Politicks," Adams accurately speculated of Louis XVI's fate in his letter, "have cost him his Crown if not his head." In that same letter to his wife Abigail, John Adams—taking note that Louis-Alexandre, Duc de La Rochefoucauld d'Anville (1743–1792), a *philosophe* and friend of America, had been stoned to death by a French mob in September 1792—observed that "[t]he Duke de la Rochefoucault too, is cutt to Pieces for his Idolatry." "If I had not washed my own hands of all this Blood, by warning them against it," Adams told his wife, "I should feel some of it upon my soul." Before signing his letter "yours kindly" followed by his initials, "J. A.," Adams expressed regret in his letter, lamenting that his own advice to the French had not been taken: "Macchiavels Advice to cutt off a numerous Nobility had more weight than mine to preserve them." "The Vengeance of Heaven for their Folly," Adams concluded in his letter, "has been revealed in more shivering Terms than in any of my numerous Examples."[113]

In the meantime, shortly before the 1787 Constitutional Convention in Philadelphia, John Adams' son, John Quincy Adams, was himself contemplating the death penalty. In February 1787, as he readied himself to graduate from Harvard in July of that year,[114] John Quincy Adams—like other college students of his time—began grappling with state-sanctioned killing as part of an academic exercise. Then aged nineteen, John Quincy Adams found himself doing "a forensic disputation" in class that he had prepared "in the course of the vacation." The topic: "Whether the infliction of capital punishments, except in cases of murder be consistent with equity?" On that subject, the young man—also thinking of the concept of proportionality—recorded this in his own diary:

> Had the question admitted other exceptions, or had it admitted none, I should have felt a greater degree of diffidence, in maintaining the affirmative. It has frequently been doubted by men who reason chiefly from speculation, whether it were equitable to punish any crime, with death, Sovereigns have attempted to abolish capital punishments entirely, but this scheme, like many others, which appear to great advantage in, theory has been found impracticable, because it has been attended with consequences very injurious to society; but if it be acknowledged, that death is the only equitable atonement which can be made for the commission of murder, I cannot see, why other crimes, equally, and perhaps still more, heinous, should not deserve a punishment equally severe. The question naturally occurs here; what is the end of punishment? Certainly, to give satisfaction, to the injured, and to insure the safety of individuals and of Society: but as the man who falls by the hand of an assassin, cannot receive satisfaction; the punishment in that case, must be inflicted only for the benefit of Society in general. No one, I presume will deny, that Treason is a crime, more dangerous to a community, than murder; as it threatens the destruction of each individual, as well as of the whole commonwealth: to inflict a milder punishment therefore upon this crime, would be destroying that proportion, in which alone, justice and equity consist. The celebrated Montesquieu observes, that the punishment should always derive from the nature of the crime, and consist in the privation of those advantages of which the criminal should have attempted to deprive others. He confesses however, that in many cases, this would not be effected: most frequently the man who robs the property of another, possesses, none himself, and therefore a corporal punishment, must supply the place of confiscation.[115]

While John Quincy Adams, in his diary entry, referenced Montesquieu—and not Beccaria—by name, he clearly had in the forefront of his mind those, like Beccaria, who had called for the abolition of capital punishments. As the diary entry of the soon-to-be-graduating student continues:

> Those who plead in favour of a lenient system of punishment, may engage the passions of their hearers, by expatiating upon the virtues of benevolence, humanity and mercy: far be it from me to derogate from the excellency of those exalted virtues; but if mildness in punishments instead of deterring men from the commission of crimes, encourages them to it, the innocent, and virtuous part of the community, who have surely the greatest claim to the benevolence of a legislator, would be the greatest sufferers.
>
> It is customary with persons who disapprove of capital punishments, to say that confinement during life to hard labour, would be a punishment, much more severe, than immediate death, and that a criminal thereby, might be rendered useful to Society, whereas a dead man is entirely lost to the community. A zealous student in surgery might deny the latter part of this proposition;[116] but I shall only reply, that admitting confinement and hard labour for life, to be a more rigorous atonement for a crime, than death it will not follow, that it is equally terrifying, and this ought to be the principal object of a legislator. The addition of confinement will be but a small restraint to the greatest part of mankind who know, that whether innocent or guilty, they must depend upon hard labour for their subsistence. But Death is more or less terrible to all men; I have frequently heard persons who supposed themselves in perfect security, express the most intrepid contempt of death, but I conceive their philosophy would be somewhat deranged if the prospect of a sudden, and violent dissolution were placed before them. In such a situation all mankind would reason like the criminal represented by the inimitable Shakespear, as being condemned to die.

Before noting that "Mr. Wigglesworth gave a public lecture this afternoon" and that "[w]e danced in the evening at White's chamber," John Quincy Adams recorded these lines from Shakespeare's *Measure for Measure*:

> Ay, but to die, and go we know not where,
> To lie in cold obstruction, and to rot;
> This sensible, warm motion, to become
> A kneaded clod, and the delighted spirit,
> To bathe in fiery floods, or to reside
> In thrilling regions of thick ribbed ice,
> To be imprison'd in the viewless winds
> And blown with restless violence round about
> The pendent world;—'tis too horrible!
> The weariest, and most loathed worldly life,
> That age, ache, penury, imprisonment
> Can lay on nature, is a paradise
> To what we fear of Death.[117]

That Beccaria's ideas continued to be discussed in the Adams family for years to come is clear. John Adams—the family patriarch—gave his son Thomas a copy of Beccaria's treatise as indicated by the following handwritten notation on the book: "Thomas B. Adams. From his Father. 1800."[118] And John Quincy Adams, who became the sixth U.S. President in 1825, would himself later oppose executions.[119] In a letter written to President James Monroe in 1818, John Quincy Adams — then serving as the United States Secretary of State — took the position that "in *every* case of capital conviction the President should decide upon a full and solemn consideration, whether he ought to grant or to withhold the exercise of this awful power of human life or death." "I include farther to the opinion that no execution ought ever to take place without such a warrant [of execution] from the President," John Quincy Adams wrote. In another letter, written in 1819, John Quincy Adams implored that punishments be proportioned to crimes, writing as follows: "By the laws of nations the punishment denounced against the crime of piracy is capital, a severity which, by the institutions of the United States, is confined to very few crimes of the most atrocious character. It would scarcely be compatible with the sentiments prevailing in this nation to extend that heaviest of all penalties to offences the malignity of which might be so different in degree, according to the circumstances under which they might be perpetrated."[120] By 1845, John Quincy Adams was supporting the efforts of the Philadelphia Society for the Abolition of Capital Punishment. "*Gladly would I co-operate with any Society whose object should be to promote the abolition of every form, by which the life of man can be voluntarily taken by his fellow creature man,*" Adams wrote.[121]

Thomas Jefferson: A Beccaria Admirer

Thomas Jefferson — the third U.S. President — began his career, like John Adams, as a lawyer. He, too, owned a copy of Beccaria's treatise in the original Italian,[122] and he would later purchase an English translation, published in London in 1809.[123] Jefferson practiced law between 1767 and 1774, and some time between 1774 and 1776,[124] Jefferson copied multiple passages from Beccaria's treatise into his legal commonplace book.[125] Jefferson kept one commonplace book dealing with equity and one dealing with legal matters, and of the 905 numbered items in Jefferson's legal commonplace book — some of which are from Montesquieu and Voltaire — twenty-six entries come from Beccaria.[126] As historian John Hostettler writes of Jefferson's respect for *On Crimes and Punishments*: "Jefferson read Beccaria's treatise in the original Italian and copied long passages into his commonplace book. This contained 26 extracts from Beccaria in Italian, all long passages cited in Jefferson's own handwriting." To say that Beccaria made a big impression on Jefferson would be to put it mildly.

Among the concepts or maxims that Jefferson recorded in Italian from Beccaria's treatise: in every criminal matter, the judge should reason syllogistically; nothing is more dangerous than the common axiom that the spirit of the laws is to be considered; there ought to be a fixed proportion between crimes and punishments; it is an admirable law which ordains that every man shall be tried by his peers; all trials should be public; an immediate punishment is more useful; the punishment of infamy should not be too frequent; and crimes are more effectually prevented by the certainty than the severity of punishment. Other passages that Jefferson copied in Italian from Beccaria's treatise were these: if punishments be very severe, men are naturally led to the perpetration of other crimes; the countries and times most notorious for severity of punishments were always those in which the most bloody and inhuman actions and the most atrocious crimes were committed; in proportion as punishments become more cruel, the minds of men, as a fluid rises to the same height with that which surrounds it, grow hardened and insensible; suicide is a crime which seems not to admit of punishment for it cannot be inflicted but on the innocent, or upon an insensible dead body; and it is better to prevent crimes than to punish them. On the latter point, Jefferson also copied passages from Beccaria's treatise advocating clear and simple laws to prevent crimes and arguing that the prevention of crimes is the fundamental principle of good legislation, which is the art of maximizing men's happiness. Jefferson also copied a passage from Beccaria's treatise stating that as punishments become milder, clemency and pardon are less necessary.[127]

In his commonplace book, Jefferson appeared interested in almost everything Beccaria had to say. In taking his notes in Italian, Jefferson thus copied long passages from a wide range of the chapters in *Dei delitti e delle pene*. Excerpts from the Italian edition that Jefferson copied come from more than twenty chapters of the treatise, with Jefferson transcribing passages from chapters relating to, *inter alia*, the interpretation of the laws, evidence, the degrees of crimes, oaths, acts of violence, the punishment of nobles, robbery, infamy, idleness, banishment, the mildness of punishments, imprisonment, suicide, bankrupts, sanctuaries, rewards for apprehending or killing criminals, attempts, accomplices, pardons, and the prevention of crime.[128] Among the passages of "false ideas of utility" copied in Italian from Beccaria's treatise, translated into English here: "Laws that forbid the carrying of arms … disarm only those who are neither inclined nor determined to commit crimes."[129] The fact that Jefferson copied so many passages from *On Crimes and Punishments* into his commonplace book plainly demonstrates that Jefferson believed Beccaria's treatise to be eminently worthy of inclusion alongside other prominent thinkers of his day.

Jefferson came of age in colonial times, an era dominated by all things British, including the English monarchy and all of its oppressive laws. Virginians had inherited English criminal laws that routinely inflicted capital and harsh corporal punishments. But Jefferson—as a young man receptive to new ideas—took a special interest, almost immediately from its publication, in Beccaria's book. "Turning to the Italian law reformer Cesare Beccaria," writes historian David Thomas Konig, "Jefferson copied into his commonplace book some time after 1774 passages whose distrust of judicial discretion sounds very much like a twentieth-century legal realist." "Jefferson," Konig notes, "chose to begin his long extract from Beccaria's essay on crimes and punishments, very significantly, with the fourth chapter, which dealt with the interpretation of laws." That chapter of Beccaria's book, in passages that Jefferson scrivened into his commonplace book, lamented that the same crimes were punished in a different manner at different times in the same tribunals; that the consequence of not consulting the constant and invariable voice of the laws was the erring instability of arbitrary interpretation; and that the disorders that may arise from a rigorous observance of the letter of penal laws are not comparable with those produced by the interpretation of them.

Anxious to implement some of Beccaria's ideas in his native Virginia, Jefferson would later draw upon *On Crimes and Punishments* in drafting his "Bill for Proportioning Crimes and Punishments in Cases heretofore Capital." In that draft legislation, which sought to restrict the death penalty's use to treason and murder and to restrict the use of corporal punishment, Jefferson cited Beccaria's treatise in four footnotes.[130] The first reference is found in a footnote on "the death of a bastard child" being characterized as murder; the second is to a section of Beccaria's treatise on suicide; the third was to support the proposition that executions shall be conducted expeditiously; and the fourth pertained to a section on the punishment of sodomy. In Jefferson's bill, treason and murder were to be punished by hanging, with the bodies of those executed for murder to be "delivered to Anatomists to be dissected." In the latter respect, Jefferson's bill sought to emulate the approach of Parliament's Murder Act of 1752, which stipulated that after murderers were executed, their bodies were to be dissected, with bodies conveyed to the Hall of Surgeons for medical research. Another section of Jefferson's bill specifically stated that "no crime shall be henceforth punished by the deprivation of life or limb, except those herein after ordained to be so punished." In one footnote to his legislation, Jefferson noted: "This takes away the punishment of cutting off the hand of a person striking another, or drawing his sword in one of the superior courts of justice."[131]

In a separate bill, Jefferson detailed what he contemplated for "malefactors condemned for labour for the Commonwealth." In that bill, "malefactors" were to be employed "in the gallies of the commonwealth, or to work in the lead mines, or on fortifications or such other hard and laborious works" as directed by "the Governor and Council, in their discretion." "And during the term of their condemnation," that bill further provided, the malefactors "shall have their heads and beards constantly shaven, and be clothed in habits of coarse materials, uniform in color and make, and distinguished from all others used by the good citizens of this commonwealth."[132] This bill, along with the bill to proportion crimes and punishments, were reported to the house of delegates by the committee for courts of justice, in November 1786, but were not passed. In the same time frame, Jefferson was also involved in the nitty gritty of prison design. After getting architectural plans from Pierre-Gabriel Bugniet, a French architect who had, in 1785, designed the Roanne prison in Lyons, Jefferson had forwarded his own ideas to Benjamin Latrobe, the designer of the Richmond, Virginia penitentiary that was ultimately built in 1800. Given the wording of Jefferson's proposed legislation, Jefferson's ideas on punishment were, at that time, very similar to those being contemplated in Philadelphia. In 1786, after a change in Pennsylvania law, prisoners known as "wheelbarrow men" started appearing on the streets of Philadelphia in irons and chains, their heads shaven and wearing coarse uniforms while they cleaned and repaired the streets to atone for their crimes.[133]

In those days, aspiring lawyers did their legal training with experienced lawyers—and in doing so were, themselves, regularly exposed to Beccaria's *On Crimes and Punishments*. In the eighteenth century, the English Inns of Court—where Beccaria's treatise drew attention from its members—controlled the admission of barristers to the practice of law. "Following the English translations of Beccaria's *Essay on Crimes and Punishments* in 1767," notes historian David Lemmings in a book about English legal culture, William Eden's *Principles of Penal Law*—a text that references Beccaria multiple times—was published in 1771. Other titles on penal reform, by progressives Samuel Romilly and Jeremy Bentham, also appeared in the 1780s, raising further issues about the status quo. A friend of William Wilberforce (1759–1833), the British legislator and evangelical Christian who campaigned relentlessly against the slave trade, Sir Samuel Romilly devoted most of his life to crusading against executions. In his first speech on criminal law reform in the House of Commons, Romilly himself acknowledged his debt to Beccaria, with other Englishmen also taking heed of Beccaria's ideas.[134] In the apprenticeship system that trained new lawyers, the apprentice—known as a "clerk" or "pupil"—would perform tasks, whether menial or otherwise, for his lawyer-mentor. The younger man, in turn, would get access to the lawyer's experience and often an extensive law library. Sometimes, Virginians—far from their mother country—would actually travel to England to pair up with a London practitioner; from 1674 to 1776, at least sixty Virginians were members of one of the English Inns of Court, with the Middle Temple being the most popular. After being called to the bar, a new barrister could argue cases in English courts and in the colony of Virginia. In Virginia, the usual apprenticeship lasted four or five years.[135]

Studying to be a lawyer was—as it is today—a rigorous endeavor. "[T]he most important aspect of an apprenticeship," historian W. Hamilton Bryson explains, "was access to the master's law library and his guidance in reading the law." "Reading law," Bryson notes, "was also frequently done independently of an apprenticeship, as Jefferson advised Philip Turpin in 1769." In a letter, Jefferson told Turpin, a relative, that it was his view that "it is the intention alone which constitutes the criminality of any act."[136] *Commonplacing*— a form of note taking developed and used in England long before Virginia's inhabitants broke away from Great Britain during the American Revolution—was itself a standard practice among legal professionals. As a student or lawyer read books and treatises of interest, entries on the points of law contained in those sources would be methodically copied into the reader's commonplace book. "The most popular title in colonial Virginia," Bryson notes, "was *Coke upon Littleton*," a treatise written by Sir Thomas Littleton but enlarged by the English jurist Sir Edward Coke. Blackstone's *Commentaries on the Laws of England*, which first appeared between 1765 and 1769, and Beccaria's *On Crimes and Punishments*, were also in high demand and carefully digested, notated, and recommended by lawyers such as Thomas Jefferson.[137]

Aside from his Beccaria-related entries, Jefferson also recorded other ideas in his commonplace book pertaining to penal reform, such as this one from William Eden's *Principles of Penal Law*: "Penal laws must not wage war with the sentiments of the human heart."[138] Eden's treatise called severe punishments "the instruments of despotism" and, in a chapter titled "Of the Infliction of Death," referred to the "cruelties" of barbarous modes of execution as "contrary to the republican spirit." While Jefferson lived in a state that, in the seven years prior to the outbreak of the Revolutionary War, saw at least 79 acquittals in capital trials, 42 applications of "benefit of clergy" to save offenders, 17 hangings and 9 pardons, Eden advocated the death penalty's restriction to seven felonies. "Nothing however, but the evident result of absolute necessity," Eden wrote in his treatise, "can authorize the destruction of mankind by the hand of man." As Eden wrote in language reminiscent of William Blackstone's post-*On Crimes and Punishments* words: "The infliction of Death is not therefore to be considered in any instance, as a mode of punishment, but merely as our last melancholly resource in the extermination of those from society, whose continuance among their fellow-citizens is become inconsistent with the public safety."[139] In Eden's book, "public utility" was emphasized as regards the rationale for punishment, with an English bill of 1778—drafted by Eden and Sir William Blackstone—providing for the construction of "Houses of Hard Labour." Eden's *Principles of Penal Law*—a book that garnered a significant readership of its own—mentions Beccaria multiple times.[140]

Thomas Jefferson—who read both Beccaria and Eden and who, when legal issues arose, consulted Blackstone, too[141]—had previously studied under Dr. William Small at the College of William and Mary in Williamsburg, Virginia. Although Jefferson completed his studies in 1762, he continued to meet with Dr. Small—a native of Scotland—until 1764, the year Beccaria's treatise first appeared in Italian. "Dr. William Small," Jefferson would later write, "fixed the destinies of my life" by exposing him to Enlightenment ideas and by persuading his friend, the prominent and highly respected lawyer George Wythe, to accept Jefferson as a student of law. With Wythe as his sponsor, Jefferson—at the age of 23, and due in part to Wythe's mentoring—was brought before the General Court of Virginia for an oral examination to gain admittance to the bar. Jefferson gained admittance in 1767, the same year Beccaria's treatise first appeared in English. Records indicate that Wythe—the much-respected Virginia jurist and law professor who the Reverend Lee Massey called "the only honest lawyer I ever knew"[142]—also owned a copy of Beccaria's book. Jefferson—who outlived Wythe—himself held on to Beccaria's treatise until his death in 1826. Indeed, an Italian version of Beccaria's treatise is listed in the auction catalog printed in 1829 for the sale of Jefferson's library following his death.[143]

George Wythe—the counselor-turned-educator and another of Beccaria's readers—made a lasting impression on Jefferson. In 1788, Jefferson called Wythe "one of the greatest men of the age"; in 1810, Jefferson referred to him as his "second father"; and near the end of his life, Jefferson wrote glowingly, "Mr. Wythe continued to be my faithful and beloved mentor in youth, and my most affectionate friend through life." Wythe, a signer of the Declaration of Independence, practiced law, and counted among his clients George Washington and fellow attorney John Blair. In 1779, Wythe also joined the faculty of William and Mary, becoming America's first law professor. Among Wythe's pupils: John Marshall, the future Chief Justice of the United States; James Monroe, the fifth President of the United States; and Henry Clay, the famed U.S. Senator from Kentucky who also served three terms as Speaker of the U.S. House of Representatives. Wythe gave Jefferson a first-class education, and Jefferson—the consummate bibliophile—came to call reading the "greatest of all amusements," observing that he could not "live without books." Jefferson would recall his time studying law with Wythe as "a time of life when I was bold in the pursuit of knowledge, never fearing to follow the truth and reason to whatever results they led."[144] After studying Beccaria's treatise and discussing the law with Wythe, Jefferson saw the world differently, and saw less of a need for executions.

Not only did Jefferson find Beccaria's ideas worthwhile, but he made sure that *On Crimes and Punishments* was on the must-read list of other young men, too. After absorbing the contents of Beccaria's treatise, carefully annotating it in his commonplace book for future reference, Jefferson thus regularly recommended it to others. For example, Jefferson wrote to John Garland Jefferson—his younger cousin—on June 11, 1790, suggesting that he study to be a lawyer by reading law rather than through a lengthy apprenticeship. "It is a general practice to study the law in the office of some lawyer," Jefferson wrote, adding: "This indeed gives to the student the advantage of his instruction." "But," Jefferson warned, "I have ever seen that the services expected in return have been more than the instructions have been worth." Jefferson then advised: "All that is necessary for a student is access to a library, and directions in what order the books are to be read." In advising his cousin, Jefferson made three lists of books. Among the books he suggested were Hawkins' *Pleas of the Crown*, Blackstone's *Commentaries*, and works by Locke, Montesquieu, Vattel and Beccaria.[145] In an 1807 letter to John Norvell (1789–1850), later a U.S. Senator from Michigan, Jefferson also recommended "Beccaria on crimes & punishments, because of the demonstrative manner in which he has treated that branch of the subject."[146]

Jefferson actually owned more than one copy of Beccaria's treatise. For example, the owner of Monticello, that brick, hilltop mansion outside Charlottesville in Virginia's Piedmont region, had a Greek edition of *Dei delitti e delle pene*. That version of Beccaria's treatise had been translated by Adamantios Koraes (1748–1833), a Greek intellectual with whom Jefferson corresponded during the last few years of his life. The Greek translation was published in Paris in 1823,[147] and was shipped to Monticello in December 1823.[148] When Jefferson's library was sold to the U.S. government in 1815 to reconstitute the Library of Congress, the sale included *On Crimes and Punishments*, *Meditazioni sulla Economia Politica da Beccaria*, and *Voltaire sur Beccaria*, a 1766 first edition self-described as *Commentaire sur le livre des délits et des peines, par un avocat de Province*. "Beccaria on crimes & punishments, either in Italian or Eng.," in fact, was written by Jefferson on a "List of Books to be Acquired by Joseph Milligan,"[149] Jefferson's preferred bookseller and leather binder in Georgetown.[150] According to E. Millicent Sowerby, the compiler of the *Catalogue of the Library of Thomas Jefferson*: "Jefferson's copy of *Dei delitti e delle pene* was missing at the time of the sale to Congress in 1815 and on March 28, 1815, he wrote to Milligan to supply a replacement copy either in Italian or English. Milligan sent a copy on April 7, 1815, price one dollar. This copy has also disappeared." After James Madison took office and occupied the Executive Mansion as President in what was then known as Washington City, Jefferson settled his accounts with Milligan—an account that included an 1809 edition of Beccaria's *Essay on Crimes and Punishments* published in New York by Stephen Gould.[151] Jefferson took books and the ideas in them seriously, and the fact that he owned more than one version of the same treatise speaks volumes about Jefferson's respect for Beccaria's book.

Jefferson's associations with Beccaria do not stop there. Jefferson himself used the French translator of Beccaria's treatise to translate his *Notes on the State of Virginia* into French. As historian Dorothy Medlin explains in her article, "Thomas Jefferson, André Morellet, and the French Version of *Notes on the State of Virginia*": "Jefferson's book originated in 1780–82 as a series of detailed responses to twenty-two queries submitted by François de Barbé-Marbois, secretary of the French legation in Philadelphia, in regard to vegetation, minerals, animals, peoples, and customs in the state of Virginia." After sending answers to Barbé-Marbois, Medlin explains, Jefferson had two hundred copies printed by Philippe-Denis Pierres in 1785 for private distribution. A Parisian bookseller, however, got his hands on one of the privately distributed copies after one recipient's death. The bookseller, sensing the opportunity to make some money, then planned a French translation. Fearful that his book would be published in French "in the most injurious form possible," as he wrote James Madison on February 8, 1786, Jefferson—who never intended his responses to be made public—went into damage-control mode. As fate would have it, André Morellet—a respected member of the Académie-Francaise who had won Voltaire's praise for his 1766 translation of Beccaria's treatise—interceded with the Parisian bookseller. Morellet offered to translate the text so that Jefferson would not be at the mercy of an unknown or unskilled translator. Jefferson, anxious to have at least some control over the final product, welcomed this "friendly proposition," then gradually warmed to the idea. "As a translation by so able a hand will lessen the faults of the original instead of their being multiplied by a hireling translator," Jefferson wrote, "I shall add to it a map, and such other advantages as may prevent the mortification of my seeing it appear in the injurious form threatened." Jefferson's embrace of Morellet as a translator must be attributed in part to Morellet's reputation as the translator of Beccaria's book.[152]

To be sure, Jefferson—who succeeded Patrick Henry as Virginia's governor—took much more than a passing or fleeting interest in Beccaria's treatise.[153] Aside from copying numerous passages from that book into his own commonplace book, Jefferson—in the midst of the American Revolution—consulted *On Crimes and Punishments* in drafting his "Bill for Proportioning Crimes and Punishments in Cases Heretofore Capital," the very title of which bears a Beccarian imprint. In that bill, painstakingly prepared and annotated for consideration by Virginia's legislature, Jefferson wrote that, to avoid the infliction of unnecessary pain, "it becomes a duty in the legislature to arrange, in a proper scale, the crimes which it may be necessary for them to repress, and to adjust thereto a corresponding gradation of punishments." Jefferson's bill—echoing the ideas of Enlightenment writers such as Beccaria, Blackstone and Eden—stated that capital punishment "should be the last melancholy resource against those whose existence is become inconsistent with the safety of their fellow-citizens." Jefferson added: "the experience of all ages and countries hath shown, that cruel and sanguinary laws defeat their own purpose." Whereas Jefferson's bill retained the death penalty for murder and treason, Virginia law at that time punished scores of offenses, including robbery and burglary, with death.[154]

Though Jefferson, in the midst of the Revolutionary War, believed murder and treason were appropriately classed as capital offenses, he didn't see executions as necessary in all such circumstances. For example, in 1781, Mann Page—an executor for the estate of John Tayloe—sent Jefferson a letter on behalf of "Billy, a Negro Man belonging to that Estate, who is now under Sentence of Death, by the Judgement of the Court of Prince William County." Page's letter stated: "The Crime for which he is condemned, and the Proceedings of the Court will be made known to you by the enclosed Papers. Not entertaining a

Doubt myself of the Illegality of the Sentence of the Court I earnestly entreat you (if it can be done) to grant a Pardon to the Fellow, but if that cannot be done, to reprieve him." The court records reflected that "Billy alias Will alias William" was "a mulatto slave belonging to John Tayloe Esqr. late of Richmond County" who was charged in April 1781 with treason. The charge stated that, "with force and arms, &c.," Billy "did feloniously and traitorously adhere to the Enemies of the Commonwealth and gave them aid and comfort" and "did in company of and conjunction with divers enemies of the commonwealth in an armed vessel feloniously and traitorously wage and levy war against the Commonwealth to the great danger of subverting thereof." The issue would come down to whether a slave — someone without legal rights and subject to a master's control — could actually be found guilty of treason.

After Billy's trial in May 1781, a Virginia court of oyer and terminer adjudged Billy guilty of the crime and sentenced him to death, ordering that the local sheriff, on the 25th of May "between the hours of Eleven and two of the same day," execute Billy "on the common gallows" by "causing the said Slave to be hanged by the neck until dead." According to the order, Billy's head was to be "severed from his body" and be "stuck up at some public cross road on a pole." The court order also adjudicated that "the said Slave is worth twenty seven thousand pounds current money." Four of the six "Gentlemen Justices" who sat in judgment in the case voted to condemn Billy for treason, but two of the judges — Henry Lee and William Carr — "were against his Condemnation because a slave in our opinion Cannot Commit Treason against the State not being Admitted to the Priviledges of a Citizen." A non-citizen, they felt, "owes the State No Allegiance" and — in the particular case at hand and before them — Lee and Carr said "there was no Positive Proof before the Court that the said Slave went Voluntarily On board of the Enemys Vessel and took up Arms."

In the aftermath of the judges' collective, but non-unanimous decision, efforts were made to save Billy's life. "On his defence," Lee and Carr wrote of Billy, "he was taken in an Oyster boat and forced on board against his will," "never took up Arms against the Country," and did not act "of his own free will." Ultimately, then-Governor Jefferson granted Billy a reprieve until both houses of the Virginia legislature determined that the "proceedings against the said slave were illegal." At that time, a 1776 Virginia law provided that the governor could "in no wise have or exercise a right of granting pardon" to any person convicted of treason, but could only suspend such a sentence "until the meeting of the general assembly, who shall determine whether such person or persons are proper objects of mercy or not." In his draft Constitution for Virginia of 1776, Jefferson himself had proposed the very Beccarian idea that there should be no "power any where to pardon crimes or to remit fines or punishments."[155] That idea, of course, was premised on laws themselves taking on a milder character.

Beccaria's treatise clearly influenced Jefferson's bill to proportion crimes and punishments, but other, far less progressive sources did, too. For example, Jefferson turned to *Coke on Littleton* — what Jefferson told James Madison in 1826 was "the universal elementary book of law students." Sir Edward Coke (1552–1634), whom Jefferson admired as an expert on "the British constitution, or in what were called English liberties," was an English barrister and judge best known for his four-volume *Institutes of the Lawes of England*. Coke was cited and quoted by Jefferson more than twenty times; Bracton's even older treatise, *De legibus et consuetudinibus Angliae*, was cited ten times; and Sir Matthew Hale's seventeenth-century treatise got seventeen references. Indeed, Jefferson cited ninth and tenth century Anglo-Saxon sources twenty-five times and felt constrained, for whatever reason, by the *lex talionis* doctrine — that Biblical notion calling for "an eye for an eye and a tooth for a tooth." In 1773, Benjamin Franklin — in a letter to his son William, capturing some flavor of the time—called *Lex Talionis* "returning Offences in kind," and in 1778, after Congress resolved to treat British prisoners in a like manner to how American prisoners were being treated by the British, Daniel Roberdeau—in a letter to John Adams—noted that "[a] lex talionis has this day unanimously passed Congress." In March 1800, in a letter to Thomas Jefferson, Thomas McKean referred to "the lex talionis" as "Moses's Law."

Jefferson's bill to proportion crimes and punishments specifically called for mandatory death sentences for treason and murder, with the proposed code linking the victim's manner of death with the proposed punishment. The bill thus called for death by poison for those who killed by poisoning; castration for male rapists and men committing sodomy; and for acts of maiming, similar disfigurement. As one provision of Jefferson's bill read: "Whosoever on purpose shall disfigure another, by cutting out or disabling the tongue, slitting or cutting off a nose, lip, or ear, branding, or otherwise, shall be maimed or disfigured in like sort." If an offender lacked the body part to be maimed or disfigured, Jefferson's bill provided that "some other part of at least equal value and estimation, in the opinion of a jury," was to be selected. The type of proportionality Jefferson's bill envisioned thus differed substantially from what Beccaria—who favored milder punishments—had proposed. As one commentator explained, Jefferson's proposed code "retained a core of brutality which suggests that Jefferson had great difficulty shaking off the dead hand of history, or at least the common law."[156]

While Beccaria's treatise had impressed Jefferson, his bill, as drafted, undeniably retained many English, common-law features and therefore contained incredibly draconian punishments for offenders, including both capital and non-lethal ones. For example, one provision called for any female committing rape or a homosexual act to be punished "by boring through the cartilage of her nose a hole of one half inch in diameter at the least." But in spite of such bizarre provisions, inspired by the draconian nature of the English common-law, Jefferson's bill sought to drastically curtail the number of capital offenses in Virginia. Even as he sought to reduce that number to just two, murder and treason, Jefferson worried privately about the implications of the *lex talionis* principle. As Jefferson explained to George Wythe in a bit of self-reflection: "The 'Lex talionis' will be revolting to the humanized feelings of modern times." "An eye for an eye, and a hand for a hand," Jefferson wrote, "will exhibit spectacles in execution, whose moral effect would be questionable."[157] The term *lex talionis*, found in the ancient Roman law of the Twelve Tables, dating to 451–450 B.C., is sometimes referred to as "the law of retaliation."[158] Wythe, the man Jefferson selected to serve as William and Mary's first law professor, had long been Jefferson's legal mentor, including most formally from 1762 to 1767. Tragically, Wythe—who, at age 35, had accepted Jefferson as a law student—is thought to have died by being poisoned by his sister's grandson who had hoped to come into an inheritance. Wythe had anti-slavery convictions, but his murderer escaped a finding of guilt because, under Virginia law, blacks could not then testify in a judicial proceeding against a white person.[159]

Since its beginnings as a British colony, Virginia—with its long history of slavery—had traditionally made a host of crimes capital in nature. In light of that history, Jefferson's bill—despite its odd, draconian provisions—consequently represented a radical, if not total departure from custom. For example, in its "Laws Divine, Moral, and Martial," put in place by Sir Thomas Gates in 1610 and enlarged by Sir Thomas Dale in 1611, the following acts, among many others, were punishable by death: treason, blasphemy, embezzlement, and speaking "impiously or maliciously against the holy and blessed Trinity … or against the known articles of the Christian faith."[160] "In contrast to Puritan New England," criminologist Mitchel Roth notes, "executions were a common occurrence in Virginia, where hundreds of crimes demanded the death penalty by the mid-1700s." "[O]f the 164 people convicted of capital crimes between 1737 and 1772," Roth writes, "125 were executed without benefit of clergy."[161] The privilege of *benefit of clergy*—as Jefferson once wrote—"originally allowed to the clergy," but later "extended to every man, & even to women," was "a right of exemption from capital punishment for the first offence in most cases."[162] Of southern, pro-death penalty attitudes and traditions, historian Stuart Banner—author of *The Death Penalty: An American History*—puts it this way: "In the South the colonies followed England in capitalizing minor property crimes." As Banner writes: "Virginia imposed the death penalty for all sorts of crimes relating to the tobacco trade—including embezzling tobacco, fraudulently delivering tobacco, altering inspected tobacco, forging inspectors' stamps, and smuggling tobacco—as well as for stealing hogs (upon a third conviction), receiving a stolen horse, and concealing property to defraud creditors."[163]

It was only after reading Beccaria's treatise that Jefferson had drafted his "Bill for Proportioning Crimes and Punishments" in the 1770s as part of his work on a revisal of Virginia's laws. Because of the Revolutionary War, that bill, however, did not come up for a vote in the Virginia legislature until 1785. By then, Jefferson was serving his country in France, mingling with the French *philosophes*. In Jefferson's absence, James Madison—Jefferson's protégé—advocated for the passage of Jefferson's bill, though it got defeated in Virginia's assembly by the narrowest of margins, just one vote. As Jefferson wrote many years after the fact:

> When proposed to the Legislature, by Mr. Madison, in 1785, it failed by a single vote. G. K. Taylor afterwards, in 1796, proposed the same subject; avoiding the adoption of any part of the diction of mine, the text of which had been studiously drawn in the technical terms of the law, so as to give no occasion for new questions by new expressions. When I drew mine, public labor was thought the best punishment to be substituted for death. But, while I was in France, I heard of a society in England, who had successfully introduced solitary confinement, and saw the drawing of a prison at Lyons, in France, formed on the idea of solitary confinement. And, being applied to by the Governor of Virginia for the plan of a Capitol and Prison, I sent him the Lyons plan, accompanying it with a drawing on a smaller scale, better adapted to our use. This was in June, 1786. Mr. Taylor very judiciously adopted this idea (which had now been acted on in Philadelphia, probably from the English model), and substituted labor in confinement for the public labor proposed by the Committee of Revisal; which themselves would have done, had they been to act on the subject again. The public mind was ripe for this in 1796, when Mr. Taylor proposed it, and ripened chiefly by the experiment in Philadelphia; whereas, in 1785, when it had been proposed to our Assembly, they were not quite ripe for it.[164]

As Jefferson's notation reflects, Virginia's criminal laws would eventually be changed by virtue of the efforts of George Keith Taylor, a member of the Virginia House of Delegates. A leading lawyer from Petersburg and the brother-in-law of John Marshall, Taylor is considered the "father of penal reform in Virginia" because of his efforts in 1796 that led to the amendment of Virginia's penal laws.[165] Taylor called the state's outdated laws "a code of carnage and horror."[166] It was said of George Keith Taylor that he "embodied the principles of Beccaria in the criminal code of a state"—the Commonwealth of Virginia—"and founded a penitentiary, the complement of that enlightened measure."[167] As *The Virginia Evangelical and Literary Magazine*, published in 1818, reported more than two decades after the change in law had taken place: "[I]t is due to ourselves to say, that from the beginning we have been warm advocates of the Penitentiary system. We remember well, with what feelings, in our youthful days, we read the speeches of George Keith Taylor, in the Virginia Legislature, on this subject."[168] A delegate from Prince George County, Taylor had forcefully argued that a punishment should fit the crime and that because punishments were too harsh some criminals—due to juries' refusal to convict for humanitarian reasons—were escaping punishment altogether.[169]

Before George Keith Taylor's legislation passed, the propriety of Virginia's death penalty—in the limelight since Beccaria's treatise was published, and especially since Madison unsuccessfully fought for the passage of Jefferson's bill in the mid-1780s—had been a topic of much discussion. One case involving a black woman, Angelica Barnett, had captivated Virginians in a unique, particularly fact-specific way. In 1793, Angelica Barnett—a free black, not a slave—had been convicted of murder after a white man, Peter Franklin, broke into her home late one night. Franklin was searching for runaway slaves, but when he found none, he assaulted Barnett in front of her family, threatening to kill her. As Franklin came towards her, Barnett hit him in the head with an axe, leading to Franklin's death four days later. After Barnett was put on trial, convicted, and sentenced to hang, three dozen of Richmond's most prominent women—including John Marshall's wife Polly—signed a public petition calling on Governor Henry "Light-Horse Harry" Lee to be merciful. To make matters worse, a prison cellmate raped Barnett and she became pregnant. After Lee, a 1773 graduate of the College of New Jersey and a Revolutionary War cavalry officer, granted a temporary stay of execution, John Marshall himself joined with leaders of the Richmond bar to request clemency. Barnett, they said, "was possessed of many of the rights of a free Citizen," including "the great right of personal immunity in her own house." "[I]t is at least reasonable to presume," that petition stated, "that many of the Circumstances alleged by the prisoner in her justification, might have been proved if her associates were not incompetent by law to give Testimony against a White person." After receiving the lawyers' petition on September 12, 1793, Governor Lee pardoned Barnett that evening, just a day before her scheduled execution.[170]

Jefferson himself was well aware—even long after his first exposure to Beccaria's treatise and the 1796 passage of penal reform in Virginia—that his fellow citizens were highly conflicted about capital punishment and still wrestling with precisely how, and to what extent, to incorporate Beccaria's principles into American law. On December 27, 1820, for instance, Jefferson replied to a letter he had received more than a year earlier from William Roscoe, an English historian and writer. Roscoe had sent Jefferson "two tracts," including one on "penal jurisprudence," and Jefferson thanked Roscoe for sending them, apologizing at the outset for his late response due to "ill health." "[T]he treatise on penal jurisprudence I read with great pleasure," Jefferson wrote, noting: "Beccaria had demonstrated general principles: but practical applications were difficult." In other words, Beccaria—the criminal law theorist—had set forth important guiding principles, but working out the details—the actual implementation of those ideas in the real world—had not been so simple. Both the Revolutionary War and the War of 1812 had only generated more complexity and impeded progress. As Jefferson added of the legislative attempts to put Beccaria's ideas into practice: "our States are trying them with more or less success." Jefferson also told Roscoe that "the great light you have thrown on the subject will, I am sure, be useful to our experiment," with Jefferson explaining: "for the thing as yet, is but in experiment."[171] Jefferson thus recognized that penal reform would be a long, arduous process, and that there would be no silver bullet to solve the problem of crime.

In 1819 in London, William Roscoe had published *Observations on Penal Jurisprudence and the Reformation of Criminals*. That book—the one Jefferson commented on—contained an appendix containing the latest reports "of the state-prisons or penitentiaries of Philadelphia, New-York, and Massachusetts." The book also specifically referred to "the celebrated work of the Marquis Beccaria," explaining that Beccaria's writings — as well as those of Montesquieu and Voltaire — had resulted in "great improvements in criminal legislation." It also noted that the Grand Duke of Tuscany had read and admired Beccaria, with Roscoe writing: "The introduction to the Edict" of the Grand Duke "is in fact an abridgment of the principles of Beccaria." In the appendix, one finds additional Beccaria references in the following documents: (1) *An Account of the Alteration and Present State of the Penal Laws of Pennsylvania* by Caleb Lownes, first published in Philadelphia in 1793; (2) *A View of the New-York State Prison* by "a Member of the Institution"; and (3) a report to the Senate and House of Representatives of the Commonwealth of Massachusetts.[172] "The opinions of Beccaria" — as one French writer, Duke de la Rochefoucauld-Liancourt, put it — "easily took root" in the "humane heart" of Caleb Lownes, the Pennsylvania reformer who relied, in part, on Beccaria's ideas in formulating his own.[173] Lownes — a charter member of the Philadelphia Society for Alleviating the Miseries of Public Prisons — was a Quaker ironmonger who, for a time, supplied nail-rods to Jefferson at Monticello.[174]

American penal reform got its start in Philadelphia, and once the Pennsylvania experiment had begun, it drove reform elsewhere, drawing the attention of Jefferson and others. Caleb Lownes, the administrator of Philadelphia's Walnut Street Prison, and Robert Turnbull, a South Carolina native studying law in Philadelphia when he toured that facility, both wrote extensively about Pennsylvania's innovative penal system. Lownes and Turnbull, historian Keally McBride notes, "cite the ideas of Beccaria with particular fervor."[175] In his pamphlet, *A Visit to the Philadelphia Prison*, Turnbull described receiving a tour of the Walnut Street Prison — a structure measuring 190 feet in length and 40 feet in depth. Noting that Pennsylvania law had abrogated the death penalty for every crime "except cool and deliberate murder," Turnbull explained how the change in the law had come about. Among the circumstances: Quaker advocacy and "the small and valuable gift of the immortal Beccaria to the world." Beccaria's treatise "had its due influence and weight," Turnbull emphasized, "for on the framing of the (then) new constitution of the state, in 1776," legislators had been "directed to proceed as soon as might be, to the reformation of the penal laws, and to invent punishments less sanguinary, and better proportioned to the various degrees of criminality." Only the "ravages of a ruinous and unnatural conflict, with the subsequent distress occasioned by it," Turnbull wrote of the Revolutionary War, had effectively "postponed the carrying into effect these humane intentions, till the year 1786, when the foundation of this long desired reform was at length laid by an act of the legislature."

In his *Travels Through the Country of North America*, the former French political leader Rochefoucauld-Liancourt wrote that "[i]t is on the subject of criminal laws that philosophy has had the most noble and useful influence in Pennsylvania; and in this respect the government may justly serve for a model to the rest of the world." Pennsylvania's prison administrators, he noted, had set forth certain objectives, including the following: "That all arbitrary proceedings, and cruelty, and injustice in the jailors, should be carefully excluded, since they dispose the mind of the prisoner to malice and revenge, instead of begetting sentiments of contrition." He took specific note of the use of prison inspections, as well as hard labor, silence and solitary confinement for crimes formerly punished with death. "The cells for solitary confinement," Rochefoucauld-Liancourt indicated, "are eight feet by six, and nine in height." "The inspectors," he emphasized, "are for the most part Quakers; and it is not to be forgotten, that it is to the society of Quakers that the public is indebted for the establishment, protection, and success of the new system." "To one of these people, whose name is Caleb Lownes," Rochefoucauld-Liancourt recorded, "is to be given the largest share of the honour of this great reform." "It was he,"

Rochefoucauld-Liancourt observed, referencing the greatness of Cesare Beccaria and John Howard, "who animated his brethren with zeal for the enlightened system of these great men." Robert Turnbull's essay also credited and singled out William Bradford and Benjamin Rush for their role in Pennsylvania penal reform.[176]

In an autobiographical statement, written in 1821, an elderly Thomas Jefferson—then in his 70s—reiterated how Beccaria and like-minded reformers had already materially influenced efforts to revise Virginia's penal laws. "When I left Congress," Jefferson wrote of 1776 and Virginia's efforts to revise its laws in the post-Declaration of Independence period, "it was in the persuasion that our whole code must be reviewed" and "adapted to our republican form of government." "[A]nd, now that we had no negatives of Councils, Governors & Kings to restrain us from doing right," Jefferson wrote of Virginia's laws and the state's revisal efforts, seeing no barriers other than public sentiment, Jefferson recorded "that it should be corrected, in all it's parts, with a single eye to reason, & the good of those for whose government it was framed." In short, Jefferson thought the consensual laws of a republican form of government should be fundamentally different than those dictated and imposed by a monarchical regime. "Early therefore in the session of 76. to which I returned," Jefferson explained of his involvement in Virginia's legislative revisal effort, "I moved and presented a bill for the revision of the laws; which was passed on the 24th. of October, and on the 5th of November Mr. Pendleton, Mr. Wythe, George Mason, Thomas L. Lee and myself were appointed a committee to execute the work." After George Mason resigned from the committee, Jefferson himself took the lead on the criminal law revisal effort.[177]

George Mason's notes—the only surviving record of a January 13, 1777 meeting of the committee—show the basic principles that the revisal committee initially agreed-upon. "The Common Law not to be medled with, except where Alterations are necessary," Mason's notes began. Mason's notes then listed a number of actions to be taken: "The Statutes to be revised & digested, alterations proper for us to be made; the Diction, where obsolete or redundant, to be reformed; but otherwise to undergo as few Changes as possible." "The Acts of the English Commonwealth to be examined." "The Laws of the other Colonies to be examined, & any good ones to be adopted." "Laws to be made on the Spur of the present Occasion, and all innovating Laws, to be limited in their Duration Criminal Law." Mason's notes also reflected plans for the punishment of particular offenses. Those notes covered the contemplated punishment for a wide array of offenses, reading: "Treason & Murder (& no other Crime) to be punished with Death, by hanging, and Forfeiture; saving Dower." "Petty-treason, Parricide, Saticide; the Body to be delivered over to Surgeons to be anatomized." "Manslaughter to be punished by Forfeiture & Labour." "Suicide not to incur Forfeiture, but considered as a Disease." "Justifiable Homicide not to be punished at all. Rape, Sodomy, Bestiality to be punished by Castration." "Other Crimes punishable by Forfeiture, Fine, Labour in public works, such as Mines, Gallies, Saltworks, Dock-Yards, Founderies, and public Manufactories."

George Mason's notes also set forth various rules of the road for criminals and criminal cases. "The Benefit of Clergy & the actual Cautery to be abolished," one read. "Corruption of Blood to be abolished in all Cases," read another. On procedural matters, Mason also jotted down these items: "Standing mute on Trial to amount to plea of not guilty, & the Court to proceed to Trial, and punishment (if guilty) or Acquittal (if innocent) in same Manner as if the Criminal had pleaded not guilty." "The Act which makes Concealment by the Mother of the Death of her bastard Child amount to Evidence of her having murdered it to be repealed." "New Trials to be allowed in Criminal Cases (in favour of the Criminal) during the Term or Session, for good Cause shewn to the Judges. Whether Pardons shall be allowed or not, in any Instance, the Committee, having not yet determined, defer to be consider'd at the next Meeting." Mason's notes reflect that Mason was to undertake the "criminal Law" portion of the revisal, but contemplated he might step out of that role. "[I]f he finds it too much," the notes read, "the other Gentlemen will take off his Hands any part he pleases."[178]

Against the backdrop of the English Revolution of 1649 and the Glorious Revolution of 1688, Beccaria's ideas inspired a fierce, new brand of republicanism. "During its short life," one historian explains, "the English republic of the 1650s left a legacy of republican writings and stimulated an enduring republican tradition." As that historian, Rachel Hammersley, writes: "The works of John Milton, Marchamont Nedham and James Harrington—written during the 1650s—were followed by those of Algernon Sidney and Henry Neville in the 1680s." "In the eighteenth century," she notes, "English republican ideas survived in the works of British commonwealthmen, such as John Trenchard, Thomas Gordon, Thomas Hollis, James Burgh, Richard Price and Joseph Priestley." In *An Essay on the First Principles of Government, and on the Nature of Political, Civil, and Religious Liberty*, published in 1768, the English scientist and thinker Joseph Priestley decided to close one section of his essay "with a few extracts from travellers, and other writers, which show the importance of political and civil liberty." One of those writers was Beccaria. "'The fear of the laws,' says the admirable author of the *Essay on crimes and punishments*," Priestley wrote, quoting Beccaria, "'is salutary, but the fear of man is a fruitful and fatal source of crimes. Men enslaved are more voluptuous, more debauched, and more cruel than those who are in a state of freedom.'"[179]

Intellectuals in Europe and America, including the Rev. Dr. Joseph Priestley, looked to Italy not only for trade and scientific advancement, but for political genius. For example, Benjamin Franklin had discussed the silk trade with the Austrian ambassador to the Court of St. James, an Italian, Count Ludovico Barbiana di Belgioioso, of a noble family from Milan who served in that role from 1769 to 1783. Dr. Franklin memorialized that communication in a letter to the Managers of the Philadelphia Silk Filature before May 1772, the same year "the Count of Belgioioso" presented "His best Compliments to Dr. Franklin" and asked Franklin where he could procure "the Glasses for the Harmonica according to His Invention." On the intellectual front, English and American thinkers also paid continuous attention to ancient Greek and Roman thinkers and to reformist titles, including *On Crimes and Punishments*. Joseph Priestley, whose own friends and admirers included John Adams, Benjamin Franklin and Thomas Jefferson, and who was fond of discussing Socrates, Plato and Aristotle as well as Jesus and his apostles, relocated to America in 1794, and referred in his own writings to both Beccaria and "[t]he *Commentary* on *Beccaria*."[180]

Likewise, the English radical, John Jebb (1736–1786), who has been described as "a warm friend of America," had read Beccaria's treatise as a reference in his theological notes in the early 1770s make clear. Jebb—the Bishop of Limerick who became a medical doctor in London—specifically refers to "the incomparable Beccaria" in a footnote of his *Address to the Freeholders of Middlesex, Assembled at Freemasons Tavern, in Great Queen Street, upon Monday the 20th of December 1779*. As Jebb said at that time: "What the incomparable Beccaria says of an enslaved people in general, holds true also with respect to those, who find themselves excluded from bearing a part in framing the Laws and directing the Public Counsels of their Country." In Anthony Page's *John Jebb and the Enlightenment Origins of British Radicalism*, it is noted that, in England, "Jebb was among the minority who believed that capital punishment should at least be greatly restricted, in comparison to the vast majority of educated men who continued to support public execution." "[A]mong Jebb's circle," Page writes, "capital punishment was seen, at the very best, as a necessary evil that should be employed with great care and reluctance."

After the Revolutionary War ended, John Jebb—with whom, in November 1783, John Adams and John Quincy Adams had dined—wrote to George Washington himself in 1785 to congratulate him on his role "in establishing the liberties of Mankind." "Our Europe," Jebb lamented in his letter, still "groans under the lash of Tyranny Civil & Religious." Across the English Channel, in Lafayette's France, however, changes in the law—as in America—would soon be afoot. Following the French Revolution, the French Declaration of the Rights of Man and Citizen would plainly echo—as one source put it—"the popular, contemporary writings of Beccaria." Indeed, the French writer Théophile Mandar, in *Des Insurrections*, argued that insurrection could be justified because liberty is essential for happiness. "Now," Mandar wrote in 1793, "the royal statues have fallen, and the busts of Sidney, of Nedham, of Beccaria, of Montesquieu, of Fénélon, of J. Locke, of J. J. Rousseau (and yours Harrington), replace these royal effigies, the stormy shadow of which insults the generations."[181]

Although a host of more traditional legal authorities also shaped Jefferson's early thinking, including his approach to his proposed Virginia penal code, Beccaria's ideas clearly influenced Jefferson's thoughts and writings throughout his adult life. In his 1821 autobiographical statement, Jefferson specifically noted that "the criminal law" fell within his portion of the committee's revisal work, but that "[o]n the subject of the Criminal law, all were agreed that the punishment of death should be abolished, except for treason and murder; and that, for other felonies should be substituted hard labor in the public works, and in some cases, the Lex talionis." "How this last revolting principle came to obtain our approbation," Jefferson reflected in 1821, "I do not remember." As Jefferson recalled in 1821: "Beccaria and other writers on crimes and punishments had satisfied the reasonable world of the unrightfulness and inefficacy of the punishment of crimes by death; and hard labor on roads, canals and other public works, had been suggested as a proper substitute. The Revisors had adopted these opinions; but the general idea of our country had not yet advanced to that point."[182] Virginia public opinion, not yet as enlightened as Jefferson's way of thinking, would thwart the state's criminal-law revisal efforts, at least until 1796. In Jefferson's America, attempts to implement Beccaria's principles were still ongoing and very much a work-in-progress.

Jefferson's Italian Neighbor, Philip Mazzei

Because of the popularity of Beccaria's treatise, Jefferson would have had plenty of fellow readers to discuss it with in his daily life. For example, Italian émigré Philip Mazzei—Jefferson's friend and neighbor in Virginia—is also known to have been a reader of Beccaria's book.[183] A world traveler, Mazzei makes specific reference to Beccaria's treatise in his memoir, *My Life and Wanderings*, which he began writing at age eighty. In that book, one finds the following passage: "A case of even harsher justice had been told to me in Constantinople, but I approved of neither. Ten or twelve years later, while I was in England, Beccaria's humane and judicious treatise on crime and punishment came out, and I heartily hailed it." In 1788, Mazzei—described by the historian Margherita Marchione as "a citizen of the world"—published a four-volume history of the United States, with Mazzei, in his memoir, highlighting his friendships with the first five presidents of the United States. "Philip Mazzei," Marchione notes, "ranks in the company of America's founding fathers and to the group of Italian immigrants who, not being able to achieve the dream of liberty within their own country, sowed its seeds throughout the world."[184]

Mazzei was born in 1730 near Florence, Italy, where he studied medicine. Mazzei practiced as a doctor at Pisa and elsewhere, then settled in London at the age of twenty-five and became a "Tuscan Language" teacher. After making influential friends in England, Grand Duke Leopold of Tuscany appointed Mazzei as his diplomatic agent there. An Italian merchant who, in the New World, cultivated relationships with John Adams, Patrick Henry, James Madison, George Mason, George Washington, and George Wythe, Mazzei— before emigrating to America—had befriended a Virginia merchant, Thomas Adams, in London, and had also gotten to know Benjamin Franklin.[185] As a result of his adventurous spirit and his time abroad, Mazzei eventually decided to make a whole new life for himself in Virginia, near Monticello, growing grapes. Upon his arrival in Virginia, Mazzei ended up purchasing a large plot of land next to Jefferson's estate, was Jefferson's guest, and engaged in a farming project—a vineyard—endorsed by Jefferson, George Washington, George Mason and Virginia's governor, Lord Dunmore.[186]

Mazzei, who grew his grapes on land adjacent to Jefferson's Monticello, was more than a gentleman farmer, however. Mazzei—who purchased and shipped arms to the Commonwealth of Virginia during the Revolutionary War—was also heavily involved in politics and foreign relations. For example, he translated the Declaration of Independence into Italian and then sent a copy to Grand Duke Peter Leopold of Tuscany.[187] An American emissary who actively corresponded with Thomas Jefferson and James Madison,[188] Mazzei had tremendous respect for Beccaria's ideas and Beccaria the man. Mazzei even suggested to John Blair in May 1785 that Beccaria be made an honorary member of the Constitutional Society of Virginia along with Florentine philosopher Felice Fontana, among other personalities of the European "Age of Enlightenment."[189] Born in Williamsburg, Virginia, John Blair had studied law in London at the Middle Temple and became a respected jurist, with George Washington appointing Blair in 1789 to serve on the U.S. Supreme Court.[190] The Constitutional Society was formed in 1784 to further "those pure and sacred principles of Liberty, which have been derived to us, from the happy event of the late glorious revolution."[191] The members of the Constitutional Society consisted of the Hon. John Blair, its president, as well as luminaries such as James Madison, John Marshall, Richard Henry Lee, Patrick Henry, Edmund Randolph and James Monroe.[192] Such men—leading figures in their communities—would have been quite conversant with Beccaria's ideas, though they did not always agree with Beccaria in toto.

During the Revolutionary War, it is hardly surprising that amidst all the suffering and bloodshed, the fate of criminals did not always top the list of American revolutionaries. They wanted to win the war, and that meant defeating the British and dealing with a host of military discipline issues, crimes and other social ills. For example, in November 1778, in the midst of the Revolutionary War, Richard Henry Lee wrote to Patrick Henry to express his concerns and frustrations over the forging of paper money. "In my opinion," Lee wrote, "these Miscreants who forge our money are as much more criminal than most other offenders, as parricide exceeds murder." Writing amid the fog of war, Lee penned these words to Patrick Henry from Chantilly, Virginia: "The mildness of our law will not deter from this tempting vice. Certain death on conviction seems the least punishment that can be supposed to answer the purpose—I believe most nations have agreed in considering and punishing the contamination of money as the highest crimes against Society are considered and punished." "Cannot the Assembly be prevailed on to amend the law on this point, and by means of light horse to secure the arrest, and punishment of these Offenders." "I hope Sir you will pardon my saying so much on this subject," Lee wrote, "but my anxiety arises from the clear conviction I have that the loss of our liberty seems at present more likely to be derived from the state of our currency than from all other causes."[193]

Jefferson, the Virginia native, and Mazzei, the Italian transplant, communicated with one another on a variety of subjects, and it is easy to imagine Beccaria's name coming up in conversation. Jefferson consulted Mazzei regarding the revisal of Virginia's laws, Mazzei regularly corresponded with Grand Duke Peter Leopold during America's Revolutionary War, and Mazzei and Jefferson became life-long friends.[194] In 1767, Mazzei had bought two "stoves" from Benjamin Franklin for Grand Duke Leopold, and it was through his warm association with what has been described as "London's 'American' circle," that Mazzei developed the idea of traveling to America. After sailing from London to the soon-to-be United States of America in 1773, Mazzei became close friends with George Washington and George Wythe, the latter of whom Mazzei described as "one of the greatest characters the world has ever produced, unexcelled in law." Americans themselves frequently described Mazzei, who called his estate adjoining Monticello *Colle* ("hill" in Italian), as "zealous" in his devotion to American independence. Like Jefferson, Mazzei believed in the universal pursuit of happiness and favored religious freedom, speaking out in church to show the justice and benefits of it. A Roman priest once accused Mazzei of printing "several works of Voltaire and Rousseau" and of shipping "forbidden books" to Italy. Mazzei's agricultural enterprise was supported by Washington and Jefferson as well as by George Mason and the Scottish peer and colonial governor Lord Dunmore, the governor of the province of Virginia from 1771 to 1775.

Philip Mazzei actively promoted liberty before and after the Revolutionary War, dining with the likes of Jefferson and George Mason and serving in the local militia, becoming, in effect, an Italian-American Founding Father. Before the war, Mazzei promoted the colonists' cause in articles published in newspapers in Florence and Tuscany in 1774 and 1775, papers that later published his translation of the Declaration of Independence in September 1776. Mazzei also penned an article in which he urged his fellow Virginia citizens to "discuss man's natural right and the grounds of a free government." As Mazzei wrote in that piece: *"All men are by nature equally free and independent. Their equality is necessary in order to set up a free government. Every man must be equal of any others in natural rights."* Worried about distinctions based on class, Mazzei concluded: "When in a nation you have several classes of men, each class must have its share in the government, otherwise one class will tyrannize the others." "In fact," writes Reneé Critcher Lyons in *Foreign-Born American Patriots*, "Mazzei wrote the *Instructions to the Freeholders of Albemarle County in Their Delegates in Convention,* in which he attempted to influence provisions of the Virginia Constitution, imploring citizens to 'restructure the relationship between the ruled and the ruler.'"

In 1778, in the midst of the Revolutionary War, Thomas Jefferson, Patrick Henry, George Mason, and John Page asked Mazzei, a trusted friend of America, to serve as a government agent. Instructed to travel to Tuscany to ask the Grand Duke for supplies and a loan, Mazzei "wholeheartedly" agreed to serve his new country. In a letter to John Hancock, Thomas Jefferson described Mazzei's role this way: "Mazzei received his appointment from Governor Patrick Henry and the Virginia Council, in January 1779. He was authorized to obtain a loan of gold and silver, not exceeding £900,000, and to purchase goods in Italy for the use of the state troops. Mazzei asked for no compensation, but only desired to have his expenses paid." Mazzei signed an oath of allegiance to the Commonwealth of Virginia on April 21, 1779, and set sail on June 19th from Hob's Hole. When Mazzei reached Norfolk, though, he discovered that the British had burned the ship he had planned to take to Europe. After boarding another ship commanded by Captain Andrew Patton, a Scotsman who turned out to be a British spy, Mazzei was captured by an awaiting British privateer and taken prisoner. Because Mazzei had surreptitiously thrown his diplomatic credentials and instructions overboard and insisted he was simply on a personal trip to Tuscany, Mazzei was eventually released, later making his way to Paris to make contact with Benjamin Franklin, his old friend.

Because of Mazzei's lack of credentials and Franklin's belief that foreign affairs should be in the hands of Congress, not individual states like Virginia, Mazzei's mission did not go as planned. Despite sending letters to Jefferson in an attempt to explain his capture and get new credentials, Mazzei never received fresh papers authorizing him to transact loans for the State of Virginia, rendering fruitless his diplomatic overtures to the Grand Duke of Tuscany. As historian Reneé Critcher Lyons explains: "Returning to Italy, Mazzei addressed eleven letters to the Grand Duke of Tuscany asking for loans for the American cause, but his pleas fell on deaf ears due to lack of credentials and the Grand Duke's insistence that Great Britain would never allow her colonies to remain independent." Mazzei did, however, write strongly worded articles to support America's quest for independence, including *The Justice of the American Cause*, *The Likelihood of a Happy Issue of the American Revolution*, *The Importance of Securing Trade with Virginia*, and *Why the American States Cannot Be Accused of Having Rebelled*. Eventually, in 1782, Virginia's new governor, Benjamin Harrison, recalled Mazzei to Virginia, to which Mazzei returned in 1783, buying an estate in Richmond upon his return in the year of the war's end.

After the war, Mazzei continued to stay engaged, helping to found Virginia's Constitutional Society before the 1787 Constitutional Convention in Philadelphia. That society sought to "do something for the instruction of the mass of the people and promulgate and defend the principles of freedom and democracy." Meetings of the Society took place at Anderson's Tavern in Richmond, with Mazzei describing the Society's purpose in a letter to its president, John Blair. "It seems to me," Mazzei wrote, "that in a truly free country, where national prosperity and happiness stand on the same foundation for everyone, the uneducated portion of the inhabitants has a right to be enlightened and advised by the educated citizens, just as a child is by his father." It was in 1785 that the always adventurous Mazzei—that tireless advocate for American interests who, at that time, had irreconcilable problems with a mistress he had married in America—left Virginia and moved to Paris while Thomas Jefferson was the U.S. ambassador there. "A few days before he left Virginia, not knowing he would never return," historian Stefania Buccini notes of Mazzei, "he had written to Madison: 'America is my Jupiter, Virginia my Venus.'" In France, Jefferson introduced Mazzei, his good-hearted Italian friend, to many prominent scientists and literary figures of the day; Mazzei himself, while in Europe, wrote and published *Recherches Historiques et Politiques sur les États-Unis de l'Amerique Septentrional* (*Political and Historical Research on the United States of America*).[195]

As America's minister to France, Thomas Jefferson had constant contact with foreigners, including Italian speakers. In a letter to William Short, for example, Jefferson—in at least one instance—emphasized of one European locale that "it is my Italian which enables me to understand the people here, more than my French." Documents also show that Jefferson had contact with Count Alessandro di Cagliostro, the alias of the Italian adventurer, freemason and occultist Giuseppe Balsamo (1743–1795), also commonly known as Joseph Balsamo. Knowledgeable in chemistry and the art of forgery, Cagliostro—once a favorite of the French nobility—studied alchemy and traveled widely in Europe with his wife in the eighteenth century, selling elixirs and constantly scheming to make money and climb the social ladder. Cagliostro reportedly once even forged a letter for Casanova, the famed Italian lover who had also discussed Italian literature with the likes of Voltaire. "Following a complex scandal known as 'the affair of the diamond necklace,' wherein Cagliostro was accused and prosecuted for attempting to defraud French nobility," one source notes of a 1785 scandal in which Cagliostro, along with con artist Jeanne de Saint-Rémy de Valois, a.k.a, Jeanne de la Motte, and her paramour, Cardinal de Rohan, were implicated, then imprisoned in the Bastille for (but ultimately acquitted of) attempting to defraud Marie Antoinette, "Cagliostro and his wife fled France for London, and then Rome." Back in Rome, the Inquisition later sentenced Cagliostro to death for being a heretic, but Cagliostro ultimately died in prison, at San Leone, after his sentence was commuted to life imprisonment.

Cagliostro's name, in fact, appears in multiple letters Thomas Jefferson wrote in 1786 while in Paris. In a May 4, 1786 letter to John Paradise, Jefferson noted that "Cardinal de Rouen is still the great topic" and that "[h]e continues in the Bastille as does Cagliostro." In another letter of that date, Jefferson also wrote this to William Stephens Smith: "I find the Cardinal de Rouen and Cagliostro in the Bastille as I left them, and there likely to remain." A few days later, on May 7, 1786, Jefferson—using a different spelling of the cardinal's name—wrote in a similar vein to Louis Guillaume Otto: "The Cardinal de Rohan and Cagliostro remain where they did, in the Bastille; nor does their affair seem as yet to draw towards a conclusion. It has been a curious matter, in which the circumstances of intrigue and detail have busied all the tongues, the public liberty none." In another letter to William Stephens Smith, Jefferson gave this final report on June 4, 1786 on the whole affair: "No news to give you but of the decision of the celebrated cause. La Villette banished. Madame la Motte condemned to be branded and whipped and to remain in a hospital all her life. But it is said the branding and whipping will be pardoned, and the hospital commuted into a convent." "The Cardinal acquitted totally," Jefferson letter continued, "[b]ut the king has taken from him his charge of Grand Aumonier and banished him to Auvergne. Cagliostro acquitted; but it is said the king will order him to leave the kingdom. Madme. Cagliostro and Mademoiselle d'Olive acquitted."

In *The Life of Joseph Balsamo, Commonly Called Count Cagliostro*, a book published in London in 1791, Beccaria's name itself comes up, with Cagliostro's Italian biographer—in the preface—calling Cagliostro "a very famous imposter." In that book, it was noted that Pope Clement XII, "of glorious memory," had "published an edict, dated January 14, 1739, in which he forbids, *under pain of death, and without any hope of pardon*, all persons from assisting or being present at the lodges of the free masons, which he terms 'pernicious associations, suspected of heresy and sedition.'" Clement XII, the book continued, had "also condemned to the same punishment all those *who engaged or solicited any one to enter into the societies, or who engaged or solicited any one to give aid, counsel, or assistance of any kind*, to their members." In a footnote to Clement XII's edict, the author of *The Life of Joseph Balsamo* commented: "Is it possible that any man can prostitute his pen by an eulogium on this cruel edict of Clement XII? Can even an inquisitor, forgetting the disproportion of the *supposed* crime to the punishment, praise this barbarous law, in the same century in which a Montesquieu and a Beccaria lived?"[196]

Meanwhile, in Philip Mazzei's own birthplace, Tuscany, penal reform was becoming a reality even in that monarchical setting. In 1786, in what became a well-known fact throughout Europe and America, Grand Duke Leopold, persuaded by Beccaria's ideas, adopted a Tuscan penal code that totally abolished capital punishment.[197] Of course, no particular locale had a monopoly on reformist ideas during the Enlightenment. Indeed, Virginians of that era—in both their everyday conversations, and in the Virginia Declaration of Rights of 1776—specifically recognized the need to avoid barbarous and cruel punishments. At Virginia's ratifying convention in 1788, Patrick Henry—after examining the proposed U.S. Constitution—argued, in particular, that a national bill of rights was needed. "[W]hen we come to punishments," Henry said, "no latitude ought to be left, nor dependence put on the virtue of representatives."[198] "In this business of legislation," Henry feared, members of Congress, if not constrained by a U.S. Bill of Rights, would lose "the restriction"—already contained in Virginia's Declaration of Rights of 1776, but not part of the proposed U.S. Constitution—"of not imposing excessive fines, demanding excessive bail, and inflicting cruel and unusual punishments." "What has distinguished our ancestors? That they would not admit of tortures, or cruel and barbarous punishments," Henry said.[199] The English Bill of Rights of 1689 — a product of the Glorious Revolution of 1688 — barred "cruel and unusual punishments," a long-standing protection for Englishmen that George Mason saw fit to replicate in the historic Virginia Declaration of Rights of 1776.[200] Without specific legal protections in place, Henry worried about the continental European "civil law" practice "of torturing, to extort a confession of the crime."[201] Under the inquisitorial system, instruments of torture, such as waterboarding and the rack, had commonly been used in Italy, France and Spain to obtain confessions.[202]

Distance made it impossible for Americans and Italians to stay completely up-to-date, in real time, on events transpiring across ocean waters. But the connections between Americans and Italian reformers is clear. For example, Philip Mazzei and others provided letters of introduction to Paolo Andreani (1763–1823), the Italian count from Milan who came to America. As a scientist, Andreani — the first Italian balloonist, gaining fame by making his assent in February 1784 outside Milan — was anxious to see Canada and America and thus sailed to North America in 1790. To facilitate that trip, Mazzei drafted a personal note in Paris in March 1790. Knowing of Andreani's interest in physics and natural history, Mazzei asked his long-time friend James Madison for guidance as to who "may be more congenial for him to meet, and who may receive reciprocal satisfaction." After leaving France for England to make final arrangements for his trip, Andreani also collected a letter of introduction in London from the eminent historian and philosopher Richard Price. Price had written *Observations on the Importance of the American Revolution* (1784) after the Revolutionary War, with Price concluding: "With heart-felt satisfaction, I see the revolution in favour of universal liberty which has taken place in *America*; — a revolution which opens a new prospect in human affairs, and begins a new era in the history of mankind."

Richard Price saw the American Revolution as a hopeful sign for the whole world. "[N]ext to the introduction of Christianity among mankind," Price wrote in his book, "the American revolution may prove the most important step in the progressive course of human improvement." "It is an event which may produce a general diffusion of the principles of humanity, and become the means of setting free mankind from the shackles of superstition and tyranny," Price emphasized before quoting Montesquieu. "I am happy to find," Price added, that the United States were taking measures to abolish slavery and "[t]he Negro trade" — human trafficking "which, as it has been hitherto carried out," Price noted, "is shocking to humanity, cruel, wicked, and diabolical." "[F]or it is self-evident," he stressed, "that if there are any men whom they have a right to hold in slavery, there may be *others* who have had a right to hold *them* in slavery." The American Revolution, Price believed, "had revived the hopes of good men and promised an opening to better times."[203]

Looking to introduce Count Andreani, the U.S.-bound Italian adventurer, to the highest echelons of American society, Price took it upon himself to draft a note to Ezra Stiles, the Yale College president, describing Andreani as "a Nobleman of character and consequence from *Milan* and a friend of liberty whose zeal and curiosity have determined him to visit the United States." Price also used the fortuitous opportunity of the planned visit to ask Count Andreani to personally deliver to Thomas Jefferson a political pamphlet written by the French revolutionary and mathematician Marquis de Condorcet. In addition, Andreani got another letter of introduction, this one from John Paradise of Oxford University, addressed to George Washington. Like Price, Paradise asked Andreani to deliver something, in his case the multi-stanza ode to America's independence by an Italian poet, Count Vittorio Alfieri. Paradise said Andreani was "a nobleman from Milan, highly distinguished by every valuable endowment, and deserving of the honour of being presented to you." To Thomas Jefferson, Paradise's American wife, Lucy Ludwell Paradise, similarly portrayed Andreani as "a learned amiable Nobleman ... worthy of every attention," asking Jefferson to "take the trouble to introduce Count Andriani by letter to our Friends in Virginia &c. &c. &c."[204]

In England, John Paradise's lively gatherings of artists and literary figures included Dr. Samuel Johnson and prominent Americans. A confidante of John Adams, Benjamin Franklin, Richard Price and Joseph Priestley, Paradise was a member of the Club of Honest Whigs, with another friend, Thomas Jefferson—including via a letter to James Madison—helping to later facilitate Paradise's emigration to Virginia. Jefferson himself sought out Paradise, a talented linguist, for his knowledge of Greek and Italian, with Jefferson writing Paradise in May 1786 from Paris: "But for myself I will only ask you to write down the Greek alphabet and the diphthongs, and opposite to each letter or diphthong, to express it's power in Italian orthography, adding perhaps an example or two of a greek word, it greek letters, and then in the Italian letters of equivalent sound." "I fix on the Italian rather than English orthography," Jefferson added, "because in the latter language the same letters have very different sounds in different words; whereas the sound of the Italian letters is always the same in the same situation." John Paradise, a founding member of the Essex Head Club that, starting in 1783, met three evenings a week at London's Essex Head Tavern, had married his wife Lucy, of a wealthy Virginia family, in 1769. Paradise himself was once described as "distinguished not only by his learning and talents, but by an amiable disposition, gentleness of manners, and a very general acquaintance with well-informed and accomplished persons of almost all nations."

In London in 1787, John Paradise's own daughter, Lucy, married an Italian, Count Antonio Barziza of Venice, with the couple's first child, Giovanni, born in 1788 in Venice, and the couple's second son, Filippo, also born in that city in 1796. Meanwhile, in America in December 1787, John Paradise and his wife Lucy stayed for four days at Mount Vernon, experiencing the same generous hospitality that the Italian botanist Luigi Castiglioni had found there. In May 1789, John Paradise's wife, Lucy, as one of Washington's prior guests, went out of her way to congratulate George Washington on his new role as the first President of the United States. As Lucy wrote at that time: "Give me leave as a Fellow Citizen to congratulate you on the Honour you have done Us, in accepting to be our President for this, our New Federal Constitution." A short time later, on July 4, 1789, John Paradise, as well as Joel Barlow and Phillip Mazzei, Americans then staying in Paris, presented Jefferson himself with a special "Fourth of July Tribute." In their tribute, all of the men expressed their collective "gratitude" and "pride" for Jefferson's services as the U.S. minister to France. It was in the following year, in April 1790, that John Paradise wrote to George Washington to present the Italian poet Alfieri's literary work—work delivered to Washington by Count Paolo Andreani, the bearer of the letter. A friend of the Paradises, Count Andreani traveled to America with a handful of introductions, including letters from John Paradise, Richard Price and John Rutledge, Jr.[205]

On June 6, 1790, Count Andreani—traveling in Luigi Castiglioni's footsteps—arrived in New York City, then the seat of the federal government. The First Congress had convened in 1789 at the newly remodeled city hall, dubbed Federal Hall, and with Congress in session, Andreani was quickly able to meet America's foremost political leaders. With Andreani staying as a guest at Vandine Ellsworth's boardinghouse on Maiden Lane, he lodged in the same place as Jefferson and Madison. Andreani praised William Duer, Alexander Hamilton, and Henry Knox as "the best men in the world" for their hospitality, with Andreani calling Madison "the most educated man that I have met here." On his visit, Andreani wrote one correspondent, Gian Mario, to say: "Here I am among good peo-ple who love foreigners, and receive them with hospitality." John Adams, though, rubbed Andreani the wrong way, and the feeling — it turned out — was mutual. Andreani de-scribed Adams as "the most pompous man that I know and the most selfish," with An-dreani adding: "God prevent that he become president!" For his part, Adams wrote that Count Andreani had failed to make a good impression, with Adams noting that he "had paid him but little Attention." On his trip, Andreani visited Ezra Stiles in New Haven, Connecticut; public buildings in Albany, New York, which became the state's capital in 1797; and, in New York City, at Federal Hall on August 13, 1790, he saw George Wash-ington give a speech and witnessed a treaty between an Indian tribe and the United States being ratified by the U.S. Senate. In Albany, Andreani took special note of the prison, writing: "When we visited it there were about twenty inmates, the majority for debts. They are badly kept, without any humanity whatsoever. The building structure con-tributes to aggravate their punishments." In the 1790s, due in part to land speculation that went awry, many people, including Revolutionary War veterans, were caught up in financial calamity and imprisoned for debt. "Andreani's awareness of the prisons," ex-plains the editors and translators of Andreani's journal, "doubtless owed much to the general Enlightenment interest in penal reform, whose principal exponent, Cesare Bec-caria, hailed from Milan and moved in the same circles as his younger compatriot."[206]

Aaron Burr and John Witherspoon

Aaron Burr, Thomas Jefferson's Vice President and the man who, over the course of 36 ballots in the U.S. House of Representatives, battled Jefferson for the presidency due to an Electoral College tie following the 1800 election, also — like Beccaria — had an at-traction to utilitarianism. Indeed, Burr — a New York lawyer and politician — also owned and relied upon Beccaria's writings.[207] As a student at the College of New Jersey, now known as Princeton, Burr (A.B. 1772) was in the same graduating class as William Brad-ford, Jr. (A.B. 1772) and just one year behind Bradford's close friend, James Madison (A.B. 1771), the future President of the United States who started his collegiate studies in 1768.[208] The president of the College of New Jersey during that time was John With-erspoon (1723–1794), a Scots Presbyterian minister. A signer of the Declaration of In-dependence, Witherspoon had come to Princeton, New Jersey, at the urging of Dr. Benjamin Rush and lawyer Richard Stockton, to lead, minister and teach at the small Presbyterian college. Popular among Princeton students, including Aaron Burr and James Madison, Witherspoon personally tutored Madison for another six months over the fall and winter of 1771–1772 after Madison graduated. A proponent of natural law, Wither-spoon served as Princeton's president from 1768 to 1794, teaching courses in divinity, history and politics, eloquence and moral philosophy.

In the Revolutionary War era, the concept of *natural law* — which reached its heyday during the Enlightenment era — was extremely popular. As Alexander Hamilton once put it: "The sacred rights of mankind are not to be rummaged for among old parchments or musty records. They are written, as with a sunbeam, in the whole volume of human na-ture, by the hand of the Divinity itself, and can never be erased or obscured by mortal power." After the Revolutionary War broke out, Witherspoon delivered a sermon on May 17, 1776, in which he spoke of "the present state of the American Colonies, and the plague of war." In preaching his message, Witherspoon spoke of British cruelty, addressing his audience as follows: "*The ambition of mistaken princes, the cunning and cruelty of oppres-*

sive and corrupt ministers, and even the inhumanity of brutal soldiers, however dreadful, shall finally promote the glory of God, and in the mean-time, while the storm continues, his mercy and kindness shall appear in prescribing bounds to their rage and fury." In a separate "Address to the Natives of Scotland, residing in America," Witherspoon specifically invoked Montesquieu, the Enlightenment writer, in these words: "The great and penetrating Montesquieu, in his Spirit of Laws, has shewn in the clearest manner, that nothing contributes so much to the prosperity of a people, as the state of society among them, and the form of their government."[209]

Princeton's academic curriculum, which Witherspoon shaped, covered a wide range of topics, including European authors and the law. In a lecture on "jurisprudence"—what he called "the method of enacting and administering civil laws in any constitution"—he alluded briefly to Montesquieu—one of Beccaria's idols—in noting: "The first preliminary remark is, that a constitution is excellent when the spirit of civil laws is such, as to have a tendency to prevent offences, and make men good, as much as punish them when they do evil." Later, Witherspoon emphasized that laws "should be so framed as to promote such principles in general as are favourable to good government" and called attention to the need to define crimes. In the late eighteenth century, students on college campuses were debating the propriety of capital and corporal punishments and—in the course of those debates—Beccaria's ideas on criminal law reform. For Witherspoon, the principle of "Public Utility" was to be the governing factor in setting punishments. "Severe laws, and severe punishments sometimes banish crimes but very often the contrary," Witherspoon advised. "[W]hen laws are very sanguinary," he said, "it often makes the subjects hate the law more than they fear it; and the transition is very easy from hating the law, to hating those who are entrusted with the execution of it." "Such a state of things," Witherspoon lectured prior to the outbreak of the Revolutionary War, "threatens insurrection and convulsions if not the dissolution of government." This intellectual climate, as Louis Masur explains in *Rites of Execution*, led to continual questions about the death penalty's efficacy. As Masur writes: "As at Yale, Princeton commencement exercises first began to address questions relating to punishment in the mid-1780s. In 1786, an oration on 'the evils of severe penal laws' was delivered. In 1787, commencement included a 'disquisition on the disadvantages of public punishments.' An oration on the impolicy of 'sanguinary punishments' was included in 1796."

As a highly educated man, Witherspoon would certainly have been familiar with Beccaria's treatise and the ongoing debate over Beccaria's views on crimes and punishments. In Witherspoon's lecture notes, one finds a short discussion of the doctrine of *lex talionis*, set forth in the law of Moses as "an eye for an eye, a tooth for a tooth." "[P]erhaps there are many instances in which it would appear very proper," Witherspoon wrote, adding: "The equity of the punishment would be quite manifest, and probably it would be as effectual a restraint from the commission of injury as any that could be chosen."[210] Yet, Witherspoon also emphasized: "it is but seldom that very severe and sanguinary laws are of service to the good order of a state." "Let the laws be just and the magistrate inflexible," he concluded his lecture, sounding a very Beccarian tone.[211] In a lecture he gave "On the Religious Education of Children" in 1789, Witherspoon called religion "more powerful than the most sanguinary laws." "Support, by your conduct and conversation, the *public credit of religion*," Witherspoon implored. Dr. Benjamin Rush—the deeply religious man who played such a crucial role in bringing Witherspoon to the school—likewise viewed the precepts and charitable impulses of Christianity as fundamentally opposed to cruel punishments. Dr. Rush explained that death penalty laws "are, in my opinion, as unchristian as those which justify or tolerate revenge."[212] A subject-catalogue of the library at the College of New Jersey, published in 1884, shows that Beccaria's treatise could be found on campus at that time—and, without a doubt, had been acquired by the college many decades earlier. That catalogue shows a "New ed." of *On Crimes and Punishments* published in Edinburgh in 1778.[213]

Aaron Burr's post-collegiate career as a lawyer gave Burr—the Princeton graduate— plenty of opportunities to consider the efficacy and morality of America's penal system. As New York's attorney general, Aaron Burr had occasion to prosecute cases involving counterfeiting, theft, forgery, rape and murder. He therefore had more than an academic interest in penal reform. Indeed, Burr was later drawn to Jeremy Bentham's 1787 plan for a prison, or "inspection-house," known as "the Panopticon"—the circular prison design that would keep inmates under constant surveillance. In 1808, Burr—who befriended Bentham in Europe after facing a treason charge in 1807—stayed for lengthy periods of time at Bentham's London residence, known as "Queen's Square Place" or the "Bird-House." Burr also stayed at Bentham's summer house near Godstone, Surrey.[214] In December 1808, after making reference to Bentham's Panopticon and speculating on its potential use in South Carolina, Burr wrote of his friend: "Jeremy Bentham has opened a new and deeper vein of political and moral science, to bring from it the most brilliant diamonds. Such a mind as his is not produced once in many centuries." "Who will be found to improve upon his ideas?" Burr asked rhetorically, adding: "I imagine he has reached the ne plus ultra, the border of the Styx; and no one can go farther, without becoming an inhabitant of the other world."[215]

It was as New York's attorney general that Burr, from a professional standpoint, had become deeply involved in criminal-law reform. In 1791, Burr prepared a report that New York's governor, George Clinton, then brought to the attention of the state legislature. At that time, New York still punished counterfeiting and forgery as capital offenses, a practice Burr opposed. "An unprejudiced mind," Burr wrote, "will not readily admit the justice or policy of sentencing to death him who forges an order for three crowns or for a pair of boots (cases which have actually come under judicial cognizance), when he who steals a thousand pounds is sentenced to be whipped." "I would advance," Burr wrote of forgery and counterfeiting, "that there are gradations in this crime, in regard both of the guilt of the offender, and of the injury and danger to the community, if not as numerous, at least as obvious, as in that of theft." "Punishments," Burr added in starkly Beccarian terms, "should be proportioned to the dangerous tendency of the crime, the degree of depravity which it denotes, the incentives to the perpetration, the facility of detection or escape, or perhaps to the result of a combined view of all these circumstances." "Gradations in crimes," he urged, "require corresponding gradations in punishments."[216]

Famously, Aaron Burr—the sitting U.S. Vice President—killed Alexander Hamilton in an 1804 duel in Weehawken, New Jersey. Although Burr was never prosecuted, his political career came to an end and, his relationship with Jefferson more strained than ever, he was eventually arrested on charges of treason in 1807. The alleged conspiracy: that Burr and James Wilkinson, a U.S. Army general and governor of the Louisiana Territory, planned to conquer Mexico, drive Spain out of the Southwest, and create an independent nation in North America. It was after being acquitted at trial of that charge that Burr took refuge abroad in London, with Burr's fascination with penal reform continuing. As Burr's biographer David Stewart notes, Burr lived at Bentham's house "for weeks at a time" and "delighted in dinners and tête-à-têtes with Bentham."[217]

In his New York legislative report, Burr—whose strong, personal bond with Bentham had yet to be formed—had embraced the utilitarian philosophy for which Bentham became famous, favoring less severe sentences even before Burr took up residence in England with Bentham. As Burr wrote in Beccarian terms: "Indiscriminate severity renders the law odious, occasions frequent convictions and frequent pardons, lead jurors to consider the consequences of their verdict, perhaps to the disregard of the facts proven, and the oaths they have taken. Thus the public sympathy is excited against public administration, and the terror of death is diminished by the hope of favor from jurors, or mercy from the chief magistrate." Burr's 1791 report, to his dismay, did not make a big legislative splash at the time. "Despite his liberal plea," Burr's biographer Nancy Isenberg writes, "Burr's fellow legislators ignored his reform agenda, suggesting that his view was perhaps too 'unprejudiced'—or, one might say, ahead of its time."[218]

Burr's correspondence, certainly, reflects his admiration for Bentham and his work, which was itself modeled in part on Beccaria's writings. "Mr. Bentham is a man of independent fortune," Burr wrote in one letter in 1808, emphasizing that Bentham "never desires nor seeks to derive any pecuniary emolument from his literary labours." "His great work on morals and legislation, the only one on that subject extant in any language which merits the name of a system," Burr continued, "has had an extensive sale in Spain, no less than seven hundred copies having been sold there, although that work is written in French." "Hence the name of Mr. Bentham," Burr wrote of his friend, "must already be familiar to the reflecting men of that country; and, being known, must be admired and respected, almost to admiration, by those who are capable of estimating his worth." In another 1808 letter, to Joseph Alston, Burr described Bentham as "that venerable sage and philosopher," "of whose literary works *you have so often heard me speak with enthusiastic admiration*." In still another letter, also written in 1808, Burr—who wrote in Bentham's library—said this: "I am very much charmed with his Panopticon; and as the State of South Carolina is just now about to erect a penitentiary, it would undoubtedly adopt his system if seasonable knowledge was given of it." "I could fill a little volume," Burr wrote his correspondent, "with anecdotes, &c., of this great and amiable man, which have fallen within my own knowledge." Writing from "Queen's Place" on September 2, 1808, Burr penned a letter to Bentham himself. "I am resolved that the Panopticon shall be known in America," Burr wrote Bentham, adding, "It will appear incredible to you that I should never have even heard of it till I read the sketch contained in Dumont's book, about three years ago." Pierre Étienne Louis Dumont, the Genevan political writer and editor, was himself enthralled with Bentham's work. He had edited, in French, Bentham's *Principles of Morals and Legislation*.[219]

James Madison

James Madison—the fourth President of the United States—was also knowledgeable of, and familiar with, *On Crimes and Punishments*.[220] In 1783, Madison even recommended Beccaria's writings to the Continental Congress—the body that had declared America's independence. During the time of the short-lived Articles of Confederation, a Continental Congress committee—chaired by Madison and whose membership also consisted of Hugh Williamson and Thomas Mifflin—reported, with Thomas Jefferson's assistance, a list of books "proper for the use of Congress."[221] In that list under the heading "Politics": "Beccaria's works."[222] At that time, politicians and jurists made frequent use of Enlightenment authors to bolster their arguments. For example, one writer, going by "Cassius" but thought to be South Carolina jurist Aedanus Burke, quoted Beccaria on confiscations in 1783 in *An Address to the Freemen of the State of South-Carolina*. The proposition for which Beccaria was quoted: "Our act of assembly which banishes so many citizens, after reducing their families to beggary, without hearing, is perhaps the most furious proscription of which we have any account in all history."[223] Lawmakers and jurists thus frequently looked to Beccaria—the young Italian philosopher—for guidance, and that was true both before and after the ratification of the U.S. Constitution.

Even in the debate over the ratification of the Articles of Confederation, Beccaria's name had come up. When the Articles of Confederation came before the South Carolina Assembly for consideration, the planter and lawyer William Henry Drayton—a delegate to the Continental Congress in the late 1770s—criticized them. In his oration on January 20, 1778, he attacked them as ambiguous and offered a different plan of confederation. "The honor and interest of America require," Drayton said, "that their grand act of confederation, should be a noble monument, free, as far as human wisdom can enable it to be from defect and flaw." "Every thing unnecessary should be critically removed— every appearance of doubt should be carefully eradicated out of it," he said. Expressing the concern that future congresses would look to "the spirit of the law," Drayton criticized that common axiom, invoking Beccaria in observing that when looking for the "spirit," what people find is "'the result of their good or bad logic; and this will depend on their good or bad digestion; on the violence of their passions; on the rank and condition of the parties; or on their connections with congress; and on all those little circumstances, which change the appearance of the objects in the fluctuating mind of man.'"[224] "Thus," Drayton said, "thought the illustrious marquis Beccaria, of Milan, a sublime philosopher, reasoning on the interpretation of laws." As Drayton continued singing Beccaria's praises:

> I must be permitted to continue his ideas, yet a little further upon this subject—they are so exactly in point. He says, "there is nothing more dangerous than the common axiom: The spirit of the laws is to be considered. To adopt it, is to give way to the torrent of opinions." "When the code of laws is once fixed, it should be observed in the literal sense." "When the rule of right which ought to direct the actions of the philosopher, as well as the ignorant, is a matter of controversy, not of fact, the people are slaves to the magistrates."—Is it not the intention of the confederation, that the people shall be free?—Let it then be adapted to the meanest capacity—let the rule of right be not matter of controversy, but of fact—let the confederation be understood according to that strict rule by which we understand penal laws. The confederation is of at least as much importance to America, as penal laws are in a small society—safety to the people is the object of both. In a word, the spirit of laws, lays down this maxim, that "in republics, the very nature of the constitution requires the judges to follow the letter of the law."[225]

It was shortly before the Articles of Confederation (1781–1789) failed that Jefferson's bill to proportion crimes and punishments finally came to a vote. Madison and Jefferson were friends, so when it came time to carry Jefferson's bill, Madison stepped forward in 1785 to take on the task, however arduous he knew it might be.[226] While Thomas Jefferson had spent a considerable amount of time drafting the Virginia bill, he had departed for France by the time Virginia's legislature actually considered it. It thus fell to Madison—in Jefferson's absence—to push for its adoption, a task that proved exceedingly difficult. The bill, Madison told fellow Virginian James Monroe in 1785, ended up being "assailed on all sides," with "Mr. Mercer" proclaiming "unceasing hostility against it."[227] Indeed, despite Madison's tireless efforts to secure the bill's passage, as well as George Wythe's support of penal reform legislation, Jefferson's bill failed to pass the Virginia legislature by a single vote.[228] A disappointed Madison lamented its demise, writing in a letter to Jefferson dated February 15, 1787, that "[t]he rage agst. Horse stealers had a great influence on the fate of the Bill." A biographical sketch of George Wythe, published in

1809, also editorialized that had the legislation passed "[t]he proportion between crimes and punishments would have been better adjusted, and malefactors would have been made to promote the interests of the commonwealth by their labor." "But the public spirit of the assembly," that biographical dictionary stated, "could not keep pace with the liberal views of Wythe."

In the post-Revolutionary War period, historians Henry Ward and Harold Greer Jr. have pointed out, Virginia — like other parts of America — experienced a rise in crime, especially horse stealing and other thefts. Years later, Jefferson himself wrote of American difficulties in preventing horse thievery. In reflecting upon the proper "scale of crimes & punishments," Jefferson noted: "in America, the inhabitants let their horses go at large, in the uninclosed lands, which are so extensive as to maintain them altogether. It is easy therefore to steal them & easy to escape. Therefore the laws are obliged to oppose these temptations with a heavier degree of punishment." In his 1787 letter to Jefferson, Madison regretted that, because of the Virginia assembly's failure to pass Jefferson's bill, "our old bloody code is by this event fully restored."[229] In that era, the English "Bloody Code" — to which Madison referred and which America's founders knew all too well — was still particularly severe. In the 1780s, notes one source, the proportion of those condemned to death who were actually hanged jumped from a prior annual average of 30 percent to more than 60 percent. In 1787, that figure skyrocketed to 80 percent.[230]

Even after the bill's rejection by a narrow majority of Virginia lawmakers, however, Thomas Jefferson — a very interested party — continued to seek information from James Madison about the bill. And Madison, in turn, was — once more — more than willing to oblige and supply the information. On June 20, 1787, Jefferson wrote to Madison: "Could you procure me a copy of the bill for proportioning crimes & punishments in the form in which it was ultimately rejected by the house of delegates?"[231] Madison's response, written on October 24, 1787 in the aftermath of the hubbub of the Constitutional Convention in Philadelphia: "You will receive herewith the desired information from Alderman Broome in the case of Mr. Burke. Also the Virga. Bill on crimes & punishments. Sundry alterations having been made in conformity to the sense of the House in its latter stages, it is less accurate & methodical than it ought to have been."[232] The Philadelphia Convention ran from May 25 to September 17, 1787, so Madison — who played an especially active role at the Convention, taking extensive notes — was incredibly busy at the time Jefferson drafted his June 1787 letter.

From their writings, it is clear that both Jefferson and Madison — like many Americans of their time — despised "barbarous treatment" and England's ferocious "Bloody Code." Before Americans ratified the U.S. Bill of Rights, Madison and Dr. Benjamin Rush had shared thoughts on criminal justice issues and, as an ex-President, Madison continued to express an interest in that subject. In 1790, Madison and Dr. Rush — both Beccaria admirers — exchanged letters on penal reform, with Madison later taking up the issue of penal reform at the federal level. As President, Madison delivered a congressional message in 1816 calling for liberalization of the country's criminal laws. "I submit to the wisdom of Congress," he said, "whether a more enlarged revisal of the criminal code be not expedient for the purpose of mitigating in certain cases penalties which were adopted into it antecedent to experiment and examples which justify and recommend a more lenient policy." And in 1827 Madison spoke of penitentiaries as a viable alternative to what he called the "cruel inflictions so disgraceful to penal codes."[233] "Reform movements of a secular nature must have interested Madison," writes historian Robert Rutland, one of the editors of Madison's papers, "for he was conversant with Beccaria's *Essay on Crimes and Punishments* and owned Benjamin Rush's attack on capital punishment as well as a tract on prison reforms printed in Philadelphia."[234]

Another illustration of Beccaria's influence is found in the writings of the famed American jurist, Joseph Story. Story, like so many Americans of his time, owned an English translation of Beccaria's *On Crimes and Punishments*.[235] In 1811, Story—nominated by James Madison to serve on the nation's highest court—became the youngest Associate Justice of the U.S. Supreme Court, serving in that position until his death in 1845.[236] In writing entries for an encyclopedia published in 1844, Story—also a prominent legal scholar at Harvard Law School—referenced Beccaria multiple times. In the entry for "Criminal Law," Story wrote: "With regard to capital punishments, more particularly, the system of deterring fell by degrees into disrepute, after the marquis Beccaria (On Crimes and Punishments, London, 1770), and a great many other learned men, had declared themselves for … [t]he system of *prevention*." In the encyclopedia entry for "Death, Punishment of," Story wrote: "The marquis Beccaria … denies that any such consent can confer this right, and therefore objects to its existence." In that same entry, Story also wrote: "Beccaria, with his characteristic humanity and sagacity, has strongly urged that the certainty of punishment is more important to deter from crimes than the severity of it."[237]

Joseph Story's *Commentaries on the Constitution of the United States*, a multiple-volume, much-reprinted treatise, also refers to Beccaria's writings. In discussing the President's power "to grant reprieves and pardons," Story—in grappling with Beccaria's ideas—wrote:

> It has been said by the Marquis Beccaria, that the power of pardon does not exist under a perfect administration of the laws; and that the admission of the power is a tacit acknowledgment of the infirmity of the course of justice. But if this be a defect at all, it arises from the infirmity of human nature generally; and, in this view, is no more objectionable than any other power of government; for every such power, in some sort, arises from human infirmity. But if it be meant, that it is an imperfection in human legislation to admit the power of pardon in any case, the proposition may well be denied, and some proof, at least, be required of its sober reality. The common argument is, that where punishments are mild, they ought to be certain; and that the clemency of the chief magistrate is a tacit disapprobation of the laws. But surely no man in his senses will contend that any system of laws can provide, for every possible shade of guilt, a proportionate degree of punishment. The most that ever has been and ever can be done, is to provide for the punishment of crimes by some general rules, and within some general limitations. The total exclusion of all power of pardon would necessarily introduce a very dangerous power in judges and juries, of following the spirit, rather than the letter of the laws; or, out of humanity, of suffering real offenders wholly to escape punishment; or else it must be holden (what no man will seriously avow) that the situation and circumstances of the offender, though they alter not the essence of the offence, ought to make no distinction in the punishment.

"A power to pardon seems, indeed," Story wrote, "indispensable under the most correct administration of the law by human tribunals; since, otherwise, men would sometimes fall a prey to the vindictiveness of accusers, the inaccuracy of testimony, and the fallibility of jurors and courts."[238]

Early U.S. Presidents all made use of the pardoning power, and it was sometimes used to set aside death sentences. Indeed, in 1823, James Madison even told G. F. H. Crockett, a Kentucky veteran and physician, "I should not regret a fair and full trial of the entire abolition of capital punishments by any State willing to make it." Madison did not agree with every single idea of Beccaria, and he told Crockett "I do not see the injustice" of capital punishment "in one case at least." The writings of Beccaria and Dr. Benjamin Rush, however, had plainly shaped Madison's views on penal reform.[239] In discussing the revisal of Virginia's laws—the project begun by Thomas Jefferson in the 1770s and continued by Madison in the following decade—Madison wrote to Thomas Grimke in the late 1820s: "One of the earliest acts of the Virginia Legislature after the State became independent provided for a revisal of the laws in force, with a view to give it a systematic character accommodated to the Republican form of Government and a meliorated spirit of legislation." In his 1828 letter, in which he thanked Grimke for "a copy of a Report on the question of reducing the Laws of S. Carolina to the form of a Code," Madison specifically described the Beccaria-inspired efforts made in Virginia decades earlier. "In the changes made in the penal law," Madison wrote, "the Revisors were unfortunately misled into some of the specious errors of Beccaria, then in the zenith of his fame as a Philosophical Legislator."[240] *On Crimes and Punishments* covered a wide range of subjects in a large number of separate chapters, so it is not clear exactly what "specious errors" Madison had in mind. What is clear, however, is that Madison was no fan of "cruel" and "unusual" punishments and was willing to contemplate the total abolition of capital punishment. Madison had vigorously supported Jefferson's efforts to reform Virginia's law, but both Jefferson and Madison were, in that respect, ahead of their time.

Hugh Henry Brackenridge

Instead of making dozens of crimes death eligible, many of America's founders, looking to what were seen as experiments with the death penalty's abolition in Russia and Tuscany, sought to substitute a far less draconian approach to punishment. In *Law Miscellanies: An Introduction to the Study of the Law*, Hugh Henry Brackenridge—a member of the Supreme Court of Pennsylvania—specifically wrote in 1814 of Beccaria's impact on the American polity. As Brackenridge stated: "Elementary writers, at the head of whom is the marquis de Beccaria, have with great plausibility, questioned the right of society to punish, by taking life at all." "They stand on surer ground," Brackenridge emphasized in his book, "who question only the necessity." "By the Russian code, and that of Tuscany," he wrote, "it has been reduced to an experiment; and capital punishment is found not necessary." "The only use of this at present," Brackenridge explained, "is to enforce a leaning of the mind towards a construction of the law, that will restrain it to the highest species of treason, and what alone ought to bear the name; a conspiracy to overthrow the government."

For Brackenridge, like Madison, ameliorating the harshness of America's penal system was a worthy goal. In *Law Miscellanies*, Brackenridge felt "emboldened" to offer his own "reflections on the subject of *capital punishment in the case of murder in the first degree;* which now remains," he noted of Pennsylvania, "the only case, in which, the punishment is *capital.*" After grappling with the meaning of a Biblical passage, "whoso sheddeth man's blood, by man shall his blood be shed," Brackenridge noted: "By our constitution, the executive magistrate is vested with *the power to pardon.*" "If the magistrate, who in this particular represents the power of society, can pardon, *he can reprieve,*" Brackenridge reasoned, asking: "Can there be any thing in his way to hold the criminal in confinement for life *under the idea of a reprieve*?" "If our magistrate has the power of reprieving in this way, it may be said, why not exercise it?" Brackenridge concluded: "though I *hold it lawful to put to death for murder,* yet I resolve it into a question of *expediency,* and, subject to *the reason of the law,* the security of the peace, and the preservation of the life of man. If, consistent with this, the criminal can be spared, it is inexpedient to put to death. If, on experience, the state of society should be found to be such as to permit this, without endangering the community, I should think capital punishment unnecessary; and it is only in a case where unavoidable, and necessary, that I should think it justifiable."

Brackenridge wrote his book between 1801 and 1814. In it, Brackenridge—Madison's contemporary—expressed his belief, like Madison, in law reform. Brackenridge himself had graduated from the College of New Jersey with James Madison in 1771, so the two knew each other well. In *Law Miscellanies*, the Pennsylvania jurist—who had originally intended to produce a "Pennsylvania Blackstone" but who eventually settled for a group of essays—specifically critiqued the present law in his home state. "[B]y the Jewish laws," Brackenridge wrote, it took "the mouth of two witnesses" for someone to be "put to death." "Under our law," Brackenridge wrote by way of contrast, "one witness is sufficient to convict." "In this respect," Brackenridge noted, "our law is more *sanguinary* than that of the Jews." As Brackenridge argued: "Might it not then be a reason for a commutation of a capital punishment for imprisonment for life, that, especially, where a conviction had taken place, on the credit of *one witness*, or *from circumstance on the evidence of more than one*. Unless the code is so ameliorated, in this particular, it is more sanguinary than even the Jewish law; for the lesser degree of evidence being sufficient to convict, makes the law more sanguinary." Pondering whether "carting to the gallows" or the use of "hard labour and confinement for life" served as the best "*example*" to others, Brackenridge speculated: "I do not take it there would be much difference as to the effect. For I count but little on the effect of a *present terror*, however *shocking the spectacle*." "The best means of preventing the catastrophe," Brackenridge wrote, "will be found in restraining the passions by a useful occupation, and impressing moral and religious instruction on the mind." "In the countries of Europe, Britain in particular, where the effect of capital punishment has been tried abundantly," he added, "it has not been effectual; not more so than transportation and exile; which in most cases has been substituted for it." "We have no Botany-bay to which we can transport," Brackenridge wrote, contemplating the fate of offenders, "but we can accomplish the same thing by confinement and hard labour."

At the College of New Jersey, Brackenridge had written a series of poems, *Satires Against the Tories*, with classmates Philip Freneau, James Madison and William Bradford. Brackenridge—the author of *Modern Chivalry* and an early American novelist—sought, like Madison, to narrow the categories of death-eligible offenders. "What then would be the amendment, in this particular, which I would propose to the penal code?" Brackenridge asked rhetorically in a state, Pennsylvania, that had already abolished the death penalty except for first-degree murder. His answer: "It would be, that, on conviction for murder in the first degree, the convict shall undergo *for life* the same punishment, which on a conviction for murder in the second degree, he shall be sentenced to undergo for years; the time specified in the act for the amelioration of the penal code of the 22d April, 1794." "This," Brackenridge concluded, "will be *imprisonment at hard labour for life; and death in case of an escape*."[241] Another Brackenridge, Hugh Henry's son Henry Marie, a self-described "Native of the West" and "Traveler, Author, Jurist" frequently referred to as "H. M. Brackenridge," himself commented on how he "referred to Beccaria" in handling a legal case.[242] Henry Marie Brackenridge (1786–1871) was a lawyer, writer and judge and also represented Pennsylvania in the U.S. House of Representatives.[243]

The Pennsylvania Abolitionists:
Benjamin Rush and Benjamin Franklin

Benjamin Franklin and Benjamin Rush were close friends, a friendship Dr. Rush first solicited in 1766, and then cherished and cultivated while studying medicine in Europe. Upon Dr. Rush's return to Philadelphia, their friendship flourished even while Franklin was in England and France. After getting to know one another, Dr. Franklin and Dr. Rush exchanged letters on everything from scientific experiments and discoveries, to the business of the American Philosophical Society, to disease and the slave trade, to the fortification of Philadelphia and Revolutionary War volunteers.[244] The two men—both extremely active in their community—would also serve together on the Pennsylvania Society for Promoting the Abolition of Slavery, with Benjamin Franklin serving as its president and Dr. Rush as one of its secretaries.[245] In his 1773 essay, "On Slave Keeping," Dr. Rush characterized the brutal hanging of slaves by their masters as cruel spectacles. As Rush wrote:

> Let us attend the place appointed for inflicting the penalties of the law. See here one without a limb, whose only crime was an attempt to regain his liberty—another led to a gallows for eating a morsel of bread, to which his labor gave him a better title than his master—a third famishing on a gibbet—a fourth, in a flame of fire!—his shrieks pierce the heavens.—O! God! Where is thy vengeance!—O! humanity—justice—liberty—religion—Where.—where are ye fled?

In 1774, Rush—driven by benevolence and his undying quest for social justice—had co-founded the Pennsylvania Society for Promoting the Abolition of Slavery, serving as that organization's secretary from 1787 to 1789 and, ultimately, its president from 1803 to 1813.[246]

Dr. Rush and Benjamin Franklin lived in the same city, Philadelphia, and they often crossed paths. Having arrived back in America in September 1785 after serving his new country in a diplomatic role, the elder Franklin—who, like Rush, had long taken an interest in penal reform—assumed another public position, serving as Pennsylvania's sixth president from October 1785 to November 1788. Although the Revolutionary War had stalled efforts to reform Pennsylvania's penal laws, an effort to change the societal approach to punishment emerged in Dr. Franklin's time as Pennsylvania's president. During Franklin's administration—on September 15, 1786, to be exact—an act was passed in Pennsylvania limiting the death penalty to four crimes: murder, treason, rape and arson.[247] That 1786 law also instituted a system of forced labor and public punishments that resulted in chained prisoners—so-called "wheelbarrow men"—appearing on the streets of Philadelphia. The notion behind Pennsylvania's "wheelbarrow law," and one that Dr. Rush whole-heartedly supported, was that society should reform criminals, not kill them. Franklin himself had closely studied the criminal justice system, and before the Revolutionary War had expressed his displeasure at England sending so many convicted criminals to America's shores. Writing from Philadelphia in 1764 to Richard Jackson, Franklin inquired about what was happening in Parliament relative to America before penning these words: "Three of your Convicts are to be executed here next Week for Burglaries, one of them suspected of a Murder committed on the Highway. When will you cease plaguing us with them?"

While Dr. Rush and Benjamin Franklin both passionately supported curtailing the death penalty's use, Pennsylvania's "wheelbarrow law" did not play out as reformers had expected. As the new law went into effect, convicts were subjected to public ridicule. At the same time, the general public was subjected to what prison reformer Robert Turnbull called "shameful scenes of drunkenness, indelicacy, and other excesses in vice."

As Turnbull put it: "The inconveniences and mischievous effects of the punishment of public labour, at length became so intolerable, that it was regarded, and with much justice, as a common nuisance." "It was in this context," historian Robert Sullivan writes, "that the notable Philadelphia physician, philosopher, and politician Benjamin Rush delivered a paper on punishment at the home of Benjamin Franklin on the evening of March 9, 1787." Having studied the principles of the Scottish Enlightenment in Edinburgh, and after witnessing the "wheelbarrow men" on the streets, Dr. Rush — constantly reading and writing and absorbing new information — advocated for a more enlightened approach. Not only had Dr. Rush read Beccaria's treatise prior to the reading of his paper, but he had also read John Howard's *The State of the Prisons* and Dufriche de Valaze's French commentary *Lois penales dan leur ordre naturel*.[248] Howard's book, which was especially influential in England and North America, was first published in 1777, with Dr. Rush calling himself "a pupil and admirer of the celebrated Mr. Howard."[249]

Dr. Rush — who sought the construction of a "house of repentance" in "a remote part of the state" — was one of America's earliest and fiercest opponents of capital punishment. A 1760 graduate of the College of New Jersey, Rush vigorously advocated for penal reform, calling for private instead of public punishments in the paper he read in March 1787 at Dr. Franklin's house. In that paper, *An Enquiry Into the Effects of Public Punishments upon Criminals, and upon Society*, Rush also noted his opposition to the death penalty for murderers and recited the purposes of punishment: to "reform" offenders, to "prevent" crimes, and to "remove" from society those shown to be "unfit to live in it." "Laws can only be respected, and obeyed," Rush believed, if they bear "an exact proportion to crimes." Lamenting the "indifference and levity with which some men suffer the punishment of hanging," Rush called for the construction of a prison with iron doors to be built in a distant part of the state. "Even murder itself is propagated by the punishment of death for murder," Rush opined, noting that Tuscany's abolition of capital punishment was a "remarkable proof" of the lack of necessity for death sentences. "The Duke of Tuscany, soon after the publication of the Marquis of Beccaria's excellent treatise upon this subject," Rush wrote, "abolished death as a punishment for murder."[250]

After Dr. Rush wrote his essay, he sent copies to his friend and fellow Pennsylvanian John Dickinson and to John Howard, the English prison reformer. Dickinson — who had, in his 1776 *Essay of a Frame of Government for Pennsylvania*, called for prohibiting "the punishing of any crime but murder, or military offenses with Death" — had previously quoted Beccaria to the effect that "an over grown republic" such as the British Empire could "only be saved from despotism by sub-dividing it" into "confederate republics." By declaring independence in 1776, Americans decided that Great Britain's despotism could no longer be tolerated. American colonists, in essence, took the sub-division of the massive British Empire into their own hands and embarked on their own nation-building exercise. When the Articles of Confederation were put in place, Americans — highly skeptical of centralized power — gave relatively few powers to the national government, deciding to leave the bulk of authority with the states themselves. Even at the 1787 Constitutional Convention in Philadelphia, delegates chose to distribute power by allocating it between the states and the federal government — and, as Montesquieu had suggested, between different branches of government. The system of checks and balances they established sought to ensure that no one branch would accumulate too much power.

At the heart of the Declaration of Independence are the notions of equality, self-determination, and the unalienable rights of man. While that document set forth what might be described as the American creed, it was the U.S. Constitution, proposed in Philadelphia in 1787 and ratified the following year, that began to flush out Americans' rights, setting forth, for example, a citizen's right to habeas corpus and the right to be free from bills of attainder and *ex post facto* laws. The six stated purposes of the U.S. Constitution — "to form a more perfect Union, establish Justice, insure domestic Tranquility, provide for the common defence, promote the general Welfare, and secure the Blessings of Liberty to ourselves and our Posterity" — are set forth in the preamble, with seven articles then laying out the structure of American government, the relationship between the federal government and the states themselves, and the process for amending the Constitution. Article I, setting forth the "legislative Powers," established the Congress, to consist of the Senate and the House of Representatives. While Article II vested the "executive Power" in "a President of the United States," to be chosen by "a number of Electors, equal to the whole Number of Senators and Representatives to which the State may be entitled in the Congress," Article III vested the "judicial Power" in "one supreme Court, and in such inferior Courts as the Congress may from time to time ordain and establish."

The other four articles — the ones that follow the division of power between the three branches of government — required that "Full Faith and Credit" be given "in each State to the public Acts, Records and judicial Proceedings of every other State" and that "[t]he Citizens of each State" receive "all Privileges and Immunities of Citizens in the several States" (Article IV); that "two thirds of both Houses" of Congress or "the Legislatures of two thirds of the several States" could propose constitutional amendments, and that such amendments would take effect after "ratified by the Legislatures of three fourths of the several States, or by Conventions in three fourths thereof" (Article V); that the Constitution, "the Laws of the United States," and "all Treaties made, or which shall be made, under the Authority of the United States, shall be the supreme Law of the Land" (Article VI); and that "[t]he Ratification of the Conventions of nine States, shall be sufficient for the Establishment of this Constitution between the States" (Article VII). After a lengthy ratification process — one that began in September 1787, and that resulted in the publication of scores of newspaper articles and pamphlets, including *The Federalist Papers* — the Constitution was ratified on June 21, 1788, when delegates in the ninth state, New Hampshire, voted 57 to 46 for it.[251]

While many early Americans, including Thomas Paine and Dr. Benjamin Rush, thought the idea of bills of rights was absurd — even dangerous — because they saw their liberties as *natural* rights, a consensus emerged in the late 1780s that a national bill of rights was advisable. "A bill of rights," Thomas Jefferson asserted, "is what the people are entitled to against every government on earth, general or particular, & what no just government should refuse or rest on inference." When the U.S. Bill of Rights was ratified on December 15, 1791, the drafters — and the people ratifying those ten amendments — thus set forth what they viewed as their natural rights, the rights that gave content to the people's right to pursue happiness. From the First Amendment, which protects the freedom of religion, speech, press and assembly and the right "to petition the Government for a redress of grievances," to the final two amendments of the Bill of Rights, which safeguard people's *unenumerated* rights, early Americans sought to ensure that their hard-won freedom from British tyranny would not ever be lost. "The enumeration in the Constitution, of certain rights," the Ninth Amendment reads, "shall not be construed to deny or disparage others retained by the people." The Tenth Amendment also made sure that "powers not delegated to the United States by the Constitution, nor prohibited by it to the States, are reserved to the States respectively, or to the people."[252]

In Philadelphia, that cradle of liberty, the state's power to take life came under special and increasing scrutiny even before the 1787 Constitutional Convention in that city. After the Revolutionary War, a robber, Aaron Doan, was attainted and sentenced to death in Bucks County, Pennsylvania in 1784 by a process of "outlawry" premised on an antiquated 1718 act, a vestige of England's Bloody Code. That prompted John Dickinson — writing in November 1784 on behalf of Pennsylvania's Supreme Executive Council, of which he was then President—to lodge a protest with the judges who made the decision in the absence of a trial by jury. That 1718 law, which went into effect in the year of William Penn's death, was titled an "Act for the advancement of justice, and more certain administration thereof." "To take away the life of a man without a fair and open trial, upon an implication of guilt," Dickinson's letter read, "has ever been regarded as so dangerous a practice, that the law requires all the proceedings in such a mode of putting to death, to be 'exceedingly nice and circumstantial' as *Blackstone* says; and 'any single minute point omitted, or misconducted, renders the whole outlawry illegal, and it may be reversed.'"

Dickinson's letter, which raised multiple questions of the judges of the Pennsylvania Supreme Court, raised serious questions, including these: "Is such a mode of attainder compatible with the letter and spirit of the Constitution of this State, which establishes, with such strong sanctions, the right of trial by jury?" "And is not this construction, *in favour of life*," writing of an interpretation of the 1718 act in question, "strengthened by the improbability, that the Legislature of *Pennsylvania* intended to make the law in this case more sanguinary here, than the law of *England* at that period, which, it is apprehended, required one or more writs of *capias*—an *exigent*—*five exactions*—at *five different* county courts—*a proclamation at the door* of a place for divine worship, &c. before an outlawry could be incurred?" A *writ of capias* is a warrant of arrest that was used in civil actions, with Dickinson's call for greater protection of rights, and for honoring the right to trial by jury in particular, resonating with many other Americans. "The Trial of all Crimes, except in Cases of Impeachment, shall be by Jury," Article III of the U.S. Constitution, as ratified in 1788, would read, with the Seventh Amendment—later ratified in 1791—further preserving the right to trial by jury in civil cases.[253]

After the judges in the Aaron Doan case responded in January 1785 that they "do not hold themselves bound to assign any reasons for their judgments," their responsive letter to Dickinson's questions stated: "If there be any thing improper in taking away the life of a man upon an attainder by a judicial outlawry, it belongs to the Legislature to alter the law in this particular; the judges cannot do it. But Council can interpose their mercy." Subsequent to this communication from the judges and after reviewing the transcript of the record in Aaron Doan's case, Pennsylvania's Supreme Executive Council determined not to issue a warrant for Doan's execution. A resolution that the Supreme Executive Council considered in January 1785 read as follows: "Resolved, That it does not appear, that a warrant can be legally issued for putting the said *Aaron Doan* to death, upon the outlawry aforesaid." Among the supporting reasons listed in the resolution: "the penalty would be so ruinous, and the precedent may be so dangerous"; "there never has been 'an instance in *Pennsylvania* of a person being executed upon outlawry *by judicial proceedings alone*,' though the 'Act for the advancement of justice, &c.' was passed near seventy years ago"; and "[b]ecause, not only would such a prosecution to death be more sanguinary, than the law then was in *England*, but would also oppose that mild system, which the constitution of this Commonwealth has adopted."

Ultimately, Benjamin Franklin—Dickinson's successor as President of Pennsylvania's Supreme Executive Council—pardoned Aaron Doan in 1787.[254] Others associated with Aaron Doan, though, were not so fortunate. Doan and his associates, including his brothers, were Tory sympathizers and, in most eyes, common criminals who lived north of Philadelphia. The "Doan gang"—as one source puts it—"harassed state officials and Whig personnel throughout the Revolution, and after." Moses Doan, a spy for the British, was the oldest of the Doan brothers, with brothers Aaron, Levi, Mahlon and Joseph, as well as a cousin, Abraham Doan, making up the core of the gang. The gang members targeted state tax collectors and payroll officers and stole and resold horses. "Prior to

1782," a Pennsylvania history explains, "state authorities, unsure of the identities of those involved, confined their punishment of the Doans to confiscating the lands of those known to have actively joined the British." "A major break for state officials came in the summer of 1782," that source continues, "when two Doan confederates, Jesse and Solomon Vickers, once captured, agreed to turn state's evidence in exchange for complete pardons." With the Vickers' confessions in hand, the Pennsylvania Supreme Court instituted the process of outlawry—a form of judicial attainder—against two of the Doans' gang, Caleb and John Paul, for their role in a Bucks County robbery. Between 1782 and 1784, seventeen men in all were charged as outlaws by Pennsylvania's Supreme Court for more than sixty offenses. While Aaron Doan was pardoned by Benjamin Franklin on the condition that Doan leave Pennsylvania forever, Abraham and Levi Doan—captured on May 15, 1787 and condemned to death—were executed on September 24, 1787, becoming the only two men to be put to death during the Revolutionary War on the basis of judicial attainders. Joseph, another of the Doan brothers, was shot and captured while robbing a tavern and was later hanged. Only after the U.S. Constitution was ratified were judicial attainders outlawed across the board in the United States.[255]

In 1787, the same year that Aaron Doan was pardoned and that Dr. Rush spoke at Benjamin Franklin's house, the Philadelphia Society for Alleviating the Miseries of Public Prisons—aimed at assisting the lowliest members of society—was founded by Rush and his fellow citizens. "The Philadelphia Society," explains historian Robert Sullivan, "was the first and most famous of those societies which were founded in the late eighteenth and early nineteenth century to bring about the reform of punishment in the United States." A committee of the Philadelphia Society was quickly appointed "to inquire into the effects of the lately enacted penal law upon the criminals now at work in our streets," and a document was produced in January 1788 calling upon the general assembly to replace "hard labor publicly and disgracefully imposed" with punishment "*by more private and even solitary labour.*" *On Crimes and Punishments* had advocated public punishments, but Dr. Rush—who had seen what that looked like on Philadelphia streets—was determined to see if private punishments might not work better.

Breaking in that major respect with Beccaria, Dr. Rush thus vocally questioned the effectiveness of public punishments. In his later writings, however, Rush continued to speak out against capital punishment, following Beccaria's anti-death penalty approach almost verbatim in terms of his language. Calling for a "scale of punishments," Dr. Rush went on to publish an anti-death penalty piece, *An Enquiry into the Justice and Policy of Punishing Murder by Death*, in the *American Museum* in July 1788, sparking a broader public debate about capital punishment. In the following months, "Philochoras"—known to be a Scottish-born minister, Robert Annan—took issue with Rush's arguments by penning a series of pieces for the *Pennsylvania Mercury*. "A Citizen of Maryland" also joined the fray, writing "An Oration Intended to Have Been Spoken at a Late Commencement, on the Unlawfulness and Impolicy of Capital Punishments, and the Proper Means of Reforming Criminals" for the *American Museum* in 1790.[256] These writings, in turn, led to only more public debate.

The more senior Dr. Franklin, for his part, regularly interacted with Dr. Rush as the two collaborated on their shared interests. The two had a cordial working relationship, and both men were enthralled and energized by the idea of reforming the criminal justice system. The two leaders, who did personal favors for one another, helped promote Beccaria's theories and put some of those theories into practice in their home state. One of Benjamin Franklin's letters to Dr. Rush, sent from Passy on October 14, 1784, even introduced Rush to Luigi Castiglioni, the botanist from Milan's innermost circle of Enlightenment thinkers. That letter began "Dear Friend," and read as follows: "The Chevr.

Castiglioni, who will deliver you this Line, is an Italian Gentleman of Character and Family, from Milan. He proposed a Tour thro' all our States. I beg leave to recommend him to your Civilities, and that you would introduce him to the Acquaintance of such of our Society as have a Tincture of Natural History and Botany in which he is particularly curious."[257] Dr. Rush did that even as the influence of Beccaria—the Milan philosopher—grew rapidly in America, a rise in popularity that would be felt in the U.S. for decades to come. In a series of lectures delivered in the 1890s by Yale University professor John Dillon, later compiled and published in Boston as *The Laws and Jurisprudence of England and America*, one finds these words: "In this country we never adopted the extreme severities of the English statutes. We were early influenced by the views of Beccaria. Instead of hanging we condemned the criminal to labor for a term of years in what we named a penitentiary. Pennsylvania led the way to this great change by a provision in her Constitution of 1776."[258]

Dr. Rush and Dr. Franklin also exchanged noteworthy letters after a speech Dr. Rush gave on February 28, 1786, to Philadelphia's American Philosophical Society, a lecture Franklin attended.[259] Dr. Rush's address, titled "An Inquiry into the Influence of Physical Causes upon the Moral Faculty," was delivered at a university hall and was dedicated to Franklin. Dr. Rush's speech was made before a large audience, including the state's Supreme Executive Council and members of Pennsylvania's General Assembly. "By the moral faculty," Rush—who constantly struggled to understand criminal behavior—told his audience at the beginning of his talk, "I mean a capacity in the human mind of distinguishing and choosing good and evil, or, in other words, virtue and vice." Over the course of his lengthy address, Dr. Rush cited "Mr. Locke" for the proposition that "some savage nations are totally devoid of the moral faculty," then methodically discussed, in separate numbered paragraphs, the effects of the following "physical causes" on the moral faculty: climate, diet, liquor, extreme hunger, diseases, idleness, excessive sleep, bodily pain, cleanliness, solitude, music, the eloquence of the pulpit, odors, light and darkness, air and medicines. "The doctrine of the influence of physical causes on morals," Rush noted, "is happily calculated," along with "the precepts of christianity," "to beget charity towards the failings of our fellow-creatures."

Though he did not specifically reference Beccaria by name in that particular oration, Rush did discuss punishments and one of Beccaria's main principles: immediate punishment. "The benefit of corporal punishments, when they are of a short duration," Rush said, "depends in part upon their being connected, by time and place, with the crimes for which they are inflicted." "Quick as the thunder follows the lightning, if it were possible," Rush added, "should punishments follow the crimes, and the advantage of association would be more certain, if the spot where they were committed were made the theatre of their expiation." "As SENSIBILITY is the avenue to the moral faculty," Rush offered, "every thing which tends to diminish it tends also to injure morals." As Rush explained: "The Romans owed much of their corruption to the sights of the contests of their gladiators, and of criminals, with wild beasts. For these reasons, executions should never be public." "Indeed," Rush told his audience, "I believe there are no public punishments of any kind, that do not harden the hearts of spectators, and thereby lessen the natural horror which all crimes at first excite in the human mind." After mentioning "CRUELTY to brute animals" as "another means of destroying moral sensibility," Rush went on to discuss the "physical remedies" used by Quakers and Methodists "in their religious and moral discipline."

For Dr. Rush, an educated citizenry was the key to curtailing crime. "VIRTUE is the soul of a republic," Rush asserted, appealing to his listeners: "Nothing can be politically right, that is morally wrong." Speaking of "learned men and learned societies," Rush contended at the American Philosophical Society gathering that "[i]t is in their power, by multiplying the objects of human reason, to bring the monarchs and rulers of the world under their subjection, and thereby to extirpate war, slavery, and capital punishments, from the list of human evils." "ILLUSTRIOUS COUNSELLORS and SENATORS of Pennsylvania!" Rush pleaded at the end of his address, "it is absolutely necessary that our government, which unites into one all the minds of the state, should possess, in an eminent degree, not only the understanding, the passions, and the will, but, above all, the moral faculty and the conscience of an individual." "[N]o necessity," Rush argued, "can ever sanctify a law, that is contrary to equity." "There is but one method of preventing crimes, and of rendering a republican form of government durable," Rush said, calling for support for public schools, "and that is, by disseminating the seeds of virtue and knowledge through every part of the state, by means of proper modes and places of education, and this can be done effectually only by the interference and aid of the legislature."[260]

Dr. Rush's lecture led to yet another round of correspondence between Dr. Franklin and Dr. Rush. After Dr. Rush's address, Benjamin Franklin wrote to his friend and asked for another small favor. "During our long acquaintance," Franklin wrote, "you have shown many instances of your regard for me, yet I must now desire you to add one more to the number, which is, that if you publish your ingenious discourse on the moral senses, you will totally omit and suppress that most extravagant encomium on your friend Franklin, which hurt me exceedingly in the unexpected hearing, and will mortify me beyond conception, if it should appear from the press." "Confiding in your compliance with this earnest request," Franklin wrote before signing his name, "I am ever my dear friend, yours most affectionately."[261] In a letter dated Friday evening, March 2, 1786, Dr. Rush replied to Franklin: "All your requests ever have, and ever shall have with me, the force of commands. The Address to your Excellency was composed before I knew the Society was to be honoured with your presence on Monday evening." "Upon my being informed of this," Dr. Rush continued, "I waited upon my friend Mr. Rittenhouse upon whose excellent judgement I could depend more than upon my own, and read to him the conclusion of the Oration, and at the same time asked him, if he thought there would be any impropriety in delivering it in your presence." As Rush reported Rittenhouse's response: "He answered 'by no means,' and his last words to me were 'not to suffer any person to persuade me to Alter one word of it.'"[262] On March 11, 1786, in another letter to Franklin, Rush noted that "[a]greeably to your request I have Suppressed the conclusion of my Oration," though Rush emphasized that "I cannot bear to think of sending it out of our State, or to Europe, without connecting it with your name." "I have therefore," Rush added, "taken the liberty of inscribing it to you, by a simple dedication," a dedication that read: "To His Excellency Benjamin Franklin Esqr President of the Supreme Executive Council of Pennsylvania. The friend and Benefactor of mankind."[263]

By the 1780s, the Beccarian principle of proportionality, like the many sturdy stands of trees Luigi Castiglioni admired on his U.S. tour, had firmly taken root in American soil and in the minds of its citizens. When Benjamin Franklin wrote a letter to his friend Benjamin Vaughan from Passy in 1785, the spreading influence of Beccaria's proportionality principle was thus plainly evident. In commenting on Martin Madan's *Thoughts on Executive Justice*—which Franklin felt had been produced by a "sanguinary" English author who "is for hanging all Thieves"—Franklin invoked, by way of contrast, a Frenchman who, in a pamphlet of his own, had advocated "proportioning punishments to Offences." *Thoughts on Executive Justice*, printed in London and "Dedicated to the Judges of Assize" and "recommended" for "All Magistrates; and to all Persons who are liable to serve on Crown Juries," expressed satisfaction with "the *severity* of our laws." "I know of none but of the most wholesome kind," Madan wrote, "for it is this alone which can deter the savage minds of those who are the objects of that *severity*, from the commission of those outrages and mischiefs against which the *severity* of our laws is levelled." Even though Madan—an English barrister who had previously advocated polygamy in a 1780 book—liked the severity of English law, he quoted "the *Marquis* of *Beccaria*" approvingly for one proposition, noting that Beccaria "observes very truly" that "a *less* punishment, which is *certain*, will do more good than a *greater*, which is *uncertain*."[264]

Franklin's letter to Benjamin Vaughn made his own sentiments clear. "To put a Man to Death for an Offence which does not deserve Death, is it not Murder?" Franklin wrote. "I read in the last Newspaper from London," Franklin added, "that a Woman is capitally convicted at the Old Bailey for privately stealing out of a Shop some Gause value 14 Shillings and threepence." Franklin queried: "Is there any Proportion between the Injury done by a Theft value 14s. 3d., and the Punishment of a Human Creature by Death on a Gibbet? Might not that Woman by her Labour have made the Reparation ordain'd by God, in paying four-fold? Is not all Punishment inflicted beyond the Merit of the Offence, so much Punishment of Innocence?"[265] In a letter to his "very dear Friend" Benjamin Vaughan, penned from Southampton in 1785, Franklin wrote: "I shall be glad of a line from you, acquainting me whether you ever received two pieces I sent you some months since; one on your penal laws, the other an account of the residence of an English seaman in China."[266] Whether Cesare Beccaria or Gaetano Filangieri influenced Dr. Franklin's views on a specific case, such as the woman convicted at the Old Bailey, is unclear. Franklin, however, had clearly imbibed Beccaria's and Filangieri's general ideas and become dissatisfied with the then-existing state of the law.

From the publication of Beccaria's *On Crimes and Punishments*—as well as other eighteenth-century books such as Michel de Servan's *Discours sur l'administration de la justice criminelle* (1767)—the whole world, in fact, began to look at executions and criminals differently. Michel de Servan (1737–1807)—a friend of Voltaire and a Beccaria admirer in his own right—was a French magistrate from Grenoble who argued in his book that the punishment of criminals should be "an example for the future rather than a vengeance for the past."[267] After Beccaria came to Paris at the invitation of Abbé Morellet, Servan—of the Parlement of Bordeaux and a friend of one of the members of the society that had invited Beccaria—advocated for reform.[268] Indeed, Beccaria's book—wherever read—never failed to generate debate and discussion, often culminating in penal reform of one sort or another. As one English commentator noted in 1880: "In France Beccaria's book became widely popular, and many writers helped to propagate his ideas, such as Servan, Brissot, Lacretelle, and Pastoret. Lacretelle attributes the whole impulse of criminal law reform to Beccaria, while regretting that Montesquieu had not said enough to attract general attention to the subject." "All the younger magistrates," that source notes, citing Morellet, "gave their judgments more according to the principles of Beccaria than according to the text of the law."[269] In the newly formed United States of America, the criminal codes themselves would change dramatically as a result of exposure to Beccaria's ideas.

Chapter 4

American Penal Reform: Reshaping the Law

Major European Influences: Montesquieu, Beccaria and Blackstone

In America, Beccaria's fame, like Montesquieu's, was at its zenith during the Revolutionary War and by the time the U.S. Constitution and the Bill of Rights were debated and ratified. The Founding Fathers had become familiar with Beccaria's treatise in the 1760s and 1770s, and many Americans had read Blackstone and Montesquieu's books, too.[1] Montesquieu, the French Enlightenment writer who inspired James Madison and the U.S. Constitution's separation of powers principle, had gained notoriety before Beccaria, with the American jurist Oliver Wendell Holmes calling Montesquieu "the precursor of Beccaria in the criminal law." In his book, *The Spirit of the Laws*—also sometimes called *The Spirit of Laws* or *Spirit of the Laws*—Montesquieu, the political theorist, specifically addressed the topic of severe punishments. "The severity of punishments," Montesquieu wrote, "is fitter for despotic governments, whose principle is terror, than for a monarchy or a republic, whose spring is honor and virtue." "In moderate governments," Montesquieu observed by way of contrast, "the love of one's country, shame, and the fear of blame are restraining motives, capable of preventing a multitude of crimes." A "good legislator," he offered, "is less bent upon punishing than preventing crimes; he is more attentive to inspire good morals than to inflict penalties."

While Montesquieu emphasized that "we shudder" in reading of "the cruelty of the sultans in administration of justice," he concluded that when people are virtuous few punishments are necessary. "Experience shows," he wrote, "that in countries remarkable for the lenity of their laws the spirit of the inhabitants is as much affected by slight penalties as in other countries by severer punishments." Calling on mankind not to be governed with "too much severity," Montesquieu offered this assessment: "If we inquire into the cause of all human corruptions, we shall find that they proceed from the impunity of criminals, and not from the moderation of punishments." "Let us follow nature," he emphasized, "who has given shame to man for his scourge; and let the heaviest part of the punishment be the infamy attending it." Montesquieu's book is full of references to *cruel* practices, with Montesquieu writing of "cruel kings," "cruel conquerors," "cruel laws" and "cruel punishments." "If an inconvenience or abuse arises in the state," Montesquieu offered at one point, "a violent government endeavors suddenly to redress it; and instead of putting the old laws in execution, it establishes some cruel punishment, which instantly puts a stop to the evil. But the spring of government hereby loses its elasticity; the imagination grows accustomed to the severe as well as the milder punishment; and as the fear of the latter diminishes, they are soon obliged in every case to have recourse to the former."[2]

Originally published in French in 1748, a 1750, English-language edition of Montesquieu's *Spirit of the Laws*, printed in London, was on the shelves of the Library Company of Philadelphia when the delegates of the Continental Congress were first granted borrowing privileges in 1774. Benjamin Franklin, in fact, had purchased the title on November 27, 1750, with Sir William Jones — the author of *An Essay on the Law of Bailments*, itself a popular American title — referring to "[t]he profound researches of Montesquieu, illuminated by a genius powerful and vivid." The "immortal" Montesquieu, that title proclaimed, had "explored the principles of a science the most important to the happiness of mankind." James Madison was familiar with the writings of both Montaigne and Montesquieu; John Adams purchased a 1752 edition of Montesquieu's *Spirit of Laws* in the 1750s; and Thomas Jefferson, in a 1771 letter, included Montesquieu's *Spirit of Laws* in a list of books for an ideal private library. Caesar Rodney, a Delaware signer of the Declaration of Independence, is also known to have owned a third English edition of the book. Montesquieu's *L'Esprit des lois* — as it was first known in French — "enjoyed a pervasive influence," two historians explain in their book, *Rethinking Leviathan*, adding that Montesquieu and Beccaria's arguments became "a staple" in discourse over the state of the penal laws.

Montesquieu's *Spirit of Laws* owed much to its author's travels and observations while abroad. After the publication in the early 1720s of his *Persian Letters*, a satire of French society, Montesquieu moved to Paris, then embarked on an extended tour through the Habsburg Empire, German principalities of the Holy Roman Empire, and Italy. It was on those trips — as well as on an extended stay in England from 1729 to 1731 — that he gathered the information for his 1734 and 1748 histories: *Considérations sur les causes de la grandeur des Romains et de leur décadence* (*Considerations on the Causes of the Greatness of the Romans and of Their Decline*) and *L'esprit des Lois* (*Spirit of the Laws*). Montesquieu's time in England observing Parliamentary debates and following political events convinced him, as one source puts it, that "English constitutional monarchy" embodied the ideals of "Freedom, toleration, moderation, and Reason." In 1786, the English penal reformer Samuel Romilly — a mutual acquaintance of Thomas Jefferson and Benjamin Vaughan — himself emphasized that "human and rational principles" had "exploded" the "absurd and barbarous notions of justice which prevailed for ages." In a letter Jefferson sent from Paris in 1788 to Angelica Schuyler Church, "Mr. Romilly of London" appears in the sentence after Jefferson takes note of "Mr. Short's departure for Italy."[3] And in *The Federalist Papers*, Madison himself wrote that "the celebrated Montesquieu" was "[t]he oracle who is always consulted and cited on the subject" of separation of powers.[4]

In England, Sir Samuel Romilly (1757–1818) — an English lawyer and member of Parliament who had studied at Gray's Inn — made his first legislative motion to amend England's criminal laws in 1808. On May 18 of that year, Romilly rose and spoke to the following effect:

> Mr. Speaker, in bringing forward a proposal for the amendment of the Criminal Law, I am fully sensible of the obstacles and difficulties to which I am exposed. I know, that, from a part of the public, at least, and more especially from that part of it, whose opinion may be supposed to have most influence on my conduct, instead of expecting praise, I must be satisfied with escaping censure. My apology, however, must be, that I have not taken up the matter suddenly or lightly; that the subject which I now presume to bring before the House, is one that has occupied my thoughts for many years. I long ago promised myself, that if ever I should have the honour of a seat in this House, I would bring forward some measures for reforming the Criminal Code; and recollecting this, I cannot but feel, that I ought rather to apologize for having delayed the proposal so long, than for bringing it forward now.

> I have always considered it a very great defect in the Criminal Code of this Country, that Capital Punishments should be so frequent; that they have been appointed, I cannot say inflicted, for so many crimes. For no principle seems to me more clear than this, that it is the certainty, much more than the severity, of punishments, which renders them efficacious. This has been acknowledged, I believe, ever since the publication of the works of the Marquis Beccaria. The impression, however, which was made in this Country by his writings, has hitherto proved unavailing; for it has not produced a single alteration in our Criminal Law; although in many other states of Europe various amendments have taken place. Indeed, if we were to take the very reverse of the principle to which I have alluded, it would be a faithful description of the English law, in its enactments and administration. It is notorious how few of those, who are condemned, actually suffer punishment. From returns which are to be found in the Secretary of State's office, it appears, that in the year 1805, there were 350 persons who received sentence of death, of whom only 68 were executed, not quite a fifth part of the number. In the year 1806, 325 received sentence of death, of whom 57 were executed; and in 1807, the number was 343, of whom there were executed 63.

In his speech, Romilly went on to observe: "I am far from being disposed either to censure or regret this relaxation of the Law; I am only inquiring whether Statutes so dispensed with can be deemed any longer essential to the well-being of the State."

Prior to making that speech, in which Romilly specifically questioned "whether a code shall continue to exist in *theory*" that was "abrogated in *practice*," the English penal reformer — who had become familiar with Beccaria's treatise decades earlier — had thus thought long and hard about the criminal law and its deficiencies. In a letter written to his brother-in-law in Switzerland on March 1, 1782, Romilly wrote: "I have lately read a second time, Beccaria on Crimes and Punishments, a favourite book, I know, of yours, and I think deservedly. But does not the author too often reason by analogy to his favourite mathematics? Are not his observations sometimes too subtle? And what do you think of the principle on which he relies so much, that crimes are to be measured by the injury they do to the State, without regard to the malignity of the will?" In another letter, Romilly had also noted the "extraordinary trial here of a clergyman, and another, gentleman, who were charged with murder, by killing an American gentleman in a duel, the one as principal, the other as second." Romilly then observed that "[t]he law with us is clear and express, that the crime is murder, however fairly the duel may have been fought." Romilly noted that the jury — which he described as "twelve tradesmen" not "under the dominion of those prejudices respecting the false point of honour which enslave those in a higher rank" — had acquitted both men. But Romilly, on the subject of duels, still found himself thinking that "in truth, one's nature recoils at the inhumanity of laws which punish with death the doing of that, which, in certain circumstances, one must be more or less than man not to do."

In another parliamentary speech, delivered on June 15, 1808, Romilly showed his close familiarization with the central ideas in Blackstone and Beccaria's writings. On that day, "Sir Samuel Romilly moved the Order of the Day for the House to resolve itself into a Committee on the Bill for abolishing the punishment of death for Privately Stealing from the person." According to a record of his speech: "He defended the Preamble of the Bill," which provided in part that "the extreme severity of Penal Laws hath not been found effectual for the prevention of Crimes." "He then proceeded," the observer noted, "to shew the necessity of a relaxation in our Criminal Code, and how its extreme rigour, by shocking the humanity of Prosecutors, of Witnesses, of Juries, and of Judges, — led them in many instances to compromise the Law and the Offence, rather than go to the extent of inflicting Capital Punishment where it was wholly disproportionate to the crime." After noting "the great Commentator on our Laws, who had enumerated no less than 160 Felonies without benefit of Clergy, to be found on the Statute Book in his day," Romilly editorialized: "What a stain upon the Legislation of this Country! What a reflection upon the Criminal Codes of other nations, over which the Law of England had been extolled as being so superior!" "A Bill had recently passed the Legislature," Romilly lamented, "adding *nine* new Capital Felonies to the former long catalogue."[5]

Long before Sir Samuel Romilly's orations in Parliament, Sir William Blackstone—that legal luminary from prestigious Oxford, and the legal commentator to whom Romilly likely alluded—also helped to legitimate Beccaria's ideas. In his 1760s *Commentaries on the Laws of England*—a much-consulted source for American colonial lawyers[6]—Blackstone, like Beccaria, frequently wrote of cruelty. "The laws of the Roman kings, and the twelve tables of the *decemviri*," he wrote, "were full of cruel punishments." "It is, it must be owned," Blackstone observed, "much *easier* to extirpate than to amend mankind; yet that magistrate must be esteemed both a weak and a cruel surgeon, who cuts off every limb, which through ignorance or indolence he will not attempt to cure." Elsewhere, Blackstone refers to a "cruel law" and "cruel edicts" and speaks of "the cool and cruel sarcasm of the sovereign." Though English law still authorized horrific punishments such as drawing and quartering, Blackstone—who gave instant credibility to Beccaria just by citing him—noted that the severity of such punishments was, in practice, often mitigated through pre-execution conduct. "[T]he humanity of the English nation," Blackstone qualified, "has authorized, by a tacit consent, an almost general mitigation of such part of these judgments as favour of torture or cruelty: a sledge or hurdle being usually allowed to such traitors as are condemned to be drawn; and there being very few instances (and those accidental or by negligence) of any person's being emboweled or burned, till previously deprived of sensation by strangling."[7]

In fact, eighteenth-century Englishmen expressed great pride in the notion that, as a society, they had *rejected* torture, at least in the manner in which they then conceived of it. For example, Jean-Louis de Lolme (1740–1806)—the Swiss and English political writer—wrote in *The Constitution of England* that "the use of Torture" was "that method of administering Justice in which folly may be said to be added to cruelty." "[T]he use of Torture," de Lolme boasted, "has, from the earliest times, been utterly unknown in England," with de Lolme editorializing that "all attempts to introduce it, whatever might be the power of those who made them, or the circumstances in which they renewed their endeavors, have been strenuously opposed and defeated." As de Lolme emphasized in his book: "[S]o anxious has the English Legislature been to establish mercy, even to convicted offenders, as a fundamental principle of the Government of England, that they made it an express article of that great public Compact which was framed at the important era of the Revolution, that 'no cruel and unusual punishments should be used.'" In reality, though, torturous practices such as *peine forte et dure*—in which an accused person was slowly pressed to death for refusing to plead to a criminal charge—had a centuries-old history. The last case of pressing to death occurred in Cambridge in 1741, but it was not until 1772 that, by statute, *peine forte et dure* was abolished, with the statute declaring that any person who should stand mute and refuse to plead when arraigned for a felony, be convicted and suffer judgment and sentence in the same manner as if convicted by verdict or confession. Not until 1827 was a refusal to plead treated, in a more modern manner, as a plea of not guilty.

Acts of torture were hardly unknown to the English law. The Tudors and early Stuarts—and the King's Star Chamber—made extensive use of torture; Jesuit priests and others were tortured extensively in England before being executed; and the Tower of London—

as every modern-day London tourist learns from the on-site yeoman warders—came to be closely associated with executions and devices of torture. "Torture," writes Geoffrey Abbott, a former Yeoman Warder of the Tower of London, "was not a punishment, but a forcible persuasion to compel the offender to admit guilt or reveal the names of accomplices." The thumbscrew—used in the Inquisition and by the English Privy Council—was not done away with until the 1680s. The last person to have a thumb compressed between iron bars by means of a screw was the Presbyterian minister William Carstairs by the Scotch Privy Council in 1685; after the Glorious Revolution of 1688, Carstairs, whose hands still bore the marks of the thumbscrew, reportedly demonstrated the device at the request of the new monarch, William of Orange. Sir Edward Coke had declared that "[t]here is no law to warrant tortures in this land nor can they be justified." But in the 1830s, David Jardine—a Middle Temple barrister—had detailed the history in England of "the application of Torture to witnesses and accused persons, for the purpose of extracting evidence and confessions." In *A Reading on the Use of Torture in the Criminal Law of England Previously to the Commonwealth*, an address delivered in 1836 and published the following year, Jardine called torture "a practice repugnant to reason, justice, and humanity—censured and condemned upon principle by philosophers and statesmen."[8]

First published in Amsterdam in 1771 as *Constitution de l'Angleterre*, *The Constitution of England* (1775) had come about after de Lolme, a Swiss lawyer, emigrated to England, where he carefully studied English law before writing his book. Avidly read by America's founders, *The Constitution of England*—several editions of which were produced—specifically equated torture with cruelty, seeing the English prohibition on "cruel and unusual punishments" as a restriction on acts of torture. Writing of "public Justice" in England and "establishing just laws among Mankind," de Lolme emphasized that "a very remarkable circumstance in the English Government (and which alone evinces something peculiar and excellent in its Nature), is that spirit of extreme mildness with which Justice, in criminal cases, is administered in England; a point with regard to which England differs from all other Countries in the World." "From the same cause," de Lolme emphasized in his book, "also arose that remarkable forbearance of the English Laws, to use any cruel severity in the punishments which experience shewed it was necessary for the preservation of Society to establish: and the utmost vengeance of those laws, even against the most enormous Offenders, never extends beyond the simple deprivation of life." "When we consider the punishments in use in the other States in Europe, we wonder how Men can be brought to treat their fellow-creatures with so much cruelty."[9]

In America, the study of Blackstone's *Commentaries*—coupled with apprenticeships—remained the primary means of acquiring a legal education until the late 1800s, making early American lawyers especially conversant with Blackstone's treatise, and thus Beccaria's ideas.[10] As one commentator explains: "By 1776, American lawyers and many of the Founding Fathers were well-versed in English law and practice through Blackstone. The *Commentaries*, in short, were widely known in America and had an enormous influence on American legal thought."[11] The death penalty scholar Welsh White, a University of Pittsburgh law professor, wrote before his death that "among those who read and acknowledged the authority of Blackstone's *Commentaries*" were John Adams, James Madison, Alexander Hamilton, John Jay and Patrick Henry.[12] In fact, any American lawyer worth his salt had spent many laborious hours pouring over—and becoming intimately familiar with—Blackstone's multi-volume treatise. "Blackstone's *Commentaries*," notes one source, "were sometimes the only law books in a colonial lawyer's office, and even after independence, Blackstone continued to influence nineteenth-century lawyers like Daniel Webster, Chancellor James Kent of New York, and Abraham Lincoln." St. George Tucker's annotated American edition of Blackstone's *Commentaries*, published in 1803, was also later a standard legal reference for American lawyers.[13]

Abraham Lincoln, America's 16th commander-in-chief, had a special affection for Blackstone's treatise, thus exposing Lincoln to Beccaria's ideas, too. In the 1830s, Lincoln had acquired Blackstone's *Commentaries*—one of only a few legal texts Lincoln had at his disposal as a young, antebellum lawyer. "One day," Lincoln reported of his days as a store-keeper, a man traveling West on a wagon asked him if he "would buy an old barrel" which the man had no room for and which Lincoln was told "contained nothing of special value." "I did not want it, but to oblige him I bought it, and paid him, I think, half a dollar for it," Lincoln said, recalling how later, in emptying it, "I found at the bottom of the rubbish a complete edition of Blackstone's 'Commentaries.'" Lincoln carefully read Blackstone's multi-volume treatise, once recalling: "I began to read those famous works, and I had plenty of time; for during the long summer days, when the farmers were busy with their crops, my customers were few and far between. The more I read, the more intensely interested I became. Never in my whole life was my mind so thoroughly absorbed. I read until I devoured them." Lincoln, in fact, was still recommending Blackstone's *Commentaries* to an aspiring lawyer decades later, with Lincoln using executions during the Civil War to curtail desertion but often refusing to carry out executions in individual soldiers' cases.[14] Hannibal Hamlin—Lincoln's first-term Vice President, serving from 1861 to 1865—was, notably, the nephew of the New Hampshire politician Samuel Livermore, a member of the First Congress who took part in the debate of the U.S. Constitution's Cruel and Unusual Punishments Clause. Hamlin had read law, settled in Maine, and was elected five times to the Maine House of Representatives as an anti-slavery Democrat. According to a biographical sketch, Hamlin "favored the abolishment of capital punishment."[15]

In his *Commentaries*, Blackstone actually used the phrase "cruel and unusual"—the very words found in the U.S. Constitution's Eighth Amendment—in two separate contexts. First, Blackstone used those words to define "murder by express malice." In detailing the elements of murder, Blackstone wrote that "the killing must be committed *with malice aforethought*, to make it the crime of murder." At one juncture, Blackstone explained: "if even upon a sudden provocation one beats another in a cruel and unusual manner, so that he dies, though he did not intend his death, yet he is guilty of murder by express malice; that is, by an express evil design, the genuine sense of *malitia*."[16] In his second reference, Blackstone referred to the concept of "cruel and unusual punishments" in discussing the English Bill of Rights. That reference was prefaced by Blackstone's discussion of criminal judgments and the possibility of an offender's "pardon" or "praying the benefit of clergy" to "arrest" a judgment.

"If all these resources fail," Blackstone wrote, "the court must pronounce that judgment, which the law hath annexed to the crime, and which hath been constantly mentioned, together with the crime itself, in some or other of the former chapters." As he explained: "Of these some are capital, which extend to the life of the offender, and consist generally in being hanged by the neck till dead; though in very atrocious crimes other circumstances of terror, pain, or disgrace are superadded: as, in treasons of all kinds, being drawn or dragged to the place of execution; in high treason affecting the king's person or government, embowelling alive, beheading, and quartering; and in murder, a public dissection." "Our statute law," Blackstone noted, "has not therefore often ascertained the quantity of fines, nor the common law ever; it directing such an offence to be punishment by fine, in general, without specifying the certain sum: which is fully sufficient, when we consider, that however unlimited the power of the court may seem, it is far from being wholly arbitrary; but it's discretion is regulated by law." "For the bill of rights," Blackstone emphasized, "has particularly declared, that excessive fines ought not to be imposed, nor cruel and unusual punishments inflicted."[17]

Blackstone, the Oxford scholar, felt strongly that English law—though harsh—was still enlightened compared to the laws of other countries.[18] "Some punishments," Blackstone wrote, "consist in exile or punishment, by abjuration of the realm, or transportation to the American colonies: others in loss of liberty, by perpetual or temporary imprisonment." "Some, though rarely," he added, "occasion a mutilation or dismembering, by cutting off the hand or ears: others fix a lasting stigma on the offender, by slitting the nostrils, or branding in the hand or face." Blackstone also noted the availability of "discretionary fines" and punishments involving the infliction of "corporal pain" such as "whipping, hard labour in the house of correction, the pillory, the stocks, and the ducking-stool."[19] A ducking stool was a chair connected to a pulley system where slanderers and women, among others, "were restrained and then repeatedly plunged into a convenient body of water."[20] "Disgusting as this catalogue may seem," Blackstone wrote of the draconian punishments still authorized by English law, "it will afford pleasure to an English reader, and do honour to the English law, to compare it with that shocking apparatus of death and torment, to be met with in the criminal codes of almost every other nation in Europe."

A significant portion of Blackstone's treatise, which highlighted alternatives to executions, was about criminal law issues. "[I]t is moreover," Blackstone explained, "one of the glories of our English law, that the nature, though not always the quantity or degree, of punishment is *ascertained* for every offence; and that it is not left in the breast of any judge, nor even of a jury, to alter that judgment, which the law has beforehand ordained, for every subject alike, without respect of persons."[21] "[W]here an established penalty is annexed to crimes," Blackstone offered, "the criminal may read their certain consequence in that law, which ought to be the unvaried rule, as it is the inflexible judgment, of his actions." It was after this discussion that Blackstone cited the "cruel and unusual punishments" clause of the English Bill of Rights, put in place in 1689 following the Glorious Revolution of 1688. "The discretionary fines and discretionary length of imprisonment, which our courts are enabled to impose," Blackstone first explained, "may seem an exception to this rule." "But," he noted, "the general nature of the punishment, *viz.* by fine or imprisonment, is in these cases fixed and determinate: though the duration and quantity of each must frequently vary, from the aggravations or otherwise of the offence, the quality and condition of the parties, and from innumerable other circumstances."[22]

By the time James Madison drafted the U.S. Bill of Rights, he would have been quite familiar with William Blackstone's *Commentaries*. Madison never became a lawyer, but he did intermittently study law. After graduating from the College of New Jersey in 1771, he stayed on "employing his times in miscellaneous studies; but not without a reference to the profession of the Law." Upon returning to Virginia, he studied law for long stretches as he contemplated becoming a member of the Bar. The law books Madison read is not clear, but in 1773 Madison wrote that he intended "to read Law occasionally and have procured books for that purpose." Madison even asked William Bradford, his closest friend from college, to send him a list of the books Bradford planned to read to become a lawyer.[23] In Pennsylvania, Bradford—destined to become a leading penal reformer—would personally lead efforts to restrict that state's death penalty to first-degree murderers. And Bradford—in the post-*On Crimes and Punishments* era—was even willing to contemplate that evidence might show one day that executions were unnecessary for those murderers, too. Bradford and Madison confided in one another, with both freely sharing ideas—including on the law—that would influence their political futures.

Blackstone's *Commentaries*, which communicated Cesare Beccaria's ideas to a much wider audience,[24] were not only highly influential in colonial and early America,[25] but specifically show up in William Bradford's correspondence with James Madison. Bradford—who later became the Attorney General of the United States—wrote in longhand of Blackstone's *Commentaries*, telling Madison of that title: "I am most pleased with & find but little of that disagreeable dryness I was taught to expect." In 1783, Madison himself recommended that Congress acquire a copy of Blackstone's *Commentaries*; in 1785, while trying to gain passage of Jefferson's Virginia bill to proportion crimes and punishments, Madison took notes on Blackstone's treatise; and at the 1787 Constitutional Convention in Philadelphia, in a debate over an *ex post facto* provision, Madison also recorded a reference to Blackstone's *Commentaries* made by John Dickinson. Though Madison, unlike John Adams, William Bradford and Thomas Jefferson, never practiced law, Madison's work as a lawmaker required that he become familiar with important legal commentators of the day, and that list included Blackstone as well as Beccaria and Montesquieu.[26]

Beccaria and Montesquieu's treatises were, in fact, both cited at important moments in early American history. For example, in the first decade of the 1800s, Pennsylvania Supreme Court Chief Justice Edward Shippen, as well as Assistant Justices Jasper Yeates and Thomas Smith, were impeached and put on trial. The charge: the "arbitrary and unconstitutional act" of sentencing Thomas Passmore to thirty days in jail and imposing a fifty dollar fine for "supposed contempt." The alleged impeachable offense: that the punishment of contempt was part of English common law, but allegedly illegal in the United States. In the course of that case, which resulted in an acquittal of all three judges, one of the lawyers, Nathaniel Boileau, argued: "the punishment inflicted on Mr. Passmore was mild and moderate, marked with humanity and forbearance." "I believe it to be a correct principle," Boileau asserted, "that punishment should always be proportioned to the crime, and that in a republic the punishments ought not to be so severe as in a monarchy." "These sentiments have some authority to support them," he said. "[A]nd as I rather give the sentiments of eminent men than my own," Boileau emphasized, "I shall refer to Beccaria on Punishments." "This is correct sound reasoning; no man of sound understanding, and if his mind is composed as mine, and I trust yours is, will contradict this doctrine," Boileau offered. "This will be further corroborated by turning to ... Montesquieu's Spirit of Laws," he added, telling his audience: "Severe punishments destroy the very germe of liberty in every country." "On principles like these was our Constitution founded," Boileau concluded, invoking section 13 of the Bill of Rights of Pennsylvania's constitution, "That excessive bail shall not be required, nor excessive fines imposed, nor cruel punishments inflicted."[27] Montesquieu and Beccaria's teachings thus infused early American law and the spirit of the American Revolution itself.

The Pennsylvania Experiment

In the Commonwealth of Pennsylvania, a Society of Friends member, Richard Wistar, has been credited with the beginnings of prison reform in that state. Before the Revolutionary War, Wistar—a Philadelphia merchant—became concerned about the grotesque conditions of the local jail. "It was a moral pest house," one commentator, Richard Vaux, later remarked of the city's jail. After some inmates in the jail had starved to death, Wistar decided to take action. He prepared soup at his house and then took it to the jail to feed the inmates. Other Quakers and concerned Philadelphia citizens soon joined this relief effort, though the Revolutionary War quickly took its toll on the charitable endeavor. On February 7, 1776, just a few months before the Continental Congress issued the Declaration of Independence, citizens in the City of Brotherly Love formed the Philadelphia Society for Assisting Distressed Prisoners. "The reform of the criminal and the introduction of the prison system," historian Harry Elmer Barnes speculates, "might have begun at that date instead of a decade later had not the British occupation of the city put an end to the activities of the society." The Revolutionary War interfered with charitable impulses in Philadelphia, but after Wistar's initial efforts, Richard Vaux explained in his history of Pennsylvania's prison system, "slow but effective measures" were nonetheless taken "to reform the penal laws and the prison system of Philadelphia."[28]

Indeed, despite the very real possibility that their own lives would be cut short by execution for treason, America's founders committed themselves to penal reform from the get-go. In Pennsylvania, a constitution with a new vision for how criminals should be dealt with was thus approved on September 28, 1776. Inspired in part by Enlightenment writers such as Beccaria, the new constitution was approved by a convention of delegates—presided over by Benjamin Franklin—that assembled in Philadelphia. That constitution included a whole host of provisions, and penal reform was among them. Section 38 provided that "[t]he penal laws as heretofore used shall be reformed by the legislature of this state, as soon as may be, and punishments made in some cases less sanguinary, and in general more proportionate to the crimes." Section 39, drafted in a similar spirit, likewise read: "To deter more effectually from the commission of crimes by continued visible punishments of long duration, and to make sanguinary punishments less necessary; houses ought to be provided for punishing by hard labour, those who shall be convicted of crimes not capital; wherein the criminals shall be imployed for the benefit of the public, or for reparation of injuries done to private persons: And all persons at proper times shall be admitted to see the prisoners at their labour."[29]

The Pennsylvania constitution of 1776—signed in Philadelphia by more than 70 men, and ratified on September 28, 1776—was drafted and shaped by the ideas of thinkers such as Thomas Paine, schoolteacher James Cannon of Philadelphia College, Philadelphia mathematician and astronomer David Rittenhouse, Dr. Thomas Young, Benjamin Franklin, jurist George Bryan, and Timothy Matlack, a brewer, ex-Quaker and the leader of the Philadelphia mechanics. These men had all given thought to the penal system, something that would occupy their thoughts for years to come, too. For example, in the memoirs of the life of David Rittenhouse, written by counselor-at-law William Barton and published in 1813, a "Professor Barton"—a reference to Dr. Benjamin Smith Barton (1766–1815), Professor of Materia Medica, Natural History and Botany, at the University of Pennsylvania— shared these remembrances of Dr. Rittenhouse from discussions they had together in 1793:

> In the month of March of the same year, I had a good deal of conversation with Mr. Rittenhouse, on the subject of penal laws. He did not think that the late judge Bradford, whose essay on this subject he greatly admired, and recommended to my perusal, was too lenient in his views of the subject. He observed, that although he had often served on juries, he thanked God, that he never had in any case where life and death were immediately involved; observing, that his conscience would *ever* reproach him, if he had, in any instance, given his verdict for death. 'Of all murders (he added) *legal* murders are the most horrid.' He did not think that death ought to be the punishment for any crime.[30]

After the adoption of Pennsylvania's constitution and the end of the Revolutionary War, Franklin himself made clear the prevailing public sentiment favoring penal reform and an overhaul of then-existing laws. "By the present criminal laws," he wrote in 1785, speaking for Pennsylvania's Supreme Executive Council, "fines are a part of the punishment for a variety of offences; applications are continually made to us by the offenders for remission of such fines; and these applications are recommended by the Magistrates, on the sole consideration that the criminals being poor and unable to pay, become, while detained in prison, a charge to the public; as this is generally the case, the imposition of fines is rendered ineffectual as a punishment, and the satisfaction due by the laws to the community from the offenders, is not made." "We, therefore, offer it to your consideration," Franklin wrote to the Pennsylvania General Assembly, "whether means may not be found to oblige them to pay by labor what they are unable to pay in money, and whether this would not tend more to the prevention of offences, those especially which are committed thro' a vicious dislike of labor." As Franklin then emphasized: "In the General Reform of our penal laws, necessary in itself, and required by the thirty-eighth section of the Constitution, this particular will properly come before you."[31]

In another communication to Pennsylvania's General Assembly, signed by Benjamin Franklin in 1788, Pennsylvania's Supreme Executive Council looked favorably upon "[l]ate experiments in Europe" as regards the reform of the penal laws. "The benefits expected from the penal laws, having not equaled the benevolent wishes of its friends and framers," that communication stated, "we recommend such alterations to be made in it as shall be calculated to render punishment a means of reformation, and the labour of criminals of profit to the State." "Late experiments in Europe," it read, alluding to the death penalty's abolition in Tuscany by Leopold II and its curtailment in Austria by Joseph II, "have demonstrated that those advantages are only to be obtained by temperance and solitude of labour."[32] Although eighteenth-century Pennsylvanians were unwilling to abandon the death penalty for all offenses, the German philosopher Georg Wilhelm Friedrich Hegel later captured, in *The Philosophy of Right*, how Beccaria's writings had shaped and aroused penal reform efforts in multiple nations. "Beccaria's efforts to abolish capital punishment," Hegel wrote in 1820, "have had good results." "Although neither Joseph II nor the French have ever been able to obtain complete abolition of the death-penalty," Hegel explained, "still we have begun to see what crimes deserve death and what do not." "Capital punishment," Hegel added, "has thus become less frequent, as indeed should be the case with the extreme penalty of the law."[33]

Pennsylvania's 1776 constitution was framed in Philadelphia under dire circumstances, with rampant rumors of an impending British invasion. As Americans risked everything for their freedom and independence and articulated the principles they held dear and were fighting for, the world was closely watching the tumultuous events unfolding in Philadelphia.[34] Luigi Castiglioni—writing after the Revolutionary War was over—had noted of America that "the most unanimous popular watchword was 'liberty.'"[35] And other Europeans, long before that, had paid close attention to America's Declaration of Independence, the American Revolution, and the progress of U.S. penal reform. For example, when word got out about Pennsylvania's new constitution, Benjamin Franklin received a congratulatory letter in 1778 from a Swiss writer and magistrate, Emanuel Wolleb-Ryhiner, in faraway Basel, Switzerland. That letter reflected that the adoption of the Pennsylvania Constitution was seen as an admirable attempt to reign in cruelty. As the letter of Wolleb-Ryhiner reads:

> I have seen in the Pennsylvania constitutions, sections 38 and 39, that you intend to reform the penal laws to render them less savage, and gladly send you the enclosed pamphlet on the same subject; hatred of cruelty and the desire for clement correction guide the author. My birth and duty as a republican commit me to hating violence and promoting humane treatment of criminals. The same principles, I hope, will prevail in more important areas, and will repel "the rough wind of North." Hail to you and our future brothers, especially if our latest news from Paris is true. I am a most devoted friend and servant, "as a gray man of 72 years," to you and all republicans.[36]

Back in Pennsylvania, the change in the state's penal code was also accompanied by a decided shift in attitudes toward criminals. For instance, the growing preference for hard labor instead of death was reflected in a petition addressed to Benjamin Franklin and Pennsylvania's Supreme Executive Council in 1788. That petition—signed by Thomas McKean and George Bryan—reads:

> We, the subscribers, do humbly certify, that the within Petitioner, John Brown, was tried before us, that he had Counsel assigned him in his challenges and to make his defence, and upon a fair hearing was convicted by an impartial jury, on evidence entirely satisfactory to us; that he was informed, that instead of the sentence of death, he was intitled to crave the punishment inflicted for such an offence by the Act of Assembly for the amendment of the penal Laws of this Sta[t]e, and that against the earnest recommendations of the court to do so, he obstinately refused, and insisted for the sentence under the former Laws being pronounced against him, which was at length passed.
>
> We conceive it proper to inform Council that the Petitioner is an old Offender, and was pardoned in the year 1785 for a Burglary, in order that they may the better be enabled to determine upon the length of time he ought to labour for the Public on condition of a Pardon, to which indulgence We have no particular objections.[37]

It would take time to reform the state's criminal code, but eventually Pennsylvania lawmakers did just that. After peace came to America in 1783 following the Treaty of Paris, Benjamin Franklin, Benjamin Rush, William Bradford and Caleb Lownes attempted to fulfill the promise of the 1776 state constitution. They accordingly led a movement to reform Pennsylvania's antiquated criminal code of 1718, which was still in effect. The resulting new law, of September 15, 1786, drastically reduced the number of capital crimes and substituted "continuous hard labor, publicly and disgracefully imposed" for the death penalty for lesser offenses. And Pennsylvania lawmakers did not stop there. In 1794, Pennsylvania became the first jurisdiction to divide murder into degrees, making only first-degree murder punishable by death. According to the Pennsylvania statute, "all murder, which shall be perpetrated by means of poison, or by lying in wait or by any other kind of wilful, deliberate and premeditated killing, or which shall be committed in the perpetration or attempt to perpetrate any arson, rape, robbery, or burglary, shall be deemed murder of the first degree." Under the statute, "all other kinds of murder shall be deemed murder in the second degree." In other words, only premeditated murders and killings committed in the context of prescribed felonies—so-called *felony murders*—were punishable by death.[38]

To achieve these reforms, Pennsylvania lawmakers organized and—to persuade their colleagues—drew heavily upon the wisdom of Enlightenment thinkers. "The Pennsylvania statute," writes legal scholar Guyora Binder, an expert on the history of felony murder, "was an outgrowth of a protracted movement to reduce and differentiate penalties inspired by such Enlightenment figures as Montesquieu and Beccaria and promoted by James Wilson, Benjamin Rush, and Pennsylvania Supreme Court Justice William Bradford." "During legislative debates," Binder writes, "murder in the course of enumerated felonies was added to the category of first-degree murder."[39] In Philadelphia—Pennsylvania's commercial center—executions had been relatively rare in the colonial period. They spiked, however, during the Revolutionary War, with forty-one men hanged between 1776 and 1783. Of the hangings, twenty-five—or 61 percent—were for property crimes, an indication of the state of the times.

Although a few executions occurred in Philadelphia after the Revolutionary War, the local populace had grown more suspect of the efficacy of state-sanctioned executions. In fact, substantial anti-death penalty agitation led to their curtailment in the lead up to the passage of Pennsylvania's 1794 law, with that agitation continuing after the law's passage.[40] From 1809 to 1811, one Italian-American in Philadelphia, James Philip Puglia, even wrote three essays that turned into a book, *Capital Punishment*. His book used "simple morality and incontrovertible logical arguments" coupled with "the principles of the Christian religion" to condemn executions. Born in Genoa of Italian and Swiss ancestry, Puglia—who spoke fluent Spanish—had been jailed for a time in Spain after his business there failed, then sailed for America, arriving in Philadelphia in July 1790 aboard the ship *Aurora*. After working as a bookkeeper and teaching Spanish, Puglia became an American citizen in May 1791 and, thanks to a new friendship with Governor Thomas Mifflin, got a job as an interpreter for the Board of Health of Pennsylvania. Puglia later wrote *The Federal Politician*, a book printed in 1795 by Francis and Robert Bailey that one historian has called "a defense of the U.S. Constitution against the excesses of popular democracy." The list of subscribers who supported that book's publication included William Bingham, a Pennsylvania U.S. Senator; former congressman Thomas Fitzsimons of Philadelphia; Alexander Hamilton, the former Secretary of the Treasury; banker and financier Robert Morris; and future President James Madison. In 1821, another publisher also published Puglia's Spanish translation of Thomas Paine's *Rights of Man*. Puglia's own life ended tragically in 1831 in Charleston, South Carolina, where he committed suicide.[41]

Although Puglia had come to America after the Revolutionary War, a number of Italians had come to America either before or during that war. Indeed, Italians themselves fought for American independence, with three Italian regiments—the Third Piedmont, the 13th Du Perche, and the Royal Italien—totaling roughly 1,500 men. Italian officers included Lieutenant James Bracco of the 7th Maryland Regiment; Captain Cosimo de Medici (Madacy) of the North Carolina Light Dragoons; 2nd Lieutenant Nicola Talliaferro of the Second Virginia Regiment; Colonel Richard Talliaferro, killed in 1781 at the Battle of Guilford Court House in North Carolina; a Captain Ferdinando Finizzi; and Giuseppe Maria Francesco Vigo (1747–1836), said to be the first Italian to become an American citizen. Vigo, a successful fur trader, served as a soldier in the Spanish army in Cuba, then came to America in the 1770s. He served as a captain, a financier and a spy during the Revolutionary War and helped settle the Northwest Territory. Vigo, who assisted General George Rogers Clark's expeditions and facilitated the capture of the British fort at Vincennes, was later, in 1800, made a colonel in the Indiana militia. Another man of European heritage, Colonel Lewis Nicola—a Revolutionary War officer of French and Italian descent—is remembered as the man who suggested that George Washington be made a king. General Washington's hasty response: "Be assured Sir, no occurrence in the course of the War, has given me more painful sensations than your information of there being such ideas existing in the Army as you have expressed, and I must view with abhorrence, and reprehend with severity."

The Talliaferro (or Taliaferro) family had especially deep roots in Virginia. George Wythe—Thomas Jefferson's mentor—married Elizabeth Taliaferro (pronounced "Tolliver") around 1775, and the couple moved into a house in Williamsburg that had been designed by Elizabeth's father, Colonel Richard Taliaferro. A prominent "gentleman architect" whose work Jefferson admired, Richard Taliaferro died in 1779 and willed the property to the Wythes after having, while alive, granted the married couple a life estate in the property. Although Elizabeth, Wythe's wife, died in 1787, Wythe continued to live in the house until 1791 when he resigned his professorship in Williamsburg and relocated to Richmond to serve as a chancery judge. Wythe himself corresponded with Jefferson about a "Major Taliaferro" in 1770, writing in March of year: "I send you some nectarine and apricot graffs and grapevines, the best I had; and have directed your messenger to call upon Major Taliaferro for some of his." Major Taliaferro later did get into Jefferson's hands "two Bundls of Grafts." Another family member, William Taliaferro—sometimes spelled Talliaferro—was the son of John Taliaferro, one of the founders of Orange County, Virginia, and the brother of Francis and John Taliaferro. In October 1776, Congress named William Taliaferro—a captain in the 2nd Virginia Regiment as of September 1775—a major of the 3rd Virginia Regiment. Originally Tagliaferro, which means "ironcutter," the Taliaferro family—of Italian descent—had put down roots in Virginia.[42]

George Washington also wrote letters in the 1740s and 1750s that reference Major Francis Talliaferro and militia leader William Talliaferro. A militia commander, William Taliaferro—as he is referred to, with a minor spelling variation, in various letters—was Washington's friend, as reflected in eighteenth-century correspondence. "Nothing could have given me more Dissatisfaction than the inclosed Letter from our Friend Colo. Wm Taliaferro," reads a September 21, 1757 letter from Charles Lewis to George Washington. The enclosed letter, signed by "W. Taliaferro" and dated September 15, 1757, was addressed to Lewis and noted that a "Lieutt Charles Smith" had, "about ½ an Hour since," "unfortunately killed a Man (to whom he was intire Stranger) by a slight Stroke on the Nose without any Malice." In writing to Washington on September 21st, Lewis has passed along the news that Smith "is to Day clear'd honourably by a call'd Court of Inquiry, neither Murder, Man Slaughter, or even Chan. Med. Found against him"—*chance-medley* referring to any kind of homicide by misadventure. The William Taliaferro who had been appointed a major in the 3rd Virginia Regiment in October 1776, was later commissioned as a lieutenant colonel in the 4th Virginia Regiment in February 1777, but was captured by the British at the Battle of Brandywine on September 11, 1777, and died the following year.

In 1775, in Orange County, a Lawrence Taliaferro also shows up in the signature block of an address to Patrick Henry along with the names of James Madison and Madison's father. In 1787, James Madison, in fact, exchanged letters with Lawrence Taliaferro shortly after the Constitutional Convention in Philadelphia, with Madison paying a visit in late 1787 to Lawrence Taliaferro's nephew, John Taliaferro, in Princeton, Madison's alma matter. A friend and supporter of Madison, Lawrence Taliaferro later urged Madison, in 1797, to run for another term in Congress. On an "Oath of Allegiance Signed by Citizens of Albemarle County" in 1777, shortly after the issuance of the Declaration of Independence, the names of "Saml. Taliaferro" and "Fran: Taliaferro" appear in a long list along with those of Thomas Jefferson and Philip Mazzei. "We whos[e] names are hereunto subscribed," the oath read, "do swear that we renounce and refuse all Allegiance to George the third King of Great Britain, his heirs and successors and that I will be faithfull and bear True Allegiance to the commonwealth of Virginia as a free and independent state."

Thomas Jefferson and James Madison were not only well acquainted with the Taliaferro family, with Jefferson's notes showing he planted "Taliaferro" apples and consumed "Taliaferro cyder," but George Wythe married into the family—and took pride in the association. In two 1786 letters, George Wythe wrote to Thomas Jefferson, attempting to get him to procure a copperplate engraving of the coat of arms of his wife's family for Richard Taliaferro, describing Taliaferro's ancestors as being from "a tuscan family," perhaps "12 or 13 miles" outside of Florence. As Jefferson, then in Paris, in turn explained to his Italian friend, Giovanni Fabbroni, in attempting to fulfill Wythe's request: "There is in the state of Virginia a family of the name of Taliaferro, which has always supposed itself of Italian extraction. The original name is probably Tagliaferro. They are informed that there is a district of country not more than four or five leagues from Florence which bears that name." As Jefferson's letter to Fabbroni continued: "They therefore conjecture that their family came from Tuscany and that their coat of arms (leurs armes) may be found in that country, especially if there be there a Herald's office where such things are registered."

Two days after getting an answer to his inquiry, Jefferson answered Wythe's letters. "I will have the copper plate immediately engraved," Jefferson wrote on August 13, 1786, adding: "They may be ready within a few days, but the probability is that I shall be long getting an opportunity of sending it to you, as these rarely occur. You do not mention the size of the plate but, presuming it is intended for labels for the inside of books, I shall have it made of a proper size for that." In his letter, Jefferson also let Wythe know that "[t]he European papers have announced that the assembly of Virginia were occupied on the re-visal of their Code of law." "This, with some other similar intelligence," Jefferson explained, "has contributed much to convince the people of Europe, that what the English papers are constantly publishing of our anarchy, is false; as they are sensible that such a work is that of a people only who are in perfect tranquility." "Our act for freedom of religion is extremely applauded," Jefferson continued, noting that European ambassadors in France had asked him for copies of it and that it had been reprinted in several books and "in the new Encyclopedie." "I think it will produce considerable good even in these countries where ignorance, superstition, poverty and oppression of body and mind in every form, are so firmly settled on the mass of the people," Jefferson advised. "I think by far the most important bill in our whole code is that for the diffusion of knowledge among the peo-ple," Jefferson observed, explaining: "No other sure foundation can be devised for the preservation of freedom, and happiness. If any body thinks that kings, nobles, or priests are good conservators of the public happiness, send them here. It is the best school in the universe to cure them of that folly." "Preach, my dear Sir, a crusade against ignorance; establish and improve the law for educating the common people," the man from Monti-cello urged Wythe.[43]

Reformers in Connecticut and New York

The death penalty in early American life, as eighteenth-century execution statistics make clear, was not reserved just for murderers. "At the close of the seventeenth century," explains historian Harry Elmer Barnes, "the barbarous English criminal code was in force in varying degrees in all of the English colonies in America, with the sole exception of the Quaker colonies of West Jersey and Pennsylvania." "The notorious 'Blue Laws' of Connecticut, adopted in 1642 and 1650," he writes, provided for fourteen capital crimes; "[t]he Hempstead Code promulgated at Hempstead, Long Island, on March 1, 1665, and introduced into New York as the Duke of York's laws," Barnes writes, "enumerated eleven capital offenses." A law passed in New York in 1788 made sixteen crimes capital offenses, and imprisonment was rarely em-ployed as a method of punishment. "Nearly all who were imprisoned for any considerable period of time were debtors," Barnes notes, explaining that imprisonment for debt was not abolished in New York until laws were passed in 1819 and 1831. The latter law came about only as a result of a concerted campaign against imprisonment for debt led by Louis Dwight of the Boston Prison Discipline Society.[44] After setting out from Boston on horseback in Oc-tober 1824 to deliver miniature bibles to prisoners, Dwight had observed prison conditions first hand throughout the United States. Dwight—who delivered the American Bible Soci-ety's bibles—later published annual reports describing in detail the deplorable conditions in state and county prisons. As Dwight ventured at one point: "There are many miseries to be relieved; many dark places, which are full of cruelty, to be exposed; many minds to be made acquainted with the facts, before the most miserable portion of the human family will be re-lieved."[45] Though Beccaria had favored imprisonment for debt in the first edition of his book, he later renounced that passage, saying, "I blush to have written so cruel a thing."[46]

In colonial and early America, non-lethal corporal punishments were as common as imprisonment for debt. In New York, Barnes writes, "[t]he stocks, pillory, whipping, branding and the ducking-stool were the normal methods used for imposing punishments." Laws passed in New York in 1732, 1736 and 1744 specifically authorized magistrates to prescribe corporal punishments for those charged with minor offenses if they could not furnish bail within forty-eight hours after arrest.[47] In Connecticut, as the biographer of American lawmaker and jurist Oliver Ellsworth (1745–1807) later wrote, "there were criminal causes involving punishments which would now seem barbarous and cruel" and "absurdly inquisitorial and excessively severe." As that biographer, William Brown, wrote:

> [W]hile Ellsworth was on the bench in Connecticut, some severe and curious sentences were handed down. At a session of the Supreme Court in January, 1785, for instance, one Moses Parker, convicted of horse-stealing, was condemned "to sit on the wooden horse half an hour; to receive fifteen stripes, pay a fine of £10; be confined in the gaol and the work house three months; and every Monday morning, for the first month, to receive ten stripes, and sit on the wooden horse as aforesaid."

The "wooden horse," the biographer noted, was simply "a log of wood, supported by four legs," with the criminal taking his "ride" in public, "booted and spurred, usually before a large crowd of amused spectators." At the same session, polygamist Judah Benjamin had ten stripes "laid upon his back; the shameful 'A' was branded on his forehead; and he was ordered to wear a halter about his neck so long as he should tarry in Connecticut, on penalty of thirty stripes if he were ever found without it."

In an earlier case reported elsewhere, Isaac Frasier—convicted of burglary in New Haven—was whipped, branded, and had his ears cropped. After being caught again in Fairfield in 1766, he received a similar punishment, only this time with an added warning: "death would be his punishment on a third Conviction." Despite that stern admonition, Frasier robbed another house. As result, he was sentenced to death, a sentence that ended up being carried out. A pastor at the execution, reflecting on the law's emphasis on vengeance, intoned, "Justice requires that you should suffer." These kind of draconian sentences, though, raised eyebrows, eventually prompting legislative and judicial reform, even as judges—in the meantime—continued applying then-existing law. "Save that the tendency of the times was away from such severity," Oliver Ellsworth's biographer wrote of the sentences handed down in Connecticut before Ellsworth, in 1796, was elevated to be Chief Justice of the U.S. Supreme Court, "it is hardly possible to define the general attitude of Ellsworth and his fellows towards these rigorous laws." But, it is clear that, in the wake of the publication of Beccaria's treatise, a public outcry against such draconian punishments did, as a general matter, follow. As Jill Lepore notes of the reaction to Isaac Frasier's punishment in *The Story of America*: "Two weeks after Frasier's death, a Hartford newspaper published an essay called 'An Answer to a very important Question, viz. Whether any community has a right to punish any species of theft with death?'" "The writer's answer—an emphatic no—borrowed extensively from Cesare Beccaria's 1764 treatise," Lepore emphasizes.[48]

Beccaria's treatise, along with Montesquieu's *Spirit of the Laws*, inspired countless advocates and reform-minded legislators.[49] For example, the Yale-educated Zephaniah Swift, a Federalist and a leading jurist in Connecticut, published a compilation of Connecticut laws in the mid-1790s in which he praised both Beccaria and Montesquieu. Montesquieu's treatise, first published in 1748, had itself inspired Beccaria's own treatise, and Pennsylvania's Beccarian experiment would likewise inspire other American states.[50] In lieu of "sanguinary punishments," Zephaniah Swift noted that Connecticut's legislature had adopted "the principle of punishing a certain class of crimes, by confinement to hard labor and coarse fare."[51] As his comments show, the penal reform efforts in Pennsylvania had, plainly, captivated the nation's attention. As Swift wrote: "The example of the State of Pennsylvania, ought to be mentioned to their honour. It is worthy the attention of every philosopher, and ought to be imitated by every government. They have substituted for all crimes excepting treason and murder in certain degrees, the punishment of *confinement to hard labour, and coarse fare*, instead of death."[52] While complete abolition eluded Connecticut reformers, the death penalty was labeled "that relic of barbarism" and Connecticut's death penalty debate reached what one historian describes as "a crescendo during the 1840s and early 1850s in which hundreds of residents petitioned the General Assembly."[53]

Swift, who became Connecticut's chief justice, was a Yale classmate of Noah Webster — the famous lexicographer who had personal relationships with George Washington, Benjamin Franklin and Benjamin Rush. Swift and Webster — along with Webster's best friend, Joel Barlow — were all members of Yale's Brothers in Unity, a literary society that had a free-lending library comprised of 163 books. And each man, in his own way, would go on to achieve great prominence. Barlow became America's Minister to France, Webster published his famous dictionary, and Swift served in Congress and became the chief justice of the Connecticut Supreme Court. The Brothers in Unity debated and discussed the pressing topics of the day, meticulously recording what they discussed in their minutes. In leafing through the leather-bond minutes of Yale's Brothers in Unity records, it is thus hardly surprising to find entries such as these, from 1796 and 1799 respectively: "Is Suicide ever justifiable?" "Ought capital punishments to be inflicted?" The older rival of the Brothers in Unity, the Linonian Society, had a dozen fewer titles, though a library catalogue of Yale's Linonian Society lists a copy of Beccaria's treatise published in Scotland in 1788.[54] With so much debate going on at Yale, it is little wonder that Jeremiah Mason — a budding lawyer — discovered Beccaria's treatise to use in his "forensic disputation" on capital punishment at his commencement. Mason was part of the Class of 1788, graduating ten years after Swift, Webster and Barlow.[55]

With its lawmakers inspired by Beccaria's ideas and Pennsylvania's example, Connecticut itself witnessed substantial penal reform efforts. "In postrevolutionary Connecticut," writes historian Lawrence Goodheart, "three prominent figures — Joel Barlow, Zephaniah Swift, and Timothy Dwight — argued from different perspectives about the need to reform the death penalty." Barlow, a Jeffersonian Republican, had written in 1792 while in London to the National Convention of France urging that the death penalty be abolished.[56] Barlow said that "punishments in modern times have lost all proportion to the crimes to which they are annexed," and he called for the "total regeneration of society." "To plead that there is a necessity for that desperate remedy," Barlow declared, "proves a want of energy on the government, or of wisdom in the nation."[57] In 1792, Barlow also released in London the second edition of his *Advice to the Privileged Orders in the Several States of Europe, Resulting from the Necessity and Propriety of a General Revolution in the Principles of Government*. In that book, Barlow emphasized that Beccaria's "compassionate little treatise, *dei delitti e delle pene*, is getting to be a manual in all languages" and noted that Beccaria's ideas on reforming criminal codes had been "pursued much farther" in America "than that benevolent philosopher, surrounded as he is by the united sabers of feudal and ecclesiastical tyranny, has dared to pursue it."[58] In another 1792 title, *The Conspiracy of Kings: A Poem Addressed to the Inhabitants of Europe from Another World*, Barlow wrote of "[t]he rights of nature and the gift of God" and penned these lines: *Where Justice reigns, and tyrants tread no more* and *Shake tyrants from their thrones, and cheer the waking world*. His poem to European readers ended with this stirring verse:

> And deign, for once, to turn a transient eye
> To that wide world that skirts the western sky;
> Hail the mild morning, where the dawn began,
> The full fruition of the hopes of man.
> Where sage Experience seals the sacred cause;
> And that rare Union, Liberty and Laws,
> Speaks to the reas'ning race "to freedom rise,
> Like them be equal, and like them be wise."[59]

Timothy Dwight — a Federalist and the grandson of famed theologian Jonathan Edwards — was Yale's president from 1795 to 1817 and a man also familiar with Beccaria's treatise. In 1813, Dwight praised Beccaria's contribution in a lecture to the senior class on the question, "Ought Capital Punishments ever to be inflicted?" While Dwight did not favor the death penalty's total abolition and found aspects of Beccaria's reasoning flawed, Dwight did profess the belief that the number of capital crimes ought to be limited.[60] In the post-Revolutionary War era, the death penalty itself had come under attack, becoming the subject of much public debate and controversy. On the very day that *The Christian Disciple* ran reformer Timothy Dwight's obituary in February 1817, that same publication ran a story in the opposite column about a man sentenced to die for murder. "This event," the publication editorialized, "calls for benevolent sympathy and serious reflection." As that publication stated: "It has become a question with many serious and reflecting men, whether it be either *useful*, or *right*, for human governments to inflict capital punishment in any case whatever; and the question probably deserves more attention than it has yet received."[61]

In the late eighteenth and early nineteenth centuries, the Enlightenment — with all of its fervor and ideas — had thus come to America. Montesquieu and Beccaria, the politician and jurist Zephaniah Swift wrote in his compilation of laws, "had immortalized their names in pleading the cause of humanity." "Our ancestors," Swift emphasized of America's colonists, "were far from being disposed to adopt the sanguinary system of their native country," saying that "[t]hey exploded the idea of inflicting death, upon crimes of a very different nature." "For a few of the most enormous crimes," he explained, "the punishment was death, and for the rest, corporal pains, and pecuniary penalties were inflicted, according to the nature of the offense."[62] For example, Swift noted: "where two, or more assemble for the purpose of doing any unlawful act against the peace, and of which the probable consequence may be bloodshed, as to beat a man, or commit a riot, and one of them kills a man, it is murder in all, because of the illegality of the act and the premeditated wickedness of the design." But as one legal commentator has pointed out, Swift also determined that English common law rules "were authoritative in Connecticut only insofar as Connecticut courts had approved them on grounds of their reason and expedience." Swift, taking a Beccarian approach, wrote that "[t]he supreme excellency of a code of criminal laws consists in defining every act that is punishable with such certainty and accuracy, that no man shall be exposed to the danger of incurring a penalty without knowing it, and which shall not give to courts … an unbounded discretion in punishment."[63]

In the fifth book of *A System of the Laws of the State of Connecticut*, titled "Of Crimes and Punishments," perhaps itself an homage to Beccaria's treatise, Swift wrote in the mid-1790s: "It is a fundamental principle, *that the sole end of punishment is the prevention of crimes, and that every punishment ought to be proportioned to the offence.*" As Swift — a member of Congress from 1793 to 1797 — argued: "It has been ascertained by experience, that mildness of punishment is better calculated to prevent crimes, than severity." "Where the laws are sanguinary, and disproportionate," Swift contended, "officers will be unwilling to prosecute, and jurors will be unwilling to convict: and if an offender should be so unfortunate as to be convicted, he will stand a chance to be deemed a proper object of pardon." "The prospect of escaping the punishment," Swift added, "will diminish its terrors, in the eyes of a criminal." "But when the punishment is mild, and proportionate to the offence," Swift conversely advised, "every person will combine in the punishment of the offender, and a mild punishment when it is certain that it will be inflicted, will operate with far greater force to deter from the commission of crimes, than severe punishments, where it is uncertain whether they will be inflicted, and the offender has a variety of chances to escape."[64] Swift felt that the list of capital crimes—homicide, treason, rape, sodomy, bestiality, dismemberment, mayhem and arson—was far too long. "The dreadful punishment of death," Swift urged, "ought only to be inflicted on those crimes which directly and immediately tend to the destruction of society and the human race, as treason, and murder."[65]

A number of early American publications also took up the cause and examined, in a circumspect way, the death penalty as a punishment. For example, in *Essays on Capital Punishments*, originally published in Connecticut in February 1810 and republished in Philadelphia in 1811, the propriety of the death penalty was vigorously questioned. In writing in response to the question, "Ought the Civil Magistrate to inflict Capital Punishments for Civil Crimes?," one essayist—writing under the pen name "PHILANTHROPOS"—wrote: "This question is very interesting to mankind; and, therefore, demands our most serious attention. In discussing it, I shall advocate the cause of humanity, and endeavour to support the negative." As the essayist, emphasizing that "all penalties ought to be proportionate to the crime," wrote in summarizing the expressed anti-death penalty position: "I shall call in question, the *right*, the *necessity*, and the *expediency* of shedding human blood: and shall endeavour to find substitutes, that would more beneficially answer the true designs of all civil punishments. I shall humbly contend, that no man, nor body of men, ought to inflict the punishment of death on any human being. And this position, I shall attempt to maintain, from reason and from scripture."

Although the essayist did not cite Beccaria, the essayist's arguments almost certainly had Beccarian origins. "In the formation of man," the essayist's first argument read, "God was graciously pleased to endow him with certain rights (such as his life, his conscience, his day of probation, &c.) which are *unalienable*." As the essayist's argument continued: "If no freeman in this state has a right to destroy his own life, or the life of any other human being; then all the freemen assembled together would have no right to do it; and they could not delegate to any person or persons, a right to do it for them: for no delegated person can have more right than all his constituents!" The essayist wrote that "[t]he true end of all punishments is fourfold": "1. To make reparation to the party injured." "2. To reform the offender." "3. To deter others from committing the like crimes." "4. To promote the peace, happiness and security of the community." "The last end," the essayist concluded, "may be attained by securing and confining the criminal: or by banishing and transporting him out of their jurisdiction." "Subjecting him to hard labour and corporeal punishments," the essayist noted, "would deter others, and might reform him." In contrast, the essayist wrote, subjecting a criminal "to death cannot reform him, nor make any reparation to the party injured." "A public execution," it was argued, again in very Beccarian language, might produce "a momentary terror in the spectators, but at the same time, it excites in them the emotions of pity, humanity and sympathy, which incline them to take the part of the sufferer, and to blame those who inflict those sufferings upon him."[66]

The influence of Beccaria and Montesquieu was felt elsewhere, too, as both farmers and city folk turned to Enlightenment writers for guidance. In New York, Thomas Eddy helped prepare the 1796 bill curtailing capital punishment and establishing prison facilities in that state.[67] He drew heavily on both Beccaria and Montesquieu in arguing for reform,[68] and expressed the belief that "[t]he Christian Religion ordains that men should love each other." After visiting Philadelphia to see its penal practices with Philip Schuyler, a Revolutionary War general and a powerful New York legislator, Eddy convinced influential figures to help change the state's antiquated penal code. Among the converted: New York's first governor, George Clinton, and Alexander Hamilton's father-in-law, Philip Schuyler, who had served as a U.S. Senator from New York from 1789 to 1791 and who was the very same man who had accompanied Eddy on his visit to Pennsylvania's prison to evaluate its success.[69] "Upon returning to New York," author Scott Christianson notes, "Eddy enlisted Cadwallader D. Colden to help him draft a comprehensive new penal code, modeled after Pennsylvania's." As an assistant attorney general, Colden would later go head to head in court with other leading lawyers such as Aaron Burr, Alexander Hamilton and Brockholst Livingston. A member of the Society for the Prevention of Pauperism in the City of New York, Colden himself praised Eddy for later serving as the superintendent of the State Prison at Newgate. "Their finished product," Christianson notes of New York's law, "abolished the death penalty in all cases except treason against the state, murder, aiding or abetting murder, and stealing from a church."[70]

In 1794, George Clinton — no doubt paying close attention to Pennsylvania reform efforts — had prepared the way for changes in New York law, reporting to the state's legislature: "[t]he sanguinary complexion of our criminal code has long been a subject of complaint."[71] As Clinton said in his speech, delivered in Albany on January 7, 1794, to a joint session of the legislature: "It is certainly a matter of serious concern, that capital convictions are so frequent, and that so little attention has been hitherto paid to a due proportion between crimes and punishments." "The greatest offences," Clinton said, "occur most frequently in those countries which have been remarkable for the severity of their punishments. Hence it is becoming the policy of modern legislators, to prevent crimes rather by the *certainty* than the *severity* of the sanction." "If you should coincide in sentiment with me, that a revision of our penal laws is entitled to attention," Clinton urged, "I have a confidence that your wisdom and humanity will lead to such improvements as the several cases may require, and a regard to public security will warrant." "Some judicious remarks of the late Attorney General, on the expediency of a reform in this particular, and which have been heretofore communicated to the legislature," Clinton added, "may assist your deliberations." By that time, Aaron Burr had finished his term as New York's attorney general and William Bradford's Beccaria-inspired essay, *An Enquiry How Far the Punishment of Death Is Necessary in Pennsylvania*, written by the former Pennsylvania attorney general, was in circulation. A footnote to a New York compilation of *Messages from the Governors* provides this detail on the call in Governor Clinton's January 1794 annual message for penal reform: "The Assembly committee to which was referred this part of the Governor's speech presented a report recommending the abolition of capital punishment in all cases except treason and willful murder, and the substitution of solitary imprisonment and hard labor." The "punishment of the pillory and whipping," it continued, "ought to be abolished," too.[72]

Even for jurists who felt constrained by the *lex talionis* principle, Beccaria's treatise had an impact. For example, DeWitt Clinton (1769–1828) — the nephew of Governor George Clinton who began studying law in 1786, later becoming a New York governor himself — cited Beccaria on the tendency of governments to concentrate power in the hands of a few.[73] DeWitt Clinton, a naturalist who became a prominent member of the New York bar, a U.S. Senator, and New York's mayor, also called for abolishing "the horrid instruments of capital punishment"[74] and earned a reputation as a judge for showing concern for the right to life. "As a criminal judge," one DeWitt Clinton biographer wrote, "it is admitted even by those who had been his political opponents, that his vigilance, his able and impartial performance of his official duties, especially in those cases involving the life of the offender, furnished a model worthy of imitation by all who occupy that highly important and responsible situation: for in him were happily united a most strict attention to the merits of the case, with the most devoted leaning to the feelings of humanity." As that biographer, David Hosack, a friend of his subject, explained in 1829:

> Mr. Clinton did not entertain the opinion expressed by some late philanthropists, that capital punishments are unnecessary or unjust. Believing with the most enlightened authorities, Beccaria, Blackstone, and the late Sir Samuel Romilly, that the certainty of punishment was the best security for the prevention of crime, our statute book bears witness to the wisdom of his counsels in mitigating the severity of the English criminal code; and during his performance of the duties of judge, as assigned to him in his office of mayor, the culprit was equally aware of the clemency of the magistrate, and of the certainty of punishment in the case of conviction; but while in his view the destruction of human life could only be expiated by the lex talionis, he was determined that the last punishment of the law should be inflicted on those who were the wanton instruments of its violation.
>
> But even then no man was more willing to listen to, or eager to discover any circumstance calculated to mitigate the crime that had been committed; to this purport we have the concurrent testimony of all who practiced in the court in which the mayor presided, while he filled that honourable and responsible office. By a gentleman who many years held an official station at his side, and of opposite political sentiments, he is represented to have been "cautious, attentive, of kind temper, patient of investigation, and discriminating with great care; and in a word, that upon all occasions he acquitted himself as the pure, impartial, patient, and upright magistrate, one of the safest men that ever presided in a criminal court, and ever uniting mercy with justice." It was also the remark of a late eminent counsel, who was frequently engaged in his court as the favourite defender of that unfortunate class found at the bar of the court of criminal jurisprudence, that in any capital trial De Witt Clinton was, in his estimation, superior to any judge he had ever known.[75]

Other New Yorkers had also come to be ambivalent about executions, sparking the movement in New York to abolish them. Alexander Hamilton, for example, thought executions necessary, but recognized that "[t]he temper of our country, is not a little opposed to the frequency of capital punishment." To prevent desertions, Hamilton expressed the view in 1799 to Lieutenant Colonel Josias Carvel Hall that "a few examples of capital punishment, perhaps one in each regiment, will be found indispensable." Hall had the idea of substituting hard labor—and perhaps branding "on some conspicuous Part of the Face" with a "hot Iron"—for death sentences for ordinary cases of desertion, reserving the punishment of death for soldiers for "the high aggravation of deserting from their Post misbehaving before the Enimy." "In European Armies Desertion is punished with Death," Hall had written to Hamilton on October 4, 1799, emphasizing that "[t]o American Habits of thinking this appears inadequate—every alleviatiting Circumstance is laid hold of the Court, & of those condemned very few are exicuted." "The Spirit of the American Constitution & Laws will not admit of runing the Gantlosse &c," Hall had added of *running the gauntlet*, a practice used in the Continental Army and by European armies to punish deserters, with the offending soldier repeatedly running between two lines of his comrades and being struck repeatedly with switches, sometimes resulting in the deserter's death.

In *The Federalist No. 74*, Hamilton—writing in the late 1780s—had himself specifically defended the Constitution's proposed presidential pardoning power, saying it was needed to avoid "sanguinary" or "cruel" results.[76] Though many Americans remained resistant to change, notice of Beccaria's writings in Hamilton's home state pre-dated the Revolutionary War, with the Rivington, New York *Gazetter* advertising Beccaria's treatise as being "in press" in 1773.[77] Though the Revolutionary War put reform efforts on hold, after the Revolutionary War ended, concrete actions were taken up fairly expeditiously to ameliorate the harsh laws that were then in place. As one source notes: "The failings of the colonial system were not lost upon New Yorkers in the aftermath of independence. They quickly moved to abolish the harsh statutory codes of colonial days."[78]

The cultural shift that took place in New York began in earnest in the 1780s and—as in Pennsylvania—solidified in the 1790s. As University of Connecticut professor Sharon Harris writes: "Although the anti-capital punishment arguments began during the 1788 legislative session, it was in 1791 that they most fully entered the political arena in such periodicals as the New York *Daily Gazette*." Dr. Samuel Latham Mitchell (1764–1831), a chemistry professor at Columbia College, published an essay on the need for cultural change, including abolition of the death penalty. Mitchell had studied medicine at the University of Edinburgh, and served in the New York State Assembly in the 1790s before becoming a U.S. Senator from New York in 1804. "The scientist Samuel Mitchell," notes Stuart Banner in *The Death Penalty: An American History*, "grouped capital punishment with slavery, duelling, and imprisonment for debt as vestiges of a lesser age, relics 'which doubtless will be done away when right reason shall gain the ascendency over the human mind.'" At the center of New York's intellectual life, Columbia itself became a popular place for debate. Formerly known as King's College, the university's early students and trustees included John Jay, Alexander Hamilton, Gouverneur Morris and Robert R. Livingston. By 1793, *The New-York Magazine* was printing multiple pieces in opposition to capital punishment, including William Bradford's *Enquiry How Far the Punishment of Death Is Necessary in Pennsylvania*—an essay that New York legislators were urged to consult in their deliberations. "Anti-capital punishment thinkers drew heavily on the writings of Voltaire and Montesquieu," but especially on Beccaria, Sharon Harris notes.[79]

Though a 1788 law in New York had prescribed imprisonment for disorderly conduct, "the true beginning of the use of imprisonment" as a method of punishing crime, writes another historian of that state's penal system, "may be dated from the passage of the act of March 26, 1796, passed on the basis of the recommendations of Governor John Jay, General Philip Schuyler, Thomas Eddy, and Ambrose Spencer, and drawn from a study of the contemporary reforms in the adjoining state of Pennsylvania."[80] Philip Schuyler—elected to the Continental Congress in 1775 before serving in the Revolutionary War as a Continental Army major general—has been described as "one of the most powerful men in the New York legislature," while Ambrose Spencer was called "the most articulate." It was Spencer—a graduate of Yale and Harvard who later served as New York's chief justice—who introduced the penal reform bill that became law in 1796. Spencer had served in the New York assembly and in the state senate between 1793 and 1802, and his second and third wives were DeWitt Clinton's sisters.[81] On January 6, 1796, then-Governor John Jay had given a speech to New York legislators in which he, like Governor George Clinton before him, pushed for legislative reform. As Jay said in his address: "It continues to be worthy of consideration how far the severe penalties prescribed by our laws in particular cases admit of mitigation; and whether certain establishments for confining, employing and reforming criminals will not immediately become indispensible."[82]

Years later, Beccaria's treatise was still being studied and regularly invoked in the state.[83] For example, one of New York's premier lawyers, David Dudley Field, was knowledgeable about Beccaria's work. In "Reminiscences of David Dudley Field," one of his friends, a Harvard Law School graduate and fellow New York lawyer A. Oakey Hall, recalled in 1894 that Field had made "ameliorating and advancing jurisprudence" his "life work." In his remembrance, Hall recalled his interactions, writing: "During thirteen years of my district-attorneyship in New York City I was honored with frequent consultations by Mr. Field in respect to the preparation, revision and final report of the codes of criminal procedure and penal code." "I beg to testify to his utter absence of pride of opinion in that work," Hall noted, recounting Field's "marvelous knowledge of the ins and outs of the science of criminal jurisprudence." As Hall reported of Field's vast knowledge: "Beccaria, Bentham (who owed so much to Beccaria), and all the English-writing authors on criminal jurisprudence from Chitty and Archbold to the days of Stephens, Wharton and Bishop, were his very familiars." Among today's lawyers, David Dudley Field is best known for codifying New York's code of civil procedure, with the eminent legal scholar Roscoe Pound comparing the importance of Field's work in that arena in the 1850s and 1860s to Beccaria's earlier efforts as regards the criminal law. "It," Pound observed of Field's work, "stands toward procedure in the world of the common law where Beccaria's treatise on Crimes and Punishments stood toward the nineteenth-century criminal law. It showed the way."[84]

A National Movement

The reform movement that started in Pennsylvania swept through the United States, influencing laws in both northern and southern states. "Between 1794 and 1798," writes law professor Stuart Banner in *The Death Penalty: An American History*, "five states abolished the death penalty for all crimes other than murder, and three of the five even abolished it for certain kinds of murder." After Pennsylvania enacted its statute, Virginia, New York and New Jersey passed their own legislative reforms, with Kentucky following suit in 1798.[85] Virginia's 1796 law made only premeditated murder and felony murders punishable by death and even treason was punishable by confinement; New York's 1796 law — modeled largely on Pennsylvania's experience — passed thanks to the support of Governor John Jay and the bill's influential allies.[86] New York, one source explained of the history of that state's penitentiary system, "was not slow to follow in the track of a more enlightened penal policy," in which Pennsylvania had "the honor of leading the way." Thomas Eddy and General Schuyler, that writer emphasized, had visited the Philadelphia prison and been so favorably impressed that they pushed for reform in their own state.[87] "Following the lead of Virginia in 1796," notes historian Michael Meranze, "all of the Southern states except North and South Carolina built new penitentiaries before the Civil War."[88] In Pennsylvania, though it never came to fruition, the state's governor, Simon Snyder, even urged the legislature to abolish capital punishment altogether in 1809 and 1811.[89]

New Jersey residents also advocated for law reform as Beccaria's treatise gained traction. In 1799, William Griffith, writing under the pseudonym "Eumenes," published *A Collection of Papers, Written for the Purpose of Exhibiting Some of the More Prominent Errors and Omissions of the Constitution of New-Jersey*. In a chapter titled "Amendments to the Judiciary System Suggested," Griffith argued for "the *independence*" of "a well organized judicature." Asking for a "*total* reorganization" of that state's judiciary in terms of judge's

compensation, "the mode of appointment," "the term of duration," "the designation of powers," and "the grades of appeal," Griffith contended: "Were these great points once attained, it would give a stability, a beauty, and a felicity to the administration of the laws,
which would render them the objects of veneration, and the means of security, instead
of being, as they are now, spectacles of contempt, and instruments of oppression." Seeing "the *uncertainty* of the laws" and "the *incompetency* of the judiciary" as major problems, Griffith feared "error, confusion, delay, and ruinous expense" until the judiciary
was reformed. "I shall conclude the very imperfect sketch which has been traced of the
defects in the judiciary of New-Jersey," he wrapped up his observations, "with a remark
and an admonition of the marquis of Beccaria, in his *twenty-third* chapter, upon 'the idea
of reformation' in the laws." As Griffith concluded his chapter, quoting Beccaria's words:
"'In short (he says) to what side fo[r]ever we turn our eyes, we are presented with a confused scene of contradictions, uncertainty, hardships, and arbitrary power: in the present age we seem universally aiming at perfection; let us not therefore neglect to perfect
the laws, on which our *lives* and *fortunes* depend."[90]

And the influence of Enlightenment writers would be keenly felt well into the nineteenth
century as penal reformers remained conversant with Montesquieu's *Spirit of the Laws*
and Beccaria's *On Crimes and Punishments*. Robert Rantoul, Jr.—the Massachusetts reformer and opponent of capital punishment—also intensely studied Beccaria and Montesquieu in the 1820s while attending Harvard College and would later invoke Beccaria's
stirring words against executions. Rantoul called Beccaria "that extraordinary man."[91] A
Harvard library catalog, published in 1830, lists three Beccaria titles, including "Dei Delitti
e delle Pene" and "On Crimes," demonstrating the ready availability of Beccaria's treatise
during that time.[92] And 1844 saw the publication, in Philadelphia, of *A Brief Statement
of the Argument for the Abolition of the Death Punishment in Twelve Essays*, more than one
of which mentioned Beccaria. "At least in part as a result of Beccaria's writings, combined
with the Enlightenment thinking that influenced the framers of the Constitution," writes
one law professor, summarizing the shift in American law, "some prominent early Americans, including Benjamin Franklin, John Jay, James Madison, and Thomas Jefferson, advocated limiting the death penalty to the most serious offenses."[93] As historian Bradley Chapin
emphasizes: "In those jurisdictions where the reformers succeeded, the influence of the
Enlightenment rationalists, of Montesquieu and Beccaria, is written all over the record."[94]

In addition to arguments appealing to reason and citing Enlightenment writers, anti-
death penalty appeals also continued to include other secular and religious arguments, including ones based on specific scriptural passages. "Although leaders of the anti-gallows
movement relied heavily on the rational arguments of Montesquieu, Voltaire, and Beccaria," writes historian David Brion Davis, "they also profited from the rise of evangelical religion and from the romantic sympathy for criminals and outcasts expressed in the fiction
and poetry of Bulwer-Lytton, Dickens, Victor Hugo, William Gilmore Simms, Sylvester
Judd, and John Greenleaf Whittier." "In 1832," notes another historian, Louis Filler, "a report to the New York legislature citing Beccaria, Franklin, and Livingston, as well as the
standard Bible arguments, and the usual appeals to precedence, in this case Russian, Tuscany, and periods in Egyptian and Roman history, introduced a bill to end capital punishment."
The novelist Victor Hugo, in an 1829 work of fiction about capital punishment, *Le Dernier
Jour d'un condamné*, made specific reference to Beccaria in his preface.[95]

In the 1830s, the State of Maine took its own concrete step toward abolition. At the
end of 1835, Edward Livingston—who had unsuccessfully tried to abolish the death
penalty in Louisiana in 1832 and 1834—wrote to Tobias Purrington, a Maine legislator.
Copies of Livingston's draft penal code were distributed to Maine's governor and state
legislators, and Purrington wrote a report incorporating Livingston's arguments. As part

of the successful effort led by Purrington and Thomas Upham, a Bowdoin professor of moral and mental philosophy, the northern state passed what came to be known as the "Maine law." Under that law, condemned criminals were confined in the state prison for one year after their sentencing proceedings and could be executed only upon a written warrant issued by the state's governor. The Maine law, as that state's governor put it in 1849, had led to the "general impression" that capital punishment had been abolished in the state; executions were rare there before the law took effect, and in his annual message to the state legislature in 1849, Governor Carlos Coolidge spoke of "the impropriety of enforcing the death penalty while such an impression exists."

Another legislative compromise—aimed at doing away with public executions while retaining capital punishment—also began to occur in the 1830s as states in New England began moving toward non-public executions. A Pennsylvania law passed in 1834 spoke of executions "within the walls or yard of the jail"; New York enacted a private execution law in 1835; and in 1836, in his annual address, Massachusetts Governor Edward Everett—expressing the sensitivities of the day—emphasized that "an increasing tenderness for human life is one of the most decided characteristics of the civilization of the day." "A grave question has been started whether it would be safe altogether to abolish the punishment of death," Everett said, continuing: "Whether it can, with safety to the community, be carried so far as to permit the punishment of death to be entirely dispensed with, is a question not yet decided by philanthropists and legislators. It may deserve your consideration whether this interesting question cannot be brought to the test of the sure teacher,—experience." As Everett, seeking an answer one way or the other to the question, concluded: "An experiment, instituted and pursued for a sufficient length of time, might settle it on the side of mercy. Such a decision would be matter of cordial congratulation. Should a contrary result ensue, it would probably reconcile the public mind to the continued infliction of capital punishment as a necessary evil."

In 1837 and 1838, Ohio's governor, Joseph Vance, also pushed for repeal, though legislative committees in that state declined to act, even as a nationwide push for private executions—finally concluded in the 1930s—continued apace. Death penalty opponents, believing public executions would spur on abolitionist sentiment, initially resisted the passage of private execution laws, though abolitionists eventually acquiesced in the passage of such laws. Their logic: the removal of public executions would effectively disprove the notion that executions somehow deterred crime. In Ohio, Governor Vance—a death penalty opponent—had called capital punishment "a relic of barbarism, that ought to be struck from the code of civilized nations." While his views did not carry the day, Ohio's shift to non-public executions was part of the national trend in that direction. "In 1844," notes one historian of Ohio's experience, "lawmakers in Columbus were so appalled by the spectacle surrounding the double hanging of Foster and Clark in February that they approved a bill in March banning public executions, instead requiring sheriffs to hold executions in or around the jail and inside enclosures tall enough to hide the gallows." On February 9, 1844, thousands of people had flocked to the gallows in Columbus, Ohio, to see convicted killers James Clark, a white man, and Esther Foster, a black woman, put to death.[96]

The advocates for total abolition of capital punishment had their first successes in the 1840s and 1850s. Michigan became the first state to abolish capital punishment for homicide in 1847, and Rhode Island and Wisconsin abolished the death penalty in the early 1850s. In Wisconsin, a crusading state senator, Marvin Bovee, led that state's fight to abolish capital punishment and later became a national leader in the anti-death penalty movement. "[T]he experience of many foreign states," Bovee would write of his abolitionist views, "has shown that the abolition of the capital penalty has increased the certainty of punishment, whilst greatly decreasing the crimes." This idea came directly from Beccaria, as Bovee made clear. "The motto of Beccaria," Bovee explained, "is of permanent truth: 'It is the certainty, rather than the severity, of punishment which constitutes its efficiency." As Bovee wrote of Beccaria's maxim: "The wisdom of this conclusion has been abundantly proved by the experience of the states where capital punishment has been totally abolished, as in Wisconsin, Rhode Island, Portugal, Tuscany, and several of the Swiss Cantons, and German Principalities; and also where the death penalty has been nearly or virtually abolished as in Russia, Austria, Bavaria, Würtemberg, Baden, Belgium, Maine, Pennsylvania, etc."

The fact that Marvin Bovee's 1869 book, *Christ and the Gallows: or, Reasons for the Abolition of Capital Punishment*, referred to Montesquieu and Beccaria shows that Enlightenment writers were still being discussed — and were still relevant to the public discourse — even after the Civil War. "The philosophy of penal legislation has in no country been more carefully investigated than in Italy," Bovee wrote in a chapter titled "Progress in Penal Legislation." As Bovee recounted: "The Marquis Beccaria, in 1764, published a work entitled, *Dei Delitti e delle Pene*, which produced a marked effect upon the public sentiment of that day. The *judicial* murder of Calas, at Toulouse, which caused a European sensation, a short time prior to the publication of Beccaria's work, occasioned, without doubt, the publication of the work referred to." "One of the French authors," Bovee continued in an allusion to the French *philosophes*, "is said to have written to a member of the Milan Literary Society: 'Now is the time to rise against religious intolerance and the exaggerated severity of penal legislation.' Beccaria, who was a member of this literary club, and a zealous reader of French authors, especially Montesquieu, Helvetius, and Condillac, was thus incited to write the work referred to, and which has made him famous in the history of penal reform."[97]

Even in the twentieth century, which brought World War I and World War II, Enlightenment writers continued to be read and consulted. A treatise on executive clemency in Pennsylvania, published in 1909 by Philadelphia lawyer William Smithers, illustrates just how influential Enlightenment writers were at that century's start. Montesquieu's *L'Esprit des Lois*, that source reports, "was recognized as a concentrated and perfected expression of ideas which for more than a century had been but outlined or partially explained by others." "The bases of rational government and the science of ruling were presented with unexcelled vigor and logic," Smithers reported of Montesquieu. Smithers' *Treatise on Executive Clemency in Pennsylvania* credited a long list of writers with effecting the change in public sentiment toward criminals. "During the latter part of eighteenth century," Smithers wrote, "the intellectual awakening of the world culminated in a general modification of views in both criminology and penology through the writings of Hobbes, Locke, Hale, Hawkins, Blackstone, Hume, Howard and Bentham in England, and Grotius, Pufendorf, La Bruyére, D'Aguesseau, Montesquieu, Voltaire, Rousseau, Thomasius and Beccaria on the continent." "From this period," Smithers explained, "the barbarous treatment of the accused before and after conviction began to abate and a new basis for criminal law grew up in which ferocity was tempered by ethical considerations." "Some writers," Smithers noted, "have denominated this the classical school of criminology in which individualism has always been prominent." "This system is fundamentally that of England and America to-day," Smithers added, emphasizing that "[e]quality of punishment for similar crimes" had become a special feature of the classical school of criminology.

Although Smithers mentioned Beccaria last in his list of writers who awakened Europe to the cause of penal reform, Smithers made clear that Beccaria deserved the most credit for the change in public attitudes. This new way of thinking, Smithers wrote, "received its greatest impetus from the work of the Marquis Beccaria who summarized the ideas of his own age including even those of Rousseau published but two years before." Taking note of the fact that *Dei delitti e delle pene* was published in 1764, Smithers wrote that Beccaria had "exercised a powerful influence" and "served to focus the philosophical and political discussions upon the many defects in the criminal law." "It has been said," Smithers wrote, "that never had so small a book created so great an effect." "Under his assault," Smithers explained, "the traditional vengeance visited upon a wrongdoer by right of the *lex talionis* wavered before the demand for rational treatment of criminals as human beings." "In the Declaration of Rights of 1789," Smithers wrote of French law, "France proclaimed the limitation of punishment by necessity and in the Constitution of 1793 declared that the law should prescribe only unavoidably necessary penalties, proportioned to the crimes for which inflicted and such as should be beneficial to society." Smithers further noted that, in the U.S., Roberts Vaux, Edward Livingston and Francis Lieber — men who lived after Beccaria — made subsequent contributions, giving added "form and direction to the American theory of punishment."[98]

Early American Pamphlets and Printers

Most significantly, Beccaria's treatise had a major impact on Americans' thinking well before America's foundational legal documents were put in place. Even before the ratification of the U.S. Bill of Rights in 1791, Beccaria's name — either by itself or right alongside Montesquieu's — was invoked in American newspapers and periodicals. For example, a 1789 edition of *The American Museum* — printed in Philadelphia by Mathew Carey and considered to be America's first literary magazine[99] — specifically referenced Beccaria. "The marquis of Beccaria," noted Dr. Benjamin Rush in *The American Museum*, "has established a connexion between the abolition of capital punishments, and the order and happiness of society."[100] As of 1787, when *The American Museum* published Dr. Rush's essay, which had been read at Benjamin Franklin's house and that mentions Beccaria's "excellent treatise," the magazine had about 1,250 subscribers,[101] among them some of the most influential men of the day.[102] "Among the nearly five hundred subscribers to *The American Museum*," one scholar, Jennings Wagoner, has noted of a time when the subscription numbers were not even quite so high, "were George Washington, Alexander Hamilton, Benjamin Franklin, James Madison, and Thomas Jefferson."

Later in life, Dr. Rush himself noted that Scotland — where he studied medicine, receiving his degree in 1768 — had given him his sense of republicanism, and that the "same republican ferment produced similar commotions … upon the subjects of education, penal laws and capital punishments, — upon each of which I published a number of essays in the 'American Museum,' the 'Columbian Magazine,' and other periodical works." "A selection of them," Rush noted, "has since been published in an octavo volume by Samuel Bradford of Philadelphia."[103] Dr. Rush was — first and foremost — a physician, and in interacting with patients, he offered both treatment advice and political prescriptions, building relationships with the people he met. "In the autumn of 1794," Dr. Rush wrote in a defense of the practice of bloodletting to combat yellow fever, "I was sent for to visit Samuel Bradford, a young man of about 20 years of age, son of Mr. Thomas Bradford, who was ill with the reigning malignant epidemic." The personal interactions between Dr. Rush and the Bradford family, including with William Bradford, Jr., would play a key role, it turned out, as Dr. Rush proselytized against the death penalty. The Bradford family had easy access to the print media, and by the time the Italian botanist, Luigi Castiglioni, visited Philadelphia in 1786, William Bradford, Jr. was already an ardent convert to Beccaria's writings.[104] The public's repeated exposure to Beccaria's enlightened ideas—prompted by publicity given to those ideas by people like Dr. Rush, Mathew Carey, and Samuel and William Bradford—would ultimately help shape American public opinion.

The connections between Dr. Rush and the Bradford family ran especially deep, as did the personal relationships between William Bradford, Jr. and luminaries such as James Madison and George Washington. Thomas Bradford (1745–1838), Dr. Rush's friend, was the eldest son of Colonel William Bradford—the official printer of the Continental Congress and the publisher of the *Pennsylvania Journal*. Thomas assisted his father in the family's newspaper business and continued working in that business after his father's death in 1791. Samuel Bradford, Thomas' son, was Dr. Rush's patient and friend, and published *The Imposter Detected*, in which he accused William Cobbett of working secretly for the British government. Both Thomas and Samuel Bradford, from the highly respected family of printers, published Dr. Rush's writings, thereby increasing the doctor's profile and prominence. Thomas Bradford's younger brother, William Bradford, Jr., was the namesake and second son of their father, Colonel William Bradford; fought in the Continental Army; became a lawyer and a jurist; developed a close friendship with Dr. Rush; and became Pennsylvania's attorney general. Later, he became the country's leading lawyer: the Attorney General of the United States.

In the spring of 1769, shortly after the first English-language version of Beccaria's treatise appeared, William Bradford, Jr. had began his studies at Princeton, where he formed his life-long friendship with his fellow student, James Madison. As one of James Madison's biographers writes of his subject's experience: "At college James was thrown together with more than one hundred classmates from different colonies. For twenty-one weeks each semester, he and the others lived at Nassau Hall. Among his closest friends was William Bradford, the son of a printer." Bradford—who, it has been written, "will long be remembered in honorable connection" with "the amelioration of the penal code and the restriction of capital punishment"—later counted President George Washington as a friend, among many other important relationships.[105] While most Pennsylvania judges had initially opposed penal reform, Bradford—joining forces with Dr. Rush, Benjamin Franklin and Caleb Lownes—fought to reform the state's sanguinary system of laws. "He associated himself to the labours of Caleb Lownes," Duke de la Rochefoucauld-Liancourt wrote of Bradford's pivotal role in the effort, "aiding him with the advice of a man versed in jurisprudence; and, having shared the difficulties, he deserved to share in the glories of the undertaking."[106]

State Constitutions and Declarations of Rights

Beccaria's words—written from afar—altered the debate in the U.S. as early Americans drew up new constitutions.[107] The Virginia Declaration of Rights, adopted by Virginia's Constitutional Convention on June 12, 1776, included the following language in its preamble: "That all men are by nature equally free and independent and have certain inherent rights, of which, when they enter into a state of society, they cannot, by any compact, deprive or divest their posterity; namely, the enjoyment of life and liberty, with the means of acquiring and possessing property, and pursuing and obtaining safety and happiness." Another portion of the Virginia Declaration spoke forthrightly of "the duty which we owe to our Creator," asserting "it is the mutual duty of all to practise Christian forbearance, love, and charity toward each other." Like the English Bill of Rights of 1689, the Virginia Declaration also declared: "That excessive bail ought not to be required, nor excessive fines imposed, nor cruel and unusual punishments inflicted." Though George Mason—seeking to ensure that Virginians would have the same rights as Englishmen—borrowed that language directly from an English antecedent, Beccaria's denunciation of cruelty colored Virginians' views of what that language actually meant in their own time.

Shortly after the Continental Congress declared America's independence, the State of Maryland also adopted a new constitution. In August 1776, Maryland delegates approved a declaration of rights that contained two separate clauses addressing cruel acts. Clause 14 read: "That sanguinary Laws ought to be avoided, as far as is consistent with the safety of the State: and no law, to inflict cruel and unusual pains and penalties, ought to be made in any case, or at any time hereafter."[108] Bills of attainder, specifically outlawed across the board by the U.S. Constitution in the late 1780s, were once used by legislative bodies to sentence people to death without the participation of juries. Bills of pains and penalties—as the U.S. Supreme Court itself has emphasized—were "simply a subspecies of bills of attainder, the only difference being that the punishment was something less than death."[109] Meanwhile, clause 22 of Maryland's 1776 declaration of rights—while differing slightly, from a textual standpoint, from the language of the English Bill of Rights of 1689—provided: "That excessive bail ought not to be required, nor excessive fines imposed, nor cruel or unusual punishments inflicted, by the courts of law." When the citizens of Massachusetts adopted their own constitution in 1780, it, too, contained a similar clause. "No magistrate or court of law," the relevant clause read, "shall demand excessive bail or sureties, impose excessive fines, or inflict cruel or unusual punishments."[110] John Adams—as legal scholars Deborah A. Schwartz and Jay Wishingrad point out—was not only "well acquainted with Beccaria" but "was involved in the formulation of the Massachusetts Bill of Rights in 1780."[111]

The Anglo-Saxon world was, in the seventeenth and eighteenth centuries, engaged in an extended and fierce debate about whether cruel punishments were permissive and absolutely necessary and, if so, which ones. A 1701 pamphlet advocating particularly brutal executions doubted that "a Community may secure it self, as it best can, without Cruelty; since one would judge so well of Human Nature, as to believe that such harsh methods would not be made use of, before they are absolutely necessary." The title of the pamphlet—*Hanging Not Punishment Enough for Murtherers, High-way Men, and House-breakers*—says about all that needs to be said about the writer's views. In contrast, a writer in *The New-York Magazine*, writing in 1794 under the pseudonym "Valentine," believed capital punishment should be eliminated entirely, illustrating the wide spectrum of eighteenth-century opinion that existed. "Would it not be a more rational punishment, instead of inflicting death on a murderer," the pseudonymous author wrote, "to condemn him to hard labor in a prison for the remainder of his life, and the product of such labor applied to the use of the widow or children of the person murdered?"[112]

This debate about capital punishment occurred in both England and America. For instance, a 1728 essay by William Hay, a member of Parliament and later appointed keeper of the records in the Tower of London, read in part: "Sanguinary Laws ought to be avoided in a State as much as possible; for although they strike a greater Terror into the Living, yet they lose another End of Punishment, which is the Amendment of the Offenders." An especially popular 1771 treatise authored by William Eden, the brother of Robert Eden, Maryland's last colonial governor, also contained this statement: "Nothing however, but the evident result of absolute necessity, can authorize the destruction of mankind at the hand of man." As that treatise, *Principles of Penal Law*, continued: "The infliction of Death is not therefore to be considered in any instance, as a mode of punishment, but merely as our last melancholly resource in the extermination of those from society, whose continuance among their fellow-citizens is become inconsistent with the public safety." Other European writings that attracted the attention of American founders such as Alexander Hamilton, Thomas Jefferson and James Madison included the radical English political philosopher William Godwin, whose *Enquiry concerning Political Justice and Its Influence on General Virtue and Happiness* was published in London in 1793. In that book, Godwin wrote of "inhuman punishments" and criticized "the number of capital offences" set forth in the English criminal law, noting that a consequence of the frequency of pardons was opening wide a door "to favour and abuse." "Hundreds of victims are annually sacrificed at the shrine of positive law and political institution," Godwin wrote, emphasizing that society's "most approved and established methods of persuading men to obedience" up to that time had been axes, chains, gibbets, racks and whips.[113]

In the United States, America's founders weighed in decidedly on the side of *avoiding* cruelty. The Northwest Ordinance, drafted by Massachusetts lawyer Nathan Dane, and agreed to in 1787, unequivocally prohibited "cruel or unusual punishments," and the Eighth Amendment—ratified in 1791—also barred "cruel and unusual punishments."[114] In *The History of the State of Rhode Island and Providence Plantations*, in a section of the book on the struggle for independence, one finds these words reflecting the impact of Enlightenment writers on American sentiment: "Questions as to Colonial rights and parliamentary wrongs were raised and considered. Grotius, Locke, Beccaria and Burlamaqui were studied and their conclusions carefully weighed and by many minds adopted." "The Dutch jurist, statesman, and poet Hugo Grotius," notes another historian, "had written in 1625 that human reason, not religious explanation, formed the basis of man's understanding of natural law." As that historian, Robert A. Ferguson, explains: "Grotius' confidence in secular inquiry and his insistence that law be presented in 'an orderly fashion' and in 'a compendious form' provided the inspiration for Samuel von Pufendorf's *Of the Law of Nature and Nations* (1673), Jean Jacques Burlamaqui's *Principles of Natural and Politic Law* (1747–1751), Baron de Montesquieu's *Spirit of Laws* (1748), William Blackstone's *Commentaries on the Laws of England* (1765–1769), and related works by such figures as Emmerich de Vattel, Lord Kames, and Cesare Beccaria."[115]

Quickly on the heels of the issuance of America's Declaration of Independence, American lawmakers thus promulgated provisions to protect offenders from governmental abuses. For example, Delaware's Declaration of Rights, adopted in September 1776, contained the following provisions: "That retrospective laws, punishing offences committed before the existence of such laws, are oppressive and unjust, and ought not to be made." "That trial by jury of facts where they arise is one of the greatest securities of the lives, liberties and estates of the people." "That in all prosecutions for criminal offences, every man hath a right to be informed of the accusation against him, to be allowed counsel, to be confronted with the accusers or witnesses, to examine evidence on oath in his favour, and to a speedy trial by an impartial jury, without whose unanimous consent he ought not to be found guilty." Section 15 of Delaware's declaration further guaranteed "[t]hat no man in the Courts of Common Law ought to be compelled to give evidence against himself," whereas section 16—modeled on similar provisions in other states—read: "That excessive bail ought not to be required, nor excessive fines imposed, nor cruel or unusual punishments inflicted." In contrast, Connecticut's Declaration of Rights, also adopted in 1776, used these words: "no Man's Person shall be restrained, or imprisoned, by any Authority whatsoever, before the Law hath sentenced him thereunto, if he can and will give sufficient Security, Bail, or Mainprize for his Appearance and good Behaviour in the mean Time, unless it be for Capital Crimes, Contempt in open Court, or in such Cases wherein some express Law doth allow of, or order the same."[116]

Many lawyers and judges—the men most steeped in law—participated in the drafting of early American constitutions, and they were very familiar, if not intimately conversant, with Beccaria's writings on the need for law reform. For instance, the drafting committee that prepared Maryland's "declaration and charter of rights, and a plan of government," had a number of members who had studied or intersected with the law as part of their professional responsibilities. Its chair, Matthew Tilghman, was a justice of the peace for Talbot County and the president of Maryland's convention. The other members of the committee were barrister Charles Carroll, a doctor's son who had studied law in England before returning to practice in Annapolis; his cousin, Charles Carroll of Carrollton, the only Roman Catholic signer of the American Declaration of Independence, who had also studied law in England; Italian-American William Paca, a successful lawyer, Maryland's first governor, and another signer of the Declaration of Independence; lawyer George Plater, educated at Virginia's William and Mary; Samuel Chase, yet another signer of the Declaration of Independence and later an associate justice of the U.S. Supreme Court; and Robert Goldsborough, another barrister.[117]

George Washington's friend, Charles Carroll of Carrollton, played an especially prominent role in the American Revolution. He counted Samuel Chase as one of his many allies, and in 1776 the Continental Congress—at Chase's urging—sent Charles Carroll of Carrollton on an important diplomatic mission to try to improve relations with French-speaking Catholics in Canada. "Should it fall into the hands of The Enemy," American patriots feared aloud, expressing concerns about British designs on their northern neighbor, "they will soon raise a Nest of Hornets on our backs that will Sting us to the quick." Chase—now most famous for having been the only U.S. Supreme Court Justice to be impeached—had recommended his friend Charles to John Adams. Chase did so because of Charles's "attachment and zeal to the Cause, his Acquaintance with the Language, Manner & Customs of France and his Religion, with the circumstances of a very great Estate." These attributes, in Chase's view, "all point him out to that all important Service."[118]

On February 15, 1776, the Continental Congress—after considering its choices—chose Dr. Benjamin Franklin, Samuel Chase and Charles Carroll of Carrollton "to proceed to Canada, there to pursue such instructions as shall be given them by Congress." It was also "Resolved" that "Mr. Carroll be requested to prevail on Mr. John Carroll"—his cousin—to accompany the committee to Canada, to assist them in such matters as they shall think useful." John Carroll (1735–1815) was the first Roman Catholic archbishop in the United States, serving in the Archdiocese of Baltimore and becoming the founder of Georgetown University. "It was through Franklin's influence," one source notes, "that Father John Carroll was made head of the American Catholic hierarchy." In America, Father Carroll would, in 1814, later rejoice at the restoration of the Society of Jesus, the religious congregation of male Catholics whose members are known as Jesuits. From 1773 to 1814, the Society of Jesus—founded by Ignatius of Loyola in 1534, and dedicated to religious and charitable work in Italy and, later, throughout the world—had been outlawed by Pope Clement XIV and the Roman Catholic Church. "Father John Carroll," notes one of his biographers, "was one of the very few English-speaking Jesuits who were at Rome during the period immediately preceding the Suppression." In Rome from 1772 to 1773, Father Carroll endured decades of anti-Jesuit sentiment, but—at long last, in 1814—happily read the papal order that restored his religious order, the suppression of which Carroll referred to as "unjust and cruel treatment."

From the day John Adams first met Charles Carroll of Carrollton on September 14, 1774, Adams had a favorable opinion, recording in his diary: "This day Mr. Chase introduced to us a Mr. Carroll of Annapolis, a very sensible gentlemen, a Roman Catholic, and of the first Fortune in America." In a letter to his wife Abigail dated February 18,

1776, John Adams described Charles Carroll of Carrollton as "a Gentleman of independant Fortune, perhaps the largest in America, 150 or 200, thousand Pounds sterling, educated in some University in France, tho a Native of America, of great Abilities and Learning, compleat Master of French Language and a Professor of the Roman catholic Religion, yet a warm, a firm, a zealous Supporter of the Rights of America, in whose Cause he has hazarded his all." In another letter of the same date, to James Warren, John Adams further emphasized of Charles Carroll of Carrollton: "He had a liberal Education in France, and is well acquainted with the French Nation. He Speaks their Language as easily as ours—and what is perhaps of more Consequence than all the rest, he was educated in the Roman Catholic Religion, and still continues to worship his Maker according to the Rites of that Church." "In the Cause of American Liberty," Adams added of Carroll, "his Zeal, Fortitude, and Perseverance have been so conspicuous that he is Said to be marked out for peculiar Vengeance by the Friends of Administration. But he continues to hazard his all: his immense fortune, the largest in America, and his Life."[119] Given Carroll's wealth and social connections, it is hardly surprising that Carroll knew of—and had read—Beccaria's treatise almost immediately after its appearance.

History shows that, by 1776, many Americans, including Catholics in Maryland, had gained a close familiarity with *On Crimes and Punishments*. Charles Carroll of Carrollton was no exception, with one historian writing that Carroll was "deeply impressed by Beccaria."[120] "[B]efore the Revolution," notes another scholar of the interest in Beccaria's treatise, "Charles Carroll of Carrollton ordered his book from abroad."[121] That founder's cousin and ally—popularly known as "Charles Carroll, Barrister"—himself had a habit of ordering new writings, frequently instructing his bookseller to send him twenty shillings' worth of the best political pamphlets. Although what writings Charles Carroll, Barrister received is not known, it is hard to imagine Beccaria's book not being on the list.[122] Indeed, in a 1767 letter, Charles Carroll of Carrollton—his relative—specifically told his own correspondent, Edmund Jenings: "the author of the essay on crimes & punishments has displayed a great fund of humanity in his little work, interspersed with many Just and Judicious observations."[123] Jenings, born in Maryland, had gone to England in 1737 with his parents and studied and lived there for the rest of his life, excepting from 1778 to 1783, years he spent in Paris and Brussels. "Educated at Eton and Cambridge," one writer records, "Jenings trained in law at the Middle Temple."[124] It was after studying law at the Middle Temple, as well as Lincoln's Inn, that the noted philosopher Jeremy Bentham—one of Beccaria's biggest disciples—was admitted to the bar in 1769.[125]

That men such as Charles Carroll of Carrollton—who spent seventeen years abroad—so quickly became familiar with Montesquieu and Beccaria's treatises shows just how swiftly Enlightenment ideas spread among American intellectuals of the time. These were men hungry for knowledge, and the humanity and rationality displayed by Beccaria appealed to Enlightenment era thinkers of all religious and political stripes. It is unclear when local Marylanders got their first shipment of Beccaria's books from Europe, but in addition to the 1767 possession of Beccaria's book by Charles Carroll of Carrollton, local records show the continuing popularity of Beccaria's treatise over time as it is listed among the 1847 *Catalogue of Books Belonging to the Library of St. John's College* in Annapolis, Maryland, just to pull out one local example.[126] For those of means, a European education meant not only rapid exposure to the latest, cutting-edge thinking on philosophy, medicine and other subjects, but to Europeans who had, themselves, already read and often embraced Beccaria's book.

The poet William Wordsworth, in 1794 correspondence with his friend William Mathews, to give a European example, suggested that they collaborate on a monthly journal called *The Philanthropist*. In that letter, Wordsworth—who crossed paths with penal reformers William Godwin and Basil Montagu—proposed "biographical papers" on figures such as Beccaria, with Wordsworth's collection of books including a 1767 edition of *On Crimes and Punishments*. Wordsworth's own writings were highly critical of England's Bloody Code and spoke of a "penal code" that was "so crowded with disproportioned penalties and indiscriminate severity that a conscientious man would sacrifice in many instances his respect for the laws to the common feelings of humanity."[127] For those in America with financial resources, certainly, Europe—the land of ancient architecture and revered philosophers—was often seen as the premier destination for educational, artistic or scientific opportunities. It was also a place where books like Beccaria's treatise might be obtained in multiple languages even more easily than in the United States.

In his case, Charles Carroll of Carrollton was educated in both France and England, studying liberal arts and both civil law and common law traditions. He sailed for France in 1748 and studied at three Jesuit institutions, the College of St. Omer, the College of Rheims and the Louis-le-Grand in Paris. It was in Paris—to quote his biographer—"that Charles first encountered, devoured, and absorbed Montesquieu's *Spirit of the Laws*." After moving to England in 1759, Charles also encountered the writings of Oxford professor Sir William Blackstone before returning to Maryland. Back at home he later took up the cause of American independence, writing under the pseudonym "First Citizen" in a state that had what one historian calls "the severest anti-Catholic laws." To his closest English friend, William Graves, Charles made clear his choice to stay in America in late 1774. "Do I ever mean to cross the [A]tlantic?" he asked rhetorically. "No," he concluded, "unless I should be transported under the obsolete act of Henry the 8th to be hanged in England for being a true American."[128] By then, the British government and the American colonists had been at odds for a decade. In 1764, the British Parliament—trying to generate revenue to pay for wars against France and Spain—passed a revenue act known as the Sugar Act, followed a year later by the hugely unpopular Stamp Act, which taxed all sorts of papers, including newspapers and documents. James Otis's *The Rights of the British Colonies Asserted and Proved* had come out in 1764, and the Virginia House of Burgesses and Boston's Sons of Liberty had vehemently opposed the much-maligned Stamp Act, which was—due to American protests—finally repealed in 1766. The Stamp Act, however, was soon replaced by duties on glass, paper and tea—part of Parliament's 1767 revenue acts known as the Townshend Acts—and what came to be known as the Intolerable or Coercive Acts of 1774, including the Boston Port Act, which closed that port in the wake of the Boston Tea Party.[129]

With American contempt for British laws hitting new heights in the 1760s and 1770s, the elimination of "sanguinary laws," often derided as the hallmark of oppressive, monarchical governments, came to be seen as a progressive, or republican, measure.[130] In fact, in eighteenth-century, English-language writings, *sanguinary* laws and punishments were routinely associated with acts of inhumanity and cruelty, including executions. To inflict "sanguinary" punishments, many Anglo-American thinkers felt, was simply not consistent with Christian values. For example, in a collection of writings put together in 1781 by Anglican clergyman John Gutch, of Oxford, one finds the following remarks by Justice Allibon in a charge to the jury "at the Assizes at Croydon": "I say, the true mark of Christianity is humility and mildness. Let me ask you from whence they have such a spirit or what will be the consequence of it to posterity; what can be the meaning that any man shall be in love with sanguinary, and bloody Laws?" "I must confess," Justice Allibon continued, "that no man can get the reputation of a good Christian by putting sanguinary Laws in execution." Although Allibon noted that "sanguinary Laws" had been "enacted" years earlier, he emphasized that "they never had a general approbation, nor no man of the Church of *England* for putting them in execution."[131]

In the eighteenth century, religious persecution—the thing often leading to the imposition of sanguinary laws—was rampant, including in much of Europe and America. In a journal entry from August 1776, William Jones, making observations on a trip to Paris, noted: "the Christians who succeeded were so cruel as to establish sanguinary laws against impiety, and put blasphemers and heretics to death."[132] William Guthrie, in a commercial grammar, likewise spoke of "cruel sanguinary executions, on account of religion" in 1780.[133] In *On Crimes and Punishments*, Beccaria himself warned against resort to "superstition," "avarice," "secret betrayals and public massacres," and of "preachers of the evangelical truth soiling with blood the hands that daily touched the God of meekness." In his chapter "On the Eradication of Heresies," Beccaria urged toleration, culling these historical examples:

> From the earliest days of Christianity, opinions were divided. The Christians of Alexandria did not think like those of Antioch on many points. The Achaians differed from the Asiatics. Such diversity has lasted throughout the ages, and will probably last forever. Jesus Christ, who could have united all of his followers in the same sentiments, did not do so. It is to be presumed, therefore, that he did not wish to do so, and that his plan was to train all his churches to be kind and charitable by permitting them to have different systems, which all joined together in recognizing him as their leader and master. All these sects, which were long tolerated by the emperors or hidden from their view, were unable to persecute each other since they were all equally subject to the Roman magistrates; they could only argue.

"Religion," Beccaria emphasized, addressing would-be rulers, "comes from God to man; the civil law comes from you to your people."[134]

Like Beccaria, America's founders—James Madison and Thomas Jefferson among them—envisioned a country in which people of different religious faiths would be tolerant of one another's beliefs. Having seen religious persecution of Baptists in Virginia, Madison exchanged letters with his friend William Bradford on the subject of "religious Toleration"; and in his home state, Jefferson drafted—and Madison helped secure the passage of—"An Act for Establishing Religious Freedom," a bill that passed the Virginia legislature in 1786. With the Virginia law as a model for the nation, the U.S. Constitution's First Amendment sought to separate church and state, promote religious tolerance, and put an end to faith-based discrimination and religious-based violence. "Congress shall make no law respecting an establishment of religion, or prohibiting the free exercise thereof," the First Amendment's opening clause reads, words now etched in stone on the Newseum's Pennsylvania Avenue, four-story façade in Washington, D.C.[135] The need for both political dissent and religious toleration, the core foundation for the First Amendment, were emphasized in Andrew Ellicott's November 14, 1810 letter to James Madison. In that letter, which quoted Voltaire, Ellicott lamented: "Political intolerance among republicans, who claim the freedom of opinion as a birth-right, and religious intolerance among christians, whose religion is founded on brotherly love, and charity, has always appeared to me a paradox, and sometimes almost induced me to believe, that there are but few real republicans, and christians in the world."[136]

If political and religious intolerance persisted in Madison's time, and they both did, the infliction of barbaric punishments—leading to a peculiar, eighteenth-century vocabulary—also remained as another, sometimes seemingly intractable societal problem. In the 1780s, the decade in which the U.S. Constitution came into force, *cruel* and *sanguinary*—that now little-used word—were often used alongside one another. William Gordon, the author of *The History of the Rise, Progress, and Establishment of the Independence of the United States of America*, wrote in 1788 of an oration, noting that "the address was stigmatized as cruel, sanguinary, and unjust."[137] A book on Morocco published in 1788 also used the phrase "sanguinary and cruel character," while a 1783 travelogue titled *Travels in India* used the phrase "cruel and sanguinary disposition."[138] *Cruel* and *sanguinary*—both frequently used in the Founding Fathers' era, whether in letters, speeches, books or pamphlets—were literally put side by side in dictionary entries.[139] Noah Webster—the creator of *An American Dictionary of the English Language*—wrote of the "sanguinary scenes" of the French Revolution, saying they "manifested a ferociousness of character, rarely found among civilized men, and impress the mind with horror."[140] In his famous dictionary, published in 1828, Webster listed two definitions for *sanguinary*: "1. Bloody; attended with much bloodshed; murderous; as a sanguinary war, contest or battle." "2. Blood thirsty; cruel; eager to shed blood." "Passion," he also noted there, "makes us brutal and sanguinary."

In his first dictionary, published in 1806, Webster had similarly defined *sanguinary* as "bloody, murderous, cruel, horrid," with *cruel* defined in that source—*A Compendious Dictionary of the English Language*—as "hardhearted, inhuman, bloody, fierce."[141] By contrast, Webster's 1828 definitions of *cruel* were more detailed, reading as follows: "1. Disposed to give pain to others, in body or mind; willing or pleased to torment, vex or afflict; inhuman, destitute of pity, compassion or kindness; fierce; ferocious; savage, barbarous, hardhearted; applied to persons or their dispositions." "2. Inhuman; barbarous; savage; causing pain, grief or distress; exerted in tormenting, vexing or afflicting." Among other examples of the use of the word *cruel*, Webster quoted the Bible—in particular, Jeremiah 6—as follows: "They are cruel, and have no mercy."[142] These are usages of *cruel* that prevailed in that era, with multiple state ratifying conventions later urging the adoption—at the federal level—of prohibitions against either "cruel or unusual" or "cruel and unusual" punishments. Delegates in Pennsylvania, New York and Rhode Island—in December 1787, July 1788, and May 1790, respectively—proposed prohibiting "cruel or unusual punishments," and in June and August of 1788 both Virginia and North Carolina delegates urged the adoption of a prohibition against "cruel and unusual punishments."[143]

From the beginning, America's founders used the words *cruel* and *sanguinary* to refer to Great Britain's laws and the harsh treatment of people, including criminals. Writing as "Novanglus" to the inhabitants of the Massachusetts-Bay Colony in February 1775, John Adams referred to Great Britain's "sanguinary laws." And in a June 1775 letter to his wife Abigail about the activities of the Continental Congress, John Adams likewise wrote of England's "hostile and sanguinary" designs as he wrote elsewhere in his letter: "I can now inform you that the Congress have made Choice of the modest and virtuous, the amiable, generous and brave George Washington Esqr., to be the General of the American Army." In "A Proclamation by the General Court," dated January 19, 1776 and in John Adams' own hand, it is further emphasized that "the Happiness of the People ... is the sole End of Government" and that efforts to obtain justice from "[t]he Administration of Great Britain" had been rejected, with a war of the most "atrocious, cruel and Sanguinary Kind" having been commenced against the colonies. In 1778 letters to John Adams, John Thaxter—a tutor for John Quincy Adams who studied law with John Adams himself—also wrote of "the sanguinary Administration of Britain," while the South Carolina native and European traveler and gadfly Ralph Izard—appointed commissioner to Tuscany by the Continental Congress, himself later serving in that body and as a U.S. Senator—spoke of "the sanguinary purposes of both Houses of Parliament."[144]

In Italy, Ralph Izard—said to be "a firm and consistent advocate for liberty" who once tried to pay Voltaire a visit—traveled to Pisa, Leghorn, Florence, Naples, Turin, Rome and Venice. While in Europe, Izard was appointed to act as a liaison to the Grand Duke of Tuscany, but was stymied in his efforts to be received at the Italian court, thus remaining in Paris for some time and failing to get a loan from the Italian power. As Izard moved about Europe, he also corresponded with, among many others, the Abbé Niccoli, the Tuscan Minister in Paris; John Strange, "*His Britannic Majesty's Resident, at Venice*"; the American diplomat Arthur Lee, who, from London, told Izard that "the die is thrown, and we must stand the hazard of the cast"; and the Scottish politician George Dempster, who, in July 1775, wrote to Izard, relating that the Continental Congress "will assume the government of America." Its "constitution," Dempster predicted, would be "of so much freedom, and so likely to preserve the power of the state, in the wisest, best and ablest hands, that it promises to exceed Rome in grandeur, and Great Britain in liberty." For his part, Izard wholeheartedly concurred, writing Dempster in early August 1775: "I make no doubt, but, if America should be driven to the necessity of disuniting herself from Great Britain, that the world would see the *finest and freest Constitution formed, that any people were ever blessed with.* The Congress, now sitting at Philadelphia, are as capable of forming such a Constitution, as any body of men on earth."

At a prior point, on October 26, 1774, Thomas Lynch—writing from Philadelphia to Izard, then in Italy—explained the ongoing work of the Continental Congress in the pre-Revolutionary War period. As Lynch wrote:

> There remains only an address to the Canadians and the petition to the King, to complete all our works, and these will soon be printed in England; should they reach you abroad, please consider whether their being translated into French and Dutch, may not have a good effect, as we shall want supplies of woollens and other goods from them, in case our mother country, (as it is called,) continues her oppression.

Writing from Naples in January 1775, Izard himself made this pointed observation, giving some sense of the political landscape in which Beccaria lived: "I have seen that the French are slaves, and I now see that there is no freedom in any state in Italy; and I know that the reason of this, is, because the people have no check over the prince." "If Parliament can take what money she pleases from us, without our consent," Izard added, drawing a parallel while elsewhere railing against tyranny, "the most ignorant cannot believe that we shall be anything but slaves; that is, we shall have a bare sufficiency for our existence left us, and the rest will be deemed superfluity, and much better employed on this side of the water than the other." "The post, from Italy to England," Izard complained on another occasion in 1775, this time writing from London to Edward Rutledge about trouble with the Italian mail, "is very uncertain, and if letters pass safely, the gentlemen at the post office very often choose to keep possession of them, if the contents do not please them." "Every letter, I am assured," Izard added, "undergoes a strict examination." In 1776, after the Revolutionary War started, censorship was to be found in England, too, with the following sentences from a May 4, 1776 letter reprinted in *Correspondence of Mr. Ralph Izard*: "I have read 'Common Sense,' the pamphlet you ask about. It is by much the cleverest, and most ingenious performance I ever saw. Almon had a copy of it, but it was taken from him."[145]

At the start of the Revolutionary War and during and after the formation of the U.S. Government following the U.S. Constitution's ratification, American revolutionaries— seeking liberty and trying to avoid oppressive laws—were themselves continually worried about the infliction of sanguinary punishments. When Thomas Jefferson wrote Edmund Pendleton on August 26, 1776, about the best means to prevent "the commission of crimes," Jefferson explained that "[i]t is only the sanguinary hue of our penal laws which

I meant to object to." In 1781, Jefferson also penned a proclamation inviting mercenary troops in the British service to desert. That proclamation read in part: "his Britannic majesty in order to destroy our freedom and happiness had commenced against us a cruel and unprovoked war, and unable to engage Britons sufficient to execute his sanguinary measures had applied for aid to foreign princes who were in the habit of selling the blood of their people for money." In the *Federalist Papers*, penned in the late 1780s, Alexander Hamilton also wrote of substituting "the violent and sanguinary agency of the sword to the mild influence of the Magistracy" and specifically worried about the justice system being "too sanguinary and cruel." One man, George Davis, in writing to James Madison from Tripoli in 1807, spoke of another's "cruel and sanguinary character" when that individual, identified as Bashaw, was "alike deaf to reason and blind to his own interest."[146]

Not only did American revolutionaries view English policies as sanguinary, but the French Revolution's bloody carnage also inspired many references to "sanguinary" behavior. Writing as "Americanus," Alexander Hamilton, for example, wrote of France's "furious and sanguinary civil war" in 1794. In October 1789, to Gouverneur Morris, who went to France on business that year and who later served as America's Minister Plenipotentiary to France from 1792 to 1794, President George Washington likewise wrote of the "alarm" caused by the infliction of "sanguinary punishments." Morris himself, writing from Paris in 1792, would speak of "[s]ome of the Sanguinary Events" which had taken place there. Two years later, in 1794, Alexander Hamilton noted that the French Revolution's "early periods" had inspired among Americans "a warm zeal for its success," "*a sentiment truly universal*"; but, he cautioned, the once unanimous support among Americans— said to be "exemplary for humanity and moderation"—had declined precipitously due to "excesses" that had degenerated French society into "a state of things the most cruel, sanguinary, and violent that ever stained the annals of mankind."[147] As part of the Reign of Terror, more than 17,000 people were condemned to death in France and more than 10,000 more died in prisons awaiting trial.[148]

Because *sanguinary* was then a commonly used word, it is hardly surprising that it continued to be used extensively in the decades after the Revolutionary War as Anglo-Americans wrestled with how to modify their penal codes. For example, in a book published in 1820, it was said that the Puritans "were the fiercest in calling for the execution of the sanguinary laws against men" and that "sanguinary proceedings" had suppressed "the Irish rebellion." Likewise, in *Thoughts on Penitentiaries*, published in Dublin in 1790, Jeremiah Fitzpatrick—the "Inspector General of Prisons"—wrote that "to obviate the infliction of sanguinary punishment," "more atrocious" offenders "have of late years been sent to colonize Botany Bay from whence, except by permission, there is no returning." With the American colonies no longer available for use, in 1779, Sir Joseph Banks—an English naturalist who had explored Australia, among many other locales—had proposed Botany Bay, in New South Wales, as a site for a new penal colony. Sir John Young also submitted a plan in 1785 for a settlement for convicts, though that scheme was rejected due to the high cost as a voyage to Botany Bay was estimated to be six times the cost of a passage to America. Only in August of 1786, desperate for a new penal colony in the Revolutionary War's wake, was Botany Bay—attractive for its potential as a naval base in the South Seas—chosen as the new site for offenders to be sent.[149]

Similarly, in George Stroud's *A Sketch of the Laws Relating to Slavery in the Several States of the United States of America*, published in 1827, Mississippi's penal code was described as "less sanguinary than that of Virginia."[150] While Maryland's 1776 "sanguinary Laws" clause has been described as "an invention of the Maryland founders,"[151] what inspired it—heart-felt public sentiment—was certainly not fabricated or insincere. On the contrary, that sentiment, shaped by an aversion to England's Bloody Code and by the writings of Montesquieu, Blackstone, Beccaria and others, arose from the Enlightenment itself. Blackstone himself had lamented the proliferation of "sanguinary laws," though England would, into the nineteenth century, maintain its reputation as an execution-prone country whose laws were considered to be—as one source put it—"uncommonly sanguinary."[152] In 1826, the American social reformer Roberts Vaux specifically commented on Pennsylvania's efforts to reform that state's criminal code. "[W]ithin less than a century past," he wrote, "learned jurists and speculative philosophers" such as Montesquieu, Blackstone, and Beccaria had "shed from their closets valuable lights upon the nature and end of punishment, and the penal laws," and thus were "justly entitled to the renown they enjoy."[153]

While the U.S. government and American states continued to punish some crimes capitally, including murder, early Americans—both in the Revolutionary War era and into the nineteenth century—simultaneously stigmatized *cruel* and *sanguinary* laws and punishments. Indeed, as reflected in Maryland's 1776 declaration of rights, Americans in the "Old Line State"—a moniker given Maryland during the Revolutionary War—renounced "sanguinary" laws just weeks after declaring their independence from Great Britain. What became known, in American patriotic circles, as the "Spirit of '76" must be gauged, certainly, in that legal and political context, with the issuance of the Declaration of Independence, in July of 1776, seen as a particularly bold move. The founders, in declaring independence, were putting themselves at extreme risk, especially since they were keenly aware, from their knowledge of English law, of the traditional, common-law punishment for treason. For centuries, English judges had ordered that traitors be hanged by the neck. To make the punishment of traitors particularly horrific, men's bodies, while dangling in the air still alive, were cut down and then disemboweled. By English custom, the traitors were then burnt alive, decapitated, and finally dismembered through a quartering of the body.[154]

It was, in fact, only as a result of a 1786 meeting in Annapolis, Maryland, the state where sanguinary laws had been renounced and where Beccaria's treatise was so well received, that the consensus emerged that another national convention had to be held. From the mid-eighteenth century through the Revolutionary War, Annapolis—the temporary capital of the United States after the signing of the Treaty of Paris in 1783—was known for its cultivated and wealthy inhabitants. It was at the Annapolis Convention in 1786 that delegates from five states—Delaware, New Jersey, New York, Pennsylvania and Virginia—called for a constitutional convention, the all-important one that convened and took place the following year in Philadelphia. Among the delegates in Annapolis: Alexander Hamilton, John Dickinson, Edmund Randolph, James Madison and St. George Tucker.[155] While Americans, still struggling to make the Articles of Confederation operational for the nation as a whole, advanced arguments for and against a new social compact, one local commentator—writing as "An Annapolitan"—thought concerns about abandoning the old regime were overblown. "I will not flatter you," that writer observed, "that this city will become the seat of congress. But should such be the event who is there will contend that Annapolis will not profit from the change?"

Writing in the *Maryland Gazette* on January 31, 1788, before the U.S. Constitution's ratification later that year, "An Annapolitan" wanted Marylanders to focus on local issues and was unafraid that national issues might get resolved elsewhere, as they soon would be in Washington, D.C., the new federal district. In the course of the writer's argument, this very Beccarian appeal was made:

> The uncertainty of the law in general, the inefficacy of the penal law, the disproportion between crimes and punishments, the delays of justice,—all these, and many others, are evils which demand their deliberation. They demand, too,

the utmost care and circumspection, with some insight into the laws and regulations of other nations. Some of these subjects have been postponed from session to session. The legislature may now apply to this important business, with their minds less occupied by the general concerns of the union, on which it is not likely that they will be competent to decide.[156]

Vermont, South Carolina and New Hampshire

In Vermont, South Carolina and New Hampshire, which adopted their own constitutions in 1777, 1778 and 1784, respectively, Americans in those places also committed themselves to making punishments less "sanguinary."[157] Vermont's provision to make "sanguinary" punishments less necessary—part of a constitution that called for "frequent recurrence to fundamental principles, and a firm adherence to justice, moderation, temperance, industry and frugality"—was derived from Section 39 of Pennsylvania's Constitution of 1776.[158] Vermont—in another important milestone—became the first American jurisdiction to abolish slavery, doing so on July 2, 1777; the anti-slavery movement would gradually continue and gain steam in other northern states as New York (1799), Pennsylvania (1780), Massachusetts and New Hampshire (1783), Connecticut and Rhode Island (1784) and New Jersey (1804) began the process of emancipation. Similar to Vermont's constitution, South Carolina's Constitution of 1778 also provided that "the penal laws, as heretofore used, shall be reformed, and punishments made in some cases less sanguinary, and in general more proportionate to the crime."[159] South Carolina's constitution, however, did not state any particular time frame for reform, making the provision more of a goal than a command. In contrast, Pennsylvania's constitution had directed that penal reform take place "as soon as may be."[160]

Still, American lawmakers were in unchartered territory, as America's penitentiary system had yet to be developed. "Although Beccaria and other advocates of classical penology were highly critical of sanguinary punishments," writes historian Rebecca McLennan, "there was nothing in the principle of proportionality *per se* to indicate how, exactly, convicted offenders should be punished—whether under a republican or any other kind of legal system." "What is clear," she explains, "is that once the war ended and the states began to transition to peacetime governance (in 1783), legislators and the citizenry began to debate in earnest the question of what a properly republican system of legal punishment might look like."[161] Desertion, in particular, had been punishable by death during the Revolutionary War, with the war's end sparking renewed reflection on the death penalty's propriety generally and for desertion in particular. The U.S. debate over the death penalty—playing out more visibly in some states than in others as war gave way to the fruits of peace—mirrored similar European debates, by enlightened men of letters, over crime and punishment.

And men, such as Beccaria, were not the only ones to recognize the need for change. Women, as well as men, had their own opinions about what should be done. Along with Abigail Adams in America, Elisabetta Caminer Turra (1751–1796), an Italian journalist, translator, poet and theatrical director, also actively promoted social change and social justice. The daughter of Domenico Caminer (1731–1795), a prolific writer, Elisabetta Caminer Turra translated more than 50 plays, including those of Voltaire. She corresponded with the Florentine, law-trained journalist Giuseppe Pelli Bencivenni, and she published a widely distributed literary and philosophical periodical, *Giornale enciclopedico* (*Encyclopedic Journal*), from 1777 to 1782, that was inspired by the French *philosophes' Encyclopédie*. "Under her direction," one source reports, "the periodical became the most progressive Enlightenment influence in the Veneto region of Italy." The Florentine journalist Giuseppe Pelli Bencivenni (1729–1808), a Florence-born lawyer who had studied law in Pisa, becoming the director of the Royal Gallery in Florence from 1775 to 1793, also reportedly "admired greatly" Cesare Beccaria's work. Together with her husband, the botanist and physician Antonio Turra (1736–1797), Elisabetta Caminer Turra owned a printing press and operated Stamperia Turra, an active publishing house in the area. "One of the complaints made against her," it has been noted of her trail-blazing work as one of Italy's first female journalists, "was her opposition to the death penalty." When challenged by an anonymous writer, she responded that the writer "praises the gallows and condemns journalists because they hope that education will make gallows less necessary. Ergo: The person who desires to see his neighbor hanged is a good Christian!"

In Europe, as in America, whether desertion should be punishable by death was very much on the agenda of reformers. In her role as a translator of plays, Elisabetta Caminer Turra—who died of breast cancer at the age of forty-four—even changed the ending of Louis-Sébastien Mercier's play, *The Deserter*, a decision she defended by reprinting a chivalrous letter from Mercier himself. In that letter, Mercier—whose plays John Quincy Adams asked his father, John Adams, for permission to buy in 1781—thanked Elisabetta, his Italian translator, for saving the life of the play's protagonist. In the original version, the protagonist had been put to death. As Mercier wrote to Elisabetta: "As in Italy, this death was not well received in France. I wanted to make a political point with my play, to enlighten my nation about the horror of this inhumane law." In writing of France, Mercier added in his letter: "I thought I would encourage her to reject the law by offering her this tableau. She could not tolerate in painting that which she permits in reality. I owe you renewed thanks for having changed this bloody catastrophe."

Elisabetta Caminer Turra's Italian translation of Mercier's play was first published in 1771, then again as part of a larger collection, in 1772. In 1771, her translated version of the play was also performed in Venice. As originally drafted, Mercier's play—as one book summarizes the original version of the plot—"recounts the story of a young French soldier (Durimel) who is placed in a regiment with an abusive colonel." As the plot summary reports: "Eventually he flees the army. As a deserter, he is subject to the death penalty, so he leaves France and seeks refuge in a small town across the German border with a widow (Madame Luzere) and her daughter (Clary), who take him in to help them tend their store." After "Durimel and Clary fall in love," the summary continues, "war erupts, Durimel's old regiment comes to the small town," and Durimel is put to death after being recognized, with Durimel's own father—in a final plot twist—"assigned to oversee the execution." In the 1780s, French theater productions were popular, and Louis-Sébastien Mercier's writings were among those well known to Americans in Paris. In his diary for February 1785, John Quincy Adams notes that he dined with Thomas Jefferson and Benjamin Franklin on separate days, went to see "equestrian exercises" with "Coll. Humphreys and Mr. Short," and that "Mr. A. went for the books arrived from London." Another entry made by John Quincy Adams in the same month indicates that he "borrowed 2 vols." of Louis-Sébastien Mercier's *Tableau de Paris*, a twelve-volume work of which Jefferson owned the first six volumes. In an 1803 letter, Jefferson himself wrote to Mercier with kind words about Margaret Bonneville, the wife of French revolutionary Nicolas de Bonneville, of the family that Thomas Paine lived with in Paris from 1797 to 1802.[162]

While Americans in Paris, including Abigail Adams and John Quincy Adams, attended French tragedies in the 1780s, following collective public sentiment in Philadelphia, the New Hampshire Constitution of 1784—the permanent replacement for that state's temporary constitution of 1776—was adopted by that state's residents. The 1784 constitution, put in place after the Revolutionary War as death penalty support softened through-out Europe and America, specifically condemned "sanguinary laws," as had Pennsylvania and Vermont. In New Hampshire, the first draft of a permanent constitution "was pro-duced"—as one Oxford University Press history puts it—"by the world's first modern constitutional convention, held in Concord, New Hampshire, in 1778." While that draft, as well as a second draft, was rejected by the people, a third draft, produced by a 1781 con-vention, did the trick, with the new constitution—modeled on the Massachusetts Con-stitution of 1780—getting ratified by voters in 1783 and going into effect in 1784. "No wise legislature," the final New Hampshire constitution stated in one proviso, "will affix the same punishment to the crimes of theft, forgery and the like, which they do to those of murder and treason." According to Article I, section 18 of that constitution: "[A] mul-titude of sanguinary laws is both impolitic and unjust. The true design of all punish-ments being to reform, not to exterminate, mankind."[163]

Blackstone's *Commentaries*—which New Hampshire lawyers would have been ex-tremely familiar with by the early 1780s—had, notably, said something very similar on the same page in which Blackstone cited Beccaria. "We may farther observe," Blackstone wrote, "that sanguinary laws are a bad symptom of the distemper of any state, or at least of its weak constitution." As Blackstone emphasized:

> A multitude of sanguinary laws (besides the doubt that may be entertained con-cerning the right of making them) do likewise prove a manifest defect either in the wisdom of the legislative, or the strength of the executive power. It is a kind of quackery in government, and argues a want of solid skill, to apply the same universal remedy, the *ultimum supplicium*, to every case of difficulty. It is, it must be owned, much *easier* to extirpate than to amend mankind: yet that mag-istrate must be esteemed both a weak and a cruel surgeon, who cuts off every limb, which through ignorance or indolence he will not attempt to cure.[164]

As Americans tried to maintain their new country's stability, especially during the time of the Articles of Confederation with their focus on state, rather than federal, power, they struggled with how to treat those accused of crimes or disloyalty. "In monarchies," Samuel Adams had once remarked, "the crime of treason and rebellion may admit of being par-doned or lightly punished; but the man who dares to rebel against the laws of a republic ought to suffer death." But in the wake of Shays' Rebellion (1786–1787) in Massachusetts, Boston lawyer James Sullivan thought that approach was wrong and spearheaded efforts to save the lives of two men involved in that rebellion. "Peace and tranquility could be re-stored without sanguinary examples," Sullivan pled to the state's Executive Council. "Ed-ucated Americans," Allan Nevins writes of this period in U.S. history, "were as well aware of the efforts of Beccaria to improve the condition of the criminal laws in Europe as they later were of the efforts of Howard to remodel the prisons of that continent." Indeed, in *The Life of the Late John Howard*, published in 1790, it was reported: "The Marquis of *Beccaria* justly remarks, that the death of a criminal is a less efficacious method of deter-ring others, than the continued example of a man *deprived of his liberty*; and that the pun-ishment of death is pernicious to society, from the example of barbarity which it affords."[165] In another book, also published in 1790, Howard's own trip to Italy, to see its prisons, had been highlighted. As Howard's observations were recorded in that source: "At Genoa, besides a prison for *debtors*, and a prison for *female criminals*, there is a great prison for *male criminals*, consisting of thirty-five rooms. I saw none of the prisoners in irons. Their daily allowance was thirteen ounces of good wheaten bread for each, besides soup."[166]

Legal commentary of the time reflects the rapidly changing public attitudes toward criminals and punishment. For instance, in 1793, shortly after the ratification of the U.S.

Bill of Rights, Nathaniel Chipman—a federal judge in Vermont—published *Sketches of the Principles of Government*. In that book, Chipman cited and quoted from Beccaria's treatise, and said that "[i]t is worthy of remark, that in the progress of society, no science has received so little improvement as that of criminal jurisprudence." Chipman wrote that "Locke, Beccaria, and many others" were "political writers, of great eminence," and included a section in his book on "Hatred and Revenge." "The passions of Hatred and Revenge," Chipman wrote, "are not, in their nature, opposed to society, though, from abuse, they become, at times, very pernicious." "Hatred," he wrote, "is a rooted aversion of one man to another, on account of a real, or supposed, fixed and intentional opposition to his interest, or happiness." "Revenge," as he defined it, "is a desire in one person, to inflict an evil on another, for a real, or supposed injury received." "The passion of revenge," Chipman wrote, "would … if laid under no restraint, become a most cruel scourge." "Malice," Chipman also observed, "is a disposition to inflict evil on others, without just cause."

In his treatise, Chipman specifically singled out Beccaria's essay, stating: "The world is more indebted to the Marquis Beccaria, for his little treatise on Crimes and Punishments, than to all other writers on the subject."[167] Chipman—whose own treatise was extremely influential, and which would be commented favorably upon by Thomas Jefferson—then wrote:

> It is true, that many circumstances of outrageous violence, with which capital and other punishments were inflicted, have, in some nations, been abolished; but it may, with equal truth, be observed, that among those nations, who boast the highest refinement, the greatest degree of improvement in their civil policy, the number of capital punishments, has been increased out of all proportion to the reform in point of cruelty. The British government, which in civil improvements, and the humanity of its laws, has gone beyond most other European nations, has proceeded with a degree of wantonness, in the enacting of capital punishments. One hundred and sixty crimes, declared to be worthy of immediate death, hardly complete the murderous catalogue.

After citing Beccaria, the jurist Chipman continued:

> A punishment annexed to a crime is, by the force of habitual association, viewed in connexion with the crime, and often serves as a measure for the degree of its guilt, which arises only from its relation to society. When, from any cause, the perpetration of a particular species of crimes has become frequent, the minds of legislators are irritated against the perpetrators, and against the crime. Determined to apply an effectual remedy, they are too prone, without adverting to the cause of the evil, to enhance the penalty, which soon becomes a new measure for the guilt of the crime.
>
> It is, however, for the interest of humanity, an excellent disposition of Providence, that in a state of any considerable degree of refinement, sanguinary laws always defeat the end of their institution. If the penalty annexed by the law, to a crime, rise above the demerit of the crime, in the estimation of the people, whose sentiments are in this case the best criterion, the law is rarely executed. Humanity, whose dictates are more readily obeyed, than the requisitions of law, is interested in the escape, or acquittal of the criminal. When the severity of the punishment excites the pity of the people, the effect of punishment is more than lost. While they pity the criminal, they forget his crime, or diminish its guilt,

and conceive an abhorrence of the law. If the criminal be detected, and condemned, he is viewed as unfortunate, rather than guilty.

In another passage, Chipman also noted: "Hangmen and public executioners are universally detested. The first impressions, which their actions make on the mind, impressions of inhumanity, and cruelty, are never effaced by reasoning on the justice of their actions, or their necessity to society."[168]

In another treatise, *Principles of Government*, Nathaniel Chipman also made reference to Beccaria's "admirable work on crimes and punishments." In that book, published in 1833, Chipman again listed Beccaria—along with Locke and Blackstone—amongst the "political writers of great eminence," and referenced the "Marquis Beccaria" more than once. "The world," Chipman recorded again, "is more indebted to the Marquis Beccaria for his little 'Treatise on Crimes and Punishments' than to all other writers on the subject." In his new treatise that reprinted some earlier material, Chipman repeated his remarks on capital punishment from *Sketches of the Principles of Government*, and again wrote with only minor, non-substantive revisions: "Hangmen and public executioners, are universally detested. The first impressions which their actions make on the mind,—impressions of inhumanity and cruelty,—are never effaced by reasoning on the justice of their actions or necessity to the community." Chipman also quoted a British lawmaker who said: "Whether hanging ever did, or can answer any good purpose, I doubt; but the cruel exhibition of every execution day, is a proof, that hanging carries no terror with it. And I am confident that every new sanguinary law operates as an encouragement to commit capital offenses; for it is not the mode, but the certainty of the punishment that creates terror."[169]

Chipman's comments—raising serious questions about the death penalty's supposed efficacy—were by no means unique. In the period after the ratification of the U.S. Bill of Rights, American books, newspapers and magazines continued regularly citing and quoting Beccaria.[170] In the December 1792 edition of *The American Museum*, for example, Beccaria's name appears in an *Address of the board of inspectors of the prison of the city and county of Philadelphia, to his excellency Thomas Mifflin, esq. governor of the state of Pennsylvania*. That lengthy address, a report commending prior prison reform efforts in Philadelphia, included a four-paragraph "extract from the excellent Beccaria."[171] Beccaria's "essay on crimes and punishments"—under the heading "miscellanies"—also appears in a January 1793 catalogue of books that Philadelphia bookseller Mathew Carey had imported. The address of the prison inspectors published in the *American Museum* spoke, in particular, of "the present system," its "salutary effects upon the criminals" and "its beneficial consequences to the community." As that address read: "we are naturally led to applaud the legislature who ventured in defiance of long established custom and prejudice, to depart from the destructive and ineffectual system of penal law, received from a government, which still continues, wantonly to sport with the lives of its subjects."

In other words, the American public—as evidenced by the address of the Philadelphia prison inspectors—were beginning to reject English common law practices in favor of a more enlightened and republican approach. Right before invoking Beccaria's words, in fact, the board of inspectors made this report to the state's governor: "Cruel and severe laws are calculated only to keep slaves in subjection; and from our experience of the good efforts, resulting from mild laws, in a free and well regulated government, we cannot avoid expressing a wish, that every thing which is of a sanguinary nature, or which may eventually deprive the state of a single citizen, may be completely expunged from our code."[172] Just as sanguinary criminal codes that took the lives of convicts were then ubiquitous, slavery was still a fact of American life at the country's founding. Some early Americans, especially in the South, feared slave revolts, which had—they knew—taken place in the eighteenth century in places as diverse as the West Indies and in New York and South Carolina. But others—whether due to their Christian beliefs, or because of what they saw as the natural rights of all human beings—came to oppose slavery on moral or Enlightenment grounds. In 1775 in Philadelphia, a hotbed of activity, a group of 24 people—16 of whom were Quakers—founded the Society for the Relief of Free Negroes Unlawfully Held in Bondage. Famously, Jefferson's *Notes on the State of Virginia* condemned slavery, though Jefferson, like other slaveholders of his time, kept—and did not free—his slaves during his lifetime.[173]

Virginia, Kentucky and Beyond

The quest to curtail sanguinary punishments, inspired in part by Beccaria's slender treatise, swept across America, north and south, in the late eighteenth and early nineteenth centuries, though it was mainly whites who reaped the rewards. Lawyers and jurists participated heavily in that social movement, and one of Thomas Jefferson's friends, John Breckinridge, a prominent Virginian who became a Kentuckian, got especially involved in the effort. In *The American Constitution as a Symbol and Reality for Italy*, writer Emiliana Pasca Noether makes this observation: "When John Breckinridge moved from Virginia to Kentucky in 1791, Beccaria accompanied him. Harry Innes, later the first federal judge on that frontier, had owned Beccaria's *Essay* since 1785." In Virginia, the home of Jefferson and Madison, reading Beccaria's treatise had long been popular. Students of the law became familiar with *On Crimes and Punishments*, and early American law professors and practitioners themselves used the treatise in their work. Indeed, St. George Tucker, a Virginia judge and William and Mary law professor, owned a copy of Beccaria's treatise—a treatise that would come in handy as he thought about the law. Tucker, Thomas Jefferson's friend and a man who liked to garden and grow trees in his spare time, had been a delegate at the Annapolis Convention. And other prominent men, in Virginia and elsewhere, took special note of Beccaria's treatise, too. As Noether emphasizes: "Examples can be multiplied. Beccaria was progressively becoming a staple in the libraries of respected lawyers and judges."[174]

Penal reform in Virginia and Kentucky, part of Virginia until it became the fifteenth state in 1792, were both influenced by Beccaria's views. In 1791, when John Breckinridge—Jefferson's close friend and fellow lawyer—was readying himself and his family for a move to Kentucky, he ordered from London a hundred and fifty books to take with him, including Beccaria's *On Crimes and Punishments*.[175] Also a close confidante of James Madison and James Monroe, Breckinridge was admitted to the Virginia bar in 1785 and practiced law in Jefferson's neck of the woods, Charlottesville, Virginia, before moving to Lexington, Kentucky in 1793.[176] Breckinridge became the Attorney General of Kentucky in 1793, won election to Kentucky's state house in 1797, and—the following year—shepherded through the legislature a massive reform of the state's antiquated criminal code.[177] The reform in Kentucky, spearheaded by Breckinridge, would come just two years after Virginia—where, thanks to the efforts of George Keith Taylor, Virginians had already overhauled their own criminal laws.[178] As one book notes of Taylor's work and progressive reputation in the legislature and the courtroom: "A frequent figure taking the cases of Indian plaintiffs in manumission suits, at least on appeal, was George Keith Taylor. Reputed to be one of the great orators of his generation, Taylor was a Federalist politician who served his native Prince George County in the state House of Delegates in the 1790s."[179]

Kentucky's penal code, like Virginia's, originally had scores of death-eligible offenses, including forgery and horse stealing, with Breckinridge asserting in a January 1798 speech that the state's then-existing code was "a scandal to reason and to humanity."[180] In 1798, Kentucky's General Assembly, inspired by Beccaria's ideas and heeding Breckinridge's call for reform, adopted a new criminal code that abolished the death penalty except for first-degree murder, slaves excepted.[181] According to the preamble to the state's new criminal code, "the reformation of the offenders, an object highly meriting the attention of the laws, is not affected at all by capital punishments, which exterminate instead of reforming, and should be the last melancholy resource against those whose existence is become inconsistent with the safety of their fellow citizens."[182] "Let us remember," Breckinridge would say, "that those unfortunate wretches are our fellow citizens" and "that to err is the lot of humanity, & that in punishing offenses, large, very large allowances ought to be made for the frailties of Human nature."[183] John Breckinridge (1760–1806) would go on to be a United States Senator from Kentucky from 1801 to 1805, and became the fifth United States Attorney General, serving under President Thomas Jefferson from 1805 to 1806.[184]

As one of the country's leading lawyers, Breckinridge was part of an organized political movement to change the country's penal laws. In late August 1793, Breckinridge had been chosen to be the chairman of the newly formed Lexington Democratic Society.[185] In November 1793, the Democratic Society called for reform of Kentucky's "sanguinary, cruel and unjust" criminal laws.[186] Those laws, the Society's resolution read, "capitally punished" a "multitude of inferior crimes ... whereby many offenders are liable to be destroyed, who might be reformed and restored good members of society." A "whereas" clause of the resolution read that "the experience of all ages hath shewn that cruel and sanguinary laws, defeat their own purpose," with the resolution adding that "when, if the punishments were only proportioned to the injury, men would feel it their inclination, as well as their duty, to see the laws observed." In other words, cruel laws led to more crime while men, by their nature, were more inclined to respect milder laws. "Resolved," the resolution concluded, "That a committee be appointed to draft a memorial to the General Assembly, requesting that a radical change may be made in our criminal code; by creating a system 'where by punishments may be proportioned to crimes, and that such punishments be made as analogous as possible to the nature of the offences.'"[187] The Democratic Society, which favored the French Revolution, had been organized in Philadelphia, with affiliates springing up in Georgetown and Paris in 1793.[188]

Another U.S. Senator from Kentucky, the famed orator Henry Clay (1777–1852), also—not surprisingly—showed familiarity with *On Crimes and Punishments*. In the case of *Cunningham v. Caldwell*, argued in February 1807, Clay—whose most famous client, Aaron Burr, he had successfully represented just the year before on a treason charge—argued as follows in a civil suit: "Even in criminal cases, the equitable principle is contended for by Beccaria, in his celebrated work on *Crimes and Punishments*, that the punishment should be proportioned to the crime."[189] Henry Clay's cousin, Cassius Clay (1810–1903), was a prominent anti-slavery crusader who also discerned a trend away from the use of executions. "The experience of mankind has fully proven, that a largely bloody code of laws has not been the most effectual to prevent crime, while the growing objections to capital punishment, and the *positive refusal of juries to convict in many instances*, warn us that some other remedy ought to be tried." Nicknamed the "The Lion of White Hall," Cassius Clay served in the Kentucky legislature, published an anti-slavery newspaper called the *True American*, and was appointed by Abraham Lincoln to serve as the Minister of Russia. "That capital punishment is not a preventive of crime was (upon investigation)," another nineteenth-century source noted, "the conviction" of Beccaria, Bentham, Cassius Clay "and hundreds of other able, thoughtful and conscientious men."[190]

From the Midwest to New England, the distaste for "sanguinary" punishments was palpable. In 1802, the State of Ohio—modeling New Hampshire's approach—adopted the following provision:

> All penalties shall be proportioned to the nature of the offense. No wise legislature will affix the same punishment to the crimes of theft, forgery and the like, which they do to those of murder and treason. When the same undistinguished severity is exerted against all offenses, the people are led to forget the real distinction in the crimes themselves, and to commit the most flagrant with as little compunction as they do the slightest offenses. For the same reasons, a multitude of sanguinary laws are both impolitic and unjust; the true design of all punishment being to reform, not to exterminate mankind.

In 1820, the State of Maine also joined the law reform chorus. Maine's constitution, put in place in that year, provides: "Sanguinary laws shall not be passed; all penalties and punishments shall be proportioned to the offence; excessive bail shall not be required, nor excessive fines imposed, nor cruel nor unusual punishments inflicted."[191]

A Maine legislative report, drafted in 1836 for the state legislature's consideration, expressly noted the definition of *sanguinary* and concluded that hanging qualified as an unconstitutional punishment. As that report stated:

> *Sanguinary* is derived from a Latin word which signifies blood, and is synonymous with the Latin *sanguinarius* and the French *sanguinaire*, both of which signify bloody, murderous, cruel. These are the definitions given by Webster, and other lexicographers; and it is in this sense that it is here used. If an objection be raised to this construction, on the ground that the law requiring the punishment of death by hanging, for certain offences, is not one requiring the blood of a fellow-being, it will be readily perceived that such an objection is unwarranted by the common use of language. If one man shall put to death another, whether by poisoning, strangulation, or suffocation, he is said to be guilty of the blood of the murdered person, and is even said to have shed his blood, although no blood has literally been spilt. It is in this sense that the advocates of the punishment of death explain and make the practical application of the passage of Scripture, "Whoso sheddeth man's blood, by man shall his blood be shed." Hence, they say, the man who has shed the blood of another should be hung upon the gallows; that is, his blood should be shed to expiate the crime. It is obviously true that the taking of life and the shedding of blood are used synonymously. In this sense, hanging a man with a halter till he is dead is as much a sanguinary punishment as decapitation. The law, therefore, prescribing this mode of punishment is a sanguinary law, and consequently unconstitutional.

Beccaria's name is found in multiple places in that report.[192]

Edward Livingston and Other Abolitionists

The influence of Beccaria was apparent even long after his death in 1794.[193] The American lawyer Edward Livingston, a member of a prominent, politically active family, also attempted to rid America of capital punishment. In drafting a proposed Code of Crimes and Punishments for the State of Louisiana, Livingston—who toiled for years to complete his work—specifically relied upon Beccaria's ideas. After being appointed by the General Assembly of Louisiana in the early 1820s to draft a "code of criminal law" founded on the notion "that punishments should be proportioned to offenses," Livingston prepared a report for that body. In his report, Livingston wrote that "[i]t would be disgusting and unnecessary to pass in review all the modes of punishment which have, even in modern times, been used, rather, it would seem, to gratify vengeance, than to lessen the number of offenses." "A spirit of enlightened legislation," he added, "taught by Montesquieu, Beccaria, Eden, and others; names dear to humanity! has banished some of the most atrocious from the codes of Europe." "If the argument were to be carried by the authority of names," Livingston emphasized, "that of Beccaria, were there no other, would ensure the victory." Livingston's report—aimed at an American legislative body—noted that, in England, the English parliament had already debated reducing the number of crimes punishable by death, some of which "every body allowed" were "manifestly cruel and absurd."[194] Although Livingston's draft penal code was never adopted, it sought to abolish capital punishment and showed Beccaria's continuing hold on America's psyche.[195]

Edward Livingston embraced the idea of codifying crimes rather than relying on the common law. He entered Princeton's Nassau Hall in 1779, studied law under John Lansing, was admitted to practice in 1785, and developed what his biographer called "a predisposition toward Roman law, which no doubt influenced his views on codification." Emperor Justinian had, in the sixth century, established what came to be known as the Justinian Code—an elaborate compilation of Roman law. Though a well-connected politician in his own right, Edward Livingston's older brother, Robert R. Livingston, had also served in the Continental Congress and was, in fact, a member of the Committee of Five that drafted the Declaration of Independence. After Edward completed his report for the State of Louisiana, he sent a copy of it to James Madison—a fellow Princeton graduate—in May 1822. The "improvement of Criminal Jurisprudence, in this part of the Union cannot but gratify those, who like you Sir, know how important that branch of Government is to the Liberties, as well as the happiness of the People," Livingston wrote to Madison in an accompanying letter.[196] In a July 1822 reply, Madison wrote back: "I should commit a tacit injustice if I did not say that the Report does great honor to the talents and sentiments of the Author. It abounds with ideas of conspicuous value and presents them in a manner not less elegant than persuasive." Madison added: "if compleat success shd. not reward your labors, there is ample room for improvements in the criminal jurisprudence of Louisiana as elsewhere which are well worthy the exertion of your best powers."[197]

To promote Edward Livingston's anti-gallows agenda, a list of death penalty opponents and critics—labeled "Testimony of Statesmen, Jurists, Philosophers, and Others, Against the Death Punishment"—was also compiled. That list not only included quotes from Blackstone, Beccaria, Bentham, Lafayette and Montaigne, but from Dr. Benjamin Rush, John Quincy Adams, Benjamin Franklin, Cassius Clay, Robert Rantoul, Jr., and Richard M. Johnson. "Fellow-citizens," the quote from Martin Van Buren's Vice President Richard M. Johnson read, "Your invitation to me to attend the anniversary meetings of the National and of the New York State Societies for the Abolition of Capital Punishment, is duly received. Under circumstances which would admit of my attendance, it would give me great pleasure to meet you and the many humane citizens who will be in your city on that noble occasion. My heart is with you."[198] The list of abolitionist sympathizers thus included extremely prominent men of the founding generation as well as those born later, such as Robert Rantoul, Jr. (1805–1852), the Massachusetts native who so vocally opposed capital punishment. In "Remarks on Education," published in *The North American Review* in 1838, Rantoul wrote that, "Beccaria, in 1767, predicted that the punishment of death would not survive that happy period, 'when knowledge instead of ignorance shall become the portion of the greater number.'"

The education and writings of Robert Rantoul, Jr. show that Beccaria's writings were still being read—and were very relevant—in the nineteenth century. While at Harvard from 1822 to 1826, Rantoul read Latin and Greek, studied German and mastered French, and became familiar with Europe's history and political institutions. According to an 1888 biographical sketch of Rantoul: "He was as intimately acquainted with Grotius and Puffendorf, Machiavelli and Beccaria, Montesquieu and Jeremy Bentham, as the foremost of his classmates were with their required classwork." Rantoul—whose father is known to have opposed capital punishment as early as 1809—cited Montesquieu, Blackstone and Beccaria in his advocacy in opposition to the gallows, with another sketch of Rantoul's life at Cambridge noting as follows: "He was at this early period profoundly interested in the science of government and legislation, and became intimately conversant with the leading continental writers in these departments, especially with Beccaria and Montesquieu." As a Massachusetts legislator, Rantoul pushed for the abolition of capital punishment in his home state, giving speeches and advocating in writing for his position.

In a Massachusetts legislative report on the abolition of capital punishment, prepared in 1836, both Montesquieu and Beccaria were specifically invoked for the maxim that "every punishment which does not arise from absolute necessity; and even every act of authority of one man over another, for which there is not an absolute necessity, is tyrannical." "Every one will agree with Beccaria," that report read, "that the question, whether the punishment of death is really necessary for the safety or good order of society, is a problem which should be solved with that geometrical precision, which the mist of sophistry, the seduction of eloquence, and the timidity of doubt are unable to resist." The report also cited Beccaria's proportionality principle and noted that Jeremy Bentham had "adopted" the "greatest happiness" principle, with the report quoting Beccaria as follows: "'If we look into history, we shall find,' says Beccaria, 'that laws which are, or ought to be, conventions between men in a state of freedom, have been, for the most part, the work of the passions of a few,—not dictated by a cool examiner of human nature, who had this only end in view, the greatest happiness of the greatest number.'"[199] As Americans of this era continued their pursuit of happiness, ridding society of capital punishment rose higher on the agenda.

The quotations accompanying Livingston's report, assembled from people throughout the United States, were calculated to engender additional public support for the abolitionist cause—a cause that counted among its supporters a growing number of leading citizens. "Dr. Benj. Franklin"—a household name whose attributed quote actually came from an essay written by Dr. Benjamin Rush that was *read* at Benjamin Franklin's house—was quoted as follows: "Laws which inflict death for murder are, in my opinion, as unchristian as those which justify or tolerate revenge."[200] "If ever any philosophy deserved the epithets of useful and practical," Edward Livingston wrote, "it was that of Dr. Franklin. His opinions must have weight, not only from his character, but from the simple, intelligible reasoning by which they are supported." Livingston then purports to quote Dr. Franklin—listing as the source, *Inquiry upon Public Punishments*—as having said the following:

> I suspect the attachment to death, as a punishment for murder, in minds otherwise enlightened upon the subject of capital punishments, arises from a false interpretation of a passage in the old testament, and that is—'He that sheds the blood of man, by man shall his blood be shed.' This has been supposed to imply,

that blood could only be expiated by blood. But I am disposed to believe, with a late commentator on this text of scripture, that it is rather a prediction than a law. The language of it is simply, that such is the folly and depravity of man, that murder, in every age, shall beget murder. Laws, therefore, which inflict death for murder, are, in my opinion, as unchristian as those which justify or tolerate revenge; for the obligations of Christianity upon individuals, to promote repentance, to forgive injuries, and to discharge the duties of universal benevolence, are equally binding upon states.[201]

The excerpted quotation, in fact, was misattributed to Dr. Franklin as the same language appears in Dr. Benjamin Rush's essay, *An enquiry into the effects of public punishments upon criminals, and upon society*. That essay, according to the *American Museum*, was "By dr. Benjamin Rush" and "Read in the society for promoting political enquiries, convened at the house of his excellency Benjamin Franklin, esq. in Philadelphia, March 9th, 1787."[202] The misattribution was later noted by anti-death penalty activist Charles Spear in his nineteenth-century book, *Essays on the Punishment of Death*. Charles Spear began his own book with an anti-death penalty quotation from Lafayette, another prominent and beloved figure in the American Revolution.[203] When Lafayette returned to the United States in 1824, he was hailed as a hero of the Revolutionary War and large crowds greeted him.[204] Spear—the man invoking Lafayette's name—was a Boston Universalist minister who edited a weekly paper, *The Hangman*; a monthly magazine, *The Prisoners' Friend*; and who formed, with others, a Massachusetts society for the abolition of capital punishment in 1844.[205] Universalists had a long-standing interest in penal reform, and Spear was one of their most committed anti-gallows activists. "[I]n the revolutionary era," writes one historian, "a number of Universalists, such as Benjamin Rush, had joined Quakers in support of penal reform and in opposition to capital punishment."[206] In England, the Society for the Abolition of Capital Punishment—supported by the Duke of Sussex and other prominent Englishmen—had earlier been founded in 1828, with petitions there leading to the abolition of the death penalty for forgery.[207]

Yet another source, a New York legislative report from 1860, reprinted the series of compiled abolitionist quotations, but added new names to the growing list of death penalty opponents. That report, taking note of the death penalty's abolition in Michigan, Rhode Island and Wisconsin, included a quote from Beccaria but focused largely on homegrown American opposition. "A large portion of our citizens believe that the death penalty ought to be abolished," the report read. The 1860 report also stated in part: "The taking of human life for murder, which for many years has been regarded as absolutely necessary to the security and well being of society, has, under the enlightened policy of free and republican institutions, come to be looked upon as quite unnecessary, and for which there can no longer be a good apology." Among the quoted names in the report: George M. Dallas, the lawyer, U.S. Senator from Pennsylvania, and eleventh Vice President of the United States, serving under President James K. Polk. Educated at the College of New Jersey before being admitted to the bar in 1813, Dallas began his career in public service as a secretary to Albert Gallatin, Thomas Jefferson's former secretary of the treasury. "Time and reflection," Dallas was quoted as saying, "have confirmed the opinion cherished by me for many years, that in our country at least, no just cause exists for the infliction of death punishment, and that its abolishment will be hereafter looked upon as evidence of the moral character of nations, as they successively shall blot it from their criminal codes."[208]

George Dallas had long been exposed to Beccaria's ideas. In 1830, a book was published in Boston titled *What Is True Civilization, or Means to Suppress the Practice of Duelling, to Prevent, or to Punish Crimes, and to Abolish the Punishment of Death*. That book, dedicated to Dallas himself and reprinting an exchange of letters between Dallas and the book's author, was written by James Sega of the University of Pavia, Beccaria's alma mater. A letter from Sega to Dallas, written in Philadelphia, had explained how Sega, an Italian, had been "driven from my country, far from all that endeareth life," and had been "brought personally to witness the evils, which society draws upon itself." "Study, long meditations, the greatest trials, feelings and chagrins," Sega wrote in English, not his native tongue, "have caused the thoughts of my childhood, and those of manhood to be embodied into the present work." "I am not entitled to the kind dedication you proposed giving to your valuable work," Dallas wrote back to Sega from Philadelphia on September 6, 1830. "That I wish it every success, and you every honor and support," Dallas added, "is certain:—but the trifling services I have been able to render do not merit so flattering a reward." "If it be in my power to be useful to you here, pray command me," Dallas concluded. In Sega's book, one finds more than thirty references to Beccaria, including to "the illustrious Beccaria."[209]

George Mifflin Dallas (1792–1864)—to use his full name—had a distinguished career in American politics. He served as the Mayor of Philadelphia from 1828 to 1829, the U.S. Attorney for the Eastern District of Pennsylvania from 1829 to 1831, a U.S. Senator from Pennsylvania from 1831 to 1833, the Attorney General of Pennsylvania from 1833 to 1835, the U.S. Minister to Russia from 1837 to 1839, the 11th Vice President of the United States from 1845 to 1849, and the U.S. Minister to the Court of St. James from 1856 to 1861. His father, Alexander Dallas—born in Kingston, Jamaica and educated in Edinburgh—was James Madison's Secretary of the Treasury and also, briefly, the Secretary of War. George Dallas got his middle name due to his father's close friendship with another abolition-leaning Pennsylvania politician, Thomas Mifflin.[210] After being elected Vice President in 1844, George Dallas agreed to address the founding convention for the American Society for the Abolition of Capital Punishment, which—not surprisingly, given his political prominence—chose him as its first president.[211] The American Society for the Abolition of Capital Punishment was organized in 1845 after state anti-gallows societies in Massachusetts and New York had been formed.[212] At its first meeting, the gallows was described as "that revolting engine of cruelty, barbarism, and vengeance." Tobias Purrington, in the 1850s, felt confident enough about the movement's prospects for success that he predicted "it will not be long before capital punishment will be banished from every State of this great and glorious Union—the consummation of which is an event devoutly to be wished by every true Christian, statesman, and philosopher."[213]

In the 1860 New York legislative report, many other prominent figures, including religious leaders and politicians, were featured, too. Their quotes—as is apparent from the way in which they were compiled—were also meant to inspire still more anti-death penalty sentiment.[214] Many of their own views were, no doubt, originally inspired by Beccaria, William Penn's abolitionist example, their own humanitarian impulses or religious beliefs, or some combination thereof.[215] One New York lawyer, John O'Sullivan, for example, had campaigned for the death penalty's abolition in the 1840s at the New York State Assembly, and at rallies and public debates. "The ancient and universal usage of all nations is sometimes urged in behalf of capital punishment," O'Sullivan wrote. "The history of all human progress," he added, "is but a record of the slow and successive conquest of reason over error." Calling for New Yorkers to change their ways, he argued: "Not even the most bigoted and narrow-minded partisan of capital punishment would pretend to claim for it any applicability to the age and social institutions in the midst of which we live." The "science of construction and discipline of penitentiaries," O'Sullivan remarked, had made executions unnecessary and nothing more than "a right of cruel and barbarian vengeance." "We have but to will it, and the immured and guarded malefactor is placed ... beyond any possibility of escape," he noted of penitentiaries. To support his position, O'Sullivan quoted St. Augustine, Benjamin Franklin, Robert Rantoul and Beccaria.[216]

The 1860 New York legislative report also quoted New York governors who had publicly supported abolitionist efforts. Governor George Clinton's 1794 quote, an abbreviated version of his legislative address, was reported as follows: "The sanguinary complexion of our criminal code has long been a subject of complaint. It is certainly a matter of serious concern that capital convictions are so frequent — so little attention paid to a due proportion of punishment — I have confidence in your wisdom and humanity." Governor Daniel Tompkins was also quoted as saying this in 1812: "I have always entertained serious doubts whether society has the right to take away life in any case. It is the vestige of barbarism." And New York Governor DeWitt Clinton was quoted, too, first in 1820: "Great good has been done by the amelioration of the criminal code."[217] And then in 1824 and 1827, respectively: "It is very desirable that the crime of murder may be accurately described first and second degree — death penalty only to the first degree." "The statuary punishments are so unequal, that they border on cruelty." And finally, Governor William H. Seward in 1842: "Every philanthropist clings to the hope that the supremacy of the laws will be maintained without exacting the sacrifice of life."[218]

These men were leading figures in American politics and certainly not fringe or anti-establishment figures. George Clinton, the first Governor of New York, became the fourth Vice President of the United States. Daniel Tompkins, New York's fourth governor, became the sixth U.S. Vice President; DeWitt Clinton, New York's sixth governor, was the Federalist nominee for the 1812 U.S. presidential election; and William Seward, New York's twelfth governor, acquired Alaska for the United States. Such political leaders, it is clear, worried about cruel acts and the proper calibration of criminal sentences, remaining highly conversant with Cesare Beccaria and his ideas about proportionality. Way back in 1787 and 1788, when DeWitt Clinton had written letters using the pen name "A Countryman," he had quoted Beccaria — the much-invoked Italian philosopher — in the December 6, 1787 edition of the *New York Journal*.[219]

In Massachusetts, the state's attorney general and future governor, James Sullivan (1744–1808), became a particularly forceful advocate for penal reform.[220] In a biography of Sullivan, published in 1859, biographer Thomas Amory recounts: "Among civilized nations ameliorations of their criminal codes have, at times, occupied the attention of humane and able minds; and Beccaria, Bentham and Romilly, are honorably distinguished by their philanthropic exertions in this direction." Sullivan, his biographer wrote, found himself "strongly prepossessed in favor of the plan of criminal jurisprudence recently introduced into Pennsylvania, and endeavoring to produce its adoption by Massachusetts."[221] Both John Hancock and Samuel Adams of Massachusetts, Amory wrote, "sympathized with these views of reform, and lent their powerful influence in bringing them about." As one source notes of what transpired around the time of Shays' Rebellion (1786–1787) in Massachusetts: "[I]n the spring elections of 1787 the people radically changed the composition of the General Court by electing as members a large number of Shays's sympathizers. John Hancock, who was known for his liberal views, was elected the new governor." That sources notes that "the people were able to realize some of the aims of the rebellion, in particular, the abolition of imprisonment for the nonpayment of debts," with fourteen death sentences eventually commuted. The two men that came closest to execution were brought to the gallows and had nooses put around their necks, with the sheriff pulling out a paper at the last minute stating that the state, "in its mercy," had pardoned them. The executions, Hancock concluded, "should be avoided for the public good." Daniel Shays himself was later pardoned, and only two men, John Bly and Charles Rose, sentenced to death in the wake of Shays' Rebellion, were ultimately executed.[222]

There was, especially in those days, with slavery and a whole host of draconian sentencing options still in place, almost endless reform to be done. In England, justices of the peace ordered that offenders' ears be cropped; courts in Massachusetts and Virginia once inflicted that punishment, too; and in the eighteenth century, brandings took place in places such as Maryland, New Hampshire, New York and Massachusetts.[223] For example, in 1754, in New York, a young man convicted of manslaughter was "burnt in the hand" and a woman was lashed "at the whipping-post."[224] In Virginia, offenders were, at one time, also punished by either loss of ears or by the slitting of the ears.[225] Only through concerted efforts did such barbaric means of punishment, including the ducking-stool, pass from the scene. While men were traditionally punished in the stocks in earlier times, ducking- or cucking-stools had been used extensively in the sixteenth and seventeenth centuries to punish women. For example, in *A Treatise of the Pleas of the Crown*, Englishman William Hawkins — under the heading "Cucking Stool" — wrote: "Sometimes called Ducking Stool, the usual punishment for a *common scold*." "Infamous punishments, such as cropping, branding, the pillory and ducking-stool," Thomas Amory notes, "were in time abolished, and punishment shown to be more efficacious when less severe and more certain."[226]

The penal reform efforts in Massachusetts typify the kinds of debates that were taking place across America — and in parts of Europe. It was in 1793 that Boston's *Independent Chronicle* published two articles by "Marcus," thought to be a pseudonym for Attorney General James Sullivan. "I very much doubt the right of any Civil Government to punish a citizen with death for any crime whatever," Marcus began. Historian Alan Rogers points out that the articles by Marcus also emphasized that because a citizen did not have the right "to dispose of his own life," the government could not assume that power. In *On Crimes and Punishments*, Beccaria had said much the same thing, with Beccaria writing that suicide "is a crime which seems not to admit of punishment, properly speaking; for it cannot be inflicted but on the innocent, or upon an insensible dead body." Marcus also insisted that the right of self-defense — a right enshrined in the criminal law for individuals put in danger of bodily harm — is "merely momentary" and not "transferable" to a republican government. It was wrong, Marcus argued, to be involved in "launching a soul into the presence of its Maker and Judge."[227]

An early editor of the *Massachusetts Centinel*, historian Alan Rogers notes, also suggested in 1784 that "taking a man's life for every trifling theft, as is done in England, is a disgrace to a civilized nation." "Humanity recoils from the idea," that editor wrote. "By the 1790s," Rogers concludes, "the pace of capital prosecutions and executions had slowed dramatically, and the people of Massachusetts recoiled from the excessive use of capital punishment."[228] One notable Massachusetts native, Abigail Adams, privately expressed the same opinion in the 1780s after she saw a captive highwayman, a young man of approximately 20 years of age, while traveling in a coach from Canterbury to London to join her husband John. "We saw the poor wretch, ghastly, and horrible, brought along on foot," she reported. Upon hearing the young man's captors tell him he would "swing" and had "but a short time" to live, Abigail recoiled in horror at the prospect of a hanging for that offense — or at least the way in which the young man was openly taunted. "Though every robber may deserve death," she said, "yet to exult over the wretched is what our country is not accustomed to. Long may it be free of such villainies and long may it preserve a commiseration for the wretched."[229]

From the founding period up until 1860, America's anti-death penalty movement remained vigorous and active, with many prominent figures joining the movement. The Civil War, however, quelled anti-gallows activity, putting an immediate stop to the movement's momentum. That war claimed more than 600,000 lives, and in the midst of all the bloodshed, the fate of criminals was, to put it mildly, not high on the agenda of U.S. lawmakers. Historian David Brion Davis found "no mention of capital punishment in the legislative journals" during the Civil War, noting that it was hard "for rationalist reformers to preach against the violence of capital punishment when reformers themselves advocated the shedding of blood." A particularly prominent U.S. anti-death penalty activist, Marvin Bovee, even delayed publication of his book *Christ and the Gallows* until 1869—four years after the Civil War came to a close. The publication date had originally been slated for 1861, but the Civil War broke out before the book was ready to be printed. "To have presented a work of this kind during the continuance of such a struggle would have been 'ill-timed,' to say the least," Bovee wrote in the book's preface after the book was finally published. As a result of the war, which saw its own share of executions on both the Union and Confederate sides, "men's finer sensibilities, which had once been revolted by the execution of a fellow human being, seemed hardened and blunted," as David Brion Davis later recorded.[230]

Beccaria's Role in Reform

The death penalty's curtailment in Pennsylvania was inspired in part by William Penn's legacy, by Beccaria's treatise, and by the writings of Dr. Benjamin Rush and jurist William Bradford, two of Beccaria's biggest disciples.[231] As for the Italian philosopher's role, Thomas McKean, the Chief Justice of the Pennsylvania Supreme Court, referred to "the great Becaria" [sic], while "[t]he celebrated work of *Beccaria*" was invoked elsewhere. Beccaria's treatise, in Pennsylvania, was "said to have served as a model for the penal code of this state, which justly excites the admiration of the civilized world."[232] And just as Philadelphians looked to Beccaria's ideas prior to the country's Constitutional Convention of 1787, Pennsylvania's penal reform efforts were passionately discussed throughout the rest of the country—and even in Italy amongst the men in Beccaria's own social circle. In his *Viaggio*, the Italian botanist Luigi Castiglioni would put in this way: "My fellow citizens cannot but be pleased at knowing how much influence the book *On Crimes and Punishments* has had in establishing the penal laws of the various American constitutions; and I am convinced that they will read with pleasure a letter written to me by the attorney general of the State of Pennsylvania upon sending me a copy of this book printed in Philadelphia a few years ago."[233] Beccaria so significantly influenced American reformers that Dr. Benjamin Rush—America's first preeminent abolitionist—has been called the "American Beccaria."[234]

That Beccaria materially changed American attitudes is reflected in writings that both mention and fail to mention his name. For example, after soliciting the views of its readers, one letter to the editor in the March 1817 edition of *The Christian Disciple*—written by "A. B."—was a lengthy piece on capital punishment. "The question, whether capital punishments be expedient or lawful, is not to be despatched as easily as many seem to imagine," that letter began. The letter writer—harkening back to the concept of necessity—expressed the view "that society has no right to inflict punishments of greater severity than its security demands." "The civil magistrate," A. B. wrote, "has no authority to inflict *one pain* which this end does not require." "The only province of the civil ruler," A. B. explained, "is, to watch over the interests of the community; and any punishment, which these interests do not require, is inflicted without authority, is gratuitous cruelty, is an act of usurpation." "From this principle," A. B. then wrote, "it follows, that if the peace and rights of the community can be secured by punishments less severe than death, then death cannot justly be inflicted, and it should no longer hold a place in our penal code." A. B. felt that "the question relating to capital punishments is to be determined, neither by abstract reasoning, nor by feeling, but by *experience*." "We must judge from *facts*, and unhappily the facts are, at present, too few, to warrant a decided judgment." The writer speculated "[t]hat capital punishments will at length be abolished," noting that "[b]reaking on the wheel, maiming, quartering, burning," and "other relicks of barbarism have passed away." Yet, the writer emphasized, "[f]riends of humanity, should, however, beware of urging a sudden and immediate abolition of punishment by death." "In our present imperfect state," the letter writer urged, "long established abuses must gradually be removed."[235]

In another article that appeared in *The Christian Disciple* a short time later, the writer took specific note of Beccaria's role in shaping the public debate. As the article titled "Capital Punishments" began:

> The public attention seems lately to have been turned to the question of the right of society to inflict capital punishment. This question was much agitated in Europe in the latter part of the last century. The Marquis *Beccaria*, in his elegant treatise on crimes and punishments, and *Voltaire*, in an essay on the same subject, discussed it with much ingenuity; and urged the policy, and developed the numerous advantages of its abolition. How honourable would it be to *America*, if this great desideratum could be effected in this country.[236]

"It has become a serious question," another 1817 piece in *The Christian Disciple* offered, "whether capital punishments are either necessary or useful, and whether some method may not be devised more beneficial both to the community and to the criminal."[237] Whether based on the precepts of Christianity, the rights of man, or reason or logic, anti-death penalty appeals regularly incorporated Beccaria's name or Beccarian features.

The writings of America's founding period, as well as those of later generations, show that Americans—from the beginning—were focused on *improving* American society. When the Declaration of Independence and early state constitutions were drafted and signed, no one would have suggested or even hinted that the state of American life or law was in a perfected state. On the contrary, America's founders and framers recognized that, following the break with Great Britain, much work remained to be done, both politically and economically and in terms of penal reform. The Founding Fathers understood that declaring independence was just the first step toward achieving freedom, and that adopting new constitutions and laws was not an endpoint, but a mechanism for facilitating and achieving greater human and scientific progress in the future. "The influence of English law practice on the American bar was inevitable," writes one legal scholar, "as the primary early sources of legal training for aspiring American lawyers were apprenticeship, reading Coke or Blackstone in the office of an English-trained barrister, and study in one of the English Inns of Court." The first Americans, however, saw English customs and practices—and the English Bloody Code in particular—as legal precedents that could be modified or disregarded altogether if facts and evidence suggested such an approach. Indeed, almost every prospective lawyer started his legal studies in the early nineteenth century by studying Tucker's *Blackstone*—an *American* text that utilized English law as a jumping off point, not the be all and end all of jurisprudential thought.[238]

Chapter 5

Rethinking Bloody Codes: The Rise of the Penitentiary

English and Early American Punishments

In England and colonial and early America, executions and severe, non-lethal corporal punishments were customary. English law authorized hangings and even boiling to death, with branding, cutting off genitals, "pulling out the tongue," and a host of other brutal punishments put to use. For example, in 1630, Alexander Leighton—a Puritan clergyman found to have libeled Anglican bishops—was almost whipped to death, subjected to the pillory, had an ear nailed to the pillory then cut off, had his cheek branded and his nose slit, and was then imprisoned. Another Puritan, William Prynne, also suffered the pillory and, before being imprisoned, was branded on the forehead and had his ears sliced off. George Jeffreys, a notorious figure known as "the Hanging Judge," presided over the Bloody Assizes of 1685 that sent scores of men to the gallows after the Monmouth Rebellion. Jeffreys served as Lord Chancellor and Lord Chief Justice of the King's Bench in the 1680s, and he sent almost three hundred prisoners to the gallows and ordered the infliction of other brutal punishments, too.

Such sentences often became notorious examples of judicial excesses and led to the English prohibition, in the English Bill of Rights of 1689, against "cruel and unusual punishments." In one instance, an English cleric, Titus Oates, was convicted of perjury for his role in the "Popish Plot hoax," a concocted charge—leading to multiple executions—that English Catholics and Jesuit priests intended to assassinate Charles II. Jeffreys and another judge, Francis Withens, thereafter expressed regret that the law did not permit Oates to be hanged for his offense. "In the national hysteria that followed Oates's sensational allegations," historian Leonard Levy recounts, "fifteen people, including the leader of the Jesuit order in England, were disemboweled, quartered, and beheaded for high treason." Instead of being executed as Jeffreys and his fellow judge would have liked, Oates himself was defrocked, ordered to pay a hefty fine, whipped from Aldgate to Newgate and then from Newgate to Tyburn, and sentenced to be imprisoned for life and to be pilloried four times a year. Only after the Glorious Revolution of 1688, which resulted in Parliament's adoption of the prohibition on "cruel and unusual punishments," was Oates' sentence remitted. In 1800, one man—expressing concerns about "a modern Jeffreys" and "the Machinists of Sedition Laws"—wrote to James Madison, one of the architects of America's Constitution and its Bill of Rights, to express optimism for "friends of republicanism" and "the genius of american Liberty."[1]

Even while living under England's harsh legal regime, many American colonists—like English supporters of republicanism—recoiled from its excesses. In a draft of an essay that would become *A Dissertation on Canon and Feudal Law*, John Adams—harkening way back to the first settlers in America—wrote in February 1765 of "Tyranny," "Cruelty," and "Tyrants," of what the early settlers faced in Europe, and of "a Resolution formed by a sensible People almost in despair." "They had become intelligent in general," Adams wrote of those who left Europe, pointing out that some of them "had been galled, and fretted, and whipped and cropped, and hanged and burned." "I always consider the settlement of America," Adams emphasized, "with Reverence and Wonder—as the Opening of a grand scene and Design in Providence, for the Illumination of the Ignorant and the Emancipation of the slavish Part of Mankind all over the Earth." "[T]hey at last resolved to fly to the Wilderness, for Refuge from the temporal and spiritual Principalities and Powers, and Plagues and scourges of their Native Country," Adams recorded, saying that "Tyranny in every shape" was the "Disdain and Abhorrence" of "the first Settlers of these Colonies."[2]

In colonial Massachusetts, Adams' place of residence, numerous acts were punished capitally or corporally, typically based on religious grounds. "Anglo-Saxon Law, Norman Law, Roman Law and Canon Law," one Scottish writer emphasized, "were all strongly influenced by the Mosaic Law." Indeed, Old Testament passages exerted tremendous influence on early colonial leaders, shaping thought about crime and punishment. For example, in the Massachusetts Bay Colony, the "Body of Liberties"—which made twelve crimes punishable by death, and which allowed for the use of "stripes"—was distributed in 1641 to towns in the colony. Biblical citations, from Deuteronomy, Exodus, Leviticus and Numbers, were listed as authority for eleven of the capital crimes, with only one capital crime— conspiring and attempting to invade or engage in insurrection or public rebellion—containing no Bible passage to support it. Leviticus 24:19–20, establishing the *lex talionis* rule, reads: "If a man injures his neighbor, what he has done must be done to him: broken limb for broken limb, eye for eye, tooth for tooth. As the injury inflicted, so must be the injury suffered." Following Massachusetts' example, Connecticut's 1642 colonial code also listed twelve capital crimes, with eleven of the offenses once again based on scriptural passages.

The Massachusetts Body of Liberties, incorporated in a later-published abridgement of the law, was, in fact, described in an introductory "Epistle" as "a modell of the Judiciall lawes of Moses with such other cases as might be referred to them." That abridgement, published in 1648 under the title, *The Book of the General Lawes and Libertyes concerning the Inhabitants of the Massachusets*, built upon the "Body of Liberties" and incorporated, in the section on "Capital Lawes," fourteen provisions from the Old Testament. An earlier draft code, written by John Cotton, was actually titled "A Model of Moses His Judicialls." The General Court of Massachusetts, a powerful institution, rejected Cotton's draft, which sought to make twenty offenses capital crimes and which asked authorities "to consider them as laws, and not faile to inflict condigne and proportionable punishments upon every man impartiallie, that shall infringe or violate any of them." But many of Cotton's draft provisions made it into the final draft of the Body of Liberties, with the number of capital crimes in colonial Massachusetts eventually rising to twenty-five toward the end of the seventeenth century. Only after the Glorious Revolution of 1688 did the colony's number of capital crimes shrink. The colony's laws were reworked in 1692, and by 1736 colonial Massachusetts had slightly more than a dozen capital crimes of widely differing types. There were violent crimes (premeditated murder, rape, dueling resulting in loss of life), political and religious ones (treason, being a Jesuit), property crimes (arson, burglary, counterfeiting, piracy, robbery and stealing), and a variety of others (bestiality, infanticide, polygamy and sodomy).[3]

In the second edition of *The History of the Colony of Massachusett's Bay*, published in 1765, Thomas Hutchinson—the Lieutenant-Governor of the Massachusetts Province— noted how early colonists were "without a code or body of laws" but that "[i]n punishing offences, they professed to be governed by the judicial law of Moses, but no farther than those laws were of a moral nature." Early punishments in the colony, as in England itself, included being put in the stocks or being severely whipped, with members of the colony approving their 1641 code—later incorporated into the 1648 colonial code—that made a dozen offenses capital in nature. "Murder, sodomy, witchcraft, arson, and rape of a child under ten years of age," Hutchinson wrote, were capital crimes in both England and the colony, with Hutchinson calling the colony's laws "more sanguinary than the English laws; for many offences were made capital here, which were not so there." "[A] man may give his wife moderate correction without exposing himself to any penalty in the law," Hutchinson wrote in an era before domestic violence was taken as seriously as it is today. After adding that "a man who struck his wife, was liable to a fine of ten pounds or corporal punishment," and that "[a] woman who struck her husband, was liable to the same penalties," Hutchinson emphasized that the latter rule "seems to leave the wife to the mercy of the husband, who ordinarily must have paid the fine himself, or suffer her to be whipped."

In detailing the Massachusetts Bay Colony's history, Hutchinson included a chapter on the colony's laws and the manner of punishment. For example, he emphasized it was, under colonial law, a capital offense to "worship of any other God besides the Lord God," noting that "[p]erhaps a roman catholic, for the adoration of the host, might have come within this law." Blasphemy, man-stealing and willful perjury, Hutchinson added, citing biblical passages, had also been made capital crimes, as was "adultery with a married woman, both to the man and woman, although the man was single." "[S]everal have suffered death upon this law," Hutchinson noted of the bar on adultery, though he clarified that "[m]ale adultery with an unmarried woman, was not capital." "Burglary and theft, in a house or fields, on the Lord's day," Hutchinson added, "were capital upon a third conviction." The punishment of rape, Hutchinson further observed, "was left to the court to punish with death or other grievous punishment, at discretion," though Hutchinson editorialized that no judge desired "to have a capital punishment left to his discretion" and that "it may be doubted whether, in any case, it can be of public utility." "Fornication," he added, "might be punished by enjoining marriage, by fine or corporal punishment."[4] In December 1767, the then-colonial lawyer John Adams himself noted that after a poor, single woman in Massachusetts had been convicted of fornication, the court sentenced her "to pay a fine of twelve shillings to his majesty, or be whipped ten stripes on her naked body, to pay costs of prosecution, and stand committed until sentence be performed."[5]

In England and colonial America, the infliction of bodily punishments—except for a time in Quaker-dominated Pennsylvania—was mostly taken for granted. Before 1681, when Charles II granted William Penn the colony of Pennsylvania, that locale's first penal code, the "Hempstead Code," included more than ten capital crimes. Among the offenses in that 1676 code: treason, premeditated murder, manslaughter, poisoning, homosexuality, bestiality, man-stealing, perjury in capital cases, and a child's assault of a parent. Arson could also result in a death sentence at the court's discretion under the Hempstead Code, with robbery and burglary carrying a death sentence after the third offense. Although William Penn's "Great Law" of 1682 overrode this 1676 code, putting in place a milder punishment regime, Pennsylvania's assembly—which revised Penn's law in 1693, 1700 and 1706—still authorized harsh punishments, including corporal ones. As Gabriele Gottlieb explains in her Ph.D. dissertation, *Theater of Death: Capital Punishment in Early America*: "A second conviction for theft, for example, carried a life sentence in prison after 1700. The same was true for the offense of sodomy with an additional penalty of a whipping every three months for offenders who were single and castration for those who were married." "The Pennsylvania assembly," Gottlieb adds, "also increased the punishments for people of color, providing the death penalty not only for murder but also for burglary, rape, and buggery."[6]

In his *Commentaries on the Laws of England*, Sir William Blackstone had detailed the English government's use of capital and corporal punishments. For example, Blackstone observed that "in case of any treason committed by a female, the judgment is to be burned alive." In another section of his treatise, on the punishment of theft for those without property themselves, Blackstone wrote: "Sir Thomas More, and the marquis Beccaria, at the distance of more than two centuries, have very sensibly proposed that kind of corporal punishment, which approaches the nearest to a pecuniary satisfaction; *viz.* a temporary imprisonment, with an obligation to labour, first for the party robbed, and afterwards for the public, in works of the most slavish kind: in order to oblige the offender to repair, by his industry and diligence, the depredations he has committed upon private property and public order." "But," Blackstone cautioned his readers, "notwithstanding all the remonstrances of speculative politicians and moralists, the punishment of theft still continues, through-out the greatest part of Europe, to be capital: and Puffendorf, together with Sir Matthew Hale, are of opinion that this must always be referred to the prudence of the legislature; who are to judge, say they, when crimes are become so enormous as to require such san-guinary restrictions." Elsewhere, Blackstone did emphasize that the English Bill of Rights of 1689 "had a retrospect to some unprecedented proceedings in the court of king's bench, in the reign of king James the second." But he also stated that "the bill of rights was only declaratory, throughout, of the old constitutional law of the land."[7]

Once English subjects themselves, America's founders thus had significant exposure to capital and corporal punishments. In 1733, Benjamin Franklin—writing in *The Penn-sylvania Gazette*—penned these words: "Yesterday, being Market Day, Watt who was con-cern'd in the Counterfeit Money, as mentioned in one of our late Papers, received part of his Punishment, being whipt, pilloried and cropt. He behaved so as to touch the Com-passion of the Mob, and they did not fling at him (as was expected) neither Snow-balls nor any Thing else." Likewise, in 1751, a court in Spotsylvania County, Virginia ordered that the sheriff take Mary McDaniel "to the Whipping post & inflict fifteen lashes on her bare back." Her offense: petty larceny for stealing "the Cloaths of Mr George Washington when he was washing in the River some time last Summer." In the 1750s, George Wash-ington himself ordered executions and other corporal punishments, including floggings. In 1756, Washington—responding to an inquiry about whether deserters should be whipped—instructed Lieutenant Colonel Adam Stephen of the Virginia Regiment: "Things not yet being rightly settled for punishing Deserters according to their crimes; you must go on in the old way of whipping stoutly." Writing to Virginia Governor Robert Dinwid-die, Washington also wrote this in 1756 as he struggled to carry out orders to build a chain of forts "on the Frontiers": "I could by no means bring the Quakers to any Terms—They chose rather to be whipped to death than bear arms, or lend us any assistance what-ever upon the Fort, or any thing of self-defence."[8]

The Club of Honest Whigs

In *Political Disquisitions*, a book written in 1774, the British Whig politician James Burgh (1714–1775), who died just a year later, penned a whole chapter titled "Of Pun-ishments" in which he also wrote of the harsh punishments of the time even as he cited Beccaria's reformist ideas. The son of a Scottish minister, Burgh ran a school in England and, in the 1760s, joined a group called the Club of Honest Whigs. That club met in Lon-don coffeehouses every other Thursday, and its evening meetings, at which politics, re-ligion and scientific matters were discussed, drew men such as John Canton, James Boswell,

Benjamin Franklin, Richard Price, Joseph Priestley and Samuel Vaughan. Priestley—like Bentham and Beccaria—was a prominent utilitarian, saying in his *Essay on the First Principles of Government* (1768) that "all people live in society for their mutual advantage; so that the good and happiness of the members, that is, the majority of the members of any state, is the greatest standard by which everything relating to that state must finally be determined." After emigrating to the United States in 1794, Priestley—an avid reader of Beccaria and the discoverer of oxygen who had left England for greener pastures—would laud his new country in a letter to his friend Theophilus Lindsey. As Priestley wrote: "I feel as if I were in another world. I never before could conceive how satisfactory it is to have the feelings I now have from a sense of perfect security and liberty, all men having equal rights and privileges, and speaking and acting as if they were sensible of it." In his two-volume *Lectures on History and General Policy*, published in London in 1793, Priestley—just a year before his departure for America—cited Beccaria's treatise on more than one occasion.

The Club of Honest Whigs, the English social group of which Priestley had been a part, debated how best to achieve the happiness of its members—and, befitting that objective, did so in a lively and festive manner. As Boswell wrote of the club meetings: "We have wine and punch upon the table. Some of us smoke a pipe, conversation goes on pretty formally, sometimes sensibly, and sometimes furiously. At nine there is a sideboard with Welsh rabbits, apple puffs, porter and beer." Composed principally of Quakers and other dissenters, the Club of Honest Whigs—as Benjamin Franklin dubbed it—was pro-American and its members often discussed political and philosophical matters. In October 1775, Benjamin Franklin—having returned to the United States—wrote to Joseph Priestley, then still in England, that "America is determined and unanimous; a very few tories and placemen excepted, who will probably soon export themselves." "My sincere respects … to the club of honest whigs," Franklin closed his letter. In a 1782 letter to Richard Price, Franklin specifically mentioned the writings "of our deceas'd Friend Mr Burgh, and others of our valuable Club." "I often think of the agreeable Evenings I used to pass with that excellent Collection of good Men, the Club at the London, and wish to be again among them," Franklin recollected later in another letter to Price, that one penned in 1784.

The opening part of Burgh's chapter on punishment, labeled "Rewards and Punishments," spoke of those two concepts as the "two principal means for drawing mankind to decency of behaviour, and deterring them from those actions which are hurtful to society." "As to punishments," Burgh wrote, "the most indispensable requisite is their being adequate." "Another essential in punishments," he emphasized, "is, that they be calculated to deter offenders, and prevent farther transgression. For this is, in fact, the sole end of punishments." Like Montesquieu had done, Burgh compared the punishment practices of different nations. "Malefactors in *Russia*," he noted, "are now condemned not to *death*, but to *work* in the mines. A regulation not less prudent than humane; since it renders this punishment of some advantage to the state." "In other countries," Burgh wrote, "they only know how to put a criminal to death with the apparatus, but are not able to prevent the commission of crimes." While Russia's empress, Burgh observed, had promised to stop putting people to death, he wrote with regret of English society: "We punish every thing with death, and with death of the same sort; so that two fellows shall go together to be hanged at *Tyburn*, the one for cutting his wife's throat, or worse, starving her to death, the other for taking a guinea of a rich man a stranger to him." In the eighteenth century, such scenes at Tyburn's scaffold had come to shock many Londoners, some of whom openly questioned the necessity for the harsh, indiscriminate punishments.

In its centuries-old history, it is estimated that tens of thousands of people were executed on London's triangular gallows at Tyburn. "For nearly 500 years," *The Rough Guide to London* reports, "Tyburn was the capital's main public execution site, its three-legged gibbet known as the 'Tyburn Tree' or the 'Triple Tree', capable of dispatching over 20 people at one go." In one execution, John Franks, a blind and elderly man, was hanged there on April 12, 1780, for stealing two damaged silver spoons from Jeremy Bentham, his former master. Bentham and his wife, Peter Linebaugh writes in his book, *The London Hanged*, testified at the Old Bailey against Franks, the servant who had once worked for them as a footman and a kitchen orderly. On the day of the execution, the first day of "the Easter Law Term," Linebaugh notes, "the grey-haired Franks was hanged reading 'his last repentant prayers with spectacles.'"

Unlike "[t]he authors of death statutes" who "belonged to the ruling and propertied classes," Peter Linebaugh emphasizes in *The London Hanged*, "[t]hose who suffered at Tyburn belonged to the propertyless and the oppressed." John Austin—a convicted murderer and highway robber—was the last such destitute person to be hanged at Tyburn's "triple tree," with his execution occurring on November 7, 1783, near London's present-day Marble Arch. The first execution in front of Newgate Prison—the notorious prison that held criminals and debtors—took place on December 9, 1783. As William Harvey's *London Scenes and London People* writes of Newgate, the new execution site: "The gallows was built with three cross-beams, for as many rows of sufferers (there were frequently from twelve to twenty)." From February to December 1785 alone, that source notes, "ninety-six persons suffered by the 'new drop,' substituted for the cart." Traditionally, prisoners had been taken, in a very public spectacle, from Newgate to Tyburn's gallows in a "death cart."

At Newgate Prison—the scaffold's new locale—condemned prisoners learned of their fate from the Bellman of St. Sepulchre, a man who, at midnight, made his rounds by candlelight, ringing a large, hand bell known as the "Execution Bell." As he passed the cells of those slated to die the following morning, he recited the following poem:

> All you that in the condemned hole do lie,
> Prepare you, for to-morrow you shall die;
> Watch all and pray, the hour is drawing near,
> That you before the Almighty must appear;
> Examine well yourselves, in time repent,
> That you may not to eternal flames be sent.
> And when St. Sepulchre's bell to-morrow tolls,
> The Lord have mercy on your souls.[9]

In England, the state's ultimate sanction thus had highly religious overtones.

James Burgh, the Scottish-born educator who also wrote *Thoughts on Education* (1747) and *The Dignity of Human Nature* (1754), was the son of a Scottish minister. Before his death, Burgh wrote about religious toleration and the preservation of liberty, with his widow, Hannah Harding Burgh, befriending Mary Wollstonecraft (1759–1797), the early English feminist. Wollstonecraft—whose brother Charles became a lieutenant in the U.S. Army—wrote novels as well as political titles such as *A Vindication of the Rights of Men* (1790), her much-celebrated response to Edmund Burke's conservative critique of the French Revolution. "The watchwords of the Revolution—liberty, fraternity, equality—spoke to her own deepest desires," Wollstonecraft's biographer emphasizes, pointing out that Wollstonecraft also described America, France's predecessor in revolution, as "the land of liberty, independence, and equality." Wollstonecraft also wrote *Thoughts on the Education of Daughters* (1787), and what became her most famous book, *A Vindication of the Rights of Women* (1792). After the latter book came out in London, John Adams' sister-in-law, Elizabeth Smith Shaw, quickly wrote to Abigail Adams to obtain a copy, with the book becoming an instant classic.

In London itself, after Mary Wollstonecraft's arrival in 1787, the radical publisher Joseph Johnson had helped her become a successful writer, giving her opportunities to write for his *Analytical Review*. That publication, established in London in 1788 and printed and produced by Johnson and the Scottish writer Thomas Christie until Johnson's 1798 conviction for seditious libel, itself promoted Beccaria's and Filangieri's ideas. As its 1791 review of Filangieri's *The Science of Legislation* reported: "The Marquis of Beccaria, by his essay on crimes and punishments, has rescued his country from the imputation of not having lately produced any great men, and the Chevalier Filangieri seems also destined to add to the laurels of modern Italy." "There is no science more useful to society," the book reviewer continued, "than that which treats of the laws by which its members ought to be governed, and no class of men are more deserving of public esteem, than those who by exerting their genius and their labours in the improvement of legislation, become the friends and benefactors of mankind." *The Analytical Review*, in 1798, also referenced Beccaria's advocacy for the "abolition of capital punishments" in a book review that spoke of "the very laudable attempt of meliorating the progress of legislation, and the defects incident to the trial and punishment of criminals."

Through Johnson, who famously hosted dinners and soirées and whose circle of friends included leading religious dissenters and Enlightenment figures such as Richard Price, William Blake and Joseph Priestley, Wollstonecraft also meet the pamphleteer Thomas Paine and, in 1791, her future husband, the English dissident and political philosopher William Godwin. "Beccaria," the biographer of Godwin notes, "enabled him to clarify his views on law and punishment," with Godwin then citing Beccaria's treatise in his own work. At Johnson's legendary dinners, the guests ate in "a little quaintly shaped upstairs room" where, on the wall, hung painter and frequent fellow guest Henry Fuseli's "The Nightmare." Johnson himself published the work of the Italian philosopher Giacinto Dragonetti, though much of the stock of Dragonetti's *A Treatise on Virtues and Rewards* was likely destroyed in a 1770 fire that, in that year, claimed Johnson's inventory of books. The novelist Mary Shelley, author of *Frankenstein* (1818), was Godwin and Wollstonecraft's daughter and later married the Romantic poet Percy Bysshe Shelley, a known reader of an Italian edition of Beccaria's treatise. In *Rambles in Germany and Italy in 1840, 1842, and 1843*, Mary Shelley herself, in discussing Italian literature, emphasized that Cesare Beccaria's daughter—the mother of the "devout Catholic" Alessandro Manzoni—"was an accomplished and active-minded woman." In that travelogue, she further described "Dei delitti e dell Pene"—Cesare Beccaria's by then classic treatise—as "the well-known work."[10]

In *Political Disquisitions*, Burgh—in his most popular book—emphatically wrote of how English laws had gone astray. "Our laws are grown to be very sanguinary," Burgh intoned, describing how death sentences were used indiscriminately. Burgh—a member of the social circle of which Joseph Johnson and Mary Wollstonecraft were a part—began by discussing the crime of murder, then described how Voltaire had criticized English law. "One would think nothing was more natural," Burgh emphasized, "than that murder be punished with death, according to *Moses*'s law, 'he, who sheddeth man's blood, by man shall his blood be shed.'" "It seems strange," Burgh editorialized in his book, "that any nation wise enough to propose punishments, should propose any other punishment for every injury, than formal retaliation, where it can be inflicted." Yet Burgh went on to say that public executions, "if they do not strike the people with fear, instead of being exemplary, do harm, by hardening them against punishment." "Whenever a people come to shew themselves unmoved, or not properly affected at those awful scenes," Burgh indicated, "a government, who had common sense, or any feeling of their proper function, would immediately put a stop to such exhibitions, and confine executions to the bounds of the prison." "In *Scotland* at an execution," he added, "all appear melancholy; many shed tears, and some faint away." Before noting that "[t]he good emperor *Antoninus* was so cautious of too great severity" that he "promised never to punish capitally a senator," Burgh called the law that made taking or killing a partridge at night punishable by public whipping a law "so cruel, that, I suppose, no magistrate will venture to put it in execution." "It is not the severity of punishments, but the certainty of not escaping, that restrains licentiousness," Burgh wrote in Beccarian-sounding language. Voltaire "makes repeated reflexions on this nation as bloody, cruel, rebellious, &c." Burgh further reported.

While writing of the death penalty's use for murderers, Burgh's invocation of Beccaria's writings shows the changing mores of that era. "If a government is mild, and a country happy under it," Burgh wrote, "banishment will be a sufficient punishment for most offences." Before emphasizing that Beccaria found capital punishment "wholly unnecessary" unless the offender's life "is clearly incompatible with the safety of the state," Burgh recounted the long history of England's use of executions: "*Henry* I. introduced hanging for theft and robbery." "Drowning was a punishment used in the time of *Edward* II. and before." "In the county palatine of Chester they used beheading instead of hanging, in the time of *Edward* I. A murderer was, in those days, dragged to execution by the relations of the murdered by a long rope." "A man was boiled to death in *Smithfield* (on an old statute since repealed) for poisoning." Such retaliatory impulses and the inclination toward private vengeance found plenty of adherents in antebellum America, too, though hanging was the usual method of execution. At one time, American executions regularly took place in the public square, with lynchings also occurring from time to time, especially in the Deep South. "Lynching," as one source puts it, "was an endemic presence in the U.S. South from the end of slavery until the late 1920s."

From a view of 30,000 feet, Beccaria's book—focused on the *prevention* of crime—thus appears to have changed the entire Anglo-American conversation about the rationale for punishment, with new state laws tailored to this new utilitarian philosophy. For example, New Hampshire's 1721 criminal code, which remained in effect until after the American Revolution, made these crimes capital offenses: willful murder, burglary, arson, rape, sodomy, bestiality, polygamy, concealing the death of a bastard child, and treason. But in 1791, the New Hampshire legislature narrowed the list of capital crimes to acts of treason, willful murder, burglary, arson at night, rape, sodomy and bestiality, thus eliminating the death penalty for polygamy and, by law, the presumption of murder for concealing the death of a child born out of wedlock. Beccaria's treatise, notes a history of capital punishment in New Hampshire, "had helped initiate" the 1791 anti-gallows debate in that state, with further reforms yet to come. In 1811, John Mason, John Goddard, and the famed lawyer Daniel Webster were appointed to revise New Hampshire's criminal laws and to establish rules for the new state prison then being built. The following year the state legislature abolished the death penalty for all crimes except murder and treason, mandating long periods of confinement at hard labor. The new law also allowed state-court judges to sentence certain offenders to solitary confinement for up to six months.[11]

Daniel Webster—like many lawyers of his time—did not oppose the death penalty in all circumstances. In fact, Daniel Webster—a lawyer's lawyer—argued both for and against the death penalty, depending on his role in the court proceedings at hand. In 1806, Webster, as a young lawyer, had unsuccessfully pleaded for a murderer's life in a courthouse in Plymouth, New Hampshire. "I made," Webster said later, "my first and the only solitary argument of my whole life against capital punishment." That murderer—following Webster's unsuccessful pleas—was hanged on August 12, 1806, before a crowd of ten thousand spectators. While Webster later spoke obliquely in an 1814 speech about how some would "run the hazard of capital punishment," it was his arguments in jury trials that got the most attention. In one murder trial, reflecting the change in rhetoric on the rationale for punishment that Beccaria's treatise had bought about, Webster made this argument:

> The criminal law is not founded in a principle of vengeance. It does not punish that it may inflict suffering. The humanity of the law feels every pain it causes, every hour of restraint it imposes, and more deeply still every life it forfeits. But it uses evil as the means of preventing greater evil. It seeks to deter from crime by the example of punishment. It restrains the liberty of the few offenders, that the many who do not offend may enjoy their liberty. It takes the life of the murderer, that other murders may not be committed.

"The law," Webster emphasized in that oration, punishes "not to satisfy any desire to inflict pain, but simply to prevent the repetition of crimes."

As a lawyer, Webster took his role as a zealous advocate very seriously, aware of the dire consequences often at stake in his cases. In *Dartmouth v. Woodward*, he defined "due process"—a term found in both the U.S. Constitution's Fifth and Fourteenth Amendments, and of utmost importance in death penalty cases—as "[t]he law which hears before it condemns; which proceeds upon inquiry and renders judgment only after trial." And no matter what side he found himself on—whether as defense counsel or as a prosecutor—Webster fought hard to persuade judges and juries. In 1830, following the murder of a wealthy merchant, Webster appeared as a private prosecutor at the behest of the murdered man's nephew as part of the public prosecutor's efforts to prosecute John "Francis" Knapp and Joseph J. Knapp, Jr. for murder. Defense counsel objected to Webster's appearance as a private prosecutor to assist the attorney general's office, questioning "the right of a private individual to retain counsel to aid the law officers of the government in effecting a conviction for a crime punishable by death." But private prosecution was not unknown to the law, and Webster was allowed to participate. Both Francis and Joseph Knapp were tried, convicted and sentenced to death.[12]

James Burgh's own writings, which were read by America's founders, reflected Beccaria's tremendous societal impact. In fact, Burgh's rationale for moving away from executions mirrored Beccaria's. As Burgh emphasized in *Political Disquisitions*, the book published long before Daniel Webster was called to the bar in 1805 after working as a clerk in Boston for jurist Christopher Gore: "When an offender is hanged, he is made an example to a few hundreds, and is forgotten. Put him in a state of slavery, confinement, or continually returning correction, during many years, or for life, and you make him a constant example to a succession of individuals during the whole period of his punishment, besides that his labour may in some degree compensate for the injury he has done society." "Too severe punishments," he added, "affect the people with compassion for the sufferer, and hatred against the laws and the administration of the laws." Worried about the effect on spectators of public executions, Burgh emphasized: "If severity were the certain means for curing some faults in a people, it does not follow that it ought to be used, because it may leave a worse distemper than it removes. It may force them out of one wrong track into another more wrong."

Burgh's *Political Disquisitions* called for a readjustment or realignment of English laws. Expressing no objection to corporal punishments, Burgh called for stricter laws in some respects and milder ones in others. As Burgh opined: "We punish many very atrocious crimes too slightly, as well as several inconsiderable crimes too severely. Perjury in *England* is only the pillory. Among the *Russians*, it is punished with severe whipping, and banishment." Burgh put it this way about the laws he felt were too lenient: "Our laws are too gentle to perjury; to adultery; to seduction of modest women; to insolvency occasioned by overtrading or extravagance; to idleness in the lower people; to bribery and corruption; to engrossing and monopolizing the necessaries of life; to giving and accepting challenges; to murder with aggravations of cruelty, &c." On the other hand, Burgh implored: "Laws ought to be so just and so mild, that they may be put in execution, which would supersede the use of the royal prerogative, and save the King the trouble of much solicitation and reflection when he refuses." Burgh specifically called for "an incorrupt legislature"; "clear and simple laws, digested in a short code"; "certainty of punishments in cases of transgressions"; and "education, useful public instruction, and a free press, with whatever else tends to spread light and knowledge among the people." "[W]e need go no farther than our own wise and judicious Quakers," Burgh said, "who do more by their manner of educating their youth, and their treatment of them in consequence of their behaviour, than all the Kings of *Europe* with their laws and sanctions piled on one another to the height of mountains."[13]

In Jefferson's America:
Capital and Corporal Punishments

In early America, lawmakers accountable to the people in their districts put in place constitutions and laws that reflected the public's continued support for executions for certain classes of offenders. For example, when New Hampshire adopted its state constitution in 1784, the death penalty, by law, was—as one source puts it—"'mandated for the crimes of treason, murder, rape, carnal knowledge between men, bestiality, burglary, arson of a dwelling and robbery.'" Although New Hampshire's 1784 constitution barred "cruel and unusual punishments" and recited that "[t]he true design of all punishments" is "to reform, not to exterminate mankind," the New Hampshire Supreme Court—in a modern-day ruling issued far from the founding era, in 2013—determined that "the death penalty was accepted by the framers as a suitable punishment for certain crimes" and that the founders' support was "reflected in the text of the New Hampshire Constitution, as adopted in 1784." Part I, Article 16 of that state constitution barred the legislature from making "any law that shall subject any person to a capital punishment ... without trial by jury," while Part II, Article 4 authorized legislators to set up courts for trying cases "whether the same be criminal or civil, or whether the crimes be capital, or not capital." Part 1, Article 15 of that constitution—reflective of the existence and reality of capital punishment—further emphasized that "[n]o subject shall be ... deprived of his life, liberty, or estate, but by the judgment of his peers, or the law of the land."[14]

Legislation drafted by Thomas Jefferson in the 1770s also contemplated the use of death sentences and other corporal punishments. A Bill for Ascertaining the Salaries and Fees of Certain Officers, drafted by Jefferson in 1779 and presented to the Virginia legislature by James Madison in 1785, had specific entries, under the heading "SHERIFF or MARSHALL," "For putting one in the stocks" and "in the pillory" and for "Whipping one" and "For executing one condemned to die." Another entry, under the heading "JAILOR" and "CONSTABLE," also referenced the act of "putting one in the stocks." Likewise, a Bill Prescribing the Punishment of Those Who Sell Unwholesome Meat or Drink, also drafted by Jefferson in 1779, provided that "a butcher that selleth the flesh of any animal dying, otherwise than by slaughter, or slaughtered when diseased, or a baker, brewer, or distiller, who selleth unwholesome bread or drink shall, on conviction the first time, be amerced; the second time he shall suffer judgment of the pillory, and the third time he shall be imprisoned and make fine; and every time after he shall be adjudged to hard labor six months in the public works." A Virginia act passed in 1789 also authorized the collection of monies for the construction of "a courthouse, prison, pillory and stocks on the lands of William Fitzhugh," indicating that corporal punishments were still in vogue— or at least being anticipated and tolerated—at that time.[15]

In his handwritten "Outline of Bill for Proportioning Crimes and Punishments," drafted in 1779, Jefferson listed "High-treason," "Petty Treason," and "Murder"—whether by "poyson," "in Duel," or "any other way"—as "Crimes whose punishmt. extends to *Life*." The entry for "High-treason" was followed by "Death <by burying alive. qu.> by hanging" and "Forfeiture of lands & goods to Commwth." The entry for "Petty Treason"— traditionally encompassing a wife killing her husband or a servant killing his master or the master's wife—was followed by "Death by hanging," "Dissection" and "Forfeitr of half lands & goods to representatives of person killed." And, in Jefferson's outline, "Murder by poyson" was to be punished by "Death by poyson" and "Forfeitre. of one half as before"; "Murder in Duel" would lead to "Death by hanging," "gibbeting, if the challenger" and "Forfeitre. of one half as before unless the Challengr fell, then to Commw."; and "Murder any other way" would warrant "Death by hanging" and "Forfeitre of half as before." The "2d offence" of "Manslaur."—an abbreviation for manslaughter—would be considered murder, and therefore also punishable by death, with the first offence punishable by "Labor for 7 years" and "Forfeitre one half as before."

Under Jefferson's outlined scheme, "Crimes whose punishment goes to *Limb*" and "Crimes punishable by *Labor* &c." also faced harsh corporal punishments or public sham- ing. Rape, polygamy and sodomy faced "Castration," while "Maiming" and "Disfiguring" faced "Retaliation" and monetary sanctions, that is, "Forfeiture of half to sufferer." Manslaughter, counterfeiting, arson, robbery, burglary, housebreaking, horse-stealing, and grand and petty larceny, on the other hand, all had "Labor" listed as the punishment, with some of those offenses also including forfeiture of estate or the payment of repara- tions. While Jefferson recorded that "nothing" should be the punishment for "Suicide," "Apos- tacy" and "Heresy," Jefferson's outline listed "Ducking" and fifteen "stripes" as the punishment for "Witchcraft &c." and contemplated shaving "*head & half the beard*" as the punishment for excusable homicide. In addition to "Labor" and "Reparation" for both types of larceny, Jefferson's outline suggested, in addition, thirty stripes and "pillory ½ an hour" for grand larceny and fifteen stripes and "pillory ¼ of an hour" for petty larceny. In other notes made by Jefferson in 1798, Jefferson—recording information from Blackstone on crim- inal prosecutions—also noted that witchcraft and kidnapping were punishable by "im- prisonment & pillory."[16]

Death sentences and corporal punishments, while sometimes imposed by English and American judges, were not always carried out in practice, however. For example, of trea- son cases in Massachusetts from 1780 to 1790, all of the sixteen capital sentences were either commuted or pardoned. In Pennsylvania, an anti-government protest occurred in 1783 in which roughly 400 disgruntled Continental Army soldiers, angered by Congress' failure to pay them, rose up in a mutiny. But Dr. Benjamin Rush—the Beccaria prose- lytizer—played a key role in getting the soldiers to back down. While the soldiers wor- ried about being punished for their actions, Dr. Rush promised to plead their case—and the causes of their discontent—before Congress if they agreed to lay down their arms. Some of the mutiny participants were later court-martialed, with two privates, a drummer and a gunner, sentenced to be whipped, and two sergeants, John Morrison and Christian Nagle, sentenced to death. After Pennsylvanians requested pardons for the men, though,

Congress pardoned all the sentenced parties. Congress' resolution, issued on September 13, 1783, specifically stated:

> [W]hereas the said prisoners appear not to have been principals in the said mutiny, and no lives having been lost, nor any destruction of property committed; now know ye, that of special grace and mere motion, and by virtue of the power and authority vested by the Articles of Confederation and perpetual union, the United States in Congress assembled, have thought fit to pardon and remit, and by these presents do grant a full, free and absolute pardon and remission to the said Christian Nagle, John Morrison, gunner Lilly, drummer Horn, Thomas Flowers and William Carman, and each of them, of all judgments or sentences of death, or other corporal punishment, pains or penalties whatsoever given or awarded by the said general court-martial.

As was often the case with pardons, Congress' universal pardon of the men was dramatically announced just before the sentences that had been originally imposed were about to be carried out.[17]

By the early nineteenth century, corporal punishments were still in use. For example, in December 1801, William Cranch—a judge of the U.S. Circuit Court for the District of Columbia—wrote to Thomas Jefferson to report that Charles Houseman, convicted of theft, had been sentenced to be "burnt in the hand" and "whip'd a certain number of stripes," a punishment that was carried out. However, correspondence involving two soldiers, John Pedon and Samuel Morris, shows that corporal punishments—at least in some circumstances—were being questioned, even among precedent- and tradition-inclined judges, by the early nineteenth century. Convicted on June 22, 1801 of stealing a hog belonging to Robert Peter, Jr., the U.S. Circuit Court for the District of Columbia sentenced the two men to be fined, placed in the pillory for a quarter of an hour, and "whipped with five stripes each." But in a letter dated June 30, 1801, William Cranch and two of his fellow judges, William Kilty and James Marshall, all of the U.S. Circuit Court for the District of Columbia, wrote to President Thomas Jefferson about Pedon and Morris, both of whom were in the service of the United States.

Cranch, the second reporter of U.S. Supreme Court decisions, then an unofficial position, was a nephew of Abigail Adams who graduated with honors from Harvard in 1787 and who was admitted to the Massachusetts bar in 1790. President John Adams, his uncle by marriage, appointed Cranch—one of the so-called "Midnight Judges"—to the District of Columbia bench under the Judiciary Act of 1801 that led to the Supreme Court's famous *Marbury v. Madison* decision, a decision that Cranch—as the Supreme Court reporter from 1801 to 1815—would later describe in his reports. When William Kilty, the Chief Judge of the Circuit Court of the District of Columbia, left his position in 1806, Cranch was selected to replace him. The first reporter of U.S. Supreme Court decisions, Alexander Dallas, was the much-respected lawyer whose son, George Mifflin Dallas, became Vice President under President James K. Polk. In a book later written by Alexander Dallas Bache (1806–1867), a graduate of West Point and an American scientist related to both George M. Dallas and Benjamin Franklin, Bache expressed his indebtedness to "the Marquis of Beccaria, one of the most strenuous friends of infant schools in Lombardy, for an account of the foundation and actual condition of the asylums of charity at Milan, in 1837." The "Marquis of Beccaria" to whom he referred, the president of a society for infant schools in Milan, was—as noted by a foreign policy quarterly—"the son of the great Beccaria," a man who—it was said—"raised his voice against the cruelty and absurdity of the criminal law and procedure in his days."[18]

The 1801 letter to President Jefferson that was signed by Cranch, Kilty and Marshall explained of the two soldiers ordered to be whipped and pilloried: "They have been tried during the present June Term and have been found guilty by the Jury of stealing a Hog the property of Mr. Peter." "The punishment," the judges noted, was "[r]estoring Four-fold the value of the Goods, Putting in the Pillory, and Whipping, not exceeding forty stripes—all of which are to be inflicted, without any discretionary Power in the Court except as to the number of stripes under that which is limited in the Law." "Altho' it does not appear that the verdict was contrary to, or without evidence so as Justify the Court in ordering a New Trial, which is applied for by the Prisoners, Yet from the nature of the Transaction as it appeared to us, We are, willing and desirous that the punishment should be lessened." "It appears that as soldiers," the judges explained, "they have not been guilty of any irregular conduct, except in the present instance" and "have heretofore sustained Good Characters and possess as We are informed the confidence of their Officers." "We should therefore, if We had the Power," the judges emphasized, "remit that part of the sentence which is of an Infamous Nature, to wit, the Pillory and stripes, and We beg leave to recommend the said John Pedon and Samuel Morris to you for the exercise of that Power of General or partial Pardon which the Constitution will enable you to Grant." On July 1st, acceding to this request, Jefferson granted Pedon and Morris a presidential pardon of their corporal punishments.[19]

"Sanguinary" Laws and Punishments

From the founding era into the nineteenth century, American citizens and English subjects alike frequently spoke out against—or at least described in print—"sanguinary" laws or punishments. For example, in his charge to a Virginia grand jury in 1791, James Wilson said that the "continuance" and "frequency" of "rigorous penalties" serve to "introduce and diffuse a hardened insensibility among the citizens; and this insensibility, in its turn, gives occasion or pretence to the farther extension and multiplication of those penalties." "Thus," Wilson explained, "one degree of severity opens and smooths the way for another, till, at length, under the specious appearance of necessary justice, a system of cruelty is established by law." "Such a system," Wilson emphasized, "is calculated to eradicate all the manly sentiments of the soul, and to substitute, in their place, dispositions of the most depraved and degrading kind." Speaking in the same year that the U.S. Bill of Rights was ratified, Wilson was blunt. "A nation broke to cruel punishments," he told jurors, "becomes dastardly and contemptible." "For, in nations, as well as individuals, cruelty is always attended with cowardice," Wilson said, calling cruelty "the parent of *slavery*." As Wilson observed in 1791, the year that, as part of the Bill of Rights, the Eighth Amendment prohibition against cruel and unusual punishments itself took effect: "In every government, we find the genius of freedom depressed in proportion to the sanguinary spirit of the laws. It is hostile to the prosperity of nations, as well as to the dignity and virtue of men."

Having studied ancient Greek and Roman history, Wilson pointed to historical examples and foreign legal systems to emphasize his points. "The laws, which Draco formed for Athens," Wilson relayed, "are said emphatically to have been written in blood." With another contemporary source, John Lemprière's *Bibliotheca Classica* (1788), recounting that "[t]he sanguinary laws of Draco were all cancelled, except that against murder," Wilson wrote this about Draco's much-maligned laws: "What did they produce? An aggravation of those very calamities, which they were intended to remove. A scene of the

greatest and most complicated distress was accordingly exhibited by the miserable Athe-
nians, till they found relief in the wisdom and moderation of Solon." Solon (c. 638–558
B.C.), the Athenian lawgiver who revised the laws of Draco (c. 600s B.C.) to make them
milder, would later be depicted in an ornamental metope located on the frieze in the
Great Hall of the U.S. Supreme Court building in Washington, D.C. A comment made
by the English clergyman George Croft in 1796 captures a sense of the times—and those
still clinging to tradition—across the pond, in England. As Croft wrote: "I had long been
accustomed to hear popular complaints against our criminal code, and had carefully perused a treatise on crimes and punishments by LORD AUCKLAND, as well as another by BEC-
CARIA. But I was not even then convinced that our laws were too sanguinary; and though
I did not think with DRACO, that small crimes should be punished with death, yet I still
am of opinion, that many offences which are made capital deserve that punishment."[20]

In early 1790s Virginia, the grand jurors were also lectured by Wilson, the U.S. Supreme
Court Justice from Pennsylvania, about American law, albeit with a decidedly international flair as he put the law in context. "It is a standing observation in China," James
Wilson stated in his 1791 charge, "that in proportion as the punishments of criminals are
increased, the empire approaches to a new revolution." Under the severe punishments of
Roman emperors, Wilson added, "Rome declined and fell." After emphasizing how few
crimes were punishable capitally in America as compared to under English law, Wilson
concluded: "The co-acervation of sanguinary laws is a political distemper of the most inveterate and the most dangerous kind. By such laws the people are corrupted; and when
corruption arises from the laws the evil may well be pronounced to be incurable; for it
proceeds from the very source, from which the remedy should flow."[21] In the nineteenth
century, another American source—in what was a common theme of writings of that
time—reported that "[a]fter the decease of Draco, his successor, the world-renowned
Solon, the prince of lawgivers, and one of the seven wise men of Greece, abrogated the
whole" of Draco's "sanguinary and ferocious code, with the exception of the article which
punished murder with death."[22]

Such sentiments on sanguinary acts—or at least variations thereof—were prevalent
in both Europe and America as the ideals of the American Revolution spread globally. In
Letters on Capital Punishment, written by Richard Wright, a Unitarian Baptist minister of
Wisbeach but using the pen name "Beccaria Anglicus," the identified intended audience
was "the English judges." A description of that title, published in London in 1807 and reviewed in *The Monthly Review*, began as follows: "A subject, in favour of which the interests of society plead equally with justice and humanity, is here urged on the attention of
the venerable persons to whom it is addressed, in a style that is highly forcible and becoming." The book review stated that "we cannot adopt, in an unqualified manner, all the
abstract propositions asserted in this tract," but it also editorialized that "we are as zealous
as the author for the leading object of it, and as fully impressed with its importance." As
the book review emphasized: "We fully agree with the author that in a well constituted society capital punishments are not only unnecessary, but 'that they are really injurious,' and
that 'vindictive laws and sanguinary punishments retard the progress of civilization.'"

"By accustoming the people to scenes of horror," the reviewer wrote of executions,
"they tend to brutalize their manners, and make them regardless of the sufferings of others." "In every other nation," the review continued, "it will be found, that the people at
large derive much of their character from the established laws and customs. If the laws
and customs be austere, ferocious, and cruel, a considerable degree of austerity, ferocity
and cruelty, will be discoverable in the people." "Capital punishments," the review continued, "retain the barbarous aspect of *vandalism*, and better assort with the manners of
savage tribes than with those of a nation which holds the first rank in the civilized world."

The book review specifically quoted "[t]hat excellent writer, Beccaria," for the proposition that severe punishments are tyrannical, with the review concluding: "Capital punishments are deprecated by this author as unnecessary to the well-being of society, as partaking of the nature of *revenge*, as subversive of the chief end of correction which is *amendment*, as making no reparation for injury committed, and as inconsistent with the spirit of the Christian Religion."[23]

Many other eighteenth- and nineteenth-century titles and periodicals — as well as sermons delivered from the pulpit — also described "sanguinary" acts or laws. In a history of the Church of England, published in 1839, Queen Elizabeth is said to have "proceeded to secure the reformation by the strong barrier of penal and sanguinary laws; making it capital, to be ordained, and to exercise spiritual functions after the ancient manner." Likewise, in an 1819 piece titled "Lines on Italy" in *The Gentleman's Magazine*, one finds the following reference: "The rough manners of the English in former years, and their sanguinary laws, afford a striking contrast with the severest punishments of modern times." In that magazine, published in London, a letter published decades earlier, in 1784, also gave this assessment: "The number of capital punishments which occur in our own nation in particular, is a circumstance that alarms the feelings of humanity...." "Did the *cruelty* of our laws," it read, "give them additional force in deterring men from incurring the penalties of them, their cruelty might perhaps admit of defence; but this does not seem to be the case." "It deserves therefore to be considered," the letter writer offered, "whether, by making *fewer crimes to be capital*, and at the same time rendering the punishments which may be appointed instead of death *more certain*, these inconveniences might not, in some measure, be avoided." In language resembling Beccaria's own recommendations, the letter writer concluded: "Let the penalties of the law be less severe, or however less sanguinary; but let them, with a very few exceptions, be invariably inflicted on conviction."[24]

In Pennsylvania, a book published in 1830, *Annals of Philadelphia*, specifically noted the significant progress that had been made in that locale as regards penal reform. In a chapter titled "Crimes and Punishments," John Watson — its author and a member of the Historical Society of Pennsylvania — put it this way: "We have been so long happily delivered from the former exhibitions of the pillory, whipping-post, ducking-stool, wheelbarrow-men, and even hanging itself, that it may serve to show the aspect of quite another age to expose the facts in the days of our forefathers, as derived from the presentments of Grand Juries, trials in the Mayor's court, or from the Gazettes." Watson noted how, in 1717, women were "publicly whipt for having an illegitimate child; and poor runaway apprentices and others, who are whipt, are charged six shillings for the unwelcome service." Watson also took notice of brutal executions that had once occurred, including that of Catharine Bevan in 1731, ordered to be burned alive. "A shocking spectacle for our country!" Watson editorialized. Watson also described the following scene, which took place in Philadelphia in 1743: "A black man, brought up to the whipping-post to be whipt, took out his knife and cut his throat before the crowd, so that he died immediately." In Watson's next chapter, on "The Excellencies of Penn's Laws," Watson's history of Philadelphia struck this more optimistic note: "There is probably no subject within the scope of our history, to which a Pennsylvanian may look with more just pride and satisfaction, than to the whole tenor of the laws instituted for the welfare of the people by the Founder and his successors." "At a single stroke of his pen," Watson wrote of Penn's Great Law of 1682, "he struck off all the sanguinary laws of his parent country respecting felonies, substituting, in lieu of death, temperate punishment and hard labour."[25]

In a lecture on capital punishment, delivered in the First Universalist Church in Philadelphia on June 20, 1830, the pastor — A. C. Thomas — himself expressed the belief that capital punishment would soon be entirely expunged from American law. His sermon, questioning the efficacy of "sanguinary" practices, sought to establish two propositions: first, "*No human tribunal possesses the right to inflict the punishment of death in any case*"; and second, "*Capital punishments are wholly unjust and inexpedient*." "Capital punishment originated in revenge," Thomas argued in his sermon, adding: "Far be it from me even to intimate that our judges in their charges, or our juries in their verdicts, are actuated by a spirit of revenge." Thomas expressly credited Beccaria's treatise, "a work from which I have derived much satisfaction," he said, "for several remarks on the subject" of capital punishment. After referring to Blackstone's *Commentaries on the Laws of England*, Thomas invoked ideas found in *On Crimes and Punishments* and Montesquieu's writings. For example, Thomas argued: "Punishments to be just must be absolutely necessary. Are capital punishments absolutely necessary?" "No — they are not," Thomas answered, saying that "in the present state of civilization" the punishment of death was no longer necessary "because we have other and more effectual means for the attainment" of deterrence. "We have prisons in which to secure the criminal," Thomas emphasized. "*Crimes are not so effectually prevented by the* SEVERITY, *or* QUANTITY, *as by the* CERTAINTY *of punishment*," Thomas told his audience, repeating a Beccarian theme. "The excellent observation of Montesquieu," Thomas concluded, "cannot be too much admired, that 'in proportion as the government is animated by the spirit of liberty, the more mild will be the punishments.'"[26]

The uses of *sanguinary*, including in the founding era, varied widely, but that word was often used to refer to laws that persecuted religious minorities, inflicted death sentences, or that imposed other harsh sentences.[27] For example, in a history of the Revolutionary War published in 1794, one finds a telling passage about Americans' desire to avoid oppressive laws: "In the reign of Charles the First, when, in consequence of repeated addresses from both houses of parliament, the king was obliged to enforce against the Roman Catholics the execution of those penal and sanguinary laws, which a more enlightened and liberal age has thought fit to repeal, Charles lord Baltimore, a Roman Catholic, and a favourite at court, obtained a grant of that part of Virginia which has since been called Maryland, as a place of refuge for himself, and his persecuted brethren of the Roman religion."[28] Charles I (1600–1649) — the monarch of England, Ireland and Scotland until his execution in 1649 — had a power struggle with Parliament; married a Roman Catholic, generating deep divisions within a society that fell into civil war; and was ultimately beheaded in front of the neo-classical Banqueting House in Whitehall, London.[29] Other sources from the founding era, or that pre-date it, reference a "cruel and sanguinary disposition,"[30] "cruel and sanguinary laws,"[31] "sanguinary tyrants,"[32] "violent and sanguinary Prosecution,"[33] "violent and sanguinary methods"[34] and "sanguinary laws."[35]

Uses of *sanguinary laws* or *sanguinary codes* — inspired in part by Draco's Grecian Code or England's Bloody Code[36] — can be found in many other places, too.[37] Unpopular for its severity, Draco's ancient code of written laws — replacing a system of oral law, handed down from one generation to the next — punished even relatively minor crimes, such as stealing an apple from an orchard, with death. "The sanguinary laws of Draco were all cancelled, except that against murder, and the punishment denounced against every offender was proportioned to his crime," reads one passage from a classical dictionary entry on Solon, the Greek lawgiver who took it upon himself to reform the Athenian constitution in 594 B.C. and who, in doing so, oversaw the repeal of many of Draco's laws.[38] England's Bloody Code, which, by 1800, made more than 200 crimes punishable by death,[39] was similarly rejected by America's Founding Fathers. Some looked to William Penn's decades-old example as a precedent for that rejection while others looked to Beccaria's *On Crimes and Punishments* as inspiration and support for their law reform efforts.

Draco's laws, described in one source as "sanguinary" and as having a "sanguinary nature," were — as explained in a collection of London-published essays — "figuratively said to be written in blood" for "it is certain they breathe a spirit calculated rather for the extinction of society, than for its reformation."[40] In the eighteenth and nineteenth centuries, when torture and executions were relatively common, intellectuals everyone were abuzz with efforts to find substitutes for harsh penalties typified by Draco's Code and the English Bloody Code. One finds, in fact, many derogatory references to "sanguinary" practices, be they in connection to monarchs,[41] councils or judges,[42] or to edicts,[43] punishments,[44] or royal policies or temperaments.[45] By the latter part of the nineteenth century, Beccaria's treatise was being credited with having transformed the criminal law. As one English source, *Notes and Queries* (1887), praised Beccaria's treatise: "The language is clear, concise, and elegant, and, although criminal law is much improved since Beccaria's time, and many reforms advocated by him have since been adopted, the work may still be perused with much pleasure and profit."[46]

Sanguinary — a word that has since largely fallen out of use — was, countless other sources show, regularly used in prior centuries to describe "bloody," "cruel" or "murderous" acts. The American Revolution itself was about breaking free of a cruel and oppressive English monarch, with "sanguinary" references particularly ubiquitous in early Anglo-American sources. In one 1795 title, *Tomahawk!*, the book — reflecting the highly charged language of that era — contained the following references, plainly ascribing negative connotations to the word's use: "the swindling, sanguinary, tyrannical *Marat*," "one of the sanguinary chiefs," "sanguinary ferocity," "sanguinary monster," "a *bullying, sanguinary*, and *destructive* manifesto," "most sanguinary," "more sanguinary," "*sanguinary* ruffian," "sanguinary errors," "sanguinary ministers," "*sanguinary* reformers," "sanguinary decrees," "sanguinary scoundrel," "sanguinary machinations," "*sanguinary* menaces," "sanguinary incroachments," "sanguinary orator" and "sanguinary cant."[47] Jean-Paul Marat — a radical journalist and physician who participated in the French Revolution, the revolution that followed America's — was himself labeled a "savage" and a "monster" who "loved carnage like a vulture." Marat was accused of being "sanguinary" for demanding aristocratic blood and participating in prison massacres.[48]

In the eighteenth century, authoritarian monarchs and tyrannical laws, which America's founders forthrightly despised, were — in source after source — termed "sanguinary." In a 1788 edition of *The History of the Decline and Fall of the Roman Empire*, for example, the historian Edward Gibbon wrote: "John the Sanguinary spread the devastations of war from the Appenine to the Hadriatic."[49] Likewise, in a 1766 history, an index entry for another source notes that emperor "Otho II, or Sanguinary," received "the epithet Sanguinary" as a result of "[h]is punishing those who deserted him in the late action."[50] Americans as well as many English citizens viewed the sanguinary policies of European monarchs as nothing short of immoral and unjust, so it is little wonder that George III's reign was described as "sanguinary" for making death a punishment for almost every offense and that so many thinkers came to despise sanguinary policies, including those that led to executions. This anti-sanguinary attitude is reflected well in the following passage from a book published in 1798: "The principles of a sanguinary policy, which first created a disproportionate inequality in society, and then punishes with death the theft it incites, is probably a perversion of ethics, and our capital punishments perhaps unqualified murders."[51]

Moved in part by Beccaria's treatise, harsh and disproportionate punishments gradually fell out of favor along with the governments, such as that of George III, that imposed them. In *The Proceedings in Cases of High Treason, Under a Special Commission of Oyer and Terminer*, one finds this blistering critique: "in all countries where severe and sanguinary punishments were encouraged, men could have no affection for the government under which they lived."[52] By issuing the Declaration of Independence, the Continental Congress decided that Americans could no longer live under such oppressive British rule. As the authors of *History of Criminal Justice* write: "Patriot leaders of the Revolution were hard-pressed to maintain law and order in the newly independent states. Despite this, there was a growing sentiment for a change in punishments. This was due in part to discontent with the continued use of British criminal law; in part, it was an interest in the new penology advocated by Beccaria and the French *philosophes*; but it was also a recognition that harsh penal laws do not, in themselves, discourage crime." As an example, that source notes: "In 1768, New York lawyer Robert R. Livingston Jr. (who would become chancellor of the newly independent state) wrote about a woman convicted of petty theft who was under sentence of death. Her execution was delayed because of her pregnancy, but would be carried out shortly after the child was born. Livingston stressed the harshness and inhumanity of a legal system that left the infant motherless." "In the same year," that book continues, commenting on the views of a British loyalist, "fellow New York lawyer, Peter Van Schaack, contemplated the penal law of the colony and concluded with resignation that, 'to preserve Society Individuals must bleed; to secure a reverence for the laws that connect that Society the Violators must suffer.'"[53]

In Anglo-American culture, the invocation of Beccaria and other writers of the Enlightenment became nothing short of a rallying cry for ending sanguinary and cruel acts. And that meant, in more specific terms, abolishing or curtailing executions or harsh corporal punishments. A review of eighteenth-century writings thus shows that *sanguinary* was frequently used to label or describe such crude or barbarous practices. In *An Account of the European Settlements in America* one finds a reference to how New England's Quakers were set in the stocks and the pillory, scourged, imprisoned and banished, and subjected to "the most sanguinary extremities," that is, after Quakers returned from banishment, they were "condemned and hanged."[54] In *Travels in the Two Sicilies in the Years 1777, 1778, 1779, and 1780*, writer Henry Swinburne also noted that "Alphonsus the Second, was a man of great military fame, but of a most sanguinary temper, the instigator and actor of all the treacheries and cruelties that sullied his father's annals."[55] And in William Preston's *A Letter to Bryan Edwards, Esquire, Containing Observations on Some Passages of His History of the West Indies*, one likewise finds reference to "the sanguinary atrocity of law, that sanctions murder and calls it policy." In that 1795 title, Preston wrote: "the progress of knowledge, and the propagation of christianity, would be more effectual, than a thousand sanguinary practices." "I can scarcely expect success in pleading the cause of humanity at a time when cruel sentiments and sanguinary rage prevail," Preston added, cautioning his readers.[56]

In the Founding Fathers' time, talk of "sanguinary" laws and practices—and the need to reform and replace them with more reasoned or Christian policies—was everywhere, especially on the tongues of American revolutionaries and other intellectuals. In *The Spirit of Laws*, first published in 1748, Montesquieu—the famous French thinker—headed one chapter "*Of the sanguinary temper of the kings of the Franks.*"[57] Similarly, in *The Theory of Moral Sentiments*, Adam Smith—the famed author of *The Wealth of Nations* whose library included works by both Beccaria and Verri—makes multiple references to "sanguinary," including in relation to punishments.[58] In a history of the Ottoman Empire, published in 1787, yet another writer made reference to a "sanguinary monarch" who issued death warrants "too rashly" and a "sanguinary general" who, it was said, "must not be permitted to put his highness's subjects to death, according to his caprice."[59] Naturally, what was considered *sanguinary*—as might be expected—varied considerably according to the writer's perspective; in an era in which monarchs regularly meted out death sentences, not all executions were necessarily seen as sanguinary *per se*. For instance, a publication called *Walker's Hibernian Magazine*, published in Dublin in 1786, included an "Account of China" and contained the following passage: "The laws of this Empire are not sanguinary; murder and high treason only, being punished with death."[60]

For America's Founding Fathers, participants in the global conversation around crime and punishment, it was no different. Some American revolutionaries, like Dr. Benjamin Rush, found *all* executions cruel and unnecessary. Others, however, took a different, less absolutist approach, only opposing executions for lower-level offenses. Even for those, like Alexander Hamilton, who did not oppose all executions, the *necessity* of the particular execution in question was a matter of special importance. In writing to Major General Henry Knox in 1782 about the case of Captain Charles Asgill, who had been condemned to die, Hamilton specifically questioned whether an execution was necessary. Asgill, the young British officer, had been selected by lot at George Washington's request to be executed in retaliation for the hanging by British loyalists of Captain Joshua Huddy of the New Jersey State Artillery. "We are told here that there is a British officer coming on from Cornwallis's army to be executed by way of retaliation for the murder of Capt Huddy," Hamilton's letter to Knox began. "As this appears to me clearly to be an ill-timed proceeding, and if persisted in will be derogatory to the national character I cannot forbear communicating to you my ideas upon the subject," Hamilton's letter continued. As Hamilton argued in his missive, urging mercy:

> A sacrifice of this sort is intirely repugnant to the genius of the age we live in and is without example in modern history nor can it fail to be considered in Europe as wanton and unnecessary. It appears that the enemy (from necessity I grant but the operation is the same) have changed their system and adopted a more humane one; and therefore the only justifying motive of retaliation, the preventing a repetition of cruelty, ceases.

"[S]o solemn and deliberate a sacrifice of the innocent for the guilty," Hamilton added, noting the "late stage" of the Revolutionary War, "must be condemned on the present received notions of humanity, and encourage an opinion that we are in a certain degree of barbarism." "Our affairs are now in a prosperous train," Hamilton wrote, "and so vigorous, I would rather say so violent a measure would want the plea of necessity." "[I]f we wreak our resentment on an innocent person," Hamilton emphasized, "it will be suspected that we are too fond of executions."

Alexander Hamilton felt so strongly about the potential fallout from an execution of Captain Asgill, a prisoner of war, that he worried about the sullying of General George Washington's reputation should an execution actually take place. As Hamilton wrote in his letter of June 7, 1782: "I am persuaded it will have an influence peculiarly unfavourable to the General's character." "If it is seriously believed that in this advanced state of affairs retaliation is necessary," Hamilton wrote of the Asgill affair, "let another mode be chose." If the execution were carried out, Hamilton gave this advice to Henry Knox—the former bookseller—to help protect Washington's reputation:

> Let under actors be employed and let the authority by which it is done be wrapt in obscurity and doubt. Let us endeavour to make it fall upon those who have had a direct or indirect share in the guilt. Let not the Commander in Chief considered as the first and most respectable character among us come forward in person and be the avowed author of an act at which every humane feeling revolts.

"[I]f we must have victims," Hamilton continued, "appoint some obscure agents to perform the ceremony, and bear the odium which must always attend even justice itself when directed by extreme severity."

In his letter, Hamilton specifically noted Knox's "liberality" and "influence" with General Washington, with Hamilton noting of Asgill's slated fate: "[I]t is said the Commander in Chief has pledged himself for it and cannot recede." "Inconsistency in this case," Hamilton then advised, "would be better than consistency," with Hamilton writing that "pretexts may be found and will be readily admitted in favour of humanity." "For my own part my Dear Sir," Hamilton concluded, "I think a business of this complexion intirely out of season. The time for it, if there ever was one, is past." Ultimately, cooler heads prevailed, with Henry Knox's biographer noting that "[m]any believed that the tactic of threatening to execute an innocent British soldier as a way to discourage acts of violence against American prisoners was misguided and unjust." General Washington himself concluded that Asgill's life should be spared, and Congress ordered Asgill's release.[61]

A friend of Paul Revere and General Washington's confidante, Henry Knox himself ended up becoming Washington's Secretary of War. Having started work as a Boston bookseller after his father, a shipbuilder, left his family for the West Indies in 1759 following the collapse of his business due in part to an act of Parliament regulating currency, Knox grew up reading books like *Plutarch's Lives*. A hard worker, he quickly impressed John and Samuel Adams, even as Parliament's Townshend Revenue Act of 1767, placing a duty on paper and other items, led to a Continental boycott of British goods such as books. When the bookshop employing Knox cancelled orders from London, business fell off, too, and Knox—who had gotten word of his father's death—became a soldier, reading more books, like Julius Caesar's *Commentaries*, as he studied military science. "With respect to General Knox," Washington later told John Adams, after Knox had risen through the ranks of the Continental Army to become a commander, "I can say with truth, there is no man in the United States with whom I have been in habits of greater intimacy; no one whom I have loved more sincerely, nor any for whom I have had a greater friendship."

Henry Knox, who regularly read Enlightenment texts, had seen first-hand, and up close, what led to the American Revolution. An eyewitness to the Boston Massacre, Knox had risked his own life to stop the bloodshed, but found himself attending the funerals of slain Bostonians after British soldiers, over Knox's protests, opened fire on local townsfolk. Knox ended up testifying at the trial of Captain Thomas Preston, a British officer represented by John Adams and Knox's former classmate Josiah Quincy, with Knox—after the boycott of British goods was lifted—opening his own bookshop. In the announcement of the store's opening, published in the *Boston Gazette*, it was reported: "This day is opened a new London Bookstore by Henry Knox, opposite William's Court in Cornhill, Boston, who has just imported in the last ships from London a large and very elegant assortment of the most modern books in all branches of Literature, Arts and Sciences (catalogues of which will be published soon) and to be sold as cheap as can be bought at any place in town." The last ad for Knox's London Bookstore, published on March 20, 1775, just a month before fighting broke out in Lexington and Concord, promoted this offering: "Just published and to be sold by Henry Knox in Cornhill, price 1 s. 6 d. *The Farmer refuted: Or a more impartial and comprehensive view of the dispute between Great Britain and the Colonies, intended as a further vindication of Congress.*"[62]

While George Washington thought executions and corporal punishments were, to some degree, warranted during the Revolutionary War, as retaliatory impulses waned at war's end, American political leaders began questioning prior assumptions about punishment practices. In particular, they began questioning the necessity—and the legitimacy—of both lethal and non-lethal corporal punishments, the public infliction of which, as regards the latter category, badly degraded, if not destroyed, one's social standing. During that era, there was an acute sensitivity to social status—and the notion of a gentleman's honor was taken so seriously that libels or even petty slights sometimes ended in deadly duels between feuding combatants. Indeed, in pre-revolutionary Europe, in an outlook and proclivity that spilled over into colonial America, social status itself often determined the nature of one's punishment for a particular offense. Nobles, notes one scholar, were not "disgraced or subjected to social infamy"; instead, they sought "to avoid public humiliation and shame" and "frequently agreed to non-publicized imprisonment as punishment." "But for the lower orders," historian Trevor Rosson emphasizes, "forced labor, public humiliation, and hangings were standard punishments, functioning as conspicuous symbols of low social status." *Public infamy*, what James Q. Whitman calls "the loss of honor and status in the eyes of the general public," thus became—in a real sense—a symbol of lowly status within the society.

With the Declaration of Independence's assertion of the "self-evident" truth that "all men are created equal," it is little wonder that American lawmakers also began questioning the need for a dual system of punishment—one for the rich and one for the poor— and for frequent executions and humiliating corporal punishments such as the pillory.[63] The Revolutionary War, historian Harry Ward notes, "underscored the brutality and capriciousness in the administration of capital punishment." Taking note of the influence of Beccaria's treatise, Ward stressed: "Henry Knox spoke for other revolutionary leaders in expressing the hope that 'dispassionate and enlightenment minds' would prevail to bring about a reduction in the number of capital penalties; otherwise the capital laws 'will be recited to sully the purity of our cause.'" As Alice F. Tyler has written: "[T]here was a fundamental incompatibility between the social forces of the American Revolution and the criminal codes of the colonial era. If the equality proclaimed in the Declaration of Independence meant anything at all, it meant equality before the law."[64]

Quakers and Puritans: Divergent Views

It was Pennsylvania's Quakers—a group repulsed by senseless violence—that perhaps most vehemently opposed cruel and sanguinary laws. William Penn had, in Pennsylvania's colonial days, already experimented with abolishing some sanguinary punishments, and the Quakers led efforts to reform penal codes in the post-Revolutionary War era, too, even as other, non-Quaker thinkers provided their own critiques of barbarous practices. "The Religious Society of Friends, often called simply Friends or Quakers," explains one encyclopedia, "is a Christian sect that emerged in mid-17th-century England in tandem with the religious upheavals of the English Civil War (1642–51)." The English Civil War— a series of armed conflicts and political controversies that pitted supporters of Charles I and Charles II against supporters of Parliament—led to the trial and execution of Charles I, the exile of his son Charles II, and the replacement of English monarchy with the Commonwealth of England (1649–1653), then a Protectorate (1653–1659) under Oliver Cromwell's rule before Charles II reclaimed the throne in 1660. The first Meeting of Friends of Philadelphia occurred in 1682, with the influx of Quaker immigration destined to shape America's death penalty debate.

In the 1820 case of *United States v. Cornell*, one federal court specifically emphasized that two Quaker jurors should have been disqualified from sitting in judgment in a capital case because they admitted being "conscientiously scrupulous of taking away life." "To compel a Quaker to sit as a juror" in such cases, the court ruled, "is to compel him to decide against his conscience."[65] Even today, American capital juries are, by law, "death-qualified," meaning those opposed to capital punishment are stripped from jury venire panels and are thereby precluded from sitting in judgment in death penalty cases. As Leslie Lytle writes of the perverse effect of this rule in *Execution's Doorstep: True Stories of the Innocent and Near Damned*: "Capital cases require death-qualified juries—juries excluding those who have a moral objection to imposing the death penalty—and statistics show that death-qualified juries are more likely to reach a guilty verdict." While the U.S. Supreme Court has, for years, sanctioned this practice, the use of death-qualified juries has the effect, in practice, of skewing the data the Supreme Court itself considers in evaluating, for the purposes of its Eighth Amendment jurisprudence, "the evolving standards of decency that mark the progress of a maturing society." It is that test, first adopted in *Trop v. Dulles* (1958), that the Court still uses to evaluate Cruel and Unusual Punishment Clause claims, relying largely on existing statutes *and jury verdicts* to gauge public sentiment.[66]

George Fox (1624–1691), the founder of Quakerism, the sect that so dominated Pennsylvania in its early years, promoted principles of social justice, creating a strong tie between Quakers and various reform movements.[67] "The doctrine of the Inner Light originated with Quaker founder, George Fox, in 1640s England," writes historian Jennifer Graber in *The Furnace of Affliction: Prisons and Religion in Antebellum America*. That doctrine, Graber notes, "affirmed that every person had the 'still, small voice' of God within." "Friends," Graber explains of Quakers, opposed executions and also committed themselves in 1774 to prohibiting slave ownership among their membership. Quakers, she observes, "traced this belief to scripture, namely John 1:9, which attested to a true light 'which lighteth every man.'" While incarcerated for blasphemy in Derby, England, Fox— a preacher often persecuted by English authorities—protested executions, as he often did during his life, urging his country's judges to "show mercy, that you may receive mercy from God the Judge of all." A friend of William Penn, Fox, for example, once wrote to judges and jurors to oppose executions for stealing, penning these words: "I am moved to write unto you to take heed of putting men to death for stealing cattle or money, etc."[68]

In America, nowhere was the Quaker influence felt more than in William Penn's Pennsylvania. As one source notes: "[I]n 1682, William Penn promulgated the 'Great Law or Body of Laws,' which was adopted by the assembly on December 7, 1682. Though the Great Law still criminalized sexual immorality, drunkenness, and profanity, it utilized imprisonment in a house of correction and/or fines instead of public physical punishment for most offenses except murder, which was still a capital offense." Of this then-novel Quaker approach, that source further explains: "William Penn was averse to jails, and the horrors he had experienced while incarcerated in London's infamous Newgate Prison pushed him to seek alternatives. Because he had been deeply impressed by Dutch workhouses (which were based on the English Bridewell system) during his tour of Holland, Penn decreed that, in Pennsylvania, all counties were to have workhouses." English *bridewells*—named after London's Bridewell Palace, which became a prison—were mainly used to hold debtors or those awaiting banishment, execution or trial. Quakers had a long tradition of caring for prisoners, in part because so many Quakers had been exiled, incarcerated or persecuted—even executed—for their own religious affiliation. But Penn's control over Pennsylvania's colonial government was tenuous, so Penn's approach to criminal justice issues—still subject to royal control—was only temporary. By May 1718, under pressure from England's monarchy, Pennsylvania returned once more to the harsh English approach to punishment that prevailed prior to William Penn's Great Law of 1682.[69]

Throughout the American colonies, the long list of capital crimes then in force—from murder and rape on down—had been inherited from English law. Those colonial laws— whether governing the Puritans or those of other religious beliefs—were often formulated or based upon Old Testament scriptural passages with which Bible-reading members of society were then so familiar. "The members of the Massachusetts Colony," historian

William Davis notes of the Puritans, "were of course believers that the Scriptures embodied the word of God and were infallible." "Consequently," Davis explains, "they believed it their duty to make every offence capital which the Bible declared should be punished by death." "Their list of capital crimes," he noted, "numbered sixteen, and nearly all were expressly based on passages of Scripture."[70] Similarly, in colonial New York, a place with a history of Dutch immigration, sixteen crimes, including murder, treason, highway robbery and forgery, were punishable by death. As historian Jennifer Graber further explains of that locale: "Other felonies, including grand larceny, embezzlement, and child rape, were punished by fines or corporal punishment for the first offense and death for the second. Recidivists of much more common crimes, including counterfeiting and horse stealing, also met their end at the gallows."[71]

In colonial Massachusetts, capital cases—from a procedural and visual perspective—often had an eerie pomp-and-circumstance about them, with colonial judges sometimes acting alone in deciding the offender's fate and ordering public executions. As one history of early American legal customs notes: around 1760 Chief Justice Thomas Hutchinson, of the Superior Court of Judicature of Massachusetts, "introduced a costume for the judges, consisting of a black silk gown, worn over a full black suit, white bands, and a silk bag for the hair" to be worn at trials. In capital trials, that source notes, the judges "wore scarlet robes, with black velvet collars and cuffs to their large sleeves, and black velvet facings to their robes."[72] Another writer notes that, in colonial America, "Puritan New Haven abolished juries altogether, even for capital crimes, relying for its criminal procedure on an inquisitorial process carried out by its magistrates, who played all the roles—charged suspects, examined witnesses, rendered judgment, and imposed punishment."[73] Though practices varied somewhat by locale, early American executions—by superstition or custom—were often carried out on Fridays. Such executions, historian Louis Masur explains in *Rites of Execution*, served a civil function, reminding spectators of the state's authority, as well as a religious one, reminding the crowd of the fate befalling sinners.[74]

A Call to Action

After the publication of Beccaria's book, which took specific aim at torture and capital punishment, American lawmakers took concrete steps to change routine practices and to curtail severe punishments. With Beccaria's treatise advocating other criminal-law reforms, too, including jury trials, those legislators—in attempting to remake American law—put in place added procedural protections for criminal defendants and explored alternatives to colonial practices. For instance, in 1790, Congress provided for the appointment of counsel "learned in the law" in capital cases, with Congress guaranteeing that lawyers would have "free access" to their clients "at all seasonable hours." The Crimes Act of 1790 also provided that "no person or persons shall be prosecuted, tried or punished for treason or other capital offence … unless the indictment for the same shall be found by a grand jury within three years next after the treason or capital offence," and that if any person "indicted of treason against the United States" shall "stand mute or refuse to plead," the court "shall notwithstanding proceed to the trial of the person or persons so standing mute … as if he or they had pleaded not guilty, and render judgment thereon accordingly." The U.S. Constitution's Sixth Amendment, ratified in 1791, further gave the accused in criminal prosecutions "the right to a speedy and public trial, by an impartial jury"; the right to confront witnesses; to have the assistance of counsel; and to be informed of the nature of the accusations. "Beccaria's ideas," notes Anne Romano in *Ital-*

ian Americans in Law Enforcement, "were incorporated into the Sixth Amendment of the U.S. Bill of Rights."[75]

Part of the reforms initiated by American lawmakers involved experimenting with places to house offenders for long periods of time. For example, in 1785, in Massachusetts, a military outpost and fortress in Boston was converted to a prison to house convicted criminals. In 1784, legislators in that state had determined that it had become "necessary to the safety of the industrious inhabitants of the Commonwealth, to provide some place other than common gaols, for the reception and confinement to hard labor of persons convicted of larcenies, and other infamous crimes." Convicts at Castle Island — located a few miles off the South Boston shore, and the first U.S. institution devoted exclusively to confining convicted inmates — performed manual labor, chiefly nail making, the same task that young slaves at Jefferson's Monticello had been assigned. The Castle Island prison — constructed in Boston Harbor and providing neither solitary confinement nor religious instruction as would be provided in Pennsylvania prisons — was soon abandoned, however, because of security issues. As one history explains of Castle Island's fatal flaw: "Inmates could escape across the ice to the mainland in the winter, and if good swimmers, could not be deterred from escape in the summer."[76]

In the 1790s, the decade that gave birth to the U.S. Bill of Rights, Americans' desire for penal reform quickened and spread throughout the country. For example, in 1793, New Jersey's Ireland-born governor, William Paterson (1745–1806), said that the English system of criminal law inherited by his state "is written in blood, and cannot be read without Horror." Paterson — a 1763 graduate of the College of New Jersey — had studied law as an apprentice with Richard Stockton, a well-known Princeton lawyer who became a signer of the Declaration of Independence. Paterson — who embraced the cause of the American Revolution, became New Jersey's first attorney general, and spent two months at the Constitutional Convention — described the then-existing system as "complicated and sanguinary in a high degree." The most effective punishments for criminals, he believed, were those that fit the crime, with Paterson expressing his belief that "the Impolicy, Inadequacy, and cruelty of the existing system of penal law" warranted a "thorough reform." Paterson had become New Jersey's governor in 1790 after the death of William Livingston (1723–1790), the man who had served in that role from 1776 until his death.[77] One of the oldest delegates at the Constitutional Convention in Philadelphia, William Livingston — born into a wealthy family in Albany, New York — had graduated from Yale College in 1741, became a lawyer in 1748, and served in both the First and Second Continental Congresses (1774–1776). His daughter Sarah would marry John Jay in 1774, and William himself served as an intellectual mentor to his nephews Edward and Robert R. Livingston and to the brilliant but volatile Alexander Hamilton.[78]

The "sanguinary punishments" clause of Vermont's constitution was specifically invoked in the early nineteenth century as efforts were made to move away from such draconian punishments. In 1807, Vermont's new governor, Israel Smith, the former chief justice of Vermont's highest court, thus argued against the infliction of outdated corporal punishments. In a speech, the newly elected governor invoked a clause in the state constitution making it his duty to lay before the General Assembly "such business as may appear" to be necessary. "Among the most important of those subjects," Smith explained, was a change in "the modes of punishment established in our criminal code." Also invoking the state constitution's "sanguinary punishments" clause, Smith emphasized: "This honorable Assembly will permit me to bring to their remembrance the thirty seventh section of the constitution of this State; it is in the following words: 'To deter more effectually from the commission of crimes, by continued visible punishments of long duration, and to make sanguinary punishments less necessary, means ought to be provided for punishing by hard labor those who shall be convicted of crimes not capital, whereby the criminal shall be employed for the benefit of the public, or for the reparation of injuries done to private persons; and all persons at proper times ought to be permitted to see them at their labor.'" "To the forcible language of the Constitution I can add nothing," Smith said, noting simply: "It is sincerely hoped the General Assembly will not permit the present session to pass away without making the necessary provisions on this subject."

In his speech, Smith called upon legislators "to substitute generally, for corporal punishments, confinement for the purpose of initiating the culprit into a habit of useful industry, or in more common phraseology, confinement to hard labor." Other states had already been utilizing prison labor and Smith wanted to follow suit. "A more intimate acquaintance with the effect produced on the conduct of culprits, in States where this mode of punishment is adopted," Smith said, "would no doubt strongly recommend the measure." "[I]n States where it has been the longest in operation," Smith noted, "there exists the most indubitable and unshaken conviction of its utility." In support of his proposal, Smith pressed his fellow citizens: "I am not insensible of the insufficiency of theoretical reasoning on abstract principles, when opposed to inveterate custom and habit. It will not be denied that corporal punishments may have had a good effect in the prevention of crimes, but this concession does not admit the inference that no other mode of punishment would be preferable." Noting that prison labor would add "a source of revenue to the State," Smith contended: "Confinement and hard labor is a mode of punishment peculiarly suited to an advanced state of society, and where the arts abound. In the infancy of government, where the arts do not exist, it is found too difficult and expensive to provide an asylum for the safe keeping of culprits, and to furnish the means and materials for their employment; but in a society and government where the arts abound, these difficulties vanish and leave the arguments drawn from feelings and humanity and the nature of man in their full force."[79]

In response to the governor's request and a legislative committee's unanimous conclusion that a state prison be built, Vermont's General Assembly authorized the construction of a state prison. Windsor was selected as the locale, with five acres of land purchased for the site and five thousand tons of stone acquired for the new structure. At a ceremony involving music and a procession of hundreds of spectators, the cornerstone for the new prison was laid in 1808 amid "the roar of cannon," with a flag of the United States unfurled for the occasion. The all-stone prison, eight-five feet by thirty-five feet in size, was finished later that year. In 1808, the Vermont General Assembly—after another call by the state's governor "to revise our criminal code of laws"—also passed "An Act Providing for the regulation of the State Prison, and altering the punishment of crimes." The law authorized the use of solitary confinement for any state prison inmate who assaulted any visitor or prison keeper or employee, with the board of visitors to consider "the nature and aggravation of the offence, and the degree of penitence discovered in the offender." Section 11 of the Act also provided that if a punishment of "pillory or whipping" was authorized by law, a court, in its discretion, could "dispense with the pillory and whipping, and in case of crimes hereafter committed," "omit the pillory and whipping" and "include in the sentence confinement to hard labor." In 1809 alone, twenty-four convicts were confined to the state prison, with their crimes ranging from counterfeiting and manslaughter to theft, rape and horse stealing.[80]

The changes brought about by the erection of the Vermont state prison were significant. "In consequence of building the State prison," notes one history, "new modes of punishing many crimes were adopted." As that history reported: "Cutting off the ears, branding, whipping, putting in the stocks and pillory had previously been well-known punishments." Indeed, a law from 1779—just three decades earlier—required "that every town in this State shall make and maintain at their own charge, a good pair of stocks, with a lock and key sufficient to hold and secure such offenders as shall be sentenced to sit therein." As the history of Vermont, written by Edward Conant, also recorded of prior times: "In Monkton a Quaker was condemned to stand a certain number of hours in the pillory for getting in hay on the Sabbath. While he stood there his wife sat by, knitting-work in hand." "In Manchester," Conant's history likewise reported, "a convict was brought to the signpost near a large hotel. He was placed on a horse-block and his head was bound fast to the sign-post. The officer cut off the lower portion of the culprit's ears and trod the pieces under his feet. Then taking a branding iron which an assistant had been heating over a kettle of coals he applied it to the convict's forehead." Just three months before the passage of the law authorizing the construction of the state prison, Conant similarly reported, a woman convicted of counterfeiting was brought high on a hill "near the center of Newfane" where stood "the whipping-post in the form of a cross." As Conant reported of what happened next:

> She was stripped naked down to her waist, her arms were tied to the arms of the cross, and thirty-nine lashes were applied to her back, partly by the sheriff and partly by an assistant. Her back became raw from the infliction and she writhed and screamed in her agony. Meanwhile multitudes were looking on from the windows of the church and academy.

"The State prison," Conant concluded, "did not come too soon; and it is well that such scenes were viewed through the windows of the meeting house and school house, else they might have continued to this day."[81]

In the post-*On Crimes and Punishments* era, American legislators also wrestled with issues such as the executive's pardoning power and how to treat suicide. They further vigorously debated the propriety of *benefit of clergy*, a medieval English doctrine that originally exempted clergy from punishment but which evolved in Anglo-American law into a mechanism by which certain offenders, particularly first-time offenders, could avoid the penalty of death.[82] In essays and surveys of the law, Beccaria's name frequently came up in such expositions. For example, in Job Tyson's *Essay on the Penal Law of Pennsylvania*, published by the Law Academy of Philadelphia in 1827, Beccaria's name appears three times. Tyson, a "Student of Law, and Member of the Law Academy," quoted William Bradford's invocation of Beccaria, cited Beccaria's treatise in a section of his essay on sodomy, and referred to Voltaire's commentary on Beccaria. In his essay, Tyson also referred to the "sanguinary temper" of "the *lex talionis*" and "the sanguinary penalties of the mother country, obtained by the act of 1718."

Along with referencing "sanguinary punishments" and the prior abolition of the death penalty for some crimes, Tyson's book cited Pennsylvania's "act of 1794, which took away this sanguinary penalty." Tyson added that the "expurgation" of the death penalty "would be a source of just and laudable pride to Pennsylvanians," and wrote: "a new era is commencing, when the penalty of death will be a stain upon our statute-book, which the humanity of our criminal code, in other respects, cannot efface." "The new penitentiary," Tyson wrote of a newly built state prison, "is surely suitable for all the purposes of rigid and inexorable justice." Pennsylvania, Tyson emphasized, "enjoys a government free and republican, the blessings of Christianity, and, as almost a necessary consequence, a vigour in legislation, which, though it has improved the laws introduced during a state of colonial vassalage, yet, it is humbly submitted, has something still to perform before perfection shall be attained."[83]

Following the Revolutionary War, state penitentiaries—an entirely new social concept—started to be built across America, with Pennsylvania legislators leading the way in terms of law reform. "Previous to the year 1786," noted one prominent commentator, John L. O'Sullivan, in 1842, "the different states of this union were governed, in the main, by the sanguinary criminal code which all as colonies had inherited from their mother-country." In 1786, O'Sullivan pointed out, Pennsylvania fashioned its new penal code, abolishing capital punishment for all felonies except arson, rape, murder and treason. Not long after, in 1790, America's first penitentiary, Philadelphia's Walnut Street Prison, opened its doors, an event coming just seven years after the Treaty of Paris, the armistice that ended America's war for independence.[84] America's founders, seeking milder punishments, had first put in place written constitutions and declarations of rights to regulate abuses of power and to set forth fundamental principles. With the Walnut Street Prison, they began the difficult task of *implementing* those principles by putting in place penitentiaries—facilities that captivated enlightened minds everywhere.

That penitentiaries were seen as an outgrowth of Beccaria's reformist ideas is made clear by *Des Prisons de Philadelphie*, a book written in the 1790s by François-Alexandre-Frédéric duc de La Rochefoucauld-Liancourt (1747–1827). That book quoted Beccaria's treatise on the title page; cited the work of William Penn, Montesquieu, Beccaria, John Howard, Caleb Lownes and William Bradford within its pages; and reprinted—in English—the Declaration of Independence and the constitutions of the American states, the instruments that had made American penal reform possible.[85] Rochefoucauld-Liancourt, a French social reformer with ties to Louis XVI, had fled to England during the French Revolution, then traveled to the United States in the mid-1790s. In 1796, François-Alexandre-Frédéric duc de La Rochefoucauld-Liancourt also authored a long pamphlet, printed in English in Philadelphia and reprinted in London, titled *A Comparative View of Mild and Sanguinary Laws; and the Good Effects of the Former, Exhibited in the Present Economy of the Prisons of Philadelphia*. That pamphlet also cited Beccaria's influence on Caleb Lownes. Before 1850, with many American penitentiaries already in place, Charles Spear—the author of *Essays on the Punishment of Death*—was telling his readers: "the great object of our labor will be to show the injustice of Capital Punishments." "Take away first this cruel, sanguinary law," Spear wrote, "and then let benevolence and justice do their work."[86] Spear, inspired by thinkers like Beccaria and Lafayette, began writing against the death penalty in the 1830s and became general agent of the newly organized Massachusetts Society for the Abolition of Capital Punishment in 1845. "I want our prisons to be more like hospitals," Spear observed.[87]

Arbitrary and sanguinary punishments were once the norm in England, capriciously handed out by infamous and bloodthirsty English judges like the much-loathed Lord Chief Justice George Jeffreys. But America's Founding Fathers and later reformers—continually expressing disdain for the arbitrary use of power—sought to usher in a new, and more rational, world order. In 1772, Benjamin Franklin, under the pen name "Silence Dogood," wrote of being "a mortal Enemy to arbitrary Government and unlimited Power." In *Poor Richard Improved* (1748), Franklin also bemoaned "arbitrary power," as he did elsewhere, too. For instance, Franklin wrote of "hating arbitrary Power of all Sorts" in 1769, and later wrote of "the arbitrary Power of a corrupt Parliament" and "Arbitrary Proceedings of Governors and other Crown Officers." George Washington also wrote of preserving "the Rights and Liberties of the people ... against the arbitrary proceedings of the military officers"; Thomas Jefferson bemoaned "arbitrary power" and "Arbitrary government"; James Madison wrote to Edmund Randolph in 1782 of "the Arbitrary Acts" that "gave birth" to "the present revolution"; and Alexander Hamilton wrote of "the arbitrary will of a prince," saying that "[t]he genius of liberty reprobates every thing arbitrary or discretionary in taxation." "[A]s we are free British Subjects," reads a 40-page pamphlet, *An Appeal to the World*, attributed to Samuel Adams, William Cooper and James Otis, "we claim all that Security against arbitrary Power, to which we are entitled by the Law of God and Nature, as well as the British Constitution." Dr. Benjamin Rush likewise wrote to John Adams of "arbitrary power"; Elbridge Gerry wrote to John Adams about "arbitrary and dangerous powers"; and John Adams himself lamented "arbitrary Will or inflexible fatality," "Arbitrary Power" and "arbitrary laws," and wrote of "an Arbitrary Government," "arbitrary lawless power," "arbitrary kings," "cruel" and "arbitrary government," "the most arbitrary Governor," and an "arbitrary" judge.[88]

The "English constitution" had always been subject to the whim of Parliament, and while English subjects had long made appeals to the "rule of law" in their dealings with British monarchs, Americans had a different conception of how government should be structured. In 1780, John Adams enshrined the American version of this Rule of Law principle by seeking, in the Massachusetts constitution he played a key role in drafting, to establish "a government of laws and not of men." That constitution recited in the preamble that "[t]he body politic is formed by a voluntary association of individuals; it is a social compact by which the whole people covenants with each citizen and each citizen with the whole people that all shall be governed by certain laws for the common good." Article I proclaimed that "[a]ll men are born free and equal, and have certain natural, essential, and unalienable rights," with Article XII—detailing criminal suspects' rights— reading: "No subject shall be held to answer for any crimes or no offence until the same is fully and plainly, substantially and formally, described to him; or be compelled to accuse, or furnish evidence against himself; and every subject shall have a right to produce all proofs that may be favorable to him; to meet the witnesses against him face to face, and to be fully heard in his defence by himself, or his counsel at his election." "And no subject," Article XII continued, "shall be arrested, imprisoned, despoiled, or deprived of his property, immunities, or privileges, put out of the protection of the law, exiled or deprived of his life, liberty, or estate, but by the judgment of his peers, or the law of the land." "And the legislature," Article XII further provided, "shall not make any law that shall subject any person to a capital or infamous punishment, excepting for the government of the army and navy, without trial by jury."[89]

Long before the Revolutionary War, Adams himself had written about the rights and liberties of Englishmen and the much-lauded British constitution, a source of tremendous pride for Englishmen of that time. As Adams recorded in January 1766 before becoming an American revolutionary: "There has been a great Inquiry, in some Parts of America, after a Diffinition of the british Constitution. Some have defined the Constitution to be the Practice of Parliament." Others, Adams wrote, "have called it, Custom," while still others had "call'd it the most perfect Combination of human Powers in society, that finite Wisdom has yet contrived and reduced to Practice, for the Preservation of Liberty, and the Production of Happiness." "Some," Adams added, have said that the King, Lords, and Commons "make the Constitution," with Adams noting that others "have said that the whole Body of the Laws are the Constitution." "I confess there is nothing in any one of these," Adams editorialized, "that is satisfactory to my Mind." "Yet," Adams added, "I cannot say that I am at any Loss about my own or any Man's Meaning when he uses those Words 'The british Constitution.'"

After concluding that "the public Good"—"the good of the whole Community"—is "the professed End of all Government," Adams wrote in 1766: "I shall take for granted what I am sure no Briton will controvert, that Liberty is essential to human Happiness— to the public Good, the Salus Populi." "And here lies the Difference between the british Constitution and other Constitutions," Adams emphasized, writing "that Liberty is its End." Adams went on to call "two Branches of popular Power"—"voting for Members of the House of Commons" and "Tryals by Juries"—as "essential and fundamental to the great End of the british Constitution, the Preservation of Liberty." In those two things, Adams wrote, "consist the security and Liberty of the People," with Adams adding: "They have no other Fortification against Power besides these, no other security against being ridden like Horses, and fleeced like Sheep, and worked like Cattle, and fed and Cloathed like Hoggs, and Hounds. Nay no other security against fines, Imprisonments, loss of Limbs, Whipping Posts, Gibbets, Bastinadoes and Racks."

Writing as "Clarendon," Adams repeated many of these themes in a letter to "William Pym" published in the *Boston Gazette* on January 27, 1766, in response to an article that was published in the *London Evening Post* and reprinted in the *Boston Evening Post*. The "Sons of Liberty," Adams wrote of the British constitution, "know the true constitution and all the resources of liberty in it, as well as in the law of nature which is one principle foundation of it." The British constitution, Adams emphasized there, "stands not on the supposition that kings are the favourites of heaven; that their power is more divine than the power of the people, and unlimited but by their own will and discretion." "It is not built," he added, "on the doctrine that a few nobles or rich commons have a right to inherit the earth, and all the blessings and pleasures of it: and that the multitude, the million, the populace, the vulgar, the mob, the herd and the rabble, as the great always delight to call them, have no rights at all, and were made only for their use, to be robbed and butchered at their pleasure." "No," Adams continued, "it stands upon this principle, that the meanest and lowest of the people, are, by the unalterable indefeasible laws of God and nature, as well intitled to the benefit of the air to breathe, light to see, food to eat, and clothes to wear, as the nobles or the king." "All men," he wrote, "are born equal: and the drift of the British constitution is to preserve as much of this equality, as is compatible with the people's security against foreign invasions and domestic usurpation."

The right to elect members of the House of Commons and "tryals by juries," Adams emphasized in the letter, "are essential and fundamental" to "the preservation of the subject's liberty." "These two powers," he wrote, employing the analogies of a human body and a functioning watch, "therefore are the heart and hungs, the main spring, and the center wheel, and without them, the body must die; the watch must run down; the government must become arbitrary, and this our law books have settled to be the death of the laws and constitution." "In these two powers," Adams reiterated, "consist wholly, the liberty and security of the people: They have no other fortification against wanton, cruel power: no other indemnification against being ridden like horses, fleeced like sheep, worked like cattle, and fed and cloathed like swine and hounds: No other defence against fines, imprisonments, whipping posts, gibbets, bastenadoes and racks." Adams reasoned: "What a fine reflection and consolation is it for a man to reflect that he can be subjected to no laws, which he does not make himself, or constitute some of his friends to make for him." "What a satisfaction is it to reflect, that he can lie under the imputation of no guilt, be subjected to no punishment, lose none of his property, or the necessaries, conveniences or ornaments of life, which indulgent providence has showered around him: but by the judgment of his peers, his equals, his neighbours, men who know him, and to whom he is known."[90]

In line with such sentiments, early American constitutions and bills of rights guaranteed the right to trial by jury—a protection Beccaria himself had endorsed—and also commonly forbid "cruel," "unusual," or "sanguinary" punishments, with eighteenth-century sources—as noted—awash with jibes and swipes at arbitrary, cruel, and sanguinary acts.[91] The phrase "sanguinary tyrant"—a phrase used by Edmund Burke in *Reflections on the Revolution in France*[92]—appears in Thomas Paine's bestseller, *Common Sense*, as does this advice from Paine himself: "Lay then the axe to the root, and teach governments humanity. It is their sanguinary punishments which corrupt mankind."[93] In *Rights of Man*, Paine wrote this of his particular disdain for executions: "In England the punishment in certain cases is by hanging, drawing and quartering; the heart of the sufferer is cut out and held up to the view of the populace. In France, under the former Government, the punishments were not less barbarous. Who does not remember the execution of

Damien, torn to pieces horses?" "The effect of those cruel spectacles exhibited to the populace," Paine added, "is to destroy tenderness or excite revenge; and by the base and false idea of governing men by terror, instead of reason, they become precedents." Paine, with his family's Quaker roots, was—like Beccaria, his literary predecessor—an ardent death penalty opponent.

In France, where Paine had been honored because of his role in the American Revolution, Paine even risked his own life by vocally opposing King Louis XVI's execution. Before Louis XVI was guillotined on January 21, 1793, in the Place de la Révolution, Paine told a friend, "If the French kill their king, it will be a signal for my departure, for I will not abide among sanguinary men." John Adams, writing to his wife Abigail on February 3, 1793, from Philadelphia, before news of Louis XVI's execution reached the City of Brotherly Love, himself recorded that he would not "exult in the Prison or Tryal of that King to whom though I am personally under no Obligation, my Country is under the greatest." In that letter, John Adams presciently emphasized that "accursed Politicks" had cost Louis XVI "his Crown if not his head" and that "[t]he Duke de la Rochefoucault too, is cutt to pieces for his Idolatry." The English-speaking Louis-Alexandre la Rochefoucauld (1743–1792), who was born into a noble family, had become a friend of Lafayette, Benjamin Franklin and John Adams, as well as of the United States, and had translated American constitutions. He was stoned to death in August 1792 in France after being recognized by an angry mob. "If I had not washed my own hands of all this Blood, by warning them against it," Adams told his wife, "I should feel some of it upon my soul." On February 3, 1793, William Short—writing from Madrid, Spain three days after news of Louis XVI's execution reached that much-closer locale—told his mentor, Thomas Jefferson, that "the assassination" of Louis XVI "seems to render war certain between France and this Country" with war "still more certain" between France and England. In fact, France declared war on Great Britain, Holland and Spain on February 1, 1793.[94]

When Louis XVI was executed, the Founding Fathers—along with the rest of the world—took notice, often recording the event in their correspondence. For example, on January 25, 1793, Gouverneur Morris—often called the "Penman of the Constitution" for his role in the drafting of that document—wrote from Paris to tell Thomas Jefferson the news:

> The late King of this Country has been publickly executed. He died in a Manner becoming his Dignity. Mounting the Scaffold he express'd anew his Forgiveness of those who persecuted him and a Prayer that his deluded People might be benefited by his Death. On the Scaffold he attempted to speak but the commanding Officer Santerre ordered the Drums to be beat. The King made two unavailing Efforts but with the same bad Success. The Executioners threw him down and were in such Haste as to let fall the Axe before his Neck was properly placed so that he was mangled. It would be needless to give you an affecting Narrative of Particulars. I proceed to what is more important having but a few Minutes to write by the present good Opportunity.

> The greatest care was taken to prevent an Affluence of People. This proves a Conviction that the Majority was not favorable to that severe Measure. In Effect the great Mass of the parisian Citizens mournd the Fate of their Unhappy Prince. I have seen Grief such as for the untimely Death of a beloved Parent. Every Thing wears an Appearance of Solemnity which is awfully distressing.

In a subsequent letter, written from Paris on February 13, 1793, Morris also reported to Jefferson that "I have had every Reason to believe that the Execution of Louis XVI has produced on foreign Nations the Effect which I had imagin'd." "The War with England," he wrote, "exists and it is now proper perhaps to consider it's Consequences."

Writing from London on January 20, 1793, the American statesman Thomas Pinckney also communicated this to Jefferson: "The news papers herewith will convey the public news up to this date. The melancholic fate of the unfortunate Louis has made a forcible impression on the public mind here...." Pinckney further noted that the French ambassador, Marquis de Chauvelin, had been ordered by the British government to leave England. Later that year, James Madison himself reported from Orange, Virginia, on Americans' reaction to the execution of Louis XVI, a former U.S. ally. Although the execution of Louis XIV diminished support for the French Revolution in some quarters, with one 1793 letter to Alexander Hamilton saying that Louis XVI's execution had changed public sentiment, Madison wrote to Thomas Jefferson on April 12, 1793 to express his own take: "The sympathy with the fate of Louis has found its way pretty generally into the mass of our citizens; but relating merely to the man & not to the Monarch, and being derived from the spurious accts. in the papers of his innocence and the bloodthirstiness of his enemies." "If he was a Traytor, he ought to be punished as well as another man," was a sentiment Madison reported "many plain men" had conveyed to him as regards the late French king. "I am persuaded," Madison told Jefferson in the aftermath of the French Revolution, that such a sentiment "will be found to express the universal sentiment whenever the truth shall be made known."[95] In August 1792, the National Assembly of France had honorifically bestowed French citizenship upon persons it believed had promoted the cause of liberty. Among the recipients: George Washington, James Madison, Alexander Hamilton, Thomas Paine, Joseph Priestley, Jeremy Bentham, William Wilberforce, and Count Giuseppe Gorani, a Milan native and *illuminista* political writer who was Cesare Beccaria's friend and a member of the *Il Caffé* social circle. Gorani's book, *Recherches sur la science de gouvernement*, had been published in Paris in 1792.[96]

The rage against "sanguinary" codes and laws took place in both Europe and America, though it percolated—then boiled over—at different times in different places as revolutionary foment spread amongst individuals and then whole states or nations. In the United States, Beccaria's reformist views gained almost immediate popularity, with the end of the Revolutionary War offering, for the first time, a real opportunity to experiment with those ideas produced by the Italian Enlightenment.[97] For example, in American states and at colleges like Yale, Beccaria's treatise was much read and admired. St. John Honeywood (1765–1798)—a native of Leicester, Massachusetts, educated at Yale College—even wrote a whole poem titled "Crimes and Punishments." Having worked as a school principal in Schenectady, New York, in the mid-1780s, Honeywood became a law student of Albany lawyer Peter W. Yates—the same man under whom the American jurist Brockholst Livingston had studied law before being admitted to the bar in 1783. The son of William Livingston, Brockholst Livingston graduated from Princeton in 1774, served in the Continental Army, went to Spain as a secretary to his brother-in-law John Jay, and ultimately became a U.S. Supreme Court Justice. After being admitted to the bar, Honeywood—the equally well-educated thinker—moved to Salem, Massachusetts, notorious for its seventeenth-century witch trials, where he became a prominent citizen. "He was one of the electors of President of the United States when Mr. Adams became the successor of General Washington," one short biographical sketch notes. A painter and a poet, Honeywood once penned these lines about John Adams: *Ardent and foremost in his country's cause, / The friend of order and of equal laws.*

In a collection of Honeywood's poems published in 1801 after his death, the opening stanzas of the lengthy "Crimes and Punishments" poem—found among the author's manuscripts and once described as "the most laboured" of his "performances"—explicitly references Beccaria and contrasts bloody monarchical punishments with milder ones. The first five stanzas of Honeywood's evocative poem give a flavor for the penal reform debate that was, at that time, consuming American legislators and the American people:

Of crimes, empoison'd source of human woes,
Whence the black flood of shame and sorrow flows,
How best to check the venom's deadly force,
To stem its torrent, or direct its course,
To scan the merits of vindictive codes,
Nor pass the faults humanity explodes,
I sing—what theme more worthy to engage
The poet's song, the wisdom of the sage!
Ah! were I equal to the great design,
Were they bold genius, blest BECCARIA! mine,
Then should my work, ennobled as my aim,
Like thine, received the meed of deathless fame.
O JAY! deserving of a purer age,
Pride of thy country, statesman, patriot, sage,
Beneath whose guardian care our laws assume
A milder form, and lose their Gothic gloom,
Read with indulgent eyes, not yet refuse
This humble tribute of an artless muse.
    Great is the question which the learn'd contest,
What grade, what mode of punishment is best;
In two famed sects the disputants decide,
These ranged on Terror's, those on Reason's side;
Ancient as empire Terror's temple stood,
Capt with black clouds, and founded deep in blood;
Grim despots here their trembling honours paid,
And guilty offerings to their idol made:
The monarch led—a servile crowd ensued,
Their robes distain'd in gore, in gore imbrued;
O'er mangled limbs they held infernal feast,
MOLOCH the god, and DRACO's self the priest.
Mild Reason's fane, in later ages rear'd,
With sunbeams crown'd, in Attic grace appear'd;
In just proportion finish'd every part,
With the fine touches of enlighten'd art.
A thinking few, selected from the crowd,
At the fair shrine with filial rev'rence bow'd;
The sage of Milan led the virtuous choir,
To them sublime he strung the tuneful lyre:
Of laws, of crimes, and punishments he sung,
And on his glowing lips persuasion hung:
From Reason's source each inference just he drew,
While truths fresh polish'd struck the mind as new.
Full in the front, in vestal robes array'd,
The holy form of Justice stood display'd:
Firm was her eye, not vengeful, though severe,
And e'er she frown'd she check'd the starting tear.
A sister form, of more benignant face,
Celestial Mercy, held the second place;
Her hands outspread, in suppliant guise she stood,
And oft with eloquence resistless sued;

But where 'twas impious e'en to deprecate,
She sigh'd assent, and wept the wretch's fate.
　　In savage times, fair Freedom yet unknown,
The despot, clad in vengeance, fill'd the throne;
His gloomy caprice scrawl'd the ambiguous code,
And dyed each page in characters of blood:
The laws transgress'd, the prince in judgment sat,
And Rage decided on the culprit's fate:
Nor stopp'd he here, but, skill'd in murderous art,
The scepter'd brute usurp'd the hangman's part;
With his own hands the trembling victim hew'd,
And basely wallow'd in a subject's blood.
Pleased with the fatal game, the royal mind
On modes of death and cruelty refined:
Hence the dank caverns of the cheerless mine,
Where, shut from light, the famish'd wretches pine;
The face divine, in seams unsightly sear'd,
The eyeballs gouged, the wheel with gore besmear'd,
The Russian knout, the suffocating flame,
And forms of torture wanting yet a name.
Nor was this rage to savage times confined;
It reach'd to later years and courts refined.
Blush, polish'd France, nor let the music relate
The tragic story of your DAMIEN's fate;
The bed of steel, where long the assassin lay,
In the dark vault, secluded from the day:
The quivering flesh which burning pincers tore,
The pitch, pour'd flaming in the recent sore;
His carcase, warm with life, convulsed with pain,
By steeds dismember'd, dragg'd along the plain.
　　As daring quacks, unskill'd in medic lore,
Prescribed the nostrums quacks prescribed before;
Careless of age or sex, whete'er befall,
The same dull recipe must serve for all;
Our senates thus, with reverence be it said,
Have been too long by blind tradition led:
Our civil code, from feudal dross refined,
Proclaims the liberal and enlighten'd mind;
But till of late the penal statutes stood
In Gothic rudeness, smear'd with civic blood;
What base memorials of a barbarous age,
What monkish whimsies sullied every page!
The clergy's benefit, a trifling brand,
Jest of the law, a holy sleight of hand:
Beneath this saintly cloak with crimes abhorr'd,
Of sable dye, were shelter'd from the lord;
While the poor starveling, who a cent purlion'd,
No reading saved, no juggling trick essoin'd;
His was the servile lash, a foul disgrace,
Through time transmitted to his hapless race;

The fort and dure, the traitor's motley doom,
Might blot the story of imperial Rome.
What late disgraced our laws yet stand to stain
The splendid annals of a GEORGE's reign.
     Say, legislators, for what end design'd
This waste of lives, this havoc of mankind?
Say, by what right (one case exempt alone)
Do ye prescribe, that blood can crimes atone?
If, when our fortunes frown, and dangers press,
To act the Roman's part be to transgress;
For man the use of life alone commands,
The fee residing in the grantor's hands.
Could man, what time the social pact he seal'd,
Cede to the state a right he never held?
For all the powers which in the state reside,
Result from compact, actual or implied.
Too well the savage policy we trace
To times remote, Humanity's disgrace;
E'en while I ask, the trite response recurs,
Example warns, severity deters.
No milder means can keep the vile in awe,
And state necessity compels the law.
But let Experience speak, she claims our trust;
The data false, the inference is unjust.
Ills at a distance, men but slightly fear;
Delusive Fancy never thinks them near:
With stronger force than fear temptations draw,
And Cunning thinks to parry with the law.
"My brother swing, poor novice in his art,
He blindly stumbled on a hangman's cart;
But wiser I, assuming every shape,
As PROTEUS erst, am certain to escape."
The knave, thus jeering, on his skill relies
For never villain deem'd himself unwise.

Honeywood's poem would later be reprinted in London and Philadelphia as part of a collection of poetry billing itself as containing "Two Thousand of the Best Pieces in the English Language."[98]

Benjamin Banneker and the Scourge of Slavery

In the founding era, African-American intellectuals also took part in efforts to reform and remake the society and the law. Particularly compelling is the story of Benjamin Banneker (1731–1806), a largely self-educated Maryland corn and tobacco farmer whose father was a freed slave. As a teenager, Banneker had the good fortune of befriending a Quaker, Peter Heinrichs, a fellow farmer. Heinrichs—of a family of means—had established a farm near the Banneker family farm and gave young Benjamin access to his personal library and provided classroom instruction. Intellectually curious throughout his

life, Banneker—whose family history included a near-fatal brush with the law—later
became a clockmaker, astronomer, surveyor and mathematician who wrote commercially
successful farmer's almanacs. Banneker's own maternal grandmother, Molly Welsh, had
worked as a dairymaid for a cruel master near Devon, England, and had been sentenced
to seven years of servitude in the colony of Maryland for allegedly stealing a pail of milk
that she had accidently spilled in 1682. She had only escaped the English death penalty
for her adjudicated theft because she could read the Bible and was granted a reprieve. Before 1691, women convicted of theft of goods worth less than 10 shillings could receive
benefit of clergy, though the ability to claim that privilege was contingent on one's ability
to recite the first verse of Psalm 51. That verse, shielding readers from the gallows, became
popularly known as the *neck verse* because it could save the accused from hanging. "Have
mercy upon me, O God, after Thy great goodness," it read.

It was after another friendly and benevolent Quaker, gristmill owner George Ellicott,
had lent Banneker books on astronomy, that Banneker—who grew up to be a very learned
man—was hired by Major Andrew Ellicott, another member of the family, to assist in marking the boundaries of the new federal district along the Potomac River. That ten-mile
square district, now known as the District of Columbia, was created through the cession
of land from Maryland and Virginia, with Banneker performing his survey work from
February through April of 1791 before returning home to Ellicott's Mills. As Thomas Jefferson, who exchanged letters with Banneker in 1791, wrote on August 30, 1791 to the French
Marquis de Condorcet: "I am happy to be able to inform you that we have now in the
United States a negro, the son of a black man born in Africa, and of a black woman born
in the United States, who is a very respectable Mathematician. I promised him to be employed under one of our chief directors in laying out the new federal city on the Patow-
mac, & in the intervals of his leisure, while on that work, he made an almanac for the next
year, which he sent to me in his own handwriting, & which I inclose to you." In a posthumously published work, Condorcet—the Enlightenment figure with whom Jefferson was
corresponding—wrote that Beccaria, that leading figure of the age, had "refuted in Italy
the barbarous maxims of Gallic jurisprudence." In the newly formed United States of
America, meanwhile, Banneker, whose intelligence, mathematical calculations and work
later earned the approval of other respected figures such as David Rittenhouse, the famed
scientist, would be celebrated by anti-slavery activists as proof of the equality of man.

On August 19, 1791, while in Maryland, Banneker wrote a moving letter to then Secretary of State Thomas Jefferson, America's future President. Banneker's letter began: "I
am fully sensible of the greatness of that freedom, which I take with you on the present
occasion; a liberty which seemed to me scarcely allowable, when I reflected on that distinguished and dignified station in which you stand, and the almost general prejudice
and prepossession, which is so prevalent in the world against those of my complexion."
"Sir, I freely and cheerfully acknowledge, that I am of the African race," Banneker wrote,
emphasizing:

> [I]t is under a sense of the most profound gratitude to the Supreme Ruler of the
> Universe, that I now confess to you, that I am not under that state of tyrannical
> thraldom, and inhuman captivity, to which too many of my brethren are doomed,
> but that I have abundantly tasted of the fruition of those blessings, which pro-
> ceed from that free and unequalled liberty with which you are favored; and which,
> I hope, you will willingly allow you have mercifully received, from the immedi-
> ate hand of that Being, from whom proceedeth every good and perfect Gift.

"I suppose it is a truth too well attested to you, to need a proof here," Banneker's letter
read, "that we are a race of beings, who have long labored under the abuse and censure

of the world; that we have long been looked upon with an eye of contempt; and that we have long been considered rather as brutish than human, and scarcely capable of mental endowment."

With Banneker hoping that a report he had gotten that Jefferson, the slaveowner, was "a man far less inflexible in sentiments of this nature, than many other," and "measurably friendly, and well disposed towards us," Banneker boldly solicited Jefferson's "aid and assistance to our relief, from those many distresses, and numerous calamities, to which we are reduced." "Now Sir, if this is founded in truth," Banneker wrote of the report that he had gotten about Jefferson's character, "I apprehend you will embrace every opportunity, to eradicate that train of absurd and false ideas and opinions, which so generally prevails with respect to us." "Sir, suffer me to recal[l] to your mind that time, in which the arms and tyranny of the British crown were exerted, with every powerful effort, in order to reduce you to a state of servitude," Banneker implored Jefferson, with Banneker observing:

> This, Sir, was a time when you clear[l]y saw into the injustice of a state of slavery, and in which you had just apprehensions of the horrors of its condition. It was now that your abhorrence thereof was so excited, that you publicly held forth this true and invaluable doctrine, which is worthy to be recorded and remembered in all succeeding ages: "We hold these truths to be self-evident, that all men are created equal; that they are endowed by their Creator with certain unalienable rights, and that among these are life, liberty, and the pursuit of happiness." Here was a time, in which your tender feelings for yourselves had engaged you thus to declare, you were then impressed with proper ideas of the great violation of liberty, and the free possession of those blessings, to which you were entitled by nature; but, Sir, how pitiable is it to reflect, that although you were so fully convinced of the benevolence of the Father of Mankind, and of his equal and impartial distribution of these rights and privileges, which he hath conferred upon them, that you should at the same time counteract his mercies, in detaining by fraud and violence so numerous a part of my brethren, under groaning captivity and cruel oppression, that you should at the same time be found guilty of that most criminal act, which you professedly detested in others, with respect to yourselves.

In his letter to America's secretary of state, Banneker specifically expressed the hope "that your sentiments are concurrent with mine, which are, that one universal Father hath given being to us all; and that he hath not only made us all of one flesh, but that he hath also, without partiality, afforded us all the same sensations and endowed us all with the same faculties; and that however variable we may be in society or religion, however diversified in situation or color, we are all of the same family, and stand in the same relation to him."

White Quakers, among them William Qualls, a Baltimore merchant, and the mill-owning Ellicott family near Banneker's farm, had, by befriending Banneker, given him unusual educational opportunities in that discrimination-ridden era. In Baltimore, Qualls had reportedly witnessed a corrupt British customs officer confiscate a large portion of Banneker's valuable tobacco crop, with Qualls then taking Banneker under his wings. Qualls introduced Banneker to Joseph Levi, a wealthy trader and investor with whom Banneker quickly bonded over their mutual love for science. While not belonging to any church, the unmarried Banneker was a religious truth seeker who occasionally attended Society of Friends meetings. Influenced by his own experiences, as well as his Quaker associations, Banneker confidently pleaded with Jefferson in his 1791 letter: "Sir, if these are sentiments of which you are fully persuaded, I hope you cannot but acknowledge, that it is the indispensible duty of those, who maintain for themselves the rights of human nature, and who possess the obligations of Christianity, to extend their power and influence to the relief of every part of the human race, from whatever burden or oppression they may unjustly labor under." "Sir," Banneker wrote, "I have long been convinced, that if your love for yourselves, and for those inestimable laws, which preserved to you the rights of human nature, was founded on sincerity, you could not but be solicitous, that every individual, of whatever rank or distinction, might with you equally enjoy the blessings thereof; neither could you rest satisfied short of the most active effusion of your exertions, in order to their promotion from any state of degradation, to which the unjustifiable cruelty and barbarism of men may have reduced them."

On August 30, 1791, Jefferson—then in Philadelphia—had quickly, if politely, written back to Banneker: "Sir, I thank you sincerely for your letter of the 19th. instant and for the Almanac it contained." Jefferson added:

> [N]o body wishes more than I do to see such proofs as you exhibit, that nature has given to our black brethren, talents equal to those of the other colours of men, & that the appearance of a want of them is owing merely to the degraded condition of their existence both in Africa & America. I can add with truth that no body wishes more ardently to see a good system commenced for raising the condition both of their body & mind to what it ought to be, as fast as the imbecillity of their present existence, and other circumstance which cannot be neglected, will admit.

Before signing off "I am with great esteem, Sir, Your most obedt. Humble servt.," Jefferson closed his letter to Banneker, the free black man, by advising, "I have taken the liberty of sending your almanac to Monsieur de Condorcet, Secretary of the Academy of sciences at Paris, and member of the Philanthropic society because I considered it as a document to which your whole colour had a right for their justification against the doubts which have been entertained of them."[99]

Banneker's almanac, supported by Quaker abolitionists anxious to disprove racial inferiority, was read widely along the East Coast. First published in 1792 by Baltimore printers Goddard & Angell, it appeared under the title *Benjamin Banneker's Pennsylvania, Delaware, Maryland and Virginia Almanack and Ephmeris, for the Year of Our Lord, 1792.* The almanac's title page stated that it contained "[t]he Motions of the Sun and Moon"; "Days for holding the Supreme and Circuit Courts of the *United States*, as also the useful Courts in *Pennsylvania, Delaware, Maryland*, and *Virginia*"; "Various Selections from the Commonplace Book of the *Kentucky Philosopher*, an *American Sage*, with interesting and entertaining essays, in Prose and Verse"; "the whole" said to comprise "a greater, more pleasing, and useful Variety than any Work of the *Kind* and *Price* in *North America*." A second edition of Banneker's almanac was later published by Philadelphia printer William Young, the same publisher that printed Beccaria's treatise in 1793, and that new edition of the almanac contained a biographical sketch of Banneker that was written by Maryland politician James McHenry, a signer of the U.S. Constitution. Having apprenticed under Dr. Benjamin Rush, the Irish-born McHenry was a physician who served in the Continental Congress and as the U.S. Secretary of War under George Washington and John Adams.

In 1783, McHenry had passionately spoken in favor of mercy for a group of Pennsylvania mutineers, including Captain Henry Carberry of Maryland and Lieutenant John Sullivan of Pennsylvania. Disgruntled soldiers court-martialed by Major General Robert Howe, the two officers—believed to have "egged on" soldiers' representatives in an upstairs room of the Doctor Franklin Tavern—had served in the Revolutionary War in the

4th Continental Dragoons and the 11th Pennsylvania Regiment. As McHenry, seeking compassion for the men, urged his colleagues, with McHenry's memoirs referring to Carberry as "Casberry":

> It is impossible that any set of men can be engaged in a business more serious or more solemn, than in deliberating upon an *act* that is to deprive a *human being* of his *life* or *character*. It will occur to the house that the operation of this act does not merely respect the *life* or character of Casberry & Sullivan, but extends beyond them, to their relations and even to all those of the same name. If a soldier falls in battle — if an honest man is killed by a robber, or murdered by his enemy, this neither injures his fame, or reflects dishonor on his relations. But the case is far otherwise if he dies under the hands of the law or the executioner. His memory thence-forward is rendered infamous, and to be his relation or to bear his name, is to carry about one a mark of indelible disgrace.
>
> ...
>
> It is certainly an extenuation of their crime, that its object was founded in justice.... But other and more urgent reasons plead that their crimes should be forgiven. Let the services and long sufferings of the army be remembered; and let the failings of these men be forgotten in their former merits and in the merits of the army. And let not the first fruits of their long and perilous contest, *our peace*, be watered with the blood of two of their companions.
>
> I hope it will not be urged that the measure is necessary for the support of our national character. Our national character can never be supported by a sacrifice of national humanity. I have always thought, and the history of all nations teach me that I am right that *acts of mercy* serve more to dignify and raise the character of a government than *acts of blood*. It is said that Draco's laws were written in blood — but no one has ever dared to praise them.

Ultimately, neither Carberry nor Sullivan was ever convicted of any offence associated with the June 1783 mutiny.[100]

The 1793 edition of Banneker's almanac, which was published from 1792 to 1797, included Banneker's correspondence with Jefferson as well as "A Plan of a Peace-Office for the United States" written by Dr. Benjamin Rush. According to Silvio Bedini, Banneker's biographer, this made Banneker's almanac "one of the most important publications of its time" as it was "distributed in great numbers and became the subject of widespread discussions at all levels." The Philadelphia printer David Lawrence also published the Banneker-Jefferson correspondence in pamphlet form in 1792. Dr. Rush's essay called for "an *office* for promoting and preserving perpetual *peace* in our country," and the appointment of "a Secretary of the Peace" who "shall be perfectly free from all the present absurd and vulgar European prejudices upon the subject of government." As Rush described the proposed post's qualifications: "let him be a genuine republican and a sincere Christian, for the principles of republicanism and Christianity are no less friendly to universal and perpetual peace, than they are to universal and equal liberty." In his essay, Dr. Rush — calling for an American edition of the Bible to be distributed to every U.S. family — asserted that "the Supreme Being alone possesses a power to take away human life, and that we rebel against his laws, whenever we undertake to execute death in any way whatever upon any of his creatures." "Let the following sentence be inscribed in letters of gold over the doors of every State and Court house in the United States," Rush wrote, seeking this inscription: "The Son of Man Came into the World, Not to Destroy Men's Lives, but to Save Them." Dr. Rush — the anti-slavery and anti-death penalty abolitionist — also made this observation:

To inspire a veneration for human life, and an horror at the shedding of human blood, let all those laws be repealed which authorise juries, judges, sheriffs, or hangmen to assume the resentments of individuals and to commit murder in cold blood in any case whatever. Until this reformation in our code of penal jurisprudence takes place, it will be in vain to attempt to introduce universal and perpetual peace in our country.[101]

Banneker and his almanac and what they represented—that African Americans had the same intellectual capacity and talents as whites—turned Benjamin Banneker into a powerful symbol of racial equality. After his appearance in the new federal district to do his surveying work, the *Georgetown Weekly Ledger* described Banneker as "an Ethiopian, whose abilities, as a surveyor, and an astronomer, clearly prove that Mr. Jefferson's concluding that race of men were void of mental endowments, was without foundation." For his own part, Banneker hoped to change American law for the better, using Jefferson's own words in the Declaration of Independence as a key component of his argument for equality. As historian Yolandea Wood argues in *Slavery in the United States*, Banneker—advocating public education and the abolition of capital punishment—"was dedicated to exploring and applying natural law for the betterment of the human race." Just as Abigail Adams' 1776 letter to her husband John, urging him, as a member of Congress, to "Remember the Ladies" in any "new Code of Laws" to be drafted, Banneker's 1791 letter to Jefferson represented an early American effort seeking justice and equality.

Although it is unclear if Banneker ever read law-related texts such as Beccaria's treatise, Abigail Adams most likely did, as the language of her "Remember the Ladies" letter seems to indicate, at least if one pays attention to the verbiage she employs in it. "Do not put such unlimited power into the hands of the Husbands," she wrote, adding: "Remember all Men would be tyrants if they could. If perticuliar care and attention is not paid to the Laidies we are determined to foment a Rebellion, and will not hold ourselves bound by any Laws in which we have no voice, or Representation." As Abigail's letter to her husband continued: "That your Sex are Naturally Tyrannical is a Truth so thoroughly established as to admit of no dispute, but such of you as wish to be happy willingly give up the harsh title of Master for the more tender and endearing one of Friend. Why then, not put it out of the power of the vicious and the Lawless to use us with cruelty and indignity with impunity." In making her final appeal, Abigail's letter concluded: "Men of Sense in all Ages abhor those customs which treat us only as the vassals of your Sex. Regard us then as Beings placed by providence under your protection and in immitation of the Supreem Being make use of that power only for our happiness."[102]

Republican Architecture:
Architects, Laws and Juries

Those involved in financing and constructing American penitentiaries, including prison architects such as Benjamin Latrobe and William Strickland, were themselves influenced by Enlightenment writers. "[I]t is clear," explains Julie Nicoletta in an article about the reform movement in early nineteenth-century America, "that the writings of European reformers, namely the Milanese jurist Cesare Beccaria's *On Crimes and Punishments* (1764) and the Englishman John Howard's *The State of the Prisons in England and Wales* (1777), drew the attention of both Europeans and Americans to the need for improving the treatment of the criminal and the insane through laws and the construction of more humane institutions." Eliane Jackson-Retondo, in studying the Massachusetts State Prison, which opened in 1805 and which was designed by Charles Bulfinch, also notes that the influence of Beccaria and Howard "could be seen in the reform rhetoric, prison discipline, and sitting of the Massachusetts State Prison at Charlestown as well as other nineteenth-century penal institutions." In *A History of Philadelphia*, published in 1839, the author Daniel Bowen specifically took note of how Dr. Benjamin Rush, in the 1780s, had followed "the suggestion of the celebrated Marquis Beccaria" in calling for the death penalty's abolition, with Bowen concluding: "From these early endeavors, have arisen the great improvements made in our Penitentiary systems, and the certainty of regulated punishments seems, so far to promise, much more in the correction of crime, than the sanguinary code, of former times."[103]

Benjamin Latrobe (1764–1820) — the architect of the U.S. Capitol, making him one of the most prominent architects of his day — spent time at Mount Vernon and was friends with a number of prominent figures, including Thomas Jefferson, Edmund Randolph and Bushrod Washington. Latrobe thought a lot about the concept of punishment and, in his journal, raised the following questions: "Is it not synonymous with revenge? As an American republican I may ask what right has any human being to prescribe laws to the actions of any other unless they be injurious to him?'" "[P]unishment," Latrobe wrote, "can only be just, as it is retaliation, as it is revenge. Punishment upon this principle — and my reasoning applies to all legislative punishments — is, in fact, a repetition of the offense, and most frequently it is a repetition with aggravation." Latrobe emphasized: "If the punishment be, as we falsely say, *just*, or exactly adequate to the crime, that is, if the pain, or evil, or inconvenience inflicted upon the criminal be equal to that occasioned by him, the moral nature of the act of punishment would stand in the place and be as *bad* as that of the crime if the crime had not preceded it." As Latrobe wrote: "We have mistaken the moral rights of communities because we have mistaken the moral rights of man. We have taken it for granted that retaliation is a law of nature because it is the propensity of educated man. But can that be a law of nature that in its mildest form *doubles* the injury committed?" Writing in the prejudice-ridden, late eighteenth century, Latrobe challenged accepted orthodoxy, observing: "Nor is it certain that the propensity is natural, because the desire of revenge may, by education, be rendered as perpetually absent from the mind of the dervish and the true Christian as it is perpetually present to that of the Cherokee and the Arab."

Benjamin Latrobe — seeing education as the way forward — wrote of considering the matter of punishment from "another point of view, and deciding upon the morality of what is called punishment by its utility." In his journal, Latrobe observed: "As far as punishment is the effect upon the punished and not the act of the punisher, so far is exclusion from the society the severest that can be suffered. It involves the society in no immoral act, and it makes unhappiness what it is in nature, in spite of human ingenuity to invert her order, synonymous with misconduct." Using words that might have come from Beccaria himself, Latrobe contrasted severe laws with the penitentiary system. "Crimes," Latrobe emphasized, "abound in every State, in proportion to the multitude and severity of the penal laws. This proves that if they be immoral, they are at the same time ineffectual. On the other hand, examine that great and first experiment in the moral science of the mind — the penitentiary house at Philadelphia."

At the U.S. Capitol — designed by James and Dolley Madison's next-door neighbor in Washington, D.C., the Quaker physician Dr. William Thornton (1759–1828) — Italian influences abound. The Capitol — later built, expanded and remodeled by Latrobe and Charles Bulfinch (1763–1844), his successor as architect of the Capitol — was influenced by ancient Greek and Roman architecture. The original plaster model for the *Statue of Freedom*—the 19-foot, 6-inch bronze female figure that sits atop the Capitol—was actually sculpted in the 1850s by the American artist Thomas Crawford while working at his studio in Rome. Ironically, slave laborers did a lot of construction work on the Capitol, with one such slave, the craftsman Philip Reid, assembling the *Statue of Freedom* at a Maryland foundry before it was installed atop the Capitol in 1863. Reid only received his freedom on April 16, 1862, the year before the actual installation of the monumental, bronze work of art, when President Lincoln signed the Compensation Emancipation Act. That act freed certain slaves for their service or labor in the District of Columbia, avoiding the awkwardness of having the *Statue of Freedom* installed at a time when Reid, one of its principal craftsmen, was still enslaved.

As part of his work on the U.S. Capitol, Latrobe turned to the Italian, Philip Mazzei, to identify artisans and sculptors. "By direction of the President of the United States," Latrobe wrote to Mazzei on March 6, 1805, "I take the liberty to apply to you for your assistance in procuring for us the aid of a good sculptor in the erection of the public buildings in this city, especially of the Capitol." "The Capitol," Latrobe wrote, "was begun at a time when the country was entirely destitute of artists and even of good workmen in the branches of architecture, upon which the superiority of public over private buildings depends." In the absence of skilled craftsmen, Latrobe turned to the well-connected Italian-American for advice. "The American consul at Leghorn, who does me the favor to forward this to you, will provide all the expenses and make the arrangements necessary to the voyage of the persons you may select," Latrobe told Mazzei. "It is proposed to place in the Chamber of Representatives a sitting figure of Liberty nine feet in height," Latrobe explained. Latrobe had wanted to procure the services of the renowned Italian sculptor Antonio Canova to create the envisioned marble figure, but Mazzei reported the disappointing news that Canova, of Venice, was unavailable.

Ultimately, two Italian sculptors—Giovanni Andrei and Giuseppe Franzoni—were brought over to America in 1806, with Franzoni, a Catholic, taking up residence on Capitol Hill with his family and dining on Sundays with Jefferson himself at the Executive Mansion. "Franzoni's eagle above the Speaker's desk was among the earliest works of monumental sculpture," one source notes. Other Italian artists, including Giuseppe Franzoni's brother Carlo, Giovanni Andrei, Luigi Persico and Enrico Causici—who did the Statue of Liberty in Statuary Hall—also came to do work on the new Capitol building, with Antonio Capellano executing a bust of George Washington. A student of Canova, Capellano was known to Thomas Jefferson and his private secretary William Short as early as the 1780s. Thomas Jefferson and Benjamin Latrobe only reluctantly abandoned plans for the gifted Antonio Canova to undertake a commission for the Capitol, the rotunda of which is decorated with John Trumbull's paintings—four large scenes from the Revolutionary War—as well as enduring works of art such as Enrico Causici's sandstone *Landing of the Pilgrims* and Constantino Brumidi's frescoed canopy, *The Apotheosis of Washington*. Notably, using plans Jefferson had created, Latrobe was also involved as the architect in the construction of the Virginia State Penitentiary in Richmond. That construction took place between 1797 and 1806.[104]

All of the early Architects of the Capitol were influenced by the European Enlightenment. Dr. Thornton, a product of the Scottish Enlightenment, had a Quaker upbringing, trained in Edinburgh to be a physician, became an American citizen in 1788, and lived in Philadelphia, becoming a member of the prestigious American Philosophical Society. A friend of Dr. John Coakley Lettsom, a fellow physician who provided Dr. Thornton with a letter of introduction to Benjamin Franklin, Thornton spent time in Paris and the West Indies before emigrating to America in 1786. In his new country, Dr. Thornton settled in Philadelphia "where his Quaker connections"—to use his biographer's words—"opened doors for him." In 1790, he married a young woman who may have been the daughter of William Dodd, the Anglican clergyman executed at Tyburn in 1777; the young woman's mother, a Mrs. Brodeau, ran a boarding school for girls on Walnut Street in Philadelphia, teaching English and French, a school sponsored by Benjamin Franklin and Robert Morris. A few months before Dodd's execution in June 1777, Dodd—known in London for his high living had, in late January 1777, written to Benjamin Franklin in Paris to ask Franklin to convey a letter, "if possible, to a worthy young Woman, who in an unfortunate Hour, went to America; and to whose fortunes and situation there I am a stranger." Appointed by Thomas Jefferson as a commissioner to the new Federal District of Washington, D.C., Dr. Thornton soon befriended George Washington.

Likewise, the well-connected Benjamin Latrobe formed a friendship with Giambattista Scandella, a Venetian physician and man of letters who spent two years in the United States. In his journal, Latrobe described Dr. Scandella as "a Venetian gentleman of the most amiable, fascinating manners, and of the best information upon almost every scientific subject, who speaks English perfectly, and who has now traveled through all the country between the St. Lawrence and James rivers." While in Philadelphia, Scandella—who had first arrived in North America in Quebec in 1796, then made his way to America—had also befriended a fellow physician, Dr. Benjamin Rush, the penal reformer. Dr. Scandella was elected to the prestigious American Philosophical Society in April 1798, with his attendance at a meeting in Philadelphia recorded the following month. Rush called Scandella—who died in America of yellow fellow, the deadly disease Rush himself had labored so hard to understand and prevent—a "learned" and "ingenious native of Venice."[105]

The other architect, Charles Bulfinch, asked by the President of the United States to visit existing penitentiaries in New York and Pennsylvania, issued a detailed report in 1826 on such establishments. "I have taken the liberty," Bulfinch wrote in his accompanying July 8, 1826, cover letter to President John Quincy Adams, "to commence the report with a sketch of the origin of such institutions, and an abstract of their history, in this country, compiled from authentic reports of the Managers and Inspectors." In the very first paragraph of his report, Bulfinch reported: "In the year 1773, the celebrated Howard commenced his examination of the state of prisons and houses of correction in England." "Previous to this," Bulfinch emphasized in the same paragraph, "the Marquis of Beccaria had published his Treatise on Crimes and Punishments, and suggested the expediency of alterations in the Penal Code, and of substituting solitary confinement and labor for the former ignominious and capital punishments." Bulfinch—the third Architect of the Capitol, also known for designing the expansion of Boston's Faneuil Hall—would himself design the first penitentiary established by the federal government, built in 1826, then enlarged in 1831, on the site of modern-day Fort McNair.[106]

Italian artists—the group of men so responsible for so many works of art at the U.S. Capitol and throughout America—took an interest, bordering on obsession, with the American Revolution. For example, Giuseppe Ceracchi—an Italian sculptor who arrived in Philadelphia in late 1790 or early 1791—wanted to create a lasting, and massive work of art, to honor America's revolution. In planning a 100-foot high marble monument depicting a Goddess of Liberty riding through the clouds in a horse-drawn chariot, a project proposed to Congress that never came to fruition, likely because of its $30,000 price tag, Ceracchi sculpted busts of more than thirty prominent Americans. Among them: George Washington, Benjamin Franklin, Thomas Jefferson, Alexander Hamilton, John Adams, John Jay, George Clinton and David Rittenhouse. In Rome, another Italian sculptor, Francesco Fazzarini, completed a full-length statue of Benjamin Franklin for The Library Company of Philadelphia, the institution that had stocked Beccaria's treatise. That statue was, Richard Juliani writes in his book *Building Little Italy*, "the first such work to arrive after the birth of the nation."[107]

In early America, juries—themselves skeptical of sanguinary punishments, familiar with Beccaria's treatise, and having little appetite for killing—were often reluctant to even convict defendants, however guilty, if death would be the punishment.[108] In 1812, a Pennsylvania legislative committee went so far as to call the law's authorization of the death for murder "the last feature of sanguinary law." As the senate committee wrote:

> Amongst the various objections to the nature of sanguinary laws which might be advanced, your committee are forcibly struck with one which they believe must render a change highly expedient. The public sentiment has now become so adverse to the punishment of death, that when our citizens are required to sit in judgment on the life of a fellow mortal, the tender sympathies of our nature are so awakened, that it is difficult to affect the conviction of those charged with the horrid crime of murder.

Other sources—whether sermons, letters or legislative reports—also described the "sanguinary law of retaliation" or, in speaking of the death penalty, labeled it a "sanguinary law" or the "present sanguinary law." In a petition asking the New York legislature to abolish capital punishment, the Society of Friends, for example, characterized the death penalty for murder as a "sanguinary practice that should long since have been numbered as among the things of a less enlightened past." The petition specifically lamented "the sanguinary law of 'blood for blood' upon our statute book."[109]

Legislators and prosecutors, faced with this civic reality, were thus forced to examine—out of necessity, if nothing else—alternative punishments. "In 1791," says one history, "the Vermont legislature switched the penalty for rape from death to imprisonment." "Consequently," that history notes of activity in another state, "when Massachusetts leaders such as Samuel Adams, John Hancock, and James Sullivan favored reforming the colonial criminal code in line with Enlightenment principles in the 1780s and 1790s, they were acknowledging the groundswell of popular reluctance to employ the death sentence." In 1794, at the burglary trial of two men in Salem, Massachusetts, one clergyman specifically observed that because "the people suppose them to be capital offenders, it is hard to supply the jury, four have already paid their fines rather than serve." After a jury was eventually empanelled, prosecutor James Sullivan would himself remark: "the Jury sat all night, but could not be prevailed upon to bring in their verdict, guilty of death, so firm are the people against sanguinary Laws." In the aftermath of Shays' Rebellion in 1787, Sullivan also argued that Massachusetts must not follow England's "sanguinary disposition." That disposition, Sullivan said, "daily gluts the grave." "[I]t was the wish of many thousands of the people," he said, "that these unhappy commotions should be settled without further loss of life."

Existing capital statutes were thus often characterized as "sanguinary," though one's viewpoint was all in the eye of the beholder. For example, the Reverend Thomas Allen—a Congregational minister from Pittsfield, Massachusetts—was a Jeffersonian who, with his son and namesake, an attorney and state legislator, "advocated imprisonment instead of the death penalty for the crime of rape." In that respect, Allen utilized his nephew's newspaper, the *Pittsfield Sun*, to attack the state's governor, a Federalist, for rejecting convicted rapist Ephraim Wheeler's pardon petitions. In particular, Allen accused his political opponents of being "peculiarly sanguinary in their temper and disposition," seeking to teach "the people" that "our sanguinary code, which grew out of monarchy," was wrong.

Allen further asserted that the time had come to reform the law so "no crime will be punishable with death, except murder." He closed his appeal by paraphrasing one of Beccaria's core principles.[110] In Great Britain, in debates in the British House of Commons, one likewise finds references to Robespierre's "sanguinary code" and "sanguinary laws."[111] A book published in London in 1785, titled *An Examination into the Rights and Duties of Jurors, with Some Strictures on the Law of Libels*, and written by a "Gentleman of the Inner Temple," expressly brought up Beccaria's name in discussing "[t]he excellence of trial by jury" and the "evils" of "arbitrary" power. "One would think the Marquis of Beccaria," that gentleman reported, citing to *On Crimes and Punishments*, "was speaking of trial by jury as it is endeavoured to be established in England."[112]

In the founding era, opposition to *arbitrary* and *sanguinary* laws and punishments became, in short, all the rage. Kings and queens—as well as their despised and much-maligned criminal codes—were given the "sanguinary" moniker.[113] In a typical reference, an English monarch was labeled "sanguinary and tyrannical."[114] And, it must be said, the eighteenth and nineteenth century uses of *sanguinary*—whether in reference to monarchs or otherwise—goes on and on, making a full recitation of references impossible.[115] In a 1795 book published in London about French politics, scores of references are found in just that one source. That book refers to "the caprice of the sanguinary Mob," "the period of the sanguinary Spanish conquests," "the sanguinary and fanatical ideas of liberty which filled the soul of the tyrant," "sanguinary doctrines," "the unexampled crimes of this sanguinary usurper," "the sanguinary measures of those days," "sanguinary court," "sanguinary tribunal," "sanguinary trial," "a vulgar and sanguinary despot," "sanguinary conspiracies," and "the horrors which have cast their sanguinary cloud over the glories of the revolution."[116] One also finds a specific reference to "the sanguinary times of the French Revolution."[117] In a report on the U.S. penitentiary system, published in New York in 1822, the report likewise contains additional references to "sanguinary horrors," "sanguinary laws," "awful and sanguinary punishments," "irrational and sanguinary laws," and "sanguinary and ignominious punishments."[118] The sanguinary label was also attached to wars,[119] whole governments,[120] populations,[121] and acts of religious persecution.[122]

And in a time consumed by revolutionary fervor, those uses of "sanguinary" were just the tip of the iceberg—by no means stray or isolated references. In still another source, a London magazine published in 1777, *sanguinary*—that then enormously popular word—is used multiple times, though its use seems to be commonly associated—as was often the case—with royal figures and tyrants. "Mary had, in order to ingratiate herself with the people, and to advance the views of her husband, suspended her persecution of the Reformers," one passage notes, adding that "her zeal and bigotry," however, "were too violent to be long restrained and Philip was not inclined, either from principle or temper, to oppose those sanguinary measures which she was now determined to pursue." "Among barbarians," notes another section of the magazine, "punishments must be sanguinary, as their bodies only are sensible of pain, not their minds." For the Founding Fathers themselves, the notions of cruelty and pain versus pleasure and happiness—concepts Beccaria and his associates wrestled with mightily—were given much thought. "As he had no regard for good men, and did not know how to distinguish them," another section of the 1777 magazine reads, "those about him were all mercenary and artful, still ready to execute his sanguinary and tyrannical commands." In describing American events, that same London magazine even referenced sanguinary actions, reading: "We proscribed the inhabitants of Boston without hearing them, and in the same manner adopted coercive and sanguinary measures against the other colonies."[123]

The Rise of the Penitentiary System

Although *sanguinary* and *cruel* are words that long pre-date the publication of Beccaria's treatise,[124] *On Crimes and Punishments* shaped Anglo-American views of what punishments should be characterized as such. Just as Beccaria's ideas were highly influential in the United States, they simultaneously shaped the legal discourse in England, leading the jurist William Blackstone and members of the British Parliament to promote the Penitentiary Act of 1779. Eventually, the English designed and built new prisons of their own to house convicts, gradually moving from a preference for execution to one for incarceration. The major proponents of reform in England were familiar with Beccaria's writings, took advice from John Howard, and convinced the British Parliament to construct new prisons in London, one for men and one for women. Although authorized in the late 1770s, the first English penitentiary, capable of housing 400 prisoners, was not built in Gloucester until 1791, with a larger prison, built in London in 1816, able to handle one thousand prisoners. In effect, Beccaria — concerned about equality of treatment and arbitrary punishments — had helped to usher in a new era of criminology. "Some writers," William Smithers wrote in 1909 in his *Treatise on Executive Clemency in Pennsylvania*, "have denominated this the classical school of criminology in which individualism has always been prominent." "This system is fundamentally that of England and America to-day," Smithers added, emphasizing that "[e]quality of punishment for similar crimes" had become a special feature of the classical school of criminology.[125]

The words *cruel* and *sanguinary*, historical documents show, were often tellingly used in juxtaposition to the term *penitentiary*.[126] For example, in the 1822 New York report, "the Penitentiary System in the United States" was contrasted with — and described as "so much superior" to "in its moral consequences" — "the old sanguinary codes of the colonies."[127] In sharp contrast to *sanguinary*, which has long meant *bloody* or *cruel*, the word *penitentiary* means "a place for repentance and amendment"[128] or "a place of penance."[129] Inmates, as one source explains, "were expected to be penitent, defined as feeling or expressing remorse for one's misdeeds or sins." The Quaker-inspired approach in Pennsylvania involved enforced silence, extreme isolation, and labor in solitary confinement.[130] On the use of solitary confinement in Philadelphia, one writer described the approach this way:

> The prisoner who is sentenced to this punishment is confined in a narrow cell; his allowance of food is much diminished; the turnkey brings it to him in the morning, and retires without speaking a word. Thus condemned to his own thoughts, he has an opportunity of reviewing his past misconduct; and its folly, if not its wickedness, are before him. While his body is reduced by the scantiness of his diet, his mind is unsupported by the stimulants of society, in short, *he must reflect*.[131]

Anchored by Enlightenment sentiment, prison reform — and the creation of a new penitentiary system — took place on both sides of the Atlantic. In England, Beccaria's treatise — as one commentator puts it — "certainly influenced the three men most responsible for the first attempt to create a national penal system," that is, Sir William Blackstone, William Eden, and John Howard.[132] "An Act to explain and amend the Laws relating to the Transportation, Imprisonment, and other Punishments, of certain Offenders" — also popularly known as the "Penitentiary Act" — was enacted in Great Britain in 1779 before the Revolutionary War drew to a close. Described as "the most forward-looking English penal measure of its time," the 74 clauses of the Penitentiary Act were — to quote one English legal historian — "primarily concerned to establish a better alternative to transportation." The fifth clause of the Act, for example, provided that "if many Offenders, convicted of Crimes for which Transportation has been usually inflicted, were ordered to solitary Imprisonment, accompanied by well-regulated Labour, and religious Instruction, it might be the Means, under Providence, not only of deterring others from the Commission of the such like Crimes, but also of reforming the Individuals, and inuring them to Habits of Industry."

America's founders, in turn, kept abreast of the writings of the Enlightenment and of the activities of English jurists, radicals and lawmakers who were pressing for penal reform. "Blackstone," explains one of his biographers, "played a pivotal role in the complex history of the Penitentiary Act from 1775 or 1776 onwards, preparing and promoting successive drafts, both outside and (via the lobbying of key MPs) within parliament." As that biographer, Wilfrid Prest, writes: "Whereas his former pupil William Eden has been regarded as prime mover in the passage of the measure by virtue of his parliamentary persona and ministerial connections, Blackstone was the indispensable 'great promotor of the design' (according to the prison reformer John Howard's first biographer writing in 1792), and at very least its 'joint Father'—his own words to Eden, in December 1778." In fact, the fate of Great Britain's Penitentiary Act—a law America's founders paid close attention to—became one of Blackstone's obsessions, with William Blackstone (1723–1780)—while on his deathbed—asking the Quaker physician John Fothergill (1712–1780), *what progress we had made in the penitentiary houses?*[133] A friend of Benjamin Franklin who published Franklin's electricity papers in 1751, the benevolent Dr. Fothergill—who, in his leisure time, was a plant collector and philanthropist—worked for the abolition of capital punishment in England along with social reformer John Coakley Lettsom, another Quaker. "I can hardly conceive that a better man has ever lived," Franklin once remarked of Dr. Fothergill.[134]

In Great Britain, shortly before his death, the much-revered Justice Blackstone even gave a charge to a grand jury about the establishment of penitentiaries under the new Penitentiary Act. As Blackstone described their function: "In these houses the convicts are to be separately confined during the intervals of their labors, debarred from all incentives to debauchery, instructed in religion and morality, and forced to work for the benefit of the public. Imagination cannot figure to itself a species of punishment in which terror, benevolence and reformation are more happily blended together." In his charge, Blackstone then asked two rhetorical questions. "What can be more dreadful to the riotous, the libertine, the voluptuous, the idle delinquent than solitude, confinement, sobriety and constant labor? Yet what can be more beneficial?" "Solitude," Blackstone said, "will awaken reflection, confinement will banish temptation, sobriety will restore vigor, and labor will beget a habit of honest industry; while the aid of a religious instructor may implant new principles in his heart, and, when the date of his punishment is expired, will conduce both to his temporal and eternal welfare." "Such a prospect," Blackstone concluded, "is truly well worth the trouble of an experiment."[135] Although the Penitentiary Act, envisioning the construction of two large prisons in London, was adopted in 1779, the resources needed to put it into practical effect were difficult to secure, and—in England—transportation of convicts to Australia was soon embraced, at least for a time, as a less costly alternative to large-scale prison construction.[136]

The Englishman John Howard—one of Dr. Benjamin Rush's idols—played a particularly pivotal role in calling for more humane treatment of offenders. The influence of Howard's writings on prison reform can be seen, for example, in a letter written after the passage of the Penitentiary Act. In that 1782 letter, to the Earl of Shelburne, Richard Price—a friend of Benjamin Franklin and the American cause—wrote: "Your Lordship will probably soon receive an application about the Penitentiary houses from an interested person who wishes to overthrow the scheme. I am informed he has already made some impressions on one of the Secretaries of State. Will you pardon me if I say, that no regard should be paid to him without consulting Mr Howard from whom the Act of Parliament which establishes the scheme took its rise; and also the three supervisors Sir Charles Bunbury, Sir Gilbert Elliot and Dr Bowdler, who are so disinterested as to intend to give up their time and attention to this business without any pay."[137]

Howard and Price were friends, corresponding with one another on multiple occasions, and Price—a much-respected figure in the United States—also, in turn, regularly corresponded with American patriots.[138] On April 24, 1781, Yale College—one of America's premier educational institutions—conferred two honorary LL.D. degrees, one on George Washington (1732–1799), America's first president, and one on Richard Price (1723–1791), the author of the 1776 tract *Observations on Civil Liberty*. That fact alone gives some indication of the high esteem with which Americans held Price, an intellectual hero of American revolutionaries. Price favored American independence on the principle of self-determination, and his book, *Observations on Civil Liberty*, sold several thousand copies within a few days of its issuance.[139]

Just as Great Britain had ardent proponents of the penitentiary system, so too did some Englishmen support the American cause. In a letter to Arthur Lee, written in 1779 and now housed in the Boston Public Library, Richard Price had forthrightly reaffirmed his support for the ideas of the American Revolution even in the midst of the Revolutionary War. As Price—who called Dr. Franklin "one of the friends in whom, while in this country, I always delighted"—wrote to Lee:

> My Pamphlets on the principles of Government and the American war were extorted from me by my judgement and my feelings. They have brought upon me a great deal of abuse; but abundant amends have been made me by the approbation of many of the best men here and abroad, and particularly by that vote of Congress to which I suppose they may have contributed.

As Price's letter to Lee continued:

> When you write to any of the members of that Assembly be so good as to represent me as a zealous friend to liberty who is anxiously attentive to the great struggle in which they are engag'd and who wishes earnestly for the sake of the world that British America may preserve its liberty, set an example of moderation and magnanimity, and establish such forms of government as may render it an Asylum for the virtuous and oppressed in other countries.[140]

At a critical time in American history, Price thus corresponded with and encouraged prominent Americans, including those deeply interested in law reform. In yet another letter, dated September 24, 1787, and sent from Hackney, near London, after the war, Richard Price wrote this to Dr. Benjamin Rush, America's best-known death penalty opponent: "I have since May last been favoured by you with two letters, and I return you many thanks for the kind attention to me which they discover." As Price's letter to Dr. Rush continued: "It is indeed highly agreeable to me to be informed of what is passing in your country. The account you give of the convention of Delegates at Philadelphia, and of the reason there was to hope for the greatest good from the wisdom and zeal of its members has been particularly encouraging to me." "You, in particular," Price wrote, "deserve the praises and thanks of your fellow-citizens for your endeavours to inform and enlighten them." In his reply to Dr. Rush's letters, Price specifically thanked Dr. Rush for Rush's "Enquiry into the effects of public punishments on criminals and society." That essay, Price wrote, "contains many just and important observations and proposals, which tho' perhaps not all practicable to the extent you mention, are proper to be offer'd to public consideration."

In his letter to Dr. Rush, Price made clear, once more, his support for the penitentiary system. As Price wrote:

> One of my best and most intimate friends (Mr. Howard) has, as all the world knows, attended with unparalleled assiduity and zeal to this subject, and his example of unspeakable benevolence is operating fast in this kingdom and likely to produce a general reformation in the state of our prisons by reducing them, agreeably to your plan, to penitentiary houses in which criminals are to be punished by solitude, silence and labour and such other treatment as shall have a tendency to reform them and at the same time to make them useful.

"There is among us," Price added, "a prevailing conviction of the importance of this; and many prisons are now building among us on this plan." In his letter, Price—though highly appreciative of Dr. Rush's writings—indicated his unwillingness to go as far as Dr. Rush in calling for the total abolition of capital punishment. "But I am not so well satisfy'd that *extermination* may not be inflicted as a punishment for vice; and there is nothing that alarms me more, or that has a greater tendency to deter men from vice, than the consideration that it is at least *possible* this may happen."[141] For many in that era, even those supportive of the American Revolution, the idea of abandoning executions altogether was a step too far.

The American Revolution nevertheless brought about tremendous change. In 1776, at the start of the Revolutionary War, American prisons—like those in Europe—were filthy places full of disease, brutality, drunkenness and promiscuity. Over time, thanks in large part to the writings of John Howard, Dr. Rush and Caleb Lownes, sentiments toward prisoners began to change. What's more, substantial and concrete efforts were made to alleviate horrid prison conditions. "A few benevolent persons in Pennsylvania, deeply deploring these evils," one writer would later note, "formed themselves into 'a society for alleviating the miseries of public prisons.'"[142] As the July 1789 edition of the *Universal Magazine* noted, that society was formed in Philadelphia for that purpose on May 8, 1787. "The gentlemen, who compose the society to which I allude," the magazine writer emphasized, "are members of various Christian denominations." Not only did those men commit themselves to penal reform, but they agreed to a written constitution—adopted very close in time to the adoption of the U.S. Constitution—memorializing their public commitment to such reform.

The printed "Constitution *of the* Philadelphia Society, *for alleviating the Miseries of Public Prisons*"—an organization financially supported by John Dickinson, the Beccaria admirer—first asserted the obligation of Christian charity. "When we consider that the obligations of benevolence, which are founded on the precepts and example of Christianity," the Society's constitution began, they are not "cancelled by the follies or crimes of our fellow-creatures." "[A]nd," that constitution continued, "when we reflect upon the miseries which penury, hunger, cold, unnecessary severity, unwholesome apartments, and guilt, (the usual attendants of prisons) involve with them, it becomes us to extend our compassion to that part of mankind, who are the subjects of these miseries." "By the aids of humanity," the Society's constitution then asserted, speaking of the prisoners sought to be served, "their undue and illegal sufferings may be prevented." The Society's constitution further sought to "preserve unbroken" the "links" which "should bind the whole family together under all circumstances" and to discover "such degrees and modes of punishment" so as to restore "our fellow-creatures to virtue and happiness."[143] The principle of treating criminals and prisoners with respect and humanity, developed and incubated in Philadelphia, thus was part of the American Revolution itself.

Pamphlets and Prisons

In 1790, in conjunction with the work of the Philadelphia Society for Alleviating the Miseries of Public Prisons, a pamphlet titled *Extracts and Remarks on the Subject of Punishment and Reformation of Criminals* was published. The first paragraph of that pamphlet laid out the organization's clear purpose and its legislative objectives: "To contribute comfort to the distressed, to promote reformation amongst the vicious, and to disseminate habits of industry amongst the indiscreet, are objects which demand the consideration of every Legislature." With reform in Pennsylvania prioritized in that pamphlet, its second paragraph contended: "The clause in the constitution of Pennsylvania which directs that punishments shall be made more proportionate to crimes, hath not been unnoticed by the assembly; but the penal laws founded on those principles, have not hitherto been attended with all those salutary effects which were hoped for by their benevolent framers." As the pamphlet continued: "That a mitigation of punishment in many cases, and a thorough reform in the internal police of gaols would prove beneficial to the community, there are strong reasons to believe; but no fair trial hath yet been made, in this state, of substituting labor and confinement for corporal punishment and death." "Arguments in favor of recurring to sanguinary systems," it was further asserted, "cannot justly be deduced from the imperfect experience derived under the present penal laws."

The 1790 pamphlet explicitly asserted that there were two ends of capital punishment: first, providing "an example of terror to others" and, second, preventing "the same person from repeating a crime." If those two objectives could be accomplished "by other means," the pamphlet reasoned, "policy and humanity will readily accede to the alternative." As to the first, the pamphlet contended:

> It may very safely be assumed as a principle that the prospect of long solitary confinement, hard labour and very plain diet, would, to many minds, prove more terrible than even an execution; where this is the case, the operation of example would have its full effect, so far as it tended to deter others from the commission of crimes.

As to the second goal, the pamphlet further asserted that an incarcerated criminal "will be prevented from a repetition of the crime, during the term of his confinement, which will be extended, according to its degree." "[I]t may very reasonably be supposed," the pamphlet continued in that respect, "that length of time, and the severity of his punishment, will either really reform his disposition towards evil practices, or will restrain him through principles of fear: thus the laws may operate as blessings on the prisoner, and the country may be benefited by the acquisition of a useful citizen."

The pamphlet, published in the year before the U.S. Bill of Rights was ratified, extracted a number of items, including information on Great Britain's Penitentiary Act, letters of the English reformer Sir Thomas Beevor written in the mid-1780s, John Howard's writings, and the "Rules, Orders and Regulations" of "*the Houses of* Correction *in the county of* Norfolk" and "*at the* House of Correction, *for the* Division *of* Bury St. Edmund's, *in the* County *of* Suffolk." In his own correspondence, which cited the influence of "Mr. Howard's book," Beevor wrote of his involvement in erecting a new, successful "penitentiary house" at Wymondham in Norfolk, England. "The house," Beevor wrote, "is constructed agreeably to the directions of the late act of parliament, and so contrived, that there are separate cells for each prisoner, airy, neat, and healthy, in which they sleep, and, when necessary, work the whole day alone." Beevor asserted that the prison was more effective than whipping and that with hard labor six days a week, prisoners earned more than twice the cost of their maintenance. An excerpt from John Howard reprinted in the pamphlet also emphasized that "[o]ur present laws are certainly too sanguinary, and are therefore ill executed," with Howard asserting: "I wish that no persons might suffer capitally but for murder—for setting houses on fire—and for house breaking, attended with acts of cruelty." Both sets of reprinted British "Rules, Orders and Regulations"—the one for Norfolk and Suffolk—specifically mentioned the use of "hard labour," as well as dietary restrictions for prisoners committed to the houses of correction.[144]

Another of the items extracted in the 1790 pamphlet was the "Edict of the Grand Duke of Tuscany for the reform of criminal law in his dominions," translated from the Italian version and issued "*by the grace of GOD*" by Peter Leopold, "PRINCE ROYAL OF HUNGARY AND BOHEMIA, ARCHDUKE OF AUSTRIA, GRAND DUKE OF TUSCANY." From those extracts, the pamphlet editorialized under the name of William White (1748–1836), the Philadelphia Society's president and an Episcopal bishop who was the chaplain for the Continental Congress, "we learn that the miseries of the unfortunate prisoner have become subjects of deep investigation in Europe and that by an observance of wholesome rules, gaols may prove the happy means of reformation, and that the criminals instead of being a burthen may be transformed into serviceable members of the community." The pamphlet concluded that the Philadelphia Society for Alleviating the Miseries of Public Prisons would "present the subject to the Legislature of Pennsylvania, hoping that the penal laws of the State may be so modeled as to promote reformation in the criminal and safety to the people." Other early leaders of the Philadelphia Society included George Duffield, a Presbyterian minister; William Rogers, a Baptist preacher; and John Oldden, a businessman. A significant number of the early members were, in fact, Quakers, with one examination of the first 175 members showing that at least 69 were of the Quaker sect.[145]

Along with *On Crimes and Punishments*, the late eighteenth century saw the publication of a large number of Enlightenment texts. In 1794, another Philadelphia penal reformer—Caleb Lownes—also wrote a pamphlet titled *An Account of the Alteration and Present State of the Penal Laws of Pennsylvania*. Published by "J. Bradford" at the corner of Main and Cross Streets in Lexington, the pamphlet noted that Lownes had "frequently been requested by respectable characters in other states" to provide answers to enquiries "about the interior management of the Gaol and Penitentiary house of Philadelphia." "It is true," Lownes wrote of reforming the system of criminal jurisprudence, "society has not been without information upon this subject." Citing Montesquieu, Beccaria and others, Lownes emphasized that such writers "have thrown considerable light upon it." "The benevolent Howard," Lownes noted, "greatly sympathized with the wretched prisoner." Howard had, Lownes said, "largely displayed the errors in principle, and the cruelties in practice of the criminal laws of most countries in Europe," with Howard—who passed away in Russia in January 1790—dying "in the prosecution of this important service," leaving the advancement of penal reform in other hands. "[B]ut a system founded upon the clear and unquestionable rights and duties of citizens of a mild and well ordered government, has not yet met the public eye," Lownes added, pointing out that Pennsylvania had "gone the farthest in the formation of such a system, of any government that has come to my knowledge."

In his account of Pennsylvania's laws, Lownes took pains to document the attempts at penal reform that had taken place since 1776. He wrote, for example, of the state's 1786 law directing that convicts be employed in cleaning streets and repairing roads. That law, Lownes wrote, required that convicts "have their *heads shaved* and be distinguished by an *infamous* habit." "This was literally complied with, but however well meant," Lownes noted, "was soon found to be productive of the *greatest evils:* and had a very opposite effect from what was contemplated by the framers of the law." The law's severity and "the disgraceful manner of executing it," he wrote, caused "a proportionate degree of depravity and insensibility and every spark of morality appeared to be destroyed." Lownes recorded that after its formation, the Philadelphia Society for Alleviating the Miseries of Public Prisons quickly grew its membership and soon became a "large and respectable" organization, with "subscriptions and donations" coming in to support its efforts. Lownes noted that instead of corporal punishments, such as stripes, the Philadelphia prison system was using solitary confinement and dietary restrictions to discipline prisoners.[146] To at least a certain extent, Pennsylvanians were thus moving away from painful punishments that operated solely on criminals' bodies and their flesh and blood, to ones that operated in more subtle ways, aiming to prevent crime by having an effect on the minds of offenders and prospective offenders.

Throughout that transition, American penal reformers looked to Beccaria even as the eighteenth century gave way to the nineteenth century. Thomas Eddy's *An Account of the State Prison or Penitentiary House, in the City of New-York*, published in 1801, contains on its title page the following quote from Beccaria: "A punishment to be just, should have only that degree of severity which is sufficient to deter others—Perpetual labour will have this object more than the punishment of death." And the first paragraph of Eddy's introduction strikes a very Beccarian tone. As the opening lines of that introduction read: "That branch of jurisprudence which treats of crimes and their punishment, is the most interesting and momentous in the whole code of laws. The peace, security and happiness of society depend on the wisdom and justice of the means devised for the *prevention* of crimes." "In no nation," Eddy wrote, "have legislators bestowed that profound attention on this subject which its importance demands." Even in England, where, Eddy noted, "secret accusations, secret and mock trials, torture, and all the cruel contrivances of superstition and despotism to confound and destroy alike the innocent and the guilty, were unknown," "there existed a scale of punishments as sanguinary and unjust as any in Europe."

In his book, Eddy emphasized how Western culture had changed but how penal codes were not necessarily keeping pace with the times. As Eddy wrote in his introduction: "While civilization and refinement were changing the condition and manners of social life, the criminal codes of the nations of Europe retained a vindictive and sanguinary spirit, the growth of a rude and barbarous age." "Benevolent and virtuous men," Eddy noted, "saw and deplored the evils produced and perpetuated by unequal and cruel punishments; but the mild voice of reason and humanity reached not the thrones of princes or the halls of legislators." After pointing out that printing presses had enabled "one man, however private and obscure," to reach "a whole people," Eddy described how three Europeans had "prepared the way for reform." "MONTESQUIEU," Eddy wrote, "exposed the errors of legislators, and unfolded sounder principles of jurisprudence." "The eloquent BECCARIA," Eddy continued, "roused the attention of civilized Europe, and, by his unanswerable appeal to reason and humanity, produced those successive efforts to meliorate the systems of penal laws, which constitute the greatest glory of the present age." "HOWARD, the active and indefatigable man," Eddy ended his list of the great triumvirate, "by exploring the prisons and dungeons of Europe, and, from their dark and unvisited recesses, bringing to light the enormous abuses and dreadful miseries produced by cruel laws and their corrupt administration, more powerfully awakened the feelings of humanity and justice, by which the legislator is enabled to complete the great work of *correction.*"

Although he gave much credit to European philosophers, Eddy—anxious to give credit where credit was due—also took note of important American penal reformers in discussing the infancy of the rapidly expanding U.S. corrections system. "[W]hile the names of MONTESQUIEU, BECCARIA and HOWARD, are repeated with gratitude and admiration," Eddy wrote, "the legislators and philanthropists of our own country deserve not to be forgotten." "WILLIAM PENN," Eddy noted, constructed an "equitable code" from which "the punishment of death was excluded, except in the single case of premeditated murder, and by which each crime received a punishment equitably proportioned to the degree of its enormity." Penn's colonial code did not last, but Eddy described how "the spirit of reform revived with the revolution" and how "the writings of BECCARIA and others" had "at length produced that system of punishment for crimes" that "reflects so much honour" on the State of Pennsylvania. In his book, Eddy argued that "crimes are most frequent where the laws are most rigorous" and "that punishments *mild* and *certain* more effectually prevent crimes than those which are sanguinary and severe." Eddy's book—adopting Beccaria's view of deterrence, and later reprinted far and wide, including in places as far away as Ireland—also specifically cited William Bradford's 1793 report on the criminal code of Pennsylvania.

As for New York, Eddy humbly wrote of his own efforts, writing that, "[i]n 1794, one of our citizens who was well acquainted with the plan and economy of the new penitentiary house in Philadelphia" became "convinced of the beneficent effects of a system which, fixing a just proportion between crimes and punishments, afforded room for the exercise of benevolence in the work of reformation." That New Yorker, Eddy emphasized, speaking of himself in the third person, procured multiple copies of Bradford's report and transmitted them to New York legislators then sitting in Albany. "The same citizen, in 1795," Eddy wrote with self-effacing modesty of his own actions, "made several visits to the prisons in Philadelphia, for the purpose of obtaining complete and satisfactory information of the operation and effects of the new system of punishment established, in which he received ample assistance from his worthy and intelligent friend CALEB LOWNES." "The result of these inquires," Eddy self-reported, "was communicated by him to General SCHUYLER, a distinguished member of the Senate of this State." "This public-spirited senator, perceiving the great importance of the subject, and the wisdom of an experiment so loudly demanded by humanity," Eddy noted of General Philip Schuyler, Alexander Hamilton's father-in-law, "visited, in company with the same person, the Philadelphia penitentiary, and witnessed, with surprise and satisfaction, the spirit of wisdom and benevolence which presided in that institution." These activities, Eddy emphasized, led to the passage in New York of the state's 1796 law that repealed the death penalty for all crimes excepting treason and murder.[147]

In *The Life of Thomas Eddy*, published in 1836, biographer Samuel Knapp wrote of Eddy's genuine and obvious affection for Beccaria, Montesquieu and Howard, and described how Eddy had pushed for "the establishment of a State or penitentiary prison" in New York as "a substitute for the profligate gaols and sanguinary punishments" of his time. In the course of describing Eddy's efforts, the biographer emphasized:

> The penal code in most of the States still has the sanguinary spirit and hard features of the English penal code, which, with all their boasted love of liberty, was written in blood. The tears of the sympathetic, and the voice of the benevolent, had made but slow progress against the apathy of the great mass of mankind, and the vindictive spirit of a few, who believe, or profess to believe, that the world should be governed by a rod of iron.

Before noting that "[t]he Friends in Pennsylvania were among the first people in the Union to make an effort to change this barbarity for some milder system," Eddy's biographer specifically detailed what the sanguinary system had produced. As Knapp wrote:

The hearts of the people were made callous by the sight of stocks, whipping-posts, and pillories, in every shire, town, and considerable village. Flagellation with the cat-o'-nine-tails, burning in the hand, or forehead, with a hot iron, cropping the ears of prisoners in the pillory, were all common sights to the youngest, as well as the oldest portion of the community.[148]

The Construction of Penitentiaries

Shortly after Dr. Benjamin Rush invoked Beccaria's name at Benjamin Franklin's house in March 1787, the Philadelphia Society for Alleviating the Miseries of Public Prisons—one of the country's first prison reform organizations—got to work.[149] And within a very short period of time, the United States—following England's lead, at least in authorizing one—witnessed the opening of its first penitentiary. In 1785, in its post-Penitentiary Act experiment, England had constructed its first, if rather small penitentiary, Wymondham Prison in Norfolk, England, a prison (or county bridewell) with 22 large cells, incorporating many of John Howard's suggested reforms. At the prison, inmates worked and slept in separate cells, and solitary confinement was put to use. In the September 1789 issue of the *American Museum* magazine, published by Mathew Carey, a lengthy description of the Wymondham facility, written by Sir Thomas Beevor, was reprinted under the title *An account of the origin, progress, and regulations, with a description of the newly-established Bridewell, or Penitentiary-House at Wymondham, in Norfolk*. A 1784 letter of Beevor reprinted with that account noted he had "read mr. Howard's book, describing the state and condition of our prisons" and been moved to act to implement reform. Such descriptions of English experimentation led Quakers to push for the adoption of similar reforms as regards Philadelphia's existing Walnut Street Jail, the new penitentiary wing of which opened in 1790 and which is considered the birthplace of the American penitentiary.

Pennsylvania's own penitentiary experiment went well, so other state legislatures soon approved their own penitentiaries, too. As one scholar has written: "The early success of Walnut Street Jail led other states to implement the penitentiary idea (New York, 1796; Virginia, 1800; Massachusetts, 1804; Vermont, 1808; Maryland, 1811; and New Hampshire, 1812)."[150] New York's 1796 law had called for two state prisons to be established—one in New York City, and one at Albany. But the idea of a penitentiary at Albany was ultimately abandoned, it being decided that the whole appropriation should go to the New York City facility. New York's Newgate Prison, which started accepting inmates on November 25, 1797, was 204 feet in length and, aside from the cells for solitary confinement on the ground floor, the whole structure consisted of 54 rooms measuring 12 x 18 feet. The state prison in Richmond, Virginia, designed for those committing such crimes as second-degree murder, manslaughter, rape, grand and petit larceny, burglary, robbery and forgery, was erected in 1800, with the Massachusetts state prison, in Charlestown, constructed of stone and divided into solitary cells, built soon thereafter in 1804. The State of Vermont built its prison at Windsor, while Maryland selected one of its major cities, Baltimore, as the site for its state prison. While New Hampshire citizens chose to construct their state prison at Concord, finishing it in 1812, the State of Ohio erected its state prison in Cincinnati in 1816. An 1822 magazine, *The Investigator*, also noted that, by then, penitentiaries also existed in New Jersey, Tennessee and Kentucky.[151]

After penitentiaries were authorized, state officials reached out to the nation's brightest minds for ideas on how to design and construct them. For example, in March 1797, Virginia Governor James Wood—the Commissioner of Prisoners for Virginia and Maryland during the Revolutionary War—wrote to Thomas Jefferson shortly after the passage of Virginia's 1796 penal reform law. "I Contemplate with great pleasure the Change which is to take place in the penal Laws of the Commonwealth," Wood wrote, adding that he felt "Much Anxiety that No time Shou'd be lost in bringing it into Complete Operation." As Wood further explained in his letter:

> The Law having Confided to the Executive, the purchase of a Sufficient Quantity of Land, and the direction of erecting the Necessary buildings for the Confinement and Accomodation of the Convicts; we feel Ourselves embarrassed from a want of Knowledge in Architecture, to fix upon the proper plan of a building to Answer the purposes of the Law.

"Our thoughts have turned On you, Sir," Wood wrote to Jefferson, "as best Qualified to give us Advice and Assistance in the Execution of this business." In requesting this advice, Wood sent Jefferson the authorizing legislation and sought a plan from Jefferson as well as his views on how much land would be needed for the project. The Virginia act had authorized the construction of "a gaol and penitentiary house" large enough "to contain with convenience two hundred convicts at least."[152]

In response, Jefferson wrote back to Wood from Monticello at the end of the month, submitting his ideas for the penitentiary's construction. As Jefferson wrote:

> When on a former occasion the Executive were pleased to apply to me (being then in France) for a plan of a Capitol, they at the same time desired one of a prison. An architect of Lyons had in 1761 proposed the idea of solitary confinement, and presented to that government an engraved plan for a prison on that idea. This was, as far as I know, the first proposition for this kind of punishment. It was *afterwards* as I believe, that a particular society adopted it in England. Pennsylvania is the 2d. and ourselves the 3d. instance of adoption. I received from the architect of Lyons (M. Bugniet) a copy of his plan, and sent it to our executive with the plans and models of the Capitol; and to adapt it to the smaller scale which suited us, I sketched a plan of a prison for us with solitary cells. These draughts probably still exist among the papers of the council. However lest they should not, as I retain the general idea in my mind, I have sketched it on paper and now inclose the sketch.... I presume others have been invited to propose plans, and have no doubt some will chance to hit on something better. If not, and this should be adopted, I would wish to be advised of it, in order to propose some details for giving to the building a plain, decent appearance, and preventing an affectation of ornament which would be entirely misplaced on a building of this character.

In fact, three other architects did submit plans, as Jefferson thought might happen. One of the three—the brother of Jefferson's love interest, Maria Cosway—was born in Livorno, Italy to English hotel-keepers, with George Hadfield serving as the U.S. Capitol superintendent from 1795 to 1798. The other two architects were Samuel Dobie, who built the state capitol in Richmond from Jefferson's design, and Benjamin Latrobe, the man whose plan for a Virginia penitentiary was ultimately adopted.[153]

Before Massachusetts, following Virginia's efforts, began its own penitentiary experiment, James Madison—making a Massachusetts-Virginia connection—was himself engaged and kept apprised of unfolding events outside his own state as regards penal reform, the subject that interested him greatly. Writing from Dorchester, Massachusetts, in 1803, Perez Morton (1751–1837)—the son of a tavern keeper who graduated from Harvard College in 1771 and became a successful lawyer—wrote to Madison:

I have to acknowledge the receipt of your kind favor, which covered the penal Laws of Virginia. Our Legislature have chosen a large Committee of both Houses to form a penal code on the penitentiary system, and a Statute for the regulation of the State prison, and report at the next Session; Of this Committee I have the honor to be one.

In April 1776, at Boston's King's Chapel, Morton also had the honor of eulogizing his fellow Freemason General Joseph Warren (1741–1775), the fallen hero killed at the Battle of Bunker Hill, after Warren's body was located in a "common grave" on the battlefield. In memorializing the Grand Master of the Ancient Grand Lodge of Massachusetts, Morton promised: "Thy memory has been embalmed in the affections of thy grateful countrymen, who, in their breasts, have raised eternal monuments to thy bravery!"[154]

The subject of a widely publicized, personal scandal in the late 1780s, Morton added that, in getting information from Madison, he did not doubt that "we shall find our Duty much facilitated" by "the Virginia code," at least as much as the "customs & habits of our People will admit." Morton had married Sarah Apthorp in 1778 and the couple had five children, but in 1788 a public rumor circulated that was reported in the press that Morton had an adulterous affair with his sister-in-law, Fanny Apthorp, who became pregnant and bore Morton's child before committing suicide. The scandalous affair would inspire Morton's neighbor, William Hill Brown, to write an early American novel, *The Power of Sympathy: or, The Triumph of Nature, Founded in Truth* (1789) about the dangers of passion and seductive behavior. In spite of the scandal, Morton—the American patriot who practiced law in Boston, and whose friends included John Adams—went on to have a distinguished career, serving as the Speaker of the Massachusetts House of Representatives before serving as the state's attorney general. He served in the latter role from 1810 to 1832, making him one of the leading lawyers of the state. Indeed, Morton rubbed shoulders with leading revolutionaries of his time, with silver Morton purchased in Boston from Paul Revere now owned by the Museum of Fine Arts in that city.[155]

Because penitentiaries were new public institutions, problems naturally arose as their administrators tried to make the prisons operate efficiently and as envisioned. Instead of just trying to recruit executioners, state and local officials turned their time and attention to how best to reform criminals. "During the 1820s," one text explains, "two models of prison operation emerged; these were the Pennsylvania and Auburn systems." As that text notes: "These two systems came into vogue as the Old Newgate Prison was closed and once it became fairly clear that the Walnut Street Jail was not a panacea for prison and/ or correctional concerns." The Old Newgate Prison, in Connecticut, first opened in 1773 in abandoned copper mines in Simsbury, was a dreadful place that finally closed its doors in September 1827. The building of two new Pennsylvania penitentiaries—the Western Penitentiary at Pittsburgh and the Eastern Penitentiary at Cherry Hill—created the "Pennsylvania system." The Western State Penitentiary, located outside of Pittsburgh and designed by architect William Strickland with 190 cells, opened its doors in 1826, almost three years prior to the building of the Eastern State Penitentiary near Philadelphia.

The Auburn and Pennsylvania systems took different approaches. "Advocates of the Pennsylvania system," Robert Hanser writes in *Introduction to Corrections*, "believed that solitary confinement was, in and of itself, sufficient punishment for offenders since human beings are social creatures and the inmate would be restricted from social activities." The Western State Penitentiary, as well as the Eastern State Penitentiary, which opened in 1829, made use of inmate labor to offset the costs of solitary confinement. As Hanser explains: "Aside from unforeseen emergencies, special circumstances, or medical issues, inmates spent 24 hours a day in their cells. Inmates in Eastern Penitentiary ate, slept, and worked within the confines of their cells." The massive Eastern State Penitentiary, designed by the Englishman John Haviland, was built on the site of a former cherry orchard, had seven cell blocks, and stood behind 30-foot stone walls. For a time, inmates at the prison were required to wear hoods, a practice intended to hide the inmate's identity from other inmates. In contrast, the "Auburn system," named after New York's Auburn Prison, which opened in 1816, was a "congregate system" in which "inmates were kept in solitary confinement during the evening but were permitted to work together during the day." After the north wing of the Auburn Prison was completed in 1825, there were 550 cells, with the cells measuring 7.5 feet long, 3.8 feet wide, and 7 feet high. The Auburn system—which attracted many adherents—was also implemented at New York's Ossining facility, later known as the Sing Sing Prison.[156]

Beccaria, while not an architect or designer of penitentiaries, had nevertheless provided the underlying intellectual impetus and justification for such institutions. As one source puts it: "Theoretical underpinnings and initiative for nineteenth-century prison reform are usually identified with Milanese jurist Cesare Beccaria and his brief yet influential work, 'An Essay on Crimes and Punishment (1764),' and John Howard's *State of the Prisons in England and Wales*." "Beccaria's treatise," that source notes, "offered theoretical basis, means, and goals for reform, while Howard's concerns identified material goals that would distinguish prisons of the past from those of the nineteenth century." In fact, the first modern correctional facility to use cellular confinement came from Italian-speaking Rome. Built in 1703, the Hospice of San Michele—a rectangular structure made up of 30 cells arranged on three tiers—was designed by the architect Carlo Fontana. John Howard himself visited that facility, where juvenile inmates—forbidden to talk—manufactured products for the Vatican. At the time Howard visited, 200 boys were confined in the institution, with the prison motto—printed above the main entry—stating its mission in plain language: "It is of little use punishing the vicious by imprisonment unless you reclaim them—make them virtuous by discipline."[157]

Nineteenth-century prisons looked and felt much different than those that existed in colonial America, and early Americans—receptive to Beccaria's and Howard's ideas, as well as those of local reformers—were anxious to try to experiment with prison reform. John Howard himself had drawn inspiration from Beccaria's *On Crimes and Punishments*, as one of his biographers emphasized in 1902 in these words: "Whether this work was known to Howard before he began his labours we cannot tell. He certainly was acquainted with it later, and greatly valued it, for he refers to it constantly in his own books." Another Howard biographer—also taking note of Howard's propensity to quote from, and often commend, *On Crimes and Punishments*—pointed out that Howard sought the repeal of "*sanguinary laws*." The influence of the books authored by Beccaria and Howard, another text emphasizes, "could be seen in the reform rhetoric" and in "prison discipline" of places such as the Massachusetts State Prison at Charlestown, the plans for which were drawn up in 1797. "However," that source notes of American penal reform, "Beccaria's treatise and Howard's recommendations would have fallen upon deaf ears if the catalysts for change had not already been present in the culture."[158]

The influence of Beccaria and other Enlightenment writers in catalyzing the penitentiary movement has long been recognized. In the *50th or Semi-Centennial Report of the Inspectors of the State Penitentiary for the Eastern District of Pennsylvania*, issued in 1880 and sent to the state's governor, legislators, and Board of State Charities, the prison inspectors specifically emphasized: "From the period when Montesquieu published 'The Spirit of the Laws,' and Beccaria his 'Essay on Crimes and Punishments' ... till 1776, the subject of penal jurisprudence was only considered in either a philosophic or speculative point of view." Filangieri and Beccaria were, that report said, speaking of Italy's two pre-eminent voices on the subject of criminal laws, among the first to draw attention to penal laws as regards society's welfare. Before making its detailed report, the Pennsylvania inspectors, led by Richard Vaux, quoted at length from *On Crimes and Punishments*, citing Beccaria's "advanced teachings." The inspectors began by quoting Beccaria's admonition, adopted from Montesquieu, that every punishment not arising from absolute necessity is tyrannical. They then quoted verbatim from Beccaria's essay over the course of four pages. "It ought not to be overlooked," the inspectors emphasized, "that Italy has thus placed herself in the foreground in efforts to instruct in the philosophy of penal legislation and penal science."[159]

Indeed, Beccaria's ideas were so influential in early America that his name was sometimes even adopted as a pen name. In 1821, an "Officer of the Virginia Penitentiary" published a book using the pseudonym "Beccaria" that was titled "An Exposition of the Penitentiary System of Punishment, but More Particularly Adapted to that of Virginia." The "Beccaria" pseudonym was listed on the very top of the title page, and the book's preface by "The Author" began:

> From early life I was impressed with the justice and humanity of the penitentiary system of punishment; and as I arrived to years of more reflection, I was sensible of the great importance it was to a government professedly republican, to administer justice equally to all its citizens, in the ratio that their conduct merited, without favor, partially or affection, which appeared impossible to me, without a well regulated penitentiary system of punishment for the commission of crimes.

"The more I became acquainted with it," the manager of the Virginia Penitentiary wrote, "the more fully was I convinced of the defects, and more clearly I saw the necessity of a change." "This necessity," the author wrote, "appeared to me strongly urged by those hostile to the system, which they denounced as being a den of thieves, impolitic and injurious to the poor, honest part of the community."

The Virginia author took particular note of problems that had been encountered in the penitentiary systems of New York and Pennsylvania, including insubordination, vice, overcrowding and rioting. But in emphasizing that "humanity is indebted to none more than to that able lawyer and profound statesman, the late George K. Taylor of Virginia, for his irresistible eloquence in support of the justice of the penitentiary system," the author wrote of how "the system, like all other works of man, was defective in its origin, and required experience to make it more efficient." As the anonymous writer noted of the penitentiary system's critics in the book's preface: "Some contended that for many crimes the offender should be hung, and for petit larceny the culprit should be publicly flogged and burnt in the hand; while others were for cropping the ears, &c., for subsequent offences committed by the same person." "These ideas being so contrary to what I believed just, at the same time carrying with it a barbarity not to be tolerated in a free and enlightened republic," the writer continued, "led me to hope that some able pen would have taken up the subject, and have done it more justice than I have been able to do with my feeble capacity." In the concluding paragraph of the preface, the author emphasized "that in no country have cruel and public and sanguinary punishment checked the commission of crimes, or produced one penitent."

In the body of that book on Virginia's penitentiary system, the anonymous author first described the development of the penitentiary system before suggesting improvements to that system. Early in the text, the author explained the penitentiary system's development, which began in Philadelphia:

Until about the latter end of the last century the philanthropic mind began to search more into the depravity of human nature, examining all the avenues to its defects, and in proportion to their magnitude apply the remedy. As they became more acquainted with the principles of criminal law, so they became acquainted with the absurdity of involving all violators of the law in one indiscriminate and cruel punishment.

"This," the author noted, "led to the establishment of the penitentiary system in the United States; that punishment might be apportioned to the degree of guilt." The author then emphasized that "philanthropic statesmen" are "endeavouring to render the condition of their country more enlightened and dignified," with the author writing: "Whatever has a tendency to increase immorality, and justifies it upon the grounds of expediency (the plea of tyrants,) has a strong affinity to cruelty, and its continuance will degrade the country, be it where it may." In short, the penitentiary was an attempt to alleviate needless acts of cruelty while simultaneously giving offenders the chance to reform or repent, even if never let out of prison.

Many of the arguments in the book—the appendices of which advocated for a national penitentiary system—tracked or resembled Beccaria's ideas. "To convicts disregarding the awfulness of death and the gallows," the author wrote, "it is no punishment to be hanged: by its frequency, the terror is lost on others, whose vicious habits are intended to be checked." "It therefore becomes cruel and inhuman," the author continued, "because no single instance of good is produced." In considering the many characters of guilt, "and how very different they are," the author asserted that "the claim on humanity and justice is irresistible, to the philanthropic mind pleading in mercy on behalf of the unfortunate beings doomed to an untimely death." Indeed, the "Beccaria" pseudonym—without fail—appears after each chapter in the book, with the Virginia writer calling the federal laws making crimes punishable by death "an erroneous idea" resulting from "a mind, narrow and confined, without any knowledge of human nature." A federal statute had authorized the death penalty since 1790, a statute that would be called into question after its passage by at least some early Americans. "[I]t is the certainty and not the severity of the punishment," the Virginian emphasized, "that keeps vice in check." That notion, the writer asserted, was supported by "every modern writer on criminal law," including Beccaria, and one "obvious to every rational understanding."

In advocating in an appendix for a "*Penitentiary System for the United States,*" the Virginia author implored his readers: "That a government, founded on the principles of the United States, should remain so long in the practice of punishing offenders against its laws, in the cruel and sanguinary way, the offspring of barbarous ages, is a matter of much surprise, with all considerate men." Proportioned and certain punishments, the anonymous writer opined, were the best mode of checking vice. "The principles of the government, and humanity," the author editorialized, "forbid that punishment to be cruel and sanguinary, but to be apportioned to the magnitude of the crime, and the injury resulting to society by a repetition of the act." In seeking the establishment of a national penitentiary system, the writer urged "abandoning the present inhuman and cruel system of taking the life of a fellow man for most offences." As the author wrote: "All the punishments should be inflicted with justice, reason and humanity—but at the same time with a certainty corresponding to the crime." Land for the nation's first federal penitentiary—referred to as the Old Arsenal Prison—was not purchased until 1826, with the conspirators convicted of assassinating President Lincoln later imprisoned and hanged in the yard at the prison. Only in 1891 did Congress authorize the country's attorney general to operate three U.S. prisons to incarcerate violators of federal law sentenced to terms of one year or more. Although construction on the penitentiary at Leavenworth, Kansas, began in 1896, that facility did not open until 1928; the U.S. penitentiary in Atlanta,

Georgia, opened in 1899, with the third prison—acquired by taking over a sixteen-year-old territorial prison on Puget Sound—known as the McNeil Island Penitentiary.[160]

The author of the 1821 book on Virginia's penitentiary system recognized, as did Beccaria himself, that change would be slow to come—a reality made clear by just how long it took to build out the federal penitentiary system. "To convince the proper authorities of the defects and the change essential to improve the system," the author wrote, "will require much time." As the author observed: "The difficulty of getting large bodies to understand collectively, things in which they do not feel immediately interested, is manifest; their progress is slow, and uncertain." The *sanguinary* system—in the writer's time—had already started to give way to the *penitentiary* system, but the kinks of the new system had yet to be worked out. There were still a host of problems with the new penitentiaries, and the lack of sufficient resources was but one issue that had yet to be dealt with as Americans entered the third decade of the nineteenth century. "Most men are convinced of the injustice and cruelty of the old system of punishment," the author continued, "and feel how inconsistent it is with the republican institutions of America; yet, few understand the principles which are sufficient to avert the danger of introducing it again into some of the states." "This is almost certain," the author warned, fearful of legislative backsliding into the sanguinary system, "unless a judicious reformation in the new and more rational system of punishment can be effected."

On the latter point, the Virginia author noted a lack of attention being paid to improving and fixing the warts of the then-existing penitentiary system. As the author wrote: "I have seen but little effort, and no progress made in improving the system. The great object has been to legislate on the fiscal concerns of these institutions...." As the author wrote of Virginia's experience: "The Virginia Legislature has at its last session made a material change in the fiscal concerns of its Penitentiary, while the most important matter connected with it was urged in vain, that of improving and arranging the buildings in order to separate the convicts at the hours of rest, and to enable them to be worked more profitably, as well as the propriety of amending the penal laws." With Virginians looking to prison labor as a means of production, the author spoke of turning Virginia's penitentiary into a self-sustaining "manufacturing institution." In an appendix, the Virginian's book—expressing concern over the state of penitentiary reform—specifically raised this question: "Have we in this enlightened age no Montesquieus, Beccarias and Howards to aid in accomplishing the work first set on foot by those benevolent men?" In other words, thinkers like Beccaria had set the standard by which others would be measured.

As to the existing state of affairs in the United States, the Virginia writer thus lamented that America was at risk of falling behind its mother country in terms of creating and building out a penitentiary system. "Governments were instituted for the good and happiness of the governed; therefore, every expedient should be resorted to, likely to improve its condition, and not endanger its safety," the author wrote. In England, it was pointed out, "the most cruel and bloody laws, that ever disgraced a country" had been put in place. "[Y]et even there," the writer said, "they have awakened from their slumbers with an eye less dim, and set about correcting the cruel and sanguinary policy that has so long stained the character of the nation." Because transportation to the British colonies in Australia had remained an attractive option even after the Revolutionary War cut off the transportation of convicts to America, Great Britain did not implement its Penitentiary Act for nearly four decades. The construction of the first large-scale English penitentiary, however, began in 1812 and opened at Millbank in 1816, a few years before the Virginia writer weighed in on the penitentiary system in Jefferson's home state. "[S]hall we, her offspring, who disclaimed and abandoned her (as a parent,) because of the multiplied injuries and tyrannical oppressions inflicted on us," the Virginia writer queried, "be now behind her in acts of benevolence?"

The Virginia writer's answer was clear. *"No,* I hope not," the author replied, gingerly urging Americas not to lag behind Great Britain—that mother country that had, through its tyrannical practices, become the nemesis of early Americans. As the Virginia writer suggested:

> [L]et those enlightened friends of humanity and domestic economy set on foot the work of reformation, in our criminal, as they have in our civil institutions, and shew to England and the world, that we are not a people making general abstract professions, and governed by laws inconsistent with ourselves, but acting on the most laudable and rational principles of doing justice to our citizens, endeavouring to correct their moral depravities and place them in a situation, where they may become useful members of society.

"In this way, too," the author concluded, "we demonstrate the absurd policy, the unjust and unchristian practice of putting it out of the power of the unfortunate culprit to make reparation for the injury he has done—before an opportunity is given him of correcting his vicious habits, and enjoying a life more usefully employed in cultivating a good understanding with penitent gratitude for the lenity shewn by the merciful and just laws of a country, whose government is founded on the purest principles of justice and humanity."[161]

The Livingston Code

The American effort to codify the criminal law—and make its rules and punishments clear to all citizens—is best illustrated by the work of Edward Livingston. Livingston, the youngest of ten children from a prominent New York family, was born in 1764, the year *Dei delitti e delle pene* first appeared in Italian, and he came of age in the midst of the American Revolution. His father, a judge of the Supreme Court of the Colony of New York, died in 1775 when Livingston was just nine years old. But Edward Livingston's older brother, Robert R. Livingston, would play a prominent role in America's quest for independence, serving, at age 29, on the committee selected by the Continental Congress to prepare the Declaration of Independence. That five-man committee—whose membership also included Thomas Jefferson, Benjamin Franklin, Roger Sherman and John Adams— put Robert R. Livingston in the company of America's most prominent revolutionaries.

Having studied at King's, now Columbia, College, and after studying law with a relative, Governor William Livingston of New Jersey, Robert R. Livingston became, for a time, a business partner of John Jay and served as New York's highest judicial officer, the Chancellor of the State of New York. He served in the latter position from 1777 to 1801, in which role he had the honor of administering the oath of office to George Washington, a fellow Freemason, at the inauguration of the first President of the United States. "Long live George Washington, President of the United States," Robert proclaimed on that august occasion, with the Bible on which the oath was taken belonging to New York's St. John's Masonic Lodge. In his inaugural address, delivered on April 20, 1789 in New York City before a joint session of Congress at Federal Hall on Wall Street, Washington declared:

> Such being the impressions under which I have, in obedience to the public summons, repaired to the present station, it would be peculiarly improper to omit in this first official act my fervent supplications to that Almighty Being who rules over the universe, who presides in the councils of nations, and whose provi-

dential aids can supply every human defect, that His benediction may conse-
crate to the liberties and happiness of the people of the United States a Government instituted by themselves for these essential purposes, and may enable every
instrument employed in its administration to execute with success the functions
allotted to his charge. In tendering this homage to the Great Author of every
public and private good, I assure myself that it expresses your sentiments not
less than my own, nor those of my fellow-citizens at large less than either. No people can be bound to acknowledge and adore the Invisible Hand which conducts
the affairs of men more than those of the United States.

While the Revolutionary War was still in progress, Robert R. Livingston's younger
brother Edward entered the junior class at Nassau Hall, now Princeton, the institution then
still being led by Dr. Witherspoon, its president. After graduating in 1781 at the age of seventeen, Edward—fluent in French and already a favorite of Lafayette, the American Revolutionary War hero—studied law with John Lansing, who later replaced Robert R.
Livingston as the Chancellor of New York, serving in that all-important role from 1801
to 1814. Edward Livingston himself was admitted to practice in 1785, and—as his biographer points out—became "strongly attracted to the civil law," studying the Code of
Justinian and commentaries on it and getting to know fellow lawyers Alexander Hamilton and Aaron Burr. Roman Emperor Justinian's sixth century A.D. *Corpus Juris*—now
depicted on a panel of bronze doors centered behind the U.S. Supreme Court's massive,
front portico entrance columns—is considered to be the first systematic codification of
Roman law. As a young lawyer, Edward Livingston also formed a lasting friendship with
James Kent, the man who would himself become Chancellor of New York, serving in that
role from 1814 to 1823. Like his older brother Robert, who was tasked in America's early
years with negotiating with the French government for the cession of Louisiana to the
United States, Edward quickly rose to prominence in American politics.[162]

Edward Livingston, born at Clermont on the banks of the Hudson River, first got voted
into office in New York. In 1794, New Yorkers elected him—then just thirty years old—
to the U.S. House of Representatives. As a member of Congress, Livingston served with
highly influential figures such as Albert Gallatin, James Madison and Andrew Jackson,
and—consistent with his long-time interest in reforming penal codes—made an early
attempt to codify and reform the nation's laws. As historian Mark Fernandez explains of
Livingston's efforts:

> Only days after taking his seat, he revealed his frustration with the sanguinary
> state of the new nation's penal laws by introducing legislation to create a penal
> code for the United States. Surprisingly liberal in its attitudes toward rehabilita-
> tion of criminals and capital punishment, Livingston's proposed legislation jibed
> with Thomas Jefferson's view on such matters, especially in its attack on the prin-
> ciple of lex talionis (retaliation) as a form of punishment, but was ultimately too
> forward-looking for other members of Congress.

Although Livingston's proposed legislation failed, Fernandez notes, Livingston—in making the effort—demonstrated "a passion for penal reform, a penchant toward codification, and an unrelenting hatred of the medieval nature of the common law."

As a member of Congress, Edward Livingston also opposed the Alien and Sedition
Acts that gave the President of the United States the power to remove aliens suspected of
treasonable intentions and made it a crime to defame legislators or the President. Arguing those acts were unconstitutional, Livingston concluded that "if we exceed our powers, we become tyrants, and our acts have no effect." Livingston also offered a series of

resolutions relative to the case of Thomas Nash, alias Jonathan Robbins. Nash had participated in a mutiny and committed a murder on the British frigate *Hermione*, but had escaped to the United States, whereupon the British government demanded his extradition under the Jay Treaty after he was taken into custody in Charleston, South Carolina. When President John Adams, through his Secretary of State Timothy Pickering, advised Thomas Bee, a South Carolina federal judge, to deliver up the prisoner, Livingston protested. With the prisoner claiming he was an American citizen who had been impressed into service in the British navy, Livingston believed the questions involved in the case—including whether Nash was entitled to a trial by jury—were exclusively for the judiciary and that the President's interference was dangerous to the judiciary's independence. "In the same Congress," one sketch of Livingston's life confirms, "Mr. Livingston moved for a committee to enquire and report whether any alterations could be made in the penal laws of the United States, by substituting milder punishments for certain crimes for which infamous and capital punishments were then inflicted." A committee was thereafter appointed, with Livingston made its chairman. But Livingston's request that the President submit to Congress detailed statements respecting the trials and convictions that had taken place under existing laws fell on deaf ears.

Although Edward Livingston became a congressman at a relatively young age, much still lay ahead for his political career despite the legislative disappointments and personal setbacks he experienced during his life. Thomas Nash was eventually court martialed and executed by the British, and a motion by Livingston that President Adams be censured for his role in the affair failed to pass. In 1801, just days after the death of his wife, a still-grieving Livingston was appointed by President Thomas Jefferson as the U.S. Attorney for the District of New York. That same year, Livingston—at the age of thirty-eight—also became the mayor of New York City. Serving in both roles, Livingston continued—albeit unsuccessfully—to try to reform New York's penal system. As one sketch of his life reports of that time:

> He proposed to the Mechanics' Society to found jointly with the city an establishment for the employment of strangers, the first month of their arrival, secondly of citizens who from sickness and casualty were out of work, third of widows and children incapable of labor, fourth of discharged convicts. The benevolence of his nature made him dwell with enthusiasm upon the results, in the suppression of mendicity, the prevention of crime, and the reformation of criminals, for which he hoped, if the measures urged by him were adopted.[163]

In 1803, Edward Livingston—whose wife and eldest son died in close proximity of one another—also fell into debt due to the dishonesty of a clerk to whom he had entrusted the collection of public funds. Hoping to rebuild his fortune in the newly acquired city of New Orleans, Livingston left New York for that southern city in December 1804, quickly rising to a position of leadership in the bar. His brother Robert R. Livingston had become the American minister to France, and the massive Louisiana Purchase—which Robert R. Livingston and James Monroe negotiated—brought new challenges and opportunities, including as regards the law itself. As one commentator explains: "Formerly a possession of France, later of Spain, then again in 1803, retransferred to France for the purpose of sale to the United States, after which much of the Spanish law remained unrepealed, the state suffered from a conflict of laws and custom." The civil law of Spain, as derived from Roman jurisprudence, was in force in New Orleans when Edward Livingston first arrived there; there were outdated laws and customs to be dealt with; and there existed a bewildering mix of Spanish, French, legislative and common law. "This medley of laws and customs," explains sociologist Elon Moore, quoting an earlier source, "'made the interpretation of criminal law perplexing, the mode of procedure uncertain, the rules of evidence largely discretionary, and the consequent miscarriage of justice frequent and inevitable.'"

Because of his skills, Edward Livingston — the Beccaria admirer — thus soon became involved in a public discussion and dispute over what law — English common law or Roman civil law — would govern the Louisiana territory. In the beginning of the 1820s, Livingston became a member of the Louisiana legislature and was elected by joint ballot of the General Assembly of Louisiana to revise the state's criminal laws. As a multi-lingual lawyer, Livingston had studied Roman, English, French, Russian, Prussian, Spanish and Tuscan laws, and he knew some of the languages in which those laws were written, giving him a distinct advantage in his work. Livingston objected to the Spanish code's medieval, fifteenth-century provisions as well as the common law's jumble of unwritten customs that resulted in arbitrary decisions. For example, someone who stole a pint of molasses from a sugarhouse was punished more harshly than one who aided the escape of a murderer. In formulating his views on the existing American penal system and how to approach his drafting assignment, Livingston also carefully studied the penitentiary systems of American states such as Massachusetts, New York and Pennsylvania. Along with his prior reading of the works of Enlightenment writers such as Beccaria, Bentham, Blackstone, Eden, Howard and Filangieri, this gave Livingston ample information to draw upon as he faced up to the arduous task ahead of him.[164]

Tragically, just as Edward Livingston was completing his work, a large portion of it was destroyed in a fire. On the night before he planned to deliver his manuscript to the printer, he had stayed up late making final edits. But after going to bed, a cry of "fire" awoke him. A spark from his study lamp had ignited the blaze, and all of his papers except sixty pages and a few "imperfect notes" were destroyed along with various books he had relied upon in doing his drafting. "Four years of labor," one commentator explains, "were completed and destroyed on the same night." Despite being sixty years of age at the time, the determined Livingston would not be deterred or allow himself to become depressed, and he immediately set out to reconstruct his work. As Livingston wrote to the Philadelphia lawyer Peter Du Ponceau just two days after the fire:

> My habits for some years past, however, have fortunately inured me to labour, and my whole life has to disappointment and distress. I therefore bear it with more fortitude that I otherwise should, and, instead of repining, work all night and correct the proof all day, to repair the loss and get the work ready by the time I had promised it to the legislature.

Livingston's letter to Du Ponceau also requested that Du Ponceau send to Livingston books by Jeremy Bentham that had been lost in the fire and that Livingston could not locate in any local library or bookstore. As Livingston wrote to Du Ponceau: "Will you do me the favor to buy, borrow, or beg them for me? The works I allude to are the French editions, published by Dumont: '*Principles of Legislation*,' 3 vols.; '*Theory of Punishments*,' 2 vols.; and '*Treatise of Judicial Proof.*'" "Your little book escaped the flames, and I saved your Bacon, though not my own," Livingston added, referencing Bacon's *Aphorisms* and trying to maintain his sense of humor.[165]

Livingston's final work product, styled "A System of Penal Law," had a Code of Crimes and Punishments, a Code of Procedure, a Code of Evidence, and a Code of Reform and Prison Discipline. Louisiana legislators refused to adopt his system, but — as his biographer notes — its publication "brought him immediate and wide fame." As that biographer emphasized:

> A great deal of barbarism characterizes the old and tenacious abuses which cling
> to the administration of penal justice: in the blind adherence to arbitrary tech-
> nical rules; in the reliance upon uncertain precedents; in the ferocity of some
> punishments, and the want of discrimination among others; in the detention of
> witnesses; and in the promiscuous confinement of the young and the old, the ten-
> der and the hardened, the innocent and the guilty.

"If, in the progress of the world, even a partial remedy for these chronic abused shall be
found in some system substantially like that of Livingston," that biographer wrote, "his
name will live to be historically and permanently associated with the names of Bacon, of
Montesquieu, of Beccaria, and of Bentham." By distributing copies of his system of penal
laws, Livingston sought to become for America what Beccaria had become for Tuscany,
the locale that made history by ridding itself of capital punishment in the wake of the
publication of *On Crimes and Punishments*.

Despite Livingston's disappointment in the failure of Louisiana lawmakers to act on
his proposal, Livingston's work was well received by others. Chief Justice John Marshall, James Madison and Thomas Jefferson favorably reacted to Livingston's work, and
Livingston himself was sought out as a speaker. In Philadelphia, Livingston's anti-death
penalty views were reprinted in Philadelphia in 1831 as legislators there considered
abolishing the death penalty; Columbia, Harvard and Transylvania conferred on Livingston Doctor of Laws degrees; and Livingston got congratulatory praise from the
likes of Victor Hugo and Czar Nicholas of Russia, King Charles of Sweden, and the
King of the Netherlands. Not only did the Institute of France elect Livingston as a new
foreign associate, but in Geneva, Switzerland, Count Jean-Jacques de Sellon—the
founder of the Geneva Peace Society who erected a monument as a tribute of respect
to those who had furthered the cause of humanity—included Livingston on one of
the monument's twelve faces. With figures such as Beccaria, the Grand Duke of Tuscany, and William Wilberforce also highlighted, the panel paying homage to Livingston
highlighted his work in demanding the death penalty's abolition in America. At a public event sponsored by the bar of New York City, Louis Kossuth—the exiled Governor
of Hungary—remarked that Livingston's code had made Livingston one of the four
Americans best known in Europe. "The code," historian George Bancroft wrote years
later of Livingston's work, "is in its simplicity, completeness, and humanity, at once
an impersonation of the man and an exposition of the American Constitution. If it
has never yet been adopted as a whole, it has proved an unfailing fountain of reforms,
suggested by its principles."[166]

Livingston—who sought the reformation, not the killing, of offenders—was a fierce
proponent of the penitentiary system. "It is," Livingston said, referring to the penitentiary system, "a great, I had almost said a godlike experiment, worthy of the free country in which it is made, honorable to the men who planned, and highly creditable to those
who conduct it." "Its progress," he added, "is regarded with an interest running into anxiety, by the friends of humanity in every quarter of the world; and its failure, from whatever cause, will check the spirit of improvement that suggested it, and restore the ancient
bloody code with all its horrors." Livingston called the penitentiary experiment "the fairest
experiment ever made in favor of humanity." In a letter to Jeremy Bentham, Edward Livingston specifically credited Bentham's work—reliant so much on Beccaria's treatise—
in influencing his own ideas. As Livingston wrote:

> Although strongly impressed with the defects of our actual system of penal law,
> yet the perusal of your works first gave method to my ideas, and taught me to
> consider legislation as a science governed by certain principles applicable to all

its different branches, instead of an occasional exercise of its powers, called forth only on particular occasions, without relation to or connection with each other.

In the place of executions, Livingston offered imprisonment for life, the same prescription offered by Beccaria. As Livingston's biographer reported of the American legislator's proposal:

> It was imprisonment for life in a solitary cell, to be painted black without and within, and bearing a conspicuous outer inscription, in distinct white letters, setting forth the culprit's name and his offence, with its circumstances, and proceeding with a fearfully graphic description of his doom:—"His FOOD IS BREAD OF THE COARSEST KIND; HIS DRINK IS WATER MINGLED WITH HIS TEARS; HE IS DEAD TO THE WORLD; THIS CELL IS HIS GRAVE; HIS EXISTENCE IS PROLONGED THAT HE MAY REMEMBER HIS CRIME, AND REPENT IT, AND THAT THE CONTINUANCE OF HIS PUNISHMENT MAY DETER OTHERS FROM THE INDULGENCE OF HATRED, AVARICE, SENSUALITY, AND THE PASSIONS WHICH LEAD TO THE CRIME HE HAS COMMITTED. WHEN THE ALMIGHTY, IN HIS DUE TIME, SHALL EXERCISE TOWARDS HIM THAT DISPENSATION WHICH HE HIMSELF ARROGANTLY AND WICKEDLY USURPED TOWARDS ANOTHER, HIS BODY IS TO BE DISSECTED, AND HIS SOUL WILL ABIDE THAT JUDGMENT WHICH DIVINE JUSTICE SHALL DECREE."

Under Livingston's approach, inmates would get religious instruction and only get such human attention as their physical needs required.[167]

In conferring with his friends and political associates about his ideas for penal reform, Livingston made his views clear even as he—like Beccaria before him—got mixed reactions to the specifics of his ideas. To his friend, the French linguist and jurist Peter Stephen Du Ponceau who had served in the American Revolutionary War and settled in Philadelphia, Edward Livingston—seeking advice—wrote in May 1821:

> My present impression is strongly against the retention of the punishment of death. I think it a most inefficient punishment in any case; it certainly has been found so in most. Is there good reason for retaining it in any? Yet in all the States it is retained for murder. Is not this owing to a secret attachment to the fanciful *lex talionis*, or, what is worse, to a vindictive spirit which the law should never indulge. Let me have your sentiments fully on this point, and on the utility, or rather the practicability, of reducing into a code all that ought to be enacted under the head of criminal law.

Livingston had, by then, long known Du Ponceau, a much-respected legal scholar. Du Ponceau had become a Pennsylvania citizen on July 25, 1781, and had served as an assistant to Robert R. Livingston while the latter served as America's Secretary for Foreign Affairs. An employment recommendation from Judge Richard Peters, of Philadelphia, had noted that Du Ponceau's native tongue was French, that he had "acquired perfectly" English, is "a good Latin scholar," "understands German, Italian, and Spanish," and "can translate Danish and Low Dutch with the help of a dictionary."

Later, Edward Livingston also had communications with both Thomas Jefferson and James Madison, seeking their views on his proposed penal code to make punishments less sanguinary. He wrote a letter to Thomas Jefferson on March 9, 1825, soliciting his input, and he also penned a letter to James Madison on March 13, 1825, seeking Madison's "general views" on "the utility of the plan." In the latter letter, Livingston asked Madison—who had been requested to set forth his own views in a reply—to consider "making them public." Such letters to America's then-elder statesmen were by no means sent out of the blue as they came from a man already well known to both men. Jefferson and Livingston had corresponded with one other for more than twenty years, and though many years often went by without a letter, Livingston knew of Jefferson's long-standing interest in penal reform. Livingston had also written to Madison more than two decades earlier, with both Jefferson and Madison also corresponding with Robert R. Livingston, Edward's older brother.

In sending Jefferson a circular on November 29, 1824, along with "the first of four codes, which forms a system of Penal Law," Edward Livingston—the man who made penal reform the cause of his life—specifically asked Jefferson to "take the trouble to peruse the work; to note in the margin such observations as occur to you for its amelioration, and to communicate them to me with your first leisure." In that circular accompanying Livingston's code, Livingston explained the importance of his Louisiana law reform work as follows: "The introduction of a body of written law, has many learned and respectable advocates in several of the States." "This first experiment, which is to test the utility of written codes in our government," Livingston emphasized, "is therefore one of general interest; and as its success depends wholly on the correctness of its principles, and the clearness and precision with which its provisions are enounced, I feel the greater confidence in asking the aid of your learning, experience, and judgment, to supply what is deficient, and to correct what is erroneous in the work."[168] At that time, American states still heavily relied on common-law crimes and the idea of a comprehensive code of laws to replace customary punishments was still a relatively novel concept, at least to the degree proposed by Livingston.

In response to Edward Livingston's requests, Thomas Jefferson and James Madison both sent letters to Livingston. On March 25, 1825, Jefferson, ensconced at Monticello, wrote a lengthy letter to Livingston. That letter stated that Jefferson was "not equal" to the "task" proposed by Livingston, with Jefferson writing:

> To examine a code of laws newly reduced to system and text, to weigh their bearings on each other in all their parts, their harmony with reason and nature, and their adaptation to the habits and sentiments of those for whom they are prepared, and whom, in this case, I do not know, is a task far above what I am now, or perhaps ever was.

"I have attended to so much of your work as has been heretofore laid before the public, and have looked, with some attention also, into what you have now sent me," Jefferson wrote, adding: "It will certainly arrange your name with the sages of antiquity." Having once himself seen his own efforts at penal reform fall one vote short in the 1780s, Jefferson closed his letter: "Wishing anxiously that your great work may obtain complete success, and become an example for the imitation and improvement of other States, I pray you to be assured of my unabated friendship and respect."

On December 27, 1825, James Madison, penning a letter from Montpellier, also wrote to Livingston, though he—like Jefferson—had little time to write a point-by-point response to Livingston's proposed code. Madison began by acknowledging receipt of Livingston's "favor of Mar. 13" that had included "a copy of the executed part of your penal Code for Louisiana." "With every disposition to comply with your request, in the full extent of it," Madison then observed, "the reflection could not escape me that I ought not to obtrude any suggestions affecting the essentials of your work, if any such should occur; and that a critical examination of its details & definitions was a task belonging to others of your friends, having a greater surplus of time, and better qualified also, by their professional studies & experience." But sharing Livingston's reform-minded and Enlightenment proclivities, Madison then clarified: "Of the great object of your undertaking, that of simplifying and humanizing the penal Code, so much in need of both, I could not express more praise than is due; and however great the merit of the portion now brought into view, it will but fulfil the expectations authorized by the ability shewn in the 'Introductory Report.'"

Madison's December 27th letter expressed both adulation and certain reservations, with Madison declining in his letter to make his own views on Livingston's code public. "It can not be doubted, I think," Madison explained, "that a legal code may be digested & reduced to writing with the great advantages of ascertaining the law where doubtful, of explaining it where obscure, of reforming it where wrong in its principles, and of rendering it at once more systematic and more concise." "But I can not overcome the doubts expressed in a former letter of the practicability, however desirable, of written enumerations & definitions so full & so precise," Madison noted, "as to supersede altogether a resort to the explanatory aids of unwritten or traditional law." "And I am still impressed, for the reasons there given," Madison added, "with the hazard of substituting for compound technical terms, new ones whatever be the skill in chusing them." "None of these doubts however," Madison emphasized, "can restrain me from joining not only in the tribute due to your enlightened and philanthropic labours; but in the sincere wish that the result of them, may receive the sanction & the experiment for which it is prepared." "As a whole," Madison added, "it must be an incalculable improvement of the existing system. And if any of the innovations so pleasing in theory should prove exceptionable in practice, the inconvenience must be limited in its space, and may be made so in its duration."

In his prior letter to Livingston, dated July 10, 1822, Madison acknowledged a letter from Livingston that—as Madison put it—was "accompanied by a copy of your Report to the Legislature of the State on the subject of a penal Code." That report to the State of Louisiana—later reprinted in 1833 and in 1872 with an introduction by Salmon Chase, the Chief Justice of the United States—had been prepared by Livingston after he received reports on England's penal reform efforts from Jeremy Bentham through the U.S. minister to England, Richard Rush. In his report, Livingston laid out what he hoped his proposed penal code would do to rectify the state of the law as it then existed, with Livingston writing:

> The incongruities which have pervaded our system will disappear; every new enactment will be impressed with the character of the original body of laws; and our penal legislation will no longer be a piece of fretwork exhibiting the passions of its several authors, their fears, their caprices, or the carelessness and inattention with which legislators in all ages and in every country have, at times, endangered the lives, the liberties, and fortunes of the people, by inconsistent provisions, cruel or disproportioned punishments, and a legislation, weak and wavering, because guided by no principle, or by one that was continually changing, and therefore could seldom be right.

Livingston's report—which invoked Beccaria's name on more than one occasion—took specific aim at England's Bloody Code, noting that "[n]o proportion was preserved between crimes and punishments."

"I should commit a tacit injustice," Madison had written to Livingston on the occasion of his prior letter in 1822, "if I did not say that the Report does great honor to the talents and sentiments of the Author. It abounds with ideas of conspicuous value and presents them in a manner not less elegant than persuasive." "The reduction of an entire code of criminal jurisprudence, into statutory provisions, excluding a recurrence to foreign or traditional codes, and substituting for technical terms, more familiar ones with or without explanatory notes," Madison wrote, "cannot but be viewed as a very arduous task." "I cannot deny, at the same time," Madison explained, however, "that I have been accustomed to doubt the practicability of giving all the desired simplicity to so complex a subject, without involving a discretion, inadmissible in free Govt. to those who are to expound and apply the law." As Madison, a practical lawmaker, expressed his concerns:

> The rules and usages which make a part of the law, tho' to be found only in elementary treatises, in respectable commentaries, and in adjudged cases, seem to be too numerous & too various to be brought within the requisite compass; even if there were less risk of creating uncertainties by defective abridgments, or by the change of phraseology.

"The risk wd. seem to be particularly incident to a substitution of new words & definitions for a technical language, the meaning of which had been settled by long use and authoritative expositions," Madison observed, cautioning Livingston: "I hope it will not be thought by this intimation of my doubts I wish to damp the enterprize from which you have not shrunk." "On the contrary," Madison urged, "I not only wish that you may overcome all the difficulties which occur to me; but am persuaded that if compleat success shd. not reward your labors, there is ample room for improvements in the criminal jurisprudence of Louisiana as elsewhere which are well worthy the exertion of your best powers, and wh will furnish useful examples to other members of the Union."[169]

In contrast to Madison and Jefferson's sympathetic communications, in February 1826, Livingston's good friend, Chancellor James Kent, expressed more traditional views. As Kent wrote to Livingston:

> I owe every obligation to you for your continued friendship, and my sense of your talents and learning has been constantly on the increase from 1786 to this day. It is very likely I shall have some old-fashioned notions and prejudices hoary with age and inflexible from habit; but I am determined to give you what I think, on the reading of all the work, and to deal out praise and censure as my judgment dictates.

In a later communication, Kent continued to express his support for capital punishment, though he sensed that the times were changing and that his own views might be out of step. As Kent wrote:

> Though I shall always be dissatisfied with any code that strips the courts of their common-law powers over contempts, and ceases to be a wholesome terror to evil-minded disposition by the total banishment of the axe, musket, or halter from its punishments, yet I admit the spirit of the age is against me, and I contentedly acquiesce.[170]

The Promise of the Penitentiary System

In the 1820s, America's still-living Founding Fathers—then of advanced age—saw substantial promise in the country's newly developed state penitentiary system. For example, in 1827, James Madison—the former President of the United States—thanked one of his many correspondents, the Philadelphia-born Quaker Roberts Vaux, for a letter "so judiciously and seasonably interposed in behalf of the Penitentiary System, an experiment so deeply interesting to the cause of Humanity."[171] In 1826, Vaux, through his Philadelphia publisher, had come out with *Notices of the Original, and Successive Efforts, to Improve the Discipline of the Prison at Philadelphia, and to Reform the Criminal Code of Pennsylvania: With a Few Observations on the Penitentiary System.*[172] In that book, Vaux pondered aloud whether, after a state penitentiary system was fully operational, "imprisonment during life" could be substituted in place of the death penalty. Writing from Montpellier to another correspondent, Madison reported to Philadelphia lawyer Thomas Wharton that, of what he had been sent and read of a "Report on the Penal Code" for Pennsylvania, he "was most attracted to what relates to the penitentiary discipline as a substitute for the cruel inflictions so disgraceful to penal codes."[173] In other words, Madison had come to favor the use of penitentiaries in place of cruel and sanguinary punishments.

In the United States, a *sanguinary* penal system was seen as one characterized by "a cruel and bloody spirit"—a spirit that was not associated with, and that was diametrically opposed to, the *penitentiary* system.[174] As one 1826 source emphasized: "Two experiments have been tried, in relation to criminal jurisprudence and prison discipline, the Sanguinary and Penitentiary Systems. In former days, a cruel and bloody spirit prevailed, characteristic of the military spirit, and severe policy of the times...." "Though in some European nations and in parts of this country, the sanguinary code still exists in form," that source reported, "it serves only to tempt the ill disposed to violate laws, which the increased humanity of the age will not suffer to be faithfully executed." Saying "[i]t deforms the statute book," the writer—whose piece was published in *The Christian Examiner and Theological Review* roughly a decade after the end of the War of 1812—concluded of the "Sanguinary" system: "As a system, it has completely failed." "The Penitentiary System," by contrast, the writer noted, "had its origin in the United States, and trial has been made of it by the principal members of the Union." As the writer explained of the penitentiary system's broad purposes: "Its object is to create habits of industry and order, to excite contrition, to effect amendment."[175] "Though the hearts of convicts will be steeled against harsh and cruel measures," the writer concluded, "we believe a generous and humane policy may operate to reclaim them."[176]

In America, the building of penitentiaries thus came to be seen as a progressive, civilizing development to be welcomed and embraced. For example, William Short—Thomas Jefferson's private secretary in Paris, and the man who succeeded Jefferson as Minister to France—wrote this in an 1823 letter to his former boss as he observed the changes that were taking place in New York:

> The country through which I have passed from Utica to this place is one of the miracles of the present time. When I passed over it sixteen years ago it was then emerging from the state of wilderness. It is now a thickly settled & highly cultivated region & I am unable to discover any of the places at which I stopped, so wunderful have been the changes.

The letter from Short, who Jefferson called his "adoptive son," then noted "all the insignia of highly improved civilization, not forgetting one of the principal, a most extensive & well built Penitentiary where was on my former journey two three small houses only."[177]

In an autobiographical statement written in 1821, Jefferson himself—in a paragraph mentioning Beccaria—had noted how "hard labor on roads, canals and other public works, had been suggested as a proper substitute" for "the punishment of crimes by death." Jefferson further noted how he had advised Virginians on "the plan of a Prison," "what is now called the Penitentiary."[178] America—"the land of the free and the home of the brave," to borrow a verse, later set to music, from Francis Scott Key's *The Star-Spangled Banner*—was seen as a country in motion. *The Star-Spangled Banner*, composed by Francis Scott Key (1779–1843) at a time when American liberty was once again being threatened, was itself the work of a lawyer. A legal adviser to Andrew Jackson, Key became the

U.S. Attorney for the District of Columbia, a position in which Key, as a prosecutor, had to make charging decisions. What has been called the "sorriest episode in Key's career" happened in 1835 after Anna Thornton, the widow of Key's close friend William Thornton, awoke one night to find her eighteen-year-old slave, Arthur Bowen, standing in her bedroom door with an axe. After she fled, Bowen was arrested, and angry whites threatened to lynch him. Violent riots ensued in Washington, D.C., and in that environment, Key sought and obtained the death penalty against Bowen for attempted murder. But after Anna Thornton pleaded with President Andrew Jackson for clemency, saying Bowen had simply been drunk, Jackson pardoned the slave. Key's own grandson, Francis Scott Key Smith, himself a lawyer, was later—as one biographical sketch notes—"the author of numerous articles on capital punishment."[179]

As the writings of Jefferson and Madison show, changes in the law were not only anticipated by America's founders, they were welcomed, even advocated for. Indeed, the very idea that America's legal system would remain static would have struck America's Enlightenment era, *forward-leaning* founders as absurd, making the whole idea of "originalism"—which has, as its premise, assessing *eighteenth-century* understandings to solve *twenty-first century* problems—highly problematic. The founders themselves, to be sure, were fascinated by history, but they made decisions in light of history without being controlled by it. Instead of submitting to British tyranny and misrule, they made their own destinies. The U.S. Constitution itself was framed not only to "secure the Blessings of Liberty" for the framers, but for persons not yet born, their "Posterity," showing the founders' heightened awareness of the rights of future generations.[180] In short, the Framers of the Constitution fully expected the law to change over time, which explains why they so often chose words and phrases with built-in flexibility, like "cruel and unusual" and "due process," in the U.S. Bill of Rights. The founders, in fact, spent their lives rejecting English laws and customs and establishing a new, uniquely American jurisprudence of their own making.

Begun as a novel experiment in Philadelphia, America's burgeoning penitentiary system—seen as a way to either curtail or even potentially eliminate death sentences or harsh corporal punishments—was itself written of as a vast improvement over the "barbarous" and "sanguinary" punishments of prior ages. "On arriving in the town," one American traveler wrote in 1819, "we found the court engaged in deciding upon the fate of a criminal, who had committed a rape." The travelers—as travelers are wont to do—then compared the criminal law of that place, the Arkansas Territory, with that of more developed states that were, by then, regularly using penitentiaries. "The legal punishment, in this and the Missouri territory, for this crime, castration!" Thomas Nuttall wrote of his travels into the Arkansas Territory, "is no less singular and barbarous, however just, than the heinous nature of the crime itself."

"The penitentiary law of confinement, so successfully tried in the states of Pennsylvania and New York, for every crime short of murder," Nuttall wrote, "is an improvement in jurisprudence, which deserves to be adopted in every part of the United States." "There is certainly a flagrant want of humanity in the multiplicity of sanguinary and stigmatizing punishments," he emphasized.[181] The movement in favor of penitentiaries would eventually catch up with Arkansas, which was admitted to the Union in 1836 and which opened its first penitentiary, doubling as a shoe manufacturing facility, soon thereafter, in 1841. But not until 1968—at a distance of more than one hundred and twenty-five years—were corporal punishments stopped through a judicial ruling. In that year, Justice Harry Blackmun, then writing for the U.S. Court of Appeals for the Eighth Circuit, ruled that the use of the strap in Arkansas prisons was unconstitutional as a "cruel and unusual punishment." "Corporal punishment," he observed, "generates hate toward the keepers who punish and toward the system which permits it."[182]

In a series of letters written in 1846 in Boston, Robert Rantoul, Jr.—capturing some of the public sentiment in the mid-nineteenth century—forthrightly made the case for abolishing capital punishment altogether. In his letters, written to the state's governor and legislators, Rantoul invoked Montesquieu's maxim that every act of punishment not warranted by "absolute necessity" is tyrannical. Rantoul also cited an array of statistics to show that the death penalty, in practice, had not curtailed violent crimes. On the contrary, Rantoul asserted that "crime diminishes in proportion as the denunciations and administration of the criminal law are rendered milder and the rule of a barbarous retaliation abandoned." "Harsh laws, beget crimes," Rantoul concluded, quoting the following observation of Jeremy Bentham: "If the legislator be desirous to inspire humanity amongst the citizens, let him set the example; let him show the utmost respect for the life of man. Sanguinary laws have a tendency to render man cruel, either by fear, by imitation, or by revenge. But laws dictated by mildness humanize the manners of a nation, and the spirit of government." In *Theory of Legislation*, Bentham had written of "[t]yrannical and sanguinary laws," and of "a writer so judicious as Beccaria," with Bentham speaking of Beccaria's work as being "dictated by the soundest philosophy." "[P]roportion," Bentham wrote in that book, "is continually outraged or forgotten, and the punishment of death is lavished upon the most trifling offences.... Thence results a system of penal law, incoherent, contradictory, uniting violence to weakness, dependent on the humour of a judge, varying from circuit to circuit, sometimes sanguinary, sometimes null." Bentham added: "Sanguinary laws have a tendency to render men cruel, by fear, by imitation, and by fostering a spirit of revenge. Mild laws humanize the manners of a nation; the spirit of the government is reproduced among the citizens."[183]

In line with Bentham's observations, Rantoul further observed in 1846 that England's government was "justly" denounced "as sanguinary" and that "[t]he proportion of convictions increases as you abandon an inhuman punishment." Mixing secular and religious arguments, Rantoul had reached the conclusion that society was harmed, not helped, by the infliction of capital punishment. As Rantoul argued after citing "the illustrious Montesquieu":

> I infer that it will be our duty, as it will be our happiness, to introduce and extend, until it shall pervade our whole legislation, the spirit of benevolence, compassion and sympathy, which is the spirit of heaven, and to banish from our code the spirit of malice, hatred and revenge, which is the spirit of hell. When men act consistently upon the belief which they now generally admit in theory, that the whole purpose of punishment is precautionary and not retributive, that brutal cruelty does not humanize him who suffers, him who inflicts, or him who beholds it; that after every instance in which the law violates the sanctity of human life, that life is held less sacred by the community among whom the outrage is perpetrated; that prisons are hospitals for the restraint of persons whose liberty would endanger the well-being of society, and for the remedial treatment of aggravated moral disease; then and not till then, will the frightful catalogue of crimes committed in civilized countries be curtailed as rapidly as the remaining obstacles of intemperance, ignorance, and extreme destitution, and those untamed passions which the spectacle of blood stimulates, will allow.

"[I]t is proved," Rantoul wrote, "that we need not violate the Divine command—Thou Shalt Not Kill, in order to protect society against the increase of crime." "[T]he blood we shed," he pleaded, "will but cause the shedding of more blood, in an endless vicious progression."[184]

The Crockett-Madison Correspondence

The attitudinal shift that took place from the earliest days of America's founding era to the early nineteenth century is typified in the pamphlet that physician G. F. H. Crockett—a member of the "K. A. Society of Hippocrates," and an "Honorary Member of the Lexington Medical Society"—sent to James Madison in 1823.[185] In that pamphlet, titled *An Address to the Legislature of Kentucky, on the Abolition of Capital Punishments, in the United States, and the Substitution of Exile for Life*, Crockett laid out his views on that subject at length.[186] Dated July 4, 1823, from Herndonsville, Kentucky, the address—in the words America's ex-President, James Madison, would have read—began as follows:

> Feeling ardently enlisted in the cause of humanity, and conscious, as I am, that the heart of every virtuous, enlightened, and philanthropic freeman, must beat with accumulated energy when he perceives the least advance made towards me-liorating the condition of his species, and investing man with those rights which *God and nature* have declared he should possess; I shall in a brief and imperfect manner, endeavor to present to your consideration, a subject, not the least im-portant which has ever engaged the attention, and elicited the talents of wise and humane legislators: viz. A project for the *abolition of capital punishment* in the United States, and the substitution of *exile for life*.

The Lexington Medical Society, of which Crockett was named the treasurer when it was first incorporated in 1821 by the Commonwealth of Kentucky's general assembly, was connected with the Transylvania University's School of Medicine. The Medical Society's avowed purpose: "cultivating to more advantage the science of medicine" and "awaken-ing in these western states, a more lively zeal for greater attainments and improvements in that important branch of knowledge.[187]

Releasing his abolitionist views on Independence Day, the anniversary of the coun-try's birth, Crockett—in his pamphlet—first acknowledged that the debate over capital punishment was not new, not by a long shot. "Though the subject of capital punishment has excited much attention during the last 20 or 30 years, both in this country and be-yond the great waters," Crockett noted, "it has attracted but little where it should have received most—That it is worthy the attention of any nation, but especially of a free peo-ple, no one can reasonably deny." Hoping to bring the debate over capital punishment from Kentucky and other states to the national level, Crockett—working toward the uni-versal abolition of executions—was nonetheless realistic about what it would take to put the nail in the death penalty's coffin. "I am aware," he wrote, "that to carry my scheme into effect, will require a concurrence of all, or at least a majority of the states." In 1823, "a let-ter from G. F. H. Crockett, enclosing an address to the Legislature on the abolition of capital punishments"—as a Kentucky legislative journal put it—was "laid before the Senate" by "[t]he Speaker" and "was read, and referred to Messrs. Flournoy, Blackburn, Marshall, T. Ward, Howard, Carneal and M'Afee."

In that same 1823 legislative journal, it was noted that the Senate had received from Kentucky's governor, John Adair, a message that the state penitentiary had been enlarged and that "[t]he great and most important object of the Legislature, in organising the Pen-itentiary, and changing the punishment for crimes, was the hope of effecting a reforma-tion in the culprit." That journal also contained a report of John Rowan and Henry Clay that noted that, "[a]t the date of the compact" that led to the creation of Kentucky, "the crime of horse-stealing, was punished, under the laws of Virginia, with death." As that re-port continued, reciting the changes in the law that had already taken place: "The state of Kentucky, very soon after it believed it possessed the power to do so, mitigated the rigor of the Virginia code in that instance, among many others, and commuted confinement in the jail and penitentiary house, for capital punishment." "The state of Kentucky," the report's authors added, "has, it is believed, in some cases of a penal character, which were punishable under the laws of Virginia at the date of the compact, with stripes or imprisonment, substituted for the punishment inflicted by those laws on the body of the culprit, an exaction upon his purse, and subjected *his lands* to the payment of the penalty."[188]

In 1792, Kentucky—following Vermont's admission in 1791—had become the fifteenth state to be admitted into the Union, and Crockett saw the potential for Kentucky to be a model for the still young nation. "[A]s the states have retained the principal part of the penal law in their own hands," Crockett noted, "the power rests with the people to amend, alter &c. the laws: and though Kentucky is but a young sister, her '*Star*' shines brilliantly in the '*Spangled banner*,' and I am only permitted to hope, that any laudable example she may propose, will be cheerfully and promptly followed by her more mature sisters." "After much anxious deliberation," Crockett offered in words that closely parallel Beccaria's, "*I am fully convinced* that *capital punishment is not absolutely necessary 'for the prevention of crimes.'*" As a medical doctor, Crockett—though not trained in the law, as Beccaria had been—felt duty bound to enter the fray over the legal system's use of executions. "Deeply sensible of my own incompetence to treat, with ability, a subject so vast, and so closely entwining itself with our political and social happiness," Crockett wrote, "I can but regret that it has not been undertaken by some one better calculated to do it justice." "Indeed," Crockett added, "I have engaged in it, not so much from a sense of its being *my* duty, but the duty of an *American*."

Acknowledging Edward Livingston's then only recently completed "labours" in drafting a plan to revise Louisiana's penal code to eliminate executions, Crockett called Livingston a "great man, this *Solon* of Louisiana." Crockett openly encouraged his own readers to read Livingston's report, which Crockett said had been prepared in "a peculiarly masterly manner." "I have not only been greatly assisted by a perusal of this interesting document," Crockett wrote, but he freely admitted that what Livingston had written had been presented in such an effective manner "as to supercede much which I would in this place, otherwise say." After taking note of "the dark ages" and "the chaos of gross darkness and error which has enveloped man," Crockett expressed his hope for mankind. "Man, by a succession of mental and spiritual efforts," he wrote, "is destined to wing his glorious flight far beyond the track of fiery suns and planets, and to approximate nearer and nearer to the Fountain of all purity and perfection." "All penal laws," Crockett emphasized, "should be founded in *equity, reason,* and *humanity*: when they transcend those bounds, they are unjust and cruel."

Crockett's address noted the need for proportionality even as he lamented the slow progress in eliminating sanguinary laws. "The penalty," Crockett wrote of criminal sanctions, "should be adapted to the nature and magnitude of the crime." "Antiquity," he added, "presents us with universally sanguinary examples; and although, in modern times, lawmakers have appeared to think more rationally, and act more humanely, the advances towards reformation have been slow, owing, principally, to the circumstance of all new governments looking too much to the codes of those who have preceded them, for a model." "That principle in human nature, which prompts us to admire, venerate, and imitate ancient systems and customs, may be carried to an unwarrantable extent," Crockett advised of this resort to legal precedents, taking solace in the fact that some progress had already been made. As Crockett wrote: "All the states inflict capital punishment: but I believe in all, reformation has had its advocates, and in some capital punishment has been abolished, except for one or two crimes; and we are not to suppose that any of them have 'stopped short in the reform of their penal law,' because they suppose they 'have arrived at the point of perfection, beyond which it would be both unwise and presumptuous to pass.'" The "free and enlightened" American states, Crockett explained, had already come to a "universal acknowledgement" that "capital punishment ought to be abolished in all cases except treason, murder, and rape." "But I presume," Crockett proclaimed, "that when the subject is candidly and impartially investigated, none will hesitate to declare it ought to be abolished in every case."

Crockett's address to the Kentucky legislature—the one Crockett hoped would make a national impact by its publication and by putting it into Madison's hands—bears Montesquieu's and Beccaria's distinctive palm prints. "The civilized part of mankind," Crockett emphasized, "have established it as a political *axiom*, 'that the sole end of punishment is to prevent the commission of crimes;' hence, punishment should be inflicted with as much precision as possible, consistent with the nature of the case." Indeed, Crockett's address—decrying laws inspired by "the bloody Draco" and bemoaning society's use of executions as "*vengeance*"—specifically brought up both Montesquieu and Beccaria. For example, after citing Montesquieu's *Spirit of Laws*, Crockett railed against "*lex talionis* laws," suggesting such laws contradicted "the religion of the New Testament!" England's "sanguinary laws," Crockett explained, "are carried sufficiently into effect to render the taking of life an ordinary every-day's occurrence, which excites little sensibility or concern." In that regard, Crockett invoked "[t]he humane and philanthropic Sir Wm. Meredith, in a speech in the British House of Commons, in 1777, on the subject of frequent executions." Meredith, Crockett reported, had said this: "It is not the mode, but the certainty of punishment, that creates terror." Crockett—surveying the legal landscape—then looked wherever he could for what he called "[e]xperiment." "Modern times," he offered, "afford three examples of leniency and humanity, which brilliantly adorn the page of history; viz: those of the empresses *Elizabeth* and *Catharine II*, of Russia, and Leopold, grand duke of Tuscany, who abolished the punishment of death in their respective dominions."

Proposing exile for life as an alternative to executions, Crockett predicted the death penalty's demise while proposing what he called his "project" to reform the nation's laws. Crockett's address confidently predicted that "if capital punishment be not abolished immediately, or within a few years," it would—should the American states "remain a republic"—be abolished "in less than fifty years." "In relation to the transportation of criminals," he mused, a "central" locale "fixed somewhere upon the Atlantic Ocean" might be chosen and inmates "might be sent to this place, from whence a vessel would carry them to their destination." After noting that "[i]t would be unjust to send our criminals into the dominions of another kingdom or state," thus necessitating the selection of "a place within our own jurisdiction," Crockett advised that "an insulated one would be preferable." After referencing a place known as "MADISON ISLAND" in the Pacific Ocean, Crockett offered this advice: "I would suggest, that all persons guilty of atrocious crimes, should be sent to this Botany Bay for life." During the War of 1812, Captain David Porter had, on America's behalf, occupied a Madison Island in the Pacific—an island also known as Nukuhiva or Sir Henry Martin's Island. The beautiful bay, where Captain Porter's ship, the *Essex*, anchored, was dubbed "Massachusetts Bay." Madison Island—the largest of the Marquesas Islands in what is known as French Polynesia—was later recommended for use as a naval and supply station.

Although Crockett noted the then-existing use of "penitentiaries," "work-houses," and "other houses or places for corrections," Crockett believed Congress should create "a national establishment" so that the "comparatively small" number of "vicious persons" would be "exiled to a great distance." As Crockett wrote of the heinous class of offenders he had in mind: "They should never be permitted to return to society, unless their innocence was made as clear as day; and none should be permitted to be accompanied by their companion, relations, or friends." "Their treatment during this wretched sequel of their lives," he further explained, "should depend, partly upon the crime of which they had been guilty, and partly upon their conduct during the same; but it should never fall short of that punishment which the crime had merited." Despite Crockett's call for a distant island— one far, far away—to house violent offenders, the idea, in Crockett's lifetime, would re- main a figment of his imagination. The McNeil Island prison—a territorial prison located in Washington's Puget Sound—did not open until 1875, and was not transferred to fed- eral control for use as a federal penitentiary until 1904. It was not until 1891, as part of Congress's Three Prisons Act, that the McNeil Island penitentiary and federal prisons in Atlanta, Georgia, and Leavenworth, Kansas, were authorized.

In the concluding paragraph of his 1823 pamphlet, Crockett—citing an earlier plea made by the anti-death penalty activist Edward Livingston—urged legislators to "look more to reason" and "utility" than to "example or the opinions of authors on the subject." "Rea- son alone, not precedent nor authority," should be their guide, Crockett said. "We are not entirely destitute of the authority of great names," Crockett emphasized, penning these words inspired by Livingston: "'A spirit of enlightened legislation' has manifested itself in the writings of 'Montesquieu, Beccaria, Eden, and a few others; names dear to humanity.'" Singling out Beccaria in particular, Crockett wrote: "Beccaria affords us high authority—indeed, we might leave that part of the subject of which he treats at issue be- tween him and its opposers." "I conclude this imperfect address, gentlemen," Crockett urged, "by expressing a hope, that it will meet with lieniency and forbearance at the hands of a liberal and magnanimous council, one in which I believe there is safety." As Crock- ett prayed: "I earnestly invoke the great Executive of the universe, to preside over your deliberations, and perpetuate the happiness of, not only the inhabitants of this great 'val- ley of the Mississippi' & the rest of United America, but of the world: and I declare that I have no interest to serve but the cause of humanity."[189]

The idea of establishing penal colonies—wherever they might be, and whoever might oversee them—was not a new one and occupied the thoughts of many early nineteenth- century reformers. For example, in 1816, one publication noted that "[t]he New-York State Prison, is overflowing with convicts." At that time, the prison had 722 inmates in a facility designed to hold 500. "The inspectors of the prison, in an address to the legisla- ture of New-York, after stating that the number of prisoners was so great as to render frequent *pardons indispensable*," the 1816 article continued, "request the legislature to rec- ommend to the general government, the establishment of a colony on the north-west coast of America, at or near Columbia River, or at Madison Island, to which convicts may be transported." "If the general government should object to this plan," the article added of the plan of reformers, "they recommend, that the New-York legislature establish such a colony, on the frontiers of the state." Having built penitentiaries, the issue of over- crowding—a natural consequence, potentially, of moving away from executions to lengthy terms of incarceration—thus reared its head, with prisons filling to capacity. In the mid- dle of the nineteenth century, 40 percent of releases from U.S. prisons were as a result of pardons.[190]

"The Spirit of the Age"

The difficulty of dealing with criminals—and the subject of how to treat them—was something that occupied and completely engaged intellectuals during the Enlightenment and thereafter. In the mid-nineteenth century, one English-speaking theologian and lecturer, Henry Rogers, even wrote two volumes of imaginary letters, one of which began by noting that the question of how to deal with criminals is "a puzzling one." "As to the plan of keeping them all in this country," he noted, "it is the very worst of all; at least, if the wretches are to be turned loose, after a term of imprisonment, on a dense population and an often glutted labour-market: this is simply the most comprehensive cruelty both to the innocent and the guilty." As Rogers wrote in his letter: "The difficulties of the question almost force one on one of two courses; either a return, under some modifications, to strictly penal settlements — a horrible alternative! — or (what, in some moods, I have thought the truest mercy, not only to society, but to criminals themselves) the plan of making all crimes of violence, — murder, highway robbery, burglary, arson, — inexpiable except by enslavement for *life*; the criminal to be employed all his days on public works, under a system of strict military law." "But it is a question of immense difficulty," Rogers opined, emphasizing: "I remember, some years ago, reading all that Bentham — all that Beccaria — all that others have said on the treatment of criminals, and thought it in-comparably the most perplexing problem in political science."[191]

Even after the Founding Fathers had all died, Beccaria's ideas on criminality thus still persisted in Europe — and in the American public's consciousness — as the ages-old de-bate over crime and punishment continued. For example, Francis Lieber — a Professor of History at South Carolina College — wrote a letter citing Beccaria, and using very Bec-carian language, that was published in 1838 by the Philadelphia Prison Society. In that letter, Lieber wrote of "the American penitentiary system," of "[d]isproportionate punishments" being "unjust," and of "cruelty," saying "I know of no other definition of cruelty than that it is the infliction of suffering for no end, or for a bad one." "Beccaria founding his argument against punishment of death on the theory of contract," Lieber wrote, "says that no man can be supposed to grant away conditionally his life, nor would it be lawful, because the right of life is inalienable." "Punishment ought to be calm in its character," Lieber argued, writing: "Strong governments, i.e. governments which have grown out of and provide faithfully for the true wants of the people, can afford to be mild. A mild punishment strikes deeper than a cruel one, for it carries the whole weight of public opinion and that of the offender himself along with it."

Lieber offered his opinions on a host of non-lethal corporal punishments, though he was reluctant to take a fully developed position on death itself, at least in his letter. "[W]hip-ping is, in my opinion," Lieber offered, "a bad punishment, not to be tolerated in a civi-lized community, which has the means of building prisons." "*Maiming*," he wrote, "is worse"; "[t]o cut the ears, split the nose, &c., are punishments which have come down to us from times when the effecting of bodily fear was the only object of punishment." "I do not wish to give here my opinion on capital punishment," Lieber added, clarifying in the short space of his letter: "not that I have not made up my mind with regard to it, or that I would hesitate one moment frankly to state my thoughts, but I should wish to give connectedly all my reasons on so grave a subject, on which many untenable arguments have been urged on both sides." "As to death with additional pains or inflammatory pro-cedures," Lieber emphasized, however, "it must be considered as entirely inadmissible." "How long is it," he wrote rhetorically, "since Beccaria and Howard dared to represent the criminal as an unfortunate man, who, though criminal, still remains a man, and to tell mankind that their penal codes and punishments were cruel and unwise?"[192]

In another letter on the penitentiary system, to South Carolina Governor Patrick Noble, Lieber looked back and simultaneously looked to the future, writing of how Americans had inherited "the English law" but that "neither the English Law, nor that of any nation, so long as that nation lives, is stationary and concluded." "The law," Lieber explained, "is a living thing; the daily and hourly application of principles to ever-changing circumstances, conditions, views and opinions." "One branch of the British law, which required great reform to suit it to the better knowledge and greater experience of mankind," he wrote, "was the penal law, of which the least praiseworthy part, or, to speak more plainly, the most objectionable, was the spirit, which had dictated the punishments for the various offenses." "Death, the '*ultimum supplicium,*' the last and extreme forfeiture, which can be demanded of man," Lieber advised of England's Bloody Code, "was gradually made to constitute the main and primary substance of the whole system of British punishment, so much so, that all the other punishments were called 'secondary,' as though the first punishment which naturally suggested itself to the penal legislator for any offence, was death, for which a minor evil would be *substituted* only upon very weighty additional considerations."[193] In other words, Lieber recognized that the law—though rooted in tradition—was bogged down in barbarity, was constantly evolving, and might and should change over time, particularly as a State itself grew more stable.

In his letter to South Carolina's governor, Lieber specifically wrote of Beccaria, Voltaire and Howard, echoing some of their ideas. "States having become larger, and governments stronger," Lieber noted, "they could afford adopting slower, as well as milder modes of punishment, less awful to the sight, in place of those which were rather founded upon quick revenge." As Lieber—later a legal advisor to President Abraham Lincoln—explained:

> Greater security produced a less sanguinary spirit in general; the age of philanthropy arose, and men like Voltaire—for whatever we may justly think of the tendency of many of his writings, we ought also to remember, how prominent and persevering an assailant of barbarous punishments, and of power persecuting innocence, he ever was, through his whole life—Beccaria and Howard appeared.

Among the "important truths" that Lieber—a man skeptical of, but not altogether opposed to, the death penalty—said had been "discovered, or more clearly and firmly established, in the course of penologic enquiries": "That it is not severity alone which gives efficacy to a punishment, but its certainty." "That punishment can be certain only, if it is, according to public feeling, and the spirit of the age, proportionate to the offence."[194] Both of those ideas—proportionality and certainty over severity—had come straight from *On Crimes and Punishments.* Elsewhere, Lieber also commented on Beccaria's idea of limiting death sentences to situations of anarchy or where the fall of a government might be at stake, along with exploration of possible alternatives to draconian sentences in the years to come.[195]

In the late nineteenth century, William Tallack—another penal reformer who served as the Secretary of the Howard Association in London from 1866 to 1901—called *On Crimes and Punishments* "[a] standard work." Tallack listed Beccaria's treatise among a group of 120 key books or pamphlets he had read on penal reform, telling a correspondent his list was not created "promiscuously" or in "hap-hazard" fashion. Tallack, who compiled a collection of John Howard's correspondence and who authored a book called *Friendly Sketches in America* (1861), called Beccaria "that excellent pioneer of penal reform." Those sketches, of the Society of Friends in America, were the result of Tallack's four-month trip through the United States in the summer of 1860, right before the onset of the Civil War. In 1871, Tallack published another book, *Humanity and Humanitarianism,* that discussed capital punishment and compared the U.S. and British prison systems. "[T]he retention of the capital punishment," Tallack reported in that book, had proven a "source of encouragement to crime" as executions "cannot be practically carried out in upwards of 90 per cent of cases." "Criminals take life almost with impunity," one jurist, Judge Brewster, had, in fact, said at the Philadelphia Quarter Sessions. The punishment for murder, Tallack emphasized, taking a stand in his own writing, "would be far more certain and easy of infliction if that penalty was altogether abrogated."[196]

That executions themselves came to be viewed as sanguinary is clear from Anglo-American letters and speeches of a now bygone era. An 1865 letter written by Dr. H. G. Lyford, a long-time medical officer of the Winchester County Gaol, conveyed the following sentiments to William Tallack:

> I beg to inform you that, having been attached to a large county prison throughout a very extended series of years, in which it was a part of my painful duties to witness on the scaffold all the executions, amounting to about forty in number, which took place during that time, affording me an almost unprecedented opportunity of making observations and reflections on this melancholy subject, I have often been desirous of reporting the result of my extended experiences to those philanthropic individuals who might feel interested in gaining every information on the effect of capital punishment, with the view of arriving at a legitimate conclusion as to the expediency of continuing or abandoning this mode of punishment.

Later reprinted in *The Scottish Law Magazine*, Dr. Lyford's letter concluded:

> Can we arrive, then, at any other conclusion but that public executions have entirely failed in accomplishing the special object for which they were instituted, and that they should therefore be at once discontinued? For under this sanguinary law doubtless murder has actually flourished.

In lieu of executions, Lyford suggested that convicted murders suffer "perpetual banishment, away from his fellow-man, in the very bowels of the earth, in the mines or in the coal fields."[197]

Such sentiments, in fact, are apparent across time, from the eighteenth century into the nineteenth century. For example, Sir William Meredith, in a speech to the House of Commons, also spoke of the sanguinary nature of executions. As Meredith told his legislative colleagues in 1777, in the very midst of the Revolutionary War:

> Whether hanging ever did, or can, answer any good purpose, I doubt: but the cruel exhibition of every execution day is a proof that hanging carries no terror with it. And I am confident that every new sanguinary law operates as an encouragement to commit capital offenses; for, it is not the mode, but the certainty of punishment, that creates terror. What men know they must endure, they fear; what they think they can escape, they despise. The multiplicity of our hanging laws has produced these two things: frequency of condemnation, and frequent pardons.

In New York, in the September 1, 1827 edition of *The Correspondent*, an article on the "*Execution of Strang*" likewise had this to say: "Atrocious as was the crime committed, I am confident that more than four fifths of the males, and all the females, had they been called on at the fatal moment to express their actual feelings, they would have declared against the execution, and in favor of a less sanguinary punishment."[198]

It was brutal, racial oppression and the scourge of slavery—other sanguinary practices not properly addressed in the Founding Fathers' time—that, in reality, led to the bloodbath of the Civil War. That war saw enormous casualties on American battlefields, but also numerous executions—especially for desertion—by both Union and Confederate forces. Prior to the Civil War, slaves were, in fact, frequently targeted for execution as a method of social control and to deter slave rebellions. When yet another war, the U.S.-Dakota War, broke out in August 1862 after Minnesota's Dakota Indians failed to receive promised annuity payments, angry white settlers—with their rage, this time, directed at Native

Americans—also demanded the death penalty. With fellow settlers having been killed in the conflict, a U.S. military commission sentenced to death more than 300 Indians who participated in what was then known as the Sioux Uprising. Ultimately, on the day after Christmas in 1862, 38 Indians were simultaneously hanged in Mankato, Minnesota, on Abraham Lincoln's orders, with Lincoln adamantly refusing to put to death more than that number. The vengeance and retaliation long associated with executions led to many of President Lincoln's most agonizing decisions. Although he detested killing and oftentimes commuted death sentences, Lincoln—if only reluctantly—also frequently followed his commanders' execution recommendations, especially to curb desertions. When Judge Advocate General Joseph Holt urged more executions, Lincoln at one point protested, "I don't think I can do it." "They say," Lincoln once remarked, "that I destroy discipline and am cruel to the Army when I will not let them shoot a soldier now and then. But I cannot see it. If God wanted me to see it, he would let me know it, and until he does, I shall go on pardoning and being cruel to the end." "Get out of the way," he told one friend as a Friday, the traditional day for executions, approached, "tomorrow is butcher day and I must go through these papers and see if I cannot find some excuse to let these poor men off."[199]

Chapter 6

An Enduring Legacy: Toward a More Perfect Union

The American Revolution: Tyranny to Liberty

In the eighteenth century, Beccaria's ideas on crime and punishment—and his view that citizens should not be subjected to torture or tyranny—became a major part of Anglo-American nomenclature. In 1779, for example, Beccaria's words got reprinted in a treatise on the elements of "Universal Law" by the English Whig barrister Capel Lofft (1751–1824). Lofft was a founding member of the Society for Constitutional Information, a British group started by Major John Cartwright (1740–1824) to promote parliamentary reform. Near the outset of the American Revolution, Cartwright, a pro-American agitator, wrote *American Independence, the Interest and Glory of Great-Britain* (1774). His Society for Constitutional Information sought, above all, to educate the public about the heritage of their political rights and liberties, with other members writing their own political pamphlets promoting American legislative autonomy.

Lofft's own name appears in a 1783 letter to Benjamin Franklin from the now little-remembered American-born sculptor Patience Wright (1725–1786), and Cartwright—an English naval officer who corresponded with Thomas Jefferson and James Madison—actively promoted universal suffrage while Americans fought for the right to govern themselves. In *The People's Barrier against Undue Influence and Corruption: or the Commons' House of Parliament According to the Constitution* (1780), Cartwright, sounding a familiar theme, wrote: "*Taxation* and *representation* ought undoubtedly to be inseparable; but then this is only *a branch* of the *general maxim*, only a *partial* application of the *universal principle*, which, considering *liberty* as the *end* of the social compact, decides, that '*law*, to bind all, must be assented to by ALL.'" In the preceding sentence, Cartwright had specifically invoked Cesare Beccaria's name, writing: "'*Commerce* and *property*,' says Beccaria, 'are not the *end* of the social compact, but the *means* of obtaining that end: so that, by making *representation* wholly dependent on *property*, we make,' according to him, 'the end subservient to the means.'"

Many colonists had spent time in England, and early Americans had sympathizers—even spies—in English society. Patience Wright, who became a Revolutionary War spy, was born into a Quaker family in New York, grew up in New York and New Jersey, then moved to Philadelphia at age sixteen. She became a gifted artist, specializing in wax portraits, and opened waxworks in Philadelphia and New York City before relocating to London. Benjamin Franklin—the globe-trotting renaissance man—was supportive of her work, and she sculpted George III and other British royals before she fell out of favor for her open support of the American cause. "It is said," one source reports, "that she passed communications to members of Congress, concealed in wax effigies she sent to America." The Society for Constitutional Information itself operated from 1780, during the Revolutionary War, to around 1795, a few years after the ratification of the U.S. Bill of Rights.

That society's membership included English radicals such as John Jebb, Thomas Brand Hollis, and Dr. Richard Price, with the society mentioned in a 1793 letter from Alexander Hamilton to George Washington.

Another of the society's members, Granville Sharp, while urging Americans to remain loyal to the Crown, favored some colonial autonomy in his *Declaration of the People's Natural Right to a Share in the Legislature.* Calling "*[f]orfeiture of life*, by hanging, too severe for the generality of the crimes now deemed *capital*," Granville—an early opponent of the slave trade—took note of the fact that "15 men" were "hanged up together upon one gallows at Newgate the very last execution-day!!!" Fellow anti-slavery activist William Wilberforce, in a letter to Christopher Wyvill, also expressed his own views on penal reform, writing: "The barbarous custom of hanging has been tried too long." "The most effective way to prevent greater crimes," he added, "is by punishing the smaller, and by endeavouring to repress that general spirit of licentiousness, which is the parent of every species of vice." Having visited Newgate Prison and joined in a British parliamentary campaign to restrict the death penalty's use, Wilberforce and his allies gathered support where they could find it. The Duke of Manchester, for example, offered these words of encouragement: "if you and other young men who are rising in the political sphere would undertake the arduous task of revising our code of criminal law ... I mean largely the number of capital punishments, I am satisfied it would go far towards bettering the people of this country."

While Beccaria's treatise became known as "the code of humanity," it was also seen as a major work of political philosophy that ranked among the greats of that era. In *A Plan of Lectures on the Principles of Nonconformity*, published in 1779, the English Dissenter and influential Baptist minister Robert Robinson, in a section titled "POLITICAL SENTIMENTS," put it this way: "MODERN nonconformity naturally leads us to study government.—SIDNEY—LOCKE—MONTESQUIEU—BECCARIA—teach the notions—WHICH we hold—of government—ALL think *the people* the origin of power—ADMINISTRATORS responsible trustees—AND the enjoyment of life—LIBERTY—and property—the right of all mankind—EXCEPT of those, whose crimes are allowed by the constitution to have disfranchised them."[1]

Beccaria's own ideas, as expressed in *On Crimes and Punishments*, not only deeply affected reform-minded Englishmen, but they stirred American revolutionaries to action even as they provided a valuable roadmap for how to frame American constitutions. Beccaria's treatise had spoken of how "natural law" was among the "moral and political principles that govern men," and Beccaria—in a chapter on "The Obscurity of the Laws"—had urged that laws be clear and in writing. "[W]ithout writing," Beccaria emphasized, "a society will never achieve a fixed form of government in which power is a product of the whole rather than the parts, and in which laws—unalterable except by the general will—are not corrupted as they wade through the throng of private interests." "If there is no stable monument to the social pact," Beccaria observed, "how will the laws withstand the inevitable onslaught of time and passions?"

For Beccaria, it was critically important to codify the laws and not rely on the whim of discretion-wielding judges. "The greater number of those who have access to and can understand the sacred code of laws," Beccaria advised, "the fewer crimes there will be, for there is no doubt that ignorance and uncertainty regarding the punishments abet the persuasive power of the passions." "[I]f the magistrate acts according to arbitrary laws that are not established by a code that circulates among all the citizens," Beccaria added, "then the door is open to tyranny, which always lies just beyond the boundaries of political liberty." "We see," Beccaria concluded, "how useful the printing press is, for it makes the public, not just a few individuals, the depositary of the sacred laws." By penning written constitutions and gradually moving away from common-law crimes to codified penal codes, early Americans had essentially taken Beccaria's advice.[2]

The idea of "Equal Justice Under Law"—the phrase engraved on the front of the U.S. Supreme Court building—has become part of the American creed, especially since the ratification of the post-Civil War Fourteenth Amendment. Alberto Burgio, who teaches the history of philosophy at the University of Bologna, has—in commenting on the equality principle—written of the idea of equality that, in fact, infuses Beccaria's treatise. "*On Crimes and Punishments* is, above all," he writes, "a book of political struggle and, on a strictly theoretical level, a work of political philosophy." As Burgio explains: "Beccaria's *garantismo*—his commitment to defending legal guarantees for citizen and 'criminal' alike—is never separated from a broader discourse on society, from a critique of the existing social structures, or from a concerted effort to construct a better political order." Traditionally, "Beccaria's masterpiece," Burgio notes of the Italian treatise and its particular emphasis on crimes and punishments, "has been read primarily, if not exclusively, as a classical text of *garantismo* in criminal law, a theory that attributes great importance to the legal and civil guarantees of individuals."

The American Revolution itself drew much inspiration from the Italian Enlightenment. In line with other Italian philosophers such as Alfonso Longo and Pietro Verri, Beccaria saw the "public good" as that which offered "the greatest sum of pleasures shared equally by the greatest number of men," with Beccaria—in his *Elementi di economia pubblica*—defining the sovereign as the "just and equitable distributor of public happiness." Longo himself wrote that the "public good" consists of the "greatest happiness possible achieved by means of the greatest equality possible," while Verri, in *Meditazioni sulla felicità* (1763) described "[t]he goal of the social pact" as "the well-being of each individual ... by means of the greatest equality possible." "Everything in Europe," Beccaria himself wrote in *Il Caffè*, at a time when titles of nobility were still prevalent, "is getting closer and becoming more similar," with there being "a stronger impulse towards equality that did not obtain in the past."[3]

The U.S. Bill of Rights, grounded in the idea of natural rights while putting to parchment, in a *written* social compact, certain key rights, closely tracks Beccaria's conception of good government, at least in broad, if not fine, brush. While America's founders looked to Montesquieu and Beccaria's ideas on how to constrain tyranny, Beccaria's own worldview of the rights of individuals had been informed by his personal travails, especially the rift with his father over his desire to marry the woman of his choice. If a society is "considered a union of families" instead of "a union of individuals," Beccaria wrote in *On Crimes and Punishments*, then—assuming "one hundred thousand people, divided into twenty thousand families, each composed of five persons, including the head of the family who represents it"—there will be "twenty thousand men and eighty thousand slaves." In that case, Beccaria contended, children "are subject to the whim of their fathers" and "the monarchic spirit will gradually permeate the republic itself, and its effects will be checked only by the conflict of individual interests, not by any feeling animated by liberty and equality." "In contrast, Beccaria wrote, "if the association is considered as consisting of individuals, then there will be a hundred thousand citizens and not a single slave." With no slaves in the republic "made up of individuals," Beccaria asserted, "the republican spirit will breathe not only in the public squares and assemblies of the nation, but also within the walls of the home, where much of man's happiness or misery is to be found."[4]

In setting up America's republic, which began with the Declaration of Independence and its focus on the right to life, liberty and the pursuit of happiness, the Founding Fathers were acutely aware of the Roman republic that preceded theirs. They studied Latin in grammar schools, and they had an easy familiarity with Roman authors and antiquity. In fact, America's founders were well versed in Roman history and shared, through their schooling as boys and their reading as adults, an abiding interest in, and a working knowledge of, Italy and its struggles and laws. For example, in a 1777 letter to Nathanael Greene, John Adams discussed "the civil Wars in Rome, in the time of Sylla," paraphrasing an account in Abbé René Aubert de Vertot's *The History of the Revolutions that Happened in the Government of the Roman Republic* (1732). In August 1779, Adams also commented candidly on "Italy," "[t]he Court of Rome," and "[t]he Priviledges of the Port of Leghorn" in a letter to the President of Congress. To his own son, John Quincy Adams, John Adams— writing from Amsterdam, and using the salutation "My dear Son"—emphasized: "You go on, I presume, with your latin Exercises: and I wish to hear of your beginning upon Sallust who is one of the most polished and perfect of the Roman Historians." "In Company with Sallust, Cicero, Tacitus and Livy, you will learn Wisdom and Virtue," Adams explained to his son.

For the founders, the glory of Rome was something they sought to emulate. When the American physician, Dr. Joseph Warren, delivered a speech at Boston's Old South Church in March 1775 to commemorate the fifth anniversary of the Boston Massacre, he even reportedly wore a toga, the wrap-around cloth, consisting of a single piece of material, that freeborn Roman male citizens wore in times of peace. The president of the revolutionary Massachusetts Provincial Congress, and appointed as a major general later that year, Dr. Warren had—while at college at Harvard—actually produced and directed in his dorm suite Addison's *Cato*, a tragic drama about the virtuous Cato who opposed Julius Caesar's despotism. That same play would inspire George Washington, who had it performed to boost morale at Valley Forge, and gave solace to Nathan Hale, the American spy who, as he faced his own execution, paraphrased Addison's words: "What pity it is that we can die but once to serve our country!"

In his March 1775 speech, delivered just months before he would be killed in action at Bunker Hill, Dr. Warren, in fact, invoked "a maxim of the Roman people"—"never to despair of the commonwealth"—then thundered: "But should America, either by force, or those more dangerous engines, luxury and corruption, ever be brought into a state of vassalage, Britain must lose her freedom also." In addressing his "fellow-citizens," Dr. Warren presciently cautioned: "You will maintain your rights, or perish in the generous struggle." Although American colonists ended up fighting for their freedom, what they sought initially was just treatment under British law. "An independence of Great Britain is not our aim," Warren advised in his March 1775 speech, saying "freedom is the prize" before proclaiming:

> No, our wish is that Britain and the colonies may, like the oak and ivy, grow and increase in strength together. But whilst the infatuated plan of making one part of the empire slaves to the other is persisted in, the interests and safety of Britain, as well as the colonies, require that the wise measures, recommended by the honorable the Continental Congress, be steadily pursued; whereby the unnatural contest between a parent honored and a child beloved may probably be brought to such an issue, as that the peace and happiness of both may be established upon a lasting basis. But if these pacific measures are ineffectual, and it appears that the only way to safety is through fields of blood, I know you will not turn your faces from your foes, but will undauntedly press forward, until tyranny is trodden under foot, and you have fixed your adored goddess Liberty on the American throne.

The role of Italian history and ideas on the American polity is clear from the books America's founders read. In 1783, when James Madison recommended books for the use of Congress, he specifically included on his list Vertot's history of Rome, as well as Louis Cousin's *Histoire Romaine*, Oliver Goldsmith's *The Roman History*, Nathaniel Hooke's *The Roman History*, Basil Kennett's *The Antiquities of Rome*, and Edward Gibbon's *The His-*

tory of the Decline and Fall of the Roman Empire. In addition, Madison recommended "Best latin Dictionary with best grammar & dictionary of each of the modern languages," a recommendation that would then have included David Francesco Lates' *A New Method of Easily Attaining the Italian Tongue* and Giuseppe Marc'Antonio Baretti's *A Dictionary of the English and Italian Languages.* Also on Madison's list: "Beccaria's works" and various books on the civil law. Among others: Francesco Guicciardini's *The History of Italy*, Pietro Giannone's *The Civil History of the Kingdom of Naples,* Paolo Sarpi's *The Maxims of the Government of Venice,* and Giovanni Battista Felice Gasparo Nani's *Histoire de la République de Venice.*

The American Revolution, like the Italian Enlightenment, was aimed at civic engagement and the dissemination of knowledge. In the late 1770s, Thomas Jefferson himself drafted "A Bill for the More General Diffusion of Knowledge," which James Madison later attempted to convince Virginia's legislature to pass. That bill began: "Whereas it appeareth that however certain forms of government are better calculated than others to protect individuals in the free exercise of their natural rights, and are at the same time themselves better guarded against degeneracy, yet experience hath shewn, that even under the best forms, those entrusted with power have, in time, and by slow operations, perverted it into tyranny." With the bill's first whereas clause expressing the view "that the most effectual means of preventing this would be, to illuminate, as far as practicable, the minds of the people at large," the bill itself sought the building of schoolhouses and made the following proposal for grammar schools: "At every of these schools shall be taught reading, writing, and common arithmetick, and the books which shall be used therein for instructing the children to read shall be such as will at the same time make them acquainted with Græcian, Roman, English, and American history." The bill's second whereas clause then struck a decidedly Beccarian chord, beginning:

> And whereas it is generally true that that people will be happiest whose laws are best, and are best administered, and that laws will be wisely formed, and honestly administered, in proportion as those who form and administer them are wise and honest; whence it becomes expedient for promoting the publick happiness that those persons, whom nature hath endowed with genius and virtue, should be rendered by liberal education worthy to receive, and able to guard the sacred deposit of the rights and liberties of their fellow citizens, and that they should be called to that charge without regard to wealth, birth or other accidental condition or circumstance.[5]

Although early American schoolchildren got lessons in Greek and Roman history, educated adults at that time knew much of that history by heart. "The basic story of the Roman republic," explains Professor Tim Sellers, an Enlightenment expert, "would have been well-known to any American political thinker." As Sellers explains of Rome's then well-known history:

> Romulus founded Rome with his brother Remus, made himself king, ruled by established (but unpublished) laws, and created a senate to advise him. The Roman *res publica* or "republic" began when the Roman people ousted Romulus's successor Tarquin, and replaced him with two annually elected consuls.

In America, the Framers of the Constitution decided to establish two legislative chambers: the U.S. House of Representatives and the U.S. Senate, the latter to, among other things, provide "advice and consent" on executive appointments and to ratify treaties. As Professor Sellers, providing the historical background of Rome, further explains: "The consuls ruled in the name of the 'senate and people of Rome', and were soon subjected to a written law code. The senate proposed all statutes, and the people enacted them, voting in carefully controlled popular assemblies." "This," Sellers observes in his book, *American Republicanism: Roman Ideology in the United States Constitution*, "was America's conception of the Roman constitution at what Americans would have considered the height of Rome's glory, power and virtue." Pseudonyms employed by early Americans, he writes, also reflected Rome's republican sensibility, with pen names like "Americanus", "Civis", "A Countryman" and "Philadelphiensis" all evoking—in Seller's words—"the same affection for Rome's citizen-farmers, who left their fields to vote and defend their liberty and country, but retained the simple virtues of the soil."

The collapse of the Roman republic, as well as the fall of England's commonwealth, a subsequent republican experiment, served as dire warnings of what could happen when power was abused. But the Roman and English precedents clearly inspired America's founders in the lead up to the Constitutional Convention in Philadelphia. That history gave early American lawmakers the idea for the U.S. Senate, often called the world's greatest deliberative body, to be balanced by an elected chief magistrate—the President of the United States—and by the U.S. House of Representatives, popularly known as "the people's house." To understand American republicanism, Professor Sellers sagely explains in his book, one must read Roman history and "the Roman authors and statesmen Americans explicitly appropriated in their pamphlets and pseudonyms" along with the European writers who had interpreted Rome's past. "Of the pseudonyms Americans adopted from historical figures," Sellers explains, "about half, including the most important ones, belonged to republican Roman heroes, such as 'Publius', 'Brutus' and 'Cato.'" For example, "'Lucius' and 'Cincinnatus'," Sellers writes, "referred to Lucius Quinctius Cincinnatus, who left his simple farm to save the republic, then returned to the plough." Other names, Sellers points out, belonged to English Commonwealth heroes and Greeks such as "Solon" and "Lycurgus."

Even the way American revolutionaries chose to honor and remember their comrades speaks volumes. In 1783, the year America's Revolutionary War ended, Continental Army officers specifically chose to honor the fifth century B.C. Roman military hero Lucius Quinctius Cincinnatus. The Society of the Cincinnati, formed by American and French Revolutionary War officers as the war drew to a close, sought to promote the ideals of the American Revolution, to maintain soldiers' fraternal bonds, and to create a fund for the relief of any indigent members. For its first president, the Society of the Cincinnati—not surprisingly—chose none other than George Washington, the American military hero who would return to his own farm at Mount Vernon after the war's conclusion. As one source, published by the Mount Vernon Ladies' Association, notes: "George Washington approved of the Society of the Cincinnati, and, like the Roman general to whom he was being compared, his thoughts focused on a return to the land." In his own resignation speech—delivered in Annapolis, Maryland, on December 23, 1783, Washington thus announced his intention to "take my leave of all the employments of public life" even as he expressed his happiness "in the confirmation of our independence and sovereignty."[6]

In the founders' time, America—under Beccaria's watchful eye—became a refuge for the dispossessed and from tyranny and oppression. In a chapter of *Miscellaneous Trifles in Prose* titled "Thoughts on the Policy of Encouraging Migration," the American publisher and immigrant Mathew Carey—in words printed in Philadelphia in 1796—specifically invoked Beccaria's name alongside that of Washington in writing of liberty itself. "Nine-tenths of the first settlers of North-America" and all of the "emigrants who have arrived since," he explained, were "*subjects of monarchies.*" "To pass from this western hemisphere, let us touch upon the bright constellation of worthies who grace the annals of liberty in the old world," Carey added, urging his readers:

> Let us contemplate and emulate the virtues of Brutus, the scourge of the Tar-
> quins; Tell, the deliverer of Switzerland; Doria, the deliverer of Genoa; Gustavas
> Vasa, the deliverer of Sweden; Paoli, the hero of Corsica; Hambden, Sidney,
> Price, Montesquieu, Raynal, Beccaria, and thousands of others, whose bosoms
> have been warmed with as pure and hallowed a spirit of liberty, benevolence,
> and philanthropy, as ever animated the most zealous republican.

After making his list of worthies, of champions of liberty, Carey added: "These have been
the '*subjects of monarchies*,' or (still worse) archducal, ducal, or aristocratical tyrannies. Yet
who is there in '*these republics*' that would not esteem it the summit of his ambition to
merit and attain the reputation they have justly acquired?"

In arguing that welcoming migration to America brought tremendous benefits, Carey
pointed to specific groups of immigrants who had already come to America's shores.
"Those Germans to whom Pennsylvania owes so much with respect to agriculture, improvements, industry, and opulence," he wrote, "were transplanted from the most despotic
soils." Yet, Carey added: "Here they became meliorated, and have furnished some of the
most active and zealous friends and supporters of America's independence." "The same,"
he emphasized, "will hold equally true of those numerous swarms of Irishmen, who both
before and during the arduous struggle, came into this country." "Their valour and conduct were displayed by sea and land—and history will bear the most honourable testimony of their heroism," Carey said of the Irish immigrants. Carey's advice:

> [S]hould the *new comer* be found to possess those qualities in a higher degree,
> let him not be exposed to neglect, abuse, or scurrility, merely because, actuated
> by a love of liberty, he has given this country a preference to his own, and aban-
> doned his friends and relatives to coalesce with the inhabitants of America, who,
> as general Washington declares in his farewel[l] address, "HAVE OPENED AN ASY-
> LUM FOR THE OPPRESSED AND DISTRESSED OF ALL NATIONS."[7]

In George Washington's now-famous farewell address, which first appeared in Philadelphia's *Daily American Advertiser* in September 1796 as Washington was preparing to step
off the public stage, he declined to seek a third term in office. Speaking of "republican liberty," Washington—appealing to "Heaven"—expressed his hope that "your union and brotherly affection may be perpetual; that the free constitution, which is the work of your
hands, may be sacredly maintained; that its administration in every department may be
stamped with wisdom and virtue; that, in fine, the happiness of the people of these states,
under the auspices of liberty, may be made complete by so careful a preservation and so
prudent a use of this blessing as will acquire to them the glory of recommending it to the
applause, the affection, and adoption of every nation which is yet a stranger to it." In
Washington's address, which has, since 1893, been read each year in the U.S. Senate on
Washington's birthday by members of different political parties, Washington—warning
against the development of factions, as had Beccaria—observed that "a government for
the whole is indispensable" to "the efficacy and permanency of your Union." Urging respect for the national government's authority and compliance with its laws, Washington
emphasized:

> The basis of our political systems is the right of the people to make and to alter
> their constitutions of government. But the Constitution which at any time ex-
> ists, until changed by an explicit and authentic act of the whole people, is sa-
> credly obligatory upon all. The very idea of the power and the right of the people
> to establish government presupposes the duty of every individual to obey the
> established government.

As Washington further emphasized:

> The necessity of reciprocal checks in the exercise of political power, by dividing and distributing it into different depositories and constituting each the guardian of the public weal against invasions by the others, has been evinced by experiments ancient and modern, some of them in our country and under our own eyes. To preserve them must be as necessary as to institute them. If in the opinion of the people the distribution or modification of the constitutional powers be in any particular wrong, let it be corrected by an amendment in the way which the Constitution designates.[8]

After Washington refused to seek a third term, one writer, Richard Dinmore, saluted "Washington, Hancock, and those immortal patriots, who bravely fought, and nobly bled, for the best blessings of humanity,—liberty." In praising George Washington, Dinmore observed that "Washington disdained prudence, repelled tyranny, secured the happiness of his country, and opened an asylum for wretched Europeans; where honest industry, untaxed, untythed; where fair ability, unoppressed, may secure to themselves the necessaries and comforts of life." In his political pamphlet, titled *An Exposition of the Principles of the English Jacobins*, Dinmore specifically credited Beccaria—along with Adam Smith, the author of *The Wealth of Nations*—for laying down the principles of freedom. As Dinmore wrote:

> By some, Adam Smith has been called the high priest of democracy; if it admits of a priesthood, Beccaria has a claim to its highest honours; he dedicated his labours to the preservation of the lives of men; he proved that even convicts might become useful members of society; and America, ever first in the practice of just principles, free America begins to adopt his maxims.

Before offering up that assessment, Dinmore spoke of poverty as a crime and called codes imprisoning honest debtors "Cruel and barbarous laws!" "Blush, my friend, for sanguinary Britain," Dinmore continued, "when you consider the number of her sons whom she annually consigns to the gallows."[9] Another writer, in 1797, also lauded the "Marquis of Beccaria," saying he had displayed "the heart of a Divinity." That author, Sir Samuel Egerton Leigh, added that "a more glorious spirit never illumed the regions of this globe."[10]

From Barbarism to Reason

The Founding Fathers lived during a time of harsh corporal punishments and in which torturous practices—and especially gruesome methods of executions—were still regularly used and permitted by law. When Paul Revere made his famous midnight ride to Lexington, one of the spectacles he reflexively took note of after passing Charlestown Neck was the place "where Mark was hung in chains." That was a reference to the familiar sight of the decomposed body of a slave named Mark who, after taking part in a plot to poison his master, was hanged in Charlestown Common. After his execution, Mark's body was then displayed for twenty years in a rusty cage, his black, rotting body shriveling up into a grotesque mummy.[11] In the eighteenth century, gibbeting, the public display of offenders' bodies or heads, as well as the public dissection of murderers' dead bodies, were still in use, as were other horrific punishments such as castration, cutting off the tongue, and nose-slitting. Before becoming President of the United States in 1829, Andrew Jackson (1767–1845) had been a U.S. Senator and served on Tennessee's highest court, the Superior Court of Law and Equity. In the latter role, Jackson—as one source puts it—"regularly joined in rendering the corporal and capital punishments characteristic of the age" and "imposed the death penalty on at least ten occasions." In American society, especially in the South, slaves in particular were often the recipients of such brutality.[12]

In civil law countries such as France and Spain, the use of judicial torture also persisted into the time of America's founding generation. In 1612, the Italian jurist Sebastian Guazzini—living in that civil law locale, where torture was used to extract confessions—called *torture* "the distress of body devised for exacting truth." "The mode of administering torture by the use of the rope," he wrote in defending the practice, "was justly invented by the Civil Law, as a mode of discovering truth, for the sake of the public welfare, to the end that crimes might not remain unpunished." "It is," Guazzini emphasized, calling torture *the queen of torment*, "always a subsidiary remedy, to be invoked only when truth cannot be discovered in any other way," for example, through the use of witnesses. In an admiralty case in 1769, John Adams himself acknowledged that torture was part of the fabric of law in many places, writing that the "Nature" of "the civil Laws" is "that before any Judgment of Death can be given against the offenders, either they must plainly *confess their offences*, (which they will never do, without Torture or Pains) or else their offences be so plainly and directly proved by Witness indifferent, such as saw their offences committed."[13]

During the Enlightenment, intellectuals began to question both the necessity and morality of such practices, with one sermon delivered in 1777 in Oxford, England—and printed at the request of English judges—emphasizing Beccaria's condemnation of the practice. "[I]t seems the duty of a happy people," the preacher James Chelsum said in his sermon titled *The Character of the Laws of England Considered*, "to contrast at all times the mildness of public punishments in this country, with the sanguinary spirit of those of neighbouring nations." As Chelsum, one of "his MAJESTY's Preachers at Whitehall," explained, citing Beccaria's "humanity" and referring to "the admirable author" of *On Crimes and Punishments* in this footnote to his published sermon:

> Look round then and behold the bloody hand of torture lifted up in other countries against the unhappy prisoner, not only as the instrument of his death, but as the instrument even of his trial; behold him condemned to the severest punishment even before conviction: behold that arbitrary and unjust mode of inquiry adopted, which has often made the innocent, in the agonies of suffering, declare himself guilty.[14]

Another sermon, "intended to have been preached in the Chapel Royal at St. James, but omitted on account of the absence of the Court during the author's month of waiting," also referenced Beccaria's treatise. That sermon, written by William Dodd—the King's chaplain—was printed in Dublin in 1777 and titled *The Frequency of Capital Punishments Inconsistent with Justice, Sound Policy, and Religion*. Dodd's sermon began by highlighting one of the Ten Commandants: "Thou Shalt Not Kill." It then noted, in a reference to Beccaria, that "[a]n able and illustrious foreigner, whose work breathes the true spirit of humanity and freedom, hath urged a variety of argument on the Topick, well known, I persuade myself, to this audience, and therefore the less necessary to be insisted on at present."[15] In Dodd's sermon, later published in London, Dodd quoted Beccaria's *On Crimes and Punishments*, then noted that "[i]t would be easy, if a complete discussion of this subject was intended, to shew at large the *injustice* of those laws which demand *blood* for the slightest offences."[16]

A number of Enlightenment figures, including Beccaria, opposed torture, but executions and devices from the Dark Ages like the rack and the thumbscrew were commonplace throughout Europe in the 1700s.[17] And in an era in which ear cropping, hangings and hand brandings, as well as the use of the stocks and the pillory, still prevailed, the novelty of Beccaria's views were not lost on him. Indeed, Beccaria began his treatise with a quote from Renaissance philosopher and English statesman Francis Bacon: "In all negociations of difficulty, a man may not look to sow and reap at once, but must prepare business, and so ripen it by degrees."[18] An English lawyer and politician, Bacon had studied law at Gray's Inn, to which he was admitted in 1576, and later served as a minister for Elizabeth I and James I; in 1605, many years before running into trouble with the House of Lords and being imprisoned for a time, Bacon had published his own treatise, *The Advancement of Learning*.[19] Beccaria—who knew well the effects of ignorance, blind adherence to custom, and the sentiments of the general public of his own time—understood all too well that change would come slowly and would meet with much resistance. The history of Rome, in fact, was full of cruel traditions and punishments. The Coliseum in Rome, which gets its name from its colossal size, was originally known as the "Amphitheatre of Titus." It was the emperor's property—a place where slaves were taken to die, where criminals were executed, and where gladiators fought to the death and for their own lives, often against wild beasts.[20]

When Beccaria's treatise found its way to America's shores, a receptive audience—feeling oppressed by the British monarchy—was eagerly waiting to receive it, impressed by its appeal to reason and humanity. In *Letters from Washington, on the Constitution, Laws and Public Characters of the United States*, written "By a Foreigner" but attributed to George Watterston, Beccaria's name is specifically mentioned. In one 1818 letter, the letter writer explicitly described American laws in Beccarian terms as "uniform and equal; not enacted for the benefit of the few and the oppression of the many." "The Constitution of this country," that letter continued, "is, I believe, universally acknowledged to be the production of human intellect, aided, perhaps, by divine inspiration." "It is," the letter writer emphasized, speaking of "the entire democratic tendency" of the U.S. Constitution, "the only constitution, literally speaking, in the world; for by a constitution I mean an original written compact, entered into by the members of society, in which a distinct and specific form of government is delineated and established." As the 1818 letter, which also cited the Declaration of Independence, Rousseau, Montesquieu, Blackstone, de Lolme and other authorities, observed:

> The constitution has been founded on the theory, that all power necessarily eminates from the people, and from long and serious reflection, I cannot but yield my assent to the correctness and reasonableness of this theory. History manifests the impolicy of taking power from the people, and condensing and accumulating it into one mass, and thus yielding up to one man or body of men, the right of regulating their political concerns. It will be found, as Beccaria very justly observes, that "in every society there is an effort continually tending to confer on *one part* the height of power and happiness, and to reduce the other to the extremes of weakness and misery; the intent of good laws is to oppose this effort, and diffuse their influence universally and equally.["] Acting on this principle, the American constitution has therefore, so circumscribed the executive authority, and so equally extended the power to the other co-ordinate branches of government, that the people are in no danger of being shackled by the trammels of despotism, or of loosing their iutrinsic [sic] and unalienable rights.

Watterston, a Federalist and the editor of *The Washington City Gazette*, was appointed to the prestigious position of Librarian of Congress in 1815 by President James Madison after dedicating a poem to Dolley Madison. It was Watterston—the third Librarian of Congress—who, utilizing Jefferson's books, had to rebuild and reorganize the library after the British burned the nation's capitol and destroyed the original library in 1814. Among the books that Watterston would catalog in that collection: Beccaria's *On Crimes and Punish-*

ments. In another 1818 letter printed in *Letters from Washington*, Watterston's book spoke of judicial independence—another cornerstone of American law—as follows:

> The independence of the Judiciary is essential to the perfection of the American government, and equally necessary with representation to the security of the people's rights. Were this branch not independent, the consequences might be such as to excite the most serious alarm, and to render the constitution a mere instrument of tyranny; it is this department literally that carries the laws which the legislative authority has enacted, into operation—those laws I mean, which concern the interests of individuals, and are of the highest importance to the peace and happiness of society.

"The judiciary," that letter continued, "stands as a check to the march of legislative omnipotence, and keeps that branch of the government within the bounds of the constitution. Should congress pass a law inconsistent with the spirit of this instrument, the judiciary interposes its authority, and sets it aside."[21] This power of judicial review, articulated by the U.S. Supreme Court in its now legendary decision of *Marbury v. Madison* (1803), has been part of the bedrock of American law since the time of Chief Justice John Marshall's ruling in that landmark case.[22]

Abuse of power of the sort Montesquieu and Beccaria warned against was a common theme in the writings of America's founders. For example, in *A Dissertation on the Canon and the Feudal Law*, published in 1765, John Adams had written disdainfully of "arbitrary government" and "cruel tyranny," and of the "oppression" exercised by kings and "*absolute monarchy.*" Calling "the *canon* and *feudal* law" the "greatest systems of tyranny," Adams equated those laws with "*ecclesiastical* and *civil* tyranny." "From the time of the reformation, to the first settlement of *America*," Adams wrote, "knowledge gradually spread in Europe, but especially in *England*; and in proportion as *that* increased and spread among the people, *ecclesiastical* and *civil* tyranny … seem to have lost their strength and weight." "The people," Adams emphasized, "grew more and more sensible of the wrong that was done them, by these systems; more and more impatient under it; and determined at all hazards to rid themselves of it; till, at last, under the *execrable* race of the *Steurarts*, the struggle between the people and the confederacy aforesaid of temporal and spiritual tyranny, become formidable, violent and bloody."

"It was this great struggle, that peopled America," Adams indicated, adding that the Puritans had become "learned" and that "[t]his people had been so vexed, and tortured by the powers of those days, for no other crime than their knowledge, and their freedom of enquiry and examination," that they emigrated to the New World. After the Puritans' arrival on American soil, Adams wrote, they built their settlements and "formed their plan both of ecclesiastical and civil government, in *direct opposition* to the *canon* and the *feudal* systems." Adams further noted that "the first Planters of these Colonies" had been persecuted, sometimes facing death sentences and tortures. As Adams wrote: "Tyranny in every form, shape, and appearance was their disdain, and abhorrence; no fear of punishment, not even of *Death* itself, in exquisite tortures, had been sufficient to conquer, that steady, manly, pertenacious spirit, with which they had opposed the tyrants of those days, in church and state."

In *On Crimes and Punishments*, Beccaria himself warned of persecuted sects degenerating into factions, offering this advice: "If you wish to prevent a sect from toppling the state, use tolerance; and imitate the wise conduct followed today by Germany, England, and Holland." As Beccaria explained: "With regard to a new sect, the only choice to make in politics is to put to death, without mercy, the leaders and their followers—men, women, and children, without exception—or to tolerate them when the sect is large. The first approach is that of a monster, the second of a wise man." Elsewhere, Beccaria emphasized the importance of everyone's "point of view" and "opinion"—the right to express oneself without fear of adverse consequences. "The true tyrant," Beccaria wrote, "always begins by controlling opinion, thereby forestalling the courage that can only shine in the clear light of truth, in the heat of passions, or in ignorance of danger." "No law," he added, "should be promulgated that cannot be enforced or that is rendered ineffectual by the nature of the circumstances." In the introductory section of *On Crimes and Punishments*, titled "To the Reader," it was specifically contended that the book's purpose was to strengthen "legitimate authority" and that those who might "wish" to "honour" Beccaria with "criticisms" should remember that "opinion in men is more powerful than force."

The U.S. Constitution's First Amendment, reflective of Beccaria's anti-tyrannical impulses, set out important protections that have been serving America well ever since. As the First Amendment reads:

> Congress shall make no law respecting an establishment of religion, or prohibiting the free exercise thereof; or abridging the freedom of speech, or of the press; or the right of the people peaceably to assemble, and to petition the government for a redress of grievances.

By protecting speech, protest, religious freedom, the rights of the press, and the people's rights to assemble and petition the government, ideas and information have flown freely, leading to accountability and innovation, scientific advance, and—ultimately—economic prosperity, one of economist Beccaria's other premier concerns. As James Madison himself once emphasized of the importance of people's rights: "A popular Government, without popular information, or the means of acquiring it, is but a Prologue to a Farce or a Tragedy; or perhaps both. Knowledge will forever ignorance: And a people who mean to be their own Governors, must arm themselves with the power which knowledge gives."

In line with Beccaria and Voltaire's specific advocacy for religious freedom, the First Amendment—through its language—also specifically ensured that there would be no official state religion. As Thomas Jefferson—the author of Virginia's earlier "Bill for Establishing Religious Freedom"—wrote to the Danbury Baptist Association in 1802, offering his own take on that amendment: "Believing with you that religion is a matter which lies solely between Man & his God, that he owes account to none other for his faith or his worship, that the legitimate powers of government reach actions only, & not opinions, I contemplate with sovereign reverence that act of the whole American people which declared that *their* legislature should 'make no law respecting an establishment of religion, or prohibiting the free exercise thereof,' thus building a wall of separation between Church & State."[23] The Virginia Act for Establishing Religious Freedom, drafted by Jefferson in 1779, but not passed by the Virginia legislature until 1786, spoke of freedom of worship and the "natural right" of every citizen, emphasizing: "though we well know this Assembly, elected by the people for the ordinary purposes of legislation only, have no powers equal to our own and that therefore to declare this act irrevocable would be of no effect in law, yet we are free to declare, and do declare, that the rights hereby asserted are of the natural rights of mankind, and that if any act shall be hereafter passed to repeal the present or to narrow its operation, such act will be an infringement of natural right."[24]

Although *On Crimes and Punishments*, along with Montesquieu, shaped the very foundation of American government, Beccaria's treatise is most remembered for his opposition to torturous practices. Beccaria, the Roman Catholic excommunicated from the church for his own views, and his early Milanese supporter, Pietro Verri, both forcefully argued for the abolition of torture, a practice now—at long last—prohibited by international law.[25] But in the eighteenth century, only limited reform on that front had taken place before Beccaria's rise to prominence. Sweden had outlawed torture for ordinary crimes in 1734, but would not do so for all purposes until 1772, just a year before the Boston Tea Party.[26] Likewise, in 1740, the more enlightened Frederick II, King of Prussia, abolished torture for all but "especially serious cases," deciding, in 1754, to completely ban judicial torture, calling it "gruesome" and "an uncertain means to discover the truth."[27] In Beccaria's dominion, Holy Roman Empress Maria Theresa of Austria (1717–1780) was slower to act, abolishing torture only in 1776, mainly at the urging of Austrian law professor Joseph von Sonnenfels. Beccaria had condemned torture as "a cruelty condoned by custom in most nations," with Sonnenfels himself later inspired by *On Crimes and Punishments* to fight for the abolition of torture and the death penalty. Sonnenfels published *On the Abolition of Torture* (1775) in the same year that, across the great blue ocean, the Second Continental Congress appointed George Washington to command America's Continental Army.[28] In a communication to the French statesman Charles Gravier, comte de Vergennes, written from Passy in 1779, John Adams, Benjamin Franklin and Arthur Lee themselves pointedly complained of American prisoners of war being thrust into "Dungeons," "loaded" with "Irons," and "exposed" to "such lingering Torments, of Cold, Hunger and Disease, as have destroyed greater Numbers, than they could have had an Opportunity of murdering." "The Savages who torture their Prisoners," they wrote of the British in Beccarian terms, "do it to make themselves terrible: in fine all the Horrors of the barbarous Ages may be introduced again and justified."[29]

Beccaria's treatise, the bestseller on more than one continent, played a significant role in curtailing such torturous practices. Beccaria's book prompted Pierre-François Muyart de Vouglans to defend the use of judicial torture in 1766, but that defense of the practice was relatively isolated. Muyart de Vouglans' treatise on French criminal law was dedicated to Louis XVI, but the use of torture—including in France—would, as it had already to some degree in England, gradually fall out of favor. The specific role that Beccaria's treatise played in putting an end to judicial torture is, on the macro level, unclear, but *On Crimes and Punishments*—in more than one locale—definitely made a big splash, generating waves, if not a tsunami, of reform against a long-entrenched practice that was already being discredited. "Based on Beccaria's essay," one criminology text explains, "King Louis XVI abolished 'preparatory' torture in 1780 and 'preliminary' torture in 1788." Likewise, Joseph von Sonnenfels, as historian Éva Balázs writes in *Hungary and the Habsburgs*, was persuaded by Beccaria's treatise, with Balázs writing: "Sonnenfels was already subscribing wholeheartedly to the conclusions of Beccaria's *On Crimes and Punishments* within a year of its publication. He condemned torture and capital punishment as not just inhumane but senseless and non-utilitarian." By contrast, legal historian John Langbein sees the role of Enlightenment writers in eliminating judicial torture as more symbolic. Critics of torture, he notes, had already expressed concerns about it before the appearance of the writings of Voltaire and Beccaria.

In tracing *judicial torture*, Langbein notes that the *law of proof*—requiring either two witnesses or a confession—emerged "in the city-states of northern Italy in the thirteenth century" and that, thereafter, continental Europe's law courts had frequently "tortured suspects to obtain evidence." Continental jurists and investigating magistrates, he explains, were guided by Medieval treatises as to whether sufficient cause existed to examine a criminal suspect under torture. As he summarizes continental European law: "Torture was permitted only when a so-called half proof had been established against the suspect. That meant either one eyewitness, or circumstantial evidence that satisfied elaborate requirements of gravity." "In the example in which a suspect was caught with the dagger and the loot," Langbein writes, "each of those indicia would have been reckoned as a quarter proof, which, cumulated to a half proof, would have been sufficient to permit the authorities to examine the suspect under torture." In contrast, the English legal system—which allowed the use of circumstantial evidence as proof—instead relied on jury trials, the judgment of one's peers, to adjudicate guilt and did not, by and large, use torture as an investigative technique.

The English did, certainly, experiment with torture in the Tudor-Stuart dynasties, with the Privy Council issuing warrants authorizing the use of torture in at least eighty-one cases from 1550 to 1640. But as Langbein emphasizes of English society, which utilized harsh bodily punishments but simultaneously took great pride in its criminal procedures: "The use of torture subsided early in the seventeenth century and appears to have lapsed after 1640." The ideas of Montesquieu and Beccaria on criminal-law proofs—even while emanating from civil law locales—nonetheless attracted attention in English legal circles, even though Englishmen themselves viewed their own country as a "torture"-free one. As Edward Christian—an English barrister, a University of Cambridge law professor, and William Wilberforce's friend—wrote in a dissertation on judicature in 1792:

> Two learned and celebrated foreigners, Montesquieu and Beccaria, have censured our laws, because in an accusation of every crime, except treason and perjury, the prisoner may be found guilty upon the testimony of one witness. The witness who affirms, and the prisoner who denies, say they, leave the proof *in equilibrio*, and it is necessary to have another witness to make the scale preponderate.[30]

In 1792, another Cambridge man, George Dyer, also spoke of "the incomparable Beccaria" on oaths, with Dyer invoking this remark of Beccaria: "There is nothing more dangerous than this common maxim, 'The spirit of the laws is to be considered.'" Dyer's take on those words: "So far as there is a necessity to explain away the letter of the law, government has no security. This must happen, where obsolete laws continue unrepealed."[31]

It became clear in the Middle Ages and in Renaissance and early modern times, as John Langbein recounts, that while the agony of torture created an incentive for suspects to speak, using torture did not necessarily translate into truthful testimony. "Cases arose recurrently," he observes, "in which the real culprit was detected after an innocent accused had confessed under torture and been convicted and executed." As a result, the use of torture declined even as a new sanction—penal servitude—emerged in the sixteenth and seventeenth centuries. "In the eighteenth century, as the law of torture was finally about to be abolished, along with the system of proof that had required it," Langbein writes of the movement against torture, "Beccaria and Voltaire became famous as critics of judicial torture by pointing to such cases, but they were latecomers to a critical legal literature nearly as old as the law of torture itself." "The two-eyewitness rule, the cornerstone of the European law of proof," Langbein emphasizes of continental Europe's unsustainable, fatally flawed law of proof and torture, "had left the criminal procedure inextricably dependent on the tortured confession."[32]

In his treatise, Beccaria himself distinguished between *perfect* and *imperfect* proofs of crime. While perfect proofs excluded the possibility of innocence, imperfect evidence did not, with Beccaria speaking of the moral certainty of proof necessary to adjudicate the guilt of the offender. "The credibility of a witness," Beccaria wrote, "must diminish in proportion to the hatred, or friendship, or close connections between him and the accused." "More than one witness is necessary," Beccaria added, "for so long as one affirms and the other denies, nothing is certain, and the right of every man to be presumed innocent prevails."[33] "It is of little surprise," one modern text on criminal procedure notes, "that the setting of concrete rules of evidence became closely associated with the tyranny of the 'inquisitorial' pre-nineteenth century procedural law." As that text explains: "Many influential writers, including Beccaria, Montesquieu and Voltaire, argued strongly against the system of proofs that had taken hold in Germany, France, and Italy, while campaigning simultaneously for the abolition of torture." Today, America's criminal procedure rules—as with various provisions in the U.S. Bill of Rights, state constitutions, and evidentiary rules—are designed to protect the rights of the accused, not to facilitate the torture of criminal suspects.[34]

Whatever its precise impact on specific European monarchs, when Beccaria wrote *On Crimes and Punishments*, he certainly recognized that torture and executions—then entrenched worldwide—would not disappear overnight. "Human sacrifices," Beccaria conceded, "were common among almost all nations," with Beccaria acknowledging that "only a few societies have refrained from use of the death penalty—and for only a brief period of time."[35] In fact, the list of abolitionist examples—some of which Beccaria himself would have had no knowledge of—was extremely short. In the first century A.D., the Buddhist King of Lanka, Amandagamani, abolished the death penalty during his reign, with successive kings following suit.[36] In 724 A.D., Japan's Emperor Shomu, a devout Buddhist, also forbade executions—as did some early Buddhist rulers in India.[37] In 818 A.D., Japanese Emperor Saga outlawed the death penalty, too, effectively abolishing it for the next 300 years.[38] In China, the country that uses the death penalty the most today, Emperor Taizong of Tang also barred executions, leading to a brief, but execution-free period there between 747 and 759 A.D.[39] Empress Elizabeth Petrovna (1709–1761), of whom Beccaria was quite familiar, had also decreed the suspension of Russian executions in the 1750s, though the death penalty itself was not formally repealed.[40] In Western Europe itself, the list of abolitionist examples was especially sparse, with executions part of the everyday routine of life. William the Conqueror had abolished the death penalty in 1066, though he did so only because he preferred mutilations of the body, such as castration, to executions.[41] To borrow a phrase from Thomas Hobbes' *Leviathan*, the life of man could be "poor, nasty, brutish, and short."[42]

Despite the stiff odds he was up against, Beccaria remained optimistic, appealing to monarchs everywhere to rid society of capital punishment, promising the sweet vindication of history even as his critics defended the use of executions. "The voice of one philosopher," he admitted, "is too weak against the clamour and the cries of so many people who are guided by blind habit." But calling upon "the few sages scattered across the face of the earth" to "echo" back to him, he countered:

> [I]f the truth should reach the throne of the monarch—despite the many obstacles that keep it at bay against his wishes—let him know that it arrives with the secret support of all mankind; and let him know that the bloody notoriety of conquerors will fall silent before him and that a just posterity will bestow him a pre-eminent place among the peaceful monuments of the Tituses, the Antonines, and the Trajans.

That few nations had barred executions, Beccaria lamented, "is consistent with the fate of great truths, which last no longer than a flash of lightning in comparison with the long and dark night that envelopes mankind." "The happy epoch," the young Cesare had written in the same era in which Benjamin Franklin and his Italian counterpart, Father Giambatista Beccaria, were experimenting with lightning and electricity, "has not yet arrived in which truth shall be—as error has heretofore been—in the hands of the greatest number."[43] After reading Cesare Beccaria's treatise, many of America's founders were, to put in mildly, enthralled, and they found themselves—in Beccaria's words—echoing back to him.

A New Paradigm of Proportionality

In America, Beccaria's treatise—whether read directly, or as filtered through Blackstone's *Commentaries* or other sources—proved highly influential in multiple respects. It led many Founding Fathers and others in early America to call for the abolition or curtailment of executions,[44] and its opposition to torture and acts of cruelty shaped American views and led to a consensus against such practices. For example, in *Cunningham v. Caldwell*, an 1807 case, the Kentucky Court of Appeals emphasized that "in criminal cases, the equitable principle is contended for by Beccaria, in his celebrated work on Crimes and Punishments, that the punishment should be proportioned to the crime." *On Crimes and Punishments* thus shaped Anglo-American law right alongside other important influences of the day such as the writings of Montesquieu, John Locke and Beccaria's fellow economist, Adam Smith. And the echoes of Beccaria's treatise were heard almost everywhere, including in America and Great Britain. A London journal, *The Literary Fly,* specifically named Beccaria along with Blackstone, Montesquieu, and Voltaire as a quartet who "have echoed to each other."[45] Those men were not, by any means, an exclusive list of those who shaped eighteenth-century law and penal reform, but Beccaria's name was certainly high on the list.

The list of books in which Beccaria's name comes up is too lengthy to recite, but Beccaria and his treatise are frequently cited in glowing terms. In *A Treatise on Courts Martial*, the third edition of which was published in London in 1786, the "Marquis of Beccaria" is called "humane and benevolent" and *On Crimes and Punishments* is called "most excellent."[46] Another title, *A Treatise on Poverty, Its Consequences, and the Remedy*, written by William Sabatier and published in London in 1797, refers to Beccaria's treatise more than a dozen times,[47] while *A Treatise on the Law of Evidence*, a standard textbook written by barrister Samuel Phillipps of London's Inner Temper, noted how Beccaria had "very justly observed" a fact relating to proofs.[48] *A Treatise on the Breeding and Management of Livestock*, published in London in 1810, even advertises Beccaria's treatise, showing that booksellers recognized that Beccaria's audience extended well beyond lawyer's offices and the law courts.[49] *On Crimes and Punishments*, in fact, helped to catalyze the American Revolution itself, then materially shaped the drafting of American constitutions and legislation.[50]

America's founders, as a whole, greatly admired the ideas produced by the Italian Enlightenment. In *Common Sense* (1776) and *Address to the Addressers* (1792), the radical Thomas Paine even quoted two sentences from a rather obscure Italian political essay, *Trattato delle virtù e dei primi*, or *Treatise on Virtues and Rewards* (1766). Those two sentences, written by the Marquis Giacinto Dragonetti, were themselves an appeal to liberty—and to the judgment of history. As Dragonetti, as quoted by Paine for his American audience, wrote: "The science of the politician consists in fixing the true point of happiness and freedom. Those men would deserve the gratitude of ages, who should discover a mode of government that contained the greatest sum of individual happiness, with the least national expense." Although Americans cited Beccaria and his treatise far more in those days, Paine called Dragonetti "that wise observer on governments."

Just as Beccaria's book changed lawmakers' conceptions of the proper "proportion between crimes and punishments," Dragonetti's book made an impact, too. Writing to John Adams from Braintree, Massachusetts, on June 13, 1776, just a few weeks before Americans declared their independence, fellow Bostonian Josiah Quincy himself quoted Dragonetti's Italian essay for the proposition that it is "within the Reach of human Wisdom … to 'fix the true Point of Happiness and Freedom' by framing, and establishing a Constitution of Government upon such Principles, as shall to endless Ages be productive of, 'the greatest Sum of individual Happiness, with the least national Expence.'" While America's founders looked to English republicans and the Scottish and French Enlightenments for ideas, they were certainly not neglecting the Italian Enlightenment as they conceived of a nation to be grounded in liberty.

The book of Giacinto Dragonetti (1738–1818), a lawyer educated in Rome and Naples under the supervision of Antonio Genovesi, was first published in Naples shortly after the appearance of Beccaria's *On Crimes and Punishments*, with a preface to the 1769 English edition noting that "Dragonetti is the author of the following treatise first published in Naples, and received an applause little inferior to that which had celebrated the name of Beccaria." In most European editions, in fact, Dragonetti's treatise was published in a single volume with Beccaria's *Dei delitti e delle pene*; "Dragonetti," one source explains, "was advertised, along with Beccaria, in the *London Chronicle*" in April and May of 1769, with the translation of Dragonetti's treatise into French and English meant "to capitalize on the publishing success recently enjoyed by Beccaria." A dictionary of political economy, published in 1901, notes that Dragonetti had "considerable knowledge of the most recent economic literature of his time" and that agriculture was of particular interest to him. "The kingdom of Naples," another source records, "threw up a whole bevy of enlightenment men who favored reform," a list that included Dragonetti and the Neapolitan lawyer, historian and legal reformer Melchiore Delfico (1744–1835), the latter of whom advised that "Equality and Liberty are reciprocal words in politics and morality." Thomas Paine, the American revolutionary, was particularly fond of quoting from Dragonetti's treatise, which one scholar speculates — because of the treatise's relative rarity — he may have brought with him as he traveled across the Atlantic from Europe.[51]

The writers of the Enlightenment often inspired and helped fuel the success of their fellow writers. Blackstone's *Commentaries* had drawn inspiration from Beccaria's treatise, and Blackstone's citation of Beccaria — coupled with America's founders direct embrace of Beccaria's treatise — helped Beccaria's ideas reach a much wider U.S. audience than it might have otherwise.[52] As one scholar, Harvey Wish, puts it, Blackstone's *Commentaries* "molded generations of susceptible American law students, many of whom were thus introduced to the penology of Beccaria."[53] The fiery orator and Virginia lawyer Patrick Henry — of "give me liberty, or give me death!" fame — cited Blackstone's *Commentaries* on multiple occasions, and it has been estimated that nearly 2,500 copies of Blackstone's *Commentaries* were in American colonies by 1776.[54] Henry and his fellow Virginians were, certainly, opponents of torture, the practice that Beccaria so despised. As legal scholar William Schabas has written of the U.S. Constitution's ratification process: "In the Virginia convention, Patrick Henry complained that the draft constitution might allow 'torture,' and he expressed concern with current practice in continental Europe, where it was widely used to extract confessions. George Mason answered that he considered the clause to prohibit torture."[55]

Early American lawyers and law professors, history shows, were in fact very familiar with — and often much influenced by — Beccaria's writings.[56] For example, in 1803, St. George Tucker — a law professor at the College of William & Mary who studied law under Jefferson's mentor, George Wythe — released his *Blackstone's Commentaries: With Notes of Reference to the Constitution and Laws, of the Federal Government of the United States, and of the Commonwealth of Virginia*. Tucker, admitted to the Virginia bar in 1775 and a Virginia delegate to the 1786 Annapolis Convention that called for the subsequent constitutional convention in Philadelphia, became famous for that book. *Tucker's Blackstone*, as it became known, contrasted English laws, as set forth in Blackstone's *Commentaries on the Laws of England*, with American laws and practices. Published in Philadelphia by William Young Birch and Abraham Small, the book was printed by Robert Carr. In it, Tucker made the following comment after Blackstone's assertion that "in every state a scale of crimes should be formed, with a corresponding scale of punishments, descending from the greatest to the least": "This was first attempted in Virginia by the committee of revisers, (Mr. Jefferson, Mr. Pendelton, and Mr. Wythe,) appointed by the general assembly of Virginia in October 1776, to prepare and report to the general assembly a code of laws for this commonwealth: treason, petit treason, and murder, were the only offences which were deemed worthy of death...."[57]

Some commentators, noting Beccaria's enormous American influence, have—in their exuberance—actually inflated or mischaracterized the nature of that influence. "Inspired by Beccaria," one writer, Edmund Clingan, editorializes, "the Bill of Rights banned cruel and unusual punishments."[58] That particular assessment, though, inflates and oversimplifies Beccaria's impact on American law. While Beccaria's treatise certainly decried cruelty and spoke of making punishments more proportionate to crimes, the text of the Eighth Amendment plainly had *English*—not Italian—origins. The prohibition against "cruel and unusual punishments" set forth in the Virginia Declaration of Rights of 1776 and the U.S. Constitution's Cruel and Unusual Punishments Clause were derivations of the English Bill of Rights of 1689.[59] What is fair to say is that Beccaria's treatise *materially informed* the Founding Fathers' views *of what actually amounted to cruelty* in that era. Responding to Beccaria's call to enact more proportionate punishments, the founders—including Thomas Jefferson, James Wilson and James Madison—began to rethink their own preconceived conceptions of cruelty and, on a state-by-state basis, crafted their own new bills and laws in attempts to put Beccaria's theoretical ideas into practice. While Beccaria's treatise was often the starting point, the devil was in the details in terms of deciding what the precise scale of punishments would be in a given locale.

The wide-ranging influence of Beccaria's ideas on American law, though complex, is nonetheless clear.[60] The Pennsylvania Constitution of 1776, a document signed by Benjamin Franklin, imposed on "the future legislature of this state" a duty to reform the "penal laws." Under that state constitution, punishments were to be made "less sanguinary" and "more proportionate" to crimes.[61] As noted earlier, the text of Section 38 of the Pennsylvania Constitution—later attributed to "the small and valuable gift of the immortal Beccaria to the world"[62]—reads: "The penal laws as heretofore used shall be reformed by the legislature of this state, as soon as may be, and punishments made in some cases less sanguinary, and in general more proportionate to the crimes." The next provision, Section 39, further clarified just how Pennsylvanians intended to do that, providing that "to make sanguinary punishments less necessary," "houses ought to be provided for punishing by hard labour, those who shall be convicted of crimes not capital."[63] Vermont's 1777 constitution contained an identical clause to the latter provision,[64] with other states choosing to phrase their constitutions or bills of rights—including their variously worded provisions barring cruel punishments—as they saw fit. If a severe punishment was not absolutely necessary, America's founders intended to do away with it.

In places such as New York and Pennsylvania, the effect on early Americans of Enlightenment writers—and of *On Crimes and Punishments* in particular—has long been recognized. In October 1783, Pennsylvania's Chief Justice Thomas McKean—a signer of the Declaration of Independence and the Articles of Confederation—wrote to Pennsylvania's then-President John Dickinson: "On considering the number of Capital offenders sentenced to death [in] the late session of Oyer and Terminer & General Gaol Delivery, I conceive it would be agreeable to the Council to spare some of their lives, if they will be enabled to discriminate properly." Likewise, in *The Plough Boy*, an agricultural journal, it was reported from Albany, New York, in June 1819 that the Massachusetts governor, John Brooks, had been reelected and that Brooks had given a speech in which he lamented "the inefficacy of sanguinary punishments in preventing crimes."

Trained as a doctor and having served in the Revolutionary War under George Washington, John Brooks (1752–1825) was the governor of Massachusetts from 1816 to 1823. Brooks, the agricultural journal noted, "seems to lean to the opinion, that the milder system of Beccaria, which we are now trying in this state, aided by the force of education, and moral and religious motives, may prove successful."[65] In 1819, Governor Brooks— as one Massachusetts history put it—"extolled the salutory benefits to be derived from imprisonment." In 1820, Brooks also emphasized that the change from corporal punishment to imprisonment was "a device of modern times" and "the commencement of a great and complicated experiment."[66] In line with that approach, Massachusetts legislators abolished branding, whipping, the stocks and the pillory in the 1804–1805 legislative session. The tattooing of recidivists within Massachusetts prisons was also discontinued in 1829.[67] In other words, whereas executions and harsh bodily punishments were the way things had been done in the past, the incarceration of offenders was seen as the wave of the future.

This line of reasoning was also apparent in a speech given on the floor of the United States Senate in 1842. During debate on a bill to provide further remedial justice in the courts of the United States, U.S. Senator Robert J. Walker (1801–1869) of Mississippi— a lawyer who became the 18th U.S. Secretary of the Treasury and the Territorial Governor of Kansas—compared the harshness of English law with the mild character of American laws. "There," Walker spoke of England, citing Blackstone, "the number of crimes punished with death is almost countless." "Here, in most of the States," Walker observed, "but a single crime (willful and deliberate murder) forfeits the life of the prisoners; and the onward march of our mild institutions is hastening under the lead of an illustrious Democrat (O'Sullivan) to adopt the principles of Beccaria and Livingston—to abolish the punishment of death, and to sweep the hangman's scaffold from American soil." John O'Sullivan, the Democrat to whom Walker referred, lived in Manhattan and sought an America without the "barbarism of the Gallows." Walker's own father, a Pennsylvania judge, took such a keen liking to Beccaria, the Italian philosopher and father of the anti-death penalty movement, that he named his third son Beccaria before his son Robert's birth.[68]

Emphasizing that "[r]eason revolts" at the "indiscriminate punishment" of crime with death, another source, a history of Lancaster County, Pennsylvania, specifically recorded in 1869 that "the humanity of the Marquis Beccaria, Montesquieu, and others, have contributed to convince the world that its welfare is best promoted by a due apportionment of the punishment to the crime, and its certain application to the offender."[69] Such assessments of Beccaria's influence, in fact, continue to appear, including by prominent criminologists and leading U.S. scholars. For example, American legal historian Lawrence Friedman has written in *A History of American Law* that the ideas of "[g]reat reformers" like Cesare Beccaria "left an imprint on the early state constitutions."[70] Beccaria's treatise, it has been emphasized again and again, influenced the views of Blackstone, who in turn influenced generations of American lawyers. For instance, an 1881 book published in London noted that "[t]he rack has been more frequently used as a state engine than has reached the knowledge of our historians; secret have been the deadly embraces of the Duke of Exeter's daughter." The rack in the Tower of London, that source noted, "was introduced by the Duke of Exeter in the reign of Henry VI., as an auxiliary to his project of establishing the civil law in this country; and in derision it was called his daughter." The book further emphasized: "lawyers are rarely philosophers"; "the history of the heart, read only in statutes and law cases, presents the worst side of human nature"; "Sir George MacKenzie, a great lawyer in the reign of James the Second, used torture in Scotland"; and the condemnation of secret, torturous practices had resulted from "philosophy combining with law," enabling "the genius of Blackstone to quote with admiration the exquisite ridicule of torture by Beccaria."[71]

In the eighteenth century, the ancient principle of *lex talionis*—found in the Old Testament as "eye for eye, tooth for tooth, hand for hand, foot for foot"[72]—was still alive and well, however. In England, it was frequently used to justify harsh corporal punishments, though it was also sometimes referred to as an "absurd Law."[73] And Beccaria's essay would contribute greatly to the latter assessment over time. In one piece in the *Medical Gazette*, titled "Military Flogging" and published on July 15, 1837, Beccaria's name came up in the context of an essay that began as follows: "No one who has ever witnessed a military flogging can think of it without horror; nor can any member of a liberal profession have a more odious duty imposed upon him than falls to the lot of the surgeon on such occasions—namely, to judge how much pain and laceration a human being can bear, without endangering his life." In that essay, "Beccaria's problem"—one confronted by military commanders who inflicted lashes—was described as follows: "given the strength of the nerves and muscles of an innocent person, it is required to find the quantity of torture necessary to make him confess himself guilty of a given crime." "Were it not that military floggings are still unjustifiably severe," the essayist wrote, "it would be needless to dwell upon these horrors—to describe the unhappy victim brought out from the hospital three and four times to receive the remainder of his punishment."[74] At that time, medical doctors—then frequent attendees at executions, often pronouncing the hour and minute of a condemned's death—were obsessed with the application of Beccaria's theories. In one book published in Cincinnati in 1835, Dr. Silas Reed's *Western Medical Gazette* contains the following passage: "With propriety does the author introduce from Beccaria, the following sentiment, that should be hung up in massy capitals in every hall of legislation: 'that the punishment of a criminal cannot be just (that is necessary) if the laws have not endeavored to prevent that crime by the best means which times and circumstances would allow.'"[75]

Among America's founders, the *lex talionis* doctrine certainly held considerable sway in the early years of the republic, though *On Crimes and Punishments* started to change that as it led to a new way of thinking about the concepts of torture, cruelty and proportionality.[76] After reading Beccaria's treatise, for example, Thomas Jefferson—while still citing ancient sources of law along with his citations to Beccaria—rethought his conception of the advisability and morality of certain punishments. While Jefferson felt constrained by the *lex talionis* principle while working on a revisal of Virginia law in the 1770s, in writing to his long-time mentor George Wythe, Jefferson expressed the view in 1778 that "[t]he lex talionis ... will be revolting to the humanized feelings of modern times."[77] "On the subject the Criminal law," Jefferson once reflected of Virginia's revisal efforts, "all were agreed that the punishment of death should be abolished, except for treason and murder; and that, for other felonies should be substituted hard labor in the public works, and in some cases, the Lex talionis." "How this last revolting principle came to obtain our approbation," Jefferson remarked, "I do not remember." Jefferson also noted of the *lex talionis* principle: "[I]t was the English law in the time of the Anglo-Saxons, copied probably from the Hebrew law of 'an eye for an eye, a tooth for a tooth,' and it was the law of several antient people. But the modern mind had left it far in the rear of it's advances."[78] In 1831, reflecting back on Jefferson and Madison's efforts to reform Virginia's criminal law in the 1770s and 1780s, John Quincy Adams likewise recorded in his diary: "With regard to the criminal law, the committee substituted for some capital punishments the lex talionis, which, on further reflection, Mr. Jefferson justly disapproves."[79] In *The Laws and Jurisprudence of England and America*, Yale University professor John Dillon summed it up nicely, recalling more than a century ago: "In this country we never adopted the extreme severities of the English statutes. We were early influenced by the views of Beccaria." As Dillon explained in 1894: "Pennsylvania led the way to this great change by a provision in her Constitution of 1776."[80]

In his little-known travelogue, *Viaggio: Travels in the United States of North America 1785–1787*, the Italian botanist Luigi Castiglioni himself emphasized that certain provisions of the Pennsylvania Constitution "are worthy of note." Among those listed, sections 38 and 39 of that constitution, the ones dealing with penal reform. In his travelogue, Castiglioni also pointed out that while adultery was once punished by death in Connecticut, the state's general assembly, in 1784, passed a law providing that adulterers shall, instead, "be severely punished by whipping on the naked body, and stigmatized, or burnt on the forehead with the letter A on a hot iron; and each of them shall wear an halter about their necks on the outside of their garments during their abode in this State so as it may be visible."[81] In fact, Nathaniel Hawthorne's famous 1850 novel, *The Scarlet Letter*, in which Hester Prynne wears an *A* for her adultery, was reflective of life in America's early legislative and judicial regimes. A New Hampshire statute against adultery, passed in 1701, required a man and woman convicted of adultery to be "Sett upon the Gallows" for an hour "with a Rope about their necks"; to have the other end of the rope "cast over the Gallows"; to be "severely whipt"; and to "for ever after weare a Capitall Letter :A: of two inches long and proportionable in Bignesse, cutt out in Cloath of a contrary Colour to their Cloaths and Sewed upon their Upper Garments, on the out Side of their Arme or on their Back in open View." Castiglioni's travelogue demonstrates that, due in part to Beccaria's treatise, Americans were, in the 1780s, gradually moving away from executions as a crime-control mechanism, even if, in some places, the reform just meant substituting harsh corporal punishments for executions.

In other places, depending on the locale, Americans also began gradually moving away from even *non-lethal* corporal punishments.[82] In January of 1793, for example, Massachusetts governor John Hancock called for an end to the punishments of "cropping and branding, as well as that of the Public Whipping Post," which he labeled "an indignity to human nature." Early legal codes and military decrees had long authorized such penal practices, making Hancock's call—and the American public's growing unease with bodily punishments—particularly notable. The Whipping Act of 1530—put in place during the reign of Henry VIII—was one such corporal punishment regime, designed to punish vagrants. As one history of punishment noted of the American colonial experience: "Public floggings in the early American colonies were used to enforce discipline, vilify evil and enhance community solidarity, and to deter others. Whipping was especially common in Virginia and other southern colonies to punish slaves and to prevent slave revolts." Early American colonists burned particular letters on offenders' hands and foreheads, with one source describing the punishments as follows: "Facial branding was more often imposed on more serious offenses at this time (e.g., blasphemy) and for repeat offenders. Rather than being physically branded, female offenders were forced to wear letters symbolizing their crimes on their clothing." Because indentured servants, slaves and the poor lacked the financial means to pay fines for misconduct, that source notes, corporal punishments—rarely inflicted on nobles—were seen as "viable alternative sanctions for these disadvantaged groups."[83]

Beccaria's treatise, once read, led to multiple and sustained calls to make punishments less intrusive on the convict's body and more proportionate to crimes. Jefferson's bill in Virginia is a prominent example in terms of its proposal to restrict the death penalty's use, but there are others, too. And of those, some—as in Pennsylvania, South Carolina, New Hampshire and Ohio—were placed right in state constitutions, provisions that are, from a practical standpoint, always much harder to amend than ordinary legislation.[84] In South Carolina, a major slaveholding state, it would, despite the 1778 constitutional provision requiring "less sanguinary" and "more proportionate" punishments, take many decades before antiquated punishments were abandoned. In that state, branding was maintained until 1833, with every person punished for manslaughter prior to 1830 branded with the letter "M." A Charleston grand jury condemned shaming punishments as "barbarous, disgusting, and unworthy of a free people," but a South Carolina legislative committee disagreed, saying in 1843 that it was "inexpedient to discard shame and disgrace" as punishments.[85] The requirement of "proportioned" penalties—despite differences in implementation according to locale—also made its way into the state constitutions of Indiana, Maine, Rhode Island, West Virginia, and Georgia. By 1868, even though the notion of avoiding *cruel* punishments has inherent in it the idea of avoiding *disproportionate* ones, nine of the thirty-seven American states at that time explicitly required in their constitutions that penalties and punishments be proportioned to the offense.[86]

Beccaria's conception of proportioning crimes and punishments, though not self-executing, deeply affected the country's moral and social leaders, even making its way into sermons in the founding era. A 1774 sermon delivered in Connecticut by Samuel Sherwood, a 1749 Yale graduate whose uncle was Aaron Burr, said this on the subject:

> Penal laws are intended for the public good: The great intention of punishing the transgressors of them is, that others may be kept in awe. And legislators have a right to annex such penalties to their just and equitable laws, as are sufficient to maintain their authority, and secure the observation of them. But yet, there is justice to be observed in proportioning punishments to crimes: and no doubt, it would be unjust, cruel and barbarous, to affix the most severe punishments that could be invented, to small and trifling offences.[87]

In 1775, Moses Mather—another Yale graduate—also delivered a sermon in Connecticut containing a reference to "crimes clearly defined and distinguished; & punishments duly proportioned to their nature and magnitude."[88]

In a similar vein, Judge Thomas Carnes's 1798 charge to a Richmond County, Georgia, grand jury struck a very Beccarian tone. A lawyer who had served as a colonel in the American Revolution, Judge Carnes had represented the State of Georgia as a member of the U.S. House of Representatives from 1793 to 1795. Carnes's charge first lauded juries "as the most certain security and protection afforded" to men for "their persons, property and reputation," then praised the accessibility of American law before specifically referencing the concept of proportionality as he spoke of the protection against cruel and unusual punishments. "It is our glory to know," Carnes spoke of the ever-inquisitive, never-resting "American mind," that "the laws of the land, fixed, known and written rules of conduct, prescribed by men of our own free choice," are "within the reach" even of "the lowest individual in the community" and "are the means made use of for the security of all that we consider valuable." Expressing the view that punishments—whether affecting "high or low" or "rich or poor"—"ought to be strictly and impartially" imposed, Carnes emphasized:

> In general we may be happy in the reflection that punishments are not cruel and unusual, but are in most instances proportioned to the crimes which they follow; and for the most part the individual base enough to commit crimes against the society which affords him protection, knows the punishment he is certainly to suffer upon detection. Taking it therefore for granted, from the nature and constitution of our government, that the nature of crimes and punishments are generally known to each individual member of the state; if justice overtakes the delinquent after a fair and impartial trial before his peers, we ought rather to rejoice at, then regret his punishment.[89]

Such thinking—both within America's judiciary and in the broader society—would have a significant impact. For example, in a memoir by New York's first attorney general, Egbert Benson (1746–1833), read before the Historical Society of the State of New-York in 1816, it noted how American punishments had already changed significantly over time. In 1691, it emphasized, a sheriff had been "ordered to prepare a ducking-stool, intended to deter from scolding, a species of excess of freedom of speech." But at a distance of several decades, the memoir cautioned: however the ducking stool "might have suited at the time, certainly now, according to some late and highly respectable opinions on the subject of crime and punishment," it was "a means of restraint too rigorous to comport with the mild and free spirit of our republican government."[90] Plainly, *On Crimes and Punishments* had made an indelible mark by the time Americans took the bold step of declaring their independence from Great Britain—an act that signaled a rejection of the frightful, anti-republican English ways of doing business.

And Beccaria's influence in religious, political and legal circles would be felt for decades to come. For example, in an 1821 issue of *The Edinburgh Review*, a writer first posed two questions: "If poaching can be extirpated by intensity of punishment, why not all other crimes? If racks and gibbets and tenter-hooks are the best method of bringing back the golden age, why do we refrain from so easy a receipt for abolishing every species of wickedness?" The writer then went on: "The best way of answering a bad argument is not to stop it, but to let it go on in its course till it leaps over the boundaries of common sense." "There is a little book called *Beccaria on Crimes and Punishments*," the writer continued, "which we strongly recommend to the attention of Mr Justice Best. He who has not read it, is neither fit to make laws, nor to administer them when made."[91] Jeremy Bentham, in *Principles of Legislation*, likewise cited Beccaria multiple times, including for the proposition that men should not be tortured.[92] In the Progressive Era, many American states— following Beccaria's advice—did away with death penalty laws altogether, though those reforms proved temporary in all but two of those states, Minnesota and North Dakota. Fear of crime, social disorder, and lynch mobs led the vast majority of Progressive Era abolitionist states to reinstate capital punishment.[93]

In some cases, Beccaria's legacy is firmly established. American courts now take it for granted that punishments should fit the crime,[94] repeatedly holding that proportionality is a relevant concept to consider in meting out punishments.[95] In 2010, for example, the U.S. Supreme Court held that "[t]he concept of proportionality is central to the Eighth Amendment."[96] The Court itself has, over the years, used the Eighth and Fourteenth Amendments to strike down a number of sentences that violate that principle, including death sentences for juvenile offenders, the insane, those with severe intellectual disabilities, non-homicidal rapists, and those who neither intended nor attempted to kill.[97] "Embodied in the Constitution's ban on cruel and unusual punishments," the Court has ruled, "is the 'precept of justice that punishment for crime should be graduated and proportioned to [the] offense.'"[98] The Vermont Supreme Court, in 1911, specifically declared that a provision of Vermont's constitution providing that "all fines shall be proportioned to the offenses" was "due … to the influence of Beccaria, whose treatise … was read with avidity by lawyers and jurists everywhere in the latter part of the eighteenth century and the earlier part of the nineteenth."[99] While jurists and academics still vigorously debate the concept of proportionality as it relates to issues of constitutional interpretation,[100] proportionality—the concept Beccaria pioneered—was embraced by America's founders and is plainly here to stay in American law.[101]

Capital Punishment and Torture

For Americans and English subjects alike, a revulsion against torture—an impulse felt even before *On Crimes and Punishments* was published—came to be seen, thanks in part to Beccaria, as one of the hallmarks of a civilized nation. William Godwin, who published an 1820 book, *Of Population*, in London, wrote that "the coast of North America" had come to be considered "the land of promise, the last retreat of independence" for worshippers. As Godwin noted of the United States of America: "Here there are no legal infliction of torture, no Bastilles and dungeons, no sanguinary laws."[102] In place of death sentences, Beccaria had envisioned—and the Founding Fathers had started to create—a prison system that would make capital punishment obsolete. "Perpetual slavery," Beccaria wrote, "has in it all that is necessary to deter the most hardened and determined, as much as the punishment of death." To those who contended that "perpetual slavery is as painful a punishment as death, and therefore as cruel," Beccaria argued: "I answer, that if all the miserable moments in the life of a slave were collected into one point, it would be a more cruel punishment than any other; but these are scattered through his whole life, whilst the pain of death exerts all its force in a moment."[103]

Ironically, even as America's founders denounced "torture" and outlawed "cruel and unusual punishments," they tolerated the brutal treatment of slaves, permitting conduct that would easily be described as torturous by today's judicial authorities. Instances of slaves and criminals being tortured in the eighteenth century are easy to find. "The first form of repression was the torture of slaves on the plantations, the method of which was left totally to the discretion of the slaveholders," writes historian Anthony Neal in *Unburdened by Conscience*. For example, one ex-slave, William Wells Brown, recalled that one of his former masters tied him up in a smoke-house and whipped him. After doing so, the master—in what was called "Virginia Play"—would light a fire and "smoke" him. Neal also takes note of "a sadistic instance in which a slaveholder took a large grey tom-cat, placed it upon the bare back of a prostrate black man, and forcibly dragged the cat by the tail from the man's shoulder, down his back, and along his bare thighs." As that "most excruciating punishment" was described in one account: "The cat sunk his nails into the flesh and tore off pieces of skin with his teeth. The man roared with the pain of this punishment." Other forms of torture included "the sweatbox," or "nigger box," the "cat-o'-nine tails," or rubbing salt in open wounds. The first method entailed the slave being put in a small box, which would then be nailed shut and placed in the hot summer sun, or, in the winter, in a cold, damp place. Kept in such boxes for days or weeks at a time, small air holes drilled into the box would be the only thing that kept slaves from suffocating. The *cat-o'-nine tails* was the terminology employed to describe the lash of a whip with nine leather straps, with every lash producing nine "licks." "Often after a severe whipping, typically performed by an overseer or slave driver," Neal reports, "the slave's raw and open wounds" would be doused with salt water, thereby aggravating the slave's pain.[104]

The West Indies, with which England and some of America's founders had ties, saw its own share of brutality. In Edward Long's *The History of Jamaica*, published in 1774, it was noted that Jamaican law punished slaves for possessing stolen goods. Slaves would "suffer death, transportation, dismembering, or other punishment, at the discretion of two justices and three freeholders." In a note after the word "dismembering," the author—in a sign of the times—wrote: "This inhuman penalty is entirely obsolete, and never of late inflicted. It is, however, reproachful to the laws, and ought to be expunged." "Fugitives were formerly punished here with amputation of their toes," Long explained, emphasizing that "[t]his execrable barbarity hindered them from *running* away." After editorializing that the "Negroes" of Jamaica have a "sanguinary, cruel temper, and filthy practices," said to include "[t]heir old custom of gormandizing on human flesh," Long's history observed: "Men are too often disposed to be cruel, of their own depraved hearts; and it becomes a Christian legislature not to inflame and encourage, but to repress as much as possible, this sanguinary disposition, by giving example throughout its penal ordinances, of justice in mercy." "The penal laws in England were always sanguinary, and still retain this savage complexion," he added later.[105]

One notorious American rogue, Stephen Burroughs, was publicly whipped on multiple occasions in the post-Revolutionary War period, and later wrote a memoir describing being convicted of counterfeiting in a case in which, at trial, he represented himself. The punishment: to stand in the pillory for one hour and to be confined to the "house of correction" for three years. Glazier Wheeler, another counterfeiter tried at the same time, received the same punishment, but also was ordered "to be cropt" and to receive "twenty stripes." In his memoir, Burroughs described one particularly painful episode of his confinement as follows: "I was ordered into another apartment, and to work went those engines of cruelty. They in the first place, made fast a flat ring around my leg, about six inches wide and an inch thick. This was connected with a chain weighing about 36lb. and ten feet in length." "The other end of the chain," he emphasized, "was fastened to the timber composing our floor, with a staple driven in with a sledge, which made the whole jail tremble." "I lay in this dismal situation about a fortnight, if I remember right," Burroughs reported. "My leg, by this time," he added, "was worn by the iron around it, till the skin was quite off."

The sheriff, Burroughs noted of another instance, confined him to "the dungeon," had him whipped for five minutes, and "hand-cuffed and pinioned" him to the floor with an iron bar. As Burroughs described the latter episode:

> This was in the month of December, in the year 1785, a remarkable cold month; and my confinement in this situation continued until January, 1786, being thirty-two days in the whole. Here I was deprived of fire, of clothing and exercise, till the time was nearly expired; and even the pitiful allowance of straw to lie on: but all this was nothing, compared with what I suffered with hunger.

"I had not been in this situation many days, before I began to experience the severe effects of the cold," Burroughs wrote of his time in the dungeon. "As I could not stand, walk nor step," he explained, "the only recourse I had to keep my feet from freezing, was rubbing them against an iron spike, a little from my feet, perhaps three inches; which had either never been driven into the floor entirely, or else had started back by some means, the space of about four inches." "After the seventh or eighth day after my confinement in this pandimonium," Burroughs added, "the pains of hunger became excruciating. Gladly would I have eaten my own flesh." As his ordeal continued, Burroughs described his dire condition before being released from the irons:

> I had now become emaciated to a skeleton. My beard had not been cut, during the time of my being in the dungeon; hence it was about two inches long. My hair had not been combed, which stood in every direction. From these circumstances, I had more the appearance of some savage beast of the forest, than any thing appertaining to the human species.

After describing his torturous confinement in the sheriff's dungeon, Burroughs — the criminal who did multiple stints behind bars — editorialized as to the "illegality" of his treatment, writing as follows:

> The fundamental principles upon which our liberties and privileges are founded, are the trial by jury, that no unnatural and cruel punishments shall be inflicted, and that a person shall never be punished, but by due course of law. These leading principles, I believe, are never to be deviated from, except in case of rebellion, when the state is in danger; then martial law may operate; and even when

martial law has its operation, it is necessary to have matters of fact established by evidence, and the voice of a majority of three, at least, to warrant a punishment.

"In the punishments inflicted on me," Burroughs wrote, "none of these preliminaries have been attended to, but I have been subjected to the arbitrary will of a petty tyrant. He punished when his inclination was for cruelty, and inflicted what kind his pleasure directed." "Where we find severe laws operating among a people, or mild laws executed in a cruel manner, we see the influence of this, upon the manners of the people, to be very great," Burroughs offered, adding: "It gradually roots out the feeling of benevolence and compassion, and in their room, implants the sentiments of cruelty and severity." "[I]f the law, or the mode of executing it, is severe and cruel," he wrote, criticizing and skewering his former jailor, the "body of mankind" will "imbibe a spirit of severity and cruelty."

In his memoir, Burroughs also described another instance in which he and other criminals were "brought to the whipping post," "stripped," and whipped with "the cat-o'ninetails." A frequent lawbreaker, Burroughs—who repeatedly suffered the consequences on multiple occasions—then described yet another punishment he received as follows: "I was then confined by a pair of heavy irons, commonly called shackles, taken to the whipping post, and there received an hundred stripes, which were laid on in a very serious manner, causing the blood to stream at every stroke, so that my shoes were filled by the time I was taken down." Yet another criminal-law sentence handed down from the bench against Burroughs was described in his memoirs in this way:

> That I should receive one hundred and seventeen stripes on the naked back; should stand two hours in the pillory; should sit one hour on the gallows, with a rope around my neck; that I should remain confined in prison three months; that I should procure bonds for good behaviour for seven years, and pay the charges of prosecution.

"True it was, I had suffered many unusual, cruel and illegal punishments since I had been under the displeasure of the government," Burroughs opined in his memoirs, with Burroughs elsewhere referring to "racks and gibbets" and "pillories and whipping posts" as "those very engines of cruelty."[106]

In England and the United States, where the populaces had first-hand experience with such barbarous punishments, Beccaria's view on the inefficacy of torture and executions gained a substantial, devoted following. One English magistrate called the Italian philosopher "[t]hat acute Reasoner, the Marquis Beccaria, who wrote after Montesquieu." Arguing that it would be more rational to punish thieves with forced labor instead of inflicting death, the English jurist then quoted Beccaria as follows: "A punishment, (says this able writer) to be just, should have only that degree of severity which is sufficient to deter others: perpetual labour will have this effect more than the punishment of death."[107] In Pennsylvania, William Bradford also wrestled with Beccaria's ideas on deterrence, writing that "[i]t is more difficult to determine what effects are produced on the mind by the terror of capital punishments; and, whether it be absolutely necessary to deter the wicked from the commission of atrocious crimes."[108] Not everyone agreed with all of Beccaria's views or with how Beccaria's principles should be implemented, but his opinions were greatly respected[109] and the question of whether executions deterred crime more effectively than imprisonment was widely debated, as was the question of whether the death penalty was justified in any event.[110]

Some of the Founding Fathers literally grew up in circumstances that made exposure to capital punishment unavoidable. The Philadelphia minister Henry Melchior Muhlenberg (1711–1787)—a Lutheran pastor from Germany who became an American missionary—tended to condemned prisoners as a spiritual advisor. Muhlenberg's children went on to play extremely prominent roles in early American law and politics. His son Peter, after serving in the Continental Army, became an ordained minister in 1768 and was elected as the Vice-President of Pennsylvania's Supreme Executive Council in 1784. He was later elected to the First Congress, the Third Congress, and the Sixth Congress, and also became a U.S. Senator in 1801. In that year, President Thomas Jefferson appointed him to serve as Pennsylvania's supervisor of revenue, and the following year Jefferson tapped Peter to serve as a Philadelphia customs collector, a role he performed until his death in 1807. Peter's brother, Frederick Augustus Muhlenberg (1750–1801), also became a Lutheran minister and politician, serving as the first Speaker of the U.S. House of Representatives. Frederick had previously served as a member of the Continental Congress, as speaker of the Pennsylvania assembly, and as president of the Pennsylvania state convention that ratified the U.S. Constitution.

The father of those congressmen, the more elder Henry Melchior Muhlenberg, had personal experience with executions. He was on hand, for instance, when burglar William Autenreid (also spelled Autenreith) and another man, John Williams, were executed in Pennsylvania in 1764. He had repeatedly visited the condemned before the execution, and he was present when their bodies were buried in a "potter's field." A few days after the execution, Henry Muhlenberg also noted in his diary that he had written "a report of the executed Autenreith's honorable origin, godless life, and criminal death." In 1765, Rev. Henry Muhlenburg also ministered to a German immigrant, Henry Halbert, alias Heinrich Albers, before Halbert was hanged at Philadelphia's Centre Square for murder. Muhlenburg recorded that the suicidal Halbert had confessed to purposely cutting the throat of a twelve-year-old boy "in order that he might lose his own life." Halbert's depressive life had been full of "drinking, whoring, cursing, swearing, breaking the Sabbath, and keeping all manner of debauched company," it was noted. After Lutheran school boys sang German hymns on execution day, Halbert—as was reported in a broadside—told the crowd:

> Attend good people, see my final end;
> Take Warning by your Dying Friend,
> I am condemned to die, and die I must,
> I die for Murder, and my Fate is just;
> I beg that God my sins may now Forgive,
> And die in Peace with all good Men that live.[111]

Once *On Crimes and Punishments* entered the public discourse, though, the question of whether life imprisonment—or, in the parlance of the day, "perpetual slavery"—could be a viable substitute for death sentences became a hot topic. This was especially so for crimes that did not involve pre-meditated or felony murder. Confinement "accompanied by labor," the English writer and schoolmaster Samuel Parr emphasized in 1809, "would, I am sure, be a most desirable substitute for many of the capital punishments which are now inflicted." "'Perpetual slavey,' says Beccaria," it was offered in one of Parr's multiple references to the Italian thinker, "'has in it all that is necessary to deter the most hardened and determined, as much as the punishment of death.'"[112] Parr concluded that "[t]he study of Beccaria and other writers on jurisprudence" had "prepared the best members of the community" to "address their legislators."[113]

And lobby governors and legislators they did, often in print or through pamphlets or speeches. Over time, such appeals became more impassioned, even strident. In 1841, New York's governor, William Seward, suggested that executions might be "an encouragement, rather than a preventative of crime." John L. O'Sullivan, the chair of a New York assembly committee, denied that the Old Testament should be a guide for legislation, with his bill for the death penalty's total abolition only narrowly rejected by a vote of 46 to 52. Thereafter, petitions for and against the death penalty poured into legislators, with petitions favoring abolition outnumbering those against that course of action. While many favored a Beccarian approach, traditionalists—including J. S. Van Rensselaer—defended the death penalty's use.[114]

When, in 1865, the U.S. Constitution's Thirteenth Amendment was finally approved, thereby abolishing "slavery" and "involuntary servitude," the drafters of that amendment carved out an exception from those prohibitions for the "punishment for crime whereof the party shall have been duly convicted."[115] This explicitly, per Beccaria's suggestion, allowed the use of prison labor, which became increasingly popular in both America and Europe in the early nineteenth century. As one source reports: "The idea of forcing prisoners into servitude was actually put into practice before the ratification of the Thirteenth Amendment. In the early 19th century, prisoners were leased out to private contractors." "The precedent-shaping exception for prison slavery" was initially set forth in the Northwest Ordinance of 1787, the authors of one book, *Prison Slavery*, explain, noting that Article 6 of that legal document regulating the Northwest Territory—an area covering Indiana, Illinois, Michigan, Ohio and Wisconsin, as well as parts of modern-day Minnesota—provided in part: "There shall be neither slavery nor involuntary servitude in the said territory, otherwise than in the punishment of crimes whereof the party shall have been duly convicted." The Northwest Ordinance, those authors explain, "was written by men adhering to social contract theory and to Cesare Beccaria's ideas on punishment, and it found its way into the Thirteenth Constitutional Amendment of 1865 and the jails and prisons of America."[116]

As Beccaria's ideas smoldered in colonial America then caught fire in the early years of the United States, the differing approaches of English and American law drew particular attention. In *The Stranger in America*, an 1807 book by a one-time Rhode Island lawyer who spent thirteen years in America, the author, Charles William Janson, wrote: "Though both the penal and common laws of England are generally adopted in the United States, the punishments differ materially." Janson spent considerable time in Philadelphia, and in taking special note of Pennsylvania's system of criminal justice, he emphasized that, in America, the punishment of death is inflicted "[i]n very few cases indeed, in any state." A later review of Janson's book, printed in England, reported that, in America, "capital punishments are rarely inflicted." "In the article of Criminal Punishments," the reviewer editorialized, "the conduct of the American Government is highly judicious, and merits universal adoption."[117] Ultimately, the publication of *On Crimes and Punishments* spelled the beginning of the end for England's Bloody Code, which was gradually replaced in the early and mid-nineteenth century as penitentiaries came into vogue alongside the continued use of exile, or transportation. In the 1960s, England—America's mother country and the originator of the "cruel and unusual punishments" language—abolished the death penalty altogether after executions dwindled and it came to light that innocent people had been executed.[118]

Historically speaking, Beccaria's enduring achievements—convincing lawmakers to begin shunning executions and to shy away from tortuous practices—were once celebrated despite being little remembered in the twenty-first century. The *Encyclopaedia Americana*, published in 1830, described Beccaria's penal reform efforts this way: "he opposes capital punishment and the torture." "This work," the encyclopedia recorded of *Dei delitti e delle pene*, "led to the establishment of more settled and more correct principles of penal law, and contributed to excite a general horror against inhuman punishments."[119] Another title, published in Baltimore in 1829, lists Beccaria among a group of "Eminent Persons,"[120] while an earlier one—published in Philadelphia in 1795 for Mathew Carey—lists Beccaria among "Men of Learning and Genius."[121] Beccaria may be little known among the general public today, but that was hardly the case decades ago. Among the Founding Fathers, Beccaria's name was not only known, it was highly revered.

One myth associated with America's founders, ironically perpetuated by Antonin Scalia, a U.S. Supreme Court Justice of Italian descent, is that the founders were highly supportive of capital punishment. In fact, due in part to Beccaria's treatise and the advocacy of its many U.S. readers, capital punishment was heavily and systematically restricted in America's first decades. While death sentences remained available for some crimes, especially murder, treason and rape, they were outlawed for many other offenses in various locales. In 1786, Pennsylvanians, in the year before they hosted the Constitutional Convention in Philadelphia, in fact abolished capital punishment for robbery, burglary and sodomy, becoming the first state to reduce its number of capital crimes in the post-war period. Other states, seeing no negative consequences from the change, then dutifully followed Pennsylvania's example after their own state-by-state debates. For example, after Virginia curtailed its capital offenses in 1796, Connecticut took arson off the list of capital crimes in 1801. In 1805, Massachusetts likewise made arson a non-capital crime along with burglary (except of a dwelling at night) and robbery (except on the highway). In a similar vein, the Territory of Indiana—not admitted to the Union until 1816—made robbery and armed burglary non-capital offenses in 1812, with rape ceasing to be a capital crime in Maine in 1829 and in Illinois in 1832. In *Democracy in America*, Alexis de Tocqueville's survey of American penal practices, it was specifically noted in 1840 that "[t]he legislators of the United States, who have mitigated almost all the penalties of criminal law, still make rape a capital offence," emphasizing that "no crime is visited with more inexorable severity by public opinion."[122]

The U.S. Constitution, in little-known clauses, itself contains provisions to suppress the death penalty's use. In particular, it outlawed *bills of attainder* and narrowly defined the concept of *treason*, an offense that had often been used in English law—and throughout the world—to squelch political or religious dissent. *Bills of attainder* and *bills of pains and penalties* were common-law exceptions to the right to trial by jury, though such legislative acts—designed to inflict punishment without the protection of a jury trial—were outlawed by Article I, sections 9 and 10 of America's new social compact, the U.S. Constitution. In May 1778, Thomas Jefferson—representing a view that America's founders collectively rejected—had himself once recommended a bill of attainder, issued against Josiah Philips and a group of outlaws. Patrick Henry, the Virginia politician, had justified that legislation because Philips, a bandit from 1775 to 1778, had allegedly "committed the most cruel and shocking barbarities" in Virginia and because the Revolutionary War was—in Henry's words—"at the most perilous stage." But men such as Edmund Randolph, Alexander Hamilton and James Madison spoke out against bills of attainder, and they were ultimately successful in forbidding their use at both the federal and state level in the U.S. Constitution. "Bills of attainder" and "ex-post-facto laws," James Madison wrote in *Federalist No. 44* of two legislative tools ultimately barred by the Constitution, "are contrary to the first principles of the social compact, and to every principle of sound legislation." In line with Madison, Bushrod Washington (1762–1829)—George Washington's nephew and a U.S. Supreme Court associate justice—also called such laws "oppressive, unjust, and tyrannical."

The Constitution's definition of *treason*—meant to make it more difficult to convict someone of that offense—also made clear that America's founders did not want the death penalty handed out with too much ease. According to Article 3, section 3:

> Treason against the United States, shall consist only in levying war against them, or in adhering to their enemies, giving them aid and comfort. No person shall be convicted of treason unless on the testimony of two witnesses to the same overt act, or on confession in open court.

Much of the debate at the 1787 Constitutional Convention focused on whether the power to punish treason would belong exclusively to the national government or would be shared concurrently with the states. The Treason Clause's agreed-upon language requiring confessions be in open court—a provision requested by Luther Martin, the Attorney General of Maryland—showed the founders' particular disdain for the civil law practice of torturing criminal suspects in secret to obtain confessions. In the aftermath of World War II, U.S. Supreme Court Justice Robert Jackson—in discussing the Treason Clause—observed that "[t]he framers' effort to compress into two sentences the law of one of the most intricate of crimes gives a superficial appearance of clarity and simplicity which proves illusory when it is put to practical application." What is clear, however, is that, in the post-*On Crimes and Punishments* era, the concept of treason morphed from one focused on disloyalty to the monarch to a lack of allegiance to a republican form of government, with two witnesses—not one—required to convict someone in the absence of a confession.[123]

And such provisions in the U.S. Constitution led, quite naturally, to a curtailment of executions. In his classic book, *Democracy in America*, in fact, Tocqueville specifically emphasized: "North America is the only country upon earth in which the life of no one citizen has been taken for a political offence in the course of the last fifty years." Saying that Americans are "extremely open to compassion," Tocqueville wrote: "in America, no one hesitates to inflict a penalty from which humanity does not recoil." But even then—perhaps especially then—there was still two Americas: one for whites and one for blacks. While Tocqueville noted that "the physical condition of the blacks is less severe" in the U.S. than in any "single European colony in the New World," he also reported that American slaves "still endure horrid sufferings" and "are constantly exposed to barbarous punishments." As Tocqueville concluded: "the same man who is full of humanity towards his fellow-creatures, when they are at the same time his equals, becomes insensible to their afflictions as soon as that equality ceases."[124]

Indeed, African Americans and other minorities in the eighteenth and nineteenth centuries were systematically excluded from the social compact itself, as a Virginia case from 1824 makes all too clear. In that Virginia Supreme Court decision, the state's cruel and unusual punishments clause was found to have no "bearing" in a legal challenge brought by "a free man of color." That state's bill of rights, the court ruled, "never was contemplated, or considered, to extend to the whole population of the State." "Can it be doubted, that it not only was not intended to apply to our slave population, but that the free blacks and mulattoes were also not comprehended in it?" the court emphasized.[125] Were the U.S. Constitution's Cruel and Unusual Punishments Clause read in an "originalist" fashion, "blacks and mulattoes" would, by extension, thus be excluded from its protections. In modern America, though, such a reading of the Constitution—the document that *all* Americans rely upon for the protection of their rights—would be absurd and wrongheaded, indeed immoral. Such an "originalist" reading would also lack any possible legitimacy, especially since the Fourteenth Amendment demands "equal protection of the laws." Just as *Brown v. Board of Education* and the Fourteenth Amendment's plain language protecting "any person" must be read to prohibit the segregation of schools and to protect women as well as men even though the Fourteenth Amendment's drafters still lived in a sexist, segregation-ridden world, the Eighth Amendment must be read in the modern era—by contemporary judges—to protect *everyone*.[126]

The late eighteenth and early nineteenth centuries saw efforts to eliminate the slave trade and slavery itself, a movement that some of America's founders championed but that not all joined as the movement picked up steam. For example, in a 1789 letter to Thomas Jefferson, who, as President, called for the abolition of the slave trade in America in 1806, Thomas Paine reported from London that "[t]he Slave Trade" issue was to come before the House of Commons and that "Mr. Wilberforce has given Notice that he shall move for a total abolition of the traffic." After becoming an evangelical Christian, the

Cambridge-educated English politician William Wilberforce (1759–1833) spearheaded the campaign against the British slave trade. Wilberforce began his crusade in 1787—the year of the Constitutional Convention in Philadelphia—by founding the Society for the Abolition of the Slave Trade. His tireless efforts led to the passage of laws, the Slave Trade Act of 1807 and the Slavery Abolition Act of 1833, that ultimately abolished the slave trade and the institution of slavery in the British Empire.[127] With a "gag" rule put in place in 1836 barring the presentation of anti-slavery petitions in the U.S. House of Representatives, a procedural barrier that John Quincy Adams argued strenuously against, slavery—still a divisive issue when, in the late 1780s, the U.S. Constitution was ratified—would not be abolished in America until the 1860s.[128]

In early America, slave codes—the predecessors of the discriminatory Black Codes passed by southern states between 1865 and 1866—routinely punished blacks more harshly than whites. Such slave codes, developed in Maryland and Virginia as early as the 1660s, frequently made the conduct of slaves capital offenses while whites received lesser punishments or no punishment at all for the same conduct. "The slave codes," notes one text, *An Introduction to Policing*, "were laws enforced by developing southern police departments to directly support slavery and the existing economic system of the South." Such slave codes persisted in the Founding Fathers' time and well into the nineteenth century; only with the ratification of the U.S. Constitution's Thirteenth and Fourteenth Amendments, barring slavery and guaranteeing equal protection of the laws, did such codes become illegal under U.S. law. The Supreme Court's infamous *Dred Scott* decision in 1857, holding that a black slave, Dred Scott, could not sue for his freedom because he was not a citizen, showed how firmly entrenched slavery still was in U.S. society at that time even though Beccaria's treatise—and the Declaration of Independence itself—spoke of equality. Indeed, only with the Supreme Court's decision in *Brown v. Board of Education* (1954) was the notorious "separate but equal" doctrine of *Plessy v. Ferguson* (1896) finally repudiated.[129]

When Tocqueville and his traveling companion, Gustave de Beaumont, were in America in the 1830s, they saw prisons not yet in existence at the time of Luigi Castiglioni's visit in the 1780s. For example, the two Frenchmen visited New York's Sing Sing Prison as well as Pennsylvania's Eastern State Penitentiary. A maximum-security prison in the town of Ossining, New York, Sing Sing is located about 30 miles from New York City along the Hudson River; in the early twentieth-century, Lewis E. Lawes—who had studied Beccaria's ideas—became Sing Sing's warden and presided over 300 executions despite his adamant opposition to corporal and capital punishment. As part of their own fact-finding mission a century earlier, Tocqueville and Beaumont also had many conversations with leading figures about capital punishment, executions and America's penal system. They spoke, for instance, with Edward Livingston, the man who had been tasked with revising Louisiana's penal code and who served as Andrew Jackson's Secretary of State.[130] Beaumont was especially impressed with Livingston, writing of an evening he spent with the Livingston family: "I mingled my square dances and waltzes with most interesting conversations with Mr. Livingston on the penitentiary system and especially on capital punishment, passing thus from the serious to the pleasant."[131]

The two Frenchmen also spoke with a Philadelphia judge and Francis Lieber—later a professor at South Carolina College and at New York's Columbia University—about the role of sheriffs at executions. The Philadelphia judge's comments largely reflect the prevailing public sentiment at that time:

> I am very much in favor of a reduction of penalties. I believe, and have observed in my practice as a judge, that milder but more certain penalties are a stronger deterrent to crime than penalties that are harsh but for that very reason less likely

to be applied. On the other hand, I am positively opposed to total abolition of the death penalty. I believe that it is essential to dissuade criminals from going beyond certain limits, such as combining murder with robbery, as they would otherwise inevitably be tempted to do by fear of arrest. I therefore believe that the death penalty should be maintained but that it should be used only in extreme cases. I have always found that *executions* had a bad effect on the public.

In a letter written from Philadelphia in 1831, Tocqueville, making his own observation, expressed the belief that "Mr. Livingston's code," drafted for Louisiana but never adopted by that state's legislature, "was designed for a social state more advanced than that of the region for which he drafted it."[132]

As evidenced by the Philadelphia judge's comments and by what happened in Louisiana, Beccaria's ideas were not always fully embraced or accepted.[133] The significance of Beccaria's treatise, however, was recognized shortly after its publication by America's first citizens.[134] Not only did Benjamin Rush, William Bradford, and Thomas Jefferson rely heavily on Beccaria's ideas in proposing to abolish or curtail death sentences, but Pennsylvania legislators — and later, lawmakers in Virginia, Kentucky and elsewhere — responded positively to law reform efforts.[135] "Beccaria's influence," writes UCLA law professor Stuart Banner in *The Death Penalty: An American History*, "was felt quickly in the debate over whether death was too harsh a penalty for property crime, but American reformers were not yet ready to follow him in advocating the abolition of capital punishment for all crimes." In 1768, Banner notes, the *Connecticut Courant* published an essay on what the newspaper called "*a very important Question*, viz. Whether any Community have a right to punish any species of theft with death?" The *Courant* concluded: "we as individuals have no right to give up our lives to the community, to be taken from us, for any species of theft whatsoever."[136] The popularity and proliferation of *On Crimes and Punishments* revealed large cracks in the theretofore-commonly-accepted wisdom that the death penalty was appropriate for all crimes, including property crimes.

By the 1780s and 1790s, as reflected by the writings of Dr. Benjamin Rush, William Bradford, and others, whether the death penalty's use was necessary for *any* crime, was a question occupying the minds of many Americans.[137] When it came to judging the death penalty's legitimacy, every category of offender was being put on the table and was up for discussion. Among the "Subjects of Discussion for the Students of Law" that the College of William and Mary law professor St. George Tucker recorded in Virginia in March of 1794: "The right of human laws to punish with Death for offences, which are not such by the law of nature."[138] Tucker's own library is known to have contained a copy of Beccaria's treatise,[139] and James Kent's *Commentaries on American Law*, published in 1826, references Beccaria, too, showing his continuing importance among respected U.S. legal commentators.[140] "The Marquis of Beccaria," still another source reported, this time on the subject of torture, "must feel with inexpressible satisfaction the advantage which his writings have afforded to mankind." "For since the publication of his benevolent treatise on crimes and punishments," it read, "torture has been abolished in several parts of Europe."[141] Recent U.S. court cases[142] and much scholarship — including in the twenty-first century — still cites Beccaria's treatise,[143] with William Schabas — an internationally renowned death penalty scholar — putting it this way in *The Death Penalty as Cruel Treatment and Torture*: "Any attempt at a brief historical review of the norm prohibiting cruel treatment and torture would not be complete without mention of the influence of Cesare Beccaria, an Italian criminologist of the eighteenth century."[144]

St. George Tucker — the early American jurist and law professor — himself acknowledged how the ideas of Montesquieu and Beccaria had, even in his time, already affected

American law. "According to Mr. Swift," Tucker noted in 1803 in a reference to Connecticut's Zephaniah Swift, "the legislature of *Connecticut*, before Montesquieu and Beccaria had immortalised their names in pleading the cause of humanity, had begun to practice upon the sublime principles which those philosophers have recommended by all the charms of eloquence and power of reason." Beccaria's suggestion that a scale of punishments be created had, by then, already been widely implemented. "Their scale," Tucker wrote of Connecticut's approach, "is death; confinement to hard labour, and coarse fare; and corporal and pecuniary pains and penalties." "The crimes for which death is the punishment," he wrote, "are treason, murder, rape, the crime against nature, mayhem, and arson, where some life is endangered." "Imprisonment and hard labour in Newgate," he added of Connecticut's prison, "are inflicted for robbery, burglary, forgery, counterfeiting, horse-stealing, arson, attempting to commit a rape, perjury, and aiding to escape from Newgate prison." Over time, American lawmakers—with each succeeding generation—would, of course, continually recalibrate the scale of punishments for various crimes as societal views changed. The death penalty was curtailed even further in the years to come, with the State of Connecticut ultimately abolishing capital punishment altogether in 2012.

St. George Tucker—Thomas Jefferson's friend and a lawyer later appointed a federal district court judge by President James Madison—singled out "the example of the state of Pennsylvania" in his writing. That state, Tucker wrote, "seems most worthy of this eulogium, and of the imitation of every other government." Pennsylvania lawmakers, he emphasized, "have substituted for all crimes, excepting treason and murder in the first degree, the punishment of confinement to hard labour and coarse fare instead of death." Tucker also noted that "the mode of inflicting the punishment, in the government and discipline of the prison," was "most effectively served" by requiring convicts to "perform the labour assigned to them" and, "[i]n case of refractory behavior," by solitary confinement. He then observed: "it is said, this mild punishment is found effectual, and that crimes are more effectually restrained by it, than heretofore by death, and other severe punishments." In a literary journal published in 1829, another author, Thomas Matthews, writing about Kentucky's penitentiary, similarly noted that Beccaria—"a celebrated writer on crimes and punishments"—had "recommended to the world a system of Penitentiary Confinement."

Tucker's book, discussing "mild punishment" as an alternative to "death" and "other severe punishments," specifically wrote of how prominent Americans favored that approach. For example, Tucker cited an account of Philadelphia's prison system published in 1796 and "an inquiry how far the punishment of death is necessary, in Pennsylvania, by the late William Bradford, Esq. printed in Carey's *Museum* for 1798." "In the year 1796," Tucker noted, "Mr. George Keith Taylor, a delegate for the county of Prince George, obtained leave to bring into the house of delegates, in Virginia, a bill to amend the penal laws of this commonwealth, formed upon the principles of the Pennsylvania law, and was happy enough to obtain a majority of the legislature in it's favor."[145] In his 1803 book, Tucker also pointed out how Virginia's penitentiary—then still a very new institution—had been financed. "The sum of thirty thousand dollars," Tucker emphasized, "was thereby granted for the erection of a spacious jail, upon the general plan of that in Philadelphia; a further grant of money has since been made, and the building is so far completed, as to be now fit for the reception of criminals; the law took effect in virtue of the governor's proclamation, that the jail was in a situation to receive criminals on the 26th of March, 1800."

Still, at that time, even as a number of progressive reforms were taking place, American states, especially in the South, could not bring themselves to jettison their two very disparate systems of justice: one for citizens and one for slaves. This, in fact, was readily acknowledged by American lawyers of the day, though only some were actively advocat-

ing for meaningful change. "And now," Tucker added after describing the 1800 penitentiary opening in his home state, "no offence whatsoever committed by any FREE PERSON
against the commonwealth of Virginia, is punishable with death, except murder in the *first*
degree; by which is meant such as may be perpetrated by poison, or by lying in wait, or
any other kind of willful, deliberate killing; or which may be committed in the perpetration or attempt to perpetrate any arson, rape, robbery, or burglary." "It is most devoutly to be wished," Tucker concluded, "that the success of this experiment in this state,
may be equal to what it has been hitherto in Pennsylvania; and that future legislatures
may be so well convinced of it's practicability, as well as of it's beneficial effects, as to extend it to SLAVES as well as FREE PERSONS, to whom it's operation is at present confined." Tucker then noted: "Several ingenious essays on the subject of capital punishments,
have, from time to time, appeared in America; of which Mr. Carey has preserved some
excellent specimens in his museum."[146]

Even before Pennsylvania restricted executions to instances of first-degree murder in 1794,
Congress itself—in the wake of the U.S. Constitution's ratification—debated what crimes
should be punishable by death. In those debates, the central idea in Beccaria's treatise—
proportionality—took center stage as it had in so many states and so many times before. For
example, in 1790, in considering the punishment of crimes against the United States, a
House committee—with Samuel Livermore sitting in the chair—considered the proper
punishment for counterfeiting. According to a contemporaneous record of the debate:

> The clause which enacts that counterfeiting the securities of the United States,
> or uttering counterfeits knowingly, shall be punished with death, by being hanged,
> it was moved, should be amended, by striking out the words "punished with
> death by being hanged," to admit a less punishment for uttering or passing than
> for counterfeiting. The degrees of criminality in the two cases were accurately de-
> fined by Mr. SHERMAN.

In the ensuing debate, Connecticut's Roger Sherman and others aired their views. As it
was reported:

> MR. WHITE observed, that he was opposed in general to inflicting death, except
> for murder, or crimes which might terminate in murder; but, in the present case,
> he thought there were degrees of guilt, and the punishment ought to be pro-
> portioned; he was, however, opposed to a capital punishment in this case, as he
> conceived it would tend to prevent convictions.

"Mr. SHERMAN," it was noted, "said he had known persons who had been convicted of this
crime, that had afterwards reformed."

But that viewpoint was not shared by everyone, and other speakers—opposing the
amendment—had a much different conception of how the concept of proportionality should
be applied in the counterfeiting context. Theodore Sedgwick of Massachusetts, for example, emphasized "the degrees of punishment ought to be proportioned to the malignity of the offence." "Persons addicted to forgery," he contended, "are seldom, if ever,
reclaimed—the security of the society, therefore, appears to depend on a capital punishment." Likewise, Thomas Fitzsimons opposed the motion, with the notetaker recording that legislator's views as follows:

> He adverted to the practice and experience of Great Britain: the injurious and
> fatal consequences to credit which result from forgery are considered in England
> in so serious a point of light, that the bank pays notes which they know to be coun-
> terfeit. Hence the inexorable rigor of the laws of that country in cases of forgery.

As Fitzsimons' views were memorialized: "He could not see so clearly, as some gentle-men appear to see, the difference between forging, and simply uttering what is known to be counterfeit—the mischief is not completed till the forgery is uttered. He enlarged on the idea of guarding public paper by every possible expedient." "Mr. SMITH and Mr. BURKE," it was reported, "were opposed to the motion," too. Those two lawmakers fo-cused on "the injuries which society was liable to from the ingenuity of these unprinci-pled persons; the extreme difficulty of guarding against their depredations rendered it highly expedient they should be cut off." Ultimately, the House committee voted down the amendment and retained the language in the bill pertaining to those uttering coun-terfeit documents.

The House committee, in considering the bill to punish crimes against the United States, also vigorously debated whether "the bodies of malefactors" should be dissected. After a member moved to strike the provision for dissection, it was argued that it "could do no good," "was wounding the feelings of the living," "was contrary" to "the practice of the several States," and "was making punishment wear the appearance of cruelty, which had a tendency to harden the public mind." On the other side, it was argued that to allow dissection "was only following a mode adopted by some of the wisest nations" and that "[i]t was making those who had injured society to contribute to its advantage by fur-nishing subjects of experimental surgery." North Carolina's Hugh Williamson, a note-taker recorded, "stated a variety of arguments in favor of the clause—and showed the very great and important improvements which had been made in surgery from experi-ments." As with advancements in the law, America's founders were focused on medical ad-vances, too. "It was attended with salutary effects," one committee member emphasized of dissection, "as it certainly increased the dread of punishment, when it is contemplated with this attendant circumstance." Ultimately, after six members spoke on each side of the question, the motion to strike the clause authorizing dissection was defeated.[147]

In setting up their own form of government and formulating legislation, the Found-ing Fathers often consulted foreign practices—whether English, Italian or otherwise. *The Federalist Papers*—written by James Madison, Alexander Hamilton and John Jay—make more than fifty references to foreign sources, and the framers were quite familiar with laws in other places. The Constitution itself references "the Law of Nations," an early moniker for international law. In his book, *Roman and Civil Law and the Development of Anglo-American Jurisprudence in the Nineteenth Century*, historian M. H. Hoeflich specifi-cally notes: "Many American law libraries (and some general libraries) in the first half of the nineteenth century had substantial holdings in civil law and Roman law. For instance, Harvard had an excellent collection through the generosity of one of its alumni, Samuel Livermore." The library of Continental Congressman Samuel Livermore, Hoeflich em-phasizes, "formed the nucleus of Joseph Story's working collection when he was writing his *Commentaries*."[148]

In an autobiographical statement written near the end of his life, Thomas Jefferson—the advocate for religious freedom and a founder of the University of Virginia—himself credited Beccaria, the Italian philosopher, with being a catalyst for his own anti-death penalty views. "Beccaria and other writers on crimes and punishments," Jefferson wrote, moving his hand across the page, "had satisfied the reasonable world of the unrightful-ness and inefficacy of the punishment of crimes by death."[149] Both John Adams and Thomas Jefferson, in fact, were close friends of America's premier abolitionist Dr. Ben-jamin Rush, the man who—along with James Madison's college classmate, William Brad-ford—played such a prominent role in spreading Beccaria's ideas throughout the United States. "I read with delight every thing which comes from your pen," Jefferson once told Rush. At Dr. Rush's death, Jefferson wrote to John Adams with his condolences: "Another of our friends of seventy-six is gone, my dear Sir, another of the co-signers of the Independence of our country. And a better man than Rush could not have left us, more benevolent, more learned, of finer genius, or more honest." Adams replied: "I know of no Character living or dead, who has done more real good in America."[150] These days, Dr. Rush is most remembered for prompting Adams and Jefferson to reconcile after a painful parting of ways, a reconciliation that sparked a remarkable set of letters between the two ex-Presidents.[151] But Jefferson, Adams and Dr. Rush also shared a mutual admiration—much less well known—for *On Crimes and Punishments*.

As America's founding era faded into the nineteenth century, Beccaria's reformist views continued to be commonly discussed, including in print and in legislative debates. For instance, one man's memoirs, first published in 1807 and compiled by a Scottish lawyer, Alexander Fraser Tytler, extensively discusses Beccaria's ideas. Those memoirs, of the Scottish judge and lawyer, the Hon. Henry Home of Kames, specifically recount: "Capital punishments have been reprobated by the Marquis de Beccaria, M. de Voltaire, and many other modern writers, as tyrannical, inhuman, and impolitic."[152] As an Italian nobleman of distinction, Beccaria was—as sources make clear—often referred to by his full name and title, Cesare Bonesana, Marquis or Marchese de Beccaria.[153] In one telling section of those Scottish memoirs, "On the Principles of Criminal Jurisprudence," containing "an Examination of the Theory of Montesquieu and Beccaria," the then-eminent jurist, Lord Kames, emphasized that "the science of Criminal Jurisprudence" remains "in a state of great imperfection." Referring to "[t]he great discrepancy of opinions entertained by the ablest writers with regard to some of the important doctrines of the science," Kames took note of "[t]he barbarity and absurdity of many of the penal laws of the most enlightened nations." That barbarity and absurdity of the laws, originally based on custom and superstition, would only gradually be recognized in Anglo-American circles, though English subjects and early American colonists were—the facts show—captivated by Beccaria's ideas even before the Revolutionary War.

If nothing else, the memoirs of Lord Kames—like other testimonials and documents from that era—highlight the rigorous moral and intellectual debate that Beccaria's treatise provoked, a debate that still continues to this day in the United States. Those particular memoirs also reflect the ambivalence and unease that many people more than two hundred years ago felt about executions as well as about the political compromise that shows up in many early American penal codes. In discussing the criminal law, Lord Kames highlighted Montesquieu's and Beccaria's ideas, took special note of Beccaria's proportionality principle, and recited Beccaria's belief that capital punishment "is neither just nor useful in a well governed state." While remarking that Beccaria's *On Crimes and Punishments* "breathes a very amiable spirit of humanity," Kames—part of a society still struggling mightily with human rights issues—felt that the punishment of death was "just vengeance against the guilty" in the case of a murderer, what he called "a noxious animal."

Kames also believed that Beccaria had erred by focusing on the prevention of crimes as the sole object of punishment. "But," Kames cautioned, "if capital punishments are both warranted by our moral feelings, and justified by good policy, the same considerations will strongly dictate, that such punishments ought not to be frequent." Quoting Sir William Blackstone's *Commentaries* for the proposition that, under England's Bloody Code, "no less than a hundred and sixty" crimes were then punishable by death, Kames lamented "sanguinary enactments." Kames also expressed the view that while "the dread of a capital punishment may be necessary to restrain the ferocity of nature which prompts to crimes of the deepest dye; it certainly will not be denied, that inferior punishments are sufficient to restrain every ordinary species of criminality."[154]

For the most part, America's founders—living in an age initially devoid of penitentiaries, the first not coming into existence until 1790 in Philadelphia—shared that sentiment. By and large, they saw executions as appropriate for killers but as too frequent and too severe, at least for certain offenses. The onset of the Revolutionary War also impacted their assessment of the propriety of particular punishments. For example, in the midst of the war, John Adams did not always fully embrace Beccaria's ideas as regards executions. In a letter dated October 1, 1776, to Colonel Daniel Hitchcock, Adams — wanting to win the war — wrote: "It is said, there was shameful Cowardice. If any Officer was guilty of it, I sincerely hope he will be punished with death." Though views were mixed, the next generation of Americans, as a collective, and even in times of peace, also found themselves unwilling to abandon capital punishment. For example, the "citizens of Albany" — in an 1842 petition — implored the New York legislature to retain capital punishment for murder. As the petition read: "The Penalties inflicted by human law, having their foundation in the intrinsick ill-desert of crime, are in their nature vindictive as well as corrective." "Beyond all question the murderer deserves to die," the petition asserted, adding in Biblical terms: "God has revealed to us His will, both through the laws of reason and conscience, and in his written word, that the murderer should be put to death."[155]

Along with its role in inspiring vigorous anti-death penalty advocacy that ultimately fell short of accomplishing total abolition, Beccaria's treatise certainly helped mold the consensus against torture that emerged in America.[156] Though torture had been abolished in a few European locales prior to the arrival of *On Crimes and Punishments*,[157] Beccaria's "monumental denunciation of torture," one commentator explains, "did so much to influence European ideas about torture and criminal justice in the eighteenth century."[158] "In a time marked by secret accusations, inadequate provisions for defending the accused, and the common use of torture," writes another commentator, "Beccaria's essay was revolutionary for its day."[159] After its publication, a variety of European states in fact abolished torture, including Denmark in 1770, Poland in 1776, and France, Tuscany, Lombardy and the Netherlands in the 1780s. In the early nineteenth century, other locales also followed suit. "[T]he real influence of writers like Voltaire and Beccaria: their work simply made torture unthinkable," one expert writes.[160] Though many Founding Fathers already vocally opposed torture before *On Crimes and Punishments* was published,[161] Beccaria's book solidified American public sentiment against the practice.[162] In a report to Louisiana's General Assembly, for example, Edward Livingston paid homage to Beccaria's "humane doctrines, and particularly of his arguments for the abolition of torture against the accused."[163]

As regards the American consensus against torture, now codified in U.S. and international law, jurists recognized Beccaria's specific influence more than two hundred years ago. Though the United States did not ratify the U.N. Convention Against Torture and Other Cruel, Inhuman or Degrading Treatment or Punishment until 1984,[164] Beccaria's name — listed "among the moderns" — was specifically cited in Vermont[165] for his opposition to torture in an 1803 case, *State v. Hobbs*. In that case, an indictment for torturing a person suspected of theft was brought against Abraham Hobbs and Return Strong. Both indicted individuals were alleged to be "persons of cruel and inhuman dispositions" who, "with force and arms," did "against the law, the constitution, and the peace and dignity of the State of Vermont," "beat, bruise, torment, torture, and burn" the body of Cato Jenkins "with fire," and, "with like force," "suspend and hang" him "by the neck." Although the jury acquitted Strong, Hobbs was found guilty, and the Vermont district court "sentenced the culprit" — Hobbs, the convicted offender — "to pay a fine to the State treasury."[166]

Vermont's Supreme Court of Judicature, after noting how "the practice of torture to extort confession had prevailed in various governments," cited Beccaria for the proposition that "in all ages and countries where this inhuman and unreasonable process has been in use, men of enlightened minds, so far as they have had occasion to mention it, have borne testimony against it."[167] In holding that "all compulsory process to enforce an acknowledgment of guilt is for ever excluded," Vermont's Supreme Court of Judicature expressly relied upon the state's Declaration of Rights. In particular, the Supreme Court of Judicature cited the tenth article of the state's Declaration of Rights, which declared:

> That in all prosecutions for criminal offences, a person hath a right to be heard by himself and his counsel; to demand the cause and nature of his accusation; to be confronted with witnesses; to call for evidence in his favour, and a speedy public trial by an impartial Jury of the country; *nor can he be compelled to give evidence against himself,* nor can any person be justly deprived of his liberty, except by the laws of the land, or the judgment of his peers.[168]

The U.S. Constitution itself, in the Fifth Amendment, prohibits compelled self-incrimination, now most popularized in American culture by the portion of the *Miranda* warning articulating the right to remain silent.[169] In its Eighth Amendment decisions, the U.S. Supreme Court has condemned "torture" and punishments involving "a lingering death," but has not, to date, outlawed the death penalty itself as a torturous or cruel and unusual punishment.[170]

At America's founding, Beccaria's opposition to torture and forced self-incrimination was shared by jurists and prominent Founding Fathers—those who shaped the U.S. Constitution and its Bill of Rights. Not only did Thomas Jefferson, the Virginian, announce his opposition to torture, but plantation owner George Mason—the author of Virginia's 1776 Declaration of Rights—specifically argued in the ratification debate over the U.S. Constitution that "torture" was prohibited by law. At Virginia's convention, one delegate, George Nicholas, questioned whether a bill of rights would effectively prevent torture. "If we had no security against torture but our declaration of rights," Nicholas said, "we might be tortured to-morrow; for it has been repeatedly infringed and disregarded."[171] In reply, Mason—who wanted a national bill of rights, like the one in his home state—argued that "the worthy gentleman was mistaken in his assertion that the bill of rights did not prohibit torture; for that one clause expressly provided that no man can give evidence against himself; and that the worthy gentleman must know that, in those countries where torture is used, evidence was extorted from the criminal himself."[172] "Another clause of the bill of rights," Mason added, "provided that no cruel and unusual punishments shall be inflicted; therefore, torture was included in the prohibition."[173] At that point, taking note of those provisions, Nicholas "acknowledged the bill of rights to contain that prohibition, and that the gentleman was right with respect to the practice of extorting confession from the criminal in those countries where torture is used."[174]

The Right to Bear Arms

In the eighteenth century, the right and men's willingness and ability to bear arms was also a topic of considerable discussion. The first state constitutions were adopted in a time of war, and justifiable fears of British attacks or a British invasion—as illustrated by the British occupation of Boston, the Revolutionary War's hard-fought battles, and the War of 1812—loomed large in the founders' minds in America's early years. "The question of arms," writes Stephen Halbrook, thus "figured prominently in eighteenth-century political economy and criminology." As Halbrook explains: "The danger to liberty of standing armies and the alternative of an armed populace was stressed in the writings of John Trenchard, Thomas Gordon, Jean Jacques Rousseau, James Burgh, and Adam Smith." Noting that Montesquieu and Beccaria offered their own views on the subject, Halbrook emphasizes that James Burgh's *Political Disquisitions* (1774) — more than 100 pages of which were devoted to stressing the virtues of an armed populace — was an especially influential Whig treatise.

Nearly everyone had an opinion on standing armies or the carrying of arms, including English and Scottish radicals, American founders, and Beccaria himself. "Nothing will make a nation so unconquerable as a militia, or every man's being trained to arms," James Burgh wrote in his treatise, adding: "A militiaman is a free citizen; a soldier, a slave for life." Adam Smith, in his *Wealth of Nations* (1776), also expressed a disdain for standing armies, writing: "Men of republican principles have been jealous of a standing army as dangerous to liberty. It certainly is so, wherever the interest of the general and that of the principal officers are not necessarily connected with the support of the constitution of the state." As Smith recounted: "The standing army of Caesar destroyed the Roman republic. The standing army of Cromwell turned the long parliament out of doors." In *On Crimes and Punishments*, Beccaria, for his part, wrote that firearm laws "are not to be considered preventative but are to be seen rather as laws that stem from a fear of crimes; they arise from the tumultuous impression made by a few isolated cases rather than from reasoned reflection on the disadvantages of a universal law." "[F]or Beccaria," Halbrook writes, "it was unreasonable to punish one for mere possession of an inanimate object, particularly an arm which the law-abiding individual could use for self-defense."[175]

Early American laws — and the men who drafted them — were plainly shaped by such treatises and the ideas in them. In Thomas Jefferson's draft Virginia constitution of 1776, Jefferson proposed that year that "[n]o free man shall be debarred the use of arms." In George Mason's Virginia Declaration of Rights, Virginians — employing at least some words reminiscent of the U.S. Constitution's Second Amendment — agreed to these words later that year: "That a well regulated militia, composed of the body of the people, trained to arms, is the proper, natural, and safe defence of a free State: that standing armies, in time of peace, should be avoided as dangerous to liberty; and that, in all cases, the military should be under strict subordination to, and governed by, the civil power." Pennsylvanians, for their part, chose these fairly similar words: "That the people have a right to bear arms for the defence of themselves and the state; and as standing armies in the time of peace are dangerous to liberty, they ought not to be kept up; And that the military should be kept under strict subordination to, and governed by, the civil power." Decades later, in *A Familiar Exposition of the Constitution of the United States*, Joseph Story — the famed jurist — described the right to bear arms this way:

> One of the ordinary modes, by which tyrants accomplish their purposes without resistance, is, by disarming the people, and making it an offence to keep arms, and by substituting a regular army in the stead of a resort to the militia. The friends of a free government cannot be too watchful, to overcome the dangerous tendency of the public mind to sacrifice, for the sake of mere convenience, this powerful check upon the designs of ambitious men.[176]

Beccaria's writings on gun ownership in *On Crimes and Punishments* continue to be cited to this day, showing up, for example, in recent, high-stakes litigation over the meaning of the U.S. Constitution's Second Amendment. The Second Amendment — ratified in 1791 — states: "A well regulated Militia, being necessary to the security of a free state, the right of the people to keep and bear Arms, shall not be infringed." In one 2012 case, *Gowder v. City of Chicago*, a federal district judge in Illinois even cited Thomas Jefferson's commonplace book, which had extensively quoted Beccaria's writings, for the following proposition: "Although the Second Amendment does not specifically reference the right to personal self-defense, it was a right that was commonly understood to be a natural right at the time of the ratification of the Second Amendment." In his commonplace book, Jefferson had transcribed these ideas from Beccaria's treatise: "Laws that forbid the carrying of arms ... disarm only those who are neither inclined nor determined to commit crimes.... Such laws make things worse for the assaulted and better for the assailants." "John Adams," the Illinois federal district judge emphasized, "specifically referenced self-defense, stating that 'Arms in the hands of citizens [may] be used at individual discretion ... in private self defense.'" [177]

In another case, *State v. Hirsch*, the Supreme Court of Oregon also made reference to Beccaria's writings in the context of firearms. In that 2005 case, the state's supreme court held that the people's right to bear arms guarantees individuals the right to defend themselves using constitutionally protected arms but that a statute making it a crime for a felon to possess a firearm is not unconstitutionally overbroad. Article 1, section 27 of the Oregon constitution—one of the provisions being interpreted in that case—provides: "The people shall have the right to bear arms for the defence of themselves, and the State, but the Military shall be kept in strict subordination to the civil power." "Beccaria," the Supreme Court of Oregon wrote, "was fiercely opposed to the notion of disarming the general populace, for fear of the now-common adage that, 'when guns are outlawed, only outlaws will have guns.'" In the founding era, with British troops on American soil, gun ownership was seen as a necessary adjunct to the preservation of liberty—and to combat British tyranny. And in Italy, in an era before studies on gun violence, fully automatic assault weapons, and deadly mass shootings at schools, movie theaters and workplaces, Beccaria had seen no reason for any laws on the subject of firearms.

Noting that "the writings of Cesare Beccaria" were influential to Thomas Jefferson, John Adams and Thomas Paine, the Oregon Supreme Court—also citing Jefferson's commonplace book in its decision—emphasized that Beccaria had written these words:

> False is the idea of utility that sacrifices a thousand real advantages for one imaginary or trifling inconvenience; that would take fire from men because it burns, and water because one may drown in it; that has no remedy for evils, except destruction. That laws that forbid the carrying of arms are laws of such a nature. They disarm those only who are neither inclined nor determined to commit crimes. Can it be supposed that those who have the courage to violate the most sacred laws of humanity, the most important of the code, will respect the less important and arbitrary ones, which can be violated with ease and impunity, and which, if strictly obeyed, would put an end to personal liberty—so dear to men, so dear to the enlightened legislator—and subject innocent persons to all the vexations that the guilty alone ought to suffer? Such laws make things worse for the assaulted and better for the assailants; they serve rather to encourage than to prevent homicides, for an unarmed man may be attacked with greater confidence than an armed man. They ought to be designated as laws not preventive but fearful of crimes, produced by the tumultuous impression of a few isolated facts, and not by thoughtful consideration of the inconveniences and advantages of a universal decree.

Long before the U.S. Bill of Rights was drafted, Jefferson had laboriously copied those words from Beccaria's treatise, albeit in the original Italian, into his commonplace book.

The Oregon Supreme Court, in taking up the issue of the right to bear arms, further noted that Thomas Paine—who shared some of Beccaria's views—had written: "Arms like laws discourage and keep the invader and the plunderer in awe, and preserve order in the world as well as property.... To protect themselves, responsible citizens must arm themselves." Paine—who also, like Beccaria, had a distaste for capital punishment, with both men seeking to reduce crime—believed in the right of self defense through arms along with other prominent Founding Fathers. As Paine, the Quaker-raised revolutionary, observed at one juncture: "[T]he peaceable part of mankind will be continually overrun by the vile and abandoned while they neglect the means of self defence." "Horrid mischief," Paine editorialized in very Beccarian terms, "would ensue were one half the world deprived of the use of them; for while avarice and ambition have a place in the heart of man, the weak will become a prey to the strong." Although the U.S. Constitution's Second Amendment was adopted as a result of many influences, the Founding Fathers—in putting that provision in the U.S. Bill of Rights—may have had Beccaria's treatise in mind as they drafted it. Without a doubt, with the Revolutionary War still in recent memory, they had in mind the preservation of their liberty—and their new republic. "The American colonial experience respecting the right to bear arms culminated in the adoption, in 1791, of the Second Amendment to the United States Constitution," the Oregon Supreme Court aptly pointed out.[178]

Infamy, Cruelty, Dueling and Suicide

As a bestselling text in eighteenth-century England and America,[179] *On Crimes and Punishments*—and its discussion of the concept of *infamy*—also shaped public discourse about infamous crimes. "Infamy," Beccaria wrote in his much-invoked treatise, "is a mark of the public disapprobation, which deprives the object of all consideration in the eyes of his fellow citizens, of the confidence of his country, and of that fraternity which exists between members of the same society."[180] For example, a sermon preached by the English writer and minister Samuel Parr at Christ Church on Easter in 1800, later reprinted as *A Spital Sermon* in London, references Beccaria's treatise multiple times. In notes on his sermon, Parr emphasized: "I think that in our moral, and perhaps our legal treatment of offenders, sufficient attention is not shown to the feeling of shame. The reader, if he pleases, may consult Beccaria in the 23d chapter, where he treats of infamy considered as a punishment, and says that 'it should not be too frequent, because the power of opinion grows weaker by repetition, nor inflicted on a number of persons at the same time, because the infamy of many resolves itself into the infamy of none." In another note to his sermon, Parr quoted and then commented on Beccaria's treatise as follows: "'Robbery,' says Beccaria, 'is commonly the effect of misery and despair, the crime of that unhappy part of mankind to whom the right of exclusive property has left but a bare existence.' I agree with Beccaria about the mitigation of punishment for robbery, unaccompanied by violence, and about the increased severity of punishment when violence *does* accompany it."[181]

Across the Atlantic, Beccaria's writings on infamy and coerced confessions also shaped the founders' understanding of—and attitudes toward—the U.S. Constitution's Fifth Amendment. The first clause of that constitutional amendment provides: "No person shall be held to answer for a capital, or otherwise infamous crime, unless on a presentment or indictment of a Grand Jury." And its third clause, which also strongly echoes Beccaria's ideas, explicitly states: "No person ... shall be compelled in any criminal case to be a witness against himself." Beccaria, a U.S. Supreme Court Justice wrote in 1956 in *Ullmann v. United States*, had opposed the use of infamy as a punishment.[182] "The punishment of infamy should not be too frequent," *On Crimes and Punishments* had declared,[183] an observation also later cited by the Supreme Court of Missouri in the second half of the nineteenth century.[184] Leonard Levy, the Pulitzer Prize-winning historian, wrote that "the Fifth Amendment was exclusively the product of English and American colonial experience." "The influence of Continental theorists," Levy emphasized, "was non-existent."[185] But reading Beccaria's treatise—it must be said—was an *integral part* of that colonial experience. And while the Fifth Amendment's language can be traced back to America's mother country, readers of Beccaria's treatise were forced to reexamine their personal conceptions of infamy and infamous punishments. Certainly, Beccaria's views on the subject colored the founders' sentiments, leading to a gradual curtailment of infamous punishments.

In America's founding era, the one shaped partly by Beccaria's writings, there were different kinds of infamy. "[I]nfamy," William Eden wrote in 1771 in *Principles of Penal Law*, consisted of two types: "the one founded in the opinions of the people respecting the mode of punishment; the other in the construction of law respecting the future credibility of the delinquent." In *Living in Infamy*, an Oxford University Press title, the historian Pippa Holloway delineates the difference. "*Infamia juris* or 'infamy in law,'" she writes, "came when the convict was subjected to a degrading punishment." William Blackstone described infamous punishments as those "that consist principally in their ignominy," listing "hard labor, in the house of correction or otherwise, as well as whipping, the pillory, or the stocks." The public nature of shaming punishments lowered a person's social status, making those subject to such punishments infamous in the community. "The latter form of infamy, *infamia facto* or 'infamy of fact,'" Holloway explains by contrast, "occurred when an individual committed a crime that violated the moral code or exhibited disregard for principles of law, order, and truth." As Holloway emphasizes: "Someone who was infamous in fact had been convicted of a crime for which he lost his reputation and status. One could become infamous of fact through a conviction for certain kinds of crime that evidenced a lack of honor, such as perjury or treason." While infamous punishments were once common in eighteenth-century England and continental Europe, not all offenders in those class-conscious societies were subjected to them. As Holloway notes: "Nobles, clerics, and wealthy men were immune from degrading punishments; these individuals, when convicted, received high-status punishments, primarily imprisonment." In that way, they "were spared infamy and the loss of citizenship rights."[186]

Titles published before Beccaria's treatise illustrate how infamous punishments were viewed in Anglo-American society in the seventeenth and eighteenth centuries. In a 1683 book, *An Impartial Collection of the Great Affairs of State*, one finds a reference to "an infamous Scaffold"; the "Pillory," "Mutilation of Members," "loss of Ears," boring "through the Tongue," and "Forehead" branding with a "Hot Iron" were all described as infamous punishments; "Mutilation of Members" was classed as a "Brand of Infamy"; and "Rebels," "Traytors" and "Thieves" were labeled "infamous Persons." Likewise, in *A Modest Defence of Publick Stews: or, An Essay upon Whoring* (1740), its author, Harry Mordaunt, wrote: "Now, there are but three Things which Men fear in this Life, *viz*, Shame, Poverty, and bodily Pain, and consequently but three Sorts of Punishments which the *Legislature* can inflict." "If the Pillory, and such like infamous Punishments," Mordaunt observed, "are more terrible for the Shame that attends them, than for the bodily Pain, it is not because such a Posture of a Man's Body, with his Neck thro' a Hole, is in itself ignominious, or that any Law can make it so, but because it publishes to the World that a Man has been prov'd to commit such a certain Action, in its own Nature scandalous, which he is asham'd to have thus publickly made known."[187]

To be sure, the Anglo-American privilege against self-incrimination had canon and common law origins pre-dating *On Crimes and Punishments*.[188] In 1645, John Lilburne, relying on the Magna Carta and the 1628 Petition of Right, asserted "it is contrary to *Law*, to force a man to answer to Questions concerning himself." In that case, Lilburne had faced a trial in England's Star Chamber and had refused to take the oath. Baron Geoffrey Gilbert, writing before 1726, also declared that while a confession was the best evidence of guilt, "this Confession must be voluntary and without Compulsion; for our Law in this differs from the Civil Law, that it will not force any Man to accuse himself." Benjamin Franklin—in 1735—had gone so far as to call the right against self-incrimination "the common Right of Mankind."

But while the Fifth Amendment plainly had English roots, Beccaria's ideas infiltrated eighteenth-century society at the highest levels, and to such an extent that it is impossible to discuss the Fifth Amendment's meaning without thinking about how Beccaria's views shaped the founders' views. After the founders had studied Beccaria's ideas, including those on infamy,[189] Americans collectively and deliberately chose to permanently enshrine in the Constitution the right against self-incrimination and the grand jury safeguard for both "capital" and "infamous" crimes.[190] As one publication, *Italian Americana*, published during America's bicentennial, in 1976, put it: "Beccaria thus anticipated the Fifth Amendment's grand jury provision, and it is of no small interest that among the longer passages which Jefferson copied from *Dei delitti e delle pene* is the attack on infamy."[191]

The U.S. Constitution's Eighth Amendment prohibition against "cruel and unusual punishments"[192]—separated by just a few lines of text from the Fifth Amendment—is also reflective of Beccaria's aversion to cruelty.[193] That language, from a textual standpoint, was plainly derived—like many of its state-law equivalents—from the English Bill of Rights of 1689 and its then-preexisting American counterpart, the Virginia Declaration of Rights.[194] In formulating Virginia's declaration in 1776 and the Eighth Amendment more than a decade later, Virginia and then American lawmakers, in barring "cruel and unusual punishments," did not look to Roman law in choosing their words; instead, they selected English or American antecedents. But Beccaria's perspective on cruelty—and what should be categorized as such—did plainly shape the Founding Fathers' views, just as *On Crimes and Punishments* shaped European sentiments.

In that respect, the evidence is everywhere. One 1791 title, published in Dublin, cited Beccaria and said that "an execution, when it takes place long after the offence committed by the sufferer," amounted to "a cruel and terrible exhibition" instead of a "just" result. And in America, *On Crimes and Punishments*—from the late 1760s onward—influenced the founders' ideas and perceptions of everything from torture and the death penalty to coerced confessions and the concept of cruelty writ large.[195] The founders—history shows—frequently spoke out against "cruelty" and "arbitrary," "cruel," "sanguinary" and "unusual" acts, laws and punishments. Though Beccaria's influence is hard to pinpoint in every specific instance, Beccaria's guiding hand can be felt time and time again in early American speeches and letters.[196] The Founding Fathers, under the spell of Beccaria's pen, contemplated and, in a fundamental way, rethought the morality of harsh penal codes. They also saw, in the future, an America with more penitentiaries and fewer pillories, death sentences and executions.

Beccaria's views on dueling—a practice once condoned by early Americans to protect their honor—also quickly attracted interest and proved influential. "Neither the great nor the rich," Beccaria had written at one juncture, "should be able to atone for an attempt against the weak and the poor by means of a cash payment." As one source reports of the immediate impact of *On Crimes and Punishments*: "[T]he first English edition was published in London in 1767, and by December of the same year, Beccaria was being quoted by the *Virginia Gazette* in an article about the best way to prevent the crime of dueling."[197] On dueling in particular, Beccaria's treatise had advised: "[T]he best method of preventing this crime is to punish the aggressor, namely, the one who has given occasion for the duel, and to acquit him who, without personal fault, has been obliged to defend what the existing laws do not assure him, that is, opinion."[198] Beccaria's ideas on dueling—along with his views on capital punishment—were repeated in a number of books, including James Burgh's *Political Disquisitions*, printed and sold in Philadelphia in 1775 by Robert Bell and William Woodhouse and in London the same year by Edward and Charles Dilly.[199]

Around the time Beccaria's treatise was first translated into English in 1767, challenges to fight in duels were taking place in the colonies. "Dr. Arthur Lee," notes historian Bruce Baird in one book, *Lethal Imagination*, "challenged James Mercer in April 1767, and Joseph Calvert challenged Thomas Burke in the summer of 1769." Lee and the anonymous author of "Essay on Honor" had defended dueling in the 1760s, celebrating "modern honour" to protect one's most valuable asset, one's reputation. "The would-be duelists," Baird recounts of events transpiring in Virginia, "had regularly engaged in libelous attacks on their opponents in the pages of the *Gazette*." "Invoking *lex talionis*," Baird notes of one specific instance, "James Mercer attacked Richard Henry Lee's libels against Mercer's brother by threatening that 'had the same facts been sworn to before a tribunal having jurisdiction, I could legally have got the author's ears condemned; indeed, had I known him in due time, I would have attempted it by force of arms.'" As Bruce Baird, the historian, writes of early American dueling proclivities in a book chapter titled "The Social Origins of Dueling in Virginia": "During the decade preceding the Revolution, as aristocratic rivalries and democratic challenges eroded the unity and control of the upper classes, dueling became more acceptable."

It is estimated that at least 75 duels took place in the British colonies and the United States during the seventeenth and eighteenth centuries. Though only 18 recorded duels occurred in the American colonies from 1619 to 1774, the pace of duels increased substantially during and after the Revolutionary War and into the nineteenth century. "Between 1775 and 1783," notes historian Matthew Byron, "23 duels occurred in the American states—five more duels than had occurred over the previous 150 years." "Between 1783 and 1799," he points out, "the United States witnessed 28 recorded duels." At least 734 duels took place in the nineteenth century, with the first decade alone witnessing 88, the fatal 1804 duel involving Vice-President Aaron Burr and Alexander Hamilton—which naturally became the talk of the whole country—among them. "By 1800," historian Bruce Baird explains of the practice of dueling, "republican rhetoric and romantic ideals of chivalric honor provided a rationale for the upsurge in dueling, but the foundations for this phenomenon were laid in the social changes of the pre-Revolutionary era."

In this cultural milieu, Beccaria's ideas on dueling were sure to draw attention, and often did in both Europe and America. In 1767, Dr. Arthur Lee and his second, Corbin Griffin, left Lee's house in Williamsburg, Virginia, with pistols to be used in a duel with Lee's nemesis, the Williamsburg attorney James Mercer. Although that duel was somehow averted, Lee—in Bruce Baird's words—had, in the "six months after his nonduel with Mercer," written to the *Virginia Gazette* to declare that honor is "that principle which the British constitution considers in the highest degree, sacred and inviolable." In that piece, as Baird writes, Lee "seconded Cesare Beccaria, the leading European authority on penal reform, that '[i]n vain have the laws endeavoured to abolish this custom (duelling) by punishing the offenders with death." Likewise, the "Marquis of Beccaria" and his "Essay on Crimes and Punishments" was specifically cited in a chapter titled "Of Duelling" by Robert Boyd in a 1787 treatise published in Edinburgh. In yet another book that discusses dueling, "Beccaria of Milan" is referred to in 1802 as a "celebrated writer."

In that era, few dueling participants faced prosecution for their actions, and those that did might be either acquitted or pardoned. For example, in 1802, Richard Dobbs Spaight—

a signer of the U.S. Constitution and a former North Carolina governor—died after injuries sustained in a duel near New Bern, North Carolina. His dueling opponent, John Stanly, served as a Federalist U.S. congressman. But after being sentenced to hang, Governor Benjamin Williams pardoned him. As a result of Beccaria's treatise, other influential writings of the day, and the public fallout from such high-profile duels involving such prominent public figures, U.S. laws, in fact, began to change. North Carolina passed an anti-dueling law in 1802, and by the end of 1803, seven American jurisdictions had laws pertaining to dueling. After Alexander Hamilton's death in July 1804, American anti-dueling efforts only intensified, with legislators consulting Beccaria's ideas on the best way to prevent duels.

As the number of American duels, 70 in the 1810s and 61 during the 1820s, rose to 81 duels during the 1830s, revisions to state and territorial laws became a major focus of legislators. And as legislative reforms took shape, some states pursued a Beccarian approach. "Following the teachings of Beccaria," one academic notes, "Tennessee removed the monetary fine from its dueling law"; likewise, that scholar emphasizes, when Massachusetts lowered the punishment for accepting a challenge to duel from 20 years imprisonment to one year imprisonment, it was "more closely following the teachings of Beccaria than any other state had up to that point." Beccaria had written that the "best method" to prevent dueling "is to punish the aggressor—that is, the person who has committed the offense that leads to a duel—and to declare innocent the man who, through no fault of his own, has been constrained to defend something that laws on the books do not assure him, that is, the opinion which others hold of him." Though defamation in Anglo-Saxon law was once punished by excision of the tongue, and libel and slander lawsuits might result in damages, duels—the centuries-old way of resolving disputes—still took place in the name of defending one's honor. The gradual disappearance of such spectacles, however, must be attributed—at least in part—to Beccaria's writings on the subject.[200]

On the topic of suicide, Beccaria's views about the boundaries of state power to punish dovetailed with his advocacy against capital punishment. "Beccaria's argument," Harvard Law School professor Carol Steiker and University of Texas law professor Jordan Steiker explain in a co-authored piece, "began with political theory: he drew on the social contract theory of Hobbes, Locke, and Rousseau to argue for a limit on the authority of the state over human life." "In Beccaria's view," they note, "governments had no authority to impose death as punishment because individuals lacked the right themselves to commit suicide and thus could not delegate such a right to the state." "To the New World architects of the first constitutional democracy, who were strongly influenced by the body of thought upon which Beccaria drew," the Steikers emphasize, "this argument was powerful." "The view that the laws governing suicide were inhumane and useless received its most eloquent expression in the works of the Italian criminologist Cesare Beccaria," adds historian Ian Dowbiggin, a professor at the University of Prince Edward Island in Canada.

Indeed, John Quincy Adams—who had likely already read Beccaria's treatise—recorded this in his diary in 1778:

> I cannot but think that Laws against suicide, are impolitic and cruel for how can it be expected, that human Laws which cannot take hold of the offender personally, should restrain from the commission of this crime, the man, who could disregard, the natural and divine Laws, which upon this subject are so deeply imprinted upon the heart?

And as the years went by, early Americans continued to ponder and wrestle with this most difficult of subjects, as another diary entry—this one in 1783, from John Quincy

Adams' diary—indicates. In that entry, John Quincy Adams recorded the following for Friday, August 15th:

> This day I dined at Passy at Dr. Franklin's with a numerous Company. In the evening I went to the Comedy at the Bois de Boulogne. *Beverlei* and le *Français a Londres* were the plays represented. Beverlei is what the French call a *Tragedie bourgeoise*, as Barnwell in English. The Subject of it is, a Man addicted to gaming, who ruins himself by it, or rather is ruined by a villain who pretends to be his Friend; and at last puts an end to his Life by Poison. It was intended to set the passion of gaming in its worst Light but the execution has not answered its Purpose, for it seems to encourage, a still worse passion; I mean suicide.[201]

The then-existing laws pertaining to suicide were, of course, just one aspect of a much broader societal cruelty that Beccaria had weighed in against in his treatise.[202] And just as Europeans took notice of Beccaria's ideas, so too did America's founders. "Like Beccaria, Jefferson believed suicide not properly punishable," emphasizes Merrill Peterson in *Thomas Jefferson and the New Nation*. In fact, in Jefferson's Bill for Proportioning Crimes and Punishments in Cases Heretofore Capital, it provided that "the law will not add to the miseries of the party by punishments or forfeiture." While English law made the forfeiture of land or goods a penalty for suicide, Jefferson sided with Beccaria in opposing forfeiture as a punishment in that context. As Jefferson wrote: "The suicide injures the state less than he who leaves it with his effects. If the latter then be not punished, the former should not." "Men," Jefferson emphasized, "are too much attracted to this life to exhibit frequent instances of depriving themselves of it." Attributing forfeiture laws to a "spirit of rapine and hostility by princes towards their subjects," Jefferson argued that such laws were "inconsistent with the principles of moderation and justice which principally endear a republican government to its citizens."

As for criminal laws punishing suicide in his time, Beccaria's own rhetoric was extremely critical, concluding that it is "useless and unjust" to punish those who commit suicide. "A person who kills himself," Beccaria wrote, "does less injury to society than one who abandons its confines forever; the former leaves his entire substance there, while the latter removes himself together with part of his possessions." Beccaria reasoned that "punishing the suicide's body by dragging it through the streets or driving a stake through the cadaver's heart was as ridiculous as whipping a statue." "To be just or effective," Beccaria wrote, "punishment must be personal." "Similarly," Beccaria wrote, "confiscating the property of the deceased was merely punishing the innocent." In Europe, Beccaria's writings led to debates about the decriminalization of attempted suicide, with France repealing the sanctions against suicides in 1790 and the British Parliament—after a long delay— ending the criminalization of suicide in 1961.

Closer in time to the publication of Beccaria's treatise, the French lawyer Jacques-Pierre Brissot de Warville also published *Theory of Criminal Laws*, receiving a prize in 1781 for the best treatment of the reform of the criminal law. A writer read by, and well known to, John Adams, Benjamin Franklin and Thomas Jefferson, Brissot de Warville—who had published an anti-British piece supportive of the American cause in 1778—thought the punishment of suicide unjustifiable. Guillotined in 1793 at the Place de la Révolution, the Frenchman wrote before his own untimely death: "Whether suicide is a crime against nature, I leave that question to the moralists. It is a crime politically speaking, but it is beyond every punishment; it ought to be prevented, never punished."[203]

In the United States, with its patchwork of states, approaches toward suicide differed, but in the late eighteenth and early nineteenth centuries, it is clear that American states began easing the common law's harsh punishment of suicide. Suicide under early English law was considered a felony, and since early colonial courts followed that law, the punishment for suicide was forfeiture of the decedent's estate. "In the wake of their war of independence from British rule," notes the *The Oxford Encyclopedia of American Political and Legal History*, "most of the former American colonies ended criminal penalties for suicide"; "over the next 140 years"—that source notes, however—"state courts and legislatures criminalized the act of helping someone to commit suicide." The abandonment of penalties for suicide was due, in part, to what has been characterized as a "growing consensus that it was unfair to punish the suicide's family" for the decedent's act. As scholar Melvin Urofsky writes of the trend in American law, "even in those few jurisdictions which at one time made attempted suicide a crime, there were no prosecutions." Today, American laws do not punish suicide or attempted suicide as a crime, though assisting suicide is a different matter. In any event, the transformation of U.S. law can be attributed, in some measure, to Beccaria's treatise. At a time when England still punished suicide attempts as a crime, the Illinois Supreme Court, in a 1903 case, even ruled that it "had never regarded the English laws as to suicide as applicable to the spirit of our institutions."[204]

Education, Pardons, Extradition
Treaties and Debtors

Among the many other topics Beccaria wrote about—and that also made an Anglo-American splash—are education, pardons, extradition treaties, and the treatment of debtors. "Beccaria," one 1910 source, *Masters of Achievement*, states, "was among the first to advocate the beneficial influence of education in lessening crime."[205] In a section titled "Of Education" in *On Crimes and Punishments*, Beccaria wrote that "the most certain method of preventing crimes is, to perfect the system of education." This kind of thinking inspired Dr. Benjamin Rush to propose a "Plan of a Federal University" in the *Federal Gazette* on October 29, 1788, a plan widely reprinted in American newspapers. As Dr. Rush wrote: "let one of the first acts of the new Congress be, to establish within the district to be allotted for them, a FEDERAL UNIVERSITY, into which the youth of the United States shall be received after they have finished their studies, and taken their degrees in the colleges of their respective states." "Should this plan of a federal university or one like it be adopted," Rush predicted, "then will begin the golden age of the United States." Rush's plan, though supported by Virginia's James Madison, Pennsylvania's James Wilson, and South Carolina's Charles Cotesworth Pinckney, never came to fruition. But public schools—emerging with strong advocates in the early nineteenth century—would become a hallmark of the American education system. Indeed, in 1786, Rush himself wrote another essay—"The Schools Are Everyone's Concern"—in which he pointed out "the influence and advantages of learning upon mankind" and quoted "the Marquis of Beccaria" as saying to this effect: "When the clouds of ignorance are dispelled by the radiance of knowledge, power trembles, but the authority of laws remains immovable."

Beccaria's views on pardons also made an impact in the United States as well as in England and France. In his chapter "Of Pardons," Beccaria wrote: "As punishments become more mild, clemency and pardon are less necessary."[206] These views, which were often reprinted elsewhere, captivated the Anglo-American and francophone legal communities. For example, in discussing "*When and how far the King may Pardon*" or grant "*Reprieves*," Joseph Chitty of London's Middle Temple—in *A Treatise on the Law of Prerogatives of the Crown*—began his section on "*Pardons, Reprieves, &c.*" as follows: "The policy of pardoning public offenders in any case has been questioned by Beccaria, who contended that clemency should shine forth in the laws, and not in the execution of them. It would certainly be impolitic to remit the punishment attached to an offence very frequently or indiscriminately."[207] On the issue of pardons, Thomas Jefferson himself took a decidedly Beccarian approach, saying, "Let mercy be the character of the law-giver, but let the judge be a mere machine."[208] Influenced by Beccaria, Jefferson expressed the view that, "when laws are made as mild as they should be," pardons—whether issued by an executive or through the doctrine of benefit of clergy—are "absurd." "The principle of Beccaria is sound," Jefferson wrote, advising: "Let the legislators be merciful but the executors of the law inexorable." In 1788, Jefferson's pro-American friend, the Frenchman known as the Marquis Nicholas de Condorcet (1743–1794), himself contributed to a supplement of Philip Mazzei's *Researches on the United States* in which the concern was expressed that "[t]he privilege of pardoning criminals" granted to the President of the United States would "open the door to intrigue and abuse of influence." "Beccaria proves clearly," it was asserted, "that this kind of mistaken humaneness is nothing other than asylum for impunity and therefore a source of crimes." While Jefferson, as Virginia's governor and America's president, issued pardons, it was only because Jefferson felt that specific American punishments were then too harsh.[209]

Although the President of the United States and most state governors have long had broad clemency powers, including the power to commute or reprieve sentences, they have not always used those discretionary powers. It was, in fact, at least in part because early American lawmakers retained capital punishment for the most serious offenses, that pardon and clemency powers were retained in the first place. Because some punishments were extremely severe, granting clemency or reprieves was necessary—indeed, the only option—to ameliorate the harshness of penal codes that men like Jefferson and Madison didn't like and thought retrograde or even barbaric in nature. George Washington, John Adams, Thomas Jefferson and James Madison, the first four U.S. Presidents, used their clemency powers from time to time, and Alexander Hamilton—George Washington's aide-de-camp—himself defended the presidential pardoning power, saying it was necessary to avoid "sanguinary" or "cruel" results.[210] On the state level, early governors also granted pardons or reprieves because of the severity of the criminal law. In Massachusetts, for instance, governors Samuel Adams and Caleb Strong pardoned three of the four men sentenced to hang for crimes other than homicide. In 1806, Governor Strong also granted a full pardon to a single woman convicted of murdering her "bastard daughter" in 1803.[211] Even those accused of treason—as was the case with eight men indicted in New Hampshire on that charge in 1786—often escaped the gallows.[212]

Although presidential and gubernatorial clemency powers remain in place to this day, an intermediate step—the abolition of "benefit of clergy"—was taken to make the application of the law more consistent. Congress abolished benefit of clergy in the United States in 1790, with Massachusetts abolishing the privilege in 1785, though it continued to be used at the trial of slaves in Virginia until 1848. In England, Parliament formally did away with that privilege in 1827, though it had fallen into disuse in the late 1770s.[213] Indeed, Beccaria's ideas on pardons were hotly debated in early America even long after they first appeared. At a constitutional convention in Albany, New York, in 1821, the issue of the gubernatorial pardoning power came up on September 11th. Some convention delegates felt that convicted murderers should not be eligible for pardons, reprieves or commutations, and should be subject to execution. "Sir, if we punish capital crimes with death," one delegate implored, "there ought never to be a commutation." On the other hand, another delegate expressed the view that the pardoning power should reside in the "chief magistrate" rather than in the hands of the legislature. "[A] power to pardon for murder," that delegate stated, "should exist some-where, because there were many cases where it was highly proper." At that point, Peter R. Livingston—another delegate—weighed in, opining that when laws are wisely ex-ecuted, "no man will escape the judgment of the law" but that, "as they are now exe-cuted, every murderer will have the expectation of being thrown upon the legislature, and there have his punishment commuted." The son of Robert J. Livingston, Peter R. Livingston (1766–1847) married Joanna Livingston, the sister of New York Chancel-lor Robert R. Livingston and penal reformer Edward Livingston. "The important point in criminal law is to make punishment certain," Livingston said, adding, "When a crim-inal is convicted, let him understand that there is no hope of pardon, and then your laws will have a salutary effect."

That line of argument then prompted Erastus Root—another convention partici-pant—to assert that "the governor might possess the power of pardon, in cases of capi-tal punishment, as fixed by our criminal code." Root, like Peter R. Livingston, emphasized that Quakers were opposed to the taking of human life, then noted that two successive governors had declared in their speeches, that because an individual could not lawfully kill himself, he could not surrender any right to others of taking his life away. "Yes," Root said, "two of your governors have gone largely into the views of the Marquis of Beccaria. Then it follows, if these governors believed, that society could not take away the life of its members, they were conscientiously bound to pardon." "But the certainty of punish-ment," Root added, "is the strongest preventive of crimes." After Martin Van Buren joined the discussion, Peter R. Livingston spoke again, with the reporter describing Livingston's speech as follows: "In reply to an observation of the honourable gentleman from Delaware (Mr. Root) that two governors had assumed the principles of the marquis of Beccaria, he would make a single remark. The governors were doubtless actuated in their conduct by conscientious motives; and if they would act so in one case, they would in another."[214]

On the issue of extraditing offenders, Beccaria took a special interest in the ratification of extradition treaties to disincentivize crime. Supporting the idea that criminals should find no amnesty from punishment, Beccaria wrote: "the conviction of finding nowhere a span of earth where real crimes were pardoned might be the most efficacious way of preventing their occurrence." At the same time, however, Beccaria also expressed con-cerns about the possible injustice of certain extraditions, especially given the oppressive state of the law with its focus on executions. "I shall not pretend to determine this ques-tion" of the propriety of whether a nation should extradite criminals, Beccaria empha-sized, "until laws more conformable to the necessities and rights of humanity, and until milder punishments, and the abolition of the arbitrary power of opinion, shall afford se-curity to virtue and innocence when oppressed; and until tyranny shall be confined to the plains of Asia, and Europe acknowledges the universal empire of reason, by which the interests of sovereigns, and subjects, are best united." In a world with harsh, arbitrary punishments in it, Beccaria was thus fearful of states handing over criminal suspects only to have those suspects tortured or executed. "This worry about the injustices of extradi-tion," explains Harvard Law School lecturer William Magnuson, "gained increasing acceptance in the nineteenth century and eventually led to an exception in extradition treaties excluding political offenders from extradition in order to prevent the very kind of political vengeance that defined ancient extradition practice."[215]

Beccaria's ideas—at least those attributed to him—also shaped European and American policymakers on the treatment of debtors. After the publication of *On Crimes and Punishments*, Beccaria seems to have taken up the issue of imprisonment for debt in a separate tract—a title that was, like his earlier treatise, soon translated into Eng-lish. In London's *Town and Country* magazine, a section titled "An Account of New

Books and Pamphlets," makes explicit reference in 1772 to a "Newbery"-released, Italian-to-English title, *Imprisonment for Debt Considered*, with the following note: "This appears to be a translation from the Italian of the marquis de Becaria [sic], author of an Essay on Crimes and Punishments, and may be called an Appendix to that work."[216]

In the translator's preface to the fully titled *Imprisonment for Debt Considered with Respect to the Bad Policy, Inhumanity, and Evil Tendency of that Practice*, "Printed for F. Newbery, at the Corner of St. Paul's Church-Yard," the translator was somewhat coy about the treatise's authorship, writing: "But some of my readers may ask me, who this benevolent author is? And indeed, had I not been insensibly led away by a subject who so nearly touched my love of humanity, I should have before told him, that it is not certainly known, whether the following sheets were written by the Marquis *Beccaria* or not." "Whether he did or did not write them," the translator added, "they may well be considered as a supplement to his work *dei delitti e delle pene*, which has been so well received here, under the title of 'An Essay on Crimes and Punishments.'"

In the actual text of *Imprisonment for Debt Considered*, the author of the treatise—not identified on the title page—wrote that "[t]he social compact, or union of men in a state of civil society, had for its end the benefit of the whole" and that "[p]rivileges granted some, to the exclusion of all others, become so many acts of injustice to the rest of the people." "Every subject," it was emphasized, "ought to appear alike in the eyes of the sovereign." All people—both "Rich and Poor"—should be "made to conform" to the "*General Will*," the author observed, calling upon "the executive power, wherever placed," to "narrowly watch over their conduct, or otherwise the Poor will be oppressed by the Rich." The author of the treatise described how "[a] Poor man borrows money of his Rich neighbour" and "promises payment on a day fixed, thinking himself certain of keeping his word." When the debtor's "hopes are, however, fatally disappointed" and "his resources fail him," the author continued, the debtor "is shut up in a prison for a Debt contracted *bona fide* with a fellow-citizen." "I have never been able to comprehend, nor ever shall, why such proceedings should obtain the sanctions of the laws?" the author concluded, announcing his opposition to a Roman legal maxim that translates as "[i]f the Debtor fails to discharge his obligation, let his body suffer for it." "Times and manners are ever changing, and laws should change with them," the author wrote, citing John Locke for support. "The great Mr. Locke was so well convinced of this truth," the treatise writer reported, "that when he formed a system of laws for Carolina, he ordered them to be observed only during the space of a century."

The writings attributed to Beccaria by Francis Newbery's publishing house influenced other thinkers, who, in turn, cited Beccaria in denouncing incarceration for non-fraudulent debtors. In *Imprisonment for Debt Considered*, the treatise author distinguished between innocent and fraudulent debtors, writing of what should be done in the case of the latter: "The Debtor or Bankrupt who has acted fraudulently, is most undoubtedly deserving of punishment; but the fraud ought first to be clearly proved, and in no case should be presumed. He will then be punished not because he is a Debtor, but as he is a criminal." "But on the other hand," the Beccaria-attributed treatise reads, "he who has contracted a debt *bona fide* ought to enjoy his personal liberty, and should not be a prisoner at the pleasure of any individual." "Imprisonment is a grievous punishment," the treatise continued, "because it deprives individuals of that portion of liberty, which every man reserved to himself, when he passed from a state of nature into that of society."[217]

Imprisonment for debt was, in fact, an issue that was of particular concern to early Americans, including to the founders themselves. At the outset of the Revolutionary War, in an October 25, 1775 letter to John Adams, Josiah Quincy worried about the closure of the courts, writing:

> How long must the Courts of Justice remain unopened, and the Law of the Land unexecuted? Shall Criminals escape the Halter? Shall Debtors defraud and starve their Creditors, and every Species of Dishonesty be countenanced and encouraged by a Delay of Justice, which is virtually a Denial of it.

"[Y]our profession," Quincy added, "has taught me that, 'It is better ten guilty should escape, than one innocent Person suffer.' But this humane Maxim shan't divert me from watching; with the Eyes of *Argos*, if I had them."[218]

Later, some of America's founders—the leading men of the day—found themselves in dire financial straights. The British-born lawyer William Duer (1743–1799), a signer of the Articles of Confederation, went bankrupt in the "Panic of 1792" and spent the rest of his life in a debtors' prison. As one source further notes: "Even two prominent signatories to the Declaration of Independence, Robert Morris and James Wilson, were later sent to debtors' prison in the United States. It is reported that by 1816, more than two thousand New Yorkers annually were incarcerated in debtors' prisons in that state alone."[219] All of this, including the spectacle of men being jailed for honest mistakes, led to sustained reform efforts. On the 1820s masthead of the *Mechanic's Free Press* of Philadelphia was listed this goal of the Workingmen's Party: "Abolition of Imprisonment for Debt."[220]

In his award-winning book, *Republic of Debtors: Bankruptcy in the Age of American Independence*, Harvard Law School professor Bruce Mann notes that Beccaria's writings specifically influenced American lawyer William Keteltas to campaign against imprisonment for debt. Keteltas—once jailed for contempt—published a newspaper from prison entitled *Forlorn Hope*, twenty-five issues of which appeared during six months of 1800. Keteltas attacked the "impolicy" of treating debtors as criminals and reprinted a chapter from Beccaria in which the Italian philosopher asked "upon what barbarous pretence" the "honest bankrupt" was imprisoned and "ranked with criminals." The Beccaria chapter, Mann notes, appeared in "On the Impolicy of Imprisonment for Debt (No. 2)," published on April 19, 1800.[221] Another piece of writing, published in *The National Register* in 1817, even appeared under the name of "BECCARIA." Published every Saturday by Joel Mead, *The National Register* ran its article titled "On Imprisonment for Debt" on March 15, 1817. The article noted that "[t]he question of imprisonment for debt has been often discussed" and that "a late act of the legislature of New-York, abolishing it altogether, in connexion with several facts upon which the propriety of abolition is supported, has produced some dissertations on the subject, of a very liberal and philanthropic character, in the New-York Evening Post."

A footnote to *The National Register* piece, citing the *New York Evening Post*, emphasized that "[t]he documents submitted to the senate by Mr. Van Beuren, on Friday, will excite no little surprise in the minds of philanthropic men who are unacquainted with the extent of miseries inflicted by merciless creditors, upon their fellow men, in this enlightened age." Martin Van Buren—as a New York state senator—had sought to abolish debtors' prisons, with the future U.S. president labeling imprisonment for debt inhuman and immoral. That footnote recounted, among other things, that "a certificate of James Bell, keeper of the debtors' goal, and under sheriff of New York," tallied "*nineteen hundred and eighty-four different persons*" committed to that prison "during the last year"; "that during the last year, there were committed to said prison for debts *under twenty five dollars, seven hundred and twenty nine persons!*"; "that nearly all of them must have *starved*, but for the bounties of the humane society and individual charity"; that the sheriff "is compelled to beg for fuel for them to keep them from freezing"; that debtors had died in prison; and that "30 of the debtors now confined, have each a wife, and in the whole 73 children." The text of *The National Register* piece further emphasized that society should move away from "precedent" in looking at such cases, saying "the question is not, as it regards imprisonment for debt, what governments have done, but what they ought to do?" "The practice of imprisonment for debt," the article concluded, "is undoubtedly a remnant of ancient barbarism."[222]

The English Common Law

American law originated in the English common law, though America's founders did not always agree with the English approach to law and punishment. In taking notes on the fourth book of William Blackstone's *Commentaries on the Laws of England*, James Madison jotted down how crimes were severely punished under the English common law. He noted how "women" were "drawn & burnt" for "*Petty Treason*"; "*Mayhem*" was "punishable antiently by lex talionis" and "cutting ear, slitting nose"; "*Rape*" "seems to have been pund. with castration & loss of eyes"; and "*Sodomy*" punishable "in very antient times of law burnt or buried alive—in times of popery subjected to ecclestl. Censures only—at present felony." In those notes, Madison further noted how "*Manslaughter*" was "felony with Clergy, with burning in hand & forfeitures of goods"; and how "*Witchcraft*" was "punished like Heresy before & after Conquest, with flames" and by "one years imprisont. & 4 times standing in pillory" for "pretending to those arts." The defining characteristic of common-law crimes was that judges, not legislators, determined the law, with English courts—over time—developing the scope of common-law crimes. In his notes, Madison specifically took notice of the following "Salutary innovations," some of which may well be allusions to Beccaria's treatise: "1. proportion", "2. perspicuity & certainty," and "3. compensation to injd. party."[223]

As American law moved from the chaos of the Revolutionary War to a more orderly administration of justice and the courts, the systematic study of law took on a greater prominence, now uninhibited by the pressing, day-to-day concerns of the war. Indeed, new American institutions—the precursors of modern-day law schools—soon began to pop up that were focused on the study of law itself. For example, in April 1824, Peter Du Ponceau—the Provost of one such institution, the Law Academy of Philadelphia—delivered a valedictory address to the students titled "A Dissertation on the Nature and Extent of the Jurisdiction of the Courts of the United States." In that dissertation, Du Ponceau—a friend and correspondent of James Madison—confronted this question: "whether the Federal Courts have a right independent of the people of the United States or their representatives, by virtue of some occult power supposed to be derived from the *common law*, to mould the Constitution as they please, and to extend their own jurisdiction beyond the limits prescribed by the national compact?" "In England, the country from whence we have derived, not only our system of jurisprudence, but most of our civil and political institutions," Du Ponceau noted at the outset, "there is a metaphysical being; called *common law*, which originally was a code of feudal customs." "The king's prerogative and the rights of the subject are alike defined and limited by the *common law*," he observed, adding:

> The various and often conflicting jurisdictions of the different tribunals in which justice is administered are also said to be derived from it, although in many instances they are known to be founded on gradual and successive assumptions of

power; but those having been established and consolidated by time are now become *common law*.

In describing the common law's historical importance, Du Ponceau's address emphasized that the common law "pervades everything, and everything is interwoven with it." As Du Ponceau explained: "Its extent is unlimited, its bounds are unknown; it varies with the successions of ages, and takes its colour from the spirit of the times, the learning of the age, and the temper and disposition of the Judges." "It has experienced great changes at different periods, and is destined to experience more," he added, saying that "[i]t is from its very nature uncertain and fluctuating; while to vulgar eyes it appears fixed and stationary." Giving examples from the past, Du Ponceau noted that under the Tudors and the first Stuarts, forced loans, monopolies, legislation by royal proclamation and even slavery "were parts of the *common law*." "At the revolution," Du Ponceau remarked, however, likely alluding to the Glorious Revolution of 1688 and the adoption of the English Declaration of Rights in that same year, the common law "shook off those unworthy fetters, and assumed the character of manly freedom for which it is now so eminently distinguished."

At the heart of any good legal system are independent, impartial and uncorrupt judges, a topic that Du Ponceau addressed from an historical perspective in his dissertation. Judges holding their offices for "good behavior," Du Ponceau wrote of the common-law system that had been built up, were "the oracles of this mystical science." "In a monarchy like England, which has no written constitution, but in which all the rights of the sovereign as well as the privileges of the people are to be deduced from the *common law*," he wrote, judges are a "useful check against the encroachments of the monarch or his ministers; hence the common law and the judicial power are in that country almost objects of idolatrous worship." "While the United States were colonies," Du Ponceau added, "they partook of this national feeling," with "[t]he grievances which induced them to separate from the mother country" considered "as violations of the *common law*." "[A]t the very moment when independence was declared," he emphasized, "the *common law* was claimed by an unanimous voice as the birth right of American citizens; for it was then considered as synonymous to the British Constitution, with which their political rights and civil liberties were considered to be identified."

But the American Revolution produced *written* constitutions, and those constitutions—first at the state level—took on immediate and real significance. Unlike Parliament's unlimited, "omnipotent power"—as one Virginia judge in the 1790s put it—written constitutions limited the powers of government and, through the social compact, gave voice to the rights of the people themselves. As Du Ponceau, the Philadelphian, explained in his dissertation:

> The revolution has produced a different state of things in this country. Our political institutions no longer depend on uncertain traditions, but on the more solid foundation of express written compacts; the common law is only occasionally referred to for the interpretation of passages in our textual constitutions and the statutes made in aid of them, which have been expressed in its well known phraseology; but there ends its political empire: it is no longer to it that our constituted authorities look to for the *source* of their delegated powers, which are only to be found in the letter or spirit of the instruments by which they have been granted.

> The common law, therefore, is to be considered in the United States in no other light than that of a system of jurisprudence, venerable, indeed, for its antiquity, valuable for the principles of freedom which it cherishes and inculcates, and justly dear to us for the benefits that we have received from it; but still in the

happier state to which the revolution has raised us, it is a SYSTEM OF JURISPRU-DENCE and nothing more. It is no longer the *source* of power or jurisdiction, but the *means* or instrument through which it is exercised. Therefore, whatever meaning the words *common law jurisdiction* may have in England, with us they have none; in our legal phraseology they may be said to be *insensible*.

Because the United States had declared its independence from England, some Americans—who had taken up arms against British forces—were naturally suspicious of allowing English laws and customs to govern in their new country. As Du Ponceau recounted:

> Various circumstances have concurred after the revolution to create doubts in the public mind respecting the operation of the common law in this country as a national system, particularly in criminal cases. The bitter feeling of animosity against England which the revolutionary war produced was not amongst the least of these causes.

"The States might recognise their own common law, but to have been subject in any case to the law of the *enemy*, seemed in some manner like a dereliction of the principle of independence," he explained. Du Ponceau himself agreed with the idea that "the common law is the general law of the land," though he said he had "never been able to understand the distinction which has been made between civil and criminal cases, nor why, when we constantly apply its principles in criminal as well as in civil trials, we should hesitate to admit its definitions or offences and distribution of punishments." "After much reflection on the subject," Du Ponceau observed, "it appears to me that these doubts have their origin in the fear, lest it should lead the federal Courts to claim and exercise too extensive a jurisdiction in criminal cases, which I think I have sufficiently shewn cannot be the case."

Du Ponceau also noted "some vague fears" of the English common law "that are entertained of certain harsh punishments which our modern manners reprove, but which still stain the page of the common law." In that respect, Du Ponceau pointed out that "the punishment of petty treason" was drawing and quartering for men and "by burning" for women. "But the 10th amendment of our Constitution," Du Ponceau assured his audience, alluding to what modern-day Americans recognized as the language of the Eighth Amendment, "has sufficiently provided that 'no cruel and unusual punishment shall be inflicted,' which word 'unusual,' evidently refers to the United States, and the time when the Constitution was made, and therefore is not to be confounded with the same clause in the English bill of rights, which referring to another period and to another country, may have been differently construed."

Rejecting the notion that the U.S. Constitution's Cruel and Unusual Punishments Clause carried the same meaning as the similarly worded clause in the English Bill of Rights of 1689, Du Ponceau wrote of what had transpired from the late seventeenth century to the late eighteenth century. He emphasized that *peine forte et dure* (the Law French phrase for "hard and forceful punishment"), also known as *pressing to death*, had been abolished along with burning in the hand in cases of manslaughter. He further noted that "milder substitutes provided by our national statutes" had been put in place, and that "corruption of blood, trial by battle, all other modes of trial, but trial by jury in criminal cases are also abolished." "[I]n short," he said, "the common law as modified by our Constitution, by our laws, manners and usages, is as wholesome and as harmless a system, in criminal as well as in civil cases, as any that can be devised."

Du Ponceau specifically took note of non-lethal corporal punishments then still in use and editorialized as to his own hopes for the law. "As to offences not capital," Du Ponceau added, "cruel and unusual punishments being forbidden by our Constitution, there remains none but fine, imprisonment and, perhaps, whipping and the pillory." "I hope," he said, "I shall hear nothing of the ducking stool and other obsolete remains of the customs of barbarous ages." Du Ponceau then offered this opinion:

> The pillory and whipping, I know, are out of use in most of the States, imprisonment at hard labour having been substituted in lieu of them. Yet Congress have thought proper to retain the latter punishment in their penal code, and we have seen it inflicted not long since in our city on an offender against the laws of the United States. It is in the power of the national Legislature to alter or amend the law in this respect, as they shall think proper; but until they do so, I see nothing inhuman in the moderate infliction of either of these penalties, nor any reason why we should reject the common law on their account.

While he worried about "the discretion of the Judges," a major concern of the Italian Cesare Beccaria, Du Ponceau said he knew "no system of laws in which some discretion" was not present. "[T]he common law," Du Ponceau emphasized, speaking of America's English heritage, "does not give jurisdiction to the federal Courts, but is merely directory of its exercise." "[T]he law in this country, as every other science," Du Ponceau firmly believed, sensing and seeing changes ahead for the law, "tends to improvement."

English judges such as Lord Chief Justice George Jeffreys—described in a 1961 encyclopedia as "the most hated judge in criminal history"—had notoriously abused their power. That sordid history, in fact, was one of the reasons that America's founders read the writings of the French and Italian Enlightenment with such interest and excitement. Although efforts to restrain judicial abuses have been a centuries-old endeavor, a certain amount of judicial discretion has always been—and will always be—inevitable, making judicial selection procedures incredibly important. But be that as it may, it was English judges' authority to inflict a wide array of punishments, ranging from death sentences to lashes, as a result of the application of common-law crimes, that came to be seen as a particular hallmark—and deficiency—of the early British legal system. Runaway discretion was seen as especially problematic, though English courts were, at times, also greatly admired for standing up to the English monarch or government ministers. In one 1757 title published in London, it was even urged that *more* discretion be given to judges, with *The Works of Sir William Temple* providing:

> [I]t may seem probable, that the more natural and effectual way in our nation, to prevent or suppress thefts and robberies, were to change the usual punishment by short and easy deaths, into some others of painful and uneasy lives, which they will find much harder to bear, and be more unwilling and afraid to suffer than the other. Therefore a liberty might at least be left to the judges and the bench, according to the difference of persons, crimes, and circumstances, to inflict either death, or some notorious mark, by slitting the nose, or such brands upon the cheeks, which can never be effaced by time or art; and such persons to be condemned either to slavery in our plantations abroad, or labour in work-houses at home; and this either for their lives, or certain numbers of years, according to the degrees of their crimes.

The advantage of written laws, of course, is that they publicly guide and thus constrain judicial discretion. In a 1785 letter to Philip Mazzei, Thomas Jefferson—writing from Paris—described American law and its development in this way: "The system of law in most of the United states, in imitation of that of England, is divided into two departments, the Common law and the Chancery." "The Common law," Jefferson told Mazzei, "is a *written law* the text of which is preserved from the beginning of the 13th. century downwards, but what preceded that is lost. It's substance however has been retained in the memory of the people and committed to writing from time to time in the decisions of the judges and treatises of the jurists, insomuch that it is still considered as a lex scripta, the letter of which is sufficiently known to guide the decisions of the courts." "In this department," Jefferson explained of the common law to his Italian-American friend, "the courts restrain themselves to the letter of the law." As Jefferson's exposition of the law's history to Mazzei continued:

> Antiently indeed, before the improvement or perhaps the existence of the court of Chancery, they allowed themselves greater latitude, extending the provisions of every law not only to the cases within it's letter, but to those also which came within the spirit and reason of it. This was called the equity of the law. But it is now very long since certainty in the law has become so highly valued by the nation that the judges have ceased to extend the operation of laws beyond those cases which are clearly within the intention of the legislators. This intention is to be collected principally from the words of the law: only where these are ambiguous they are permitted to gather further evidence from the history of the times when the law was made and the circumstances which produced it.

In 1801, in a letter written to John Colvin from Monticello, Jefferson—in writing about the law—also added this caveat in responding to his correspondent's question:

> The question you propose, Whether circumstances do not sometimes occur which make it a duty in officers of high trust to assume authorities beyond the law, is easy of solution in principle, but sometimes embarrassing in practice. [A] strict observance of the written laws is doubtless *one* of the high duties of a good citizen: but it is not *the highest*. [T]he laws of necessity, of self-preservation, of saving our country when in danger, are of higher obligation. [T]o lose our country by a scrupulous adherence to written law, would be to lose the law itself, with life, liberty, property, & all those who are enjoying them with us; thus absurdly sacrificing the end to the means.... [I]n all these cases the unwritten laws of necessity, of self-preservation, & of the public safety controul the written laws....

Since America's founding, the role of American judges has been controversial, just as Abraham Lincoln's suspension of the writ of habeas corpus during the Civil War—an action taken, in line with Jefferson's views, to preserve the Union—has attracted the attention of countless scholars and historians. Thomas Jefferson himself praised the abilities of individual judges, but grew distrustful of the federal courts—more particularly, the Federalist judges who had been appointed before his term—even though the U.S. Constitution itself had authorized Congress to create those courts. In the early years of the republic, judges did not always even issue written opinions, simply announcing their decisions from the bench. This meant that, when decisions were made, there was no written decision to be analyzed later, thus necessitating the role of the so-called "court reporter." William Cranch—an early reporter of U.S. Supreme Court decisions in that era—was, he said, eventually "rescued from much anxiety, as well as responsibility, by the practice which the court has adopted of reducing their opinions to writing, in all cases of difficulty or importance."

In the preface to his first volume of reported Supreme Court cases, William Cranch attributed "MUCH of that *uncertainty of the law*, which is so frequently, and perhaps so justly, the subject of complaint in this country," to "the want of American reports" of the decisions. "Uniformity," Cranch asserted of litigated matters in U.S. courts, "cannot be expected where the judicial authority is shared among such a vast number of independent tribunals, unless the decisions of the various courts are made known to each other." "It is therefore much to be regretted," Cranch added, "that so few of the gentlemen of the bar have been willing to undertake the task of reporting." As Cranch, using fairly Beccarian language, explained the importance of written reportage of judicial decisions:

> In a government which is emphatically styled a government of laws, the least possible range ought to be left for the discretion of the judge. Whatever tends to render the laws certain, equally tends to limit that discretion; and perhaps nothing conduces more to that object than the publication of reports. Every case decided is a check upon the judge. He cannot decide a similar case differently, without strong reasons, which, for his own justification, he will wish to make public. The avenues to corruption are thus obstructed, and the sources of litigation closed.

Modern democracies are complicated, and the varied and conflicting interests of citizens and politician's constituents can lead to messy disputes, including over federal and state laws and the U.S. Constitution itself. Although everyone agrees that American judges must interpret written constitutions and statutes and apply, as applicable, common-law rules, judges' decisions are—to say the least—not always popular. On the role of judges, the current U.S. Supreme Court Chief Justice John Roberts famously spoke at his U.S. Senate confirmation hearing of judges being "umpires" whose job it is "to call balls and strikes and not to pitch or bat." Yet, charges and cries of "activist judges" are inevitably made, largely because judges, applying the law, must *make* decisions—decisions that, because they cannot be dodged, may be unpopular, perhaps even by a majority of the population. Indeed, in proper cases, through the power of judicial review, American judges—interpreting the Constitution—are *required* by their oaths to strike down unconstitutional laws, thus checking the power of lawmakers when they overstep their authority.

The very idea of the U.S. Bill of Rights, in fact, is that the people have certain inherent rights that no government or governmental official—or even the tyranny of a majority—can take away. As U.S. Supreme Court Justice Robert Jackson once famously wrote:

> The very purpose of a Bill of Rights was to withdraw certain subjects from the vicissitudes of political controversy, to place them beyond the reach of majorities and officials and to establish them as legal principles to be applied by the courts. One's right to life, liberty, and property, to free speech, a free press, freedom of worship and assembly, and other fundamental rights may not be submitted to vote; they depend on the outcome of no elections.[224]

In congressional debates over the U.S. Bill of Rights, James Madison—in making the case for a national bill of rights—himself said that "if all power is subject to abuse," "then it is possible the abuse of the powers of the General Government may be guarded against in a more secure manner than is now done." While Madison worried that "paper barriers" might be insufficient to protect people's individual liberties, he thought that, at the very least, a Bill of Rights would have a "tendency to impress some degree of respect for them, to establish the public opinion in their favor, and rouse the attention of the whole community."[225]

As the years went by, of course, the U.S. Bill of Rights—initially viewed by some American founders, perhaps even skeptically, as merely a "parchment barrier"—has roused the attention of Americans, just as Madison predicted. Although the parchment-engrossed provisions of the Bill of Rights—along with subsequent additions, like the Thirteenth and Fourteenth Amendments—were written with quill and ink, they have come to be seen as critical and enforceable safeguards for the individual rights and liberties of all Americans. The word "privacy," for example, nowhere appears in the actual text of the Constitution. Yet, the Supreme Court—interpreting a Constitution that, in the Ninth and Tenth Amendments, explicitly states that some rights are "reserved" to, or "retained" by, "the people"—has rightfully recognized that American citizens do, in fact, possess that right. While some "originalists" may question the rulings in cases like *Griswold v. Connecticut* (1965), *Roe v. Wade* (1973), and *Lawrence v. Texas* (2003), when Supreme Court Justices issue their rulings, they are doing exactly what they are appointed to do: issue rulings that decide what the law is.[226]

Just as modern-day litigants and legal scholars debate the meaning of the Constitution, early American lawmakers and academics did too. After being sent a copy of Du Ponceau's *Dissertation on the Nature and Extent of the Jurisdiction of the Courts of the United States*, James Madison—who himself wrestled with the role of judges in American life—wrote back to Du Ponceau in August 1824 to offer a partial critique and to identify common ground. While Madison praised Du Ponceau's ability as a writer, Madison—of his own mind—took issue with at least certain aspects of Du Ponceau's analysis. "I must say," Madison wrote, "that I have not been made a convert to the doctrine that the 'Common Law' as such is a part of the law of the U. S. in their federo-national capacity. I can perceive no legitimate avenue for its admission beyond the portions fairly embraced by the Common law terms used in the Constitution, and by acts of Congress authorized by the Constitution as necessary & proper for executing the powers which it vests in the Government." Writing from Montpellier, Madison emphasized: "That the Constitution is predicated on the existence of the Common Law cannot be questioned; because it borrows therefrom terms which must be explained by Com: Law authorities: but this no more implies a general adoption or recognition of it, than the use of terms embracing articles of the Civil Law would carry such an implication." "[W]hatever may have been the mode or the process by which the Common law found its way into the colonial codes," Madison argued, "no regular passage appears to have been opened for it into that of the [U.] S. other than through the two channels above mentioned."

Madison, as a Virginian, thus parted ways with Du Ponceau, a Pennsylvanian, on how traditional English common-law authorities should be viewed. "If the Common Law has been called our birthright," Madison wrote, "it has been done with little regard to any precise meaning." After referring to "the Statute law of England," "the English Constitution itself," and "our ancestors" who emigrated "during the Dynasty of the Stuarts," Madison added of the natural-rights orientation of the American social compact: "As men our birthright was from a much higher source than the common or any other human law and of much greater extent than is imparted or admitted by the common law. And as far as it might belong to us as British subjects it must with its correlative obligations have expired when we ceased to be such." But after making his critique, Madison concluded his letter by highlighting what he called an "important" point on which he fully agreed with Du Ponceau. "It has always appeared to me," Madison observed, "impossible to digest the unwritten law or even the penal part of it, into a text that would be a compleat substitute." As Madison wrote:

> A Justinian or Napoleon Code may ascertain, may elucidate, and even improve the existing law, but the meaning of its complex technical terms, in their application to particular cases, must be sought in like sources as before; and the smaller the compass of the text the more general must be its terms & the more necessary the resort to the usual guides in its particular applications.

Were the common law abolished, Du Ponceau himself had warned, "[n]ot all the codes of all the Benthams" could "fill up the immense chasm which would be produced by its absence."[227] The English common law had been around for centuries, and no legal system, as both Madison and Du Ponceau agreed, could start entirely from scratch.

In England and America, traditionally considered *common law* as opposed to *civil law* countries, statutes have long co-existed with judicial decisions articulating legal rules. Great Britain has had written statutes for centuries, and the U.S. Congress and state legislatures have been passing new laws since their formation. Indeed, in both countries, substantial efforts were made to *codify* crimes even before the publication of Beccaria's *On Crimes and Punishments*. For example, in 1648, the New England Puritans in colonial Massachusetts—having come to America aboard the *Mayflower* in 1620—codified the criminal law in accordance with their own values and views. The Massachusetts "Laws and Liberties" were based on the Bible and authorized capital punishment for, among other things, adultery, bestiality, blasphemy, cursing a parent, murder, rape, sodomy and treason. Over time, secular reasons were also offered as justifications for particular statutory punishments, with common-law crimes and defenses as well as legal terminology developed at common law supplementing those statutory enactments. "The notion of common-law crimes," as criminologist Joel Samaha notes, "persisted on American soil, though Beccaria's treatise—among other Enlightenment texts—prompted renewed efforts to change the Great Britain-inherited status quo." As Samaha writes: "The 18th-century Enlightenment, with its emphasis on reason and natural law, inspired reformers to put aside the piecemeal 'irrational' common law scattered throughout judicial decisions and to replace it with criminal codes based on a natural law of crimes."[228] Edward Livingston's attempt to create a comprehensive penal code would become a prominent early nineteenth-century example of this trend in American law.

In a report written in 1800, James Madison himself expressed his concerns about the prospect of English common law being incorporated wholesale into federal law. "If it be understood that the common law is established by the Constitution," Madison wrote, "it follows that no part of the law can be altered by the Legislature; such of the statutes already passed as may be repugnant thereto would be nullified, particularly the Sedition Act itself, which boasts of being a melioration of the common law; and the whole code, with all its incongruities, barbarisms, and bloody maxims, would be inviolably saddled on the good people of the United States." The Sedition Act—one of the subjects of Madison's wrath—made it a crime to "write, print, utter or publish" any "false, scandalous, and malicious" statement against the U.S. government, Congress, or the President of the United States. Making the case for the unconstitutionality of the Alien and Sedition Acts, Madison criticized the notion of federal common-law crimes. "If aliens had no rights under the constitution," Madison wrote at one point, "they might not only be banished, but even capitally punished, without a jury or the other incidents to a fair trial." "[A]lien friends," Madison declared, "were never meant to be subjected to banishment by any arbitrary and unusual process."[229]

Among the materials that Madison relied upon in drafting his 1800 report were notes written in the prior year by the American lawyer Edmund Randolph, a man who also worried about the indiscriminate incorporation of English law into American law. In his notes, Randolph raised this "General Question": "Is the common law of England the law of the United States?" One of Randolph's subordinate questions then asked: "Can the judiciary of the U S exercise a jurisdiction in any Crimes or misdemesnors described in the common law without a *constitutional* or special *Legislative* adoption in pursuance of the Constitution?" Randolph's notes reflected his view that "[t]he Common law is not adopted by the Constitution, either from its nature or specially," but that "Congress may indeed in the execution of any of its penal powers borrow provisions from the Common law as it may from British Statutory law, the civil law, or any other foreign laws." On the subordinate question posed, Randolph gave this response: "The negative of this question is uncontrovertable" because "Congress cannot resort" to the common law "as a source of Criminal power independent of the Constitution."[230] In other words, while the English common law might inform Americans' understanding of certain *legal terms of art*, it was not a separate source of *judicial power*, at least as regards the then newly formed federal judiciary.

The Codification of American Law

One of Dr. Benjamin Rush's own sons, the lawyer-diplomat and presidential confidante Richard Rush, became Attorney General of the United States in 1814. In that role, serving his father's friend President James Madison, Richard Rush had the idea for compiling *The Laws of the United States*, a project that, under his leadership, came to fruition. The publication of the *Laws of the United States*, compiled by J. B. Colvin, was authorized by Congress on April 18, 1814, and published in 1815 by Bioren & Duane, of Philadelphia, and Roger Weightman, of Washington, D.C.[231] The federal laws were arranged in chronological order, and the act of Congress authorized the purchase of a thousand copies. As one source notes of Richard Rush's contribution: "he superintended the publication of *The Laws of the United States from 1789 to 1815* (1815), the first codification of the laws of the United States." "Bioren & Duane's edition," one source reports, "was, for a long time, the standard collection of acts of Congress." It was a five-volume set, with the fifth volume containing the index, making it possible to find the law more easily. Roger Weightman (1787–1876) had learned to be a printer from Andrew Way and William Duane, bought the latter's bookstore and printing office in 1807, and had sold books and stationery to Thomas Jefferson.

On the 50th anniversary of the Declaration of Independence, July 4, 1826, it was Weightman — then the mayor of Washington, D.C. — who read to the assembled crowd a letter from Thomas Jefferson, who lay dying in Virginia. Jefferson's letter described the Declaration of Independence as "the signal of arousing men to burst the chains under which monkish ignorance and superstition had persuaded them to bind themselves, and to assume the blessings and security of self-government." "All eyes are opened, or opening, to the rights of man," Jefferson's letter observed. In words paraphrasing the last words on the scaffold of Richard Rumbold, an English colonel executed for treason in 1685, Jefferson's letter further proclaimed: "the light of science has already laid open to every view the palpable truth, that the mass of mankind has not been born with saddles on their backs, nor a favored few booted and spurred, ready to ride them legitimately, by the grace of God." "For ourselves," Jefferson concluded in this letter, written to be read on the Fourth of July, "let the annual return of this day forever refresh our recollections of these rights, and an undiminished devotion to them."[232] On July 4, 1826, the same day Weightman read the letter, John Adams — ninety years old at his death — uttered his own, now famous last words, "Thomas Jefferson lives." Unbeknownst to Adams, Jefferson had died that very day a few hours earlier.[233]

By codifying its laws, but letting judges continue to cite precedents to interpret terms used in those laws, the U.S. charted a middle course between the code-based *civil law* and the discretion-dependent *common law*. In 1821, in an address at the opening of the Law Academy of Philadelphia before the members of the Society for the Promotion of Legal Knowledge, Peter Du Ponceau explicitly contrasted the *civil law* — what he called "a science founded on principles" — with the *common law*, said to rest "on a different foundation." In his speech, Du Ponceau said both systems, though different, "assimilate more than is generally believed." "The fruits of the study of the civil law, which has lately become fashionable among us," he observed, "are already to be perceived in erudite works of jurisprudence, and in the able decisions of federal and State Judges who have shown by their examples what advantages may be derived from an acquaintance with that beautiful system of moral philosophy applied to human affairs."

In establishing the Law Academy to promote the study of law, part of an American movement to formalize legal education through the creation of law schools, Du Ponceau emphasized: "The common law, the civil law, the law commercial and maritime, the law of nature and nations, the constitutional and federal law of our country, and the jurisprudence of the different States, form together the aggregate of the great body of American law." "It is impossible," Du Ponceau added, "that such a vast, such a diversified field of knowledge can be well or successfully cultivated without the aid of academical instruction."[234] In fact, not only did legal instruction and training occur during the Revolutionary War, but American law schools were already operating before the end of the eighteenth century. Over time, apprenticeships would give way to more formal law school training, the model of legal education that prevails today.

From New England to the Old Dominion, the need for law instruction in the eighteenth and early nineteenth centuries was clear. George Wythe, Jefferson's mentor, started teaching law through his affiliation with the College of William and Mary in the 1770s before the Revolutionary War's end. And in Litchfield, Connecticut, Judge Tapping Reeve also offered instruction in law as early as 1774. His brother-in-law, Aaron Burr, would be his first pupil after he opened his home to law students, with the Litchfield Law School — a one-room building — opening its doors in 1784. That law school, at which James Gould also taught, operated until 1833 and had more than one thousand law graduates. James Wilson — the Beccaria disciple and signer of both the Declaration of Independence and the U.S. Constitution — started teaching law at the College of Philadelphia in 1790; Columbia College started its law school in 1793, with Transylvania University opening its law school shortly thereafter, in 1799. The University of Maryland and Harvard College also started law programs in 1816, with other law schools to follow in the years to come. These institutions and courses of study would provide a substitute for the prior training in English law that had taken place at the British Inns of Court.[235]

Before codifying U.S. laws, Richard Rush — the son of the physician-signer of the Declaration of Independence who so valued education — had graduated from Princeton in 1797. He studied law with William Lewis, a prominent member of the Philadelphia Bar, then became Attorney General of Pennsylvania in 1811. Like William Bradford, Jr. before him, the attorney generalship of Pennsylvania proved to be a stepping-stone for him to become the nation's top law enforcement official.[236] After being appointed to the Court of St. James in 1817, Richard Rush would, in Europe, befriend Jeremy Bentham, a man equally interested in law and who drafted legal codes for Italy, France, Portugal and Spain. Bentham — over the course of his life — became nothing short of an evangelist for penal reform, frequently bringing up Beccaria's name. For example, in 1814, Jeremy Bentham wrote to Alexander I, the Russian czar, emphasizing that, "among the *dead*," the names of "*Montesquieu, Beccaria* and *Blackstone*" had been mentioned "with honour" in a preface to "a complete *penal* code" promulgated by "the French *Emperor*." The Napoleonic Code, to which Bentham referred, had been promulgated in 1804. Indeed, in writing to Jeremy Bentham in 1821, professor Toribio Núñez, Bentham's Spanish translator, paid Bentham perhaps the biggest compliment of all, calling him a "Genius of good" and saying that Bentham had "completed what was attempted by the estimable *Beccaria*." In his own writings, Bentham also wrote fondly of "the celebrated Dr. Rush," the ambassador's father and his fellow Beccaria admirer.[237]

The Laws of the United States was authorized at a tumultuous time in American history. The War of 1812 (1812–1815), a military conflict between the United States and the British Empire, would once more test British might against the American people. In that conflict, trading with the enemy became a prevalent problem, though no federal statute existed to adequately address it. In spite of that fact, Attorney General Richard Rush nevertheless resisted calls for localities to issue indictments based on federal common-law jurisdiction. In writing to the United States Attorney in Massachusetts, Rush said: "I must declare that I do not think the common law applicable in such a case to the Government of the United States." As Rush reasoned: "I do not think that a Federal Republic like ours, resting upon, as its only pillars, the limited political concessions of distinct and independent sovereign States, drew to itself, by any just implication, at the moment of its circumscribed structure, the whole common law of England, with all or any portion of its dark catalogue of crimes and punishments." That English code, Rush remarked, made "scarcely less than two hundred" actions subject to "capital infliction," thereby "imprinting more of human blood upon the gibbet than is known to the same extent of population in any other portion of Europe." Rush thereby railed against the English Bloody Code in the same way that James Madison had to Thomas Jefferson at an earlier time. "Against the incorporation of such a code, even with the limitations that might be implied, upon the jurisprudence of the Union," Rush wrote, "I perceive serious and insurmountable objections."[238]

Richard Rush's skepticism of the death penalty in particular is also reflected in his own handwritten notes. On November 24, 1816, Richard Rush—then still serving as James Madison's United States Attorney General—wrote out a list of "Crimes punishable by existing laws of the U. States with death." The compiled list set forth fourteen offenses, consisting as follows: (1) treason, (2) murder, (3) robbery, (4) running away with, or yielding up to a pirate a ship or vessel or goods to the value of fifty dollars, (5) a seaman laying violent hands upon his commanders to hinder his fighting in defense of the ship or goods committed to his charge, (6) a seaman making a revolt on board a ship, (7) piracy, (8) accessory before the fact to murder, (9) accessory before the fact to robbery, (10) accessory before the fact to piracy, (11) forgery of any indenture, certificate or other public security of the United States, (12) setting at liberty or rescuing any person convicted of treason, (13) setting at liberty or rescuing any convicted murderer or other person convicted of any other capital crime, and (14) the willful destruction of a vessel at sea. "In running through the statute book this morning," Rush summarized, "I find the foregoing list of offences punishable capitally." "It is possible I may have passed some over, but most probably the list presents the whole," Rush added, hedging his bets in the era before computer-assisted legal research.

In describing the list of capital crimes he had compiled, Rush noted: "It is a long one. Considering the very few offences known to the laws of the U. States, those punished with death exist, in a greater proportion, than in England." Contrasting federal law with that of American states, Rush continued: "Neither rapes, nor arsons, nor burglaries, nor many others of a high grade, are, as yet, at all provided for." "In short, as far as we have gone," Rush wrote, "we have copied, closely enough, the bloody code of England," with Rush expressing concern about lawmaking inspired by the "spirit" of Draco, the notorious ancient Greek lawgiver. "If so much severity be right in itself, it certainly does not conform to the analogy of the mitigated codes of, I believe, nearly all the states of the Union; a mitigation agreed, I also believe, to have been productive of good effects," Rush noted. "The offences I have underscored seem not to call for so heavy a doom," Rush wrote, underscoring the following offenses: (1) robbery, (2) "running away with, or yielding up (to a pirate) ... goods to the value of fifty dollars," (3) a "[s]eaman making a revolt in the ship," (4) accessory before the fact to murder, (5) accessory before the fact to robbery, (6) accessory before the fact to piracy, (7) forgery of any indenture, certificate, or other public security of the United States, (8) "[s]etting at liberty or rescuing any person convicted of … any other capital crime" other than treason or murder, and (9) the "wilful destruction of a vessel at sea." In other words, Richard Rush wanted to see the list of federal capital crimes winnowed substantially as his native Pennsylvania and other states had already done.

In an explanatory note after compiling the list of federal capital offenses, Richard Rush questioned: "Why should the two systems, operating in the same community, so differ, merely because a citizen may happen to be upon one side, or the other, of an ideal jurisdictional line?" After raising this question about the divergence of federal and state approaches, Rush then ventured as follows: "Perhaps some explanation of the greater harshness of that of the U. States may be found in this: that most of its capital crimes, (from the search I have made since last evening I should say all but one) were made so by the old act of April 30, 1790." Congress enacted that act before Pennsylvania and other states had taken the novel step of dividing murder into degrees, with the states thereby making fewer homicides punishable by death. "Now, it is since this epoch," Rush wrote, "that, both in Europe and in our own country, but especially in the latter, the progress of humane and enlightened reform has been so considerable." Rush signed the note, dated November 24, 1816, "R. R."[239] As a practicing lawyer, Richard Rush himself was certainly no stranger to capital trials. Rush—along with another lawyer, Nicholas Biddle—had defended John Joyce and Peter Matthias, two men found guilty of strangling Sarah Cross, a widowed shopkeeper who lived in Philadelphia in Black-Horse Alley. Both Joyce and Matthias had been born as Maryland slaves, with Matthias having bought his freedom and whose first employer in Philadelphia was none other than Richard Rush's father, Dr. Benjamin Rush. The Reverend Richard Allen—a founder and minister of the "Mother" Bethel Church, an African Methodist Episcopal Church—attended those condemned men to their public executions in March 1808.[240]

Still another note found in Richard Rush's papers, prepared in advance of James Madison's annual message to Congress, reads as follows: "If the federal government, in its corporate capacity, draw not to itself the common law, as applicable to criminal matters, a chasm would seem to exist in this part of our system." "All offences, not specially provided for by statue," Rush wrote, "must be left without punishment in places, of which the number is not inconsiderable, where the U. States possess an exclusive jurisdiction." In the latter regard, Rush listed arsenals, dock yards, navy yards, forts, and light houses, as well as the families or individuals living within the confines of those places. "If, moreover," Rush added, "there be any offences already known to the statute, without a penalty being annexed, a necessity arises, under the same hypothesis, of defining the punishment as well as the crime." "It is right that an attention should be awakened to these topicks commensurate with their urgency," Rush advised, suggesting that it might be "expedient" to remedy "deficiencies" in "our penal system" and "to examine whether it might, in some particulars, be rendered, with due wisdom, less sanguinary."[241]

In a later published memoir about his overseas service as the Minister to the Court of St. James,[242] a book dedicated to James Madison, Richard Rush heaped praise upon Madison. In that memoir, Rush—the son of the legendary penal reformer—also included a lengthy entry about dining at Jeremy Bentham's house on July 27, 1818. "The company was small, but choice," Rush wrote, noting that Sir Samuel Romilly and "Mr. Mill," among others, were in attendance. Richard Rush also recorded that, on January 22, 1819, "Mr. Bentham came to see me." The two men discussed the suicide of Sir Samuel Romilly, with Bentham telling Rush that Romilly's death "leaves a chasm in parliament" in "the field of philosophical jurisprudence, but particularly as regards the criminal code, to mitigate and improve which, was a grand object of his parliamentary labours."[243] While serving as minister to Great Britain, John Quincy Adams—Richard Rush's immediate predecessor—had also held long conversations with Bentham as the two men walked about London. Adams would describe Bentham as "somewhat eccentric in his deportment, but of great ingenuity and benevolence." James Madison and Bentham had themselves exchanged letters on law reform, with Bentham sending Madison a collection of his writings and, in 1811, offering to work on a penal code for the United States of America.[244]

After working on codifying laws in other nations, Bentham launched what author Philip Schofield, in *Utility and Democracy*, calls a "sustained campaign to secure an invitation to codify aimed at the United States of America." "Between 1811 and 1817," Schofield notes, Bentham "pursued three avenues of approach, appealing separately to the President, the Governors of the individual states, and the people." Although Madison did not take Bentham up on his offer, perhaps wary of accepting the assistance of what another called "a foreign hand," Madison wrote to Bentham of the "very distinguished character you have established with the world by the inestimable gifts which your pen has made to it." In 1816, in a belated response to Bentham, with the five-year delay caused by the War of 1812 and the time pressures of the presidency, Madison wrote: "a digest of our laws on sound principles, with a purgation and reduction to a text, of the unwritten part of them, would be an invaluable improvement." "[T]he task," Madison added, "could be undertaken by no hand in Europe so capable as yours." In a "P.S.", Madison—who had taken his time in responding to Bentham's offer—thanked Bentham "for the valuable collection of your works which accompanied your letter."

When Bentham did not get an immediate response from President Madison, he did not give up. In 1814, the ever-persistent Bentham—who never lost his interest in Beccaria—also wrote to Simon Synder, Pennsylvania's governor. In that letter, Bentham spoke of a letter written by Albert Gallatin, the Swiss-American politician who represented Pennsylvania in Congress before becoming the 4th U.S. Secretary of the Treasury. Gallatin once described how Pennsylvania's penal code "is already much improved, and naturally daily improving." "The great reforms of the penal code, which, to the lasting honor of Pennsylvania, originated in that State," Gallatin recorded elsewhere, "had already been carried into effect, principally under the auspices of William Bradford." While Bentham received positive responses from Synder and New Hampshire's governor, William Plumer, neither Pennsylvania nor New Hampshire legislators ended taking up Bentham on his offer to provide codification assistance. In his own writings, Bentham spoke of "the laudable commencements of *Beccaria*," and mentioned "*Montesquieu, Beccaria*, and *Blackstone*" in a letter to Russia's Emperor.[245] Over the course of his life, Bentham corresponded with other prominent Americans, too. Among them: Aaron Burr, John Quincy Adams, Richard Rush and DeWitt Clinton, men who shared a similar interest in penal reform.[246]

Beccaria's name, in fact, showed up almost everywhere in the early nineteenth century as American lawmakers and jurists grappled with pressing legal issues. "Perhaps the most intellectually rigorous attack on the concept of common law crimes at the state level," writes historian Kunal Parker, "was John Milton Goodenow's *Historical Sketches of the Principles and Maxims of American Jurisprudence, in Contrast with the Doctrines of English Common Law on the Subject of Crimes and Punishments* (1819)." Born in 1782, Goodenow studied law, practiced law in Ohio, and then served in Congress before becoming a judge on the Ohio Supreme Court in 1830. It was after a judicial ruling in Ohio in 1817 that crimes under English common law could be punished in the state that Goodenow wrote his book strongly protesting that approach. Goodenow's treatise refers to Beccaria multiple times, with Goodenow writing at one point: "desiring my reader, without delay, to read, if he has not done it already, the Marquis Beccaria on Crimes and Punishments."

Among the many things that Goodenow wrote in his book, copies of which he distributed himself: "Suppose our legislature are so humane (and the day, I hope, is not distant) as to abolish *capital* punishment for murder."[247] In short, the provisions of the English Bloody Code were seen as inconsistent with American values.

At the federal level, American legislators never managed to completely eliminate capital punishment. It was not, however, for a want of trying on the part of congressmen such as Edward Livingston, the New Yorker who served as a Louisiana congressman from 1823 to 1829, as a U.S. Senator from 1829 to 1831, as President Andrew Jackson's secretary of state from 1831 to 1833, and as America's minister to France from 1833 to 1835. After becoming a U.S. Senator, Livingston introduced a bill at the national level proposing a penal code along the same lines as he had proposed for Louisiana. "In introducing the system," his biographer noted of Livingston's actions, "he asked the particular attention of senators to two of its features, — provisions for defining and punishing, by positive law, offences against the law of nations; and the total abolition of the penalty of death." "The work was printed by the Senate, for further consideration," that biographer emphasized, but noted that the subject was never taken up by Congress. Livingston's views on the death penalty — rejected by the U.S. Congress — would be transmitted worldwide, however, with some of his thoughts published in the 1830s as *Remarks on the Expediency of Abolishing the Punishment of Death, by Edward Livingston*. Livingston himself engaged in an extensive letter-writing campaign, and in 1847, the New York State Society for the Abolition of Capital Punishment brought out *Argument of Edward Livingston Against Capital Punishment*.[248]

U.S. Supreme Court Justice Joseph Story — a close friend of Daniel Webster — believed that the Judiciary Act of 1789 authorized federal judges to define and punish common law crimes. But the U.S. Supreme Court, of which he was a part, expressly rejected that view in 1812, holding that Congress must criminalize the act, provide a penalty for it, and give the federal courts jurisdiction over the offense in order for a federal court to convict someone of a federal crime. In the 1812 case of *United States v. Hudson*, a case in which two defendants were charged with common-law criminal seditious libel on the President and Congress for accusing them in the *Connecticut Currant* of paying the French emperor Napoleon Bonaparte $2 million to sign a treaty with Spain, the only legal question presented in the case was "whether the Circuit Courts of the United States can exercise a common law jurisdiction in criminal cases." In determining that they could not, the U.S. Supreme Court, with Associate Justice William Johnson authoring the Court's opinion, ruled: "Certain implied powers must necessarily result to our Courts of justice from the nature of their institution. But jurisdiction of crimes against the state is not among those powers." *United States v. Coolidge*, another Supreme Court case, also rejected federal court jurisdiction over common-law crimes in 1816, effectively settling the issue, at least from the Court's perspective.[249]

With Justice Story viewing Congress' Crimes Act of 1790 as inadequate because of its failure to criminalize various acts falling within the federal government's legitimate scope of legislative authority, he sought to remedy the omissions and deficiencies he saw. The Supreme Court's unwillingness to create federal common-law crimes had, in Story's view, left gaping holes in federal law, leading Justice Story to take matters into his own hands by drafting new federal crimes legislation for the consideration of Congress. The original version of the Crimes Act of 1825, drafted by Story with the assistance of Daniel Webster, a frequent Supreme Court advocate, consisted of seventy sections and sought to put in place a more systematic code of federal criminal law. Webster — Story's legislative ally — argued 223 cases before the U.S. Supreme Court between 1814 and 1852, making him a familiar face during oral arguments. "The Criminal Code of the United States is singularly defective and inefficient," Story said, noting that "few, very few of the practical crimes, if I may say so, are now punishable by statutes, and if the courts have no general common law of jurisdiction (which is a vexed question) they are *wholly dispunishable.*" As Story reasoned: "The State Courts have no jurisdiction of crimes committed on the high seas or in places ceded to the United States. *Rapes, arsons, batteries, and a host of other crimes, may in these places, be committed with impunity.*" Although the original bill drafted by Justice Story, circulated for approval to his Supreme Court colleagues, twice passed the Senate, the House of Representatives refused to pass the legislation. "The disfavor with which all legislation conferring adequate powers upon the Federal courts has frequently been regarded in the Southern and Southwestern parts of the country," one source explains of the House's disapproval, "prevented its enactment."

But thanks to the help and legendary oratorical skills of Justice Story's close friend, the congressman Daniel Webster, the Crimes Act of 1825—slimmed down to twenty-six sections and praised for the "clearness and lucidity" of its drafting—became law in that year. Formally titled "An Act more effectually to provide for the punishment of certain crimes against the United States, and for other purposes," the federal legislation that Justice Story conceived and that Webster sponsored was the first omnibus federal crime bill since 1790. After a lengthy series of debates about the proper division of jurisdiction between the state and federal courts, as well as about the propriety of various penalties set forth in the legislation, the bill as finally enacted in 1825 defined a series of new federal crimes, conferred jurisdiction on the federal courts over those crimes, modified or increased existing punishments, and permitted the use of fines, imprisonment and hard labor but no longer allowed the use of stripes or the pillory. In explicit recognition of the penitentiary system that American states had already created, section 15 of the Crimes Act of 1825, as adopted, explicitly provided as follows: "That, in every case where any criminal convicted of any offence against the United States shall be sentenced to imprisonment and confinement to hard labor, it shall be lawful for the court by which the sentence is passed, to order the same to be executed in any state prison, or penitentiary within the district where such court is holden."[250]

In debate over the Crimes Act of 1825, Daniel Webster—then a Congressman from Massachusetts—had first moved the U.S. House of Representatives to take up the bill in January 1825. After his bill was brought up in committee, however, it came under immediate attack from its critics. For example, one congressman, William Cox Ellis of Pennsylvania, moved to strike out the words "or rape" from the bill, believing that rape should not be a capital offense. "This crime," he said, "was, by the penal codes of most of the states of the Union, punished in a manner different from murder; and, however infamous the former crime might be, he thought there ought to be a gradation in its punishment below that of the latter." After another member offered his support for Ellis's Beccarian-sounding motion, Webster replied that "the Committee on the Judiciary did not consider themselves as instructed to re-modify the penal policy of the United States" and "had no authority to do so." "Should the time come when the Government should see fit to abolish capital punishments entirely," Webster said, "it was competent to do so—but the present bill would be found, upon the whole, to be a mitigation of the laws as they previously stood."

After the motion of Representative Ellis was lost, Edward Livingston of Louisiana—the man long taken with Beccaria's views—also took issue with Daniel Webster's approach, as did Representative James Buchanan of Pennsylvania. Buchanan—a future President of the United States—began by saying that he "highly approved of the general features of this bill" as "[i]t was a disgrace to our system of laws, that no provision had ever been made for the punishment of the crimes which it embraced, when committed in places within the exclusive jurisdiction of the United States." But Representative Buchanan "thought, however, that the penalty of death was too severe to be annexed to the description of crimes contained in the section under consideration." As Buchanan argued: "Vengeance belongs not to man. We should, therefore, be careful not to inflict punishments of a nature more severe than the safety of society requires. In all cases where the character of the crime does not involve such a degree of moral depravity in the criminal as to preclude a reasonable hope of his reformation, it would be both unjust and cruel, in the extreme, to deprive him of life." Pointing to one provision of the bill declaring that a passenger on board a vessel who steals goods valued at $1,000 shall suffer death, Buchanan queried: "Is not this punishment out of all proportion with the crime? Is it necessary for the safety of society that death should be the penalty in such a case?" "What," Buchanan asked, "is the consequence of annexing cruel punishment to crimes?" His reply to his own question:

> The people of the United States are humane and compassionate, and when the feelings of society are in opposition to the laws, you cannot carry them into execution. The humanity of juries is interposed between the criminal and punishment. The highest crimes thus often pass unpunished; and the chance of escape is in proportion to the enormity of the offence.

"It is the interest of society, therefore," Buchanan concluded, successfully striking out one provision of the bill that provided for the death penalty's infliction, "that, in the degree of punishment, justice should be tempered with mercy."

On January 24, 1825, as congressional debate over Daniel Webster's bill intensified, Representative Charles Wickliffe of Kentucky also sought to recommit the bill to the Judiciary Committee and sought to strike out the punishment of death for the crime of arson. Wickliffe—it was reported at the time—"expressed himself as opposed to capital punishments, except in cases of murder and treason" and "felt satisfied that the public sentiment of this country, in this respect, coincided with his own." "The objects of punishment," Wickliffe said, were two: "first, the reformation of the offender, and, secondly, the benefit of society." Wickliffe went on to say that capital punishment "obviously defeats the first of these objects" and that he "doubted greatly whether such an example which presented the offender as suffering the penalty of death under the United States' laws, for offences, some of which were not made capital and penal by the laws of any of the states, was calculated to have a salutary effect on the public mind." As Wickliffe reasoned: "where the feelings of society revolt against the severity of any penal enactment, it usually happens that the law is practically defeated, and the offender suffered to escape, through the lenity of courts and juries." "As relates to those offences against life, limb, or property, committed without the limits of the states," Wickliffe concluded of the federal crimes legislation, he "would willingly go with the gentleman from Massachusetts, in legislating for their punishment, provided some proportion was preserved between the punishment and the crime."

In reply to Wickliffe's arguments, Daniel Webster rose to defend the bill's provisions authorizing the death penalty's use. As it was reported of the debate, Webster "regretted, as much as any of the gentlemen could do, the necessity of capital punishments, and he did not know that he was not prepared to say, that a system might be formed in which it should be dispensed with altogether." "But such was not the present system of our laws," Webster continued, adding: "We punish the crimes of treason, murder, and rape, with death, and so long as this punishment was retained at all, he conceived that the crime of arson merited it as richly as either of the other offences." Webster's expressed "reasons for this opinion": "No human code, proceeding on just principle, could undertake to administer any part of that moral retribution, which belonged to the General Government of the

Universe. The great objects of human punishments is to deter, by example, from the commission of crimes." As Webster emphasized in the legislative debate: "Laws do not, or ought not, to proceed on a vindictive principle. Offenders are punished, not to take vengeance of them, but that others may not offend, in like manner." "The true inquiry, therefore," Webster told his colleagues, "is, what degree of punishment is likely to the purpose of prevention, and to secure the safety of lives and property."

Webster's remarks prompted yet another rejoinder from Representative Arthur Livermore of New Hampshire, a lawyer who was the son of former Congressman and U.S. Senator Samuel Livermore — the man who had, as a member of the First Congress, questioned on vagueness grounds the inclusion of the Cruel and Unusual Punishments Clause in the U.S. Bill of Rights. "The clause seems to express a great deal of humanity, on which account I have no objection to it; but as it seems to have no meaning in it, I do not think it necessary," Samuel Livermore had said when what became the Eighth Amendment was first proposed in Congress. "[I]t is sometimes necessary to hang a man, villains often deserve whipping, and perhaps having their ears cut off," Samuel Livermore had said at the time, fearing that the clause might in the future be used to bar such punishments and adding only this proviso: "If a more lenient mode of correcting vice and deterring others from the commission of it could be invented, it would be very prudent in the Legislature to adopt it; but until we have some security that this will be done, we ought not to be restrained from making necessary laws by any declaration of this kind." In 1825, the reporter recorded Arthur Livermore's own comments on another federal proposal, the bill's arson provisions, as follows: "Mr. LIVERMORE, after making a few remarks on capital punishments, and the limits within which they should be confined, expressed a hope that the Committee on the Judiciary would further consider that subject, and would be prepared, on to-morrow, to modify this section in such a manner as to remove the burning of some of these objects from under the punishment of death and assign to them a lighter penalty." After Arthur Livermore's motion was agreed to, the House adjourned for the day.

The next day, January 25, 1825, the U.S. House of Representatives again took up Daniel Webster's bill, with Webster managing it. At the outset, Webster said "that, in compliance with the suggestion of the honorable member from New Hampshire, (Mr. LIVERMORE,) he had divided the offences in the bill, into two classes, to the first of which only, the punishment of death was to be applied." At that point, "Mr. WICKLIFFE consented to withdraw the amendment which he had offered to the bill," noting, however, "that he was not thereby to be understood as giving his consent that the punishment of death should be assigned to any of the crimes specified in the bill." As the debate proceeded, "Mr. WEBSTER then proposed an amendment to the first section of the bill, so as to make the burning of any store, barn, or stable, a capital offence, only when such store, barn, &c. was parcel of a dwelling house, or mansion house."

After the House of Representatives voted 76 to 61 in favor of an Indiana congressman's motion to amend the bill to allow courts to imprison offenders in the nearest state prison or penitentiary if the federal district where the offender was convicted had no such prison or penitentiary, Edward Livingston joined the fracas on the House floor. In particular, Livingston sought to strike out language authorizing the death penalty and asked to replace it with language authorizing the imposition of a fine and imprisonment at hard labor. Livingston then gave "an extended and eloquent argument" against capital punishment, criticizing "sanguinary" punishments and expressing his "solemn conviction" that "it was not proper to take away human life as a punishment for any crime whatever." After several members commented on Livingston's floor speech, some favorably and some not, the question was then called on Livingston's proposed amendment but it failed to pass.

From Livingston's perspective, however, all was not lost. At the end of 1824, the year before Edward Livingston and his allies unsuccessfully battled Daniel Webster, the U.S. House of Representatives had agreed to a resolution proposed by Representative William Cox Ellis of Pennsylvania. That resolution provided that "the Committee on the District of Columbia be instructed to inquire into the condition of the Jails of Washington and Alexandria" and "the expediency of erecting a Penitentiary house for the District of Columbia in the city of Washington." As support for that resolution, Ellis had said that "in all well governed communities, the means of repressing and punishing crimes, had been a subject of the first importance in their legislation" and that "the modes of punishment and reformation of offenders against the laws, had long been an object of great solicitude among the most enlightened men of Europe." "This subject," Ellis emphasized, "had drawn to its consideration the first talents of modern times," with Ellis specifically singling out the work of Beccaria and Howard.

Noting that the "experiment made in Pennsylvania" with respect to its penitentiary system had led to "the melioration of punishments in New York, and many other states," Ellis sought through his resolution to similarly change "the laws of Congress" because the laws then in place at the federal level focused only on punishment and not at all on the reformation of offenders. "Every humane and enlightened visitor, who comes to remark upon the character of this place, and to carry away a report and portraiture of the city and the administration of the government of the United States," Ellis emphasized on the House floor in Washington, D.C., "would say that reformation was necessary." Born in Pennsylvania, William Cox Ellis (1787–1871) graduated from the Friends' School near Pennsdale, Pennsylvania, then studied and practiced law before being elected to Congress.[251]

Beccaria's Lasting Legacy

The importance of Beccaria's influence in America—and, in particular, on its founders and laws—is aptly summarized in Sydney George Fisher's *The Struggle for American Independence*. Beccaria's treatise, Fisher writes, "caused a great stir in the world" and "exercised great influence on the colonists." American political leaders, Fisher notes, read that "eloquent volume" along with Montesquieu's *Spirit of the Laws* and the writings of other influential European thinkers such as Jean-Jacques Burlamaqui. Just as European intellectuals sought out Beccaria and actively consulted his treatise as they thought about penal reform, Americans did too. As Fisher explains:

> Beccaria, though not writing directly on the subject of liberty, necessarily included that subject, because he dealt with the administration of the criminal law. His plea for more humane and just punishments, and for punishments more in proportion to the offence, found a ready sympathy among the Americans, who had already revolted in disgust from the brutality and extravagant cruelty of the English criminal code.

Beccaria's foundational doctrine—that "every act of authority of one man over another for which there is not absolute necessity is tyrannical"—made, as Fisher writes, "a most profound impression in America."

Another of Beccaria's core principles—that "in every human society there is an effort continually tending to confer on one part the highest power and happiness, and to reduce the other to the extreme of weakness and misery"—also became, in Fisher's words, "the life-long guide of many Americans." "It was," Fisher explains, "the inspiration of the 'checks and balances' in the national Constitution" and "can be traced in American thought and legislation down to the present time."[252] The idea that power should not be concentrated in one place — but should be distributed across institutions, with the people themselves remaining at the controls — was a central focus of American revolutionaries, and in that respect, Beccaria had much to offer. For example, one Anti-Federalist, lawyer Abraham Yates, Jr. — a New York sheriff and a member of Albany's common council from 1753 to 1773 — wrote a series of essays in opposition to a stronger central government in the 1780s. As one historian, Jackson Turner Main, explains of a piece Yates wrote under the signature of "Rough Hewer, Jr." in the *New York Packet* on April 21, 1785: "Abraham Yates, Jr., called upon Montesquieu and Beccaria to testify that republicanism could exist only in small states and pointed out that in both Switzerland and the Netherlands, local governments retained control over finances." In the United States, much local control and autonomy is built into the legal system, with power divided between the federal, state and local units of government.

In the U.S. Constitution, the result of the compromise reached in Philadelphia, while the federal government was delegated certain powers, the states — and the people themselves — retained others, with the people having both enumerated and unenumerated constitutional rights. "We the People of the United States, in Order to form a more perfect Union," the Constitution's preamble begins before setting out its intended goals, each of which, as Minnesota Senator Hubert Humphrey once noted, begins with a verb, suggesting the need for active citizen participation and vigilance: "establish Justice, insure domestic Tranquility, provide for the common defence, promote the general Welfare, and secure the Blessings of Liberty to ourselves and our Posterity."[253] In his own treatise, Beccaria — using slightly different language — had, more than two decades earlier, expressed his own views on the ideal social order, describing how people "deposited" authority "in the hands of the sovereign" as a "lawful administrator" to handle the "deposit." Beccaria's theory of the social compact would get repeated in political essays written by the likes of Richard Hey, whose *Observations on the Nature of Civil Liberty, and the Principles of Government* was published in London in 1776. "I have given the printed translation, though it is not a literal one," Hey explained of Beccaria's social compact theory before quoting Beccaria's treatise in the original Italian.[254]

"Laws," Beccaria wrote in *On Crimes and Punishments*, seeing the absolute necessity of punishment as its only justification, "are the conditions under which men, naturally independent, unite themselves in society." According to the first chapter of the 1785 Newbery edition of *On Crimes and Punishments*: "Weary of living in a continual state of war, and of enjoying a liberty which became of little value, from the uncertainty of its duration, they sacrificed one part of it, to enjoy the rest in peace and security. The sum of all these portions of the liberty of each individual constituted the sovereignty of a nation." The Constitution, as one American lawyer, Richard Sipe, explained in the *Indiana Law Journal* in 1946, "echoes" that worldview when it says in the Tenth Amendment to the U.S. Bill of Rights: "The powers not delegated to the United States by the Constitution, nor prohibited by it to the States, are reserved to the States respectively, or to the people."[255]

In this respect, Beccaria's writings — along with those of Montesquieu — shaped the very outline and structure of American government. America's founders dispersed power between the legislative, executive and judicial branches and chose not to place it solely in the hands of an executive — let alone a king. Indeed, *the people* — through elections and their ability to pick their own representatives — remain the source of all American political power. In *Letters from the Federal Farmer*, printed in pamphlet form after being published between November 1787 and January 1788 in the Poughkeepsie *Country Journal*, the anonymous author expressed specific concerns about the concentration of power in the seventh letter. That particular letter saw "the various governments instituted by mankind" as being "reducible to two principles"—"force and persuasion." "By the former men are compelled, by the latter they are drawn," the letter writer observed, adding: "We denominate a government despotic or free as the one or other principle prevails in it." As the seventh letter read in part: "In despotic governments one man, or a few men, independent of the people, generally make the laws, command obedience, and enforce it by the sword: one-fourth part of the people are armed and obliged to endure the fatigues of soldiers to oppress the others and keep them subject to the laws." "I have been sensibly struck," the letter writer observed shortly before the U.S. Constitution's ratification, "with a sentence in the Marquis Beccaria's treatise: this sentence was quoted by Congress in 1774, and is as follows:—'In every society there is an effort continually tending to confer on one part the height of power and happiness and to reduce the others to the extreme of weakness and misery; the intent of good laws is to oppose this effort and to diffuse their influence universally and equally.'"[256] Repeated again and again by Americans in the founding era, that sentence—in essence—encapsulates the whole impetus behind the American Revolution, also serving to the lay the groundwork for the American notions of equal justice and equal opportunity.

In fact, in the Revolutionary War period, prominent Americans regularly sought out Beccaria's views as America's ongoing experiment with law reform unfolded following the issuance of the Declaration of Independence. In a letter written on July 6, 1778, "To his Excellency the Marquis de Rosignan, Envoy from the Court of Turin, at Berlin," Arthur Lee—an American diplomat who served as a U.S. commissioner to the French, Spanish and Prussian courts—first wrote: "I hope you will not forget, that the constitution of our government having for their direct and ultimate object the security of the rights and the promotion of happiness of all their citizens alike, it is the duty of every lover of mankind to contribute his aid in bringing them to perfection." Referring to "the privilege of citizenship," to be "open to all men," Lee—who had studied medicine at the University of Edinburgh and who had also studied and practiced law in London—then specifically sought out his correspondent's views, as well as those of Beccaria. As Lee wrote: "I may therefore entertain the hope, that in some of your leisure hours you will favour me with your observations on our forms of government, most of which you will see collected in the Affairs Etrangers. It seems to me that I have understood you were in habits of friendship with the Marquis Beccaria. If so, you will have an opportunity on your return to Italy of adding his sentiments to your observations."

In his letter, Lee sought to explain how state governments worked with the hope of soliciting Beccaria's views on the proper operation of government. "The general object and operation of our governments are, the security of life, personal liberty, and property, by laws made by legislatures annually constituted by the people at large, and applied by juries chosen by lot," Lee explained. "But," he added, "the detail of operations to carry these views into execution, is what creates the difficulty, and often frustrates the best purposes." As an example, Lee brought up commerce and punishment practices, two topics sure to be of interest to Beccaria himself. After all, Beccaria was an economist as well as a penal reformer. "As it is infinitely more desirable to *prevent* than to *punish* crimes, what would be the most effectual regulations for that purpose?" Lee inquired. Lee then posed a serious of questions, questions that the leaders of the new republic had to address:

> Are charitable foundations, hospitals, &c. as beneficial by the relief they give to real distress, as they are injurious in creating distress, by encouraging the worst of all evils, idleness? How can one best reconcile a speedy administration of justice, with a clear discovery of the facts on which it ought to be founded? Are appeals necessary? For if the first jurisdiction is competent, why should it not be final? if it is not, why should it judge at all?[257]

Of greatest significance, perhaps, *On Crimes and Punishments* convinced American legislators to codify their criminal codes and to experiment with new penal codes restricting executions. The notion of common-law crimes, both at the state and federal level, became a controversial subject in early America, with judge-made rules and unwritten English customs giving way to new ways of thinking about the law. "The defining characteristic of common law crimes," one source explains of England's common law heritage, "is that they are made by judges, rather than legislative bodies." In America, though, the use of written legal codes, adopted by the people's representatives, became more popular, though judicial decision-making, especially in interpreting those codes, continued to survive. Both Coke and Blackstone spoke of "customs" and "common law" as being a part of English law, but with America's formation in 1776, everything about the law was up for grabs, with the Founding Fathers having to decide how much, if any, English law and custom they wanted to incorporate into their own laws. Ultimately, early Americans—first in the states, then at the federal level—chose to put in place systems of government that would rely upon regular elections of representatives, be they at the local, state or national level. Through those chosen representatives, Americans then adopted comprehensive statutory criminal codes, albeit ones that were built on their understanding of common-law principles and the legal terminology that had been developed by English tribunals in past centuries. As such statutory codes were put in place, they superseded the notion of common-law crimes.

American lawyers today still occasionally cite English precedents in their cases, though suspicion—even hatred—of English authorities was rampant after the Revolutionary War. An 1801 New Jersey law forbade that state's lawyers from even citing in that state's courts any decision, opinion or exposition of common law made or written in Great Britain since July 1, 1776, and the law made any violator subject to punishment. In 1808, the State of Kentucky also passed legislation forbidding the citation of English cases, though Henry Clay—who opposed the idea—got the proscription limited to those judicial decisions delivered since the day the American colonies declared their independence. Pennsylvanians similarly voted to forbid the citation of any English cases handed down since July 4th, 1776, a law that remained on the books for more than twenty years. But while the notion of common-law crimes largely gave way to statutory codes in American law, aspects of England's common law system still remain in the United States. For example, common-law *defenses* to crimes, such as insanity and self-defense, continue to be viable even in places that have done away with common-law crimes. And in civil actions, at least where the elements of causes of action have not been codified, common-law legal principles continue to apply in everything from contracts to tort cases.[258]

What Beccaria's treatise also did is encourage early Americans, including the founders themselves, to make sure the laws—of whatever source—were clear and accessible to the public at large. An informed citizenry, they realized, was the key to making their new republic work. An article titled "Knowledge of the Law," published in *The Whig Almanac* in 1850, specifically emphasized that "[e]very person is bound to know the law, whether life, liberty, or property, is involved." "He is bound," that article read, using the male pronoun at a time when women still had few rights, "to understand the nice and subtle distinctions of the common law, as well as its plainest rules, and to conform his actions to the letter and spirit of the statutes, whether the language in which they are written is plain or doubtful." As that article reported: "In most of the States, our fellow-citizens are required to obey the constitutions, the statutes passed by Congress, the state laws or statutes, the common law, and what is called equity, or the rules and orders of a court of chancery." "In Ohio," the article pointed out, however, "there are no common-law crimes: a man can only be held to answer in the courts for an offence defined and set forth in its statute-book." In fact, an entire pamphlet was published in 1919 titled *Why Are There No Common Law Crimes in Ohio?* "In New York, in 1846," the article in *The Whig Almanac* continued, "a convention, while amending the constitution, provided for the appointment of three commissioners as a board to codify or arrange in writing, in plain language, the whole body of the common law." "De Witt Clinton," the article noted, "earnestly urged on the legislature of 1825 the great work of codification, so that the rules which men must abide by might be rendered more clear and distinct."[259] The codification of all U.S. laws— the project overseen by Richard Rush—represented an attempt to publicize and make clear for all what the laws actually were, itself a very Beccarian idea.

Not everyone, of course, thought so highly of Beccaria's ideas, especially the notion of eliminating executions altogether. American lawmakers—accustomed to applying English laws from their days as English subjects—were generally unwilling to accept the notion that all executions should cease. When the First Congress, of which James Madison was a member, passed the Judiciary Act of 1789, for example, it was taken for granted that some death penalty laws would remain on the books. "[I]n cases punishable with death," one section read, "the trial shall be had in the county where the offence was committed, or where that cannot be done without great inconvenience, twelve petit jurors at least shall be summoned from thence." "[U]pon all arrests in criminal cases," yet another provision provided, "bail shall be admitted, except where the punishment may be death."[260] Such provisions implied that death sentences would be forthcoming. A legislative report on capital punishment, presented in the first half of the 1800s, even said that "arguments against the right of society to take away life" amounted to "nothing more than the well known sophism of the Marquis Beccaria." "For the infancy of the human race," that source reported, "there comes down to us an unbroken line of testimony, delivering it as the universal judgment of mankind, that the murderer should be put to death."[261] The U.S. Bill of Rights, in provisions intended to provide *protections* to capital suspects at a time when death sentences were *mandatory* upon conviction of certain crimes, itself contains the words "capital," "life" and "limb." Such words—like the provisions of the Judiciary Act of 1789—contemplated the use of executions and harsh, non-lethal corporal punishments, though they hardly can be said to represent commands that such punishments continue *in perpetuity*.[262]

In early America, the death penalty was seen as an appropriate punishment for murders, rapists and those disloyalty or levying war against the state, with British loyalists occasionally hanged for treason.[263] The first federal crime bill, passed by the First Congress on April 30, 1790, came into existence only after American jurists, such as U.S. Supreme Court Associate Justice William Cushing, lamented the lack of congressional action. While Article III of the U.S. Constitution had created "one supreme Court" and authorized "such inferior courts as the Congress may from time to time ordain and establish," Congress did not pass its first crime bill concurrently with its passage of the Judiciary Act of 1789—the implementing legislation that established the structure of the lower federal courts. Writing to John Lowell on April 4, 1790, Justice Cushing, one of George Washington's first appointments to the Court, lamented that the bill respecting federal crimes and punishments had been "sleeping sometime" because of other matters pending before Congress. "I am urging the completion of it," Cushing wrote, "without which I do not know in what predicament our Courts will be in as to carrying into Execution punishments for pyracies & felonies on the h. Seas & some other matters."

The first crime act—authored by U.S. Senator (and future U.S. Supreme Court Justice) Oliver Ellsworth—made certain federal offenses punishable by death. Because the federal government's powers under the U.S. Constitution were limited in scope, however, only a limited number of acts—seventeen—were categorized as federal offenses. Of those, only six — treason, murder, piracy, accessory to piracy, forgery, and rescue of a person found guilty of a capital crime — were categorized as capital crimes.[264] In an era when punishments swiftly followed the crime, it didn't take long before the first execution under federal law took place. In June 1790 in Maine, Thomas Bird — a sailor convicted of piracy and murdering his captain — was executed under the auspices of federal law after George Washington rejected Bird's clemency request. From 1790 to the first codification of the U.S. Code in 1815, the list of federal crimes punishable by death had expanded to those described by Richard Rush in his handwritten notes.[265] Yet the list of federal capital offenses — and the procedure for the imposition of death sentences — fluctuated over time as new lawmakers assumed their offices. In 1897, for example, Congress passed a law titled "An Act to reduce the cases in which the penalty of death may be inflicted." That law provided in section 1 that "in all cases where the accused is found guilty of the crime of murder or of rape ... the jury may qualify their verdict by adding thereto 'without capital punishment'" and "whenever the jury shall return a verdict qualified as aforesaid the person convicted shall be sentenced to imprisonment at hard labor for life."[266] While the number of federal offenses punishable by death was expanded in the 1990s, the execution of federal offenders is rare, as is the number of death sentences and executions in the states. A December 2013 article in *The New York Times* reported that "for the second straight year, only nine states put prisoners to death."[267]

The seeds planted by Beccaria's treatise in the fertile soil of the American Revolution sprouted rapidly, then grew in fits and starts over time, leading Americans to where they are today. One principle of Beccaria, that *certainty* rather than *severity* should govern penal laws, has been repeated multiple times by American courts.[268] For example, in *Commonwealth v. Anthes*, the Supreme Judicial Court of Massachusetts wrote: "An eminent and judicious writer on criminal law (Beccaria on Crimes) has said, that certainty in the infliction of punishments is much more essential to their efficacy, than the severity of them."[269] Another related principle — that punishment should quickly follow the crime — also drew the attention of early Americans. In a letter to Colonel Timothy Pickering, William Bradford — Madison's close friend — wrote on February 7, 1790: "It is the opinion of Beccaria, and all enlightened philosophers on this subject, that punishment should follow the crime as quickly as possible."[270] Thomas Jefferson himself footnoted Beccaria's treatise after drafting this provision in his Virginia bill to proportion crimes and punishments: "Whenever sentence of death shall have been pronounced against any person for treason or murder, execution shall be done on the next day but one after such sentence, unless it be Sunday, and then on the Monday following."[271] It is hard to conceive of a punishment following a crime much more quickly than that.

In railing against secret accusations and the arbitrary, pre-trial detention of people, Beccaria's treatise also found sympathetic readers in the United States. In that vein, America's founders — though eighteenth-century conceptions of justice, rough and swift as they were — saw fit to ensure through the U.S. Bill of Rights that judicial proceedings would remain orderly and be public and as free of arbitrariness as possible. The Fifth Amendment to the U.S. Constitution provides: "No person shall be held to answer for a capital, or otherwise infamous crime, unless on a presentment or indictment of a grand jury." Likewise, the Sixth Amendment to the Constitution provides:

> In all criminal prosecutions, the accused shall enjoy the right to a speedy and public trial, by an impartial jury of the state and district wherein the crime shall have been committed, which district shall have been previously ascertained by law, and to be informed of the nature and cause of the accusation; to be confronted with the witnesses against him; to have compulsory process for obtaining witnesses in his favor, and to have the Assistance of Counsel for his defence.

And in line with English traditions dating back to the Magna Carta, the U.S. Constitution's Fifth Amendment also guaranteed "due process of law," while the Eighth Amendment expressly provided for the right to bail, at least where the defendant did not present a danger to the community if released on a pretrial basis.[272] All of this was done as America's founders sought to perfect the Union that they formed in 1776.[273]

Of particular importance, *On Crimes and Punishments*—written in a civil law locale—nudged American jurists and lawmakers away from common-law crimes and toward a codification of offenses at both the state and federal levels. "Beccaria," Kate Stith and José A. Cabranes emphasize in their book *Fear of Judging*, "had been adamantly opposed to any leeway permitted judges to interpret the law." "Only the laws," Beccaria believed, "can determine the punishment of crimes; and the authority of making penal laws can reside only with the legislator, who represents the whole society united by the social compact." "[T]he authority to interpret penal law can scarcely rest with criminal judges," Beccaria had written in his treatise, "for the good reason that they are not lawmakers." "In every criminal case," Beccaria explained, "the judge should come to a perfect syllogism: the major premise should be the general law; the minor premise, the act which does or does not conform to the law; and the conclusion, acquittal or condemnation." Not only did America's newly empowered federal government codify crimes in 1790, but in the nineteenth century, most American states replaced common-law crimes with detailed criminal codes. "The abolition of common law crimes in the federal courts and eventually in all state courts as well," writes Melvin Urofsky in *A March of Liberty*, citing Beccaria's influence, "comprised part of a larger reform movement in criminal law."[274]

In assessing Beccaria's impact globally, Beccaria's ideas made a major contribution. His rejection of torture is now reflected in the U.N. Convention against Torture and Other Cruel, Inhuman or Degrading Treatment or Punishment. His rejection of the death penalty is reflected in multiple U.N. General Assembly resolutions and in the increasing number of countries—especially Western and industrialized democracies—that have turned away from executions. According to statistics compiled by Amnesty International, only one in ten countries worldwide carried out death sentences in 2012, and in the Americas that year, the United States was the *only* country to carry out an execution. Though thirty-two American states continue to retain capital punishment on the statute books, only nine of the fifty American states had executions in 2012, meaning the death penalty is now largely a dormant practice in many places.[275] At the international level, the humane treatment of prisoners—something Beccaria also urged—is also now dealt with by the U.N. Standard Minimum Rules for the Treatment of Prisoners. And Beccaria's views on the need for an independent judiciary and open and public trials are similarly reflected in U.S. law and in the International Covenant on Civil and Political Rights, ratified by the United States in 1992. Most importantly, the universality of rights—an outgrowth of the natural-law movement of which Beccaria was a part—has now been enshrined in international law. With the 1948 adoption by the U.N. General Assembly of the Universal Declaration of Human Rights, the countries of the world—without dissent—recognized in the very first article: "All human beings are born free and equal in dignity and rights." Another article specifically declared that "[e]veryone has the right to life, liberty and security of person," with Eleanor Roosevelt—a major participant in the adoption of that provision—opposing any explicit reference to the death penalty in the Universal Declaration of Human Rights.[276]

Ironically, the modern U.S. death penalty, with death row inmates spending an average of more than twelve years on death row before execution,[277] runs directly counter to one of the central principles—"immediate Punishment"—advocated by Beccaria.[278] Hundreds of American death row inmates have languished in their cells for more than 25 years, and the average time spent on death row for the 46 inmates executed in 2010 was 14 years.[279] In contrast, America's founders took a decidedly Beccarian approach to the timing of punishment,[280] with Thomas Jefferson—taking the idea to an extreme—calling for particularly speedy punishment upon conviction.[281] The founders lived in a society in which appeals were limited and rare and in which punishments were carried out in days or weeks or perhaps months, with that idea of swift punishments—then firmly entrenched—carrying over into later generations. For instance, in the nineteenth century, J. J. Hooker, the chair of the Joint Select Committee on Freedman, called for "a speedy and rigid enforcement of the criminal laws." Likewise, in the early twentieth century, a West Virginia attorney general's report noted that only "speedy and rigid enforcement" of the penal laws "will produce the desired result."[282] Such sentiments on speedy punishment, reinforced in part by Beccaria's writings, were thus pervasive in the founding era and among American minds thereafter.

The Founding Fathers would, no doubt, be much surprised—indeed, likely shocked and horrified—by the long delays now associated with state-sanctioned executions. America's founders recognized that societies evolve, just as twenty-first-century Americans' understanding of the concept of due process has evolved from the bygone days of few or perfunctory appeals and speedy executions.[283] "I like the dreams of the future better than the history of the past," Thomas Jefferson once wrote to John Adams, adding: "When we have lived our generation out, we should not wish to encroach on another."[284] Elsewhere, Jefferson reiterated that "the earth belongs to the living and not the dead," announcing that "[t]he will and the power of man expire with his life, by nature's law." In 1824, Jefferson—noting that future generations "may change their laws and institutions to suit themselves"—specifically emphasized in a letter to Major John Cartwright that "[n]othing then is unchangeable but the inherent and unalienable rights of man." Though not seeking to control the outcome of modern-day legal controversies, America's founders fervently believed that a punishment should follow as quickly as possible after a crime. That principle, in the case of American executions, has fallen by the wayside, even as America's death penalty has become associated with a bevy of problems, from arbitrariness, to the conviction of the innocent, to racial bias in capital charges and the infliction of death sentences.[285] The whole European Union, in fact, now views America's death penalty as a violation of basic human rights.

Given his own views on the death penalty and extradition treaties, however, Beccaria himself, were he alive, might not be so surprised that other nations, in light of the U.S. retention of capital punishment, are now refusing to extradite offenders to America unless assurances are obtained that the death penalty will not be sought. In a number of cases, foreign legal and judicial systems have determined that it would be a violation of human rights instruments to send offenders to the United States and subject them to the prospect of capital charges or lengthy confinement on death row prior to execution. For example, in 1989 in *Soering v. United Kingdom*, the European Court of Human Rights focused on what has become known as the "death row phenomenon" in deciding not to extradite an individual to Virginia without assurances that the death penalty would not be sought. The "death row phenomenon" focuses on the horrid conditions on death row and their impact on death row prisoners due to the sheer length of confinement prior to execution. Likewise, in 2001, the Canadian Supreme Court held that, except in extraordinary cases, extradition of offenders to the United States without assurances would constitute a violation of the requirement of fundamental justice set forth in section 7 of the Canadian Charter of Rights and Freedoms.

In strongly worded dissents, Justice Stephen Breyer and, before his retirement, Justice John Paul Stevens, both expressed a desire for the U.S. Supreme Court to take up the issue of whether extended stays on death row violate inmates' constitutional rights. In his dissent from a denial of certiorari in *Lackey v. Texas*, Justice Stevens framed the issue as "whether executing a prisoner who has already spent some 17 years on death row violates the Eighth Amendment's prohibition against cruel and unusual punishment." "Such a delay, if it ever occurred," Stevens dissented, "certainly would have been rare in 1789, and thus the practice of the Framers would not justify a denial of petitioner's claim." "Where a delay, measured in decades, reflects the State's own failure to comply with the Constitution's demands," Justice Breyer has written, "the claim that that time has rendered the execution inhuman is a particularly strong one." Dissenting in a case where a Florida inmate spent more than twenty-three years on death row, Breyer called the inmate's claim "a serious one" and emphasized that such a delay in the carrying out of the sentence "is unusual—whether one takes as a measuring rod current practice or the practice in this country and in England at the time our Constitution was written."[286] To date, however, the Supreme Court has refused to review such a case. When it does, one of Beccaria's principles—and perhaps more than one—is likely to come up again.

Conclusion

On Crimes and Punishments has aptly been described as "a founding work in modern penology."[1] For America's Founding Fathers, Beccaria's treatise was certainly a seminal, landscape-changing work, one very much in line with the precepts of the American Revolution. America's founders quoted the treatise, they repeatedly relied upon it, and they regularly excerpted or borrowed Beccaria's ideas and arguments.[2] George Washington purchased Beccaria's treatise and made use of its ideas while leading the Continental Army; Thomas Jefferson copied lengthy sections of it into his commonplace book and recommended the treatise to others; and John Adams pulled a moving line out of *On Crimes and Punishments* to dramatically use in a Massachusetts courtroom following the Boston Massacre. Indeed, in the debates over the U.S. Constitution itself, Beccaria's name often appears in the mix. Thus, at New York's 1788 ratifying convention, Melancton Smith (1744–1798)—a former member of the Continental Congress—passionately invoked Beccaria in the course of opposing an approach to the law that risked perpetuating the gap between rich and poor. "'In every human society,'" Smith quoted from *On Crimes and Punishments*, "'there is an effort continually tending to confer on one part the height of power and happiness, and to reduce the other to the extreme of weakness and misery.'"[3]

Despite their Italian origins, Beccaria's ideas quickly filtered out into American society, with *On Crimes and Punishments* even inspiring the lengthy, later published eighteenth-century ode to the book by the American lawyer and poet St. John Honeywood. No less a figure than historian Garry Wills, in *Inventing America: Jefferson's Declaration of Independence*, has argued that it was the works of Francis Hutcheson and Cesare Beccaria that undergirded the Declaration of Independence's true origins.[4] While scores of Enlightenment writers shaped the founders, references to Italian thinkers—and Rome and its history—abound. Historians, explains legal historian Tim Sellers, "cannot avoid the constant references to republican Rome, and American citations to Livy, Cicero, Sallust and Tacitus." A University of Baltimore law professor, Sellers emphasizes that a host of European figures, from Beccaria, Burlamaqui, de Lolme, Grotius and Locke, to Montesquieu, Pufendorf, Rousseau, Vattel and Voltaire, "were important influences on American constitutional thought," with those thinkers sharing "a republican Roman sensibility." "Roman republicanism," Sellers notes, "shaped the language and values of any American who had been to grammar school, just as it shaped the thinking of the Europeans"—like Beccaria—"they admired."[5]

John Adams—who passionately quoted Beccaria's words in open court—was so well versed in Roman history that he often dropped references to it into his own writings. "If we look into History," Adams argued as early as 1755, citing ancient Rome's example during America's colonial days, "we shall find some nations rising from contemptible beginnings, and spreading their influence, 'till the whole Globe is subjected to their sway." Noting that "[i]mmortal Rome was at first but an insignificant Village," Adams—a consummate student of government and politics, and no doubt pondering even then how the dictatorial fate of the Roman republic might have been averted—wrote of Rome's decline. "When they reach'd the summit of Grandeur," Adams cautioned, "some minute and unsuspected Cause commonly effects their Ruin, and the Empire of the world is trans-ferred to some other place." By 1774, on the cusp of the Revolutionary War, Adams—sensing that it was America's time, and having already read *On Crimes and Punishments*—wrote that a "comprehensive Knowledge of Arts and Sciences, and especially of Law and History, of Geography, Commerce, War, and Life, is necessary for an American States-man, at this Time as was ever necessary for a British or a Roman Senator, or a British or Roman General." By then, a working knowledge of Beccaria's treatise—itself quoted that year by the Continental Congress—was indispensable.

America has, since its inception, been a country focused on free enterprise and eco-nomic opportunity—a country of immigrants and seekers and strivers, the proverbial land of "the American Dream." In *On Crimes and Punishments*, Cesare Beccaria—the Italian economist and political philosopher—himself wrote of economic competition, repub-licanism and equality of treatment. On the topic of trade and intellectual discourse, Bec-caria took specific note of how "commerce has become dynamic thanks to the philosophical truths made widely available by the printing press," saying "a quiet war of industry has bro-ken out among nations, the most humane sort of war and the most worthy of reasonable men." For North American colonists, a liberty-loving people seeking fair trade, a seat at the table of power, and a just say in the matter of their own taxation, Beccaria's words about tyranny and fair treatment struck an exposed nerve. When coupled with the shining ex-ample of Rome's ancient civilization, a *res publica* begun with the overthrow of the Roman monarchy, Americans began to contemplate—in a very real way—the possibility of a separation from their mother country.[6]

Prior to 1768, the colonists had already endured much British oppression and imposition. The British Parliament passed the Sugar Act in 1764, followed by the notorious Stamp Act of 1765. Although the Stamp Act was repealed in 1766, the Townshend Act of 1767 there-after imposed duties on seventy-two items, including glass, paint, paper and tea. In 1768, the year after Beccaria's treatise was translated into English, the American revolutionary John Dickinson—in urging merchants, in response, to boycott British goods—thus naturally looked, like Adams, to Roman history for inspiration. At that time, Dickinson—a known Beccaria admirer—said this in the face of the colonists' economic hardships: "I would beg Leave to ask whether any People in any Age or Country ever defended and preserved their Liberty from the Encroachment of Power without suffering present Inconveniences." "The Roman people," he observed in response to his own rhetorical question, "suffered them-selves to be defeated by their Enemies, rather than submit to the Tyranny of the Nobles."[7]

With George III and the British Parliament responsible for colonists' economic inse-curity, American colonists—in the lead up to the Revolutionary War—saw their freedom and honor, as well as their very livelihoods, at stake. The colonists viewed themselves, first and foremost, as Englishmen, but Englishmen had rights, and their rights were being ignored. In framing the debate, Dickinson and his fellow American colonists initially wanted, above all else, to simply reclaim the liberties they felt they had lost through ne-glect and inattention. In a speech delivered in 1772, for example, the future American martyr, Dr. Joseph Warren of Boston, took the opportunity, like Adams and Dickinson before him, to speak of the Roman love of liberty. "It was," he said, "this noble attachment to a free constitution which raised ancient Rome from the smallest beginnings to the bright summit of happiness and glory to which she arrived." "[A]nd it was," Dr. Warren warned, sensing the gathering storm, "the loss of this which plunged her from that sum-mit into the black gulph of infamy and slavery."[8]

The republican, forward-leading ideas in Beccaria's treatise—about everything from happiness and tyranny to the need for a more rational system of criminal justice—thus came at an opportune time. America's founders, already intoxicated by visions of ancient Rome's once glorious republic, avidly read Beccaria's words, then began—if only as a matter of last resort—the American Revolution when their demands for equal treatment were not met. As Americans sought, through war, to realize what Jefferson—in the Declaration of Independence—deftly called "the pursuit of Happiness," they had in mind not only their working knowledge of Roman history and republicanism, but an easy familiarity with Beccaria's treatise and John Locke's *Essay on Human Understanding*, a 1689 work that used the exact phrase "pursuit of happiness" multiple times. Indeed, before 1776, many other Europeans—among them, the lexicographer Dr. Samuel Johnson, the pro-republican philosopher Richard Price, the writer William Wollaston, and the Scottish jurist Francis Hutcheson—had themselves used that now-familiar phrase. In America, Pennsylvania's James Wilson—one of Beccaria's biggest disciples and one of only six signers of both the Declaration of Independence and the U.S. Constitution—himself wrote in a 1774 essay that "the happiness of the society is the first law of every government."[9]

Beccaria's principles were disseminated far and wide, from the bustling cities of Europe to the farms and plantations of a then-predominantly agricultural America. Like Thomas Paine's *Common Sense*, Beccaria's treatise was highly accessible, with America's founders viewing their conflict with the British through its lens. In a letter to the President of Congress, written from Amsterdam in 1781, John Adams even trotted out a principle that can be found front and center in Beccaria's treatise—"the greatest happiness of the greatest Number"—in describing the impulse, or motivating factor, behind the American Revolution itself. "The American Revolution," Adams wrote, had "given Rise to this assuming Pride of the People as it is called in Europe." "Multitudes," Adams emphasized, "are convinced that the People should have a Voice, a share, and be made an integral part" of governing; "that the Government should be such a mixture, such a Combination of the Powers of one, the few and the many, as is best calculated to check and controul each other, and oblige all to co-operate in this one democratical principle, that the End of all Government is the happiness of the People: and in this other, that the greatest happiness of the greatest Number is the point to be obtained." "The principles," Adams added, "are now so widely spread, that Despotisms, Monarchies and Aristocracies must conform to them in some degree in practice, or hazard a total Revolution in Religion and Government throughout all Europe." "The longer the American War lasts," Adams predicted in the midst of the Revolutionary War, "the more the Spirit of American Government will spread in Europe, because the Attention of the World will be fixed there, while the War lasts."[10]

Having suffered the tyranny of British rule, early American jurists and political leaders proved to be an especially receptive audience for Beccaria's treatise, with the influence of *On Crimes and Punishments* only accelerating after the war's end in 1783. When Luigi Castiglioni visited America during the mid-1780s, William Bradford, Jr.—the man who rose to become the country's top lawyer—took the time in 1786 to effusively praise Beccaria's book in his lengthy letter to the roving naturalist.[11] It was just a few months later, on March 9, 1787, that a group of leading Philadelphia citizens, the Society for Promoting Political Enquires, gathered in Benjamin Franklin's home to discuss how to better treat prisoners at Philadelphia's Walnut Street Jail—the local prison that would later become America's first penitentiary. That group's secretary was none other than William Bradford, Jr., and the society—organized shortly before Philadelphia's all-important Constitutional Convention of 1787—met that day to hear Dr. Benjamin Rush's ideas for criminal justice reform.[12] Dr. Rush's paper, "An Inquiry into the Effects of Public Punishments upon Criminals and upon Society," specifically invoked both Beccaria and Voltaire, the popular French writer who had, two decades earlier, effusively praised Beccaria's treatise, piggybacking off its success.[13] In effect, American penal reform would advance in lockstep with American constitutionalism and its unique brand of republicanism.

When the Revolutionary War started, the United States was a loose collection of thirteen former colonies united mainly by their collective disdain for British misrule. The issuance of the Declaration of Independence, now celebrated every year throughout America with parades, picnics and loud displays of fireworks, represented the Founding Fathers' reasoned assessment that England's monarchy and the British Parliament would never heed the colonists' long-asserted calls for fair treatment and a voice in their own lives and affairs. The Articles of Confederation, drafted beginning in June 1776, created a plan of confederation for the consideration of Congress, with John Dickinson serving as the chair of the thirteen-man committee, one from each colony, tasked with preparing that plan — a plan initially presented to the Continental Congress on July 12, 1776. Along with Dickinson, the committee consisted of Samuel Adams, Josiah Bartlett, Button Gwinnett, Joseph Hewes, Stephen Hopkins, Francis Hopkinson, Robert R. Livingston, Thomas McKean, Thomas Nelson, Edward Rutledge, Roger Sherman and Thomas Stone. With a final draft approved by the Second Continental Congress in 1777 in York, Pennsylvania, and later ratified in 1781, the Articles of Confederation established a "perpetual Union" between the states — a union based on "a firm league of friendship with each other, for their common defense, the security of their liberties, and their mutual and general welfare."[14]

The ideas exchanged in Philadelphia in America's founding era — whether at Benjamin Franklin's house, at local taverns, or at the Constitutional Convention in 1787 — would eventually blossom, leading not only to the ratification of the U.S. Constitution but to a series of American penitentiaries. Those penitentiaries would better protect Americans from violent crime — thus promoting the general welfare — while simultaneously reducing the need for corporal punishments and executions. In Humphrey Marshall's *The History of Kentucky*, published in 1824, one finds a particularly telling description of Kentucky's 1798 legislative session, said to be "memorable in the history of amelioration and reform" for its reduction of capital crimes. "The sentiment upon which that reform is predicated," Marshall recorded, "had manifested itself and been spreading by insensible degrees among the people of the country, for some years." "It was," he wrote, "a sentiment of humanity, combined with liberality, which induced different philosophers, half a century before, to turn their eyes on the penal code of Europe and America." "Being by various writers taxed with impolicy, as well as with cruelty," Marshall noted of America's prior punishment practices, once modeled on England's Bloody Code, "it was proposed to be mitigated, by a system of reform, founded upon the principle, of proportioning punishments to their relative crimes." "Of all those who took up the pen on this interesting subject," Marshall noted, "none handled it with a more truly philisophic [sic] spirit, than the Marquis of Bacaria [sic]; whose book on crimes and punishments, not only enlightened his own country, but extending its benign rays throughout the civilized world, became the first, it is believed, to make converts in the United States; where its principles have in a manner become predominant." It was out of such sentiment, Marshall concluded nearly 200 years ago, that America's penitentiary system grew.[15]

The U.S. victory in the Revolutionary War — establishing the American republic, based at least in part on its ancient Roman predecessor — emboldened America's first lawmakers. Fresh off the victory over Great Britain's monarchy, the last two decades of the eighteenth century were heady times for American revolutionaries. The Society for Promoting Political Enquiries, consisting of fifty members and constituting just one of many intellectual societies of the time, had been formed in February 1787, just a month before Dr. Rush's talk at Benjamin Franklin's house and just a few months before the Constitutional Convention delegates assembled in the City of Brotherly Love.[16] Among the society's members—men already quite familiar with Roman republicanism and Beccaria's ideas—were some of the most influential figures of the day: Tench Coxe, Francis Hopkinson, Jared Ingersoll, Thomas Mifflin, Robert Morris, David Rittenhouse, Benjamin Rush, Edward Shippen, Charles Vaughan, Samuel Vaughan, Jr., and James Wilson. Meeting on a weekly basis to study political science at the home of its eminent president, Benjamin Franklin, this society—the American equivalent of the Milanese Academy of Fists—would try to tackle the pressing issues of the day. The society's vice-presidents were Pennsylvania politician George Clymer, a signer of the Declaration of Independence, and William Bingham, a wealthy businessman then serving as a Pennsylvania delegate to the Continental Congress.[17]

It was in this context that Benjamin Rush injected Beccaria's name into the public discourse once more, this time in favor of the abolition of capital punishment. At its March 1787 meeting, Dr. Rush—always striving to improve American society—would announce his total abolition to capital punishment shortly before the Constitutional Convention got underway. "I have said nothing upon the manner of inflicting death as a punishment for crimes," Rush said, "because I consider it as an improper punishment for *any* crime." As Rush explained: "Even murder itself is propagated by the punishment of death for murder. Of this we have a remarkable proof in Italy." "The duke of Tuscany soon after the publication of the marquis of Beccaria's excellent treatise upon this subject," Dr. Rush emphasized, arguing from the historical precedent just months before Philadelphia's Constitutional Convention, "abolished death as a punishment for murder."[18]

On Crimes and Punishments, which the Continental Congress itself invoked in 1774 before declaring America's independence, was—history reveals—a game-changing book in the late eighteenth century. Everyone from Continental Army soldiers and veterans, to American judges and lawyers, to early U.S. presidents read and cited Beccaria's treatise in those extremely turbulent, bygone days. Beginning in the 1760s, Beccaria's book—then fresh off the presses—enveloped the whole of Europe and America like a thunderstorm, flooding the terrain with new ideas and affecting Anglo-American law in ways big and small. Along with writings on Roman and English republicanism, it thus influenced American thought in the lead up to the Declaration of Independence and prior to the drafting of the U.S. Constitution and the U.S. Bill of Rights. It also, just as plainly, inspired others to create the then-novel English and American penitentiary systems. As Rexford Newcomb, of the University of Southern California, wrote of post-Revolutionary War America in an article for *The American Architect* about the history of penitentiaries:

> With the signing of the Paris Treaty and the return of the country to a more peaceful state, the attention of the people was drawn to the reform of penal codes. A wave of reform was sweeping over the whole world, due to the reports of Howard and the work of Beccaria, to say nothing of the writings of Blackstone.[19]

"For my part," Peter Du Ponceau, the Provost of the Law Academy of Philadelphia later emphasized in 1824, reflecting the sentiment of the age, "I am inclined to think that a good legislator ought to possess the combined knowledge and talents of the lawyer, the philosopher, and the statesman."[20]

In the midst of their efforts to chart a new course for American law—one that would model Rome's republican heyday while steering clear of the shoals of England's notorious "Bloody Code"—the Founding Fathers carefully studied Beccaria's writings in Italian and in translation. They drew upon Beccaria's ideas as they drafted legislation in the post-colonial period, and in their constitutions, the documents that would provide the foundation and framework for the American Rule of Law for generations to come, they voiced their collective disapproval of "cruel," "unusual" and "sanguinary" punishments even while disagreeing on which specific acts should be so classified. Beccaria had warned against inflicting the same punishment on "someone who kills a pheasant" as on "someone who murders a man or who falsifies an important document." A failure to draw a distinction, he said, would destroy "moral sentiments" that were "the work of many centuries and much blood and developed very slowly and with great difficulty in the human heart." As Americans read Beccaria's words, they clearly took Beccaria's advice into account as they wrestled, on a state-by-state basis, with how to structure their own scales of crimes and punishments.

Beccaria's treatise became so influential among America's intelligentsia that, in 1823, the Supreme Court of Pennsylvania felt compelled to even try to divine Beccaria's unspecified views. "The Marquis of Beccaria gives no direct opinion as to the right of a sovereign to demand the delivery of the fugitive, but from the whole scope and spirit of his thoughts, it is plainly to be seen, that he was against it," the court wrote.[21] The homage to Beccaria was typical for the age. It is almost impossible, in fact, to consider the American Revolution and take stock of it without consulting *On Crimes and Punishments*. That treatise—as well as the name of its Italian author—became part and parcel of the lingo of the American Revolution itself. Sadly, far too many histories of the American Revolution—and, for that matter, of the Constitution's origins—fail to mention Beccaria at all, for his influence was immense.

In drafting America's written constitutions, the Founding Fathers struggled mightily to answer this question, as John Adams put it in *A Defence of the Constitutions of Government of the United States of America*: "What combination of powers in society, or what form of government, will compel the formation of good and equal laws, an impartial execution, and faithful interpretation of them, so that the citizens may constantly enjoy the benefit of them, and be sure of their continuance"? "[T]his became," as law professor Tim Sellers puts it, quoting the Roman historian Titus Livius and the English republican theorist James Harrington, "the search to establish an '*imperium legum*' or 'the empire of laws and not of men.'" Referring to another, now more much obscure Italian thinker, Sellers adds:

> The Venetian Donato Gianotti observed in a passage repeated by the English-man James Harrington a century later, and again by the American John Adams, at the time of his own Revolution, that they all belonged to the timeless party of justice, fighting over the centuries to establish government under law ('*de jure*'), in the public interest, against arbitrary ('*de facto*') government, maintained in the interest of those in charge.

Plainly, Beccaria's push for "a fixed code of laws"—and his call for "blind and impartial laws" and a legal regime not tilted "for the comfort of a few" or driven by "the passions of the few"—made a favorable impression on the American polity. In speaking out against "arbitrary discretion of judges," Beccaria's treatise also found an especially welcome audience in American circles.

Cesare Beccaria's ideas—along with those of reformers such as Gaetano Filangieri and the Mexican-born jurist Manuel de Lardizábal y Uribe—were part of a grand global conversation to establish a better system of justice, one that made its way from Europe to the Americas as the American discontentment with British tyranny reached fever pitch. In 1776, Lardizábal—in an effort that would itself get noticed by Americans—had been tasked with reviewing Spanish criminal jurisprudence. Influenced by Beccaria, as Americans had been, Lardizábal produced his *Discurso sobre las penas contrahido á las leyes criminales de España, para facilitar su reforma* (1782), published in Madrid six years later. That Spanish language work on penology, in fact, ended up in Thomas Jefferson's library, with Lardizábal concluding that "after learning the value of life and the liberty of man," humanity "could no longer avoid the indispensable necessity of reforming criminal laws."

In this republic of letters, Lardizábal himself reached out to Jefferson in 1786 and 1788 through, respectively, the French journalist and penal reformer Jacques-Pierre Brissot de Warville, author of *Théorie des lois criminelles* (1781), and the U.S. ambassador to Spain, William Carmichael. Jefferson ended up communicating directly with Lardizábal's brother Miguel, from whom Jefferson sought to obtain Spanish books on America. "Do you see Don Miguel de Lardizabal ever?" Jefferson wrote to Ambassador Carmichael in June 1788, adding, "If you do be so good as to present my compliments to him, and to remind him of my catalogue of books, in which he was so kind as to promise me his aid." As Aniceto Masferrer, a University of Valencia professor of the history of law, writes of the reformist sentiment in the Founding Fathers' time: "The lack of proportion between crime and punishment was one of the most consistent criticisms made by Enlightenment thinkers against the Ancién Regime."[22] The laws on crimes and punishments produced by America's founders, in fact, were a direct response to that criticism, much of which they leveled themselves after the appearance of Beccaria's treatise.

Not surprisingly, perhaps, Beccaria's cultural influence would extend through—and well beyond—the Founding Fathers' own time. Awards are still given in Beccaria's honor, and Beccaria's name is still found in American atlases. In 1807, Beccaria Township, in the Commonwealth of Pennsylvania, was specifically named in honor of Cesare Beccaria, and—thanks to a naturalist—Beccaria even had a mollusk, the Scottish mollusca *Rotália Beccárii*, named after him.[23] In 1812, another unit of local government, a Pennsylvania county, was itself renamed in honor of William Bradford, Jr., Beccaria's ardent American disciple, while in 1814, Rush Township—also in Pennsylvania—was named after Dr. Benjamin Rush, another steadfast Beccaria admirer.[24] Bradford County, Pennsylvania, it has been noted, was ceremoniously named for the late United States Attorney General, a descendant of the printer William Bradford who came from England to Philadelphia in 1685 "as a printer of books for the Society of Friends in the colonies."[25] Even in the decades leading up to the Civil War, Beccaria's treatise continued to garner praise. For example, in 1847, the Supreme Court of Georgia—at a distance of eighty years from the book's first translation into English—called *On Crimes and Punishments* an "admirable little treatise." Today, at least among criminologists and legal historians, Beccaria's little treatise—reprinted to this day—still rightfully demands the time and attention of its twenty-first century readers.[26]

Any study of American law or the history or principles of the American Revolution would thus be woefully incomplete without a considered exploration of Beccaria's impact. As *On Crimes and Punishments* grew in popularity, early Americans rethought their conceptions of societal happiness and also moved away from *common-law* crimes in favor of *codified* criminal codes—codes that were easier for people to understand and that reflected a more humane American character than their English counterparts. Indeed, Beccaria's fame grew to such an extent that his name later appeared in multiple U.S. Supreme Court opinions, the decisions handed down by the highest court in the land. Beccaria's writings were invoked in *Payne v. Tennessee*, a 1991 case holding that the Constitution allows the introduction of victim impact evidence, as well as in a 1972 concurring opinion in *Furman v. Georgia*, the landmark case that temporarily halted American executions based on the Eighth and Fourteenth Amendments. In *Ullmann v. United States*, a 1956 case, Justices William O. Douglas and Hugo Black likewise invoked Beccaria's name, arguing in dissent that "[t]he Fifth Amendment was designed to protect against infamy as well as prosecution." Beccaria, they wrote, had long been "well known" in America, with the two dissenters writing that the Italian thinker "was the main voice against the use of infamy as punishment."[27]

The American Revolution, to be sure, brought about radical changes in law and social policy, but it did not achieve all at once everything that some of its most ardent, battle-hardened soldiers and patriots sought. The rights clause of America's Declaration of Independence, for example, forcefully proclaims that "all men are created equal" and it articulated the "unalienable Rights" to "Life, Liberty and the pursuit of Happiness." But that document, despite its lofty, aspirational language, was penned in the era of slavery, a dark, ugly chapter in American history. The U.S. Constitution, which established the enduring foundation for America's government, was itself the product of an unseemly, sordid compromise, tolerating slavery even as it set up the pillars for America's system of checks and balances. In the battle over the meaning of the Constitution itself, this fact—that the founders tolerated *slavery*—should not be lost on today's judges as they consider the relative weight to be given to eighteenth-century Americans. The legitimacy of any constitution depends upon how it treats people, and the black mark of American slavery certainly casts a long shadow on the project of "originalism," however conceived or articulated as looking for "original meaning" or "original intent."

Although some American founders, including Dr. Benjamin Rush, vehemently opposed slavery and wanted to outlaw it, eighteenth-century slaveholders debating the Constitution's text insisted on states' rights to engage in the slave trade, at least until 1808. As the Constitution, as finally worded, obliquely read without actually using the word *slave*: "The Migration or Importation of such Persons as any of the States now existing shall think proper to admit, shall not be prohibited by the Congress prior to the Year one thousand eight hundred and eight, but a Tax or duty may be imposed on such Importation, not exceeding ten dollars for each Person." Another section of the Constitution, elevating slaveholders' private interests above the revolutionary ideals of liberty and equality, even callously counted each slave as "three fifths" of a person for purposes of apportioning taxes and representation.[28] It should go without saying that, in light of these facts, with eighteenth-century lawmakers choosing to totally disenfranchise both minorities and women, one should approach *with extreme skepticism* any suggestion that "original" understandings of the Constitution should govern modern, twenty-first century judicial decision making.

With human bondage and the slave trade stubbornly entrenched in eighteenth-century law, America's founders—still struggling to stamp out the evils of slavery—never reached a consensus on whether killers, traitors and rapists should be executed or, as suggested by Beccaria, spared from the gallows. The battle over the "peculiar institution" of slavery would continue past the infamous *Dred Scott* decision in 1857 and through the bitterly contested Civil War, fought from 1861 to 1865 and pitting North against South, abolitionists against slave owners, and—at times—brother against brother. It would take hundreds of thousands of casualties and President Abraham Lincoln's dogged determination and leadership, as well as a series of Reconstruction Amendments to the U.S. Constitution, to outlaw slavery, even begin to protect minority rights, and to install the concept of "equal protection of the laws" into American law. Like the Revolutionary War, the price of liberty in Lincoln's time was bloodshed. "If there is no struggle," the abolitionist leader Frederick Douglass said before the Civil War's bloodbath, "there is no progress." As Douglass explained: "Those who profess to favor freedom, and yet depreciate agitation, are men who want crops without plowing up the ground. They want rain without thunder and lightning. They want the ocean without the awful roar of its many waters." Only after slavery's abolition in the mid-1860s could American lawmakers—to borrow Beccaria's words—start to see their "own nation," at least in a preliminary way, as "a family of brothers."[29]

To be sure, *a majority* of the Founding Fathers—the men who fought the British, put in place the first federal criminal laws, and agitated for law reform—thought executions necessary to deter crime and foster law and order. As a result, they passed and signed into law, in their own time, *legislation* and *statutes* that authorized the punishment of death. But even then, in that den of racial and gender inequality, others, such as Dr. Benjamin Rush, took an opposite view and saw the death penalty—America's other "peculiar institution," as NYU law professor David Garland describes it—as immoral, unchristian and unnecessary. Indeed, it is significant that neither the U.S. Constitution nor early American state constitutions ever stated anything to the effect that the death penalty shall be deemed lawful *for all time*. On the contrary, early American constitutions simply prohibited *cruel, unusual* and *sanguinary* punishments, leaving it to future jurists to decide what so qualifies, in all likelihood because the founders made themselves clear—again and again—that every new generation had to govern themselves. And so, America's death penalty debate—like its debate over slavery and women's rights—was left unfinished and unresolved during America's founding era.

What the founders thought necessary *in their time* does not, of course, answer the inquiry—whether posed as a legal or factual one—of what is necessary *in our own time*. Still, the founders' probing eighteenth-century questions—Are executions necessary? And do penitentiaries render death sentences obsolete?—are worth considering, if only because they inform our own conceptions of what, within the U.S. Constitution's Eighth Amendment and similar state-law equivalents, is *cruel* and *unusual*. After all, early Americans themselves—in line with Montesquieu and Beccaria—repeatedly expressed the view that any punishment that goes beyond "absolute necessity" is "tyrannical." This was a core principle—and one that applied to *every punishment*, whether corporal or capital in nature. They made their own assessments of the validity of punishments in their time as the penitentiary system was still being created. But twenty-first century Americans—including American jurists—are entitled to make their own judgments in that regard, too. Certainly, societal conceptions of cruelty can change, and what is considered normal or routine in one era can become considered unusual in another.

In modern America, with the availability of supermax prisons and the universality of life-without-parole sentencing schemes, executions can—as a matter of fact and constitutional law—no longer be considered necessary. Non-death penalty states get along without the death penalty just fine, and even the U.S. Government and the U.S. military have gone for years at a time without executing anyone. In the U.S., in fact, there are approximately 15,000 murders committed every year. Yet, in the past few years, there have been fewer than 100 death sentences handed out per year and less than 50 executions carried out per year. Those statistics, all by themselves, show that the death penalty is not necessary—let alone *absolutely necessary*, as America's founders thought required to justify any punishment.

Plus, the sheer arbitrariness reflected in America's state-run death penalty lottery—the capricious decisions that get made about who lives and who dies—runs afoul of "due process" and "equal protection" principles. Racial disparities, now centered largely on race-of-the-victim discrimination, continue to plague the death penalty, just as racism did in the founding era. And the punishment's massive geographic disparities—with most executions occurring in one region, the South, and even then, arising out of discretionary prosecutorial decisions from a tiny percentage of U.S. counties—only exacerbates the unfairness of the system as a whole. One academic, James Liebman of Columbia University, has even found that *68 percent* of death sentences imposed between 1973 and 1995 were eventually overturned for some reason or another, showing just how error-infested the whole death penalty enterprise has become. This should bother even the most

ardent "originalist" given that the founders themselves regularly decried "arbitrary" results and outcomes—the very thing now being produced, and tolerated, by America's
twenty-first century death penalty regime.[30]

The law, in constant need of revision to adapt itself to the times, has always been imperfect, and that was certainly the case in the late eighteenth century. Minorities were not guaranteed the right to vote until the Fifteenth Amendment's ratification in 1870 and the passage
of the Voting Rights Act of 1965. Even now, discrimination against minority voters remains
a recurring problem in various locales. Women—another group excluded from eighteenth-
century social compacts—were not guaranteed the right to vote under federal law until the
Nineteenth Amendment's ratification in 1920. In the employment context, women still earn
substantially less money, on average, than men; and in the political sphere, women are still
underrepresented in the halls of Congress. Just as Jefferson and other founders felt morally
conflicted about slavery, often unwilling to free their slaves even as they acknowledged slavery's barbarity, America's founders also felt great ambivalence about state-sanctioned killing
even as they tolerated and sanctioned the practice.[31] What modern-day U.S. Supreme Court
Justices do with these facts—and they are facts—is for them to decide.

In revolutionary America, Beccaria's book—in truth—became much more than a respected little treatise. It became a revered, must-read book, one that denounced tyranny
and that articulated the principles of liberty and happiness. Through its reasoned approach
to law, it became a rallying cry for American revolutionaries and a guide for lawmakers.
Along with the residual influence of William Penn's humanistic Quaker experiment in Pennsylvania, it inspired constitutions and penal laws of a more proportionate, republican character throughout the United States. "Americans," writes historian Harry Ward, "had already
become familiar with European writers of the Enlightenment and their appeal for more humane criminal codes," and that was especially true of Cesare Beccaria's *On Crimes and Punishments*. The Revolutionary War, Ward notes, highlighting the hanging of two elderly
Quakers in Philadelphia in 1778 for collaborating with the enemy, "underscored the brutality
and capriciousness in the administration of capital punishment." "For a republican society,"
Ward emphasizes, alluding to the equality principle of America's Declaration of Independence, "the unevenness in the rate of handing down capital sentences did not make sense."[32]

In fact, to American revolutionaries, *On Crimes and Punishments* became, like the
writings of Voltaire, Bentham and Blackstone, synonymous with the Enlightenment itself. George Wickersham, the Attorney General of the United States during William
Howard Taft's presidency, put it nicely, saying this in 1911 of the Italian penal reformer:
"Modern humane consideration of crime, which began with the writings of Beccaria, has
established the postulate that punishment, or the consequence of crime, must be proportioned to the injury done to society by the offense."[33] "The Enlightenment notion that
the punishment should be proportional to the crime, first heralded by Cesare Beccaria,"
another commentator, Robert Dumond, similarly wrote, "set the stage for penal and legislative reforms that were a radical departure from the prevailing practice of capital punishment for a broad spectrum of crimes and substituted the penitentiary movement in its
place."[34] In 1911, the State of Minnesota—along with several other American states during the Progressive Era—abolished capital punishment for all crimes, included premeditated murder, in what was then a high-water mark for American's anti-gallows movement.[35]

The British monarchy, dating back centuries, had frequently executed common criminals as well as high-profile political dissidents. By declaring independence, American
revolutionaries, like Henry VIII's sixteenth-century wives, two of whom were executed,
had reason to fear for their own lives if captured by George III's forces and taken as prisoners. Having declared America's sovereignty, America's founders were immediately classified as traitors to the British Empire and—quite literally—put their own lives on the

line. In fact, on the day in 1776 that the Continental Congress declared America's independence, Dr. Benjamin Rush was present to observe the frame of mind of American revolutionaries, and he later recalled the "sleepless nights" leading up to that august occasion. In a letter to John Adams, Dr. Rush later reflected on how the "solemnity" of the event was broken only momentarily by Benjamin Harrison, a rotund Virginia planter who offered a bit of gallows humor that day. In his letter, Rush wrote: "Do you recollect the pensive and awful silence which pervaded the house when we were called up, one after another, to the table of the President of Congress to subscribe what was believed by many at that time to be our own death warrants?" "The silence and gloom of the morning," Rush recalled, writing after a Fourth of July celebration in 1811 and thinking back to that fateful day in 1776, "were interrupted only for a moment by Colonel Harrison of Virginia, who said to Mr. Gerry at the table: 'I shall have a great advantage over you, Mr. Gerry, when we are all hung for what we are now doing. From the size and weight of my body I shall die in a few minutes, but from the lightness of your body you will dance in the air an hour or two before you are dead.'" "This speech procured a transient smile," Dr. Rush remembered of the exchange between Harrison and the slender Massachusetts merchant Elbridge Gerry, "but it was soon succeeded by the solemnity with which the whole business was conducted."

Across the newly formed United States of America, the fear of being executed by the British—with whom fighting had already commenced, first at Lexington and Concord, Massachusetts, and then at places like Fort Ticonderoga and Bunker (Breeds) Hill—was thus palpable. In 1776, John Adams wrote that "it requires a Faith, which can remove Mountains, to believe that Liberty and Safety, can ever hereafter be enjoyed by America, in any Subjection to the Government of Great Britain." In the same letter, to Horatio Gates, Adams pondered what would happen if the war "terminates in downright Submission," with Adams making reference to "Persecution and Imprisonment, scorn and Insult, Blocks, Halters, Gibbets." Legend has it that before John Hancock—the president of the Second Continental Congress—actually signed the Declaration of Independence, he insisted, "We must be unanimous. There must be no pulling different ways. We must all hang together." Benjamin Franklin, with his signature wit, reportedly replied: "Yes, we must, indeed, all hang together, or, most assuredly, we shall all hang separately."[36] Despite these well-founded fears, the quest for a more just society led enlightened thinkers—including the Founding Fathers themselves—to remake the law against all odds.

In his published address to the students of the Law Academy of Philadelphia in 1824, Peter Du Ponceau—Baron von Steuben's Revolutionary War aide, Lafayette's friend, and James Madison's correspondent—was still emphasizing, even decades after the Revolutionary War, that the "science" of jurisprudence "ought to be studied, particularly in this country." "The conflict of opinions" of "liberal and learned jurists," Du Ponceau told his audience, "will produce truth, and truth at last will find its way every where." As Du Ponceau—the aging Continental Army veteran—observed:

> The law should be treated as every other science; its theories should be scanned, and its defects pointed out; the excellent principles with which it abounds should be confronted with the decisions in which they have been either forgotten or misapplied, and this course should be pursued until the whole system at last shall be founded on the basis of universal justice. For justice, not in form merely, but in substance is a debt which is due by every government to its citizens.

"Mild punishments" had already replaced "the former sanguinary code," Du Ponceau proclaimed of England's disgraceful Bloody Code, adding that "the interior economy of prisons, and penitentiaries has been suited to the humanity of the age."[37]

The eighteenth century, which gave birth to American law, was an entirely different world from that which exists today. America's founders wrote letters, not e-mails, and they traveled by horse, carriage or ship, not in automobiles and planes. They had swords and muskets, not assault rifles or AK-47s; they stored information in closets not on computers or in the cloud; and they feared standing armies and not cyber attacks. In the 1760s, when the audacious Italian philosopher Cesare Beccaria, then in his mid-twenties, dared to write *On Crimes and Punishments*, the American colonies had yet to proclaim their independence and still had in place an array of antiquated laws modeled on England's "Bloody Code" or provisions of the Old Testament. The American colonies were mired in slavery and the African slave trade, and the American Revolution had not yet begun.

By the 1790s, the decade of Beccaria's death and the birth of the U.S. Bill of Rights, American slaves were still being held in bondage and subjected to the lash, with the French Revolution—with all its turmoil and bloodshed—raising more questions still about "sanguinary" conduct. The late eighteenth century would prove to be a time of much violence, with revolutions and executions taking place side by side as elites—the establishment—still clung to centuries-old traditions. The French and British monarchies both came under assault in the late eighteenth century while Beccaria's ideas—both feared and embraced, depending on the audience—rose to prominence. In that time, indiscriminate executions—the product of arbitrary and capricious governments—were themselves closely associated with tyrannical regimes.

Following the Revolutionary War, when Americans, in peacetime, had a chance to rework their laws in a manner more in line with the ideals of the American Revolution, they began to question, in earnest, the need for executions, once thought to be an indispensable part of any criminal justice system. They drafted new constitutions with a Beccarian flair, and in responding to Edmund Burke's 1790 attack on the French Revolution, Thomas Paine—the author of *Common Sense*—tried to contextualize why, after the storming of the Bastille, "four or five persons were seized by the populace, and instantly put to death." "Whom has the National Assembly brought to the scaffold?" Paine asked rhetorically in *Rights of Man* (1791), speaking of France's national assembly. "None," he replied, though he noted that, when the Bastille had been taken, the Governor of the Bastille and the Mayor of Paris had been put to death, with their heads—along with those of a minister, Joseph-François Foulon de Doué, and his son-in-law, Berthier de Sauvigny—"stuck upon spikes, and carried about the city." "[I]t is upon this mode of punishment that Mr. Burke builds a great part of his tragic scene," Paine asserted. In discussing the French Revolution, the conflict that followed America's own revolution, Paine then offered: "Let us therefore examine how men came by the idea of punishing in this manner." "They learn it," Paine contended, "from the governments they live under, and retaliate the punishments they have been accustomed to behold." "The heads stuck upon spikes, which remained for years upon Temple-bar," Paine noted of the place where severed heads had been exhibited in London, "differed nothing in the horror of the scene from those carried about upon spikes at Paris: yet this was done by the English government." "It is their sanguinary punishments which corrupt mankind," Paine emphasized.[38]

In 1790s America, racial oppression and violence remained widespread, including in relation to penal codes. At that time, even America's northern states still had slaves living among a populace that had, just two decades earlier, vehemently professed its love of liberty. While Americans had fought the British government in a life-or-death contest to achieve freedom and self-determination, American slaves were largely forgotten, as least by a majority of American lawmakers. In describing then-existing conditions in New York City, Luigi Castiglioni—the Italian botanist—wrote this in his *Viaggio*, first published in Milan in 1790 but not translated into English until the 1980s:

> The negroes are very numerous and many of them slaves, but in general they are treated gently and not crushed by labor. Many would think it much better for the safety of the city not to have so many of them, since there have already been plots, among others one a few years ago, when they planned to burn down the city in order to kill the male inhabitants and marry the widows.

In order to quell slave revolts, eighteenth-century judges—living amidst a populace still clinging to slavery—often resorted to the lash, or worse yet, executions. Sometimes, authorities even used gibbeting or burning slaves to death to send a particularly chilling message to other slaves. When Gabriel—a literate Virginia slave—tried to foment a slave rebellion in 1800, making a flag that read "Death or Liberty," he was—without a second thought, even though he was fighting for *his* freedom—hanged by state authorities for his role in organizing the plot. Only in 2007 did Virginia Governor Tim Kaine officially acknowledge the injustice, issuing an informal pardon to the long-dead Gabriel and his co-conspirators because Gabriel's motivation had been "his devotion to the ideals of the American Revolution."[39]

In writing of slavery, Castiglioni himself naturally compared what he saw of the American experience with what he had come to know as part of the Italian Enlightenment, with Italian city-states having had their own lengthy struggles with slavery and forced labor. "Surely it is a matter of surprise and pity for a European to read about the sale of slaves here in the newspapers," Castiglioni observed, "and all the more so if these notices are compared with those put out for the sale of horses, from which they differ not a bit." Of slaves in Virginia, where Castiglioni had traveled, too, just a decade and half before Gabriel's rebellion, Castiglioni had described the "severe labour" expected of slaves from "day-break" to "dusk," with Castiglioni reprinting an article from the *American Museum* about how a disobedient slave would be "tied up." The slave, that article reported, would receive "a number of lashes on his bare back, most severely inflicted, at the discretion of those unfeeling sons of barbarity, the overseers, who are permitted to exercise an unlimited dominion over them." "[T]he law," that article noted, "directs a negro's arm to be struck off, who raises it against a white person, should it be only in his own defence." Castiglioni further noted how South Carolina plantation owners "often vent their ill temper on the poor negroes, who, to the shame of mankind, are scarcely reputed to be human beings, and for the slightest failing are exposed to the lash of a slave driver, when the master himself does not take the barbaric pleasure of tormenting them."

Since the Founding Fathers' time, the way people live—including the way people get from place to place in their daily lives—has changed dramatically, with there being a much greater awareness of the universality of human rights—and a better appreciation for the principle of equality—than ever existed before. When Luigi Castiglioni traveled to America by ship, his trip across the ocean took thirty-four days and, once he arrived, he traveled—as Jefferson did in Italy—by mule, horse or carriage, using his hand-written letters of introduction, the preferred mode in that age, to gain entrée to important scientists and political figures of the day. In Cambridge, Massachusetts, Castiglioni observed of Harvard College, that venerable institution founded in 1636:

> The building, made of brick, is very large, and 100 self-supporting students live there. There are six professors: one for theology, one for mathematics and natural philosophy, another for oriental languages, a professor of anatomy and surgery, one of theoretical and practical medicine, and, finally one for chemistry and materia medica.

"The library," Castiglioni recorded, "is furnished with about 10,000 volumes, among which are the ancient classical authors and the most renowned of modern philosophers, in addition to an adequate collection of curious and handsome books." Today, Harvard has approximately 21,000 students, 2,100 faculty members, more than 10,000 academic appointments in affiliated teaching hospitals, and its library collection—of which Beccaria's *On Crimes and Punishments* is still a part—contains about 17 million volumes.

When Luigi Castiglioni traveled across America, making his notes on American plants and American life, the U.S. Supreme Court—an institution created by the U.S. Constitution's ratification in 1788—had yet to even come into existence. After the Constitution's creation of what came to be known as "The Court of Last Resort," the Supreme Court itself actually lacked its own building—a place to permanently call home. Located for a time on the ground floor of the U.S. Capitol building, the Supreme Court's designated meeting space from 1810 to 1860 was the place that had served as the U.S. Senate chamber from 1800 to 1808. Only after the Senate chamber was moved to the second floor was a chamber for the Supreme Court's oral arguments—one designed by architect Benjamin Latrobe—constructed in that space, work that was finally completed in 1819 under the direction of Charles Bulfinch, Latrobe's successor as Architect of the Capitol.

Appropriately, when the U.S. Supreme Court finally got its own space, a hand-me-down from the Senate, it was an Italian artist who created its centerpiece. "Facing the bench is the relief *Justice*, sculpted by Carlo Franzoni in 1817," a U.S. Capitol brochure for "The Old Supreme Court Chamber" reads of the now restored courtroom and its only piece of permanent decoration—a work of art created in plaster by the Italian sculptor a couple of years before his death in 1819. "The allegorical group," the brochure explains of Franzoni's relief of three carvings, "is dominated by the figure of Justice with scales upraised in her left hand, her right hand resting on an unsheathed sword." "At the feet of Justice," the tourist brochure continues, "an eagle guards several bound volumes representing the written laws." "The third figure, signifying the new nation," the brochure concludes, "is a winged youth seated before a rising sun and holding a large tablet symbolizing the Constitution."[40]

In *On Crimes and Punishments*, Beccaria—asserting that lawmakers "ought to allow men and their brothers to enjoy in peace that small portion of happiness" set aside for them to enjoy—argued that "[t]he lawmaker ought to be a wise architect who raises his building on the foundation of self-love" so that "he will not be forced at every moment to separate the public good from the good of individuals." At the 1787 Constitutional Convention in Philadelphia, James Madison—one of the architects of the U.S. Constitution, the document hammered out in that city—had recorded Benjamin Franklin's own comments about a "rising sun" decades before Carlo Franzoni began executing his relief of *Justice*. During the Convention at Pennsylvania's State House, Franklin had commented about the sun that a craftsman had painted on the upper back slat of a Chippendale chair George Washington sat in as the Convention's president. Timing his anecdote with the signing of the U.S. Constitution, Franklin's comments—as recorded by Madison—speak for themselves. "Whilst the last members were signing it," Madison's note begins, "Doctr. Franklin looking towards the Presidents Chair, at the back of which a rising sun happened to be painted, observed to a few members near him, that Painters had found it difficult to distinguish in their art a rising from a setting sun." "I have, said he," Madison relayed next of Franklin's captured remark, "often and often in the course of the Session, and the vicissitudes of my hopes and fears as to its issue, looked at that behind the President without being able to tell whether it was rising or setting: But now at length I have the happiness to know that it is a rising and not a setting Sun."[41]

The current U.S. Supreme Court building, the white marble edifice designed by the American architect Cass Gilbert (1859–1934) to resemble an ancient Roman temple, was not completed until 1935. The words "EQUAL JUSTICE UNDER LAW," carved above the building's entrance, serve as a daily reminder to its visitors that the Supreme Court's mission is to do justice and to ensure that all American citizens, rich or poor, black or white, and regardless of background or orientation, are to be treated equally under the law. For the Supreme Court chamber itself, Adolph Weinman (1870–1952), a German-born Beaux-Arts sculptor who came to America as a teenager, was selected by Cass Gilbert to design the friezes that now adorn the upper walls of the courtroom. In accordance with the common practice of the time, Weinman — the artist — was permitted to choose the symbols and figures to be created.

The allegorical figures, along with the carvings of real historic figures, run the gamut, and date back many centuries. The East Wall Frieze — located directly above the Court's bench — includes two male figures, the *Majesty of Law* with a law book at his side, and the *Power of Government* holding the *fasces*, an ancient Roman symbol of authority. A pylon carved with Roman numerals I through X divides the two male figures, representing the U.S. Constitution's first ten amendments, popularly known as the U.S. Bill of Rights. The West Wall Frieze, by contrast, depicts an allegorical representation of "Good vs. Evil." On one side, the "Powers of Good": *Defense of Virtue, Charity, Peace, Harmony* and *Security.* On the other side, the "Powers of Evil": *Vice and Crime, Corruption, Slander, Deception,* and *Despotic Power.*[42]

Cesare Beccaria is nowhere depicted on the courtroom friezes, but Sir William Blackstone — one of the jurists Beccaria did influence — is, depicted on the North Wall Frieze, wedged in between an allegorical figure, *Right of Man,* and a depiction of John Marshall, the influential fourth Chief Justice of the United States. Drawn from an array of civilizations, the South and North Wall Friezes mostly depict ancient lawgivers. There is Menes, an Egyptian king, and Hammurabi, the King of Babylon. And there is Octavian, the first emperor of the Roman Empire, and Justinian, the Byzantine emperor who ordered the codification of Roman law and published *Corpus Juris Civilis,* also known as the Justinian Code. In addition to the Chinese philosopher Confucius, Moses, and the Islamic prophet Muhammad, one finds a number of kings — from Roman Emperor Charlemagne, the King of the Franks, and Louis IX, King of France, to Solomon, the King of Israel — on the north- and south-facing friezes. There, too, one finds King John (1166–1216), whose seal is affixed to the Magna Carta — that early symbol of English liberty. Also depicted on the South and North Wall Friezes are Napoleon (1769–1821), the Emperor of France who ordered the recodification of French law; Draco and Solon, the Athenian lawgivers; and Huig de Groot (1583–1645) — the Dutch scholar and lawyer better known as Hugo Grotius — who holds in his hands *De jure belli ac pacis* (*Concerning the Law of War and Peace*), an early and influential book on international law.[43]

As the struggle over the meaning of the U.S. Constitution continues in the elegant U.S. Supreme Court building, the forward-looking mentality of America's founders should not be overlooked. The founders themselves not only fought for law reform in their time, but they fully expected more changes to occur in the future. For example, writing to a young William Munford from Monticello in 1799, Thomas Jefferson laid out his views on the progressive nature of human knowledge. "I believe also, with Condorcet," Jefferson wrote, that the mind of man "is perfectible to a degree of which we cannot as yet form any conception." Jefferson saw room for advancement in anatomy, chemistry, geometry, medicine, surgery and other branches of science, telling Munford: "I join you therefore in branding as cowardly the idea that the human mind is incapable of further advances." Such thinking, Jefferson wrote, "is precisely the doctrine which the present despots of the earth are inculcating," with despots peddling the misguided idea, especially as regards "religion & politics," that "we are to look backwards then and & not forwards for the improvement of science." Despots, Jefferson said, espoused the view "that it is not probable that any thing better will be discovered than what was known to our fathers," and that advances were to be found "amidst feudal barbarisms and the fires of Spital-fields."

The very idea of Jeffersonian democracy and the American republic is thus premised on the notion that things can always be made better, and that the people of the United States of America are constantly striving to make it so. "[B]ut thank heaven," Jefferson wrote to Munford, then of college age, that "the American mind is already too much opened, to listen to these impostures." So long as "the art of printing" was with Americans, he emphasized, "science can never be retrograde" for "what is once acquired of real knowledge can never be lost." As Jefferson, the revolutionary, relayed to Munford in his letter, expressing his values: "to preserve the freedom of the human mind then & freedom of the press, every spirit should be ready to devote itself to martyrdom; for as long as we may think as we will, & speak as we think, the condition of man will proceed in improvement." Jefferson, in his own hand, thus recognized, in a recurring theme, that each successive generation was responsible for making its own contributions and advances. "[T]he generation which is going off the stage," he wrote, "has deserved well of mankind for the struggles it has made, & for having arrested that course of despotism which had overwhelmed the world for thousands & thousands of years." But "if there seems to be danger that the ground they have gained will be lost again," Jefferson warned, "that danger comes from the generation" that followed his own, with the man from Monticello seeing any forces opposing the advancement of "freedom and science" as a "monstrous" phenomenon.

In *On Crimes and Punishments*, Cesare Beccaria—in his chapter on "Interpretation of the Laws"—expressed the view that "the authority to interpret penal laws cannot rest with criminal judges, for the simple reason that they are not legislators." But Beccaria—like Jefferson—knew the law itself would change over time and should not be tied to barbaric or antiquated customs. "Judges," Beccaria wrote, "have not received laws from our ancient forefathers as if they were a family tradition or a will that leaves to posterity the sole task of obedience; they receive them, rather, from living society or from the sovereign who represents it as the legitimate depositary of the current sum of the will of everyone." The U.S. Constitution—establishing the structure for the operation of America's republic—puts "We the People" in the preeminent position. The Constitution and its Bill of Rights, however, sets specific limits—in writing, no less—on how the people can treat criminals and criminal suspects. By setting forth, in the Constitution, explicit rights for criminal defendants and limits on the majority's authority, America's founders sought to check, in effect, the dark impulses of human nature. As Beccaria himself had warned in his treatise: "Left to their most natural feelings, men prefer cruel laws, although given that they are subject to these very laws, it would be in the interest of each individual that laws be moderate, for the fear of being injured is greater than the desire to do harm."[44]

The Eighth Amendment, ratified in 1791, famously bars "cruel and unusual punishments"—a prohibition that was put in place when Beccaria's star was still rising but when gruesome corporal punishments such as ear cropping and the pillory were also still in use. Slaves, seamen and soldiers could all be viciously subjected to the lash or other inhumane corporal punishments in the founders' time. For example, after a slave named Ned was found guilty of stealing the contents of Thomas Jefferson's trunk from a boat docked in the James River Canal basin in Richmond, the slave was sentenced in 1809 to be "burnt in his left hand and receive thirty-nine lashes on his bare back at the public whipping post."[45] Jefferson himself oversaw a nailery at Monticello, an operation set up in 1794 that used slave labor to make up to 10,000 nails a day. The laborers—"my own negro boys," in Jefferson's words—were boys aged 10 to 16 "who would otherwise be idle." "[T]he small ones," as Jefferson learned when he was serving in Philadelphia as America's second U.S. Vice President, were being whipped by an overseer. "I had him severely flogged in the presence of his old companions," Thomas Jefferson wrote to Reuben Perry of one nailor, James Hubbard, a slave that had run away from Jefferson's plantation.[46] In a different context, President James Madison, in 1815, received a letter from an anonymous writer describing himself as "ONCE A SOLDIER, NOW A CITIZEN AND A REPUBLICAN." That letter, written from Georgia and describing another then-routine practice, complained about the brutal whipping of U.S. Infantrymen for "mere trivial crimes."[47]

As is clear from Luigi Castiglioni's *Viaggio*, early American social customs differed radically from those of the twenty-first century, with corporal punishments — including the lash — commonly in use in eighteenth-century America.[48] Instead of riders like Paul Revere sent out by horseback to deliver messages, today's world is peppered with texts and Tweets and Facebook posts, and iChats, Snapchats and Instagrams. E-mail and Skype now allow for instantaneous global communications, and a transatlantic trip — booked on Expedia.com — can be made in hours, not weeks. Beccaria's own place in history, thanks largely to the publication and translation of *On Crimes and Punishments*, was ensured two and a half centuries ago, well before the age of computers and high-tech devices. His book, along with others by Thomas Paine and Montesquieu, created the intellectual climate for the American and French Revolutions — and the Declaration of Independence and the U.S. Constitution. When Peter Du Ponceau concluded his 1824 address to the Law Academy of Philadelphia, he ended, tellingly, with a rhetorical flourish focused on Enlightenment principles, encouraging Philadelphia's rising crop of lawyers to study "general jurisprudence" and "the eternal and immutable principles of right of wrong." "Sound theories," he offered, "will take the place of false ones, and the rules of genuine logic will direct their application to particular cases." "All this," he added, "will be done gradually and insensibly, and the benefit of it will be felt by our remotest posterity."

Thomas Jefferson — who felt that "the earth belongs to the living, and not to the dead," a belief he freely shared with men like James Madison — once wrote that he was not "an advocate for frequent and untried changes in laws and constitutions." Jefferson, however, expressed the strongly held view that "laws and institutions must go hand in hand with the progress of the human mind." "We might as well require a man to wear still the coat which fitted him when a boy, as civilized society to remain ever under the regimen of their barbarous ancestors," Jefferson wrote to Samuel Kercheval from Monticello in 1816, a clear acknowledgment that, in his mind, past practices did not validate the legitimacy or morality of current societal punishments. Peter Du Ponceau — the Philadelphian — likewise declared, in a similar vain, that he was not "a friend to rash and sudden innovation; "on the contrary," he said, he was "well convinced that amendments in the laws ought to be gradual" and that "the delicate chisel, and not the rough axe, is the instrument to be employed." But as a lawyer like Jefferson, Du Ponceau saw law reform of the kind advocated by Montesquieu and Beccaria as nothing short of a professional duty. "The true principles of jurisprudence, in order to fructify," Du Ponceau wrote, "ought first to take root in the minds of the members of the legal profession." "Then, and not till then," he advised, "will false principles gradually give way, as the ripe fruit falls from the tree."

Just as Thomas Jefferson encouraged William Munford to read Enlightenment texts, Peter Du Ponceau — in his address — pointed to Enlightenment writers, telling Philadelphia's law students that "we ought to invite each other to reflection on these important subjects by learned treatises and free discussions, and the labours of the jurist ought not to be confined to mere compilations." "In short," Du Ponceau said, taking a very Beccarian approach, "jurisprudence ought to be treated as a philosophical science." As Du Ponceau argued:

> If Montesquieu had not written, the distinction between the three powers of government would be yet unknown, and their limits undefined. If Beccaria had not written, the torture and its horrid concomitants would not have disappeared from the face of Europe, and sanguinary codes would not almost every where have given way to mild punishments.

Citing changes to the common law suggested by Blackstone, Du Ponceau's concluding two lines offered this specific prediction:

> The common law is destined to acquire in this country the highest degree of perfection of which it is susceptible, and which will raise it in all respects above every other system of laws, ancient or modern. But it will not have fully reached that towering height, until the maxim shall be completely established in practice as well as in theory, THAT PURE ETHICS AND SOUND LOGIC ARE ALSO PARTS OF THE COMMON LAW.[49]

In preparing a "Course of Reading for William G. Munford" in December 1798, Jefferson had, under the heading "Politicks," methodically listed out Locke, Sydney, Montesquieu, Beccaria, *The Federalist Papers*, Chipman, and "Burgh's disquisitions" as sources that should be consulted. The recipient, William Green Munford, was the youngest son of a law enforcement officer, a county sheriff, with the young student's life still very much ahead of him. In 1799, as one century was about to give way to the next, the Italian émigré Carlo Bellini — a close friend of Jefferson and Philip Mazzei and a College of William and Mary faculty member — referred to the young man as "Monford," calling him "an ornament to human nature." Jefferson, the young man's acquaintance, carefully advised Munford on his studies, even looking through Philadelphia bookshops for books to send him. Writing to Munford from Philadelphia, also in 1799, Jefferson noted: "I have been to most of the bookstores here and collected such of the books mentioned in the catalogue as could be found here." On the list: "Stewart's philosophy of the human mind," "Vattel's law of nations," "Smith's wealth of nations," "Nicholson's philosophy," "Chipman's sketches on government," and "Condorcet's progress of the human mind." Jefferson called "the little book of Chipman" a "very excellent elementary book" — a law book that, like so many of the age, referred to Beccaria's own little treatise.[50]

So important was Beccaria's influence on early American law that "it would be impossible" — as one modern criminology textbook puts it — "to discuss the nature of punishment in the United States," or, for that matter, in Europe, "without acknowledging the profoundly influential work of Cesare Beccaria in his short treatise, *On Crimes and Punishments*."[51] In 1784, when John Adams' own book, *History of the Dispute with America*, was printed for "J. Stockdale" in London, among the "NEW PUBLICATIONS" advertised for sale in that title: "AN ESSAY on CRIMES and PUNISHMENTS, with a View of and Commentary upon Beccaria, Rousseau, Voltaire, Fielding, and Blackstone" by "M. Dawes, Esq."[52] Much later, constitutional historian Irving Brant himself emphasized — not in an eighteenth-century ad, but in a modern scholarly text — that Beccaria "did more than any other man to arouse Europe to the monstrous nature of torture and other forms of compulsory self-incrimination."[53] And that influence extended well beyond those particular issues, with another author, James Simpson, encapsulating Beccaria's impact in a book published in Boston in 1834. "Much of the modern improvement of criminal legislation," Simpson wrote, "has been influenced by Beccaria's views." Stressing that Beccaria "wrote much in advance of his own age," Simpson — in the nineteenth-century's third decade—ventured to say that Beccaria's ideas "are yet in advance of Europe, and even Britain," but that "America is acting up to them more nearly."[54]

That observation—that Beccaria's ideas had gained greater traction in America than in Europe—was certainly then true, with America's own founders often leading the way with their advocacy for Beccarian ideas and overseeing the construction of penitentiaries. Today, though, the situation—as least as regards penal reform and the death penalty in particular—is oddly inverted. Europe is now an execution-free zone, thanks in part to the European Union's human rights regime. America's penal system, meanwhile, has been critiqued as one of "mass incarceration" and U.S. laws, at least at the federal level and in a majority of the fifty states, still authorize state-sanctioned killing. The death penalty's fate in America is still uncertain, though the history of the death penalty does seem to be one of successive restrictions on its use, suggesting that, one day, it will be done away with entirely. Whether it gradually withers away over the course of years, or is, more dramatically, declared unconstitutional by the U.S. Supreme Court, is, frankly, unknowable and yet to be seen.

In Europe itself, the death penalty's abolition took place over time, with much anti-death penalty agitation after the Holocaust and World War II. Italy abolished the death penalty for all crimes during peacetime in 1947; the 1949 Constitution of the Federal Republic of Germany stated succinctly that "capital punishment is abolished"; and, in the United Kingdom, Parliament's Abolition of Death Penalty Act of 1965 imposed a moratorium that was made permanent in 1969.[55] Now, as signatories to Protocols 6 and 13 of the European Convention on Human Rights, European countries have acceded to treaties to ensure the death penalty is never used again in Europe, either in peacetime or in time of war. The United States—in stubbornly retaining capital punishment and using executions, however sporadically—has, for its part, actually submitted reservations to international treaties in an attempt to allow for the death penalty's continued use. At least as regards executions, European nations have thus far more faithfully realized Beccaria's vision than the United States.

In *On Crimes and Punishments*, Beccaria wrote about torture and the death penalty in separate chapters. Increasingly, though, the death penalty is viewed as a form of *torture*, a concept long associated with the intentional infliction of physical or psychological harm. The United States of America ratified the U.N. Convention against Torture on October 21, 1994,[56] making an international public commitment—along with its European counterparts—to abandon that practice. It was in part because of that treaty's ratification that the Bush Administration's use of waterboarding in terrorism investigations drew such a stern rebuke from the international community. Yet, while other nations throughout the world have moved away from executions, the U.S. government, the U.S. military, and many U.S. states have failed to abandon them. This has resulted in a prominent U.N. official, Juan Méndez, taking aim at executions as a species of torture.[57]

The U.S. Supreme Court held in 1976, America's bicentennial year, that the Eighth Amendment's Cruel and Unusual Punishments Clause was itself drafted to proscribe "torture" and other barbarous punishments. Eighteenth-century conceptions of torture differ substantially, however, from how that concept is viewed by human rights advocates today. Whereas eighteenth-century lawmakers generally thought of torture as an Inquisitorial *pre-trial* practice, a modern conception of torture does not limit its use to pre-trial practices. In any event, the Supreme Court has not yet lumped death sentences and executions with torturous practices, in part, perhaps, because of the definition of *torture* in the Convention against Torture itself. In that treaty, *torture* is defined as "any act by which severe pain or suffering, whether physical or mental, is intentionally inflicted on a person," but then is said to exclude "pain or suffering arising only from, inherent in or incidental to lawful sanctions."[58] In effect, pain and suffering—even if intentionally inflicted—is purportedly exempted from the definition of torture if a *government*, as opposed to a *private party*, inflicts it. If the treaty is read in this manner, this bizarrely sets *a lower bar* for the conduct of governments than the citizens who, as part of the social compact, authorize governments in the first place.

To date, the U.S. Supreme Court has declined to declare the death penalty unconstitutional under the Eighth Amendment's Cruel and Unusual Punishments Clause even though *non-lethal* corporal punishments have long been abandoned by the U.S. penal system.[59] Instead, the Supreme Court has simply restricted the categories of death-eligible offenders, forbidding the death penalty's use on juveniles, the insane, the severely intellectually disabled, and those who have neither killed nor attempted to kill. The U.S. Government, as well as thirty-two American states, still have death penalty laws on the books, putting the United States in the company of a few other countries such as China, Iran and Saudi Arabia—mostly a rouges' gallery of totalitarian regimes—that still execute people. The once apartheid-ridden South Africa, through its Constitutional Court, itself abandoned the death penalty altogether back in the mid-nineties, emphasizing the importance of human dignity and the right to life.[60]

When early foreigners, including in the eighteenth century, visited Philadelphia, they invariably paid a stop to the then-novel Walnut Street Prison, with one article, "The Rage for Going to America," noting that, in that institution, "[a] real attempt had been made to combine Quaker ideas on penology with those of the great Italian, Beccaria."[61] The question that modern American lawmakers and jurists must ask themselves, in the twenty-first century, is this: should Beccaria have written about torture and the death penalty not in *separate* chapters, but as two related subjects as part of a *single* chapter? In other words, do death sentences and executions—when the concept of *torture* is fairly considered from a common sense perspective—just amount to another gruesome sub-species of the broader concept of torture, as normally understood in a layperson's sense? Death sentences and executions certainly inflict pain, be it physical or psychological, or both, in a deliberate manner, and when executions are compared to other, *non-lethal* acts already classified as torture, it is hard to conceive of any reason why *lethal* acts should not be classified as torture, too.

Despite all the progress that has been made in the world in the realm of human rights, torture and summary and state-sanctioned executions, it must be acknowledged, still persist in many parts of the world.[62] In the United States, death sentences—as in authoritarian countries, mostly in Asia, the Middle East, and North Africa—thus continue to be handed out by state officials, albeit less frequently than in past decades. The number of American death sentences, in fact, fell from 315 in 1996 to 80 in 2011, and American executions—which have also declined significantly in number—are now largely a southern phenomenon. The number of U.S. executions fell from 98 in 1999 to 43 in 2011, 43 in 2012 and 39 in 2013, and of the 1,379 American executions that have taken place since 1976, the vast majority, 1,126, were carried out in just one geographic area, the South. Indeed, more than half of those executions, 736, took place in just three southern states: Texas, Virginia and Oklahoma. Although the U.S. Bill of Rights safeguards the nation as a whole, just *two percent* of U.S. counties, a 2013 report by Richard Dieter of the Death Penalty Information Center points out, have been responsible for *the majority* of cases leading to executions since 1976, with racial disparities in the death penalty's infliction remaining a continuing problem. If there is ever to be "Equal Justice Under Law"—as the Supreme Court's motto promises—the death penalty, plain and simple, must be declared unconstitutional. Right now, offenders are, plainly, *not* being treated equally, with race and geography playing the dominant roles in determining who lives and who dies.[63]

Although Beccaria argued 250 years ago that the speed and certainty of a punishment is more important than its severity, the American executions that occur now are taking place, on average, roughly *fifteen years* after the commission of the crimes for which they are being meted out.[64] In that respect, the modern American judicial and criminal justice system has strayed just about as far as possible from the Founding Fathers' Beccaria-inspired conception of punishment. In the founders' time, consistent with Beccaria's advice, punishments—including capital punishments—were usually inflicted in a matter of days or weeks after a crime had occurred. And at that time, the English or American death penalties, certainly, could not then be fairly described as "unusual," as English common law and early American statutes made death the *mandatory* penalty for certain crimes. Because of their mandatory character, death sentences were, in fact, the *usual* means of punishing a number of offenses.

By contrast, American death sentences—now imposed by juries on a *discretionary* basis—are currently handed out in a discriminatory and capriciously haphazard fashion. In essence, the principles that Beccaria espoused—and that the founders themselves embraced—have been turned on their head. Moreover, the world's tectonic plates—with European countries leading the way—have shifted under the feet of modern American lawmakers and jurists as human rights principles have rapidly spread around the globe. In the past few decades, a plethora of nations—from Australia to Canada and from nations in Africa to Europe—have adamantly refused to even extradite offenders to the United States in the absence of assurances that the death penalty would not be sought. Their rationale: long delays in the carrying out of such sentences, coupled with harsh conditions of confinement and concerns over the death penalty itself. Bottom line: the death penalty has, increasingly, come to be seen as cruel or inhuman treatment or punishment, a violation of human dignity, or even torture.[65] Were he alive today, Beccaria would no doubt be deeply troubled by the continuance of executions and by death sentences being carried out a decade and a half—and in some cases, more than three decades—after the crimes for which the punishments were imposed.

Beccaria's famous treatise, *On Crimes and Punishments*, set America's anti-death penalty movement in motion. While it is impossible to say what America's founders would make of twenty-first century death penalty practices were they still alive, the modern-day legal battles over the Eighth Amendment's meaning can be attributed mainly to the founders' conscious choice to broadly prohibit certain *types* of punishments. Instead of locking future generations into their own era-specific mores, the founders deliberately chose—as the language they crafted makes clear—to broadly prohibit "cruel and unusual punishments" in the Eighth Amendment. Indeed, some founders, including Thomas Jefferson, openly acknowledged that such eighteenth-century mores—then permitting slavery and brutal whippings and often predicating punishment on the rigid *lex talionis* doctrine— would not hold up well over time.[66]

Alexis de Tocqueville, the French writer who wrote *Democracy in America* after studying America's penal system in the 1830s, himself contrasted the "mildness" of America's then-existing criminal laws with the "terrible powers" of European societies. As Tocqueville wrote in 1840: "In no country is criminal justice administered with more mildness than in the United States. Whilst the English seem disposed carefully to retain the bloody traces of the Middle Ages in their penal legislation, the Americans have almost expunged capital punishment from their codes."[67] The past, of course, is the past, and the history of American law cannot be changed. The future, however, is a different matter, and "originalists" and "living constitutionalists" alike must contemplate *for themselves* whether the death penalty is constitutional *in our time*. The founders themselves would demand no less.

What is crystal clear—and what this book shows—is that Beccaria's treatise profoundly affected our forefathers' conceptions of cruelty and their views on everything from gun ownership to the proper proportion between crimes and punishments. America's founders and framers, it is equally clear, made a deliberate choice in that era dominated by Enlightenment ideas to use generic, non-specific proscriptions against "cruel," "unusual" or "sanguinary" punishments in their constitutions and bills of rights. As a result, the right to be free from "sanguinary" or "cruel and unusual" punishments, as with, say, the rights to "due process" or "equal protection," read like value-laden statements instead of bullet-point listings of what specific acts are forbidden or permitted. This naturally means that, like it or not, it is up to *living* American judges—as the arbiters of what the U.S. Constitution and state-law equivalents mean—to decide what so qualifies. And in doing so, they must utilize a provision of law—the Fourteenth Amendment's guarantee of "equal protection of the laws"—that was nowhere to be found in the founding era. While the equality principle set forth in the Declaration of Independence was a ray of sunlight in Thomas Jefferson's still slave-ridden society, the rights clause of that landmark instrument in the history of the world has not been read by U.S. courts to confer binding, legally enforceable protections.

Just as American judges have already determined that punishments such as breaking on the wheel and crucifixion would be classified as "cruel and unusual punishments,"[68] twenty-first century judges must, ultimately, evaluate for themselves whether death sentences and executions should be so classified. In prior cases, the U.S. Supreme Court has thus far consistently rejected challenges to modes of executions. In 1879, in *Wilkerson v. Utah*, the Supreme Court rejected an Eighth Amendment challenge to execution by firing squad. In 1890, *In re Kemmler*, the Court upheld the constitutionality of the electric chair. And in 2008, in *Baze v. Rees*, the Court upheld Kentucky's three-drug lethal injection protocol. In one 1987 case, the Court, in its 5–4 decision in *McCleskey v. Kemp*, even rejected an Eighth and Fourteenth Amendment challenge to Georgia's death penalty despite credible, essentially unrebutted statistics showing it was being administered in a racially discriminatory manner. Since 1976, more than 75 percent of murder victims in cases resulting in an execution were white, even though, nationally, only 50 percent of murder victims are generally white.[69]

To date, some U.S. Supreme Court Justices have read the Eighth Amendment's language as if it were forever locked in the eighteenth century—as if the text had been handed down by the Founding Fathers, Sermon on the Mount style, with a stipulation that it be read and understood only as America's founders would have read and understood it. For example, Justices Clarence Thomas and Antonin Scalia lamented in a 1992 dissent in *Hudson v. McMillian* that the Cruel and Unusual Punishments Clause had been "cut" loose from "its historical moorings." "The Eighth Amendment," they contended, "is not, and should not be turned into, a National Code of Prison Regulation."

Justice Scalia—who has taken the position that, for him, "the constitutionality of the death penalty is not a difficult, soul-wrenching question"—has further emphasized that, in his judgment, the Eighth Amendment "is addressed to always-and-everywhere 'cruel' punishments, such as the rack and the thumbscrew." But this kind of thinking both ignores the founders' own much-expressed preference for human progress and the ratification of the Fourteenth Amendment, which fundamentally reshaped American law. In fact, such an "originalist" approach minimizes the Supreme Court's role as a neutral, independent arbiter to define what "cruel and unusual punishments" are by, in effect, bizarrely contending that *eighteenth-century practice* should *predetermine* twenty-first century legal rulings. In fact, the law, as it must, is constantly evolving, as the U.S. Supreme Court itself has recognized in multiple majority opinions with its "evolving standards of decency" test—the test it currently employs in evaluating Eighth Amendment cruel and unusual punishments claims.[70]

In American life, Cesare Beccaria's legacy—including his call for clear and precise laws—still endures in ways large and small, even beyond his call for the death penalty's abolition. *On Crimes and Punishments* fundamentally changed the way Americans thought about law and proportionality, with the notion of equality of treatment eventually finding expression in American law in the Fourteenth Amendment's post-Civil War guarantee of "equal protection of the laws." The Criminal Justice Section of the Philadelphia Bar Association, in a gesture of respect and recognition, has even paired up with The Justinian Society, a group of Italian-American lawyers, judges and law students, to give out the Cesare Beccaria Award in his honor. Established in 1994, the Beccaria Award goes each year to a jurist, scholar or practitioner for outstanding contributions to the cause of justice and the advancement of legal education. In 2007, the Philadelphia Bar Association—taking things a step further—unveiled a bust of Cesare Beccaria, an art form popular with America's founders, to be permanently installed in the Jury Assembly Room. The bust, placed in an appropriate spot given Beccaria's own support for jury trials, was the brainchild of the late Philadelphia lawyer Michael Rainone, a past president of the National Italian American Bar Association, the Lawyers' Club of Philadelphia, and the Philadelphia Trial Lawyers Association.[71]

Still cited by American jurists and law professors, *On Crimes and Punishments*—despite its age—certainly has not lost its currency. Indeed, Beccaria's Italian fingerprints, not wiped away since the Founding Fathers' era, remain detectable in American law, if only, at times, in partial prints. It is thus particularly fitting that another Italian, Constantino Brumidi, should be the artist who painted *The Apotheosis of Washington*, the stunning fresco that adorns the ceiling of the U.S. Capitol dome. After being arrested in 1851, accused of taking part in a revolt, Brumidi was pardoned on the condition that he leave Italy, with the liberty seeking Brumidi—who dedicated himself to decorating the U.S. Capitol's walls and ceilings with frescoes—eventually becoming a U.S. citizen. In the Capitol's Senate-side "Brumidi Corridors," Brumidi's beautiful work—completed during the 1850s through the 1870s—can still be admired.[72]

Known as the Michelangelo of the U.S. Capitol, Brumidi—like Beccaria—is one of many Italians who shaped U.S. history. Another Italian—the explorer Amerigo Vespucci (1454–1512)—actually, as a result of a Latin translation of his name by an amateur German mapmaker—became America's namesake. When Martin Waldseemüller, the cartographer, was mapping the New World, he decided to name the landmass after Amerigo Vespucci, who had sailed along the coast of South America. The plaster cast for the Statue of Freedom that now sits atop the U.S. Capitol was itself shipped from Rome in 1858, with the completed bronze statute—depicting a female figure wearing a toga-like robe and helmet adorned with nine stars and an eagle's head and feathers—hoisted into place in 1863 in the midst of the Civil War.[73]

The much-celebrated Beccaria, mindful of the difference between cutting-edge thinking on human progress and the traditions of national judiciaries, once expressed the view that every country's judicial system lags behind the progress of civilization by two or three hundred years.[74] In the long arc of Western civilization, the concept of human rights, stretching back to the Magna Carta and even farther than that, has ancient origins,[75] though progress—and change—has often been slow to come. There have been many struggles and many setbacks, with continuous battles—both epic and small—having been fought in that realm for centuries. The quest of Americans to end torturous practices, establish the Rule of Law, and move toward more humane and civilized punishments, have, however, all taken place against the backdrop of Beccaria's ideas. In writing about clear laws and mild punishments, *On Crimes and Punishments* set American law—as well as the world's human rights movement—on a course not unlike those mapped out by Vespucci as a navigator. In arguing for the death penalty's abandonment, Beccaria recognized that he would face treacherous seas and unforeseeable obstacles, but he still raised his sails, confident that gusts of wind would take him to his desired destination, a better world for himself, or at least for those who would come after him.[76]

Over the past 250 years, the American public's reliance on the ideas in Beccaria's treatise has varied with the times. The treatise garnered high praise in the eighteenth and nineteenth centuries, with Englishmen, colonial subjects and American citizens alike making use of its ideas.[77] But despite continued resistance from some quarters to jettison the centuries-old institution of state-sanctioned killing, Beccaria's abolitionist views—already the law in twenty-first century Europe—may yet prevail throughout the globe. The death penalty—the vestige of a bygone era in which non-lethal corporal punishments once prevailed alongside death sentences—is already under siege in America, in its courts, and in the remaining retentionist countries, like North Korea, in which it persists. The World Coalition Against the Death Penalty, formed to pressure governments to abolish capital punishment altogether, now holds global meetings every three years to mark the progress of the anti-death penalty movement.

The arguments against the death penalty, presented at such gatherings, however, have changed little since Beccaria's time. Because of the world's experience with capital punishment over the past 250 years, though, American lawmakers and judges—in assessing its inefficacy—have that much more history to examine, including the death penalty's persistent and recurring discriminatory and arbitrary application. While predictions of the death penalty's demise have often proved premature, Jeremy Bentham—the English social reformer so inspired by Beccaria—once offered this sage assessment: "The more we examine the punishment of death, the more we shall be induced to adopt the opinion of Beccaria. This subject is so well discussed in his work that there is scarcely any necessity for further investigation."[78] As American jurists and policymakers continue to oversee and administer death penalty schemes, those words seem as prescient as ever.

In the modern era, *On Crimes and Punishments* thus remains as relevant as it was at the zenith of its fame in the eighteenth century, and still stands—as one source puts it— "as one of the lasting contributions of the Enlightenment to the modern world."[79] Because of the printed word and the transmission of ideas across ages and generations, the reverberations and echoes of Beccaria's humane voice, however faint now to Millennials and Generation Xers, can still be heard. Though silenced by his death in Milan in 1794 before America's penitentiary system could become fully operational, Beccaria's humanistic voice— through his writings—has been present through the decades and can, like a compass, still guide future generations. Beccaria's little book, in fact, continues to inspire the anti-death penalty movement and a progressive agenda around the globe. As the abolition movement stands at the two-and-a-half-century milestone, the nagging question that remains is this: will Americans—at long last—finally heed Beccaria's advice and abolish capital punishment once and for all, just as they did away with another human rights abuse—slavery— in the nineteenth century? When one examines America's abandonment of *non-lethal* corporal punishments within prisons, as well as the bevy of problems that continue to plague America's death penalty, the answer becomes clear: capital punishment should be sent the way of the stocks, the pillory and the whipping post.

As for Beccaria's overall influence on American law, the extent of that influence is immeasurable. As University of Chicago professor Bernard Harcourt has written, *On Crimes and Punishments* served as "a manifesto for legal reform centered on the Enlightenment values of rationality, proportionality, legality, lenience, and the rule of law." It shaped American law, led to the birth of the penitentiary system, and "[o]ver the centuries"— to quote Harcourt—became "a placeholder for the classical school of thought in criminology and deterrence-based public policy, for death penalty abolitionism, as well as for liberal ideals of legality and the rule of law." As England's Bloody Code gave way to the much-replicated Pennsylvania experiment with milder punishments, American lawmakers—in large part due to Beccaria's treatise—mapped out a new course for U.S. society, the likes of which, bolstered by the Italian philosopher's reasoned arguments, had not been seen since the days of William Penn and the Quaker's use of less severe punishments. "In becoming a classic text that has been so widely and varyingly cited, though perhaps little read today," Harcourt emphasizes of its broad cultural significance, "*On Crimes and Punishments* may be used as a mirror on the key projects over the past two centuries and a half in the domain of penal law and punishment theory."

Before the American Revolution, arbitrary and tyrannical punishments, oppressive English laws, and assertions of absolute monarchical power were ubiquitous, causing widespread fear and discontentment among American colonists. With Beccaria's treatise resting on a social contract theory that departed from those espoused by his intellectual predecessors, including Hobbes and Rousseau, Beccaria asserted that individuals—the members of that social compact—only relinquished "the smallest possible portion" of their freedom to ensure their security within society. As Beccaria wrote: "The sum of these smallest possible portions constitutes the right to punish." In expressing limits to a sovereign's right to punish, Beccaria—disapproving of acts of cruelty, and inspiring men such as John Adams, James Madison and Thomas Jefferson in the process—saw unnecessary punishments as tyrannical and unjust. In arguing for proportion between crimes and punishments, Beccaria—seeking, like his American counterparts, a more rational system of justice—sought more rigorous enforcement of clear and precise laws, but felt milder punishments, and not arbitrary punishments or executions, were the best means of enforcing the social contract. Before Jefferson's Declaration of Independence spoke of "unalienable" rights, and before America's framers, in the U.S. Constitution, collectively wrote of "We the People," Beccaria's novel model of state power and sovereignty captivated—and appealed to—America's founders, thereby forever shaping the development of American law.[80]

Notes

Introduction

1. Bessler, Cruel and Unusual, 31; Hostettler, Cesare Beccaria, x; Cees Maris & Frans Jacobs, eds., Law, Order and Freedom: A Historical Introduction to Legal Philosophy 168 (Dordrecht, Netherlands: Springer, Jacques de Ville, trans. 2011).

2. Israel, Democratic Enlightenment, 339–40; Maestro, Cesare Beccaria and the Origins of Penal Reform, 42–43; Massaro, Cesare Beccaria; Bellamy, On Crimes and Punishments, xxix; Fisher, *The Birth of the Prison Retold*, 1278.

3. Bailyn, The Ideological Origins of the American Revolution, 27, 29, 149–50; 1 Bailyn, Pamphlets of the American Revolution, 23.

4. David J. Siemers, The Antifederalists: Men of Great Faith and Forbearance 146 n.8 (Lanham, MD: Rowman & Littlefield Publishers, 2003).

5. McBride, Punishment and Political Order, 90; Rebecca Stefoff, *Furman v. Georgia*: Debating the Death Penalty 29 (Tarrytown, NY: Marshall Cavendish Benchmark, 2008).

6. Bessler, Cruel and Unusual, 55–56; Pauley, *The Jurisprudence of Crime and Punishment*, 114–19; Gottlieb, Theater of Death, 192.

7. Massie, Catherine the Great, 344–45, 348; Hostettler, Cesare Beccaria, x.

8. Darren Staloff, Hamilton, Adams, Jefferson: The Politics of Enlightenment and the American Founding 256 (New York: Hill and Wang, 2005).

9. Schabas, The Abolition of the Death Penalty in International Law, 5.

10. Foucault, Discipline & Punish, 13; James M. Donovan, Juries and the Transformation of Criminal Justice in France in the Nineteenth & Twentieth Centuries 65 (Chapel Hill: University of North Carolina Press, 2010); Michael Tonry, Thinking about Crime: Sense and Sensibility in American Penal Culture 72 (Oxford: Oxford University Press, 2004); Luann Brennan, Restoring Justice to the Juvenile Justice System, Master's thesis, Wayne State University (2006), p. 18.

11. Todd R. Clear, George F. Cole & Michael D. Reisig, American Corrections 37 (Belmont, CA: Wadsworth, 10th ed. 2013).

12. Tonry, The Handbook of Crime and Punishment, 740.

13. Bessler, Cruel and Unusual, 48–49; Hunt, Inventing Human Rights, 80–81. Blackstone's treatise, a widely available exposition of English law and practice, was a primary resource for American lawyers. Chipman, Sketches of the Principles of Government, 237; 1 Flanders, The Lives and Times of the Chief Justices, 35.

14. Banner, The Death Penalty, 92.

15. Bessler, *Revisiting Beccaria's Vision*, 205.

16. Jeremy Bentham, A Fragment on Government; Being an Examination of Whit Is Delivered, On the Subject of Government in General in the Introduction to Sir William Blackstone's Commentaries (1776); 1 Cohen & Cohen, Readings in Jurisprudence and Legal Philosophy, 346 n.46.

17. J. H. Burns & H. L. A. Hart, eds., Jeremy Bentham, A Fragment on Government 13–14 (Cambridge: Cambridge University Press, 2001) (1776).

18. Colquhoun, A Treatise on the Police of the Metropolis, 282, 300, 314.

19. Noether, The American Constitution as a Symbol and Reality for Italy, 36.

20. Bessler, Cruel and Unusual, 47, 50–51, 53–55; McBride, Punishment and Political Order, 90; Caso, We, the People, 14; *see also* 1 Claude H. Van Tyne, The Causes of the War of Independence: A History of the Founding of the American Republic 344 (Boston: Houghton Mifflin Co., 1922) ("John Hancock owned ... Beccaria on Crimes"); *Kitty Preyer and Her Books* ("George Washington, John

Adams and Thomas Jefferson all were familiar with Beccaria's work, and it influenced their thinking about crime and punishment.").

21. Bessler, Cruel and Unusual, 53; Sullivan, *The Birth of the Prison*, 333.

22. Rush, An Enquiry into the Effects of Public Punishments upon Criminals; William Federer, The Ten Commandments and Their Influence on American Law: A Study in History 19 (St. Louis, MO: Amerisearch, 2003).

23. Bessler, Cruel and Unusual, 53.

24. Criminologists still study Beccaria's ideas. As a 1989 text notes: "An examination of nine of the leading textbooks on criminology, which, together, are read by 180,000 young men and women annually as part of their introductory instruction in criminology, reveals that all of these books discuss Beccaria." 2 William S. Laufer & Freda Adler, eds., Advances in Criminological Theory 2 (New Brunswick, NJ: Transaction Publishers, 1990); id. at 3 ("American criminology students on the graduate level will not only read the *Essay* itself, or the splendid Beccaria biography by Elio Monachesi (1960), but also critical analyses, such as those contained in recent articles by the American Beccaria scholar David B. Young…, who is particularly concerned with fathoming the inconsistencies between Beccaria's utilitarianism and his retributism.").

25. Catherine Drinker Bowen, John Adams and the American Revolution 371–72, 394–95 (Old Saybrook, CT: Konecky & Konecky, 1950).

26. 20 John P. Kaminski, Gaspare J. Saladino & Richard Leffler, eds., The Documentary History of the Ratification of the Constitution 1082 (Madison: State Historical Society of Wisconsin, 2004); Jean Paul de Lagrave, Voltaire's Man in America 48 (Montreal: R. Davies Multimedia Pub. 1997).

27. Amar, America's Constitution, xi.

28. William F. Northen, ed., Men of Mark in Georgia 163–64 (Atlanta, GA: A. B. Caldwell, 1907); 1 Lawrence S. Rowland, Alexander Moore & George C. Rogers, Jr., The History of Beaufort County, South Carolina 301 (Columbia: University of South Carolina Press, 1996).

29. Bessler, Cruel and Unusual, 47–53.

30. Adam Smith, An Inquiry into the Nature and Causes of the Wealth of Nations (London: W. Strahan & T. Cadell, 1776).

31. Lynn McDonald, The Early Origins of the Social Sciences 155–56 (Montreal, Quebec: McGill-Queen's University Press, 1993).

32. Pinker, The Better Angels of Our Nature, 539.

33. Bessler, Cruel and Unusual, 141–45.

34. Bellamy, On Crimes and Punishments, 113; Jeannette Covert Nolan, The Shot Heard Round the World: The Story of Lexington and Concord (New York: Julian Messner 1963).

35. Constance M. Greiff, Independence: The Creation of a National Park 13 (Philadelphia: University of Pennsylvania Press, 1987).

36. Journal of the Proceedings of the Congress, Held at Philadelphia, September 5, 1774, at 105–113 (Washington, DC: Government Printing Office, 1904).

37. Bessler, Cruel and Unusual, 47–53; Sullivan, *The Birth of the Prison*, 339–41.

38. Robert J. Cottrol, *Finality with Ambivalence: The American Death Penalty's Uneasy History*, 56 Stan. L. Rev. 1641, 1650 (2004).

39. Bellamy, On Crimes and Punishments, 3, 7, 113.

40. Pauline Maier, Ratification: The People Debate the Constitution, 1787–1788 (New York: Simon & Schuster, 2010); Ronald P. Formisano, For the People: American Populist Movements from the Revolution to the 1850s, at 58–59 (Chapel Hill: North Carolina University Press, 2008); Morton Keller, America's Three Regimes: A New Political History 58 (Oxford: Oxford University Press, 2007).

41. Biographical Directory of the United States Congress, 1774–2005, at 2169 (Washington, DC: U.S. Government Printing Office, 2005) (entry for John Williams); Francis Childs' Notes of the New York Ratification Debates (June 21, 1788), *available at* http://www.consource.org/document/francis-childs-notes-of-the-new-york-ratification-debates-1788-6-21/; Melancton Smith's Notes of the New York Ratification Convention Debates (June 21, 1788), *available at* http://www.consource.org/document/melancton-smiths-notes-of-the-new-york-ratification-convention-debates-1788-6-21/.

42. The Debates and Proceedings of the Convention of the State of New York, Assembled at Poughkeepsie, on the 17th of June, 1788: To Deliberate on the Form of Government Recommended by the General Convention at Philadelphia on the 17th September, 1787, at 30–33 (New York: Francis Childs, 1788); Thomas, On Crimes and Punishments, 80; Edgar J. McManus, Black Bondage in the North 173–74 (Syracuse, NY: Syracuse University Press, 1973).

43. "Brutus," "To the Citizens of the State of New York" (Oct. 18, 1787), *in* Ketcham, The Anti-

Federalist Papers, 275–76; Noah Pickus, True Faith and Allegiance: Immigration and American Civic Nationalism 192 n.14 (Princeton: Princeton University Press, 2005).

44. *E.g.*, Biographical Anecdotes of the Founders of the French Republic, and of Other Eminent Characters, Who Have Distinguished Themselves in the Progress of the Revolution 109 (London: R. Phillips, 1797) ("In this tract, he [M. de la Rochefoucauld Liancourt] points out the difference between mild and sanguinary laws, by a reference to the actual practice of Pennsylvania, in consequence of which the number of offenders has been lessened full one half! No whips, or chains, are to be seen there."); id. at 264 ("The other was on Death, considered as a punishment. In this, all the modern governments were justly reproached for the sanguinary laws still prevalent in their criminal codes, and doubts were hinted, as to the right claimed by society of cutting off the life of an individual.").

45. Thomas Jefferson, Third Draft of the Virginia Constitution (1776), *reprinted in* 1 Julian P. Boyd ed., The Papers of Thomas Jefferson 359 (Princeton: Princeton University Press, 1950).

46. Noether, The American Constitution as a Symbol and Reality for Italy, 26.

47. Northwest Ordinance (July 13, 1787), § 5; Laws Passed in the Territory of the United States Northwest of the River Ohio, from the Commencement of the Government to the 31st of December, 1791, at 17–21 (Philadelphia: Francis Childs & John Swaine, 1792); *see also* Brent G. Filbert & Alan G. Kaufman, Justice and Procedure in the Sea Services 4 (Annapolis, MD: U.S. Naval Institute, 1998) ("In June 1775, the Continental Congress appointed a committee to prepare rules and regulations for the government of the Continental army. George Washington sat as a member of this committee, which adopted a set of sixty-nine articles known as the American Articles of War. Another committee of the Continental Congress revised this code in 1776 to more closely match the British Articles of War of 1774. John Adams, Thomas Jefferson, and John Rutledge were members of this panel.").

48. Congressional Serial Set 4 (Washington, DC: U.S. Government Printing Office, 1901).

49. Bessler, Cruel and Unusual, 187–88; Bessler, *The Public Interest and the Unconstitutionality of Private Prosecutors*, 515–16.

50. Jonas Hanway, Solitude in Imprisonment, intro. & 3–4 (1776); Jan Alber, Narrating the Prison: Role and Representation in Charles Dickens' Novels, Twentieth-Century Fiction, and Film 17 (Youngstown, NY: Cambria Press, 2007); Laurie Throness, A Protestant Purgatory: Theological Origins of the Penitentiary Act, 1779, at 51–52 (Hampshire, UK: Ashgate, 2008); Third Report of the Inspectors Appointed under the Provisions of the Act 5 & 6 Will. IV. c. 38 to Visit the Different Prisons of Great Britain 71–73 (London: W. Clowes and Sons, 1838) (referring to Beccaria's writings and Hanway's).

51. http://www.britannica.com/EBchecked/topic/1269536/The-Founding-Fathers-and-Slavery (listing slaveholders and non-slaveholders).

52. Henry Wiencek, *Master of Monticello*, Smithsonian, Oct. 2012, pp. 40–49; Thomas Jefferson to Thomas Mann Randolph, Jan. 23, 1801, *available at* www.founders.archives.gov.

53. Stephanie Kermes, Creating an American Identity: New England, 1789–1825, at 19 (New York: Palgrave MacMillan, 2008); Jay P. Dolan, In Search of an American Catholicism: A History of Religion and Culture in Tension 15 (Oxford: Oxford University Press, 2002); Raven, London Booksellers and American Customers, 6–18.

54. Pace, Luigi Castiglioni's Viaggio, xvii–xviii, 3, 11, 337; J. T. S. Wheelock, *Alessandro Verri's Unpublished "Osservazioni" on Isidoro Bianchi's* Elogio storico di Pietro Verri, Forum Italicum: A Quarterly of Italian Studies 270, 295 n.7 (1974); 1 George Washington Greene, The Life of Nathanael Greene: Major-General in the Army of the Revolution 56 (Boston: Houghton, Mifflin & Co., 1890); http://archive.org/stream/viaggioneglista00castgoog#page/n7/mode/2up (reproducing original Italian edition of Luigi Castiglioni's *Viaggio*).

55. Bessler, Cruel and Unusual, 300, 306; Maura Lyons, William Dunlap and the Construction of an American Art History 101–102 (Amherst: University of Massachusetts Press, 2005); Pace, Luigi Castiglioni's Viaggio, 335–38; Pace, Benjamin Franklin and Italy, 284; http://onlinelibrary.wiley.com/store/10.1111/j.2050-411X.2000.tb00282.x/asset/j.2050-411X.2000.tb00282.x.pdf?v=1&t=hfro4j4i&s=d7cebf4bac2b70d0ef00d308e11a911dbe86dda8.

56. Pace, Luigi Castiglioni's Viaggio, xxiv, xxviii, xxxii, 14–15, 23, 26, 112, 221; *see also* Giovanni Di Capua & Luigi Saibene, Luigi Castiglioni Nel Paese Degli Uomini Liberi (Rubbettino Editore, 2005).

57. Jill Lepore, The Story of America: Essays on Origins 302 (Princeton: Princeton University Press, 2012).

58. Shackelford, Thomas Jefferson's Travels in Europe, 1, 31.

59. Abbé de Mably, Remarks Concerning the Government and Laws of the United States of Amer-

ica: In Four Letters, Addressed to Mr. Adams 2 (New York: Burt Franklin, 1785).

60. Jon Meacham, Thomas Jefferson: The Art of Power 191 (New York: Random House, 2012); Pace, Luigi Castiglioni's Viaggio, 336.

61. Herbert A. Johnson, Nancy Travis Wolfe & Mark Jones, History of Criminal Justice 16 (Newark, NJ: Matthew Bender & Co., 4th ed. 2008) ("Beginning with the major work of Beccaria, a new school of thought evolved concerning the function that punishment should play in the criminal justice system.").

62. Keith Hayward, Shadd Maruna & Jayne Mooney, eds., Fifty Key Thinkers in Criminology 6 (New York: Routledge, 2010); 1 Cohen & Cohen, Readings in Jurisprudence and Legal Philosophy, 346 n.46.

63. "Account of the late Marquis Beccaria," 6 The Monthly Magazine and British Register 260 (London: R. Phillips, 1798) (October 1798 issue containing a "eulogium of the late Marquis Beccaria").

64. Cornell, A Well Regulated Militia, 20; U.S. Const., amend. XIII; State v. Hirsch, 114 P.3d 1104, 1332 & n.48 (Or. 2005).

65. Payne v. Tennessee, 501 U.S. 808, 819–20 (1991); Bessler, *Revisiting Beccaria's Vision*, 284–85; Michael Mello, Against the Death Penalty: The Relentless Dissents of Justices Brennan and Marshall (Boston: Northeastern University Press, 1996).

66. Hostettler, Cesare Beccaria, 26.

67. The Society for the Diffusion of Knowledge about the Punishment of Death, The Second Supplement to the Penny Cyclopædia of the Society for the Diffusion of Useful Knowledge 432 (London: Knight & Co., 1858); Robert Southey and His Age: The Development of a Conservative Mind 77, 196 (Oxford: Clarendon Press, 1960); 1 Leon Radzinowicz, A History of English Criminal Law and Its Administration from 1750: The Movement for Reform, 1750–1833, at 345, 349 (New York: Macmillan Co., 1948).

68. Garry Wills: Lincoln and Gettysburg: The Words that Remade America (New York: Simon & Schuster, 2012); Terence Ball, ed., Lincoln: Political Writings and Speeches 113 (Cambridge: Cambridge University Press, 2013); Roger Billings and Frank J. Williams, eds., Abraham Lincoln, Esq.: The Legal Career of America's Greatest President 106 (Lexington: The University Press of Kentucky, 2010); Nicholas Buccola, The Political Thought of Frederick Douglass: In Pursuit of American Liberty 46 (New York: New York University Press, 2012).

69. 2 Edwin Wiley, Irving E. Rines & Albert Bushnell, eds., Lectures on the Growth and Development of the United States 357 (New York: American Educational Alliance, 1916); Sydney George Fisher, Struggle for American Independence 26, 35 (Philadelphia: J. B. Lippincott Co., 1908). Some of the many translations of *On Crimes and Punishments* are listed in the bibliography.

70. Dred Scott v. Sandford, 60 U.S. 393 (1857). Respondent's real name was Sanford.

71. Bessler, Cruel and Unusual, 171, 176–77.

72. Asher, Goodheart & Rogers, Murder on Trial, 6 ("Jurors in murder trials, lawyers, and legislators in the early American republic were enormously influenced by a book published by Italian nobleman, Cesare Beccaria.").

73. *E.g.*, A Catalogue of the Books Belonging to the New-York Society Library; Together with the Charter and By-Laws of the Same 95 (New York: C. S. Van Winkle, 1813) (listing Beccaria's treatise among its holdings); 27 Transactions of the First International Congress on the Enlightenment 1495 (Geneva: Institut et Musee Voltaire, 1963) ("[T]he Catalogue of Books belonging to the South Carolina College Library (1807) listed 'Beccaria on Crimes.'").

74. Manasseh Dawes, An Essay on Crimes and Punishments, with a View of, and Commentary Upon Beccaria, Rousseau, Voltaire, Montesquieu, Fielding, and Blackstone (1782) (printing in London for "C. Dilly" and "J. Debrett (successor to Mr. Almon)" and authored by "M. Dawes, of the Inner Temple, Esq."); Chipman, Sketches of the Principles of Government ("From the Press of J. Lyon" in Rutland and "Printed for the Author," with the author being Nathaniel Chipman, "Judge of the Court of the United States, for the District of Vermont."); *see also* Richard Hey, Observations on the Nature of Civil Liberty, and the Principles of Government 35 (London: T. Cadell, 1776) (referencing Beccaria); Thomas Percival, A Socratic Discourse on Truth and Faithfulness 11 (Warrington, England: Whieldon and Butterworth, 1781) (same); John McArthur, A Treatise of the Principles and Practice of Naval Courts-Martial 13, 133 (Warrington, England: Whieldon and Butterworth, 1792) (citing Beccaria); Howard, The State of the Prisons in England and Wales, 29 (quoting Beccaria); Case of Peter Finnerty, Including a Full Report of All the Proceedings Which Took Place in the Court of King's Bench Upon the Subject ii n.*, x, xxvi, 34 n.†, 47 (London: J. McCreery, 1811) (referencing Beccaria multiple times); 2 Montagu, Opinions of Different Authors, 9, 24, 33, 35, 39, 64, 109, 145, 173 (same); 7 Forbes Winslow, ed., The Journal of Psychological Medicine and Mental Pathology 35, 44 (London: John Churchill, 1854); 1 D. Antonio Puigblanch, The Inquisition Unmasked:

Being an Historical and Philosophical Account of that Tremendous Tribunal, Founded on Authentic Documents; and Exhibiting the Necessity of Its Suppression, as a Means of Reform and Regeneration 220 (London: Baldwin, Cradock, and Joy, 1816) (citing Beccaria's treatise). For a discussion of Beccaria's influence in England in the eighteenth century, see Anthony J. Draper, *Cesare Beccaria's Influence on English Discussions of Punishment, 1764–1789*, 26 History of European Ideas 177 (2000).

75. Catalogue of Books for MDCCCXXXVI: On Sale by Thomas Rodd, No. 2, Great Newport Street, Long Acre, London (London: Compton and Ritchie, 1837), Part II, p. 2 (listing three copies of Beccaria's treatise); A Catalogue of Books Selling by Richard Priestley, No. 143, High Holborn 354 (London: J. F. Dove, 1819) (a London catalog listing an Italian edition of Beccaria's treatise); A Catalogue of Books, in Various Branches of Literature, Now Selling by J. Parker, in the Turle (Oxford: W. Baxter, 1818) (listing 1769 and 1807 editions of Beccaria's treatise); W. Bent, The London Catalogue of Books, with Their Sizes and Prices 66, 77 (London: M. Brown, 1799) (listing two copies of Beccaria's book in a catalogue printed in London for "W. Bent, Paternoster Row" by "M. Brown"); Bibliotheca Smithiana: A Catalogue of Books, &c. Second Day's Sale, Tuesday 8 (London: S. Baker & G. Leigh, 1773) (listing a copy of Beccaria's treatise for sale in an auction by Baker & Leigh as Lot No. 168); Joseph Butterworth (and son), A General Catalogue of Law Books 172 (London: Joseph Butterworth and Son, 6th ed. 1819) (listing Beccaria's treatise).

76. George W. Carey, ed., The Political Writings of John Adams 158–59 (Washington, DC: Regnery Publishing, 2000).

77. Montagu, Thoughts on the Punishment of Death for Forgery, 7, 15, 70.

78. 2 The Punishment of Death: A Selection of Articles from *The Morning Herald*, with Notes iii, 55, 95, 243, 248, 267, 278 (London: Hatcher & Son/Smith, Elder & Co., 1837).

79. In an 1814 letter to his friend Thomas Jefferson Hogg, an English barrister, the English romantic poet Percy Bysshe Shelley was partially impressed yet a bit dismissive, writing in part: "I have begun to learn Italian again. I am reading Beccaria, 'Dei delitti e pene.' His essay seems to contain some excellent remarks, though I do not think that it deserves the reputation it has gained." 1 Roger Ingpen, ed., The Letters of Percy Bysshe Shelley 417–20 (London: Sir Isaac Pitman & Sons, 1912) (quoting Percy Bysshe Shelly to Thomas Jefferson Hogg, Mar. 16, 1814).

80. *E.g.*, William G. Shade, ed., Revisioning the British Empire in the Eighteenth Century: Essays from Twenty-five Years of the Lawrence Henry Gipson Institute for Eighteenth-Century Studies 135 (Cranbury, NJ: Associated University Presses, 1998).

81. Bessler, Cruel and Unusual, 176–84.

82. Bessler, *Revisiting Beccaria's Vision*, 198 (discussing Beccaria's views on infamy); William Magnuson, *The Domestic Politics of International Extradition*, 52 Va. J. Int'l L. 839, 849 n.47 (2012) (noting that Beccaria argued that dueling should be strictly punished and that "Beccaria took a keen interest in the spread of extradition treaties, for he believed they might serve an important role in disincentivizing crime").

83. A. H. Stewart, American Bad Boys in the Making 223 (New York: Hermann Lechner, 1912).

84. Paul A. Rahe, Montesquieu and the Logic of Liberty: War, Religion, Commerce, Climate, Terrain, Technology, Uneasiness of Mind, the Spirit of Political Vigilance, and the Foundations of the Modern Republic xviii (New Haven: Yale University Press, 2009) (noting that Montesquieu's *De l'Esprit des lois* "had a profound effect on Cesare Beccaria").

85. Pinker, The Better Angels of Our Nature, 147–48, 180.

86. Bellamy, On Crimes and Punishments, xvii.

87. John Aikin, A View of the Life, Travels, and Philanthropic Labors of the Late John Howard, Esquire (Philadelphia: W. W. Woodward, 1794); David Williams, Condorcet and Modernity 10, 15, 42–43 (Cambridge: Cambridge University Press, 2004).

88. Bessler, Cruel and Unusual, 50–53, 93, 141, 167–68; 1 L. Kinvin Wroth & Hiller B. Zobel, eds., Legal Papers of John Adams cxxviii (Cambridge: Harvard University Press, 1965); Foster, In Pursuit of Equal Liberty, 157; *see also* Rogers, Murder and the Death Penalty in Massachusetts, 31, 38, 101 (noting the use of Beccaria's treatise by Adams and another lawyer).

89. Bessler, Cruel and Unusual, 94–95, 174–76; Bessler, *The Anomaly of Executions*, 302 n.27; 1 William Canton, A History of the British and Foreign Bible Society 120 (London: John Murray, 1904). Not until 1832 was the death penalty abolished in England for stealing a horse or a sheep. Id.

90. Willard Sterne Randall, Thomas Jefferson: A Life 418 (New York: HarperCollins, 1994); C. G. Oakes, Sir Samuel Romilly, 1757–1818: "The Friend of the Oppressed," 22, 71 (London: G. Allen & Unwin, 1935); Samuel Romilly, Observations on a Late Publication, Intituled, Thoughts on Executive Justice (London 1786), *reprinted in* 2 Crimmins, The Death Penalty; Samuel Romilly, Observations on the Criminal Law of England as it relates to Capital Punishments, and on the Mode in which it is

Administered (1810), *reprinted in* 3 Crimmins, The Death Penalty; Barbara B. Oberg & J. Jefferson Looney, eds., The Papers of Thomas Jefferson Digital Edition (Univ. of Virginia Press, Rotunda, 2008), http://rotunda.upress.virginia.edu/founders/TSJN-01-13-02-0344 (letter from Benjamin Vaughan referencing "our mutual acquaintance Mr. Romilly"); 3 Charles Francis Adams, ed., The Works of John Adams (Boston: Little, Brown and Co., 1856) (diary entry for "15. Saturday" of 1786 reads in part: "Dined with Mr. Brand Hollis, in Chesterfield Street.... Our company were Price, Kippis, Bridgen, Romilly, and another, besides Jefferson, Smith, and myself."); Caroline Robbins, *Thomas Brand Hollis (1719–1804): English Admirer of Franklin and Intimate of John Adams*, 97 Proceedings of the American Philosophical Society 239, 239 & n.1 (1953).

91. Wilf, Law's Imagined Republic, 138–46; Bessler, Cruel and Unusual, 266; Richard Rush to James Madison, Nov. 24, 1816, *available at* www.founders.archives.gov (remarks upon Commodore Patterson's letter to the secretary of the navy, dated New Orleans, Aug. 15, 1816). Thomas Paine himself advocated for the abolition of executions. Bessler, Cruel and Unusual, 54, 106–8, 110–11; *see also* White, John Jay, 92 ("Paine's opposition to capital punishment led him to support King Louis XVI's exile to America").

92. Ellen Holmes Pearson, Remaking Custom: Law and Identity in the Early American Republic 25–26, 182 (Charlottesville: University of Virginia Press, 2011).

93. U.S. Const., amend. V (ratified Dec. 15, 1791).

94. U.S. Const., amend. VIII (ratified Dec. 15, 1791). For a discussion of the language variants of early American state constitutions, see Bessler, Cruel and Unusual, 177–81.

95. Wood, Empire of Liberty, 492.

96. Hostettler, Cesare Beccaria, x–xi; Beirne, *Inventing Criminology*, 25.

97. Colvin, Penitentiaries, Reformatories, and Chain Gangs, 48 (noting that Beccaria's ideas were "instrumental in drastically reducing moral offenses from the statute books and scaling back capital punishment"); Roth, Crime and Punishment, 90 (noting a reduction in executions).

98. Hunt, Inventing Human Rights, 38–39; Anthony Santoro, Exile & Embrace: Contemporary Religious Discourse on the Death Penalty 6, 42 182 (Boston: Northeastern University Press, 2013).

99. Christof Heyns, "A 'Struggle Approach' to Human Rights," *in* Arend Soeteman, ed., Pluralism and Law 171 (Dordrecht, The Netherlands: Kluwer Academic Publishers, 2001); Beirne, *Inventing Criminology*, 31 ("On more than one occasion, Beccaria openly acknowledged his profound indebtedness to the humanist writings of the French *philosophes*."); id. at 38 ("Beccaria was inspired by the ideas of the founder of the Scottish Enlightenment, the Glaswegian philosopher Francis Hutcheson, and by Hutcheson's pupil Hume"); *see also* id. ("Nearly every page of *Dei delitti* is marked, I suggest, by Hutcheson's towering influence on Beccaria's thinking."); id. at 39 ("just as much of the specific content of Beccaria's famous treatise is taken from Hutcheson's (1755) *System* so, too, is much of the structure of its argumentation"); Carl Ubbelohde, "The Reform of the Pennsylvania Penal Code and Prisons, 1776–1800," University of Wisconsin-Madison, Master of Science thesis (1950), p. 15 ("Beccaria, by his own admission, had been led to his ideas by reading Montesquieu's *Persian Letters* and *The Spirit of the Laws*.").

100. Hostettler, Cesare Beccaria, 26.

101. Jeremy Bentham, A Fragment on Government preface n.*g* (1776).

102. Mary Sokol, Bentham, Law and Marriage: A Utilitarian Code of Law in Historical Contexts (London: Continuum International, 2011).

103. Colvin, Penitentiaries, Reformatories, and Chain Gangs, 49; Hall, The Oxford Companion to American Law 631 (noting that two penitentiaries opened in Pennsylvania: the Western Penitentiary, in Pittsburgh in 1826, "a round building modeled after Bentham's Panopticon," with cells "arranged like spokes around a hub, from which the prisoners could be constantly watched," and the Eastern Penitentiary in Philadelphia, which opened in 1829 and which "consisted of seven wings, also connected to a central hub").

104. Eden, Principles of Penal Law, 235, 264, 296; Howard, The State of the Prisons in England and Wales, 29–30, 74 n.*; *see also* Lemmings, Professors of the Law, 218 n.53 ("Following the English translation of Beccaria's *Essay on Crimes and Punishments* in 1767, William Eden's *Principles of Penal Law* was published in 1771, Romilly's *Observations on a Late Publication entitled "Thoughts on Executive Justice"* in 1786, and Bentham's *Introduction to the Principles of Morals and Legislation* in 1789."); Mark Goldie & Robert Wokler, eds., The Cambridge History of Eighteenth-Century Political Thought 567 (Cambridge: Cambridge University Press, 2006) (noting that in later editions of John Howard's *The State of the Prisons in England and Wales* he acknowledged the influence of writers such as Beccaria and Eden).

105. Marcia Coyle, The Roberts Court: The Struggle for the Constitution 3–4 (New York: Simon

& Schuster, 2013).

106. Thomas, On Crimes and Punishments, 61.

107. Jay Winik, The Great Upheaval: America and the Birth of the Modern World 1788–1800, at 169 (New York: HarperCollins, 2008).

Chapter 1

1. Douglas, *God and the Executioner*, 146–50.

2. David G. Chardavoyne, A Hanging in Detroit: Stephen Gifford Simmons and the Last Execution under Michigan Law 143 (Detroit, MI: Wayne State University Press, 2003); Banner, The Death Penalty, 89 ("English radicals of the 1640s and 1650s argued unsuccessfully for an end to the death penalty for property crimes like robbery and burglary. Some of the Quakers went even further and advocated abolishing the death penalty for all crimes."); Masur, Rites of Execution, 4 ("In the 1640s some Englishmen, most notably Levellers, demanded the abolition of the death penalty."). Beccaria is also credited with founding the modern field of criminology. Thomas, On Crimes and Punishments, xvi; Rachel A. Van Cleave, *Rape and the Querela in Italy: False Protection of Victim Agency*, 13 Mich. J. Gender & L. 273, 280 (2007); Paolucci, On Crimes and Punishments, ix. In truth, Beccaria was not the first thinker to question the death penalty's efficacy—though he was the first to gain international renown for his anti-death penalty stance. For example, two years before Beccaria's book was published, a Spanish Benedictine, Martín Sarmiento (1695–1772), maintained that the death penalty should be abolished because criminals are "more useful to society alive than dead." Sarmiento's writings on a wide variety of subjects, however, were all published after his death, except for one piece of writing unrelated to the death penalty. James J. Megivern, The Death Penalty: An Historical and Theological Survey 537 n.11 (Mahwah, NJ: Paulist Press, 1997); Germán Bleiberg, Maureen Ihrie & Janet Pérez, eds., Dictionary of the Literature of the Iberian Peninsula 1497–98 (Westport, CT: Greenwood Press, 1993); *see also* E. Christian Brugger, Capital Punishment and Roman Catholic Moral Tradition 233 n.155 (South Bend, IN: University of Notre Dame Press, 2003) ("It is true that the Anabaptists, Socinians and Quakers (Society of Friends) were abolitionist long before the mid-eighteenth century, but because of their exclusivity and countercultural patterns of life, they had little noticeable effect on the wider debate.").

3. Friedman, A History of American Law, 207.

4. Bellamy, On Crimes and Punishments, 31.

5. Larry Siegel & Clemens Bartollas, Corrections Today 26–27 (Belmont, CA: Wadsworth, 2011); Melusky & Pesto, Capital Punishment, 11.

6. 2 Charles Phineas Sherman, Roman Law in the Modern World 470–84 (New Haven: New Haven Law Book Co., 1922).

7. David S. Kidder & Noah D. Oppenheim, The Intellectual Devotional Biographies: Revive Your Mind, Complete Your Education, and Acquaint Yourself with the World's Greatest Personalities 13 (New York: Rodale, 2010); Mitchel P. Roth, Crime and Punishment: A History of the Criminal Justice System 11 (Belmont, CA: Wadsworth, 2005).

8. 1 Morris R. Cohen & Felix S. Cohen, Readings in Jurisprudence and Legal Philosophy 346 n.46 (New York: Little, Brown and Co., 1951) (*"On Crimes and Punishments* ... is probably the most influential essay ever written on the subject."); id. ("The essay was widely read and was translated into 22 languages shortly after its publication in 1764."); Hostettler, Cesare Beccaria, 22 ("The book went through six editions in 18 months and was translated into 22 languages.").

9. George W. Carey, The Political Writings of John Adams, 110–11, 146, 173, 259 (Washington, DC: Regnery Publishing, 2000).

10. Rep. Henry Hyde, Forfeiting Our Property Rights: Is Your Property Safe from Seizure? 18 (Washington, DC: Cato Institute, 1995).

11. Carlo Luigi Golino, ed., Italian Quarterly, Vols. 8–9, p. 84 (1965); Stanley Sadie, Mozart: The Early Years 1756–1781, at 149 (Oxford: Oxford University Press, 2006).

12. Newman & Marongiu, On Crimes and Punishments, lx–lxi; Pierpaolo Polzonetti, Italian Opera in the Age of the American Revolution 49 (Cambridge: Cambridge University Press, 2011); Frank A. Kafker, Notable Encyclopedias of the Late Eighteenth Century: Eleven Successors of the Encyclopédie 73 (Oxford: Voltaire Foundation, 1994).

13. Carlo Luigi Golino, ed., Italian Quarterly, Vols. 8–9, p. 85 (1965).

14. 4 Arts and Ideas in Eighteenth-Century Italy: Lectures Given at the Italian Institute 1957–1958, at 37 (Rome: Edizioni di Storia e Letteratura, 1960); 16 G. Long, ed., The Penny Cyclopaedia: Society for the Diffusion of Useful Knowledge 409 (London: Charles Knight & Co., 1840).

15. Marjorie Elizabeth Plummer & Robin Barnes, eds., Ideas and Cultural Margins in Early Modern Germany: Essays in Honor of H. C. Erik Midelfort 75 (Surrey, England: Ashgate Publishing Ltd., 2009); Maestro, Cesare Beccaria and the Origins of Penal Reform, 127; Shlomo Giora Shoham, Paul Knepper & Martin Kett, eds., International Handbook of Victimology 119 (Boca Raton, FL: CRC Press, 2010); Austin Sarat & Christian Boulanger, eds., The Cultural Lives of Capital Punishment: Comparative Perspectives 64–65 (Stanford, CA: Stanford University Press, 2005); Israel, Democratic Enlightenment, 339; Harriet Rudolph & Helga Schnabel-Schüle, eds., 48 Trierer Historische Forschungen Justiz 126 (Kliomedia, 2003).

16. Ulrike Gleixner & Marion W. Gray, Gender in Transition: Discourse and Practice in German-Speaking Europe, 1750–1830, at 68 n.7 (Ann Arbor: University of Michigan Press, 2006).

17. Thomas, On Crimes and Punishments, xxvii–xxviii.

18. Shackelford, Thomas Jefferson's Travels in Europe, 37–41.

19. Nicholas Cronk, The Cambridge Companion to Voltaire 43–44, 226 (Cambridge: Cambridge University Press, 2009); Roland Mortier, "Diderot and Penal Law: Objections to Beccaria," in François Jost, Aesthetics and the Literature of Ideas: Essays in Honor of A. Owen Aldridge 203–04 (Cranbury, NY: Associated University Presses, 1990).

20. Hostettler, Cesare Beccaria, xii.

21. Daniel Heartz, Haydn, Mozart and the Viennese School 1740–1780, at xxiv (New York: W. W. Norton & Co., 1995); 1 Derek Beales, Joseph II: In the Shadow of Maria Theresa, 1741–1780, at 236–37 (Cambridge: Cambridge University Press, 1987); Eyewitness Travel Guide: Austria 42 (London: Dorling Kindersley, 2012).

22. Maestro, Cesare Beccaria and the Origins of Penal Reform, 5–6, 9.

23. Thomas, On Crimes and Punishments, xvi–xvii, xl–xli.

24. Hostettler, Cesare Beccaria, xii.

25. Cliff Eisen & Simon P. Keefe, eds., The Cambridge Mozart Encyclopedia 176, 289–90, 307, 386–87, 462, 480 (Cambridge: Cambridge University Press, 2006).

26. 4 Charles Knight, The English Cyclopaedia: A New Dictionary of Universal Knowledge 99 (London: Bradbury and Evans, 1857); see also id. (Count Firmian "encouraged men of learning, and protected them against the cabals of their enemies").

27. Lynn McDonald, The Early Origins of the Social Sciences 155 (Montreal: McGill-Queen's University Press, 1993).

28. Szabo, Kaunitz, 1, 11, 16–19, 181–84.

29. Maestro, Cesare Beccaria and the Origins of Penal Reform, 112, 122. The last drawing and quartering in England took place in 1817. Leonard R. N. Ashley, George Peele 212 (New York: Twayne Publishers, 1970).

30. 12 The New International Encyclopedia 783 (New York: Dodd, Mead & Co., 2d ed. 1930).

31. Thomas, On Crimes and Punishments, xxi. For additional biographical information about Beccaria, see Hostettler, Cesare Beccaria; Maestro, Voltaire and Beccaria as Reformers of Criminal Law; Phillipson, Three Criminal Law Reformers. Further sources about Beccaria can be found in Gregory Hanlon's Early Modern Italy 1550–1800: A Comprehensive Bibliography of Titles in English and French (10th ed., Summer 2012), available at http://c.ymcdn.com/sites/www.rsa.org/resource/resmgr/files/ghbibliooct252012.pdf.

32. Richter, The Political Theory of Montesquieu, 60, 95; Anne M. Cohler, Basia C. Miller & Harold S. Stone, eds., Montesquieu, The Spirit of the Laws xxxv–xxxvi (Cambridge: Cambridge University Press, 1989); David Wallace Carrithers, ed., Montesquieu, The Spirit of Law: A Compendium of the First English Edition 480 (Berkeley, CA: University of California Press, 1977); J. C. D. Clark, ed., The Memoirs and Speeches of James, 2nd Earl Waldegrave, 1742–1762, at 319 (Cambridge: Cambridge University Press, 1988).

33. David W. Carrithers, "Montesquieu and the Liberal Philosophy of Jurisprudence," in David W. Carrithers, Michael A. Mosher & Paul A. Rahe, eds., Montesquieu's Science of Politics: Essays on The Spirit of Laws 292 (Lanham, MD: Rowman & Littlefield, 2001).

34. Richter, The Political Theory of Montesquieu, 60.

35. Hunt, Inventing Human Rights, 30, 32, 35–36, 38.

36. James Madison to James Madison, Sr., Nov. 23, 1792; Ralph Ketcham, James Madison: A Biography 389 (Charlottesville: University Press of Virginia, 1990); 2 Lynn Hunt, Thomas R. Martin,

Barbara H. Rosenwein, R. Po-Chia Hsia & Bonnie Smith, eds., The Making of the West: Peoples and Cultures 642–43 (New York: Bedford/St. Martin's, 2009).

37. 1 Marrone, Encyclopedia of Italian Literary Studies, 146, 1977–78; Reill & Wilson, Encyclopedia of the Enlightenment, 6, 205, 486, 566–67, 574, 611; 26 G. Long, The Penny Cyclopædia of the Society for the Diffusion of Useful Knowledge 272 (London: Charles Knight and Co., 1843); Christine Suzanne Getz, Music in the Collective Experience in Sixteenth-Century Milan 1–3 (Burlington, VT: Ashgate, 2005); Stefano D'Amico, Spanish Milan: A City within the Empire, 1535–1706 (New York: Palgrave Macmillan, 2012); George Holmes, The Oxford Illustrated History of Italy 364 (Oxford: Oxford University Press, 1997); 1 Henry Dunning MacLeod, A Dictionary of Political Economy: Biographical, Bibliographical, Historical, and Practical 252–59 (London: Longman, Brown, Longmans, and Roberts, 1863); Stephen J. Pfohl, Images of Deviance and Social Control: A Sociological History 55 (New York: McGraw-Hill, 1985); 1 Alessandro Verri, Roman Nights; or The Tomb of the Scipios v–viii (New York: E. Bliss & E. White/Philadelphia: H. C. Carey & I Lea, 1825).

38. Thomas, On Crimes and Punishments, xxii–xxiii; 37 American Society for Microbiology & Society for American Bacteriologists, Bacteriological Reviews 284 (1974); Elena Riva, Carlo Verri Patrizio, Prefetto e Possidente (Milan: Guerini e Associati, 2005); Hostettler, Cesare Beccaria, 23–24; *see also* Johann Georg Zimmermann, Essay on National Pride: To Which Are Added Memoirs of the Author's Life and Writings 176 (London: C. Dilly, 1797) ("The modern Italian philosophers break the bands of hierarchy and despotism, with an almost unexampled boldness. We need only read the work of a noble Italian, on the reformation of Italy, the treatise on crimes and punishments of the immortal Beccaria, the Coffee-house, an Italian weekly publication, in comparison with which the English Spectator seems to be only written for women; the reflections of an Italian on the church in general, on the regular and secular clergy, and the head of the church; and we shall be ashamed of harboring the thought that Italy is totally deprived of genius."); Johann Georg Zimmermann, Essay on National Pride 211 (J. Wilkie, 1771) (referencing Beccaria's treatise).

39. Maestro, Cesare Beccaria and the Origins of Penal Reform, 9–10, 20; Maestro, Voltaire and Beccaria as Reformers of Criminal Law, 54; Thomas, On Crimes and Punishments, xxiii, 166 n.37; 1 Marrone, Encyclopedia of Italian Literary Studies, 146–47, 1980–1981; Egle Becchi, Formare alle professioni: Sacerdoti, principi, educatori 341 (Milano, Italy: FrancoAngeli, 2009); Robert Darnton, The Business of Enlightenment: A Publishing History of the *Encyclopédie* 1775–1800, at 34–35 (Cambridge: Harvard University Press, 1986); Peter Bondanella & Julie Conway, eds., Cassell Dictionary of Italian Literature 608 (London: Cassell, 1996).

40. Nancy F. Koehn, Brand New: How Entrepreneurs Earned Consumers' Trust from Wedgwood to Dell 208 (Cambridge: Harvard Business Press, 2001).

41. Thomas, On Crimes and Punishments, xvii; Maestro, Cesare Beccaria and the Origins of Penal Reform, 6, 8–9. The latter society is also translated as the Academy of Fisticuffs. Young, On Crimes and Punishments, x.

42. 1 Marrone, Encyclopedia of Italian Literary Studies, 146.

43. Andrew Burnaby, Travels through the Middle Settlements in North-America in the Years 1759 and 1760: with Observations upon the State of the Colonies x–xi (London: T. Payne, 1775); Benjamin Franklin to Jared Eliot, Feb. 13, 1750 (n.2); Andrew Burnaby to George Washington, Jan. 4, 1760; Andrew Burnaby to George Washington, June 23, 1760; Andrew Burnaby to George Washington, Apr. 14, 1761; George Washington to Andrew Burnaby, July 27, 1761; Andrew Burnaby to George Washington, Dec. 14, 1763; Andrew Burnaby to George Washington, Apr. 29, 1765; George Washington to Samuel Athawes, June 1, 1774 ("my old acquaintance & friend Mr Burnaby (for whom I entertained a very sincere esteem)"); Andrew Burnaby to George Washington, Apr. 9, 1778, *available at* www.founders.archives.gov.

44. 2 Carlo Calisse, A History of Italian Law 456–57 (Washington, DC: Beard Books, 2001); Shackelford, Thomas Jefferson's Travels in Europe, 19; The Italian American Experience: An Encyclopedia 604 (New York: Garland Publishing, 2000).

45. André Morellet to David Hume, Sept. 8, 1766; Voltaire to Etienne Noël Damilaville, Sept. 16, 1766; Jean François Marmontel to Voltaire, Oct. 28, 1766; André Morellet to Voltaire, Nov. 15, 1766; Voltaire to Jean le Rond d'Alembert, Dec. 2, 1766; Paul Henri Thiry, baron d'Holbach, to Voltaire, Dec. 4, 1766, *available at* Electronic Enlightenment, Electronic Enlightenment Project, Bodleian Libraries, University of Oxford, www.e-enlightenment.com.

46. Hostettler, Cesare Beccaria, 22–23; Phillipson, Three Criminal Law Reformers, 4; Donata Chiomenti Vassalli, Giulia Beccaria: La Madre del Manzoni 13 (Milano: Casa Editrice Ceschina, 1956).

47. Hostettler, Cesare Beccaria, 6–8; Groenewegen, Eighteenth-Century Economics, 8.

48. Hostettler, Cesare Beccaria, 22–23; 1 Marrone, Encyclopedia of Italian Literary Studies, 145;

Groenewegen, Eighteenth-Century Economics, 8; 1 Macleod, A Dictionary of Political Economy, 252.

49. Bernard E. Harcourt, Beccaria's *On Crimes and Punishments*: A Mirror on the History of the Foundations of Modern Criminal Law, Institute for Law and Economics Working Paper Series (July 22, 2013), *available at* http://papers.ssrn.com/sol3/papers.cfm?abstract_id=2296605.

50. Thomas, On Crimes and Punishments, xvii–xviii.

51. Young, On Crimes and Punishments, xviii; Maestro, Cesare Beccaria and the Origins of Penal Reform, 9, 12; Peter Brand & Lino Pertile, eds., The Cambridge History of Italian Literature 378–79 (Cambridge: Cambridge University Press, rev. ed. 1996); Thomas, On Crimes and Punishments, xxii–xxiii.

52. Young, On Crimes and Punishments, x.

53. 1 Marrone, Encyclopedia of Italian Literary Studies, 1977–78.

54. 1 Marrone, Encyclopedia of Italian Literary Studies, 146.

55. Thomas, On Crimes and Punishments, xix, xxxvii. The inaugural edition appeared in June 1764 around the same time that *On Crimes and Punishments* was published. Young, On Crimes and Punishments, xix; Maestro, Cesare Beccaria and the Origins of Penal Reform, 46. Beccaria started working on his book in March 1763, and the first edition of *On Crimes and Punishments*, published anonymously, began circulating in July 1764, first in Tuscany and then in Lombardy. Thomas, On Crimes and Punishments, at xxii–xxiii.

56. Szabo, Kaunitz, 34–35.

57. Paolo Frisi to Benjamin Franklin, May 30, 1784; Benjamin Franklin to Paolo Frisi, Sept. 26, 1784.

58. Pace, Luigi Castiglioni's Viaggio, xxiii; Thomas Hockey, ed., Biographical Encyclopedia of Astronomers 393 (New York: Springer, 2007).

59. Pace, Benjamin Franklin and Italy, 88.

60. 2 The Select Circulating Library Containing the Best Popular Literature, Including Memoirs, Biography, Novels, Tales, Travels, Voyages, &c. 167 (Philadelphia: Adam Waldie, 1837).

61. Thomas, On Crimes and Punishments, xxvii.

62. Israel, Democratic Enlightenment, 357–58.

63. Marraro, *Count Luigi Castiglioni*, 473.

64. Thomas, On Crimes and Punishments, xviii; Maestro, Cesare Beccaria and the Origins of Penal Reform, 6, 47–50.

65. Brand & Pertile, The Cambridge History of Italian Literature, 427.

66. Young, On Crimes and Punishments, x; Ferdinando Meacci, ed., Italian Economists of the 20th Century 163, 168 (Northampton, MA: Edward Elgar Publishing, 1998).

67. Sophus A. Reinert, "The Italian Tradition of Political Economy: Theories and Policies of Development in the Semi-Periphery of the Enlightenment," *in* Jomo K. Sundaram & Erik S. Reinert, eds., The Origins of Development Economics: How Schools of Economic Thought Have Addressed Development 25 (New Delhi: Tulika Books, 2005).

68. Thomas, On Crimes and Punishments, xxii–xxiii, 166 n.36; Maestro, Cesare Beccaria and the Origins of Penal Reform, 20; *Special Collections Focus: New Acquisitions*, Legal Miscellanea (Jacob Burns L. Libr., Washington D.C.), Autumn 2004, at 1–2, *available at* http://www.law.gwu.edu/Library/Friends/Documents/Legal_Miscellanea/FriendsNwsltr_F04.pdf; Paolucci, On Crimes and Punishments, xiv.

69. Bessler, Cruel and Unusual, 39; Hostettler, Cesare Beccaria, 21; Stephen G. Tibbetts, Criminological Theory: The Essentials 43 (Thousand Oaks, CA: SAGE Publications, 2012) (noting that Beccaria's book remained on the list of condemned works until the 1960s and that the Roman Catholic Church excommunicated Beccaria when it became known that he wrote it).

70. Jeffrey Merrick & Dorothy Medlin, eds., André Morellet (1727–1819) in the Republic of Letters and the French Revolution 188–89 (New York: Peter Lang, 1995); Israel, Democratic Enlightenment, 349.

71. Maestro, Cesare Beccaria and the Origins of Penal Reform, 20; Young, On Crimes and Punishments, xiv; Thomas, On Crimes and Punishments, xxii–xxiii; Paolucci, On Crimes and Punishments, xiii–xiv.

72. Thomas, On Crimes and Punishments, xxv–xxvi.

73. Mitch Stokes, Galileo 171–73 (Nashville, TN: Thomas Nelson, Inc., 2011).

74. Ross King, Machiavelli: Philosopher of Power 138 (New York: HarperCollins, 2007).

75. Hostettler, Cesare Beccaria, 21.

76. Thomas, On Crimes and Punishments, 30.

77. Bellamy, On Crimes and Punishments, 48.

78. Thomas, On Crimes and Punishments, xxvi, 32–37.

79. These words come from the 1775 English translation of *On Crimes and Punishments* that John Adams later gave to his son Thomas. Cesare Beccaria, An Essay on Crimes and Punishments iii–iv, vii–viii (4th ed. 1775), *available at* http://archive.org/stream/essayoncrimespun1775becc#page/n3/mode/2up. Modern translations of Beccaria's treatise differ somewhat. Herbert J. Storing, ed., The Complete Anti-Federalist 353–54 n.61 (Chicago, IL: University of Chicago Press, 1981).

80. An Essay on Crimes and Punishments, Translated from the Italian; with a Commentary Attributed to Mons. De Voltaire, Translated from the French (London: J. Almon, 1767), *available at* http://archive.org/stream/anessayoncrimes02beccgoog#page/n4/mode/2up; Bellamy, On Crimes and Punishments, xxxi; *see also* Maestro, Cesare Beccaria and the Origins of Penal Reform, 5 ("Born in Milan on March 15, 1738, he was the first son of aristocratic though not very wealthy parents, Giovanni Saverio and Maria Beccaria. His full name and title were Marchese Cesare Beccaria Bonesana."). There are multiple English translations of Beccaria's *On Crimes and Punishments*. Thomas, On Crimes and Punishments, xxx. A recent translation, published in 2008 by the University of Toronto Press, is part of the Lorenzo Da Ponte Italian library series. A French translation, prepared André Morellet, was completed in 1765, and German, Swedish, Russian, Spanish and early English translations were often based on that French translation, which radically reorganized Beccaria's book. *Id.* at xxvii–xxx; Maestro, Cesare Beccaria and the Origins of Penal Reform, 40–43. The French translation of Beccaria's book, prepared by Morellet, was not even sent to Beccaria until after its publication in France. Bellamy, On Crimes and Punishments, 119–20 n.4; Maestro, Cesare Beccaria and the Origins of Penal Reform, 40. What has been described as the "authoritative Italian edition" of *Dei delitti e delle pene*—one that Beccaria himself had a hand in revising—came out in 1766 as Beccaria's fame was spreading around the globe. Only two other English translations of that authoritative Italian text exist. Thomas, On Crimes and Punishments, xxx & n.48 (citing Bellamy, On Crimes and Punishments & Young, On Crimes and Punishments).

81. Thomas, On Crimes and Punishments, 17–19.

82. The Historian: The Magazine for Members of the Historical Association, Issues 1–12 (1986), p. 6.

83. 1 A Sexton of the Old School, Dealings with the Dead 207 (Boston: Dutton and Wentworth, 1856).

84. Aharon Barak, Proportionality: Constitutional Rights and Their Limitations 175–76 (Cambridge: Cambridge University Press, 2012); Nicholas M. McLean, *Livelihood, Ability to Pay, and the Original Meaning of the Excessive Fines Clause: Rediscovering the Eighth Amendment's "Economic Survival Norm,"* 40 Hastings Const. L. Q. 833 (2013); The Magna Carta, paras. 20–21 (1215), *available at* http://www.constitution.org/eng/magnacar.htm.

85. An Act Declaring the Rights and Liberties of the Subject and Settling the Succession of the Crown (1689), *available at* http://avalon.law.yale.edu/17th_century/england.asp.

86. E. Thomas Sullivan and Richard S. Frase, Proportionality Principles in American Law: Controlling Excessive Government Actions 163–64 (Oxford: Oxford University Press, 2009).

87. Thomas, On Crimes and Punishments, 3–4, 7, 21, 42–43, 46, 98, 100–101, 114.

88. Bellamy, On Crimes and Punishments, 49, 63–64; Thomas, On Crimes and Punishments, 99.

89. Schabas, The Abolition of the Death Penalty in International Law, 5; Hugo Adam Bedau, *Interpreting the Eighth Amendment: Principled vs. Populist Strategies*, 13 T.M. Cooley L. Rev. 789, 805 (1996) ("The original impetus to abolish the death penalty two hundred years ago in Europe was fueled by Cesare Beccaria's little book, *On Crimes and Punishments*, and by Jeremy Bentham in England.").

90. Thomas, On Crimes and Punishments, 2, 26, 51, 55.

91. Larry J. Siegel, Criminology 620 (Belmont, CA: 11th ed. 2009).

92. Thomas, On Crimes and Punishments, 51–52; *see also* Cesare Beccaria, An Essay on Crimes and Punishments 103 (4th ed. 1775), *available at* http://archive.org/stream/essayoncrimespun1775becc#page/n3/mode/2up.

93. Thomas, On Crimes and Punishments, 51, 55–57, 61. The concept of "natural rights" was, of course, well-known to the Framers of the U.S. Constitution. *See* Terry Brennan, *Natural Rights and the Constitution: The Original "Original Intent"*, 15 Harv. J.L. & Pub. Pol'y 965, 971–74 (1992).

94. David P. Forsythe, ed., Encyclopedia of Human Rights 397 (Oxford: Oxford University Press, 2009).

95. Sigmund, St. Thomas Aquinas on Politics and Ethics, xiii, 48, 69; 1 Anton C. Pegis, ed., Basic Writings of St. Thomas Aquinas xlviii (Indianapolis, IN: Hackett Publishing Co., 1997).

96. 5 The Works of John Locke 309, 339, 344, 387 (London: O. Otridge and Son, 11th ed. 1812); Brian Tierney, The Idea of Natural Rights 80 (Grand Rapids, MI: Wm. B. Eerdmans Publishing Co., 2001).

97. S. G. Hefelbower, The Relation of John Locke to English Deism 4 (Chicago, IL: The University of Chicago Press, 1918).

98. Joseph M. Flora & Lucinda H. MacKethan, eds., The Companion to Southern Literature: Themes, Genres, Places, People, Movements, and Motifs 720–721 (Baton Rouge: Louisiana State University Press, 2002); 2 Yossi Dotan, Watercraft on World Coins: America and Asia, 1800–2008, at 55 (Portland, OR: The Alpha Press, 2010).

99. Elaine K. Ginsberg, "The Patriot Pamphleteers," *in* Everett Emerson, ed., American Literature, 1764–1789: The Revolutionary Years 23 (Madison: University of Wisconsin Press, 1977); Ellen Frankel Paul, Fred D. Miller, Jr. & Jeffrey Paul, eds., Natural Rights: Liberalism from Locke to Nozick 11 (Cambridge: Cambridge University Press, 2005); U.S. Const., amend. V; Thomas Jefferson to John Trumbull, Feb. 15, 1789; Poor Richard Improved, 1748; James Madison Papers, Notes on a Brief System of Logick, 1766–1772; Adams' Minutes of the Trial and Notes for His Argument: Middlesex Inferior Court, Charlestown, March 1768; Adams' Minutes of the Trial: Worcester Inferior Court, Worcester, May 1769; Thomas Jefferson to Robert Skipwith, with a List of Books for a Private Library, Aug. 3, 1771, *available at* www.founders.archives.gov.

100. Kevin Dooley & Joseph Patten, Why Politics Matters: An Introduction to Political Science 73 (Stamford, CT: Cengage Learning, 2014).

101. Francis Hutcheson, An Inquiry into the Original of Our Ideas of Beauty and Virtue 123, 135, 206, 221, 229, 243, 247, 254, 265, 267, 269, 285, 288–89, 301 (London, R. Ware, J., et al., 5th ed. 1753).

102. Beirne, "Inventing Criminology," 794–95 & nn.24, 26.

103. 2 Francis Hutcheson, A System of Moral Philosophy 95, 102, 284, 337 (London: R. and A. Foulis, 1755); *see also* id. at 331 ("The other sort of sanctions are punishments; the peculiar end of which is the deterring all from like vicious practices, and giving publick security against others, as well as the offenders. When this right of punishing which belonged to all in natural liberty, is conveyed in a civil state to the magistrate, he obtains the sole right in all ordinary cases, and has the direct power of life and death over criminals.").

104. Thomas, On Crimes and Punishments, 61.

105. Bellamy, On Crimes and Punishments, 77; Beirne, "Inventing Criminology," 794 ("Nearly every page of *Dei delitti* is marked, I suggest, by Hutcheson's towering influence on Beccaria's thinking. It is found in the common metaphors of expression used in *Dei delitti* and in Hutcheson's (1755) *System of Moral Philosophy*.").

106. Decl. of Independence (July 4, 1776).

107. Thomas, On Crimes and Punishments, 55. Dr. Benjamin Rush — Thomas Jefferson's friend and correspondent — felt much the same way, saying capital punishment "lessens the horror of taking away human life" and thus "tends to multiply murders." Banner, The Death Penalty, 104.

108. Thomas, On Crimes and Punishments, 26, 51, 56.

109. McLynn, Crime and Punishment in Eighteenth-Century England, xi–xii, 257; 1 George Harris, The Life of Lord Chancellor Hardwicke 130, 143, 159–61, 166, 232 (London: Edward Moxon, 1847).

110. Thomas, On Crimes and Punishments, 102; Banner, The Death Penalty, 101.

111. Bessler, Cruel and Unusual, 85–86.

112. Steven H. Jupiter, *Constitution Notwithstanding: The Political Illegitimacy of the Death Penalty in American Democracy*, 23 Fordham Urb. L.J. 437, 478 n.198 (1996); Lynn Hudson Parson, John Quincy Adams 234 (Lanham, MD: Rowman & Littlefield, 2001); Sigmund, St. Thomas Aquinas on Politics and Ethics, 70; John Quincy Adams to William Cranch, Nov. 6, 1785, *available at* www.founders.archives.gov.

113. Cesare Beccaria, An Essay on Crimes and Punishments 104–106, 112 (4th ed. 1775), *available at* http://archive.org/stream/essayoncrimespun1775becc#page/n3/mode/2up.

114. Christoph Burchard, *Torture in the Jurisprudence of the Ad Hoc Tribunals*, 6 J. Int'l Crim. Just. 159, 160 (2008); *see also* Paola Gaeta, *When Is the Involvement of State Officials a Requirement for the Crime of Torture?*, 6 J. Int'l Crim. Just. 183 (2008) (discussing the definition of torture).

115. Cesare Beccaria, An Essay on Crimes and Punishments 57, 62–63, 67 (4th ed. 1775), *available at* http://archive.org/stream/essayoncrimespun1775becc#page/n3/mode/2up.

116. Bellamy, On Crimes and Punishments, 79–82.

117. *See* Matthew Lippman, *The Development and Drafting of the United Nations Convention Against Torture and Other Cruel, Inhuman or Degrading Treatment or Punishment*, 17 B.C. Int'l & Comp. L. Rev. 275, 281–82 (1994).

118. Thomas, On Crimes and Punishments, 32.

119. Thomas, On Crimes and Punishments, 30, 63.

120. Respectfully Quoted: A Dictionary of Quotations 183 (North Chelmsford, MA: Courier Dover Publications, 2010).

121. James Q. Whitman, The Origins of Reasonable Doubt 1, 4, 202 (New Haven: Yale University Press, 2008).

122. Thomas, On Crimes and Punishments, 32–37, 59–63, 65, 119, 139.

123. Robert Bartlett, Trial by Fire and Water: The Medieval Judicial Ordeal (Oxford: Clarendon Press, 1988); Thomas Jefferson to James Fishback (Draft), Sept. 27, 1809, *available at* www.founders.archives.gov.

124. Ellen Frankel Paul & Howard Dickman, eds., Liberty, Property, and the Foundations of the American Constitution 50 (Albany: State University of New York Press, 1989); Allen Jayne, Jefferson's Declaration of Independence: Origins, Philosophy, and Theology 128–29 (Lexington: University Press of Kentucky, 1998).

125. Kevin J. Hayes, The Road to Monticello: The Life and Mind of Thomas Jefferson 338 (Oxford: Oxford University Press, 2008).

126. John H. Langbein, The Origins of Adversary Criminal Trial 340 (Oxford: Oxford University Press, 2003).

127. Terance D. Miethe & Hong Lu, Punishment: A Comparative Historical Perspective 43–44 (Cambridge: Cambridge University Press, 2005); 2 Hampshire Notes and Queries 73 (Winchester: The Observer Office, 1884) (reprinted from the *Winchester Observer & County News*); Gregg Stebben, Everything You Need to Know About Religion 115 (New York: Pocket Books, 1999).

128. T. C. Smout, ed., Anglo-Scottish Relations from 1603 to 1900, at 75–77, 79 (Oxford: Oxford University Press, 2005).

129. Bessler, Cruel and Unusual, 56, 140–41, 184; Dorothy Medlin, *Thomas Jefferson, André Morellet, and the French Version of Notes on the State of Virginia*, 35 Wm. & Mary Q. 85 (1978).

130. Thomas, On Crimes and Punishments, 26, 52, 54; *see also* id. at 21 ("[T]he violation of the right to security acquired by each citizen must be assigned some of the most severe punishments provided for by the law"); *id.* at 22 ("Attacks against the security and liberty of the citizens are thus among the greatest crimes.").

131. *E.g.*, 6 New York Review 130–31 & n.* (New York: Alexander V. Blake, 1839).

132. Thomas, On Crimes and Punishments, xlvi, 10–11, 53–54.

133. James Mackintosh, Vindiciæ Gallicæ. Defense of the French Revolution and Its English Admirers, against the Accusations of the Right Hon. Edmund Burke 121 (London: G. C. J. and J. Robinson, 2d ed. corr. 1791).

134. The Federalist No. 47 (Jan. 3, 1788); Bessler, *Revisiting Beccaria's Vision*, 207. A search of documents on The Constitutional Sources Project website pulls up sixty documents — many from the 1780s — pertaining to Montesquieu.

135. Madan, Thoughts on Executive Justice, 11.

136. Newman & Marongiu, On Crimes and Punishments, 57, 117.

137. McLynn, Crime and Punishment in Eighteenth-Century England, 308.

138. Bessler, Death in the Dark, 29, 37–80; Thomas ed., Cesare Beccaria, On Crimes and Punishments, 52–54. For Beccaria, a government's stability or instability was of great importance in considering what the punishment should be. *Id.* at 85.

139. Pinker, The Better Angels of Our Nature, 63–64.

140. William Bradford, An Enquiry How Far the Punishment of Death Is Necessary in Pennsylvania 5, 9, 20–43, 56 (Philadelphia: T. Dobson, 1793).

141. *See* Opinion of the Undersigned Members of the Committee Charged with the Reform of the Criminal System in Austrian Lombardy for Matters Pertaining to Capital Punishment (1792), *reprinted in* Thomas, On Crimes and Punishments, 153–59.

142. Thomas, On Crimes and Punishments, xvii, 153–55, 178–79 n.1. Scotti, a ministry of justice official, was one of Beccaria's pupils when Beccaria taught economics at the Scuole Palatine in Milan, and Risi was associated with the Accademia dei Trasformati, the first academy Beccaria had joined prior to joining the Academy of Fists. "[W]e should suppress the death penalty" in favor of "perpetual enslavement," the minority report concluded, recommending that prisons be set up in several cities "so as to make sure that the punishment is clear for all to see." *Id.* at 155, 158.

143. Bellamy, On Crimes and Punishments, 30, 35, 48, 50, 53, 56, 83, 85–86.

144. Melvin E. Page, Colonialism: An International Social, Cultural, and Political Encyclopedia 461–62 (Santa Barbara, CA: ABC-CLIO, 2003); Bessler, Cruel and Unusual, 100–101.

145. James Harrington, The Common-Wealth of Oceana (London: F. Streater, 1656); Bessler,

Cruel and Unusual, 103; Linda K. Kerber, Toward an Intellectual History of Women 287 & n.66 (Chapel Hill: University of North Carolina, 1997); George A. Peck, Jr., The Political Writings of John Adams xxii (Indianapolis, IN: Hackett Publishing Co., 2003); John Adams to James Sullivan, May 26, 1776, *available at* http://press-pubs.uchicago.edu/founders/documents/v1ch13s10.html.

146. Bellamy, On Crimes and Punishments, 7; *compare* id. at xviii (noting that Beccaria's exact words were 'the greatest (*massima*) happiness shared among the greater (*maggior*) number").

147. http://hlsl5.law.harvard.edu/bracton//index.htm.

148. John Sainsbury, John Wilkes: The Lives of a Libertine 71–74 (Hampshire, UK: Ashgate, 2006); Martin Van Creveld, Wargames: From Gladiators to Gigabytes 272 (Cambridge: Cambridge University Press, 2013); Geoffrey Brennan, Lina Eriksson, Robert E. Goodin & Nicholas Southwood, Explaining Norms 123 (Oxford: Oxford University Press, 2013); McLynn, Crime and Punishment in Eighteenth-century England, ch. 8; Young, On Crimes and Punishments, 86 n.1.

149. Bellamy, On Crimes and Punishments, 9–12, 14–15, 17, 21–23, 26–28, 35, 54, 87–90, 92–95, 101, 103–06; David Lee Russell, Oglethorpe and Colonial Georgia: A History, 1733–1783, at 195 (Jefferson, NC: McFarland & Co., 2006).

150. Gowder v. City of Chicago, No. 11 C 1304, 2012 WL 2325826 *6 n.3 (N.D. Ill., June 19, 2012); Halbrook, The Founders' Second Amendment, 132.

151. Bellamy, On Crimes and Punishments, 113.

152. U.S. Const., amend. VI; Thomas J. Gardner & Terry M. Anderson, Criminal Law 25 (Belmont, CA: Wadsworth, 11th ed. 2012).

153. Harcourt, The Illusion of Free Markets, 55; Stefano Castelvecchi, Sentimental Opera: Questions of Genre in the Age of Bourgeois Drama 95–96, 257 (Cambridge: Cambridge University Press, 2013); Pauley, *The Jurisprudence of Crime and Punishment*, 131.

154. Lorraine Daston, Classical Probability in the Enlightenment 344 (Princeton: Princeton University Press, 1988).

155. 11 Rt. Hon. John Morley, The Works of Voltaire: A Contemporary Version 30–31 (Paris: E. R. DuMont, 1901); Commentaire sur le livre des délits et des peines (1766). Another edition of Voltaire's commentary was also printed in Geneva in 1767. Commentaire sur le livre des délits et des peines (1767).

156. Harcourt, The Illusion of Free Markets, 55; Matthew A. Pauley, *The Jurisprudence of Crime and Punishment*, 131; Thomas L. Hankins, Jean d'Alembert: Science and the Enlightenment 14, 66 (Oxford: Oxford University Press, 1970); Diary entry of John Adams, Feb. 21, 1765; Thomas Jefferson to Robert Skipwith, Aug. 3, 1771; Diary entry of John Adams, Apr. 28, 1778, *available at* www.founders.archives.gov. In a letter to Abigail Adams, John Adams asked his wife, "Have you ever read J. J. Rousseau?" "If not, read him—your Cousin Smith has him," Adams urged his wife. John Adams to Abigail Adams, Dec. 2, 1778.

157. Maestro, Cesare Beccaria and the Origins of Penal Reform, 43. A more complete history of Beccaria's book—and additional information about the editions and translations of it—can be found elsewhere. *See, e.g.*, Bellamy, On Crimes and Punishments, xli–xliv, xlvi–xlvii; Banner, The Death Penalty, 91.

158. Davidson, Voltaire in Exile, 153–54.

159. Thomas, On Crimes and Punishments, 113–15, 128–29, 132; Maestro, Voltaire and Beccaria as Reformers of Criminal Law, 79, 95, 169, 177; Maestro, Cesare Beccaria and the Origins of Penal Reform, 45; Hostettler, Cesare Beccaria, 30. *See* William Windle Carr, Poems on Various Subjects 175 (London, 1791):

> At an inn, where we lodged together, between Milan and Turin, a gentleman, who was returning from Ferney on a visit to Voltaire, whom I afterwards understood to be the Marquis of Beccaria, amongst others, told me the following story of him.—A traveller, taking his leave of him, in his way to Rome, asked him if he had any commands to that Capital. Voltaire holla'd out with his usual vivacity—"*Oui, Monsieur, me renvoyez les oreilles du grand inquisiteur.*" When this gentleman arrived at Rome, the story was whispered about, and came at last to the ears of the Pope, who sent for him, and very politely inquired of him if he had no message from Ferney; with some hesitation he acknowledged his commission, and told his holiness frankly what Voltaire had desired of him; the Pope, smiling, intreated him, if he returned by Ferney, to carry Voltaire his blessing, and to acquaint him, *Que l'inquisiteur n'a ni des oreilles ni des yeux.*

160. Wayne Andrews, Voltaire 104–105 (New York: New Directions Books, 1981).

161. Maestro, Voltaire and Beccaria as Reformers of Criminal Law, 110; Jacques Lagrange, ed., Michel Foucault: Psychiatric Power, Lectures at the Collège de France 1973–1974, at 17 n.3 (New

York: Picador, 2003); Richard Vogler, A World View of Criminal Justice 47–48 (Burlington, VT: Ashgate Publishing Co. 2005).

162. Adams, Bureaucrats and Beggars, 306 n.85.

163. 2 Carlo Calisse, A History of Italian Law 460 (Washington, DC: Beard Books, 1928); Sipe, *Cesare Beccaria*, 38.

164. Harcourt, The Illusion of Free Markets, 55, 60; François Jean de Beauvior, Marquis de Chastellux to Jeremy Bentham, July 3, 1778 & Paul Henri Thiry, baron d'Holbach to David Garrick, Feb. 9, 1766, *available at* Electronic Enlightenment, Electronic Enlightenment Project, Bodleian Libraries, University of Oxford, www.e-enlightenment.com; 1 Lord Fitzmaurice, Life of William Earl of Shelburne Afterwards First Marquess of Lansdowne 424, 429–30 (London: MacMillan and Co., 2d rev. ed., 1912).

165. Thomas, On Crimes and Punishments, xxviii; Maestro, Cesare Beccaria and the Origins of Penal Reform, 74, 95–96; Paolucci, On Crimes and Punishments, xi; Bellamy, On Crimes and Punishments, 129; Israel, Democratic Enlightenment, 344–45; Marrone, Encyclopedia of Italian Literary Studies, 1979; Harcourt, The Illusion of the Free Markets, 255–56 n.48; 1 Macleod, A Dictionary of Political Economy, 252; John Macdonell & Edward Manson, eds., Great Jurists of the World 507 (New York: Little, Brown & Co., 1914); Ronald Grimsley, Jean d'Alembert, 1717–83, 218 (Oxford: Clarendon Press, 1963); Peter Hanns Reill & Ellen Judy Wilson, Encyclopedia of the Enlightenment 293 (New York: Facts on File, rev. ed. 2004); Sipe, *Cesare Beccaria*, 28, 31, 38–41; *see also* Max Pearson Cushing, Baron d'Holbach: A Study of Eighteenth Century Radicalism in France 76 (New York: Columbia University, Ph.D. thesis, 1914) (noting in a 1766 letter from "Holbach to Wilkes," sent from Paris, that "Marquis Beccaria is going to leave us very soon being obliged to return to Milan: Count Veri will at the same time set out for England.").

166. Hostettler, Cesare Beccaria, 57; W. F. Reddaway, ed., Documents of Catherine the Great xxiv (CUP Archive, 1971); *see also* 1 Secret Memoirs of the Court of Petersburg: Particularly Towards the End of the Reign of Catharine II, at 105 n.† (London: C. Whittingham, 1800) ("The Instruction for a Code is so literally taken from Montesquieu and Beccaria, that Mr. F**** de B****, who undertook to translate it, thought he could not do better than copy the text of these celebrated writers.").

167. Bessler, Cruel and Unusual, 33; Maestro, Cesare Beccaria and the Origins of Penal Reform, 134.

168. 2 Jackson J. Spielvogel, Western Civilization: A Brief History 401 (Boston: Cengage Learning, 8th ed. 2012).

169. 12 Thomas Holcroft, trans., Correspondence: Letters Between Frederic II and Mess. D'Alembert, De Condorcet, Grimm and D'Arget 401–402, 408–409 (London: G. G. J. and J. Robinson, 1789).

170. Benjamin Franklin to John Waring, Dec. 17, 1763; Marquis de Condorcet to Benjamin Franklin, Dec. 1773; Benjamin Franklin to Benjamin Rush, July 25, 1774; Thomas Jefferson to James Madison, July 31, 1788; John Adams to Thomas Jefferson, June 28, 1812, *available at* www.founders.archives.gov.

171. "Account of the late Marquis Beccaria," 6 The Monthly Magazine and British Register 260 (London: R. Phillips, 1798) (October 1798 issue containing a "eulogium of the late Marquis Beccaria").

172. Szabo, Kaunitz, 184 & n. 148 (citing Voltaire to Kaunitz, July 3, 1766, *in* The Complete Works of Voltaire, Vol. CXIV (Banbury, 1973), pp. 295–96).

173. Szabo, Kaunitz, 184–85.

174. Maestro, Cesare Beccaria and the Origins of Penal Reform, 35–39.

175. Thomas, On Crimes and Punishments, xxiii–xxiv, xxvi; Maestro, Cesare Beccaria and the Origins of Penal Reform, 28–29; *see also* Paolucci, On Crimes and Punishments, xi ("The Church of Rome had placed the treatise on the Index in 1766, condemning it for its extremely rationalistic presuppositions.").

176. Bellamy, On Crimes and Punishments, 22–23.

177. Maestro, Cesare Beccaria and the Origins of Penal Reform, 35.

178. Thomas, On Crimes and Punishments, xxvi.

179. Israel, Democratic Enlightenment, 357–58.

180. Michael Tavuzzi, Renaissance Inquisitors: Dominican Inquisitors and Inquisitorial Districts in Northern Italy, 1474–1527, at 28, 56, 36, 278, 257 (Lieden, The Netherlands: Koninklijke Brill, 2007). The Beccaria family has a long history in Italy. After Emperor Henry VII came to Lombardy in 1310, that northern Italian region submitted itself to his rule. "When Henry had departed, however, the strong Matteo Visconti immediately assumed possession of Milan, in 1311; and two years later he took possession of Pavia, which thus became a member of the Visconti dominions,—with the family of the Beccaria as viceroys." Egerton R. Williams, Jr. Lombard Towns of Italy 229 (London: Smith, Elder & Co., 1914).

181. Thomas, On Crimes and Punishments, xxiv–xxv, 7–8, 100, 102–112, 172 n.8, 175; John Adams to Edmund Jenings, June 20, 1780; John Adams Diary, "1779. March 4," *available at* www.

founders.archives.gov.

182. Mario Rosa, "The Catholic *Aufklärung* in Italy," *in* A Companion to the Catholic Enlightenment in Europe 232 (The Netherlands: Koninklijke Brill, 2010).

183. Thomas, On Crimes and Punishments, 128–29; Iain McDaniel, Adam Ferguson in the Scottish Enlightenment 47–48 (Cambridge: Cambridge University Press, 2013); Immanuel Kant, Metaphysical Elements of Justice 141–42 (John Ladd, trans., 2d ed. 1999).

184. Thomas, On Crimes and Punishments, xxvii; *see also* Schwartz & Wishingrad, *The Eighth Amendment*, 812.

185. Paolucci, On Crimes and Punishments, xi; Thomas, On Crimes and Punishments, 172 n.6; Maestro, Cesare Beccaria and the Origins of Penal Reform, 4, 36–37.

186. Maria Theresa Habsburg (the Holy Roman Empress) of Austria and Grand Duke Leopold of Tuscany both expressed their admiration for Beccaria's ideas. Paolucci, On Crimes and Punishments, x; Bellamy, On Crimes and Punishments, xxxvii.

187. Young, On Crimes and Punishments, xxviii–xxix.

188. Lorraine Daston, Classical Probability in the Enlightenment 343 (Princeton: Princeton University Press, 1988).

189. Maestro, Cesare Beccaria and the Origins of Penal Reform, 68–71, 153–55.

190. Richard Sennett, Flesh and Stone: The Body and the City in Western Civilization 298–99 (New York: W. W. Norton & Co., 1994); Gregory Fremont-Barnes, ed., Encyclopedia of the Age of Political Revolutions and New Ideologies, 1760–1815, at 318 (Westport, CT: Greenwood Press, 2007); Mark Jones & Peter Johnstone, History of Criminal Justice 145 (Waltham, MA: 5th ed., 2012); 9 Albert Henry Smyth, ed., The Writings of Benjamin Franklin 637 (New York: Macmillan & Co. 1907); Ted Gottfried, Capital Punishment: The Death Penalty Debate 96 (Berkeley Heights, NJ: Enslow Publishers, 1997); Joscelyn Godwin, The Theosophical Enlightenment 152 (Albany: State University of New York Press, 1994).

191. Michael Walzer, ed., Regicide and Revolution: Speeches at the Trial of Louis XVI, at 81, 156 (New York: Columbia University Press, 1992); William E. Nelson, Marbury v. Madison, *Democracy, and the Rule of Law*, 71 Tenn. L. Rev. 217, 227 (2004); William Falconer, Remarks on the Influence of Climate, Situation, Nature of Country, Population, Nature of Food, and Way of Life, on the Disposition and Temper, Manners and Behaviour, Intellects, Laws and Customs, Form of Government and Religion, of Mankind 9, 33, 98–103, 158, 459, 486–88, 496 (London: C. Dilly, 1781); *see also* Scott M. Malzahn, *State Sponsorship and Support of International Terrorism: Customary Norms of State Responsibility*, 26 Hast. Int'l & Comp. L. Rev. 83, 86 (2002).

192. Thomas, On Crimes and Punishments, xxix; Paolucci, On Crimes and Punishments, x; *see also* Daye v. State, 769 A.2d 630, 637 (Vt. 2000) (noting "the influence of Cesare Beccaria" on the Pennsylvania Constitution of 1776); Fisher, *The Birth of the Prison Retold*, 1278 ("Beccaria was enormously influential in Britain").

193. "Perfecting the Prison: United States, 1789–1865," *in* Norval Morris & David J. Rothman, eds., The Oxford History of the Prison: The Practice of Punishment in Western Society 102 (Oxford: Oxford University Press, 1995).

194. Thomas, On Crimes and Punishments, xxix; Maestro, Cesare Beccaria and the Origins of Penal Reform, 124, 135; Laurence A. Grayer, *A Paradox: Death Penalty Flourishes in U.S. While Declining Worldwide*, 23 Denv. J. Int'l L. & Pol'y 555, 557 (1995).

195. Maestro, Cesare Beccaria and the Origins of Penal Reform, 122, 136.

196. 1 John Macdonell & Edward Manson, Great Jurists of the World 514 (Boston: Little, Brown, 1914); Robert W. Shaffern, Law and Justice from Antiquity to Enlightenment 205, 208 (Plymouth, UK: Rowman & Littlefield, 2009).

197. Continental Congress to the Inhabitants of the Province of Quebec, Oct. 26, 1774; Diary of John Adams (Oct. 4, 1774), *available at* http://www.masshist.org/digitaladams/aea/cfm/doc.cfm?id=D22; Journal of the Proceedings of the Congress, Held at Philadelphia, September 5, 1774, at 118–20 (Philadelphia: William & Thomas Bradford, 1774); Extracts from the Votes and Proceedings of the American Continental Congress, Held at Philadelphia on the 5th of September, 1774, at 57–58 (New London, CT: Timothy Green, 1774) ("Published by order of the Congress"); Extracts from the Votes and Proceedings of the American Continental Congress, Held at Philadelphia on the 5th of September, 1774, at 36–37 (Annapolis, MD: Anne Catharine Green, and Son, 1774).

198. David Thomas Konig, ed., Divising Liberty: Preserving and Creating Freedom in the New American Republic 195 (Stanford: Stanford University Press, 1995).

199. Jeremy Black, George III: America's Last King 360 (New Haven, CT: Yale University Press, 2006); *accord* Nancy Jean Curtin, The Origins of Irish Republicanism: The United Irishmen in Dublin and

Ulster, University of Wisconsin — Madison (1988), p. 241.

200. John Dickinson, An Essay on the Constitutional Power of Great-Britain over the Colonies in America; with the Resolves of the Committee for the Province of Pennsylvania iii–vii, 9–127 (Philadelphia: William & Thomas Bradford, 1774); William H. Ukers, All About Coffee (MobileReference, 2010) (unpaginated). I am especially grateful to the John Dickinson Writings Project, led by its director and editor Jane E. Calvert, for providing information about John Dickinson's role in the American Revolution. According to Calvert, there are two drafts of the letter to the inhabitants of the province of Quebec by people other than Dickinson, though neither of those drafts reference Beccaria.

201. Decl. of Independence (July 4, 1776); John Powell, ed., Biographical Dictionary of Literary Influences: The Nineteenth Century, 1800–1914, at 220 (Westport, CT: Greenwood Press, 2001).

202. 1 Marrone, Encyclopedia of Italian Literary Studies, 1978.

203. Hostettler, Cesare Beccaria, 23; Reill & Wilson, Encyclopedia of the Enlightenment, 611. Pietro Verri wrote Observations on Torture in 1777, but it was not published until after Verri's death in 1804. 1 Marrone, Encyclopedia of Italian Literary Studies, 1980. In his Discourse on Happiness (1781), Pietro Verri argued that public and private happiness could be achieved by maximizing pleasure and minimizing pain. Roland Sarti, Italy: A Reference Guide from the Renaissance to the Present 15–16, 257, 615 (New York: Facts on File, 2004). It was through Pietro and Alessandro Verri that Beccaria became familiar with works by Montesquieu and others. Id. at 146; Keith Hayward, Shadd Maruna & Jayne Mooney, eds., Fifty Key Thinkers in Criminology 3–4 (2010).

204. Brand & Pertile, The Cambridge History of Italian Literature, 427; Hales, La Bella Lingua, 226; compare 3 Frank N. Magill, ed., Cyclopedia of World Authors 1353 (Pasadena, CA: Salem Press, 1997) ("Alessandro (Francesco Tommaso Antonio) Manzoni, widely rated as one of Italy's outstanding novelists on the basis of a single book, The Betrothed, was born in Milan in 1785, presumably the son of Pietro Manzoni and his wife Giulia Beccaria, although there is some evidence to show that he was in fact the son of Giovanni Verri, one of his mother's lovers.").

205. Buccini, The Americas in Italian Literature and Culture, 173–74; 8 Carl E. Rollyson & Frank N. Magill, eds., Critical Survey of Long Fiction 3895 (Pasadena, CA: Salem Press, 2d ed. 2000); 50 The North American Review 315–16 (1840); Southern California Quarterly, p. 136 (1977); Hales, La Bella Lingua, 226–27; 2 The Monthly Miscellany or Gentleman and Lady's Complete Magazine, for the Year 1774, at 367 (London: R. Snagg, 1774); Nagel's Encyclopedia-Guide 71 (Geneva: Nagel Publishers, 1987); Natalia Ginzburg, The Manzoni Family 16 (New York: Arcade Publishing, 1989).

206. Roy Sydney Porter, Richard & Maria Cosway: Regency Artist of Taste and Fashion 91 (1995); Burnell, Divided Affections, 360.

207. 1 Gaetana Marrone, Encyclopedia of Italian Literary Studies 146, 1706 (2006); 5 Ainsworth B. Spofford, ed., The Twentieth Century Cyclopedia 400 (1902); 27–29 American Association of Teachers of Italian, Italica: Bulletin of the American Association of Teachers of Italian 159 (1950); Hales, La Bella Lingua, 225.

208. Alessandro Manzoni, The Betrothed (I Promessi Sposi) 4 (Stilwel, KS: Digireads.com, 2008).

209. 2 Kelly Boyd, ed., Encyclopedia of Historians & Historical Writing 759–61 (Chicago, IL: Fitzroy Dearborn Publishers, 1999); Sandra Bermann, trans., Alessandro Manzoni, On the Historical Novel: Del Romanzo Storico 4 (Lincoln: University of Nebraska Press, 1984).

210. Bessler, Cruel and Unusual, 139.

211. Edward Eldefonso, Alan Coffey & Richard C. Grace, Principles of Law Enforcement: An Overview of the Justice System 329 (New York: John Wiley & Sons, 1982); 4 The Encyclopaedia Britannica, or Dictionary of Arts, Sciences, and General Literature 559 (Edinburgh: Adam and Charles Black, 8th ed. 1854); Hostettler, Cesare Beccaria, 33.

212. Supplements of the Bulletin of the History of Medicine 288, 305 (Baltimore, MD: Johns Hopkins, 1944).

213. Hostettler, Cesare Beccaria, 32–33.

214. Natalia Ginzburg, The Manzoni Family 15 (New York: Arcade Publishing, 1989).

215. Newman & Marongiu, On Crimes and Punishments, lxviii.

216. 4 The Encyclopaedia Britannica, or Dictionary of Arts, Sciences, and General Literature 559 (Edinburgh: Adam & Charles Black, 8th ed. 1854).

217. 1 Selections from the Most Celebrated Foreign Literary Journals and Other Periodical Publications 1, 45 (London: J. Debrett, 1798).

218. 2 General Biography; or Lives, Critical and Historical, of the Most Eminent Persons of All Ages, Countries, Conditions, and Professions 71, 180 (London: J. Johnson, 1801).

219. Milan (English Edition): History, Map and Guide 67 (Firenze: Casa Editrice Bonechi, 2007);

Nancy J. Scott, Vincenzo Vela, 1820–1891, at 272, 519 (New York: Garland Publishing Co., 1979); Karl Bædeker, Italy: Handbook for Travellers (First Part: Northern Italy, including Leghore, Florence, and Ancona, and the Island of Corsica) 118–19 (Leipsic: Karl Bædeker, 3d ed. 1874); Hostettler, Cesare Beccaria, 33; Pasquale Troncone, The Right of a State to Punish by Death: A Case of the Political Contamination of the Science of Penal Legislation (Rome: ARACNE editrice, Oct. 2012), *available at* www.aracneeditrice.it/pdf/9788854854390.pdf.

220. Maestro, Cesare Beccaria and the Origins of Penal Reform, 122, 135; Helen Borowitz & Albert Borowitz, Book Review, 45 Md. L. Rev. 1066, 1070 n.8 (1986) (reviewing Samuel Y. Edgerton, Jr., Pictures and Punishment: Art and Criminal Prosecution During the Florentine Renaissance (1985)).

221. Adams, Bureaucrats and Beggars, 248.

222. Joan Fitzpatrick & Alice Miller, *International Standards on the Death Penalty: Shifting Discourse*, 19 Brook. J. Int'l L. 273, 336 n.289 (1993) (citing Hugo Adam Bedau, Death Is Different: Studies in the Morality, Law, and Politics of Capital Punishment 85–86 (1987)); Maestro, Cesare Beccaria and the Origins of Penal Reform, 140–41; *see also* Hugo Adam Bedau, *Bentham's Utilitarian Critique of the Death Penalty*, 74 J. Crim. L. & Criminology 1033, 1033–36 (1983) (describing Bentham's writings against capital punishment, including in his book, *Rationale of Punishment*).

223. http://www.gettyimages.com/detail/news-photo/portrait-of-giulio-bonesana-beccaria-son-of-cesare-beccaria-news-photo/122216111; Sylvanus Urban, The Gentleman's Magazine, March 1858 ("At Milan, aged 80, the Marquis Beccaria, son of the celebrated author of 'Crimes and Punishments.'").

224. Newman & Marongiu, On Crimes and Punishments, lviii; Maestro, Voltaire and Beccaria as Reformers of Criminal Law, 93; Maestro, Cesare Beccaria and the Origins of Penal Reform, 5; "Centennial of the Cabinet of Di Brera, Milan," XLII American Journal of Numismatics, No. 4, p. 131 ("Among the important acquisitions during Cattaneo's time were the collections of the Marquis Giulio Beccaria…."); *see also* The Linguistic Writings of Alessandro Manzoni: A Textual and Chronological Reconstruction 65 (Cambridge, England: W. Heffer & Sons, 1950) ("Giulio Beccaria, the husband of Antonietta Curioni and brother of Giulia, had a villa at Gessate.").

225. *See* Thomas, On Crimes and Punishments, x.

Chapter 2

1. On Beccaria's American influence and Enlightenment texts in American circles generally, see David Lundberg & Henry May, *The Enlightened Reader in America*, 28 American Quarterly 262 (Summer 1976) and Donald S. Lutz, *The Relative Influence of European Writers on Late Eighteenth Century American Political Thought*, 78 Am. Political Sci. Rev. 189 (1984).

2. Cesare Beccaria, An Essay on Crimes and Punishments (1767); *see also* Cosmo Mythogelastick Professor, Makarony Fables; with the New Fable of the Bees (London: J. Almon, 2d ed. 1768) (advertisement reading: "*Next Month will be published* … Printed for J. ALMON, opposite Burlington-House, in Piccadilly; of whom may be had … 4. An Essay on Crimes and Punishments; translated from the Italian of the Marquis Beccaria of Milan; price 4s 6d bound.").

3. Cesare Beccaria, An Essay on Crimes and Punishments iii–iv (1767).

4. John Brewer, Party Ideology and Popular Politics at the Accession of George III, at 61, 174, 215 (Cambridge: Cambridge University Press, 1976); Charles Knight, Biography or Third Division of "The English Encyclopedia" 70 (London: Bradbury, Evans, & Co., 1872); Brett F. Woods, ed., Letters from France: The Private Diplomatic Correspondence of Benjamin Franklin 1776–1785, at 129 (New York: Algora Publishing, 2006); Memoirs of John Almon, Bookseller of Piccadilly (1790); [Novanglus Papers, 1774–1775]; Three Public Notices Concerning the Petition from the Continental Congress, Jan. 17–18, 1775; John Adams to Abigail Adams; La Rochefoucauld to Benjamin Franklin, Mar. 26, 1777; John Adams to Edmé Jacques Genet, June 8, 1778; John Adams to Thomas Digges, Apr. 15, 1780, *available at* www.founders.archives.gov; oll.libertyfund.org (reprinting "Novanglus" letters). John Adams' "Novanglus" letters were published in 1775 just prior to the outbreak of the Revolutionary War. *See* http://democraticthinker.wordpress.com/2010/05/17/the-novanglus-essays/.

5. 1 Moncure Daniel Conway, ed., The Writings of Thomas Paine 169 (New York: G. P. Putnam's Sons, 1894); A Clear Idea of the Genuine and Uncorrupted British Constitution in an Address to the Inhabitants of the Province of Quebec from the Forty-nine Delegates in the Continental Congress in Philadelphia; September 5, to October 10, 1774 (London, 1774); Thomas Paine to Benjamin Franklin, June 20, 1777, *available at* www.founders.archives.gov.

6. Benjamin Franklin to John Almon, Nov. 7, 1774; Benjamin Franklin to Jacques Barbeu-Dubourg, Dec. 5, 1774; John Almon to Benjamin Franklin, Dec. 6, 1774, *available at* www.founders.archives.gov.

7. Take Your Choice! xvi, 10, 22–23, 25–26 (London: J. Almon, 1776); John Cartwright, The Legislative Rights of the Commonality Vindicated, or, Take Your Choice! 33, 37 (London: J. Almon, 2d. ed. 1777) (reprinting the same quotes from Beccaria); A Committee of Boston Merchants to Benjamin Franklin, Dec. 29, 1769, *available at* www.founders.archives.gov.

8. Samuel Estwick, A Letter to the Reverend Josiah Tucker, D.D. Dean of Glocester, in Answer to His Humble Address and Earnest Appeal, &c. 43 (London: J. Almon, 1776); *see also* 2 William Thomas Ayres, A Comparative View of the Differences Between the English and Irish Statute and Common Law 234 (Dublin/London: Edward Brooke, 1780) ("The proper end and measure of those punishments, and how far the power of legislators extends to inflict penalties for offences, are subjects which are amply discussed in Grotius, Puffendorff, Montesquieu, Hale, Beccaria, and De Lolme, each of whom will convey pleasure and instruction well worth the pains of their perusal."); 2 Edward Topham, Letters from Edinburgh: Written in the Years 1774 and 1775: Containing Some Observations on the Diversions, Customs, Manners and Laws, of the Scotch Nation 97 (Dublin: W. Watson, et al., circa 1780) (referring to "[t]he Marquis Beccaria" and "his excellent Treatise on Crimes and Punishments"); Letters from Edinburgh; Written in the Years 1774 and 1775: Containing Some Observations on the Diversions, Customs, Manners, and Laws of the Scotch Nation, During a Six Months Residence in Edinburgh 292 (London: J. Dodsley, 1776) (referring to "[t]he Marquis Beccaria" and "his excellent Treatise on Crimes and Punishments").

9. Sheldon S. Cohen, British Supporters of the American Revolution, 1775–1783: The Role of the 'Middling Level' Activists 28, 31 (Woodbridge, UK: The Boydell Press, 2004); Benjamin Franklin to Thomas Digges, May 30[–31], 1779; Thomas Digges to Benjamin Franklin, Jan. 9, 1780; Thomas Digges to John Adams, Mar. 3, 1780; Thomas Digges to John Adams, Apr. 14, 1780, *available at* www.founders.archives.gov.

10. George S. Street, The Ghosts of Piccadilly 261 (London: Archibald Constable & Co., 1907); Debrett's Peerage and Baronetage 17 (London: Kelly's Directories, 1995).

11. Judith Phillips Stanton, ed., The Collected Letters of Charlotte Smith 148 n.5 (Bloomington: Indiana University Press, 2003); A Catalogue of Books Printed for, and Sold by Charles Dilly, in London 2, 14, 16, 18–19 (1787).

12. Cesare Beccaria, An Essay on Crimes and Punishments (Dublin: John Exshaw, 1767); A Dictionary of Members of the Dublin Book Trade 1550–1800, at 190 (Cambridge, England: The Bibliographic Society, 2000).

13. Cesare Beccaria, An Essay on Crimes and Punishments (London: F. Newbery, 2d ed. 1769).

14. 2 John Morgan, The Attorney's Vade Mecum, and Client's Instructor, Treating of Actions: (such as Are Now Most in Use.) of Prosecuting and Defending Them: Of the Pleadings and Law 72 (Dublin: William Power, 1792) (Morgan, a barrister of the Inner Temple, cites the "*Harlam Ed.* 1780" of Beccaria's treatise); Charles Watkins, Reflections on Government in General, with Their Application to the British Constitution 27, 33, 60 (London: W. and C. Spilsbury, 1796) (citing Beccaria multiple times); 1 M. de la Croix, A Review of the Constitutions of the Principal States of Europe, and of the United States of America 79 (London: G. C. J. and J. Robinson, 1792) (citing Beccaria's "Treatise on Offences and Punishments"); Abbe Rochon, A Voyage to Madagascar, and the East Indies 82 (London: G. C. J. and J. Robinson, 1792) (citing "[t]he Marquis of Beccaria" and "his excellent treatise on *Crimes and Punishments*"); 2 William Godwin, An Enquiry Concerning Political Justice, and Its Influence on General Virtue and Happiness 256 (Dublin: Luke White, 1793) ("the humane and benevolent Beccaria"); Stephen Payne Adye, A Treatise on Courts Martial: To Which Is Added, an Essay on Military Punishments and Rewards 231, 263 (London: J. Murray, 3d ed. 1786) (referring to "the humane and benevolent Marquis of Beccaria"); 2 John Disney, The Works of Theological, Medical, Political, and Miscellaneous of John Jebb, M.D. F.R.S. with Memoirs of the Life of the Author 160, 482–83, 563 (London: T. Cadell, J. Johnson & T. Stockdale, 1787) (referring to "the excellent Beccaria"); 13 Arthur Young, Annals of Agriculture, and Other Useful Arts 244 (Bury St. Edmund's: J. Rackham, 1790) (referring to Beccaria and "his excellent treatise"); A Catalogue of Books for Sale or Circulation, by William P. Blake, at the Boston Book-Store, No. 59, Cornhill (Boston: William P. Blake, 1793) (listing "Beccaria on crimes and punishments" for sale for one dollar); "Tristram Shandy," A Sentimental Dialogue Between Two Souls, in the Palpable Bodies of an English Lady of Quality and an Irish Gentleman ii (1768); 2 George Watson, ed., The New Cambridge Bibliography of English Literature 1660–1800, at 954 (Cambridge: Cambridge University Press, 1971); *see also* The New Foundling Hospital for Wit: Being a Collection of Several Curious Pieces, in Verse and Prose i–ii (Lon-

don, 1768) (advertising Beccaria's treatise under the heading, "This day are published,").

15. *See* Cesare Beccaria, An Essay on Crimes and Punishments (5th ed. 1777); "John Exshaw," Gallery C, http://www.galleryc.net/artist-image/maps/exshaj000001-lecture.html; An Essay on Crimes and Punishments (Dublin: John Exshaw, 5th ed., 1777).

16. Hostettler, Cesare Beccaria, xvi; Shirley Granahan, John Newbery: Father of Children's Literature 6–9 (Edina, MN: ABDO Publishing Co., 2010); E. Jennifer Monaghan, Learning to Read and Write in Colonial America 321 (Amherst: University of Massachusetts Press, 2007); Welsh, A Bookseller of the Last Century, 8, 21, 23, 59, 67–70, 82–84, 87–88, 117, 119, 126–35, 144, 276 (listing titles published by Francis Newbery and John Newbery, describing the business at St. Paul's Churchyard, and noting that Francis Newbery, the son, and Francis Newbery, the nephew, succeeded John in different aspects of the business).

17. Cesare Beccaria, An Essay on Crimes and Punishments iii–iv (Dublin: John Exshaw, 1767); Cesare Beccaria, An Essay on Crimes and Punishments iii–iv (London: F. Newbery, 2d ed. 1769); Walsh, A Bookseller of the Last Century, 21.

18. Cesare Beccaria, An Essay on Crimes and Punisments [sic] (1770).

19. Bruce L. R. Smith, Jeremy D. Mayer & A. Lee Fritschler, Closed Minds? Politics and Ideology in American Universities 26 (Washington, DC: The Brookings Institution, 2008) ("[P]rominent Pennsylvanians studied in England, which was considered a highly desirable path to success in life before the Revolution, helping the sons of wealthy merchants to establish a career in trade.").

20. Cesare Beccaria, An Essay on Crimes and Punishments (3d ed. 1770).

21. A. L. Brown & Michael Moss, The University of Glasgow: 1451–1996 (Edinburgh: Edinburgh University Press, 1996).

22. Manuel & Manuel, James Bowdoin and the Patriot Philosophers, 45, 48–51; Conrad Edick Wright, Revolutionary Generation: Harvard Men and the Consequences of Independence 70 (Amherst: University of Massachusetts Press, 2005); William Allen, A Decade of Addresses, Delivered, from 1820 to 1829, to the Senior Classes at Bowdoin College; Together with an Inaugural Address 267 (Concord: Horatio Hill & Co., 1830).

23. Alyn Brodsky, Benjamin Rush: Patriot and Physician 40–50 (New York: St. Martin's Press, 2004).

24. Jürgen Martschukat, "A Horrifying Experience? Public Executions and the Emotional Spectator in the New Republic," *in* Jessica C. E. Gienow-Hecht, ed., Emotions in American History: An International Assessment 186 (New York: Berghahn Books, 2010).

25. Sher, The Enlightenment and the Book, 269.

26. Catalogus Librorum in Bibliotheca Cantabrigiensi Selectus, Frequentiorem in Usum Harvardinatum, Qui Gradu Baccalaurei in Artibus Nondum Sunt Donati 7, 9, 16, 24 (Boston: Edes & Gill, 1773).

27. 1 Giuseppe Gorani, Il Vero Dispotismo, avviso 227, 231 (Londra, 1770); 2 Giuseppe Gorani, Il Vero Dispotismo, avviso 255 (Londra, 1770); Robert Aldrich & Garry Wotherspoon, eds., Who's Who in Gay & Lesbian History: From Antiquity to World War II, at 220–21 (New York: Psychology Press, 2002); Sudhir Hazareesingh, ed., The Jacobin Legacy in Modern France 165 (Oxford: Oxford University Press, 2002).

28. The Annual Register, or a View of the History, Politics, and Literature, for the Year 1767, at 316–20 (London: J. Dodsley, 2d ed. 1772); William Eden, Principles of Penal Law 180, 235, 264, 287, 296 (London: B. White & T. Cadell, 1771); William Eden, Principles of Penal Law 163, 288, 311, 323 (Dublin: John Milliken, 3d ed. 1772); Consideration on Criminal Law xxii (Dublin: H. Saunders, et al., 1772); M. De Voltaire, The Man of Forty Crowns 69 (London: T. Becket & P. A. D'Hondt, 1768); Giacinto Dragonetti, A Treatise on Virtues and Rewards (London: Johnson and Payne; J. Almon, 1769); *see also* "Civilian," Free Thoughts on Seduction, Adultery, and Divorce 37 (London: J. Bell, 1771) ("[t]he celebrated Marquis de Beccaria"); Samuel Denne, A Letter to Sir Robert Ladbroke, Knt. Senior Alderman, and One of the Representatives of the City of London 74 (London: J. and W. Oliver, 1771) ("the benevolent Marquis Beccaria").

29. Cæsar Beccaria Bonesaria, A Discourse on Public Oeconomy and Commerce 30–31, 43–44 (London: J. Dodsley & J. Murray, 1769); Raven, London Booksellers and American Customers, 94, 114, 116.

30. The Patriots of North-America: A Sketch with Explanatory Notes 1, 26 (New York, 1775); Arthur Lee, A Speech Intended to Have Been Delivered in the House of Commons, in Support of the Petition from the General Congress at Philadelphia 33 (London: J. Almon, 1775).

31. Cesare Beccaria, An Essay on Crimes and Punishments (4th ed. 1775). In 1785, another edition of Beccaria's treatise was also printed in London for "E. Newbery." Cesare Beccaria, An Essay on Crimes and Punishments (4th ed. 1785).

32. Hostettler, Cesare Beccaria, xvi.

33. 3 Samuel Ward, A Modern System of Natural History: Containing Accurate Descriptions, and Faithful Histories, of Animals, Vegetables, and Minerals (London: F. Newbery, 1775) (advertisement).

34. William Sparrow Simpson, Gleanings from Old S. Paul's 266 (London: Elliot Stock, 1889); The Life of Mr. Richard Savage, Son of the Earl Rivers (London: F. Newbery, 4th ed. 1777) (advertisement).

35. Halbrook, A Right to Bear Arms, 136 n.181.

36. Lyndall Gordon, Vindication: A Life of Mary Wollstonecraft 53 (New York: Harper Perennial, 2005); http://www.history.com/this-day-in-history/john-adams-appointed-to-negotiate-peace-terms-with-british.

37. 5 J. W. M. Gibbs, comp., The Works of Oliver Goldsmith 407 (London: George Bell and Sons, 1886).

38. John M. Murrin, et al., Liberty, Equality, Power: A History of the American People 127 (Boston, MA: Wadsworth, 5th ed. 2011); Cash, John Wilkes, 399 n.6; Ann Lyon, Constitutional History of the United Kingdom 290–92 (London: Cavendish Publishing, 2003); 1 John Almon, ed., The Correspondence of the Late John Wilkes, with His Friends, Printed from the Original Manuscripts, in Which Are Introduced Memoirs of His Life viii, 14–15, 33–34, 38–39, 52–56, 62–64, 91–133, 139–41, 154–55, 157, 165, 178 (London: Richard Phillips, 1805); An Essay on Woman, in Three Epistles (London: Printed for the Author, 1763); Benjamin Franklin to William Franklin, Apr. 16, 1768 & Benjamin Franklin to Joseph Galloway, May 14, 1768, available at www.founders.archives.gov. Benjamin Franklin became aware of The North Briton itself very quickly and was well aware of the dispute between Wilkes and Lord Bute and the controversy surrounding North Briton No. 45. David Hall to Benjamin Franklin, June 23, 1763; Benjamin Franklin to John Whitehurst, June 27, 1763; Benjamin Franklin to William Strahan, June 28, 1763; Benjamin Franklin to William Strahan, Aug. 8, 1763; William Strahan to Benjamin Franklin, Aug. 18, 1763; John Sargent to Benjamin Franklin, Nov. 8, 1763; Henton Brown to Benjamin Franklin, Nov. 26, 1763; Benjamin Franklin to Richard Jackson, June 25, 1764, available at www.founders.archives.gov.

39. Horace Bleackley, Life of John Wilkes 183–227 (London: John Lane, 1917); Jerry White, A Great and Monstrous Thing: London in the Eighteenth Century 457, 516–17, 526 (London: Random House, 2012); Merrill Jensen, The Founding of a Nation: A History of the American Revolution, 1763–1776, at 317–20 (Indianapolis, IN: Hackett Publishing Co., 2004); John Sainsbury, John Wilkes: The Lives of a Libertine 1, 234 (Hampshire, UK: Ashgate, 2006).

40. Pauline Maier, From Resistance to Revolution: Colonial Radicals and the Development of American Opposition to Britain, 1765–1776, at 176–77 (New York: W. W. Norton & Co., 1991); Neil Forsyth, ed., Reading Contexts 45–46 (Tübingen: Narr, 1988) (Volume 4 of Swiss papers in English language and literature); "A Friend to Civil and Religious Liberty," The North Briton, from No. I to No. XLVI, at i, lxxiii (London: W. Bingley, 1769); Cash, John Wilkes, 1–4, 31, 158, 170–80, 249, 292; 1–2 The North Briton (Revised and Corrected by the Author): Illustrated with Explanatory Notes 260–68 (Dublin: John Mitchell & James Williams, 1764); 2 The Adams Papers: Papers of John Adams 353–54 (Cambridge, MA: Harvard University Press, 1977). A different John Wilkes (1750–1810), an English printer and bookseller in the County of Sussex, published Encyclopædia Londinensis (1810), in which he wrote of "the inhumanity and mistaken policy" of "the local constitutions of other nations" that "have been sufficiently pointed out by Montesquieu, Beccaria, and other ingenious writers." 5 John Wilkes, Encyclopædia Londinensis; or, Universal Dictionary of Arts, Sciences, and Literature 361 (London: J. Adlard, 1810).

41. E.g., Joshua Cooke, A Catalogue of Books, Containing Several Libraries Lately Purchased Which Will Begin to Be Sold (at the Prices Printed in the Catalogue) 70 (London: Rivington's, 1804); Thomas Payne, Bookseller, A New Catalogue for the Year 1797, of a Valuable Collection of Books Ancient and Modern, in Various Languages, and in Every Branch of Literature 161, 265 (London, 1797).

42. Tobias Kelly, This Side of Silence: Human Rights, Torture, and the Recognition of Cruelty 198 (Philadelphia: University of Pennsylvania Press, 2012).

43. M. de Voltaire, Prix de la justice et de l'humanité 16–17, 34 (Géneve, 1778); 4 Dr. J. Campbell, Lives of the British Admirals: Containing a New and Accurate Naval History, from the Earliest Periods (London: Alexander Donaldson, 1779) (advertisement); James Boswell, The Decision of the Court of Session, upon the Question of Literary Property; in the Cause of John Hinton of London, Bookseller, Pursuer; against Alexander Donaldson and John Wood, Booksellers in Edinburgh, and James Meurose Bookseller in Kilmarnock, Defenders (1774); A Catalogue of Books Printed for Alexander Donaldson Bookseller in Edinburgh; and Sold at His Shop Near Norfolk-street, in the Strand, London, and at Edinburgh (1764); Yamada Shoji, "Pirate" Publishing: The Battle over Perpetual Copyright in Eighteenth-Century Britain 135 (Kyoto: International Center for Japanese Studies, Lynne E. Riggs, trans., 2012).

44. 3 Edward Craig, ed., Routledge Encyclopedia of Philosophy 330 (Taylor & Francis, 1998); Robert Crawford, Scotland's Books: A History of Scottish Literature 364 (Oxford: Oxford University

Press, 2009).

45. Sher, The Enlightenment and the Book, 206, 316, 348, 381–82, 385, 388, 453; Laurel Brake & Marysa Demoor, eds., Dictionary of Nineteenth-Century Journalism 46–47 (Gent: Academia Press, 2009).

46. 1 Ezra Greenspan, ed., Book History 55, 60, 92 (University Park, PA: The Pennsylvania State University Press, 1998).

47. Richardson, A History of Early American Magazines, 237, 243, 253, 256–58 & n.89; William Montgomery Meigs, Life of Josiah Meigs (Philadelphia, 1887).

48. Masur, Rites of Execution, 85; Richardson, A History of Early American Magazines, 237.

49. Green, Mathew Carey, 3–5, 7–9, 27; Earl L. Bradsher, Mathew Carey: Editor, Author and Publisher 1–10 (New York: Columbia University Press, 1912); John R. Vile, The Constitutional Convention of 1787: A Comprehensive Encyclopedia of America's Founding 516 (Santa Barbara, CA: ABC-CLIO, 2005); Peter Okun, Crime and the Nation: Prison Reform and Popular Fiction in Philadelphia, 1786–1800, at 37 (New York: Psychology Press, 2002) ("Benjamin Rush's denunciation of capital punishment, was reprinted in the American Museum and subsequently published in pamphlet form (1792)."); Benjamin Rush, "Address to the People of the United States," The American Museum, Jan. 1787, pp. 8–11; Benjamin Rush, "Plan of a Federal University," The American Museum, Nov. 1788, pp. 442–43; see also Banner, The Death Penalty, 332 nn.24 & 32 (noting Benjamin Rush's authorship of "An Enquiry Into the Justice and Policy of Punishing Murder By Death" and "Rejoinder to a Reply to the Enquiry Into the Justice and Policy of Punishing Murder By Death," both published in The American Museum).

50. Richardson, A History of Early American Magazines, 323–24 & n.242 (noting pamphlets and essays published by Mathew Carey in the American Museum, including "An Enquiry into the Justice and Policy of Punishing Murder by Death" (July 1788) and a reply to Dr. Rush, "Observations on Capital Punishments" (Nov., Dec. 1788)); id. at 324 (noting that "one, who signed himself 'Alfred,' of Baltimore, wished capital punishment limited to convictions of murder"); id. at 359 (noting that "The Politician," in 1789, "argued for the abolition of capital punishment").

51. "To the Patrons of Fine Arts," Philadelphia, Jan. 5, 1787, The Historical Society of Pennsylvania; American Broadsides: Prints and Maps 24 (Philadelphia: Rosenbach Co., 1948).

52. Stanley L. Klos, President Who? Forgotten Founders 8, 220–21 (Carnegie, PA: Estoric.com, 2004); Catalogue of the Loan Exhibition of Historical Portraits and Relics 174 (New York: Committee on Centennial Celebration of the Inauguration of Washington, 1889); 2 Merrill Jensen, ed., The Documentary History of the Ratification of the Constitution 38 (Madison, WI: State Historical Society of Wisconsin, 1978); John K. Alexander, The Selling of the Constitutional Convention: A History of News Coverage 12 (Madison, WI: Madison House Publishers, 1990); 31 Proceedings of the American Antiquarian Society (April 13, 1921–October 19, 1921) 111 (Worcester, MA: American Antiquarian Society, 1922); 11 Samuel Hazard, ed., Pennsylvania Archives 124 (Philadelphia: Joseph Severns & Co., 1855) (reprinting Robert Smith's letter of March 12, 1787 to Hon. Charles Biddle, "V. P. S. Ex. Council"); http://www.baumanrarebooks.com/rare-books/58118.aspx (handbill by Philadelphia printer Robert Smith issued shortly after the U.S. Constitution was publicly announced on September 17, 1787).

53. Robert Morris Skaler, Society Hill and Old City 31 (Charleston, SC: Arcadia Publishing, 2005); Philadelphia: A Guide to the Nation's Birthplace 263 (Harrisburg, PA: The Telegraph Press, 1937); Roger W. Moss, Historic Landmarks of Philadelphia 87 (Philadelphia: University of Pennsylvania Press, 2008); Letter from Samuel R. Wood to Thomas Kittera, Esq. 4–12 (Philadelphia: J. W. Allen, 1831); Blake McKelvey, American Prisons: A History of Good Intentions 1 (Montclair, NJ: Patterson Smith, 1977).

54. 3 Thomas Lynch Montgomery, ed., Pennsylvania Archives, 1018 (Harrisburg, PA: Harrisburg Publishing Co., 1907).

55. Julia A. Stern, The Plight of Feeling: Sympathy and Dissent in the Early American Novel 271 (Chicago: The University of Chicago Press, 1997); James Tyson, Selected Addresses on Subjects Relating to Education, Biography, Travel, Etc. 278 (Philadelphia: P. Blakiston's Son & Co., 1914); Dr. Benjamin Rush, An Account of the Bilious remitting Yellow Fever, as It Appeared in the City of Philadelphia, in the Year 1793, at 29 (Philadelphia: Thomas Dobson, 1794).

56. William Bradford, An Enquiry into How Far the Punishment of Death Is Necessary in Pennsylvania (Philadelphia: T. Dobson, 1793).

57. Elmer James Ferguson & John Catanzariti, eds., The Papers of Robert Morris, 1781–1784, at 47–48 (Pittsburgh, PA: University of Pittsburgh Press, 1975); Colleen McDannell, Material Christianity: Religion and Popular Culture in America 89 (New Haven: Yale University Press, 1998); Sher, The Enlightenment and the Book, 528–29, 713; id. at 530 ("With rare exceptions, such as octavo editions of Beccaria's Essay on Crimes and Punishments and Miscellanies by M. de Voltaire (consisting of

three philosophical tales), which appeared in 1778, Bell limited his Enlightenment publications during the early years of the war to smaller works."); 3 James Burgh, Political Disquisitions; or, An Enquiry into Public Errors, Defects, and Abuses 125–26, 169 (Philadelphia: Robert Bell and William Woodhouse, 1775).

58. 2 Robert A. Gross & Mary Kelley, eds., An Extensive Republic: Print, Culture, and Society in the New Nation, 1790–1840, at 138 (Chapel Hill: The University of North Carolina Press, 2010); Karen Nipps, Lydia Bailey: A Checklist of Her Imprints 2, 4, 17, 41, 261 (University Park, PA: The Pennsylvania State University Press, 2013).

59. 6 The Monthly Review; or, Literary Journal 341 (London: R. Griffiths, 1791).

60. Madeleine B. Stern, Studies in the Franco-American Booktrade during the Late 18th and Early 19th Centuries 38 (London: Pindar Press, 1994); Benjamin Franklin V, Boston Printers, Publishers and Booksellers: 1640–1800, at 377 (Boston: G. K. Hall, 1980); Madeleine B. Stern, Books and Book People in 19th-Century America 68 (New York: R. R. Bowker Co., 1978).

61. 1 The Correspondent: A Selection of Letters from the Best Authors; Together with Some Originals, Adapted to All the Periods and Occasions of Life 83–84 (London: T. Cadell, Jr. & W. Davies, 1796).

62. Hoeflich, Legal Publishing in Antebellum America, 172 & n.5.

63. 2 Reports of Judicial Decisions in the Constitutional Court, of the State of South-Carolina, Held at Charleston and Columbia During the Years 1812, 13, 14, 15, and 16, at 961, 965 (Charleston: W. R. H. Treadway, 1823); A Collection of Cases Decided by the General Court of Virginia, Chiefly Relating to the Penal Laws of the Commonwealth Commencing in the Year 1789, and Ending in 1814, at 338 (Philadelphia: James Webster, 1815); Hoeflich, Legal Publishing in Antebellum America, 37–40; Saul S. Friedman, Jews and the American Slave Trade 115 (New Brunswick, NJ: Transaction Publishers, 2000); Jacob Rader Marcus, United States Jewry, 1776–1985, at 192 (Detroit, MI: Wayne State University Press, 1989).

64. 1 Kemp P. Battle, History of the University of North Carolina: From Its Beginning to the Death of President Swain, 1789–1868, at 72, 80–81, 85 (Raleigh, NC: Edwards & Broughton Printing Co., 1907).

65. 25 The Senator: or, Parliamentary Chronicle Containing an Impartial Register: Recording, with the Utmost Accuracy, the Proceedings and Debates of the Houses of Lords and Commons. Being the Fourth Session in the Eighteenth Parliament of Great-Britain: Held in the Years 1788, 1800, at 853 (London: W. Stratford & H. D. Symonds, 1800).

66. Sarat & Martschukat, Is the Death Penalty Dying?, 177.

67. 4 Alexander Chalmers, The General Biographical Dictionary: Containing an Historical and Critical Account of the Lives and Writings of the Most Eminent Persons in Every Nation 300 (London: J. Nichols and Son, 1812).

68. Manasseh Dawes, An Essay on Crimes and Punishments, with a View of, and Commentary upon Beccaria, Rousseau, Voltaire, Montesquieu, Fielding, and Blackstone iii, 11, 52–53, 63–64, 75, 121, 123, 143, 221 (London: C. Dilly & J. Debrett, 1782). Beccaria's influence on English reformers such as William Eden, Henry Dagge, and Manasseh Dawes is discussed elsewhere. Beirne, "Inventing Criminology," 780 n.6 (citation omitted).

69. Joseph A. Amato, Victims and Values: A History and a Theory of Suffering 88 (Westport, CT: Greenwood Press, 1990); 2 Louis-Sébastien Mercier, Memoirs of the Year Two Thousand Five Hundred 1–11, 170 (Dublin: W. Wilson, trans. W. Hooper, 1772); 1 M. Mercier, Fragments of Politics and History 156–57 (London: H. Murray, 1795).

70. 2 Daniel R. Coquillette & Neil Longley York, eds., Portrait of a Patriot: The Major Political and Legal Papers of Josiah Quincy Junior (The Law Commonplace Book) 68, 185–86, 227 (Boston: Colonial Society of Massachusetts, 2007).

71. 39 Sylvanus Urban, The Gentleman's Magazine, and Historical Chronicle 310 (London: D. Henry & F. Newbery, 1769).

72. Rules of the Carlisle Library Company: with a Catalogue of Books Belonging Thereto 15 (Carlisle, PA: George Kline, 1797) (listing "Beccaria on crimes and punishments"); Robert Gray, Letters during the Course of a Tour Through Germany, Switzerland and Italy, in the Years M.DCC.XCI, and M.DCC.XCII, with Reflections on the Manners, Literature, and Religion of Those Countries 308 (London: F. & C. Rivington, 1794); The Trial of the Rev. Thomas Fyshe Palmer, Before the Circuit Court of Justiciary, Held at Perth, on the 12th and 13th September, 1792, at 43 (Edinburgh: W. Skirving, 1793) ("the greatest constitutional writers that we know of, every book that I have been able to lay my hand upon from Grotius[,] Puffondorf, the Marquis de Beccaria, and downwards, all say that the people have a right to hold speculative opinions, and that they are entitled to use them in any way or manner they please"); 3 Thomas Moore, The Works of Lord Byron: With His Letters and Jour-

nals, and His Life 298–301 (London: John Murray, 1839); George Dyer, The Complaints of the Poor People of England 59 (London, 1793); *see also* George Dyer, The Complaints of the Poor People of England 25 (London: J. Ridgway, 2d ed. 1793) ("Punishment should be adjusted according to the rule laid down by Beccaria, Montesquieu, and since by the very ingenious Mr. David Williams, in a work well deserving the study of the British youth, viz. in proportion to the injury done to society.").

73. An Essay on Crimes and Punishments, Translated from the Italian of Caesar Bonesana, Marquis Beccaria, to Which Is Added, a Commentary, by M. D. Voltaire (Philadelphia: Philip H. Nicklin, 1819); Catalogue of the New-York State Library 23 (Albany, NY: Charles Van Benthuysen, 1850); A Catalogue of the Library of the Department of State of the United States 30 (Washington, DC: United States Dept. of State Library, 1825); 2 Joseph K. Angell, ed., The United States Law Intelligencer and Review 346 (Philadelphia: P. H. Nicklin & T. Johnson, 1830).

74. Catalogue of the Library of the American Philosophical Society, Held at Philadelphia for Promoting Useful Knowledge 141 (Philadelphia: American Philosophical Society, 1824) (listing a 1785 "London" edition of *On Crimes and Punishments*).

75. Thomas C. Upham, A Philosophical and Practice Treatise on the Will 184–85 (1834).

76. "Capital Punishments," The Christian Disciple, Vol. 5, No. 5, pp. 144–47 (Boston: Joseph T. Buckingham, 1817); James Marten, ed., Children and Youth in a New Nation 230 (New York: New York University Press, 2009).

77. Virginia Historical Society, http://vhs4.vahistorical.org/starweb/vhs/servlet.starweb.

78. Hunter Family Papers, 1766–1918, Mss1 H9196 a FA2, Virginia Historical Society, http://www.vahistorical.org/arvfind/hunter.htm; http://www.worthpoint.com/worthopedia/1794-ds-col-rev-war-brother-general-293970957.

79. W. Hamilton Bryson, Essays on Legal Education in 19th Century Virginia 117 (Getzville, NY: William S. Hein & Co., 1998).

80. 3 Thomas Condit Miller & Hu Maxwell, West Virginia and Its People 1235 (New York: Lewis Historical Publishing Co., 1913).

81. Robert Nelson Corwin, ed., Fiftieth Year Record of the Class of Eighty-Seven: Yale College, 1887–1937, at 179 (New Haven: The Class, 1938).

82. E-mail from Scott Pagel, Associate Dean for Information Services, The George Washington University Law School (Jan. 22, 2014) (on file with author).

83. Harcourt, The Illusion of Free Markets, 37, 55; 5 The Popular Encyclopedia; or, "Conversations Lexicon" 61 (Glasgow: Blackie & Son, 1846); Jeremy Bentham, A View of the Hard-Labour Bill: Being an Abstract of a Pamphlet, Intituled, "Draught of a Bill, to Punish by Imprisonment and Hard Labour, Certain Offenders; and to Establish Proper Places for Their Reception": Interspersed with Observations Relative to the Subject of the Above Draught in Particular, and to Penal Jurisprudence in General (1778), *available at* http://oll.libertyfund.org.

84. Michel Foucault, Abnormal: Lectures at the Collège de France 1974–1975, at 28 n.15 (New York: Picador, 2003); Michel Foucault, Discipline & Punish: The Birth of the Prison 9 (New York: Vintage Books, Alan Sheridan, trans., 1995).

85. Jeremy Bentham, The Rationale of Punishment 32 (London: Robert Heward, 1830); Hugo Adam Bedau, Killing as Punishment: Reflections on the Death Penalty in America 78, 81 (Boston: Northeastern University Press, 2004); 3 The New International Encyclopedia 149 (New York: Dodd, Mead & Co., 2d ed. 1918).

86. James v. Commonwealth (Jan. 3, 1825), *reprinted in* 12 Thomas Sergeant & Wm. Rawle, Jr., eds., Reports of Cases Adjudged in the Supreme Court of Pennsylvania 220 (Philadelphia: Thomas Davis, 2d ed. 1846).

87. Jeremy Bentham, The Rationale of Punishment 77–79 (London: Robert Heward, 1830); 3 The New International Encyclopedia 149 (New York: Dodd, Mead & Co., 2d ed. 1918). Under English and early American law, corporal punishments had been commonplace, though certain procedural protections were put in place before corporal punishments could be inflicted. Patrick T. Conley & John Kaminski, ed., The Bill of Rights and the States: The Colonial and Revolutionary Origins of American Liberties 35 (Madison, WI: Madison House, 1992) ("A decree by the General Assembly in 1677 established the principle that in Virginia 'noe law can compell a man to sweare against himselfe in any matter wherein he is lyable to corporall punishments.'"); id. at 107 ("'Cruel and Barbarous' punishments were forbidden by the oft reaffirmed Declaration of Rights of 1650, that did not rule out banishment, pillory, branding, and flogging.").

88. Susan Vandiver Nicassio, Tosca's Rome: The Play and the Opera in Historical Perspective 109 (Chicago, IL: The University of Chicago Press, 2001).

89. Jeremy Bentham, The Rationale of Punishment 168, 178–79, 191–96 (London: Robert Heward, 1830); Bessler, Cruel and Unusual, 49.

90. Jeremy Bentham to Rev. John Forster, Apr./May 1778, *available at* Electronic Enlightenment, Electronic Enlightenment Project, Bodleian Libraries, University of Oxford, www.e-enlightenment.com.

91. Jeremy Black, Fighting for America: The Struggle for Mastery in North America, 1519–1871, at 129 (Bloomington: Indiana University Press, 2011); Emma Christopher, A Merciless Place: The Fate of Britain's Convicts after the American Revolution 81–82 (Oxford: Oxford University Press, 2010); Andrew Jackson O'Shaughnessy, The Men Who Lost America: British Leadership, the American Revolution and the Fate of the Empire 64 (New Haven: Yale University Press, 2013); Richard Borkow, George Washington's Westchester Gamble: The Encampment on the Hudson & the Trapping of Cornwallis 53 (Charleston, SC: The History Press, 2011); Joseph C. Morton, The American Revolution 94–95 (Westport, CT: Greenwood Press, 2003).

92. Jeremy Bentham, An Introduction to the Principles of Morals and Legislation (Oxford: Clarendon Press, 1789).

93. John Stuart Mill, On Liberty 46, 59 (London: John W. Parker and Son, 2d ed. 1859); W. J. Mander, ed., The Oxford Handbook of British Philosophy in the Nineteenth Century 348 (Oxford: Oxford University Press, 2014).

94. Anthony Walsh & Craig Hemmens, Introduction to Criminology: A Text/Reader 27 (Thousand Oaks, CA: SAGE Publications, 2d ed. 2011).

95. 3 The New International Encyclopedia 149 (New York: Dodd, Mead & Co., 2d ed. 1918); Jefferson P. Selth, Firm Heart and Capacious Mind: The Life and Friends of Etienne Dumont 152, 154 (Lanham, MD: University Press of America, 1997); 2 Association of American Law Schools, John MacDonell & Edward Manson, eds., The Continental Legal History Series: Great Jurists of the World 509–10 (Boston: Little, Brown, & Co., 1914); 1 David Levinson, ed., Encyclopedia of Crime and Punishment 513 (Thousand Oaks, CA: Sage Publications, 2002).

96. Jeremy Bentham, The Rationale of Punishment 10 (London: Robert Heward, 1830) (advertisement).

97. Charles Rappleye, Robert Morris: Financier of the American Revolution 78, 240, 278–81 (New York: Simon & Schuster, 2010); 8 Elliot H. Goodwin, The New Cambridge Modern History: The American and French Revolutions, 1763–93, at 430 (Cambridge: Cambridge University Press, 1976); Michael Lee Lanning, The American Revolution 100: The People, Battles, and Events of the American War for Independence, Ranked by Their Significance 165 (Naperville, IL: Sourcebooks, 2008); Bessler, Cruel and Unusual, 91, 110–11.

98. Shackelford, Jefferson's Adoptive Son, 23–26; Shackelford, Thomas Jefferson's Travels in Europe, 20, 29; Ellen Strong Bartlett, "John Trumbull, the Patriot Painter," *in* The Bay State Monthly: An Illustrated Monthly 607 (Boston: Warren F. Kellogg, 1895–1896); William Howard Adams, The Paris Years of Thomas Jefferson 25 (New Haven: Yale University Press, 2000); Bizaredel & Rice, *"Poor in Love Mr. Short,"* 516–17, 520–21, 529; 1 Legal Papers of John Adams cxii (Cambridge: Harvard University Press, 1965); Sanderson Beck, Confederation and a Constitution 1784–89, *available at* http://www.san.beck.org/13-6-Confederation.html.

99. George L. Clark, A History of Connecticut: Its People and Institutions 498 (New York: G. P. Putnam's Sons, 2d ed. 1914); Vernon Louis Parrington, The Connecticut Wits lvi (Hamden, CT: Archon Books, 1966).

100. Robert E. Shalhope, The Roots of Democracy: American Thought and Culture, 1760–1800, at 118 (Lanham, MD: Rowman & Littlefield, 1990); Everett Emerson, ed., American Literature, 1764–1789: The Revolutionary Years 233 (Madison: University of Wisconsin Press, 1977); 1 Kenneth Ray Ball, A Great Society: The Social and Political Thought of Joel Barlow 30, 98 (Madison: University of Wisconsin, 1967) (thesis).

101. John Trumbull, M'Fingal: A Modern Epic Poem, in Four Cantos iii–v, 7, 18, 58, 90 (Boston: Manning & Loring, 1799) (printed for Ebenezer Larkin); http://www.bartleby.com/96/59.html.

102. Cesare Beccaria, An Essay on Crimes and Punishments (London: F. Newbery, 3d ed. 1770) (call number: BEIN 1997 1382); "Memoir of the Late Hon. Christopher Gore, of Waltham, Mass.," *in* 3 Collections of the Massachusetts Historical Society 191–204 (Cambridge: E. W. Metcalf and Co., 1833); Rogers, Murder and the Death Penalty in Massachusetts, 50–52; Ellen Strong Bartlett, "John Trumbull, the Patriot Painter," *in* The Bay State Monthly: An Illustrated Monthly 607–28 (Boston: Warren F. Kellogg, 1895–1896); Conrad Edick Wright, Revolutionary Generation: Harvard Men and the Consequences of Independence 131 (Amherst: University of Massachusetts Press, 2005).

103. Ray Raphael, Founders: The People Who Brought You a Nation 359–60 (New York: The New Press, 2009); Shackelford, Thomas Jefferson's Travels in Europe, 29, 65, 68, 164–65; Frank E. Griz-

zard, Jr., George Washington: A Biographical Companion 310–12 (Santa Barbara, CA: ABC-CLIO, 2002); Catalogue of the Very Important Collection of Studies and Sketches Made by Col. John Trumbull (Sometime Aide-to-Camp to Gen Washington) 34 (1896). In *The Problem of Cain: A Study in the Treatment of Criminals*, a William Trumbull—a lawyer—later quoted Beccaria's adage that "[c]ertainty of punishment is of much greater value than severity." William Trumbull, The Problem of Cain: A Study in the Treatment of Criminals 39 (1890).

104. Donald Sassoon, The Culture of the Europeans: From 1800 to the Present 169 (2006); Dan Edelstein, The Enlightenment: A Genealogy 181 n.43 (2010); Philip Schofield, Catherine Pease-Watkin & Cyprian Blamires, eds., Rights, Representation, and Reform: Nonsense upon Stilts and Other Writings on the French Revolution 59 n.1 (Oxford: Oxford University Press, 2002).

105. 2 Bernard Sarrans, Memoirs of General Lafayette and of the French Revolution of 1830, at 75–76 (London: Richard Bentley, 1832); Wendell Phillips, Speeches, Lectures, and Letters 106 (Boston: Lee and Shepard, 1905); *compare* Dane Archer & Rosemary Gartner, Violence & Crime in Cross-National Perspective 119 (New Haven: Yale University Press, 1984) (quoting Lafayette as follows: "I shall continue to demand the abolition of the death penalty until I have the infallibility of human judgments demonstrated to me."); Clara Elizabeth Fanning, comp., Selected Articles on Capital Punishment 129 (Minneapolis, MN: The H. W. Wilson Co., 1909) (quoting Lafayette as follows: "I shall persist in demanding abolition of the punishment of death, until I have the infallibility of human judgment demonstrated to me.").

106. Beirne, "Inventing Criminology," 780 n.5; Peterson, Thomas Jefferson and the New Nation, 299, 302, 311–12, 314–16, 319–20, 322–23, 326, 334, 371, 373, 381. Morellet also had a close friendship with Benjamin Franklin, with Morellet first meeting Franklin in 1772 at a house party. Isaacson, Benjamin Franklin, 364, 499; Letter from Benjamin Franklin to Abbé André Morellet, Dec. 10, 1788. Franklin, writing from Passy, called Morellet—the translator—"a vary sagacious Man." Letter from Benjamin Franklin to Samuel Cooper, May 15, 1781.

107. Jean Paul de Lagrave, Voltaire's Man in America 32 (Westmount, Canada: Robert Davies Multimedia, 1997); Voltaire, An Essay on Universal History, the Manners, and Spirit of Nations, from the Reign of Charlemaign to the Ages of Lewis XIV, at 130–31 (London: J. Nourse, 2d ed. 1759); Anthony J. Draper, *Cesare Beccaria's Influence on English Discussions of Punishment, 1764–1789*, 26 History of European Ideas 177, 180 n.12, 168–90 (2000).

108. Willard Sterne Randall, Thomas Jefferson: A Life 389, 390–92, 404, 427, 430 (New York: Henry Holt and Co., 1993).

109. Peterson, Thomas Jefferson and the New Nation, 380.

110. Shackelford, Thomas Jefferson's Travels in Europe, 21.

111. Schabas, The Abolition of the Death Penalty in International Law, 5, 10; Michael Dudley, Derrick Silove & Fran Gale, Mental Health and Human Rights: Vision, Praxis, and Courage 60 (2012); *see also* Maestro, Cesare Beccaria and the Origins of Penal Reform, 135 ("One of the most active members of the French assembly in the movement for penal reforms was General Lafayette who some years before had returned to France from America."); id. at 152 (noting that "the Declaration of the Rights of Man" incorporated "several of Beccaria's principles").

112. Jean Brissaud, A History of French Public Law 543 (Washington, DC: Beard Books, 2001).

113. Schabas, The Abolition of the Death Penalty in International Law, 5; Isaacson, Benjamin Franklin, 364.

114. Roger Smith, The Norton History of the Human Sciences 330 (New York: W. W. Norton & Co., 1997); David Williams, ed., The Enlightenment 61 (Cambridge: Cambridge University Press, 1999); John Hostettler, Champions of the Rule of Law 74 (Hampshire, UK: Waterside Press, 2011); Gregory Fremont-Barnes, ed., Encyclopedia of the Age of Political Revolutions and New Ideologies, 1760–1815, at 190 (Westport, CT: Greenwood Press, 2007); Alexander Leslie Klieforth & Robert John Munro, The Scottish Invention of America, Democracy and Human Rights: The History of Liberty and Freedom from the Ancient Celts to the New Millennium 297–98 (Lanham, MD: University Press of America, 2004).

115. Allison Lee Palmer, Historical Dictionary of Neoclassical Art and Architecture 80 (Lanham, MD: Scarecrow Press, 2011).

116. Shackelford, Thomas Jefferson's Travels in Europe, 4, 89.

117. Burnell, Divided Affections, xxiii, 2–4, 162–63, 373, 489; Scharff, The Women Jefferson Loved, 204–208 (discussing Jefferson's relationship with Maria Cosway, who was born in Florence, Italy, and who had been "a child prodigy in music, painting, and languages").

118. Shackelford, Thomas Jefferson's Travels in Europe, 69–70, 73–74.

119. Pace, Luigi Castiglioni's Viaggio, 185–86 & 301 n.9; Jon Kukla, Mr. Jefferson's Women 86 (New York: Vintage Books, 2008).

120. John D. Bessler, Writing for Life: The Craft of Writing for Everyday Living 170 (Minneapolis, MN: Bottlecap Books, 2007).

121. Shackelford, Thomas Jefferson's Travels in Europe, 84.

122. Catalogue of the Library of Congress in the Capitol of the United States of America 348, 427 (Washington, DC: Langtree and O'Sullivan, 1840) (printed for Congress); Ernest Hatch Wilkins, The Invention of the Sonnet and Other Studies in Italian Literature 295–96 (Roma: Edizioni di Storia e Letteratura, 1959).

123. Thomas Jefferson to John Minor, Aug. 30, 1814, including Thomas Jefferson to Bernard Moore [ca. 1773?]; Benjamin Franklin to Giambatista Beccaria, Aug. 11, 1773; Rev. James Madison to James Madison, June 11, 1787; Philip Mazzei to James Madison, Feb. 4, 1788; The Federalist No. 70 [Mar. 15, 1788]; John Adams to Abigail Adams, May 24, 1789; Edward Newenham to George Washington, Mar. 10, 1791; A Course of Reading for Joseph C. Cabell, Sept. 1800; John Adams to Thomas Jefferson, Feb. 3, 1812, *available at* www.founders.archives.gov; Corinne Comstock Weston, English Constitutional Theory and the House of Lords 1556–1832, at 86 (New York: Routledge, 2010).

124. U.S. Const., amends. V & VIII.

125. Jean Louis de Lolme, The Constitution of England: or, An Account of the English Government 169–81 (London: C. G. J. and J. Robinson, new ed. corrected 1789).

126. Thomas Jefferson to Edmund Randolph, Feb. 3, 1794; Thomas Jefferson to John Page, Aug. 30, 1795.

127. Bakewell, How to Live, 3, 61–62, 78, 85–85.

128. Lisa Silverman, Tortured Subjects: Pain, Truth, and the Body in Early Modern France 158, 165 (Chicago: The University of Chicago Press, 2001).

129. Bakewell, How to Live, 178, 190–91, 222–23, 299, 353–54; Montaigne, "Of Cruelty," http://www.readbookonline.net/readOnLine/22099/.

130. Joseph Guerin Fucilla, The Teaching of Italian in the United States: A Documentary History 62 (New York: Arno Press, 1975) ("Jefferson's attachment to things Italian is not only demonstrated by the books he owned and read. He was instrumental in having Charles Bellini appointed first professor of Modern Languages, including Italian, in 1779, at the College of William and Mary."); *see also* id. at 60 ("In the early days of 1764 he seems to have been deep in the study of Italian. On February 4 he bought Baretti's *Italian-English Dictionary*...."); id. at 62 (noting that Jefferson's "first great library" contained "111 Italian titles").

131. Thomas Jefferson to Charles Bellini, Sept. 30, 1785; 3 Gianclaudio Macchiarella, ed., Preserving and Promoting Italian Language and Culture in North America 55 (Lewiston, NY: Soleil Pub., 1997).

132. Marchione, The Fighting Nun, 123; *Charles Bellini, First Professor of Modern Languages in an American College*, 5 Wm. & Mary College Q. Hist. Mag. 1, 1 (1925).

133. Marchione, The Fighting Nun, 63; Hawke, Benjamin Rush, 51.

134. Will & Ariel Durant, Rousseau and Revolution: A History of Civilization in France, England, and Germany from 1756, and in the Remainder of Europe from 1715 to 1789, at 145 (New York: Simon and Schuster, 1967).

135. Thomas Jefferson to John Banister, Jr., June 19, 1787; Thomas Jefferson to John Adams, July 1, 1787, *available at* www.founders.archives.gov; Elizabeth Cometti, ed., Seeing America and Its Great Men: The Journal and Letters of Count Francesco dal Verme, 1783–1784, at xvii (Charlottesville: University Press of Virginia, 1969); Pace, Benjamin Franklin and Italy, 285; Shackelford, Thomas Jefferson's Travels in Europe, 189; Thomas Jefferson's Monticello, Journey through France and Italy (1787), http://www.monticello.org/site/research-and-collections/journey-through-france-and-italy-1787.

136. 39 The Papers of Benjamin Franklin 516–17 (New Haven: Yale University Press, 2009); Elias Boudinot to George Washington, July 8, 1783; George Washington to Jonathan Trumbull, Sr., Aug. 4, 1783; John Langdon to George Washington, Aug. 30, 1783; George Washington to William Fitzhugh, Sept. 24, 1783; George Washington to William Paca, Sept. 24, 1783; John Adams to John Hancock, Apr. 28, 1783, *available at* www.founders.archives.gov.

137. Pace, Luigi Castiglioni's Viaggio, 86, 95–97, 111–13; Stephen A. McLeod, ed., Dining with the Washingtons: Historic Recipes, Entertaining, and Hospitality from Mount Vernon 12 (Chapel Hill: University of North Carolina Press, 2011); Tench Tilghman to George Washington, Dec. 13, 1785, *available at* www.founders.archives.gov.

138. Twelve Years a Slave: Narrative of Solomon Northup: A Citizen of New-York, Kidnapped in Washington City in 1841, and Rescued in 1853, from a Cotton Plantation Near the Red River, in Louisiana 110, 165, 179 (New York: Miller, Orton & Mulligan, 1855).

139. Frank E. Grizzard, Jr. & D. Boyd Smith, Jamestown Colony: A Political, Social, and Cultural History 24–25 (Santa Barbara, CA: ABC-CLIO, 2007); A Guidebook to Virginia's Historical Markers 143 (Charlottesville: University of Virginia Press, 1994); Richard L. Jones, Dinwiddie County, Carrefour of the Commonwealth: A History 236 (Board of Supervisors of Dinwiddie County, 1976); Pace, Luigi Castiglioni's Viaggio, 116; George Washington to Fielding Lewis, Apr. 20, 1773; Plan of Philip Mazzei's Agricultural Company, 1774; George Washington to John Banister, Apr. 21, 1778; Thomas Jefferson to John Banister, Jan. 30, 1781; John Banister to Thomas Jefferson, Feb. 20, 1781; Thomas Jefferson to John Banister, Feb. 24, 1781; Thomas Jefferson to John Banister, Jr., Oct. 15, 1785; Thomas Jefferson to John Banister, Jan. 26, 1786, *available at* www.founders.archives.gov.

140. Pace, Luigi Castiglioni's Viaggio, 145, 147, 149, 158, 165, 194–95, 213, 225, 227; Juliani, Building Little Italy, 13.

141. Juliani, Building Little Italy, 3, 5–7, 13, 28–30; Lawrence Lewis, Jr., A Memoir of Edward Shippen, Chief Justice of Pennsylvania: Together with Selections from His Correspondence (Philadelphia: Collins, 1883).

142. 16 Herbert B. Adams, ed., John Hopkins University Studies in Historical and Political Science 11, 15, 17 (Baltimore: The Johns Hopkins Press, 1897); 1 Henry S. Randall, The Life of Thomas Jefferson 472–73 (New York: Derby & Jackson, 1858); Marco Beretta & Alessandro Tosi, Linnaeus in Italy: The Spread of a Revolution in Science 164–66 (Canton, MA: Science History Publications/USA 2007); The William Howard Adams, Paris Years of Thomas Jefferson 113–14 (New Haven: Yale University Press, 2000); Shackelford, Thomas Jefferson's Travels in Europe, xxxiv, 75, 89–90, 95–97, 101; John B. Boles, ed., America: The Middle Period; Essays in Honor of Bernard Mayo 27 (Charlottesville: University Press of Virginia, 1973); Lawrence S. Kaplan, Thomas Jefferson: Westward the Course of Empire 56 (Wilmington, DE: Scholarly Resources, 1999); Shackelford, Jefferson's Adoptive Son, 5, 31, 34–36, 95, 97–98, 114.

143. Brian W. Dotts, The Political Education of Democratus: Negotiating Civic Virtue during the Early Republic 191 (Lanham, MD: Lexington Books, 2012).

144. Edmund Jennings Lee, ed., Lee of Virginia 1642–1892: Biographical and Genealogical Sketches of the Descendants of Colonel Richard Lee 194–95 (Westminster, MD: Heritage Books, 2008); Thomas Jefferson to Francis dal Verme and Others, July 13, 1788; Gaudenzio Clerici to Thomas Jefferson, July 14, 1787; Thomas Jefferson to Gaudenzio Clerici, *available at* www.founders.archives.gov.

145. Shackelford, Jefferson's Adoptive Son, 35–39; William Short to Thomas Jefferson, Oct. 28, 1788; *John Rutledge, Jr. (1766–1819)*, Biographical Directory of the United States Congress, http://bioguide.congress.gov/scripts/biodisplay.pl?index=R000553.

146. Robert K. Ratzlaff, John Rutledge, Jr.: South Carolina Federalist, 1766–1819, at 36, 41, 54, 62, 223 (New York: Arno Press, 1982); Pier Francesco Asso, ed., From Economists to Economists: The International Spread of Italian Economic Thought, 1750–1950, at 308 (Florence, Italy: Polistampa, 2001); Elizabeth Cometti, ed., Seeing America and Its Great Men: The Journal and Letters of Count Francesco dal Verme, 1783–1784, at xix (Charlottesville: University of Virginia Press, 1969); Bizardel & Rice, *"Poor in Love Mr. Short,"* 527–31.

147. Shackelford, Thomas Jefferson's Travels in Europe, 28–29.

148. Paul R. Baker, The Fortunate Pilgrims: Americans in Italy, 1800–1860, at 17 (Cambridge: Harvard University Press, 1964); Journal of Dr. John Morgan of Philadelphia from the City of Rome to the City of London 1764, at 20–26, 28, 31–32, 43–44, 131–32, 151, 219–29 (Philadelphia: J. B. Lippincott Co., 1907); Pace, Benjamin Franklin and Italy, 69.

149. Brands, The First American, 325, 444–45; Giambatista Beccaria to Benjamin Franklin, May 20, 1771; *see also* 1 Jared Sparks, The Works of Benjamin Franklin 234 (Boston: Hillard, Gray, rev. ed. 1840) (noting that "Beccaria, the celebrated Italian electrician," who had corresponded with Benjamin Franklin before he left America for England, "sent to him a long communication, containing an account of some new experiments in electricity illustrative of the Franklinian hypothesis").

150. I. Bernard Cohen, Benjamin Franklin's Science 9, 107, 138, 216 n.35, 241 n.125 (Cambridge: Harvard University Press, 1996).

151. Benjamin Franklin, Experiments and Observations on Electricity, Made at Philadelphia in America 161, 409, 415 (London: David Henry, 1769) (listed on the title page as "sold by FRANCIS NEWBERY, at the Corner of St. Paul's Church-Yard"); Joseph Priestley, The History and Present State of Electricity with Original Experiments xxvii, xxx, 7, 51, 140, 187, 193–94, 196–98, 201–202, 206, 245 (London: J. Dodsley, et al., 2d ed., 1769).

152. 2 Joseph Priestley, Experiments and Observations on Different Kinds of Air vi, x, xvii–xviii (London: J. Johnson, 2d ed., 1776); Joseph Priestley, Observations on Respiration and the Use of the Blood 12, 17 (London, 1776).

153. *See, e.g.*, The Private Life of the Late Benjamin Franklin, LL.D. 184–85 (London: J. Parsons, 1793) ("The most illustrious foreigners have testified their admiration of his philosophic labours. Beccaria, so celebrated for his Essay on 'Crimes and Punishments,' to his curious treatise, intitled, 'Elettrico Artificiale,' has prefixed a complimentary letter to Dr. Franklin, in which he considers him as 'the father of electricity,' and speaks of his discoveries with enthusiasm.").

154. Pace, Benjamin Franklin and Italy, 1, 7–9, 20–22, 50, 53–55, 66, 125–26, 132, 275; Charles Toth, Liberté, Egalité, Fraternité: The American Revolution and the European Response 104 (Troy, NY: Whitston Publishing Co., 1989); Gioanni de Bernardi to Benjamin Franklin with Franklin's Note for a Reply: Résumé, Mar. 20, 1779, *available at* www.founders.archives.gov.

155. Ferrone, The Politics of Enlightenment, 10, 50, 57, 80, 120, 203.

156. Geerdt Magiels, From Sunlight to Insight: Jan IngenHousz, the Discovery of Photosynthesis and Science in the Light of Ecology 17–19, 28, 32, 117, 136 (Brussels: VUBPRESS, 2010); 12 The Encyclopædia Britannica, or Dictionary of Arts, Sciences, and General Literature 380–81 (Edinburgh: Adam & Charles Black, 8th ed. 1856).

157. Benjamin Franklin to Philip Mazzei, Dec. 27, 1775; Pace, Benjamin Franklin and Italy, 4; Declaration of the Causes and Necessity of Taking up Arms, July 6, 1775, http://www.nationalcenter.org/1775DeclarationofArms.html.

158. Giuliano Pancaldi, Volta: Science and Culture in the Age of Enlightenment 93 (Princeton: Princeton University Press, 2005); Margherita Marchione, ed. & S. Eugene Scalia, trans., Philip Mazzei: My Life and Wanderings 222 (American Institute of Italian Studies, 1980); Pace, Benjamin Franklin and Italy, 4.

159. Alexander DeConde, Half Bitter, Half Sweet: An Excursion into Italian American History 18–19, 21–22 (New York: Scribner, 1971); 2 Richard C. Cole, ed., The General Correspondence of James Boswell, 1766–1769, at 73–74 (New Haven: Yale University Press, 1997); Elisabeth A. Roark, Artists of Colonial America 177 (Westport, CT: Greenwood Press, 2003); A Journal of Samuel Powel (Rome, 1764) 25 (Studio per Edizioni, 2001); Julie Aronson & Marjorie E. Wieseman, Perfect Likeness: European and American Portrait Miniatures from the Cincinnati Art Museum 98 (New Haven: Yale University Press, 2006); Glenn Weaver, The Italian Presence in Colonial Virginia 57 (Center for Migration Studies, 1998); In Pursuit of Refinement: Charlestonians Abroad, 1740–1860, at 29 (Columbia: University of South Carolina Press, 1999); Maurie Dee McInnis, Henry Benbridge, 1743–1812: Charleston Portrait Painter 7 (Charleston, SC: Gibbes Museum of Art, 2000); www.amphilsoc.org; "Cultural Relations Between Italy and the American Colonies," Center for Migration Studies, Vol. 16, pp. 143–46 (July 2000), *available at* http://onlinelibrary.wiley.com/doi/10.1111/j.2050-411X.2000.tb00282.x/abstract.

160. Howard R. Marraro, *Italo-Americans in Pennsylvania in the Eighteenth Century*, 7 Pennsylvania History 159, 160 (1940); Adolph Caso, ed., Alfieri's Ode to America's Independence 9–15 (Boston: Branden Press, 1976); Courtland L. Bovée, Contemporary Public Speaking 156 (San Diego, CA: Collegiate Press, 2d ed. 2003).

161. Bolt, The Librettist of Venice, 61–63, 128, 225, 269; Ernest Hatch Wilkins, The Invention of the Sonnet and Other Studies in Italian Literature 304 (Roma: Edizioni di Storia e Letteratura, 1959); Sheila Hodges, Lorenzo Da Ponte: The Life and Times of Mozart's Librettist ix–x, 168 (Madison: University of Wisconsin Press, 2002); 2 Libretti Londinesi: Lorenzo Da Ponte 974 (Il Polifilo, 2007); Pierpaolo Polzonetti, Italian Opera in the Age of the American Revolution (Cambridge: Cambridge University Press, 2011); Maurice Lever, Beaumarchais: A Biography xiii, 74, 109, 116, 127, 273 (New York: Farrar, Straus and Giroux, 2004); 1 Elizabeth S. Kite, Beaumarchais and the War of American Independence 35, 37 (Boston: The Gorham Press, 1918); Luciano Mangiafico, Italy's Most Wanted: The Top 10 Book of Roman Ruins, Wonderful Wines, and Renaissance Rarities (Washington, DC: Potomac Books, 2007); Abigail Adams to Lucy Cranch, Jan. 5, 1785; Larry Wolff, Paolina's Innocence: Child Abuse in Casanova's Venice 27–28 (Stanford: Stanford University Press, 2012). Item "1511" of a 1796 Lackington, Allen & Co. catalogue lists a 1775 edition of "Beccaria on Crimes and Punishments" as "*scarce*, 3s." 1 Lackington, Allen, & Co.'s Catalogue 46 (1796).

162. Thomas Katheder, The Baylors of Newmarket: The Decline and Fall of a Virginia Planter Family 99 (Bloomington, IN: iUniverse, 2009); William M. Thayer, From Boyhood to Manhood: The Life of Benjamin Franklin 435–36 (New York: Hurst & Company, 1889); Kevin J. Hayes, The Road to Monticello: The Life and Mind of Thomas Jefferson 34–35, 39, 105 (Oxford: Oxford University Press, 2008); Lynn Hudson Parsons, John Quincy Adams 13–14 (Lanham, MD: Rowman & Littlefield Publishers, 2001); Debbie Levy, James Monroe 40 (Minneapolis, MN: Lerner Publications Co., 2005); Alyn Brodsky, Benjamin Rush: Patriot and Physician 51 (New York: St. Martin's Press, 2004).

163. Thomas, On Crimes and Punishments, xv, xxviii.

164. Thomas J. Schaeper, The Life of Jacques-Donatien Leray de Chaumont, 1725–1803, at 39–40 (New York: Berghahn Books, 2007).

165. Hartnett, Executing Democracy, intro.

166. Historical Handbook and Guide to Oxford 270 (Oxford, UK: Shrimpton & Son, 1878); James M. O'Toole & David Quigley, eds., Boston's Histories: Essays in Honor of Thomas H. O'Connor 33 n.2 (Boston: Northeastern University Press, 2004); 1 Legal Papers of John Adams lii (Cambridge: Harvard University Press, 1965).

167. Thomas A. Foster, Sex and the Eighteenth-Century Man: Massachusetts and the History of Sexuality in America 148 (Boston, MA: Beacon Press, 2006); *see also* Patricia Bradley, Slavery, Propaganda, and the American Revolution 19 (Jackson: University of Mississippi Press, 1998) (discussing the issue of rape, race and the death penalty in Massachusetts).

168. Register and North Carolina Gazette (Raleigh, NC), Nov. 11, 1830.

169. Hartnett, Executing Democracy, intro.; 11 American Antiquarian Society, Proceedings of the American Antiquarian Society 6–7 (Worcester, MA: American Antiquarian Society, 1898).

170. Countess of Elizabeth Chudleigh Bristol, The Laws Respecting Women 301–302, 306 (London: J. Johnson., 1777). *The Laws Respecting Women* also quoted from *On Crimes and Punishments*. Id. at vii, n. *d*.

171. Maestro, *Benjamin Franklin and the Penal Laws*, 551; "The Speech of Miss Polly Baker," The General Advertiser, Apr. 15, 1747, *available at* Benjamin Franklin Papers, www.franklinpapers. org.

172. "A Narrative of the Late Massacres," Jan. 1764, *available at* Benjamin Franklin Papers, www. franklinpapers.org; Maestro, *Benjamin Franklin and the Penal Laws*, 552–53.

173. Moir, Capital Punishment, 30–31; Bessler, Cruel and Unusual, 42, 48; Simon Harvey, ed., Voltaire, Treatise on Tolerance and Other Writings 119–21 (Cambridge: Cambridge University Press, 2000); Lisa Silverman, Tortured Subjects: Pain, Truth, and the Body in Early Modern France 157–59, 165 (Chicago: The University of Chicago Press, 2001); Alexander J. Nemeth, Voltaire's Tormented Soul: A Psychobiographic Inquiry 179 (Cranbury, NJ: Associated University Presses, 2008); Travis C. Pratt, Travis W. Franklin & Jacinta M. Gau, Key Ideas in Criminology and Criminal Justice 8 (Thousand Oaks, CA: SAGE Publications, 2011).

174. Maestro, *Benjamin Franklin and the Penal Laws*, 554; Benjamin Franklin to Samuel Cooper, Apr. 14, 1770; Benjamin Franklin to Henry Bouquet, Sept. 30, 1764; *see also* Edwin Wolf II & Kevin J. Hayes, The Library of Benjamin Franklin 816 (entry 3537) (Philadelphia: American Philosophical Society/Library Company of Philadelphia, 2006).

175. Joe Walker Kraus, Book Collections of Five Colonial College Libraries: A Subject Analysis, Ph.D. dissertation, University of Illinois 217 (1960) ("On criminal law the library possessed writings of … Beccaria"); Hoeflich, Legal Publishing in Antebellum America, 119–20 (in the context of an 1848 auction of a deceased judge's library, noting that the judge, "[l]ike many of his contemporaries," "owned a copy of a translation of Beccaria's work on criminal law, attesting to the importance of this Italian jurist's influence on the development of American criminal law and penology"); Catalogue of the Books Belonging to the Loganian Library 78 (Philadelphia: C. Sherman and Co., 1837) (listing a 1778 edition of Beccaria's treatise); Catalogue of the Books Belonging to the Mercantile Library Company of Philadelphia 17 (Philadelphia: Mercantile Library Company of Philadelphia, 1840) (listing an 1819 edition of Beccaria's treatise). In its 1828 catalogue, the Mercantile Library of Philadelphia also reported owning a copy of *On Crimes and Punishments*. Mercantile Library of Philadelphia, Catalogue of the Mercantile Library of Philadelphia 9 (Philadelphia: I. Ashmead & Co., 1828).

176. *E.g.*, A Catalogue of Several Valuable Collections of Books, Lately Purchased; including the Libraries of John Parsons, Esq., and The Rev. Mr. Thompson, M.A., Lately Deceased 126, 257 (London, 1782) (listing books to be sold "By Robert Faulder, Bookseller"); Catalogue of Books in the Library of Robert Ferguson of Raith, Esquire 19 (1817) (listing a 1780 edition of "Delitti e delle Pene" under the topic of "international law"); Cesare Beccaria, An Essay on Crimes and Punishments (new ed. corrected 1778) (printed for Alexander Donaldson and sold at his shops in London and Edinburgh); Cesare Beccaria, An Essay on Crimes and Punishments (new ed. 1778) (printed by Bell & Murray in Edinburgh for W. Gordon and W. Creech); Cesare Beccaria, An Essay on Crimes and Punishments (new ed. 1788) (printed by James Donaldson in Edinburgh); Cesare Beccaria, An Essay on Crimes and Punishments (1801) (printed in London by E. Hodson for J. Bone); Cesare Beccaria, Essay on Crimes and Punishments (5th ed. rev. & corrected 1804) (printed in London for H. D. Symonds); Cesare Beccaria, An Essay on Crimes and Punishments (1807) (printed in Edinburgh for Bell & Bradfute).

177. David W. Robson, Educating Republicans: The College in the Era of the American Revolution 73 (Westport, CT: Greenwood Press, 1985) (listing "Beccaria" among the holdings of the Har-

vard Library in 1773); Joe W. Kraus, The Harvard Undergraduate Library of 1773, College and Research Libraries 247, 252 (July 1961) (noting that Harvard's 1773 library contained "Cesare Beccaria's Dei delitti e delle pene," among other works).

178. Brown & Brown, The Hanging of Ephraim Wheeler, 196–97 & 339 n.23; *accord* Catalogue of Books in the Library of Williams College, Williamstown 33 (1821) (listing Beccaria's treatise).

179. Cornell, A Well-Regulated Militia, 225 n.19.

180. Catalogue of Books in the Second Social Library, Deerfield: With the Bye Laws of the Company; and the Rules and Regulations Under Which Books Are Loaned from the Library 2 (Walpole, NH: Thomas & Thomas/D. Newhall, 1803) (listing Beccaria's treatise); George Burrell, A Catalogue of the Library of the Athenaeum, Liverpool 350 (Liverpool: Harris and Co., 1820) (listing a 1766 edition of *Dei delitti e delle pene*); Catalogue of Books Belonging to the Dialectic Society, Chapel-Hill, February, 1821, at 9 (Hillsborough, NC: D. Heartt, 1821) (listing Beccaria's treatise); 1 Documents of the Senate of the State of New-York 6 (Albany: E. Croswell, 1831) (listing "Beccaria on Crimes" in a "Catalogue of Books" belonging to "the State Library"); Catalogue of Books in the Portsmouth Athenaeum 24 (Portsmouth, NH: Charles W. Brewster, 1849) (listing a 1793 edition of Beccaria's treatise); Alphabetical Catalogue of the Library of Congress 92–93 (1864) (listing an 1829 edition of *Dei delitti e delle pene*, an 1856 edition of *Des Délits et des Peines*, and a 1785 edition of *On Crimes and Punishments*).

181. A Catalogue of the Books Belonging to the Charleston Library Society 62 (Charleston: A. E. Miller, 1826) (entries 811 and 812).

182. "All Matters and Things Shall Center There": A Study of Elite Political Power in South Carolina, 1763–1776, Ph.D. dissertation, Georgetown University, Faculty of the Graduate School of Arts and Sciences (Oct. 19, 2009), p. 41.

183. The South Carolina Historical Magazine, Vols. 76–77, p. 71 (1975).

184. New Select Catalogue of Benjamin Guild's Circulating Library, Containing Principally Novels, Voyages, Travels, Poetry, Periodical Publications, and Books of Entertainment at the Boston Book-Store, No. 59, Cornhill 6 (Boston: Benjamin Guild, 1789); C. K. Bolton, Proprietary and Subscription Libraries, p. 2, *located in* William Bishop, Library of Congress (American Library Association Publishing Board, 1911); John Quincy Adams to John Adams, May 17, 1781 & John Thaxter to Abigail Adams, July 21, 1781, *in* 4 L. H. Butterfield & Marc Friedlaender, eds., The Adams Papers: Adams Family Correspondence 116, 460 (Cambridge: The Belknap Press of Harvard University Press, 1973); Voltaire in America, 1744–1800, p. 38; Mary Smith Cranch to Abigail Adams, May 15, 1790, *in* 9 Margaret A. Hogan, et al., eds., The Adams Papers: Adams Family Correspondence 60, 76 (Cambridge: The Belknap Press of Harvard University Press, 2009); Abigail Adams to John Adams, Apr. 15, 1780, *available at* www.masshist.org (noting Benjamin Guild's background in footnote 1). The Grand Duke of Tuscany, Benjamin Guild learned from Dr. Thomas Bond of the American Philosophical Society on a 1779 trip to Philadelphia, had offered the society anything "that Italy could afford." Manuel & Manuel, James Bowdoin and the Patriot Philosophers, 27.

185. Catalogue of Books in the Library of Yale College 69 (New Haven: Oliver Steele & Co., 1808); Catalogue of Books in the Boston Atheneum 28 (Boston: William L. Lewis, 1827).

186. A. London Fell, Origins of Legislative Sovereignty and the Legislative State 63, 85, 247 (Westport, CT: Greenwood Press, 1983).

187. http://orbis.library.yale.edu; http://hollis.harvard.edu.

188. American Antiquarian Society, http://catalog.mwa.org/vwebv/holdingsInfo?searchId=3704&recCount=10&recPointer=12&bibId=472639 (catalog entry).

189. White Knights Library: Catalogue of that Distinguished and Celebrated Library 7 (Pall-Mall: Mr. Evans, 1819) (listing a 1780 edition of Beccaria's treatise among books to be sold at auction by "Mr. Evans" at his house); Catalogue of the Library of David Constable, Esq. Advocate 9 (Edinburgh: D. Speare, 1828) (listing books to be sold by auction, including "Beccaria on Crimes and Punishments," by "D. Speare, at His Sale Rooms, No. 80, Prince's Street").

190. James Vallance, A Catalogue of the Library of the Late Right Honourable Denis Daly 5 (Dublin: John Archer, 1792); A Catalogue of the Library of Richard Wright, M.D. 84 (Scotland Yard: T. and J. Egerton, 1787); A Catalogue of the Greater Portion of the Library of the Late Edmond Malone, Esq. 4 (London: Wright and Murphy, 1818); A Catalogue of the Library of George Hibbert, Esq. of Portland Place 38 (London: W. Nicol, 1829).

191. Hoeflich, *Translation & the Reception of Foreign Law*, 771.

192. Pace, Luigi Castiglioni's Viaggio, xii.

193. Davis, *The Movement to Abolish Capital Punishment in America*, 26.

194. Abigail Adams to Abigail Adams Smith, Feb. 10, 1793, *available at* www.founders.archives.gov.

195. Bessler, Cruel and Unusual, 54, 86, 86–90; id., ch. 3, e-note 36.

196. Pace, Luigi Castiglioni's Viaggio, xi, xl; Anthony J. Pansini, The Federalist, Continued xxi, xxxii–xxxiii (1995); Meskell, *The History of Prisons in the United States from 1777 to 1877*, 844; Henry Reeve, trans., Alexis de Tocqueville, Democracy in America (New York: George Dearborn & Co., 1838). One source was located indicating that Giovanni Francesco Cigna, an eminent Italian physician and anatomist, born in Mondovi in 1734, was "a nephew of Beccaria the jurist." Cigna—elsewhere described as the nephew of the Italian chemist "Gianbatista Cesare Beccaria"—became a professor of anatomy at Turin and published treatises on electricity and respiration before dying in 1790. 1 Joseph Thomas, Universal Pronouncing Dictionary of Biography and Mythology 650 (1915); Joe Jackson, A World on Fire: A Heretic, An Aristocrat, and the Race to Discover Oxygen (2007). Cigna—a student of Giambatista Beccaria who experimented with the "rubbing of ribbons" and "the electricity of glasses"—is referenced in a 1766 letter from Giambatista Beccaria to Benjamin Franklin. Giambatista Beccaria to Benjamin Franklin, Oct. 11, 1766, *available at* http://franklinpapers.org/ franklin/framedVolumes.jsp?tocvol=40. Franklin himself exchanged letters on one occasion with Cigna, also known as Gian Francesco Cigna. *See* Gian Francesco Cigna to Benjamin Franklin, "28 juilliet 1783" & Benjamin Franklin to Gian Francesco Cigna, July 5, 1785, *available at* http://franklin papers.org/franklin/framedVolumes.jsp?tocvol=40. Other information indicates that Beccaria's grandson, Alessandro Manzoni (the child of Cesare Beccaria's daughter Giulia, who preferred to sign his name "Alessandro Manzoni Beccaria"), had an uncle, Giulio Beccaria. Mary Vance Young, "Alessandro Manzoni-Beccaria, Romanticist," *in* 13 The Romanic Review 337 n.22, 352 & n.83, 353 n.85 (1922); Newman & Marongiu, On Crimes and Punishments, lxvii; Federica-Brunori Deigan, trans., Alessandro Manzoni's *The Count of Carmagnola* and *Adelchis* 1 (Baltimore, MD: The Johns Hopkins University Press, 2004).

197. Pace, Luigi Castiglioni's Viaggio, xvi–xviii.

198. Pace, Benjamin Franklin and Italy, 26, 35; Belfiglio, *Italian Culture in Eighteenth-Century Philadelphia*, 76.

199. Pace, Luigi Castiglioni's Viaggio, xi, 64, 218–19, 225, 227.

200. Voltaire, Letters Concerning the English Nation (London: J. and R. Tonson, et al., 1778).

201. Tamasak Wicharaya, Simple Theory, Hard Reality: The Impact of Sentencing Reforms on Courts, Prisons, and Crime 26 (Albany: State University of New York Press, 1995); Jeffy R. Self, America's God and Its Founding Fathers 13 (New York: Vantage Press, 2008).

202. Buckner F. Melton, Jr., The Quotable Founding Fathers: A Treasury of 2,500 Wise and Witty Quotations from the Men and Women Who Created America 48–49 (Washington, DC: Brassey's, Inc., 2004).

203. Schiavo, The Italians in America Before the Civil War, 32 ("Very little is known of Castiglioni, who was a member of a noble family of Milan, Italy, where he was born in 1757 and where he spent most of his life."); *compare* Howard R. Marraro, *Count Luigi Castiglioni: An Early Italian Traveller to Virginia (1785–1786)*, 58 Va. Mag. of History & Biography 473, 473 (1950) ("Very little is known of the life of Count Castiglioni. Born in Milan in 1756, of an old and distinguished noble family, Count Castiglioni early in life showed a keen interest in the natural sciences, particularly in botany…").

204. Loretta Innocenti, Franco Marucci & Paola Pugliatti, eds., Semeia: Itinerari per Marcello Pagnini 270 (1994) ("the Verris were Castiglioni's uncles, and Pietro his brother-in-law").

205. Buccini, The Americas in Italian Literature and Culture, 2, 149; Pace, Luigi Castiglioni's Viaggio, xii–xviii, xxiv, 5, 112, 230–31, 286 n.6.

206. 1 Jeremy Belknap, The History of New-Hampshire 47–48, 52, 68 (Dover: S. C. Stevens and Ela & Wadleigh, 1831); Manasseh Culter to Jeremy Belknap, June 29, 1785, *reprinted in* 4 Collections of the Massachusetts Historical Society 297–301 (Boston: Massachusetts Historical Society, 1891).

207. William Willis, ed., Journals of the Rev. Thomas Smith, and the Rev. Samuel Deane, Pastors of the First Church in Portland: With Notes and Biographical Notices 254, 256 (Portland: Joseph S. Bailey, 1849). The Rev. Samuel Deane also recorded these entries for July 8 and July 29, 1785, respectively: "I walked with Count Castiglioni." "Count Castiglioni set out westward. Gov. Hancock arrived." Id. at 358.

208. A. J. Morrison, ed., Travels in Virginia in Revolutionary Times 61 (Lynchburg, Va.: J. P. Bell Co., 1922); *see also* George Washington Diary Entry, Dec. 25, 1785, *available at* www.founders.archives. gov ("Count Castiglioni, Colo. Ball, and Mr. Willm. Hunter came here to dinner.").

209. Dexter, The Literary Diary of Ezra Stiles, 236.

210. 1 Emily Ellsworth Fowler Ford, comp. & Emily Ellsworth Ford Skeel, ed., Notes on the Life of Noah Webster 145, 212 (New York: Privately Printed, 1912).

211. *See* Pace, Luigi Castiglioni's Viaggio, xxxix–xl n.64:

> While I have not had the opportunity to verify the relations of the Beccaria and Castiglioni families, such a union of nobility and wealth is by no means outside the bounds of either possibility or probability, given the mores and socioeconomic imperatives of the Milanese patriciate. It is noteworthy in this connection that William Bradford, presenting Luigi Castiglioni with a copy of a recent American translation of Beccaria's masterpiece, called it "a new proof of the veneration that my fellow citizens entertain for the sentiments *of your relative.*"

212. *Id.* at xxiv (undated note). *But compare* id. at xxiv–xxv (Antonio Pace's "General Introduction"). Antonio Pace says this of the undated note:

> The inaccuracies and exaggerations in Vaughan's memorandum could be owing to misunderstanding on his part. More likely, they are a byproduct of Castiglioni's strategy for winning concessions. In the first place, Luigi was not a count—at least not until Napoleon so dubbed him in 1810.... The title of count was borne properly for the family by Luigi's elder brother Alfonso, upon whom it had been conferred by Maria Theresa in 1774. One must conclude that Castiglioni found it expedient to usurp his brother's title as a social lubricant during his travels, for which purpose it clearly served him well.
>
> ....
>
> On the other hand, Vaughan's assertion that Castiglioni was "related to Father Beccaria" can be plausibly explained as owing to a mutual misunderstanding. One imagines that Vaughan was the first to bring up the name of Beccaria in some allusion to the Piedmontese professor of physics Giambatista Beccaria, who would have been known to him through the polemic of some years earlier over Franklin's electrical theories. Castiglioni, on his part, hearing the same surname, would presumably have associated it at once with his own countryman, the famous penologist Cesare Beccaria.

Id. at xxiv–xxv.

213. Id. at xxxii (noting Castiglioni "spent four days with Washington at Mount Vernon" and inferring that "Castiglioni met in person and associated more or less intimately with such notables as John Adams, Samuel Adams, John Hancock, Robert Morris, Charles Thomson, Nathanael Greene, Henry Knox, and Benjamin Lincoln"); 3 The Encyclopædia Britannica: A Dictionary of the Arts, Sciences, Literature and General Information 602 (Cambridge, England: Cambridge University Press, 11th ed. 1910).

214. Pace, Luigi Castiglioni's Viaggio, 185.

215. William Short correspondence, 1787–1838 (Mss.B.Sh83), http://www.amphilsoc.org/mole/view?docId=ead/Mss.B.Sh83-ead.xml.

216. 2 Memoirs of the American Academy of Arts and Sciences 162–65 (Boston: Isaiah Thomas & Ebenezer T. Andrews, 1793); Robert A. Silverman, Terence P. Thornberry, Bernard Cohen & Barry Krisberg, eds., Crime and Justice at the Millennium: Essays by and in Honor of Marvin E. Wolfgang 392 (New York: Springer, 2002).

217. 1 Transactions of the American Philosophical Society, Held at Philadelphia, for Promoting Useful Knowledge ix, xiii (2d ed. corrected 1789); Martin P. Snyder, City of Independence: Views of Philadelphia Before 1800, at 166 (New York: Praeger Publishers, 1975); 1 Whitfield J. Bell, Jr., Patriot-Improvers: Biographical Sketches of Members of the American Philosophical Society, 1743–1768, at 28–29 (Philadelphia: American Philosophical Society, 1997); Juliani, Building Little Italy, 13–14; 90 American Philosophical Society, Proceedings of the American Philosophical Society Held at Philadelphia for Promoting Useful Knowledge 395 (Philadelphia: American Philosophical Society, 1946); *see also* id. at 392, 395–96 ("The summer of 1786 found Castiglioni back in Philadelphia for a protracted stay, and all signs indicate that he came to know intimately many of the resident members of the American Philosophical Society.").

218. Thomas Dionysius Clark, Travels in the Old South: The Expanding South, 1750–1825, at 93 (Norman: University of Oklahoma Press, 1969).

219. Meskell, *The History of Prisons in the United States from 1777 to 1877*, 844.

220. Bessler, Cruel and Unusual, 85–91; *see also* 10 Samuel Hazard, ed., Hazard's Register of Pennsylvania 118 (1833) (reprinting Bradford's remark about Beccaria).

221. Rogers, Murder and the Death Penalty in Massachusetts, 414 n.65; Harris, Executing Race, 66.

222. Pace, Luigi Castiglioni's Viaggio, xl, 313–14; Jack D. Marietta & G. S. Rowe, Troubled Experiment: Crime and Justice in Pennsylvania, 1682–1800, at 211–12 (Philadelphia: University of Pennsylvania Press, 2006).

223. Desmond Gregory, Napoleon's Italy 21 (Cranbury, NJ: Associated University Presses, 2001); *see also* Thomas Sadler, ed., Diary, Reminiscences, and Correspondence of Henry Crabb Robinson,

Barrister-at-Law 133 (Boston: Houghton, Mifflin and Co., 1898) (noting in a July 22, 1830 diary entry: "Beccaria and Filangieri are their prime writers, economists as well as philanthropists.").

224. Ferrone, The Politics of Enlightenment, 13–14.

225. Pace, Benjamin Franklin and Italy, 141, 156; Gustavo Costa, Book Review, 11 Eighteenth-Century Studies 380, 381 (Spring 1978) (reviewing Marcello Maestro, Gaetano Filangieri and His "Science of Legislation"); Samuel Paterson to Alexander Hamilton, Feb. 16, 1793 ("I have Sent you … a Translation on Legislation from the Italian of Filangieri"), *available at* www.founders.archives.gov.

226. Pace, Benjamin Franklin and Italy, 147–48, 151–54; Maestro, *Benjamin Franklin and the Penal Laws*, 557.

227. Marcello T. Maestro, Gaetano Filangieri and His Science of Legislation 31, 42 (Philadelphia: American Philosophical Society, 1976); Maestro, *Benjamin Franklin and the Penal Laws*, 551.

228. Johann Wolfgang von Goethe, Italian Journey, 1786–1788, at 191–92 (London: Penguin Books, 1970); *see also* id. at 192 (Goethe adds in his March 5, 1787 entry of the time he spent with Filangieri: "Soon after we met, he introduced me to the work of an older writer, whose profound wisdom is so refreshing and edifying to all Italians of this generation who are friends of justice. His name is Giambattista Vico, and they rank him above Montesquieu. From a cursory reading of the book, which was presented to me as if it were sacred writ, it seems to me to contain sibylline visions of the Good and the Just which will or should come true in the future.").

229. Moir, Capital Punishment, viii, xvii, xxiv, xxviii, 30–31, 35–36 & n.2, 38; Benjamin Franklin to Gaetano Filangieri, Jan. 11, 1783; Ferrone, The Politics of Enlightenment, 14, 237 n.6; Peter Bondanella & Julia Conway Bondanella, eds., Cassell Dictionary of Italian Literature 213–14 (London: Cassell, 1996); Maestro, *Benjamin Franklin and the Penal Laws*, 551, 554–57 & n.7; 5 The American Review: A Whig Journal of Politics, Literature, Art and Science 359 (New York: George H. Colton, 1847); Forty-Sixth Annual Report of the Inspectors of the State Penitentiary for the Eastern District of Pennsylvania, to the Senate and House of Representatives of the Commonwealth of Pennsylvania, for the Year 1875, at 8–12 (Philadelphia: Sherman & Co., 1876); Tommaso Astarita, Between Salt Water and Holy Water: A History of Southern Italy 215 (New York: W. W. Norton & Co., 2005); *see also* Pace, Benjamin Franklin and Italy, 142 ("Franklin's decision to sponsor in 1783 a translation of the constitutions of all the thirteen colonies into the universally known French language was a genial idea. Rendered in their entirety by his old friend and masonic brother Louis-Alexandre Duc de la Rochefoucauld d'Anville, the state constitutions quickly became a sort of breviary of eighteenth-century libertarian principles…. The American constitutions were required reading for any enlightened prince who desired to keep abreast of modern currents, and those who were not furnished with copies as a result of Franklin's official distribution in Paris made haste to acquire their own.").

230. Benjamin Franklin to Gaetano Filangieri, Oct. 14, 1787.

231. Pace, Benjamin Franklin and Italy, 157.

232. Maestro, *Benjamin Franklin and the Penal Laws*, 561–62.

233. Ferrone, The Politics of Enlightenment, 228 n.27.

234. Moir, Capital Punishment, 39, 41.

235. Cotlar, "Every Man Should Have Property," *in* Young, Nash & Raphael, Revolutionary Founders, 345.

236. John Dickinson, An Essay on the Constitutional Power of Great-Britain over the Colonies in America; with the Resolves of the Committee for the Province of Pennsylvania, and Their Instructions to Their Representatives in Assembly 350–51 (Philadelphia, 1774).

237. Raven, London Booksellers and American Customers, 154–55, 186–88, 214, 434 n.245.

238. Lorenzo Sears, John Hancock: The Picturesque Patriot 109 (Boston: Little, Brown, and Company, 1912).

239. Daniel L. Dreisback & Mark David Hall, eds., Faith and the Founders of the American Republic 240 (Oxford: Oxford University Press, 2014); *see also* John Hancock's Life and Speeches: A Personalized Vision of the American Revolution, 1763–1793, at 188–89 (Lanham, MD: The Scarecrow Press, 1996) (discussing Hancock's views on capital punishment).

240. Benjamin H. Irvin, Clothed in Robes of Sovereignty: The Continental Congress and the People Out of Doors 203 (Oxford: Oxford University Press, 2011); Lewis R. Harley, The Life of Charles Thomson: Secretary of the Continental Congress and Translator of the Bible from the Greek 8, 15–16, 63, 85–132 (Philadelphia: George W. Jacobs & Co., 1900); Benjamin Franklin to Charles Thomson & Thomas Mifflin, Jan. 27, 1769, *available at* www.founders.archives.gov; Brands, The First American, 112–13; http://www.librarycompany.org/collections/index.htm (the Library Company's online catalog, WolfPAC, contains the listed editions).

241. Raven, London Booksellers and American Customers, 158.

242. Davis, *The Movement to Abolish Capital Punishment*, 25.

243. Edict of the Grand Duke of Tuscany, for the Reform of Criminal Law in his Dominions 1–2, 27–28 (1789).

244. Joseph Gurney, comp., The Whole Proceedings on the Trials of Two Informations Exhibited ex Officio by the King's Attorney-General Against George Gordon, Esq. Commonly Called Lord George Gordon 30 (1787).

245. "The Original Shaker Communities in New England," *in* 22 New England Magazine: An Illustrated Monthly 303–304 (1900) ("*From the Plumer Papers.*").

246. Parker P. Simmons, James Otis's Speech on the Writs of Assistance (1761) (A. Lovell & Co., 1902), p. 1 ("James Otis's speech on the Writs of Assistance is conveniently regarded as the first in the chain of events which led directly and irresistibly to revolution and independence."); James Otis, The Rights of the British Colonies Asserted and Proved (1763), *available at* www.oll.libertyfund.org.

247. James Otis, A Vindication of the British Colonies (London: J. Almon, 1769).

248. Preyer, "Two Enlightened Reformers of the Criminal Law," *in* Blackstone in America, 259 n.23.

249. May, The Enlightenment in America, 118.

250. Noether, The American Constitution as a Symbol and Reality for Italy, 26.

251. Anthony L. Bleecker, New York Society Library, http://www.nysoclib.org/collection/ledger/people/bleeker_anthony; William Linn, New York Society Library, http://www.nysoclib.org/collection/ledger/people/linn_william; Marinus Oudenarde, New York Society Library, http://www.nysoclib.org/collection/ledger/people/oudenarde_marinus.

252. David J. Rothman, The Discovery of the Asylum: Social Order and Disorder in the New Republic 59–60 (Piscataway, NJ: Transaction Publishers, rev. ed. 2009).

253. Charles C. Soule, Abbreviations Used in Law Books: Reprinted from the Lawyer's Reference Manual of Law Books and Citations 13 (1897).

254. Allen D. Boyer, ed., Shaping the Common Law: From Glanvill to Hale, 1188–1688, at 101, 135–36 (Palo Alto, CA: Stanford University Press, 2008).

255. Mark Goldie & Robert Wokler, eds., The Cambridge History of Eighteenth-Century Political Thought 556 (Cambridge: Cambridge University Press, 2006).

256. Wai Chee Dimock, Residues of Justice: Literature, Law, Philosophy 11, 16 (Berkeley, CA: University of California Press, 1997); Immanuel Kant, The Philosophy of Law: An Exposition of the Fundamental Principles of Jurisprudence as the Science of Right (Edinburgh: T. & T. Clark, trans. W. Hastie 1887); Otfried Höffe, Categorical Principles of Law: A Counterpoint to Modernity 152 (University Park, PA: Pennsylvania State University Press, Mark Migotti, trans. 2002); Moir, Capital Punishment, 42; 1 Emanuel Kant, The Metaphysic of Morals Divided into Metaphysical Elements of Law and Ethics 107 (London: William Richardson, 1799).

257. *E.g.*, Francis L. Hawks, ed., The Pictorial Cyclopaedia of Biography: Embracing a Series of Original Memoirs of the Most Distinguished Persons of All Times 84 (New York: D. Appleton and Co., 1856) (the entry for Beccaria reads as follows: "author of a celebrated treatise on crimes and punishments, which is regarded as one of the best works ever written on legislation"); The Foreign Review, and Continental Miscellany, Vol. IV, p. 208 (London: Black, Young, and Young, 1829) (noting that *Dei delitti e delle pene* "has eclipsed so many other titles").

258. Dwight C. Kilbourn, The Bench and Bar of Litchfield County, Connecticut, 1709–1909: Biographical Sketches of Members, History, and Catalogue of the Litchfield Law School 92, 171–72 (Clark, NJ: The Lawbook Exchange, Ltd., 2006) (listing law books sold to Seth P. Beers on July 5, 1804).

259. 22 REAL: The Yearbook of Research in English and American Literature 153 (2006).

260. A Letter of a Remonstrance to Sir Robert Gifford, Knight, His Majesty's Attorney General 37 (London: Hayward and Roscoe, 1820).

261. Wai Chee Dimock, Residues of Justice: Literature, Law, Philosophy 16 (Berkeley: University of California Press, 1997); 3 Madeline House, Graham Storey & Kathleen Tillotson, The Letters of Charles Dickens 105, 110, 123, 181 (Oxford: Oxford University Press, 1974).

262. 1 Charles Dickens, Miscellaneous Papers from 'The Morning Chronicle,' 'The Daily News,' 'The Examiner,' 'Household Words' 'All the Year Round,' Etc. and Plays and Poems 30–51 (London: Chapman & Hall, 1911).

263. Charles Dickens, Pictures from Italy 6, 47 (London: Bradbury & Evans, 1846); Caleb Smith, The Prison & the American Imagination 59–62 (New Haven: Yale University Press, 2009); Peter O.

Nwankwo, Criminology and Criminal Justice Systems of the World: A Comparative Perspective 60–61 (Bloomington, IN: Trafford Publishing, 2011).

264. John Lomas, ed., The City Hall Reporter, and New-York Law Magazine 27–28 (New York: James Ormond, Oct. 1833); 1 David Hoffman, A Course of Legal Study, Addressed to the Students and the Profession Generally 432–34 (Baltimore: Joseph Neal, 2d ed. 1836); *see also* 2 David Hoffman, A Course of Legal Study, Addressed to the Students and the Profession Generally 423, 852 (Baltimore: Joseph Neal, 2d ed. 1836) (listing Beccaria's treatise).

265. Gary L. Mcdowell, The Language of Law and the Foundations of American Constitutionalism 18 (Cambridge: Cambridge University Press, 2010); David Hoffman, A Course of Legal Study: Respectfully Addressed to the Students of Law in the United States 218–19, 225–29 (Baltimore, MD: Coale and Maxwell, 1817).

266. Cotlar, Tom Paine's America, 115 & 236 n.9.

267. Joseph Callo, John Paul Jones: America's First Sea Warrior xviii, 40 (Annapolis, MD: Naval Institute Press, 2006).

268. May, The Enlightenment in America, 235; Philip S. Foner, The Democratic-Republican Societies, 1790–1800: A Documentary Sourcebook of Constitutions, Declarations, Addresses, Resolutions, and Toasts 15 (Westport, CT: Greenwood Press, 1796); Cotlar, "Every Man Should Have Property," *in* Young, Nash & Raphael, Revolutionary Founders, 337–39, 343–44; "From Officers of the American Squadron: Affidavit," Oct. 30, 1779, Benjamin Franklin Papers, http://franklinpapers.org/franklin/framedVolumes.jsp.

269. John O'Brien, A Treatise on American Military Laws, and the Practice of Courts Martial 222 (Philadelphia: Lea & Blanchard, 1846).

270. *E.g.*, 6 Dane, General Abridgement and Digest of American Law, 625, 629–30, 636–37; William Rawle, A View of the Constitution of the United States (2d ed. 1829), *available at* http://press-pubs.uchicago.edu/founders/documents/a3_2_1s84.html; Joseph Story, Commentaries on the Constitution (1833), *available at* http://press-pubs.uchicago.edu/founders/documents/a2_2_1s30.html.

271. Thomas Jefferson to James Madison, July 27, 1804; Thomas Jefferson to William Rawle, May 15, 1793; Alexander Hamilton to William Rawle, Jan. 6, 1793; George Washington [Diary Entry: 20 October 1794], *available at* www.founders.archives.gov.

272. John Clarke Ridpath, Charles K. Edmunds & G. Mercer Adam, James Otis: The Pre-Revolutionist 78 (2006); 3 Mercy Otis Warren, History of the Rise, Progress and Termination of the American Revolution 356–57 (Boston: Manning and Loring, 1805).

273. Mercy Otis Warren: Selected Letters 44 (Athens, GA: University of Georgia Press, 2009).

274. Maestro, *A Pioneer for the Abolition of Capital Punishment*, 465, 467; Craig Parkinson, The Pendulum of Politics: Today's Politics from Yesterday's History 2 (Bloomington, IN: AuthorHouse, 2011).

275. Peter Gay, The Enlightenment, The Science of Freedom 440 (New York: W. W. Norton & Co., 1977).

276. Mark Bevir, ed., Encyclopedia of Political Theory 110 (Thousand Oaks, CA: SAGE Publications, 2010) ("Enlightened reforming absolute monarchs including Catherine the Great of Russia and Frederick II of Prussia were ... attracted to Beccaria's rationalistic and modernizing approach.").

277. Bhikhu Parekh, ed., Jeremy Bentham: Critical Assessments 433 (London: Routledge, 1993); *see also* id. at 43 (quoting Bentham as follows: "I was beginning to get gleams of practical philosophy. Montesquieu, Barrington, Beccaria, and Helvetius, but most of all Helvetius, set me on the principle of utility."); *compare* James E. Crimmins, Utilitarian Philosophy and Politics: Bentham's Later Years 57 (London: Continuum International, 2011) (dating Bentham's commonplace entry referencing Beccaria to 1783, noting how "shaky" Bentham's memory was by that date, and noting: "More plausible than Bentham's claim to have first seen the utilitarian formula in Priestley are his occasional attributions to the Italian law reformer Cesare Beccaria.").

278. 7 Tait's Edinburgh Magazine for 1840, at 456 (Edinburgh: William Tait, 1840) ("Memoirs of Jeremy Bentham").

279. Decl. of Independence (July 4, 1776); Marilyn C. Baseler, "Asylum for Mankind": America 1607–1800, at 126 (1998).

280. *E.g.*, Cassius ["Supposed to be Written by Aedanus Burke, Esquire, one of the Chief Justices of the State of South-Carolina"], An Address to the Freeman of the State of South-Carolina 18 (1783) (printed and sold by Robert Bell in Philadelphia) ("*Beccaria makes the following remarks on confiscation ...*").

281. Bessler, Cruel and Unusual, 63.

282. Masur, Rites of Execution, 52; 3 Dexter, The Literary Diary of Ezra Stiles, 328; Memoir, Autobiography and Correspondence of Jeremiah Mason 12, 41–42, 302, 323, 325, 356, 362, 443, 447 (Kansas

City, MO: Lawyers' International Publishing Co., 1917); Goodheart, The Solemn Sentence of Death, 269 n.2 (noting that the "serialized publication of Beccaria's book can be found" in the *New Haven Gazette* "from Jan. 12, 1786, through Aug. 3, 1786"); *see also* id. at 69–70 ("Much of Beccaria's agenda for just laws, prevention of crime, proportionate punishment, and rehabilitation of offenders resonated with similar sentiment in Connecticut. An editorial endorsement of the Italian reformer in the *Gazette* instructed citizens that 'a mild penal system is a political advantage,' a measure of good government."); Lyon Norman Richardson, A History of Early American Magazines, 1741–1789, at 258 n.89 (1931) (noting dates from "Feb. 23" to "Aug. 3, 1786," and relevant page numbers, in which "Beccaria's *Essay on Crimes and Punishments*" was "begun in the newspaper" and "concluded in the magazine"); Catalogue of a Valuable and Useful Collection of Books in the Various Departments of Science, [Many of Which Have Been Recently Imported,] for Sale by E. L. Carey & A. Hart, Corner of Chesnut and Fourth Streets, Philadelphia, p. 33 (undated catalogue listing "Beccaria on Crimes" in the "Law" section," with the catalogue appended to Davy Crockett, An Account of Col. Crockett's Tour to the North and Down East, in the Year of Our Lord One Thousand Eight Hundred and Thirty-Four (1835), published by "E. L. Carey and A. Hart"; Ernest L. Bogart, Peacham: The Story of a Vermont Hill Town 198–99 (2010) (noting that an advertisement in *The Watchman* on May 16, 1811, offered for sale ten books on law, including Beccaria's treatise).

283. Jill Lepore, The Story of America: Essays on Origins 302 (Princeton: Princeton University Press, 2012).

284. Memoir, Autobiography and Correspondence of Jeremiah Mason 443, 447 (Kansas City, MO: Lawyers' International Publishing Co., 1917); *Mason, Jeremiah (1768–1848)*, Biographical Directory of the United States, http://bioguide.congress.gov.

285. Preyer, "Cesare Beccaria and the Founding Fathers," *in* Blackstone in America, 242 ("Booksellers in Boston and New York were advertising the volume in 1771, 1772, and 1773. A circulating library in Annapolis and the Harvard College library contained copies by the latter year."); *see also* Banner, The Death Penalty, 91.

286. Palmer, "All Matters and Things Shall Center There," 41.

287. Cesare Beccaria, An Essay on Crimes and Punishments (1777); Ray Raphael, A People's History of the American Revolution: How Common People Shaped the Fight for Independence 220 (New York: HarperCollins, 2002); 7 George G. Rogers, Jr. & David R. Chesnutt, eds., The Papers of Henry Laurens 3 (Columbia: University of South Carolina Press, 1979); Lorenzo Sabine, The American Loyalists: Or, Biographical Sketches of Adherents to the British Crown in the War of the Revolution 181 (Cambridge: Cambridge University Press, 2012). In 1773, the Rivington *Gazetter* in New York advertised Beccaria's book as "in press." Adolph Caso, They Too Made America Great: Lives of the Italian Americans 56 (Boston: Branden Books, 1978). A copy of that edition, if it was ever printed, has not been located. Caso, We, the People, 307. Notably, a reference is found to a 1773 edition of Beccaria's *On Crimes and Punishments* in an early twentieth-century bibliography of works printed in the United States, suggesting that the book was in fact printed. 4 Charles Evans, American Bibliography: A Chronological Dictionary of All Books Pamphlets and Periodical Publications Printed in the United States of America (Chicago: The Blakely Press, 1907) (see entry 12665, listing Beccaria's treatise "Printed by James Rivington" in 1773 in "New-York").

288. 1 Hugh Amory & David D. Hall, eds., A History of the Book in America: The Colonial Book in the Atlantic World 233 (Cambridge, UK: Cambridge University Press, 2007). In what one antiquarian book dealer describes as "a matter of some debate," an earlier edition of Beccaria's book may have been printed in New York in 1773, though the book dealer describes that edition—which, again, has never been found—as "ghosts." Law Books by the Lawbook Exchange, Ltd., http://www.find-a-book.com/member/detail.php3?custnr=&lang=&membernr=1661&booknr=368187001.

289. M. H. Hoeflich, Roman and Civil Law and the Development of Anglo-American Jurisprudence in the Nineteenth Century 56 (Athens: University of Georgia Press, 1997); Eric Dabney & Mike Coker, Historic South Carolina: An Illustrated History 52 (San Antonio, TX: Historical Publishing Network, 2006).

290. Everton, The Grand Chorus of Complaint, 56.

291. Cesare Beccaria, An Essay on Crimes and Punishments (1778).

292. Benjamin Franklin to David Hume, Sept. 27, 1760; Benjamin Franklin to David Hume, Jan. 21, 1762; Benjamin Franklin to David Hume, May 19, 1762; Benjamin Franklin to William Franklin, Jan. 30, 1772; David Hume to Benjamin Franklin, Feb. 7, 1772, *available at* www.founders.archives.gov.

293. David Hume, Essays and Treatises on Several Subjects 6–8 (London: A. Millar, A. Kincaid & A. Donaldson, new ed. 1758).

294. Sher, The Enlightenment and the Book, 530; The Life of David Hume, Esq: The Philosopher and Historian, Written by Himself (Philadelphia: Robert Bell, 1778); A Philosophical and Religious Dialogue in the Shades, Between Mr. Hume and Dr. Dodd: With Notes by the Editor 9 (London: Hopper and Davis, 1778); Mark Blaug, ed., David Hume (1711–1776) and James Steuart (1712–1780) iv (Brookfield, VT: Elgar, 1991); James Fieser, ed., Early Responses to Hume's Life and Reputation xxvi (Bristol, England: Thoemmes Continuum, 2d ed. 2005); Brian P. Block & John Hostettler, A History of the Abolition of Capital Punishment in Britain 32 (Winchester, UK: Waterside Press, 1997); 8 Joseph Woodfall Ebsworth, ed., The Roxburghe Ballads: Illustrating the Last Years of the Stuarts 332 (Hertford: Stephen Austin and Sons, 1895) (printed for The Ballad Society); William Dodd, Thoughts in Prison, in Five Parts, viz. The Imprisonment, the Retrospect, Public Punishment, The Trial, Futurity: To Which Are Added, His Last Prayer, Written in the Night before His Death 99 (London: J. G. Barnard, 1809).

295. Hoeflich, Legal Publishing in Antebellum America, 32, 131, 133. David Hall, another prominent Philadelphia bookseller, sold an English edition of Blackstone's Commentaries in 1769. Id. at 131.

296. Bessler, Cruel and Unusual, 48–49; Kathryn Preyer, "Two Enlightened Reformers of the Criminal Law: Thomas Jefferson of Virginia and Peter Leopold, Grand Duke of Tuscany," in Blackstone in America, 259 ("Blackstone's references to Beccaria's theories undoubtedly communicated them to a wider American audience than may have read the original."); John H. Langbein, "Blackstone, Litchfield, and Yale: The Founding of the Yale Law School," in Anthony T. Kronman, ed., History of the Yale Law School 41 n.46 (New Haven: Yale University Press, 2004).

297. Thomas Paine, Common Sense (1776); "Subscribers in Virginia to Blackstone's Commentaries on the Laws of England, Philadelphia, 1771–1772," 1 William and Mary College Quarterly Historical Magazine 183–85 (July 1921). Dr. Benjamin Rush was the one who convinced Paine to get in touch with Bell, a prosperous businessman with a reputation for republicanism. Everton, The Grand Chorus of Complaint, 56.

298. Cesare Beccaria, An Essay on Crimes and Punishments (new ed. corrected 1793); see also Suter, Earnest & Earnest, The Hanging of Susanna Cox, 51 ("The treatise became so popular, Philadelphia printers published two editions, one in 1778 and another in 1793.").

299. 2 Robert A. Gross & Mary Kelley, eds., A History of the Book in America: An Extensive Republic: Print, Culture, and Society in the New Nation, 1790–1840, at 24, 81 (2010).

300. Cesare Beccaria, An Essay on Crimes and Punishments (1809) (published by Stephen Gould in New York); Cesare Beccaria, An Essay on Crimes and Punishments (1809) (published in Boston by Farrand, Mallory and Co.); Cesare Beccaria, An Essay on Crimes and Punishments (2d Am. ed. 1819) (published in Philadelphia by Philip H. Nicklin; printer: A. Walker, 24 Arch St.; translated from the French by Edward D. Ingraham); Hoeflich, Legal Publishing in Antebellum America, 172 n.3 (noting that translations of Beccaria's book were published in New York City in 1819 by Stephen Gould; and in Boston in 1809 by Farrand & Mallory).

301. Bessler, Cruel and Unusual, 54; Mark L. Jones, Fundamental Dimensions of Law and Legal Education: An Historical Framework—A History of U.S. Legal Education Phase I: From the Founding of the Republic Until the 1860s, 39 J. Marshall L. Rev. 1041, 1163 n.431 (2006) (noting that Beccaria's name appears in moot court briefs of the Winchester Law School in Winchester, Virginia, which operated from 1824 to 1831).

302. Maestro, A Pioneer for the Abolition of Capital Punishment, 467.

303. 2 Gordon S. Wood & Louise G. Wood, eds., Russian-American Dialogue on the American Revolution 161 & n.115 (Columbia: University of Missouri Press, 1995) (citing Gilbert Chinard, ed., The Commonplace Book of Thomas Jefferson: A Repertory of His Ideas on Government (Baltimore, 1926), pp. 298–316).

304. Kastenberg, An Enlightened Addition to the Original Meaning, 50–51, 55–56, 58, 61–62; Maestro, Cesare Beccaria and the Origins of Penal Reform, 18–19, 44–45.

305. Arthur Isak Applbaum, Professional Detachment: The Executioner of Paris, 109 Harv. L. Rev. 458, 477 n.55 (1995) (quoting Voltaire's commentary in the South Carolina, David Bruce-published, 1777 edition of Beccaria's treatise).

306. Caso, We, the People, 322 ("the 1777 edition published in Charlestown, South Carolina, has the name of Voltaire and not that of Beccaria"; "[t]he fact that Beccaria's book became widely known under the name of Voltaire is significant at least in the promulgation of those ideas").

307. Denis Lacorne, Religion in America: A Political History 1, 18 (New York: Columbia University Press, George Holoch, trans., 2011); 16 The Literary Digest: A Repository of Contemporaneous Thought and Research 253 (New York: Funk & Wagnalls Co., 1898); see also Gertrude Himmelfarb, The Roads to Modernity: The British, French, and American Enlightenments 216 (2005) ("Voltaire

was the only *philosophe* well known in America before the Revolution").

308. *See* "A Commentary on the Book of Crimes and Punishments," *in* Cesare Beccaria, An Essay on Crimes and Punishments i, iv–v, xx–xxi, xxxvi, xxxviii (4th ed. 1775), *available at* http://archive.org/stream/essayoncrimespun1775becc#page/n3/mode/2up.

309. 1 Geoffrey Treasure, ed., Who's Who in British History: Beginnings to 1901, at 719–20 (Chicago, IL: Fitzroy Dearborn Publishers, 1998); Lon Cantor, What Makes America Great? Land of Freedom, Honor, Justice, and Opportunity 84 (Lincoln, NE: iUniverse, 2003); "A Commentary on the Book of Crimes and Punishments," *in* Cesare Beccaria, An Essay on Crimes and Punishments xxxviii (4th ed. 1775), *available at* http://archive.org/stream/essayoncrimespun1775becc#page/n3/mode/2up.

310. Id. at xlii–xliii, xlviii, lxi–lxii.

311. Richard A. Harris & Daniel J. Tichenor, eds., A History of the U.S. Political System: Ideas, Interests, and Institutions 81–82 (2010) (an Anti-Federalist quotes Beccaria in 1788); Cornell, A Well Regulated Militia, 225 n.19 (noting that Donald Lutz, in a study of the patterns of citation to various thinkers in published writings in the founding period, found that Beccaria accounted for one percent of citations in the 1770s and three percent in the 1780s); Gordon S. Wood, Empire of Liberty: A History of the Early Republic, 1789–1815, at 404 (2009) (noting there were "ample quotations from the eighteenth-century Italian legal reformer Cesare Beccaria" in the founding era) (citing "On the Present States of America," 10 Oct. 1776, *in* Peter Force, ed., American Archives, 5th Ser. (Washington, DC, 1837–46), 2:969 & William Henry Drayton, Speech to General Assembly of South Carolina, Jan. 20, 1778, *in* Hezekiah Niles, ed., Principles and Acts of the Revolution in America 359 (New York, 1876)); M. E. Bradford, A Better Guide Than Reason: Federalists and Anti-Federalists 128–29 (1994); 4 Murray N. Rothbard, Conceived in Liberty: The Revolutionary War, 1775–1784, at 256 (Auburn, AL: Mises Institute, 1999) (noting that the radical leader, William Henry Drayton, quoted Beccaria); Josiah Quincy & Eliza Susan Quincy, eds., Memoir of the Life of Josiah Quincy, Junior, of Massachusetts Bay: 1744–1775, at 323 (3d ed. 1875) (quoting Beccaria in observations on the Boston port bill); Reports of the Proceedings and Debates of the Convention of 1821, Assembled for the Purpose of Amending the Constitution of the State of New York 131 (1821) ("[W]e had had two governors in succession, who, at the opening of the legislature, declared in their speeches, that because an individual could not lawfully take away his own life, he could not surrender his right to others of taking it away. Yes, two of your governors have gone largely into the views of Beccaria.").

312. Robert H. Webking, The American Revolution and the Politics of Liberty 41 (Baton Rouge: Louisiana State University Press, 1988); John Dickinson's Draft Letter to the Inhabitants of the Province of Quebec, Oct. 24–26, 1774.

313. The John Dickinson Writings Project, http://dickinsonproject.rch.uky.edu/about.php (quoting Benjamin Rush, Travels Through Life: An Account of Sundry Incidents & Events in the Life of Benjamin Rush).

314. Journal of the Continental Congress, Oct. 26, 1774; 32 Charles Elliott, ed., The Canadian Law Times 231 (1912); John Dickinson's Draft Letter to the Inhabitants of the Province of Quebec, Oct. 24–26, 1774; "Candidus" [James Chalmers], Plain Truth; Addressed to the Inhabitants of America, Containing, Remarks on a Late Pamphlet entitled Common Sense (Philadelphia: R. Bell, 1776); 2 Jonathan Elliot, comp., The Debates in the Convention of the State of New York, on the Adoption of the Federal Constitution 247 (1836) (statement of Melancton Smith); 1 Herbert J. Storing, ed., The Complete Anti-Federalist 38, 40, 72, 77, 159, 353–54 n.61 (Chicago: The University of Chicago Press, 1981) (Beccaria is quoted by John De Witt and "A Countryman," with Herbert Storing noting the specific passage was quoted by the Continental Congress and several Anti-Federalists); 1 Joseph Gales, comp., Annals of Congress: The Debates and Proceedings in the Congress of the United States 862 (1834) ("Mr. Jackson" quotes "[t]he accurate Marquis Beccaria" on August 31, 1789).

315. Henry Zouch, Remarks upon the Late Resolutions of the House of Commons, respecting the Proposed Change of the Poor Laws 53 (Leeds: G. Wright, 1776); 3 Noah Webster, A Grammatical Institute of the English Language Comprising, an Easy, Concise and Systematic Method of Education, Designed for the Use of Schools in America 167 (Hartford, CT: Barlow & Babcock, 1785).

316. John P. Kaminski & Richard Leffler, eds., Federalists and Antifederalists: The Debate Over the Ratification of the Constitution 194–95 n.* (Lanham, MD: Madison House Publishers, 2d rev. ed., 1998); 20 Merrill Jensen, John P. Kaminski, Gaspare J. Saladino, & Richard Leffler, eds., The Documentary History of the Ratification of the Constitution 1082 (Madison, WI: State Historical Society of Wisconsin, 2004); 7 The Town and Country Magazine; or, Universal Repository of Knowledge, Instruction, and Entertainment for December, 1776, at 620–21 (London: A. Hamilton, 1776).

317. Yvan Lamonde, The Social History of Ideas in Quebec 1760–1896, at 12–13 (Montreal, Quebec: McGill-Queen's University Press, 2013); Henry C. Van Schaack, The Life of Peter Van Schaack,

LL. D. 110, 121–22 (1842). In those observations, Peter van Schaack also quoted Beccaria as follows: "'Can there be a more melancholy spectacle,' (says the humane Beccaria,) 'than a whole family overwhelmed with misery from the crime of their chief?'" Id. at 114.

318. Bessler, Cruel and Unusual, 56.

319. Rudiments of Law and Government, Deduced from the Law of Nature (1783), *reprinted in* 1 Charles S. Hyneman & Donald S. Lutz, eds., American Political Writing During the Founding Era: 1760–1805 (Indianapolis, IN: Liberty Fund, 1983).

320. 2 W. Hooper, trans., A Treatise on Man, His Intellectual Faculties and His Education: A Posthumous Work of M. Helvetius 239–40 (London: B. Law & G. Robinson, 1777).

321. 3 A. F., Student of the Inner Temple, The Criminal Recorder; or, Biographical Sketches of Notorious Public Characters; Including Murderers, Traitors, Pirates, Mutineers, Incendiaries, Defrauders, Rioters, Sharpers, Highwaymen, Footpads, Pickpockets, Swindlers, Housebreakers, Coiners, Receivers, Extortioners, and Other Noted Persons Who Have Suffered the Sentence of the Law for Criminal Offenses (London: James Cundee, 1804).

322. The British Controversialist, and Literary Magazine 311 (London: Houlston and Wright, 1864).

323. Maestro, *A Pioneer for the Abolition of Capital Punishment*, 468.

Chapter 3

1. Craig Hanyan, De Witt Clinton: Years of Molding, 1769–1807, at 30 (New York: Garland, 1988) ("Clinton next turned to Beccaria to apply this well-known argument to men living under government."); id. at 33 ("The other five letters, certainly De Witt Clinton's, are littered with references to 'Mr. Beccaria'…."); Carmona v. Ward, 576 F.2d 405, 427 (2d Cir. 1978) (Oakes, J., dissenting) (Appendix) (describing Beccaria's influence).

2. Suter, Earnest & Earnest, The Hanging of Susanna Cox, 51.

3. Banner, The Death Penalty, 91; *see also* Rebecca Stefoff, *Furman v. Georgia*: Debating the Death Penalty 29 (Marshall Cavendish, 2007) ("Copies of Beccaria's book were sold in the American colonies. Thomas Jefferson, George Washington, and John Adams all owned the book, and it appeared in several colonial newspapers."); Kathryn Preyer, "Two Enlightened Reformers of the Criminal Law: Thomas Jefferson of Virginia and Peter Leopold, Grand Duke of Tuscany," *in* Blackstone in America, 259 ("by 1769, George Washington urged his nephew to read the *Essay*").

4. 27 Transactions of the First International Congress on the Enlightenment 1495 (1963); Catalogue of Books for Master Custis Referred to on the Otherside, Viz, *available at* http://etext.virginia.edu/etcbin/toccer-new2?id=WasFi02.xml&images=images/modeng&data=/texts/english/modeng/parsed&tag=public&part=341&division=div1 (citing *The Writings of George Washington*, Vol. 2; *see also* Frances Laverne Carroll & Mary Meacham, The Library at Mount Vernon 96–97 (Beta Phi Mu, 1977); Bernhard Knollenberg, George Washington, the Virginia Period, 1732–1775, at 74, 212 (Durham, NC: Duke University Press, 1964).

5. Augustine Birrell, Frederick Locker-Lampson: A Character Sketch 33–34 (Constable, 1920).

6. George Mason to George Washington, Apr. 9, 1768.

7. 1 Griffin, Catholics and the American Revolution, 332.

8. George Washington to Continental Congress, Aug. 31, 1778; *see also* George Washington Papers, General Orders, Sept. 22, 1775; General Orders, Oct. 3, 1775; Minutes of the Conference, Oct. 18–24, 1775; General Orders, Nov. 15, 1775; General Orders, Apr. 25, 1776; General Orders, Apr. 27, 1776; General Orders, May 2, 1776; General Orders, May 3, 1776; General Orders, May 27, 1776; General Orders, June 2, 1776; General Orders, June 5, 1776; General Orders, June 6, 1776; General Orders, June 9, 1776; General Orders, June 11, 1776; General Orders, June 16, 1776; General Orders, July 7, 1776; General Orders, Sept. 11, 1776, *available at* www.founders.archives.gov (noting various prisoners convicted of offenses ordered to be whipped).

9. 1 Griffin, Catholics and the American Revolution, 127–29.

10. Major General Israel Putnam to George Washington, July 19, 1777 & General Orders, Sept. 14, 1778, *available at* www.founders.archives.gov.

11. Robert Shackleton, The Book of Boston 16, 275 (Philadelphia, PA: The Penn Publishing Co., 1916).

12. Elio Monachesi, *Pioneers in Criminology IX — Cesare Beccaria (1738–1794)*, 46 J. of Crim. L. & Criminology 439, 441–43, 448 (1956).

13. 1 William Henry Smith, The St. Clair Papers: The Life and Public Services of Arthur St. Clair 106 n.1 (Cincinnati, OH: Robert Clarke & Co., 1882); 1 The National Cyclopædia of American Biography: Being the History of the United States 48–50 (New York: James T. White & Co., 1898); Alexander Hamilton to John Laurens, Oct. 11, 1780, *available at* www.founders.archives.gov; Willard O. Mishoff, *Business in Philadelphia during the British Occupation, 1777–1788*, 61 Pa. Mag. of. Hist. & Biog. 165 (1937); Mark Jacob & Stephen H. Case, Treacherous Beauty: Peggy Shippen, the Woman Behind Benedict Arnold's Plot to Betray America 25–30 (Guilford, CT: Globe Pequot Press, 2012). In an academy in Geneva, where he studied mathematics, music, drawing and other liberal arts, André met Pierre-Eugene Du Simitiere, the man who proposed that the phrase *E Pluribus unum* (Out of many, one) be incorporated into the design of the Great Seal of the United States. Id. at 30. Du Simitiere did the French translation of the 1774 address of Congress to the inhabitants of Quebec, charging eight dollars for his services. Lettre adressé aux habitans de la Province de Quebec ci-devant le Canada, de la part du Congres General de l'Amérique Septentrionale, tenu à Philadelphie (Philadelphie: de Fleury Mesplet, 1774); *see also* John C. Van Horne, Pierre Eugene Du Simitiere: His American Museum 200 Years after an Exhibition at the Library Company of Philadelphia, 1314 Locust Street, Philadelphia, Pa. July to October 1985, at 2:24 (1985).

14. Bessler, Cruel and Unusual, 126–33 (discussing Washington's views on executions).

15. Brookhiser, What Would the Founders Do?, 34–35.

16. M. William Phelps, Nathan Hale: The Life and Death of America's First Spy (New York: St. Martin's Press, 2008); Alexander Rose, Washington's Spies: The Story of America's First Spy Ring (New York: Random House, 2007).

17. Bessler, Cruel and Unusual, 128, 132; Robert G. Smith, A Brief Account of the Services Rendered by the Second Regiment Delaware Volunteers in the War of the Rebellion 140 (Wilmington: The Historical Society of Delaware, 1909); Major General John Sullivan to George Washington, Aug. 7, 1777, *available at* www.founders.archives.gov; George Washington to John Sullivan, Aug. 10, 1777, *available at* www.memory.loc.gov.

18. George Washington to Samuel Huntington, Feb. 3, 1781, *reprinted in* 7 Jared Sparks, ed., The Writings of George Washington: Being His Correspondence, Addresses, Messages, and Other Papers, Official and Private 395–96 (Boston: Ferdinand Andrews, 1840).

19. Thomas A. Lewis, For King and Country: The Maturing of George Washington, 1748–1760, at 222 (Minneapolis, MN: Castle Books, 2009).

20. Bessler, Cruel and Unusual, 126–33.

21. Id. at 151–53; Philip J. Schwarz, Twice Condemned: Slaves and the Criminal Laws of Virginia, 1705–1865, at 15 (Union, NJ: The Lawbook Exchange, 1998).

22. Proceedings of the Massachusetts Historical Society 127 (Boston: Massachusetts Historical Society, 1996).

23. Hartnett, Executing Democracy.

24. Henry Knox to Nicholas Fish, Apr. 10, 1786; Henry Knox to Arthur St. Clair, Apr. 19, 1791; Alexander Hamilton to James McHenry, July 29, 1799.

25. Charles Spear, Essays on the Punishment of Death vii (Boston: Charles Spear, 3d ed. 1844). Charles Spear himself quotes from Beccaria. Id. at 23; *see also* id. at 82 (noting Beccaria's role in the death penalty's abolition in Tuscany); id. at 201 (referencing Blackstone, Beccaria and Montesquieu).

26. Memoirs of the Life of the Late Charles Lee, Esq. to Which Are Added His Political and Military Essays 121 (1792).

27. Masur, Rites of Execution, 56–58; Bessler, Cruel and Unusual, 128, 137–38; Sheila L. Skemp, William Franklin: Son of a Patriot, Servant of a King 263 (Oxford: Oxford University Press, 1990).

28. George Washington to Charles Asgill, Nov. 13, 1782, *available at* www.founders.archives.gov.

29. Arthur D. Pierce, Smugglers' Woods: Jaunts and Journeys in Colonial and Revolutionary New Jersey 274 (New Brunswick, NJ: Rutgers University Press, 1960).

30. John C. Fredriksen, Revolutionary War Almanac 281 (New York: Facts On File, 2006); 2 J. J. Boudinot, ed., The Life, Public Services, Addresses and Letters of Elias Boudinot, LL.D.: President of the Continental Congress 45, 218–29 (Boston, MA: Houghton, Mifflin and Co., 1896); *see also* Joseph Lee Boyle, "Their Distress is almost intolerable": The Elias Boudinot Letterbook, 1777–1778 (Heritage Books, 2002).

31. Brenda Haugen, Ethan Allen: Green Mountain Rebel 74–75 (Minneapolis, MN: Compass Point Books, 2005); 4 Frank N. Magill, ed., Dictionary of World Biography: The 17th and 18th Centuries 35 (New York: Salem Press, 1999); Ethan Allen's Narrative of the Capture of Ticonderoga, and of His Cap-

tivity and Treatment by the British 6, 13–14, 29, 33 (Burlington, VT: C. Goodrich & S. B. Nichols, 5th ed. 1849); Willard Sterne Randall, Ethan Allen: His Life and Times 434 (New York: W. W. Norton, 2011).

32. Draft of a Declaration on the British Treatment of Ethan Allen, 2 January 1776, *available at* www.founders.archives.gov.

33. John Adams to Jean Luzac, Nov. 30, 1780, *available at* www.founders.archives.gov.

34. 1 George Washington Greene, The Life of Nathanael Greene: Major-General in the Army of the Revolution 55, 253 (New York: G. P. Putnam and Son, 1867); 2 Richard K. Showman, ed., The Papers of General Nathanael Greene 342 (Chapel Hill: University of North Carolina Press, 2005); Theodore Thayer, Nathanael Greene: Strategist of the American Revolution 117 (New York: Twayne Publishers, 1960); Alexander Rose, Washington's Spies: The Story of America's First Spy Ring 46 (New York: Bantam Books, 2006).

35. 5 Andrew Hilen, ed., The Letters of Henry Wadsworth Longfellow 335 (Cambridge: Harvard University Press, 1982); Encyclopedia Britannica, Vol. 12 (1911); Melvin H. Buxbaum, Critical Essays on Benjamin Franklin 186 (Boston, MA: G. K. Hall & Co., 1987); 3 Storia d'Italia di Carlo Botta continuata da quella di Francesco Guicciardini sino all'anno 1789 con ischiarimenti e note 480 (Milano: Giovanni Silvestri, 1843); George Washington Greene, History and Geography of the Middle Ages for Colleges and Schools 77 (New York: D. Appleton and Co., 1857); George Washington Greene, Historical Studies 140, 448 (New York: George P. Putnam, 1850); George Washington Greene, The German Element in the War of American Independence vi–viii (New York: Hurd and Houghton, 1876).

36. 1 John Fiske, Essays, Historical, and Literary 57–72 (New York: The MacMillan Co., 1902).

37. Langworthy, Memoirs of the Life of the Late Charles Lee, 117, 121, 124.

38. Thomas L. Purvis, Colonial America to 1763, at 73, 80, 123–24, 310–11 (New York: Facts on File, Inc., 1999).

39. Bessler, Cruel and Unusual, 34, 46.

40. Langworthy, Memoirs of the Life of the Late Charles Lee, 80–81; *see also* Plain Facts in Five Letters to a Friend, on the Present State of Politics 84 (London: J. S. Jordan, 1798) (quoting the views of Charles Lee and his citation to Beccaria). In Russia, Beccaria's ideas attracted substantial interest from the monarchy. Massie, Catherine the Great, 345–46. Catherine had read Voltaire as a teenager, and her predecessor, Elizabeth Petrovna, had taken steps of her own to halt executions even before the publication of *On Crimes and Punishments.* Cyril Bryner, *The Issue of Capital Punishment in the Reign of Elizabeth Petrovna*, 49 Russian Review 389, 390 (1990).

41. Langworthy, Memoirs of the Life of the Late Charles Lee, 82.

42. 1 Robert A. Rutland, The Papers of James Madison 128 (Chicago: The University of Chicago Press, 1991).

43. 2 John M'Arthur, Principles and Practice of Naval and Military Courts Martial 3, 46, 54, 144 (London: A. Strahan, 2d ed. 1805).

44. Armstrong Starkey, War in the Age of Enlightenment, 1700–1789, at 25 (Westport, CT: Praeger, 2003); U.S. Const., Art. III, § 3.

45. Alexander Hamilton to James McHenry, Dec. 1799, *available at* www.founders.archives.gov.

46. General Orders, Jan. 4, 1800, *available at* www.founders.archives.gov.

47. Bessler, Cruel and Unusual, 51–53.

48. Robert Green McCloskey, ed., The Works of James Wilson (1967) ("Would you prevent crimes? says the Marquis of Beccaria: let the laws be clear and simple: let the entire force of the nation be united in their defence: let them, and them only, be feared."), *available at* http://press-pubs.uchicago.edu/founders/documents/a2_2_1s23.html.

49. Albert James Harno, Legal Education in the United States: A Report Prepared for the Survey of the Legal Profession 24 (Clark, NJ: The Lawbook Exchange, 2004); 3 Bird Wilson, ed., James Wilson, Lectures on Law, Delivered in the College of Philadelphia, in the Years One Thousand Seven Hundred and Ninety, and One Thousand Seven Hundred Ninety One 3, 9, 13 (1804); *see also* id. at 154–55 (discussing Beccaria's views on criminal confessions); id. at 44 (discussing Beccaria's views on proportionality and a "scale of crimes"); id. at 173 ("The Marquis of Beccaria is of opinion, that the objection against the competency of a witness should be confined altogether to his interest; and that his infamy should not exclude him.").

50. "James Wilson's Charge to the Grand Jury of the Circuit Court for the District of Virginia" (delivered in Richmond, Virginia, on May 23, 1791), *in* 2 Maeva Marcus, ed., The Documentary History of the Supreme Court of the United States, 1789–1800: The Justices on Circuit, 1790–1794, at 166–70, 190 (1988). A reference to Beccaria also appears in a grand jury charge delivered by another jurist in 1848. *See* "The Enforcing of Objectionable Laws" (a charge to the grand jury of the U.S. Circuit Court

delivered in 1848), *in* 2 Writings of Levi Woodbury, LL. D.: Political, Judicial and Literary 24 (1852). Grand jury charges were customarily delivered by leading judges, and—as one commentator notes— "[f]or broader jurisprudential points, widely read works such as Montesquieu's *Spirit of Laws*, Beccaria's *Essay on Crimes and Punishment[s]*, and Francis Bacon's *Works* often appeared." 2 Marcus, *supra*, at 5.

51. Bessler, Cruel and Unusual, 53; "A Charge Delivered to the Grand Jury in the Circuit Court of the United States, for the District of Virginia, in May 1791," *in* 1 Kermit L. Hall & Mark David Hall, eds., Collected Works of James Wilson (Indianapolis, IN: Liberty Fund, 2007).

52. "James Wilson's Charge to the Grand Jury of the Circuit Court for the District of Massachusetts" (delivered in Boston, Massachusetts, on June 7, 1793), *in* 2 Maeva Marcus, ed., The Documentary History of the Supreme Court of the United States, 1789–1800: The Justices on Circuit, 1790–1794, at 396, 402 (New York: Columbia University Press, 1988).

53. 3 Bird Wilson, ed., James Wilson, Lectures on Law, Delivered in the College of Philadelphia, in the Years One Thousand Seven Hundred and Ninety, and One Thousand Seven Hundred Ninety One 390 (1804); *see also* id. at 155 (invoking Beccaria on "oaths").

54. Bessler, Cruel and Unusual, 179.

55. 1 Kermit L. Hall & Mark David Hall, eds., Collected Works of James Wilson, *available at* www.oll.libertyfund.org.

56. 1 Robert Green McCloskey, ed., The Works of James Wilson 63, 263, 370, 442, 495, 501, 535, 594–95, 614–15, 624, 634, 693–94, 705, 821 (Cambridge: The Belknap Press of Harvard University Press, 1967).

57. Bessler, Cruel and Unusual, 58.

58. Landa M. Freeman, Louise V. North & Janet M. Wedge, eds., Selected Letters of John Jay and Sarah Livingston Jay 46 (Jefferson, NC: McFarland & Co., 2010).

59. 1 William Jay, The Life of John Jay: With Selections from His Correspondence and Miscellaneous Papers 390 (New York: J. & J. Harper, 1833); Cyndi Banks, Punishment in America: A Reference Handbook 40 (Santa Barbara, CA: ABC-CLIO, 2005).

60. "Charge to Grand Juries by Chief-Justice Jay," *in* 3 Henry P. Johnston, ed., The Correspondence and Public Papers of John Jay, 1782–1793, at 387, 391–92 (1793).

61. Sullivan, *The Birth of the Prison*, 334.

62. George Pellew, John Jay 98–99 (Boston: Houghton, Mifflin & Co., 1895).

63. Walter Stahr, John Jay: Founding Father 345 (London, UK: Bloomsbury Academic, 2006).

64. Living in Prison: A History of the Correctional System with an Insider's View 46 (Westport, CT: Greenwood Publishers, 2004).

65. Mitchel P. Roth, Prisons and Prison Systems: A Global Encyclopedia xxxiii (Westport, CT: Greenwood Press, 2006).

66. Thomas Eddy, An Account of the State Prison or Penitentiary House, in the City of New-York 6, 9, 15 n.* & 64 (1801).

67. Thomas Eddy to Thomas Jefferson, Feb. 9, 1802, *available at* www.founders.archives.gov.

68. Dennis Sullivan, The Punishment of Crime in Colonial New York: The Dutch Experience in Albany during the Seventeenth Century 240 (New York: Peter Lang, 1997).

69. 1 The Colonial Laws of New York from the Year 1664 to the Revolution 59 (Clark, NJ: The Lawbook Exchange, 2006).

70. Herbert A. Johnson, John Jay: Colonial Lawyer 57 (Washington, DC: Beard Books, 1989).

71. Pieter Spierenburg, The Spectacle of Suffering: Executions and the Evolution of Repression 168–69 (Cambridge: Cambridge University Press, 1984).

72. Edwin Burrows & Mike Wallace, Gotham: A History of New York City to 1898, at 366 (Oxford: Oxford University Press, 1998); Scott Christianson, 500 Years of Imprisonment in America 340 n.198 (Boston: Northeastern University Press, 1998); *see also* Harry Elmer Barnes, *The Historical Origin of the Prison System in America*, 12 Journal of the American Institute of Criminal Law and Criminology 35, 40 (1921) (noting that attempts to reform criminal jurisprudence in New York, including in the eighteenth century, "center mainly about the writings and activities of Beccaria and Howard and the Pennsylvania reformers, such as Bradford, Rush, Vaux, Lownes, and others").

73. Roger K. Newman, ed., The Yale Biographical Dictionary of American Law 445 (New Haven: Yale University Press, 2009); 2 Benson J. Lossing, Harpers' Popular Cyclopædia of United States History from the Aboriginal Period 1181 (New York: Harper & Brothers, rev. enlarged ed. 1893); David A. Adler, George Washington: An Illustrated Biography 220 (2004); Mark J. Rozell, William D. Pederson & Frank J. Williams, eds., George Washington and the Origins of the American Presidency 17 (Westport, CT: Praeger, 2000); Thomas Jefferson's autobiographical statement (Jan. 6, 1821 entry);

Philip J. Schwarz, Twice Condemned: Slaves and the Criminal Laws of Virginia, 1705–1865, at 25 n.35 (Union, NJ: The Lawbook Exchange, 1998) ("For petitions against executions, see Edmund Randolph to Governor Beverley Randolph, January 14, 1790, in Miscellaneous Manuscripts, Chicago Historical Society (CWRD microfilm M-97)...."); Hartnett, Executing Democracy; Bessler, Cruel and Unusual, 57. Bradford died just a year later, in 1795, and was replaced as Attorney General by Charles Lee, an American lawyer from Virginia (not to be confused with General Charles Lee) and the younger brother of General Henry "Light Horse Harry" Lee. Id.; Maeva Marcus, ed., The Documentary History of the Supreme Court of the United States, 1789–1800, at 288 (New York: Columbia University Press, 1994).

74. Suter, Earnest & Earnest, The Hanging of Susanna Cox, 51; Hartnett, Executing Democracy.

75. Jacob Axelrad, Philip Freneau: Champion of Democracy (Austin: University of Texas Press, 2013); Fred Lewis Pattee, Century Readings for a Course in American Literature 27–38 (New York: The Century Co., 1919); Philip Freneau's Poem on Thomas Jefferson's Retirement, Feb. 1809, *available at* www.founders.archives.gov.

76. 2 Octavius Pickering, The Life of Timothy Pickering xiii, 434 (Bedford, MA: Applewood Books, 2009).

77. Bessler, Cruel and Unusual, 85; Harris, Executing Race, 66, 126.

78. Kevin R. C. Gutzman, James Madison and the Making of America 3–8 (2012) (citing Madison-Bradford correspondence); Schiavo, The Italians in America Before the Civil War, 29.

79. Suter, Earnest & Earnest, The Hanging of Susanna Cox, 52.

80. Bessler, Cruel and Unusual, 88–91.

81. William Bradford, An Enquiry How Far the Punishment of Death Is Necessary in Pennsylvania (Philadelphia: T. Dobson, 1793), p. 3.

82. Janice E. McKenney, Women of the Constitution: Wives of the Signers 126 (Lanham, MD: Scarecrow Press, 2013); Jack D. Marietta & G. S. Rowe, Troubled Experiment: Crime and Justice in Pennsylvania, 1682–1800, at 213 (Philadelphia: University of Pennsylvania Press, 2006).

83. Journal of the Senate of the Commonwealth of Pennsylvania 39 (Philadelphia: Zachariah Poulson, Jr., 1793); The American Museum: or, Annual Register of Fugitive Pieces, Ancient and Modern, for the Year 1798, at 5–39 (1799).

84. Bessler, Cruel and Unusual, 86–87, 90; Harris, Executing Race, 66; Edwin R. Keedy, *History of the Pennsylvania Statute Creating Degrees of Murder*, 97 U. Pa. L. Rev. 759 (1949).

85. 3 Frank M. Eastman, Courts and Lawyers of Pennsylvania: A History, 1623–1923, at 777 (New York: The American Historical Society, 1922).

86. 2 J. J. Boudinot, ed., The Life, Public Services, Addresses and Letters of Elias Boudinot, LL.D.: President of the Continental Congress 48–49 (Boston: Houghton, Mifflin & Co., 1896).

87. Bernard S. Katz & C. Daniel Vencill, eds., Biographical Dictionary of the United States Secretaries of the Treasury, 1789–1995, at 304–05 (Westport, CT: Greenwood Press, 1996); Henry Wheaton, Some Account of the Life, Writings, and Speeches of William Pinkney 550, 558 (New York: J. W. Palmer & Co., 1826).

88. United States v. Flemmi, 195 F. Supp.2d 243, 253 (D. Mass. 2001).

89. Adams' Copy of the Information and Draft of His Argument, Court of Vice Admiralty, Boston, Oct. 1768–Mar. 1769, Founding Families: Digital Editions of the Papers of the Winthrops and the Adamses, C. James Taylor, ed., Boston: Massachusetts Historical Society, 2007, *at* http://www.masshist.org/publications/apde/portia.php?id=LJA02d043. Adams' argument continued as follows:

> Treason is justly punished with death because it is an attempt to overthrow the whole Frame of the Government, and the Government can never be overturned without the slaughter of many Hundreds of Lives and the Ruin of many Thousands of Fortunes. If a Man will murder his Fellow subject it seems but equall that he should loose his own Life. But in this Case what is the Crime? Landing a few Casks of Wine. Admitting the Crown to have the clearest Right to the Duties it is but unjustly taking away a small sum of Money from the Crown, and one would think that the forfeiture of £100 would be an equal Punishment for withholding £100 in Duties. But surely the Forfeiture of an whole Cargo of Wines worth Ten Thousand Pounds, for withholding one hundred Pounds in Duties would be a great Disproportion between the Crime and Punishment. To carry it one step further, and subject the ship, as well as Cargo to Confiscation, but above all to subject the Master to £1000, and every Person concerned to a forfeiture of threble value, is such a stretch of security as renders this Act more Penal, than any Statute vs. Rape, Robbery, Murder or Treason.

Id.

90. 1 Frank Moore, American Eloquence: A Collection of Speeches and Addresses 285 (New York: D. Appleton, 1857).

91. The Trial of William Wemms, James Hartegan, William M'Cauley, Hugh White, Matthew Killroy, William Warren, John Carrol, and Hugh Montgomery, Soldiers in His Majesty's 29th Regiment of Foot 140, 148–49 (undated) ("Boston Printed"; "London reprinted, for T. Evans"; "*Taken in Short-Hand by* John Hodgson, *and published by Permission of the Court*"); The Trial of the British Soldiers, of the 29th Regiment of Foot, for the Murder of Crispus Attucks, Samuel Gray, Samuel Maverick, James Caldwell, and Patrick Carr, on Monday Evening, March 5, 1770, at 6, 89, 95 (Boston: William Emmons, 1824); Bernard Bailyn, The Ideological Origins of the American Revolution 27 (Cambridge: Harvard University Press, 1992) (noting Josiah Quincy, Jr.'s use of Beccaria).

92. Bernard Schwartz, A Book of Legal Lists: The Best and Worst in American Law 241 (Oxford: Oxford University Press, 1997).

93. Josiah Quincy, Memoir of the Life of Josiah Quincy Jun. of Massachusetts: By His Son, Josiah Quincy 394 (Boston: Cummings, Hilliard, & Co., 1825); Josiah Quincy, Memoir of the Life of Josiah Quincy, Junior, of Massachusetts Bay: 1744–1775, at 324–25 (Boston: Little, Brown, and Co., Eliza Susan Quincy, ed., 3d ed. 1875).

94. Boston Public Library, More Books: Being the Bulletin of the Boston Public Library 5 (1926).

95. Paul C. Nagel, John Quincy Adams: A Public Life, a Private Life 102, 153, 214 (New York: Knopf, 1997); Hostettler, Cesare Beccaria, 137; *see also* 4 James B. Longacre & James Herring, comp., The National Portrait Gallery of Distinguished Americans 12 (Philadelphia: James B. Longacre, 1839) ("The writer of this article has often heard from individuals, who had been present among the crowd of spectators at the trial, the electrical effect produced upon the jury, and upon the immense and excited auditory, by the first sentence with which he opened his defence; which was the following citation from the then recently published work of Beccaria."). The argument of John Adams—and his use of Beccaria's words at the beginning of that argument—was to be studied for years to come. William Sullivan, An Address to the Members of the Bar of Suffolk, Mass. at Their Stated Meeting on the First Tuesday of March, 1824, at 30 (1825).

96. Bessler, Cruel and Unusual, 179; Proceedings of the Massachusetts Historical Society 160 (Boston: Massachusetts Historical Society 1987); Schwartz & Wishingrad, *The Eighth Amendment, Beccaria, and the Enlightenment*, 814 n.148; *see also* Catalogue of the John Adams Library in the Public Library of the City of Boston 23 (Boston: Trustees of the Public Library of the City of Boston, 1917) (noting that John Adams owned a 1780 Italian edition of *Dei delitti e delle pene* and an English translation of that treatise).

97. Founding Families: Digital Editions of the Papers of the Winthrops and the Adamses, C. James Taylor, ed., Boston: Massachusetts Historical Society, 2007, at http://www.masshist.org/publications/apde/portia.php?id=DJA01d476. John Adams' June 1770 diary entry is his first reference to Beccaria. Robert C. Baron & Conrad Edick Wright, eds., The Libraries, Leadership, & Legacy of John Adams and Thomas Jefferson 287 n.20 (Boston, MA: Fulcrum Publishing/Massachusetts Historical Society, 2010).

98. 4 Charles Francis Adams, ed., The Works of John Adams, Second President of the United States 443 (Boston: Charles C. Little & James Brown, 1851).

99. George W. Carey, ed., The Political Writings of John Adams 159 (Washington, DC: Regnery Publishing, 2000); *see also* Philip Mazzei to James Madison, Feb. 4, 1788, *available at* www.founders.archives.gov (a footnote to the letter notes that, in it, "Mazzei was evidently referring to the pamphlet by a 'Farmer of New-Jersey,' *Observations on Government, Including Some Animadversions on Mr. Adams's Defence of the Constitutions . . . and on Mr. De Lolme's Constitution of England* (New York, 1787). Contemporaries attributed the authorship to Gov. William Livingston of New Jersey, but the 'farmer' in fact was John Stevens, later famous as an inventor.").

100. 2 Joseph Priestley, Lectures on History and General Policy 190, 303–04 (Philadelphia: P. Byrne, 1803); Daniel J. Boorstin, The Lost World of Thomas Jefferson 17–19 (Chicago: The University of Chicago Press, 1993); Peter Watson, Ideas: A History of Thought and Invention, From Fire to Freud 577 (New York: HarperPerennial, 2006).

101. Federal Judicial Center, History of the Federal Judiciary, http://www.fjc.gov/servlet/nGetInfo?jid=2348&cid=999&ctype=na&instate=na.

102. Charles Lanman, Dictionary of the United States Congress and the General Government; Compiled as a Book of Reference for the American People 351 (Hartford: T. Belknap and H. E. Goodwin, 5th ed. 1868); John H. Morison, Life of the Hon. Jeremiah Smith, LL.D.: Member of Congress during Washington's Administration, Judge of the United States Circuit Court, Chief Justice of Hew Hampshire, Etc. 184–85, 199, 201–203, 500–501 (Boston: Charles C. Little and James Brown, 1845).

103. 1 L. H. Butterfield, ed., Legal Papers of John Adams lii, 354 (Boston: Massachusetts Historical Society, 1965); James Grant, John Adams: Party of One 86 (New York: Farrar, Straus and Giroux,

2005); 1 L. H. Butterfield, ed., Diary and Autobiography of John Adams 354 (New York: Atheneum, 1964) (discussing the Samuel Quinn case).

104. Caso, We the People, 101.

105. Bessler, Cruel and Unusual, 59–60, 136–37. Adams sometimes did so against the advice of his cabinet. Paul Douglas Newman, Fries's Rebellion: The Enduring Struggle for the American Revolution 182–83 (Philadelphia: University of Pennsylvania Press, 2004).

106. No. 33: Catalogue des Livres Nouveaux (Du Samedi 17 Août 1776); Diary of John Adams, "Personal Expenditures, February–July 1780," *available at* http://www.masshist.org/publications/apde/portia.php?id=DJA02d544 (entries for July 7–8, 1780). In 1778, John Adams had recorded in his diary that "the best Italien Dictionary and Grammar are those of Veneroni." Diary of John Adams, *available at* http://www.masshist.org/publications/apde/portia.php?id=DJA02d409 (May 30, 1778 entry); *see also* Diary of John Adams, *available at* http://www.masshist.org/publications/apde/portia.php?id=DJA04d093 (May 30, 1778 entry) ("Having some Inclination to look a little into the Italian Language, I asked him which was the best Dictionary and Grammar of it. He said those of Veneroni…."). Signor Giovanni Veneroni published a popular Italian grammar. Giovanni Veneroni, The Complete Italian Master; Containing the Best and Easiest Rules for Attaining that Language (London: J. Nourse, 1763) (listing Signor Veneroni as "Italian Secretary to the Late French King"); *see also* Thompson Cooper, A New Biographical Dictionary: Containing Concise Notices of Eminent Persons of All Ages and Countries 1146 (London: George Bell & Sons, 1873) ("Veneroni, Giovanni, a grammarian, whose real name was Vigneron, which he Italianized, in order to pass for a native of Florence, though he was born at Verdun. He taught Italian with reputation at Paris, where he published a grammar (1710) and dictionary of that language, which still hold their rank among useful books.").

107. Dei Delitti e Delle Pene, Edizione Sesta Di nuovo corretta ed accresciuta ("Harlem, Et se vend A Paris, Chez Molini Libraire, Quai des Augustins," 1766); Newman & Marongiu, On Crimes and Punishments, lxii; Catalogue of the John Adams Library in the Public Library of the City of Boston 19 (Boston: Trustees of the Public Library of the City of Boston, 1917); Edward Planta, A New Picture of Paris; or, The Stranger's Guide to the French Metropolis 429 (London: Samuel Leigh, 15th ed., 1827); Jamie Cox Robertson, A Literary Paris: Hemingway, Colette, Sedaris, and Others on the Uncommon Lure of the City of Light 94 (Avon, MA: Adams Media, 2010); http://data.bnf.fr/122 30833/giovanni_claudio_molini/; http://cesar.org.uk/cesar2/places/places.php?fct=edit&location_UOID=200627; Benjamin Franklin to Jean Chappe d'Auteroche, Jan. 31, 1768, *available at* www.founders.archives.gov; Mariana Starke, Information and Directions for Travellers on the Continent 373–75 (Paris: A. and W. Galignani, 5th ed. 1826); Mariana Starke, Travels in Europe Between the Years 1824 and 1828 Adapted to the Use of Travellers Comprising an Historical Account of Sicily 493 (London: John Murray, 1828); Robert M. S. McDonald, ed., Light and Liberty: Thomas Jefferson and the Power of Knowledge (Charlottesville: University of Virginia Press, 2012); Italica, Vols. 25–26, p. 95 (1948); Ben Thomas & Timothy Wilson, eds., C. D. E. Fortnum and the Collecting and Study of Applied Arts and Sculpture in Victorian England 172–73 (Oxford: Oxford University Press, 1999); John Adams to John Bondfield, July 7, 1780; Kevin J. Hayes, The Road to Monticello: The Life and Mind of Thomas Jefferson 69–70, 148, 282, 285 (Oxford: Oxford University Press, 2008); Hans Erich Bödeker, Histoires du livre 114, 124, 135 (Institut Mémoires de l'édition contemporaine, 1995); Ernst Erich Noth, Books Abroad iii, 208 (Norman: University of Oklahoma Press, 1935); Tom O'Neill, Of Virgin Muses and of Love: A Study of Foscolo's Dei Sepolcri 111 (Foundation for Italian Studies, University College Dublin—Irish Academic Press, 1981). Those studying Italian were often directed to Beccaria's treatise as a book to read. Henry Marius Tourner, A New Introduction to the Italian Language, Grounded on Reason and Authority xxxi (Edinburgh: Neill & Co., 1794) (listing Beccaria among the Italian writers to be read "for subject, and style, and language").

108. Bessler, Cruel and Unusual, 179–80; Catalogue of the John Adams Library in the Public Library of the City of Boston vii–viii, 35, 93, 112–13, 171, 176, 218, 235 (Boston: Trustees of the Public Library of the City of Boston, 1917); 2 Benjamin Rush, Medical Inquiries and Observations 29, 31, 44–46, 53–54, 56 (Philadelphia: J. Conrad & Co., 2d ed. 1805).

109. Luigi Ricci, trans., Niccolò Machiavelli, The Prince 60, 65 (London: Grant Richards, 1903) (1532); 1 Leslie J. Walker, trans., The Discourses of Niccolò Machiavelli 53 (New York: Routledge, 2013); Paola Rapelli, Symbols of Power in Art 362 (Los Angeles, CA: The J. Paul Getty Museum, 2011).

110. James Madison Papers, Commonplace Book, 1759–1772 & Notes on Banks [ca. Feb. 1], 1791; Robert R. Livingston to Benjamin Franklin, Jan. 7, 1782; Thomas Jefferson to Boinod & Gaillard, Apr. 26, 1784; Report on Books for Congress, [Jan. 23,] 1783; Abigail Adams to Richard Cranch, May 10, 1787, *available at* www.founders.archives.gov; Founding Families: Digital Editions of the Pa-

pers of the Winthrops and the Adamses, ed. C. James Taylor, Boston: Massachusetts Historical Society, 2007, *at* http://www.masshist.org/publications/apde/portia.php?mode=p&id=DJA03p194. In 1800, John Adams gave an English translation of Beccaria's treatise to his son Thomas Boylston Adams. Id. A copy of that Italian-to-English translation, a 1775 edition printed for "F. Newbery" in London, is accessible online. *See* http://archive.org/stream/essayoncrimespun1775becc#page/n3/mode/2up.

111. Robert J. Allison, The Boston Tea Party (Carlisle, MA: Commonwealth Editions, 2007); Studies on Voltaire and the Eighteenth Century 1499 (Institut et Musee Voltaire, 1963) (Volume 27 of Transactions of the First International Congress on the Enlightenment); Founding Families: Digital Editions of the Papers of the Winthrops and the Adamses, C. James Taylor, ed., Boston: Massachusetts Historical Society, 2007, *at* http://www.masshist.org/publications/apde/portia.php?mode=p&id=DJA03p194.

112. Diary of John Adams, Vol. 3 (entry for "24 [*i.e.* 23] July," 1787), *available at* Massachusetts Historical Society, Digital Editions: Adams Papers, http://www.masshist.org/publications/apde/portia.php?id=DJA03d188.

113. John Adams to Abigail Adams, Feb. 3, 1793, *available at* www.founders.archives.gov; *see also* Thomas Jefferson to William Duane, Apr. 4, 1813, *available at* www.founders.archives.gov (referencing receipt of "the Commentary on Montesquieu," with Jefferson emphasizing that "[i]t is true that I am tired of practical politics, and happier while reading the history of antient, than of modern times"). Writing in the midst of the War of 1812, Jefferson wrote William Duane in 1813:

> [T]he total banishment of all moral principle from the Code which governs the intercourse of nations, the melancholy reflection that after the mean, wicked and cowardly cunning of the Cabinets of the age of Machiavel had given place to the integrity and good faith which dignified the succeeding one of a Chatham and Turgot, that this is to be swept away again by the daring profligacy, and avowed destitution of all moral principle of a Cartouche and a Blackbeard, sickens my soul unto death. I turn from the contemplation with loathing, and take refuge in the histories of other times, where if they also furnished their Tarquins, their Catilines & Caligulas, their stories are handed to us under the brand of a Livy, a Sallust and a Tacitus, and we are comforted with the reflection that the condemnation of all succeeding generations has confirmed the censures of the historian, and consigned their memories to everlasting infamy, a solace we cannot have with the Georges & Napoleons, but by anticipation.

Id.

114. James E. Lewis Jr., John Quincy Adams: Policymaker for the Union 5 (Wilmington, DE: Scholarly Resources, 2001).

115. Diary of John Quincy Adams, Volume 2 (entry for Feb. 13, 1787), *available at* Massachusetts Historical Society, Digital Editions: Adams Papers, http://www.masshist.org/publications/apde/portia.php?id=DQA02d338.

116. The bodies of executed criminals were sometimes publicly dissected. Cheung, Public Trust in Medical Research?, 37–38.

117. Diary of John Quincy Adams, Volume 2 (entry for Feb. 13, 1787), *available at* Massachusetts Historical Society, Digital Editions: Adams Papers, http://www.masshist.org/publications/apde/portia.php?id=DQA02d338.

118. Halbrook, A Right to Bear Arms, 132 n.181.

119. Bessler, Cruel and Unusual, 63–64, 273–74.

120. 5 Worthington Chauncey Ford, ed., Writings of John Quincy Adams 439, 544 (New York: Macmillan, 1916).

121. Bessler, Cruel and Unusual, 274.

122. Robert A. Ferguson, Law & Letters in American Culture 53 (Cambridge: Harvard University Press, 1984); *see also* http://tjportal.worldcat.org/title/dei-delitti-e-delle-pene/oclc/11196153&referer=brief_results.

123. Thomas Jefferson's Monticello, http://www.monticello.org/site/jefferson/laws-forbid-carrying-armsquotation; http://tjportal.monticello.org/cgi-bin/Pwebrecon.cgi?BBID=80719. This copy was later sold to the Library of Congress. Sowerby, Entry 2349, 3:21, *available at* http://www.monticello.org/site/jefferson/laws-forbid-carrying-armsquotation; Index of Catalogue of the Library of Thomas Jefferson (compiled with annotations by E. Millicent Sowerby (Library of Congress, 1952–59), *available at* http://catdir.loc.gov/catdir/toc/becites/main/jefferson/52060000.idx.html#B; *see also* James Gilreath & Douglas L. Wilson, eds., Thomas Jefferson's Library: A Catalog with the Entries in His Own Order (Washington, DC: Library of Congress, 1989), ch. 24 (listing Beccaria's treatise).

124. Blinka, *Jefferson and Juries*, 40; Tomlins & Mann, The Many Legalities of Early America, 116; Saul K. Padover, Jefferson 17 (New York: North American Library, 1952); Dumbauld, *Thomas Jef-*

ferson's Equity Commonplace Book, 1259. A reference to Beccaria's *On Crimes and Punishments* also appears in the commonplace book of Josiah Quincy, Jr. Daniel R. Coquillette, *The Legal Education of a Patriot: Josiah Quincy Jr.'s Law Commonplace (1763)*, 39 Ariz. St. L.J. 317, 367, 369 (2007); *see also* Patrick J. Charles, *Restoring "Life, Liberty, and the Pursuit of Happiness" in Our Constitutional Jurisprudence: An Exercise in Legal History*, 20 Wm. & Mary Bill Rts. J. 457, 498 n.249 (2011) ("The lasting impression of Beccaria on this point is evidenced by its notation in Josiah Quincy's Political Commonplace Book.").

125. Bessler, Cruel and Unusual, 54; Chinard, The Commonplace Book of Thomas Jefferson, 298–317.

126. Dumbauld, *Thomas Jefferson's Equity Commonplace Book*, 1258–59; Chinard, The Commonplace Book of Thomas Jefferson, 298–317; http://memory.loc.gov/ammem/collections/jefferson_papers/mtjser5.html.

127. John Hostettler, Champions of the Rule of Law 86 (Hampshire, U.K.: Waterside Press, 2011).

128. Chinard, The Commonplace Book of Thomas Jefferson, 298–317.

129. Sally De Witt Spurgin, The Power to Persuade: A Rhetoric and Reader for Argumentative Writing 160 (Upper Saddle River, NJ: Prentice Hall, 1993).

130. David Thomas Konig, "Legal Fictions and the Rule(s) of Law: The Jeffersonian Critique of Common-Law Adjudications," *in* Tomlins & Mann, The Many Legalities of Early America, 116; John Hostettler, Champions of the Rule of Law 86 (Hampshire, U.K.: Waterside Press, 2011).

131. 1 Thomas Jefferson Randolph, ed., Memoirs, Correspondence, and Private Papers of Thomas Jefferson: Late President of the United States 124–28 (London: Henry Colburn & Richard Bentley, 1829); Bessler, Cruel and Unusual, 144–45; Cheung, Public Trust in Medical Research?, 37–38.

132. Dubber, "An Extraordinarily Beautiful Document," 135.

133. George W. Munford, comp., Third Edition of the Code of Virginia: including Legislation to January 1, 1874, at 1261 (Richmond, VA: James E. Goode, 1873); B. L. Rayner, Life of Thomas Jefferson 145 (Boston: Lilly, Wait, Colman, & Holden, 1834); Richard F. Hamilton, The Social Misconstruction of Reality: Validity and Verification in the Scholarly Community 177 (New Haven: Yale University Press, 1996); Masur, Rites of Execution, 78.

134. Hostettler, Cesare Beccaria, 61; 2 Memoirs of the Life of Sir Samuel Romilly, Written by Himself 1810 (London: John Murray, 1840); Harry Potter, Hanging in Judgment: Religion and the Death Penalty in England from the Bloody Code to Abolition 34 (Norwick, U.K.: SCM Press, 1993).

135. David Lemmings, Professors of the Law: Barristers and English Legal Culture in the Eighteenth Century 218 & n.53 (Oxford: Oxford University Press, 2000); Eden, Principles of Penal Law, 235, 264, 296.

136. Paul Rosenzweig, *Reflections on the Atrophying Pardon Power*, 102 J. Crim. L. & Criminology 593, 601 (2012).

137. W. Hamilton Bryson, "The History of Legal Education in Virginia," History of the Marshall-Wythe School of Law, Paper 8, http://scholarship.law.wm.edu/history/8, at 155, 157–62, 164, 168–69 (1979). Jeremy Bentham was a barrister of Lincoln's Inn. Bernard William Kelly, A Short History of the English Bar 107–108 (London: Swan Sonnenschein & Co., 1908).

138. Harold Hellenbrand, The Unfinished Revolution: Education and Politics in the Thought of Thomas Jefferson 109 (Newark: University of Delaware Press, 1990).

139. Eden, Principles of Penal Law, 12, 21–22; Preyer, Crime, the Criminal Law and Reform in Post-Revolutionary Virginia, 61 & n.27.

140. Eden, Principles of Penal Law, 235, 264, 296; Gertrude Himmelfarb, Victorian Minds: A Study of Intellectuals in Crisis and Ideologies in Transition 39 (Chicago, IL: Ivan R. Dee, 1995).

141. Thomas Jefferson to Henry Tazewell, Jan. 27, 1798 ("I devoted yesterday evening to the extracting passages from Law authors showing that in Law-language the term crime is in common use applied to *misdemeanors*, & that *impeachments*, even when for *misdemeanors* only are *criminal prosecutions*. These proofs were so numerous that my patience could go no further than two authors, Blackstone & Wooddeson.")

142. Aleck Loker, Profiles in Colonial History 105 (2008).

143. J. E. Morpurgo, Their Majesties' Royall Colledge: William and Mary in the Seventeen and Eighteenth Centuries 94 (Williamsburg, VA: College of William and Mary, 1976); The Library of George Wythe at 13, *available at* https://digitalarchive.wm.edu/bitstream/handle/10288/13433/GeorgeWytheLibrary.pdf?sequence=1 ("Thomas Jefferson owned the New York: 1809 edition that was sold to the Library of Congress in 1815, but it did not survive to know who may have previously owned it. He also had owned the Italian edition … that was missing when he sold his library to the Library of Congress in 1815. Since

the New York edition was published long after Wythe had died, then the edition that Wythe may have owned may have been the unknown edition in Italian. There is an Italian copy listed in the auction catalog printed in 1829 for the sale of Jefferson's library following his death: *#629*."); Catalogue: President Jefferson's Library: A Catalogue of the Extensive and Valuable Library of the Late President Jefferson 11 (1829) (listing the Italian version of Beccaria's treatise as lot number "629" for the auction to be held "at the Long Room, Pennsylvania Avenue, Washington City" by Nathaniel P. Poor).

144. James L. Golden & Alan L. Golden, Thomas Jefferson and the Rhetoric of Virtue 4–6 (Oxford: Rowman & Littlefield Publishers, 2002); W. Cleon Skousen, The Making of America: The Substance and Meaning of the Constitution (C&J Investments, 1985); Aleck Loker, Profiles in Colonial History 105 (Williamsburg, VA: Solitude Press, 2008); Robert Aitken & Marilyn Aitken, Law Makers, Law Breakers and Uncommon Trials 105 (Chicago, IL: American Bar Association, 2007).

145. W. Hamilton Bryson, "The History of Legal Education in Virginia," History of the Marshall-Wythe School of Law, Paper 8, http://scholarship.law.wm.edu/history/8, at 175–76 (1979).

146. Thomas Jefferson to John Norvell, June 11, 1807.

147. "Adamantios Koraes," Thomas Jefferson's Monticello, http://www.monticello.org/site/jefferson/adamantios-koraes. Jefferson called him Adamantios Coray. For further information on Jefferson and Koraes, see Nicholas D. Diamantides, "An Elective Encounter: The Koraes-Jefferson Connection," *in* Modern Greek Studies Yearbook 37905 (1994–1995): 587–602; Andrew S. Horton, *Jefferson and Korais: The American Revolution and the Greek Constitution*, 13 Comparative Literature Studies 323–329 (1976).

148. Ioannis D. Evrigenis, *A Founder on Founding: Jefferson's Advice to Koraes*, 1 The Historical Rev. 157, 177–78 (2004).

149. 8 J. Jefferson Looney, ed., The Papers of Thomas Jefferson: Retirement Series (October 1814 to August 1815) 388 (Princeton: Princeton University Press, 2012).

150. Gordon S. Brown, Incidental Architect: William Thornton and the Cultural Life of Early Washington, D.C., 1794–1828, at 52 (Athens, OH: Ohio University Press, 2009).

151. Andrew Burstein & Nancy Isenberg, Madison and Jefferson 471 (New York: Random House, 2010); 8 J. Jefferson Looney, ed., The Papers of Thomas Jefferson: Retirement Series 388, 673 (Princeton: Princeton University Press, 2011); 3 E. Millicent Sowerby, Catalogue of the Library of Thomas Jefferson 21 (Charlottesville: University Press of Virginia, 1953); Catalogue of the Library of Congress 171, 181, 189 (Washington, DC: Duff Green, 1830).

152. Dorothy Medlin, *Thomas Jefferson, André Morellet, and the French Version of Notes on the State of Virginia*, 35 William & Mary Q. 85, 85–89, 91 (1978).

153. Robert A. Silverman, Terence P. Thornberry, Bernard Cohen & Barry Krisberg, eds., Crime and Justice at the Millennium: Essays by and in Honor of Marvin E. Wolfgang 384 (Norwell, MA: Kluwer Academic Publishers, 2002) ("Thomas Jefferson knew of Beccaria's essay and in his first inaugural address proposed what he called 'Equal and exact justice to all men'"); *see also* 8 H. A. Washington, ed., The Writings of Thomas Jefferson: Being His Autobiography, Correspondence, Reports, Messages, Addresses, and Other Writings, Official and Private 21–22 (New York: Riker, Thorne & Co., 1854) (Jefferson's "Special Message" of January 28, 1802, to the "*Gentlemen of the Senate and House of Representatives*" reads in part: "[I]t will be worthy the consideration of the legislature, whether the provisions of the law inflicting on Indians, in certain cases, the punishment of death by hanging, might not permit its commutation into death by military execution, the form of the punishment in the former way being peculiarly repugnant to their ideas"); id. at 229 (Jefferson's January 9, 1809 letter "*To the Deputies of the Cherokee Upper Towns*" gives this advice to Cherokee Indians: "All of you being equally free, no one has a right to say what shall be law for the others. Our way is to put these questions to the vote, and to consider that as law for which the majority votes. The fool has as great a right to express his opinion by vote as the wise, because he is equally free, and equally master of himself."); id. at 230 (Jefferson's January 9, 1809 letter "*To the Deputies of the Cherokee Upper Towns*" further notes: "In our States, generally, we punish murder only by death, and all other crimes by solitary confinement in a prison."); id. at 1–4 (in his first inaugural address of March 4, 1801, Jefferson addressed his "*Friends and Fellow Citizens*" and spoke of "equal rights, which equal laws must protect"; spoke of the Union's "republican form" and said "We are all republicans, we are all federalists"; and called for "[e]qual and exact justice to all men, of whatever state or persuasion, religious or political").

154. 1 Thomas Jefferson Randolph, ed., Memoir, Correspondence, and Miscellanies, from the Papers of Thomas Jefferson 120–21 (Boston: Gray and Bowen, 2d ed. 1830); James Headley, *Proportionality Between Crimes, Offenses, and Punishments*, 17 St. Thomas L. Rev. 247, 250 (2004). Identical language is found in a Kentucky law passed in 1798. "An Act to amend the Penal Laws of this Commonwealth" (approved Feb. 10, 1798), *reprinted in* 2 C. S. Morehead & Mason Brown, eds., A

Digest of the Statute Laws of Kentucky, of a Public and Permanent Nature 1264 (Frankfort, KY: Albert G. Hodges, 1834).

155. Mann Page to Thomas Jefferson, Enclosing Court Proceedings against a Slave, Together with Jefferson's Reprieve, May 13, 1781, *available at* www.founders.archives.gov; Harry M. Ward, The War for Independence and the Transformation of American Society 57 (London: Routledge, 1999).

156. Benjamin Franklin to William Franklin, July 14, 1773; Daniel Roberdeau to John Adams, Jan. 21, 1778; Thomas McKean to Thomas Jefferson, Mar. 7, 1800, *available at* www.founders.archives. gov; Blinka, *Jefferson and Juries*, 90; Dubber, "An Extraordinarily Beautiful Document," 133–34.

157. Bessler, Cruel and Unusual, 141–42.

158. James F. Davis, Lex Talionis in Early Judaism and the Exhortation of Jesus in Matthew 5.38–42, at 1, 97 (New York: T&T Clark International, 2005).

159. Davison M. Douglas, *The Jeffersonian Vision of Legal Education*, 51 J. Legal Educ. 185, 200 (2001); L. Carroll Judson, A Biography of the Signers of the Declaration of Independence, and of Washington and Patrick Henry 60 (Philadelphia: J. Dobson, 1839); Fawn M. Brodie, Thomas Jefferson: An Intimate History 60–61 (New York: W. W. Norton & Co., 1974); Jan Ellen Lewis & Peter S. Onuf, eds., Sally Hemings and Thomas Jefferson: History, Memory, and Civic Culture 58 (Charlottesville: University of Virginia Press, 1999).

160. Ed Southern, ed., The Jamestown Adventure: Accounts of the Virginia Colony, 1605–1614, at 178–93 (Salem, NC: John F. Blair, 2004).

161. Mitchel P. Roth, Crime and Punishment: A History of the Criminal Justice System 67 (Belmont, CA: Wadsworth, 2005).

162. Bessler, Cruel and Unusual, 268. For example, two of the men convicted of manslaughter at the Boston Massacre trial "prayed the benefit of clergy, which was allowed; and were burnt in the hand in open court, and discharged." William Sullivan, Address to the Members of the Bar of Suffolk, Mass. at Their Stated Meeting on the First Tuesday of March, 1824, at 32 (Boston: Press of the North American Review, 1825).

163. Banner, The Death Penalty, 8.

164. John P. Foley, ed., The Jeffersonian Cyclopedia: A Comprehensive Collection of the Views of Thomas Jefferson 422 (New York: Funk & Wagnalls Co., 1900); Kevin J. Hayes, The Road to Monticello: The Life and Mind of Thomas Jefferson 420 (Oxford: Oxford University Press, 2008).

165. Suzanne Lebsock, The Free Women of Petersburg: Status and Culture in a Southern Town, 1784–1860, at 206 (1985); Edward A. Wyatt, IV, *George Keith Taylor, 1769–1815, Virginia Federalist and Humanitarian*, 16 Wm. & Mary College Q. His. Mag. 1, 1 (1936).

166. George Keith Taylor, *Substance of a Speech Delivered in the House of Delegates in Virginia, on the Bill to Amend the Penal Laws of This Commonwealth* (Richmond: Samuel Pleasants, 1796); R. A. Burchell, ed., The End of Anglo-America: Historical Essays in the Study of Cultural Divergence 88 (Manchester University Press, 1991).

167. Scott, Memoirs of Lieut.-General Scott, 26–27.

168. The Virginia Evangelical and Literary Magazine 553 (1818).

169. Michael L. Nicholls, Whispers of Rebellion: Narrating Gabriel's Conspiracy (Charlottesville: University of Virginia Press, 2012).

170. Jean Edward Smith, John Marshall: Definer of a Nation 161–62 (New York: Henry Holt, 1996); Charles Royster, Light-Horse Harry Lee (New York: Random House, 2013).

171. Thomas Jefferson to William Roscoe, Dec. 27, 1820, *reprinted in* 15 Albert Ellery Bergh, ed., The Writings of Thomas Jefferson 302 (Washington, DC: The Thomas Jefferson Memorial Association, 1907).

172. William Roscoe, Observations on Penal Jurisprudence, and the Reformation of Criminals 3, 31, 54, 65–66 & n.*, 70, 72, 74 n.*, 86, 90, Appendix (London: T. Cadell & W. Davies, 1819).

173. 4 Duke de la Rochefoucault Liancourt, Travels through the United States of North America, the Country of the Iroquois, and Upper Canada, in the Years 1795, 1796, and 1797, at 43 (London: R. Phillips, 2d ed. 1800).

174. Bessler, Cruel and Unusual, 82; Edwin Morris Betts, Thomas Jefferson's Farm Book 426–27 (Redmond, WA: Laing Communications, 1999).

175. Keally McBride, Punishment and Political Order: Law, Meaning, and Violence 90, 97–98 (Ann Arbor: University of Michigan Press, 2007); Negley K. Teeters, Caleb Lownes of Philadelphia, 1754–1828: Administrator of the First Penitentiary in the World—the Walnut Street Jail (Philadelphia: Pennsylvania Prison Society, 1963).

176. Robert J. Turnbull, A Visit to the Philadelphia Prison, in a Letter to a Friend, *reprinted in*

The Belfast Monthly Magazine, Vol. 4, No. 22 (May 31, 1810), pp. 327–344; 2 Rochefoucault Liancourt, Travels through the United States of North America, 336–46.

177. Thomas Jefferson, Autobiography Draft Fragment, Jan. 6–July 27, 1821.

178. Plan for the Committee to Revise the Laws (Jan. 13, 1777), *available at* http://www.consource.org/document/plan-for-the-committee-to-revise-the-laws-1777-1-13/; Dubber, "An Extraordinarily Beautiful Document," 129–30.

179. Gideon Freudenthal & Peter McLaughlin, eds., The Social and Economic Roots of the Scientific Revolution: Texts by Boris Hessen and Henryk Grossman 63 (Dordrecht, Netherlands: Springer, 2009); Joseph Priestley, "An Essay on the First Principles of Government, and on the Nature of Political, Civil, and Religious Liberty" (1768), *available at* http://oll.libertyfund.org/simple.php?id=1767; Peter Miller, ed., Political Writings: Joseph Priestley 38 (Cambridge: Cambridge University Press, 1993).

180. Mary Ellen Bowden & Lisa Rosner, eds., Joseph Priestley: Radical Thinker 44–48 (Philadelphia: Chemical Heritage Foundation, 2005); Isabel Rivers & David L. Wykes, eds., Joseph Priestley, Scientist, Philosopher, and Theologian 209 (Oxford: Oxford University Press, 2008); Joseph Priestley, Lectures on History and General Policy; To Which Is Prefixed an Essay on a Course of Liberal Education for Civil and Active Life 462 (London: Thomas Tegg, 1826); 2 Thomas Cooper, Memoirs of Dr. Joseph Priestley, to the Year 1795, Written by Himself: with a Continuation, to the Time of His Decease, By His Son, Joseph Priestley 46, 54, 66, 93, 626, 628, 651, 663, 665, 721, 761, 796–803, 814–16 (London: J. Johnson, 1807); Benjamin Franklin to the Managers of the Philadelphia Silk Filature [before May 10, 1772]: Extracts; The Count of Belgioioso: Two Letters to Benjamin Franklin, Sept. 30, 1772, *available at* www.founders.archives.gov.

181. Rachel Hammersley, French Revolutionaries and English Republicans: The Cordeliers Club, 1790–1794, at 1, 81 (Suffolk, UK: The Boydell Press, 2005); Théophile Mandar, Des Insurrections, Ouvrage Philosophique et Politique 435–36 (Paris, 1793); Anthony Page, John Jebb and the Enlightenment Origins of British Radicalism 228, 230 (Westport, CT: Praeger Publishers, 2003); Charles Forster, The Life of John Jebb, D.D. F.R.S: Bishop of Limerick, Ardfert and Aghadoe (London: James Duncan, 2d ed. 1836); John Jebb, An Address to the Freeholders of Middlesex, Assembled at Freemasons Tavern, in Great Queen Street, upon Monday the 20th of December 1779, Being the Day Appointed for a Meeting of the Freeholders, for the Purpose of Establishing Meetings to Maintain and Support the Freedom of Election 16–17 (London: J. Dixwell, T. Cadell & J. Almon, 1779); Ralph C. Hancock & L. Gary Lambert, The Legacy of the French Revolution 194, 202 (Oxford: Rowman & Littlefield, 1996); John Jebb to George Washington, June 4, 1785; John Adams to John Quincy Adams, June 6, 1784, *available at* www.founders.archives.gov. In 1800, Benjamin Rush wrote this to Thomas Jefferson of "Dr. Jebb": " 'No good effort is lost' was a favorite Saying of the late Dr. Jebb." Benjamin Rush to Thomas Jefferson, Oct. 6, 1800, *available at* www.founders.archives.gov.

182. Thomas Jefferson, Autobiography Draft Fragment, Jan. 6–July 27, 1821; Scott, Memoirs of Lieut.-General Scott, 26. A further description of Virginia's penal reform debate — and James Madison's role in advocating for Jefferson's bill — can be found elsewhere along with a description of George Keith Taylor's subsequent bill. *See* Bessler, Cruel and Unusual, 156–57.

183. Caso, We, the People, 252–58; Schiavo, The Italians in America Before the Civil War, 161–66, 175–77; Chiara Cillerai, " 'A continual and almost exclusive correspondence': Philip Mazzei's Transatlantic Citizenship," *in* Theresa Strouth Gaul & Sharon M. Harris, eds., Letters and Cultural Transformations in the United States, 1760–1860, at 17, 21 & n.8 (Surrey, UK: Ashgate Publishing Ltd., 2009).

184. Salvatore J. LaGumina, Frank J. Cavaioli, Salvatore Primeggia & Joseph A. Varacalli, eds., The Italian American Experience: An Encyclopedia 361–62 (New York: Routledge, 2000); Margherita Marchione, ed. & S. Eugene Scalia, trans., Philip Mazzei: My Life and Wanderings 99 (American Institute of Italian Studies, 1980).

185. Schiavo, The Italians in America Before the Civil War, 175–76; Masini & Gori, How Florence Invented America, 115–17, 131, 138, 152, 156–57. For more information on Philip Mazzei, see H. R. Marraro, ed., *Philip Mazzei on American Political, Social and Economic Problems*, 15 J. of Southern Hist. 354 (1949).

186. Masini & Gori, How Florence Invented America, 119, 121.

187. Kathryn Preyer, "Two Enlightened Reformers of the Criminal Law: Thomas Jefferson of Virginia and Peter Leopold, Grand Duke of Tuscany," *in* Blackstone in America, 264 n.39; Irving Brant, James Madison: The Virginia Revolutionist 343, 347–50 (Indianapolis, IN: Bobbs-Merrill, 1941).

188. Luciano J. Iorizzo, Italian Immigration and the Impact of the Padrone System 12 (1980); *see also* Schiavo, The Italians in America Before the Civil War, 171 ("Towards the end of 1778 Jefferson

asked Mazzei if he would go to Europe and arrange a loan for the state. Governor Patrick Henry, George Mason, John Page and others had approved the idea and thought that Mazzei was the best man for the job. Mazzei accepted, signed the Oath of Allegiance to the Commonwealth of Virginia on April 21, 1779, and on June 19, 1779 ... he sailed for France.").

189. 2 Filippo Mazzei, Memorie della vita e delle peregrinazioni del Fiorentino Filippo Mazzei con documenti storici sulle sue missioni politiche come agente degli Stati-Uniti d'America e del re Stanislao di Polonia 296, 299 (Lugano: Tipografia Della Svizzera Italiana, 1846).

190. 7 Maeva Marcus, ed., The Documentary History of the Supreme Court of the United States, 1789–1800, at 59 (New York: Columbia University Press, 2003).

191. Masini & Gori, How Florence Invented America, 133–37; Marchione, The Fighting Nun, 124 (referencing Mazzei's letter of May 12, 1785, to John Blair); *see also* Caso, They Too Made America Great, 47 (noting that Mazzei "helped to introduce Cesare Beccaria's humanitarian philosophy, which pervades such documents as the Declaration of Causes (1775), the Declaration of Independence (1776), the Constitution, and the Bill of Rights"; that Mazzei "worked on and translated the Declaration of Causes"; and that Benjamin Franklin, in a letter to Mazzei about the Declaration, wrote: "I am myself much pleased, that you have sent a Translation of our Declaration to the Grand Duke; because having high esteem of the Character of that Prince ... I should be happy to find that we stood well in the opinion of that court.").

192. Rules of the Constitutional Society of Virginia (ca. 14 June 1784), *available at* http://www.consource.org/document/rules-of-the-constitutional-society-of-virginia/.

193. Letter from Richard Henry Lee to Patrick Henry, Nov. 15, 1778, *in* James Curtis Ballagh, ed., The Letters of Richard Henry Lee 451–52 (New York: The MacMillan Co., 1911).

194. Howard R. Marraro, ed., Philip Mazzei: Virginia's Agent in Europe 14 (New York: New York Public Library, 1935); Schiavo, The Italians in America Before the Civil War, 166; Howard R. Marraro, Mazzei's Correspondence with the Grand Duke of Tuscany During His American Mission, pp. 1–48, *available at* http://archive.org/stream/mazzeiscorrespon00mazz#page/n0/mode/2up.

195. Buccini, The Americas in Italian Literature and Culture 1700–1825, at 138–40, 144, 149; Reneé Critcher Lyons, Foreign-Born American Patriots: Sixteen Volunteer Leaders in the Revolutionary War 5–17 (Jefferson, NC: McFarland & Co., 2014).

196. David J. Ley, Insatiable Wives: Women Who Stray and the Men Who Love Them 124–25 (Lanham, MD: Rowman & Littlefield); Outlines of the French Revolution Told in Autographs 12 (New York: New York Public Library, 1905); 6 The Penny Cyclopædia of the Society for the Diffusion of Useful Knowledge 129 (London: Charles Knight and Co., 1836); The Life of Joseph Balsamo, Commonly Called Count Cagliostro: Containing the Singular and Uncommon Adventures of that Extraordinary Personage from His Birth Till His Imprisonment in the Castle of St. Angelo iv, 90–92 (London: C. & G. Kearsley, 1791); Derek Parker, Casanova 118 (Charleston, SC: History Press, 2002); Thomas Jefferson to John Paradise, May 4, 1786; Thomas Jefferson to William Stephens Smith, May 4, 1786; Thomas Jefferson to Louis Guillaume Otto, May 7, 1786; Thomas Jefferson, June 4, 1786; Thomas Jefferson to William Short, Mar. 29, 1787, *available at* www.founders.archives.gov.

197. Bessler, Cruel and Unusual, 46.

198. *Furman*, 408 U.S. at 259 (Brennan, J., concurring); Joseph A. Melusky & Keith Alan Pesto, Capital Punishment 69–70 (Santa Barbara, CA: ABC-CLIO, 2011).

199. *Furman*, 408 U.S. at 260 (Brennan, J., concurring).

200. Bessler, Cruel and Unusual, 94–95, 177.

201. *Furman*, 408 U.S. at 260 n.2. (Brennan, J., concurring)

202. Culombe v. Connecticut, 367 U.S. 568, 588 n.30 (1961); Margaret C. Jacob, James R. Jacob, Myrna Chase & Theodore H. Von Laue, Western Civilization: Ideas, Politics, and Society from the 1400s, at 434 (Independence, KY: Cengage Learning, 9th ed. 2009); Jean Kellaway, The History of Torture and Execution: From Early Civilization Through Medieval Times to the Present 58–59 (Guilford, CT: The Lyons Press, 2003).

203. Richard Price, Observations on the Importance of the American Revolution, and the Means of Making It a Benefit to the World 1–2, 6, 83 (Dublin: L. White, et al., 1785); Richard Price, Observations on the Importance of the American Revolution (Boston: Powers and Willis, 1784).

204. Marino & Tiro, Along the Hudson and Mohawk, 9, 11; Heather Ewing, The Lost World of James Smithson: Science, Revolution, and the Birth of the Smithsonian 16, 71–72 (New York: Bloomsbury, 2007); Justin D. Murphy, Military Aircraft, Origins to 1918: An Illustrated History of Their Impact 6 (Santa Barbara, CA: ABC-CLIO, 2005).

205. Pat Rogers, The Samuel Johnson Encyclopedia 137, 229, 286–87 (Westport, CT: Greenwood Press, 1996); John Paradise & William Jones to Benjamin Franklin, May 20, 1779; John Paradise &

William Jones to Benjamin Franklin, June 1, 1779; Richard Price to Benjamin Franklin, Oct. 14, 1779; John Paradise to Benjamin Franklin, Oct. 2, 1780; Benjamin Franklin to Thomas Digges, Oct. 9, 1780; Benjamin Franklin to Richard Price, Oct. 9, 1780; William Hodgson to Benjamin Franklin, May 8, 1781; Thomas Jefferson to James Madison, Apr. 25, 1786; John Paradise to Thomas Jefferson, May 23, 1786; Thomas Jefferson to John Paradise, May 25, 1786; Thomas Jefferson to Archibald Cary and Others, May 29, 1786; Thomas Jefferson to John Paradise, Aug. 8, 1786; Lucy Paradise Barziza to Abigail Adams, Jan. 12, 1788; John Paradise to Thomas Jefferson, [ca. June 1788]; Jefferson's Affidavit concerning John and Lucy Ludwell Paradise, July 6, 1788; Lucy Paradise to George Washington, May 12, 1789; A Fourth of July Tribute to Jefferson, July 4, 1789; Thomas Jefferson to John Paradise, July 5, 1789; John Paradise to George Washington, Apr. 2, 1790; John Paradise to Thomas Jefferson, Apr. 2, 1790; Abigail Adams to Lucy Ludwell Paradise, Sept. 6, 1790, *available at* www.founders.archives.gov.

206. Marino & Tiro, Along the Hudson and Mohawk, 13–15, 19; Christianson, With Liberty for Some, 101.

207. Isenberg, Fallen Founder, 509 n.21 (citing Burr's inventory of his book collection and Burr's use of Beccaria's ideas).

208. "Princeton University in the American Revolution," Princeton University, http://www.princeton.edu/main/about/history/american-revolution/; McGinty, 'An Animated Son of Liberty', 363; William P. Litynski, "Prominent Students & Alumni of Princeton University," http://www.scribd.com/doc/77951495/List-of-Princeton-University-Graduates. Other prominent Princeton graduates whose lives intersected, in one way or another with the issue of capital punishment, included Charles Lee (A.B. 1775), United States Attorney General from 1795 to 1801; Edward Livingston (A.B. 1781), U.S. Secretary of State from 1831–1833; Richard Rush (A.B. 1797), Dr. Benjamin Rush's son and the U.S. Attorney General from 1814 to 1817; and George M. Dallas (A.B. 1810), Vice-President of the United States from 1845–1849. Id.

209. John Witherspoon, The Dominion of Providence over the Passions of Men: A Sermon Preached at Princeton, on the 17th of May, 1776, 9, 49 (Philadelphia, 2d ed./Glasgow, reprinted: Booksellers in Town and Country, 1777).

210. McGinty, 'An Animated Son of Liberty', 69, 104, 121, 123, 138, 157–59, 166, 203, 250–54, 287, 291, 340, 352–53, 358, 363, 366, 369; Brookhiser, Alexander Hamilton, 24; Charles Rice, 50 Questions on the Natural Law: What It Is and Why We Need It 40–43 (San Francisco, CA: Ignatius Press, 1999).

211. Masur, Rites of Execution, 159–60, 174 (citing Princeton University Archives, *Sources for Commencement Notices* and *Faculty Minutes*).

212. Bessler, Cruel and Unusual, 72; Daniel L. Dreisbach, Mark D. Hall & Jeffry H. Morrison, eds., The Founders on God and Government 130, 143 & n.44 (Oxford: Rowman & Littlefield, 2004); Catherine Pease-Watkin & Philip Schofield, eds., The Collected Works of Jeremy Bentham, On the Liberty of the Press, and Public Discussion and Other Legal and Political Writings for Spain and Portugal 182 (Oxford: Oxford University Press, 2012).

213. Subject-Catalogue of the Library of the College of New Jersey, at Princeton 151 (New York, 1884).

214. 1 Davis, The Private Journal of Aaron Burr, 27–28, 32–33, 35, 38–43, 47, 60, 67, 72–73, 86, 113, 125–26, 134–35, 151, 179–80 (containing the private journal entries of Aaron Burr, as well as various letters, depicting the relationship that developed between Jeremy Bentham and Burr from 1808 to 1809).

215. 1 Davis, The Private Journal of Aaron Burr, 114.

216. Bessler, Cruel and Unusual, 50–51; 1 Mary-Jo Kline & Joanne Wood Ryan, eds. Political Correspondence and Public Papers of Aaron Burr 72–76 (Princeton: Princeton University Press, 1983).

217. David O. Stewart, American Emperor: Aaron Burr's Challenge to Jefferson's America 280–81, 292 (New York: Simon & Schuster, 2011); R. Kent Newmyer, The Treason Trial of Aaron Burr: Law, Politics, and the Character Wars of the New Nation 25 (Cambridge: Cambridge University Press, 2012).

218. Bessler, Cruel and Unusual, 50–51 (noting Burr's use of Beccaria's ideas).

219. 1 Davis, The Private Journal of Aaron Burr, 32, 38–39, 46–48, 82–83; *see also* id. at 88 ("Evening with Bentham; conversed of tattooing, and how to be made useful; of infanticide; of crimes against Nature, &c., &c."); id. at 93 ("my great and good friend Bentham"); id. at 98 ("I have been living all this while with my great and good friend Bentham."); id. at 100 ("My amiable friend Bentham is a botanist."); id. at 147 ("Went to bed, but my head got so awake and so full of Bentham that I could not sleep."); id. at 166 (in a letter dated January 23, 1809, to Bentham, Burr wrote: "Every hour of every day I have conversed with you. In solitude, in company, at dinners, routes, balls...."); id. at

178 ("I have seen nobody, having secluded myself except to my venerable and enlightened friend Bentham, and three or four Scotchmen, whom I can meet familiarly.").

220. Robert A. Rutland, Madison's Bookish Habits (1980) (unpaginated pamphlet) ("Completing the list of Madison's key works were Montesquieu's *Spirit of the Law*, and the whole raft of eighteenth-century writers who were the advance guard of modern liberalism—headed by John Locke and including Richard Hooker, James Harrington, Algernon Sidney, Edward Montagu, Cesare Beccaria, John Millar, Adam Smith, James Burgh, Richard Price, and Joseph Priestley.").

221. Madison's Treasures, "An Attempt to Establish a Library of Congress, 1783," Library of Congress, *available at* http://www.loc.gov/exhibits/madison/objects.html.

222. Journal of the Continental Congress, Jan. 24, 1783. Among the books listed under the heading "Law" is "Blackstone's *Commentaries*," which—as noted earlier—itself refers to Beccaria's writings. Id.

223. "Cassius" ["Supposed to be written by Aedanus Burke, Esquire, One of the Chief Justices of the State of South-Carolina"], An Address to the Freemen of the State of South-Carolina 18 (Philadelphia: Robert Bell, 1783).

224. Merrill Jensen, The Articles of Confederation: An Interpretation of the Social-Constitutional History of the American Revolution 1774–1781, at 186 (Madison: University of Wisconsin Press, 1940).

225. Jon L. Wakelyn, ed., America's Founding Charters: Primary Documents of Colonial and Revolutionary Era Governance xiii, 880, 883 (Westport, CT: Greenwood Press, 2006).

226. Mary Sarah Bilder, *James Madison, Law Student and Demi-Lawyer*, 28 Law & Hist. Rev. 389, 430–31 (2010).

227. Bessler, Cruel and Unusual, 156–57; James Madison to James Monroe, Dec. 17, 1785 ("The Bill proportioning crimes & punishments was the one at which we stuck after wading thro' the most difficult parts of it."); James Madison to Thomas Jefferson, Dec. 4, 1786 ("The bill proportioning crimes & punishments on which we were wrecked last year, has after undergoing a number of alterations, got thro' a Committee of the Whole; but it has not yet been reported to the House, where it will meet with the most vigorous attack.").

228. James Madison to George Washington, Dec. 24, 1786 ("Several bills also and particularly the bill relating to crimes & punishments, have been rejected and require reconsideration from another Assembly. This last bill after being purged of its objectionable peculiarities was thrown out on the third reading by a single vote."); James Madison to Thomas Jefferson, Feb. 15, 1787 (stating that "the Bill on crimes & punishments, which after being altered so as to remove most of the objections as was thought, was lost by a single vote").

229. James Madison to Thomas Jefferson, Feb. 15, 1787; Bessler, Cruel and Unusual, 142; Hartnett, Executing Democracy; William Allen, An American Biographical and Historical Dictionary, Containing an Account of the Lives, Characters, and Writings of the Most Eminent Persons in North America from Its First Discovery to the Present Time 629 (Cambridge: Hilliard & Metcalf, 1809).

230. Ian Marsh, Criminal Justice: An Introduction to Philosophies, Theories and Practice 67 (London: Routledge, 2004).

231. Thomas Jefferson to James Madison, June 20, 1787.

232. James Madison to Thomas Jefferson, Oct. 24, 1787.

233. Bessler, Cruel and Unusual, 158–59; Letter from James Madison to Edmund Pendleton, Oct. 31, 1780 ("Congress have felt a becoming resentment of the barbarous treatment of the gentlemen in captivity at Charleston, and have directed General Washington to require of Clinton an explanation of the matter."); Wilf, Law's Imagined Republic, 139, 156; *see also* id. at 139 ("Between 1688 and 1815, an immense number of capital crimes dominated English statute books. While in 1688 fewer than 50 offences were punished with death, by 1776, there were nearly 200. This sanguinary criminal legislation has been called the 'Bloody Code'").

234. Robert A. Rutland, Madison's Bookish Habits (1980) (unpaginated pamphlet).

235. Hoeflich, *Translation & the Reception of Foreign Law*, 769.

236. R. Kent Newmyer, Supreme Court Justice Joseph Story: Statesman of the Old Republic 64, 496 (Chapel Hill: University of North Carolina Press, 1985).

237. Morris L. Cohen, comp., Joseph Story, Joseph Story and the *Encyclopedia Americana* v–vi, x–xv, 31, 142–43 (Clark, NJ: The Lawbook Exchange, 2005) (1844).

238. 2 Joseph Story, Commentaries on the Constitution of the United States 362–63 (Boston: Little, Brown and Co., 3d ed. 1858).

239. Bessler, Cruel and Unusual, 156, 158.

240. James Madison to Thomas S. Grimke, Jan. 15, 1828.

241. Brackenridge, Law Miscellanies, 237–43, 497; Marder, A Hugh Henry Brackenridge Reader, 4–5, 17, 22.

242. H. M. Brackenridge, Recollections of Persons and Places in the West 154 (Philadelphia: J. B. Lippincott & Co., 2d ed. 1868).

243. William F. Keller, The Nation's Advocate: Henry Marie Brackenridge and Young America (Pittsburgh: University of Pittsburg Press, 1956); *Henry Marie Brackenridge (1786–1871)*, http://bioguide.congress.gov/scripts/biodisplay.pl?index=B000732.

244. Benjamin Rush to Benjamin Franklin, Oct. 22, 1766; Benjamin Rush to Benjamin Franklin, Oct. 14, 1770; Benjamin Franklin to Benjamin Rush, Mar. 22, 1768; Benjamin Franklin to Benjamin Rush, Feb. 14, 1773; Benjamin Rush to Benjamin Franklin, May 1, 1773; Benjamin Franklin to Benjamin Rush, July 14, 1773; Benjamin Rush to Benjamin Franklin, [after Sept. 15, 1773]; Benjamin Franklin to Benjamin Rush, July 22, 1774; Benjamin Franklin to Benjamin Rush, July 25, 1774; Benjamin Franklin to Benjamin Rush, June 26, 1776; Benjamin Franklin to Benjamin Rush, June 17, 1778; Benjamin Franklin to Benjamin Rush, June 30, 1778; Benjamin Franklin to Benjamin Rush, Dec. 26, 1783; *see also* Letter from Benjamin Franklin to Smith, Wright, & Gray, Feb. 13, 1769 (Franklin requests that "Dr. Benjamin Rush, a young Physician" and "a particular Friend of mine" be extended "a Letter of Credit on Paris" for which Franklin agreed to be "answerable to you for what he may take up there on such Letter"); Benjamin Franklin to Benjamin Rush, Feb. 14, 1773 ("believe me ever Your affectionate Friend and humble Servant"); Benjamin Franklin to Benjamin Rush, Jan. 7, 1775 ("My best Wishes attend you, being ever, dear Sir, Your affectionate Friend and most obedient Servant"); Benjamin Franklin to Benjamin Rush, Mar. 12, 1784 ("Dear Friend").

245. Constitution of the Pennsylvania Society for Promoting the Abolition of Slavery, Apr. 23, 1787, *available at* Benjamin Franklin Papers, Benjamin Franklin to Benjamin Rush, Mar. 1786.

246. Hartnett, Executing Democracy.

247. Maestro, *Benjamin Franklin and the Penal Laws*, 551.

248. Sullivan, *The Birth of the Prison*, 333–35; Benjamin Franklin to Richard Jackson, May 1, 1764; Robert J. Turnbull, A Visit to the Philadelphia Prison, in a Letter to a Friend, *reprinted in* The Belfast Monthly Magazine, Vol. 4, No. 22 (May 31, 1810), p. 329.

249. Hawke, Benjamin Rush, 364–65.

250. Sullivan, *The Birth of the Prison*, 339; Jack P. Greene, The Constitutional Origins of the American Revolution 164 (Cambridge: Cambridge University Press, 2011); Bessler, Cruel and Unusual, 66, 69–83; Hartnett, Executing Democracy.

251. Workers of the Writers' Program of the Works Progress Administration in the State of New Hampshire, New Hampshire: A Guide to the Granite State 43 (Boston: Houghton Mifflin Co., 1938); Susan E. Marshall, The New Hampshire State Constitution 4 n.7 (Oxford: Oxford University Press, 2011); U.S. Const., art. I, §§ 9–10; U.S. Const., art. III, § 2.

252. U.S. Const., amend. X; Calvert, Quaker Constitutionalism and the Political Thought of John Dickinson, 258; Bessler, Cruel and Unusual, 93, 95–96, 163–65.

253. U.S. Const., amend. VII.

254. Letter of John Dickinson, Nov. 22, 1784; Letter of Thomas McKean, George Bryan and Jacob Rush, Jan. 15, 1785; Proceedings of the Supreme Executive Council of Pennsylvania, Jan. 1785; Philip Hamburger, Law and Judicial Duty 516 n.22 (Cambridge: Harvard University Press, 2009); Powers and Duties of Constables in Pennsylvania 16 (Harrisburg: Commonwealth of Pennsylvania, Dept. of Community Affairs, 1974).

255. G. S. Rowe, Embattled Bench: The Pennsylvania Supreme Court and the Forging of a Democratic Society, 1684–1809, at 164–66 (Cranbury, NJ: Associated University Presses, 1994); Scott Bruce, It Happened in Philadelphia 20–25 (Guilford, CT: TwoDot, 2008).

256. Bessler, Cruel and Unusual, 66, 69–83; Hartnett, Executing Democracy; Jessica C. E. Gienow-Hecht, ed., Emotions in American History: An International Assessment 186 (New York: Berghahn Books, 2010); Sullivan, *The Birth of the Prison*, 340–41; U.S. Const., Art. I, §§ 9–10.

257. Benjamin Franklin to Benjamin Rush, Oct. 14, 1784.

258. John F. Dillon, The Laws and Jurisprudence of England and America: Being a Series of Lectures Delivered Before Yale University 368 (Boston: Little, Brown, and Co., 1894).

259. 1 Whitfield J. Bell, Jr., Patriot-Improvers: Biographical Sketches of Members of the American Philosophical Society, 1743–1768, at 28 (Philadelphia: American Philosophical Society, 1997).

260. Benjamin Rush, An Inquiry into the Influence of Physical Causes upon the Moral Faculty: Delivered Before a Meeting of the American Philosophical Society, Held at Philadelphia on the Twenty-seventh of February, 1786, by Benjamin Rush, M.D. 1, 8, 11–19, 21–22, 24, 27–28 (Philadelphia:

Haswell, Barrington, and Haswell, 1839); id. "Introductory Notice" of George Combe (Feb. 15, 1839).

261. Benjamin Franklin to Benjamin Rush, Mar. 1786.

262. Letter from Benjamin Rush to Benjamin Franklin, Mar. 3, 1786.

263. Letter from Benjamin Rush to Benjamin Franklin, Mar. 11, 1786.

264. Letter from Benjamin Franklin to Benjamin Vaughan, Mar. 1785; Martin Madan, Thelyphthora; or, A Treatise on Female Ruin, in Its Causes, Effects, Consequences, Prevention, and Remedy; Considered on the Basis of the Divine Law (London: J. Dodsley, 1780); Madan, Thoughts on Executive Justice, 8–11, 62–63; *see also* id. at 131–32 (noting that Montesquieu and Beccaria, among other writers "on the subject of laws," "all contend for the certainty of punishment, in order to render laws respected and efficacious").

265. Maestro, Cesare Beccaria and the Origins of Penal Reform, 132 ("Benjamin Franklin, who was then living in Europe as American minister to France, spoke often of the cruelty and absurdities in the existing legal systems."); Alexander DeConde, Half Bitter, Half Sweet: An Excursion into Italian-American History 20 (New York: Scribner, 1971) ("[o]ther Italian intellectuals who exchanged ideas with Franklin were the Marchese Cesare Beccaria").

266. Letter from Benjamin Franklin to Benjamin Vaughan, July 1785, *available at* Benjamin Franklin Papers, http://franklinpapers.org/franklin/framedVolumes.jsp.

267. Sara Maza, Private Lives and Public Affairs: The Causes Célèbres of Prerevolutionary France 237 (Berkeley: University of California Press, 1993); Jean-Sylvain Bailly, De L'Examen Du Magnétisme Animal (Geneva: Slatkine, 1784); Charles Prud'homme, Michel De Servan (1737–1807) Un Magistrat Reformateur (Charleston: Nabu Press, 2012).

268. Max Pearson Cushing, Baron D'Holbach: A Study of Eighteenth Century Radicalism in France, Ph.D. Thesis, Columbia University 20 (New York, 1914).

269. Cesare Beccaria, Crimes and Punishments 34 (London: Chatto & Windus, James Anson Farrer, trans. 1880).

Chapter 4

1. Robert E. Shalhope, The Roots of Democracy: American Thought and Culture, 1760–1800, at 118 (Oxford: Rowman & Littlefield, 2004); *see also* The Literary Fly, No. VIII, Mar. 6, 1779 ("Montesquieu, Beccaria, Voltaire, Blackstone" are said to have "echoed to each other," "the first ornaments of the age").

2. Charles-Louis De Montesquieu, The Spirit of the Laws 81–86, 88, 129, 200, 222, 246, 272, 280 (New York: Hafner Press, 1949); Oliver Wendell Holmes, Collected Legal Papers 264 (New York: Harcourt, Brace and Co., 1920).

3. Brewer & Hellmuth, Rethinking Leviathan, 366–67; Hoeflich, Legal Publishing in Antebellum America, 182; Sir William Jones, An Essay on the Law of Bailments 29–30 (London, printed; Philadelphia, re-printed, 1804); Franklin and Hall: Account with Benjamin Franklin, 1750–1754; James Madison Papers, Commonplace Book, 1759–1772; John Adams [Summer 1759]; Thomas Jefferson to Robert Skipwith, with a List of Books for a Private Library, Aug. 3, 1771; Benjamin Vaughan to Thomas Jefferson, Aug. 2, 1788; Thomas Jefferson to Angelica Schuyler Church, Sept. 21, 1788; Thomas Jefferson to Benjamin Vaughan, Sept. 13, 1789; Thomas Jefferson to Jean Antoine Gautier, June 8, 1792, *available at* www.founders.archives.gov.

4. Edwin Wolf II & Marie Elena Korey, eds., Quarter of a Millennium: The Library Company of Philadelphia 1731–1981, at 221 (Philadelphia: The Library Company of Philadelphia, 1981); Reill & Wilson, Encyclopedia of the Enlightenment, 398; *see also* Otfried Höffe, Democracy in an Age of Globalisation 68 (Dordrecht, The Netherlands: Springer, 2007) ("In the history of ideas the separation of powers is commonly traced back to Milton, Locke, Montesquieu, Hume, the *Federalist Papers*, as well as to Kant. There were predecessors, however, such as Donato Gianotti in the sixteenth century, the last eminent political thinker of the Florentine republic.") (citations omitted).

5. 1 The Speeches of Sir Samuel Romilly in the House of Commons xxix–xxx, 38–50 (London: James Ridgway and Sons, 1820).

6. James E. Pfander & Daniel D. Birk, *Article III and the Scottish Judiciary*, 124 Harv. L. Rev. 1613, 1614 n.1 (2011) ("First published in England between 1765 and 1769, when Blackstone held the Vinerian chair at Oxford, the *Commentaries on the Laws of England* enjoyed remarkable success in America.").

7. 4 William Blackstone, Commentaries on the Laws of England: A Facsimile of the First Edition of 1765–1769, at 17–18, 138, 151, 370, 399 (1769) (1979).

8. John Hostettler, A History of Criminal Justice in England and Wales 86, 111 (Hampshire, UK: Waterside Press, 2009); David Jardine, A Reading on the Use of Torture in the Criminal Law of England Previously to the Commonwealth 1, 12–13 (London: Baldwin and Cradock, 1837); Ayanna Thompson, Performing Race and Torture on the Early Modern Stage (New York: Routledge, 2008), ch. 1; Tegg's Dictionary of Chronology: or, Historical and Statistical Register, from the Birth of Christ to the Present Time 689 (London: William Tegg and Co., 5th ed. 1854); 1 Joseph Irving, The Book of Dumbartonshire: A History of the County, Burghs, Parishes, and Lands, Memoirs of Families, and Notices of Industries Carried on in the Lennox District 271 (Edinburgh and London: W. and A. K. Johnston, 1879); John MacKintosh, Scotland 236 (London: G. P. Putnam's Sons, 1890); Edward J. White, Legal Antiquities: A Collection of Essays upon Ancient Laws and Customs 189–90 (St. Louis, MO: F. H. Thomas Law Book Co., 1913).

9. J. L. de Lolme, The Constitution of England, or, an Account of the English Government 340–41 (1777); J. L. de Lolme, The Constitution of England; or, an Account of the English Government 378, 380–81, 383–86 (London: C. G. J. and J. Robinson, Corrected ed., 1789) (citing English Bill of Rights, Art. X).

10. Jessica J. Sage, *Authority of the Law? The Contribution of Secularized Legal Education to the Moral Crisis of the Profession*, 31 Fla. St. U. L. Rev. 707, 714 (2004).

11. Guy I. Seidman, *The Origins of Accountability: Everything I Know about the Sovereign's Immunity, I Learned from King Henry III*, 49 St. Louis U. L.J. 393, 479 (2005).

12. Welsh S. White, *Fact-Finding and the Death Penalty: The Scope of a Capital Defendant's Right to Jury Trial*, 65 Notre Dame L. Rev. 1, 4 n.24 (1989) (citing Dennis R. Nolan, *Sir William Blackstone and the New American Republic: A Study of Intellectual Impact*, 51 N.Y.U. L. Rev. 731, 743–45 (1976)).

13. Kopel, *The Second Amendment in the Nineteenth Century*, 1370–72; Melusky & Keith Pesto, Capital Punishment, 30.

14. Roger Billings & Frank J. Williams, eds., Abraham Lincoln, Esq.: The Legal Career of America's Greatest President 106 (Lexington: University Press of Kentucky, 2010); Allen C. Guelzo, Abraham Lincoln: Redeemer President 77 (Cambridge, UK: Wm. B. Eerdmans Pub. Co., 2003); Norman Hapgood, Abraham Lincoln: The Man of the People 36–37 (New York: The Macmillan Co., 1901); Robert J. Johnson, Jr., Trial by Fire: Abraham Lincoln and the Law, Ph.D. dissertation, Graduate Faculty in History, The City University of New York (2007), p. 74; Abraham Lincoln to James T. Thornton, Dec. 2, 1858, *available at* The Abraham Lincoln Papers at the Library of Congress, memory.loc.gov.

15. The New England Historical and Genealogical Register xlviii (Boston: New-England Historical Genealogical Society, 1900).

16. 4 Blackstone, Commentaries on the Laws of England, 198–99; *compare* id. at 200. In *Pleas of the Crown*, Sir Matthew Hale had written in 1678: "In Cases of Murder, there must be Malice; and if a Man assaults another with a dangerous Weapon, tho' without Provocation, 'tis express Malice from the nature of the Fact, which is Cruel." Sir Matthew Hale, Pleas of the Crown: Or, A Methodical Summary of the Principal Matters relating to that Subject 19 (1716) (1678).

17. 4 William Blackstone, Commentaries on the Laws of England: A Facsimile of the First Edition of 1765–1769, at 368–72 (1769) (1979).

18. William Blackstone (1723–1780) was the Vinerian Professor of Civil Law who, in the 1760s, arranged for Oxford University Press to print his *Commentaries*. Lionel Bently & Jane C. Ginsburg, *"The Sole Right … Shall Return to the Authors": Anglo-American Authors' Reversion Rights from the Statute of Anne to Contemporary U.S. Copyright*, 25 Berkeley Tech. L.J. 1475, 1499 (2010).

19. 4 Blackstone, Commentaries on the Laws of England, 370.

20. Meskell, *The History of Prisons in the United States from 1777 to 1877*, 841–42.

21. 4 Blackstone, Commentaries on the Laws of England, 370–71. Death sentences at that time were mandatory. Scott W. Howe, Furman's *Mythical Mandate*, 40 U. Mich. J.L. Reform 435, 472 (2007) ("mandatory death sentences were allowed at the time of the founding").

22. 4 Blackstone, Commentaries on the Laws of England, 371.

23. Bilder, *James Madison, Law Student and Demi-Lawyer*, 390–98, 402–403.

24. Bessler, Cruel and Unusual, 84–91; *see also* Bessler, *Revisiting Beccaria's Vision* (describing Cesare Beccaria's influence on American penal reform).

25. Preyer, "Cesare Beccaria and the Founding Fathers," *in* Blackstone in America, 241 ("Blackstone's references to Beccaria in his *Commentaries on the Laws of England*, published between 1765 and 1769 and widely available in the colonies, may have communicated Beccaria's theories to a wider audience than read the original.").

26. 4 Blackstone, Commentaries on the Laws of England, 395, 398–99. Thomas Jefferson regularly recommended that aspiring lawyers read Blackstone's *Commentarie*s. Bessler, Cruel and Unusual, 54.

27. 1 Charles Warren, History of the Harvard Law School and of Early Legal Conditions in America 199 (New York: Lewis Pub. Co., 1908); William Hamilton, ed., Report of the Trial and Acquittal of Edward Shippen, Esquire, Chief Justice, and Jasper Yeates and Thomas Smith, Esquires, Assistant Justices, of the Supreme Court of Pennsylvania, on an Impeachment Before the Senate of the Commonwealth 328–29 (Jan. 1805); The Diary of William Maclay and Other Notes on Senate Debates 441 (Baltimore: Johns Hopkins University Press, 1988); G. S. Rowe, Embattled Bench: The Pennsylvania Supreme Court and the Forging of a Democratic Society, 1684–1809, at 253 (Cranbury, NJ: Associated University Presses, 1994); Randy J. Holland, The Delaware State Constitution: A Reference Guide 61 (Westport, CT: Greenwood Press, 2002).

28. Richard Vaux, The Pennsylvania Prison System, *reprinted in* 21 Proceedings of the American Philosophical Society 651–52 (1884) (read before the American Philosophical Society, June 20, 1884); David H. McElreath, Linda Keena, Greg Etter & Ellis Stuart, Introduction to Corrections 15–16 (Boca Raton, FL: CRC Press, 2012); Barnes, *The Historical Origin of the Prison System in America*, 45.

29. Pa. Const. (Sept. 28, 1776). The Philadelphia delegates had first assembled on July 15, 1776.

30. 4 Samuel Hazard, ed., The Register of Pennsylvania: Devoted to the Preservation of Facts and Documents, and Every Other Kind of Useful Information Respecting the State of Pennsylvania 209–13 (Philadelphia: Wm. F. Geddes, 1829); Hawke, Benjamin Rush, 143; Halbrook, A Right to Bear Arms, 21–22; Brian W. Dotts, The Political Education of Democratus: Negotiating Civic Virtue during the Early Republic 140–41 (Lanham, MD: Lexington Books, 2012); Bernard Schwartz, The Great Rights of Mankind: A History of the American Bill of Rights 72–74 (Lanham, MD: Madison House, 2002); 1 Murray N. Rothbard, Conceived in Liberty 1371 (Auburn, AL: Ludwig von Mise Institute, 2011); 3 William Barton, Memoirs of the Life of David Rittenhouse: Late President of the American Philosophical Society 603, 607–608, 614 (Philadelphia: Edward Parker, 1813); Luigi Luzzatti, God in Freedom: Studies in the Relations Between Church and State 684 (New York: Cosimo, Alfonso Arbib-Costa, trans. 2005); *see also* John Spencer Walters, U.S. Government Publication: Ideological Development and Institutional Politics from the Founding to 1970, at 16 (Oxford: Scarecrow Press, 2005) ("There is no certainty as to who authored the 1776 Pennsylvania Constitution, though James Cannon often is cited as a contributor. Its supporters hoped to make this document irreproachable by ascribing authorship to Benjamin Franklin.... Most historians agree that this constitution was largely the work of such scarcely remembered men as Timothy Matlack, George Bryan, and David Rittenhouse.").

31. "Benjamin Franklin and the Pennsylvania Supreme Executive Council to the Pennsylvania General Assembly," Nov. 11, 1785, *available at* Benjamin Franklin Papers, http://franklinpapers.org/franklin/framedVolumes.jsp.

32. "The Pennsylvania Supreme Executive Council to the Pennsylvania General Assembly," Feb. 21, 1788, *available at* Benjamin Franklin Papers, http://franklinpapers.org/franklin/framedVolumes.jsp; Bessler, Cruel and Unusual, 46.

33. S. W. Dyde, trans., Georg Wilhelm Friedrich Hegel, Hegel's Philosophy of Right 98 (London: George Bell & Sons, 1896).

34. Rosalind L. Branning, Pennsylvania Constitutional Development 10 (Pittsburgh: University of Pittsburgh Press, 2004) ("No Pennsylvania constitution was framed under more dramatic circumstances than the constitution of 1776, drafted by a convention meeting in Philadelphia at a time when the brave tones of Liberty Bell had scarcely ceased to reverberate through the city, when Continental soldiers and British troops were locked in uncertain struggle, and rumors of the impending invasion of the capital city were daily conversation.").

35. Pace, Luigi Castiglioni's Viaggio, 48.

36. Letter from Emanuel Wolleb-Ryhiner to Benjamin Franklin, Jan. 3, 1778 (sent from "Basel"), *available at* Benjamin Franklin Papers, http://franklinpapers.org/franklin/framedVolumes.jsp (source listed as American Philosophical Society); "Wolleb-Ryhiner, Emanuel (1706–1788)," Packard Humanities Institute: The Papers of Benjamin Franklin, *available at* http://216.129.112.195/franklin/framedNames.jsp?ssn=001-78-6360.

37. Thomas McKean and George Bryan to Benjamin Franklin and the Pennsylvania Supreme Executive Council, Apr. 5, 1788, *available at* Benjamin Franklin Papers, http://franklinpapers.org/franklin/framedVolumes.jsp.

38. Binder, Felony Murder, 148; David C. Brody, James R. Acker & Wayne A. Logan, Criminal Law 357–58 (Gaithersburg, Md.: Aspen Publishers, 2001); Barnes, *The Historical Origin of the Prison System in America*, 46; Bessler, Cruel and Unusual, 79, 89; Samuel Roberts & Robert E. Wright, Di-

gest of Select British Statutes, Comprising Those Which, According to the Report of the Judges of the Supreme Court Made to the Legislature, Appear to Be in Force in Pennsylvania 79 (1847) (noting that, in 1786 in Pennsylvania, "[i]n conformity with" the constitutional provision that punishments should be rendered less sanguinary and more proportionate to crimes, "the crime against nature, robbery, and burglary, became punishable by imprisonment at hard labour, instead of death").

39. Binder, Felony Murder, 128–29.

40. Gottlieb, Theater of Death, 104–106.

41. Juliani, Building Little Italy, 21–27, 335.

42. Mary Mostert, Banner of Liberty: The Threat of Anarchy Leads to the Constitution of the United States 85 (Provo, UT: CTR Publishing, 2005); Armand Santilli, Và Pensiero: Fly, My Thoughts, On Winds of Gold 53–54 (Bloomington, IN: AuthorHouse, 2006); Frank W. Alduino & David J. Coles, Sons of Garibaldi in Blue & Gray: Italians in the American Civil War 7 (Youngstown, NY: Cambria Press, 2007); Bill Yenne, Tommy Gun: How General Thompson's Submachine Gun Wrote History 15 (New York: St. Martin's Press, 2009); Frederick Harling & Martin Kaufman, The Ethnic Contribution to the American Revolution 57, 59 (Westfield, MA: Westfield Bicentennial Committee, 1976); Sebastian A. Santucci, My Wartime Italian Roots and My Canadian Dream 82–83 (Bloomington, IN: Xlibris Corp., 2000); Salvatore J. LaGumina, Frank J. Cavaioli, Salvatore Primeggia & Joseph A. Varacalli, eds., The Italian American Experience: An Encyclopedia 662–63 (New York: Garland Publishing, 2000); The London Quarterly and Holborn Review (1933), p. 420; George Washington to Lawrence Washington, May 5, 1749; Memorandum Respecting the Militia, May 14, 1756; Memorandum Respecting the Militia, May 17, 1756, *available at* www.founders.archives.gov; http://www.niaf.org/blog/blogmanager/blogmanager.asp?post=italians-role-in-american-revolution.

43. Michael Olmert, Official Guide to Colonial Williamsburg 85 (Williamsburg: The Colonial Williamsburg Foundation, 3d ed. 1998); Ralph G. Giordana, The Architectural Ideology of Thomas Jefferson 33–35 (Jefferson, NC: McFarland & Co., 2012); William Taliaferro to Charles Lewis, Sept. 15, 1757; Charles Lewis to George Washington, Sept. 21, 1757; George Wythe to Thomas Jefferson, Mar. 9, 1770; Mrs. Drummond to Thomas Jefferson, Mar 12, 1771; Address to Captain Patrick Henry and the Gentlemen Independents of Hanover, May 9, 1775; George Washington to John Hancock, Oct. 5, 1776; Oath of Allegiance Signed by Citizens of Albemarle County [1777]; George Washington to Edmund Pendleton, Apr. 12, 1777; George Wythe to Thomas Jefferson, Jan. 10, 1786; George Wythe to Thomas Jefferson, Feb. 10, 1786; Thomas Jefferson to Giovanni Fabbroni, May 24, 1786; Thomas Jefferson to George Wythe, Aug. 13, 1786; James Madison to Lawrence Taliaferro, ca. Nov. 18, 1787; Lawrence Taliaferro to James Madison, Dec. 16, 1787; Lawrence Taliaferro, Jan. 4, 1797; Thomas Jefferson's Notes on Household Consumption, June 3, 1809–Oct. 23, 1811; Thomas Jefferson's Notes on Monticello Plantings, Mar. 16, 1811; Thomas Jefferson to James Mease, June 29, 1814, *available at* www.founders.archives.gov.

44. Barnes, "The Historical Origin of the Prison System in America," 38–39.

45. Denis R. Caron, A Century in Captivity: The Life and Trials of Prince Mortimer, a Connecticut Slave 105–112 (Lebanon: University of New Hampshire Press, 2006).

46. U. M. Rose, "Beccaria and Law Reform," 34 Am. L. Rev. 524, 542 (1900).

47. Barnes, "The Historical Origin of the Prison System in America," 39; William Garrott Brown, The Life of Oliver Ellsworth 109–11 (New York: The Macmillan Co., 1905). A grand jury charge U.S. Supreme Court Chief Justice Oliver Ellsworth wrote and delivered while riding the circuit does give a flavor for his views at that time. As Ellsworth instructed grand jurors:

> Your duty may be deemed unpleasant, but it is too important not to be faithfully performed. To provide in the organization that reason shall prescribe laws, is of little avail, if passions are left to control them. Institutions without respect, laws violated with impunity, are, to a Republic, the symptoms and the seed of death. No transgression is *too small*, no transgressor *too great*, for animadversion. Happily for our laws, they are not written in blood, that we should blush to read them, or hesitate to execute them. They breathe the spirit of a parent, and expect the benefits of correction, not from *severity* but from *certainty.*.... The national laws are the national ligatures and vehicles of life. Though they pervade a country as diversified in its habits as it is vast in extent, yet they give to the whole harmony of interest and unity of design.... Let there be vigilance, constant diligence, and fidelity for the execution of laws— of laws made by all and having for their object the good of all. So let us rear an empire sacred to the rights of man and commend a government of reason to the nations of the earth.

Id. at 245–46.

48. Jill Lepore, The Story of America: Essays on Origins 301 (Princeton: Princeton University Press, 2012).

49. Brewer & Hellmuth, Rethinking Leviathan, 366–67. Beccaria himself had borrowed many of Montesquieu's ideas. Hon. Danes Barrington, Observations on the More Ancient Statutes, from Magna Charta to the Twenty-First of James I, at 442 (London: W. Bowyer & J. Nichols, 1769) ("[t]he Marquis *Beccaria* … seems to have adopted most of *Montesquieu's* ideas").

50. Bessler, Cruel and Unusual, 33, 36; Goodheart, The Solemn Sentence of Death, 71.

51. Zephaniah Swift, A System of the Laws of the State of Connecticut 295 (1795–1796). "For this purpose," Swift wrote, "New-Gate prison was erected." Id. at 295–96; Goodheart, The Solemn Sentence of Death, 71.

52. Zephaniah Swift, A System of the Laws of the State of Connecticut 294 (1795–1796); R. A. Burchell, ed., The End of Anglo-America: Historical Essays in the Study of Cultural Divergence 4 (Manchester: Manchester University Press, 1991) ("In terms which suggested the influence of Beccaria and other eighteenth-century critics of the excessive use of the death penalty, Pennsylvanians specified in the 1776 radical constitution that the object of punishment was deterrence and that its form should be public, while the 1784 New Hampshire constitution adopted the principle of proportionality in punishments.").

53. Goodheart, The Solemn Sentence of Death, 107.

54. Kendall, The Forgotten Founding Father, 33–34, 137–39; Catalogue of the Society of Brothers in Unity, Yale College, Founded A. D. 1768, at 17–18 (New Haven, CT: Brothers in Unity, 1854); Catalogue of the Library of Linonian Society 18 (New Haven, CT: Yale College, 1846).

55. Clarence Deming, Yale Yesterdays 138–40 (New Haven, CT: Yale University Press, 1915); 2 Anson Phelps Stokes, Memorials of Eminent Yale Men: A Biographical Study of Student Life and University Influences During the Eighteenth and Nineteenth Centuries 247–52 (New Haven, CT: Yale University Press, 1914) (providing a sketch of the life of Jeremiah Mason); Yale Clubs, Brothers in Unity Records, Yale University, Secretary's records, Minutes of meetings (1783–1803), Group No. 40-A-5, Box 8, Folder No. 36.

56. Goodheart, The Solemn Sentence of Death, 71.

57. Brown & Brown, The Hanging of Ephraim Wheeler, 193 & 337 n.9 (citing Joel Barlow, *A Letter to the National Convention of France on the Defects in the Constitution of 1791* (1792), *in* Charles S. Hyneman & Donald S. Lutz, eds., American Political Writing during the Founding Era, 1760–1815, at 833–34 (Indianapolis, IN: Liberty Press, 1983)); Goodheart, The Solemn Sentence of Death, 71.

58. 1 Joel Barlow, Advice to the Privileged Orders in the Several States of Europe, Resulting from the Necessity and Propriety of a General Revolution in the Principle of Government 131 (London: J. Johnson, 1792); 1 Joel Barlow, Advice to the Privileged Orders in the Several States of Europe, Resulting from the Necessity and Propriety of a General Revolution in the Principle of Government 131 (London: J. Johnson, 3d ed. 1793); Cotlar, Tom Paine's America, 236 n.9.

59. Joel Barlow, The Conspiracy of Kings: A Poem Addressed to the Inhabitants of Europe from Another World (London: J. Johnson, 1792), *available at* Early Americas Digital Archive.

60. Goodheart, The Solemn Sentence of Death, 71–73.

61. The Christian Disciple, Vol. V, No. 2 (Feb. 1817), p. 64.

62. Zephaniah Swift, A System of the Laws of the State of Connecticut 295 (1795–1796); *accord* William A. Carroll & Norman B. Smith, American Constitutional Rights 505 (1991) (noting that Pennsylvanians and the "[t]he draftsmen of Virginia's Declaration of Rights," influenced by the books written by Montesquieu and Beccaria, "appear to have been influenced more by contemporary European philosophers than by English legal history").

63. Binder, Felony Murder, 126–27, 131.

64. Zephaniah Swift, A System of the Laws of the State of Connecticut 293 (1795–1796); 4 Franklin Bowditch Dexter, Biographical Sketches of the Graduates of Yale College with Annals of the College History 60 (New York: Henry Holt and Co., 1907).

65. Goodheart, The Solemn Sentence of Death, 71–72; Zephaniah Swift, A System of the Laws of the State of Connecticut 296–97 (1795–1796).

66. Essays on Capital Punishments 157–58, 161–62 (Philadelphia: Brown & Merritt, 1811) (republished from Poulson's Daily Advertiser), *available at* The Historical Society of Pennsylvania.

67. Donald Braman, *Punishment and Accountability: Understanding and Reforming Criminal Sanctions in America*, 53 UCLA L. Rev. 1143, 1172 & n.113 (2006).

68. *E.g.,* Thomas Eddy, An Account of the State Prison or Penitentiary House, in the City of New-York 6 (New York: Isaac Collins and Son, 1801); Lewis, From Newgate to Dannemora, 5; *see also* Samuel Lorenzo Knapp, The Life of Thomas Eddy: Comprising an Extensive Correspondence with Many of the Most Distinguished Philosophers and Philanthropists of This and Other Countries 58 (New York: Conner & Cooke, 1834) ("In 1801, Mr. Eddy published an account of the State Prison of New

York. His mottos were taken from Beccaria and Montesquieu...."); O. F. Lewis, The Development of American Prisons and Prison Customs, 1776–1845, at 43 (Albany: Prison Association of New York, 1922) ("Eddy was a most diligent student of penal principles. His own philosophy of criminal treatment was based upon Beccaria, Montesquieu, Penn, Howard and other writers.").

69. Graber, The Furnace of Affliction, 25–26; Edwin G. Burrows & Mike Wallace, Gotham: A History of New York City to 1898, at 366 (Oxford: Oxford University Press, 1999); J. E. Granrud, Five Years of Alexander Hamilton's Public Life 1786–1791, at 45 (Private edition, 1894).

70. Scott Christianson, With Liberty for Some: 500 Years of Imprisonment in America 94 (Boston: Northeastern University Press, 1998); Henry Cabot Lodge, The Democracy of the Constitution and Other Addresses and Essays 215 (New York: Charles Scribner's Sons, 1915); Hugh Barbour, et al., eds., Quaker Crosscurrents: Three Hundred Years of Friends in the New York Yearly Meetings 85 (Syracuse, NY: Syracuse University Press, 1995); Mark E. Kann, Taming Passion for the Public Good: Policing Sex in the Early Republic (New York: New York University Press, 2013), ch. 3, n.27.

71. Banner, The Death Penalty, 98.

72. The Speeches of the Different Governors to the Legislature of the State of New-York 41–44 (Albany: J. B. Van Steenbergh, 1825); Proceedings of the New York State Historical Association 379 & n.4 (Cooperstown, NY: New York State Historical Association, 1943); 2 Charles Z. Lincoln, ed., State of New York Messages from the Governors: Comprising Executive Communications to the Legislature and Other Papers Relating to Legislation from the Organization of the First Colonial Assembly in 1683 to and Including the Year 1906, at 332, 336 & n.3 (Albany, NY: J. B. Lyon Co., 1909).

73. Evan Cornog, The Birth of Empire: DeWitt Clinton and the American Experience, 1769–1828, at 20 (Oxford: Oxford University Press, 1998) ("Clinton — stepping out of his Countryman's character — then cites the Italian jurist and legal philosopher Cesare Beccaria on the tendency of governments to concentrate power in the hands of the few, to the detriment of the many, and says he fears that 'this is the case with the new constitution men,' who have given such great power to the 'president-general' and the Senate.").

74. John L. Brooke, Columbia Rising: Civil Life on the Upper Hudson from the Revolution to the Age of Jackson 245 (Chapel Hill: The University of North Carolina Press, 2010).

75. David Hosack, Memoir of De Witt Clinton xiv–xv, 28, 31, 34–35, 41–42, 45, 53–54 (New York: J. Seymour, 1829).

76. Bessler, Cruel and Unusual, 133, 135; Harry M. Ward, George Washington's Enforcers: Policing the Continental Army 158 (Carbondale, IL: Southern Illinois University Press, 2006); Josias Carvel Hall to Alexander Hamilton, Oct. 4, 1799, *available a*t www.founders.archives.gov.

77. Caso, They Too Made America Great, 56.

78. 1 Crime and Punishment in New York: An Inquiry into Sentencing and the Criminal Justice System: Report to Governor Hugh L. Carey 8 (1979).

79. Banner, The Death Penalty, 100; Harris, Executing Race, 126; www.columbia.edu/content/history.html.

80. Barnes, "The Historical Origin of the Prison System in America," 38–39.

81. Masur, Rites of Execution, 86; Morgan Lewis to James Madison, 8 Apr. 1811 (n.1), *available at* www.founders.archives.gov.

82. The Speeches of the Different Governors to the Legislature of the State of New-York 47–51 (Albany: J. B. Van Steenbergh, 1825).

83. Report on the Penitentiary System in the United States, Prepared Under a Resolution of the Society for the Prevention of Pauperism in the City of New York 40, 86 (1822) ("[o]n reading the celebrated work of the Marquis Beccaria," the Grand Duke of Tuscany "entirely abolished capital punishments").

84. A. Oakey Hall, Reminiscences of David Dudley Field, 6 Green Bag 209–11 (1894); The Code of Civil Procedure of the State of New-York, *in* 1 New York Field Codes 1850–1865, at x (Union, NJ: The Lawbook Exchange, 1998).

85. Banner, The Death Penalty, 98.

86. Binder, Felony Murder, 148–49; 2 Rochefoucault Liancourt, Travels Through the United States of North America, 44; 1 Grossberg & Tomlins, The Cambridge History of Law in America, 206; Barnes, "The Historical Origin of the Prison System in America," 40.

87. Natural History of New York 182 (Albany, New York: D. Appleton & Co., 1842).

88. 1 Grossberg & Tomlins, The Cambridge History of Law in America, 208.

89. Banner, The Death Penalty, 131; Davis, *The Movement to Abolish Capital Punishment in America*, 28.

90. Eumenes [William Griffith], Being a Collection of Papers, Written for the Purpose of Exhibiting Some of the More Prominent Errors and Omissions of the Constitution of New-Jersey, Established on the Second Day of July, One Thousand Seven Hundred and Seventy-Six; and to Prove the Necessity of Calling a Convention for Revision and Amendment, 113–16 (Trenton, NJ: G. Craft, 1799); Rosemarie Zagarri, The Politics of Size: Representation in the United States, 1776–1850, at 55 (Ithaca, NY: Cornell University Press, 1987).

91. Hamilton, Memoirs, Speeches and Writings of Robert Rantoul, Jr., 4–5, 440, 444, 452, 461; see also James M. O'Toole & David Quigley, eds., Boston's Histories: Essays in Honor of Thomas H. O'Connor 28 ("In the winter of 1793 two articles were published in Boston's Independent Chronicle that gave voice to the people's antipathy toward the Commonwealth's use of capital punishment. 'Marcus' — perhaps a pseudonym for Attorney General James Sullivan — articulated a compelling argument against the death penalty."); id. at 35 n.40 ("'Marcus' borrowed from Cesare Beccaria's Essay on Crimes and Punishments").

92. 3 A Catalogue of the Library of Harvard University in Cambridge, Massachusetts 62 (1830).

93. Lyn Suzanne Entzeroth, The End of the Beginning: The Politics of Death and the American Death Penalty Regime in the Twenty-First Century, 90 Or. L. Rev. 797, 801 (2012).

94. A Brief Statement of the Argument for the Abolition of the Death Punishment in Twelve Essays 17, 19, 26 (Philadelphia: Gihon, Fairchild & Co., 1844) (mentioning Beccaria in Essays VIII, X and XII); Bradley Chapin, Felony Law Reform in the Early Republic, 113 Pa. Mag. of Hist. & Biography 163, 164 (1989).

95. Victor Brombert, Victor Hugo and the Visionary Novel 25–26 (Cambridge: Harvard University Press, 1984); Davis, The Movement to Abolish Capital Punishment in America, 29–31; Filler, Movements to Abolish the Death Penalty in the United States, 127.

96. Davis, The Movement to Abolish Capital Punishment in America, 31–34, 36; Filler, Movements to Abolish the Death Penalty in the United States, 127–28; Michael Dow Burkhead, A Life for a Life: The American Debates over the Death Penalty 33 (Jefferson, NC: McFarland & Co., 2009); 2 The Commonwealth of Massachusetts: Bulletins for the Constitutional Convention 1917–1918, at 261 (Boston: Wright & Potter, 1919); Bessler, Death in the Dark, 41, 66; Evan J. Mandery, ed., Capital Punishment in America: A Balanced Examination 500 (Sudbury, MA: Jones & Bartlett Learning, 2d ed. 2012); Andrew Welsh-Huggins, No Winners Here Tonight: Race, Politics, and Geography in One of the Country's Busiest Death Penalty States 9–10, 18 (Athens, OH: Ohio University Press, 2009).

97. Bessler, Death in the Dark, 44–45; Bovee, Christ and the Gallows, 191, 197, 217.

98. Smithers, Treatise on Executive Clemency in Pennsylvania, 25–26, 107–108; Antony Taylor, The Prison System and Its Effects — Wherefrom, Whereto, and Why? 16 (Hauppauge, NY: Nova Science Publishers, 2008).

99. Green, Mathew Carey, 20.

100. 5 The American Museum: or Repository of Ancient and Modern Fugitive Pieces 63, 65 (1789) (Mathew Carey dedicated this volume, dated "Philadelphia, January 30, 1789," of The American Museum "To His Excellency Thomas Mifflin, Esq. President of the Commonwealth of Pennsylvania"); Banner, The Death Penalty, 332 (listing Benjamin Rush as the author).

101. David Paul Nord, Communities of Journalism: A History of American Newspapers and Their Readers 196 n.24 (Champaign: University of Illinois Press, 2001); 2 The American Museum, or Repository of Ancient and Modern Fugitive Pieces, &c. Prose and Poetical 151 (1787).

102. Jared Gardner, The Rise and Fall of Early American Magazine Culture: The History of Communication 105 (Champaign: University of Illinois Press, 2012).

103. Jennings L. Wagoner, Jr., Jefferson and Education 51, 285–86 (Chapel Hill: University of North Carolina Press, 2004).

104. Pace, Luigi Castiglioni's Viaggio, 313–14.

105. Benjamin Rush, Medical Inquiries and Observations: Containing an Account of the Bilious Remitting and Intermitting Yellow Fever, as It Appeared in Philadelphia in the Year 1794, at 207 (Philadelphia: Thomas Dobson, 1796); 1 L. H. Butterfield, ed., Letters of Benjamin Rush 669, 692, 701, 889, 963, 976 (Princeton: Princeton University Press, 1951); Brodsky, Benjamin Rush, 41–42; Henry Simpson, The Lives of Eminent Philadelphians, Now Deceased 123, 136–38, 143–49 (Philadelphia: William Brotherhead, 1859); Jeremy Roberts, James Madison 17–18 (Minneapolis, MN: Lerner Publications, 2004); Marcus Daniel, Scandal & Civility: Journalism and the Birth of America Democracy 346 n.45, 348, 352 (Oxford: Oxford University Press, 2009); 1 Robert Huish, Memoirs of the Late William Cobbett, Esq. M. P. for Oldham 137 (London: John Saunders, 1836).

106. 2 Rochefoucault Liancourt, Travels through the United States of North America, 346.

107. Alfred F. Young, Gary B. Nash & Ray Raphael, eds., Revolutionary Founders: Rebels, Radi-

cals, and Reformers in the Making of the Nation 344–45 (2012) (noting that in Wilmington, Delaware, Robert Coram—around 1790—read Beccaria's treatise after joining the Wilmington Library Company); Merle Curti, The Growth of American Thought 40–41 (New Brunswick, NJ: Transaction Publishers, 3d ed. 1964) (noting that, in 1800, when St. Louis had a population of just 669 people, fifty-six heads of families owned books, and that the library of Auguste Chouteau included the works of Voltaire and Beccaria); Stuart Banner, *Written Law and Unwritten Norms in Colonial St. Louis*, 14 Law & Hist. Rev. 33, 46 n.50 (1996) ("Auguste Chouteau, probably the wealthiest man in Upper Louisiana, owned the first French edition (1766) of Beccaria's *Traite de delits et des peines*"); Zechariah Chafee, Jr., Book Review, 57 Harv. L. Rev. 399, 421 (1944) (reviewing Daniel J. Boorstin, ed., Delaware Cases, 1792–1830 (1943) ("Eighteenth-century Delaware lawyers were evidently investing heavily in treatises and reports imported from England, either directly or through booksellers in Philadelphia.").

108. Bessler, Cruel and Unusual, 177–78.

109. Carmell v. Texas, 529 U.S. 513, 537 n.27 (2000); Nixon v. Administrator of Gen. Services, 433 U.S. 425, 474 (1977).

110. Bessler, Cruel and Unusual, 178, 180.

111. Schwartz & Wishingrad, *The Eighth Amendment, Beccaria, and the Enlightenment*, 825 n.199.

112. Harris, Executing Race, 66 & 195 n.181 (citing The New-York Magazine, Jan. 1794, p. 36).

113. 1 William Godwin, An Enquiry Concerning Political Justice and Its Influence on General Virtue and Happiness 9, 40–41 (London: G. G. J. & J. Robinson, 1793); Alexander Hamilton to James A. Bayard, 16 Jan. 1801; Nathaniel Niles to James Madison, 9 June 1801; Samuel R. Demaree to Thomas Jefferson, 13 Feb. 1814, *available at* www.founders.archives.gov.

114. Cogan, The Complete Bill of Rights, 617; Bessler, Cruel and Unusual, 191; Hanging Not Punishment Enough for Murtherers, High-way Men, and House-breakers (1701), *reprinted in* The Opinions of Different Authors upon the Punishment of Death 123 (Basil Montagu ed. 1809); William Hay, An Essay on Civil Government: Treating Summarily of Its Necessity, Original, Dissolution, Forms, and Properties 44–45 (London, 1728); Baron William Eden Auckland, Principles of Penal Law 21–22 (London: B. White & T. Cadell, 1771).

115. 2 Thomas Williams Bicknell, The History of the State of Rhode Island and Providence Plantations 709 (New York: American Historical Society, 1920); Robert A. Ferguson, Law and Letters in American Culture 42 (Cambridge: Harvard University Press, 2004).

116. Cogan, The Complete Bill of Rights, 613; Delaware Declaration of Rights, Sept. 11, 1776.

117. Dan Friedman, The Maryland State Constitution: A Reference Guide 2–3 (2006); 1 Oswald Tilghman, History of Talbot County, Maryland, 1661–1861, at 428 (1915); George A. Hanson, Old Kent: The Eastern Shore of Maryland 141, 145–47, 260, 280 (Baltimore, MD: Clearfield, 1876); McDermott, Charles Carroll of Carrollton, 15; Lewis A. Leonard, Life of Charles Carroll of Carrollton 259–60 (New York: Moffat, Yard and Co., 1918); Caso, They Too Made America Great, 57–59; Adolph Caso, Alfieri's Ode to America's Independence 16 (Boston: Branden Press, 1976); Russell R. Esposito, The Golden Milestone: Over 2500 Years of Italian Contributions to Civilization 10, 296 (New York: New York Learning Library, 3d ed. 2000); J. D. Warfield, The Founders of Anne Arundel and Howard Counties, Maryland 244 (1905); Maryland: A Guide to the Old Line State 422 (University of Maryland/Federal Works Agency/Works Projects Administration, 1940); Christopher Weeks, Where Land and Water Intertwine: An Architectural History of Talbot County, Maryland 80 (Baltimore, MD: The Johns Hopkins University Press, 1984); Michael F. Trostel, Mount Clare, Being an Account of the Seat Built by Charles Carroll, Barrister, Upon His Lands at Patapsco (Baltimore: National Society of the Colonial Dames of America in the State of Maryland, 1981); Joseph Taggart, Biographical Sketches of the Eminent American Patriots 60–62 (Kansas City, MO: The Burton Co., 1907); Halbrook, A Right to Bear Arms, 63; Charles A. Rees, *Remarkable Evolution: The Early Constitutional History of Maryland*, 36 U. Balt. L. Rev. 217, 239–40 (2007); Dan Friedman, *Tracing the Lineage: Textual and Conceptual Similarities in the Revolutionary-Era State Declarations of Rights of Virginia, Maryland, and Delaware*, 33 Rutgers L.J. 929, 1003 (2002); Dan Friedman, *The History, Development, and Interpretation of the Maryland Declaration of Rights*, 70 Temp. L. Rev. 945, 948 (1997).

118. Birzer, American Cicero, xiii, 80, 84; *see also* id. at 96 ("Others enjoyed Charles's company as well, as Charles recorded meeting with John Dickinson, his fellow student from the Inner Temple in London and someone whom Charles had praised in his First Citizen letters."); id. at 107 (quoting a letter in which John Adams discusses the commitment of Charles Carroll of Carrollton to "the Cause of American Liberty").

119. Birzer, American Cicero, 96, 105–107; Paul R. O'Neill & Paul K. Williams, Georgetown University 9 (Charleston, SC: Arcadia Publishing, 2003); Pennsylvania History, Vols. 26–27, p. 270; 2

Peter Guilday, The Life and Times of John Carroll: Archbishop of Baltimore (1735–1815) 447, 524, 527–66, 828 (New York: The Encyclopedia Press, 1922).

120. 1 Harvey Wish, Society and Thought in Modern America: A Social and Intellectual History of the American People from 1865, at 209 (New York: David McKay Co., 1966).

121. Nevins, The American States during and after the Revolution, 455.

122. McDermott, Charles Carroll of Carrollton, 93; W. Stull Holt, "Charles Carroll, Barrister: The Man," Maryland Historical Magazine, Vol. 31, no. 2 (June 1936).

123. Letter of Charles Carroll of Carrollton to Edmund Jenings (Aug. 13, 1767), *in* 1 Hoffman, Mason & Darcy, Dear Papa, Dear Charley, 431 & n.2; *compare* Letter of Charles Carroll of Carrollton to Edmund Jennings (Aug. 13, 1767), *in* Thomas Meagher Field, ed. & comp., Unpublished Letters of Charles Carroll of Carrollton, and His Father, Charles Carroll of Doughoregan 142 (New York: The United States Catholic Historical Society, 1902) ("I have received your kind letter of the 3rd. of last May with ye essay on crimes and punishments, and the tracts relating to ye Roman Catholics, for which I am much obliged to you. The author of ye essays on crimes and punishments has displayed a great fund of humanity in his little work, interspersed with many facts and judicious observations. The comment is plainly ye production of Voltaire's pen; his sarcastic wit and humour are so peculiar that ye easily distinguish in works.").

124. 1 Hoffman, Mason & Darcy, Dear Papa, Dear Charley, 273.

125. Jeffrey A. Bell, ed., Industrialization and Imperialism 1800–1914: A Biographical Dictionary 26 (Westport, CT: Greenwood Press, 2002).

126. Catalogue of Books Belonging to the Library of St. John's College, Annapolis, MD, 10 (Riley & Davis, 1847).

127. Duncan Wu, Wordsworth's Reading 1770–1799, at 12, 80, 171 (Cambridge: Cambridge University Press, 1993); Quentin Bailey, Wordsworth's Vagrants: Police, Prisons, and Poetry in the 1790s, at 4 n.9, 62–68, 91 (Surrey, UK: Ashgate Publishing, 2011).

128. Birzer, American Cicero, x, 2–28, 39–40, 42, 48–50, 53–56, 79.

129. Everett Emerson, ed., American Literature, 1764–1789: The Revolutionary Years ix–xv (Madison: University of Wisconsin Press, 1977).

130. 1 John Gough, A History of the People Called Quakers 337, 370, 376, 388–89, 461, 480, 487, 496 (Dublin: Robert Jackson, 1789) (making reference to "sanguinary laws," "sanguinary measures," "sanguinary law," "sanguinary proceedings," and the infliction of "sanguinary punishment").

131. 1 John Gutch, Collectanea Curiosa; or Miscellaneous Tracts, Relating to the History of Antiquities of England and Ireland 395 (Oxford: Clarendon Press, 1781).

132. 1 William Jones, Observations in a Journey to Paris By Way of Flanders, in the Month of August 1776, at 183 (London: G. Robinson, 1777).

133. William Guthrie, A New Geographical, Historical, and Commercial Grammar and Present State of the Several Kingdoms of the World 311 (London: C. Dilly, 1780).

134. Thomas, On Crimes and Punishments, 17, 117–19.

135. U.S. Const., amend. I; James Madison to William Bradford, Dec. 1, 1773; Virginia Statute for Religious Freedom, The Monticello Classroom, http://classroom.monticello.org/kids/resources/profile/262/Virginia-Statute-for-Religious-Freedom/.

136. Andrew Ellicott to James Madison, Nov. 14, 1810.

137. 1 William Gordon, The History of the Rise, Progress, and Establishment of the Independence of the United States of America 458 (London: Charles Dilly, 1788).

138. 2 M. Chenier, trans., The Present State of the Empire of Morocco 272 (London: G. G. J. and J. Robinson, 1788); William Hodges, Travels in India, During the Years 1780, 1781, 1782, & 1783, at 55 (London: William Hodges, 1783).

139. 1 Diccionario Espanol e Ingles 203 (Londres: A Costa de Piestre y Delamolliere, 1786) (defining "Cruento" as "cruel, sanguinary"); Joseph Baretti, ed., A Dictionary of Spanish and English and English and Spanish (2d ed. 1778) (entry for "Cruento" in unpaginated text reads "cruel, sanguinary"); Abel Boyer, Dictionnaire Royal François-Anglois et Anglois-François 538 (1780) (defining "Sanguinaire" as "*Blood-thirsty, bloody, cruel, sanguinary*").

140. Kendall, The Forgotten Founding Father, 272.

141. Noah Webster, A Compendious Dictionary of the English Language (1806). That dictionary defined *unusual* as "uncommon, rare." Id.

142. Noah Webster, An American Dictionary of the English Language (1828). This dictionary defined unusual as "Not usual; not common; rare." Id.

143. Cogan, The Complete Bill of Rights, 613.

144. Harlow G. Unger, John Quincy Adams 40–43 (Philadelphia: Da Capo Press, 2012); 11 Walter Lynwood Fleming, ed., The South in the Building of the Nation: A History of the Southern States Designed to Record the South's Part in the Making of the American Nation 540 (Richmond, VA: The Southern Historical Publication Society, 1909); John Adams, To the Inhabitants of the Colony of Massachusetts-Bay, Feb. 6, 1775; John Adams to Abigail Adams, June 11/17, 1775; A Proclamation by the General Court, Jan. 19, 1776; John Thaxter to John Adams, Jan. 20, 1778; Ralph Izard to John Adams, Dec. 22, 1778, *available at* www.founders.archives.gov.

145. 1 Correspondence of Mr. Ralph Izard, of South Carolina, From the Year 1774 to 1804; with a Short Memoir vii, xii, 14–15, 18–19, 37–41, 44–48, 67–69, 72, 75–76, 91, 96–99, 108–15, 156, 202, 212–13 (New York: Charles S. Francis & Co., 1844); 2 James Parton, Life and Times of Benjamin Franklin 257–58 (New York: Mason Brothers, 1864); *see also* Phillips Russell, Benjamin Franklin: The First Civilized American 270 (New York: Cosimo, Inc., 2005) (noting that Ralph Izard hung around Paris waiting for the Grand Duke of Tuscany to receive him, but that Tuscany never did receive him).

146. Thomas Jefferson to Edmund Pendleton, Aug. 26, 1776; Proclamation Inviting Mercenary Troops in the British Service to Desert, Feb. 2, 1781; George Davis to James Madison, Aug. 7, 1807, *available at* www.founders.archives.gov.

147. The Federalist No. 15, Dec. 1, 1787; The Federalist No. 74, Mar. 25, 1788; George Washington to Gouverneur Morris, Oct. 13, 1789; Americanus No. I, Jan. 31, 1794; Gouverneur Morris to George Washington, Oct. 23, 1792; The French Revolution [1794], *available at* www.founders. archives.gov.

148. Linda S. Frey & Marsha L. Frey, The French Revolution 27 (Westport, CT: Greenwood Press, 2004).

149. Godwin, Of Population, 382, 387; Jeremiah Fitzpatrick, M.D. Knt., Thoughts on Penitentiaries 9 (Dublin: H. Fitzpatrick, 1790); Gordon Beckett, A Population History of Colonial New South Wales: The Economic Growth of a New Colony 301 (Singapore: Trafford Publishing, 2013).

150. Stroud, A Sketch of the Laws Relating to Slavery in the Several States of the United States of America, 110.

151. Dan Friedman, The Maryland State Constitution: A Reference Guide 25 (2006),

152. 3 Charles F. Partington, ed., The British Cyclopaedia of the Arts, Sciences, History, Geography, Literature, Natural History, and Biography 560 (London: Wm. S. Orr & Co., 1838).

153. Roberts Vaux, Notices of the Original, and Successive Efforts, to Improve the Discipline of the Prison at Philadelphia, and to Reform the Criminal Code of Pennsylvania 48 (Philadelphia: Kimber and Sharpless, 1826).

154. Melusky & Pesto, Capital Punishment, 31 ("In addition to reading Beccaria and Blackstone, the signers of the Declaration of Independence in 1776 had personal reasons to study the death penalty. They knew their English law and history, and despite the high rate of royal pardons in lesser matters, they knew that if they had lost the war, they would have been lucky to be hanged as traitors, if lucky.").

155. Alessandro Ferrara, Justice and Judgment: The Rise and the Prospect of the Judgment Model in Contemporary Political Philosophy 114 (Thousand Oaks, CA: SAGE Publications, 1999).

156. 1 Conway W. Sams & Elihu S. Riley, The Bench and Bar of Maryland: A History 204–205 (Chicago, IL: The Lewis Pub. Co., 1901).

157. Bessler, Cruel and Unusual, 102–103, 179–80; Vermont Const. (1777), Art. XXXV.

158. William C. Hill, The Vermont State Constitution: A Reference Guide 133 (Westport, CT: Greenwood Press, 1992); Sydney George Fisher, The Evolution of the Constitution of the United States 205 (Philadelphia: J. B. Lippincott, 1900); Vt. Const., ch. I, art. XVI (1777).

159. S.C. Const. of 1778, art. XL; Les Washington, Generations: A Commentary on the African Immigrants and Their American Descendents 363 (Lincoln, NE: Writers Club Press, 2002).

160. William Clarence Webster, A Comparative Study of the State Constitutions of the American Revolution 95 (1897).

161. Rebecca M. McLennan, The Crisis of Imprisonment: Protest, Politics, and the Making of the American Penal State, 1776–1941, at 22–23 (Cambridge: Cambridge University Press, 2008).

162. Sama, Elisabetta Caminer Turra, 1–38, 61, 66 & nn.20, 85; *see also* id. at 106, 118–19 & nn.24, 79; John Quincy Adams to John Adams, Feb. 11, 1781; John Quincy Adams' Diary [February 1785]; Margaret B. Bonneville to Thomas Jefferson, *available at* www.founders.archives.gov. Elisabetta's contemporaries, including Giovanni Scola (1736–1820), were Enlightenment intellectuals with connections to Beccaria's social circle. Scola himself has been described as "a lawyer, a journalist, a Freemason, and a representative of the municipal government in Vicenza after the fall of the Venetian Republic." As that source reports: "An admirer of the philosophy of d'Alembert, Giambattista Vico, Pietro Verri, and Francesco Antonio Grimaldi, Scola was himself an active participant in the Republic of Letters,

especially through his collaboration (1777–81) with Elisabetta Caminer Turra on the *Giornale enci-clopedico."* For example, Scola had written a positive review of *On Man* (*De l'homme,* 1773). Sama, Elisabetta Caminer Turra, 7 n.18 & 31 n.110.

163. Friedman, A History of American Law, 207; Susan E. Marshall, The New Hampshire State Constitution 4 (Oxford: Oxford University Press, 2011); Abigail Adams to Mercy Otis Warren, Sept. 5, 1784; Abigail Adams to Elizabeth Cranch, Dec. 3, 1784; John Quincy Adams' Diary [Jan.], 28, [1785], *available at* www.founders.archives.gov.

164. 4 Blackstone, Commentaries on the Law of England, 17–18.

165. Nevins, The American States during and after the Revolution, 455; The Life of the Late John Howard, Esq. with a Review of His Travels 43 (J. Ridgway, 1790); Rogers, *"A Long Train of Hideous Consequences",* 16–17, 28; *see also* Asher, Goodheart & Rogers, Murder on Trial, 6 ("Although some American patriots worried that the traditional fragility of a republic necessitated a death penalty in order to maintain order, others such as Benjamin Rush of Pennsylvania and Attorney General James Sullivan of Massachusetts denounced capital punishment as monarchical and touted the benefits of Beccaria's enlightened approach to punishment.").

166. John Howard, Extracts Selected from the Writings and Observations of the Late John Howard, Esq. 28 (Newcastle: W. Thompson, 1790).

167. Chipman, Sketches of the Principles of Government, 14 & n.*, 41, 45, 48, 73, 193 & n.*, 198 n.*; *see also* id. at 70 (referring to Locke and Beccaria in the category of "eminent writers and states-men" who "we venerate … as men" and who "have extended and improved the most important sci-ence, the science of government").

168. Chipman, Sketches of the Principles of Government, 165, 198–200; id. at 223 ("We con-ceive an officer to do his duty, when he executes a criminal condemned to death, by the sentence of the laws."); Thomas Jefferson to Dr. Joseph Priestley, Nov. 29, 1802, *in* 9 Paul Leicester Ford, ed., The Works of Thomas Jefferson 405 (New York: Cosimo, 2009) (1905) (Jefferson stated that "Chipman's Sketches on the principles of government," among other sources, "would furnish the principles of our constitution and their practical development in the several parts of that instrument"); Paul S. Gillies, *Nathaniel Chipman and the Common Law,* 35 Vt. B.J. 8, 9 (Summer 2009) ("After statehood was achieved in 1791, Chipman was appointed Vermont's first U.S. District Judge. As he had little to do in that job, he used the time to produce *Sketches of the Principles of Government,* published in 1793, a book that has been called the first systematic study of law written in America.").

169. Nathaniel Chipman, Principles of Government: A Treatise on Free Institutions 2, 61, 154, 210, 213–16 (Burlington, VT: Edward Smith, 1833).

170. *E.g.,* James Mease, The Picture of Philadelphia, Giving an Account of Its Origin, Increase and Improvements in Arts, Sciences, Manufactures, Commerce and Revenue 162 (Philadelphia: T. Kite, 1811) ("In the year 1788, Dr. Rush published a second pamphlet, entitled 'an inquiry into the justice and pol-icy of punishing murder by death,' in which he adopted and defended the opinion of the Marquis of Bec-caria, by denying the right of government to punish even the crime of deliberate murder by death.").

171. The American Museum, or, Universal Magazine 341, 345 (Dec. 1792).

172. *See* "Mathew Carey, No. 118, Market-Street, Philadelphia, *Has imported from London, Dublin, and Glasgow,* An Extensive Assortment of Books," p. 12 (Jan. 1793).

173. Willie Lee Rose, ed., A Documentary History of Slavery in North America 67–68 (Athens, GA: University of Georgia Press, 1999); Tim McNeese, The Abolitionist Movement: Ending Slavery 28–30 (New York: Chelsea House, 2008); Gelien Matthews, Caribbean Slave Revolts and the British Abolitionist Movement 41–42 (Baton Rouge: Louisiana State University Press, 2006).

174. Noether, The American Constitution as a Symbol and Reality for Italy, 26; Williamsburg: A Seasonal Sampler 8 (Williamsburg: The Colonial Williamsburg Foundation, 2000).

175. Illinois v. Kentucky, 500 US. 380, 387 (1991); Kleber, The Kentucky Encyclopedia, 116; Richard Beale Davis, Intellectual Life in Jefferson's Virginia, 1790–1830, at 82 (1964).

176. 14 Martha J. Lamb, ed., The Magazine of American History with Notes and Queries 190–200 (New York: Historical Publication Co., 1885).

177. Kleber, The Kentucky Encyclopedia, 116.

178. Gail McKnight Beckman, Three Penal Codes Compared, 10 Am. J. Legal Hist. 148 (1966).

179. Peter Wallenstein, Tell the Court I Love My Wife: Race, Marriage, and Law—and American History 32 (New York: Palgrave Macmillan, 2002).

180. Klotter, The Breckinridges of Kentucky, 27; *see also* id. at 208 ("After observing a public ex-ecution in the city, he called for private ones—if there must be such. Breckinridge had serious doubts whether the death penalty ought ever to be inflicted.").

181. Klotter, The Breckinridges of Kentucky, 27; *see also* 2 Marshall, The History of Kentucky, 238 (describing the 1798 Kentucky legislative session).

182. 1 William Elsey Connelley & Ellis Merton Coulter, History of Kentucky 314 (Chicago: The American Historical Society, 1922).

183. Harrison & Klotter, A New History of Kentucky, ch. 7.

184. Diane B. Boyle, Senators of the United States: A Historical Bibliography 31 (Washington, DC: Government Printing Office, 1995); Robert Sobel, Biographical Directory of the Executive Branch, 1774–1989, at 40 (Westport, CT: Greenwood Press, 1990); Kleber, The Kentucky Encyclopedia, 117; Merrill D. Peterson, Thomas Jefferson and the New Nation: A Biography 804–805 (Oxford: Oxford University Press, 1970).

185. Klotter, The Breckinridges of Kentucky, 17.

186. Lowell H. Harrison, John Breckinridge: Jeffersonian Republican 86 (1969).

187. Thomas D. Clark, ed., The Voice of the Frontier: John Bradford's Notes on Kentucky 207–208 (Lexington: The University Press of Kentucky, 1993).

188. Robert Davidson, History of the Presbyterian Church in the State of Kentucky 101 (New York: Robert Carter, 1847); Harrison & Klotter, A New History of Kentucky, ch. 6.

189. Cunningham v. Caldwell, 1807 WL 528 *5 (Ky. App., 1807); Heller, Democracy's Lawyer, 74 (noting Henry Clay's involvement in the case).

190. H. Edward Richardson, Cassius Marcellus Clay: Firebrand of Freedom 10, 33–34, 46–59, 89, 131 (Lexington: University Press of Kentucky, 1976); Marvin H. Bovee, Reasons for Abolishing Capital Punishment (Chicago: A. J. Cox and Co., 1878); James Harold Romain, Gambling: Or, Fortuna, Her Temple and Shrine 177–78 (Chicago: The Craig Press, 1891).

191. Ohio Const., art. VIII, § 14 (1802); Maine Const., art. 1, § 9 (1820).

192. "Report on Capital Punishment, Made to the Maine Legislature in 1836," *reprinted in* Tobias Purrington, Report on Capital Punishment, Made to the Maine Legislature in 1836, at 12, 14–16, 28–29 (3d ed. 1852).

193. Dario Melossi, Controlling Crime, Controlling Society: Thinking about Crime in Europe and America 33 (Cambridge, UK: Polity Press, 2008).

194. 1 The Complete Works of Edward Livingston on Criminal Jurisprudence vi, 1–7, 31, 36–37, 56, 116 (New York: The National Prison Association of the United States of America, 1873).

195. Mark T. Carleton, Politics and Punishment: The History of the Louisiana State Penal System 4 (Baton Rouge, LA: Louisiana State University Press, 1971).

196. Hunt, Life of Edward Livingston, 39–42; Fernandez, From Chaos to Continuity, 74–75; Edward Livingston to James Madison, May 19, 1822; Francis Fukuyama, The Origins of Political Order: From Prehuman Times to the French Revolution 268 (New York: Farrar, Straus and Giroux, 2011). The letter was written from New Orleans. Id.

197. James Madison to Edward Livingston, July 10, 1822.

198. Edward Livingston, Capital Punishment: Argument of Edward Livingston (undated text), *available at* http://books.google.com/books.

199. 3 D. Hamilton Hurd, ed., History of Essex County Massachusetts, with Biographical Sketches of Many of Its Pioneers and Prominent Men xli (Philadelphia: J. W. Lewis, 1888); Hamilton, Memoirs, Speeches and Writings of Robert Rantoul, Jr., 1, 5, 73, 108, 426, 432–33, 436, 440, 444, 452, 461, 847; *see also* id. at 4 (noting that Rantoul "became intimately conversant with the leading continental writers" on "the science of government and legislation," "especially with Beccaria and Montesquieu").

200. Edward Livingston, Capital Punishment: Argument of Edward Livingston (undated text), *available at* http://books.google.com/books.

201. Edward Livingston, A System of Penal Law, for the State of Louisiana 130–31 (1833); *see also* 1 The Complete Works of Edward Livingston on Criminal Jurisprudence 215–17 (New York: The National Prison Association of the United States of America, 1873) (attributing the quote to Dr. Franklin).

202. 2 The American Museum, or Repository of Ancient and Modern Fugitive Pieces, &e. Prose and Poetical 142, 151 (1787).

203. Charles Spear, Essays on the Punishment of Death, title page, 83 n.† (Boston: Charles Spear/London: John Green, 2d ed. 1844) ("We had occasion to remark, in our first essay, that the sentiments were attributed, by Livingston and other eminent jurists, to Franklin himself. If it were intentional, it was probably thought to add to their authority, forgetting that the name of Rush will always be dear to all the lovers of humanity; as he was among the first in America to urge the mitigation of our penal code and the abolition of slavery.").

204. 1 A. Levasseur, Lafayette in America in 1824 and 1825, at 38, 98, 113 (Philadelphia: Carey and Lea, John D. Godman, trans. 1829).

205. Davis, From Homicide to Slavery, 36 & n.70.

206. Ann Lee Bressler, The Universalist Movement in America, 1770–1880, at 83–84 (Oxford: Oxford University Press, 2001).

207. John Macrae Moir, ed., Capital Punishment, Based on Professor Mittermaier's 'Todesstrafe' 29–30 (London: Smith, Elder and Co., 1865).

208. State of New York, "Report of the Select Committee on the Petitions for a Repeal of the Death Penalty in this State," No. 82 (Feb. 16, 1860), in 3 Documents of the Assembly of the State of New-York, Eighty-Third Session—1860, at 2–3, 9–10, 15–17, 21–26 (1860).

209. James Sega, What Is True Civilization, or Means to Suppress the Practice of Duelling, to Prevent, or to Punish Crimes, and to Abolish the Punishment of Death, vii, ix, 3–5, 7, 11, 24, 53–54, 57, 65, 78, 81, 100–101, 105, 117, 135–36, 151, 156, 159–60, 178, 198, 208–210, 212, 217, 226 (Boston: William Smith, 1830).

210. Susan Dallas, ed., Diary of George Mifflin Dallas while United States Minister to Russia 1837 to 1839, and to England 1856 to 1861, at 3–4 (Philadelphia: J. B. Lippincott Co., 1892).

211. Michael Kronenwetter, Capital Punishment: A Reference Handbook 168–69 (Santa Barbara, CA: ABC-CLIO, Inc., 2d ed. 2001).

212. Davis, *The Movement to Abolish Capital Punishment in America*, 42, 36, 44; Filler, *Movements to Abolish the Death Penalty in the United States*, 129; Hugo A. Bedau, "General Introduction, in James A. McCafferty, ed., Capital Punishment 8 (Piscataway, NJ: Transaction Publishers, 2010); *see also* Matthew J. Grow, "Liberty to the Downtrodden": Thomas L. Kane, Romantic Reformer 38 (New Haven, CT: Yale University Press, 2009) ("In 1844, a New York Society for the Abolition of Capital Punishment was founded, followed the next year by organizations in Massachusetts and Philadelphia and a national group, the American Society for the Abolition of Capital Punishment.").

213. Paul Christian Jones, Against the Gallows: Antebellum American Writers and the Movement to Abolish Capital Punishment 3 (Iowa City: University of Iowa Press, 2011).

214. State of New York, "Report of the Select Committee on the Petitions for a Repeal of the Death Penalty in this State," No. 82 (Feb. 16, 1860), in 3 Documents of the Assembly of the State of New-York, Eighty-Third Session—1860, at 21–26 (1860).

215. Davis, From Homicide to Slavery, 23.

216. Robert D. Sampson, John L. O'Sullivan and His Times 9, 96, 98, 100 (Kent, OH: The Kent State University Press, 2003).

217. State of New York, "Report of the Select Committee on the Petitions for a Repeal of the Death Penalty in this State," No. 82 (Feb. 16, 1860), in 3 Documents of the Assembly of the State of New-York, Eighty-Third Session—1860, at 25 (1860). George Clinton was also quoted as saying this in 1802: "The wisdom of substituting imprisonment instead of death has been in a great measure realized." Id.

218. Id. at 25–26 (quoting DeWitt Clinton).

219. John Robert Irelan, History of the Life, Administration and Times of Thomas Jefferson, Third President of the United States 350–52 (Chicago, IL: Fairbanks and Palmer Publishing Co., 1886); Ray W. Irwin, Daniel D. Tompkins: Governor of New York and Vice President of the United States (New York Historical Society, 1968); 1 Jennings B. Sanders, A College History of the United States 255 (Evanston, IL: Row, Peterson, 1962); Claus-M. Naske & Herman E. Slotnick, Alaska: A History of the 49th State 60–61 (Norman: University of Oklahoma Press, 2d ed. 1987); Evan Cornog, The Birth of Empire: DeWitt Clinton and the American Experience, 1769–1828, at 19–20 (Oxford: Oxford University Press, 2000); 22 John P. Kaminski & Gaspare J. Saladino, eds., The Documentary History of the Ratification of the Constitution 1794 (Madison: Wisconsin Historical Society Press, 2008).

220. 3 W. Bernard Peach, ed., The Correspondence of Richard Price 71 n.1 (Durham, NC: Duke University Press, 1994).

221. 1 Amory, Life of James Sullivan, 295–96.

222. Gordon S. Wood & Louise G. Wood, eds., Russian-American Dialogue on the American Revolution 262 (Columbia: University of Missouri Press, 1995); Leonard L. Richards, Shays's Rebellion: The American Revolution's Final Battle 39–42 (Philadelphia: University of Pennsylvania Press, 2003).

223. Jane Kamensky, Governing the Tongue: The Politics of Speech in Early New England 251 (Oxford: Oxford University Press, 1997); George Lee Haskins, Law and Authority in Early Massachusetts: A Study in Tradition and Design 277 n.57 (Lanham, MD: University Press of America, 1960); Matthew Pate & Laurie A. Gould, Corporal Punishment Around the World 20 (Santa Barbara, CA: ABC-CLIO, 2012).

224. 2 William Dunlap, History of the New Netherlands, Province of New York, and State of New York, to the Adoption of the Federal Constitution clxxix (New York: Carter & Thorp, 1840).

225. Alice Morse Earle, Curious Punishments of Bygone Days 148 (Bedford, MA: Applewood Books, 1896).

226. 1 Amory, Life of James Sullivan, 296; Alfred Creigh, History of Washington County: From Its First Settlement to the Present Time 16–18 (Harrisburg, PA: B. Singerly, 2d ed., rev. & corr. 1871); 1 William Hawkins, A Treatise of the Pleas of the Crown; or, A System of the Principal Matters Relating to that Subject, Digested Under Proper Heads 624 (Thomas Leach, ed., 6th ed. 1777); *see also* id. at 352 n.3 (in another section of his treatise, Hawkins also made reference to a "usual" punishment, writing in that unrelated context: "The usual mode of punishment at present is by pillory, fine, imprisonment, and surety for the good behaviour.").

227. Rogers, *"A Long Train of Hideous Consequences"*, 28–29; Adolph Caso, ed., Cesare Beccaria, An Essay on Crimes and Punishments 77 (International Pocket Library, 2d ed. 1992) (originally published as "fourth ed." in London and "Printed for F. Newberry, 1775").

228. Rogers, *"A Long Train of Hideous Consequences"*, 28. As Rogers writes of the Massachusetts experience:

> From 1780 to 1784 fifty-five people were prosecuted for committing capital crimes, whereas from 1790 to 1794 only eighteen persons stood before the Supreme Judicial Court accused of a capital crime. Likewise, twenty people were executed in the 1780s, but the number fell to ten in the 1790s and dropped even further during the first three decades of the nineteenth century.

Id. at 27.

229. Id. at 28; James M. O'Toole & David Quigley, eds., Boston's Histories: Essays in Honor of Thomas H. O'Connor 35 n.37 (Boston: Northeastern University Press, 2004); Woody Holton, Abigail Adams 197 (New York: Free Press, 2009).

230. Bessler, Death in the Dark, 46.

231. Bessler, Cruel and Unusual, 53–54, 272.

232. Kathryn Preyer, "Cesare Beccaria and the Founding Fathers," *in* Blackstone in America, 245–46; 2 David Bailie Warden, A Statistical, Political, and Historical Account of the United States of North America: From the Period of Their First Colonization to the Present Day 77 (Edinburgh: Archibald Constable and Co., 1819) (citing letter from Pennsylvania's William Bradford, Jr. to Luigi Castiglioni).

233. Pace, Luigi Castiglioni's Viaggio, 313 n.39.

234. Sarat & Martschukat, Is the Death Penalty Dying?, 21.

235. "Capital Punishments," The Christian Disciple, Vol. V, No. 3 (Mar. 1817), p. 74–76, 78–79.

236. "Capital Punishments," The Christian Disciple, Vol. V, No. 5 (May 1817), p. 144.

237. "A Plan for Securing and Reforming Convicts," The Christian Disciple, Vol. V, No. 5 (May 1817), p. 135; *see also* "Facts Interesting to Humanity," The Christian Disciple, Vol. V, No. 3 (Mar. 1817), p. 95 ("A resolution is before the legislature of Pennsylvania, for the abolition of capital punishments in all cases.").

238. Jason J. Kilborn, *Who's In Charge Here? Putting Clients in Their Place*, 37 Ga. L. Rev. 1, 14 n.62 (2002); Kopel, *The Second Amendment in the Nineteenth Century*, 137.

Chapter 5

1. Levy, Origins of the Bill of Rights, 234–37; Andrew Delahunty & Sheila Dignen, Adonis to Zorro: Oxford Dictionary of Reference and Allusion 193 (Oxford: Oxford University Press, 2010).

2. Fragmentary Draft of a Dissertation on Canon and Feudal Law, Feb. 1765 & John G. Jackson to James Madison, Sept. 25, 1800, *available at* www.founders.archives.gov.

3. Gottlieb, Theater of Death, 79–81; Levy, Origins of the Bill of Rights, 231.

4. Thomas Hutchinson, The History of the Colony of Massachusett's Bay, from the First Settlement Thereof in 1628, until Its Incorporation with the Colony of Plimouth, Province of Main, &c. by the Charter of King William and Queen Mary, in 1691, at 435–45 (London: M. Richardson, 2d ed. 1765); Henry W. Farnam, Chapters in the History of Social Legislation in the United States to 1860, at 15 (Union, NJ: The Lawbook Exchange, 2000) (1902).

5. John Adams Papers, Record: Plymouth Court of General Sessions, Plymouth, December 1767, *available at* www.founders.archives.gov.

6. Gottlieb, Theater of Death, 82–85.

7. 4 William Blackstone, Commentaries on the Laws of England: A Facsimile of the First Edition of 1765–1769, at 238, 368–72 (1769) (1979).

8. Washington Papers, Court Case, Dec. 3, 1751; Adam Stephen to George Washington, Jan. 18, 1756; George Washington to Robert Dinwiddie, Aug. 4, 1756; George Washington to Adam Stephen, Feb. 1, 1756; Franklin Papers, Extracts from the Gazette, 1733; George Washington to Robert Dinwiddie, Jan. 12, 1757, *available at* www.founders.archives.gov.

9. Peter Linebaugh, The London Hanged: Crime and Civil Society in the Eighteenth Century 74, 361–62 (London: Verso, 2003); London as It Is To-Day: Where to Go, and What to See, during the Great Exhibition 51 (London: H. G. Clarke & Co., 1851); 2 Joseph Priestley, Lectures on History and General Policy 179, 300 (London: J. Johnson, 1793); Robert Bard, Tyburn: The Story of London's Gallows (Gloucestershire, UK: Amberly Publishing, 2012); Jean Kellaway, The History of Torture and Execution: From Early Civilization through Medieval Times to the Present 46–47 (Guilford, CT: The Lyons Press, 2003); Top Ten of Britain: 250 Quintessentially British Lists (London: Octopus Books, 2009); Bolt, The Librettist of Venice, 275; Ernest W. Pettifer, Punishments of Former Days 89 (Winchester, UK: Waterside Press, 1992); William Harvey, London Scenes and London People: Anecdotes, Reminiscences, and Sketches of Places, Personages, Events, Customs, and Curiosities of London City, Past and Present 273 (London: W. H. Collingridge, 1864); Herbert Fry, London: Bird's-Eye Views of the Principal Streets 153 (London: W. H. Allen and Co., 1887); Rob Humphreys, The Rough Guide to London (London: Penguin Books, 2012).

10. Diane Jacobs, Her Own Woman: The Life of Mary Wollstonecraft 11, 37, 108, 110, 166, 286–87, 292 (New York: Citadel Press Books, 2001); Daniel I. O'Neill, The Burke-Wollstonecraft Debate: Savagery, Civilization, and Democracy 109–10 (University Park, PA: Pennsylvania State University Press, 2007); Luigino Bruni, The Genesis and Ethos of the Market 209 (New York: Palgrave Macmillan, 2012); David H. Weinglass, Prints and Engraved Illustrations by and after Henry Fuseli xix (London: Scolar Press, 1994); David Wootton, ed., Republicanism, Liberty and Commercial Society, 1649–1776, at 414 n.136 (Stanford, CA: Stanford University Press, 1994); Peter H. Marshall, William Godwin 83 (New Haven: Yale University Press, 1984); 10 The Analytical Review, or History of Literature, Domestic and Foreign, on an Enlarged Plan 87 (London: J. Johnson, 1791); 26 The Analytical Review, or History of Literature, Domestic and Foreign, on an Enlarged Plan 517 (London: J. Johnson, 1798); 2 William Godwin, An Enquiry Concerning Political Justice, and Its Influence on General Virtue and Happiness 712, 716 (London: G. C. J. & J. Robinson, 1793); H. J. Jackson, Romantic Readers: The Evidence of Marginalia 19 (New Haven: Yale University Press, 2005); Elizabeth Smith Shaw to Abigail Adams, Dec. 29, 1793; 2 Mary Wollstonecraft Shelley, Rambles in Germany and Italy in 1840, 1842, and 1843, at 190–202 (London: Edward Moxon, 1844); 1 Roger Ingpen, The Letters of Percy Bysshe Shelley 419–20 (London: Sir Isaac Pitman & Sons, 1912); Alexander Hamilton to James McHenry, May 23, 1800, *available at* www.founders.archives.gov.

11. Austin Sarat & Thomas R. Kearns, eds., Law's Violence 154 (Ann Arbor: University of Michigan Press, 1995); Helen P. Bruder & Tristanne Connolly, Sexy Blake 38 (New York: Palgrave Macmillan, 2013); Mary Hilton, Women and the Shaping of the Nation's Young: Education and Public Doctrine in Britain 1750–1850, at 75 (Hampshire, UK: Ashgate, 2007); John Mee, Conversable Worlds: Literature, Contention, & Community 1762 to 1830, at 81 (Oxford: Oxford University Press, 2011); 1–2 Kenneth Neill Cameron, ed., Shelley and His Circle, 1773–1822, at 49 (New York: The Carl and Lily Pforzheimer Foundation, 1961); Quentin J. Blaine, "Shall Surely Be Put to Death:" Capital Punishment in New Hampshire, 1623–1985, 27 New Hampshire Bar Journal 134 (1986), *reprinted in* http://www.nhbar.org/uploads/pdf/BJ-Spring2011-Vol52-No1-Pg5.pdf.

12. Henry Cabot Lodge, Daniel Webster 34–35 (Boston: Houghton, Mifflin and Co., 5th ed. 1885); Eva A. Speare, Stories of New Hampshire 72 (Somersworth, NH: New Hampshire Pub. Co., 1975); 1 George Ticknor Curtis, Life of Daniel Webster 378–84 (New York: D. Appleton and Co., 5th ed. 1893); Leigh H. Irvine, By Right of Sword: A Defense of Capital-Punishment, Based on a Searching Examination of History, Theology, and Philosophy 36 (New York: Baker & Taylor Co., 1915); Maurice G. Baxter, One and Inseparable: Daniel Webster and the Union 17 (Cambridge: Harvard University Press, 1984); Issam A. Awad, ed., Philosophy of Neurological Surgery 163 (Park Ridge, IL: American Association of Neurological Surgeons, 1995); Letters of Daniel Webster 56 (New York: Haskell House Publishers, 1902); 1 Fletcher Webster, ed., The Private Correspondence of Daniel Webster 51–52 (Boston: Little, Brown and Co., 1857); Robert V. Remini, Daniel Webster: The Man and His Time 79 n.8 (New York: W. W. Norton, 1997); The Granite Monthly: A New Hampshire Magazine, Vol. L (New Series, Volume XIII), p. 100.

13. Margaret Canovan, *The Un-Benthamite Utilitarianism of Joseph Priestley*, 45 Journal of the History of Ideas 435, 440 (1984); Craig R. Smith, Daniel Webster and the Oratory of Civil Reli-

gion 25–26 (Columbia: University of Missouri Press, 2005); 3 Burgh, Political Disquisitions, 159–164; Verner W. Crane, *The Club of Honest Whigs: Friends of Science and Liberty*, 23 Wm. & Mary Q. 210 (1966); Robert E. Schofield, The Enlightened Joseph Priestley: A Study of His Life and Work from 1773 to 1804, at 18 (University Park, PA: Pennsylvania State University Press, 2004); Charles Tanford, Ben Franklin Stilled the Waves: An Informal History of Pouring Oil on Water with Reflections on the Ups and Downs of Scientific Life in General 38–39 (Oxford: Oxford University Press, 2004); Stanley Finger, Doctor Franklin's Medicine 132 (Philadelphia: University of Pennsylvania Press, 2006); Benjamin Franklin to John Canton, Mar. 14, 1764; Benjamin Franklin to Joseph Priestley, Oct. 3, 1775; Joseph Priestley to Benjamin Franklin, Feb. 13, 1776; Richard Price to Benjamin Franklin, Oct. 14, 1779; Benjamin Vaughan to Benjamin Franklin, Mar. 5, 1782; Benjamin Franklin to Richard Price, June 13, 1782; Benjamin Franklin to Richard Price, Aug. 16, 1784.

14. State of New Hampshire v. Michael Addison, No. 2008–945 (Nov. 6, 2013) (slip op.) (citing An Act for the punishment of certain Crimes, Laws 1792, *reprinted in* 5 Laws of New Hampshire 596–99 (Henry Metcalf ed. 1916)).

15. A Bill for Ascertaining the Salaries and Fees of Certain Officers, 18 June 1779, *available at* www.founders.archives.gov; *see also* A Bill to Prevent Forestalling, Regrating, and Engrossing, and Sales by Auction, 18 June 1779; Lund Washington to George Washington, Apr. 28, 1790 (n.4), *available at* www.founders.archives.gov (containing a provision relating to standing in the pillory).

16. Outline of Bill for Proportioning Crimes and Punishments, &c., 1779; Enclosure: Notes on Criminal Prosecutions and Impeachment [26 January 1798], *available at* www.founders.archives.gov.

17. Hindus, Prison and Plantation, 103; 25 Gaillard Hunt, ed., Journals of the Continental Congress 1774–1789, at 565–66 (Washington, DC: Government Printing Office, 1922); Peter S. Onuf, ed., Congress and the Confederation 443–45 (Taylor & Francis, 1991); Mary A. Y. Gallagher, *Reinterpreting the "Very Trifling Mutiny" at Philadelphia in June 1783*, 119 Pa. Mag. of History and Biography 3, 28 (1995).

18. 20 The Foreign Quarterly Review 270 (London: Black and Armstrong, 1838); Joseph Henry, Memoir of Alexander Dallas Bache: Read Before the National Academy 183 (1869); Alexander Dallas Bache, Report on Education in Europe, to the Trustees of the Girard College for Orphans 159 (Philadelphia: Lydia R. Bailey, 1839); Biographical Dictionary of Federal Judges (entry for "Cranch, William"), *available at* http://www.fjc.gov/servlet/nGetInfo?jid=2813&cid=999&ctype=na&instate=na.

19. William Cranch to Thomas Jefferson, Dec. 19, 1801; William Kilty, James Marshall, and William Cranch to Thomas Jefferson, June 30, 1801, *available at* www.founders.archives.gov.

20. George Croft, A Short Commentary, with Strictures, on Certain Parts of the Moral Writings of Dr. Paley & Mr. Gisborne 246 (Birmingham: Thomas Pearson, 1796); *see also* 2 Rev. W. Beloe, trans., The Attic Nights of Aulus Gellius 119 (London: J. Johnson) ("Some admirable remarks upon the punishment which ought to be inflicted for theft, are to be found in the Marquis Beccaria; Blackstone also has some excellent observations on this subject, from which it may be concluded that he was no friend to extreme and sanguinary punishments."); *compare* Observations on the Life and Character of Alfred the Great 11 n.* (London, 1794) ("Ever since the first dawn of reason I have been uniformly of opinion, that death is a punishment which on no account ought to be inflicted upon a fellow creature, except in case of murder; there the divine law is express. 'Whoso sheddeth man's blood, by man shall his blood be shed.' My sentiments on this subject were still more confirmed, by reading the Marquis of Beccaria's Treatise on Crimes and Punishments; which I beg the reader to peruse.").

21. "A Charge Delivered to the Grand Jury in the Circuit Court of the United States, for the District of Virginia, in May 1791," *in* 1 Kermit L. Hall & Mark David Hall, eds., Collected Works of James Wilson (Indianapolis, IN: Liberty Fund, 2007); John Lemprière, Bibliotheca Classica (1788; London: George Routledge & Sons, 1890); Information Sheet, "Exterior Portrait Medallions and The Great Hall Metopes," Office of the Curator, Supreme Court of the United States; *see also* 1 William Fordyce Mavor, Universal History, Ancient and Modern 21 (1804) ("He commenced his reform, by abrogating all the sanguinary laws of Draco, except that which related to murder, for which he thought no punishment could be too severe."); 15 William Mavor, Universal History, Ancient and Modern 134, 151, 156, 160, 174, 179, 186, 217, 223, 229, 241, 244, 254, 277, 341, 348 (London: Richard Phillips, 1802) (referring to "a most sanguinary war," "a sanguinary war," "a sanguinary battle," "several sanguinary battles," "sanguinary conflicts," "a most sanguinary conflict," "sanguinary tyrant," "violent and sanguinary measures," "sanguinary intentions," and "sanguinary tribunals"); id. at 221–22 ("This prince, though only sixteen years of age, commenced his reign with such cruel and sanguinary measures as induced his subjects to brand him with the epithet of 'Cruel.'").

22. Twenty-Ninth Annual Report and Documents of the New-York Institution for the Instruction of the Deaf and Dumb 92 (New York: Egbert, Hovey & King, 1848).

23. Dictionary of Anonymous and Pseudonymous English Literature 333 (New York: Haskell House Publishers, 1926–1934); The Monthly Review; or Literary Journal, Enlarged 320–21 (London: T. Becket, 1808).

24. Bessler, Cruel and Unusual, 49, 52, 70, 86–88, 92, 110–11, 135–36, 139, 141, 144, 148, 178–80, 192, 214, 305; Jeremy Bentham, Theory of Legislation 114, 344–45, 428 (R. Hildreth, trans. 1882); *see also* Letter dated July 3 from "E.P." to "Mr. Urban" (dated July 3), *in* 56 Sylvanus Urban, The Gentleman's Magazine: and Historical Chronicle 514 (1784) ("The number of capital punishments which occur in our own nation in particular, is a circumstance that alarms the feelings of humanity.... Did the *cruelty* of our laws give them additional force in deterring men from incurring the penalties of them, their cruelty might perhaps admit of defence; but this does not seem to be the case.... It deserves therefore to be considered whether, by making *fewer crimes to be capital*, and at the same time rendering the punishments which may be appointed instead of death *more certain*, these inconveniences might not, in some measure, be avoided. Let the penalties of the law be less severe, or however less sanguinary; but let them, with a very few exceptions, be invariably inflicted on conviction."); J. Holland, "Lines on Italy," *in* 126 The Gentleman's Magazine: and Historical Chronicle from July to December, 1819, at 65 (1819) ("A weaken'd race with sanguinary laws"); id. at 396 (another portion of that magazine contains the following reference: "The rough manners of the English in former years, and their sanguinary laws, afford a striking contrast with the severest punishments of modern times."); id. at 154 (noting that Queen Elizabeth "proceeded to secure the reformation by the strong barrier of penal and sanguinary laws; making it capital, to be ordained, and to exercise spiritual functions after the ancient manner"); 2 Rev. M. A. Tierney, ed., Dodd's Church of England: From the Commencement of the Sixteenth Century to the Revolution in 1688, at 154 (London: Charles Dolman, 1839); *see also* id. at 49 (stating, in a section discussing Edward IV's religion, that "he seemed not" inclined "to shed blood on that account; and, therefore, no sanguinary, but only penal, laws were executed upon such as stood off," with an editorial note pertaining to Dodd's language, "*such as stood off*," reading: "but the burnings of Bocher and Von Paris will shew that, in other instances, even Edward's unwillingness to shed blood might be subdued by the zeal and the importunties of such a prelate as Cranmer"); id. at 105 ("Now, whether the legislature, in queen Mary's reign, acted prudently in reviving the sanguinary laws, and whether they had a sufficient provocation and inducement to put them in execution, depends altogether upon the circumstances of those times; and particularly, on the behaviour of the persons who had rendered themselves obnoxious."); id. at 128–29 ("He was seconded by Anthony Brown, lord viscount Montague, and again by Mr. Atkinson, in the house of commons, who made it appear, that it was contrary to the hitherto avowed principles of the reformers, that sanguinary laws should be pressed upon the catholics. 'I desire, said he, it may be remembered, that people, who suffer for refusing this oath, are not to be considered as common malefactors, thieves, and murderers. They don't offend from wicked intention, and malice prepense. No, it is conscience, and good meaning, which makes them clash with the law. I don't deny, but they may be mistaken; but, when this happens, the case is still harder: for, if we let the penalty loose upon them under such mispersuasion, we bar recollection, and destroy both body and soul.'").

25. John F. Watson, Annals of Philadelphia, Being a Collection of Memoirs, Anecdotes, & Incidents of the City and Its Inhabitants from the Days of the Pilgrim Founders 257–262 (Philadelphia: E. L. Carey & A. Hart, 1830).

26. "A Lecture on Capital Punishment," The Sentinel, and Star in the West (Cincinnati), July 31, 1830 (newspaper edited by J. Kidwell, J. C. Waldo, and S. Tizzard).

27. 1 Thucydides, The History of the Peloponnesian War lv (William Smith, trans. 1753) ("The punishment of death hath never effectually awed the tempers of mankind.... Men should be retained in their duty by mild discretionary precautions; severe and sanguinary proceedings never answer the purpose.") (quoting speech of Diodotus); id. at 254 ("To keep men firm in their duty, we should scorn the expedient of severe and sanguinary laws, since mild discretionary caution would better answer the purpose.") (quoting Diodotus); Shannon E. Duffy, "An Enlightened American: The Political Ideology of Thomas Hutchinson on the Eve of the Revolutionary Crisis," Dissertation, University of Maryland, College Park 96 (2008) (quoting Thomas Hutchinson, the last royal governor of Massachusetts, as saying that "sanguinary laws against particular doctrines or tenets in religion are not to be defended"); Address of the Branch Council for Great Britain 82 (2d ed. 1839) ("The colonists settled here, imitated the policy of the established church, whose doctrine they professed, by passing the most sanguinary laws against the Catholics."); id. at 83 ("The laws of Charles II, which completed the spoliation of the Catholics by stripping them of the little left untouched by his predecessors, had been extended to the colonies; to these, severe as they were, additions were made in the reign of Anne;

but the new lawgivers of Maryland, not content with so sanguinary a code, consummated the malice of English legislation against the Catholic Church, by introducing statutes of a still more exterminating character.").

28. 1 C. Stedman, The History of the Origin, Progress, and Termination of the American War 9 (London: J. Murray, 1794).

29. C. V. Wedgwood, A King Condemned: The Trial and Execution of Charles I, at 146–93 (London: Tauris Parke, 2011); The Riverside Dictionary of Biography 162–63 (Boston: Houghton Mifflin Harcourt, 2005).

30. William Hodges, Travels in India, During the Years 1780, 1781, 1782, & 1783, at 55 (London: William Hodges, 1783); *compare* Sylvanus Urban, The Gentleman's Magazine 415 (1746) ("a cruel sanguinary disposition").

31. 17 The Monthly Review: or, Literary Journal, Enlarged 114 (1795) ("He has fallen a martyr to cruel and sanguinary laws, or at least to the merciless sentence of lawyers....").

32. 17 The Monthly Review: or, Literary Journal, Enlarged 248, 530 (1795).

33. 2 The London Magazine, or, Gentleman's Monthly Intelligencer 572 (1733) ("[t]he violent and sanguinary Prosecution of the *Popish Plot*").

34. 3 Memoirs of Maximilian de Bethune, Duke of Sully, Prime Minister to Henry the Great 28 (London: J. Rivington and Sons, 5th ed. 1778).

35. John Walker, The Universal Gazetteer (1795) (entry for "England"); *see also* François-Alexandre-Frédéric duc de La Rochefoucauld-Liancourt, A Comparative View of Mild and Sanguinary Laws; and the Good Effects of the Former, Exhibited in the Present Economy of the Prisons of Philadelphia (2d ed. 1796).

36. Morris L. Cohen, comp., Joseph Story, Joseph Story and the *Encyclopedia Americana* 143 (Clark, NJ: The Lawbook Exchange, 2005) (1844) (in an 1844 encyclopedia entry, Justice Story, Associate Justice of the U.S. Supreme Court, wrote: "The codes of most civilized nations abound with capital punishments. That of Great Britain, a nation in which the public legislation has a deep infusion of popular opinion, is thought to be uncommonly sanguinary. Blackstone, in his Commentaries (vol. iv, 18), admits that, in his time, not less than *one hundred and sixty crimes* were, by the English law, punishable with death.").

37. 2 Mathew Bacon, A New Abridgment of the Law, Alphabetically Digest Under Proper Titles (Dublin: Luke White, 1793) (noting, in an unpaginated text, that "our Law does not punish the Stealing of Corn or Grass growing, or Apples on a Tree" with "Death" and explaining that "it was not necessary to guard this Sort of Property with such Sanguinary Laws"); "Power of Congress over the District of Columbia," *in* 1 The Plaindealer 452 (1836) (quoting a writer from the *Baltimore Chronicle* as saying: "The Constitution and the Bill of Rights of Maryland forbid the legislature to do many acts which the Constitution of the United States does not prohibit Congress. Among others they declare that no sanguinary laws shall be enacted...."); 3 The Christian Examiner and Theological Review 27 (1826) ("The construction of the prisons and the state of the prisoners are as might be expected, where such sanguinary laws prevail."); "By a citizen of Maryland," "An oration intended to have been spoken at a late commencement, on the unlawfulness and impolicy of capital punishments, and the proper means of reforming criminals," The American Museum, or, Universal Magazine 8 (1790) ("The advocates for sanguinary statutes have asserted, that 'they are founded upon natural reason;' for that 'by the law of nature, a murderer is put to death.' Here I would ask those gentlemen to explain themselves."); id. at 69 ("But it has been said, that religion authorises capital punishments. And here we are presented with a long list of sanguinary laws...."); id. at 70 ("what a horrid spectre would a sanguinary statute appear!"); id. ("No one will pretend to adduce, from the new testament, any positive injunction of inflicting death for crimes. It is only alleged, that, as it does not expressly abolish the penal law of the Jews—and as there are several instances of inspired men submitting to the sanguinary laws of the Romans, and enjoining submission upon their disciples, therefore such laws must be approved by the Holy Ghost."); id. ("let us beware, lest, forsaking the spirit, and viewing with microscopic eye a few minute points of the letter, we prop a fabric of sanguinary jurisprudence, which must soon melt away before the strong beams of religious truth, and leave us objects of pity and derision to succeeding generations"); id. at 71 ("The plan of building morality upon the gallows, implies this capital mistake, that the human mind has no principle of action, but fear.... Penal laws consult political expediency more than morality. Nay, by annexing the same punishment of theft and parricide, they tend to confound the different degrees of guilty, and blunt the moral sense. These remarks would shew, *a priori*, the inefficacy of our sanguinary laws for the prevention of crimes."); 5 Biographia Britannica: or, The Lives of the Most Eminent Persons 3429 (London: W. Meadows, et al., 1760) (referencing "sanguinary laws against the Clergy"); id. at 3019 ("san-

guinary temper"); id. at 3076 ("our sanguinary temper"); id. at 3396 n.*X* ("sanguinary proceedings").

38. J. Lempriere, Bibliotheca Classica: or, A Classical Dictionary, Containing a Full Account of All the Proper Names Mentioned in Antient Authors (London: T. Cadell, 1788) (entry for "Solon"); Information Sheet, "Constitution Friezes: South and North Walls," Office of the Curator, Supreme Court of the United States.

39. Rudolph J. Gerber, *Death Is Not Worth It*, 28 Ariz. St. L.J. 335, 336 (1996); *compare* The Edinburgh Annual Register, for 1819, at 158 (Edinburgh: Archibald Constable and Co., 1823) ("Before the period of which we are now speaking (1819), the Statute Law of England contained no less than *two hundred* capital felonies, although, for the seventy years immediately preceding, execution had been enforced on only *twenty-five* of that immense number.").

40. 1 The Observer: Being a Collection of Moral, Literary and Familiar Essays 153, 157 (1786). That commentator would further observe:

> If the principle of punishment does not consist in revenging what is past, but in preventing the culprit from repeating and the community from suffering the like or any other offence from the same person, it may well be doubted if death need be inflicted in any case; the terror example, not the spirit of revenge, must constitute the necessity of such a mode of punishment, if any necessity exists; but if punishments may be devised, by which guilty persons shall be made to atone to society without cutting them from it, and if these punishments may be such as shall deter and terrify the evil-minded equally with death itself, policy, independent of religion, will be interested to adopt them.

Id. at 157.

41. 3 A. Hawkins, The History of the Turkish, or Ottoman Empire, from Its Foundation in 1300, to the Peace of Belgrade in 1740, at 25 (Exeter: R. Thorn, 1787) ("the emperor, grown jealous of Bajazet, made their mother fear that this monarch, already too sanguinary, would put to death a rival who was more dangerous, because Bajazet affected lenity and kindness, as much as his brother did severity").

42. A True and Exact Relation of the Death of Two Catholicks, Who Suffered for Their Religion at the Summer Assizes, Held at Lancaster in the Year 1628, at 27 (London, 1737) ("[t]he Behavior of a Sanguinary Judge increased the Martyr's Glory"); Case of Great Britain and America, Addressed to the King and Both Houses of Parliament 37 (London, 2d ed. 1769) ("What then are the ultimate objects of the most oppressive laws, and most sanguinary councils?"). The later source was reprinted by William and Thomas Bradford at the London Coffee-House. 4 Charles Evans, American Bibliography: A Chronological Dictionary of All Books Pamphlets and Periodical Publications Printed in the United States of America (Chicago: The Blakely Press, 1907) (see entry 11193).

43. 3 The Lives of Saints: Collected from Authentick Records of Church History 344 (London: Thomas Meighan, 1729) ("sanguinary Edicts"); 4 The Lives of Saints: Collected from Authentick Records of Church History 118 (London: T. Osborne, 2d ed. 1750) ("[a]s soon as the sanguinary Edict was published, the two Converts were seized and carried before *Sabinus*"); id. at 221 ("[t]he Sanguinary Edict reached Alexandria at the Beginning of 250"); *see also* id. at 45–46 ("*Maximus* then commanded the Officers who attended the Court to see him stript, bound, and severely whipt. This sanguinary Order was executed as soon as given...."); id. at 389 ("[h]is sanguinary Views were providentially defeated").

44. 2 William Robertson, The History of the Reign of the Emperor Charles V, at 458 (London: A. Strahan, T. Cadell & W. Davies, 1769) ("The sanguinary punishments frequent under other governments were unknown.").

45. 5 John Langhorne & William Langhorne, trans., Plutarch's Lives 344 (London: C. Bathurst, et al., 1794) ("Ochus was the most cruel and sanguinary of princes"); Walker's Hibernian Magazine: or, Compendium of Entertaining Knowledge 295 (Dublin: Thomas Walker, 1786) ("The Duke repented that he had granted him his protection; when Crichton, looking on his sanguinary success with disdain, offered to stake 1500 pistoles, and mount the stage against him."); id. at 338 ("that sanguinary wretch will not be turned loose again like a tyger to gut his insatiable thirst for blood"); id. at 348 ("It would be superfluous to enter into a detail of the horrors produced by the fanaticism of this young nobleman and his sanguinary followers."); id. at 377 ("Although this sanguinary man was commonly known by the name of Scotch Andrew, he was not a native of Scotland...."); id. ("He continued to play an active and sanguinary part, till these insurgents were quelled, and then he saved himself from the search of justice, by sculking up and down the country.").

46. Notes and Queries: A Medium of Intercommunication for Literary Men, General Readers, Etc. 258–59 (London: John C. Francis, 1887).

47. Tomahawk! or, Censor General 50, 52, 65, 136, 155, 222, 269, 293, 312, 315, 317, 323–25, 382, 418, 433 (1795).

48. The History of Robespierre, Political and Personal 35 (London: C. Whittingham, 1794).

49. 7 Edward Gibbon, The History of the Decline and Fall of the Roman Empire 209 (London: A. Strahan & T. Cadell, new ed. 1788).

50. 65 The Modern Part of an Universal History, from the Earliest Account of Time (London: C. Bathurst, et al., 1766).

51. The Real Calumniator Detected: Being Candid Remarks on Mr. King's Apology; or, Reply to His Calumniators 14 (London: J. Downes, 1798); 3 Cyrus Redding, Personal Reminiscences of Eminent Men (London: Saunders, Otley & Co., 1867).

52. William Ramsey, comp., The Proceedings in Cases of High Treason, Under a Special Commission of Oyer and Terminer, Which Was First Opened at Hicks's Hall, Oct. 2, 1794, and Afterwards Continued at the Sessions House, in the Old Bailey 728 (1794); Delahay Gordon, A General History of the Lives, Trials, and Executions of All the Royal and Noble Personages 265 (London: J. Burd, 1760).

53. Herbert A. Johnson, Nancy Travis Wolfe & Mark Jones, History of Criminal Justice 171 (Newark, NJ: Matthew Bender & Co., 4th ed. 2008); compare id. ("[B]oth of these young men must have suspected that excessive punishments did not deter crime. A 1767 notice in the New York Mercury described a hanging of pickpockets at the public execution ground, and went on to advise that as the hanging took place one man in the assembled crowd had his pocket picked.").

54. 2 Edmund Burke, An Account of the European Settlements in America 150–51 (London: R. and J. Dodsley, 3d ed. 1760).

55. 1 Henry Swinburne, Travels in the Two Sicilies in the Years 1777, 1778, 1779, and 1780, at 39 (London: T. Cadell and P. Elmsly, 2d ed. 1790).

56. William Preston, A Letter to Bryan Edwards, Esquire, Containing Observations on Some Passages of His History of the West Indies 19, 28, 38 (London: J. Johnson, 1795).

57. 1 Charles de Secondat Montesquieu, The Spirit of Laws (Edinburgh: Donaldeon and Reid, 3d ed. 1762); Bessler, Cruel and Unusual, 33.

58. John Cunningham Wood, ed., Adam Smith: Critical Assessments 102 (London: Routledge, 1996); Adam Smith, The Theory of Moral Sentiments 175 (London: Millar, Kincaid & Bell, 3d ed. 1767) (noting that "the sovereign," "[i]n the punishment of treason," "resents the injuries done to himself" and "as he judges in his own cause, he is very apt to be more violent and sanguinary in his punishments than the impartial spectator can approve of"); compare id. at 226 ("his observations upon the conduct of others, have taught him how horrible all such sanguinary revenges appear"); id. at 319 (in a discussion of "savage nations" and the "passions of a savage," noting that when the "savage" gives way to "vengeance" and "symptoms of anger," it "is always sanguinary and dreadful").

59. 3 A. Hawkins, The History of the Turkish, or Ottoman Empire, from Its Foundation in 1300, to the Peace of Belgrade in 1740, at 29–30 (Exeter: R. Thorn, 1787) ("he sometimes procured the recall of the death warrants which this sanguinary monarch had issued too rashly"); id. at 57 ("Mehemet suppressed this sanguinary order"); id. at 80 ("the sanguinary disposition of Amurath"); id. at 82 ("His sanguinary humour made him at times both unjust and cruel."); id. at 113 ("a prince as sanguinary as effeminate"); id. at 330 ("As sanguinary and absolute as Mustapha was, he, durst not take on him to order new executions...."); id. at 358 ("a timid, sanguinary general must not be permitted to put his highness's subjects to death, according to his caprice").

60. Walker's Hibernian Magazine: or, Compendium of Entertaining Knowledge 28 (Dublin: Thomas Walker, 1786).

61. Puls, Henry Knox, 171; Bessler, Cruel and Unusual, 68–94, 137–38; Alexander Hamilton to Henry Knox, June 7, 1782, available at www.founders.archives.gov.

62. Puls, Henry Knox, 1–25.

63. Trevor Rosson, Booknote, 31 Am. J. Crim. L. 317, 323 (2004) (reviewing James Q. Whitman, Harsh Justice: Criminal Punishment and the Widening Divide Between America and Europe (Oxford: Oxford University Press, 2005)).

64. Harry M. Ward, The War for Independence and the Transformation of American Society 240–41 (London: UCL Press, 1999).

65. Albert Cook Myers, Quaker Arrivals at Philadelphia 1682–1750: Being a List of Certificates of Removal Received at Philadelphia Monthly Meeting of Friends (Baltimore, MD: Genealogical Publishing Co., 2007); Nancy Black Sagafi-Nejad, Friends at the Bar: A Quaker View of Law, Conflict Resolution, and Legal Reform 50, 72 (Albany, NY: State University of New York Press, 2011); 58 The Atlantic Reporter 498 (St. Paul, MN: West Publishing Co., 1904).

66. Leslie Lytle, Execution's Doorstep: True Stories of the Innocent and Near Damned 236 (Boston: Northeastern University Press, 2008); Joel Samaha, Criminal Law 72 (Belmont, CA: Wadsworth, 11th ed. 2013).

67. Brian A. Pavlac, A Concise Survey of Western Civilization: Supremacies and Diversities Throughout History 221 (Plymouth, UK: Rowman & Littlefield, 2011); William Young, International Politics and Warfare in the Age of Louis XIV and Peter the Great 166, 190, 193 (Lincoln, NE: iUniverse, 2004).

68. Graber, The Furnace of Affliction, 22–23; William Tallack, George Fox, the Friends, and the Early Baptists 171 (London: S. W. Partridge, 1868); John H. Ferguson, Politics Quaker Style: A History of the Quakers from 1624 to 1718, at 19 (San Bernardino, CA: The Borgo Press, 1995); George Fox, An Autobiography 36, 105, 161 (NuVision Publications, 2007).

69. Wilbur R. Miller, ed., The Social History of Crime and Punishment in America: An Encyclopedia 762, 1475 (Thunder Oaks, CA: SAGE Publications, 2012); Larry K. Gaines & Roger Leroy Miller, ed., Criminal Justice in Action 429 (Independence, KY: Cengage Learning, 7th ed., 2012); Paul Ibell, Theatreland: A Journey through the Heart of London's Theatre 12 (London: Continuum, 2009). Notably, John Penn (1760–1834), the grandson of Pennsylvania's founder, inherited a 75 percent interest in the Province of Pennsylvania after the death of his father, Thomas Penn, in 1775. John Penn had his property confiscated by the Pennsylvania legislature, though he was later compensated for his loss. A minor at the time he briefly became the 5th and last chief proprietor of Pennsylvania (1775–1776), John Penn returned to England with the loss of his position. Although he lived in Philadelphia for a few years after the Revolutionary War, he ultimately went back to England and became a writer. In *Further Thoughts on the Present State of Public Opinion* (1800), Penn, in a book printed for the bookseller to "Her Majesty," announced his respect, but opposition to, Beccaria's ideas. As Penn wrote: "'I would *not* proceed further, nor venture on such untried experiments as the philosophers of the present day, or even a Beccaria would recommend.' Thus I may appear, perhaps, still less inclined to innovation in our laws, than a queen's solicitor general, the judicious Blackstone, who speaks with the respect I do of Beccaria's ideas, but dwells more on them." Penn, Further Thoughts on the Present State of Public Opinion, 26.

70. William T. Davis, History of the Judiciary of Massachusetts 32 (Boston: The Boston Book Co., 1900).

71. Graber, The Furnace of Affliction, 25.

72. Charles Warren, History of the Harvard Law School and of Early Legal Conditions in America 47, 55 (New York: Lewis Publishing Co., 1908).

73. Maeva Marcus, ed., Origins of the Federal Judiciary: Essays on the Judiciary Act of 1789, at 174 (Oxford: Oxford University Press, 1992).

74. Bessler, Legacy of Violence, 136; Bessler, Cruel and Unusual, 266, 271; Robert J. Tórrez, Myth of the Hanging Tree: Stories of Crime and Punishment in Territorial New Mexico 26 (Albuquerque: University of New Mexico Press, 2008); *see also* April Moore, Folsom's 93: The Lives and Crimes of Folsom Prison's Executed Men, part VII (Fresno, CA: Craven Street Books, 2013) ("There is no recorded explanation why executions in the United States took place only on Fridays. Historians believed that after Christ's crucifixion occurred on that day, ecclesiastical courts began fixing Friday for legal executions. The custom continued in England and was brought to the United States.").

75. Bessler, Cruel and Unusual, 122; U.S. Const., amend. VI; Anne T. Romano, Italian Americans in Law Enforcement 23 (Xlibris Corp., 2010); An Act for the Punishment of certain Crimes against the United States, §§ 29–31.

76. Wilbur R. Miller, ed., The Social History of Crime and Punishment in America: An Encyclopedia 762 (Thunder Oaks, CA: SAGE Publications, 2012); O. F. Lewis, The Development of American Prisons and Prison Customs 1776–1845, at 68 (Albany, NY: Prison Association of New York, 1922); 1 The American Magazine of Useful and Entertaining Knowledge 531 (Boston: The Boston Bewick Co., 1835); McMurry & Adams, People, Power, Places, 120.

77. Markus D. Dubber & Lindsay Farmer, eds., Modern Histories of Crime and Punishment 146 n.55 (Stanford, CA: Stanford University Press, 2007); William Paterson: Lawyer and Statesman, 1745–1806, at 205 (New Brunswick, NJ: Rutgers University Press, 1979); R. A. Burchell, ed., The End of Anglo-America: Historical Essays in the Study of Cultural Divergence 88 (Manchester, UK: Manchester University Press, 1991); Maxine N. Lurie, ed., A New Jersey Anthology 130 (New Brunswick, NJ: Rutgers University Press, 2010).

78. Joseph C. Morton, Shapers of the Great Debate at the Constitutional Convention of 1787: A Biographical Dictionary 173–77 (Westport, CT: Greenwood Press, 2006).

79. 52 Vermont History 243 (Vermont Historical Society, 1984); Zadock Thompson, History of Vermont, Natural, Civil, and Statistical 93 (Burlington, VT: Chauncey Goodrich, 1842); 5 E. P. Walton, ed., Records of the Governor and Council of the State of Vermont 393–94 (Montpelier, VT: Steam Press of J. & J. M. Poland, 1877).

80. John Russell, Jr., An Authentic History of the Vermont State Prison: From the Passing the Law for Its Erection in 1807, to July, 1812, at 6–24 (Windsor, VT: Preston Merrifield, 1812).

81. Edward Conant, The Geography, History, Constitution and Civil Government of Vermont 135–36 (Rutland, VT: The Tuttle Co., 3d ed., 1896).

82. Laura I. Appleman, *The Lost Meaning of the Jury Trial Right*, 84 Ind. L.J. 397, 399, 416–17, 420 (2008); Karin E. Gedge, Without Benefit of Clergy: Women and the Pastoral Relationship in Nineteenth-Century American Culture 53 (New York: Oxford University Press, 2003).

83. Job R. Tyson, Essay on the Penal Law of Pennsylvania 2, 14–15, 18, 32, 34–35, 64, 68–69 (Philadelphia: Law Academy of Philadelphia, 1827).

84. Natural History of New York 181–82 (New York: D. Appleton & Co. 1842) (containing a "Note" on the subject of "penitentiary disciple" furnished by "Hon. John L. O'Sullivan").

85. Bessler, Cruel and Unusual, 94–95; François-Alexandre-Frédéric duc de La Rochefoucauld-Liancourt, Des Prisons de Philadelphie 1–2, 25–27, 38, 63, 65–66, 74, 94 (Amsterdam: J. van Gulik & W. Holtrop, 2d ed. 1799).

86. Charles Spear, Essays on the Punishment of Death 15 (London: John Green, 2d ed. 1844); François-Alexandre-Frédéric duc de La Rochefoucauld-Liancourt, A Comparative View of Mild and Sanguinary Laws; and the Good Effects of the Former, Exhibited in the Present Economy of the Prisons of Philadelphia 24 (Philadelphia printed/London: Darton and Harvey, 1796).

87. http://www25.uua.org/uuhs/duub/articles/charlesspear.html.

88. An Appeal to the World: or a Vindication of the Town of Boston 29 (Boston: Edes and Gill, 1769) ("Published by Order of the Town"), *available at* https://www.masshist.org/dorr/volume/2/sequence/1037; Silence Dogood, No. 2, Apr. 16, 1722; Poor Richard Improved, 1748; George Washington to Robert Dinwiddie, Sept. 23, 1756; John Adams to Samuel Quincy, Apr. 22, 1761; John Adams Papers, June 8, 1762 entry; "A Dissertation on the Canon and the Feudal Law," No. 1, Aug. 12, 1765; "A Dissertation on the Canon and the Feudal Law," No. 2, Aug. 19, 1765; Adams' Original Draft, Sept. 24, 1765; "A Dissertation on the Canon and the Feudal Law," No. 4, Oct. 21, 1765; Benjamin Franklin to Samuel Cooper, Apr. 27, 1769; Benjamin Franklin to Samuel Cooper, June 8, 1770; Benjamin Franklin to Noble Wimberly Jones, Apr. 2, 1772; John Adams to Abigail Adams, June 30, 1774; John Adams, Thoughts on Government, Apr. 1776; Jefferson's "Original Rough Draught" of the Declaration of Independence, June 11–July 4, 1776; The Declaration of Independence as Adopted by Congress, June 11–July 4, 1776; Benjamin Rush to John Adams, Aug. 8, 1777; John Adams to the President of the Congress, Dec. 8, 1778; John Adams to Robert Treat Paine, Dec. 8, 1778; Elbridge Gerry to John Adams, Oct. 12, 1779; Alexander Hamilton to James Duane, Sept. 3, 1780; James Madison to Edmund Randolph, Apr. 9, 1782; Alexander Hamilton, The Continentalist No. VI [July 4, 1782], *available at* www.founders.archives.gov.

89. Mass. Const., preamble & arts. I & XII (1780); 2 Daniel Neal, The History of the Puritans, or, Protestant Non-Conformists, From the Death of Queen Elizabeth to the Beginning of the Civil War in the Year 1642, at 134 (Dublin: Brice Edmond, 1755); Giles Jacob, A New Law-Dictionary: Containing the Interpretation and Definition of Words and Terms Used in the Law (Savot: E. and N. Nutt, et al., 1729) (entry for "Custom"); *see also* George Fox, The Law of God, the Rule of Law-makers: The Ground of All Just Laws, and the Corruption of English Laws and Lawyers Discovered (Giles Calvert, 1658); Ronald M. Peters, Jr., The Massachusetts Constitution of 1780: A Social Compact 57 (Amherst: University of Massachusetts Press, 1974).

90. John Adams, Diary Entry for Jan. 18, 1766; John Adams Papers, The Earl of Clarendon to William Pym, Jan. 27, 1766, *available at* www.founders.archives.gov; The Earl of Clarendon to William Pym, *in* The Works of John Adams, *available at* www.oll.libertyfund.org.

91. Teresia Constantia Muilman, A Letter Humbly Address'd to the Right Honourable the Earl of Chesterfield 17 (London: Teresia Constantia Muilman, 1750) ("sanguinary Acts of Cruelty"); 4 The Town and Country Magazine: or, Universal Repository of Knowledge, Instruction, and Entertainment 483 (1772) ("The military should never be called in upon any trifling occasion, where peace-officers would be sufficient to quell a tumult or disperse a mob. A minister who acts otherwise displays a sanguinary disposition, and seems to sport with the lives of his fellow subjects.").

92. Edmund Burke, Reflections on the Revolution in France, and on the Proceedings in Certain Societies in London Relative to that Event 56 (London: J. Dodsley, 1790).

93. Thomas Paine, Common Sense: Addressed to the Inhabitants of America 6, 14 (1776).

94. Bessler, Cruel and Unusual, 106–108, 110–11; White, John Jay, 92; Harry Harmer, Tom Paine: The Life of a Revolutionary 88 (London: Haus Publishing, 2006); Stacy Schiff, A Great Improvisation: Franklin, France, and the Birth of America 85–86, 409 (New York: Owl Books, 2005); Paul R. Han-

son, Historical Dictionary of the French Revolution 182–83 (Oxford: Scarecrow Press, 2004); John Adams to Abigail Adams, Feb. 3, 1793; William Short to Thomas Jefferson, Feb. 3, 1793; Alexander Hamilton to George Washington, Apr. 5, 1793; Thomas Jefferson to James Madison, Mar. 25, 1793, *available at* www.founders.archives.gov (discussing France's declaration of war and noting in a footnote that "the execution of Louis XVI on 21 Jan. became known in Philadelphia by 15 Mar.") (quoting Parson, Diary of Jacob Hiltzheimer, p. 190).

95. Gouverneur Morris to Thomas Jefferson, Jan. 25, 1793; Gouverneur Morris to Thomas Jefferson, Feb. 13, 1793; James Madison to Thomas Jefferson, Apr. 12, 1793; William Heth to Alexander Hamilton, June 14, 1793; Thomas Pinckney to Thomas Jefferson, Jan. 30, 1793, *available at* www.founders.archives.gov.

96. Sudhir Hazareesingh, ed., The Jacobin Legacy in Modern France: Essays in Honour of Vincent Wright 165–70 (Oxford: Oxford University Press, 2002); The National Assembly of France to George Washington, Aug. 26, 1792; Jean Marie Roland to Alexander Hamilton, Oct. 10, 1792, *available at* www.founders.archives.gov.

97. Brown & Brown, The Hanging of Ephraim Wheeler, 196.

98. Rufus Wilmot Griswold, The Poets and Poetry of America 65–67 (Philadelphia: Parry and McMillan, 16th ed. 1855); 2 S. O. Beeton & W. M. Rossetti, eds., Encyclopædia of English and American Poetry: From Cædmon and King Alfred's Boethius to Browning and Tennyson (London: Ward, Lock & Tyler, 1873); 1 The American Review, and Literary Journal, for the Year 1801, at 297–303 (New York: T. & J. Swords, 1801); 14 The New International Encyclopædia 247 (New York: Dodd, Mead and Co., 2d ed. 1915).

99. Outlines of an Historical View of the Progress of the Human Mind: Being a Posthumous Work of the Late M. de Condorcet 257 (London: J. Johnson, 1795); Copy of a Letter from Benjamin Banneker to the Secretary of State with His Answer 3–11 (Philadelphia: Daniel Lawrence, 1792); Benjamin Banneker to Thomas Jefferson, Aug. 19, 1791; Thomas Jefferson to Benjamin Banneker, Aug. 30, 1791, *available at* www.founders.archives.gov; Thomas Jefferson to M. de Condorcet, Aug. 30, 1791; Charles A. Cerami, Benjamin Banneker: Surveyor, Astronomer, Publisher, Patriot 2, 36–46 (New York: John Wiley & Sons, 2002); Thomas J. Gardner & Terry M. Anderson, Criminal Law 158 (Belmont, CA: Thomson Higher Education, 10th ed. 2009); http://www.oldbaileyonline.org/static/Gender.jsp. The phrase "the imbecility of their present condition" is also found in Blackstone's *Commentaries.* St. George Tucker, Blackstone's Commentaries with Notes of Reference to the Constitution and Laws, of the Federal Government of the United States; and of the Commonwealth of Virginia 291 (Philadelphia: William Young Birch & Abraham Small, 1803).

100. Peter Thompson, Rum Punch and Revolution: Taverngoing & Public Life in Eighteenth-Century Philadelphia 178 (Philadelphia: University of Pennsylvania Press, 1999); 15 Gregg L. Lint, et al., eds., The Adams Papers: Papers of John Adams 121 n.11 (Cambridge: The Belknap Press of Harvard University Press, 2010); Bernard C. Steiner, The Life and Correspondence of James McHenry: Secretary of War under Washington and Adams 57–58 (Cleveland, OH: The Burrows Brothers Co., 1907).

101. Benjamin Rush, Essays, Literary, Moral and Philosophical 183–88 (Philadelphia: Thomas & William Bradford, 1806); Carter G. Woodson, The Negro in Our History 69–70 (1922); Molefi Kete Asante, 100 Greatest African Americans: A Biographical Encyclopedia 48–50 (Amherst, NY: Prometheus Books, 2002); Henry Louis Gates Jr. & Evelyn Brooks Higginbotham, eds., African American Lives 44–45 (Oxford: Oxford University Press, 2006); 2 Paul Finkelman, ed., Encyclopedia of African American History 1619–1895: From the Colonial Period to the Age of Frederick Douglass 115–16 (Oxford: Oxford University Press); Dick Russell, Black Genius: Inspirational Portraits of African-American Leaders (New York: Skyhorse Publishing, 2009), ch. 18; Benjamin Brawley, ed., Early Black American Writers: Selections with Biographical and Critical Introductions 75–86 (New York: Courier Dover Publications, 2012); Charles E. Shaw, The Untold Stories of Excellence: From a Life of Despair and Uncertainty to One that Offers Hope and a New Beginning 64–67 (Xlibris Corp., 2011); Richard Newman, "Good Communications Corrects Bad Manners": The Banneker-Jefferson Dialogue and the Project of White Uplift," *in* John Craig Hammond & Matthew Mason, eds., Contesting Slavery: The Politics of Bondage and Freedom in the New American Nation 69 (Charlottesville: University of Virginia Press, 2011); *see also* Silvio A. Bedini, The Life of Benjamin Banneker (New York: Scribners, 1972); Myra Weatherly, Benjamin Banneker: American Scientific Pioneer (Minneapolis: Compass Point Books, 2006).

102. 1 Junius P. Rodriguez, ed., Slavery in the United States: A Social, Political, and Historical Encyclopedia 186–87 (Santa Barbara, CA: ABC-CLIO, 2007); 1 Robin D. G. Kelley & Earl Lewis, ed., To Make Our World Anew: A History of African Americans to 1800, at 158 (Oxford: Oxford University Press, 2005); Abigail Adams to John Adams, Mar. 31, 1776.

103. Julie Nicoletta, *The Architecture of Control: Shaker Dwelling Houses and the Reform Movement in Early-Nineteenth-Century America*, 62 Journal of the Society of Architectural Historians 352, 371 (2003); Daniel Bowen, A History of Philadelphia, with a Notice of Villages, in the Vicinity 180 (Philadelphia: Daniel Bowen, 1839).

104. http://www.aoc.gov/philip-reid-and-statue-freedom; Vivien Green Fryd, "The Italian Presence in the United States Capitol" & Barbara A. Wolanin, "Constantino Brumidi's Frescoes in the United States Capitol," *in* Irma B. Jaffe, The Italian Presence in American Art, 1760–1860, at 132–34 (New York: Fordham University Press, 1989); Carl Sifakis, The Encyclopedia of American Prisons 128 (New York: Facts on File, 2003); Latrobe, The Journal of Latrobe, xvii, xxii–xxv, 12–13, 50, 76–78, 123, 150–51; Brown, Incidental Architect, 30; Eric Foner, The Story of American Freedom 93–94 (New York: W. W. Norton & Co., 1998); Michael W. Fazio & Patrick A. Snadon, The Domestic Architecture of Benjamin Henry Latrobe 15, 194, 244, 255, 259 (Baltimore: The Johns Hopkins University Press, 2006); 1 Pennsylvania: Biographical Dictionary 20 (St. Clair Shores, MI: Somerset Publishers, 3d ed. 1999); 6 Records of the Columbia Historical Society 217 (Washington, DC: Columbia Historical Society, 1903); 17 Proceedings of the American Academy of Arts and Letters and the National Institute of Arts and Letters 108 (1967); Jefferson and the Arts: An Extended View 215 (Washington, DC: National Gallery of Art, 1976); The National Catholic Almanac 142 (Paterson, NJ: St. Anthony's Guild 1948); Shackelford, Thomas Jefferson's Travels in Europe, 191; www.aoc.gov/capitol-buildings/about-us-capitol-building; Thomas Jefferson to William Short, Feb. 28, 1789; William Short to Thomas Jefferson, Mar. 26, 1789; William Lee to James Madison, Apr. 4, 1817; Antonio Capellano to James Madison, Sept. 5, 1817; James Madison to Antonio Capellano, Sept. 8, 1817, *available at* www.founders.archives.gov.

105. Brown, Incidental Architect, 1–25; Benjamin Latrobe, The Notes and Sketches of an Architect, Naturalist and Traveler in the United States from 1796 to 1820, at 43 (Carlisle, MA: Applewood Books, 2007); Juliani, Building Little Italy, 14–16; A Public Notice by Franklin and Robert Morris, Dec. 5, 1775 (printed in *The Pennsylvania Gazette*) & William Dodd to Benjamin Franklin, Jan. 29, 1777, *available at* www.founders.archives.gov.

106. Report of Charles Bulfinch on the Subject of Penitentiaries (Washington, DC: Gales & Seaton, 1827); Paul K. Williams, Images of America: Southwest Washington, D.C. 26 (Charleston, SC: Arcadia Publishing, 2005).

107. Juliani, Building Little Italy, 11–12.

108. Bessler, Cruel and Unusual, 325.

109. Journal of the Senate of the Commonwealth of Pennsylvania, Vol. XXII (Feb. 22, 1812), pp. 278–79; Marmaduke Blake Sampson, Criminal Jurisprudence Considered in Relation to Mental Organization 18 (London: Samuel Highley, 1841); Report from the Select Committee on the Subject of Capital Punishment to the New York State Assembly (May 4, 1846), *in* The United States Magazine and Democratic Review, Vol. 20, No. 103 (Jan. 1847), p. 72; "The Influence of the Religious Teachings of the Age on Questions of Social and Political Progress," The Reasoner, Vol. 6, No. 155 (May 16, 1849); George G. Macy, Petition of the Society of Friends Against the Death Penalty to the Legislature of New York (Mar. 27, 1872), p. 3, *in* Documents of the Assembly of the State of New York, Vol. 8, No. 118.

110. Brown & Brown, The Hanging of Ephraim Wheeler, 196, 237, 260; Carole Owens, Pittsfield: Gem City in the Gilded Age 20, 59 (Charleston, SC: The History Press, 2007).

111. The Parliamentary Register; or History of the Proceedings and Debates of the House of Commons 220 (1796) ("the sanguinary code of Roberspierre [sic]"); id. at 547 ("It is thus, said Mr. Sheridan, that you blaspheme and violate your statute books with oppressive and sanguinary laws, which afterwards you dare not execute."); id. at 708 ("Mr. Hume … was extremely sorry to see the catalogue of capital crimes, and sanguinary punishments. An increase of the penal code of any country, to use the language of a great writer, spoke a distemper in the State."); id. ("In appealing to history Mr. Jekyll begged the House to look at the effect of sanguinary laws in Roman times; under their Kings various were the penal enactments; and how long did the kingly government exist? The Porcion law abrogated their bloody institutions, and the Republic flourished."); id. at 719 (referencing "sanguinary laws" and "sanguinary law"); id. at 722 ("Mr. FOX … admitted that laws were necessary; but he did not think that sanguinary and severe laws were the most efficacious for that purpose.").

112. A Gentleman of the Inner Temple, An Examination into the Rights and Duties of Jurors; with Some Strictures on the Law of Libels 35–36 & n.11 (London: T. Whieldon, 1785).

113. The Book of Martyrs: or, The History of Paganism and Popery 360 (1764) ("[t]his bad conduct of the queen-regent, and what follows, must be imputed to the sanguinary counsels"); *accord* 1 Maryland Medical and Surgical Journal, and Official Organ of the Medical Department of the Army

and Navy of the United States 84 (1840) ("the sanguinary Queen of England"); 20 John Bell, Bell's British Theatre, Consisting of the Most Esteemed English Plays 26 (London: John Bell, 1780) ("Of the King's wrath; some sanguinary purpose").

114. 4 John Reeves, History of the English Law, from the Time of the Saxons, to the End of the Reign of Philip and Mary 272–73 (London: E. Brooke, 1787); id. at 144 ("The alteration made in the law of crimes and punishments in this reign seems as remarkable.... The criminal code begun now to assume a sanguinary appearance, which every reign since has been heightening."); id. at 566 (referencing a "sanguinary" reign "in criminal proceedings").

115. *E.g.*, Augustin Barruel, Memoirs, Illustrating the History of Jacobinism 267 (London: T. Burton, 1797) ("The Elector's Tribunal could not by any calumny be accused of being sanguinary, as not one of the adepts was condemned to death."); id. at 359 ("many a sanguinary scene"); id. at 434 ("these sanguinary Legislators"); id. at 442 ("this sanguinary tribe" and "in sanguinary rage, thirsting after murder, and particularly after the blood of the Queen"); id. at 543–44 ("the sanguinary butcher of the bloody September"); id. at 560 ("sanguinary rage"); id. at 591 ("sanguinary rage"); id. at 13 ("sanguinary chiefs"); id. at 16 ("its cruel and sanguinary object"); id. at 19 ("sanguinary zeal"); id. at 41 ("bearing on pikes in sanguinary triumph the heads of the best men of England"); J. L. Blake, A General Biographical Dictionary, Comprising a Summary Account of the Most Distinguished Persons of All Ages, Nations and Professions 56, 161, 207, 234, 277, 350, 480, 518, 532, 542, 602, 606, 787, 797, 811, 907, 942, 948 (New York, 2d ed. 1839) (referencing "a sanguinary inquisition," "a sanguinary faction," "the sanguinary conduct of Marat," "one of the most sanguinary characters of the French revolution," "a sanguinary assembly," Robespierre's "sanguinary" conduct, "the sanguinary tribunal," "sanguinary terrorists," "the sanguinary revolution," "sanguinary tyrants," "sanguinary accomplices," "the sanguinary cannibals of Paris," "the sanguinary Robespierre," "sanguinary monster," "sanguinary proceedings," "the sanguinary Marat," and "sanguinary judges").

116. 1 Helen Maria Williams, Letters Containing a Sketch of the Politics of France 2, 40, 55, 81, 131, 203, 211, 228, 235, 240, 243, 247, 276 (London: G. G. and J. Robinson, 1795).

117. The Literary Gazette; and Journal of the Belles Lettres, Arts, Sciences, &c. for the Year 1830, at 4 (1830).

118. Report on the Penitentiary System in the United States, Prepared under a Resolution of the Society for the Prevention of Pauperism in the City of New York 6 n.c, 8, 12, 47, 84–85, 90 (New York: Mail on Day, 1822). It also took note of the "sanguinary predecessors" of Russian Empress Elizabeth, quoted a reformer on "the effects of a barbarous and sanguinary Code of laws," and referenced provisions in Pennsylvania's 1776 constitution and New Hampshire's 1784 constitution to make punishments "less sanguinary" or to reduce the "multitude of sanguinary laws." Id. at 14, 87, 93, appendix, p. 2. The appendix further referenced "a sanguinary and disproportionate punishment," a "sanguinary law," "sanguinary punishments," "sanguinary crimes," "sanguinary measures," and "sanguinary enactments." Id., appendix, pp. 15, 55, 67, 84, 88.

119. 2 The London Magazine 496 (1784) ("the longest and most sanguinary war that ever afflicted a nation"); 17 The Monthly Review; or, Literary Journal, Enlarged 202 (1802) ("a distant and sanguinary war"); *see also* id. at 315 ("the sanguinary administration of Robespierre"); id. at 530 ("sanguinary tyrants").

120. 7 The Parliamentary Register: or, History of the Proceedings and Debates of the Houses of Lords and Commons 28 (1799) (containing a reference to "the sanguinary Government of France"); *see also* id. at 730 ("While, then, we deplore the late abominable excesses, it is our duty to prevent the return of the sanguinary scenes, by a Union of national interest, likely to reconcile and command the affections of the people."); 52 James Boswell, The Scots Magazine 39 (1790) (referencing "a sanguinary and vindictive government"); id. at 584 (referencing "sanguinary laws" in discussing "the laws of Draco"); id. at 642 ("They have seen the French rebel against a mild and lawful monarch, with more fury, outrage, and insult, than ever any people has been known to rise against the most illegal usurper, or the most sanguinary tyrant.").

121. Thomas Birch, The Life of the Most Reverend Dr. John Tillotson, Lord Archbishop of Canterbury 302 (London: J. and R. Tonson, et al., 1752) ("a confederacy of cruel and sanguinary men").

122. John Quincy Adams, Answer to Pain's Rights of Man 21 (London: Owen, Picadilly, 1793) ("the Parliament had mitigated the severity of a sanguinary and tyrannical law of persecution against the Roman Catholics"); *compare* Brantz Mayer, ed., Journal of Charles Carroll of Carrollton, During His Visit to Canada in 1776, as One of the Commissioners from Congress 33 (1876) ("And 'we think the legislature of Great Britain is not authorized by the constitution to establish a religion fraught with sanguinary and impious tenets,' &c.").

123. 60 The Universal Magazine of Knowledge and Pleasure 65, 178, 188, 215 (London: John Hinton, 1777).

124. *E.g.*, "Felons and Rattlesnakes," *The Pennsylvania Gazette*, May 9, 1751, *in* Benjamin Franklin Papers ("In some of the uninhabited Parts of these Provinces, there are Numbers of these venomous Reptiles we call Rattle-Snakes; Felons-convict from the Beginning of the World: These, whenever we meet with them, we put to Death, by Virtue of an old Law, *Thou shalt bruise his Head*. But as this is a sanguinary Law, and may seem too cruel; and as however mischievous those Creatures are with us, they may possibly change their Natures, if they were to change the Climate; I would humbly propose, that this general Sentence of *Death* be changed for *Transportation*."); Letter from Benjamin Franklin to Benjamin Vaughan, Mar. 1785 (in writing about *Thoughts on Executive Justice*, Franklin remarked: "That it is better 100 guilty Persons should escape, than that one innocent Person should suffer, is a Maxim that has been long and generally approv'd, never that I know of controverted. Even the sanguinary Author of the *Thoughts* agrees to it...."). The word *sanguinary* is even found in a collection of Aesop's fables. Sir Roger L'Estrange, Fables of Aesop and Other Eminent Mythologists: With Morals and Reflections 442 (8th ed. corrected 1738) ("But let the Oppression be never so Sanguinary, there's no Appeal left from the Tyranny....").

125. Smithers, Treatise on Executive Clemency in Pennsylvania, 107; Antony Taylor, The Prison System and Its Effects—Wherefrom, Whereto, and Why? 16 (Hauppauge, NY: Nova Science Publishers, 2008).

126. Roberts Vaux, Notices of the Original, and Successive Efforts, to Improve the Discipline of the Prison at Philadelphia, and to Reform the Criminal Code of Pennsylvania: With a Few Observations on the Penitentiary System 44 (1826) (noting that, in 1821, in an effort "to impress the general assembly with the necessity of a penitentiary in this section of the state," a "Memorial of the Philadelphia Society for alleviating the Miseries of Public Prisons" read in part: "In the performance of the duties which they believed to be required of them by the dictates of Christian benevolence, and the obligations of humanity, they investigated the conduct and regulations of the jail, and likewise the effects of those degrading and sanguinary punishments, which were at that period inflicted by the laws of this Commonwealth.").

127. Report on the Penitentiary System in the United States, Prepared under a Resolution of the Society for the Prevention of Pauperism in the City of New York 20 (1822).

128. Frederick Howard Wines, Punishment and Reformation: A Study of the Penitentiary System 350 (New York: T. Y. Crowell & Co., 1910).

129. "Report of the Warden," Appendix to the House Journal of the Forty-Fourth General Assembly of the State of Tennessee, First Session, 1885, at 12 (1885); *compare* 15 Louisiana History 364 (1974) ("The word 'penitentiary' means a place where the guilty may have an opportunity to become penitent.").

130. Matt DeLisi & Peter J. Conis, American Corrections: Theory, Research, Policy, and Practice 45 (Burlington, MA: Jones & Bartlett Learning, 2d ed. 2013).

131. Thomas Fowell Buxton, An Inquiry, Whether Crime and Misery Are Produced or Prevented, by Our Present System of Prison Discipline 96–97 (London: John & Arthur Arch, 1818).

132. Richard Herrick Condon, The Reform of English Prison, 1773–1816, Ph.D. thesis, Brown University, 1962, p. 17.

133. Wilfrid Prest, William Blackstone: Law and Letters in the Eighteenth Century 297, 301 (Oxford: Oxford University Press, 2008). Blackstone himself sentenced convicts to death, so he was no stranger to capital punishment. Id. at 265.

134. Walter Isaacson, Benjamin Franklin: An American Life 496 (New York: Simon & Schuster, 2003); Masur, Rites of Execution, 74.

135. 50th or Semi-Centennial Report of the Inspectors of the State Penitentiary for the Eastern District of Pennsylvania for the Year 1879, at 14–15 (Philadelphia: McLaughlin Brothers, 1880) (citing 19 Geo. 3, ch. 74).

136. Daniel V. Botsman, Punishment and Power in the Making of Modern Japan 118 (Princeton, NJ: Princeton University Press, 2005).

137. 2 D. O. Thomas, ed., The Correspondence of Richard Price (March 1778–February 1786) 133–34 (Cardiff: University of Wales Press, 1991).

138. 3 W. Bernard Peach, ed., The Correspondence of Richard Price (February 1786–February 1791) 37–39, 69–71, 138 (Durham, NC: Duke University Press, 1994).

139. 2 W. Bernard Peach & D. O. Thomas, eds., The Correspondence of Richard Price 195–96 (Cardiff: University of Wales, 1991); 1 The Annual Biography and Obituary for the Year 1817, at 577–80 (London: Longman, Hurst, Rees, Orme and Brown, 1817); Ronald Hamowy, The Encyclopedia of Libertarianism 388–89 (Thousand Oaks, CA: SAGE Publications, 2008).

140. 2 D. O. Thomas, ed., The Correspondence of Richard Price (March 1778–February 1786) 35–36 (Cardiff: University of Wales Press, 1991).

141. 3 W. Bernard Peach, ed., The Correspondence of Richard Price (February 1786–February 1791) 145–47 (Durham, NC: Duke University Press, 1994).

142. Thomas Fowell Buxton, An Inquiry, Whether Crime and Misery Are Produced or Prevented, by Our Present System of Prison Discipline 90–91 (London: John & Arthur Arch, 1818); see also id. at 90 (noting in a section of the book titled the "Prison of Philadelphia": "About the year 1776, the prisons in America were in a situation very similar to that of the generality of English prisons at the present moment.").

143. "A Description, with a Perspective View, of the Jail, in Philadelphia," Universal Magazine, July 1789, at 17–20 (available at The Library Company of Philadelphia); Milton E. Flower, John Dickinson, Conservative Revolutionary 264 (Charlottesville: University Press of Virginia, 1983).

144. Extracts and Remarks on the Subject of Punishment and Reformation of Criminals 3–20 (1790); William Carpenter, Anecdotes of the French Revolution, of 1830, at 265 (London: William Strange, 1830); Options to Improve and Expand Federal Prison Industries, Hearing Before the Subcommittee on Crime of the Committee on the Judiciary, House of Representatives, 105th Congress, 1st Sess., Serial No. 107 (Oct. 30, 1997), p. 36.

145. Extracts and Remarks on the Subject of Punishment and Reformation of Criminals 14–15, 23 (1790); John N. Norton, The Life of the Rt. Rev. William White, D. D., Bishop of Pennsylvania 10, 96 (New York: Church Book Society, 1856); 2 Pennsylvania Prison Society, The Journal of Prison Discipline and Philanthropy 1–3 (Philadelphia: James M. Campbell, 1846); Michael Meranze, Laboratories of Virtue: Punishment, Revolution, and Authority in Philadelphia, 1760–1835, at 143 n.29 (Chapel Hill: The University of North Carolina, 1996).

146. Caleb Lownes, An Account of the Alteration and Present State of the Penal Laws of Pennsylvania, Containing Also an Account of the Gaol and Penitentiary House of Philadelphia and the Interior Management Thereof 3–5, 13 (Lexington: J. Bradford, 1794).

147. An Account of the State Prison or Penitentiary House, in the City of New-York 5–8, 11–13, 16 (New York: Isaac Collins and Son, 1801) (listed on the title page as written "by one of the inspectors of the prison"); The Belfast Monthly Magazine, Vol. 7, No. 37 (Aug. 31, 1811), pp. 83–90. Eddy noted that "AMBROSE SPENCER, Esq. particularly distinguished himself as a most zealous friend to the proposed reform," and that by the 1796 law "two state-prisons were directed to be built; one at New-York, and the other at Albany." In his book, Eddy then noted: "The plan of a prison at Albany was afterwards relinquished, and the whole of the money appropriated for both prisons was directed to be applied to the one in the city of New-York." Id. at 13; see also Samuel L. Knapp, The Life of Thomas Eddy 58 (New York: Conner & Cooke, 1834) ("In 1801, Mr. Eddy published an account of the State Prison of New York. His mottos were taken from Beccaria and Montesquieu; in fact, his whole theory of crimes and punishments is drawn from those great friends of liberty, Beccaria, Montesquieu, Howard, Penn, and other celebrated reformers of this and a former age.").

148. Samuel L. Knapp, The Life of Thomas Eddy, Comprising an Extensive Correspondence with Many of the Most Distinguished Philosophers and Philanthropists of This and Other Countries 8, 40–42, 52 (London: Edmund Fry and Son, 1836).

149. Negley K. Teeters, They Were in Prison: A History of the Pennsylvania Prison Society, 1787–1937, Formerly the Philadelphia Society for Alleviating the Miseries of Public Prisons (Philadelphia: John C. Winston, 1937).

150. Mitchel P. Roth, Crime and Punishments: A History of the Criminal Justice System 89 (2d ed. 2011); The Fifth Report of the Committee of the Society for the Improvement of Prison Discipline, and for the Reformation of Juvenile Offenders 81–83 (London: J. and A. Arch, 1823); 6 The American Museum: or Repository of Ancient and Modern Fugitive Pieces 223–26 (Philadelphia: Mathew Carey, 1789); see also Philip R. Popple & Leslie Leighninger, Social Work, Social Welfare, and American Society 325 (Boston: Allyn and Bacon, 2d ed. 1993) ("Prison construction proceeded at a fast pace with the first, the Walnut Street jail, being built in Philadelphia in 1790, Newgate state prison built in New York in 1796, the New Jersey penitentiary completed in 1797, prisons in Virginia and Kentucky built in 1800, and facilities completed within a few years in Vermont, New Hampshire, and Maryland.").

151. 5 William Bengo Collyer, Thomas Raffles & James Baldwin Brown, eds., The Investigator: or, Quarterly Magazine 393–95 (London: Henry Fisher, 1822); Ellen Susan Bulfinch, ed., The Life and Letters of Charles Bulfinch, Architect: With Other Family Papers 154 (Boston: Houghton, Mifflin and Co., 1896).

152. James Wood to Thomas Jefferson, Mar. 3, 1797, available at www.founders.archives.gov.

153. James Wood to Thomas Jefferson, Mar. 3, 1797 (note) & Thomas Jefferson to James Wood, Mar. 31, 1797, available at www.founders.archvies.gov.

154. Blanche M. G. Linden, Silent City on a Hill: Picturesque Landscapes of Memory and Boston's Mount Auburn Cemetery 97 (Amherst: University of Massachusetts Press, 2007).

155. William Hill Brown, The Power of Sympathy xxxviii (New York: Penguin Books, 1996) (first published by Isaiah Thomas in 1789); Perez Morton to James Madison, July 18, 1803, *available at* www.founders.archives.gov; http://www.mfa.org/collections/object/ladle-42322.

156. Robert D. Hanser, Introduction to Corrections 27–31 (Thousand Oaks, CA: SAGE Publications, 2013); Francis X. Dolan, Eastern State Penitentiary 7–8 (Charleston, SC: Arcadia Publishing, 2007); Meskell, *The History of Prisons in the United States*, 852–58; *see also* David A. Jones, History of Criminology: A Philosophical Perspective 51 (Westport, CT: Greenwood Press, 1986) ("Inspired directly by Beccaria, Alexander Maconochie and John Haviland came to create major penal institutions in the early nineteenth century.").

157. Mitchel P. Roth, Prisons and Prison Systems: A Global Encyclopedia 235 (Westport, CT: Greenwood Press, 2006).

158. McMurry & Adams, People, Power, Places, 120; Edgar C. S. Gibson, John Howard 63–64 (Boston: Knight & Millet, 1902); John Field, The Life of John Howard; with Comments on His Character and Philanthropic Labours 166, 168 (London: Longman, Brown, Green, and Longmans, 1850).

159. 50th or Semi-Centennial Report of the Inspectors of the State Penitentiary for the Eastern District of Pennsylvania for the Year 1879, at 8, 11–14 (Philadelphia: McLaughlin Brothers, 1880).

160. Brigette Polmar & Norman Polmar, Washington, DC's Most Wanted: The Top 10 Book of Tourist Treasures, Powerful Politicians, and Capital Wonders (Sterling, VA: Potomac Books, 2010); The Waking Dream: Photography's First Century 320 (New York: The Metropolitan Museum of Art, 1993); John E. Holman & James F. Quinn, Criminal Justice: Principles and Perspectives 295 (St. Paul, MN: West Publishing Co., 1996); James McGrath Morris, Jailhouse Journalism: The Fourth Estate Behind Bars 76 (Piscataway, NJ: Transaction Publishers, 1998).

161. An Exposition of the Penitentiary System of Punishment, but More Particularly Adapted to that of Virginia, Comprising a Series of Numbers Published in the Richmond Enquirer, with Some General Remarks on the Defects, Their Remedies, and the Advantages that Would Result from a Well Regulated System iii–iv, 5–10, 12, 15–18, 23, 30, 36–40, 43, 45, 52 (Richmond, VA: Shepherd & Pollard, 1821) (available at The Library Company of Philadelphia); The New Book of Knowledge 482 (Grolier, 1992); William Trumbull, The Problem of Cain: A Study in the Treatment of Criminals 40–41 (New Haven, CT: Tuttle, Morehouse & Taylor, 1890).

162. Joint Congressional Committee on Inaugural Ceremonies, Inaugural Addresses of the Presidents of the United States 1–5 (New York: Cosimo, 2008); Hunt, Life and Services of Edward Livingston, 1–3, 5; Hunt, Life of Edward Livingston, 11, 15–16, 20–21, 38–39, 41–45, 57, 119, 198–99, 326–27, 408; Frederic de Peyster, A Biographical Sketch of Robert R. Livingston: Read Before the N.Y. Historical Society, October 3, 1876, at 16–17 (New York: New York Historical Society, 1876); "The Bronze Doors," Information Sheet, Office of the Curator, Supreme Court of the United States.

163. Mark F. Fernandez, From Chaos to Continuity: The Evolution of Louisiana's Judicial System, 1712–1862, at 75 (Baton Rouge: Louisiana State University Press, 2001); Hunt, Life and Services of Edward Livingston 5–11; Hunt, Life of Edward Livingston, 59–60, 64, 76–81, 83–84; 6 Maeva Marcus, ed., The Documentary History of the Supreme Court of the United States, 1789–1800, at 526 n.17 (New York: Columbia University Press, 1998); Moore, *The Livingston Code*, 344 n.*a*.

164. Hunt, Life and Services of Edward Livingston, 12–20; Hunt, Life of Edward Livingston, 255, 259, 268; Moore, *The Livingston Code*, 344–48.

165. Moore, *The Livingston Code*, 348–49.

166. Henry Barnard, "A Visit to the Count de Sellon, Founder and President of the Geneva Peace Society," 10 American Advocate of Peace 81–83 (Sept. 1836); Moore, *The Livingston Code*, 355–60.

167. Hunt, Life of Edward Livingston, 94–97 & n.*, 266, 269, 273, 275.

168. Robley Dunglison, A Public Discourse in Commemoration of Peter S. Du Ponceau, LL.D, Late President of the American Philosophical Society, Delivered Before the Society Pursuant to Appointment, on the 25th of October, 1844, at 16–17 (Philadelphia: American Philosophical Society, 1844); Edward Livingston to Thomas Jefferson, Mar. 9, 1825; Edward Livingston to Thomas Jefferson, Mar. 25, 1824; Edward Livingston to Thomas Jefferson, Nov. 29, 1824 (Printed Circular on Penal Law for the State of Louisiana); Thomas Jefferson to Robert R. Livingston, Mar. 16, 1802; Robert R. Livingston to Thomas Jefferson, May 4, 1802; James Madison to Robert Livingston, Apr. 18, 1803; James Madison to Robert Livingston, July 29, 1803; Edward Livingston to James Madison, Mar. 25, 1801; Edward Livingston to James Madison, Apr. 30, 1801; Edward Livingston to James Madison, July 22, 1801; Edward Livingston to James Madison, Sept. 3, 1801, *available at* www.memory.loc.gov.

169. 1 The Complete Works of Edward Livingston on Criminal Jurisprudence: Consisting of Penal Law for the State of Louisiana and for the United States of America v–viii, 8–9, 31, 37, 56 (New York: National Prison Association of the United States of America, 1873); James Madison to Edward Livingston, Dec. 27, 1825 & James Madison to Edward Livingston, July 10, 1822, *available at* The James Madison Papers, www.memory.loc.gov.

170. Hunt, Life of Edward Livingston, 287–88, 280–81; 7 H. A. Washington, ed., The Writings of Thomas Jefferson: Being His Autobiography, Correspondence, Reports, Messages, Addresses, and Other Writings, Official and Private 402–405 (New York: Derby & Jackson, 1859). Jefferson had also written to Edward Livingston the year before. Id. at 342.

171. Bessler, Cruel and Unusual, 159.

172. Roberts Vaux, Notices of the Original, and Successive Efforts, to Improve the Discipline of the Prison at Philadelphia, and to Reform the Criminal Code of Pennsylvania: With a Few Observations on the Penitentiary System (1826).

173. Id. at 62–63. As Vaux wrote:

> When the positive security of society shall have been provided for, by penitentiaries placed under such management as has been suggested, it may become a question with the Legislature, whether, for the penalty of death now imposed on murder in the first degree, imprisonment during life may not be substituted. There is an aversion in Pennsylvania from inflicting death; and the difficulty of convicting when the crime is so great as to be visited with that punishment, is such as to defeat in many instances the purposes of justice.

Id.

174. 3 The Christian Examiner and Theological Review 204 (1826). One source, from 1790, defined "Sanguinary" as "bloody, cruel." Thomas Morell, An Abridgement of the Last Quarto Edition of Ainsworth's Dictionary, English and Latin (London: Charles Rivington, 3d ed. 1790) (entry for "Sanguinary"). Another, from 1781, similarly defined "Sanguinary" as "bloody, cruel, delighting in shedding of blood." Thomas Dyche & William Pardon, A New General English Dictionary; Peculiarly Calculated for the Use and Improvement of Such as Are Unacquainted with the Learned Languages (London: Toplis and Bunney, 1781) (entry for "Sanguinary"). Another, from 1780, defined "Sanguinary" as "Cruel, bloody, murtherous." Thomas Sheridan, A General Dictionary of the English Language (London: J. Dodsley & C. Dilly, 1780) (entry for "Sanguinary"). And still another, from 1764, defined "Sanguinary" as "blood-thirsty, cruel." Nathan Bailey, An Universal Etymological English Dictionary (London: R. Ware, et al., 20th ed. 1764) (entry for "Sanguinary").

175. 3 The Christian Examiner and Theological Review 204–205 (1826). The writer added:

> Let no one, filled with honest disgust at the abuses of the Penitentiary System, defend a return to the barbarous practices of former times. Sanguinary laws neither terrify nor reform, but only harden the heart. The history of the English criminal code, which made upwards of two hundred crimes capital, demonstrates the inutility of legal severity. Mild laws, and the certain infliction of punishment, are much more effectual.

Id. at 205. Although the writer saw some "truth" in the view that "Penitentiaries" had become "seminaries of vice and crime," the writer editorialized: "Bad as it is, we are satisfied that the other system was infinitely worse. It has been stated, that it has proved three times as efficacious in preventing crimes as the Sanguinary practice." Id. at 206.

176. Id. at 212. The writer further noted that since the District of Columbia's creation, Maryland and Virginia "have since changed the whole system of their criminal jurisprudence, by substituting confinement to hard labor for the cruel practice of branding, whipping, &c." Id. at 209.

177. William Short to Thomas Jefferson, July 28, 1823.

178. Thomas Jefferson, Autobiographical Draft Fragment, Jan. 6–July 27, 1821.

179. Henry B. F. MacFarland, District of Columbia: Concise Biographies of Its Prominent and Representative Contemporary Citizens, and Valuable Statistical Data (1908–1909), at 434 (Washington, DC: The Potomac Press, 1908); Steve Vogel: Through the Perilous Fight: Six Weeks that Saved the Nation 409–10 (New York: Random House, 2013).

180. U.S. Const., preamble.

181. Thomas Nuttall, A Journal of Travels into the Arkansas Territory During the Year 1819, at 248 (Savoie Lottinville, ed., 1999); *compare* 60 The Critical Review: or, Annals of Literature 160 (1785) ("in those countries where the punishment has been certain and severe, crimes have been more sanguinary").

182. Bessler, Cruel and Unusual, 242; Workers of the Writers' Program of the Works Progress Administration in the State of Arkansas, comp., Arkansas: A State Guide 393 (1941); Paul Miller, State Capitol Week in Review, June 3, 2004, http://www.areawidenews.com/story/1421154.html.

183. Jeremy Bentham, Theory of Legislation 114, 344–45, 428 (R. Hildreth, trans. 1882).

184. "Hon. Robert Rantoul, Jr.'s Letters on the Death Penalty," *reprinting* Letter of Robert Rantoul, Jr., Feb. 4, 1846; Letter of Robert Rantoul, Jr., Feb. 6, 1846; Letter of Robert Rantoul, Jr., Feb. 10, 1846; Letter of Robert Rantoul, Jr., Feb. 12, 1846; Letter of Robert Rantoul, Jr., Feb. 14, 1846.

185. Bessler, Cruel and Unusual, 158.

186. G. F. H. Crockett, An Address to the Legislature of Kentucky, on the Abolition of Capital Punishments, in the United States, and the Substitution of Exile for Life (Georgetown, KY: N. L. Finnell, 1823); *see also* Journal of the House of Representatives of the United States, Being the First Session of the Nineteenth Congress: Begun and Held at the City of Washington, December 5, 1825, and in the Fiftieth Year of the Independence of the United States 152 (Washington, DC: Gales & Seaton, 1825) (one entry for January 16 reads: "Mr. James Johnson, of Kentucky, presented an essay on the abolition of capital punishments, and the substitution of exile for life at hard labor, in the form of an Address to the Congress of the United States, by G. F. Crockett, M. D. Member of the K. A Society of Hypocrates, and Honorary Member of the Lexington Medical Society; which said Essay or Address, was referred to the Committee on the Judiciary.").

187. Acts Passed at the First Session of the Thirtieth General Assembly for the Commonwealth of Kentucky 420–21 (Frankfort: Kendall and Russell, 1821). A Colonel Joseph Crockett was one of the founders of Transylvania University, an institution founded in 1798. Robert Peter & Johanna Peter, Transylvania University: Its Origin, Rise, Decline, and Fall 72 (Louisville, KY: John P. Morton and Co., 1896); Biographical Sketch of Colonel Joseph Crockett: A Paper Read Before the Filson Club at Its Meeting, April 6, 1908 (printed in 1909 as Part Second of Sketches of Two Distinguished Kentuckians, Filson Club Publications No. 24, p. 42; *see also* 24 The Baptist Missionary Magazine 20 (Board of Managers of the Baptist General Convention (Boston: John Putnam, 1844) (noting that, in Philadelphia, on April 24, 1844, "[p]reliminary to the opening of the Convention, a large number of brethren from different parts of the country met for devotional exercises," among them, "G. F. H. Crockett, of Mississippi"); 16 State Trials: A Collection of the Important and Interesting Criminal Trials which Have Taken Place in the United States, from the Beginning of Our Government to 1920, at 85 (Wilmington, DE: Scholarly Resources, 1972) ("*The Intelligencer*, Jan. 6, 1852, mentions the presence in the city of Dr. G. F. H. Crockett who is on his way from Kentucky to Liberty, Clay County, Missouri to settle. He was probably a relative to Joseph B. Crockett and stopped over to see him."); 24 Bulletin of the History of Medicine 185 (Baltimore, MD: Johns Hopkins University Press, 1950) (noting "a communication from Dr. G. F. H. Crockett of Mississippi proposing a medical school and setting forth principles and standards for its organization and administration"; "[c]hief among Crockett's qualifications was the statement that he had graduated at Transylvania University in 1822"); 3 The Papers of Mirabeau Buonaparte Lamar 50 (Austin, TX: Von Boeckmann-Jones Co., 1927) (Crockett writes of being an "officer in the U.S. army about 2½ during the late war with G. Britain—have spent 19 years in Kentucky & 4½ in this state—am a graduate of the medical department of Transylvania University, in 1822—have been in practice ever since—am 44 years old—and have as good testimonials of my standing in Society & my profession as I wish to possess"); 82 Texas Medicine 49 (Texas Medical Association, 1986) ("The first mention of a medical school for Texas occurred in 1839 when Dr. G. F. H. Crockett of Mississippi wrote the president of the Texas republic, Mirabeau B. Lamar, about the possibility of opening a school there."); Pat Ireland Nixon, The Medical Story of Early Texas: 1528–1853, at 390 (Lancaster, PA: Lancaster Press, 1946) ("The same year there came to Lamar the suggestion that a medical school be established in the Republic of Texas. The suggestion came in a letter from Dr. G. F. H. Crockett of Mississippi which contains the first mention of a medical school in Texas.").

188. Journal of the Senate of the Commonwealth of Kentucky: Begun and Held in the Town of Frankfort, on Monday the Third Day of November, in the Year of Our Lord 1823, at 6, 55, 59, 133 (Frankfort, KY: Amos Kendall and Co., 1823).

189. G. F. H. Crockett, An Address to the Legislature of Kentucky, on the Abolition of Capital Punishments, in the United States, and the Substitution of Exile for Life (Georgetown, KY: N. L. Finnell, 1823), pp. 1–5, 7–8.

190. 1 Philo Pacificus, The Friend of Peace, 15–16 (Boston: Joseph T. Buckingham, 1816); James Morton Callahan, American Relations in the Pacific and the Far East 1784–1900, at 25–29 (Baltimore, MD: The Johns Hopkins Press, 1901); Jeffrey Geiger, Facing the Pacific: Polynesia and the U.S. Imperial Imagination 38–39 (Honolulu: University of Hawai'i Press, 2007); Edward Walter Dawson, The Isles of the Sea 169, 195 (Hartford, CT: Betts & Co., 1886); Michael Newton, Criminal Justice: Prison and the Penal System 60 (New York: Chelsea House, 2010); 3 David Levinson, ed., Encyclopedia of Crime and Punishment 1131 (Thousand Oaks, CA: Sage Publications, 2002).

191. Henry Rogers, Selections from the Correspondence of R. E. H. Greyson, Esq. 153–54 (London: Longman, Green, Longman, and Roberts, 3d. ed. 1861) (letter to "Alfred West, Esq." dated "Sutton, Oct. 1847").

192. Lieber, A Popular Essay on Subjects of Penal Law, iii, 6, 12, 16, 32–33, 36, 50, 56, 93.

193. Francis Lieber to His Excellency P. Noble, Governor of South Carolina (Nov. 1839). "This severity," Lieber wrote, "remained almost unchanged as late as the year 1819." "It was a bloody code," Lieber said, "and because bloody, at once injudicious and barbarous." Id.

194. Id.; John Fabian Witt, Lincoln's Code: The Laws of War in American History 181, 226 (New York: Free Press, 2012). John Howard's influential book on prison reform cited Beccaria's treatise multiple times. John Howard, The State of the Prisons in England and Wales, with Preliminary Observations, and an Account of Foreign Prisons and Hospitals 15, 42, 72, 118 (London: T. Cadell, J. Johnson & C. Dilly, 3d ed. 1784).

195. See, e.g., "Irish Parliamentary Intelligence," House of Commons ("*Thursday, May 4*"), *in* The Hibernian Magazine, or Compendium of Entertaining Knowledge 492 (1781):

> Mr. Holmes called the attention of gentlemen to what he judged to be an object of importance as well as to the humanity as the policy of a state,—he meant the operation of the criminal laws.—It was a matter interesting to every man, in a constitution envied for its formation, there was a strange disproportion in crimes and punishments. So much, indeed, as not to be paralleled in any other state, ancient or modern. The Romans seldom inflicted death, but where the safety of the common wealth was concerned; and even the barbarism of Russia could furnish no instances of those sanguinary abolitions of human beings, in the reigns of the two last Empresses, but where the political safety was in question. He stated, that this death-dealing maxim had so far prevailed in our laws, as to furnish 160 declared felonies, without benefit of clergy.... He declared he was actuated by principles of humanity only, by moving, That a committee be appointed to inspect into the present state of our criminal laws, and to make such reports to this house, as shall seem necessary for a reform of the same.

196. Documents of the Senate of the State of New York: Ninety-Fourth Session 605, 613 (Albany: The Argus Co., 1871); William Tallack, Penological and Preventative Principles, with Special Reference to Europe and America 139 (London: Wertheimer, Lea & Co, 1889); Philip Priestley & Maurice Vanstone, eds., Offenders or Citizens? Readings in Rehabilitation (New York: Willan Publishing, 2010); William Tallack, Friendly Sketches in America (London: A. W. Bennett, 1861); William Tallack: Letters and Memories (London: Methuen & Co., 1905); William Tallack, Humanity and Humanitarianism: With Special Reference to the Prison Systems of Great Britain and the United States, the Question of Criminal Lunacy, and Capital Punishment 8–9 (London: F. B. Kitto, 1871).

197. Letter of H. G. Lyford (Sept. 1, 1865), *in* The Scottish Law Magazine 65–66 (Nov. 1865).

198. 19 William Cobbett, The Parliamentary History of England from the Earliest Period to the Year 1803, at 235 (1814); "Execution of Strang," The Correspondent, Vol. 2, No. 6 (Sept. 1, 1827), p. 90.

199. Bessler, Legacy of Violence, 25–65; Ella Lonn, Desertion during the Civil War 181 (Lincoln: University of Nebraska Press, 1998) (1928); Steven E. Woodworth, ed., The Art of Command in the Civil War 50–51 (Lincoln: University of Nebraska Press, 1998). Some U.S. laws actually continue to allow the use of *private prosecutors*, that is, attorneys hired and paid for by the murder victim's family to assist in the prosecution of the accused. Bessler, The Public Interest and the Unconstitutionality of Private Prosecutors, 515–40.

Chapter 6

1. 1 Capel Lofft, Elements of Universal Law, and Particularly of the Law of England: Being the First Volume of a Translation of a Work, intitled Principia Juris Universalis 146, 150, 158–59 (London: His Majesty's Law Printers, 1779); 1 Capel Lofft, Principia cum Juris Universalis tum Præcipue Anglicani 197, 202, 209, 285 (London: W. Owen & E. & C. Dilly, 1779); David Lemmings, ed., The British and Their Laws in the Eighteenth Century (Woodbridge, UK: Boydell Press, 2005); John W. Osborne, John Cartwright 25–26, 44, 48, 52–53 (Cambridge: Cambridge University Press, 1972); Memoirs of Thomas Brand-Hollis, Esq. 13 (London: T. Gillet, 1808); Dorothy A. Mays, Women in Early America: Struggle, Survival and Freedom in a New World 430 (Santa Barbara, CA: ABC-CLIO, 2004); Patience Wright to Benjamin Franklin, July 30, 1782; Patience Wright to Benjamin Franklin,

Mar. 21, 1783; Alexander Hamilton to George Washington, May 2, 1793, *available at* www.founders. archives.gov; Women's Project of New Jersey, Past and Promise: Lives of New Jersey Women 41–44 (Scarecrow Press, 1997); John Cartwright, The People's Barrier against Undue Influence and Corruption: or the Commons' House of Parliament According to the Constitution 28 (London: J. Almon, 1780); Stanley Wientraub, Iron Tears: America's Battle for Freedom, Britain's Quagmire: 1775–1783, at 221 (New York: Simon & Schuster, 2005); Eugene Charlton Black, The Association: British Extra-parliamentary Political Organization, 1769–1793, at 175 (Cambridge: Harvard University Press, 1963); 3 Thomas Jefferson Randolph, ed., Memoirs, Correspondence, and Private Papers of Thomas Jefferson: Late President of the United States 403 (London: Henry Colburn & Richard Bentley, 1829); 9 Gaillard Hunt, ed., The Writings of James Madison: 1819–1836, at 181–83 (New York: G. P. Putnam's Sons, 1910); A Plan of Lectures on the Principles of Nonconformity: For the Instruction of Catechumens 49, 60 (Cambridge: T. Fletcher, 3d ed. 1779); Jack P. Greene & J. R. Pole, A Companion to the American Revolution 252 (Malden, MA: Blackwell Publishers, 2000); William Hague, William Wilberforce: The Life of the Great Anti-Slave Trade Campaigner 98–99, 108, 447 (Orlando, FL: Houghton Mifflin Harcourt, 2007); David J. Vaughan, Statesman and Saint: The Principled Politics of William Wilberforce 252 (Nashville, TN: Cumberland House Publishing, 2002); Stephen Tomkins, William Wilberforce: A Biography 55 (Oxford, England: Lion Hudson, 2007); Granville Sharp, An Account of the Constitutional English Polity of Congregational Courts 240, 386 (London: B. White & C. Dilly, 2d ed. 1786); Paul Finkelman, ed. Slavery, Race, and the American Legal System 1700–1872, at 37 (Clark, NJ: The Lawbook Exchange, 2007).

2. Thomas, On Crimes and Punishments, 6, 16, 25; *see also* Eric Slauter, The State as a Work of Art: The Cultural Origins of the Constitution 72 (Chicago: The University of Chicago Press, 2009) ("By 1787, in criticizing the writings of Adams and Jean Louis de Lolme, John Stevens felt compelled to use scare quotes when describing 'the constitution of England.' Prefiguring Paine's attack on Burke in *The Rights of Man*, Stevens observed that no constitution could be said to exist if it could not be produced in a textual form. 'In vain have Englishmen boasted of a constitution; in vain shall we search their records for an original compact. No one part of the government can be said to be unalterably fixed and established. The parliament are without any controul whatever; they are, in the language of their lawyers OMNIPOTENT; and I think Coke tells us they can do every thing except making a man a woman.'").

3. Thomas, On Crimes and Punishments, xxxii–xxxiv, xxxvii, l.

4. Id. at 47–48. Under Roman law, adult, property-owning men traditionally had power over the household. In the early Roman republic, the *paterfamilias* — or "father of the family" — had absolute power, including, though rarely exercised, over the life or death of his wife, any children, his slaves, and any livestock. Sama, Elisabetta Caminer Turra, xvi.

5. Eran Shalev, Rome Reborn on Western Shores: Historical Imagination and the Creation of the American Republic 114–50 (Charlottesville: University of Virginia Press, 2009); Caroline Winterer, The Culture of Classicism: Ancient Greece and Rome in American Intellectual Life 1780–1910, at 26 (Baltimore, MD: The Johns Hopkins University Press, 2002); Samuel A. Forman, Dr. Joseph Warren: The Boston Tea Party, Bunker Bill, and the Birth of American Liberty 31 (Gretna, LA: Pelican Pub. Co., 2012); John Adams to Nathanael Greene, May 24, 1777; A Bill for the More General Diffusion of Knowledge, June 18, 1779; John Adams to the President of the Congress, Aug. 4, 1779; John Adams to John Quincy Adams, May 18, 1781; Report on Books for Congress [Jan. 23] 1783, *available at* www.founders.archives.gov.

6. Sellers, American Republicanism, 5–10, 17, 20–22; Carol Borchert Cadou, The George Washington Collection: Fine and Decorative Arts at Mount Vernon 108 (Manchester, VT: Hudson Hills Press, 2006); Charles Morris, The World's Great Orators and Their Orations 26–28 (Philadelphia: John C. Winston Co., 1917); Washington's Resignation Speech (Final Draft) — Annapolis, MD — Dec. 23, 1783, *available at* http://msa.maryland.gov/msa/intromsa/pdf/booklet.pdf; http://www.society ofthecincinnati.org/about/history.

7. Mathew Carey, Miscellaneous Trifles in Prose 111–16, 119–20 (Philadelphia: Lang and Ustick, 1796).

8. Washington's Farewell Address to the People of the United States, 106th Cong., 2d Sess., Senate Document, No. 106-21 (Washington, DC: Government Printing Office, 2000), pp. 5, 12–16, 19; Thomas, On Crimes and Punishments, 118.

9. Richard Dinmore, Jr., An Exposition of the Principles of the English Jacobins; with Strictures on the Political Conduct of Charles J. Fox, William Pitt and Edmund Burke; Including Remarks on the Resignation of George Washington 13–14, 19–20 (Norwich: John March, 1796); Richard Dinmore, Jr., An Exposition of the Principles of the English Jacobins; with Strictures on the Political Conduct of Charles James Fox, William Pitt and Edmund Burke; Including Remarks on the Resignation of George

Washington 13 (Norwich: J. March, 3d ed. 1797). In the eighteenth century, Beccaria's name often came up in discussions of poverty and how best to remedy it. William Sabatier, A Treatise on Poverty, Its Consequences, and the Remedy 182, 185, 189–90, 193, 195, 199, 205, 207, 209, 222–23, 238, 243–44 (London: John Stockdale, 1797); Some Observations on the Bill Now Pending in Parliament, for the Better Support and Maintenance of the Poor: Prepared for the Use of the Trustees of the Poor of the Parish of Kensington, and Published by Their Direction 2 (London: John Stockdale, 1797).

10. 2 Munster Abbey, A Romance: Interspersed with Reflections on Virtue and Morality 85 (Edinburgh: John Moir, 1797).

11. Bessler, Cruel and Unusual, 270–71.

12. Anne-Marie Kilday, Women and Violent Crime in Enlightenment Scotland 133 (Suffolk, UK: The Boydell Press, 2007); Brian P. Block & John Hostettler, Hanging in the Balance: A History of the Abolition of Capital Punishment in Britain 30 (Winchester, UK: Waterside Press, 1997); Roger K. Newman, ed., The Yale Biographical Dictionary of American Law 285 (New Haven: Yale University Press, 2009); Garland, Peculiar Institution, 114; Jon Butler, Becoming America: The Revolution Before 1776, at 42 (Cambridge: Harvard University Press, 2001); 2 William Connor Sydney, England and the English in the Eighteenth Century 306–307 (London: Ward & Downey, 1891); W. Michael Byrd & Linda A. Clayton, An American Health Dilemma: A Medical History of African Americans and the Problem of Race 230 (New York: Routledge, 2000).

13. Darius Rejali, Torture and Democracy 36 (Princeton: Princeton University Press, 2007); Edward Peters, Torture 251 (Philadelphia: University of Pennsylvania Press, 1985); Adams' Argument and Report, Special Court of Admiralty, Boston, May 1769, *available at* Massachusetts Historical Society, Digital Editions, http://www.masshist.org/publications/apde/portia.php?id=LJA02d073. The first Spanish legal text to abolish torture was the 1812 Constitution of Bayonne. Aniceto Masferrer, "The Liberal State and Criminal Law Reform in Spain," *in* Mortimer Sellers & Tadeusz Tomaszewski, eds., The Rule of Law in Comparative Perspective 39 (Dordrecht, The Netherlands: Springer, 2010).

14. James Chelsum, The Character of the Laws of England Considered: A Sermon Preached on Thursday, March 6, 1777, in St. Mary's Church, Oxford, at the Assizes, before the Honourable Mr. Baron Eyre and Mr. Baron Perryn, and Before the University 10 (Oxford: Daniel Prince, 1777).

15. William Dodd, The Frequency of Capital Punishments Inconsistent with Justice, Sound Policy, and Religion 5, 11, 17–19 (Dublin: William Hallhead, 1777).

16. William Dodd, The Frequency of Capital Punishments Inconsistent with Justice, Sound Policy, and Religion: Being the Substance of a Sermon 11 & n.* (undated pamphlet, printed for "W. Faden," "B. Law," and "C. Dilly," thought to be published in the 1760s; the title page refers to "William Dodd, LLD" as "Chaplain to the King").

17. *See* Frankenberg, *Torture and Taboo*, 413; Parker B. Potter, Jr., *Antipodal Invective: A Field Guide to Kangaroos in American Courtrooms*, 39 Akron L. Rev. 73, 83 (2006); Margaret Jane Radin, *The Jurisprudence of Death: Evolving Standards for the Cruel and Unusual Punishments Clause*, 128 U. Pa. L. Rev. 989, 1031 (1978); Foucault, Discipline & Punish, 3–6, 12–13; Maestro, Cesare Beccaria and the Origins of Penal Reform, 14–15; *see also* Daines Barrington, Observations on the More Ancient Statutes from Magna Charta to the Twenty-First of James I, at 498 (London: J. Nichols, 5th ed. 1796) ("The Marquis *Beccaria*, who seems to have adopted most of *Montesquieu's* ideas, makes use of the following argument against the use of torture....").

18. Thomas, On Crimes and Punishments, xxi, 3; Bellamy, On Crimes and Punishments, xxxiii, 1.

19. Perez Zagorin, Francis Bacon 3, 5, 18, 22 (Princeton, NJ: Princeton University Press, 1998).

20. Livaudais v. Municipality No. 2, 16 La. 509, 1840 WL 1413 (1840); Rachel Stevens, *The Trafficking of Children: A Modern Form of Slavery, Using the Alien Tort Statute to Provide Legal Recourse*, 5 Whittier J. Child & Fam. Advoc. 645, 652 (2006); *accord* Fik Meijer, The Gladiators: History's Most Deadly Sport (New York: St. Martin's Griffin, 2007).

21. Julia Elizabeth Kennedy, George Watterston: Novelist, "Metropolitan Author," and Critic, Ph.D. thesis, Catholic University of America (1933), pp. 8, 16; Catalogue of the Library of the United States 94 (Washington, DC: Jonathan Elliot, 1815); Letters from Washington, on the Constitution and Laws; with Sketches of Some of the Prominent Public Characters of the United States 9, 12, 15–16, 20–22, 29–30 (Washington, DC: Jacob Gideon, Jr., 1818) (said to be "written during the winter of 1817–18 by a foreigner").

22. Marbury v. Madison, 5 U.S. 137 (1803).

23. U.S. Const., amend. I; James Madison to W. T. Barry, Aug. 4, 1822; Thomas, On Crimes and Punishments, 5, 14, 26, 66, 118–19; John Adams, "A Dissertation on the Canon and the Feudal Law," No. 1 (Aug. 12, 1765) & No. 2 (Aug. 19, 1765), *available at* Massachusetts Historical Society, Digital

Editions: Papers of John Adams, Vol. 1; Thomas Jefferson to the Danbury Baptist Association, Jan. 1, 1803, *available at* www.founders.archives.gov.

24. An Act for Establishing Religious Freedom (1786).

25. Isaac A. Linnartz, *The Siren Song of Interrogational Torture: Evaluating the U.S. Implementation of the U.N. Convention Against Torture*, 57 Duke L.J. 1485, 1491–93 (2008).

26. *See* Thomas, On Crimes and Punishments, 173 n.10; Heikki Pihlajamäki, *The Painful Question: The Fate of Judicial Torture in Early Modern Sweden*, 25 Law & Hist. Rev. 557, 574 (2007); Caleb A. Wall, The Historic Boston Tea Party of December 16, 1773 (Worcester, MA: F. S. Blanchard & Co., 1896).

27. Maestro, Cesare Beccaria and the Origins of Penal Reform, 18–19, 126–27, 136; Thomas, On Crimes and Punishments, 173 n.11; Frankenberg, *Torture and Taboo*, 408.

28. Thomas, On Crimes and Punishments, 32; Bessler, Cruel and Unusual, 98.

29. Benjamin Franklin, Arthur Lee & John Adams, The Commissioners to the Comte de Vergennes, Jan. 9, 1779, *available at* Massachusetts Historical Society, Digital Editions, http://www.masshist.org/publications/apde/portia.php?id=PJA07d242.

30. Edward Christian, A Dissertation Shewing that the House of Lords in Cases of Judicature Are Bound by Precisely the Same Rules of Evidence, as Are Observed by All Other Courts 22 (Cambridge: J. Archdeadon, 1792).

31. George Dyer, An Inquiry into the Nature of Subscription to the Thirty-Nine Articles 41, 101, 108, 111 (London: J. Johnson, 1792).

32. Éva H. Balázs, Hungary and the Habsburgs 1765–1800: An Experiment in Enlightened Absolutism 77 (Budapest, Hungary: Central European University Press, 1987); Silverman, Thornberry, Cohen & Krisberg, Crime and Justice at the Millennium, 391; Michelle Farrell, The Prohibition of Torture in Exceptional Circumstances 211 (Cambridge: Cambridge University Press, 2013); Friedland, Seeing Justice Done, 214; John H. Langbein, "The Legal History of Torture," *in* Sanford Levinson, ed., Torture: A Collection 93–101 (Oxford: Oxford University Press, 2004).

33. Imogene L. Moyer, Criminological Theories: Traditional and Nontraditional Voices and Themes 20 (Thousand Oaks, CA: SAGE Publications, 2001).

34. John D. Jackson & Sarah J. Summers, The Internationalisation of Criminal Evidence: Beyond the Common Law and Civil Law Traditions 61 (Cambridge: Cambridge University Press, 2012).

35. Thomas, On Crimes and Punishments, 57.

36. C.H.S. Jayawardene, *The Death Penalty in Ceylon*, 3 Ceylon J. Hist. Soc. Stud. 166, 185 (1960).

37. David T. Johnson, *Japan's Secretive Death Penalty Policy: Contours, Origins, Justifications, and Meanings*, 7 Asian-Pac. L. & Pol'y J. 62 n.27 (2006) (citing Damien P. Horigan, *Of Compassion and Capital Punishment: A Buddhist Perspective on the Death Penalty*, 41 Am. J. of Juris. 271, 283–85 (1996)).

38. Taylor Young Hong, *Televised Executions and Restoring Accountability to the Death Penalty Debate*, 29 Colum. Hum. Rts. L. Rev. 787, 794 n.32 (1998).

39. Charles Benn, China's Golden Age: Everyday Life in the Tang Dynasty 8 (Oxford: Oxford University Press, 2002).

40. *See* Thomas, On Crimes and Punishments, 174 n.15; Andrew A. Gentes, Exile to Siberia, 1590–1822: Corporeal Commodification and Administrative Systematization in Russia 51, 78 (New York: Palgrave Macmillan, 2008); Maria Kiriakova, *The Death Penalty in Russia 1917–2000: A Bibliographic Survey of English Language Writings*, 30 Int'l J. Legal Info. 482, 486–87 (2002). Though Beccaria praised the Russian empress as providing "the leaders of all peoples an illustrious example worth at least as much as many conquests bought with the blood of her country's sons," the "reality"—as one commentator wrote—was that Russia's death penalty "was replaced by terribly cruel punishments which often resulted in the convict's death." As that author writes: "In fact, convicts were beaten with the *knut*, their nostrils were torn, and then their forehead and cheeks were branded with an iron. Many died and those who survived were usually deported to do forced labour in Siberia." Thomas, On Crimes and Punishments, 52 & 174 n.15.

41. Millett, *Will the United States Follow England*, 551. Henry I ultimately reinstated the death penalty in 1108 and the death penalty was not abolished again in England until 1965. *Id.*

42. Maxine Sheets-Johnstone, The Roots of Morality 302 (University Park, PA: Pennsylvania State University, 2008).

43. Thomas, On Crimes and Punishments, 57; Friedland, Seeing Justice Done, 214; Michael Brian Schiffer, Draw the Lightning Down: Benjamin Franklin and Electrical Technology in the Age of Enlightenment 56–57, 172 (Berkeley, CA: University of California Press, 2003); Benjamin Franklin, Experiments and Observations on Electricity, Made at Philadelphia in America by Benjamin Franklin, L. L. D. and F. R. S. (London: David Henry, 1769) ("sold by FRANCIS NEWBERY, at the Corner of St. Paul's Church-Yard").

44. William Tudor to John Adams, July 7, 1776 ("I have carefully read the military Code which regulates the British Army, and heartily wish it could be adopted by the Continental Government, with a very few Alterations, such as making fewer Crimes punishable capitally and limiting the Number of Lashes to 1 or 200. The General joins with me in this Opinion.").

45. Wilfrid Prest, William Blackstone: Law and Letters in the Eighteenth Century 308 (Oxford: Oxford University Press, 2008); Cunningham v. Caldwell, 3 Ky. 123, 1807 WL 528, at *5 (1807).

46. Stephen Payne Adye, A Treatise on Courts Martial: To Which Is Added, An Essay on Military Punishments and Rewards 231, 261 (London: J. Murray, 3d ed. 1786).

47. William Sabatier, A Treatise on Poverty, Its Consequences, and the Remedy 182, 188–89, 192–96, 198–99, 201–202, 205, 207, 214, 223, 230, 243–44 (London: John Stockdale, 1797); *see also* 1 Thomas Ruggles, The History of the Poor; Their Rights, Duties, and the Laws Respecting Them 76–77 (London: J. Deighton, 1793) (describing *Dei delitti e delle pene* as an "excellent treatise").

48. S. M. Phillipps, A Treatise on the Law of Evidence 112 (London: J. Butterworth and Son, 2d ed. 1815).

49. Richard Parkinson, Treatise on the Breeding and Management of Livestock 11 (London: Cadell and Davies, 1810).

50. Early American state constitutions prohibited "cruel and unusual," "cruel or unusual," "cruel" or "sanguinary" punishments. Bessler, Cruel and Unusual, 178–81. Such provisions—part of ongoing efforts to reform American's penal laws—were adopted by political leaders who plainly admired Beccaria's treatise. Daye v. State, 769 A.2d 630, 637 & n.3 (Vt. 2000) (noting Beccaria's influence on Benjamin Franklin in Pennsylvania, which ultimately lead "to the enactment of § 39 of the Pennsylvania Constitution of 1776").

51. A. Owen Aldridge, Thomas Paine's American Ideology 70–71 (Cranbury, NJ: Associated University Presses, 1984); 1 R. H. Inglis Palgrave, ed., Dictionary of Political Economy 637 (London: MacMillian and Co., 1901); Desmond Gregory, Napoleon's Italy 21 (Cranbury, NJ: Associated University Presses, 2001); David Wooton, ed., Republicanism, Liberty, and Commercial Society, 1649–1776, at 36–38, 415 n.142 (Stanford: Stanford University Press, 1994); Benjamin Vincent, Specimen Pages, Prospectus, & Opinions of the Press of Haydn's Dictionary of Dates 126 (London: Edward Moxon and Co., 13th ed. ed. 1868); Luigino Bruni, The Genesis and Ethos of the Market 137–39 (New York: Palgrave Macmillan, 2012); Josiah Quincy to John Adams, June 13, 1776, *available at* www.founders. archives.gov. One of the chapters in Beccaria's treatise is specifically titled "of the proportion between crimes and punishments." Cesare Beccaria, On Crimes and Punishments, ch. 6 (4th ed. 1784); *see also* United States v. McCusker, Nos. CRIM A. 92-33-04 & CIV. A. 95-3494, 1995 WL 613103 *4 (E.D. Pa. 1995) ("Since the time of Beccaria, criminal sentencing law has emphasized the need for 'a certain conformity between crime and punishment.'") (citing Leon Radzinowicz, A History of English Criminal Law and Its Administration from 1750: The Movement for Reform 1750–1833, at 281–83 (New York: Macmillan Co., 1948)); United States v. Nehas, 368 F. Supp. 435, 439 n.11 (W.D. Pa. 1973) ("[t]he principle of proportionality between crime and punishment has been recognized at least since the time of Beccaria").

52. State v. Wheeler, 175 P.3d 438, 443 & n.4 (Or. 2007).

53. 1 Harvey Wish, Society and Thought in America 211 (New York: Longmans, Green and Co., 1950).

54. Kevin J. Hayes, The Mind of a Patriot: Patrick Henry and the World of Ideas 97 (Charlottesville: University of Virginia Press, 2008); David J. Vaughan, ed., Give Me Liberty: The Uncompromising Statesmanship of Patrick Henry 85 (Nashville, TN: Cumberland House Publishing, 1997); Kathryn Preyer, "Cesare Beccaria and the Founding Fathers," *in* Blackstone in America, 241 n.8; Herbert E. Sloan, Principle and Interest: Thomas Jefferson and the Problem of Debt 244–45 (Charlottesville: University of Virginia Press, 1995) (noting that Virginia libraries often contained works by Blackstone and Montesquieu).

55. Schabas, The Death Penalty as Cruel Treatment and Torture, 19.

56. *E.g.*, John Theodore Horton, James Kent: A Study in Conservatism, 1763–1847, at 120 (2000) (listing "Beccaria's Crimes and Punishments" among law books listed for sale in American newspapers in the 1790s).

57. St. George Tucker, Blackstone's Commentaries: With Notes of Reference to the Constitution and Laws, of the Federal Government of the United States, and of the Commonwealth of Virginia (1803), *available at* http://www.constitution.org/tb/tb5.htm.

58. Edmund Clingan, An Introduction to Modern Western Civilization 47 (Bloomington, IN: iUniverse, 2011).

59. Bessler, Cruel and Unusual, 174–76.

60. Joseph A. Melusky & Keith Alan Pesto, Capital Punishment 31 (Santa Barbara, CA: Greenwood, 2011) ("After separating from England, the constitutions and criminal codes adopted by the American states tended to announce their adoption of the philosophies of Locke and Montesquieu, Blackstone and Beccaria."); Richard B. Morris, The Forging of the Union, 1781–1789, at 169 (New York: Harper & Row, 1987) ("[I]t is clear that American reformers sought to adapt to their respective states the notions of Italy's great penological reformer, Cesare Beccaria, and of England's John Howard.").

61. Friedman, A History of American Law, 207; Pennsylvania Constitution (1776).

62. 4 The Belfast Monthly Magazine 327–28 (1810) (discussing "A Visit to the Philadelphia Prison, in a Letter to a Friend, by Robert J. Turnbull, of South Carolina").

63. Pennsylvania Constitution (1776), §§ 38–39.

64. Vermont Constitution (1777), § XXXV ("to make sanguinary punishments less necessary; houses ought to be provided for punishing, by hard labour, those who shall be convicted of crimes not capital").

65. G. S. Rowe, Embattled Bench: The Pennsylvania Supreme Court and the Forging of a Democratic Society, 1684–1809, at 163 (Cranbury, NJ: Associated University Presses, 1994); Henry Homespun, Jr., The Plough Boy, June 12, 1819, Vol. 1, No. 2, *reprinted in* 1 The Plough Boy: From June 5, 1819 to May 27, 1820 (Albany: John O. Cole, 1819–20), p. 14.

66. Edwin Powers, Crime and Punishment in Early Massachusetts 1620–1692: A Documentary History 193, 243 (Boston: Beacon Press, 1966). Other early Massachusetts governors also advocated "some amelioration of the capital laws," including Caleb Strong in 1804. Id. at 311.

67. Hindus, Prison and Plantation, 100–101.

68. Hartnett, Executing Democracy (discussing O'Sullivan); Speech of Hon. Robert J. Walker, of Mississippi, on the Bill to Provide Further Remedial Justice in the Courts of the United States: Delivered in the Senate of the United States, June 21, 1842, at 18 (Washington, DC: The Globe Office, 1842); Biographical Directory of the United States Congress, http://bioguide.congress.gov/scripts/biodisplay.pl?index=W000067 (entry for "Walker, Robert John"); Robert John Walker: A Politician from Jackson to Lincoln 4 (New York: Columbia University Press, 1961) ("He admitted that the great Italian penologist … had influenced his thought. So much so that he named his third son, who died before Robert's birth, Beccaria.").

69. J. I. Mombert, An Authentic History of Lancaster County, in the State of Pennsylvania 97 (Lancaster, PA: J. E. Barr & Co., 1869).

70. Friedman, A History of American Law, 207.

71. 2 Isaac Disraeli, Curiosities of Literature 377–78 (London: Frederick Warne & Co. 1881); *see also* 2 Isaac Disraeli, Curiosities of Literature 121–22 (New York: Thomas Y. Crowell, 1881).

72. Thomas M. Franck, *Proportionality in International Law*, 4 Law & Ethics Hum. Rts. 229, 241 n.49 (2010); *see also* Leigh Goodmark, *The Punishment of Dixie Shanahan: Is There Justice for Battered Women Who Kill?*, 55 U. Kan. L. Rev. 269, 288 (2007) ("Retribution is the oldest moral underpinning for criminal punishments, dating back to the Code of Hammurabi, developed by the Babylonians around the eighteenth century B.C. The lex talionis, or law of retribution, limited all sentences to punishment proportionate to the crime—an eye for an eye, a life for a life.").

73. 4 Blackstone, Commentaries on the Laws of England, 14; Thomas Wood, A New Institute of the Imperial or Civil Law 263 (London: J. and J. Knapton, et al., 4th ed. corr. 1730).

74. 20 The London Medical Gazette: Being a Weekly Journal of Medicine and the Collateral Sciences 596–600 (London: Longman, Orme, Brown, Green & Longmans, 1837).

75. 2 The Western Medical Gazette: A Monthly Journal Devoted to Medicine and the Collateral Sciences (Cincinnati, OH: A Pugh, 1835).

76. Markus Dirk Dubber, *Toward a Constitutional Law of Crime and Punishment*, 55 Hastings L.J. 509, 538–39 (2004) ("Jefferson's own view of proportionality oddly combined strict adherence to the lex talionis and a Beccarian interest in balancing the anticipated pains of punishment against the anticipated pleasures of crime"); *see also* 11 William Holdsworth, A History of English Law 578 (Boston: Little, Brown and Co., 1938) ("Beccaria made men reflect upon the theory of punishment.").

77. Steven H. Jupiter, *Constitution Notwithstanding: The Political Illegitimacy of the Death Penalty in American Democracy*, 23 Fordham Urb. L.J. 437, 477 (1996).

78. Paul Leicester Ford, ed., The Autobiography of Thomas Jefferson, 1743–1790, at 69 (Philadelphia: University of Pennsylvania Press, 2005).

79. Bessler, Cruel and Unusual, 63–64.

80. John F. Dillon, The Laws and Jurisprudence of England and America: Being a Series of Lectures Delivered Before Yale University 368 (Boston: Little, Brown and Co., 1894).

81. Pace, Luigi Castiglioni's Viaggio, 221, 253.

82. Friedman, Crime and Punishment in American History, 40.

83. Bessler, Cruel and Unusual, 54; Terance D. Miethe & Hong Lu, Punishment: A Comparative Historical Perspective 35–36, 90 (Cambridge: Cambridge University Press, 2005).

84. Ohio. Const. of 1802, art. VIII, § 14.

85. Hindus, Prison and Plantation, 102; S.C. Const. (1778), art. XL.

86. Ind. Const. of 1816, art. I, § 16; Me. Const. of 1819, art. I, § 9; R.I. Const. of 1842, art. I, § 8; W. Va. Const. of 1861–1863, art. II, § 2; Ga. Const. of 1868, art. I, § 21; *compare* Calabresi & Agudo, *Individual Rights Under State Constitutions When the Fourteenth Amendment Was Ratified in 1868*, 83.

87. Samuel Sherwood, "Scriptural Instructions to Civil Rulers, and all Free-born Subjects" (1774), *available at* http://www.consource.org/document/scriptural-instructions-to-civil-rulers-by-samuel-sherwood/.

88. Moses Mather, "America's Appeal to the Impartial World" (1775), *available at* http://www.consource.org/document/americas-appeal-to-the-impartial-world-by-moses-mather/ (a sermon delivered in Hartford, Connecticut).

89. 1 Stanton D. Krauss, ed., Gentlemen of the Grand Jury: The Surviving Grand Jury Charges from Colonial, State, and Lower Federal Courts Before 1801, at 214–15 (Durham, NC: Carolina Academic Press, 2012).

90. Egbert Benson, Memoir Read Before the Historical Society of the State of New-York, December 31, 1816, at 79 (Jamaica: Henry C. Sleight, 2d ed. 1825).

91. The Edinburgh Review, or Critical Journal: for March 1821.... July 1821, at 133–34 (Edinburgh: Heirs of David Willison, 1821).

92. Jeremy Bentham, Principles of Legislation: From the Ms. of Jeremy Bentham 20, 128, 190, 285, 288, 296 (Boston: Wells and Lilly, John Neal, trans. & M. Dumont, ed. 1830).

93. Bessler, Legacy of Violence, 174–77; Galliher, Koch, Keys & Guess, America Without the Death Penalty, 79.

94. Payne v. Tennessee, 501 U.S. 808, 820 (1991); *see also* BMW of North Am., Inc. v. Gore, 517 U.S. 559, 575 n.24 (1996) ("The principle that punishment should fit the crime 'is deeply rooted and frequently repeated in common-law jurisprudence.'") (quoting Solem v. Helm, 463 U.S. 277, 284 (1983)); People v. Babcock, 666 N.W.2d 231, 262–63 (Mich. 2003) ("As in any civilized society, punishment should be made to fit the crime and the criminal.") (citing Beccaria).

95. *Babcock*, 666 N.W.2d at 262–63 ("The relevancy of proportionality is obvious.") (citing Beccaria).

96. Graham v. Florida, 130 S. Ct. 2011, 2021 (2010); *accord* Miller v. Alabama, 132 S. Ct. 2455, 2463 (2012).

97. *E.g.*, *Miller*, 132 S. Ct. at 2475 ("the mandatory sentencing schemes before us violate this principle of proportionality"); *Graham*, 130 S. Ct. at 2034 ("The Constitution prohibits the imposition of a life without parole sentence on a juvenile offender who did not commit homicide."); Kennedy v. Louisiana, 554 U.S. 407, 420 (2008) ("The Court further has held that the death penalty can be disproportionate to the crime itself where the crime did not result, or was not intended to result, in death of the victim.").

98. *Graham*, 130 S. Ct. at 2021 (quoting Weems v. United States, 217 U.S. 349, 367 (1910)). A closely divided U.S. Supreme Court has held that the Eighth Amendment contains a "narrow proportionality principle," that "does not require strict proportionality between crime and sentence" but which "forbids only extreme sentences that are 'grossly disproportionate' to the crime." *Graham*, 130 S. Ct. at 2021 (quoting Harmelin v. Michigan, 501 U.S. 957, 997 (1991).

99. State v. Burlington Drug Co., 78 A. 882, 885 (Vt. 1911). Other professionals, such as physicians, also remained familiar with Beccaria's writings in the nineteenth century. Alonzo Calkins, M.D., "Felonious Homicide: Its Penalty, and the Execution Thereof Judicially," p. 4 (1878) (citing Beccaria in a paper ordered for publication after being read before the Medico-Legal Society of the City of New York, Sept. 25, 1873).

100. *E.g.*, John F. Stinneford, *Rethinking Proportionality under the Cruel and Unusual Punishments Clause*, 97 Va. L. Rev. 899 (2011); Kevin White, *Construing the Outer Limits of Sentencing Authority: A Proposed Bright-Line Rule for Noncapital Proportionality Review*, 2011 B.Y.U. L. Rev. 567 (2011); Richard G. Singer, *Proportionate Thoughts about Proportionality*, 8 Ohio St. J. Crim. L. 217 (2010).

101. *See generally* Youngjae Lee, *Why Proportionality Matters*, 160 U. Pa. L. Rev. 1835 (2012); William W. Berry III, *Practicing Proportionality*, 64 Florida L. Rev. 687 (2012); William W. Berry III, *Promulgating Proportionality*, 46 Ga. L. Rev. 69 (2011); *see also* Gregory S. Schneider, *Sentencing Proportionality in the States*, 54 Ariz. L. Rev. 241 (2012).

102. Godwin, Of Population, 376.

103. Burroughs, Memoirs of the Notorious Stephen Burroughs, 180, 183, 237, 107; Memoirs of Stephen Burroughs: A New and Revised Edition 167 (Amherst, MA: M. N. Spear, 1858).

104. Anthony W. Neal, Unburdened by Conscience: A Black People's Collective Account of America's Ante-Bellum South and the Aftermath 16–18 (Lanham, MD: University Press of America, 2009).

105. 2 Edward Long, The History of Jamaica: or, General Survey of the Antient and Modern State of that Island 381–82, 485 & n.*b.*, 496 (1774).

106. Mark C. Carnes, ed., American National Biography 62 (Oxford: Oxford University Press, 2005); Burroughs, Memoirs of the Notorious Stephen Burroughs, 114–130, 134–41, 156, 180, 183, 237, 252; Sketch of the Life of the Notorious Stephen Burroughs 85, 104 (Philadelphia: David Hogan, 1811).

107. Colquhoun, A Treatise on the Police of the Metropolis, 282.

108. The American Museum: or, Annual Register of Fugitive Pieces, Ancient and Modern for the Year 1798, at 8–9 (1799) (reprinting *An Enquiry How Far the Punishment of Death Is Necessary in Pennsylvania*); William Allen, An American Biographical and Historical Dictionary, Containing an Account of the Lives, Characters, and Writings of the Most Eminent Persons in North America from Its First Discovery to the Present Time 95–96 (Cambridge: Hilliard & Metcalf, 1809) (noting that William Bradford's 1793 essay "had much influence in meliorating the criminal laws and hastening the almost entire abolition of capital punishments not only in Pennsylvania, but in several other states, where the interests of humanity have at last prevailed over ancient and inveterate prejudices").

109. The Memoirs of Charles Westcote 74 (London, 2d ed. 1807) ("You presume rightly in supposing I have studied Beccaria. I love him as a writer: I reverence his memory: he did honour to the country that give him birth. But, however excellent the opinions of the marquis—however much he sympathized with the feelings of the sufferer, in his aim to discover the punishment that would have the greatest possible effect on the spectator, with the least possible pain to the delinquent; he has been guilty of the grossest error by supposing that slavery would better answer the end of example."); id. ("Beccaria was a humane man: but slavery is no ingredient of humanity."); *see also* id. at 77 ("Beccaria affirms the terror of death to make so slight an impression, that it has not force enough to withstand that forgetfulness natural to mankind, even in the most essential things; especially when assisted by the passions: but, that perpetual slavery has in it all that is necessary to deter the most hardened and determined as much as the punishment of death").

110. Basil Montagu, comp., The Opinions of Different Authors upon the Punishment of Death 13, 22–23, 109, 136, 181, 253, 296, 301 (London: Longman, Hurst, Rees & Orme, 1809).

111. Donald A. Ritchie, The Congress of the United States: A Student Companion 146 (Oxford: Oxford University Press, 3d ed. 2006); Gottlieb, Theater of Death, 27–28, 143; "Muhlenberg, John Peter Gabriel (1746–1807)," http://bioguide.congress.gov/scripts/biodisplay.pl?index=M001066.

112. 2 Philopatris Varvicensis [Samuel Parr], Characters of the Late Charles James Fox 436–37 (1809). This source mentions Beccaria's name, or cites Beccaria in footnotes, more than thirty-five times. Id. at 323, 327, 348, 362–63, 394, 402, 421, 423, 434, 437, 452–54, 464, 476–77, 480–82, 485–87, 494, 506–508, 517, 519, 798, 802, 807.

113. Id. at 494. The pseudonym "Philopatris Varvicensis" was identified as belonging to Samuel Parr in a subsequently published memoir. 4 John Johnstone, comp., The Works of Samuel Parr, LL.D.: Prebendary of St. Paul's, Curate of Hatton, &c. with Memoirs of His Life and Writings, and a Selection from His Correspondence 2 (Longman, Rees, Orme, Brown and Green, 1828).

114. David Brion Davis, From Homicide to Slavery: Studies in American Culture 31–32 (Oxford: Oxford University Press, 1986).

115. U.S. Const., amend. XIII.

116. Northwest Ordinance, art. 6; Junius P. Rodriguez, Slavery in the Modern World: A History of Political, Social, and Economic Oppression 460 (Santa Barbara, CA: ABC-CLIO, 2011); Society for the Diffusion of Knowledge upon the Punishment of Death and the Improvement of Prison Discipline, Description of the Tread Mill Invented by Mr. William Cubitt, of Ipswich, for the Employment of Prisoners, and Recommended by the Society for the Improvement of Prison Discipline (London: Longman, Hurst, Rees, Orme, and Brown, 1822); The Society for the Improvement of Prison Discipline, and for the Reformation of Juvenile Offenders, Rules for the Government of Gaols, Houses of Correction, and Penitentiaries (London: T. Bensley, 2d ed. 1821); Barbara Esposito & Lee Wood, Prison Slavery 38–39 (Silver Spring, MD: Committee to Abolish Prison Slavery, 1982); *see also* id. at 43 (noting that Nathan Dane was "primarily responsible for passing Article 6" of the Northwest Ordinance and that Dane mentioned Melancton Smith of New York and R. H. Lee of Virginia as committee members "in hearty sympathy with him" who "very materially assisted in the preparation of the Northwest Territory Ordinance").

117. The Monthly Review, or Literary Journal 53–54, 58, 60–61 (1807); *see also* W. Plees, An Account of the Island of Jersey; Containing a Compendium of Its Ecclesiastical, Civil, and Military, History 239–41 (Southampton: T. Baker, 1817) (quoting Janson's *Stranger in America* on capital punishment in America).

118. Markus D. Dubber & Lindsay Farmer, eds., Modern Histories of Crime and Punishment 45–46 (Stanford: Stanford University Press, 2007); John H. Langbein, The Origins of Adversary Criminal Trial 6 (Oxford: Oxford University Press, 2003); J. David Hirschel & William Wakefield, Criminal Justice in England and the United States 175 (Westport, CT: Greenwood, 1995).

119. 2 Francis Lieber, ed., Encyclopaedia Americana: A Popular Dictionary of Arts, Sciences, Literature, History, Politics and Biography 24–25 (Philadelphia: Carey and Lea, 1830).

120. William Darby, Mnemonika or the Tablet of Memory 286 (Baltimore: Edward J. Coale, 1829); *see also* J. Willoughby Rosse, Blair's Chronological Tables: Revised and Enlarged 642, 663 (London: H. G. Bohn, 1856) (listing Beccaria's birth and the 1764 publication of *On Crimes and Punishments* by "marquis Beccaria" among a list of "Events and Eminent Men.").

121. 2 William Guthrie, A New System of Modern Geography: or, a Geographical, Historical, and Commercial Grammar 30 (Philadelphia: Mathew Carey, 1795).

122. Banner, The Death Penalty, 131; Stone & Mennell, Alexis de Tocqueville on Democracy, Revolution and Society, 129; U.S. Const., art. I, sec. 9; U.S. Const., art. III, sec. 3.

123. Brian F. Carso, Jr., "Whom Can We Trust Now?": The Meaning of Treason in the United States, from the Revolution through the Civil War 71–74 (Lanham, MD: Lexington Books, 2006).

124. Stone & Mennell, Alexis de Tocqueville on Democracy, Revolution and Society, 106; Bessler, Cruel and Unusual, 275.

125. Bessler, Cruel and Unusual, 188–89.

126. Brown v. Board of Education, 347 U.S. 483 (1954); U.S. Const., amend. XIV.

127. 2 George Thomas Kurian & James D. Smith III, eds., The Encyclopedia of Christian Literature 641 (Lanham, MD: Scarecrow Press, 2010); John P. Kaminski, Thomas Jefferson: Philosopher and Politician 29 (Madison: Parallel Press, 2005); Triumph & Tragedy in History: National History Day 2007, at 50–53 (College Park, MD: University of Maryland, 2006); Thomas Paine to Thomas Jefferson, Feb. 16, 1789; James Smith to George Washington, June 22, 1792; Caesar A. Rodney to Thomas Jefferson, Mar. 30, 1811, *available at* www.founders.archives.gov.

128. Justin Buckley Dyer, Natural Law and the Antislavery Constitutional Tradition 74 (Cambridge: Cambridge University Press, 2012).

129. John S. Dempsey & Linda S. Forst, An Introduction to Policing 10 (Clifton Park, NY: Delmar, 6th ed. 2012); Lawrence M. Friedman & Harry N. Scheiber, eds., American Law and the Constitutional Order: Historical Perspectives 209 (Cambridge: Harvard University Press, 1998) ("Every southern state defined a substantial number of felonies carrying capital punishment for slaves and lesser punishment for whites."); Molefi Kete Asante & Ama Mazama, Encyclopedia of Black Studies 120 (Thousand Oaks, CA: SAGE Publications, 2005) (discussing "Black Codes").

130. Bessler, Cruel and Unusual, 275; Ralph Blumenthal, Miracle at Sing Sing: How One Man Transformed the Lives of America's Most Dangerous Prisoners 79–80, 109–10, 122, 124, 128, 235 (New York: St. Martin's Press, 2004); Zunz, Alexis de Tocqueville and Gustave de Beaumont in America, 155 n.201 (noting that Edward Livingston, who was directed to revise Louisiana's penal code and who served as Secretary of State from 1831 to 1833, was "exceptionally helpful to Tocqueville and Beaumont's study of American prisons and was the only person Tocqueville thanked by name in the preface to his first volume of *Democracy in America*").

131. Jon Meacham, American Lion: Andrew Jackson in the White House 412 n.168 (New York: Random House, 2009).

132. Zunz, Alexis de Tocqueville and Gustave de Beaumont in America, 156, 238–40, 387.

133. Goodheart, The Solemn Sentence of Death, 108 (noting that, in the 1840s, the Reverend Jonathan Cogswell, a professor at the Theological Institute of Connecticut, published *A Treatise on the Necessity of Capital Punishment*, and called Beccaria "a corrupt magistrate" with a "weak, sophistical argument"); *see also* John Thomas Scharf, History of Delaware: 1609–1888, at 571 (Philadelphia: L. J. Richards & Co., 1888) (a profile of Caesar Rodney, a 1790 graduate of the University of Pennsylvania who was admitted to the New Castle, Delaware bar in 1793, contains the following story: "Old-fashioned lawyers sometimes thought he got out of bounds. Chief Justice Read, when he quoted 'Beccaria on Crimes and Punishments,' stopped him, saying, 'that book is no authority in any court.'"); William Thompson Read, Life and Correspondence of George Read: A Signer of the Declaration of Independence 231 (Philadelphia: J. B. Lippincott & Co., 1870) (containing the same anecdote).

134. Bessler, Cruel and Unusual, 48 (noting the comments of Bentham, Blackstone and Voltaire on Beccaria's treatise).

135. Id. at 66–91, 150–51; Heller, Democracy's Lawyer, 26 ("In 1797, under the active leadership of John Breckinridge, Kentucky reformed its criminal laws, revoking the death penalty except for first-degree murder.").

136. Banner, The Death Penalty, 93–94.

137. Carol S. Steiker & Jordan M. Steiker, *Entrenchment and/or Destabilization? Reflections on (Another) Two Decades of Constitutional Regulation of Capital Punishment*, 30 Law & Ineq. 211, 216 (2012) ("Many of our founders—including James Madison, Thomas Jefferson, Benjamin Franklin, and Benjamin Rush—were familiar with Cesare Beccaria's pathbreaking critique of the death penalty and accordingly advocated restriction or abolition of capital punishment.").

138. St. George Tucker Notebook, Law Lectures, Book 7, p. 43 (notes for "Mar. 1794"), *available at* https://digitalarchive.wm.edu/handle/10288/13361; *compare* St. George Tucker Notebook, Law Lectures (circa 1790s), Book 8, p. 12, *available at* https://digitalarchive.wm.edu/handle/10288/13361 (listing as a subject "The punishment of Death in capital cases" before a section of his notes on slavery).

139. Richard Beale Davis, Intellectual Life in Jefferson's Virginia, 1790–1830, at 94 (Knoxville, TN: Newfound Press, 1964).

140. 1 James Kent, Commentaries on American Law 265 (New York: O. Halsted, 1826); 1 James Kent, Commentaries on American Law 284 (Boston: Little, Brown, 12th ed. 1873) (edited by Oliver Wendell Holmes, Jr.) ("The Marquis Beccaria has contended, that the power of pardon does not exist under a perfect administration of law....").

141. Coxe, Account of the Prisons and Hospitals, 32 n.*; *compare* Penn, Further Thoughts on the Present State of Public Opinion, 26 (making a reference to Beccaria, then writing: "Thus I may appear, perhaps, still less inclined to innovation in our laws, than a queen's solicitor general, the judicious Blackstone, who speaks with the respect I do of Beccaria's ideas, but dwells more on them.").

142. United States v. Blake, 89 F. Supp.2d 328, 341–42 (E.D.N.Y. 2000) ("This work would affect policy to the present day.") (citing *On Crimes and Punishments*); *accord* State v. Gaylord, 890 P.2d 1167, 1185 (Haw. 1995) (citing Beccaria's treatise); Commonwealth v. O'Neal, 339 N.E.2d 676, 678 (Mass. 1975) (same).

143. Panel Discussion, *Human Rights and Human Wrongs: Is the United States Death Penalty System Inconsistent with International Human Rights Law?*, 67 Fordham L. Rev. 2793 (1999) (discussing Beccaria's influence); Schwartz & Wishingrad, *The Eighth Amendment, Beccaria, and the Enlightenment*, 783.

144. Schabas, The Death Penalty as Cruel Treatment and Torture, 18.

145. St. George Tucker, Blackstone's Commentaries: With Notes of Reference to the Constitution and Laws, of the Federal Government of the United States, and of the Commonwealth of Virginia (1803), *available at* http://www.constitution.org/tb/tb5.htm; George St. Tucker to Thomas Jefferson, May 2, 1798, *available at* www.founders.archives.gov (signed "S G Tucker"); American Law School Review, Vol. 1, p. 313 (St. Paul, MN: West Publishing Co., 1911); Thomas J. Matthews, ed., The Transylvanian, or Lexington Literary Journal 208 (1829); David Ariosto, "Connecticut Becomes 17th State to Abolish Death Penalty," CNN, Apr. 25, 2012, http://www.cnn.com/2012/04/25/justice/connecticut-death-penalty-law-repealed/. *Tucker's Blackstone*—as it was known—had "widespread circulation, both as a text-book and otherwise." 1 Charles Warren, History of the Harvard Law School and of Early Legal Conditions in America 211 (New York: Lewis Publishing Co., 1908).

146. American Museum, vol. II, p. 142; vol. III, pp. 395, 509–516; vol. IV, pp. 78, 444, 547; vol. V, pp. 63, 121; vol. VII, pp. 6, 69, 135, 193; vol. VIII, pp. 153, 202; vol. X, pp. 215, 267; Museum for 1798, p. 1. In *The Life of Thomas Jefferson*, George Tucker—then a Professor of Moral Philosophy at the University of Virginia—noted that when a young man in Philadelphia asked Jefferson for advice on a course of political reading, "he good-naturedly sat down to give a full answer to the other's inquiries." Among the things that Tucker reported Jefferson as having said: "He recommends Locke, Sidney, Priestley, Chipman and the Federalist; together with Beccaria on Crimes, Smith's Wealth of Nations, and Say's Political Economy." 2 George Tucker, The Life of Thomas Jefferson, Third President of the United States 264 (London: Charles Knight and Co., 1837).

147. Joseph Gales, Sr., comp., The Debates and Proceedings in the Congress of the United States 1571–74 (Washington, DC: Gales and Seaton, 1834) (Gale & Seaton's History, "Punishment of Crimes," debate of April 5, 1790).

148. Bessler, Cruel and Unusual, 98, 198; M. H. Hoeflich, Roman and Civil Law and the Development of Anglo-American Jurisprudence in the Nineteenth Century 56 (Athens, GA: University of Georgia Press, 1997).

149. Thomas Jefferson, Autobiography Draft Fragment, Jan. 6–July 27, 1821.

150. Bessler, Cruel and Unusual, 93; Andrew Burstein, The Inner Jefferson: Portrait of a Grieving Optimist 186 (Charlottesville: University Press of Virginia, 1995).

151. Lester J. Cappon, ed., The Adams-Jefferson Letters: The Complete Correspondence Between Thomas Jefferson and Abigail and John Adams (Chapel Hill: University of North Carolina Press, 1988).

152. 3 Alexander Fraser Tytler, Memoirs of the Life and Writings of the Honourable Henry Home of Kames 110–11, 118, 131–32, 134–35, 143, 346 (Edinburgh: T. Cadell & W. Davies, 2d ed. 1814).

153. Russell Pond, Introduction to Criminology 14 (Winchester, UK: Waterside Press, 1999).

154. 1 Alexander Fraser Tytler, Memoirs of the Life and Writings of the Honourable Henry Home of Kames 73–103 (Edinburgh: William Creech, 1807) (Appendix No. X).

155. John Adams to Col. Daniel Hitchcock, Oct. 1, 1776; Friedman, A History of American Law, 281–82.

156. Karen J. Greenberg, ed., The Torture Debate in America 40–41, 122 (Cambridge: Cambridge University Press, 2006); see also Matthew Lippman, The Development and Drafting of the United Nations Convention Against Torture and Other Cruel, Inhuman or Degrading Treatment or Punishment, 17 B.C. Int'l & Comp. L. Rev. 275, 281 (1994) ("In 1764, Italian criminologist Cesare Beccaria drafted the most comprehensive and influential critique of torture. Although Beccaria's arguments were not novel, he provided an intellectual justification which quickened the currents of reform."); Aniceto Masferrer, The Liberal State and Criminal Law Reform in Spain, 3 IUS Gentium 19, 39 (2010) (noting that Beccaria's arguments against torture were echoed in Spain); Khouzam v. Ashcroft, 361 F.3d 161, 163 (2d Cir. 2004) (describing Beccaria as one of the "critics" of torture).

157. William F. Schulz, ed., The Phenomenon of Torture: Readings and Commentary 25 (2007) ("Prussia all but terminated judicial torture in 1740; it was used for the last time in 1752 and authoritatively abolished in 1754."); Bessler, Cruel and Unusual, 33 ("Sweden had outlawed torture for ordinary crimes in 1734, but would not do so for all purposes until 1772 after Gustavus III came to power."); Cesare Beccaria, On Crimes and Punishments 92 (David Young trans. 1986) ("Torture in common criminal cases was abolished in Sweden in 1734, but Gustavus III, claiming Beccaria as his mentor, abolished it altogether in 1772.") (translator's note).

158. Scott Horton, "William Wilberforce: Progenitor of the Global Human Rights Movements," in George Hunsinger, ed., Torture Is a Moral Issue: Christians, Jews, Muslims, and People of Conscience Speak Out 255 (Cambridge, UK: Wm. B. Eerdmans Publishing Co., 2008).

159. Scott Bloom, Spare the Rod, Spoil the Child? A Legal Framework for Recent Corporal Punishment Proposals, 25 Golden Gate U. L. Rev. 361, 366 n.40 (1995).

160. Edward Peters, Torture 90–91, 100 (Philadelphia: University of Pennsylvania Press, expanded ed. 1996); see also id. at 91 ("Bavaria abolished torture in 1806, Wurttemburg in 1809. Torture was abolished in Norway in 1819, in Hanover in 1822, in Portugal in 1826, in Greece in 1827, in Gotha in 1828.").

161. E.g., Bessler, Cruel and Unusual, 56.

162. John Adams, "A Dissertation on the Canon and the Feudal Law," No. 2, Aug. 19, 1765, available at Massachusetts Historical Society, Digital Editions: Papers of John Adams, Vol. 1.

163. 1 The Complete Works of Edward Livingston on Criminal Jurisprudence vi, 31, 36, 56 (New York: The National Prison Association of the United States of America, 1873).

164. G.A. res. 39/46, annex, 39 U.N. GAOR Supp. (No. 51) at 197, U.N. Doc. A/39/51 (1984), entered into force June 26, 1987; Sanford Levinson, ed., Torture: A Collection 140 (Oxford: Oxford University Press, 2004).

165. 2 Royall Tyler, Reports of Cases Argued and Determined in the Supreme Court of Judicature of the State of Vermont 380 (New York: I. Riley, 1810). Royall Tyler was the Chief Judge of the Supreme Court of Judicature.

166. 1803 WL 184 (Vt. 1803).

167. 2 Royall Tyler, Reports of Cases Argued and Determined in the Supreme Court of Judicature of the State of Vermont 381 (New York: I. Riley, 1810). After citing Beccaria's On Crimes and Punishments, the Vermont Supreme Court noted: "Judge Blackstone, in his Commentaries, quotes from this author what he styles an exquisite piece of raillery. He says the Marquis has proposed this problem with a gravity and precision that are truly mathematical." Id. at 382.

168. Id. at 832. This prohibition, Vermont's Supreme Court of Judicature ruled, governed "not only … our judicial proceedings, but all attempts of individuals to extort confession by bodily suffering." Id. at 383.

169. Gary L. Stuart, Miranda: The Story of America's Right to Remain Silent 40 (Tucson: University of Arizona Press, 2004).

170. Schabas, The Death Penalty as Cruel Treatment and Torture, 21.

171. Bessler, Cruel and Unusual, 188.

172. 2 Kate Mason Rowland, The Life of George Mason, 1725–1792, at 419 (1892) (June 1788 debate). Beccaria himself opposed torture because he felt that practice is a "sure way to acquit robust scoundrels and to condemn weak but innocent people." Lippman, *The Development and Drafting of the United Nations Convention Against Torture*, 282.

173. Id. Although George Mason was not a lawyer, he studied with—and was mentored by—his uncle John Mercer, a highly respected lawyer. Mercer had an impressive library that included many legal treatises, giving Mason an appreciation for such books. *See* Robert Allen Rutland, George Mason, Reluctant Statesman 7 (Baton Rouge: Louisiana State University Press, 1989):

> Good libraries were rare in the colony, and at Marlborough, a few miles down river from Dogue's Neck, Mercer owned one of the best. Book collector as well as lawyer, Mercer introduced the lad to shelves that held hundreds of the classics and almost every important legal treatise of the time, ranging from Coke's commentaries on Littleton to Mercer's own abridgment of the laws of Virginia.

174. 3 Jonathan Elliot, comp., The Debates in the Several State Conventions on the Adoption of the Federal Constitution 452 (Philadelphia: J. B. Lippincott Co., 2d ed. 1891).

175. Halbrook, That Every Man Be Armed, 30–34; Thomas, On Crimes and Punishments, 78.

176. Halbrook, A Right to Bear Arms, 53; Robert J. Cottrol, ed., Gun Control and the Constitution: Sources and Explorations on the Second Amendment 266 (Oxford: Taylor & Francis, 1994); An Account of the Numbers of Men Able to Bear Arms in the Provinces and Towns of France, Taken by the King's Orders in 1743, at 1, 2, 6, 16–17 (London: M. Cooper, 1744); 1 John Entick, The General History of the Late War: Containing It's Rise, Progress, and Event in Europe, Asia, Africa, and America 379 (London: Edward Dilly and John Millan, 1763); Cornell, *A New Paradigm for the Second Amendment*, 165.

177. U.S. Const. amend. II; Gowder v. City of Chicago, 2012 WL 2325826 *6 n.3 (N.D. Ill. 2012).

178. State v. Hirsch, 338 Or. 622, 625, 665, 671–72 & nn. 2, 48 (2005); Don B. Kates & Clayton E. Cramer, *Second Amendment Limitations and Criminological Considerations*, 60 Hastings L.J. 1339, 1367–68 (2009); David Thomas Konig, *Thomas Jefferson's Armed Citizenry and the Republican Militia*, 1 Alb. Gov't L. Rev. 250, 260–61 (2008); Cornell, *A New Paradigm for the Second Amendment*, 162–63.

179. Meltsner, Cruel and Unusual, 34 ("By far the most influential European critic of capital punishment was the Italian jurist Cesare Beccaria."); *see also* William J. Novak, The People's Welfare: Law and Regulation in Nineteenth-Century America 308 n.5 (1996) ("Beccaria's *Essay on Crimes and Punishments* (1764) greatly impressed, among others, John Adams, Thomas Jefferson, and Nathaniel Chipman, as well as American criminal law reformers Benjamin Rush, William Roscoe, and Edward Livingston.").

180. Cesare Beccaria, An Essay on Crimes and Punishments 85 (4th ed. 1775).

181. Samuel Parr, A Spital Sermon Preached at Christ Church, upon Easter Tuesday, April 15, 1800, at 145–6 (London: J. Mawman, 1801).

182. U.S. Const., amend. V (ratified Dec. 15, 1791); Ullmann v. United States, 350 U.S. 422, 451–52 (1956) (Douglas, J., dissenting) ("The Beccarian attitude toward infamy was a part of the background of the Fifth Amendment."); id. at 452 ("Beccaria, whose works were well known here and who was particularly well known to Jefferson, was the main voice against the use of infamy as punishment."); *see also* Frederick A.O. Schwarz Jr. & Aziz Z. Huq, Unchecked and Unbalanced: Presidential Power in a Time of Terror (New York: The New Press, 2011), ch. 4 (noting Beccaria's influence on the founders in shaping the Fifth Amendment).

183. Cesare Beccaria, An Essay on Crimes and Punishments 86 (4th ed. 1775).

184. Blair v. Ridgely, 1867 WL 4732 *7 (Mo. 1867) ("The learned Beccaria, after conceding that infamy is a punishment frequently inflicted for the commission of crime, adds the following sensible remarks touching its employment: 'The punishment of infamy should not be too frequent.... '").

185. Levy, *The Right Against Self-Incrimination*, 10.

186. Pippa Holloway, Living in Infamy: Felon Disfranchisement and the History of American Citizenship 4–5 (Oxford: Oxford University Press, 2014).

187. 2 John Nalson, An Impartial Collection of the Great Affairs of State, from the Beginning of the Scotch Rebellion in the Year MDCXXXIX to the Murther of King Charles I, at 199, 571, 574–75, 588–89 (London: Tho. Dring, et al., 1683); Harry Mordaunt, A Modest Defence of Publick Stews: or, An Essay upon Whoring 37 (London: T. Read, 1740).

188. United States v. Balsys, 524 U.S. 666, 674, 685 n.9 (1998); Michigan v. Tucker, 417 U.S. 433, 440 (Mich. 1974); McKune v. Lile, 536 U.S. 24, 56–57 (2002) (Stevens, J., dissenting); State v. Davis,

256 P.3d 1075, 1079–81 (Or. 2011); State v. Rees, 748 A.2d 976, 982 (Me. 2000); John H. Langbein, *The Historical Origins of the Privilege Against Self-Incrimination at Common Law*, 92 Mich. L. Rev. 1047, 1048 (1994); Eben Moglen, *Taking the Fifth: Reconsidering the Origins of the Constitutional Privilege Against Self-Incrimination*, 92 Mich. L. Rev. 1086, 1100–1102 (1994); Vincent Martin Bonventre, *An Alternative to the Constitutional Privilege Against Self-Incrimination*, 49 Brook. L. Rev. 31, 33–34 (1982).

189. Levy, *The Right Against Self-Incrimination*, 6 n.22, 8, 12, 27 n.92; James M. Lawler, ed., Dialectics of the U.S. Constitution: Selected Writings of Mitchell Franklin 144 (2000) ("Jefferson studied Beccaria's discussion of infamy in the Italian text, as his extracts from Beccaria show.").

190. Nathaniel Chipman, Sketches of the Principles of Government 166 (June 1793) ("In the administration of criminal law, the institution of a grand jury has a very leading influence, in a free government. To guard the innocent from the infamy and oppression of a public accusation....").

191. Italian Americana (1976), p. 87.

192. U.S. Const., amend. VIII (ratified Dec. 15, 1791).

193. *On Crimes and Punishments* makes multiple references to the concept of cruelty. Bessler, Cruel and Unusual, 55–56.

194. Bessler, Cruel and Unusual, 174, 177–78; *see also* Schabas, The Death Penalty as Cruel Treatment and Torture, 18 ("A committee chaired by George Mason was entrusted with preparing the document that became the Virginia Bill of Rights. Adopted on June 12, 1776, it was largely inspired by the English Bill of Rights of 1689.").

195. Twenty Essays on Literary and Philosophical Subjects 248 (Dublin: Richard White, 1791) ("[T]he minds of the common people cannot easily, at such a distance of time, connect the punishment with the action that has occasioned it, and are tempted to consider an execution, when it takes place long after the offence committed by the sufferer, rather in the light of a cruel and terrible exhibition, than as the just consequence of a particular violation of the laws of society.") (citing Beccaria, Montesquieu, Blackstone, and Voltaire, among others). Beccaria spoke out against confessions obtained through torture from criminal suspects. Stephen C. Thaman, *A Comparative Approach to Teaching Criminal Procedure and Its Application to the Post-Investigative Stage*, 56 J. Legal Educ. 459, 465 n.33 (2006); David Luban, *Liberalism, Torture, and the Ticking Bomb*, 91 Va. L. Rev. 1425, 1435 (2005).

196. *E.g.*, Bessler, Cruel and Unusual, 52–53, 61, 86, 101, 108–9, 111, 122, 124–25, 130–31, 135–36, 146, 159–60, 181, 183–84, 186, 296, 299, 312, 322; U. M. Rose, "Beccaria and Law Reform," Address Delivered as President of the Arkansas State Bar Ass'n at its Meeting Held at Little Rock on Jan. 3, 1900, *in* George B. Rose, Addresses of U. M. Rose with a Brief Memoir by George B. Rose 207 (Chicago: George I. Jones, 1914) (emphasizing that Beccaria's treatise "has had an immense influence in shaping the laws which at present prevail in all of the civilized countries of the earth").

197. Byron, Crime and Punishment, 59; *Kitty Preyer and Her Books*.

198. Michael Louis Corrado, *Responsibility and Control*, 34 Hofstra L. Rev. 59, 74 n.71 (2005).

199. 3 James Burgh, Political Disquisitions; or, An Enquiry into Public Errors, Defects, and Abuses 125, 168–69 (Philadelphia: Robert Bell and William Woodhouse, 1775); 3 "J. B.," Political Disquisitions; or, An Enquiry into Public Errors, Defects, and Abuses 125, 168–69 (London: Edward and Charles Dilly, 1775).

200. Robert Boyd, The Office, Powers, and Jurisdiction, of His Majesty's Justices of the Peace, and Commissioners of Supply 505 n.5 (Edinburgh: E. Balfour and J. Murray, 1787); 2 Alexander Campbell, A Journey from Edinburgh through Parts of North Britain 93 (London: T. N. Longman and O. Rees, 1802); Bruce C. Baird, "The Social Origins of Dueling in Virginia," *in* Michael A. Bellesiles, ed., Lethal Imagination: Violence and Brutality in American History 87–98 (New York: New York University Press, 1999); Byron, Crime and Punishment, 6, 12 n.15, 21, 23–27, 47–60, 63; Theodore F. T. Plucknett, A Concise History of the Common Law 483 (Union, NJ: The Lawbook Exchange, 5th ed., 2001); Beau Baez III, Tort Law in the USA 68 (The Netherlands: Kluwer Law International, 2010).

201. Diary entry of John Quincy Adams, Aug. 15, 1783, *available at* www.founders.archives.gov.

202. Ian Dowbiggin, A Concise History of Euthanasia: Life, Death, God, and Medicine 33 (Lanham, MD: Rowman & Littlefield, 2007); Diary of John Adams (entry for Jan. 29, 1788), *available at* http://www.masshist.org/publications/apde/portia.php?id=DQA02d689; *see also* 2 A Full Inquiry into the Subject of Suicide 108 (London: J. F. and C. Rivington, 1790) ("The author of an 'Essay on Crimes and Punishments'—the Marquis Beccaria of Milan, has a short chapter (C. xxxii) on the punishment of suicide.").

203. 2 Charles Moore, A Full Inquiry into the Subject of Suicide: To Which Are Added (as Being Closely Connected with the Subject) Two Treatises on Duelling and Gaming 108 (London: J. F. & C. Rivington, 1790) (quoting extensively from Beccaria's chapter on suicide); Lieven Vandekerckhove, On Punishment: The Confrontation of Suicide in Old-Europe 127 (Leuven, Belgium: Leuven University Press,

2000); Norman St. John-Stevas, Life, Death and the Law: Law and Christian Morals in England and the United States 251 (Washington, DC: Beard Books, 2002); Eloise Ellery, Brissot de Warville: A Study in the History of the French Revolution 386 (Boston: Houghton Mifflin Co., 1915); John Adams to Edmund Jenings, Oct. 23, 1780; Jacques-Pierre Brissot de Warville to Benjamin Franklin, Dec. 22, 1781; Liste des Livres de Mr. Franklin, Dec. 31, 1781–Jan. 8, 1782; Brissot de Warville to Benjamin Franklin, Mar. 7, 1782; Thomas Jefferson to Brissot de Warville; Lafayette to Thomas Jefferson, Aug. 30, 1786; Brissot de Warville to Thomas Jefferson, Nov. 10, 1786, *available at* www.founders.archives.gov; *see also* J. P. Brissot de Warville & Etienne Claviere, The Commerce of America with Europe; Particularly with France and Great Britain; Comparatively Stated, and Explained xxi (London: J. S. Jordan, 1794) ("to those persons who have read Beccaria's Essay on Crimes and Punishments, it will not appear that Brissot has added much novelty to the subject"); 2 J. P. Brissot de Warville, New Travels in the United States of America: Including the Commerce of America with Europe; Particularly with France and Great Britain xxi (London, 1794) (same); J. P. Brissot, The Life of J. P. Brissot, Deputy from Eure and Loire, to the National Convention 13 (Dublin: Zachariah Jackson, 1794) ("With the exception of some points, most successfully investigated by *Beccaria* and *Servan*, no writer had, hitherto, considered the whole of these laws under a philosophical point of view. *I* dared to undertake the task; *I* delineated a general plan; and, in the year 1780, my *Theory of Criminal Laws* appeared in two octavo volumes.").

204. 1 Donald T. Critchlow & Philip R. Vandermeer, eds., The Oxford Encyclopedia of American Political and Legal History 62 (Oxford: Oxford University Press, 2012); American College of Legal Medicine, Legal Medicine 315 (Philadelphia: Mosby, 6th ed. 2004); Carol S. Steiker & Jordan M. Steiker, *Cost and Capital Punishment: A New Consideration Transforms an Old Debate*, 2010 U. Chi. Legal F. 117, 126 (2010); Kristina Ebbott, *A "Good Death" Defined by Law: Comparing the Legality of Aid-in-Dying Around the World*, 37 Wm. Mitchell L. Rev. 170, 177 n.51 (2010); Jessie K. Liu, *Victimhood*, 71 Mo. L. Rev. 115, 126 (2006); Melvin I. Urofsky, *Leaving the Door Ajar: The Supreme Court and Assisted Suicide*, 32 U. Rich. L. Rev. 313, 330 (1998); Daniel M. Crone, *Historical Attitudes Toward Suicide*, 35 Duq. L. Rev. 7, 30, 37–38 (1996); Earl A. Groliman, Suicide: Prevention, Intervention, Postvention 16 (Boston: Beacon Press, 1988); Burnett v. People, 68 N.E. 505, 510 (Ill. 1903); Norman St. John-Stevas, Life, Death and the Law: Law and Christian Morals in England and the United States 234, 242, 251 (Washington, DC: Beard Books, 1961); Merrill D. Peterson, Thomas Jefferson and the New Nation: A Biography 128 (Oxford: Oxford University Press, 1970); Elizabeth Price Foley, The Law of Life and Death 156 (Cambridge: The Belknap Press of Harvard University Press, 2011).

205. Henry W. Ruoff, ed., Masters of Achievement: The World's Greatest Leaders in Literature, Art, Religion, Philosophy, Science, Politics and Industry 555 (Buffalo, NY: The Frontier Press Co., 1910).

206. Eve Kornfeld, Creating an American Culture 1775–1800: A Brief History with Documents 120–24 (Boston, MA: Bedford/St. Martin's, 2001); Arthur J. Newman, ed., In Defense of the American Public School 12 (Cambridge, MA: Schenkman Publishing Co., 1978); William J. Reese, America's Public Schools: From the Common School to "No Child Left Behind" 2, 12 (Baltimore, MD: The Johns Hopkins University Press, 2011); Cesare Beccaria, An Essay on Crimes and Punishments 174–75 (4th ed. 1775), *available at* http://archive.org/stream/essayoncrimespun1775becc#page/n3/mode/2up.

207. Joseph Chitty, A Treatise on the Law of the Prerogatives of the Crown and the Relative Duties and Rights of the Subject 88 (London: Joseph Butterworth and Son, 1820).

208. Merrill D. Peterson, Thomas Jefferson and the New Nation: A Biography 126 (Oxford: Oxford University Press, 1970).

209. Paul Leicester Ford, ed., The Writings of Thomas Jefferson: 1784–1787, at 168–69 (New York: G. P. Putnam's Sons, 1894); Guillaume Ansart, ed. & trans., Condorcet: Writings on the United States 10–11, 57 (University Park, PA: Pennsylvania State University Press, 2012).

210. Bessler, Cruel and Unusual, 59–60, 128, 135–37.

211. Brown & Brown, The Hanging of Ephraim Wheeler, 192.

212. 1 Jeremy Belknap, The History of New-Hampshire 403 (Dover: S. C. Stevens and Ela & Wadleigh, 1831); John Farmer, Catechism of the History of New-Hampshire, from Its First Settlement to the Present Period 74 (Concord, NH: Hoag and Atwood, 1830) (noting that after 200 men tried to force New Hampshire's legislature into a paper money system, "[e]ight were arraigned at the superior court on an indictment for *treason*; but no one suffered *capital punishment*").

213. Bessler, Cruel and Unusual, 157, 268; Allyson N. May, The Bar and the Old Bailey, 1750–1850, at 180 (Chapel Hill: University of North Carolina Press, 2003); Shannon M. Barton-Bellessa, ed., Encyclopedia of Community Corrections 24 (Thousand Oaks, CA: SAGE Publications, 2012).

214. L. H. Clarke, A Report of the Debates and Proceedings of the Convention of the State of New-York; Held at the Capitol, in the City of Albany, on the 28th day of August, 1821, at 2, 67–69 (New York: J. Seymour, 1821).

215. William Magnuson, *The Domestic Politics of International Extradition*, 52 Va. J. Int'l L. 839, 849 n.47 (2012).

216. The Town and Country Magazine; or Universal Repository of Knowledge, Instruction, and Entertainment for the Year 1772, Vol. IV, at 99 (London: A. Hamilton, 1772); *see also* Imprisonment for Debt Considered, With Respect to the Bad Policy, Inhumanity, and Evil Tendency of that Practice (London: F. Newbery, 1772).

217. Steven Laurence Kaplan, The Bakers of Paris and the Bread Question 1700–1775, at 394–95 (Durham, NC: Duke University Press, 1996).

218. Josiah Quincy to John Adams, Oct. 25, 1775, *available at* www.founders.archives.gov.

219. Mann, Republic of Debtors, 88, 101, 120, 146–47; Charles Jerome Ware, Legal Consumer Tips and Secrets: Avoiding Debtors' Prison in the United States 179 (Bloomington, IN: iUniverse, 2011).

220. William A. Sullivan, *Philadelphia Labor during the Jackson Era*, 15 Pennsylvania History 305, 313 (Oct. 1948).

221. Mann, Republic of Debtors, 103–105.

222. The National Register (Washington, D.C.), Mar. 15, 1817; Caroline Evensen Lazo, Martin Van Buren 22, 51 (Minneapolis, MN: Lerner Publications Co., 2005).

223. Edmund Randolph's Notes on the Common Law [ca. September] 1799, *available at* www.founders.archives.gov (quoting Madison's notes in an editorial note).

224. Brian McGinty, The Body of John Merryman: Abraham Lincoln and the Suspension of Habeas Corpus 1 (Cambridge: Harvard University Press, 2011); 1 William Cranch, Reports of Cases Argued and Adjudged in the Supreme Court of the United States, in August and December Terms, 1801, and February Term, 1803, at iii–v (New York: C. Wiley, 2d ed. rev. 1812); Bryan A. Garner, Garner on Language and Writing 440 (Chicago, IL: American Bar Association, 2009); Sandra Day O'Connor, Out of Order: Stories from the History of the Supreme Court 56 (New York: Random House, 2013); Henry J. Abraham, Justices, Presidents, and Senators: A History of U.S. Supreme Court Appointments from Washington to Bush II, at 185 (Lanham, MD: Rowman & Littlefield, 5th ed. 2008); Thomas Jefferson to Philip Mazzei, Nov. 1785; Thomas Jefferson to John B. Colvin, Sept. 20, 1810, *available at* www.founders.archives.gov.

225. Bessler, Cruel and Unusual, 170.

226. U.S. Const., amends. IX & X; Griswold v. Connecticut, 381 U.S. 479 (1965); Roe v. Wade, 410 U.S. 113 (1973); Lawrence v. Texas, 539 U.S. 558 (2003); Robert A. Licht, ed., The Framers and Fundamental Rights 37, 128 (Lanham, MD: American Enterprise Institute, 1991).

227. Peter S. Du Ponceau, A Dissertation on the Nature and Extent of the Courts of the United States (Philadelphia: Abraham Small, 1824); James Madison to Peter Du Ponceau, Aug. 1824, *available at* The James Madison Papers, www.memory.loc.gov; A Collection of Cases Decided by the General Court of Virginia, Chiefly Relating to the Penal Laws of the Commonwealth Commencing in the Year 1789, and Ending in 1814, at 24, 33, 35–36, 40, 45, 48, 56, 59–60, 66, 70–74 (Philadelphia: James Webster, 1815); 3 The Works of Sir William Temple, Bart 56 (London: J. Clark, et al. 1757): *accord* 3 The History of the Works of the Learned: or, An Impartial Account of Books Lately Printed in all Parts of Europe 636 (London: H. Rhodes, et al. 1701) ("That for the more Effectual suppression of Thefts and Robberies, it would be proper to change the usual Punishment by short and easie Deaths, into some others of painful and uneasie Lives, which they will find much harder to bear, and be more unwilling and afraid to suffer than the other.").

228. The Concise of Encyclopedia of Crime and Criminals 201 (New York: Hawthorn Books, 1961); Joel Samaha, Criminal Law 31 (Belmont, CA: Thomson Wadsworth, 9th ed. 2008); D. Scott Broyles, Criminal Law in the USA 42 (Dordrecht, The Netherlands: Kluwer Law International, 2011); Wilbur R. Miller, ed., The Social History of Crime and Punishment in America: An Encyclopedia 994 (Thousand Oaks, CA: SAGE, 2012); Lydialyle Gibson, *Going Dutch*, The Univ. of Chi. Mag. 42, 44 (Nov./Dec. 2013).

229. 6 Gaillard Hunt, ed., The Writings of James Madison 379–80 (New York: G. P. Putnam's Sons, 1906); The Report of 1800, [7 January] 1800, *available at* www.founders.archives.gov.

230. Edmund Randolph's Notes on the Common Law [ca. September] 1799, *available at* www.founders.archives.gov.

231. 7 Justin Winsor, ed., Narrative and Critical History of America 296 (Boston: Houghton, Mifflin and Co., 1888); Catalogue of the Library of the United States Senate 443 (Washington, DC: Government Printing Office, 1910).

232. Bernard S. Katz & C. Daniel Vencill, eds., Biographical Dictionary of the United States Secretaries of the Treasury 1789–1995, at 304–05 (Westport, CT: Greenwood Press, 1996); Bessler, Cruel and Unusual, 148.

233. 1 A Digest of the Reports of the United States Courts, and of the Acts of Congress xix (New York: Diossy & Co., 1871); 2 House Reports (Public), 66th Congress, 2d Session (December 1, 1919–June 5, 1920), at 3 (Washington, DC: Government Printing Office, 1920); Ellen Frankel Paul, Fred D. Miller, Jr. & Jeffrey Paul, eds., Natural Rights: Liberalism from Locke to Nozick 28 (Cambridge: Cambridge University Press, 2005); Randy Howe, ed., The Quotable John Adams 270 (Guilford, CT: The Lyons Press, 2008); Thomas Jefferson to Roger C. Weightman, June 24, 1826; Roger C. Weightman to Thomas Jefferson, 12 Oct. 1811, *available at* www.founders.archives.gov.

234. Peter S. Du Ponceau, An Address Delivered at the Opening of the Law Academy of Philadelphia, Before the Trustees and Members of the Society for the Promotion of Legal Knowledge, in the Hall of the Supreme Court, on Wednesday, the 21st of February, 1821.

235. "First Law School in America," 24 Lancaster L. Rev. 63 (1907); Daniel J. Kornstein, Partial Verdicts: Essays on Law and Life 347–50 (Bloomington, IN: AuthorHouse, 2008); Marian C. McKenna, Tapping Reeve and the Litchfield Law School 40 (Oceana Publications, 1986); Mark L. Jones, *Fundamental Dimensions of Law and Legal Education: An Historical Framework—A History of U.S. Legal Education Phase I: From the Founding of the Republic Until the 1860s*, 39 J. Marshall L. Rev. 1041, 1063–69 (2006).

236. 2 S. Austin Allibone, A Critical Dictionary of English Literature and British and American Authors Living and Deceased 1893 (Philadelphia: J. B. Lippincott, 1899).

237. Bessler, Cruel and Unusual, 92; Alfred W. McCoy & Francisco A. Scarano, Colonial Crucible: Empire in the Making of the Modern American State 89 (Madison: University of Wisconsin Press, 2009); The Professional Protection Officer: Practical Security Strategies and Emerging Trends 437 (Burlington, MA: Butterworth-Heinemann, 2010); 9 Stephen Conway, ed., The Collected Works of Jeremy Bentham: The Correspondence of Jeremy Bentham (January 1817 to June 1820) 116, 129, 137–38, 409 (New York: Oxford University Press, 1989); Jeremy Bentham to Alexander I, czar of Russia, Jan. 1814 & Translation from Spanish into English of Toribio Núñez to Jeremy Bentham, Dec. 20, 1821, *available at* Electronic Enlightenment, Electronic Enlightenment Project, Bodleian Libraries, University of Oxford, www.e-enlightenment.com.

238. 1 Charles Warren, The Supreme Court in United States History 439 (Boston: Little, Brown, and Co., 1922).

239. Richard Rush Papers, 1812–1847, Box 1, The Historical Society of Pennsylvania.

240. The Annual Report of the Library Company of Philadelphia for the Year 1969, at 25–26 (Philadelphia: The Library Company of Philadelphia, 1970); Negley K. Teeters & Jack H. Hedblom, "… Hang by the Neck …": The Legal Use of Scaffold and Noose, Gibbet, Stake, and Firing Squad from Colonial Times to the Present 286 (Springfield, IL: Charles C. Thomas, 1967); Richard S. Newman, Freedom's Prophet: Bishop Richard Allen, the AME Church, and the Black Founding Fathers 151–53, 200 (New York: New York University Press, 2008).

241. Richard Rush Papers, 1812–1847, Box 1, The Historical Society of Pennsylvania.

242. 23 The Encyclopaedia Britannica: A Dictionary of Arts, Sciences, Literature and General Information 857 (11th ed. 1911).

243. Richard Rush, Memorandum of a Residence at the Court of London 75–76, 344–50, 490–94 (2d ed. 1833).

244. 4 John Bowring, comp., The Works of Jeremy Bentham 467–68, 507–514 (Edinburgh: William Tait, 1838) (citing Jeremy Bentham to James Madison, Oct. 1811; James Madison to Jeremy Bentham, May 8, 1816 & Jeremy Bentham to James Madison, Sept. 1817); William Twining, ed., Bentham: Selected Writings of John Dinwiddy 22 (Stanford, CA: Stanford University Press, 2004); Everett S. Brown, *Jeremy Bentham, 1748–1832*, 55 Mich. Alumnus Q. Rev. 55, 61 (1948).

245. Henry Adams, The Life of Albert Gallatin 84 (Philadelphia: J. B. Lippincott & Co., 1879); 4 John Bowring, comp., The Works of Jeremy Bentham 467–75, 479, 514, 573 (Edinburgh: William Tait, 1838); Philip Schofield, Utility and Democracy: The Political Thought of Jeremy Bentham 243–44 (Oxford: Oxford University Press, 2006).

246. Bhikhu Parekh, Jeremy Bentham: Critical Assessments 287–90 (London: Routledge, 1993).

247. John Milton Goodenow, Historical Sketches of the Principles and Maxims of American Jurisprudence: In Contrast with the Doctrines of English Common Law on the Subject of Crimes and Punishments 160, 339, 399–400 (New York: Arno Press, 1972) (1819); Kunal M. Parker, Common Law, History, and Democracy in America, 1790–1900: Legal Thought Before Modernism 103 (Cambridge: Cambridge University Press, 2011); *Goodenow, John Milton (1782–1838)*, www.bioguide.congress.gov; *John Milton Goodenow*, www.supremecourt.ohio.gov/SCO/formerjustices/bios/goodenow.asp.

248. Hartnett, Executing Democracy, ch. 2, n. 3; Hunt, Life of Edward Livingston, 352–53.

249. United States v. Hudson, 11 U.S. 32 (1812); David L. Hudson Jr., The Handy Supreme Court Answer Book 95 (Canton, MI: Visible Ink Press, 2008); Jack David & Robert B. McKay, eds., The Blessings of Liberty: An Enduring Constitution in a Changing World 15 (New York: Random House, 1989); 1 G. Edward White, Law in American History: From the Colonial Years Through the Civil War 231–32 (Oxford: Oxford University Press, 2012); Kermit L. Hall, ed., The Oxford Companion to the Supreme Court of the United States 984 (Oxford: Oxford University Press, 2d ed. 2005).

250. George C. Holt, "The Defects of the United States Criminal Law," in 53 The Independent (New York), Sept. 26, 1901; Crimes Act of 1825, 18th Cong., Sess. II, ch. 65 (approved Mar. 3, 1825); Robert V. Remini, Daniel Webster, The Man and His Time 119 (New York: W. W. Norton & Co., 1997); 1 Charles Richmond Henderson, ed., Correction and Prevention 16–17 (New York: Charities Publication Committee, 1910); The Roosevelt Panama Libel Case against the New York World and Indianapolis News 94–95 (New York: The New York World, 1910).

251. Bessler, Cruel and Unusual, 186; Biographical Dictionary of the United States Congress 1774–2005, at 1014 (Washington, DC: U.S. Government Printing Office, 2005); U.S. House of Representatives, Dec. 27, 1824 & Jan. 7, 10, 24–25, 1825, Gales & Seaton's Register, pp. 59–60, 152–58, 165–68, 188–89, 335–41, 348–56, 363–65, reprinted in 1 Register of Debates in Congress, Comprising the Leading Debates and Incidents of the Second Session of the Eighteenth Congress (Washington, DC: Gales & Seaton, 1825). The distinguished lawyers Henry Clay and John J. Crittenden—the latter of whom served as the United States Attorney General—later teamed up to defend a different Charles Wickliffe, a young man put on trial in Kentucky in 1829 for killing the editor of the Kentucky Gazette in Lexington. Robert Wickliffe, the boy's father, had been running for office when his opponent published a defamatory article in the Gazette over the signature "Dentatus." When the editor declined to identify the author, an altercation ensued, and a young Charles Wickliffe shot and killed the editor. The defense successfully put on by Clay and Crittenden was excusable homicide premised on self-defense. After his acquittal, the hot-headed Charles Wickliffe was later killed in a duel by George Trotter, the editor of the Gazette who had succeeded the editor that Wickliffe had shot and killed. John J. Crittenden: The Struggle for the Union 38 (Westport, CT: Greenwood Press, 1974); 1 Calvin Colton, ed., Works of Henry Clay: Comprising His Life, Correspondence and Speeches 112–15 (New York: Henry Clay Publishing Co., 1896).

252. 1 Sydney George Fisher, The Struggle for American Independence 25–26 (Philadelphia: J. B. Lippincott Co., 1908); Clorinda Donato, ed., The Letters of Fortunato Bartolomeo De Felice to Pietro Verri, 107 MLN 74, 77, 92, 108 (1992) (published by The Johns Hopkins University Press).

253. Jackson Turner Main, The Anti-Federalists: Critics of the Constitution, 1781–1788, at 80 n.25 (Chapel Hill: University of North Carolina Press, 1961); John P. Kaminski & Gaspare J. Saladino, The Documentary History of the Ratification of the Constitution: Ratification of the Constitution by the States: New York 10, 115 (State Historical Society of Wisconsin, 2003); Abraham Yates, Jr., American National Biography, http://www.nysm.nysed.gov/albany/bios/y/ayjranb.html.

254. Richard Hey, Observations on the Nature of Civil Liberty, and the Principles of Government 35–36 (London: T. Cadell, 1776).

255. Sipe, Cesare Beccaria, 31.

256. Letters from the Federal Farmer, No. 7, 31 Dec. 1787, available at http://oll.libertyfund.org.

257. Richard Henry Lee, Life of Arthur Lee, LL.D. 157–159 (Boston: Wells and Lilly, 1829).

258. D. Scott Broyles, Criminal Law in the USA 42 (The Netherlands: Kluwer Law International, 2011); Benjamin N. Cardozo, Judicial Process 58–59 (New Haven: Yale University Press, 1921); 3 John Bach McMaster, A History of the People of the United States, from the Revolution to the Civil War 417–18 (New York: D. Appleton and Co., 1892); Orrin K. McMurray, Foreign Influences in English and American Law, 23 Case and Comment 531, 533 (Dec. 1916).

259. The Whig Almanac and United States Register 54 (1850); Alexander Hadden, Why Are There No Common Law Crimes in Ohio? (The Cleveland Law Library Association, 1919).

260. Bessler, Cruel and Unusual, 121.

261. 14 Princeton Review 332–33 (Apr. 1842) (reprinting legislative report).

262. U.S. Const., amend. V.

263. Henry J. Young, Treason and Its Punishment in Revolutionary Pennsylvania, The Pennsylvania Magazine of History and Biography, July 1966, pp. 287–313; Paul S. Clarkson & R. Samuel Jett, Luther Martin of Maryland 44 (Stoughton, WI: Books on Demand, 1987) ("To check the Tory depredations, particularly on the Eastern Shore, the Maryland General Assembly in 1777 decreed the death penalty for any person levying war against either the state or the Continental Congress.").

264. Lawrence M. Friedman, Crime and Punishment in American History 71 (New York: Basic

Books, 1993); Obi N. I. Ebbe, ed., Comparative and International Criminal Justice Systems: Policing, Judiciary, and Corrections 42 (Boca Raton, FL: CRC Press, 3d ed. 2013); Robert A. Katzmann, ed., Judges and Legislators: Toward Institutional Comity 50 (Washington, DC: The Brookings Institution, 1988); An Act for the Punishment of Certain Crimes against the United States, Apr. 30, 1790, 1 Stat. 112.

265. Tim Sample & Steve Bither, Maine Curiosities: Quirky Characters, Roadside Oddities & Other Offbeat Stuff 192 (Guilford, CT: The Globe Pequot Press, 2d ed. 2006); Bessler, Cruel and Unusual, 131–32.

266. 2 William A. Richardson, ed., Supplement to the Revised Statutes of the United States: Legislation of the Fifty-Fourth Congress, First Session 538 (Washington, DC: Government Printing Office (1896); Winston v. United States, 172 U.S. 303 (1899).

267. Erik Eckholm, *In Death Penalty's Steady Decline, Some Experts See a Societal Shift,* N.Y. Times, Dec. 19, 2013, p. A23.

268. People ex rel. Colorado Bar Ass'n v. Irwin, 152 P. 905, 908 (Colo. 1915) (quoting Blackstone's reference to Beccaria's principle); Eureka County Bank Habeas Corpus Cases, 126 P. 655, 661 (Nev. 1912) (referencing Beccaria's certainty principle); Ex parte Smith, 111 P. 930, 936 (Nev. 1910) (same); Ex parte Davis, 110 P. 1131, 1134 (Nev. 1910) (same); Ex parte Rickey, 100 P. 134, 141 (Nev. 1909); Ex parte Deidesheimer, No. 990, 1879 WL 3488 *4 (Nev. 1879).

269. 1885 WL 7316 *26 (1885).

270. 2 Charles W. Upham, The Life of Timothy Pickering 434 (Boston: Little, Brown, and Co., 1873).

271. 1 Thomas Jefferson Randolph, ed., Memoirs, Correspondence, and Private Papers of Thomas Jefferson, Late President of the United States 127 & n.* (London: Henry Colburn & Richard Bentley, 1829).

272. U.S. Const. amends. V, VI and VIII.

273. Declaration of Independence (July 4, 1776).

274. Kate Stith & José A. Cabranes, Fear of Judging: Sentencing Guidelines in the Federal Courts 200 n.33 (Chicago: The University of Chicago Press, 1998); John Henry Merryman & Rogelio Pérez-Perdomo, The Civil Law Tradition: An Introduction to the Legal Systems of Europe and Latin America 125 (Stanford, CA: Stanford University Press, 3d ed. 2007); Michael Willrich, City of Courts: Socializing Justice in Progressive Era Chicago 71 (Cambridge: Cambridge University Press, 2003); Melvin I. Urofsky, A March of Liberty: A Constitutional History of the United States 156 (New York: Alfred A. Knopf, 1998).

275. Amnesty International, Death Sentences and Executions 2012 (2013), pp. 5–6.

276. 2 William S. Laufer & Freda Adler, eds., Advances in Criminological Theory 10–11 (New Brunswick, NJ: Transaction Publishers, 1990); International Covenant on Civil and Political Rights, December 16, 1996, 999 UNTS 171, entered into force March 23, 1976 (ratified by the United States on September 8, 1992); Schabas, The Abolition of the Death Penalty in International Law, 43; Mary Ann Glendon, A World Made New: Eleanor Roosevelt and the Universal Declaration of Rights xv (New York: Random House, 2002); Universal Declaration of Human Rights, arts. 1, 3.

277. Elizabeth Rapaport, *A Modest Proposal: The Aged of Death Row Should Be Deemed Too Old to Execute*, 77 Brook. L. Rev. 1089, 1114 (2012).

278. *See* Cesare Beccaria, An Essay on Crimes and Punishments 74 (4th ed. 1775) ("The more immediately after the commission of a crime, a punishment is inflicted, the more just and useful it will be. It will be more just, because it spares the criminal the cruel and superfluous torment of uncertainty….").

279. David Von Drehle, Report: Death Penalty Use and Support Is Dropping, TIME, Dec. 21, 2010, http://www.time.com/time/nation/article/0,8599,2039273,00.html.

280. George Pellew, John Jay 98–99 (Boston: Houghton, Mifflin and Co., 1895).

281. Bessler, Cruel and Unusual, 142.

282. Christopher Waldrep, Roots of Disorder: Race and Criminal Justice in the American South, 1817–80, at 105 (Champaign: University of Illinois Press, 1998); 1 West Virginia Governor's Message Submitted to the Legislature of 1907 with the Accompanying Reports and Documents Covering the Two Fiscal Years Oct. 1, 1904 to Sept. 30, 1906 (1907).

283. *See, e.g.,* Jason Parkin, *Adaptable Due Process*, 160 U. Penn. L. Rev. 1309 (2012).

284. Joyce Appleby & Terence Ball, eds., Jefferson: Political Writings 51–53 (Cambridge: Cambridge University Press, 1999).

285. Paul Zummo, Thomas Jefferson's America: Democracy, Progress, and the Quest for Perfection, Ph.D. dissertation, Catholic University of America, Washington, D.C. (2008), p. 117; Joyce Appleby & Terence Ball, eds., Jefferson: Political Writings 385 (Cambridge: Cambridge University Press, 1999).

286. Lilian Chenwi, Towards the Abolition of the Death Penalty in Africa: A Human Rights Perspective 91–92, 122–38 (Pretoria: Pretoria University Law Press, 2007); Bessler, Cruel and Unusual, 228; Schabas, The Death Penalty as Cruel Treatment and Torture, 125.

Conclusion

1. David Johnston, A Brief History of Justice 233 (West Sussex, UK: Wiley-Blackwell, 2011).

2. 1 J. Mitchell Miller, ed., 21st Century Criminology: A Reference Handbook 11 (Thousand Oaks, CA: SAGE Publications, 2009) ("The drafters of the U.S. Constitution were greatly influenced by Beccaria; the sections of the Bill of Rights that address crime and justice in particular reflect his principles and guidelines.").

3. Joseph L. Esposito, Pragmatism, Politics, and Perversity: Democracy and the American Party Battle (Lanham, MD: Lexington Books, 2012).

4. Patrick J. Charles, Restoring "Life, Liberty, and the Pursuit of Happiness," *in* Our Constitutional Jurisprudence: An Exercise in Legal History, 20 Wm. & Mary Bill of Rts. J. 457, 474–75 (2011).

5. Sellers, American Republicanism, 20–21.

6. Jackson J. Spielvogel, Western Civilization 127 (Boston, MA: Wadsworth, 8th ed., 2012).

7. Alvin Rabushka, Taxation in Colonial America 752–55 (Princeton: Princeton University Press, 2008).

8. Thomas, On Crimes and Punishments, 9; Carl J. Richard, The Founders and the Classics: Greece, Rome, and the American Enlightenment 77–78 (Cambridge: Harvard University Press, 1994).

9. Leonard W. Levy, Seasoned Judgments: The American Constitution, Rights, and History 16–17 (New Brunswick, NJ: Transaction Publishers, 1997); John R. Vile, The Men Who Made the Constitution: Lives of the Delegates to the Constitutional Convention of 1787, at 348 (Lanham, MD: Scarecrow Press, 2013). Sir William Blackstone, in his *Commentaries on the Laws of England*, wrote "that man should pursue his own happiness." Likewise, Richard Bland, a Virginia delegate to the Continental Congress, cited Wollaston's use of "pursuit of happiness" in his 1766 *Inquiry into the Rights of the British Colonies*, with early Americans seeking their own path to happiness.

10. John Adams to the President of Congress, Oct. 25, 1781, *available at* www.founders.archives.gov.

11. Pace, Luigi Castiglioni's Viaggo, 313–14.

12. Teeters, The Cradle of the Penitentiary, 29; George S. Bridges, Joseph G. Weis & Robert D. Crutchfield, eds., Criminal Justice: Readings 383 (Thousand Oaks, CA: SAGE Publications, 1996); Katy Ryan, ed., Demands of the Dead: Executions, Storytelling, and Activism in the United States 146 (Iowa City: University of Iowa Press, 2012); Robert Jay Lifton & Greg Mitchell, Who Owns Death? Capital Punishment, the American Conscience, and the End of Executions 28 (New York: HarperCollins, 2002); 3 The Philomathic Journal, and Literary Review 319 (1825).

13. Harry Hayden Clark, ed., Thomas Paine: Representative Selections xcvii (New York: American Book, 1944); Rush, Essays, Literary, Moral and Philosophical, 140, 158 (reprinting "An Enquiry into the Effects of Public Punishments upon Criminals, and upon Society," read at the Society for Promoting Political Enquiries, convened at the house of Benjamin Franklin in Philadelphia on March 9, 1787).

14. Merrill Jensen, The Articles of Confederation: An Interpretation of the Social-Constitutional History of the American Revolution 1774–1781, at 249 (Madison: University of Wisconsin Press, 1940); 6 Journals of the Continental Congress 1774–1789, at 1123 (Washington, DC: Government Printing Office, 1906); Duncan Watts, Dictionary of American Government and Politics 13 (Edinburgh: Edinburgh University Press, 2010); J. H. Schooler, A Complete Analysis of American History with Especial Reference to the Political Institutions of the United States 74 (Newark, OH: Advocate Printing Co., 1903); Karen Price Hossell, The Articles of Confederation 16 (Chicago, IL: Heinemann Library, 2004).

15. 2 Marshall, The History of Kentucky, 238.

16. 2 William Guthrie, A New System of Modern Geography: or, A Geographical, Historical, and Commercial Grammar 442 (Philadelphia: Matthew Carey, 1795).

17. Jeffrey A. Smith, Franklin & Bache: Envisioning the Enlightened Republic 92 (Oxford: Oxford University Press, 1990); Gordon S. Wood, The Americanization of Benjamin Franklin 216 (New York: Penguin Books, 2005); 3 W. Bernard Peach, ed., The Correspondence of Richard Price (February 1786–February 1791) 129 nn.1–2 (Durham, NC: Duke University Press, 1994); 1 Frank Warren Crow, The Age of Promise: Societies for Social and Economic Improvement in the United States, 1783–1815,

at 74 (University of Wisconsin, 1952).

18. Rush, Essays, Literary, Moral and Philosophical, 158.

19. Rexford Newcomb, *The Evolution of the Prison Plan—Part II*, American Architect, Vol. 110 (1917), p. 277; *see also* Rexford Newcomb, *The Evolution of the Prison Plan—Part I*, American Architect, Vol. 110 (1916), p. 244 ("While Beccaria was fighting for revised penal legislation in Italy and France, John Howard, in England, was beginning prison reform.").

20. Peter S. Du Ponceau, A Dissertation on the Nature and Extent of the Courts of the United States (Philadelphia: Abraham Small, 1824).

21. Commonwealth v. Deacon, 1823 WL 2218 *4 (Pa. 1823); *see also* 2 William Draper Lewis, ed., Great American Lawyers: A History of the Legal Profession in America 159 (Philadelphia: The John C. Winston Co., 1907) (noting that William Tilghman, the chief justice of Pennsylvania's supreme court, "laboriously" studied and then cited "the Marquis of Beccaria," among others, "in the case of Commonwealth vs. Deacon").

22. Thomas, On Crimes and Punishments, 9, 15, 68, 71, 79; Mortimer Sellers, "An Introduction to the Rule of Law in Comparative Perspective" & Aniceto Masferrer, "The Liberal State and Criminal Law Reform in Spain," *in* Mortimer Sellers & Tadeusz Tomaszewski, eds., The Rule of Law in Comparative Perspective 2–4, 27, 31 (Dordrecht, The Netherlands: Springer, 2010); Robert M. Buffington, Criminal and Citizen in Modern Mexico 12 (Lincoln: University of Nebraska Press, 2000); Brissot de Warville to Thomas Jefferson, Nov. 10, 1786; Thomas Jefferson to William Carmichael, Dec. 26, 1786; Miguel de Lardizábal y Uribe to Thomas Jefferson, Jan. 17, 1787; William Carmichael to Thomas Jefferson, May 29, 1788; Thomas Jefferson to William Carmichael, June 3, 1788; William Carmichael to Thomas Jefferson, July 24, 1788, *available at* www.founders.archives.gov.

23. William MacGillivray, A History of the Molluscous Animals of Scotland, and Found in the North-Eastern District, Particularly in the Shires of Aberdeen, Kincardine, and Banff 24, 35 (London: H. G. Bohn, 2d ed. 1844) (describing the "*Rotália Beccárii*" as a "Shell orbicular, depressed, convex above; of four or five obliquely lobate turns, the last with about twelve lobes. Named after Beccaria, an Italian philosopher.").

24. "The History of Rush Township," http://www.rushtownship.com/rushtownshiphistory.html; Lewis Cass Aldrich, ed., History of Clearfield County, Pennsylvania 70–71, 444 (Syracuse, NY: D. Mason & Co., 1887); *accord* John F. Meginness, History of the Great Island and William Dunn, Its Owner, and Founder of Dunnstown 180–81 (Williamsport, PA: Gazette and Bulletin Printing House, 1894).

25. The Annual: Bradford County Historical Society 30–31 (Towanda, PA: Bradford Star Print, 1912); *see also* Henry C. Bradsby, History of Bradford County, Pennsylvania: With Biographical Selections 191–92, 201 (Chicago: S. B. Nelson & Co., 1891).

26. Ezekiel v. Dixon, 1847 WL 1321 *7 (Ga. 1847).

27. Bessler, *Revisiting Beccaria's Vision*, 284–85.

28. U.S. Constitution, Art. I, §§ 2, 9.

29. U.S. Const., amends. XIII, XIV & XV; Frederick Douglass on Slavery and the Civil War 42 (Mineola, NY: Dover Publications, 2003); Thomas, On Crimes and Punishments, 82.

30. Joseph A. Melusky & Keith A. Pesto, eds., Cruel and Unusual Punishments: Rights and Liberties under the Law 143 (Santa Barbara, CA: ABC-CLIO, 2003); Facts about the Death Penalty, Death Penalty Information Center, Feb. 27, 2014; http://www.deathpenaltyinfo.org/dpic-death-penalty-county-underscores-geographic-disparities; http://www.fbi.gov/about-us/cjis/ucr/crime-in-the-u.s/2012/crime-in-the-u.s.-2012/tables/4tabledatadecoverviewpdf/table_4_crime_in_the_united_states_by_region_geographic_division_and_state_2011-2012.xls.

31. Paul Finkelman, Slavery and the Founders: Race and Liberty in the Age of Jefferson 190 (Armonk, NY: M. E. Sharpe, 2d ed. 2001); Garland, Peculiar Institution; U.S. Const., amends. XV (ratified Feb. 3, 1870) & XIX (ratified Aug. 18, 1920); Voting Rights Act of 1965, 42 U.S.C. §§ 1973–1973aa-6.

32. Harry M. Ward, War for Independence and the Transformation of American Society 240 (London: Routledge, 1999).

33. George W. Wickersham, "The Parole of United States Prisoners," p. 223, *in* Proceedings of the Annual Congress of the American Prison Association (Indianapolis: Wm. B. Burford, 1911).

34. Robert W. Dumond, *The Impact of Prisoner Sexual Violence: Challenges of Implementing Public Law 108-79—The Prison Rape Elimination Act of 2003*, 32 J. Legis. 142, 145 (2006).

35. John D. Bessler, *The "Midnight Assassination Law" and Minnesota's Anti-Death Penalty Movement, 1849–1911*, 22 Wm. Mitchell L. Rev. 577 (1996).

36. Bessler, Cruel and Unusual, 102–03; David A. Adler, B. Franklin, Printer 115 (New York: Holiday House, 2001); John Adams to Horatio Gates, Apr. 27, 1776, *available at* www.founders.archives.gov.

37. Peter S. Du Ponceau, A Dissertation on the Nature and Extent of the Jurisdiction of the Courts

of the United States (Philadelphia: Abraham Small, 1824).

38. Thomas Paine, Rights of Man: Being an Answer to Mr. Burke's Attack on the French Revolution 33–36 (London: J. S. Jordan, 7th ed. 1791).

39. Bessler, Cruel and Unusual, 151; S. Jill Miller, The ABC's of the Underground Railroad: The Secret Code Revealed 69 (Bloomington, IN: AuthorHouse, 2009).

40. "The Old Supreme Court Chamber 1810–1860," United States Senate, S. Pub. 106–12; http://www.senate.gov/artandhistory/art/artifact/Sculpture_25_00001.htm.

41. John R. Vile, The Constitutional Convention of 1787: A Comprehensive Encyclopedia of America's Founding 681 (Santa Barbara, CA: ABC-CLIO, 2005).

42. Jeanne Fogle, Washington, D.C.: A Pictorial Celebration 22 (New York: Sterling Publishing Co., 2005); Anne Hempstead, The Supreme Court 14 (Chicago, IL: Heinemann, 2006); Kermit L. Hall, ed., The Oxford Companion to the Supreme Court of the United States 890 (Oxford: Oxford University Press, 2d ed., 2005); "Courtroom Friezes: East and West Walls," Office of the Curator, Supreme Court of the United States.

43. "Courtroom Friezes: South and North Walls," Office of the Curator, Supreme Court of the United States.

44. Thomas, On Crimes and Punishments, 13–14, 70.

45. Samuel J. Harrison to Gibson & Jefferson, 16 July 1809, *available at* www.founders.archives.gov.

46. Alan Pell Crawford, Twilight at Monticello: The Final Years of Thomas Jefferson 87 (New York: Random House, 2008); Henry Wiencek, Master of Monticello, Smithsonian 46–49, 92, 95 (Oct. 2012); Thomas Jefferson to Caleb Lownes, Dec. 18, 1793; Thomas Jefferson to James Lyle, July 10, 1795 & Thomas Jefferson to Reuben Perry, Apr. 16, 1812, *available at* www.founders.archives.gov.

47. Anonymous to James Madison, 27 September 1815, *available at* www.founders.archives.gov.

48. Thomas Jefferson to William G. Munford, June 18, 1799; Pace, Luigi Castiglioni's Viaggio, xxxiv, 11, 23, 19, 23, 26–27, 33, 96–97, 111, 164–65, 194–95; Steven A. Epstein, Speaking of Slavery: Color, Ethnicity, & Human Bondage 51–54 (Ithaca, NY: Cornell University Press, 2001); "About Harvard," Harvard University, http://www.harvard.edu/harvard-glance.

49. Paul K. Saint-Amour, The Copywrights: Intellectual Property and the Literary Imagination 125 (Ithaca, NY: Cornell University Press, 2003); John P. Kaminski, ed., Citizen Jefferson: The Wit and Wisdom of an American Sage 85 (Lanham, MD: Rowman & Littlefield, 2006); Peter Stephen Du Ponceau, A Dissertation on the Nature and Extent of the Jurisdiction of the Courts of the United States, Being a Valedictory Address Delivered to the Students of the Law Academy of Philadelphia, at the Close of the Academic Year, on the 22nd April, 1824 (Philadelphia: Abraham Small, 1824), p. 60 (quoted in Jennifer Denise Henderson, "A Blaze of Reputation and the Echo of a Name": The Legal Career of Peter Stephen Du Ponceau in Post-Revolutionary Philadelphia, M.A. thesis, Florida State University, College of Arts and Sciences, p. 96 (2004)); Hoeflich, *Translation & the Reception of Foreign Law*, 770 (noting that when Peter Du Ponceau's library was sold after his death in 1844, a copy of a translation of Beccaria was among the books).

50. American National Biography Online, www.anb.org (listing for "Bellini, Carlo (c. 1735–June 1804)"); Course of Reading for William G. Munford, 5 Dec. 1798; Thomas Jefferson to William G. Munford, 27 Feb. 1799, *available at* www.founders.archives.gov.

51. Travis C. Pratt, Travis W. Franklin & Jacinta M. Gau, Key Ideas in Criminology and Criminal Justice xi (Thousand Oaks, CA: SAGE Publications, 2011).

52. John Adams, History of the Dispute with America, from Its Origin in 1754, Written in the Year 1774 (London: J. Stockdale, 1784); *see also* Thomas Day, Reflexions upon the Present of England, and the Independence of America (London: J. Stockdale, 2d ed. 1782) (advertising the book by "M. Dawes, Esq." *An Essay on Crimes and Punishments, with a View of and Commentary upon Beccaria, Rousseau, Voltaire, Montesquieu, Fielding, and Blackstone*).

53. Irving Brant, The Bill of Rights: Its Origins and Meaning 32–33 (Indianapolis, IN: Bobbs Merrill, 1965).

54. James Simpson, Necessity of Popular Education, as a National Object; with Hints on the Treatment of Criminals, and Observations on Homicidal Insanity 179 n.† (Boston: Marsh, Capen & Lyon, 1834). "The humane and profound Beccaria, a century ago," Simpson wrote, "denounced capital punishment *in toto*, and so much *shocked* an unprepared age, that he concealed his name." Id. at 203.

55. Thomas Banchoff, "Human Rights, the Catholic Church, and the Death Penalty in the United States," *in* Thomas Banchoff & Robert Wuthnow, eds., Religion and the Global Politics of Human Rights 289 (Oxford: Oxford University Press, 2011).

56. Donald W. Jackson, Michael C. Tolley & Mary L. Volcansek, eds., Globalizing Justice: Criti-

cal Perspectives on Transnational Law and the Cross-Border Migration of Legal Norms 99 n.40 (Albany: State University of New York Press, 2010).

57. 1 Paul Finkelman, ed., Encyclopedia of American Civil Liberties 223 (New York: Routledge, 2006); Alan W. Clarke, Rendition to Torture 38–40 (Piscataway, NJ: Rutgers University Press, 2012).

58. U.N. Convention against Torture and Other Cruel, Inhuman or Degrading Treatment or Punishment, 10 Dec. 1984, A/RES/39/46; Estelle v. Gamble, 429 U.S. 97, 102 (1976); *see also* Furman v. Georgia, 408 U.S. 238, 319 (1972) (Marshall, J., concurring) ("our Founding Fathers intended to outlaw torture and other cruel punishments").

59. John W. Palmer, Constitutional Rights of Prisoners 40–44 (New Providence, NJ: Matthew Bender & Co., 9th ed. 2010); William M. Oliver & James F. Hilgenberg, Jr., A History of Crime and Criminal Justice in America 103, 300 (Durham, NC: Carolina Academic Press, 2d ed. 2010).

60. *Facts about the Death Penalty*, Death Penalty Info. Ctr., Dec. 12, 2013, at 1. In 2011, 21 countries were known to have carried out executions and, in that year, at least 63 nations imposed death sentences. "Figures on the Death Penalty," Amnesty International, *available at* http://www.amnesty.org/en/death-penalty/numbers.

61. Caroline Robbins, *The Rage for Going to America*, 28 Pennsylvania History 231, 249 (1961).

62. Sangmin Bae, When the State No Longer Kills: International Human Rights Norms and Abolition of Capital Punishment 110 (2008); Darius Rejali, Torture and Democracy 12 (Princeton: Princeton University Press, 2007).

63. *Facts about the Death Penalty*, Death Penalty Info. Ctr., Dec. 12, 2013, at 1, 3; *Facts about the Death Penalty*, Death Penalty Info. Ctr. (May 6, 2014); Richard C. Dieter, "The 2% Death Penalty: How a Minority of Counties Produce Most Death Cases at Enormous Cost to All" (Washington, DC: Death Penalty Information Center, Oct. 2013).

64. Emily Beckett, Assistant AG Discusses Death Penalty Appeals Process, The Clanton Advertiser, http://www.clantonadvertiser.com/2013/02/01/assistant-attorney-general-discusses-death-penalty-appeals-process/.

65. Bessler, Cruel and Unusual, 290.

66. Baze v. Rees, 553 U.S. 35 (2008); Motion and Memorandum of Law in Support of Motion to Strike State's Notice of Intention to Seek Sentence of Death Because Maryland's Death Penalty Law Is a Sanguinary Law and Violates Article 16 of the Maryland Declaration of Rights (dated Aug. 2, 2011), State v. Maryland v. Lee Edward Stephens, Case No. K08-646 (Circuit Court for Anne Arundel County), *available at* http://www.circuitcourt.org/images/pdfstephens/2011-08-03_defendants_motion_to_strike_death_penalty_as_a_sanguinary_law.pdf.

67. Bessler, Cruel and Unusual, 274–75.

68. Schabas, The Death Penalty as Cruel Treatment and Torture, 159.

69. Wilkerson v. Utah, 99 U.S. 130 (1879); In re Kemmler, 136 U.S. 436 (1890); McCleskey v. Kemp, 481 U.S. 279 (1987); Baze v. Rees, 553 U.S. 35 (2008); "Facts about the Death Penalty," Death Penalty Information Center (Feb. 13, 2014), p. 1.

70. Bessler, Cruel and Unusual, 4, 26; Hudson v. McMillian, 503 U.S. 1 (1992) (Thomas, J., dissenting).

71. Criminal Justice Section, Philadelphia Bar Ass'n, http://criminaljusticesection.wordpress.com/2009/11/17/gaeton-alfano-receives-beccaria-award/; www.justinian.org/beccaria.php; http://www.philadelphiabar.org/page/NewsItem?appNum=3&newsItemID=1000649; "Philadelphia Lawyer, and Advocate of Italian-American Advancement, Dies," http://thelegalintelligencer.typepad.com/tli/2012/10/philadelphia-lawyer-and-advocate-of-italian-american-advancement-dies.html.

72. Simon Cox, Decoding the Lost Symbol: The Unauthorized Expert Guide to the Facts Behind the Fiction 31–34 (New York: Touchstone, 2009).

73. Robert Viscusi, Buried Caesars and Other Secrets of Italian American Writing 81–82 (Albany, NY: State University of New York Press, 2006); Ann Richmond Fisher, Explorers of the New World Timeline 30–31 (Dayton, OH: Teaching & Learning Co., 2007); "The Statue of Freedom," U.S. Capitol brochure, CVC#12-078; *see also* John W. Hessler, ed. & trans., The Naming of America: Martin Waldseemüller's 1507 World Map and the Cosmographiae Introductio (London: Giles, 2008).

74. People v. Melvin, 2 Wheeler C.C. 262, Yates Sel. Cas. 112, 174 (N.Y. Sup. 1810); 13 John D. Lawson, ed., American State Trials: A Collection of the Important and Interesting Criminal Trials Which Have Taken Place in the United States, from the Beginning of Our Government to the Present Day 632 (1921); *see also* Prize Essays on a Congress of Nations 243 (Boston: Whipple & Damrell, 1840) ("It is an observation of the Marquis of Beccaria, that the customs of nations are always one or two centuries behind their refinements.").

75. *See generally* Micheline R. Ishay, The History of Human Rights: From Ancient Times to the Globalization Era (Berkeley: University of California Press, 2008).

76. Richard Pierre Claude & Burns H. Weston, eds., Human Rights in the World Community: Issues and Action 83, 385 (Philadelphia: University of Pennsylvania Press, 3d ed. 2006).

77. *E.g.*, Newton Martin Curtis, To Define the Crime of Murder, Provide Penalty Therefor, and to Abolish the Punishment of Death: Speech of Gen. Newton Martin Curtis, of New York, in the House of Representatives, Thursday, June 9, 1892, at 26 (1892) (noting that the advocates of abolition "including the greatest names in European and American history," including Beccaria, Sir Samuel Romilly, Jeremy Bentham, Edward Livingston, and Robert Rantoul, Jr., and that "the greatest credit" will be given to them "when this principle shall have been adopted, as it surely will be, by the Christian nations of the earth").

78. Id. at 36; *see also* id. (quoting Bentham as saying the following: "Sanguinary laws have a tendency to render men cruel, either by fear, by imitation, or by revenge. But laws dictated by mildness humanize the manners of a nation and the spirit of government.").

79. Peter Hanns Reill & Ellen Judy Wilson, Encyclopedia of the Enlightenment 46, 189 (New York: Facts on File, rev. ed. 2004).

80. Bernard E. Harcourt, Beccaria's *On Crimes and Punishments*: A Mirror on the History of the Foundations of Modern Criminal Law, Institute for Law and Economics Working Paper Series (July 22, 2013).

"We have managed to squeak by for more than two hundred years without a consensus approach to constitutional interpretation," notes constitutional law scholar C.J. Peters. "Still," Peters emphasizes, "it is profoundly strange that we agree so broadly that the Constitution is the supreme law of the land but diverge so widely on how to determine just what that law requires of us." Christopher J. Peters, *What Lies Beneath: Interpretive Methodology, Constitutional Authority, and the Case of Originalism*, 2013 BYU L. Rev. 1251, 1255 (2013).

The Birth of American Law has sought to shed light on the origins of American law not for its own sake or because of a belief that any one book could ever settle that centuries-old interpretive debate. Rather, *The Birth of American Law* has sought to give ordinary Americans a better understanding of the historical origins of the American Revolution and the U.S. Constitution so that they will be better informed as regards the intellectual climate that gave rise to the Declaration of Independence, the U.S. Constitution and the Bill of Rights.

Certainly, Cesare Beccaria's influence on the Founding Fathers should not be forgotten as Americans continue to debate the meaning of the U.S. Constitution. Beccaria's name appears in early congressional debates, including at the First Congress, and his ideas—studied intently in the founding era—deserve to be remembered. *E.g.*, Proceedings and Debates of the House of Representatives of the United States, at the First Session of the First Congress, Begun at the City of New York, March 4, 1789, 1 Annals of Cong. 830 (1789–1790) ("Mr. Jackson," in debate in August 1789, argues: "The accurate Marquis Beccaria points out a danger which it behooves us to guard against. In every society, says he, there is an effort continually tending to confer on one part the height of power and happiness, and to reduce the other to the extreme of weakness and misery. The intent of good laws is to oppose this effort and diffuse their influence universally and equally."); id. ("This celebrated writer," Jackson continued of Beccaria, "pursues the principle still further, and confirms what we urge on our side against the unnecessary establishment of inferior courts. He asserts, with the great Montesquieu, that every punishment which does not arise from absolute necessity is tyrannical; a proposition which may be made more general thus, every act of authority of one man over another for which there is not an absolute necessity is tyrannical."); John Dickinson's Draft Letter to Quebec [October 24–26? 1774], 1 Letters Del. Cong. 236–37 (1774–1775) (quoting Beccaria); 1 Joseph Simpson & M. Dawes, Reflections on the Natural and Acquired Endowments Requisite for the Study of Law 53 n.* (5th ed. corr., 1793) ("Before the student enters on the study of criminal law, he will do well to make himself acquainted with Beccaria, Rousseau, Voltaire, Montesquieu, Fielding, and Blackstone, on the important subject of Crimes and Punishments."); *see also* William O. Foster, James Jackson: Duelist and Militant Statesman, 1757–1806, at 35 (Athens, GA: University of Georgia Press) ("Jackson's essays, addresses, and letters indicate a wide acquaintanceship with the works of such political scientists as Vattel, Grotius, Beccaria, Locke, Rousseau, Montesquieu, and Blackstone."); Proceedings and Debates of the House of Representatives of the United States, at the First Session of the Second Congress, Begun at the City of Philadelphia, October 24, 1791, 3 Annals of Cong. 283 (1791–1793) (in December 1791 debate over whether "Post Office Department" employees should suffer death for robbing the mail, a "Mr. Murray" spoke and "adverted to the principles advanced by Montesquieu, Beccaria, and others, who had written so ably on crimes and punishments"); Proceedings and Debates of the House of

Representatives of the United States, at the Second Session of the Fifth Congress, Begun at the City of Philadelphia, Monday, November 13, 1797, 7 Annals of Cong. 1084–87 (1797–1798) (in February 1798 debate, a "Mr. HAVENS" stated: "It must be evident to every one that peace, independence, and equality, must constitute the happiness of every country; but it was notorious that the leading men in most countries had been opposed to these, for their own ends. *Beccaria*, he said, in his Essay on Crimes and Punishments, had laid it down as a certain principle, that there were in every society such a class of men. In England, perhaps, this was more evident than in any nation. A set of men appeared early in that country to render the Executive Power a Government of despotism. The doctrines of passive obedience and the divine right of Kings, continued to be asserted for one whole reign.").

It has been 250 years since Beccaria's ideas first appeared in print, published anonymously for fear of reprisal. *See* Francesca Bregoli, "Hebrew Printing in Eighteenth-Century Livorno: From Government Control to a Free Market," *in* Joseph R. Hacker & Adam Shear, eds., The Hebrew Book in Early Modern Italy 171 (Philadelphia: University of Pennsylvania Press, 2011) ("In the past twenty years, scholars have widely explored the importance of the printing business in the port of Livorno in connection to the history of the Italian Enlightenment and to the circulation of reformist ideas. Between the middle of the 1740s and the rise of Napoleon, the period that roughly corresponded to the phase of state reforms initiated by the Lorraine house in Tuscany, Livorno was a center of production and distribution of enlightened ideas in Italy and beyond, thanks to the open support, or silent approval, of the ruling dynasty. It was in Livorno that Cesare Beccaria was able to publish his groundbreaking legal essay *Dei delitti e delle pene* (On Crimes and Punishments) in 1764, and the port city was home to the second Italian edition of Diderot and D'Alembert's *Encyclopédie* (1770–78)."); *see also* Newman & Marongiu, On Crimes and Punishments, lix ("Beccaria eventually 'produced' the first version of the book between March 1763 and January 1764. It is probable that most of the work was done in Pietro Verri's apartment in Milan after Beccaria's summer vacation, in about two months during the fall of 1763. The final manuscript was ready on February 29, 1764 and sent to Verri's publisher in Livorno, Giuseppe Aubert, on April 12...."); id. at lix–lx ("The first edition of the book ... appeared in July of the same year in Livorno's printing office of Coltellini. The volume consisted of an Introduction, forty-one unnumbered chapters, 104 numbered pages, bore no bibliographical information, except the year and (in a few rare copies) an enclosed *errata corrige*. It was published anonymously, for security reasons, fearing some reprisal from catholic authorities.").

After it was published, *Dei delitti e delle pene*—as one scholar so aptly put it—"was immediately hailed as a new Evangel, was translated into all European languages, and won for its author the highest honors." Mary Vance Young, "Alessandro Manzoni-Beccaria, Romanticist," 13 The Romanic Review 331, 353 n.85 (1922); *see also* John B. Romeiser, "A Philosophe on Crime and Punishment: Diderot's Response to Beccaria," 6 French Literature Series: Authors and Philosophers 48 (1979) ("Beccaria's treatise shook the d'Holbachian circle, especially Diderot, in its zealous plea for the rights of the individual and blanket condemnation of torture and the death penalty. Diderot's interest in the Italian philosopher extends over six years, beginning with the translation of a letter from the Scot, Allan Ramsay, in January 1766, a series of marginal notes he made in a copy of Morellet's translation of *Dei delitte* the same year, and terminating in 1771...."); Scott Burnham & Michael P. Steinberg, eds., Beethoven and His World 36 (Princeton, NJ: Princeton University Press, 2000) ("The European conscience regarding prisons had been awakened by Cesare Beccaria in Italy, whose great essay on prison reform, issued originally in 1764, was widely read and highly influential. Beccaria was quoted with approval by writers and heads of state throughout the later eighteenth and down into the nineteenth century.").

In the years and decades following the publication of Beccaria's treatise, many early Americans—as well as many Europeans—rethought their views on the relationship between states and individuals and questioned the necessity of harsh bodily punishments, including the need for state-sanctioned executions. For example, in writing to then-U.S. Secretary of State Edmund Randolph in 1795, the U.S. Minister to France, James Monroe, wrote from Paris about the fate of prisoners from an "emigrant army" taken captive after "about 4,000 were slain" in a battle. "By the law," Monroe emphasized, many of the prisoners were "doomed to suffer capital punishment." "[B]ut," Monroe added, "it is to be hoped, as many of them are weak and misguided men, its rigour will be moderated, at least in regard to them." James Monroe to Edmund Randolph, Aug. 1, 1795, *in* 2 Stanislaus Murray Hamilton, ed., The Writings of James Monroe 331, 334 (New York: G. P. Putnam's Sons, 1899); *see also* Alfonso Scirocco, Garibaldi, Citizen of the World: A Biography 4 (Princeton, NJ: Princeton University Press, 2007) (noting that the Italian revolutionary, soldier and politician Giuseppe Garibaldi "declared himself a follower of Cesare Beccaria" and that "[h]is book collection included Gaetano Filangieri's *Scienza della legislazione*").

In the anti-death penalty essay, "*On the Punishment of Death*," written for a 1794 edition of the *New-York Magazine*, one eighteenth-century writer—going by "Valentine"—began by quoting this sentiment: "*When the Penalty exceeds the Offence, it is not the Criminal, but Human Nature that suffers.*" Invoking the name of John Howard, a much-revered Beccaria disciple, "Valentine" then wrote: "The seventeenth century has much to boast of, yet there are great improvements to be made; and among many important objects, the knowledge and diffusion of *Liberty* and the *Rights of Man*—the prevention of *crimes*, and infliction of *punishments*, are not the least. A few general observations against the punishment of death shall be the subject of the present essay; and while I write, may the philanthrophic genius of *Howard* inspire my pen." "Would it not be a more rational punishment, instead of inflicting death on a murderer," Valentine queried, "to condemn him to hard labor in a prison for the remainder of his life, and the product of such labor to be applied to the use of the widow or children of the person murdered?" Advocating for the use of the penitentiary system, Valentine then offered: "Preserve liberty and equality, encourage virtue and industry, promote education, and there will be but few crimes among us; and, when a crime is committed, let us punish like *men*—not like *tyrants*." 5 The New-York Magazine; or, Literary Repository 35–37 (New York: Thomas and James Swords, 1794).

The editors of the *New-York Magazine*, published in the 1790s, themselves opposed the death penalty, with scholar Sharon M. Harris emphasizing that the magazine's editors—Thomas and James Swords—consistently took a "progressive" stance against capital punishment. With the subscribers of the *New-York Magazine* including President George Washington and Vice-President John Adams, Harris writes of the magazine's editorial sentiment: "As with its essays on antislavery, the editors' opposition to capital punishment remained consistent over the years of the magazine's publication. The ideals of the American Revolution, an emergent liberal theology, and the development of the penitentiary all influenced the change in attitudes about capital punishment in the years from the Revolution to the 1790s." Sharon M. Harris, "The *New-York Magazine*: Cultural Repository," *in* Mark L. Kamrath & Sharon M. Harris, eds., Periodical Literature in Eighteenth-Century America 339, 341, 352 (Knoxville: The University of Tennessee Press, 2005); *see also* id. at 355 ("[T]he premier poet of the *New-York Magazine* was Margaretta V. Bleecker Faugeres.... Bleecker Faugeres's political perspectives complemented those of the magazine—she was opposed to slavery and to capital punishment...."); Kristin Boudreau, The Spectacle of Death 20, 29 (Amherst, NY: Prometheus Books, 2006) (reprinting the frontispiece to a poem titled "The Ghost of John Young" by "Mrs. Faugeres" that recites the execution in 1797 of Young, "The *HOMICIDE*," for the murder of Robert Barwick, "*a Sherif's Officer*," and which—in the language on the frontispiece—has as its purpose "shewing how inconsistent sanguinary Laws are, in a Country which boasts of her Freedom and Happiness").

While modern-day historians and constitutional scholars have long neglected or overlooked Cesare Beccaria's influence on the American Revolution, that influence was profound—and has been hiding in plain sight. Indeed, many early Americans—along with scores of educated and reform-minded Europeans—had well-worn copies of Beccaria's *On Crimes and Punishments* in their libraries and regularly used the Italian philosopher's ideas in crafting their own political and legal arguments. *E.g.*, Wilkins Updike, A History of the Episcopal Church in Narragansett, Rhode Island 422 (Boston, MA: The Merrymount Press, 1907); 3 Charles Phillips, Vacation Thoughts on Capital Punishments 2, 23, 38, 41–42, 60, 98 (London: William & Frederick, 1857). The spirit of American republicanism—and America's focus on individual rights—can be attributed, in fact, at least in part to Beccaria's treatise, that eighteenth-century bestseller. *See* 2 Martin van Gelderen & Quentin Skinner, eds., Republicanism: A Shared European Heritage 269 (Cambridge: Cambridge University Press, 2002) ("To find a radical formulation of individual autonomy we have to turn to Cesare Beccaria's *Dei delitti e delle pene* (1764), Chapter 26 of which, entitled 'Of the Spirit of Family', seems a digression prompted by the custom of confiscating the property of convicted criminals. Beccaria condemned this practice which, in punishing the guilty individual, also struck at the innocent members of his family, especially the children who had nothing to do with the offences committed by their father.").

What historical documents reveal is that the Founding Fathers were plainly fascinated by Cesare Beccaria's ideas, the products of the Italian Enlightenment, of which *On Crimes and Punishments* was a part, and the penitentiary system advocated by Beccaria's many ardent converts and disciples. After George Washington's death, for instance, an inventory of items at Mount Vernon took note of Jeremy Bentham's *Panopticon* and copies of Mathew Carey's *American Museum*. Worthington Chauncey Ford, ed., Inventory of the Contents of Mount Vernon 1810, at 16, 28 (Cambridge: The University Press, 1909). It is also clear that, in August 1792, the American diplomat Thomas Pinckney, while in London, sent Thomas Jefferson Bentham's *Panopticon*—a book about the proper functioning of a penitentiary. A separate sheet in Pinckney's handwriting notes that President George Washington, who appointed Pinckney as the U.S. minister to Great Britain, would also be receiving a copy of Bentham's book, explaining its later presence at Mount Vernon. As Pinckney's note reads: "Three copies of Mr. Bentham's Panopticon presented by Mr. Benjn. Vaughan—one for the President—one for the Secretary of State and one for the Chief Justice." *See* Thomas Pinckney to Thomas Jefferson, Aug. 29, 1792 (editorial note), *available at* www.founders.archives.gov. While Thomas Jefferson's notes on his 1787 trip to southern France and northern Italy are focused on geographic features and the agricultural products of the regions and cities he visited, it is crystal clear that America's founders—both before and after Philadelphia's Constitutional Convention—were also taken with an array of intellectual exports from Europe, be they from Roman historians or English, French, Italian, Scottish or Swiss philosophers. *See* Notes of a Tour into the Southern Parts of France, &c., Mar. 3–June 10, 1787, *available at* www.founders.archives.gov.

Cesare Beccaria's own French translator, the Abbé André Morellet (1727–1819), actually developed an especially close friendship with America's senior statesman, Benjamin Franklin, with the two men even working together on Dr. Franklin's famous stove. Morellet—who translated important documents for Franklin as well as a scandalous manual unearthed in Italy that had been used by the Inquisition—regularly dined with Franklin, and the witty Morellet even penned a drinking song in Franklin's honor. Upon returning to America, Dr. Franklin—happily at home again in Philadelphia—wrote to André Morellet in April 1787 on the eve of the Constitutional Convention, making this optimistic report to his French friend: "Whatever may be reported by the English in Europe, you may be assured that our People are almost unanimous in being satisfied with the Revolution. Their unbounded Respect for all who were principally concern'd in it, whether as Warriors or Statesmen, and the enthusiastic Joy with which the Day of the Declaration of Independence is every where annually celebrated, are indisputable Proofs of this Truth." *See* Edward Peters, Inquisition 182-83 (Berkeley, CA: University of California Press, 1989); Philipp Blom, A Wicked Company: The Forgotten Radicalism of the European Enlightenment 63, 217–20 (New York: Basic Books, 2013); The Abbé André Morellet's Song in Honor of Franklin [1779]; Benjamin Franklin to André Morellet, Apr. 22, 1787; Claude-Anne Lopez, Mon Cher Papa: Franklin and the Ladies of Paris 284–92 (New Haven: Yale University Press, 1990).

Though Beccaria's name is now little remembered in twenty-first century America, the influence of the Italian Enlightenment on American law—including its emphasis on human dignity and maximizing people's happiness—can be felt to this day. *See* Richard Bellamy, Croce, Gramsci, Bobbio and the Italian Political Tradition 54 (Colchester, UK: ECPR Press, 2013) (noting Beccaria defined the public good as "the greatest sum of pleasures, divided equally amongst the greatest number of people"); Derek Bok, The Politics of Happiness: What Government Can Learn from the New Research on Well-Being 4 (Princeton, NJ: Princeton University Press, 2010) ("A whole series of political theorists—Cesare Beccaria, Claude-Adrien Helvétius, and Francis Hutcheson, among others—proposed the promotion of happiness and the avoidance of pain as the proper aim of personal and public morality.... In the United States, Jefferson famously included the pursuit of happiness in the Declaration of Independence, and more than half the states inserted the phrase in their constitutions.").

As Americans and the U.S. Supreme Court continue to debate the U.S. Constitution's meaning, Cesare Beccaria's legacy may—in the future, and whether explicitly acknowledged or not—continue to shape that contentious public debate. Already, in an Eighth and Fourteenth Amendment case involving the potential execution of a convicted killer with severe intellectual disabilities, Justice Anthony Kennedy—in a 5–4 decision—emphasized the importance of human dignity to constitutional interpretation. "The Eighth Amendment," he wrote of the Supreme Court's jurisprudence, "'is not fastened to the obsolete but may acquire meaning as public opinion becomes enlightened by a humane justice.'" *See* Hall v. Florida, No. 12-10882 (May 27, 2014), slip op., p. 5. "To enforce the Constitution's protection of human dignity," Justice Kennedy noted, "this Court looks to the 'evolving standards of decency that mark the progress of a maturing society.'" "The Eighth Amendment's protection of dignity," he concluded, "reflects the Nation we have been, the Nation we are, and the Nation we aspire to be." Id. at 5–6. In holding that a Florida law barring the introduction of evidence of intellectual disability where the petitioner had an IQ score of 71 "contravenes our Nation's commitment to dignity and its duty to teach human decency as the mark of a civilized world," Justice Kennedy's majority opinion proclaimed that States "may not deny the basic dignity the Constitution protects." Id. at 22.

While Cesare Beccaria's name nowhere appears in Justice Kennedy's majority opinion, the questions raised by Beccaria's *On Crimes and Punishments* in the eighteenth century have continuing vitality today, especially in light of America's long-standing abandonment of *non-lethal* corporal punishments. *See generally* Bessler, "The American Enlightenment"; Bessler, *The Anomaly of Executions*; John D. Bessler, *The Death Penalty in Decline: From Colonial America to the Present*, 50 Crim.

L. Bull. 245 (2014). Indeed, in an earlier 5–4 decision, Justice Kennedy—writing for the majority of the Court in the context of another contentious case, again involving a man sentenced to death—had previously offered his own introspective remarks on America's continued use of capital punishment, the issue that so captivated early American readers of *On Crimes and Punishments*. As Justice Kennedy—perhaps channeling, but not citing Beccaria's treatise—forcefully wrote in that case: "When the law punishes by death, it risks its own sudden descent into brutality, transgressing the constitutional commitment to decency and restraint." Kennedy v. Louisiana, 554 U.S. 407, 420 (2008).

Bibliography

Books

Akhil Reed Amar, America's Constitution: A Biography (New York: Random House, 2006).

Thomas C. Amory, Life of James Sullivan: With Selections from His Writings (Boston: Phillips, Sampson and Co., 1859).

Robert Asher, Lawrence B. Goodheart & Alan Rogers, eds., Murder on Trial, 1620–2000 (Albany, NY: State University of New York Press, 2005).

Bernard Bailyn, The Ideological Origins of the American Revolution (Cambridge, MA: The Belknap Press of Harvard University Press, enlarged ed. 1992).

Bernard Bailyn, ed., Pamphlets of the American Revolution, 1750–1776 (Cambridge, MA: The Belknap Press of Harvard University Press, 1965).

Sarah Bakewell, How to Live, or, A Life of Montaigne in One Question and Twenty Attempts at an Answer (New York: Other Press, 2010).

Stuart Banner, The Death Penalty: An American History (Cambridge, MA: Harvard University Press, 2002).

Richard Bellamy, ed., Cesare Beccaria, On Crimes and Punishments and Other Writings, trans. Richard Davies (Cambridge: Cambridge University Press, 1995).

John D. Bessler, Cruel and Unusual: The American Death Penalty and the Founders' Eighth Amendment (Boston: Northeastern University Press, 2012).

John D. Bessler, Death in the Dark: Midnight Executions in America (Boston: Northeastern University Press, 1997).

John D. Bessler, Kiss of Death: America's Love Affair with the Death Penalty (Boston: Northeastern University Press, 2003).

John D. Bessler, Legacy of Violence: Lynch Mobs and Executions in Minnesota (Minneapolis: University of Minnesota Press, 2003).

Guyora Binder, Felony Murder (Stanford, CA: Stanford University Press, 2012).

Bradley J. Birzer, American Cicero: The Life of Charles Carroll (Wilmington, DE: ISI Books, 2010).

William Blackstone, Commentaries on the Laws of England: A Facsimile of the First Edition of 1765–1769 (1765–1769) (1979).

Rodney Bolt, The Librettist of Venice: The Remarkable Life of Lorenzo Da Ponte, Mozart's Poet, Casanova's Friend, and Italian Opera's Impresario in America (New York: Bloomsbury Publishing, 2006).

Hugh Henry Brackenridge, Law Miscellanies: An Introduction to the Study of the Law (Philadelphia: P. Byrne, 1814).

Peter Brand & Lino Pertile, eds., The Cambridge History of Italian Literature (Cambridge: Cambridge University Press, rev. ed. 1996).

H. W. Brands, The First American: The Life and Times of Benjamin Franklin (New York: Anchor Books, 2002).

John Brewer & Eckhart Hellmuth, eds., Rethinking Leviathan: The Eighteenth-Century State in Britain and Germany (Oxford: Oxford University Press, 1999).

Alyn Brodsky, Benjamin Rush: Patriot and Physician (New York: Macmillan, 2004).

Richard Brookhiser, Alexander Hamilton: American (New York: Touchstone, 1999).

Richard Brookhiser, What Would the Founders Do? Our Questions, Their Answers 34–35 (New York: Basic Books, 2007).

Gordon S. Brown, Incidental Architect: William Thornton and the Cultural Life of Early Washington, D.C., 1794–1828 (Athens, OH: Ohio University Press, 2009).

Irene Quenzler Brown & Richard D. Brown, The Hanging of Ephraim Wheeler: A Story of Rape, Incest, and Justice in Early America (Cambridge, MA: Belknap Press of Harvard University, 2003).

Stefania Buccini, The Americas in Italian Literature and Culture 1700–1825, trans. Rosanna Giammanco (University Park, PA: Pennsylvania State University Press, 1997).

James Burgh, Political Disquisitions; or, An Enquiry into Public Errors, Defects, and Abuses (Philadelphia: Robert Bell and William Woodhouse, 1775).

Carol Burnell, Divided Affections: The Extraordinary Life of Maria Cosway, Celebrity Artist and Thomas Jefferson's Impossible Love (Lausanne, Switzerland: Column House, 2007).

Stephen Burroughs, Memoirs of the Notorious Stephen Burroughs (Boston: Charles Gaylord, 1835).

Jane E. Calvert, Quaker Constitutionalism and the Political Thought of John Dickinson (Cambridge: Cambridge University Press, 2009).

Arthur H. Cash, John Wilkes: The Scandalous Father of Civil Liberty (New Haven: Yale University Press, 2006).

Adolph Caso, We, the People: Formative Documents of America's Democracy (Boston: Branden Publishing Co., 1995).

Philip Cheung, Public Trust in Medical Research?: Ethics, Law and Accountability (Oxford: Radcliffe Publishing, 2007).

Gilbert Chinard, ed., The Commonplace Book of Thomas Jefferson: A Repertory of His Ideas on Government (Baltimore, MD: Johns Hopkins Press, 1926).

Nathaniel Chipman, Sketches of the Principles of Government (Rutland, VT: J. Lyon, June 1793).

Scott Christianson, With Liberty for Some: 500 Years of Imprisonment in America (Boston: Northeastern University Press, 1998).

Neil H. Cogan, ed., The Complete Bill of Rights: The Drafts, Debates, Sources, and Origins (Oxford: Oxford University Press, 1997).

Morris R. Cohen & Felix S. Cohen, Readings in Jurisprudence and Legal Philosophy (New York: Little, Brown and Co. 1951).

Patrick Colquhoun, A Treatise on the Police of the Metropolis (London: H. Fry, 2d ed. 1796).

Mark Colvin, Penitentiaries, Reformatories, and Chain Gangs: Social Theory and the History of Punishment in Nineteenth-Century America (New York: St. Martin's Press, 1997).

Saul Cornell, A Well Regulated Militia: The Founding Fathers and the Origins of Gun Control in America (New York: Oxford University Press, 2006).

Seth Cotlar, Tom Paine's America: The Rise and Fall of Transatlantic Radicalism in the Early Republic (Charlottesville: University of Virginia Press, 2011).

William Coxe, Account of the Prisons and Hospitals in Russia, Sweden, and Denmark with Occasional Remarks on the Different Modes of Punishments in Those Countries (London: T. Cadell, 1781).

James E. Crimmins, ed., The Death Penalty: Debates in Britain and the U.S., 1725–1868 (London: Continuum International, 2004).

Nathan Dane, General Abridgement and Digest of American Law, with Occasional Notes and Comments (Boston: Cummings, Hilliard, 1823).

David Brion Davis, From Homicide to Slavery: Studies in American Culture (Oxford: Oxford University Press, 1986).

Matthew L. Davis, ed., The Private Journal of Aaron Burr, During His Residence of Four Years in Europe; with Selections from His Correspondence (New York: Harper & Brothers, 1838).

Franklin Bowditch Dexter, ed., The Literary Diary of Ezra Stiles, D.D., LL.D., President of Yale College (New York: Charles Scribner's Sons, 1901).

William Eden, Principles of Penal Law (London: B. White & T. Cadell, 1771).

Michael J. Everton, The Grand Chorus of Complaint: Authors and the Business Ethics of American Publishing (Oxford: Oxford University Press, 2011).

James Anson Farrer, trans., Cesare Beccaria, Crimes and Punishments (London: Chatto & Windus, 1880).

Mark F. Fernandez, From Chaos to Continuity: The Evolution of Louisiana's Judicial System, 1712–1862 (Baton Rouge, LA: Louisiana State University Press, 2001).

Vincenzo Ferrone, The Politics of Enlightenment: Constitutionalism, Republicanism, and the Rights of Man in Gaetano Filangieri (London: Anthem Press, Sophus A. Reinert, trans., 2012).

Henry Flanders, The Lives and Times of the Chief Justices of the Supreme Court of the United States (New York: James Cockcroft & Co., 1875).

Joseph S. Foster, In Pursuit of Equal Liberty: George Bryan and the Revolution in Pennsylvania (University Park, PA: Pennsylvania State University Press, 1994).

Michel Foucault, Discipline & Punish: The Birth of the Prison (New York: Vintage, Alan Sheridan trans., 1979).

Paul Friedland, Seeing Justice Done: The Age of Spectacular Capital Punishment in France (Oxford: Oxford University Press, 2012).

Lawrence M. Friedman, A History of American Law (New York: Simon & Schuster, 3d ed. 2005).

Lawrence M. Friedman, Crime and Punishment in American History (New York: Basic Books, 1993).

John F. Galliher, Larry W. Koch, David Patrick Keys & Teresa J. Guess, America Without the Death Penalty: States Leading the Way (Boston, MA: Northeastern University Press, 2002).

David Garland, Peculiar Institution: America's Death Penalty in the Age of Abolition (Cambridge, MA: The Belknap Press of Harvard University Press, 2010).

William Godwin, Of Population: An Enquiry Concerning the Power of Increase in the Numbers of Mankind (London: Longman, Hurst, Rees, Orme and Brown, 1820).

Lawrence B. Goodheart, The Solemn Sentence of Death: Capital Punishment in Connecticut (Amherst: University of Massachusetts Press, 2011).

Jennifer Graber, The Furnace of Affliction: Prisons and Religion in Antebellum America (Chapel Hill: University of North Carolina Press, 2011).

James N. Green, Mathew Carey: Publisher and Patriot (Philadelphia: Library Company of Philadelphia, 1985).

Martin I. J. Griffin, Catholics and the American Revolution (Ridley Park, PA: Martin I. J. Griffin, 1907).

Peter Groenewegen, Eighteenth-Century Economics: Turgot, Beccaria and Smith and Their Contemporaries (London: Routledge, 2002).

Michael Grossberg & Christopher Tomlins, eds., The Cambridge History of Law in America 206 (Cambridge: Cambridge University Press, 2008).

Stephen P. Halbrook, A Right to Bear Arms: State and Federal Bills of Rights and Con-stitutional Guarantees (Westport, CT: Greenwood Press, 1989).

Stephen P. Halbrook, That Every Man Be Armed: The Evolution of a Constitutional Right (Albuquerque: University of New Mexico Press, rev. updated 2013).

Stephen P. Halbrook, The Founders' Second Amendment: Origins of the Right to Bear Arms (Chicago: Ivan R. Dee, 2008).

Dianne Hales, La Bella Lingua: My Love Affair with Italian, the World's Most Enchant-ing Language (New York: Broadway Books, 2009).

Kermit L. Hall, ed., The Oxford Companion to American Law (New York: Oxford Uni-versity Press, 2002).

Luther Hamilton, ed., Memoirs, Speeches and Writings of Robert Rantoul, Jr. (Boston: John P. Jewett and Co., 1854).

Bernard E. Harcourt, The Illusion of Free Markets: Punishment and the Myth of Nat-ural Order (Cambridge: Harvard University Press, 2011).

Sharon M. Harris, Executing Race: Early American Women's Narratives of Race, Society, and the Law (Columbus: Ohio State University Press, 2005).

Lowell H. Harrison & James C. Klotter, A New History of Kentucky (Lexington, KY: The University Press of Kentucky, 2009).

Stephen John Hartnett, Executing Democracy: Capital Punishment & the Making of America, 1683–1807 (East Lansing: Michigan State University Press, 2010).

David Freeman Hawke, Benjamin Rush: Revolutionary Gadfly (Indianapolis, IN: Bobbs-Merrill, 1971).

J. Roderick Heller III, Democracy's Lawyer: Felix Grundy of the Old Southwest (Baton Rouge, LA: Louisiana State University Press, 2010).

Michael Stephen Hindus, Prison and Plantation: Crime, Justice, and Authority in Mass-achusetts and South Carolina, 1767–1878 (Chapel Hill: University of North Carolina Press, 1980).

H. M. Hoeflich, Legal Publishing in Antebellum America (New York: Cambridge Uni-versity Press, 2010).

Ronald Hoffman, Sally D. Mason & Eleanor S. Darcy, eds., Dear Papa, Dear Charley: The Peregrinations of a Revolutionary Aristocrat, as Told by Charles Carroll of Carrollton and His Father, Charles Carroll of Annapolis, with Sundry Observations on Bastardy, Child-Rearing, Romance, Matrimony, Commerce, Tobacco, Slavery, and the Politics of Revolutionary America (Chapel Hill: University of North Carolina Press, 2001).

John Hostettler, Cesare Beccaria: The Genuis of 'On Crimes and Punishments' (Hamp-shire, UK: Waterside Press, 2011).

John Howard, The State of the Prisons in England and Wales, with Preliminary Obser-vations, and an Account of Some Foreign Prisons (London: William Eyres, 1777).

Carleton Hunt, Life and Services of Edward Livingston: Address of Carleton Hunt, May 9, 1903 (New Orleans, LA: J. G. Hauser, 1903).

Charles Haven Hunt, Life of Edward Livingston (New York: D. Appleton and Co., 1864).

Lynn Hunt, Inventing Human Rights: A History (New York: W. W. Norton & Co., 2007).

Walter Isaacson, Benjamin Franklin: An American Life (New York: Simon & Schuster, 2003).

Nancy Isenberg, Fallen Founder: The Life of Aaron Burr (New York: Penguin Books, 2007).

Jonathan I. Israel, Democratic Enlightenment: Philosophy, Revolution, and Human Rights 1750–1790 (Oxford: Oxford University Press, 2011).

Richard N. Juliani, Building Little Italy: Philadelphia's Italians Before Mass Migration (University Park, PA: Pennsylvania State University Press, 1998).

Mark E. Kann, Punishment, Prisons, and Patriarchy: Liberty and Power in the Early American Republic (New York: New York University Press, 2005).

Joshua Kendall, The Forgotten Founding Father: Noah Webster's Obsession and the Creation of an American Culture (New York: Berkley Books, 2010).

Ralph Ketcham, ed., The Anti-Federalist Papers and the Constitutional Convention Debates: The Clashes and Compromises that Gave Birth to Our Form of Government (New York: Signet Classic, 2003).

John E. Kleber, ed., The Kentucky Encyclopedia (Lexington, KY: The University of Press of Kentucky, 1992).

James C. Klotter, The Breckinridges of Kentucky (Lexington, KY: The University Press of Kentucky, 2006).

Edward Langworthy, Memoirs of the Life of the Late Charles Lee, Esq. to Which Are Added His Political and Military Essays (London: J. S. Jordan, 1792).

Benjamin Latrobe, The Journal of Latrobe: The Notes and Sketches of an Architect, Naturalist and Traveler in the United States from 1796 to 1820 (Carlisle, MA: Applewood Books, 1876).

David Lemmings, Professors of the Law: Barristers and English Legal Culture in the Eighteenth Century (Oxford: Oxford University Press, 2000).

Leonard W. Levy, Origins of the Bill of Rights (New Haven: Yale University Press, 1999).

W. David Lewis, From Newgate to Dannemora: The Rise of the Penitentiary in New York, 1796–1848 (Ithaca, NY: Cornell University Press, 2009).

Francis Lieber, A Popular Essay on Subjects of Penal Law, and on Uninterrupted Solitary Confinement at Labor, as Contradistinguished to Solitary Confinement at Night and Joint Labor by Day, in Letter to John Bacon, Esquire (Philadelphia: Philadelphia Society for Alleviating the Miseries of Public Prisons, 1838).

Henry Dunning Macleod, A Dictionary of Political Economy: Biographical, Bibliographical, Historical, and Practical (London: Longman, Brown, Longmans, and Roberts, 1863).

Martin Madan, Thoughts on Executive Justice, with Respect to Our Criminal Laws, Particularly on the Circuits (London: J. Dodsley, 1785).

Marcello T. Maestro, Cesare Beccaria and the Origins of Penal Reform (Philadelphia: Temple University Press, 1973).

Marcello T. Maestro, Voltaire and Beccaria as Reformers of Criminal Law (New York: Octagon Books, 1972).

Bruce H. Mann, Republic of Debtors: Bankruptcy in the Age of American Independence (Cambridge, MA: Harvard University Press, 2009).

Frank E. Manuel & Fritzie P. Manuel, James Bowdoin and the Patriot Philosophers (Philadelphia: American Philosophical Society, 2004).

Margherita Marchione, The Fighting Nun: My Story (Madison, NJ: Fairleigh Dickinson University Press, 2000).

Daniel Marder, ed., A Hugh Henry Brackenridge Reader, 1770–1815 (Pittsburgh: University of Pittsburgh Press, 1970).

Cesare Marino & Karim M. Tiro, eds. and trans., Along the Hudson and Mohawk: The 1790 Journey of Count Paolo Andreani (Philadelphia: University of Pennsylvania Press, 2006).

Gaetana Marrone, ed., Encyclopedia of Italian Literary Studies (New York: Routledge, 2007).

Humphrey Marshall, The History of Kentucky (Frankfort, KY: Geo. S. Robinson, 1824).

Giancarlo Masini & Iacopo Gori, How Florence Invented America: Vespucci, Verrazzano, & Mazzei and Their Contribution to the Conception of the New World (New York: Marsilio Publishers, 1998).

Dominic R. Massaro, Cesare Beccaria — The Father of Criminal Justice: His Impact on Anglo-American Jurisprudence (Cecina, Italy: Universitas Internationalis Coluccio Salutati, 1991).

Robert K. Massie, Catherine the Great: Portrait of a Woman (New York: Random House, 2011).

Louis P. Masur, Rites of Execution: Capital Punishment and the Transformation of American Culture, 1776–1865 (Oxford: Oxford University Press, 1989).

Henry F. May, The Enlightenment in America (Oxford: Oxford University Press, 1978).

Keally McBride, Punishment and Political Order: Law, Meaning, and Violence (Ann Arbor: The University of Michigan Press, 2007).

Scott McDermott, Charles Carroll of Carrollton: Faithful Revolutionary (New York: Scepter Publishers, 2002).

J. Walter McGinty, 'An Animated Son of Liberty': A Life of John Witherspoon (Bury St. Edmunds, UK: 2012).

Frank McLynn, Crime and Punishment in Eighteenth-Century England (London: Routledge, 1989).

Sally McMurry & Annmarie Adams, eds., People, Power, Places: Perspectives in Vernacular Architecture (Knoxville: University of Tennessee Press, 2000).

Marilyn McShane & Frank P. Williams III, eds., Criminal Justice: Contemporary Literature in Theory and Practice (New York: Garland Publishing, 1997).

Michael Meltsner, Cruel and Unusual: The Supreme Court and Capital Punishment (New Orleans: Quid Pro, LLC, 2011).

Joseph A. Melusky & Keith Alan Pesto, Capital Punishment (Santa Barbara, CA: ABC-CLIO, 2011).

John Macrae Moir, ed., Capital Punishment, Based on Professor Mittermaier's 'Todesstrafe' (London: Smith, Elder and Co., 1865).

Basil Montagu, comp., Opinions of Different Authors upon the Punishment of Death (London: Longman, Hurst, Rees, Orme, and Brown, 1812).

Basil Montagu, Thoughts on the Punishment of Death for Forgery (London: William Pickering, 1830).

Allan Nevins, The American States during and after the Revolution, 1775–1789 (New York: Macmillan, 2d ed. 1924).

Graeme R. Newman & Pietro Marongiu, trans., Cesare Beccaria, On Crimes and Punishments (Lexington, KY: Seven Treasures Publications, 5th ed. 2009).

Emiliana Pasca Noether, The American Constitution as a Symbol and Reality for Italy (Lewiston, NY: Edwin Mellen Press, 1989).

Antonio Pace, Benjamin Franklin and Italy (Philadelphia: American Philosophical Society, 1958).

Antonio Pace, ed. and trans., Luigi Castiglioni's Viaggio: Travels in the United States of North America 1785–1787 (Syracuse, NY: Syracuse University Press, 1983).

Henry Paolucci, trans., Cesare Beccaria, On Crimes and Punishments (Indianapolis: Bobbs-Merrill, 1963).

John Penn, Further Thoughts on the Present State of Public Opinion; Being a Continuation of A Timely Appeal to the Common Sense of the People of Great Britain in General, and of the Inhabitants of Buckinghamshire in Particular, on the Present Situation of Affairs (London: J. Hatchard & W. Bulmer and Co., 1800).

Merrill D. Peterson, Thomas Jefferson and the New Nation: A Biography (Oxford: Oxford University Press, 1970).

Coleman Phillipson, Three Criminal Law Reformers: Beccaria, Bentham, Romilly (Glen Ridge, NJ: Patterson Smith, 1970).

Steven Pinker, The Better Angels of Our Nature: Why Violence Has Declined (New York: Penguin Books, 2011).

Mark Puls, Henry Knox: Visionary General of the American Revolution (New York: Palgrave Macmillan, 2008).

James Raven, London Booksellers and American Customers: Transatlantic Literary Community and the Charleston Library Society, 1748–1811 (Columbia: University of South Carolina Press, 2002).

Peter Hanns Reill & Ellen Judy Wilson, Encyclopedia of the Enlightenment (New York: Facts on File, Inc., rev. ed. 2004).

Lyon Norman Richardson, A History of Early American Magazines, 1741–1789 (New York: Octagon Books, 1931).

Melvin Richter, The Political Theory of Montesquieu (Cambridge: Cambridge University Press, 1977).

Duke De La Rochefoucault Liancourt, Travels Through the United States of North America, the Country of the Iroquois, and Upper Canada in the Years 1795, 1796, and 1797 (London: R. Phillips, 1799).

Alan Rogers, Murder and the Death Penalty in Massachusetts (Amherst, MA: University of Massachusetts Press, 2008).

Mitchel P. Roth, Crime and Punishment: A History of the Criminal Justice System (Belmont, CA: Wadsworth, 2011).

Benjamin Rush, Essays, Literary, Moral and Philosophical (Philadelphia: Thomas and William Bradford, 1806).

Catherine M. Sama, ed. & trans., Elisabetta Caminer Turra: Selected Writings of an Eighteenth-Century Venetian Woman of Letters (Chicago: The University of Chicago Press, 2003).

Austin Sarat & Jürgen Martschukat, eds., Is the Death Penalty Dying?: European and American Perspectives (Cambridge: Cambridge University Press, 2011).

William A. Schabas, The Abolition of the Death Penalty in International Law (3d ed. 2002).

William A. Schabas, The Death Penalty as Cruel Treatment and Torture: Capital Punishment Challenged in the World's Courts (Boston: Northeastern University Press, 1996).

Virginia Scharff, The Women Jefferson Loved (New York: HarperCollins, 2010).

Giovanni Schiavo, The Italians in America Before the Civil War (New York: Vigo Press, 1934).

Winfield Scott, Memoirs of Lieut.-General Scott, LL. D. (New York: Sheldon & Co., 1864).

M. N. S. Sellers, American Republicanism: Roman Ideology in the United States Constitution (New York: New York University Press, 1994).

George Green Shackelford, Jefferson's Adoptive Son: The Life of William Short, 1759–1848 (Lexington, KY: The University Press of Kentucky, 1993).

George Green Shackelford, Thomas Jefferson's Travels in Europe, 1784–1789 (Baltimore, MD: The Johns Hopkins University Press, 1995).

Richard B. Sher, The Enlightenment and the Book: Scottish Authors and Their Publishers in Eighteenth-Century Britain, Ireland and America (Chicago: University of Chicago Press, 2007).

Paul E. Sigmund, ed. & trans., St. Thomas Aquinas on Politics and Ethics (New York: W. W. Norton & Co., 1988).

Robert A. Silverman, Terence P. Thornberry, Bernard Cohen & Barry Krisberg, eds., Crime and Justice at the Millennium: Essays by and in Honor of Marvin E. Wolfgang (Dordrecht, The Netherlands: Kluwer Academic Publishers, 2002).

William W. Smithers, Treatise on Executive Clemency in Pennsylvania (Philadelphia: International Printing Co., 1909).

John Stone & Stephen Mennell, eds., Alexis de Tocqueville on Democracy, Revolution and Society (Chicago: The University of Chicago Press, 1980).

George M. Stroud, A Sketch of the Laws Relating to Slavery in the Several States of the United States of America (Philadelphia: Kimber and Sharpless, 1827).

Patricia Earnest Suter, Russell Earnest & Corinne Earnest, The Hanging of Susanna Cox: The True Story of Pennsylvania's Most Notorious Infanticide & the Legend That's Kept It Alive (Mechanicsburg, PA: Stackpole Books, 2010).

Franz A. J. Szabo, Kaunitz and Enlightened Absolutism 1753–1780 (Cambridge: Cambridge University Press, 1994).

Negley Teeters, The Cradle of the Penitentiary: The Walnut Street Jail at Philadelphia, 1773–1835 (Philadelphia: Pennsylvania Prison Society, 1955).

Aaron Thomas, ed., Cesare Beccaria, On Crimes and Punishments and Other Writings, trans. Aaron Thomas and Jeremy Parzen (Toronto: University of Toronto Press, 2008).

Christopher L. Tomlins & Bruce H. Mann, eds., The Many Legalities of Early America (Chapel Hill: University of North Carolina Press, 2001).

Michael H. Tonry, The Handbook of Crime and Punishment (New York: Oxford University Press, 2000).

Charles Walsh, A Bookseller of the Last Century: Being Some Account of the Life of John Newbery, and of the Books He Published, with a Notice of the Later Newberys (London: Griffith, Farran, Okeden & Welsh, 1885).

Casey White, John Jay: Diplomat of the American Experiment (New York: The Rosen Publishing Group, 2006).

Steven Wilf, Law's Imagined Republic: Popular Politics and Criminal Justice in Revolutionary America (Cambridge: Cambridge University Press, 2010).

Gordon S. Wood, Empire of Liberty: A History of the Early Republic, 1789–1815 (New York: Oxford University Press, 2009).

Alfred F. Young, Gary B. Nash & Ray Raphael, eds., Revolutionary Founders: Rebels, Radicals, and Reformers in the Making of the Nation (New York: Vintage Books, 2012).

David Young, trans., Cesare Beccaria, On Crimes and Punishments (Indianapolis: Hackett Publishing Co., 1986).

Olivier Zunz, ed., Alexis de Tocqueville and Gustave de Beaumont in America: Their Friendship and Their Travels (Charlottesville: University of Virginia Press, Arthur Goldhammer, trans. 2010).

Book Chapters

Piers Beirne, "Inventing Criminology: The 'Science of Man' in Cesare Beccaria's Dei Delitti E Delle Pene (1764)," in 3 Marilyn McShane & Frank P. Williams III, eds., Criminal Justice: Contemporary Literature in Theory and Practice (New York: Garland Publishing, 1997).

John D. Bessler, "The American Enlightenment: Eliminating Capital Punishment in the United States," in Lill Scherdin, ed., Capital Punishment: A Hazard to a Sustainable Criminal Justice System? (Farnham: Ashgate, 2014).

Seth Cotlar, "Every Man Should Have Property": Robert Coram and the American Revolution's Legacy of Economic Populism, in Alfred F. Young, Gary B. Nash & Ray Raphael, eds., Revolutionary Founders: Rebels, Radicals, and Reformers in the Making of the Nation (New York: Vintage Books, 2012).

Markus D. Dubber, "An Extraordinarily Beautiful Document": Jefferson's "Bill for Proportioning Crimes and Punishments" and the Challenge of Republican Punishments, in Markus D. Dubber & Lindsay Farmer, eds., Modern Histories of Crime and Punishment (Stanford: Stanford University Press, 2007).

Kathryn Preyer, "Cesare Beccaria and the Founding Fathers," *in* Mary Sarah Bilder, Maeva Marcus & R. Kent Newmyer, eds., Blackstone in America: Selected Essays of Kathryn Preyer (Cambridge: Cambridge University Press, 2009).

Alan Rogers, "'A Long Train of Hideous Consequences': Boston, Capital Punishment, and the Transformation of Republicanism, 1780–1805," *in* James M. O'Toole & David Quigley, eds., Boston's Histories: Essays in Honor of Thomas H. O'Connor (Boston: Northeastern University Press, 2004).

Articles

Harry Elmer Barnes, *The Historical Origin of the Prison System in America*, 12 Journal of the American Institute of Criminal Law and Criminology 35 (Chicago, IL: Northwestern University Press, 1921).

Valentine J. Belfiglio, *Italian Culture in Eighteenth-Century Philadelphia*, 23 Italian Quarterly 75 (1982).

John D. Bessler, *Revisiting Beccaria's Vision: The Enlightenment, America's Death Penalty, and the Abolition Movement*, 4 Nw. J.L. & Soc. Pol'y 195 (2009).

John D. Bessler, *The Anomaly of Executions: The Cruel and Unusual Punishments Clause in the 21st Century*, 2 Br. J. Am. Leg. Studies 297 (2013).

John D. Bessler, *The Death Penalty in Decline: From Colonial America to the Present*, 50 Crim. L. Bull. 245 (2014).

John D. Bessler, *The Public Interest and the Unconstitutionality of Private Prosecutors*, 47 Ark. L. Rev. 51 (1994).

John D. Bessler, *Tinkering Around the Edges: The Supreme Court's Death Penalty Jurisprudence*, 49 Am. Crim. L. Rev. 1913 (2012).

Mary Sarah Bilder, *James Madison, Law Student and Demi-Lawyer*, 28 Law & Hist. Rev. 389 (2010).

Yvon Bizardel & Howard C. Rice, Jr., *"Poor in Love Mr. Short,"* 21 Wm. & Mary Q. 516 (1964).

Daniel D. Blinka, *Jefferson and Juries: The Problem of Law, Reason, and Politics in the New Republic*, 47 Am. J. Legal Hist. 35 (2005).

Steven G. Calabresi & Sarah E. Agudo, *Individual Rights Under State Constitutions When the Fourteenth Amendment Was Ratified in 1868: What Rights Are Deeply Rooted in American History and Tradition?*, 87 Tex. L. Rev. 7 (2008).

Saul Cornell, *A New Paradigm for the Second Amendment*, 22 Law & Hist. Rev. 161 (2004).

David Brion Davis, *The Movement to Abolish Capital Punishment in America, 1787–1861*, 63 American Historical Review 23 (Oct. 1957).

Davison M. Douglas, *God and the Executioner: The Influence of Western Religion on the Death Penalty*, 9 Wm. & Mary Bill Rts. J. 137 (2000).

Edward Dumbauld, *Thomas Jefferson's Equity Commonplace Book*, 48 Wash. & Lee L. Rev. 1257 (1991).

Louis Filler, *Movements to Abolish the Death Penalty in the United States*, The Annals of the American Academy 124 (Nov. 1952).

George Fisher, *The Birth of the Prison Retold*, 104 Yale L.J. 1235 (1995).

Günter Frankenberg, *Torture and Taboo: An Essay Comparing Paradigms of Organized Cruelty*, 56 Am. J. Comp. L. 403 (2008).

M. H. Hoeflich, *Translation & the Reception of Foreign Law in the Antebellum United States*, 50 Am. J. Comp. L. 753 (2002).

Joshua E. Kastenberg, *An Enlightened Addition to the Original Meaning: Voltaire and the Eighth Amendment's Prohibition Against Cruel and Unusual Punishment*, 5 Temp. Pol. & Civ. Rts. L. Rev. 49 (1995).

David B. Kopel, *The Second Amendment in the Nineteenth Century*, 1998 B.Y.U. L. Rev. 1359 (1998).

Leonard W. Levy, *The Right Against Self-Incrimination: History and Judicial History*, 84 Political Science Quarterly 1 (1969).

Matthew Lippman, *The Development and Drafting of the United Nations Convention Against Torture and Other Cruel, Inhuman or Degrading Treatment or Punishment*, 17 B.C. Int'l & Comp. L. Rev. 275 (1994).

Marcello Maestro, *A Pioneer for the Abolition of Capital Punishment: Cesare Beccaria*, 34 Journal of the History of Ideas 463 (July–Sept. 1973).

Marcello Maestro, *Benjamin Franklin and the Penal Laws*, 36 Journal of the History of Ideas 551 (1975).

Howard R. Marraro, *Count Luigi Castiglioni: An Early Italian Traveller to Virginia (1785–1786)*, 58 Va. Mag. Hist. & Biography 473 (Oct. 1950).

Matthew W. Meskell, *The History of Prisons in the United States from 1777 to 1877*, 51 Stan. L. Rev. 839 (1999).

Frederick C. Millett, *Will the United States Follow England (and the Rest of the World) in Abandoning Capital Punishment?*, 6 Pierce L. Rev. 547 (2008).

Elon H. Moore, *The Livingston Code*, 19 Am. Inst. Crim. L. & Criminology (Fall 1928).

Matthew A. Pauley, *The Jurisprudence of Crime and Punishment from Plato to Hegel*, 39 Am. J. Juris. 97 (1994).

Kathryn Preyer, *Crime, the Criminal Law and Reform in Post-Revolutionary Virginia*, 1 Law and Hist. R. 53 (1983).

Deborah A. Schwartz & Jay Wishingrad, *The Eighth Amendment, Beccaria, and the Enlightenment: An Historical Justification for the* Weems v. United States *Excessive Punishment Doctrine*, 24 Buff. L. Rev. 783 (1975).

Richard V. Sipe, *Cesare Beccaria*, 22 Ind. L.J. 27 (1946).

Robert R. Sullivan, *The Birth of the Prison: The Case of Benjamin Rush*, 31 Eighteenth-Century Studies 333 (1998).

Essays, Pamphlets & Theses

Matthew A. Byron, Crime and Punishment: The Impotency of Dueling Laws in the United States (Ph.D. thesis, University of Arkansas, 2008).

Gabriele Gottlieb, Theater of Death: Capital Punishment in Early America, 1750–1800 (Ph.D. thesis, University of Pittsburgh, 2005).

Aaron J. Palmer, "All Matters and Things Shall Center There": A Study of Elite Political Power in South Carolina, 1763–1776 (Ph.D. thesis, Graduate School of Arts and Sciences, Georgetown University, Washington, D.C., Oct. 19, 2009).

Kitty Preyer and Her Books, Daniel R. Coquillette Rare Book Room, Boston College Law Library (Fall 2006) (unpaginated pamphlet), *available at* http://www.bc.edu/content/dam/files/schools/law_sites/library/pdf/RBR_items/pdf/ExhibitCatalogPreyer.pdf.

Benjamin Rush, An Enquiry into the Effects of Public Punishments upon Criminals, and upon Society, Mar. 9, 1787.

Index

"A. B.," 270–71

"A. F.," 149

Abbott, Geoffrey, 223

Abelard, Peter, 29

abolition: anti-death penalty movement, 3–4, 14, 16–18, 25–26, 39, 50–51, 74, 88–89, 96, 103–4, 126–27, 131, 136, 149, 157, 171–72, 181–82, 195, 208–9, 212, 224, 228–30, 237–44, 259, 262–71, 279–80, 299, 311, 336, 343–47, 368, 379–81, 384–85, 417–18, 420, 435, 440, 449–50, 454; anti-slavery movement/sentiment, 16, 92, 189, 211, 256, 261–62, 354, 382–83, 438; of Austrian death penalty, 4, 66, 104, 228, 243; of benefit of clergy, 193, 400; of common-law crimes, 427; and "fair and full trial of the entire abolition of capital punishments by any State willing to make it," 208; of Germany's death penalty, 449; of imprisonment for debt, 232, 268, 403; of Italy's death penalty, 26; for non-homicide offenses, 15, 21, 221–22, 280, 381, 461; of Russian executions, 4, 209; of slavery/slave trade, 14, 21, 200, 256, 380, 382–83; of torture, 28, 45, 62–63, 74, 222, 364–67, 384, 389; of Tuscany's death penalty, 4–5, 66, 104, 136–37, 161, 199, 209, 212, 228. *See also specific countries, crimes, organizations, and states*

Abolition of Death Penalty Act of 1965, 449

abuse of power, 8, 17–19, 363

Académie-Francaise, 187

Academy of Fists, 32–35, 71, 435, 469

Academy of the Transformed, 31

Accademia dei Pugni, 32

Accademia dei Trasformati, 31, 469

accomplices, 56, 183

Account of the Alteration and Present State of the Penal Laws of Pennsylvania, An, 192, 322

Account of the Bilious remitting Yellow Fever, as It Appeared in the City of Philadelphia, in the Year 1793, An, 90

Account of the European Settlements in America, An, 4, 290

Account of the Manners and Customs of Italy, 137

Account of the origin, progress, and regulations, with a description of the newly-established Bridewell, or Penitentiary-House at Wymondham, in Norfolk, An, 325

Account of the State Prison or Penitentiary House, in the City of New-York, An, 323–24

Achaians, 251

Act for Establishing Religious Freedom, An, 251, 364

Act for the Punishment of Certain Crimes Against the United States, An, 9

Act to reduce the cases in which the penalty of death may be inflicted, An, 426

Adair, John, 344

Adams, Abigail, 100, 119, 125, 179–80, 248, 252, 256, 278, 284, 302; in England, 80, 269; in France, 257; on "good Government," 127; on John Adams' study of Italian republics, 179; and "Remember the Ladies" letter, 11, 311; and Rousseau, 470

Adams, John, xiii, 11, 19, 26, 62, 66, 87, 108, 257, 278; and Abigail Adams, 11, 180, 302, 311; and American Academy of Arts and Sciences, 130; on arbitrariness, 25, 300, 363; and Benjamin Guild, 125; and Benjamin Rush, 5, 178, 299–300, 387–88, 441; books/library of, 174, 178–79; and Boston Massacre trial, 5, 174, 292, 431; on "British constitution," 300–1; bust of, 314; on canon and feudal law, 363; and Cesare Beccaria, xi, 4–5, 17–18, 36, 43–44, 80, 146, 159, 174–77, 179, 246, 392, 432, 455, 501, 503; and Charles Carroll of Carrollton, 248–49; as "Clarendon," 301; on confessions, 361; on corporal punishments, 52, 300–1; on cruelty, 273, 363; on custom, 300; and Daniel Roberdeau, 189; death of, 412; on death penalty, 26, 121, 300–1, 389; and Declaration of Independence, 332; as defense counsel, 5, 80, 121, 174, 431; on "despots," 100; diary of, 179, 502; as diplomat, 100, 106; and Duke de la Rochefoucauld, 175, 302; on "Dungeons"/ "Irons," 365; in England, 19, 80, 269; on England's "hostile and sanguinary" designs, 252; on English "Cruelty and Barbarism," 159; on Enlightenment writers, 63; on equality, 63, 301, 436; on "faithful interpretation" of laws, 436; on fines, 300–1; in France, 80, 100, 175; and Francesco dal Verme, 108–9, 114; and George Keith Taylor, 175; and George Washington, 292; on "good and equal laws," 436; on happiness, 252, 300, 433; and Henry Knox, 292; on "impartial execution"

of laws, 436; on imprisonment, 300–1; and Jacques-Pierre Brissot de Warville, 398; and James McHenry, 309; and James Warren, 249; and Jean-Louis de Lolme, 106, 175; and Jeremiah Smith, 175; and John Almon, 77; and John Hancock, 173–74; and John Jebb, 195; and John Locke, 41; and John Paradise, 201; and John Quincy Adams, 180, 195, 356; and John Trumbull, 101; and Joseph Priestley, 194; and Josiah Quincy, 403; on juries/jury trials, 300–1; on "king-killing," 100; on "laws of Draco," 26; on "laws of God," 301; on laws of nature, 301; as lawyer, 5, 80, 121, 174, 182, 226, 431; on liberty, 300–1; on loss of limbs, 300–1; on Louis XVI, 100, 179–80, 302; and Luigi Castiglioni, 13; and Machiavelli, 179–80; and Massachusetts constitution, 19, 63, 77, 178, 246, 300; and Mercy Otis Warren, 142; and Montesquieu, 17–18, 220; and Nathanael Greene, 356; on necessity for punishment, 178; as "Novanglus," 75, 252; and Paolo Andreani, 202; pardons/ uses of clemency of, 400; and Perez Morton, 327; and Philip Mazzei, 196; on power, 300; as President, 19, 80, 173, 175–76, 284, 334; on "Pride of the People," 433; on prisoners of war, 365; on proportionality, 174, 179, 500; on Revolutionary War, 441; on rights, 63; and Roman/Italian history, 179, 431–32; and Rousseau, 59, 175, 470; and St. John Honeywood, 303; and Samuel Quinn, 176; on "sanguinary laws," 252; on social compact, 52–53, 300; on "Solon's reputation for wisdom and integrity," 26; on "Spirit of American Government," 433; study of French, 120; study/use of Italian, 17, 108, 175–79, 502; study/knowledge of Roman history, 356; on "the People," 252, 363; and Thomas Adams, 181; on Thomas Nash, 334; on torture,

300–1, 361; on treason, 500; as treaty commissioner, 14; on tyranny, 273–74; on tyrants/tyranny, 173, 179, 363; on "unbridled majorities," 100; as Vice President, 9; on voting/suffrage, 52–53, 300; and William Blackstone's *Commentaries*, 223; on whipping, 275; writings of, 17, 26, 77, 175, 179, 436, 448; on "young woman" convicted of "trifling theft," 26

Adams, John Quincy, 125, 257; and American Academy of Arts and Sciences, 130; and anti-slavery efforts, 383; and Benjamin Franklin, 257; and Cesare Beccaria, 174; on death penalty, 180–82, 264; on executive clemency, 182; on gaming, 397–98; as Harvard graduate, 180; and Jeremy Bentham, 416; and John Adams, 174, 195, 356; and John Jebb, 195; on laws against suicide, 397; on lex talionis, 372; as minister to Great Britain, 173, 416; and Montesquieu, 180–81; on natural law, 397; on proportionality, 180, 182; as Secretary of State, 182; study of French, 120; study of Italian, 108; study of Latin, 356; study of Roman history, 356; on suicide, 43, 397–98; and Thomas Jefferson, 257; tutoring of, 252; as President, 181, 314

Adams, Samuel, 11, 13, 87, 137, 258, 268, 292, 299, 434; pardons of, 400; and penal reform, 315

Adams, Thomas, 196

Adams, Thomas Boylston, 146, 181, 503

Addison, Joseph, 30, 105, 356

Address of the board of inspectors of the prison of the city and county of Philadelphia, 260

Address to the Addressers, 368

Address to the Freeholders of Middlesex, 194

Address to the Freemen of the State of South Carolina, An, 205

Address to the Inhabitants of Quebec, 5, 7–8, 66–67, 75, 147–48, 162; drafts of, 473; French translation of, 147–48, 497; German translation of, 147

Address to the Legislature of Kentucky, on the Abolition of Capital Punishments, An, 344–47

Adelphic Union Library, 125

adultery: branding for, 122, 373; as capital crime, xv, 275, 373, 411; as crime "difficult to prove," 44–45; and English law, 282; and scarlet letter, 373; setting on the gallows for, 373

Advancement of Learning, The, 362

Adventures of Sappho, The, 71

Advice and Consent Clause, 357

Advice to the Privileged Order in the Several States of Europe, 234

affair of the diamond necklace, 198–99

affairs of honor. *See* duels/dueling

Africa, 307, 450–51. *See also* North Africa; *specific countries*

African American(s): enslavement of, 11, 382, 442; exclusion from testifying, 189; exclusion from social compact, 382; intellectuals, 16, 306–9, 311; lynching of, 112; punishment of, 383. *See also* racial discrimination; slave trade; slavery; slaves

African slave trade, 442. *See also* slave trade

Age of Reason, 19. *See also* Enlightenment; reason

Agogna River, 113

Alaska, 268

Albany, New York, 202, 237, 296, 324–25, 370, 389, 400, 422, 538

Albemarle County, Virginia, 231

Albergo Croce Bianco, 114

Albergo Reale, 113

Albers, Heinrich, 379

Aldgate, 273

Alexander, 70

Alexander I (Russian czar), 413

Alexander VI (Pope), 178

Alexandria, 251

Alexandria, Virginia, 106, 110

Alexandrine, Charlotte, 116

Alfieri, Vittorio, 73, 106, 119, 176, 201

Alien and Sedition Acts, 333, 411
Allen, Ethan, 158–59
Allen, John, 13, 118
Allen, Richard, 415
Allen, Thomas, 315–16
Allen, William, 85
Allen, William (chief justice), 13, 15, 118
Allibon, Richard, 250
Almon, John, 75–77, 81–82, 91–92, 138
Alphonsus II, 290
Alsop, Richard, 101
Alston, Joseph, 205
Amandagamani (King), 367
Amar, Akhil, xii, 5
amercements, 37. *See also* fines
America. *See* United States
America, 88
American Academy of Arts and Sciences, 130
"American Antiquities," 101
American Bible Society, 158, 232
American colonies, 3, 11, 49, 68, 70, 99, 117, 120, 161, 190, 202, 225, 232, 254, 294, 316, 363, 369, 373, 380, 396, 399, 405, 424, 434, 442; transportation to, 52. *See also* penal colonies
American colonists, 78, 80, 120, 144, 147, 212, 235, 250, 356, 373, 432, 434, 455; as claiming rights of Englishmen, 68–69; assertion of rights of, 67–69; grievances of, 68
American Dictionary of the English Language, An, 252
American Dream, 432
American independence, 26, 72, 99, 101, 103, 119, 121, 126, 145, 148, 152, 171, 197–98, 200, 205, 228, 230, 246, 250, 271, 319, 359, 368, 405. *See also* Declaration of Independence; Revolutionary War
American Independence, the Interest and Glory of Great-Britain, 353
American law: accessibility of, 374; birth of, 442; as breathing "the spirit of a parent," 515; body of, 413; Cesare Beccaria's effect on, xiv–xv, 5–6, 191, 226,

261, 371, 373, 380, 437, 448, 453–54; codification of, 173, 412–14, 425, 427; and corporal punishments, 480; future of, 451; and judicial review, 363; as "not enacted for the benefit of the few and the oppression of the many," 362; as "not written in blood," 515; origins of, 404, 407–8; study of, 437; transformation of, xi–xii, 6, 13–14, 18, 21, 23, 241, 454; as unequal, 311; as "uniform and equal," 362. *See also* law; *specific states*; United States
American Museum, The, 88, 112, 172, 215, 244, 260, 266, 325, 385–86, 443
American Philosophical Society, 34, 118–120, 129, 211, 216, 313–14
American Revolution, xii, xiv–xv, 3, 5, 12, 15, 20–21, 66, 70, 76, 82, 85, 87, 90–91, 100–1, 103, 126, 131, 142, 147, 151, 160, 168–70, 175, 185, 187, 196, 200–1, 226, 228, 248–49, 266, 280, 286, 289–90, 292–93, 296, 302, 314, 319–20, 332, 353, 355, 357–58, 368, 374, 396, 405, 423, 426, 431, 433, 436, 438, 442–43, 447, 455, 473, 564
American revolutionaries, xi–xii, 6–7, 22, 66, 100, 138, 148, 161, 170, 196, 253–54, 290–91, 293, 300, 319, 327, 332, 354, 369, 422, 432, 434, 440–41; aided by French, 100, 119–20; Luigi Castiglioni's impressions of, 13
American Society for the Abolition of Capital Punishment, 264, 267
American Weekly Mercury, 121–22
"Americanus," 254, 358
Aminta, 177
Amnesty International, 427
Amory, Thomas, 268–69
"Amphitheatre of Titus," 362
amputation: of ear(s), 167; of hand, 167, 184; of toes, 376. *See also* ear cropping
Amsterdam, 125, 223, 356, 433
Analytical Review, The, 279
Anarchiad, The, 101
anarchy, 69, 137, 232; and duels, 55; state/ times of, 44, 349

Anderson's Tavern, 198

André, John (Major), 103, 153–54, 497

Andreani, Paolo, 106, 119, 200–2

Andrei, Giovanni, 313

Anglo-Saxon law, 274

Anglo-Scottish Union of 1707, 47

animals: slaughter of, 107; use in executions, 129, 216

Annals of Philadelphia, 287

Annan, Robert, 215

Annapolis, Maryland, 66, 248–49, 255, 358; convention in, 255, 261, 369

"Annapolitan," 255–56

Anne (Queen), 47

anti-dueling laws, 397

Anti-Federalist(s), 422

anti-gallows movement. *See* abolition

Antiquities of Rome, The, 356

anti-slavery sentiment/societies. *See* abolition

Antoinette, Marie (Queen), 29, 119, 180, 199

Antoninus (Emperor), 280, 367

Aphorisms, 335

apostasy, 283

Apotheosis of Washington, The, 313, 453

Appeal to Justice and Interests of the People of Great Britain, in the Present Disputes with America, An, 76

Appeal to the World, An, 299

appointment of counsel, 295

apprenticeships, 413

Apthorp, Fanny, 327

Apthorp, Sarah, 327

Aquinas, St. Thomas, 39, 41, 43

arbitrariness, 299, 301, 316, 335, 395, 436; and Bill of Rights, 426; and death penalty, 26, 428, 439, 454; and due process, 439; and enforcement/interpretation of law, 54, 57, 183, 224, 335–36; and English law, 49, 83–84; and equal protection, 439; and executions, 442; founders' disdain of, 440; of government/law(s), 72, 300–1, 354, 392, 436, 442; of judges, 56, 152–53, 300, 436; of kings, 300; and pre-trial

detention, 426; of punishments/proceedings, 155, 192, 226, 299, 317, 361, 378, 395, 401, 455; and tyrants, 378. *See also* death sentences; Due Process Clause(s); Eighth Amendment; execution(s); Fourteenth Amendment

arbitrary power, 67, 72, 80, 145, 175, 192, 224, 241, 299–300, 316, 401

Archbold, John Frederick, 240

Archduke of Austria, 137, 322

Argentina, 94

Argument of Edward Livingston Against Capital Punishment, 417

aristocracy, 73, 359, 433

Aristotle, 194

Arkansas: corporal punishments in, 342; Territory, 342

armed populace, 390–91. *See also* right to bear arms; Second Amendment

armonica, 117, 194

Arnold, Benedict, 153, 170

Arouet, François-Marie. *See* Voltaire

arson, 229, 386, 414, 418; abolition for, 172, 381; as capital crime, 9, 26, 236, 274–75, 280, 282, 299, 322; fines for, 9; imprisonment for, 9; labor for, 383; and life sentences, 348; pillory for, 9; whipping for, 9

Articles of Confederation, 112, 116, 205–6, 255, 284, 370, 403, 434; approval/ratification of, 206, 212, 434; and state vs. federal power, 258

Articles of War, 9, 152, 162

Asgill, Charles, 157–58, 291–92

Asia, 401, 450; death sentences in, 450. *See also specific countries*

Asiatics, 251

assassination: attempted, 46; as capital crime, 42, 46

assassin(s), 38, 180

assault: as capital crime, 275

assault weapons, 392

assistance of counsel, 106, 247, 295, 426

asylums, 56

Athens, Greece, 285–86; lawgivers of, 445

Atlanta, Georgia, 347; penitentiary in, 330

Atlantic Ocean, xi, 4, 17, 74, 123, 250, 317, 346, 393

attainder: bills of, 170, 213, 215, 246; concept of, 27, 214; judicial, 215; references in Constitution, 381. *See also* bills of attainder; Bill of Attainder Clause(s)

attempted crimes, 56, 183. *See also specific crimes*

attorneys. *See* counsel, defense; prosecutors

Attorney(s) General. *See specific individuals and states*; United States

Aubert, Giuseppe, 27, 31

Auburn Prison, 328

"Auburn system," 327–28

Aurora, 230

Austin, John, 278

Australia(n): exploration of, 254; penal colonies, 52, 318, 331; refusal to extradite without assurances death penalty will not be sought, 451

Austria(n), 30, 126–27, 137, 179, 365; administration, 31, 34; ambassador, 84, 108; coffeehouses in, 31; and control of northern Italy, 30; death penalty's curtailment in, 4, 66, 104, 228; Empire, 28; penal laws/reform, 51; rulers, 33–34, 118, 137; torture abolished in, 63

Autenreid (Autenreith), William, 379

Auvergne, France, 199

axe(s), 39, 41, 65, 176, 247, 302, 340, 342. *See also* executioners

Babylon, King of, 445. *See also* Hammurabi; Code of Hammurabi

Bache, Alexander Dallas, 284

Bacon, Francis, 41, 141, 335–36, 362, 499

Bad State of the Milanese Currency, 30

Baden, 243

bail, 85, 106; and Constitution, 427; corporal punishments in lieu of, 233; excessive, 200, 226, 246–47, 263; right to, 427

Bailey, Francis, 89–90, 230

Bailey, Robert, 230

Bailyn, Bernard, 3

Baird, Bruce, 396

Bakewell, Sarah, 107

Balázs, Éva, 365

Ball, Burgess, 110

Ball, Kenneth, 101

Balsamo, Giuseppe, 198–99. *See also* Cagliostro, Alessandro di

Baltimore, Maryland, 110, 140, 308, 380; Archdiocese of, 248; state prison in, 325

Banat, 63

Bancroft, George, 336

banishment, 52, 60, 129, 183, 205, 236, 280–81, 290, 294, 411. *See also* exile; transportation

Banister, John, 112

Banister, Jr., John, 108, 112

Banister, Sr., John, 112

bankruptcy: punishment of, 42, 56, 183, 282, 402–4

Banks, Joseph, 129, 254

Banneker, Benjamin, 306–11

Banner, Stuart, 190, 239–40, 384

Banqueting House, 288

barbarians, 123

barbarism/barbarity, 10, 112, 121, 139, 157–60, 189, 220, 234, 243, 251, 267–68, 271, 301, 323, 342–43, 349, 360, 365, 371, 374, 378, 381, 388, 400, 404, 407, 411, 443; of English criminal code, 232, 324; of executioners, 164; "of men," 309; and modes of execution, 185; as part of definition of "cruel," 252; of slavery, 361, 376; and torture, 47. *See also* "Bloody Code"

Barbé-Marbois, François de, 187

Barber of Seville, The, 119

Barbò, Anna, 73

Barbò, Barnaba, 73

Baretti, Giuseppe M. A., 107, 137, 176, 357

Barlow, Joel, 88, 101, 201, 234

Barnard, Nathaniel, 173

Barnes, Harry Elmer, 226, 232–33

Barnett, Angelica, 191

Baron d'Holbach, 33, 59–60, 83

Baron von Steuben, 153, 441

Barré, Isaac, 60

Barrington, William, 161

Bartlett, Josiah, 434

Barton, Benjamin Smith, 227

Barton, William, 137, 227

Barziza, Antonio, 201

Basel, Switzerland, 228

Bashaw, 254

Basilica di Sant'Eustorgio, 63

"bastard" child: birth of, 123; death of, 183, 193, 400; concealment of, 193

Bastille prison, 60, 95, 199; governor of, 442; storming of, 442. *See also* French Revolution

bastinadoes, 301. *See also* whipping

Batacchi, Joseph, 103

Batoni, Pompeo, 105

battery, 418

Bavaria, 243; penal code of, 139

Bayley, Mary, 47

Baze v. Rees, 452

bearing false witness, as capital crime, 26

Beaumarchais, Pierre-Augustin Caron de, 119–20

Beaumont, Elie de, 124

Beaumont, Gustave Auguste de, xv, 139, 383

Beauvior, François Jean de, 60

Beccaria, Annibale, 73

Beccaria, Cesare, 93, 199, 202, 218, 240, 265, 322, 363, 422, 473, 477, 521, 532; as "a brother," 146; as "able and illustrious foreigner," 361; as "able writer," 4; on "absolute necessity" for punishment, 16, 38, 48, 51, 54, 329, 421–22; and Academy of Fists, 33; on accomplices, 56, 183; on acts of violence, 183; as "acute Reasoner," 4, 378; as "admirable author," 361; as "admired by many of the British Dissenters and American radicals," 114; on adultery, 44–45; "advanced teachings" of, 329; as "amiable and eloquent champion of the rights of humanity," 140; as among "greatest constitutional writers," 93; on anarchy, 43–44, 49, 349; and André Morellet, 36, 218; on "arbitrary discretion of judges," 56, 436; on "arbitrary laws," 57; on "arbitrary power," 80; on attempted crimes, 56, 183; on asylums, 56; awards in honor of, 437, 453; background of, xii, 28–36, 62, 71–74, 129–30; on banishment, 52, 183; on "barbaric and useless tortures," 42; on "barbarous and useless torments," 38; as "beneficent genius," 146; as "benevolent," 80, 164, 166, 331; as "benevolent philosopher," 234; on "blind and impartial laws," 56; on "blind habit," 367; on bounties, 56; bust of, 453; on card games, 35; and "cause of humanity," 235; "celebrated," 5, 50, 79–80, 147, 167, 172, 270, 312, 369, 385, 396; as "celebrated author," 73; "celebrated work of," 192; censorship/criticism of, 35, 62–63, 176; on certainty vs. severity of punishment, 7, 18, 38, 94, 182, 208, 238, 243, 349, 426, 450, 482; "characteristic humanity and sagacity" of, 208; children of, 73; citation in U.S. courts, 15, 384, 391–93, 437; cited by the Continental Congress, 148, 432, 435; on "clear" laws, 54–55, 183, 354, 455; on commerce/currency, 30, 59, 61, 76, 353, 432; commentary on, 92, 142, 194, 448; as "compassionate author," 59; on "comprehensive" laws, 80; on confessions/false confessions, 44–46, 166, 393; on confiscations, 205, 398; confused with "Father Beccaria," 130; on "connexion between the abolition of capital punishments, and the order and happiness of society," 244; on "constant and fixed voice of the law," 54; on corporal punishments, 51–53; on counterfeiting, 56; on credibility of witnesses, 366; on crimes, 166; criminologists' study of, xi, 5,

458; on cruelty/cruel laws, 6, 38–39, 42, 56, 182, 194, 232, 246, 368, 370, 446, 455, 554; on "dangerous" revolutionaries, 43–44, 49–51; death of, 14, 64–65, 73–74, 442, 454; on death penalty, xi, 3, 25, 36–39, 41–44, 47–51, 90, 96, 133, 142, 161–62, 208–9, 244, 258, 264–65, 268, 280, 295, 348, 365, 367, 378, 388–89, 397, 428, 449, 454; on debtors/bankrupts, 56, 183, 232, 399, 401–3; as "declared enemy of the Supreme Being," 63; "deeply impressed by," 249; on degrees of crime, 183; on despotism, 69, 165; on deterrence, 18, 37, 39, 44, 47–50, 168, 258; on discretion of judges, 56, 407; as displaying "the heart of a Divinity," 360; on dueling, 18, 55–56, 90, 92, 395–97; as economist, 6, 35, 364, 432; on education, 6, 18, 57, 399; as "elegant writer," 4; "eloquent," 164, 166, 168; as "eminent and judicious writer on criminal law," 426; on Empress Elizabeth, 545; as "enemy of Christianity," 63; as "Eminent Person," 380; "enlightened," 18; as entitled to "highest honours," 360; on equality, 66, 355, 383; "estimable," 413; on evidence, 165, 183; "excellent," 148, 260; as "excellent pioneer of penal reform," 349; as "excellent writer," 287; excommunicated from church, 364; on executioners, 39; on exile, 53; on extraditions/extradition treaties, 56, 399, 401, 428, 436; as "extraordinary man," 241; on factions/sects, 363–64; on "false" ideas of utility, 57, 392; as "familiar to every reader conversant with criminal law," 140; as "famous penologist," 489; on "fear" of man, 57, 165, 194; on "fear of the laws," 57, 164, 194; on fines, 51; as "first evangelist of Reason," 4; on "fixed code of laws," 436; as founder of criminology, 463; Francis Hutcheson's influence on, 41; on freedom, 51, 56, 194, 265; on freedom of religion,

364; as "friend to humanity," 147; general/common axioms of, 206; on "general will," 39, 63, 354, 402; "genius of," 69, 136; as "glorious spirit," 360; on goal of "good laws"/legislation, 8, 66, 86; on "good of individuals," 444; in grand jury charges, 498–99; "great," 270, 284; "great eminence" of, 259–60; as "great friend of man," 87; as "great lover of men of letters," 73; on "great truths," 367; and "greatest happiness" principle, 19, 53, 56, 142–43, 265, 433; on "greatest sum of pleasures," 355; on gun laws/firearms, 14, 18, 57, 183, 390–93; on happiness, 7–8, 16, 18, 54, 56, 66, 147–48, 183, 244, 265, 355, 362, 423, 431, 444; on "hard crimes to prove," 44; on "harsh" punishments, 38–39; on "Heresies," 251; on honor, 165; as honorary member of Constitutional Society of Virginia, 196; house of, 73–74; "humane," 92, 146, 496; "humane and benevolent," 368; "humane and profound," 562; "humane doctrines" of, 389; as "humane philosopher," 159; "humanity of," 371; on idleness, 183; "illustrious," 9, 206, 267; "immortal," 3, 35, 192, 370; "immortal work of," 74; "immortalised," 385; as impetus for penitentiary system, 328, 454; on imprisonment, 44, 183; "incomparable," 194, 366; on industry, 77, 80; on "inequality," 51; on infamy, 18, 44–45, 182–83, 393–95, 437–38; influence of, xi–xvi, 3–22, 25–27, 36–39, 48–49, 57–66, 68–69, 74, 79–81, 87–94, 101, 104, 109, 131–34, 138–49, 151–53, 169, 171–75, 186–96, 205, 209–10, 212, 216, 219, 221–22, 225–27, 229, 233–41, 243–44, 247, 249–50, 257–58, 261–68, 270–71, 290, 293, 295–96, 298, 311–12, 323–24, 328–30, 346–49, 353–55, 359, 362–65, 367–68, 370, 372, 375, 378, 384–85, 387–89, 391–93, 395–99, 401, 413,

416, 421–28, 431–37, 448, 451–52, 455, 479; as "ingenious writer," 4; on innocence, 44; on "intensity" of punishment, 49; on "intent of good laws," 147–48, 362, 423; on interpretation of laws, 54–55, 183, 206, 427, 446; on judicial discretion, 55; on judges, 427, 446; "judicious," 343; as "judicious author," 146; on jury trials, 18, 36, 51, 182, 295, 316, 453; on justice, 7, 54; "justly-celebrated," 65; on labor, 44, 51, 378; on lawlessness/threat thereof, 43, 49; on laws as "contracts amongst free men," 53; on laws "as conventions between men in a state of freedom," 265; on laws as "residue of the most barbarous centuries," 7; "laudable commencements of," 416; as "learned and celebrated," 366; "Learning and Genius" of, 380; "led the way," 164, 171; on legislation/legislators, 183, 427, 446; on "lenient" laws/punishments, 38, 56; on liberty/freedom, 80, 165, 422, 455; on life sentences, 47–49; as "lover of humanity," 59; on "magistrates," 43; as "man of great genius," 34; as "man of pre-eminent talents," 141; "masterly hand of," 69–70, 136; on "mild" punishments, 38, 56, 94, 183; "milder system of," 371; on misery, 8, 16, 56, 66, 76, 147, 174, 355, 362, 421, 423, 431, 496; on "moderate" laws, 446; mollusk named after, 437; on "monarchic spirit," 355; Montesquieu's influence on, 29, 36, 38, 48, 54, 153, 203, 378, 473; "motto of," 243; on murder, 44; as name "dear to humanity," 264; on natural law/rights, 39, 42; on necessity for punishment(s)/execution(s), xi, 37, 43–44, 47–48, 50–51, 57, 66, 161, 179, 280; as "Newtoncino," 37; on nobles, 183; on number of witnesses, 366; on oaths, 166, 183, 366; on "Obscurity of the Laws," 354; on odors, 35; on "opinion"/"point of view," 364; on "overgrown"/"confederate" re-

publics, 69, 165, 212; on pain, 45–46; and Paolo Frisi, 36–37; on pardons/clemency, 38, 56, 165, 183, 208, 399–401; on "passions of the judge," 165; on penitence, 166; on people as source of power, 354; on "perpetual slavery"/"permanent penal servitude," 38, 47–49, 51–52, 376, 378–80, 469; on "personal liberty," 39; "philosophic," 162; as "pillar of enlightened opinion," 169; and "pinnacle of fame," 14; poem about, 303–6; on poor, 51, 76, 395; as "poor philosopher," 63; on poverty, 51, 544; on power, 8, 16, 66, 147, 174, 362, 421, 423, 431; on "precise" laws, 54, 455; on pre-trial detention, 51; on prevention of crime, 18, 25, 44, 47, 56–57, 165, 182–83, 208, 280, 388, 395, 399; "principles of," 166, 171–72, 378, 401; on prison labor, 380; as "profound and amiable philosopher," 145; on "proofs," 45, 162, 165, 366–68; on property, 42, 76, 353, 393; on proportionality, xi, 16, 22, 25, 37, 47, 57, 99, 133, 162, 182, 262, 268, 349, 368, 370, 373–75, 388; on prosecutors, 165; on "public good," 355, 444; on "public peace," 51; on public punishments, 57; on public trials, 165, 182; on punishments, 15, 37, 45, 54, 57, 148, 179, 182–83, 265, 354, 378, 427; on purpose of punishment, 25, 47; as "received by the intelligent as an Angel from heaven," 4; on religious toleration, 251; "renowned," 115; on representation, 353; on republicanism, 53, 80, 355; "respect" for ideas of, 532; on "revolutions in despotick states," 165; on "reward of industry," 51; on rewards, 56, 183; on rich, 51, 76, 395; on right to life, 7, 42; on right to punish, 455; on "rights of humanity," 401; on robbery, 183, 393; on role of judges, 54; as "Rousseau of the Italians," 64; on "rule of law," 50; "sagacious," 80; on sanctuaries, 183; "satisfied the reasonable world of the unrightfulness and inefficacy of the punishment of crimes by death," 195, 387; on scale of crimes and punishments, 37–38, 166, 385; sculptures/monuments of, 73–74; on serious vs. minor crimes, 42, 56; on "simple" laws, 80; on slavery/enslavement, 45, 57, 194, 355; "small and valuable gift of," 192, 370; on smuggling, 35, 56; on social contract, 53–54, 76, 348, 353, 402, 422, 427, 455; as "socialista," 58; on sodomy, 44–45; "sophism of," 425; "sophistry" of, 64; "specious errors of," 209; on speedy punishment, 38, 57, 171, 182, 426–27, 450; on speedy trials, 36; on "spirit of the law," 54, 182, 366; as "stating most beautifully and clearly the essential principles of liberty," 16; study of, 148, 241, 247, 265; on style, 35; as "sublime philosopher," 206; on suicide, 51, 182–83, 269, 397–99; on "superstition," 251; as "teacher of laws in Italy," 58; "the great Italian," 450; on thefts, 51; "Theory of," 388; on tolerance, 363; on torment to offender's bodies, 25–26, 38, 42, 44; on torture, xi, 3, 36, 38, 42, 44–46, 51, 74, 142, 295, 353, 361, 364–68, 371, 384, 389–90, 427, 449, 553; town named after, 437; on truth, 39; and two-witness rule, 162, 366; on tyranny/tyrants, 14–16, 51, 77, 353, 364, 421; U.S. Supreme Court citations of, 15, 437; on "useless severity," 38; "usual humanity" of, 162; and Voltaire, 59; on war, 42, 422; on "weak and corrupt judges," 38; on weak/weakness, 8, 16, 51, 66, 147, 174, 362, 367, 421, 423, 431; as "wicked man," 63; as "wise," 3; wives of, 60–61, 73; the "world" as "indebted to," 259–60; as "world celebrity," 59; on written laws, 354; writings of, 10, 99, 168, 205, 208, 221, 241, 248, 255, 299, 324, 335, 357, 384, 402, 428, 435; and "zenith of his fame as a Philo-sophical Legislator," 157, 209, 219. *See also On Crimes and Punishments*

Beccaria, Francesco, 73
Beccaria, Giambatista (Giambattista) (Father), 116–17, 130, 135, 367, 488–89
Beccaria, Gian, 33
Beccaria, Gioacchino, 63
Beccaria, Giovanni Saverio, 33
Beccaria (Manzoni), Giulia, 33, 71–72, 105, 160, 488
Beccaria, Giulio Bonesana, 73–74, 488
Beccaria, Maddalena, 73
Beccaria, Maria, 33, 73
"Beccaria Anglicus," 286
Beccaria family, 73, 471, 489
Beccaria Township, Pennsylvania, 437
Becket, T., 91
Bedau, Hugo Adam, 95–96
Bedini, Silvio, 310
Bee, Thomas, 334
Beers, Seth, 139
Beevor, Thomas, 321, 325
beheading, 40, 154, 224, 273, 280; machine, 64–65. *See also* decapitation; guillotine
Beinecke Rare Book & Manuscript Library, xiii, 102
Beirne, Piers, 41
Belfiglio, Valentine, 128
Belgioioso, Ludovico Barbiana di, 194
Belgium, 62, 243
Belknap, Jeremy, 129
Bell, James, 403
Bell, John, 88
Bell, Robert, 90, 144–45, 396, 494
Bell & Murray, 87–88
Bellamy, Richard, 19
Bellini, Charles ("Carlo"), 107–8, 448
Bellman of St. Sepulchre, 278
Benbridge, Henry, 118
Bencivenni, Giuseppe Pelli, 256–57
benefit of clergy: abolition of, 193, 400; doctrine/privilege of, 190, 222, 298, 307, 400, 542; as "holy sleight of hand," 305; to "arrest" a judgment, 224; use of, 185, 307, 404, 506

Benjamin, Judah, 233

Benson, Egbert, 374

Bentham, Jeremy, xii–xiii, 19, 60, 95–100, 263, 336, 410; and Aaron Burr, 22, 99, 204–5, 416; admitted to the bar, 249; background of, 95–97; and Benjamin Rush, 413; and Cesare Beccaria, 4, 15, 22, 95–100, 142, 240, 336, 343, 375, 416, 454; on corporal punishments, 96; on cruelty, 343; on death penalty, 74, 95–97, 264, 454; and Edward Livingston, 336; as "familiar to every reader conversant with criminal law," 140; and "greatest happiness" principle, 19, 142–43, 265; on hard labor, 96; and honorary French citizenship, 303; house of, 204, 415; "inestimable gifts" of, 416; influence of, 265, 348; and James Madison, 22, 416; and John Franks, 278; and John Quincy Adams, 416; on mild laws, 343; and Montesquieu, 95; on Napoleonic Code, 413; and offers to draft American penal codes, 416; and Panopticon, 22, 168, 204–5; and penal reform, 95–100, 184, 268, 413; on proportionality, 95; on revenge, 343; and Richard Rush, 339, 413, 415–16; on "sanguinary laws," 343; on solitary confinement, 96; on torture, 375; writings of, 141, 243, 335, 440

Berlin, Germany, 423

Bernard, Francis, 131

Bernardi, Gioanni de, 117

bestiality: as capital crime, 236, 274–75, 280, 282, 411; castration for, 193

Betrothed, The, 30, 72

Bevan, Catharine, 287

Beven, Joseph, 121

"beyond a reasonable doubt" standard, 45

Bianconi, Carlo, 105

Bible(s), 25, 40, 90, 137, 168, 188, 209, 232, 241, 252, 274–75, 294–95, 310, 332, 389, 411; Jeremiah 6, 252; John 1:9, 294; Psalm 51, 307; reprieves for

reading, 307. *See also* New Testament; Old Testament

Biblioteca Ambrosiana, 74

Bibliotheca Classica, 285

Biddle, Charles, 89

Biddle, Nicholas, 415

Bill for Ascertaining the Salaries and Fees of Certain Officers, 282

Bill for Establishing Religious Freedom, 364

Bill for Proportioning Crimes and Punishments, xi, 3, 183–84, 187–91, 206–7, 226, 283, 373, 398, 426

Bill for the More General Diffusion of Knowledge, 357

Bill of Attainder Clause(s), 213, 246

Bill of Rights, 22, 296, 342, 370, 390, 422, 445–46; as absurd/dangerous, 213; adoption of, 22, 296, 442; applicability to states, 21; and arbitrariness, 426; and Cesare Beccaria's influence, 6, 15, 564; debates over, 409; depicted in U.S. Supreme Court building, 445; drafting of, xv, 127, 136, 392–93, 435; and English law, 17; flexible language of, 342, 420; insistence on, 199–200; and James Madison, 127, 273, 409; and natural rights, 355; as "paper"/"parchment" barrier, 409; and Patrick Henry, 199–200; purpose of, 409; ratification of, 17–18, 50, 106, 146, 171, 207, 213, 219, 244, 258–60, 285, 321, 353; as safeguarding individual rights/liberties, 213, 367, 409, 425, 450; text of, 422, 425–27. *See also specific amendments*

Bill Prescribing the Punishment of Those Who Sell Unwholesome Meat or Drink, 282

bills of attainder: in England, 170; prohibition of, 213, 246, 381; use of, 246, 381. *See also* Bill of Attainder Clause(s)

bills of pains and penalties, 246, 381

bills of rights: and English law, xv; and natural rights, 410; and right to trial by jury, 301; variant wording of, 370,

452. *See also* Bill of Rights; *specific jurisdictions*

Billy, 187–88

Binder, Guyora, 229

Bingham, William, 230, 435

Bioren & Duane, 412

Birch, William Young, 369

Bird, Thomas, 426

Bishop, Joel Prentiss, 240

Bishop of Gloucester, 82

Bishop of Limerick, 194

Black, Hugo, 57–58, 437

Black, Jeremy, 67

black codes, 383. *See also* slave codes

Blackbeard, 503

Black-Horse Alley, 415

Blackmun, Harry, 342

blacks. *See* African Americans; racial discrimination

Blackstone, William, xii, 12, 98, 125, 164, 185, 187, 210, 214, 264–65, 271, 287, 424, 532, 552; on arbitrariness, 224; and Cesare Beccaria, 4, 79, 142, 258, 317, 369, 371, 445; commentary on, 92, 448; on corporal punishments, 225; on "cruel and unusual punishments," 224; on cruelty, 222; on death penalty, 371; on discretion, 224–25; on English Bill of Rights, 224–25; on fines, 225; "genius of," 371; "great eminence" of, 260; on happiness, 560; on imprisonment, 225, 283; on infamous punishments, 394; influence of, 4, 67, 219, 221–26, 238, 362, 368–69, 413, 416; on innocence, 45; on kidnapping, 283; and penitentiaries, 317–18; on pillory, 283; on "sanguinary laws," 255; treatise/commentary of, 12, 16, 91, 125, 138–39, 141, 145, 185–86, 222–26, 247, 258, 276, 368, 388, 404, 457; as William Eden's mentor, 99; on witchcraft, 283; writings of, 159, 243, 250, 255, 335, 435, 440. *See also Commentaries on the Laws of England*

Blair, John, 186, 196, 198

Blake, William, 279

Bland, Richard, 560

Blasco, Domenico di, 33

Blasco, Teresa di, 33, 35, 60–61, 71, 73

blasphemy, 251, 294; as capital crime, 189, 275, 411; corporal punishment for, 373

Bleackley, Horace, 84–85

Bleak House, 139

Bleecker, Anthony, 138

blood: acts of, 310; corruption of, 193, 406; "effusion of," 149, 158; "expiated by," 266; for blood, 97, 159; laws written in, 26, 93, 515; shedding of, 40, 42, 65, 137, 159, 196, 209, 236, 252, 263, 265, 270, 438; spilling of, 46, 76, 147; tainted, 27. *See also* "Bloody Code"; corruption of blood; sanguinary

bloodletting, 244

Bloody Assizes of 1685, 273

"Bloody Code," 6, 10, 20, 43, 49, 57, 65, 152, 164, 207, 213, 250, 254, 271, 288–89, 339, 349, 380, 388, 414, 417, 434–35, 441–42, 454, 540, 542; criticism of, 20; as "crowded with disproportioned penalties and indiscriminate severity," 250; as "dark catalogue of crimes and punishments," 414; as ineffective at preventing crime, 262; as label for England's criminal laws, 43; as "written in blood," 324. *See also* England

Bly, John, 268

"Body of Liberties," 274

Bohemia, 137, 322; torture abolished in, 63

Boileau, Nathaniel, 226

boiling to death, 273, 280

Bois de Boulogne, 398

Bologna, Italy, 116

Bonaparte, Napoleon, 417, 503. *See also* Napoleon

Bonducci, Andrea, 27

Bonesana, Cesare, 141, 388. *See also* Beccaria, Cesare

Bonesana, Gian Beccaria, 33

Bonhomme Richard, 141
Bonneville, Margaret, 257
Bonneville, Nicolas de, 257
Book of the General Lawes and Libertyes concerning the Inhabitants of the Massachusets, The, 274
Bordeaux: Parlement of, 218
Borgia, Cesare, 178
boring through nose, 189
boring through tongue, 129, 394
Borzacchini, Marcel, 176, 179
Boston, Massachusetts, 12, 75, 78, 86–87, 90–91, 94, 102–3, 109, 122, 129, 138, 173, 216, 258, 266, 269, 281, 327, 343, 356, 368, 432; books/bookstores in, 125, 156, 292, 448; British occupation of, 68, 390; Cesare Beccaria quoted in, 179; Court of Vice Admiralty, 173; grand jury charge in, 164; harbor, 163; inhabitants of, 316; King's Chapel, 327; Museum of Fine Arts, 327; prisons in, 296; Sons of Liberty in, 68, 179, 250
Boston Atheneum, 125
Boston Bookstore, 125
Boston Common, 103, 152
Boston Evening Post, 301
Boston (frigate), 120
Boston Gazette, 292, 301
Boston Harbor, 296
Boston Massacre, 5, 85–86, 292; fifth anniversary of, 356; trial, 80, 174, 431, 506; and "electrical effect produced upon the jury" by Cesare Beccaria's words, 174
Boston Port Act of 1774, 174, 250
Boston Prison Discipline Society, 232
Boston Public Library, 80, 174, 319
Boston Tea Party, 68, 174, 179, 250, 365
Boston Weekly Post-Boy, The, 123
Boswell, James, 276–77
Botany Bay, 210, 254, 346
botched executions, 65
Botta, Carlo, 72, 160
Boudinot, Elias, 109, 158
bounties, 56
Bouquet, Henry, 124

Bourbon government, 134
Bourdeaux, 48
Bovee, Marvin, 242–43, 270
Bowdler, Thomas, 319
Bowdoin II, James, 78
Bowdoin III, James, 78
Bowdoin College, 94, 242
Bowen, Arthur, 342
Bowen, Catherine Drinker, 5
Bowen, Daniel, 312
Boyd, Robert, 396
Boylston, Ward Nicholas, 78
Bracco, James, 230
Brackenridge, Henry Marie, 210
Brackenridge, Hugh Henry, 170, 209–10
Bracton, Henry de, 53–54
Bradford, Andrew, 121
Bradford, Gamaliel, 178
Bradford, Isaac, 121
Bradford, John, 322
Bradford, Samuel, 244–45
Bradford, Thomas, 68, 244–45, 530
Bradford, William (printer), 68, 113, 245, 437, 530
Bradford, William, Jr. (lawyer): and Aaron Burr, 170; anti-death penalty efforts of, 6, 50, 239, 385; background of, 170, 173, 225; and Benjamin Rush, 43, 173, 244–45; and Cesare Beccaria, 13–14, 22, 50, 126–27, 131, 136, 144, 170–72, 237, 245, 270, 298, 384, 426, 437; on criminology, 127; on cruelty, 131; death of, 500; and death penalty, 90, 171–73, 239, 244–45, 384–85; on deterrence, 378; and George Washington, 170, 245; and James Madison, 13, 127, 158, 170–71, 178, 225–26, 245, 251, 387, 426; as judge, 227; as lawyer, 170, 173, 226, 237, 245; and Luigi Castiglioni, 13–14, 127, 131–32, 144, 171, 244–45, 489; and Montesquieu, 50; on necessity for punishments, 43, 131, 172, 378; and penal reform, 19, 50, 131, 170, 193, 229, 237, 244–45, 299, 324, 416; as Pennsylvania attorney general, 127, 173,

245, 413; on prevention of crime, 172; at Princeton, 170–71, 202, 210, 225, 245; on proportionality, 172; on punishment, 131; on "sanguinary" punishments, 50, 172; on "severity of our criminal law," 171–72; on speedy punishments, 171; and Timothy Pickering, 171; on tyranny, 131; as United States Attorney General, 170, 225, 245, 413, 433, 500; on speedy punishments, 426; and William Blackstone's *Commentaries*, 225–26; writings of, 43, 127, 171–72, 324. *See also Enquiry How Far the Punishment of Death Is Necessary in Pennsylvania*

Bradford County, Pennsylvania, 437

Braintree, Massachusetts, 368

branding, 122, 131, 189, 199, 233, 269, 273, 373–74; abolition of, 371; as "cruel," 540; cheek, 273, 407; facial, 162, 225, 238, 297, 373, 394, 407, 545; on forehead, 122, 233, 273, 298, 325, 373, 545; hand, 122, 225, 325, 329, 361; as infamous punishment, 394; and use of "Hot Iron," 394

Brandywine, battle of, 89, 231

Brant, Irving, 448

breaking on the wheel, 28, 38, 64–65, 72, 92, 124, 146, 271, 305; as "cruel and unusual punishment," 452; in France, 107; in Tuscany, 161–62

Breckinridge, John, 261–62

Brentford, England, 84

Breslau, 27

Breyer, Stephen, 428–29

bribery, 282

Bridewell Palace, 294

bridewells, 10, 294, 325

Brief Statement of the Argument for the Abolition of the Death Punishment in Twelve Essays, A, 241

Brissot de Warville, Jacques-Pierre, 218, 398, 437

Bristol, England, 40

Britain. *See* Great Britain

British Army, 153, 160; executions by, 154

British colonies, 4, 19, 138, 331, 396

"British constitution," 75, 147, 188, 299–301, 396, 405

British East Florida, 32

British Empire, 7, 69, 99, 148, 383, 414, 440

British goods: boycott of, 292, 432

British loyalists, 20, 26, 148, 153, 157, 291, 425

British Navy, 334

British Parliament, 20, 32, 47, 55, 68, 77, 81–87, 92, 101–2, 138, 144, 147–48, 161, 164, 168, 170, 174, 183, 211, 220–22, 246, 250, 252–53, 264, 273, 288, 292–93, 300, 317–18, 321, 354, 391, 400, 405, 432, 434, 449; House of Commons, 30, 76, 83–86, 106, 148, 184, 252, 300–1, 316, 346, 350, 382; House of Lords, 82, 106, 164, 252, 362; "omnipotent power" of, 405; publication of debates of, 82

British penitentiaries/prisons, 99–100, 169, 273, 278, 294, 321, 325, 354

British prisoners, 189

British radicalism, 194

British subjects, 72, 76, 81, 95, 106, 123, 145, 276, 285, 299–300, 375, 388, 410, 425

British West Florida, 98

Briton, The, 81

Brodeau, Mrs., 314

Brookhiser, Richard, 154

Brooks, John, 370–71

Broome, John, 207

Brothers in Unity, 234

Brown, Daniel, 154

Brown, John, 229

Brown, William Hill, 327

Brown, William Wells, 376

Brown University, 160

Brown v. Board of Education, 382–83

Bruce, David, 144

Brumidi, Constantino, 313, 453

"Brumidi Corridors," 453

Brussels, 249

brutalization effect, of executions, 37, 49

Brutus, 359

"Brutus," 9, 358

Bryan, George, 227, 229

Bryson, W. Hamilton, 184–85

Buccini, Stefania, 198

Buchanan, James, 418–19

Buckingham, Joseph, 94

Buckingham Palace, 84

Bucks County, Pennsylvania, 213, 215

Buddhism, 367

Buffon, Georges-Louis Leclerc (Comte de), 32, 59

"buggery": as capital crime, 275. *See also* sodomy

Bugniet, Pierre-Gabriel, 184, 326

Bulfinch, Charles, 312–14, 444

Bunbury, Charles, 319

Bunker (Breeds) Hill, battle of, 7, 327, 356, 441

Burgh, Hannah Harding, 278

Burgh, James, 90, 276–82; on dueling, 396; as English republican, 194; as "familiar to every reader conversant with criminal law," 140; on right to bear arms, 390–91; writings of, 448

Burgio, Alberto, 355

burglary, 229, 386, 414; abolition for, 136, 381; branding for, 122, 233; as capital crime, 187, 274–75, 280, 282; ear cropping for, 233; execution for, 211; fines for, 9; imprisonment for, 9, 325, 385; labor for, 283; and life sentences, 348; whipping for, 9, 233. *See also* robbery; theft

Burke, Aedanus, 205, 387

Burke, Edmund, 4, 48, 77, 103, 278, 301, 442

Burke, John, 207

Burke, Thomas, 396

Burke, William, 4

Burlamaqui, Jean-Jacques, 15–16, 39, 41, 46, 67, 79, 125, 247, 421, 431

Burnaby, Andrew, 32

Burney, Charles, 28

burning: alive, 29, 222, 255, 271, 274, 276, 287, 404; on forehead, 373; in hand(s), 269, 284, 404, 446, 506; as punishment, 129; of slaves, 443, 446; at stake, 29, 46–47; to death, 26, 46–47, 167, 406. *See also* branding; women

Burr, Aaron, 374; and battle for the presidency, 202; duel with Alexander Hamilton, 204, 396; and Edward Livingston, 333; friendship with Jeremy Bentham, 22, 99, 204–5, 416; as New York lawyer, 202, 204, 237; and penal reform, 204–5; on proportionality, 204; as Princeton student/graduate, 170, 202, 204; as pupil of Tapping Reeve, 413; and Thomas Jefferson, 202, 204; and treason charge, 204, 262; as Vice President, 99, 202, 396

Burroughs, Stephen, 377–78

Burrows, Edwin, 169

Bury St. Edmund's, England, 321

burying alive, 404

Bush, George W., 449

Byron, George Gordon (Lord), 93

Byron, Matthew, 396

Cabranes, José A., 427

Caesar, Julius, 70, 75, 115, 292, 356, 391

Cagliostro, Alessandro di, 198–99. *See also* Balsamo, Giuseppe

Calais, France, 83

Calas, Jean, 28, 59–60, 64, 81, 107, 123–24, 146, 243

Calas, Marc-Antoine, 60, 124

Calas, Pierre, 60

Caligula, 503

Calisse, Carlo, 60

Calvert, Jane, 473

Calvert, Joseph, 396

Cambridge, England, 222

Cambridge, Massachusetts, 79, 124, 265, 443

Cambridge University, 63, 78, 249, 366, 383

Caminer, Domenico, 256

Canada, 66, 82, 152, 158, 200, 248, 397; refusal to extradite without assurances death penalty will not be sought, 428, 451. *See also* Quebec

Canadian Charter of Rights and Freedoms, 428

Canadian Supreme Court, 428

Canadians, 66, 148, 253

"Candidus," 147

Cannon, James, 227

canon law, 46, 274, 394

Canova, Antonio, 313

Canterbury, 269

Canton, John, 276

Capellano, Antonio, 313

capital crimes, xv, 295, 400, 414; in army, 156; in colonial America, 189–90, 232, 274–75, 294–95; in England, 15, 131, 190, 273, 275, 540; in Europe, 15, 273; in France, 4; under federal law, 9–10, 414–15, 426; reduction of, 167, 169, 229, 235–36, 280, 381, 434; under Roman law, 46; for whites vs. blacks, 383. *See also specific crimes and jurisdictions*

capital litigation/prosecutions, 269; error rate in, 439

capital punishment. *See* death penalty; death sentence(s); execution(s)

Capital Punishment, 135, 230

Capital Punishment Within Prisons Bill, 49

capital sentencing. *See* death sentence(s); judge(s); juries

capital statutes. *See* capital crimes; *specific jurisdictions*

Caracciolo di Brienza, Giuseppe, 120

Caramanico, Principe di, 108

Caraminici, Prince, 109

Carazzi, Isabella de, 55

Carberry, Henry, 309–10

Cardinal de Bernis, 115

Cardinal de Retz, 178

Cardinal de Rohan, 198–99

Carey, 121–22

Carey, Mathew, 12, 90, 244–45, 260, 325, 358–59, 385–86; and Benjamin Franklin, 88; libel case against, 88; as publisher of *American Museum* magazine, 88, 172

Carli, Gianrinaldo, 34

Carlisle Commission, 99

Carlisle, Pennsylvania, 93

Carlisle Library Company, 93

Carman, William, 284

Carmichael, William, 437

Carnes, Thomas, 374

Carr, Robert, 369

Carr, William, 188

Carrithers, David, 29

Carroll, Charles (barrister), 248–49

Carroll, Charles (of Carrollton), xv, 248–50; and Cesare Beccaria's treatise, xiii, xv, 249; and Montesquieu's treatise, 250

Carroll, John, 248

Carstairs, William, 223

Cartouche, Louis Domingue, 503

Cartwright, John, 76, 353, 428

Casa Belgioiosa, 108, 114

Casa Candiani, 108, 114

Casa Roma, 108

Casanova, 198

Cash, Arthur, 87

"Cassius," 205

Castiglioni, Alfonso, 114–15, 489

Castiglioni, Luigi, 12–14, 32, 114–15, 171, 488; and American Academy of Arts and Sciences, 130; and American Philosophical Society, 34, 130; on American social customs, 447; background of, 35, 110–11, 130, 216, 489; and Benjamin Franklin, 12–14, 34, 127–30, 215–16; and Benjamin Lincoln, 13; and Benjamin Rush, 12, 34, 129–30, 215–16; as botanist, 12–13, 34, 115, 128, 130, 171, 201, 215, 244, 270, 373, 442; and Cesare Beccaria's influence, 12, 270; and Cesare Beccaria's social circle, 12; and Charles Thomson, 13; on corporal punishments, 373; in England, 12, 35; in Europe, 12, 35, 128–30; family of, 114–15, 129, 489; in France, 12, 35; and George Washington, 12, 110–12, 129; in Georgia, 12, 111, 129; and Giuseppe Mussi, 130; and Henry Knox, 13; and James Madison, 13; and Jeremy Belknap, 129; and John Adams, 13; and John Banister, 112; and John Hancock, 13, 129; on liberty, 228; in Massachusetts, 109–10, 443–44; at Monticello, 105, 108; at Mount Vernon, 110–11, 129–30, 201; and Nathanael Greene, 12–13; in New York, 109–10, 201; and North American trip, 12–13, 34–35, 108–9, 113, 127–29, 201, 216–17, 383, 433, 443–44; and On Crimes and Punishments, 270; and Order of St. Stephen, 34, 110; and Paolo Frisi, 34–35, 127–28; in Pennsylvania, 108, 112–13, 128, 130, 244–45; on Pennsylvania constitution, 373; and Robert Morris, 13; and Samuel Adams, 13; on slavery, 110, 443; and Società Patriottica, 130; in South Carolina, 111–12; and Thomas Jefferson, 14; in Vermont, 128–29; villa of, 114; travelogue of, 12–13; in Virginia, 14, 105, 110–12, 130, 443; and William Bradford, Jr., 13, 131–32, 144, 171, 489; and William Short, 130. See also Viaggio

Castiglioni, Madame, 115–16
Castiglioni, Maria, 31
Castiglioni-Litta, Paola, 130
Castle, John, 121
Castle Island, 296
castration: punishment of, 29, 193, 273, 275, 283, 360, 367, 404; for bestiality, 193; for rape, 189, 193, 342; for sodomy, 193
Catalogue of Books Belonging to the Library of St. John's College, 249
"Catalogue of Books for Master Custis," 151

Catalogue of the Library of Thomas Jefferson, 186
Catherine II (Empress), 3–4, 61–62, 64, 98, 137, 346, 498. See also Russia
Catholic(s), 12, 29, 72, 88, 107, 123–24, 151, 248–49, 273, 279, 313. See also Roman Catholic(s)
Catiline, 503
"Cato," 358
Cato, 356
cat-o'-nine tails, 325, 376, 378
Caucasians. See whites
Causici, Enrico, 313
cautery, 193. See also branding
censorial jurisprudence, 4, 19, 99
Ceracchi, Giuseppe, 314
Cesare Beccaria Award, 453
chains, 48, 59, 247; hanging in, 360; use of, 111, 184, 211, 377
Chalmers, James, 147
Chamber of Counts, 31
chance-medley, 231
Chantilly, Virginia, 196
Chapel Royal at St. James, 361
Chapin, Bradley, 241
Chapin, Rev. Dr., 143
Character of the Laws of England Considered, The, 361
Charlemagne, 103, 445
Charles (King of Sweden), 336
Charles I (King), 288, 293
Charles II (King), 47, 273, 275, 293
Charles V (Emperor), 30
Charles VI (Roman Emperor), 28–29
Charleston (Charles Town) Library Society, 125, 136–37
Charleston, South Carolina, 6, 90–91, 115, 149, 230, 334; grand jury, 374
Charlestown, Massachusetts, 325, 328
Charlestown, South Carolina, 144
Charlestown Common, 360
Charlestown Neck, 360
Charlottesville, Virginia, 130, 186, 261
Chase, Salmon, 339
Chase, Samuel, 11, 248
Chastellux, Marquis de, 60

Château de La Roche-Guyon, 27

Chauvelin, Marquis de, 303

checks and balances, 16, 20, 212, 360, 363, 421–22, 433, 438

Chelsum, James, 361

Chiari, Pietro, 177

child rape, 275, 295. *See also* rape

children. *See* juveniles

Childs, Francis, 8

Chile, 94

China, 218, 286; death sentences/executions in, 291, 367, 450

Chipman, Nathaniel, 259–60, 448, 551

Chitty, Joseph, 240, 399

chivalry, codes of, 55; and "chivalric honor," 396

Christ and the Gallows, 243, 270

Christ Church, 393

Christian, Edward, 366

Christian Disciple, The, 94, 235, 270–71

Christian Examiner and Theological Review, The, 341

Christian(ity), 25, 200, 251, 257, 298; beliefs, 261; Benjamin Rush's views on, 203, 310; and condemnation of executions, 25, 230; faith, 189; "earliest days of," 251; evangelical, 382; "forbearance, love, and charity," 245; "humility and mildness" as "true mark of," 250; "legislature," 376; "obligations of," 266, 309; as "part of the common law," 176; and penal reform, 320; precepts of, 216, 271; "propagation of," 290; "pure principles of," 169; and religious intolerance, 251; and slave trade, 184; "spirit of," 287; Thomas Jefferson's views on, 5, 169; tribunals, 175; "true," 312; values, 250; and view that "men should love each other," 237; "world," 46. *See also* Bible; New Testament; Old Testament; religion

Christian(s), 102, 267; kingdoms, 138; and opposition to executions, 25; spiritual advisor(s), 378. *See also* religious persecution

Christianson, Scott, 237

Christie, Thomas, 279

Christin, Charles-Gabriel Frédéric, 28

Christmas Carol, A, 139

Church, Angelica Schuyler, 220

church and state: separation of, 30, 251

Church of England, 250, 287

Cicero, 81, 125, 356, 431

Cigna, Giovanni Francesco, 488

Cincinnati, Ohio, 372; state prison in, 325

"Cincinnatus," 358

Cincinnatus, Lucius Quinctius, 110, 358

Circuit Court of Justiciary, 93

circumstantial evidence, 365–66

"Citizen of Maryland," 215

citizens: "liberty and happiness of," 167; "liberties of," 357; and loss of rights, 394; natural rights of, 40–41, 234, 245, 261, 357; "Privileges and Immunities" of, 213; "rights and duties of," 322

citizenship, privileges of, 11

City-Hall Reporter, and New-York Law Magazine, The, 140

Civil History of the Kingdom of Naples, The, 357

civil law, 29, 106–7; books on, 357, 387; as code-based, 412; countries/locales, 124, 361, 427; as "science founded on principles," 412; study of, 333, 413; and torture, 200, 361, 371, 382; tradition, 250; versus common law, 17, 335, 410–12

Civil War, 11, 21–22, 224, 240, 243, 269–70, 349–50, 355, 408, 437–38, 453

"Civilian," 80

civility, 7

"Civis," 358

"Clarendon," 301

Clark, George, 101

Clark, George Rogers, 230

Clark, James, 242

Clark, Jr., John, 159–60

Clay, Cassius, 262–64

Clay, Henry, 186, 262, 344, 424, 558

Clayton, Robert, 135

Clear Idea of the Genuine and Uncorrupted British Constitution, A, 75, 77

clemency, executive: acts of, 38, 176, 185, 191, 214–15, 229, 238; commutations/pardons, 30, 56, 111, 128, 154–55, 165, 188, 193, 210, 224, 236, 268, 283–85, 342, 399–401, 443, 453; in Europe, 29; frequent use of, 152, 204, 247, 347, 350–51, 396–97; as "less necessary" with "mild" punishments, 56, 183, 208, 399–400; Machiavelli on, 178; petitions/pleas for, 84, 145, 154, 191, 342; power of, 163, 208–9, 239, 298, 400–1; rejection of, 26, 145, 315, 426; in Rome, 178; treatise on, 243, 317. *See also* pardons; President(s); reprieves

Clement XII (Pope), 199

Clement XIII (Pope), 64

Clement XIV (Pope), 248

Clerici, Gaudenzio, 114–15

Clermont, New York, 333

Clingan, Edmund, 370

Clinton, DeWitt, 237–39, 268, 416; and citation of Cesare Beccaria, 237, 268; on codification of laws, 425

Clinton, George, 110, 169, 204, 237, 239, 268, 524; bust of, 314

close confinement, 83

Club of Honest Whigs, 201, 276–77

Clymer, George, 435

coarse fare/food, 234, 337, 385. *See also* dietary restrictions

Cobbett, William, 245

Cobenzl, Philipp von, 62

Code Duello, 55

Code of Draco, 26, 288–89, 310; as "sanguinary," 289

Code of Hammurabi, 26, 547

Codex Theresianus, 29

codification: of criminal codes, 55, 264, 425, 427, 437; and Edward Livingston's efforts, 264; and Jeremy Bentham's efforts, 416

Coercive Acts of 1774, 174, 250

Coffeehouse, The, 30. *See also Il Caffé*

coffeehouses, 31, 60, 68, 276

Cogswell, Mason, 101

Coke, Edward, 91, 139, 164, 185, 188, 223, 271, 424, 553

Coke (up)on Littleton, 185, 188, 553

Colbhart, Matthias, 152

Colden, Cadwallader D., 237

collateral consequences, 37

Colle, 197

Collection of Cases Decided by the General Court of Virginia, A, 91

Collection of Papers, Written for the Purpose of Exhibiting Some of the More Prominent Errors and Omissions of the Constitution of New-Jersey, A, 240–41

College of New Jersey, 120, 127, 170, 173, 191, 202–3, 210, 212, 225, 266, 296

College of Philadelphia, xv, 5, 116, 413

College of Rheims, 250

College of St. Omer, 250

College of William and Mary, 25, 100, 107, 114, 169, 185–86, 189, 248, 261, 369, 384, 413, 448

Colosseum (Rome), 26, 362

Coltellini, Marco, 27

Columbia College/University, 119, 239, 332, 336, 383, 413, 439

Columbia River, 347

Columbian Magazine, The, 88, 244

Columbus, Ohio, 242

Column of Infamy, 72

Colvin, J. B., 412

Colvin, John, 408

Comédie Italienne, 101

Comity Clause. *See* Privileges and Immunities Clause

Commentaire sur le (livre) Traité des Délits et des Peines, 27, 58, 95, 186. *See also* Voltaire

Commentaries on American Law, 384

Commentaries on the Constitution of the United States, 142, 208, 387

Commentaries on the Laws of England, 139, 247, 276, 287, 388; and Abraham Lincoln, 16, 223–24; and Alexander Hamilton, 223; in America, 91, 125,

138, 186, 223–26, 258, 368–69, 404, 494, 552; citation of Cesare Beccaria's treatise in, 4, 16, 79, 258, 368–69, 510; in colonial America, 145, 185, 222–23, 369; and Daniel Webster, 223; fourth book of, 404; on happiness, 560; influence of, 223–26, 368–69; and James Kent, 223; and James Madison, 223; and John Adams, 223; and John Jay, 223; and Patrick Henry, 223; and St. George Tucker, 223, 369–70

commerce, 423, 432. *See also* trade

commercial law, 413

common law: authorities, 264, 410; as "birth right" of Americans, 405, 410; and Christianity, 176; as "code of feudal customs," 404; and colonial codes, 410; and Congress, 411; and Constitution, 404, 410–12; crimes, xv, 16–17, 58, 166, 338, 354, 404, 411, 415–17, 424–25, 427, 437; courts, 247; and custom(s), 20, 335; defenses, 411, 424; as "destined to acquire in this country the highest degree of perfection of which it is susceptible," 448; as discretion-dependent, 412; and forced loans, 405; as "general law of the land," 406; "harsh punishments" that "still stain the page of," 406; "idolatrous worship" of, 405; as "irrational," 411; jurisdiction, 406–7, 411–12, 414; as "law of the *enemy*," 406; and "learning of the age," 405; and "long"/"immemorial" usage, 68–69; and manslaughter, 9; "medieval nature of," 333; as "modified by our Constitution, by our laws, manners and usages," 406; and monopolies, 405; "not to be meddled with, except where Alterations are necessary," 193; as part of body of American law, 413; "pervades everything," 405; powers of contempt, 340; principles of, 424; and "principles of freedom," 405; and "privileges of the people," 405; "pure ethics" and "sound logic" as part of, 448; rejection of parts

of, 406; and "rights of the sovereign," 405; and "rights of the subject," 404; and self-incrimination, 394; and slavery, 405; and "spirit of the times," 405; "system," 20, 405–6; and suicide, 398; as supplementing statutes, 411; and "temper and disposition" of judges, 405; tradition(s), 6, 189, 250, 405; and "uncertain traditions," 405; and unwritten customs, 335; and U.S. courts/law, 407–11, 414; use in interpreting written constitutions, 405, 410; versus civil law, 412; versus natural law, 410; violations of, 405; "whole body of," 425. *See also* English common law

Common Sense, 5, 20, 70, 75, 113, 144–45, 147, 301, 368, 433, 442

commonplacing, 184–85

Commonwealth of Oceana, The, 53

Commonwealth v. Anthes, 426

commutation(s). *See also* clemency, executive

Company of the Redwood library, 125

Comparative View of Mild and Sanguinary Laws, A, 299

Compendious Dictionary of the English Language, A, 252

Compensation Emancipation Act, 313

Complaints of the Poor People of England, The, 93

Conant, Edward, 298

concealing death of "bastard" child: as capital crime, 280

Concerning Artificial and Natural Electricity, 116

Concerning the Law of War and Peace, 445

Concord, Massachusetts, 7, 292, 441

Concord, New Hampshire, 258; prison in, 325

Concord Square, 72

Condillac, Etienne, 31, 243

conditions of confinement, 232, 320. *See also* death row

Condorcet, Jean-Antoine Nicolas de Caritat de (marquis), 19, 61–62, 65, 200,

309, 400, 445, 448; and Cesare Beccaria, 307; and Thomas Jefferson, 307

confession(s): coerced/extorted, 200, 389,
395, 552; as evidence of guilt, 395;
false, 44; in open court, 162, 382; and
torture, 28, 46, 361, 365–66, 372, 390;
and Treason Clause, 162; versus refusal to plead when arraigned, 222;
voluntary, 395

confinement, 163, 234, 236, 240, 297, 318,
326, 328, 336, 342, 385; as alternative
to death sentences, 155, 163, 234, 321;
for life, 181, 281; as substitute for corporal punishments, 321. *See also* close
confinement; imprisonment; incarceration

Confrontation Clause, 295

Confucius, 445

"congregate system," 328

Congress, 90, 110, 115, 198, 234, 292, 334,
410–11, 416–17, 421, 424; and appointment of counsel, 295; benefit of
clergy abolished by, 400; and creation
of federal courts, 408; and crimes/pun-
ishments, 9, 58, 386–87; and criminal-law jurisdiction, 411–12; and
federal penitentiaries, 330–31, 346–47;
First, 9, 158, 201, 224, 379, 420, 425,
564; and freedom of speech/religion,
251; James Madison's messages to, 207,
415; laws of, 412; and *Laws of the
United States*, 173, 412, 414; members
of, 199, 333, 353; pardons of, 283–84;
and Pennsylvania mutiny, 283–84;
President of, 356, 441; Sixth, 379;
Third, 379; and U.S. courts, 425. *See
also* Continental Congress; *specific
members*

Connecticut, 88, 101–2, 122, 139, 202,
385–86; adultery in, 373; "Blue Laws,"
88, 232; colonial code, 274; corporal
punishments in, 385; courts, 235;
death penalty, 385; death penalty abolition efforts in, 234, 236, 385; Declaration of Rights, 247; emancipation
of slaves in, 256; executions in, 233;
governor, 101, 103; grand jury charge
in, 167; hard labor in, 385; legal instruction in, 413; legislature, 101,
233–34, 373, 385; penal codes/reform
in, 233–34, 381; prison(s) in, 327, 385;
private execution law, 49; punishments
in, 233, 385; sermons in 374; Superior Court, 101; Supreme Court, 234;
Supreme Court of Errors, 101; Wits,
101

Connecticut Courant, 384

Connecticut Currant, 417

conscience: as natural/unalienable right,
236

Considerations on Criminal Law, 79

*Considerations on the Causes of the Great-
ness of the Romans and of Their Decline*, 220

*Considerations on the Injustice and Impolity
of Punishing Murder by Death*, 126–27

Conspiracy of Kings, The, 234

Constantine (Emperor), 25

Constantinople, 81, 195

Constitution, 14–15, 201, 390, 422, 427,
447, 452; adoption of, 18, 126, 212,
251, 320; Article I, 10, 213; Article II,
213; Article III, 213–14, 425; Article
IV, 213; Article V, 213; Article VI, 213;
Article VII, 213; and Bill of Rights,
199–200; and bills of attainder, 213,
215, 246, 381; and "beyond a reasonable doubt" standard, 45; and Cesare
Beccaria's influence, 3, 6, 15, 20, 564;
and checks and balances, 16, 20,
362–63; and common law, 410–11; as
compromise, 438; defense of, 230; "democratic tendency" of, 362; and division of power, 362; drafting/design of,
47, 126, 136, 435; and evidentiary protections, 162; and ex post facto laws,
213, 381; and executive power, 213;
framers/framing of, xi, 357; and "Full
Faith and Credit," 213; and future generations, 8; and grand jury safeguard,
395; and habeas corpus, 213; interpretation of, 14–15, 409–10; and in-

terpretative theories, 14–15, 410, 451, 564; and James Madison, 273; and judicial power, 213; and "Law of Nations," 387; and legislative power, 213; and "living constitutionalism," 451; as majoritarian check, 446; and "originalism," 438, 440, 451; preamble of, 213, 342, 422, 446; and presidential pardoning power, 239; printing/publication of, 89; process for amending, 213, 360; as "production of human intellect," 362; as prohibiting self-incrimination, 395; proposed, 135; and ratification debates, 48; ratification of, 5–11, 17, 58, 206, 212–15, 219, 253, 255, 295, 369, 379, 383, 386, 390, 423, 434, 444; as "sacredly obligatory upon all," 359; and separation of powers, 219; signing/signers of, 13, 22, 397, 413, 433, 444; and slavery/slave trade, 380, 383; as social compact, 381; "Spirit of the American," 238; supremacy of, 213, 564; and Supreme Court, 444; and "three fifths" clause, 438; translation into Italian, 135; and treason, 381; and treaties, 213; and unenumerated rights, 213, 410; as "written compact," 362. *See also* Bill of Rights; Constitutional Convention; *specific amendments, clauses, and states*

Constitution de L'Angleterre, 106, 223

Constitution of England, The, 106, 222–23

Constitutional Convention, 6–7, 106, 126, 163, 165, 170, 179–80, 198, 207, 212–13, 226, 231, 270, 319, 358, 381, 383, 433–35, 444; attendees of, xv, 296; debate at, 381–82; states/delegates calling for, 255

constitutional interpretation: theories of, 14–15, 564. *See also specific theories*

constitutional monarchy, 104, 220

Constitutional Society of Virginia, 196, 198

contenement, 37

Continental Army, 110, 116, 138, 152–55, 157, 161, 163, 172, 230, 238–39, 245,

283, 292, 303, 358, 365, 379, 431, 435, 441

Continental Congress, xv, 5, 7–9, 80, 109, 112, 116, 120, 137, 151–52, 156, 158, 205–6, 239, 252–53, 356, 379, 431, 560; and Articles of Confederation, 434; books recommended for, xv, 205; and British prisoners, 189; and Canadian diplomatic mission, 248; chaplain of, 322; and citation of Cesare Beccaria's treatise, 148, 432, 435; and Declaration of Independence (1776), 5, 20, 66, 70–71, 99, 137, 143, 193, 226, 246, 264, 290, 332, 441; delegates/members of, 172, 220, 309, 387, 435; First, 136, 296; letter/address to the inhabitants of Quebec (1774), 5, 7–8, 66–67, 75, 147–48, 162, 473, 497; letter to the people of Great Britain (1774), 72; loans provided to, 100; and member's book borrowing privileges, 220; official printer of, 245; President of, 147, 155, 170; proceedings of, 75; Second, 118, 161, 296, 365, 434, 441; secretary of, 137

contrition, 192, 341

Convention Against Torture and Other Cruel, Inhuman or Degrading Treatment or Punishment, 389, 427; text of, 449; U.S. ratification of, 449

Coolidge, Carlos, 242

Cooper, Samuel, 124

Cooper, William, 299

Copernicanism, 36

Coram, Robert, 141

Coray, Adamantios, 505. *See also* Koraes, Adamantios

Corda, 96

Cornell, Saul, 14, 125

corporal punishments, 6, 10, 16, 51–53, 103, 122, 167, 180, 183, 275–76, 281, 283, 323, 342, 371, 373, 383, 434, 447; abandonment/abolition of, 297; in America, 121, 360; "benefit of," 216; in colonial America, 233; as common/ "usual," 96, 480; as "cruel and unusual," 342; debates about, 92, 203; to deter, 236; in England, 372; in Europe, 121; in Italy, 96; in military, 155; on necessity for, 439; non-lethal, 6, 10, 51, 169, 233, 273, 348, 373, 406, 425, 450, 454; as outdated, 296; in prisons, 454; to reform, 236; to shame/humiliate, 293; as substitute for executions, 321, 373; use of, 51, 283–85, 292, 295, 301, 361, 446. *See also* branding; ducking stool; ear cropping; limb(s), deprivation of; pillory; whipping

corpses: dissection of, 183, 193, 224, 387, 503. *See also* gibbeting

Corpus Juris Civilis, 333, 445

Corradini, Gertrude, 83

correction(s), 312, 323–24, 327; house(s) of, 74, 225, 294, 314, 321–22, 346, 377, 394

Correspondence of Mr. Ralph Izard, 253

Correspondent, The, 91, 350

corruption, 203, 282, 286, 308, 445; in Europe, 8, 153, 216, 323

corruption of blood, 26–27, 193, 406

Corsica, 359

Cortlandtown, New York, 152

Così fan tutte, 119

Cosway, Maria, 72–73, 101, 105, 326

Cosway, Richard, 101, 105

Cotton, John, 274

Cottrol, Robert, 7

Council of Economy, 31

counsel, defense. *See* assistance of counsel

counterfeiting, 56, 196, 204, 377; abolition for, 172; as capital crime, 26, 204, 274, 295; corporal punishments for, 276, 283, 298; debated by Congress, 386–87; imprisonment for, 297, 385; and U.S. Constitution, 386

"Countryman," 268, 358

Course of Legal Study, A, 140–41

Court of Common Pleas, 83

Court of King's Bench, 19, 75, 84–86, 146, 273, 276

Court of St. James, 173, 194, 413, 415

Courtanvaux, Marquis de, 177

courts: "fallibility of," 208. *See also* federal courts; United States; *individual states*

courts-martial proceedings, 151–52, 155, 162–63, 309, 334

Cousin, Louis, 356

cowardice, 389

Cox, Susanna, 171

Coxe, Tench, 435

Cranch, Mary Smith, 125

Cranch, Richard, 179

Cranch, William, 43, 284–85, 408–9

Crawford, Thomas, 313

Creech, William, 87

"crime against nature," 172, 398; as capital crime, 385

crimes: codification of, 54, 333, 354, 411, 427; "infamous," 395, 426. *See also specific crimes*

Crimes Act of 1790, 9, 295, 330, 415, 417–18, 425–27

Crimes Act of 1825, 417–18

criminal procedure, 46, 240, 284, 295, 366–67

Criminal Recorder; or, Biographical Sketches of Notorious Public Characters, The, 149

criminals: attitudes toward, 10, 21, 49, 121, 142, 228. *See also specific offenders*

criminology: "classical school of," 243, 317, 454; field/founding of, xi

"Crisis," 75–76

Critical Review, 179

Crittenden, John, 558

Crockett, G. F. H., 208, 344–47

Croft, George, 286

Cromwell, Oliver, 293, 391

Cronk, Nicholas, 27

cropping. *See* ear cropping

Cross, Sarah, 415

Cross of Malta, 71

Croydon, England, 250

crucifixion, 26; as "cruel and unusual punishment," 452

"cruel": definition/meaning of, 252; as "[d]isposed to give pain to others," 252; as "hardhearted, inhuman, bloody, fierce," 252; as "inhuman, destitute of pity, compassion or kindness," 252; sanctions, 37; used in juxtaposition to "penitentiary," 317; as "willing or pleased to torment, vex or afflict," 252. *See also* punishment(s)

"cruel and unusual": built-in flexibility of, 17, 342; "pains and penalties," 246. *See also* punishment(s)

"cruel and unusual punishments": bar against, 20, 22, 199–200, 285, 370, 374–76, 395, 406, 429, 446, 449, 452; concept of, 224; and "death row phenomenon," 427–29; death sentences/executions as, 439–40; and English law, 222, 224, 380; exclusion of blacks from protection of, 382; as general/broad language, 451; methods of execution as, 452; as restricting torture, 223, 390; in state constitutions/declarations, 17–18, 21, 246, 252, 282, 382, 390; and Supreme Court's reading of, 390; William Blackstone's references to, 224–25. *See also* Cruel and Unusual Punishments Clause; Eighth Amendment; English Bill of Rights; *specific states and cases*

Cruel and Unusual Punishments Clause, 15, 22, 95, 375, 382, 429, 446, 449–52; debate over, 224; as derived from English law, 17, 370, 406; and "evolving standards of decency" test, 294; as "not to be confounded with the same clause in the English bill of rights," 406; vagueness of, 420; and use of general terms, 17. *See also* Eighth Amendment; English Bill of Rights; *specific cases*

"cruel nor unusual punishments," 263

"cruel or unusual punishments": in Northwest Ordinance, 247; in state constitutions/declarations, 19, 21, 178, 246–47, 252

cruelty: acts of, 172, 378; animal, 216; as "attended with cowardice," 285; as "austere, ferocious, and cruel," 286; aversion to/avoidance of, 246–47; as

"barbarous," 252; of British, 202, 434; Cesare Beccaria's aversion to, 395, 451; concept/consideration of, 6, 17, 316, 372, 395, 451; as "dastardly and contemptible," 285; definition of, 348; "engines of," 377–78; of "existing system," 296; founding fathers' views of, 370; "impressions of," 260; of jailors, 192; John Adams on, 273; judicial, 18; of laws, 287; Montaigne on, 107; as "parent of slavery," 285; "revolting engine of," 267; Roman, 178; "strong affinity to," 330; "system of," 285; and "unequal" punishments, 268

Cuba, 230

cucking-stool(s), 269. *See also* ducking stool(s)

Cunningham v. Caldwell, 262, 368

cursing parent, as capital crime, 411

Cushing, Thomas, 5, 148

Cushing, William, 425

Custis, John Parke, 151

custom(s), 54–55, 57, 189, 300, 334, 388; "among the Jews," 164; antiquated, 446; barbaric, 446; "of barbarous ages," 407; blind adherence to, 362; English, 255, 424; French, 60, 334; "of our People," 327; and punishments, 16, 442; Spanish, 334; unwritten, 335

Cutler, Manasseh, 129

cutting off ears. *See* ear cropping

cutting off nose(s), 189

cutting out tongue, 189, 360

Da Ponte, Lorenzo, 119

da Vinci, Leonardo, 74

Dagge, Henry, 79, 479

D'Aguesseau, Henri-François, 243

Daily American Advertiser, 359

Daily News, The, 139

Dakota Indians, 350–51

Dale, Thomas, 189

d'Alembert, Jean-Baptiste le Rond, 32–33, 35, 58–60

Dallas, Alexander, 267, 284

Dallas, George Mifflin, 266–67, 284

Daly, Denis, 126

damages, awards of, 149

Damiens, Robert-François, 46, 95, 103, 305

Damilaville, Etienne Noël, 33

Dana, Eleutheros, 88

Danbury Baptist Association, 364

Dane, Nathan, 142

Danish, 337

d'Aquino, Giacomo, 108

Dark Ages, 361

Dartmouth College, 125

Dartmouth v. Woodward, 281

Datson, Lorraine, 64

d'Auteroche, Jean Chappe, 177

Davis, David Brion, 126–27, 137, 241, 270

Davis, George, 254

Davis, William, 295

Dawes, Manasseh, 92, 448, 479

De jure belli ac pacis, 445

De legibus et consuetudinibus Angliae, 188

De l'esprit, 32

De l'esprit des lois, 29, 61. *See also L'Esprit des lois*

de Lolme, Jean-Louis, 106–7, 222–23, 362, 431; and John Adams, 175; and Cesare Beccaria's treatise, 106–7

Dealings with the Dead, 37

Deane, Samuel, 488

Deane, Silas, 120

death penalty: as "abhorrent and disagreeable to our natures," 157; as "absurd policy," 332; as "absurd punishment for dueling," 90; as "almost universally reckoned too severe," 96; as arbitrary, 428, 454; as "barbarous," 286; and call for "revision of those laws which inflict capital punishment for many inferior crimes," 87; categorical restrictions on, 450; as constitutional, 390, 450, 452; as "contrary to the order and happiness of society," 43; as "contrary to the popular habits of thinking," 163; for "crimes of revolt against the state," 66; as cruel, 96, 419, 439, 451; debates about, xv, 34, 43, 143, 203, 234–36, 239, 246, 256, 378–80, 439; as discriminatory, 454; as disproportionate, 419; as "encouragement to crime," 349; as "example of barbarity," 44, 258; as "example of cruelty," 39, 96; as "example" to others, 210; exemption from, 190; as "futile excess of punishments," 39; and geographic disparities, 439, 450; "horrid instruments of," 237; as human rights issue, 451, 454; as immoral, 439; as "impolitic," 388; "in theory" vs. "in practice," 221; as "inhuman," 388, 451; irrevocability of, 52; as "just vengeance against the guilty," 388; as "last and extreme forfeiture," 349; as "last melancholy resource," 187, 246, 262; as "less efficacious method of deterring others," 258; as "most inefficient punishment," 337; as "necessary"/"necessity," 131, 171–72, 210, 266, 419; as "necessary evil," 242; as "neither just nor useful in a well governed state," 388; as "pernicious to society," 258; and question of "necessity" for, 90, 93, 154, 209–10, 242, 384; as "really injurious," 286; as "relic of barbarism," 234, 242; and reluctance to impose, 227; as "sanguinary law," 315; as "sanguinary practice," 315; simple vs. afflictive, 96; substitutes for, 48, 137, 190, 195, 210, 229, 234, 321, 341, 372, 379, 385; as torture, 449–51; as "tyrannical," 388; as "unchristian," 203, 265, 332, 439; as unconstitutional, 449–50; as unjust, 51, 238, 419; as unnecessary, 43, 49, 51, 131, 171–72, 209–10, 212, 238, 257, 266, 286, 288, 343, 439; as unusual, 439; use of, 361; as "vandalism," 286; as "wholly disproportionate to the crime," 222; as "wholly unjust and inexpedient," 288; as "wholly unnecessary" except where the offender's life "is clearly incompatible with the safety of the state," 90, 280. *See also* abolition; capital statutes; death sentence(s); execution(s); *specific jurisdictions*

Death Penalty Information Center, 450

death-qualification, of juries, 293–94

death row: conditions on, 427–28; lengths of stay on, 427–29

death row inmates: average time spent on death row, 428; pregnant, 121, 169

"death row phenomenon," 428

death sentence(s): alternatives to, 10, 21, 48, 137, 161, 190, 195, 210, 229, 234, 238, 321, 341, 349, 372, 376, 379, 385; annual number of, 450; arbitrariness of, 26, 428, 450; in colonial America, 363; commutation of, 268; as cruel, 19–20, 140, 452; declining number of, 427, 439; discretionary, 451; as discriminatory, 439, 450; disproportionality of, 204; and error rate, 439; frequency of, 237; ineligibility for, 375; and Inquisition, 27; mandatory, 21, 153, 189, 425, 451; as necessary, 40, 139–40; number of countries imposing, 427, 563; as obsolete, 439; pronouncement/imposition of, 40, 169, 233, 290, 426; as punishment, 282, 363, 407, 425; rarity/infrequency of, 221, 426, 451; remission of, 145, 208, 268, 283–84, 351; restriction/curtailment of, 128, 149, 172, 342, 349, 381, 384, 395; as sanguinary, 20, 103, 279, 288, 290; as torture, 449–50; as "*ultimum supplicium*," 140, 258, 349; in U.S., 10, 450–51; as unnecessary, 40, 140, 212, 439; as unusual, 452; as usual, 451; worldwide, 451. *See also* death penalty; *names of specific people*

death warrants, 182

Debrett, John, 77, 91–92

debtors: abolition of imprisonment for, 232, 268, 403; fraudulent, 402–3; imprisonment/punishment of, 36, 56, 232–33, 239, 258, 294, 360, 399, 401–4; innocent/honest, 360, 402; prison(s) for, 202, 401–4. *See also* bankruptcy

decapitation, 26, 164. *See also* beheading; guillotine

Decemviri, 222. *See also* Twelve Tables

Decius (Emperor), 25

Declaration of Independence, 362; Abraham Lincoln's reverence for, 16; and Cesare Beccaria's influence, 3, 6, 15, 20, 66, 142, 431, 433, 447, 564; and Committee of Five, 264, 332; drafting/issuance of, 6–7, 20, 22, 70, 136, 143, 148, 193, 226, 231, 247, 255, 264, 271, 290, 332, 423, 434; equality principle of, 66, 212, 293, 383, 440; and European interest, 228; fiftieth anniversary of, 412; at Lafayette's house, 104; origins of, 15, 431; public reading of, 7; reprinting of, 299; rights clause of, xvi, 7, 16, 42, 70, 143, 438, 452; and "rights of man," 212, 412; signing/signers of, xv, 5, 13–14, 19, 55, 71, 103, 115, 137, 202, 248, 296, 370, 403, 413, 433, 435, 441; text of, 22, 42, 70–71, 186, 293, 308, 438; translation of, 196–97; and "unalienable rights," 212, 455

Declaration of the Causes and Necessity of Taking up Arms, 118

Declaration of the People's Natural Right to a Share in the Legislature, 354

declarations of rights, 299. *See also specific jurisdictions*

DeConde, Alexander, 118

defamation, 56, 333, 397. *See also* libel; slander

Defence of the Constitutions of Government of the United States of America, A, 17, 26, 77, 175, 179, 436

Dei delitti e delle pene, xi, 3, 21, 26–27, 29, 34–36, 38–39, 41, 47, 58, 61, 71, 73, 75, 79, 103, 119, 124, 126, 135, 140, 160, 183, 186, 241, 243–44, 279, 332, 369, 380, 395, 402, 461, 467; as "manual in all languages," 234; Molini edition of, 176; and translation into French, 47, 58. *See also On Crimes and Punishments*

Delaware, 66, 255, 441; constitution, 141; courts in, 309; "cruel or unusual punishments" clause, 247; declaration of rights, 247; "excessive bail" clause, 247; "excessive fines" clause, 247; River, 163

Delfico, Melchiore, 369

Dell' Elettricismo Naturale ed Artificiale, 130

democracy, 230, 360, 397, 409, 416, 446

Democracy in America, 13, 127, 381–82, 451

Democratic Society, 262

Dempster, George, 253

Denmark: torture abolished in, 389

Denoffee, William, 103

deodand, 27

Derby, England, 294

Des délits et des peines, 60, 96. *See also On Crimes and Punishments*

Des Insurrections, 195

Des Prisons de Philadelphie, 299

Descartes, 93

Deserter, The, 257

desertion: as capital crime, 163, 224, 238, 256; to/from British Army, 152, 254; crime of, 163; in "European Armies," 238; executions for, 133, 155–56, 224, 238; in France, 58; lashes/whipping for, 151, 156, 276; Louis-Sébastien Mercier's play about, 257; pardons for, 224; punishment of, 133, 151, 154

despotism, 69–70, 80–81, 133, 161, 165, 219, 304–5, 356, 359, 362, 423, 433, 445; "cruel contrivances of," 323; of Great Britain, 212; "instruments of," 185; and "sanguinary punishments," 172; "unchecked and unbounded," 68

deterrence, 6, 18, 37, 39, 42, 44, 46, 49–50, 167–68, 208, 236, 258, 281, 288, 321, 323–24, 376, 378, 383, 420, 454; as end of punishment, 47–48, 236, 277, 420

Deuteronomy, 274

Devon, England, 307

Dexter, Aaron, 129

Dickens, Charles, 139–40

Dickinson, John, 5, 66–70, 118, 432; as Annapolis delegate, 255; and Articles of Confederation, 434; and Benjamin Rush, 147, 212; and Cesare Beccaria, 5, 69–70, 136, 147–48, 212, 432, 473; on death penalty, 212; on military offenses, 212; and Montesquieu, 147; on natural law, 67; as "Penman of the Revolution," 5, 147; as President of Pennsylvania's Supreme Executive Council, 213–14; and Thomas McKean, 370; and William Blackstone's *Commentaries*, 226

dictionaries: defining "cruel," 252; defining "sanguinary," 252, 540; defining "unusual," 520; Italian, 107, 176, 357, 502

Dictionary of the English and Italian Languages, A, 357

Diderot, Denis, 19, 32, 58–59, 64, 107, 123

dietary restrictions: for prisoners, 10, 317, 321–23. *See also* coarse fare/food

Dieter, Richard, 450

Digest of the Laws of Actions and Trials at Nisi Prius, 91

Digges, Thomas, 77

dignity, 302; of man/men, 14, 285; as right, 427; "of the nation," 164

Dignity of Human Nature, The, 278

Dijon, France, 113

Dillon, John, 216, 372

Dilly, Charles, 75, 77, 92, 396

Dilly, Edward, 77, 396

Dinmore, Richard, 360

Dinwiddie, Robert, 156, 276

Diocletian (Emperor), 25

Discipline and Punish, 95

Discours sur l'administration de la justise criminelle, 59, 218

Discourse on Happiness, 71, 473

Discourse on Nature of Pleasure and Pain, 71

Discourse on Public (O)Economy and Commerce, 6, 80, 93

Discourse on the Origin and Basis of Inequality Among Men, 59

discretionary power, 20, 275; and courts-martial proceedings, 163; and death sentences, 19, 21, 275; and fines/terms of imprisonment, 224; of judges, 123, 155, 224, 235, 354, 407, 436; lack of, 285; and pardons, 400; of prosecutors, 439; "regulated by law," 224

discrimination: faith-based, 251. *See also* minorities; racial discrimination

Discurso sobre las penas contrahido á las leyes criminales de España, para facilitar su reforma, 436

disease: in prisons, xv, 141, 321; study of, 126, 216

disembowelment, 4, 164, 167, 222, 224, 255

disfigurement, 189, 283. *See also* branding; ear cropping; maiming

dismemberment, 225, 255; as capital crime, 236; of slaves, 376. *See also* drawing and quartering

disorderly conduct, 239

disproportionality: between crimes/punishments, 93, 222, 255, 259, 289, 339, 348, 437, 540. *See also* proportionality

dissection, 183, 193, 224. *See also* public dissection

Dissertation on the Canon and the Feudal Law, A, 273, 363

Dissertation on the Nature and Extent of the Jurisdiction of the Courts of the United States, A, 404–7, 410

District of Columbia. *See* Washington, D.C.

disturbing fish pond, as capital crime, 20

Doan, Aaron, 213–15

Doan, Abraham, 214–15

Doan, Joseph, 214–15

Doan, Levi, 214–15

Doan, Mahlon, 214

Doan, Moses, 214

Dobie, Samuel, 326

Dobson, Thomas, 89–90

Doctor Franklin Tavern, 309

Dodd, William, 145, 314, 361

Dodsley, James, 80

domestic violence, 275

Don Giovanni, 119

Donaldson, Alexander, 87–88

Donaldson, James, 88

Dorcester, Massachusetts, 326

Doria, Andrea, 359

Double Jeopardy Clause, 425

Douglas, Davison, 25

Douglas, William O., 437

Douglass, Frederick, 16, 438

Dowbiggin, Ian, 397

dower, 193

dowry, 33

Draco, 26, 122, 285–89, 304, 310, 346, 445; "spirit" of, 414

Dragonetti, Giacinto, 79, 279, 368–69; as "wise observer on governments," 368

drawing and quartering, 4, 29, 46, 164, 167, 222, 224, 255, 271, 273, 404, 406

Drayton, William Henry, 206

Dred Scott v. Sandford, 383, 438

drowning, death by, 280

Dryden, John, 81

Du Ponceau, Peter, 335, 337, 404–7, 410–13, 435, 441, 447–48

Du Simitiere, Pierre-Eugene, 497

Duane, William, 412, 503

Dublin, Ireland, 30, 77, 79, 92, 126, 254, 291, 361, 395

Duchy of Milan, xi, 30–31, 62–63. *See also* Milan, Italy

ducking, punishment of, 96, 269, 283

ducking stool(s), 96, 225, 233, 269, 287, 375, 407

"due process," 40, 281, 427, 439, 452; as barring arbitrariness, 439; built-in flexibility of, 342, 452; as concept, 281, 428; in France, 104

Due Process Clause(s), 40, 281, 427. *See also* Fifth Amendment; Fourteenth Amendment

duels/dueling, 18, 55–56, 90, 92, 204, 221, 239, 292, 396; in America, 396–97; between nobles, 55; as capital crime,

274, 283; crime of, 395; laws pertaining to, 397; origins of, 55

Duer, William, 201, 403

Duffield, George, 322

Duke of Exeter, 371

Duke of Manchester, 354

Duke of Portland, 109

Duke of Sussex, 266

Duke of Tuscany, 5, 66, 74, 115, 137, 161–62, 177, 192, 196–99, 253, 322, 336, 346; and Cesare Beccaria's treatise, 162, 435. See also Leopold, Peter

Duke of York, 116; laws of, 232

Dumond, Robert, 440

Dumont, Pierre Étienne Louis, 99–100, 205, 335

Duncan, Elizabeth, 43

dungeon(s), 92, 365, 376–77; of Europe, 323

Dunlap, John, 89

Duomo of Milan, 74

Dutch: immigration, 295; translations, 253

Dwight, Louis, 232

Dwight, Theodore, 101

Dwight, Timothy, 101, 234–35

Dyer, George, 93, 366

e pluribus unum, 137

ear cropping, 6, 102, 129, 162, 169, 233, 269, 273–74, 276, 297–98, 325, 329, 348, 361, 373, 376, 404, 420, 446; as infamous punishment, 394

Earl of Bute, 81–82

Earl of Carlisle, 99

Earl of Chatham, 503. See also Pitt, William

Earl of Hardwicke, 43

Earl of Huntington, 92

Earl of Shelburne, 60, 104, 318

East India Company, 179

Eastern State Penitentiary, 139–40, 327–28, 383

Economic Society of Berne, 61

Eddy, Robert, 246

Eddy, Thomas, 236–37, 239–40, 323–24, 538; background of, 168–69; and Cesare Beccaria, 237; and Thomas Jefferson, 168–69

Eden, William, 79, 98–99, 184–85, 187, 246, 347; and Cesare Beccaria, 22, 104, 185, 479; on infamy, 394; as name "dear to humanity," 264; and penitentiaries, 317–18; writings of, 141, 335

Edict of the Grand Duke of Tuscany, for the Reform of Criminal Law, 137, 192, 322

Edinburgh, 47, 64, 78, 87–88, 239, 313, 396; and David Hume, 144; publication of Cesare Beccaria's treatise in, 204

Edinburgh Review, The, 375

education, 6, 18, 136, 265, 282, 308, 357; of "common people," 232; in Europe, 11–13, 63, 78, 112, 249–50; importance of, 49, 399; legal, 413; to prevent crime, 49, 216–17; public, 141, 311, 399; to reduce "desire of revenge," 312; of women, 30

Edward I (King), 280

Edward II (King), 280

Edwards, Ignatious, 156

Edwards, Jonathan, 235

Egypt: history of, 241; king of, 167, 445

Eighth Amendment, xii, 6, 20, 22, 224, 395, 439, 451–52; as absolute prohibition, 382; and "barbaric" punishments, 6, 449; and cruelty, 6, 20–22, 247, 285, 395, 446; and death penalty, 390, 437, 450; and "death row phenomenon," 428–29; and death sentences, 375, 437, 452; debates surrounding meaning of, 420, 451; and "disproportionate" punishments, 222; and electric chair, 452; English origins of, 17–18, 224, 370, 395; and "evolving standards of decency," 294, 452; and "excessive" sanctions, 427; and executions, 15, 449, 452; and firing squad, 452; flexible language of, 451; and insane, 375, 450; and intellectual disabilities, 375; and juvenile offenders, 375, 450; and less culpable offenders, 375, 450; and lethal injection, 452; and mandatory sentences, 451; and methods of execution, 452; and non-homicidal offenders, 375, 450; and proportionality, 375; as protecting rights, 382, 427; and racial discrimination, 452; and rapists, 375; ratification of, 247, 285, 446; text of, 406; and torture, 390, 449; and victim impact evidence, 15. *See also* Cruel and Unusual Punishments Clause; *specific cases*

El Dorado, 40

elections, 8, 84, 86, 202, 268, 409, 422, 424

Electoral College, 202

electricity/lightning, study of, 116, 118, 128, 318, 367, 488

electrocution(s): constitutionality of, 452

Elements of the Civil Law, 125

Elements of the Philosophy of the Human Mind, 448

Elizabeth (Empress), 4, 161–62, 346, 367, 498, 542, 545

Elizabeth I (Queen), 40, 52, 287, 362

Elizabethtown, New Jersey, 119

Ellicott, Andrew, 251, 307

Ellicott, George, 307

Ellicott's Mills, Maryland, 307

Elliot, Gilbert, 319

Ellis, William Cox, 418, 421

Ellis Island, 163

Ellsworth, Oliver, 130, 233, 425, 515

Ellsworth, Vandine, 201

embezzlement, 295; as capital crime, 189

Empress's Palace, 98

Encyclopaedia Americana, 380

Encyclopaedia Britannica, 73

Encyclopædia Universalis, 33

Encyclopédie, 27, 32, 35, 58–59, 107, 232, 256

"Encyclopedists," 29, 58, 60–61, 133

England, xv, 3, 12–13, 32, 41, 64, 75, 77–79, 81, 83, 100, 106, 109, 112–13, 124, 141, 158, 200, 204, 220, 223, 243, 250, 253, 276–77, 286, 299, 303, 332, 353, 363, 371, 380, 394–95, 404, 429, 532; Alessandro Verri in, 117; André Morellet in, 95; anti-death penalty efforts in, 246, 266, 318; benefit of clergy abolished in, 400; Benjamin Franklin in, 117, 211; "Bloody Code" of, 6, 10, 20, 43, 49, 57, 65, 152, 164, 207, 213, 250, 254, 271, 288–89, 324, 339, 349, 380, 388, 414, 417, 434–35, 441–42, 454, 540, 542; capital crimes in, 15, 190, 273, 275, 371, 540; and Cesare Beccaria's influence, 3–4, 17–19, 36, 93, 104, 137, 142, 148–49, 195, 316–17, 366, 393, 399; Church of, 287; coffeehouses in, 31, 276; as "common law" country, 16, 49, 411; commonwealth of, 293, 358; and conflict with American colonists, 69, 103, 113, 252–53; corporal punishments in, 269, 273–75, 281, 372; "criminal Judicature in," 106; "cruel and bloody laws" of, 331; "cruel and sanguinary policy" of, 331; death penalty in, 194, 269, 301; death penalty abolished in, 380, 449; duels in, 55; executions in, 29, 36, 46–47, 49, 66, 121, 139, 255, 273, 277–78, 280; felonies in, 99; history of, 223, 357, 363; "hostile and sanguinary" designs of, 252; and Inns of Court, 184, 271, 413; John Adams in, 101, 179; and John Howard's influence, 212, 317; John Paradise in, 106, 201; jury trials in, 366; "justice" in, 223; law(s) of, 131, 214, 216, 222, 406–7, 414, 424; "liberties of the people of," 68; Luigi Castiglioni in, 32; monarchy of, 26, 40, 70, 97, 138, 288, 293, 405–6, 434; Montesquieu's influence in, 4, 220; Paolo Andreani in, 200; penal reform in, 4, 36, 128, 220–21, 246–47, 264, 266, 317–18, 339, 380; Philip Mazzei in, 195–96; prisons/penitentiaries in, 19, 22, 98–100, 311, 314, 317–18, 320–22, 325–26, 328, 331; private execution law of, 49; punishments in, 16–17, 274–75, 299, 301, 361, 394, 399; Quakers in, 128, 277, 294, 302, 318;

as "sanguinary," 315, 343, 346, 377; Star Chamber in, 395; statute law of, 410–11; study of law in, 184–85, 248–50; Thomas Jefferson in, 101; and torture, 46, 323, 365–66; and transportation, 52; U.S. minister to, 339; and use of transportation, 52, 122, 161, 317–18, 331; and West Indies, 376. *See also* "Bloody Code"; Glorious Revolution of 1688

English Bill of Rights of 1689, 17, 37, 86, 200, 224, 245–46, 273, 276, 370, 395, 406; "cruel and unusual punishments" clause of, 222, 224–25, 273, 380

English bridewells, 10, 294, 325

English Channel, 60, 84, 129, 195

English Civil War, 293

English common law, 57, 189, 226, 235, 260, 335, 380, 404–8, 411–12, 414, 416, 424, 451; American reactions to, 20, 57–58, 414; and colonial lawyers' training, 16; and torture, 46. *See also* English law

English Commonwealth, 193, 358

"English constitution," 86, 106, 410; as unwritten, 405

English constitutional monarchy, 220

English Declaration of Rights, 405. *See also* English Bill of Rights; Glorious Revolution of 1688

English law: and adultery, 282; as "always sanguinary," 377; and bankruptcy/insolvency, 282; and bribery, 282; "brutality and extravagant cruelty of," 421; Cesare Beccaria's influence on, 4, 21; common-law rights/tradition, 16–17, 20, 57, 424; and corporal punishments, 225, 273, 480; and corruption, 282; criticism of, 279; and custom, 342, 424; and death sentences, 221, 273, 307; as "defective to a degree both gross and cruel," 167; as evolving/nonstatic, 348; "excellence of," 36; and idleness, 282; influence of, 131, 223, 271, 425; laudation of, 135; as "less than perfect," 36; and lex talionis, 372; and

monopolies, 282; and murder, 282; as oppressive, 455; and perjury, 281–82; and proportionality, 37; and royal decree(s), 97; as sanguinary, 254–55; and seduction of women, 282; severity of, 218; study of, 223, 335, 413; and suicide, 398–99; and theft, 19; and torture, 365; transformation of, xi; and treason, 255; as "uncommonly sanguinary," 255; versus American law, 286, 348. *See also* "Bloody Code"; British Parliament

English Revolution of 1649, 194

English workhouses, 10

Englishmen, rights of, 20, 81, 300

Enlightenment, 3, 5–7, 11, 15–20, 22, 25, 27, 29, 41, 46, 49, 54, 60–61, 65, 67, 70, 75, 78, 94, 100, 104, 106–7, 121, 126, 143–45, 148, 165, 174, 185, 187, 196, 199, 202–3, 215, 227, 229, 235–36, 241, 243, 247, 249, 255, 257, 261, 279, 290, 292, 315, 317–18, 322, 328, 342, 347, 357, 361, 365, 369–70, 411, 437, 440, 447, 452, 454. *See also* French Enlightenment; Italian Enlightenment; Scottish Enlightenment

Enquiry concerning Political Justice and Its Influence on General Virtue and Happiness, 247

Enquiry How Far the Punishment of Death Is Necessary in Pennsylvania, 50, 90, 127, 131, 171–72, 237, 239, 324, 385

Enquiry Into the Effects of Public Punishment upon Criminals, and upon Society, An, 212, 319

Enquiry into the Justice and Policy of Punishing Murder by Death, An, 215

"Equal Justice Under Law," 355, 444, 450

equal opportunity, 423

Equal Protection Clause, 21–22, 438; text of, 21

"equal protection of the laws," 21, 382–83, 438–39, 452–53. *See also* Fourteenth Amendment

equal rights, 277

equality, 8, 11, 15, 21, 63, 197, 438; and Abraham Lincoln, 16; between rich and poor, 112; as birthright, 245, 301; and distribution of rights and privileges, 308–9; Immanuel Kant's views of, 139; of justice, 423; principle of, 66, 70, 139, 212, 301, 355, 382, 440, 443; as right, 67, 300–1, 427; and punishments, 21, 243; as "reciprocal" with liberty, 369; Thomas Jefferson's views of, 112; of treatment, 433, 453. *See also* Declaration of Independence

equity, 136, 180, 182, 203, 217, 345

errors: in capital cases, 439. *See also* innocence

Essay Concerning Human Understanding, An, 40, 46

Essay of a Frame of Government for Pennsylvania, 212

Essay on Crimes and Punishments, An. See On Crimes and Punishments

Essay on Crimes and Punishments, with a View of and Commentary upon Beccaria, Rousseau, Voltaire, Fielding, and Blackstone, An, 448

Essay on Human Understanding, 433

Essay on Man, 82

"Essay on Odors," 35

Essay on the Constitutional Power of Great-Britain over the Colonies in America, An, 68

Essay on the First Principles of Government, and on the Nature of Political, Civil, and Religious Liberty, An, 142, 194, 277

Essay on the Law of Bailments, An, 220

Essay on the Penal Law of Pennsylvania, 298

Essay on Toleration, 41

Essay on Universal History, An, 103

Essay on Woman, An, 82–83, 85–86

Essays, Moral, Political and Literary, 145

Essays on Capital Punishments, 236

Essays on the Mind, 32

Essays on the Principles of Morality and Natural Religion, 87

Essays on the Punishment of Death, 157, 266, 299

Essex, 346

Essex Head Club, 201

Essex Head Tavern, 201

Establishment Clause, 251, 364

Ethiopia, 167

Eton College, 63, 249

"Eumenes," 240

Europe, 14, 17, 28, 49, 100, 104–5, 108, 110–12, 117, 119, 126, 128–30, 132, 158, 160–62, 170, 197–98, 204, 217, 232, 253, 265, 273–74, 293, 322, 336, 363, 401, 413–14, 416, 433; army discipline in, 238; books from, 11, 144, 156, 249; capital crimes in, 15, 257, 276; and Cesare Beccaria's ideas/treatise, xiii, 3, 17–18, 35–36, 62, 65–66, 74, 79, 92, 106, 124, 142, 144, 146, 164, 249, 258, 348, 355, 367, 435–36, 449, 454; "celebrated literati in," 164; corruption in, 8, 153; corporal punishments in, 120–21, 361, 367; death penalty in, 120–21, 210, 367, 449; duels in, 55; educational opportunities in, xv, 5, 11–12, 63, 78, 112, 211, 250; as execution–free zone, 449; executions in, 46–49, 210, 367; intellectuals/intellectual climate in, 78, 157, 194, 286, 303, 421; "[l]ate experiments in," 228; murders in, 50; penal codes/reform in, 64, 98, 120, 133, 137, 145, 168, 199, 221, 225, 258, 264, 269, 282, 323, 415, 434; poverty in, 57; prison labor, 380; prisons in, 320; punishments in, 223, 394; and refusal to extradite offenders, 451; religious persecution in, 251; salons/literary societies in, 32; "sanguinary" laws of, 168, 323; "stirred to excitement," 58; torture in, 46–47, 200, 365–66, 369, 448; war(s) in, 81, 244. *See also specific countries, monarchs and wars*

European Convention on Human Rights, 449

European Court of Human Rights, 428

European Union, 428; human rights regime, 449

Evening Chronicle, The, 89, 126

Everett, Edward, 242

"evolving standards of decency," 294, 452. *See also* Eighth Amendment

Ex Post Facto Clause(s), 213, 226, 381

ex post facto laws, 213, 381

Examination into the Rights and Duties of Jurors, with Some Strictures on the Law of Libels, An, 316

"excessive": bail/fines, 37, 106, 199–200, 222, 224, 226, 246–47, 263; punishment, 59, 122, 233

executioners, 41, 176; "cruelty" of, 260; depicted in frontispiece to *On Crimes and Punishments*, 39; and executions, 5, 121; in France, 302; "inhumanity" of, 260; and judges "fond of spilling human blood," 147; public, 59, 260; recruitment of, 121–22, 327; reference in Declaration of Independence, 71; and torture, 164; as "universally detested," 260. *See also* hangmen

execution(s): ambivalence toward, 16–17, 238; annual number of, 439, 450; arbitrary nature of, 442, 450; "bad effect" of, 384; botched, 65; British, 334; as brutalizing, 37, 42, 49, 286–87; in colonial times, xv; as constitutional, 452; as cruel, 250–51, 291, 452; as "cruel and abominable," 167; as "cruel and terrible exhibition," 395; curtailment/reduction of, xi, 6, 16–17, 19, 21, 142, 154–55, 170, 269, 290, 368, 424, 434; as customary/common, 273, 289, 442; declining number of, 269, 395, 427, 450; as de-humanizing, 37; delays in carrying out, 427–29, 450–51; dragging condemned to, 280; during Civil War, 270, 351; during French Revolution, 65; in early America, 207; in England, 36, 46–47; in foreign countries, 36, 46–47, 334, 563; in France, 46; frequency of, 157–58, 293, 346; on Fridays, 295, 351; and

geographic disparities, 439, 450; as "impolitic," 167; as indiscriminate, 442; inefficacy of, 378; as inflicting pain and suffering, 450; as infusing "disgust at the barbarous severity of government," 167; as "inhuman," 167; mandatory, 425; methods/modes of, 65, 360, 452; on "necessity"/"absolute necessity" for, 39, 43, 54, 152, 164, 179, 185, 187, 209–10, 329, 439; number of countries carrying out, 563; opposition to, 25, 42, 104, 140, 172, 181–82, 184, 230, 241, 268, 294, 301, 344–45, 367, 380; and political dissidents, 25; private, 216, 242, 279; public, 46, 49, 95, 121, 194, 216, 236, 242, 278–81, 295, 302, 415; public sentiment on, 131; rarity of, 426; of religious minorities, 25; in Rome, 25–26, 107; for sake of "Example," 154; as sanguinary, 251, 350; in 1780s, 207; "should not be aggravated by any sufferings," 164; of slaves, 156, 362, 443; in South, 439, 450; in Spain, 47; substitutes for, 10, 39, 49, 122, 155, 337, 346–47, 371, 373, 395; summary, 450; support for, 282, 292, 389; suspension of, 15, 367; threat of, 122; as torture, 450; as unconstitutional, 15, 263, 449–50; in U.S., 10; as unjust, 54; as unnecessary, 36, 39, 50, 225, 291, 439, 442; as unusual, 452; use of, 276, 280; of women, 46–47, 63, 102, 121, 171, 242; worldwide use of, 367. *See also specific jurisdictions; names of specific people*

executive appointments, 357

executive branch. *See* President(s); United States

executive clemency. *See* clemency, executive

Executive Mansion, 186, 313

exile, 53, 149, 210; for life, 344, 346; as punishment, 52, 161, 225, 300, 380; of Quakers, 294; as substitute for executions, 161, 201. *See also* banishment; transportation

Exodus, 15, 274

exonerations. *See* innocence

Experiments and Observations on Different Kinds of Air, 116

Experiments and Observations on Electricity, 116

exporting rice, as capital crime, 108

Exposition of the Penitentiary System of Punishment, but More Particularly Adapted to that of Virginia, An, 329

Exposition of the Principles of the English Jacobins, An, 360

Exshaw, John, 77–78

Extracts and Remarks on the Subject of Punishment and Reformation of Criminals, 321

extradition: assurances obtained before, 428, 451; refusals to allow, 428, 451; treaties, 56, 399, 401, 428. *See also specific countries*

eyes: gouging/loss of, 129, 404

eyewitness testimony, 365

Fabbroni, Adamo, 115

Fabbroni, Giovanni, 115, 231

Facchinei, Ferdinando, 63–64

factions, 124, 359, 363

Fairfield, Connecticut, 233

Falconer, William, 65

false confessions, 44, 72. *See also* confession(s)

Familiar Exposition of the Constitution of the United States, A, 391

Faneuil Hall, 314

Farrand, William, 91

Farrand & Mallory, 91

fasces, 445; as Roman symbol of authority, 445

Fazzarini, Francesco, 314

federal courts, 404, 406, 408, 418; and common-law crimes, 58, 411–12; jurisdiction of, 58, 406–7, 411–12, 415, 417–18. *See also* Supreme Court; United States

federal death penalty, 414–15, 426. *See also* United States

"Federal Farmer," 422

Federal Gazette, 399

federal government. *See* United States

Federal Hall, 201–2, 332

federal judges, 413; views on common-law crimes, 417; and written opinions, 408–9

federal penitentiaries, 314, 316, 325, 330–31, 346–47

Federal Politician, The, 230

federalism, 212, 422

Federalist Papers, 168, 213, 220, 254, 387, 448, 551; *No. 44*, 381; *No. 47*, 48; *No. 70*, 106; *No. 74*, 239

Federalist(s), 102, 170, 233, 235, 261, 268, 362, 397; judges, 408; newspaper, 89; policies, 101

Fell, A. London, 125

"Fellow Citizen," 76

felo de se, 43. *See also* suicide

felonies: as capital crimes, 222, 229, 372, 414–15; in England, 222; punishment of, 27, 195, 229, 295, 372, 399, 404, 425. *See also* felony murder; *specific crimes*

felony murder, 229, 240, 379, 384, 386

Fénelon, François de Salignac de La Mothe, 30, 195

Ferdinando IV (King), 133

Ferguson, Robert A., 247

Fernandez, Mark, 333

Ferney, France, 59, 470

Ferrara, Italy, 116

Ferrone, Vincenzo, 136

Feuerbach, Paul Johann Anselm Ritter von, 139

Field, David Dudley, 240

Fielding, Henry, 92; commentary on, 448; Italian translation of, 177

Fifteenth Amendment, 440

Fifth Amendment, 20, 281, 395; and "due process of law" protection, 427; grand jury provision, 395; origins of, 394–95; and protection against infamy, 437; provisions/text of, 40, 393, 395, 426;

and self-incrimination prohibition, 390

Filangieri, Gaetano, xi, 117, 119, 132–36, 160, 178, 218, 279, 329, 335, 436

Filler, Louis, 241

fine(s): for arson, 9; for burglary, 9; discretionary, 224–25; and English law, 224, 273; excessive, 199, 224, 246–47; as "far from being wholly arbitrary," 224; for kissing, 88; monetary, 397; and nobles, 373; proportionate, 375; as punishment, 9, 51, 103, 123, 133, 188, 193, 224, 275, 283, 295, 301, 389, 407, 418; remission of, 227

Finizzi, Ferdinando, 230

firing squad(s): constitutionality of, 452; as execution method, 153

Firmian, Karl Joseph von (Carlo di), 28–30, 35, 62–64, 126

First Amendment, 20, 213, 251, 364; text of, 213, 251, 364

"First Citizen," 250

First Congress. See Congress

Fisher, Sydney George, 15–16, 421

Fishkill, New York, 168

Fitzhugh, William, 283

Fitzmaurice, William, 104

Fitzpatrick, Jeremiah, 254

Fitzsimons, Thomas, 230, 386–87

flagellation, 325

flogging, 10, 167, 276, 372–73; public, 329. See also whipping

Florence, Italy, 13, 27, 105, 115–16, 177, 196–97, 231, 252, 257

Florida: colonies in, 32, 98; death row, 429

Flowers, Thomas, 284

Fontana, Carlo, 328

Fontana, Felice, 196

forced labor, 51–52, 211, 293, 378, 545; to prevent crime, 49. See also slavery

forced loans, 405

forfeiture: of goods, 161, 345, 398, 404; of land/property, 27, 161, 193, 215, 345, 398; as punishment, 9, 283, 398

forgery, 196, 204, 262–63; abolition for, 15, 266; as capital crime, 18, 204, 295, 414–15, 426; debated by Congress, 386–87; imprisonment for, 325, 385; punishment of, 258

forgiveness, 266; "Side of," 155

Forlorn Hope, 403

Formation of Thunder, Lightning, and of Various Other Meteors Explained According to the Ideas of Mr. Franklin, The, 117

fornication, 275

Forster, John, 97–98

Fort Cumberland, 156

Fort Duquesne, 177

Fort Independence, 163

Fort McNair, 314

Fort Mifflin, 163

Fort Ticonderoga, 441

Fort Vincennes, 230

Foster, Esther, 242

Foster, Thomas, 121

Fothergill, John, 318

Foucault, Michel, 95

Foulon de Doué, Joseph-François, 442

Founding Fathers. See individual founders/ framers

Fourteenth Amendment, 281, 355, 375, 452–53; and death sentences, 375, 437; as ensuring equality of treatment, 21, 382, 452; ratification/approval of, 22, 383, 409, 452; text of, 382; and women's rights, 382. See also Due Process Clause(s); Equal Protection Clause

Fourth of July, 20, 142, 201, 412, 424, 434, 441

Fox, George, 294

Fragment on Government, A, 4, 22, 98

"Fragment on Style," 35

Fragments of Politics and History, 93

Framers. See individual framers

France, 12–14, 28–32, 50, 104–5, 113, 115–16, 170, 179, 199–201, 232, 248–50, 254, 257, 278, 305, 334, 336, 398, 413; abolition/abolition efforts in, 4, 103; aid from, 120; balloon ascents in, 119; Benjamin Franklin in,

12, 34, 77, 108–9, 127, 211, 215, 365, 398; Benjamin Guild in, 125; capital crimes in, 4; Cesare Beccaria's influence in, 3–4, 31, 61, 64, 95, 99–100, 103, 137, 195, 218, 244, 399; as civil law country, 361; coffeehouses in, 31, 60; confessions/torture in, 200; Constituent/National Assembly of, 65, 104, 180, 234, 303, 442; desertion in, 58; duels in, 55; emperor of, 445; executions in, 29, 46, 95, 100, 103, 107, 124, 180, 254, 302; James Monroe in, 120; and Jeremy Bentham, 413; John Adams in, 14, 80; John Wilkes in, 81–83; king of, 100, 110, 119, 302, 445; Luigi Castiglioni in, 35; lynching in, 107; minister to, 78, 80, 106, 108, 120, 140, 198, 201, 234, 334, 341, 417; and law/penal reform, 195; prison(s) in, 190; punishments in 301; religious intolerance in, 107; and Revolutionary War assistance, 100, 119–20; south of, 116; system of proofs in, 367; Thomas Jefferson in, 14, 101, 103, 105, 157, 190, 206, 326; Thomas Paine in, 302; torture abolished in, 104, 389; torture in, 361, 365, 367; U.S. minister to, 106; Voltaire's advocacy in, 64, 123–24, 366–67. *See also* French Enlightenment; French Revolution; Paris, France

Frankenstein, 279

Franklin, Benjamin, xi, 62, 77, 85, 108, 117, 157, 241, 284; and Alessandro Verri, 117; and Alexander Dallas Bache, 284; as *American Museum* subscriber, 244; and American Philosophical Society, 118; and André Morellet, 60, 95, 104, 482; on "arbitrary" power, 299; and Benjamin Rush, 5, 211–12, 215–17; and Benjamin Vaughan, 45, 130, 217–18; bust of, 314; and Canada, 248; and Capel Lofft, 353; and Cesare Beccaria, xi, 124, 218; and Charles Thomson, 137; and Club of Honest Whigs, 277; at Constitu-

tional Convention, 444; on corporal punishments, 276; and David Hume, 144; on death penalty, 7, 211, 241, 264, 268; on Declaration of Independence, 332, 441; as diplomat, 100, 211; and Dr. Guillotin, 65, 118; and Dr. John Fothergill, 318; and Duke de la Rochefoucauld, 302; on "Dungeons"/ "Irons," 365; in England, 211; and Francesco dal Verme, 108–9, 114; in France, 14, 100, 106, 141, 211; and Francis Bailey, 90; and Gaetano Filangieri, xi, 132–36, 218; and Giambattista Beccaria, 116–17, 135; house of, 4, 212, 215, 244, 265, 325, 433–34; on innocence, 45; and interest in Italian culture, 113; and Jacques-Pierre Brissot de Warville, 398; and Jan Ingenhousz, 118; and Jean Claude Molini, 177; and John Almon, 75–77; and John Carroll, 248; and John Coakley Lettsom, 313; and John Locke, 40; and John Morgan, 116; and John Paradise, 201; and John Paul Jones, 141; and John Quincy Adams, 257; on John Wilkes, 84–85; and Joseph Banks, 129; and Joseph Priestley, 194, 277; on "[l]ate experiments in Europe," 228; on lex talionis, 188–89; and Library Company of Philadelphia, 125, 137; on London mobs, 84–85; and Ludovico Barbiana di Belgioioso, 194; and Luigi Castiglioni, 12–13, 34, 127–30, 215–16; and Luigi Pio, 134–35; and Mathew Carey, 88; as minister to France, 106; and Montesquieu, 220; and Noah Webster, 234; and Paolo Frisi, 34; pardon(s) of, 215; at Passy, 12, 34, 77, 108–9, 127, 215, 365, 398; and Patience Wright, 353; and penal reform, xi, 88, 122–23, 229, 245; and Pennsylvania constitution, 227–28, 370; and Pennsylvania General Assembly, 228; petition addressed to, 229; and Philip Mazzei, 118, 196–98; as President of Pennsylvania's Supreme

Executive Council, 214, 217; as printer, 11–12; on prisoners of war, 365; quote misattributed to, 265–66; and Richard Jackson, 211; and Richard Price, 277, 318–19; and Robert Coram, 141; and Robert R. Livingston, 109, 178; on self-incrimination, 395; and Society for Promoting Political Enquiries, 434–35; statue of, 315; study of electricity/lightning, 116–17, 318, 367, 488–89; study of French, 116, 120; study/use of Italian, 116, 118, 120, 124, 134–36; study of Spanish, 120; and *The North Briton*, 81; and Thomas Jefferson, 118; and Thomas Mifflin, 137; and Thomas Paine, 75; on torture, 47; on transportation, 52; as treaty commissioner, 14; and Voltaire, 124, 146; and William Dodd, 314; on William Penn, 40; and William Strahan, 137; and William Thornton, 313

Franklin, Peter, 191

Franklin, William, 84–85, 157, 188

Franks, John, 278

Franzoni, Carlo, 313, 444

Franzoni, Giuseppe, 313

Frase, Richard, 37

Frasier, Isaac, 233

Frederick II (King), 28–29, 61–62, 66, 79, 156, 365; and Cesare Beccaria, 61–62; and Voltaire, 61

free enterprise, 432

Free Exercise Clause, 364

Free Thoughts on Seduction, Adultery, and Divorce, 80

freedom, 7, 54, 56, 69, 72, 133–34, 179, 228, 235, 254, 271, 305, 368, 438, 442, 446; as birthright, 40, 59, 67, 245, 300, 356, 427; Benjamin Banneker on, 307; "blessings" of, 67; as "English subject's Prerogative," 81; "genius of," 285; ideal of, 220; "perfect," 40; preservation of, 232; principles of, 168, 360; as "prize," 356; relinquishing "smallest possible portion" of, 455; "spirit of," 168, 361;

as "spirit or soul" of constitution, 69; state of, 265

freedom of assembly, 213, 364, 409

freedom of religion/worship, 63, 87, 213, 251, 364, 409

freedom of press, 145, 213, 282, 364, 409

freedom of speech, 63, 213, 251, 364, 375, 409

Freeman's Journal, The, 90, 170

freemasons, 199, 332

French: books, 120; Code of 1791, 3–4; Constitution of 1793, 244; court, 423; Declaration of Rights of 1789, 244; emperor, 417; law(s), 60, 244, 334–35, 445; mastery/"Master" of, 116, 249, 265; and *Notes on the State of Virginia*, 187; and *On Crimes and Punishments*, 3, 27, 47, 95, 103, 144, 187; penal reform, 104; society, 254; spoken in Milan, 34; study/use of, 91, 95, 105, 113, 116, 120, 144, 153, 160, 314, 333; translation of letter to the inhabitants of Quebec, 148; translation of state constitution, 135; writers, 29, 32–33, 35, 59, 74, 92–93, 100, 243, 451

French Academy of Medicine, 64

French and Indian War(s), 44, 82, 124, 156

French Declaration of the Rights of Man and of the Citizen, 104, 195

French Enlightenment, 29, 103, 120, 219, 369, 407

French National/Constituent Assembly, 4, 100, 104

French National Convention, 65, 180, 234

French *philosophes*, 4, 19, 27, 32–33, 35, 58, 61, 64, 73, 83, 87, 100, 103, 126, 133, 161, 180, 190, 243, 256, 290. *See also specific individuals*

French Polynesia, 346

French Revolution, xiv, 4, 20, 48, 59, 64–65, 100, 102, 170, 195, 252, 262, 278, 289, 299, 303, 358, 442, 447; American views of, 254; and "liberty, fraternity, equality," 278; "sanguinary times of," 316

French Riviera, 113

Freneau, Philip, 170–71, 210

Frequency of Capital Punishments Inconsistent with Justice, Sound Policy, and Religion, The, 361

Friedman, Lawrence, 25, 371

Friendly Sketches in America, 349

Friends. *See* Quakers; Society of Friends

Fries's Rebellion, 7

Frisi, Paolo, 34–37, 127–28

Fromond, Giovanni Francesco, 118

Full Faith and Credit Clause, 213

Furman v. Georgia, 15, 437

Further Thoughts on the Present State of Public Opinion, 532

Fuseli, Henry, 279

future generations: consideration of, 8, 20, 342, 446, 454; and U.S. Constitution, 8, 342. *See also* posterity

Gabriel's Rebellion, 443

Gage, Thomas, 161

Galiani, Ferdinando, 35, 133

Galicia, 63

Galileo, 36

Gallatin, Albert, 266, 333, 416

galleys, 162. *See also* forced labor; slavery

Galloway, Joseph, 85

gallows, 10, 17, 49, 73, 102–3, 107, 121, 138, 154–55, 176, 188, 242, 257, 263, 265, 268, 273, 295, 330, 360, 373, 400; barbarism of, 371; carting to, 210; in England, 277–78; hill, 152; humor, 441; and "neck verse," 307; "portable," 103; sitting on, 102, 373, 378; in Tuscany, 161. *See also* hanging(s)

gaols, 233, 296, 322, 326. *See also* penitentiaries; prisons

Garland, David, 439

Garrick, David, 60

Gates, Horatio, 441

Gates, Thomas, 189

gender inequality, 11, 439. *See also* discrimination; women

General Advertiser, The, 122

General History of the Christian Church, 175

General Hospital of Milan, 116

general warrant(s), 82, 84

Geneva, Switzerland, 29, 59, 79, 99, 106, 116, 153, 205, 336, 470, 497

Geneva Peace Society, 336

Genoa, Italy, 108, 114, 116, 139, 230, 258, 359

Genovesi, Antonio, 35, 117, 133, 369

Gentleman's Magazine, The, 93, 287

Geoffrin, Marie Thérèse Rodet, 60

George III (King), 14, 67–68, 70, 75, 81–84, 86–87, 144–45, 173, 231, 289, 353, 432, 440, 503; administration of, 81; "Cruelty" of, 143; and Declaration of Independence, 70–71, 143; reign of, 143, 306; "long train of abuses" of, 70–71; portraits of, 103; tyranny of, 81

George III: America's Last King, 67

George Washington University, 7, 94

Georgetown, 186, 262

Georgetown University, 248

Georgetown Weekly Ledger, 311

Georgia, 110–11, 447; attorney general, 111; constitution, 374; death penalty in, 452; duel in, 55; grand jury charge, 374; Luigi Castiglioni in, 12, 111, 129; penitentiaries in, 6, 347; Supreme Court, 437

German Element in the War of American Independence, The, 160

German(y), 105, 363, 378; and Cesare Beccaria, 4, 27, 467; customs, 160; death penalty abolished in, 449; immigration, 359; language, 153, 160, 337; philosopher, 228; principalities, 220, 243; states, 28; study of, 265; system of proofs in, 367

Germantown, Pennsylvania, 129, 154; battle of, 89

Gerry, Elbridge, 52, 178, 300, 441

Gettysburg Address, 16

Giannone, Pietro, 36, 357

Gianotti, Donato, 436

gibbeting, 162, 218, 247, 283, 301, 360, 375, 378, 414, 441, 443

Gibbon, Edward, 289, 356

Gilbert, Cass, 444–45

Gilbert, Geoffrey, 395

giving intelligence to the enemy, 152

gladiators, 107, 216, 362

Glasgow, Scotland, 41, 78–79, 144, 146

Glorious Revolution of 1688, 41, 70, 194, 200, 223, 225, 273–74, 405

Gloucester, England, 317

God, 5, 16, 54, 85, 118, 176, 227, 251, 275, 296, 299, 344; as "Almighty Being"/ "the Almighty," 332, 337; Cesare Beccaria's invocation of, 33, 51, 55, 63–64; duty to, 68; as endowing "man" with "certain rights," 236; "gift of," 234; glory of, 203; "grace of," 412; infallibility/"infallible law of," 138, 295; "laws of," 42, 301; "Nature's," 42, 70; as possessing authority "over life and death," 43; serving, 41; will of, 389; word of, 295. *See also* Bible; natural law; religion; religious persecution

Goddard, John, 280

Goddard & Angell, 309

Godstone, Surrey, 204

Godwin, William, 247, 249, 279, 376

Goethe, Johann Wolfgang von, 133–34

Goldsborough, Robert, 248

Goldsmith, Oliver, 356

Golphintown, Georgia, 111

Gomez, Benjamin, 92

Goodenow, John Milton, 416–17

Goodheart, Lawrence, 234

Gorani, Giuseppe, 79, 303

Gordon, Thomas, 194, 390

Gordon, William (printer), 87

Gordon, William (historian), 77, 251

Gore, Christopher, 102, 281

Gottlieb, Gabriele, 275

gouging of eyes, 304

Gould, James, 413

Gould, Stephen, 91–92, 186

Gould & Treadway, 91

"government of laws," 175, 409

governors. *See* clemency, executive; *specific governors*

Gowder v. City of Chicago, 391

Graber, Jennifer, 294–95

Grammatical Institute of the English Language, A, 148

Grand Duke of Tuscany, 66, 74, 115, 118, 137, 161–62, 177, 192, 196–99, 253, 322, 336, 346; and Cesare Beccaria's treatise, 162, 435. *See also* Leopold, Peter

grand juries: charges/indictments, 20, 164, 167, 175–76, 285–87, 318, 374, 393, 498–99, 515; requirement of, 106, 395, 426

Grand Jury Clause, 395, 426

"Grand Tours," 13

Grandi, Giuseppe, 74

Graves, William, 250

Gravier, Charles, 365

Gray, Robert, 93

Gray's Inn, 220, 362

Great Britain, 5, 29, 50, 72, 75, 253, 317–19, 331–32, 424; absence of written constitution in, 405; administration/government of, 252, 411; Cesare Beccaria's treatise in, 4, 26, 37, 316, 368; common law of, 411, 424; counterfeiting in, 386; despotism of, 212; duels in, 55; executions in, 210; "glory and prosperity" of, 70; independence from, 5–6, 65, 70, 72, 126, 173, 212, 356, 375; king/monarchy of, 231, 434; minister(s) to, 102, 416; penal code/ laws in, 10, 101, 252; Penitentiary Act of, 317–19, 321, 331; and proportionality of punishments, 37; and reconciliation attempts, 32, 67–70, 98–99, 147; and relationship to colonies, 50, 70, 198, 292; and Revolutionary War, 67, 100, 119–20, 148, 159, 185, 198, 271, 375; rights in, 20; "sanguinary laws" of, 252; taxation policies of, 70; trampling on "the rights of mankind," 148; written statutes of, 411. *See also* British Parliament; England

Great Charter. *See* Magna Carta

"Great Law of 1682," 128, 275, 287, 294
Great Seal of the United States, 137, 497
Greece, 286
Greek, 137; alphabet, 201; architecture, 313; authors, 93; history, 175, 285, 357; lawgiver(s), 26, 288, 414; laws, 26; pseudonyms, 7, 358; study of, 105, 160, 201, 265; translation of Cesare Beccaria's treatise, 186
Green Mountain Boys, 158
Greene, George Washington, 72, 159–60
Greene, Nathanael, 12–13, 72, 153, 159–60, 356; as "Fighting Quaker," 12; and ownership of Beccaria's treatise, 12, 159–60; and William Blackstone, 12
Greenwich Village, 167, 169
Greer Jr., Harold, 207
Grenoble, France, 218; Parlement of, 60
Grenville, George, 82
Griffin, Corbin, 396
Griffin, Martin, 151
Griffith, William, 240–41
Griffiths, R., 91
Grimaldi, Francesco Antonio, 521
Grimke, Thomas, 209
Griswold v. Connecticut, 410
Groot, Huig de, 445. *See also* Grotius, Hugo
Grotius, Hugo, 39, 41, 67, 75, 93, 174, 243, 247, 265, 431, 445
Gualdo, John, 113
Gualdrasco, Italy, 33
Guarini, Giovanni Battista, 177
Guazzini, Sebastian, 361
Guicciardini, Francesco, 178, 357
Guide pour le voyage d'Italie en poste, 105
Guild, Benjamin, 125
Guillotin, Dr. Jospeh-Ignace, 64–65, 118
guillotine, 4; use of 29, 302, 398. *See also* beheading
gun ownership, 18, 390–93, 451
gun violence, 392
Gunpowder Plot, 164
Gunston Hall, 151
Gutch, John, 250

Guthrie, William, 251
Gwinnett, Button, 55, 434

habeas corpus: curtailment of, 15; petitions/proceedings, 83; privilege/writ of, 213, 408; right to, 26, 69; suspension of, 408
Habsburgs, 28, 30, 35, 44, 61, 118, 220, 365; laws of, 29
Hadfield, George, 326
Hague, The, 84
Haines, Charles Glidden, 178
Halbert, Henry, 379
Halbrook, Stephen, 390–91
Hale, Matthew, 188, 243, 276, 513
Hale, Nathan, 154, 356
Hales, Dianne, 71
Hall, A. Oakey, 240
Hall, Josias Carvel, 238
Hall, Thomas, 91
Hall & Nancrede, 91
Hall of Surgeons, 183
Hall-Stevenson, John, 77
halter(s), 233, 340, 373, 403, 441; "round his neck," 163. *See also* noose(s); rope; scaffold
Hambden, John, 359
Hamburg, Germany, 27
Hamilton, Alexander, 8, 11, 16, 247; and affiliation with Columbia College, 239; and American Academy of Arts and Sciences, 130; as *American Museum* subscriber, 244; as Annapolis delegate, 255; on arbitrariness, 299; on bills of attainder, 381; bust of, 314; and Charles Asgill, 157, 291–92; on "cruel and sanguinary" punishments, 254; death of, 397; on death sentences, 163, 238; on desertions, 163, 238; on desirability of revising Articles of War, 162; duel with Aaron Burr, 396–97; and Edward Livingston, 333; on executions and their frequency, 157–58, 163, 291; and *Federalist Papers*, 387; on French Revolution, 254; and Gaetano Filangieri, 132; as George Wash-

ington's aide-de-camp, 400; on hard labor, 163; and Henry Knox, 291–92; and honorary French citizenship, 303; and Jean-Louis de Lolme, 106; as lawyer, 237; on Louis XVI's execution, 303; on Major John André, 153–54; on natural rights, 202; on opposition to "frequency of capital punishment," 238; and Paolo Andreani, 201; on penal reform, 162; and Philip Schuyler, 237, 324; on presidential pardoning power, 239, 400; on "sacred rights of mankind," 202; as Secretary of the Treasury, 88, 230; and Society for Constitutional Information, 354; on traitors, 163; and William Blackstone's *Commentaries*, 223; and William Livingston, 296; and William Rawle, 142

Hamlin, Hannibal, 224

Hammersley, Rachel, 194

Hammurabi, 445

Hancock, John, 11, 13; and Cesare Beccaria, 4, 136; and corporal punishments, 373; on Declaration of Independence, 441; fighting for liberty, 360; and Francesco dal Verme, 109; and John Adams, 173–74; and John Wilkes, 87; and Luigi Castiglioni, 129, 488; pardons of, 268; and penal reform, 268, 315, 373; and Thomas Jefferson, 197

Hanging Not Punishment Enough for Murtherers, High-way Men, and Housebreakers, 246

hanging(s), 6, 17, 73, 121, 164, 263, 274, 287, 291, 330, 361, 420; as "benefit to nobody but the executioner," 146; in chains, 360; in Connecticut, 143; as "cruel exhibition," 350; under English law, 255, 273, 278, 280; in Europe, 47; as "example," 281; as execution method, 193, 224, 280, 283, 293, 329, 354, 386; for forgery, 15; of Major John André, 153–54; in Massachusetts, 102–3; under military law, 152, 155–56; in Minnesota, 351; in Philadelphia, 229; as punishment, 212;

of Quakers, 290; for robbery, 269; of slaves, 156, 211, 443; for theft/stealing, 26; in 1780s, 207; for treason, 425, 441; as usual method of execution, 280; in Virginia, 156, 185, 443

Hangman, The, 266

hangmen, 74, 122, 146, 153, 260, 305–6, 311. *See also* executioners

Hanser, Robert, 327

Hanway, Jonas, 10

happiness: Benjamin Rush's views on, 43, 244; Cesare Beccaria's views on, 7–8, 18, 47, 54, 56, 66, 147–48, 316, 362, 421, 423, 431–32, 444; as "chief end" of mankind, 46; of community, 36, 236; "desire of," 67; "established upon a lasting basis," 356; as "first law of every government," 433; founders' views on, xv, 7–8, 316; Gaetano Filangieri's views on, 134; of "generations yet unborn," 8; "greatest happiness" principle, 19, 53, 56, 142–43, 174, 265, 433; "greatest Sum of individual," 368–69; James Wilson's views on, 164–66; Jeremy Bentham's views on, 98, 142–43, 265; John Adams' views on, 300; John Dickinson's views on, 67, 69; John Locke's views on, 40, 46; Joseph Priestley's views on, 142–43, 277; and law, 164; and liberty/freedom, 167, 195, 254, 264, 300, 368, 440; in Lombardy, 28–29; Montesquieu's views on, 220; Nathaniel Chipman's views on, 259; "of the citizens," 167; "of mankind," 220; "of the governed," 331; "of the People," 40, 252, 264, 333, 359, 433; maximizing, 183; Philip Mazzei's views on, 197–98; Pietro Verri's views on, 31, 35, 71, 473; preservation of, 232; principle of, 440; private, 473; "Production of," 300; "promotion of," 423; public, 232, 355, 357, 473; pursuing/ "pursuit of," xvi, 16, 46, 70, 143, 197, 213, 236, 245, 265, 356, 433, 438, 560; restoration of "fellow-creatures" to,

320; securing, 360; societal, 43, 67, 98, 259, 277, 311, 320, 323, 345, 347, 360, 363, 433, 437; as "sole End of Government," 252; Thomas Jefferson's views on, 159, 183, 232, 254; "true point of," 368; William Godwin's views on, 247; writings on, 247

Harcourt, Bernard, 33, 58, 95, 454–55

hard labor, 10, 20, 39, 96, 112, 132, 149, 163, 181, 192, 195, 210, 225, 227–29, 233, 236–38, 246, 280, 283, 297, 321, 370, 372, 385, 407, 418; "as efficacious" as death, 172; "for life," 426; as "infamous" punishment, 394; as substitute for corporal punishments, 540; as substitute for executions, 10, 20, 39, 341; use in England, 98, 185, 321–22

Harrington, James, 53, 194–95, 436

Harris, Sharon, 239

Harrison, Benjamin, 137, 198, 441

Hartford, Connecticut, 233

Hartford Wits, 101

Hartnett, Stephen John, 156

Harvard College, 91, 102–3, 124–25, 239, 265, 284, 326, 336, 356, 387, 413; and Cesare Beccaria's treatise, 79, 241, 444; description of, 443–44

Harvard Law School, 140, 208, 240, 397, 401, 403

Harvey, William, 278

hatred: as "pernicious," 259; of "cruelty," 228; of "medieval" practices, 333; of "severe punishments," 281; "spirit of," 343; of tyrants, 119

Haviland, John, 328

Hawkins, William, 243, 269

Hawthorne, Nathaniel, 373

Hay, William, 246

Hayes, Kevin, 177

head: shaving of, 163, 184, 322

Hebrew law, 372

Hegel, Georg Wilhelm Friedrich, 228

Heidelberg University, 21

Heinrichs, Peter, 306

Helvétius, Claude Adrien, 31–32, 59–60, 97–98, 149, 243

Hemings, Critta, 11

Hemings, James, 11

Hempstead, Long Island, 232

Hempstead Code, 232, 275

Henry, Patrick, 196, 231; and Bill of Rights, 199; on bills of attainder, 381; and Constitutional Society of Virginia, 196; on "cruel and unusual punishments," 200; on "excessive bail," 200; on "excessive fines," 199; and "give me liberty, or give me death," 369; as governor, 187; and Philip Mazzei, 196–97; on punishments, 199; on torture, 13, 200, 369; and William Blackstone's *Commentaries*, 223

Henry I (King), 280

Henry VI (King), 371

Henry VII (Emperor), 471

Henry VIII (King), 250, 373, 440

Henry Martin's Island, 346

hereditary nobility, 8

heresy, 36, 64, 199, 283, 404; as capital crime, 40

heretics, 25; punished by death, 251

Hermione, 334

Herndonsville, Kentucky, 344

Hewes, Joseph, 434

Hey, Richard, 422

Heyns, Christof, 21

high treason, 135, 273, 283. *See also* treason

highway robbery, 103, 278; as capital crime, 295; execution(s) for, 102, 269, 278; and life sentences, 348; as non-capital crime, 103. *See also* robbery

Histoire de la République de Venice, 357

Histoire d'Elisabeth Canning et de Jean Calas, 107

Histoire Romaine, 356

Historical Sketches of the Principles and Maxims of American Jurisprudence, 416

Historical Society of Pennsylvania, 287

Historical Society of the State of New-York, 374

History and Geography of the Middle Ages for Colleges and Schools, 160

History and Present State of Electricity with Original Experiments, The, 116

History of Italy, The, 178, 357

History of Kentucky, The, 434

History of Naples, 36

History of New-Hampshire, The, 129

History of Philadelphia, A, 312

History of the Affairs of Europe in this Present Age, but More Particularly of the Republick of Venice, The, 178

History of the Colony of Massachusett's Bay, The, 274

History of the Column of Infamy, 72

History of the Decline and Fall of the Roman Empire, The, 289, 356–57

History of the Dispute with America, 448

History of the Revolutions that Happened in the Government of the Roman Republic, 356

History of the Rise, Progress, and Establishment of the Independence of the United States of America, The, 77, 251

History of the State of Rhode Island and Providence Plantations, The, 247

History of the War of Independence of the United States of America, 72, 160

Hitchcock, Daniel, 389

Hobbes, Thomas, 39, 46, 54, 243, 367, 397, 455; and John Adams, 175

Hobbs, Abraham, 389

Hob's Hole, Virginia, 197

Hoeflich, M. H., 91–92, 387

Hoffman, David, 140–41

Hogg, Thomas Jefferson, 461

Holcombe, Henry, 6

Holland, 100, 294, 302, 363

Hollis, Thomas Brand, 19, 178, 194, 354

Holloway, Pippa, 394

Holmes, Oliver Wendell, 219

Holocaust, 449

Holt, Joseph, 351

Holy Roman Emperor, 28, 66

Holy Roman Empire, 34, 220. *See also* Roman Empire

Holy Roman Empress, 365. *See also* Theresa, Maria

Holy See, 115. See also Vatican

Home, Henry, 388. *See also* Lord Kames

Homer, 30, 93

homicide(s): by misadventure, 231; as capital crime, 26, 48, 236, 415; "excusable," 283; "justifiable," 174, 193. *See also* murder(s)

homosexuality: abolition of death penalty for, 381; as capital crime, xv, 26, 236, 274–75, 280, 404, 411; castration for, 189, 193, 283; punishment of, 44–45, 183. *See also* sodomy

Honeywood, St. John, 303–6, 431

honor, 55–56, 67, 71, 165, 292, 394, 396–97

hoods: wearing of, 140

Hooke, Nathaniel, 356

Hooker, J. J., 428

hooks, 162

Hopkins, Lemuel, 101

Hopkins, Stephen, 434

Hopkinson, Francis, 434–35

Horace, 178

horsestealing: as capital crime, 295, 344; crime of, 207, 214, 233, 262; imprisonment for, 385; punishment of, 233, 283, 297; "rage" against, 206

Hosack, David, 238

Hosmer, Parker, 163

Hospice of San Michele, 328

Hostettler, John, 15, 104, 182

Hotel de Choiseul, 177

Hôtel d'Orléans, 177

Hôtel Langeac, 101

House of Commons, 30, 76, 83–86, 148, 184, 252, 300–1, 316, 346, 350, 382. *See also* British Parliament

House of Lords, 82, 164, 252, 362. *See also* British Parliament

housebreaking, 102, 283, 322. *See also* burglary

Houseman, Charles, 284

houses of correction, 74, 225, 294, 314, 321–22, 346, 377, 394

Howard, Frederick, 99

Howard, John, 18–19, 258, 299, 323–24, 331; as "active and indefatigable man," 323; as "benevolent," 331; and Benjamin Rush, 212; "celebrated," 314; and Cesare Beccaria, 22, 317, 328, 542; correspondence of, 349; on cruelty, 348; death of, 322; influence of, 169, 193, 212, 243, 299, 311–12, 317, 323–24, 328, 349, 421; as "intelligent and indefatigable friend to the distressed," 98; in Italy, 258; on penal codes, 348; as penal reformer, 130, 318–19, 322, 325, 435; and penitentiaries, 317–20, 325; "unspeakable benevolence" of, 320; visits to prisons, 19, 98, 258, 323, 328; writings of, 19, 22, 98, 212, 243, 258, 311, 320–22, 325, 328, 335, 435

Howard Association, 349

Howe, Robert, 310

Hubbard, James, 447

Huddy, Joshua, 157, 291

Hudson River, 168–69, 333

Hudson v. McMillian, 452

Hugo, Victor, 74, 241, 336

human beings: as "born free," 427; criminals as, 244; discrimination against, 111, 443; as "equal in dignity and rights," 427; natural rights of, 261; "sanguinary abolitions of," 542; as "social creatures," 327. *See also* people

human dignity, 450; violation of, 451. *See also* dignity; Eighth Amendment

human nature, 17, 42, 70, 158, 175, 246, 345; "cool examiner of," 265; "dark impulses of," 446; "depravity of," 330; "frailties of," 262; "indignity to," 373; "infirmity of," 208; "ornament to," 448; "rights of," 309; "worst side of," 371; writings on, 32, 278

human rights, 15, 21, 29, 388, 427–28, 449–51, 453; abuses, 454; universality of, 443; violation of, 428. *See also* Universal Declaration of Human Rights

human trafficking, 200. *See also* slave trade

humanity, 67–68, 70, 76, 149, 157–58, 174, 181, 208, 211, 223, 226, 236–37, 254, 262, 268–69, 286, 321, 324, 336, 345, 362, 382, 434, 437; advocate for, 141; "[a]ll the punishments should be inflicted with," 330; "blessings of," 360; cause of, 43, 120, 235–36, 290, 336, 347, 385; Cesare Beccaria's "appeal to," 168; "claims of," 157; "claim on," 330; "defender of," 36; displayed by Cesare Beccaria, 4, 249; "enlightened friends of," 332; of "English nation," 222; "feelings of," 238, 250, 287, 323; "friends of," 271, 336; as "indebted to" George Keith Taylor, 329; "interest of," 259; "less shocking to," 152; "love of," 402; "names dear to," 264; "notions of," 291; "of juries," 419; "of Prosecutors, of Witnesses, of Juries, and of Judges," 221; "of the age," 341; "of the law," 281; "of the penitentiary system of punishment," 329; penal code as "scandal to," 262; principles of, 200, 330, 332; rights of, 118, 140, 172, 401; "sacred laws of," 57; "Side of," 167; "spirit of," 361; and "spirit of the law," 174; toward prisoners, 158; "voice of," 323; "want of," 342; writers "respected for their," 164. *See also* natural law; natural rights

Humanity and Humanitarianism, 349

Hume, David, 31–33, 41, 46–47, 59, 146; autobiography of, 144; and Benjamin Franklin, 144; influence of, 4, 156; as pupil of Francis Hutcheson, 41; writings of, 144–45, 243

humiliation of offenders. *See* corporal punishments

Humphrey, Hubert, 422

Humphreys, David, 101, 106, 257

Hungary, 137, 322, 365; governor of, 336

Hunt, Lynn, 29–30

Hunter, Adam, 94

Hunter, James, 94

Hunter, William, 110

Huntington, Samuel, 155

Hutcheson, Francis, 39, 46, 74, 431, 433; on "bad effect" of "horrid spectacles of torture," 42; on death penalty, 41–42, 48; influence on Beccaria, 22, 41; as "obscure Philosopher," 41; on "perpetual slavery," 42

Hutchinson, Thomas, 274–75, 295

Hyde Park, 55, 83

Hyde Park Corner, 84

Hyneman, Charles, 4

idleness, 10, 183, 216, 282, 318

idolatry, 180, 302

Ignatius of Loyola, 248

ignominy, 162, 394. *See also* infamy

Il Caffé, 30, 33–35, 79, 303, 355, 466

Il Pastor Fido, 177

Il Principe, 36

Il Vero Dispotismo, 79

Iliad, The, 30

Illinois, 391–92; abolition efforts in, 381; as part of Northwest Territory, 380; Supreme Court, 399

Illuminismo, 126. *See also* Enlightenment; Italian Enlightenment

Imbonati, Carlo, 71

Imbonati, Giuseppe Maria, 31–32

immersion in water, 96. *See also* ducking

immigration: to America, 8, 201, 277, 313, 358–59, 363, 410; Dutch, 295; German, 359; Irish, 359; Italian, 32, 119, 196; Quaker, 293

immunities, 213, 300

impalement, 64

Impartial Collection of the Great Affairs of State, An, 394

impeachment, 214, 226, 248

impiety, 61, 64; laws against, 251

Imposter Detected, The, 245

imprisonment, 97, 129, 181, 183, 283, 295, 301, 317, 345, 404, 407, 418, 420, 441; "a device of modern times," 371; as corporal punishment substitute, 371, 407; as death penalty substitute, 5, 10, 39, 190, 315, 378; for debt, 36, 160, 232–33, 239, 268, 401–4; discretionary

terms of, 225; for dueling, 397; non–publicized, 293; perpetual, 49, 62, 83, 96, 379; as punishment, 129, 232, 328, 385, 394, 402, 426; solitary, 10, 318; temporary, 225, 276; term of, 348. *See also* life imprisonment; prison(s)

Imprisonment for Debt Considered, 402

In re Kemmler, 452

inalienable rights, 21, 348. *See also* unalienable rights

incarceration, 5, 39, 99, 128, 133, 347, 371, 402; mass, 449. *See also* imprisonment; life imprisonment; prison(s)

income inequality, 8

indentured servants, 57, 161, 373. *See also* involuntary servitude

independence. *See* Declaration of Independence; Revolutionary War

Independence Day, 344

Independence Hall, 7, 16. *See also* State House

Independent Chronicle, 269

Index Librorum Prohibitorum, 176

Index of Forbidden Books, 35, 63

India, 367

Indiana: abolition efforts in, 381; constitution, 374; militia, 230; as part of Northwest Territory, 380; Territory, 381

Indiana Law Journal, 61, 422

Indians. *See* Native Americans

indictments. *See* grand juries

individual rights. *See specific rights*

ineffective assistance of counsel. *See* counsel, defense; Sixth Amendment

inequality, 8, 51, 59, 289, 439. *See also* minorities; women

"infamous" crimes/punishments, 133, 300, 310, 334, 393–95, 426

infamy, 18, 67, 123, 162–63, 183, 293; concept of, 393–95; different kinds of, 394; as "mark" of "public disapprobation," 393; protection against, 437–38; public, 293; as punishment, 45, 393, 438; "purgation of," 44; as "stain," 45 infanticide: as capital crime, 274

Ingenhousz, Jan, 118

Ingersoll, Jared, 435

Ingraham, Edward D., 94

inhumanity: "appearance of," 154; of "brutal soldiers," 203; of capital punishment, 104, 250; "impressions of," 260; of imprisonment for debt, 402; "instinct to," 107; "of laws which punish with death," 221

injustice, 51, 54, 120, 132, 136, 166, 192, 401; of capital punishment, 104, 107, 126–27, 208, 299, 361; of extraditions, 401; of "laws" demanding "blood for the slightest offences," 361; of "old system of punishment," 331; of slavery, 308. See also miscarriage(s) of justice

inmates. See death row inmates; prison(s)

Inner Light, doctrine of, 294

Inner Temple, 92, 149, 316, 368

Innes, Harry, 261

innocence: of accused, 167; and "beyond a reasonable doubt" standard, 45; protection of, 45, 401; "protestations of," 154; "Punishment of," 218; and torture, 44, 361, 366, 372, 553; versus guilt, 59, 61–62, 336, 392; and wrongful convictions, 346, 403, 428

Inns of Court, 184, 271, 413. See also Gray's Inn; Lincoln's Inn; Inner Temple; Middle Temple

Inquiry into the Effects of Public Punishments upon Criminals and upon Society, An, 266, 433

Inquiry into the Influence of Physical Causes upon the Moral Faculty, An, 216

Inquiry into the Legality of Capital Punishments, 91

Inquiry into the Original of Our Ideas of Beauty and Virtue, 41

Inquiry into the Rights of the British Colonies, 560

Inquiry upon Public Punishments, 265

Inquisition(s), 21, 27, 35, 47, 63, 199, 223; "horrors of," 12; tyranny of, 366. See also Roman Inquisition; Scottish Inquisition; Venetian Inquisition

inquisitorial system, 200, 366

insane: bar on executing, 375, 450

insanity, 424

insolvency, 282. See also bankruptcy; debtors

Institutes of the Lawes of England, 188

Instruction of Her Imperial Majesty Catherine the Second for the Commission Charged with Preparing a Project of a New Code of Laws, 3

Instructions to the Freeholders of Albemarle County in Their Delegates in Convention, 197

intellectually disabled: bar on executing, 375, 450

International Covenant on Civil and Political Rights, 427

international law, 445; and capital punishment, 104; and torture, 364, 389; and universal rights, 427; use by founders, 387. See also "Law of Nations"; treaties

interrogations. See confessions; self-incrimination

Intolerable Acts, 20, 174, 250

Introduction to Natural Philosophy, 448

Introduction to the Principles of Morals and Legislation, 99

Introductory Views of the Rationale of Evidence, 99

Investigator, The, 325

involuntary servitude, 21, 307, 380

Iran: executions in, 450

Ireland, 12, 77, 79, 88, 128, 324; and Code Duello, 55; duels in, 55; emigrants from, 359; monarch of, 288; republicanism in, 67, 77

irons, use of, 159, 184, 258, 365, 377–78

Isenberg, Nancy, 205

Israel: king of, 445

Israel, Jonathan, 61

Italian: architectural influences, 312–13; artistic influences, 314–15, 444, 453; books, 79, 105, 119, 124, 176–77;

booksellers, 176–77; and Declaration of Independence, 196; as "fine Language," 118; history, 30, 178–79; immigrants, 32, 113, 195–98, 230–31, 267, 448; language, 71, 176, 179, 182–83, 201, 337, 357; law, 60; literature, 30, 71, 177, 279; monk, 63; opera, 119; opera house, 177; poet(s), 73, 106, 119, 176, 201; prison(s), 328; scientists/botanists, xi, 12–13, 17, 116, 119, 127, 171, 200, 216, 244, 270, 373; society, 51, 119; states, 4, 13, 27, 49, 443; study/use of, 91, 95, 105, 107–8, 113, 116, 124, 144, 153, 160, 176–79, 201, 337, 435, 502; republics, 178–79. *See also specific city-states/republics*

Italian-English Dictionary, 107

Italian Enlightenment, xi, xiv, 17, 30–31, 35, 108, 114, 119–20, 303, 355, 357, 368–69, 407, 443. *See also specific individuals*

Italian Journey, 133

Italian Riviera, 113

Italy, 29–30, 58–60, 69, 100–1, 105, 113–15, 118, 134, 136, 161, 194, 196–98, 253, 257, 261, 287, 307, 326, 329, 356, 365, 423, 435, 443, 453; "antient republican spirit" of, 80; aristocratic families in, 73; books from, 176–77; books on, 105, 137, 139, 178, 356–57; coffeehouses in, 31, 60; confessions/torture in, 200; corporal punishments in, 96; death penalty abolished in, 26, 449; duels in, 55; "in the foreground in efforts to instruct in the philosophy of penal legislation and penal science," 329; and Jeremy Bentham, 413; Jesuits in, 248; Montesquieu in, 220; *On Crimes and Punishments* in, 31, 64, 243, 270, 392; penal reformers in, 329; persecution in, 160; prior to unification, 18, 28; system of proofs in, 365, 367; ties to France and Great Britain, 29, 34; torture in, 200; travel in, 13, 78, 93, 95, 108, 113–16, 118, 220, 252–53, 258,

279, 443; wars of, 12. *See also* Italian Enlightenment; Tuscan(y)

Izard, Ralph, 118, 252–53

Jackson, Andrew, 333, 341–42, 360–61, 383, 417

Jackson, Clare, 47

Jackson, Richard, 211

Jackson, Robert, 382, 409

Jackson-Retondo, Eliane, 312

Jacobins, 179

jail(s). *See* prison(s); Walnut Street Jail

Jamaica, 267, 376; slave laws of, 87, 376

James I (King), 40–41, 81, 362

James II (King), 146, 276, 371

James River, 314, 446

Janson, Charles William, 380

Japan: abolition efforts in, 367

Jardine, David, 223

Jay, John, 8, 11, 102, 110, 130, 169, 296, 303–4, 332; and affiliation with Columbia College, 239; bust of, 314; as Chief Justice of the U.S. Supreme Court, 167–68; on death penalty, 241; and *Federalist Papers*, 387; and penal reform, 167–68, 239–40; and Peter van Schaack, 148; and William Blackstone's *Commentaries*, 223

Jay, Sarah, 167–68

Jay, William, 167

Jay Treaty, 334

Jebb, John, 194–95, 354, 507

Jefferson, John Garland, 186

Jefferson, Martha, 11, 100, 105

Jefferson, Thomas, 16, 19, 62, 107–8, 115, 136, 185, 247, 261, 266, 311, 342, 400; and Aaron Burr, 202, 204; and Adam Smith, 551; and Adamantios Koraes, 186, 505; on affair of the diamond necklace, 199; and American Academy of Arts and Sciences, 130; as *American Museum* subscriber, 244; and André Morellet, 27, 103–4, 187; and Angelica Schuyler Church, 220; and Antonio Canova, 313; and Antonio Capellano, 313; on apostasy, 283; on "arbitrary" power, 299; on arson, 283; on "art of avoiding pain," 46; on "barbarous ancestors," 447; on benefit of clergy, 400; and Benjamin Banneker, 307–10; and Benjamin Latrobe, 312; and Benjamin Rush, 5, 387–88, 468, 507; and Bill for Establishing Religious Freedom, 364, 387; and Bill for Proportioning Crimes and Punishments, 3, 6, 183–84, 187–91, 206–7, 226, 283, 373, 398, 426; and Bill for the More General Diffusion of Knowledge, 357; on Bill of Rights, 213; on bills of attainder, 381; book recommendations of, 185, 448, 551; and books "for the use of Congress," 205; on burglary, 283; on burying alive, 283; bust of, 314; and "Carlo" Bellini, 108, 448; and Cesare Beccaria, xi, 3–4, 6, 14, 19, 46, 57, 70, 125, 138, 146, 159, 182–83, 185–87, 195, 341, 372, 384, 387, 392, 395, 426, 448, 455, 551; and Christianity, 5; on "civilized society," 447; and *Coke on Littleton*, 188; and Committee of Revisors, 3, 190, 193, 195, 270, 372; on common law, 408; commonplace book of, xiv, 6, 57, 146, 182–84, 186, 391–92, 431; on corporal punishments, 282–83; on counterfeiting, 283; on "cruel and sanguinary laws," 187; on "cruel and unprovoked war," 254; on cruelty, 370; and David Hume, 46; death of, 412; on death penalty, 3, 7, 9, 156, 187–88, 195, 241, 282–83, 333; and Declaration of Independence, 6–7, 15, 22, 42, 46, 70, 308, 311, 332, 431, 433, 452, 455; and Declaration of the Causes and Necessity of Taking up Arms, 118; on despots, 445–46; as diplomat, 100, 106; as distrustful of federal courts, 408; and draft Virginia constitution, 188, 391; on "dreams of the future," 428; on duels, 283; and Edmund Pendleton, 253–54; on education, 112; and Edward Livingston, 142, 334,

336–38, 340, 540; in England, 19, 101; on equality, 112; and Ethan Allen, 159; and foreign languages, 105, 107, 120, 146; on forfeiture of land/goods, 283, 398; on Fourth of July, 412; in France, xiii, 14, 100–1, 104–5, 108, 113–14, 130, 140, 177, 198–99, 206, 231; and Francesco dal Verme, 108, 114; and Francis Hutcheson, 46; and freedom of religion, 232, 364, 387; and French Revolution, 104; on future generations, 428, 446–47; on Gabriel's rebellion, 156; and George Wythe, 185–86, 189, 230–32, 369–70, 372, 413; on gibbeting, 283; and Giovanni Fabbroni, 115, 231; and Giuseppe Franzoni, 313; and Gouverneur Morris, 302; on gun laws, 183; on hard labor, 195; "Head" and "Heart" letter of, 73; on heresy, 283; on horse-stealing, 207, 283; on housebreaking, 283; on human knowledge, 445–46; on imprisonment, 190, 283; on "inherent and unalienable rights of man," 428; on interpretation of laws, 183; in Italy, xi, 108, 113–14, 443; and Jacques-Pierre Brissot de Warville, 398; and James Madison, 66, 142, 187–88, 190–91, 206–7, 209, 303, 414, 447; and James Monroe, 156; and James Wood, 325–26; and Jean Claude Molini, 177; and Jean-Jacques Burlamaqui, 46; and Jean-Louis de Lolme, 106; and John Adams, 428; and John and Lucy Paradise, 105–6, 199, 201; and John Banister, 112; and John Breckinridge, 261–62; and John Cartwright, 353; and John Hancock, 197; and John Locke, 41, 46, 186, 551; and John Quincy Adams, 257; and John Trumbull, 101, 103; and Joseph Priestley, 175, 194, 551; on judges, 446; on kidnapping, 283; on labor, 283; and Lafayette, 100, 103–4, 157; on larceny, 283; as lawyer, 182, 185, 226; on "laws and institutions," 447; on lex talionis, 188–89, 195, 372, 451; library/books of, 105, 136, 179, 185–86, 362, 436; on "light of science," 412; on loss of limbs, 283; and Louis XVI, 14; and Louisiana Purchase, 142; and Louis-Sébastien Mercier, 257; and Luigi Castiglioni, 14, 105; and Machiavelli, 179; on maiming/disfiguring, 283; on manslaughter, 283; and Maria Cosway, 72–73, 101, 105; and Marquis de Condorcet, 307; and Mathew Carey, 88; and Miguel de Lardizábal, 437; as Minister to France, 104, 108, 140, 157, 198, 341; and Montaigne, 107; and Montesquieu, 41, 182, 186, 220, 448; and Monticello, 11, 107–8, 130, 156, 177, 192, 196, 296, 326, 338, 446–47; on murder, 283; nailery of, 11, 192, 446; and Nathaniel Chipman, 259, 551; on "nature's law," 428; and *Notes on the State of Virginia*, 32, 187, 261; and Paola Andreani, 200–1; on pardons, 188; pardons/clemency decisions of, 183, 188, 284–85, 400; and penal reform, xi, 3, 6, 9, 190–91, 193, 232, 372, 507; and penitentiaries/prisons, 10, 313; and Peyton Randolph, 169–70; in Philadelphia, 309; and Philip Freneau, 170–71; and Philip Mazzei, 107–8, 114, 119, 177, 195–98, 407–8; on pillory, 283; plantation of, 14; on polygamy, 283; as President, 11, 19, 182, 284, 307, 334, 379, 382, 400; on prevention of crime, 183; on prisons/penitentiaries, 326, 341; on "progress of the human mind," 447; and proportionality, 182, 187–90, 373; and "public labor," 190; on rape, 189, 283; and "reason," 193; and religious freedom/tolerance, 251, 364, 387; on "republican government," 398; on retaliation, 159; and Reuben Perry, 447; and Richard Taliaferro, 230; on right to bear arms, 391–92; on "rights of man," 412; on robbery, 283; and Robert R. Livingston, 338; and Roger Weightman, 412; and Rousseau, 59; and St. George Tucker, 261, 385; on sale of unwholesome food/drink, 282; and Samuel Kercheval, 447; and Samuel Romilly, 220; on "sanguinary" punishments, 73; on science, 445–46; as Secretary of State, 170, 307; on self-government, 412; on slave trade, 382; as slaveowner, 11, 22, 308, 446–47; and slavery, 187–88, 261, 440; on sodomy, 283; on solitary confinement, 190; on smuggling, 108; on speedy punishments, 426, 428; on stripes, 283; on study of law, 186; study/use of Italian, 105, 108, 146, 177, 182–83, 201; on studying in Europe, 112; on suicide, 283, 398; on "sword of the law," 128; and Taliaferro family, 231; and Thomas Eddy, 168–69; and Thomas Hobbes, 46; and Thomas McKean, 189; and Thomas Paine, 382; and Thomas Pinckney, 303; on torture, 46–47, 390; on treason, 187–88, 283; as treaty commissioner, 14; trunk of, 446; on "unalienable" rights, 428; and University of Virginia, 387; as Vice President, 447; views on pardons, 400; on Virginia penal reform, 190; and Voltaire, 182; on "wars & persecutions," 46; on whipping, 11; and William Blackstone, 46, 138, 185; and William Carmichael, 437; and William Duane, 503; and William Eden, 185; and William Munford, 445–48; and William Rawle, 142; and William Roscoe, 191; and William Short, 114–15, 198, 220, 302, 313, 341; and William Thornton, 314; on witchcraft, 283; on written vs. unwritten laws, 408

Jeffreys, George, 19, 146, 273, 299, 407

Jenings, Edmund, 63, 249

Jenkins, Cato, 389

Jensen, Merrill, 85–87

Jersey Chronicle, The, 170

Jesuit(s), 12, 73, 248, 273; and Cesare Beccaria, 28, 30; torture/execution of, 222

Jesus, 194, 251; Cesare Beccaria's invocation of, 33; and his apostles, 194

Jew(s): "custom" of, 164; early American, 92, 110; law of, 210

Jim Crow laws, 112

John (King), 37, 445

John the Sanguinary, 289

Johnson, Herbert, 169

Johnson, Joseph, 279

Johnson, Richard M., 264

Johnson, Samuel, 60, 77–78, 201, 433

Johnson, William, 417

Johnstone, George, 98

Joint Select Committee on Freedman, 428

Jones, John Paul, 141

Jones, William, 251

Jones, William (Sir), 220

Joseph II (Emperor), 28–29, 62, 66, 74, 126, 133, 228

Journals of the Continental Congress, xv

Joyce, John, 415

Judah, Naphtali, 92

Judd, Sylvester, 241

judge(s): colonial, 295; as check on power, 363; and constitutional interpretation, 14, 452; and "dangerous power" of, 208; and death sentences, 311; discretion of, 55–56, 275, 407–9; garb of, 174; as guardians of rights, 237–38; independence of, 262; as "mere machine," 400; role of, 54, 409–10, 452; and "spirit of revenge," 288; as "umpires," 409; "weak and corrupt," 38; wearing wigs, 174. *See also* federal judges

judicial activism, 409

judicial discretion, 55–56, 275, 407–9

judicial independence, 240, 334, 363, 408–9, 427

judicial outlawry, 85, 213–14

judicial review, use of, 409; as check on legislative/majoritarian power, 363, 409

judicial selection, 407, 409

judicial torture, 29, 46–47, 62, 124, 361, 366; in France, 361; as "gruesome," 365; in Spain, 361; as "uncertain means to discover the truth," 365; as "vestige of barbarity," 47. *See also* torture

judiciary. *See* federal judges; judge(s); *specific courts*

Judiciary Act of 1789, 417, 425

Judiciary Act of 1801, 284

Juliani, Richard, 113, 315

Julie, or the New Héloïse, 29

Junius, 175

juries, 246; as check on power, 300; and "dangerous power" of, 208; death–qualified, 293–94; and death sentences, 311; discretion of, 451; "fallibility of," 208; "humanity of," 419; impartial, 295, 426; "lenity of," 419; and reluctance/refusal to convict, 191, 205, 236, 262, 315; as "security and protection," 374; selection of, 293–94, 315; and "spirit of revenge," 288; and unanimity requirement, 45; and victim impact evidence, 15, 437

jurisdiction: federal, 417–18. *See also* common law

jurisprudence, 245; American, 342, 414; censorial, 4, 19, 99; criminal, 238, 240, 259, 264, 268, 322–23, 339–41, 388, 540; and "establishment of truth and justice," 174; Gallic, 307; general, 447; "improvement in," 342; "in a state of great imperfection," 388; lecture on, 203; "of the mother country," 167; penal, 328; as "philosophical science," 448; principles of, 447; Roman, 334; science of, 441. *See also* law; American law; English law

jury trial, right to, 18, 26, 106, 214, 282, 300–1, 334, 406, 453; common-law exceptions to, 381; in England, 221, 316; as "fundamental" protection, 377; as "one of the greatest securities of the lives, liberties and estates of the people," 247; as "very useful one," 51

"just deserts," 139. *See also* retribution

justice, 16, 211, 223, 234, 256, 260, 286, 323, 330, 332, 445; administration/conceptions of, 51, 54, 102, 107, 149, 157, 219–20, 222, 233, 336, 377, 403, 423, 426; "[a]ll the punishments should be inflicted with," 330; as "basis of civil policy and jurisprudence," 174; "divine," 337; as due to citizens, 441; "equally to all its citizens," 329; "establish," 213; "in proportioning punishments," 374–75; "of the penitentiary system of punishment," 329; and liberty, 67; "principles of," 332; reference in U.S. Constitution, 422; "tempered with mercy," 419; "universal," 441

Justices. *See specific Justices*

justices of the peace, 148, 248, 269

Justinian (Emperor), 25, 178, 264, 333, 445

Justinian Code, 25–26, 264, 333, 410, 445

Justinian Society, The, 453

juveniles: bar on executing, 375, 450

K. A. Society of Hippocrates, 344

Kaine, Tim, 443

Kansas: penitentiary in, 347; territorial governor, 371

Kant, Immanuel, 64, 139

Kaunitz-Rietberg, Wenzel Anton, 29, 34, 62–63

Kennett, Basil, 356

Kent, James, 223, 333, 340, 384

Kentucky, 186, 208, 309, 419; admission to Union, 345; anti-death penalty efforts in, 240, 262; attorney general, 261; Court of Appeals, 368; governor, 344; and law forbidding citation of English cases, 424; legislature, 261–62, 344, 346, 434; lethal injection protocol, 452; penal reform in, 240, 261–62, 344–45, 384, 505; penitentiary in, 325, 344–45, 385

Kercheval, Samuel, 447

Keteltas, William, 403

Key, Francis Scott, 341–42

kidnapping, 283

killer(s). *See* murderer(s)

killing. *See* execution(s); homicide(s); murder(s)

killing animal, as capital crime, 20, 280

Kilty, William, 284–85

Kimbrough, Elijah, 121–22

King, Rufus, 102

King George's War, 44

King of Lanka, 367

Kingdom of Naples, 134, 369. *See also* Naples

King's Arms Tavern, 84

King's Bench, Court of, 75, 84–86, 146, 273, 276

King's Bench Prison, 85

King's College, 239, 332. *See also* Columbia College/University

kings: "arbitrary," 300; "cruel," 219; and death penalty, 367; "divine right" of, 301; depicted in U.S. Supreme Court chamber, 445; European, 282; on execution of, 161; laws of, 282; power of, 103, 193, 363; Roman, 222; royal prerogative of, 282; "sanguinary" behavior of, 290, 316; "tyrannical" acts of, 316; versus "power of the people," 301, 422; versus "public happiness," 232. *See also* monarchs; *specific kings*

Kingston, Jamaica, 267

Knapp, John "Francis," 281

Knapp, Jr., Joseph J., 281

Knapp, Samuel, 324

Knight, Joseph, 88

Knox, Henry, 13, 156–57, 201, 291–93

knut, 305, 545

Koehn, Nancy, 31

Konig, David Thomas, 183

Koraes, Adamantios, 186, 505

Kossuth, Louis, 336

La Bruyére, Jean de, 243

La Nouvelle Héloïse, 33

La Scienza della legislazione, xi, 132–36, 178

La Storia di Tom Jones, 177

labor: to "beget a habit of honest industry," 318; "constant," 318; crimes punishable by, 283; to deter others, 44; "for the public," 147, 276; inmate, 327; perpetual, 323, 378; prison, 39, 331, 380; "profitable," 10; public, 137, 155, 190, 193, 195, 215; punishment of, 14, 51, 190, 193, 207, 283, 297; to "repair" injury, 44, 276; as reparation for injury, 218, 246; "severe," 443; "solitary," 215; "strenuous and continuous," 131; as substitute for corporal punishments, 321; as substitute for death sentences, 96, 163, 216, 314, 321, 379; "well-regulated," 318. *See also* hard labor; forced labor; involuntary servitude; slave labor

Lackey v. Texas, 429

Lackington, Allen & Co., 119

Lacretelle, Pierre-Louis, 218

Lafayette, Marquis de, 12, 100–104, 302, 333, 441; anti-death penalty views of, 103, 157, 264, 266, 299; and Cesare Beccaria, 104, 157; and French Declaration of the Rights of Man and of the Citizen, 104; and George Washington, 104–5; and law/penal reform, 195; and Thomas Jefferson, 100, 104, 157; and trip to America, 266

Lagrave, Jean Paul de, 104

Lambertenghi, Luigi, 31

Lancaster, Pennsylvania, 90, 123, 371

Landing of the Pilgrims, 313

Langbein, John, 365–66

Lansing, John, 264, 333

larceny: flogging for, 329; grand, 295, 325; petit, 325, 329; petty, 276, 283; imprisonment for, 325

Lardizábal, Miguel de, 437

Lardizábal y Uribe, Manuel de, 436–37

Larkin, Ebenezer, 102

Larousse, 33

lashes, 112, 131, 151, 298, 372, 376, 407, 442–43, 446–47; fifteen, 102; for desertion, 156; ninety-nine, 163; one hundred, 151, 155–56; one thousand, 151; thirty-nine, 151, 446; thirty-three, 163. *See also* whipping

Last Day of a Condemned Man, The, 74

Last Supper, The, 74

Last Words, 103

Lates, David Francesco, 357

Latin, 79, 453; authors, 93; and Magna Carta, 37; study of, 105, 160, 265, 337, 355–57; translation of *felo de se*, 43

Latrobe, Benjamin, 184, 311–14, 326, 444

Laurens, Henry, 108–9, 125

Laurens, John, 153–54

Lausanne, Switzerland, 27, 59

Law Academy of Philadelphia, 298, 404, 412–13, 435, 441, 447

Law French, 406

Law Miscellanies, 209–10

"Law of Nations," 138, 152–53, 387, 413, 417

Law of Nations, The, 448

law schools, 404, 413. *See also specific schools*

Lawes, Lewis E., 383

Lawrence, David, 310

Lawrence v. Texas, 410

law(s): as "arbitrary," 57, 80, 152, 336; as "barbaric," 152; as clear, 55, 57, 133, 165, 183, 282, 354, 374, 424, 453, 455; as "cruel" where "charity is wanting," 146; on equality of, 235; as imperfect, 440; interpretation of, 206; letter of, 206, 208; as "a living thing," 348; of nature, 67, 70, 138, 149, 152, 299, 312, 384, 413; "of necessity," 408; "of the land," 282, 300, 390, 403; as precise, 19, 54–55, 133, 339, 452, 455; "principles of," 69; and reason, 209; as "repressive," 152; "rules and usages" of, 340; as "science," 441; of "self-preservation," 408; as simple, 57, 165, 183, 282; "spirit" of, 206, 208; study of, 113, 129, 140–41, 184–86, 189, 209, 223–26, 248, 252, 257, 264, 404, 413, 421, 437, 447–48; uncertainty of, 152, 241, 255, 408; and uniformity, 408. *See also* American law; common law;

English law; jurisprudence; natural law

Laws and Customs of England, The, 54

Laws and Customs of Scotland in Matters Criminal, 47

Laws and Jurisprudence of England and America, The, 216, 372

"Laws Divine, Moral, and Martial," 189

Laws of the United States from 1789 to 1815, The, 173, 412, 414

"Laws respecting Crimes and Punishments" (1787), 9

Laws Respecting Women, The, 123

lawyers. *See* assistance of counsel; counsel, defense; prosecutors

Lawyers' Club of Philadelphia, 453

Le Dernier Jour d'un condamné, 241

Leavenworth, Kansas, 347; penitentiary in, 330

Lectures on History and General Policy, 175, 277

Lee, Arthur, 76, 80, 319; as American diplomat, 253, 423; and duel, 396; on "Dungeons"/"Irons," 365; on prisoners of war, 365

Lee, Charles (Attorney General), 500

Lee, Charles (General), 66, 157, 160–62, 500; and Cesare Beccaria's treatise, 160–62

Lee, Charles (Mr.), 106

Lee, Henry, 154, 188, 191, 500

Lee, John, 160

Lee, Richard Henry, 76, 115, 148, 196, 396

Lee, Thomas L., 193

Leeds, England, 148

legal education, 223–26, 413. *See also* law schools; law(s)

Legal Publishing in Antebellum America, 91

legal terms, 411–12. *See also* common law; *specific terms*

Leghorn, 3, 13, 27, 31–32, 110, 116–18, 136, 252, 356; American consul at, 313. *See also* Livorno

legislation. *See specific bills/laws*

Leicester, Massachusetts, 303

Leigh, Samuel Egerton, 360

Leighton, Alexander, 273

Lemmings, David, 184

Lemprière, John, 285

L'Enfant, Pierre, 104–5

Leo V (Emperor), 25

Leopold II (Emperor), 74, 228

Leopold, Peter (Pietro) (Grand Duke), 66, 74, 115, 137, 161–62, 196–97, 346; and admiration of Cesare Beccaria's treatise, 162; edict of, 322

Lepore, Jill, 14, 233

Les Aventures de Télémaque, 30

L'Esprit des lois, 220, 243. *See also De l'esprit des lois*

lethal injection(s), 452

Letter of a Remonstrance to Sir Robert Gifford, Knight, His Majesty's Attorney General, A, 139

Letter to Bryan Edwards, Esquire, A, 290

Letter to the Inhabitants of Quebec, 5, 7–8, 66–67, 75, 147–48, 162; drafts of, 473; French translation of, 147–48, 497; German translation of, 147

Letters Concerning the English Nation, 128

Letters during the Course of a Tour Through Germany, Switzerland and Italy, 93

Letters from a Farmer in Pennsylvania, 5

Letters from a Pennsylvania Farmer, 118

Letters from Italy, 137

Letters from the Federal Farmer, 422

Letters from Washington, on the Constitution, Laws and Public Characters of the United States, 362–63

Letters on Capital Punishment, 286

Lettsom, John Coakley, 313, 318

Levellers, 25

Levi, Joseph, 308

Leviathan, 367

Levinson, Sanford, xii

Leviticus, 274

Levy, Leonard, 273, 393–94

Lewis, Charles, 231

Lewis, Nicholas, 105

Lewis, William, 413

lex talionis: as "absurd law," 372; doctrine of, 15, 97, 139, 188–89, 195, 203,

237–38, 274, 298, 333, 346, 372, 396, 404, 451, 547; "secret attachment to the fanciful," 337; versus "rational treatment of criminals as human beings," 244; "vindictive spirit" of, 337

Lexington, battle of, 78, 441

Lexington, Kentucky, 261–62, 322

Lexington, Massachusetts, 7, 292, 360, 441

Lexington Democratic Society, 262

Lexington Medical Society, 344

Leyden Gazette, 98

libel, 55, 82, 397; as capital crime, 26; as cause of duels, 55, 292

liberty, 7, 11, 16, 68, 84–85, 87, 106, 119, 128, 138, 152, 170, 211, 235, 253, 273, 277, 281, 356, 358–59, 368, 377, 407, 422, 424, 432, 441, 453; "absolute power over," 43; advocate for, 141; American, 142, 249, 369, 409–10; "Annual Parliaments and," 76; Benjamin Banneker on, 307; and Bill of Rights, 15–16; "Blessings of," 213, 342, 360, 422; of British subjects, 161; champions of, 359; "Civil and Religious," 87; and Constitution, 15–16; "danger to," 390; "dangerous to," 391; "defence of," 152; "depository of," 133; deprivation of, 49, 258, 390; dream of, 195; as "end of the social compact," 353; enjoyment of, 245; "equal," 53; and essential for happiness, 195; "every friend of," 68; "extreme," 145; "extreme political," 165; foundation of, 46; "genius of," 299; "happy," 117; "highest possible degree of," 176; "human," 58; and "human Happiness," 300; "and Laws," 235; loss of, 44, 162, 196, 225; love/lovers of, 75, 83, 145, 324, 359, 432, 442; of man, 195, 437; "nation jealous of its," 172; as natural right, 40, 67; "not to be sported away with impunity," 83; "of the citizens," 167; "of the People," 264, 300–1, 333; "of the Press," 145; "personal," 39, 52, 392, 402, 423; "pillars of," 138; "political and civil," 194; as "popular watchword," 228; preser-vation/security of, 40, 278, 300–1, 392–93; "principles of," 152, 440; "public," 84; "rational," 101; "received from our ancestors," 67; as "reciprocal" with equality, 369; and representative bodies, 8; right to, 16, 67, 69–70, 143, 282, 300, 308, 354–55, 409, 427, 438; "sacred principles of," 196; slaves quest for, 334; "spirit of," 288, 359; "to transmit to our posterity," 67; universal, 200; versus despotism, 133, 145; "of Whigs and Englishmen," 81; "zealous friend to," 319. *See also* Declaration of Independence; Universal Declaration of Human Rights

Liberty, 173

Liberty Bell, 7

libraries. *See specific libraries*

Library Company of Philadelphia, 125, 137, 220, 315

Library of Congress, 105, 186; librarian of, 362

licentiousness, 145, 280, 354

Lieber, Francis, 244, 348–49, 383, 542

Liebman, James, 439

life: deprivation/taking of, 7, 40, 183, 223, 263, 282; enjoyment of, 245; "forfeiture of," 354; as natural/unalienable right, 236; "no right to dispose of," 43; "offenses against," 419; as "poor, nasty, brutish, and short," 367; protection of, 149; right to, 16, 40, 42, 69–70, 143, 236, 308, 354–55, 409, 424, 427, 438, 450; security of, 423; value of, 437. *See also* Declaration of Independence; Due Process Clause(s); Universal Declaration of Human Rights

life imprisonment, 10, 21, 48, 146, 199, 210; commutation to, 199, 210; as "perpetual"/"permanent" servitude, 47–49, 96; as substitute for death penalty, 20, 47, 49, 167, 181, 210, 246, 281, 337, 341, 379, 524, 540; without parole, 439

Life of David Hume, Esq.; The Philosopher and Historian, Written by Himself, The, 144–45

Life of Joseph Balsamo, Commonly Called Count Cagliostro, The, 199

Life of Mr. Richard Savage, The, 80

Life of Nathanael Greene, The, 159

Life of the Late John Howard, The, 258

Life of Thomas Eddy, The, 324

"life or limb," 41, 55, 149, 183; crimes punishable by, 283; unalienable right to, 41

Lilburne, John, 394–95

Lilly, Gabriel, 11

limb(s): loss/deprivation of, 112, 183, 211, 258, 301, 443; "offenses against," 419; protection of, 149. *See also* ear cropping; "life or limb"

Lincoln, Abraham, 11, 262, 313, 349, 351, 408, 438; assassination of, 330; and Cesare Beccaria, 16; and Civil War executions, 224; on Declaration of Independence, 16; and William Blackstone's *Commentaries,* 16, 223–24

Lincoln, Benjamin, 13, 158

Lincoln Memorial, 16

Lincoln's Inn, 96, 249

Lindsey, Theophilus, 277

Linebaugh, Peter, 278

Linn, William, 138

Linnaeus, 114, 129

Linonian Society, 234

Litchfield, Connecticut, 413

Litchfield Law School, 413

Literary Fly, The, 368

Litta, Amelia, 115

Littleton, Thomas, 185, 553

Livermore, Arthur, 420

Livermore, Samuel, 224, 386–87, 420

Liverpool, England, 75

living constitutionalism, 15, 22, 451

Livingston, Brockholst, 237, 303

Livingston, Edward, 103, 241, 244, 296; and Aaron Burr, 333; and Alexander Hamilton, 333; on Alien and Sedition Acts, 333; background of, 140, 263–64, 332–35, 417; as "benevolent and powerful legislator," 140; on Benjamin Franklin, 265–66; and Cesare Beccaria's influence, 264, 339, 389, 418; on death penalty, 140, 241, 265, 333–34, 336, 383, 417, 420; draft code of, 140, 241, 264, 335–36, 338–39, 384, 411; honorary degrees awarded to, 336; influences on, 333, 335, 347; and James Kent, 333, 340; and James Madison, 142, 264, 337–40; and Jeremy Bentham, 336; on life imprisonment, 337; in Louisiana, 140, 241, 264, 345, 417; as Minister to France, 140, 334, 417; in New York, 140, 417; as penal reformer, 263–64, 333–35, 337–38, 371, 383, 401, 411, 417, 420–21; and Peter Du Ponceau, 335, 337; at Princeton, 333; on proportionality, 264; report/drafting of, 264, 345, 384; on solitary confinement, 337; and study of civil law, 333; and Thomas Jefferson, 142, 334, 337–38, 340, 540; on Thomas Nash, 333–34; on torture, 389; on "tyrants," 333; on vengeance, 264

Livingston, Joanna, 401

Livingston, Peter R., 401

Livingston, Robert J., 401

Livingston, Robert R., 8, 239, 296, 333–34, 337, 401; and Benjamin Franklin, 109, 178; in Continental Congress, 264, 332, 434; and James Madison, 338; and John Jay, 169, 332; as New York's chancellor, 290, 333; and Thomas Jefferson, 338

Livingston, Sarah, 296

Livingston, William, 158, 296, 303, 332

Livius, Titus, 436

Livorno, 3, 27, 31, 58, 118, 326. *See also* Leghorn

Livy, Titus, 93, 356, 431, 503

Locke, John, 30, 39, 47, 54, 148, 195, 247; background of, 39–40; on changing nature of law, 402; "great eminence" of, 259–60; influence of, 4, 15–16,

40–42, 63, 67, 70, 75, 216, 259, 368, 397, 431, 433; on pain/pleasure, 46; on people as origin of power, 354; on "pursuit of true and solid happiness," 46; and Thomas Jefferson, 186, 448, 551; writings of, 77, 79, 87, 159, 243

Lofft, Capel, 353

Logan, Mr., 129

Lois penales dan leur ordre naturel, 212

Lomas, John, 140

Lombard(y), xi, 28, 30, 33–35, 41, 51, 62, 73, 118, 126–27, 284, 466, 471; authorities, 79; capital, 114; law, xi; torture abolished in, 389

London, England, 4–5, 8, 15, 18–19, 32, 34, 40, 52, 65, 81, 84, 87, 92–93, 95, 99, 108–9, 112, 116, 118–19, 122–24, 128, 130, 137, 142, 145, 148, 153, 184, 200–1, 223, 234, 247, 253, 261, 279, 287–89, 294, 299, 303, 306, 314, 316, 319, 353, 361, 371, 376, 393, 396, 407, 423, 441, 503; Aaron Burr in, 204; Alessandro Verri in, 61; and "American circle," 197; Benjamin Franklin in, 144; books/booksellers in, 11, 75–78, 80, 87, 292, 368; and Bridewell Palace, 294; and Cesare Beccaria's treatise, 5, 36, 44, 75–81, 87, 94, 125–26, 138, 149, 182, 368, 395; Christopher Gore in, 102; and Club of Honest Whigs, 276–77; coffeehouses in, 276; executions in, 277–78; John Adams in, 179, 269; John Blair in, 196; John Paradise in, 105; John Trumbull in, 103; and Joseph Johnson, 279; Maria Cosway in, 105; Mary Wollstonecraft in, 279; mayor of, 87, 157; mob violence in, 84–85; Philip Mazzei in, 196; prisons in, 273, 278, 294, 317–18, 331, 354; sale of Italian books in, 177; severed heads exhibited in, 442; and slave trade, 382

London Bookstore, 156, 292

London Chronicle, 369

London Coffee-House, 68, 89, 113, 530

London Courant, 77

London Evening Post, 301

Long, Edward, 376

Long Island, 232

Longfellow, Henry Wadsworth, 160

Longo, Alfonso, 34, 355

Lord Auckland, 286

Lord Baltimore, 288

Lord Bute, 81–84

Lord Byron, 93

Lord Coke, 91

Lord Dunmore, 196–97

Lord Kames, 87, 247, 388

Lord Mansfield, 75, 83, 85

Lord Sandwich, 82

Lord Suffolk, 98

Lord Talbot, 55

Lord Viscount Chewton, 79

Loreto, Italy, 107

loss of citizenship rights, 394

Louis IX (King), 445

Louis XII (King), 30

Louis XV (King), 46, 95, 103

Louis XVI (King), 65, 100, 110, 119, 299; and abolition of torture, 365; execution of, 4, 62, 100, 179–80, 302–3; as "best king in Europe," 100; and Thomas Jefferson, 14

Louis-le-Grand, 250

Louisiana: acquisition of, 82; attempted penal reform in, 140, 241, 263–64, 338, 384, 417; general assembly/legislature, 264, 335–36, 339, 384, 389; penal code, 345, 383; Purchase, 142, 333–34; Territory, 204, 335

Low Dutch, 337

Lowell, John, 425

Lownes, Caleb, 192, 299; "humane heart" of, 192; and penal reform, 229, 245, 322–24; writings of, 320

"Lucius," 358

Lucretius, 178

Ludwell (Paradise), Lucy, 105–6, 201

Luttrell, Henry Lawes, 86

Lutz, Donald, 4

Luzac, Jean, 159

"Lycurgus," 358

Lyford, H. G., 350
Lynch, Thomas, 253
lynch mobs, 375
lynching(s): in America, 112, 280; in France, 107; threats of, 342
Lyon, Ann, 82–83
Lyons, France, 95; prison at, 184, 190, 326
Lyons, Reneé Critcher, 197–98
Lytle, Leslie, 293

Mably, Abbé de, 14
Macdonald, James, 59
Machiavelli, Niccolò, 36, 53, 66, 175, 178–80, 265, 503
Mackenzie, George, 47, 371
Mackintosh, James, 48
Madame Cagliostro, 199
Madame Castiglioni, 115–16
Madan, Martin, 49, 217–18
Madeira, Portugal, 173
Mademoiselle d'Olive, 199
Madison, Dolley, 312, 362
Madison, Fanny, 30
Madison, James, 19, 29–30, 62, 231, 247, 254, 261, 342, 400; on "abolition of capital punishments," 208; administration of, 267; and Alien and Sedition Acts, 411; as *American Museum* subscriber, 244; and Andrew Ellicott, 251; as Annapolis delegate, 255; on "arbitrary" acts, 299, 411; on banishment, 411; and Benjamin Rush, 5, 207, 399; and Bill for Proportioning Crimes and Punishments, 6, 190–91, 206–7; and Bill for the More General Diffusion of Knowledge, 357; and Bill of Rights, 127, 225, 273, 409; on bills of attainder, 381; book recommendations of, xv, 179, 205, 226, 356–57; on certainty of punishment, 404; and Cesare Beccaria, xi, 157, 207, 357, 455; classic works read by, 178; on codes/bloody code, 410, 414; on common law, 410–11; commonplace book of, 178; congressional message of 1816, 207; as congressman, 333, 425; and Constitution, 273, 410–11; at Constitutional Convention, 207, 444; and Constitutional Society of Virginia, 196; on corporal punishments, 282, 404; and "cruel and unusual punishments," 209; on cruelty, 370; on death penalty, 7, 208–10, 241, 282, 404; and Edmund Randolph, 158; and Edward Livingston, 142, 336–40; on education, 399; and 1800 report, 411; on ex post facto laws, 226, 381; and *Federalist Papers*, 220, 381, 387; and G. F. H. Crockett, 208, 344–47; and honorary French citizenship, 303; and Hugh Henry Brackenridge, 210; and Jean-Louis de Lolme, 106; and Jeremy Bentham, 22, 416; and John Breckinridge, 261; and John Cartwright, 353; and John Locke, 40; and John Paradise, 201; and Joseph Story, 208; as lawmaker, 226; and Lawrence Taliaferro, 231; on Louis XVI's execution, 303; and Luigi Castiglioni, 13; and Machiavelli, 178–79; and Montaigne, 220; and Montesquieu, 48, 220; on natural law, 410; noting "ample room for improvements in the criminal jurisprudence," 264; on "our old bloody code," 207; and Paolo Andreani, 119, 200–1; pardons/clemency decisions of, 400; and penal codes/reform, 190, 207–9, 326–27, 372, 410, 507; on penitentiaries/penitentiary system, 10, 207, 326–27, 340–41; and Perez Morton, 326–27; and Peter Du Ponceau, 404, 410, 441; and Philip Freneau, 170; and Philip Mazzei, 107–8, 119, 196, 198; on "popular Government," 364; as President, 173, 186, 207, 230, 340, 362, 385, 412, 416; at Princeton, 170, 202, 210, 231, 245, 264; on proportionality, 404; as "Publius," 48; on religious tolerance, 251; on rich vs. poor, 66; and Richard Rush, 173, 414–15; and Robert R. Livingston, 338; and St. George Tucker, 385; on separation of

powers, 48, 220; as slaveowner, 11, 22; on social compact, 381; on "sound legislation," 381; study of French, 120; study of Italian, 108; and Taliaferro family, 231; and Thomas Grimke, 209; and Thomas Jefferson, 66, 142, 187–88, 190–91, 206–7, 209, 303, 414, 447; on tyranny, 48; on "unusual process," 411; on unwritten law, 410; and William Blackstone's *Commentaries*, 223, 226, 404; and William Bradford, Jr., 13, 127, 158, 171, 178, 225–26, 245, 251, 387, 426; and William Livingston, 264; and William Thornton, 312

Madison, James, Sr., 29, 231

Madison Island, 346–47

Madrid, Spain, 302, 436

Maestro, Marcello, 122–24, 133–34, 142, 146, 149

magistrate(s): and "arbitrary laws," 354; chief, 205, 208, 358, 400; "civil," 174, 236, 270; English, 85, 217, 222, 378; French, 48, 218; government, 40, 227, 238, 280, 295; as "inflexible," 203; "investigating," 365; Italian, 30, 33, 73; power of, 41, 209; restrictions on, 246; Roman, 251; Swiss, 228; "the people as slaves to," 206; versus executioners, 147; "vigilance" of, 38; "wise," 43

Magna Carta, 37, 86, 394, 427, 445, 453

Magnuson, William, 401

maiming, 41, 189, 271, 283, 348. *See also specific corporal punishments*

Main, Jackson Turner, 422

Maine, 224; anti-death penalty efforts in, 381, 241–43; constitution, 263, 374; and "cruel nor unusual punishments" clause, 263; and "excessive bail" clause, 263; and "excessive fines" clause, 263; execution(s) in, 426; governor(s), 241–42; House of Representatives, 224; legislative report, 263; legislature, 224, 241–42; and penal reform, 263; and proportionality between crimes/

punishments, 263; and "Sanguinary laws" clause, 263

majoritarian power, 52; abuse of, 100, 409

Malesherbes, Guillaume-Chrétien de Lamoignon de, 58, 60

malice, 192, 231; aforethought, 224; as "disposition to inflict evil on others," 259; express, 224

Malone, Edmond, 126

Man of Forty Crowns, The, 79

Manchester, Vermont, 298

Mancini, Pasquale Stanislao, 74

Mandar, Théophile, 195

mandatory death sentences, 21, 189, 282, 425, 451; repeal/abandonment of, 21

Mandeville, Bernard, 175

Manhattan, 159

Mankato, Minnesota, 351

Mann, Bruce, 403

Mann, Horace, 13

manslaughter, 9, 231; branding for, 122, 269, 373–74, 404; as capital crime, 275, 283; convictions for, 506; forfeiture of goods for, 404; imprisonment/punishment for, 193, 283, 297, 325

"manstealing," as capital crime, 275

Mantua, Italy, 116

Manual of Political Economy, 99

Manzoni, Alessandro, 30, 71–73, 160, 279, 488

Manzoni, Pietro, 71

Marat, Jean-Paul, 289

Marble Arch, 278

Marbury v. Madison, 284, 363

Marchant, Henry, 116

Marchesi, Pompeo, 73

Marchione, Margherita, 195

"Marcus," 269

Marelli, Giuseppe, 12

Mario, Gian, 202

maritime law, 413

Mark: hung in chains, 360

Marmontel, Jean François, 33

Marquesas Islands, 346

Marraro, Howard, 119

Marriage of Figaro, The, 119

Marshall, Humphrey, 434

Marshall, James, 284–85

Marshall, John, 186, 191, 363, 445; brother-in-law of, 190; and Constitutional Society of Virginia, 196; and Edward Livingston, 336

Marshall, Polly, 191

Marshall, Thurgood, 15

M'Arthur, John, 162

martial law, 377–78

Martin, Karl Anton, 62

Martin, Luther, 382

Martin, Samuel, 55, 83

Martineau, Harriet, 139

Martschukat, Jürgen, 79

Mary I (Queen), 316

Maryland, 11, 102, 255, 306–7; anti-Catholic laws in, 250; attorney general, 382; branding in, 269; Catholics in, 248–49; Cesare Beccaria's treatise in, 249; colony of, 246, 307; Commissioner for Prisoners, 325–26; constitution, 246; courts in, 309; and "cruel and unusual pains and penalties" clause, 246; declaration of rights, xiii, 246, 248, 255; governor, 246, 248; hard labor/incarceration in, 540; prison(s)/penitentiaries in, 325; Quakers in, 306–9; as refuge, 288; and "sanguinary Laws" clause, xiii, 246, 254; slaves/slave codes in, 383, 415

Maryland Gazette, 255

Masferrer, Aniceto, 437

Masi, Tommaso, 27

masks: wearing of, 140

Mason, George: background of, 553; and Committee of Revisors, 193–94; on "cruel and unusual punishments," 246, 390; and George Washington, 151; and Philip Mazzei, 196–97; in ratification debate, 390; on torture, 369, 390; and Virginia Declaration of Rights, 151, 200, 246, 390–91; on Washington, D.C., 10

Mason, Jeremiah, 143, 234

Mason, John, 280

Mason, Mary Elizabeth, 143

mass incarceration, 449

mass shootings, 392

Massachusetts, 5, 11–12, 52, 88, 93, 101–2, 109, 136, 142, 258, 264–65, 368, 386, 414, 418–19, 431, 441; anti-death penalty efforts in, 265, 267, 547; anti-dueling law, 397; attorney general, 268, 327; bar, 284; Bay Colony, 44, 131, 252, 274–75, 294–95; benefit of clergy abolished in, 400; bill of rights, 246; Body of Liberties, 274; branding in, 269, 371, 373; colonial codes, 274–75, 315, 411; Commonwealth of, 192, 296; constitution, 19, 63, 77, 175, 178, 246, 258, 300; corporal punishments in, 371, 373; "cruel or unusual punishments" clause, 19, 178, 246; death penalty in, 269; ear cropping in, 269, 373; emancipation of slaves in, 256; "excessive bail" clause, 246; "excessive fines" clause, 246; executions in, 102–3, 121, 268, 360; Executive Council, 258; fighting in, 7; General Court, 252, 268, 274; governor(s), 78, 102, 109, 242, 268, 370–71, 373, 400, 547; grand jury charges in, 164, 167; "Laws and Liberties," 411; laws of, 411; legislative report, 265; legislature, 102–3, 131, 192, 327, 371; penal reform, 268–69; prison(s)/penitentiary in, 191, 296, 312, 325–28, 335, 371; private execution law, 49; Provincial Congress, 356; Puritans in, 411; rebellion in, 7; Society for the Abolition of Capital Punishment, 299; Superior Court of Judicature, 295; Supreme Judicial Court, 426, 525; treason cases in, 283; U.S. District Attorney for, 102; and witch trials, 303

Massachusetts Centinel, 122, 269

Massacre of St. George's Fields, 86

Massey, Lee, 185

Massie, Robert K., 3

Masur, Louis, 143, 203, 295

Mather, Moses, 374

Mathews, William, 249

Matlack, Timothy, 227

Matthews, Thomas, 385

Matthias, Peter, 415

Maxims of the Government of Venice, The, 357

May, Henry, 138

Mayflower, 411

mayhem, as capital crime, 236, 385, 404

Mazzei, Philip, 107–8, 112, 114, 118–19, 231; background/life of, 195–99, 201; and Benjamin Franklin, 118, 197; and Carlo Bellini, 448; and Cesare Beccaria, 195–96; and George Washington, 197; and George Wythe, 197; and history of the U.S., 195; and Italian artists, 313; and James Madison, 198; memoir of, 118, 195; and Paolo Andreani, 200; on pardons, 400; and Thomas Jefferson, 115, 118, 177, 195–98, 407–8; and "Tuscan" language, 177, 196

McBride, Keally, 192

McCleskey v. Kemp, 452

McCloskey, Robert, 165

McDaniel, Mary, 276

McHenry, James, 162, 309–10

McIntosh, Lachlan, 55

McKean, Thomas, 113, 189, 229, 270, 370, 434

McKechnie, William, 37

McKelvey, Blake, 89

McLennan, Rebecca, 256

McLynn, Frank, 49

McNeil Island prison/penitentiary, 331, 347

Mead, Joel, 403

Measure for Measure, 181

Mechanic's Free Press, 403

Medical Gazette, 372

Medical Inquiries and Observations upon the Diseases of the Mind, 178

Medici (Madacy), Cosimo de, 230

Medieval law(s)/practices, 27, 46, 55, 298, 335, 365

Meditations on Happiness, 31, 35

Meditations on Political Economy, 71

Meditazioni sulla Economia Politica da Beccaria, 186

Meditazioni sulla felicità, 31, 355

Medlin, Dorothy, 187

Meigs, Josiah, 88

Memoirs of the Year Two Thousand Five Hundred, 92

men: duels by, 55; and violent crime, 50

Méndez, Juan, 449

Menes (King), 445

Meranze, Michael, 240

Mercer, James, 396

Mercer, John, 553

Mercer, John Francis, 206

Mercier, Louis-Sébastien, 92–93, 257

mercy, 167, 178, 181, 205, 214, 222, 268, 294, 348, 419; absence of, 252; acts of, 310; as "character of the law-giver," 400; of husband, 275; "justice in," 377; "measure of," 96; "side of," 155, 242. *See also* clemency, executive

Meredith, William, 346, 350

Merrimack River, 43

mesmerism, 65

Mesplet, Fleury, 148

method(s) of execution, 4, 96, 360; and Eighth Amendment, 452; Roman, 26. *See also specific methods*

Mexico, 204; and penal reform, 436–37

M'Fingal, 101

Michelangelo, 453

Michigan, 186; death penalty's abolition in, 242, 266; as part of Northwest Territory, 380

Middle Ages, 39, 55, 366, 451

middle class, participation of, 8

Middle East, 450; death sentences in, 450. *See also specific countries*

Middle Temple, 63, 112–13, 142, 184, 196, 223, 249, 399

Middlesex, County of, 84, 86–87

Middleton, Henry, 7, 147

"middling class," 8

"Midnight Judges," 284

Midwest, 263. *See also specific states*

Mifflin, Thomas, xv, 137, 205, 230, 260, 267, 435; as delegate to Continental Congress, 172; and General Charles Lee, 161; as Pennsylvania governor, 170–71, 173; from Quaker family, 172

Milan, Italy, 30–31, 34–35, 63–64, 73–74, 93, 105, 108–9, 113–18, 127, 129–30, 435, 469–71, 489; Alessandro Manzoni in, 72–73; Alessandro Verri in, 128; balloon ascent in, 119, 200; as capital of Lombardy, 126; Cesare Beccaria in, xi, 3, 14, 19, 28–29, 32, 35, 55, 60–62, 64–65, 73, 75, 78, 80, 93, 124, 202, 206, 216, 304, 311, 328, 364, 396, 454; coffeehouses/salons in, xi, 130; and connections to French intellectuals, 35; court of Inquisition in, 27; currency problems in, 35; Francesco dal Verme in, 109, 113–15; Gioanni de Bernardi in, 117; Giovanni Francesco Fromond in, 118; Giuseppe Gorani in, 303; infant schools in, 284; literary society in, 124, 243; Luigi Castiglioni in, 12, 35, 113, 115, 127, 129–30, 215–16; monuments to Cesare Beccaria in, 73–74; noble families in, 34, 79, 109, 194, 489; Paolo Andreani in, 119, 200–2; Paolo Frisi in, 35, 127; "Patriotic Society" of, 31; Pietro Verri in, 128, 130, 364; population of, 34; "sage of," 304; and Spanish rule, 29; Supreme Economic Council of, 61; thinkers in, 215; Thomas Jefferson in, 108, 113–14; Viaggio published in, 442

mild laws/punishments, 74, 81, 94, 167, 175, 183, 214, 236, 260, 282, 303, 324, 343, 378, 383, 399–400, 448, 451, 540

military: commission, 351; conflicts, 44; discipline, 152, 162, 196; executions, 155–56, 224, 439; and flogging/whipping, 163, 372, 446–47; justice, 151, 154; law, 9, 348; leaders, 19; and proposed colony, 161; punishments, 162; and Quakers, 172; "spirit," 341; as subordinate to civil power, 391–92; training, 152; treatises, 141. See also specific individuals

military law/offenses, 9. See also Articles of War; courts-martial proceedings; desertion

militia(s), 391; "well regulated," 391

Mill, John Stuart, 99

Millbank Prison, 331

Milligan, Joseph, 186

Milton, John, 194

Minnesota: death penalty's abolition in, 375, 440; as part of Northwest Territory, 380; and U.S.-Dakota War, 350–51

minorities: discrimination against, 6, 10, 382, 438–39; exclusion from social compact, 52, 382; religious, 25, 288; right to vote, 440. See also African Americans; racial discrimination; slavery; slaves

Miranda warning, 390

miscarriage(s) of justice, 7, 107, 335. See also innocence

Miscellaneous Trifles in Prose, 358

Miscellanies by M. de Voltaire, 144

misdemeanors, 411

Mississippi, 371; penal code, 254; River, 347

Missouri: Supreme Court, 393; territory, 342

Mitchell, Samuel Latham, 239

"mitigating" factors/circumstances, 238

Mittermaier, Karl J. A., 135–36

Modern Chivalry, 210

Modern System of Natural History, A, 80

modes of execution, 185, 452. See also methods of execution; specific modes

modes of punishment. See specific methods

Modest Defence of Publick Stews, A, 394

Moir, John Macrae, 135

Molini, Frederick, 177

Molini, Giovan Claudio (Jean Claude), 176–77; Paris bookshop of, 177

Molini, Giuseppe, 176–77

Moloch, 304

mollusk: named after Cesare Beccaria, 437

Monachesi, Elio, 152–53

monarchs: and "ancient laws," 39; Austrian, 28, 66; British/English, 20, 26, 67, 70, 82, 138, 183, 220, 223, 288–89, 293–94, 300, 316, 362, 402, 405, 407, 434, 440, 442; "barbarous usages" of, 169; "cruel," 68; and despotism, 165; disloyalty to, 382; European, 61, 66, 126, 132, 217, 367, 433; French, 442; and "monarchic spirit," 355; oppressive laws of, 183, 193; power of, 178, 455; Prussian, 61, 64, 66; Roman, 432; Russian, 3, 64; "sanguinary" behavior of, 9, 289–90, 303–4, 315–16; and "severity of punishments," 219; subjects of, 358–59; and torture, 304–5; tyranny/cruelty of, 7, 20, 316, 363; and use of death sentences/executions, 9, 48–49, 290; and use of pardons, 258; and use of punishment, 26, 169, 219, 226, 258, 303. *See also specific monarchs*

monarchy: "constitutional," 104, 220; as governmental system, 6, 9, 43–44; limited, 30, 69

Mondovi, Italy, 488

money in politics, 8

Monkton, Vermont, 298

Monluc, Blaise, 107

Monmouth Rebellion, 273

monopolies, 405; and necessaries of life, 282

Monroe, James, 120, 156, 173, 182, 186, 196, 206, 261, 334

Montagu, Basil, 15, 18, 249

Montaigne, Michel Eyquem de, 93, 107, 220, 264

Montesquieu, Charles de, 20, 25, 31, 47, 68, 93, 125, 132, 145, 148, 195, 199, 218, 220, 265, 322, 336, 363, 422, 477; background of, 48; as "benevolent," 331; and "cause of humanity," 235; "celebrated," 180, 220; cited by Continental Congress, 148; commentary on, 92; on cruelty, 219; on death penalty, 48; "genius" of, 220; in grand jury charges, 499; "great," 48; "great and penetrating," 203; "humanity of," 371; "illustrious," 9, 343; "immortal," 29, 48, 147, 220; "immortalised," 385; influence of, 3–4, 9, 15, 20, 48, 50, 67, 70, 95, 99, 120, 133–34, 138, 143, 169, 180–81, 203, 219–20, 226, 229, 233, 236–37, 239, 241, 243–44, 249, 323–24, 328, 345, 347, 359, 362, 366, 368, 378, 384, 413, 416, 431; influence on Cesare Beccaria, 22, 36, 38, 48, 54, 329, 473; influence on Jeremy Bentham, 95; as "learned and celebrated," 366; "led the way," 171; as name "dear to humanity," 264; as "oracle" on separation of powers, 220; on people as origin of power, 354; popularity of, 48; as "precursor of Beccaria in the criminal law," 219; printing/sale of, 87–88, 92; "profound researches of," 220; and proportionality, 133; on punishments/necessity for, 38, 48, 179, 265, 277, 329; referenced in *Federalist No. 47*, 48; and Richard Price, 200; and separation of powers, 15, 48, 212, 219–20, 422, 448; study of, 91, 265; "Theory of," 388; and Thomas Jefferson, 41, 182, 186, 448; travels of, 220; and two-witness rule, 162; views/writing of, 29, 41, 48, 79, 100, 104, 120, 124, 145, 178, 192, 226, 241, 243, 247, 250, 255, 288, 290, 299, 343, 346, 390, 421, 441, 447. *See also Spirit of the Laws*

Montgolfier, Jacques, 119

Montgolfier, Joseph, 119

Monthly Review, The, 91, 286

Monticello, 11, 14, 105, 107–8, 114, 130, 156, 177, 186, 192, 196–97, 232, 296, 326, 338, 408, 445–47

Montigny, Jean-Charles Philibert Trudaine de, 60

Montpellier, 338, 341, 410

Montreal, 158

Moore, Clement, 119

Moore, Elon, 334

Mordaunt, Harry, 394

More, Thomas, 66, 137, 276

Morellet, André, 19, 60, 123, 467; and Benjamin Franklin, 104, 482; and Cesare Beccaria, 36, 218; and David Hume, 33; and Thomas Jefferson, 103; translation of Beccaria's *On Crimes and Punishments*, 27, 58–60, 95, 103–4, 120, 187; translation of Jefferson's *Notes on the State of Virginia*, 27, 47, 104, 187; and Voltaire, 33

Morgan, John, 116

Morocco, 252

Morris, Gouverneur, 239, 254; as "Penman of the Constitution," 302

Morris, Robert, 13, 90, 230, 314, 403, 435

Morris, Samuel, 284–85

Morrison, John, 283–84

Morton, Joseph, 99

Morton, Perez, 102, 326–27

Mosaic law, 189, 274

Moscow, Russia, 98, 161

Moses, 445; law(s) of, 189, 203, 274, 279

"Mother" Bethel Church, 415

Motte, Jeanne de la, 198–99

Mount Vernon, 32, 106, 110–11, 129–30, 201, 312, 358

Mount Vernon Ladies' Association, 358

Mozart, Wolfgang Amadeus, 28, 119

Muhammad, 445

Muhlenberg, Frederick Augustus, 9, 379

Muhlenberg, Henry Melchior, 378–79

Muhlenberg, Peter, 379

Mullen, Patrick, 151

Munford, William, 445–48

municipal privileges, 133

Murder Act of 1752, 183

murder(s), 19, 39, 47, 168, 180, 183, 196, 204, 221, 231, 263, 418, 500; accessory to, 414; aggravated, 97, 282; aiding and abetting, 237; "by express malice," 224; as capital crime, 7, 9, 16, 42, 92, 133, 135, 169, 187, 189, 193, 234, 236–37, 240, 255, 274–75, 280, 282, 288, 294–95, 299, 316, 322, 324, 370, 372, 381, 384–85, 389, 411, 414, 419, 425–26; in "cold blood," 123; "cool and deliberate," 192; degrees of, 127, 209–10, 229, 415; "deliberate," 229, 371, 386; in Europe, 50; execution(s) for, 291; and federal law, 414–15; felony, 229, 240, 379, 384, 386; first-degree, 209, 229, 262, 268, 385–86; "judicial," 243; and life sentences, 348; and malice, 513; and mandatory death sentences, 189; number of, 439; premeditated, 167, 171, 229, 240, 324, 379; as "propagated by the punishment of death," 212, 435; punishment of, 235, 258, 265; and retaliation, 139; and "revelation," 92; second-degree, 210, 229, 268, 325; in Tuscany, 162; victims, 452; "willful," 237, 371, 386; "with malice aforethought," 224. *See also* homicide(s)

murderer(s), 97, 124, 171, 389, 438; dissection of, 360; execution of, 26, 232; as "noxious animal," 388; and pardons, 401. *See also* death row inmates; *specific individuals*

Murphy, John, 154

Murray, John, 80, 88

Murray II, John, 93

Mussi, Giuseppe, 113, 130

mutilation(s), 131, 162, 225, 367; as infamous punishment, 394. *See also* maiming

mutiny, 283, 334

My Life and Wanderings, 118, 195

Nagle, Christian, 283–84

Nakaz, 3, 98

Nancrede, Joseph, 91

Nani, Giovanni Battista Felice Gasparo, 178, 357

Naples, Italy, 35, 39, 55, 61, 78–79, 115–17, 133–35, 252–53, 369; punishments in, 96

Napoleon (Emperor), 413, 417, 445; code of, xiv, 410, 413, 445; era of, 78

Narrative of the Capture of Ticonderoga, and of His Captivity and Treatment by the British, 158

Narrative of the Late Massacres, A, 123

Nash, Thomas, 334

Nassau Hall, 89, 245, 264, 333. *See also* College of New Jersey; Princeton University

national defense/security, 9, 43, 49

National Italian American Bar Association, 453

National Register, The, 403–4

Native Americans, 261, 312; clashes with colonists, 50; execution of, 350–51; and manumission suits, 261; punishment of, 129; treaty with, 202

natural law, 39–40, 104, 135, 138, 202, 247, 299, 311–12, 354; of crimes, 411; founders' embrace of, 16, 67, 70, 411; movement, 427; theorists, 39–40, 42

natural rights, 39, 41, 67, 197, 213, 234, 261, 300, 344, 355, 357, 364, 410; founders' embrace of, 42; "life, liberty, and estate" as, 40; self-defense as, 391–92

Neal, Anthony, 376

"necessaries," monopolization of, 282

Necessary and Proper Clause, 410

Necker, Suzanne Churchod, 60

Ned, 446

Nedham, Marchamont, 194–95

Nelson, Thomas, 434

Nemesis Theresiana, 29, 62

Neptune, 12

Netherlands, The, 125, 422; king of, 336; torture abolished in, 63, 389

Neville, Henry, 194

Nevins, Allan, 258

New Bern, North Carolina, 397

New England, 189, 263, 411, 413; Cesare Beccaria's influence in, 92. *See also specific states*

New Hampshire, 44, 125, 129, 175–76, 224, 400, 420; adultery in, 373; anti-death penalty efforts in, 280; attorney general, 143; branding in, 269; chief justice of, 138; colonial code, 280; constitution, 256–58, 282, 373; corporal punishments in, 269, 373; death penalty in, 280, 282; emancipation of slaves in, 256; governor, 176, 416; grand jury charge in, 167; legislature, 280, 416; prison(s)/penitentiary in, 325; private execution law, 49; ratification convention, 213; Supreme Court, 282; Supreme Court of Judicature, 167

New Haven, Connecticut, 88, 102, 143, 202, 233, 295

New-Haven Gazette, The, 88, 143

New Jersey, 88, 109, 119, 158, 240, 255, 332, 353; anti-death penalty efforts in, 240; attorney general, 296; constitution, 240; dueling in, 204; emancipation of slaves in, 256; governor, 296; judiciary, 241; and law forbidding citation of English cases, 424; penitentiary in, 325; private execution law, 49; State Artillery, 291

New-Jersey Magazine, and Monthly Advertiser, The, 88

New London, Connecticut, 66

New Method of Easily Attaining the Italian Tongue, A, 357

New Orleans, 334

New Select Catalogue of Benjamin Guild's Circulating Library, 125

New South Wales, 254

New Testament, 90, 346

New World, 32, 112, 129, 131, 140, 196, 382, 397; mapping of, 453; settlement of, 363

New York, 11, 44, 80, 92, 119, 122, 170, 202, 239, 255, 316, 353, 383, 422, 425; act of 1796, 237; anti-death penalty efforts in, 238, 240, 267, 324; Attorney General, 204, 237, 374; bar, 237, 240; branding in, 233, 269; capital offenses in, 204, 232; Cesare Beccaria's treatise in, 148, 186, 370; chancellor, 290, 332–33; City, 91, 110, 138, 140–41, 154, 169, 201–2, 237, 240,

325, 332, 334, 336, 353, 383, 442; colonial, 169, 232, 239, 295, 332; corporal punishments in, 233, 269; courts-martial proceedings in, 152; debtors' prison, 202, 403–4; emancipation of slaves in, 256; executions in, 153–54, 350, 383; governor, 167–68, 204, 237, 239, 268, 379; grand jury charge in, 167; harbor, 163; Historical Society, 120; imprisonment for debt abolished in, 232; legislative reports, 266–68, 317; legislature, 110, 148, 169, 204–5, 237, 239, 241, 267, 315, 324, 347, 379, 389, 403, 425; Manumission Society, 8; mayor, 237, 334; penal reform in, 168–69, 204–5, 236–40, 324, 421; prison(s)/penitentiaries in, 167–69, 191, 202, 240, 314, 324–25, 328–29, 335, 341–42, 347, 383, 538; private execution law, 49, 242; Quakers in, 168–69, 353; ratifying convention/debate, 8–9, 148, 252, 431; and "reverence for the laws," 290; Senate, 324; slaves in, 261; Society library, 125, 138; State Library, 94; State Prison, 347; State Society for the Abolition of Capital Punishment, 264, 417; Supreme Court, 332; U.S. Attorney for, 334; U.S. Senator, 102, 237; use of pillory/stocks in, 233; whipping in, 233

New York *Daily Gazette*, 239
New York Evening Post, 403
New York Gazette, The, 123
New York Journal, 268
New-York Magazine, The, 131, 171, 239, 246
New York Packet, 422
New York Times, The, 426
New York University, 439
New York Weekly Journal, The, 123
Newbery, E., 476
Newbery, F., 77, 80, 94, 402, 503
Newbery, Francis (son of John), 78, 80–81
Newbery, Francis (nephew of John), 78, 80–81

Newbery, John, 78, 80
Newcomb, Rexford, 435
Newfane, Vermont, 298
Newgate Prison (Connecticut), 327, 385
Newgate Prison (England), 169, 273, 278, 294, 354
Newgate Prison (New York), 168, 237, 325
Newport, Rhode Island, 125
Newseum, 251
newspapers. *See specific newspapers*
Newton, Isaac, 34, 37, 40–41, 117
Niccoli, Abbé, 253
Nicholas (Czar), 336
Nicholas, George, 390
Nicholson, William, 448
Nicklin, Philip, 93
Nicola, Lewis, 230
Nicoletta, Julie, 311
"nigger box," 376
Nineteenth Amendment, 440
Ninth Amendment, 213, 410
Noble, Patrick, 348
nobles: duels between, 55–56; in England, 84; French, 95, 104, 107, 302; Italian, xi, 12–13, 32–34, 36, 38, 79, 108–10, 115, 127, 129, 132, 194, 200–1, 388; and punishment(s), 183, 293, 373, 394; and social standing, 293; "Tyranny of," 432; versus people's rights, 301; versus "public happiness," 232. *See also specific nobles*
Noether, Emiliana Pasca, 138, 261
nonviolent crimes, 15, 42, 51. *See also specific crimes*
noose(s): around neck, 102, 268
Norfolk, Virginia, 197
Norfolk County, England, 321–22, 325; penitentiary/houses of correction in, 321–22, 325
Norman law, 274
Normandy, 27
North Africa: death sentences in, 450. *See also specific countries*
North America, 66, 75, 119, 148, 156, 158, 204, 309; colonies in, 4, 432; colonization of, 40, 50, 128, 358; com-

passion in, 382; duels in, 55; fighting in, 44; John Howard's influence in, 212; as "retreat of independence," 376; travel to, 11, 34, 113, 200

North American Review, The, 119, 140, 265

North Briton, The, 81–83, 85–87

North Carolina, xv, 230, 240, 387; anti-dueling law of, 397; and Cesare Beccaria's treatise, 92; and corporal punishments, 92; duel in, 397; executions in, 121–22; governor, 397; Light Dragoons, 230

North Dakota, abolition in, 375

North Korea, executions in, 454

Northen, William, 6

Northup, Solomon, 112

Northwest Ordinance of 1787, 9, 247, 380

Northwest Territory, 9, 230, 380

Norvell, John, 186

Norwich, Connecticut, 143

nose: boring through, 189; cutting off, 189; slitting/splitting of, 189, 225, 273, 348, 360, 404, 407, 545

Notes and Observations on the Book Entitled 'On Crimes and Punishments', 63

Notes and Queries, 289

Notes on the State of Virginia, 27, 32, 47, 104, 114, 186, 261

Notices of the Original, and Successive Efforts, to Improve the Discipline of the Prison at Philadelphia, and to Reform the Criminal Code of Pennsylvania, 340–41

Nova Scotia, 44

"Novanglus," 75, 252

novel(s): American, 210, 327, 373; English, 177, 278–79; French, 33, 241; influence of, 21, 29–30, 327; Italian, 71–72

Nugent, Thomas, 29

Nukuhiva, 346

Numbers, book of, 274

Núñez, Toribio, 413

Nuova guida di Milano, 105

Nuttall, Thomas, 342

Oates, Titus, 273

oaths, 106, 166, 366

Observations on Civil Liberty, 319

Observations on Penal Jurisprudence and the Reformation of Criminals, 191

Observations on Respiration and the Use of the Blood, 116

"Observations on the Banishing Act of the Senate and Assembly of the State of New-York, 1778," 148

Observations on the Importance of the American Revolution, 200

Observations on the Nature of Civil Liberty, and the Principles of Government, 422

Observations on the Several Acts of Parliament, 75

Observations on Torture, 71, 473

Octavian, 445

Of Population, 376

Of the Law of Nature and Nations, 247

offenders. *See* death row inmates; *specific offenders*

offenses. *See specific crimes*

Ogilvie, William, 174

Ohio, 416; anti-death penalty efforts in, 242; and common-law crimes, 424–25; constitution, 263, 373; executions in, 242; governor(s), 242; as part of Northwest Territory, 380; prison in, 325; private execution law, 242; and proportionality of crimes/punishments, 263; River, 177; and "sanguinary laws" clause, 263; Supreme Court, 416

Oklahoma, executions in, 450

Old Arsenal Prison, 330

Old Bailey, 146–47, 218, 278

Old South Church, 356

Old Testament, 25, 265, 274, 294, 372, 379, 442

Old World, 131, 156

Oldden, John, 322

Oldham, James, 11

On Crimes and Punishments, 173–74, 203, 207, 225, 235, 288, 316, 498; abbreviation for, 139; as "admirable little treatise," 437; as "admirable work," 260;

advertisement of, 77, 80, 89–91, 102, 144–45, 239, 368–69; in America, xi, 3–5, 12, 17, 79–80, 102, 120, 125, 131, 136–37, 144, 146, 156, 159–60, 203–4, 216, 219, 249, 259–60, 311, 317, 349, 362, 367–68, 370, 381, 384, 387–88, 394, 423–24, 427, 435–36, 440, 448–49, 454, 546, 552; anonymous publication of, 18, 35, 58, 64, 466; "benign rays" of, 434; and Bill for Proportioning Crimes and Punishments, 183–84, 187; in bookstores, 13, 17, 125, 138–39; "breathes the true spirit of humanity and freedom," 361; as "canonical text," 136; "caused a great stir in the world," 421; as "celebrated and influential work," 135; as "celebrated Essay," 91, 93; as "celebrated Treatise," 93; as "celebrated work," 262, 368; censorship of, 35, 62–63, 176; as "classic text," 455; as "code of humanity," 354; commentary on, 17; as "common among lettered persons of Pennsylvania," 131; as "compassionate little treatise," 234; drafting/revision of, 31, 33–34, 130, 367, 442, 466–67; editions of, xiii, 27, 31, 43, 59, 74–81, 87–91, 93–94, 102, 124–26, 135, 144, 146, 176, 186, 208, 250, 270, 279, 368–69, 422, 466, 470, 476, 493, 503; as "elegant treatise," 94; as "eloquent volume," 421; in England, 3–4, 65, 75–79, 82, 95, 104, 137, 286, 289, 317, 361, 369, 454; in Europe, 311, 367–68, 435, 448–49; as "excellent book," 146; as "excellent little work," 141; as "excellent treatise," 5, 212, 244, 435; as "favourite book," 221; as "founding work in modern penology," 431; in France, 3–4, 27, 31–32, 58, 64–65, 95, 100, 120, 137, 176, 218, 467; frontispiece to, 39; in Germany, 4, 27, 467; as "golden treatise," 159; "great fund of humanity" displayed in, 249; as "humane and judicious treatise," 195; as "humanitarian system," 131; in grand

jury charges, 499; as "incomparable treatise," 161; influence of, 3–22, 25–27, 36–39, 48–49, 57–66, 68–69, 74, 79–81, 87–94, 104, 109, 120, 131, 135–49, 151–53, 159–60, 167, 169, 171–75, 186–95, 205, 209–10, 212, 219, 221–22, 225–26, 233–40, 243–44, 249–51, 259, 261–62, 270–71, 277, 279, 281, 289, 293, 298, 311, 317, 328–30, 349, 362–65, 367–73, 381, 387–89, 391–93, 395–99, 416, 422–28, 431–35, 440, 453–55; in Italy, 31, 95, 116; in Ireland, 77, 79; "Just and Judicious observations" of, 249; as "le code de l'humanité," 59; in libraries, 13, 17, 93–94, 124–25, 136–39, 141, 144, 204, 234, 261, 315, 362–63; as "long admired in secret," 131; "merit of," 79; as "most excellent," 368; as "most excellent book of humanity," 77; as "most influential essay ever written on the subject," 14; "never had so small a book created so great an effect," 244; poem about, 303–6; popularity of, 5, 11–13, 18–19, 79, 126, 141, 144, 153, 156–57, 195, 216, 303, 369, 384, 393, 437, 451; and "Preface of the Translator," 36, 75; as producing "a revolution in the human mind, in government, and in courts of justice," 14; publication of, 14, 35, 58, 87, 116, 128, 136, 218, 314, 336, 375, 380, 384, 411, 447; recommendation of, 186; in Russia, 3, 467, 498; in Scotland, 78–79, 234; serializing of, 88; in Spain, 4, 467; "spirit of humanity" of, 388; as "standard work," 349; as "strongly recommended," 375; study of, 91, 140–41, 261; subscription proposal for, 89–90, 126; in Sweden, 27, 467; translation(s) of, xi, xiii, 3, 26–27, 35–36, 58, 63, 65, 71, 74–82, 91, 93–95, 120, 124, 131, 135, 144, 176, 179, 182–83, 187, 208, 396, 432, 437, 447, 467, 470, 489, 503; use in studying Italian, 502; as "well-

known work," 279; as "work of polit-
ical philosophy," 355; at Yale, xiii. *See
also Dei delitti e delle pene*
On Liberty, 99
On Man, 522
On the Abolition of Torture, 365
*Opinions of Different Authors on the Pun-
ishment of Death, The*, 15
Orange, Virginia, 303
Orange County, Virginia, 231
*Oration, Pronounced at Salem, on the
Fourth Day of July, 1804, An*, 142
ordeals by fire/water, 45–46
Order of St. Stephen, 34, 110
Oregon Supreme Court, 392–93
original intent, 438
original meaning, 438
originalism, 15, 22, 438, 440, 451–52; pro-
ponents of, 410, 440
Ossining, New York, 383; prison in, 328
O'Sullivan, John L., 298–99, 371, 379
O'Sullivan, John O., 267–68
Otho II, 289
Otis, George Alexander, 72
Otis, James, 138, 142, 178, 250, 299
Otranto, Italy, 35
Otto, Louis Guillaume, 199
Ottoman Empire, 290
Oudenarde, Marinus, 138
outlawry, 86, 214
overcrowding, 329
Oxford, England, 121, 250, 361
Oxford University, 78, 96, 99, 105, 112,
142, 159, 200, 222, 225, 250, 258, 394

Paca, William, 248
Pace, Antonio, xi, 13, 117, 126, 128, 133,
489
Pacific Ocean, 346
Padua, Italy, 105, 116
Page, Anthony, 194
Page, John, 197
Page, Mann, 187
pain: avoidance/minimization of, 270, 473;
bodily, 216, 394; concept of, 46, 316;
corporal, 235; fear of, 394; infliction

of, 26, 45–47, 93, 96, 225, 270, 312;
physical, 449–50; psychological/men-
tal, 449–50; "superadded" to execution, 224; and torture, 45–46. *See also*
torture
Paine, Thomas, 11, 92, 161; abolitionist
views of, 100, 462; and American independence, 148; and Benjamin Rush,
5, 145, 494; on Bill of Rights, 213; and
Cesare Beccaria, 4, 392–93; and *Common Sense*, 20, 70, 75, 113, 144–45,
147, 301, 433, 442; "Crisis" series,
75–76; in England, 279; on executions,
301–2, 392; in France, 257, 302; on
French Revolution, 301–2, 442; and
Giacinto Dragonetti, 368–69; and
honorary French citizenship, 303; influence of, 16; and Louis XVI, 100,
302; and Pennsylvania constitution,
227; on punishment, 128, 442; and
Rights of Man, 230, 301–2; on "san-
guinary punishments," 442; on self-
defense, 393; on slave trade, 382; and
Thomas Jefferson, 382; writings of,
447
"pains and penalties," 246, 381; Maryland's
prohibition on, 246
Palatine School, 61
Palazzo di Brera, 73
Pall Mall, 91
Palma, John, 113
Palmer, Aaron, 125
Palmer, Edmund, 152
Palmer, Thomas Fyshe, 93
Panetti v. Quarterman, 248–49
Panic of 1792, 403
Panopticon, 22, 99, 168, 204–5
Panopticon, or the Inspection House, The,
99
Paoli, Pasquale, 359
Paolucci, Henry, 58–59
Papers of James Madison, The, 162
Paradise, John, 105–6, 199–201
Paradise, Lucy, 105–6, 201

pardoning power, 208–9, 298, 401; gubernatorial, 401; presidential, 182, 239, 400. *See also* clemency, executive

pardons, 30, 56, 183, 188, 193, 208, 236, 283–85, 399–401; as "absurd," 400; as "dangerous," 165; and English law, 224; frequent, 204, 247, 347, 350; requests for, 188, 283, 191; use of, 154–55, 185, 191, 224, 229, 268, 284, 342, 347, 400, 443

Parini, Giuseppe, 34, 73

Paris, France, 12, 26–27, 32, 65, 73, 93, 95, 104, 108, 112, 114–15, 118, 124, 201, 249, 314; Academy of Sciences, 309; Alessandro Verri in, 60–61, 71; Americans in, 257; Benjamin Franklin in, 88, 100, 106, 127, 141; cafés of, 59; and Cesare Beccaria's treatise, 27, 35, 175, 186; and Cesare Beccaria's visit, 59–61, 71, 218; Charles Carroll of Carrollton in, 250; Christopher Gore in, 102; citizens of, 302; David Hume in, 59; and Democratic Society, 262; diplomat(s) in, 120; and Gaetano Filangieri's treatise, 135; Giulia Beccaria in, 71–72; Gouverneur Morris in, 254; hot air balloons in, 119; John Adams in, 100, 175–76, 179; John Trumbull in, 101–3; John Wilkes in, 83; Louis XVI's execution in, 302–3; Luigi Castiglioni in, 127; Luigi Pio in, 134; Mathew Carey in, 88; mayor of, 442; mob violence in, 442; Montesquieu in, 48, 220; operas/plays in, 119; Philip Mazzei in, 198; Ralph Izard in, 253; salons in, 58, 160; Thomas Jefferson in, xiii, 100, 105, 114, 177, 341, 407; Thomas Paine in, 257; Tuscan minister in, 253; William Short in, 100, 116, 130, 341; William Thornton in, 313

Parisian Gazette littéraire de l'Europe, 58

Parker, Kunal, 416

Parker, Moses, 233

Parliament. *See* British Parliament

parliamentary reform, 353

Parma, Italy, 27–28, 116

parole, ineligibility for. *See* life imprisonment

Parr, Samuel, 379, 393, 549

parricides, 38, 193, 196

Parsons, Samuel Holden, 9

Passmore, Thomas, 226

Passy, 12, 34, 77, 108–9, 127, 135, 141, 217, 365, 398

Pastoret, Claude-Emmanuel de, 140, 218

Paternoster Row, 78, 177

Paterson, Samuel, 132

Paterson, William, 296

pathology, study of, 126

Patriotic Society of Milan, 31, 34

Patriots of North-America, The, 80

Patton, Andrew, 197

Paul, Caleb, 215

Paul, John, 215

Pauley, Matthew, 58

Pavia, Gioacchino Beccaria de, 63

Pavia, Italy, 28, 30, 35, 63, 108, 129, 267, 471

Payne v. Tennessee, 15, 437

peace, 36, 164, 229, 258, 310, 356, 391, 445; of community, 236; office to promote, 310; of society, 323; time(s) of, 44, 163, 389, 442, 449. *See also* Treaty of Paris

Peace of Amiens, 72

Pedon, John, 284–85

Peekskill, New York, 152

peine forte et dure, 222, 405. *See also* pressing to death

penal codes. *See specific jurisdictions*

penal colonies, 52, 318, 331

penal reform. *See specific individuals and jurisdictions*

Pendleton, Edmund, 47, 145, 193, 253, 370

Pendleton, John Strother, 94

Pendleton, Nathaniel, 111

penitence, 166

penitentiaries, xv, 5–6, 10, 20, 22–23, 89–90, 99–100, 110, 122, 128, 139, 168–69, 172, 184, 190–91, 205, 216,

240, 254, 256, 267–68, 273, 298–99, 311–14, 317–18, 320–31, 341–42, 344–47, 380, 383, 385, 388, 395, 418, 420–21, 433–35, 439–41; as alternative to "cruel inflictions so disgraceful to penal codes," 207, 341; as "attracting visitors," 139; building of, 5, 22, 168, 325–32, 341, 449; circular design for, 22, 204; as experiment, 140, 325–26, 336, 340; federal, 330–31, 346–47; as "indispensable," 168; as "one of the byproducts of the intellectual and humanitarian movements of the eighteenth century," 89; as outgrowth of Cesare Beccaria's ideas, 299; as "substitute for the profligate gaols and sanguinary punishments," 324; as "suited to the humanity of the age," 441; versus "sanguinary" punishments, 317; "well built," 341; as "world famous," 139. *See also* prison(s); *specific states*; United States

Penitentiary Act of 1779, 317–19, 321, 325, 331

penitentiary system, 10, 20, 190, 192, 240, 256, 312, 317, 320, 327, 329–31, 335–36, 341–42, 348, 383, 385, 418, 421, 435, 439, 454, 540; "abuses of," 540; birth of, 454; as contrasted with "the old sanguinary codes of the colonies," 317; to "create habits of industry and order," 341; to "effect amendment," 341; to "excite contrition," 341; as "experiment so deeply interesting to the cause of Humanity," 340; as "fairest experiment ever made in favor of humanity," 336; as "godlike experiment," 336; improvements in, 312; "kinks" in, 331; in lieu of "bloody code of earlier days," 6; national, 330–31; as "place for repentance and amendment," 317; promise of, 340–42; proponents of, 319; "well-regulated," 329; as "worthy of the free country in which it is made," 336

Penn, John, 532

Penn, Thomas, 532

Penn, William, 32, 128, 168, 214, 267, 270, 275, 287–88, 293–94, 299, 400, 440, 455; colonial code of, 324. *See also* "Great Law of 1682"

Pennsdale, Pennsylvania, 421

Pennsylvania, 5–6, 40, 66, 88, 112–13, 126, 130, 142, 172, 210, 217, 239, 255, 258, 266, 286, 370, 378, 380, 399, 418, 421, 424, 532; act of 1718, 213–14, 229, 298, 359, 371, 417, 433, 444; act of 1786, 171, 184, 211, 229; act of 1794, 172, 210, 229–30, 298, 386, 415; anti-death penalty efforts in, 6, 171, 192, 210, 240, 243, 270, 298–99, 435, 540; assembly, 215, 228, 275, 321, 379; Attorney General, 13, 237, 267, 270, 413; Board of Health, 230; capital offenses in, 131, 540; Cesare Beccaria's influence in, vii, 4, 13–14, 19, 131–32, 270, 370–71; colony/province of, 13, 67–68, 168, 232, 275, 294, 324, 532; Commonwealth of, 90, 171, 214, 226, 437; constitution, 131, 164, 192, 214, 216, 226–29, 256, 321, 370, 372–73; and Continental Congress, 136; and corporal punishments, 287; Court of Common Pleas, 167; courts in, 167, 171, 309; and "cruel punishments" clause, 226; dividing murder into degrees, 127, 209–10, 229; emancipation of slaves in, 256; example of, 385; executions in, 171, 229, 379, 440; "experiment," 421, 454; governor, 113, 170–71, 240, 260, 328, 416; hard labor in, 385; judges, 245; "led the way"/ "leading the way," 216, 240; legislative report, 171, 328; legislature, 131–32, 171, 214, 216, 315, 322, 328, 384–85, 532; life imprisonment in, 210; mutiny in, 309–10; penal reform/laws in, 170–73, 192–93, 211, 216, 225–28, 233, 237, 240, 255, 270, 321–22, 324, 381, 416; penitentiaries/prisons in, 89–90, 139, 168, 172, 191–92, 226–27, 237, 240, 296, 298–99, 312, 314, 322,

324–29, 335, 340–42, 385, 388, 433; private execution law in, 49, 242; and proportionality, 164, 321; punishments in, 131; Quakers in, 128, 169, 192, 261, 266, 275, 293–94, 317, 322, 325, 340, 440, 455; ratifying convention/debate, 252, 379; rebellion in, 7; and "sanguinary" punishments, 164, 192; Society for Promoting the Abolition of Slavery, 211; slaves in, 415; solitary confinement in, 327–28; Supreme Court, 96, 113, 170, 209, 214–15, 226, 229, 270, 436; Supreme Executive Council, 89, 214, 216–17, 227–29, 379; "system," 327–28; U.S. Senator, 230, 267; "wheelbarrow" law, 211, 322–23

Pennsylvania Evening Herald, 88

Pennsylvania Gazette, The, 52, 113, 276

Pennsylvania Journal, 245

Pennsylvania Mercury, 215

Pennsylvania Packet and the General Advertiser, 113

people: as a body, 174; and duty "to obey the law," 359; "free," 71; and "general will," 402; "of the United States," 419; rights of/retained by, 213, 364, 405, 410; as source of political power, 70, 165, 354, 362, 422, 446

People's Barrier against Undue Influence and Corruption, The, 353

People's Republic of China. *See* China

perjury: as capital crime, 26, 275; and English law, 273, 281; hard labor for, 385; imprisonment for, 385; and lack of honor, 394; and Titus Oates, 273

"perpetual" slavery/penal servitude, 42, 51–52, 62, 376, 469; as substitute for death sentences, 379. *See also* life imprisonment; slavery

Perry, Reuben, 447

Persian Letters, 29, 88, 125, 220

Persico, Luigi, 313

Perth, Scotland, 93

Peter, Jr., Robert, 284–85

Peters, Christopher J., 564

Peters, Richard, 337

Petersburg, Virginia, 112, 190

Peterson, Merrill, 398

petit treason: as capital crime, 370

petition, right to, 213, 364

Petition of Right of 1628, 394

Petitjean, 113

Petrovna, Elizabeth (Empress). *See* Elizabeth (Empress)

Pettinella, Diambra de, 55

petty larceny/theft, 26, 290. *See also* larceny

petty treason, 283, 404; punishment of, 193, 406

Philadelphia, 5, 7, 22, 32, 39, 66, 88, 94, 99, 108, 113, 115–16, 118–19, 121, 125, 128, 130, 135, 144, 148, 158, 170, 172, 179, 207, 211, 214, 216, 227–28, 230, 236, 241, 243–45, 257, 261, 267, 287, 299, 306, 309–10, 313, 320, 323, 335–37, 359, 378–80, 383–84, 412, 415, 433–34, 447, 453, 532; bar, 94, 173, 413, 447, 453; bookshops/booksellers, 260, 396, 448; British occupation of, 227; and Cesare Beccaria's treatise, 89–91, 126, 144–47, 270; Centre Square, 379; charitable impulses in, 227; coffee-house, 68; College, 227; and Constitutional Convention, xi, 6–7, 47, 106, 126, 163, 165, 170, 179–80, 198, 207, 212–13, 226, 231, 255, 296, 319, 358, 381, 383, 422, 433–35, 444; and Continental Congress, 253; and corporal punishments, 287; and Democratic Society, 262; executions in, 229, 379, 440; "experiment" in, 190, 340, 342; fortification of, 211; French legation in, 187; and Gaetano Filangieri, 132; and Independence Hall, 16; Italians in, 113, 119; law academy, 298, 447; mayor of, 267; mechanics, 227; militia, 90; and Montesquieu's treatise, 145; and news of Louis XVI's execution, 302; printers/printing in, 89–90, 92; prison inspectors, 260; prison(s)/jail(s)/

penitentiaries in, 89–90, 139, 168, 172, 191–92, 226–27, 237, 299, 312, 322, 324–25, 327, 329, 340–41, 385, 388, 433; Quakers, 169, 261, 293, 314, 322, 324–25, 340; Quarter Sessions, 349; and religious toleration, 124; society, 153; solitary confinement in, 317; wax-works in, 353; and "wheelbarrow" men, 184; yellow fever epidemic in, 90, 244. *See also* Constitutional Convention; Pennsylvania; Walnut Street Jail/Prison

Philadelphia Advertiser, The, 126

Philadelphia Bar Association, 453

Philadelphia Prison Society, 348

Philadelphia Silk Filature, 194

Philadelphia Society for Alleviating the Miseries of Public Prisons, 168, 192, 215, 320–23, 325; constitution of, 320

Philadelphia Society for Assisting Distressed Prisoners, 226–27

Philadelphia Society for the Abolition of Capital Punishment, 182

Philadelphia Trial Lawyers Association, 453

"Philadelphiensis," 358

Philanthropist, The, 249

"Philanthropos," 236

Philip (King), 316

Philips, Josiah, 381

Phillipps, Samuel, 368

Phillips, Richard, 15

"Philochoras," 215

"Philopatris Varvicensis," 549

Philosophical and Miscellaneous Papers, 77

Philosophical and Religious Dialogue in the Shades, Between Mr. Hume and Dr. Dodd, A, 145

Philosophy of Law, The, 139

Philosophy of Right, The, 228

Piazza Beccaria, 74

Piccadilly, 75, 77, 92

Pickering, Timothy, 171, 334, 426

pickpocketing, at executions, 49

Pictures from Italy, 139

Pierres, Philippe-Denis, 187

pillory: abolition/abandonment of, 287, 371, 407, 418, 454; for working on the Sabbath, 298; as infamous punishment, 269, 394; "moderate infliction of," 407; standing in, 298, 377–78, 404; use of, 9–10, 102, 121, 169, 225, 233, 237, 273, 276, 281–85, 290, 293, 297, 325, 361, 395, 407, 446

Pinckney, Charles, 125

Pinckney, Charles Cotesworth, 11, 399

Pinckney, Thomas, 303

Pinckney, William, 102

Pinker, Steven, 6, 19

Pinkney, William, 173

Pio, Luigi, 134–35

piracy: accessory to, 414–15, 426; as capital crime, 42, 182, 274, 414–15, 426; punishment of, 425

pirates: yielding up goods to, 414; yielding up ship/vessel to, 414

Pisa, Italy, 116, 196, 252, 257

Pitt, William, 81–82

Pittsburgh, Pennsylvania, 327

Pittsfield, Massachusetts, 315

Pittsfield Sun, 315

Place de la Révolution, 180, 302, 398

Placentia, Italy, 116

plain diet, 321. *See also* course fare

Plain Truth, 147

Plan of Lectures on the Principles of Nonconformity, A, 354

Plater, George, 248

Plato, 93, 178, 194

Pleas of the Crown, 186, 513

pleasure: "barbaric," 111, 443; concept of, 43, 46, 50, 54, 316; "greatest sum of," 355; maximizing, 473; Montaigne on, 107

Plessy v. Ferguson, 383

Pliny, 93

Plough Boy, The, 370

Plumer, William, 138, 416

Plutarch, 93, 178

Plutarch's Lives, 94, 292

Plymouth, Massachusetts, 176

Plymouth, New Hampshire, 280

poaching, 375

poisoning: as capital crime, 42, 189, 275, 280, 283; killing by, 189, 229, 263, 283, 385, 398

Poland: torture abolished in, 389

Poli, Giuseppe Saverio, 117

Political and Historical Research on the United States of America, 198

Political Disquisitions, 90, 276, 279–80, 391, 396, 448

political intolerance, 251

Polk, James K., 266, 284

Polybius, 175

polygamy, 218; abolition for, 280; as capital crime, 274, 280; punishment of, 233, 283

poor, 51–52, 66, 112, 293, 329, 395, 401, 431, 445; and corporal punishments, 373; criminals, 227; and disproportionality between crimes and punishments, 93. *See also* poverty

Poor Laws and Pauper Management, 99

Poor Richard Improved, 40, 299

Pope, Alexander, 82

Pope(s), 60, 64, 116; and papacy's ban on Cesare Beccaria's treatise, 63; and Voltaire, 470. *See also specific Pope(s)*

"Popish Plot," 273

popular democracy, 230; "excesses of," 230

Porter, David, 346

Portugal, 413; death penalty's abolition in, 243

possessing stolen goods, 376

post-conviction proceedings. *See* habeas corpus

posterity, 213, 245; appeals to, 52, 67–68; reference in U.S. Constitution, 342, 422. *See also* future generations

Potomac River, 307

Potter, Thomas, 82

Poughkeepsie *Country Journal*, 422

Pound, Roscoe, 240

poverty, 51, 57, 178–79, 232, 360, 544; fear of, 394; treatise on, 368. *See also* poor

Powel, Samuel, 116

power: abuse of, 8, 17, 177, 357, 363, 407, 409; "accumulation of," 48; "always follows Property," 53; arbitrary, 80, 145, 175, 192, 241, 299–300, 316; balance of, 53, 106; Cesare Beccaria on, 8, 16, 66, 147, 174, 362, 421, 423, 431; checking, 17; concentrated, 20, 422; and "constitution for a free country," 8; "cruel," 45; and death penalty laws, 9, 40, 43, 91; as derived from "consent of the governed," 70; as derived from "the people," 165, 354, 362; "despotic," 80; discretionary, 285; executive, 111, 213, 258, 402; of federal courts, 58; of federal government, 10; of Great Britain, 67–68, 70; judicial, 213, 363, 405, 409; "lawless," 81; legislative, 213, 407; of Pope, 60; reserved "to the people," 422; "reserved to the States," 422; "Sovereign," 179; state, 121, 167, 397; and torture, 47; "unlimited," 299. *See also* checks and balances; pardoning power; separation of powers

Power of Sympathy, The, 327

Prange, James, 89

pregnant offenders: and reprieves, 121, 169, 290

prejudice, racial. *See* racial discrimination

premeditation. *See* murder(s)

Prescott, W. H., 119

President(s), 358, 360, 400, 417–18, 435; and Cesare Beccaria's treatise, 3, 120, 151; power to pardon/reprieve, 182, 208–9; U.S., 201–2, 205, 208. *See also specific presidents*

pressing to death, 222, 406

Prest, Wilfrid, 318

Preston, Thomas, 292

Preston, William, 290

pre-trial detention, 18, 51, 60, 426–27

prevention of crime, 18, 25, 44, 46–47, 56, 163, 165, 175, 182–83, 208, 212, 217, 237, 262, 280, 321, 323, 334, 345–46, 372, 399, 401, 420, 423, 530; and "a largely bloody code of laws," 262; and "best method of," 395; "by making examples of the guilty," 49; "extreme severity of Penal Laws hath not been found effectual for," 221; as goal of "good legislator," 219; "inefficacy of sanguinary punishments in," 370; as "noblest end and aim of criminal jurisprudence," 164; and penitentiary vs. sanguinary system, 540; as "sole end of punishment," 172, 235; as "the sole object of punishment," 388; through education/forced labor, 49, 57

Price, Richard, 194, 200–1, 277, 279, 318–19, 354, 433; influence of, 359; and John Adams, 175; and Yale College's honorary degree, 319

Priestley, Joseph, 116, 142, 194, 201, 277, 279, 303; and André Morellet, 60; background of, 175; and Cesare Beccaria, 175; and John Adams, 175; and Thomas Jefferson, 175

Prince of Wales, 105

Prince, The, 36, 178

Prince George County, Virginia, 191, 261

Prince William County, Virginia, 187

Princeton, New Jersey, 202

Princeton University, 89, 127, 138, 231, 264, 296, 202, 204, 303, 333, 413; academic curriculum of, 203; commencement exercises, 203. *See also* College of New Jersey

Principles and Practice of Naval and Military Courts-Martial, 162

Principles of Government, 260

Principles of Legislation, 335, 375

Principles of Morals and Legislation, 205

Principles of Natural and Politic Law, 247

Principles of Natural Law, 125

Principles of Penal Law, 22, 79, 98, 184–85, 246, 394

printing presses: availability of, 432; manufacture of, 11–12; usefulness of, 354

prison discipline, 140, 328, 341

Prisoners' Friend, The, 266

prisoners of war, 141, 158–59, 291, 365

prison(s): American, 49, 89, 109–11, 121, 167–69, 172, 178, 191–92, 202, 226–27, 237, 260, 280, 283, 288, 296–99, 311–12, 320–21, 323–25, 327–28, 341–42, 380, 403–4, 433, 450; building/design of, 5, 10, 22, 95, 99, 184, 204, 212, 311, 320, 325, 348; conditions, xv, 36, 232; English, 19, 22, 36, 76, 85–86, 103, 278–79, 294, 314, 317–18, 321, 325; European, 19, 98, 258, 323; federal, 330–31, 347; French, 190, 198–99, 254, 326; horror/filth of, 36; as "hospitals," 343; as "indispensable," 168; Italian, 30, 33, 36, 199, 258; lack of, 16; maximum-security, 439; as "penitentiaries," 128; proliferation of, 23; reports on, 191; ships, 141, 158–59, 170; supermax, 439; use of, 10, 18. *See also* conditions of confinement; imprisonment; life imprisonment; penitentiaries

privacy, right to, 410

private execution laws: passage of, 49, 242

private executions. *See* execution(s)

private prosecution, 281, 542

privileges, 300; municipal, 133

Privileges and Immunities Clause, 213

Privy Council, 46, 223, 366; and use of torture, 47

Prix de la justice et de l'humanité, 87

Proceedings in Cases of High Cases, The, 289

Progressive Era, 375, 440

proof, law of, 59, 365–67

property, 53, 72, 136, 353–54, 374, 419–20, 423–24; "absolute power over," 43; "acquiring and possessing," 245; deprivation of, 40, 300; "offenses against," 419; private, 276; right to, 26, 43, 69, 354, 408–9; as "social right," 42

property crimes: as capital crimes, 190, 229, 274, 384; abolition for, 381. *See also* burglary; forgery; larceny; robbery; stealing; theft proportionality: between crimes and punishments, xi, 36–38, 57, 95, 122, 131, 133, 145, 147, 155, 164, 166, 174, 179, 182, 204, 207, 217–18, 235–37, 244, 255–56, 262–64, 324, 368, 371, 374, 385, 419, 434, 451; and Cesare Beccaria's treatise, 22, 25–26, 99, 189, 268, 349, 368, 370, 372, 386, 388, 421, 451, 453, 455; concept/principle of, 37, 48, 133, 162, 179–80, 217, 256, 265, 268, 372, 374–75, 386, 404; and Eighth Amendment, 375; Immanuel Kant's views of, 139; need for, 345; in state constitutions, 192, 263, 321, 373–75; types of, 189; under French law, 244

prosecutors, 165; charging/discretionary decisions, 10, 525; private, 281, 542

Protestant(s), 28, 107, 110, 123, 202

Prussia, 28, 30, 61, 64, 66, 79, 127, 153, 156, 179; abolition of torture in, 61; king/court of, 365, 423; laws of, 61, 335

Prynne, Hester, 373

Prynne, William, 273

Psalm 51, 307

pseudonym(s): "Beccaria" used as, 329–30; Greek, 7, 358; Roman, 7, 358. *See also* *specific pseudonyms*

public dissection, of corpses, 224, 283, 360, 387, 503

public education. *See* education

public executions, 46, 49, 95, 121, 194, 236, 242, 278–81, 295, 302, 415; gradual disappearance of, 49; laws barring, 49, 242. *See also* execution(s)

public good, 93, 300, 333, 355, 374, 444

public humiliation, 293. *See also* shame

public labor, 137, 155, 190, 193, 195, 212. *See also* hard labor; labor

public opinion: changing, 163; on death penalty/executions, 97, 195, 245, 315, 350; on "infamous" punishments, 310; on justice, 100; on mild punishments, 348; on penal reform, 131, 153; on rape, 381

public punishments. *See* punishments

public schools, 399

public shaming, 283, 374, 394

public trial(s), 165, 295; right to, 426

"Publius," 48, 358

Pufendorf, Samuel von, 39, 41, 67, 75, 93, 99, 125, 174, 243, 247, 265, 276, 431

Puget Sound, 331, 347

Puglia, James Philip, 230

Punishment of Death, The, 18

punishment(s): as "absolutely necessary," 43, 171–72, 246, 288, 378, 439; "absolute necessity" for, 38, 54, 131, 156, 185, 246, 265, 329, 343, 345, 422, 439; as "absurd," 264; antiquated, 373; arbitrary, 155, 192, 299, 317; barbarous/barbaric, 6, 200, 233, 243, 251, 342, 374, 378, 382; "better proportioned," 192; bodily, 366, 371, 373; "certain," 167, 218, 324, 330; "certainty of," 238, 242–43, 260, 282; certainty vs. severity, 7, 38, 122, 164, 176, 208, 218–19, 221, 236–38, 280, 288, 330, 349, 450, 482, 515, 540; "condigne," 274; of contempt, 226; "corrective," 122; "cruel," 6, 10, 21, 38, 47, 96, 138, 182, 187, 200, 203, 209, 219, 222–23, 233, 239, 246–47, 255, 263–64, 285, 301, 323, 329–30, 339, 341, 348, 374, 376–78, 436, 439, 452, 546; "cruel and unusual," 17, 20–22, 199–200, 222, 252, 285, 370, 374–76, 395, 406, 429, 446, 449, 452, 546; "cruel nor unusual," 263; "cruel or unusual," 19, 21, 178, 246–47, 252; of debtors, 36, 56, 232–33, 239, 258, 294, 360, 399, 401–4; and degree of guilt, 259; delays in imposing, 168; discretionary, 235, 275, 443; disgraceful, 56, 123, 132, 163, 215, 224, 229, 374; degrading, 389, 394, 427; "disgusting," 225; disproportionate, 147, 222, 234–35, 250, 289, 339, 348, 374, 542; "draconian," 225; equal, 22, 139, 243, 317; "excessive," 122; "excessively severe," 233; extending to "Labor," 283; extending to "Life," 283; extending to

"Limb," 283; "exterminating," 122; "hard and forceful," 406; "harsh," 38–39; as having "lost all proportion to the crimes to which they are annexed," 234; "heavier degree of," 207; humiliating, 169, 293; "ignominious," 314; "illegal," 378; immediate, 131, 216, 427; "indiscriminate," 277, 371; and "indiscriminate severity," 250; "infamous," 133, 269, 300, 310, 334, 393–95; "inhuman," 247, 330, 380; involving "lingering death," 390; "just," 148; "least possible in the given circumstances," 104; "less sanguinary," 164, 187, 192, 227, 254, 256, 287, 337, 370, 373, 415, 442; mandatory, 21, 131, 153, 189, 425, 451; as "manifestly cruel and absurd," 264; "melioration of," 421; "mild," 37, 56, 94, 164, 167, 175, 181, 183, 208, 226, 235–36, 288, 303, 324, 334, 348–49, 383, 385, 441, 448, 454; "moderate," 122, 164, 167, 226; modes/methods of, 224, 304; "more proportionate," 164, 227, 256, 370, 373; on necessity for, 9, 43–44, 57, 65–66, 104, 131, 148, 157, 167, 171, 209, 227, 236, 246, 265, 343, 345, 372, 384, 530; painful, 224, 323; private, 242; "prompt," 104, 155; proportionate, 25, 37–38, 57, 95, 104, 131, 133, 145, 147, 164, 167, 172, 192, 204, 208, 217–18, 227, 236, 256, 262–63, 265, 268, 270–71, 274, 321, 330, 349, 368, 371, 373–74, 419, 434, 440; public, 5, 57, 95, 104, 131–32, 203, 211–12, 215–16, 229, 233, 236, 278, 281, 288, 302, 329, 415, 446; purpose of, 343; "rigorous," 175; "sanguinary," 17, 21, 50, 103, 172, 227, 233, 235, 239, 250, 255, 261, 263, 293, 296, 299, 301, 303, 323–24, 329–30, 341–43, 370, 373, 439, 441, 452, 546; scale of, 37–38, 207, 215, 323, 370, 385, 420, 436; "severe," 37, 94, 175, 180, 182, 203, 219, 226, 235, 281, 287, 324, 374, 385, 419; shaming, 233, 374, 394; shaving beard/eyebrow/head, 163, 184, 283, 322; "smallest possible," 131; speedy, 38, 57, 164, 171, 426–28, 450–51; and "spirit of the age," 349; "stigmatizing," 342; "true design of," 263; "true end of," 236; as "tyrannical," 142, 148, 175, 265, 287; "uncertain," 218; "unequal," 323; "unjust," 179, 374; "unnatural," 377; "unusual," 17, 200, 209, 247, 263, 301, 378, 436, 439, 452; "usual," 222; "visible," 296. *See also* Bloody Code; "cruel and unusual punishments"; "cruel or unusual punishments"; Cruel and Unusual Punishments Clause; corporal punishments; death penalty; execution(s)

Punitive Acts, 174

Puritan(ism), 40, 189, 254, 273, 294–95, 411

Purrington, Tobias, 241–42, 267

"pursuit of Happiness," 143, 433; right to, 16, 79, 308, 355, 438. *See also* Declaration of Independence; happiness

Putnam, Israel, 152

Quakers, 12–13, 15, 25, 110, 113, 118, 127, 216, 302, 312–13, 393; and assistance of prisoners, 158; banishment of, 290; and Benjamin Banneker, 306–9; in England, 128, 277, 282, 294, 318; execution of, 129, 290, 440; immigration of, 293; and incarceration/ penitentiary system, 10, 128, 340; in Maryland, 306–9; in Massachusetts, 129; in New England, 290; in New York, 168–69, 353; as opposing taking of life, 401; and penal reform, 450; in Pennsylvania, 128, 169, 192, 226–27, 261, 266, 275, 293–94, 314, 322, 324, 440, 455; and solitary confinement, 317; in Vermont, 298; whipping of, 276

Qualls, William, 308

Quebec, 5, 7–8, 66–67, 75, 81, 147–48, 162, 314, 473, 497; battle of, 7

Quebec Act of 1774, 148

queens: "sanguinary" behavior of, 316; "tyrannical" acts of, 316. *See also* monarchs; *specific queens*
Quincy, Elizabeth, 125
Quincy, Josiah, 93, 174, 178, 292, 368, 403
Quinn, Samuel, 121, 176

race: of defendants/victims, 439, 452; and oppression/violence, 442. *See also* minorities; racial discrimination
racial discrimination, 11, 308, 428; and death penalty, 121, 450, 452; and murder victims, 439, 452; in punishment, 10. *See also* Fourteenth Amendment; minorities
racial inequality, 11, 382, 439. *See also* discrimination; racial discrimination
rack(s), 45, 92, 167, 247, 301, 375; as cruel, 452; labeled "Duke of Exeter's daughter," 371; use of, 6, 64, 200, 361, 371, 378
Rainone, Michael, 453
Raleigh, North Carolina, 121–22
Raleigh, Walter, 40–41
Rambles in Germany and Italy in 1840, 1842, and 1843, 279
Ramsay, Allan, 21, 64
Ramsay, David, 114
Randolph, Beverly, 179
Randolph, Edmund, 107, 158, 299, 312; as Annapolis delegate, 255; as Attorney General of United States, 169–70; on bills of attainder, 381; and Cesare Beccaria, 170; on common law, 411–12; and Constitutional Society of Virginia, 196
Randolph, John, 169
Randolph, Peyton, 147, 169
Randolph, Thomas Mann, 11
Rantoul, Robert, 241, 264–65, 268, 343
rape, 204, 229, 386, 414, 418, 438, 500; abolition for, 172, 381; attempted, 385; as capital crime, 26, 236, 274–75, 280, 294, 299, 315, 381, 385, 411, 419, 425–26; castration for, 189, 193, 283, 342, 404; child, 275, 295; executions for,

121; imprisonment for, 325; as infamous crime, 418; as non-capital crime, 315; punishment of, 189, 297, 315, 404; and U.S. Supreme Court, 374
ratification debates/conventions, 7–10, 48, 369. *See also* Constitution; *specific states*
Rationale of Judicial Evidence, The, 99
Rationale of Punishment, The, 95–97
Rawle, Francis, 13
Rawle, William, 142
Raynal, Guillaume Thomas François, 359
Read, James, 90
Read, Joseph, 68
Reading, Pennsylvania, 171
Reading on the Use of Torture in the Criminal Law of England Previously to the Commonwealth, A, 223
reason, 32, 36, 193, 223, 235–36, 271, 338, 345, 347, 362, 371, 401; "[a]ll the punishments should be inflicted with," 330; Cesare Beccaria's "appeal to," 168; Enlightenment's focus on, 411; "human," 217; ideal of, 220; penal code as "scandal to," 262; "perfection of," 76; "power of," 385; "right," 239; versus "unreason," 49; "voice of," 323
Reasonableness of Christianity, The, 46
rebellion, 274, 311; as capital crime, 97, 103; crime of, 258; Irish, 254; slave, 11, 156, 443. *See also specific rebellions*; treason
rebels, 64, 69, 100, 119; as "infamous Persons," 394
Recherches Historiques et Politiques sur les États-Unis de l'Amerique Septentrional, 198
Recherches sur la science de gouvernement, 303
recidivists, 295; tattooing of, 371
Reconstruction Amendments, 21, 438. *See also* Fifteenth Amendment; Fourteenth Amendment; Thirteenth Amendment
Reed, Silas, 372
Reeve, Tapping, 413
Reflections on the Revolution in France, 301

reformation: of offenders, 18, 122, 164, 168, 212, 222, 236, 246, 262, 318, 321–22, 332, 334, 336, 419; as "object highly meriting the attention of the laws," 262; as "object of great solicitude among the most enlightened men of Europe," 421; as "true design of all punishment," 263

Réfutation des principes hasardés dans le Traité des délits et des peines, 59

regicides, punishment of, 46

Register and North Carolina Gazette, 121

rehabilitation, 5, 333

Rehnquist, William, 15

Reid, Philip, 313

Reign of Terror, 65, 160, 254. *See also* French Revolution

religion, 76, 136, 175, 211, 216, 251, 308, 433, 445, 530; as "more powerful than the most sanguinary laws," 203; established/organized, 32, 72; "public credit of," 203; punishments based on, 274, 294–95; state, 123. *See also* Bible; Catholic(s); God; Protestant(s)

religious arguments: on death penalty, 40, 209, 241, 263, 343, 361

religious conformity, 47

religious freedom, 197, 364. *See also* religious toleration

religious instruction: of offenders, 210, 318, 337

religious intolerance, 107, 243, 251

religious persecution, 46, 251, 288, 294

religious toleration, 25, 124, 251, 278, 363–64

Remarks Concerning the Government and Laws of the United States of America, 14

Remarks on Several Parts of Italy, 105

Remarks on Some of the Provisions of the Laws of Massachusetts, Affecting Poverty, Vice, and Crime, 178

Remarks on the Expediency of Abolishing the Punishment of Death, 417

Remarks upon the Late Resolutions of the House of Commons, respecting the Proposed Change of the Poor Laws, 148

"Remember the Ladies" letter, 11, 311

Remembrancer, The, 75, 77

Remus, 357

Renaissance, 17, 74, 362, 366

reparation: "applied to the use of the widow or children of the person murdered," 246; of injuries, 227, 283; as punishment, 218; to the injured party, 236, 283

repeat offenders, 373. *See also* recidivists

repentance, 212, 266, 278, 317, 330, 337

Reply to a Document entitled Notes and Observations on the Book of Crimes and Punishments, 71

Report on the Penitentiary System in the United States, 178

Reports of Judicial Decisions in the Constitutional Court, of the State of South-Carolina, 91

representative democracy, 8

representatives: number of, 8; right to choose, 86; and taxation, 353

reprieves, 121–22, 188, 208–9, 307, 399–400; for work as executioners, 121

Republic of Letters, 437, 521; "Venerable Sages and Fellow Citizens in the," 178

republicanism, 9, 14, 53, 73, 101, 147, 161, 170, 193–94, 206, 209, 234, 244, 251, 256, 258, 260, 269, 273, 329, 355, 357–58, 375, 382, 398, 431–33, 435, 440; American, 358, 434; and capital punishment, 14; and dueling, 396; English, 77, 369, 436; and "hating violence and promoting humane treatment of criminals," 228; ideals of, 7; and "institutions of America," 331; Irish, 67, 77; and liberty, 359; and local control, 422; principles of, 391; in Rome, 432–33; and "severity of punishments," 219; spread of, 12, 119; "spirit" of, 185; and virtue, 216; "zealous," 359. *See also specific republics* reputation, 165, 250, 374, 394, 396

res publica, 54, 357, 432

rescuing condemned: convicted of murder, 414; convicted of other capital offense, 414; convicted of treason, 414; as capital crime, 414, 426

Researches on the United States, 400

retaliation: "barbarous," 343; concept of, 292, 333; and executions, 291, 351, 442; imprisonment as, 103; law of, 157, 189, 279–80, 312; and murder, 139; as punishment, 283, 291–92; "resort to," 159; "Right of," 139; question about legitimacy of, 157; "sanguinary law of," 315

retribution, 15, 139, 547; "moral," 419; theory of, 37

revenge: concept/principle of, 156, 259, 343, 530; death penalty as, 288; nature of, 287–88; as "pernicious," 259; "spirit of," 288, 343, 530; thoughts/impulses of, 140, 192, 302; toleration of, 203, 265–66; and punishment, 312, 349. *See also* vengeance

Revere, Paul, 292, 327, 360, 447

Revolution Square, 72

Revolutionary War, 3, 7–8, 12–13, 16, 18–20, 58, 65–67, 76, 78, 80, 82, 88–90, 98–101, 103, 105, 110, 112–13, 119, 122, 124, 136–37, 141, 148–49, 151–52, 154–60, 162, 167–70, 178, 185, 187, 191–92, 195–97, 200–1, 203, 207, 211, 213, 215, 219, 226–30, 235, 237, 239, 253–56, 258, 266, 288, 291–93, 298, 300, 302, 313, 317, 319–20, 326, 331, 333, 337, 350, 353, 358, 371, 377, 381, 388–90, 393, 396, 399, 402, 404, 406, 413, 423–24, 432–35, 438, 440–42, 532

rewards for apprehending criminals, 56, 183

Rhode Island, 116, 125, 380; constitution, 374; death penalty's abolition in, 242–43, 266; emancipation of slaves in, 256; House of Representatives, 160; ratifying convention/debate, 252

rich, 51–52, 66, 112, 115, 293, 301, 402, 431, 444; and payment of fines, 395. *See also* poor; wealth

Richard I (King), 97

Richardson, Lynn, 88

Richmond, Virginia, 94, 191, 198, 230, 313, 325–26, 446; penitentiary in, 184

Richmond County, Georgia, 374

Richmond County, Virginia, 188

right to bear arms, 14, 390–93; Cesare Beccaria's views on, 14, 57; Thomas Jefferson's views on, 14, 57, 392; versus George III's compelling "our fellow Citizens taken Captive on the high Seas to bear Arms against their Country," 71; versus Quakers' refusal to bear arms, 113

right to life: in Bill of Rights, 409; Cesare Beccaria's views on, 42; concern for, 238; Daniel Tompkins, on, 268; in Declaration of Independence, 308; as natural right, 39–40; Robert Robinson on, 354; in state constitutions/declarations, 282, 300; Thomas Jefferson on, 408

right to remain silent, 390

right to vote: denial of, 11, 53; exercise of, 76; of minorities, 11, 440; of women, 11, 53, 440

rights: enumerated, 422; of individuals, 148; of man/"of mankind," 148, 271; retained by people, 410; unenumerated, 213, 422; universality of, 427. *See also* Bill of Rights; natural rights; *specific rights*

Rights of Man, 301, 442; Spanish translation of, 230

Rights of the British Colonies Asserted and Proved, The, 138, 250

Riot Act, 85

rioting, 329, 342. *See also* slave riot(s)/rebellion(s)

Risi, Paolo, 51, 469

Rittenhouse, David, 217, 307, 435; bust of, 314; on capital punishment, 227;

on penal laws, 227; and Pennsylvania constitution, 227

Rivington, New York *Gazetter*, 239

robbery, 229, 276, 386, 500; abolition for, 381; accessory to, 414–15; acts of, 167; as capital crime, 42, 102–3, 187, 274–75, 280, 282, 384, 407, 414; death sentences for, 121; as "effect of misery and despair," 393; executions for, 280; imprisonment for, 325, 385; punishment of, 283. *See also* burglary; theft

Robbins, Jonathan, 334. *See also* Nash, Thomas

Roberdeau, Daniel, 189

Roberts, John (Chief Justice), 409

Robertson, Archibald Gerald, 94

Robertson, Donald, 120

Robespierre, Maximilien, 4, 65, 316

Robinson, Robert, 354

Rochefoucauld, Duchesse de La, 116

Rochefoucauld, Louis-Alexandre la, 180, 302

Rochefoucauld-Liancourt, François-Alexandre-Frédéric duc de La, 175, 192–93, 245, 299

Rodney, Caesar, 220

Roe v. Wade, 410

Rogers, Alan, 102, 269, 525

Rogers, Henry, 348

Rogers, William, 322

Roman architecture, 313

Roman authors, 358. *See also specific authors*

Roman Catholic Church, 64, 248–49

Roman Catholic(s), xv, 28, 73, 88, 123, 248–49, 275, 288, 364; Volunteers, 151. *See also* Catholic(s)

Roman Coliseum, 26, 362

Roman constitution, 358

Roman emperors, 145, 286, 432

Roman Empire, 25, 220, 445

Roman generals, 432

Roman gladiators, 107, 216, 362

Roman government, 145

Roman history, 241, 285, 355–57, 362, 431–33, 436

Roman History, The, 356

Roman Inquisition, 35, 63

Roman law, xi, 26, 46, 55, 189, 222, 274, 333–35, 395, 402, 445, 543; books on, 387; compilation of, 264; and corporal punishments, 96; and executions, 129; as "full of cruel punishments," 222; and torture of slaves, 47. *See also* Justinian Code

Roman Nights, 30

Roman pseudonyms, 7, 358

Roman republic(anism), 7, 355, 358, 391, 431, 435, 543

Roman senate/senators, 357–58, 432

Romano, Anne, 295

Rome, Italy, 26–27, 75, 78, 95, 108, 112, 115–16, 118, 199, 252, 279, 369, 431, 470; Alessandro Verri in, 61, 71; ancient civilization/republic of, 432–33; anti-Jesuit sentiment in, 248; cellular confinement in, 328; citizens of, 356, 358; civil wars in, 356; executions in, 25–26; fall of, 125, 286; founding of, 357; glory/grandeur of, 253, 356, 358, 432; "imperial," 306; in Machiavelli's time, 178; Maria Cosway in, 105; punishments in, 542; slavery in, 145; Thomas Crawford's studio in, 313; torture in, 36; tyranny in, 145

Romilly, Samuel, 4, 15, 19, 238, 268, 415; and Cesare Beccaria, 19, 184, 221; death of, 415; on death penalty, 184, 221–22; on duels, 221; as member of Parliament, 220–21; and penal reform, 184, 220–22

Romulus, 357

Roosevelt, Eleanor, 427

Root, Erastus, 401

rope(s): around neck, 102, 373; cast over gallows, 373; lack of, 111; use in corporal punishments, 96; and torture, 361. *See also* hanging(s); noose(s)

Roscoe, William, 191–92

Rose, Charles, 268

Rosignan, Sigard, 423

Rosson, Trevor, 293

Rotália Beccárii, 437

Roth, Mitchel, 189

Rothman, David, 65–66, 138

"Rough Hewer, Jr.," 422

Rousseau, Jean-Jacques, 3, 16, 31, 54, 58–60, 63, 87, 104, 107, 195, 244, 470; and Cesare Beccaria, 33; commentary on, 92, 448; on death penalty, 63; influence of, 41, 175, 243, 362, 397, 431; and John Adams, 59, 175, 470; on liberty, 390; and Philip Mazzei, 197; social contract theory of, 29, 153, 455; on standing armies, 390; writings of, 79

Rowan, John, 344

Royal Society of London, 129

Rudiments of Law and Government, Deduced from the Law of Nature, 149

Rule of Law, 16, 19, 50, 300, 435, 453–54

Rumbold, Richard, 412

running the gauntlet, 238–39

Rush, Benjamin: and American Academy of Arts and Sciences, 130; as "American Beccaria," 270; background of, 5, 244; anti-slavery views of, 310; and Benjamin Franklin, 5, 211–12, 215–17, 325; on Bill of Rights, 213; and Bradford family, 244–45; and Cesare Beccaria, 4–5, 19, 22, 42, 79, 116, 126–27, 207, 212, 244–45, 270, 312, 325, 384, 387, 413, 433, 435, 437; and Christianity, 5, 203, 216, 310; on corporal punishments, 216; on cruelty, 216, 291; on death penalty, 5, 43, 74, 78–79, 88–89, 126–27, 203, 211–12, 217, 244, 264, 291, 310, 320, 384, 435, 439, 468; on Declaration of Independence, 441; on education, 216–17, 399; father of Richard Rush, 20, 173, 412–13, 415; on "good and evil," 216; on happiness, 244; and James Madison, 5, 207–9; and James McHenry, 309; and John Adams, 5, 178, 299–300, 387–88, 441; and John Dickinson, 147, 212; and John Howard, 212, 318; and John Morgan, 116; and John Witherspoon, 202–3; on liberty, 43; and

Louis XVI, 100; and Luigi Castiglioni, 12, 34, 129–30, 215–16; and Mathew Carey, 88; on "moral faculty," 216–17; and Noah Webster, 234; on peace, 310; and penal laws/reform, 5–6, 193, 212, 229, 244–45, 266, 310–11, 433; and Pennsylvania mutiny, 283; "Plan of a Federal University," 399; on prevention of crime, 212, 217; as Princeton graduate, 212; on prison(s)/penitentiaries, 212; on property, 43; on proportionality, 212; on public vs. private punishments, 212, 215–16, 266, 433; as "pupil and admirer of the celebrated Mr. Howard," 212; on republicanism, 217, 310; on revenge, 203; and Richard Price, 319–20; on "scale of punishments," 215; as signer of Declaration of Independence, 19; on slavery, 211, 217, 438; on social compact, 43; and Society for Promoting Political Enquiries, 266, 434–35; on solitary confinement, 216; on speedy punishments, 216; study of French, 120; study of Italian, 108; and Thomas Dobson, 90; and Thomas Jefferson, 5, 387–88, 468, 507; and Thomas Paine, 5, 145, 494; on vice, 216; on virtue, 216–17; and Voltaire, 146, 433; on war, 217; on "wheelbarrow" law, 211–12; and William Bradford, Jr., 43; writings of, 88, 90, 178, 208, 319–20; and yellow fever epidemic, 90, 244

Rush, Richard, 20; as Attorney General of the United States, 173, 414–15; and codification of U.S. law, 173, 412–13, 425; as Comptroller of the Treasury, 173; as Dr. Benjamin Rush's son, 173; on federal common-law jurisdiction, 414; on death penalty laws, 173, 414–15; and James Madison, 173; and Jeremy Bentham, 339, 415–16; as minister to Great Britain, 173, 339, 415–16; and penal reform, 416; as practicing lawyer, 173, 415; as Princeton graduate, 173

Rush Township, Pennsylvania, 437

Russia: anti-death penalty efforts in, 4, 209, 243, 346, 367; "barbarism of," 542; and Cesare Beccaria's influence, 3–4, 61–62, 64, 79, 98; czar/ruler of, 336, 416; duels in, 55; empress of, 98, 277; executions in, 367; and labor in mines, 277; and *On Crimes and Punishments*, 3; penal laws/punishments in, 62, 64, 281, 335, 413, 545; U.S. minister to, 267; John Howard's death in, 322

Rutgers College, 138

Rutland, Robert, 207

Rutledge, Edward, 11, 253, 434

Rutledge, John, 114–15

Rutledge, Jr., John, 114–15, 201

Sabacos (King), 167

Sabatier, William, 368

sacrilege, as capital crime, 26

Saga (Emperor), 367

Sainsbury, John, 83

St. Augustine, 268

St. Clair, Arthur, 9

St. George's Fields, 85–86

St. James's Park, 52

St. Lawrence River, 314

St. Paul's Church, 144

St. Paul's Churchyard, 78, 80–81, 87, 94, 402

St. Petersburg, Russia, 62, 98

St. Sepulchre, 278

Saint-Lambert, Jean-François, 58

Salem, Massachusetts, 12, 142, 303, 315

Salerni, Carlo, 35

Sallust, 356, 431, 503

Salzburg, Austria, 28

Samaha, Joel, 411

"sanguinary": as "attended with much bloodshed," 252; as "blood-thirsty," 540; as "bloody," 10, 317, 540; as "blood for blood," 315; as "bloody, murderous, cruel," 252, 263; "Britain," 360; as "cruel," 10, 252, 317, 540; definition/uses of, 72, 252–54, 263, 288–91, 298, 301, 315–17, 345,

349–50, 376, 395, 400, 442, 540; as "delighting in shedding of blood," 540; as "derived from a Latin word which signifies blood," 263; as "eager to shed blood," 252; laws/codes/punishments, xiii, 10, 20–21, 50, 103, 129, 138, 140, 147, 164, 168, 172, 187, 192, 203, 210, 214, 217, 233, 235, 237, 246, 250–55, 258–63, 268, 275, 279, 285–90, 293, 296, 298–99, 301, 303, 315–17, 322–23, 328–29, 333, 341–43, 345–46, 350, 370, 376, 388, 420, 439, 441–42, 448, 452, 540, 546; "men," 302; motives, 158; as "murderous," 252; as "murtherous," 540; results, 239; "spirit," 324, 361; system, 9, 235, 321, 331, 341; statutes, 76; used in juxtaposition to "penitentiary," 317

Santoro, Anthony, 21

Sarmiento, Martín, 463

Sarpi, Paolo, 357

saticide, 193

Satires Against the Tories, 210

Saudi Arabia, executions in, 450

Sauvigny, Berthier de, 442

Saxony, 103

Say, Jean-Baptiste, 551

scaffold, 74, 96, 302, 350, 442; as "infamous," 394. *See also* gallows; hanging(s)

Scalia, Antonin, 381, 452

Scandella, Giambattista, 314

scarlet letter, 373; and branding for adultery, 233

Scarlet Letter, The, 373

Schabas, William, 104, 369, 384

Schaeper, Thomas, 120

Schenectady, New York, 303

Schofield, Philip, 416

Schuyler, Philip, 168–69, 237, 239–40, 324

Schuylkill River, 151

Schwartz, Deborah A., 246

Science of Legislation, The, 132–36, 279

Scola, Giovanni, 521–22

scolding, crime of, 96, 296, 375

Scopoli, Giovanni, 35, 129

Scotland, 12, 77–79, 88–89, 163, 203, 244, 279; Benjamin Rush's studies in, 78–79; and Lord Kames, 388; monarch of, 288; prisons in, 19; torture in, 47, 371. *See also* Scottish Enlightenment

Scotland Yard, 126

Scott, Dred, 383

Scottish Enlightenment, 21, 29, 41, 78–79, 87, 146, 212, 313, 369

Scottish Inquisition, 47

Scotti, Francesco Gallarati, 51, 469

Scottish Law Magazine, The, 350

scripture, 236, 266; passages of, 40, 209, 263, 265–66, 274–75, 279; punishments based on, 294–95. *See also* Bible; New Testament; Old Testament

Scuola Palatine, 34, 469

seamen: laying violent hands on commander, 414; revolting on board, 414; punishment of, 446

Second Amendment, 14, 391–93

secret accusations/trials, 323, 389, 426

security: "against arbitrary Power," 299; "best"/"best means of," 64, 238; of community, 236; national, 43, 49; "perfect," 277; "personal," 111; public, 237, 414; right to, 427; of society, 36, 42, 54, 323, 386, 455. *See also* Universal Declaration of Human Rights

Sedgwick, Theodore, 386

sedition, 61, 64, 93, 199, 273. *See also* Alien and Sedition Acts

Sedition Act, 333, 411

seditious libel, 82–83, 279, 417. *See also* libel; slander

seduction of women, 282

Sega, James, 267

segregation, 382

Seine River, 100

seizure of papers, 84

Select Society of Edinburgh, 64

self-defense, 149, 269, 391–93, 424, 558

self-determination, 20, 212, 442; right to, 70

self-government, 412

self-incrimination, 390, 448; privilege against, 394; protection against, 390, 393, 395

Sellers, Tim, xii, 357–58, 431, 436

Sellon, Jean-Jacques de, 336

sentence(s). *See* death sentence(s); imprisonment; life imprisonment

Sentimental Dialogue Between Two Souls, in the Palpable Bodies of an English Lady of Quality and an Irish Gentleman, A, 77

Sentimental Journey through France and Italy, A, 137

serfdom, 132. *See also* slavery

separate-but-equal doctrine, 383

separation of church and state, 30, 251

separation of powers: concept of, 219–20; and Jean-Louis de Lolme, 106; and Montesquieu, 48, 220, 448; in U.S. Constitution, 219, 422

Servan, Joseph Michel Antoine, 59–60, 218

servitude, 149. *See also* forced labor; involuntary servitude

Seven Years' War, 79, 81–82, 124

Seventh Amendment, 214

Seward, William H., 268, 379

sewing up in sack, as punishment, 129

Shackelford, George Green, xi, 105, 113–16

shackles, 39; use of, 378. *See also* irons

Shakespeare, 71, 87, 181

shame, 111, 163, 170, 175, 293, 304, 374, 443; fear of, 394; feelings of, 393; public, 88, 293. *See also* public humiliation

Sharp, Granville, 354

Sharp, Samuel, 137

shaving beard, as punishment, 283

shaving head, as punishment, 283, 322

Shaw, Elizabeth Smith, 278

Shays, Daniel, 268

Shays' Rebellion, 7, 258, 268, 315

Shelley, Mary, 279

Shelley, Percy Bysshe, 279, 461

Sher, Richard, 79

Sherman, Roger, 332, 386, 434

Sherwood, Samuel, 374

Shippen, Edward, 113, 226, 435

Shippen, Joseph, 13, 118

Shippen, Peggy, 153

Shippen, Thomas Lee, 114–15, 130

Shomu (Emperor), 367

shooting, death by. *See* firing squad(s)

shooting rabbit, as capital crime, 20

Short, William, 100, 114–15, 313; in
    France, 100–1, 114–15, 130, 257; in
    Italy, 114–15, 220; in Spain, 302; and
    Thomas Jefferson, 114–15, 198, 341

Shury, Charles, 121

Siberia, 545

Sidney, Algernon, 75, 125, 194–95, 354,
    359, 551. *See also* Sydney, Algernon

Signing of the Declaration of Independence,
    102

silence, 192, 317. *See also* solitary con-
    finement

"Silence Dogood," 299

Simms, William Gilmore, 241

Simpson, James, 448–49, 562

Simsbury, Connecticut, 327

Sing Sing Prison, 328, 383

Sioux Uprising, 350–51

Sipe, Richard, 61, 422

Sixth Amendment, 58, 295–96, 426

*Sketch for a Historical Picture of the Progress
    of the Human Mind*, 448

*Sketch of the Laws Relating to Slavery in the
    Several States of the United States of
    America, A*, 254

Sketches of the Principles of Government,
    259–60, 448; as "very excellent ele-
    mentary book," 448

slander, 55, 225, 397, 445; as cause of duels,
    55

slave codes, 383

slave labor, 111–12, 211, 443, 446–47

slave riot(s)/rebellion(s), 11, 110, 350, 373,
    443; executions for, 156, 443; fear of,
    260

slave trade, 57, 184, 200, 382–83, 438, 442;
    abolition of, 382–83; in Great Britain,
    382–83; and U.S. Constitution, 438

Slave Trade Act of 1807, 383

slavery, 16, 178, 189, 217, 239, 260, 269,
    382, 439, 451; abolition of, 21, 280,
    294, 438; and common law, 405; cru-
    elty of, 47, 200; "death" as "better
    than," 75; and forced labor, 110–12;
    and founders, 11, 22, 110, 438; as
    human rights violation, 454; institu-
    tion of, 11; for life, 47, 162, 348; "Long
    Parliaments and," 76; opposition to,
    261; permanent/perpetual, 42, 47–48;
    as punishment for crime, 14, 21,
    47–48, 469; scourge of, 350; for "term
    of years," 162; and treason, 188; "un-
    happy moments of," 47. *See also* serf-
    dom; Thirteenth Amendment

Slavery Abolition Act of 1833, 383

slaves: bar on testimony of, 47; and bene-
    fit of clergy, 400; brutalization of,
    10–11, 111–12, 376, 442–43; colonists
    "degraded" into, 69; and Constitution,
    6; corporal punishments for, 373;
    emancipation of, 256; execution of,
    11, 26, 110, 156, 211, 350, 362, 443; in
    northern states, 442–43; ownership
    of, 110, 294, 415, 442–43; punish-
    ment/mistreatment of, 6, 385–86,
    446–47; in southern states, 385–86,
    446–47; torture of, 47; versus repub-
    licanism, 355; whipping of, 11, 376,
    442, 446–47

slitting the ears, 269. *See also* ear cropping

slitting the nostrils. *See* nose

Small, Abraham, 369

Small, William, 185

smallpox, 118

Smith, Abigail Adams, 127

Smith, Adam, 6, 79, 290, 360, 368, 551;
    on standing armies, 390–91

Smith, Catharine, 121

Smith, Charles, 231

Smith, Elihu, 101

Smith, Francis Scott Key, 342

Smith, Israel, 296–97

Smith, Jeremiah, 138, 175–76

Smith, Melancton, 8–9; and Cesare Beccaria, 8, 148, 431
Smith, Robert (architect), 89
Smith, Robert (printer), 89–90, 126
Smith, Thomas (jurist), 226
Smith, Thomas (Rev.), 129
Smith, William, 103
Smith, William, 156
Smith, William (Rep.), 387
Smith, William Stephens, 199
Smithers, William, 243–44, 317
Smollett, Tobias, 81
smuggling, 35, 56; as capital crime, 108
Snyder, Simon, 240
social clubs, 31. *See also specific clubs*
social compact: American, 381, 410; and Cesare Beccaria's views, 53–54, 353, 402, 427; concept of, 306; and death penalty, 348; and Dr. Benjamin Rush's views, 43; eighteenth-century, 440; English, 222; as excluding blacks, 382; as excluding women/children, 52–53; liberty as end of, 353; in Massachusetts, 300; Pietro Verri's views on, 355; and rights of people, 405; theory, 64, 153, 380, 397, 422, 450, 455
Social Contract, The, 29, 58–59, 63
social status, 292–93, 394
Società dei Pugni, 30. *See also* Academy of Fists
Società Patriottica, 130
Society for Constitutional Information, 353
Society for Promoting Political Enquiries, 266, 433–35
Society for the Abolition of Capital Punishment, 266
Society for the Abolition of the Slave Trade, 383
Society for the Prevention of Pauperism in the City of New York, 237
Society for the Promotion of Legal Knowledge, 412
Society for the Relief of Free Negroes Unlawfully Held in Bondage, 261

Society of Fists, 30. *See also* Academy of Fists
Society of Friends, 113, 128, 172, 226, 293–94, 308, 315, 324, 349, 421, 437. *See also* Quakers
Society of Jesus, 248. *See also* Jesuit(s)
Society of Supporters of the Bill of Rights, 86–87
Society of the Cincinnati, 358
Socrates, 99, 194
sodomy: abolition for, 381; as capital crime, xv, 26, 236, 274–75, 280, 282, 404, 411; castration for, 189, 193, 283; and citation to Cesare Beccaria's treatise, 298; as crime "difficult to prove," 44–45; punishment of, 183. *See also* "buggery"
Soering v. United Kingdom, 428
solitary confinement: in America, 127, 296, 325–28, 337; cells for, 192, 325; in England, 318, 325; in Europe, 190, 325–26; "long," 321; St. George Tucker's views on, 385; as substitute for corporal punishments, 323; as substitute for executions, 10, 237, 314; Thomas Jefferson's views on, 190, 326; use of, 10, 192, 317
solitude, 127, 140, 172, 216, 318, 320. *See also* silence, solitary confinement
Solitude in Imprisonment, 10
Solomon, 445
Solon, 26, 286, 288, 345, 445; code of, 26
"Solon," 358
Sonnenfels, Joseph von, 62, 365
Sons of Liberty, 68, 137, 179, 250, 301
Sophocles, 93
Sorbonne, 58, 95
South: capital offenses in, 190; Cesare Beccaria's influence in, 92; in Civil War, 438; colonies in, 190, 373; death penalty in, 190; discrimination in, 10–11, 385–86; executions in, 386, 450; lynchings in, 112, 280; penitentiaries in, 240; slavery/slave codes in, 260, 361, 383; and slave revolts, 373. *See also* slaves; slavery; *specific states*

South Africa, 21; apartheid in, 450; Constitutional Court of, 450; death penalty declared unconstitutional in, 450

South America, 97, 453

South Carolina, 7, 11, 111, 114–15, 118, 192, 204–5, 230, 240, 252, 333, 399; branding in, 373–74; case reporter, 91; College, 144, 348, 383; constitution, 256, 373; execution(s) in, 6; governor, 348–49; laws of, 209; legislature, 205–6, 374; penitentiary, 6, 205; and "proportionate" punishments, 256; plantation owners, 147, 443; and "sanguinary" punishments, 256; slaves in, 261; state convention, 6

South Carolina, 141

South-Carolina Weekly Gazette, 144

Southampton, England, 218

Sowerby, E. Millicent, 186

Spaight, Richard Dobbs, 396–97

Spain, 28, 30, 82, 204, 250, 302–3, 334, 413; abolition efforts in, 463; ambassador to, 437; and Cesare Beccaria, 4, 63; confessions/torture in, 200, 361; court of, 423; duels in, 55; execution(s) in, 29, 47; James Philip Puglia in, 230; and Jeremy Bentham, 205; minister to, 78; treaty with, 417

Spanish: books, 437; language, 337; law(s), 334–35; use/study of, 160, 230

Spanish Empire, 30

Spear, Charles, 157, 266, 299

Spectator, The, 30

Speech of Miss Polly Baker, The, 88, 122–23

speedy trial(s), 295; right to, 247, 426

Spelmen, Henry, 137

Spencer, Ambrose, 239, 538

Spirit of the Laws, The, 3–4, 9, 91–92, 145, 178, 203, 247, 346, 421; in grand jury charges, 499; influence of, 29, 41, 48, 219–20, 226, 233, 249–50, 328; publication of, 29, 233, 290; study of, 241

Spital Sermon, A, 393

Spotsylvania County, Virginia, 276

Springfield, Massachusetts, 122

spying, executions for, 103, 152–53

Stafford County, Virginia, 94

Staloff, Darren, 3

Stamp Act of 1765, 20, 68, 82, 250, 432

standing armies, 174, 390–91, 442

standing mute, 193, 222

Stanly, John, 397

Star Chamber, 222, 395

Star-Spangled Banner, The, 341, 345

Starkey, Armstrong, 162

state constitutions, 21, 245–48, 257–58, 263, 271, 299, 435, 440, 546; adoption of, 390; as based on "the most enlightened philosophy," 14; Cesare Beccaria's influence on, 270, 354, 368, 371, 442; and "cruel" punishments, 17–18, 21, 172, 439; and "cruel and unusual punishments," 17, 21, 282, 439; and "cruel or unusual punishments," 21; and "dignity of man," 14; French translation of, 135; and proportionality, 21, 172, 256, 263, 373–75; "humane principles" of, 14; and jury trials, 282, 301; as safeguarding individual rights/liberties, 367; and "sanguinary" laws/punishments, 17–18, 21, 192, 256, 263, 439; translation of, 302; and "unusual" punishments, 17, 439. *See also specific states*

state courts. *See individual states/courts*

State House (Philadelphia), 444

state legislators. *See specific legislators*; legislation

state of nature, 40, 135, 165, 402

State of the Prisons in England and Wales, The, 22, 212, 311, 328

state penitentiaries. *See* penitentiaries

state prison(s). *See* prison(s)

State Prisons and the Penitentiary System, 178

State v. Hirsch, 392

State v. Hobbs, 389

Statuary Hall, 313

Statue of Freedom, 313, 453

Statue of Liberty, 313

statutory penal codes, xv, 20

stealing: as capital crime, 26, 137–38, 237, 274, 288, 294; from church, 237;

whipping for, 88. *See also* burglary; horsestealing; robbery; theft
Steele, Richard, 30
Stefoff, Rebecca, 3
Steiker, Carol, 397
Steiker, Jordan, 397
Stephen, Adam, 156, 276
Stephen's Chapel, 101. *See also* British Parliament
Sterne, Laurence, 137, 160
Stevens, John Paul, 428–29
Stewart, David, 204
Stewart, Dugald, 448
Stiles, Ezra, 116, 129, 200, 202
Stith, Kate, 427
Stockdale, John, 448
stocks, 102, 169, 325, 371, 454; as "infamous" punishment, 394; use of, 121–22, 167, 169, 225, 233, 269, 275, 282–83, 290, 297, 361
Stockton, Richard, 202, 296
Stone, Thomas, 434
stoning to death, 302
Story, Joseph, 387, 391, 417–18; citation of Cesare Beccaria, 142; on David Hoffman's *A Course of Legal Study*, 140; as Harvard professor, 140; and Jeremiah Mason, 143; ownership of Cesare Beccaria's treatise, 208; as U.S. Supreme Court Justice, 208; writings/views of, 142
Strahan, William, 137
Strange, John, 253
Stranger in America, The, 380
strangling, 222
strangulation, 263
strap, 342, 376; as unconstitutional, 342. *See also* lashes; whipping
strappado, 96
Street, George, 77
Strickland, William, 311, 327
strict constructionism, 22
stripes, 96, 233, 274, 283–85, 323, 345, 376, 378, 418. *See also* lashes; whipping
Strong, Caleb, 400, 547

Strong, Return, 389
Stroud, George, 254
Stuart, John, 81–82
Stuart dynasty, 81, 222, 363, 366, 405, 410
suffering: physical, 449; psychological/mental, 449
suffocation, death by, 263
Suffolk County, England, 321–22; house of correction in, 321–22
suffrage: movement, 11, 52–53, 440; universal, 353. *See also* voting
Sugar Act of 1764, 250, 432
suicide: assisted, 399; attempted, 398–99; and Cesare Beccaria's treatise, 51, 182–83, 269, 397–99; consideration of, 298; as "Disease," 193; decriminalization of, 398–99; Dr. Benjamin Rush's views on, 43; and dragging body through streets, 60, 398; laws against, 397–99; of Marc-Antoine Calas, 60, 124; and French law, 60; as "mortal sin," 43; Thomas Jefferson's views on, 283; as "totally wrong," 43
Sullivan, James, 52–53, 258, 268–69; and penal reform, 315
Sullivan, John (Lieutenant), 309–10
Sullivan, John (Major General), 154
Sullivan, Robert, 167, 212, 215
Sullivan, Thomas, 37
sultans: cruelty of, 219
Summa Theologiae, 43
Summary View of the Rights of British America, A, 169–70
superstition: beliefs based on, 200, 232, 388; "cruel contrivances of," 323; and "ignorance," 12, 36; "of our ancestors," 10
Supreme Court, 58, 115, 138, 208, 233, 248, 303, 379, 417–18, 425; as arbiter of the law, 452; building/chamber, 286, 333, 355, 444–45; and "beyond a reasonable doubt" standard, 45; on bills of attainder/bills of pains and penalties, 246; citation of Cesare Beccaria, 15, 437; on common-law crimes, 58; creation of, 425, 444; on death penalty,

15, 375, 390, 450; and death-qualified juries, 294; and "death row phenomenon," 427–29; and Eighth Amendment, 22, 294, 390; on electrocution, 452; and "evolving standards of decency," 294, 452; on firing squad, 452; and Fourteenth Amendment, 383; Great Hall, 286; and habeas corpus, 15; on insane, 375, 450; on intellectually disabled, 375, 450; and judicial independence/review, 363; on juvenile offenders, 375, 450; on less culpable offenders, 375, 450; on lethal injection, 452; on "lingering" deaths, 390; members of, 196; motto, 450; old chamber of, 444; on proportionality, 375; on racial discrimination, 452; on rape, 375; reporter, 284; on torture, 390, 449; and victim impact evidence, 15, 437. *See also specific cases and Justices*

Supreme Economic Council of Milan, 61
"sweatbox," 376
Sweden, 359; king(s) of, 336, 559; torture abolished in, 45, 365
Swift, Zephaniah, 88, 233–36, 385
Swinburne, Henry, 290
Swiss cantons, 243
Switzerland, 106, 161, 221, 228, 336, 358, 422. *See also* Swiss cantons
Sydney, Algernon, 63, 79; and Thomas Jefferson, 448. *See also* Sidney, Algernon
Sylla, 356
Synder, Simon, 416
System of Moral Philosophy, A, 41–42
System of the Laws of the State of Connecticut, A, 235
Szabo, Franz A. J., 29, 34, 62–63

Tableau de Paris, 257
Tacitus, 145, 356, 431, 503
Taft, William Howard, 440
Tagliaferro family, 231
Taizong of Tang (Emperor), 367
Take Your Choice!, 76
Talbot County, Maryland, 248

Tale of Two Cities, A, 139
Taliaferro, Elizabeth, 230
Taliaferro, Francis, 231
Taliaferro, John, 231
Taliaferro, Lawrence, 231
Taliaferro, Richard, 230–31
Taliaferro, Samuel, 231
Taliaferro, William, 231
Tallack, William, 349–50
Talliaferro, Francis, 231
Talliaferro, Nicola, 230
Talliaferro, Richard, 230
Talliaferro, William, 231
Tappan, New York, 153
Tarpeian Rock, 26
Tarquin(s), 357, 359, 503
Tasso, Torquato, 177
taxation, 8, 299, 353, 432; without representation, 26, 32, 142
Tayloe, John, 187–88
Taylor, George Keith, 261; bill/legislation of, 190–91, 507; as embodying "principles of Beccaria," 190; and John Adams, 175; and penal reform, 190–91, 261, 385; and penitentiary system, 329
Taylor, John, 125
Tell, William, 359
Temple, William, 407
Temple Bar, 442
Ten Commandments, 361; "Thou Shalt Not Kill," 343, 361
Tennessee: anti-dueling law, 397; fines in, 397; penitentiary in, 325; Superior Court of Law and Equity, 360–61
tenter-hooks, 375
Tenth Amendment, 213, 410, 422
terror, 304, 318, 350; of death, 205; effect of pardons on, 236; and life imprisonment vs. executions, 210; "lost" through "frequency" of hanging, 330; and methods of execution, 224; momentary, 236; "of example," 167; and "Sanguinary Laws," 246; and severity of punishments, 219; "to evil-minded

disposition," 340; "to others," 321; versus "resentment," 154

terrorism, 449

Tessé, Adrienne Cathérine de Noailles de, 101

Texas: executions in, 450

textualism, 22

Thaxter, John, 125, 252

Théâtre des Italiens, 177

theft, 137, 147, 204, 207, 263, 307, 389; abolition efforts for, 17, 19; branding for, 122; as capital crime, 26, 48, 137–38, 160, 169, 233, 275, 280, 289–90, 384, 407; from church, 169, 237; petty, 138, 290; and proportionality of punishment, 218; punishment of, 49, 102, 233, 258, 280, 284–85, 297, 378; "trifling," 269

Theodosian Code, 25

Théorie des lois criminelles, 437

Theory of Criminal Laws, 398

Theory of Legislation, 343

Theory of Moral Sentiments, The, 290

Theory of Punishments, 335

Theresa, Maria (Empress), 28–29, 31, 33–34, 44, 62–64, 118, 126, 130, 365, 489. *See also* Austria; Habsburgs

thieves: as "infamous Persons," 394

Thirteenth Amendment, 14, 21; approval/ratification of, 380, 383, 409

Thiry, Paul-Henri (Baron d'Holbach), 33, 59–60, 83

Thomas, A. C., 287–88

Thomas, Aaron, 120

Thomas, Clarence, 452

Thomas, Isaiah, 88

Thomasius, Christian, 243

Thomson, Charles, 13, 68, 137

Thornton, Anna, 342

Thornton, William, 312–14, 342

Thoughts in Prison, 145

Thoughts on Education, 278

Thoughts on Executive Justice, 49, 217

Thoughts on Penitentiaries, 254

Thoughts on the Education of Daughters, 278

Thoughts on the Punishment of Death for Forgery, 18

Three-fifths Clause, 438

Three Prisons Act, 347

Thucydides, 178

thumbscrew: as cruel, 452; use of, 223, 361

Tilghman, Matthew, 248

Tilghman, Tench, 110–11

Titus (Emperor), 362, 367

tobacco: notes/certificates, 190; embezzling/smuggling of, 190; use of, 40

Tocqueville, Alexis de, xv, 13, 127, 139, 381–84, 451

toes: amputation of, 376

toga(s), 356, 453

toleration: "apostles of," 48; ideal of, 220. *See also* religious toleration

Tomahawk!, 289

Tompkins, Daniel, 268

tongue: boring through, 129, 394; cutting/pulling out, 129, 273, 360, 397

Tonry, Michael, 4

Tories, 102, 111, 167, 210; during Revolutionary War, 277; execution/killing of, 153; spying by, 153; sympathizers of, 214

Tortuna, Italy, 108

torture, 51, 60, 64, 74, 137, 142, 323, 372, 427; as "abhorrent and disagreeable to our natures," 157; abolition of, 45, 62, 74, 364–67, 384, 389; and Bill of Rights, 200, 390; "bloody hand of," 361; citation of Cesare Beccaria with respect to, 361, 389; common law vs. civil law, 107; and confessions/false confessions, 28, 44, 361, 366, 372, 389–90, 382; consensus against, 21, 369, 376, 389–90; of criminals, 164, 376–78; as cruel, 44–45, 365; death sentences as, 449–51; definition of, 449–50; in England, 222–23; executions as, 450–51; in Europe, 28, 46–47, 223, 305, 366, 384, 389; "for bringing the Verity to Light," 47; forms of, 305; founders' views of, 200, 378, 389, 395; in France, 46; "horrid concomitants" of, 448; "horrid spectacles" of, 42; and infliction of pain/suffering, 38, 44–46, 449–50; and innocence, 553; instruments of, 47, 200, 223; and international law, 364, 389, 449–50; as investigative technique, 366; judicial, 29, 46–47, 62, 124, 361, 365–66; lethal vs. non-lethal acts of, 450; "monstrous nature of," 448; as "practice repugnant to reason, justice, and humanity," 223; and Patrick Henry, 13, 200; physical, 449–50; "practiced in the age of Beccaria," 48; "preliminary," 365; "preparatory," 365; and "proofs," 45; psychological/mental, 449–50; as "queen of torment," 361; revulsion against, 375; "ridicule of," 371; in Rome, 36; in Scotland, 371; of slaves, 376; in Tuscany, 161; and tyranny, 363; use of, 222–23, 389; warrants, 46. *See also* judicial torture

Tothill Field Prison, 103

Toulouse, France, 59, 64, 107, 123–24, 243; parliament of, 60

Tower of London, 40, 82–83, 222–23, 246, 371

Town and Country, 148, 401

Townshend Revenue Act(s) of 1767, 250, 292, 432

trade, 32, 194, 432. *See also* commerce

Traité des délits et des peines, 27, 58, 95, 120. *See also On Crimes and Punishments*

Traité sur la tolerance, 107, 124, 178

traitors, 170, 438; classification as, 440; execution/hanging of, 26, 255; as "infamous Persons," 394; punishment of, 255

Trajan (Emperor), 367

transatlantic book trade, 11, 144, 156, 249

"Transfuge," 58

transportation: British use of, 52, 98, 122, 161, 210, 225, 317–18, 331; as punishment, 10, 98, 225, 236, 380; of slaves, 376; as substitute for executions, 210

Transportation Act of 1718, 161

Transylvania University, 336, 344, 413

Trattato delle virtù e dei primi, 368

Tratto dei Delitti e delle Pene, 160. *See also Dei delitti e delle pene*

Travels in India, 252

Travels in Italy, 114

Travels in the Two Sicilies in the Years 1777, 1778, 1779, and 1780, 290

Travels Through the Country of North America, 192

Travels through the Middle Settlements of North America, 32

Treadway, W. R. H., 91

treason, 73, 135, 180, 263, 400; against the United States, 381; and Alien and Sedition Acts, 333; as capital crime, 7, 9, 16, 26, 133, 160, 169, 183, 187, 189, 193, 224, 227, 234, 236–37, 274–75, 280, 282, 291, 295, 299, 324, 370, 372, 381, 385, 411, 414, 419, 426, 500; and charge against Aaron Burr, 204; and common law, 255; concept of, 381; and congressional debate, 381–82; and "conspiracy to overthrow the government," 209; crime of, 258, 283; death sentences/executions for, 291, 412; definition of, 381; and English law, 255; high, 273, 283, 291; "highest species of," 209; imprisonment for, 240; and lack of honor, 394; petty, 283; "pretended," 159; punishment of, 258; rescuing person convicted of, 414; and slavery, 188; trials for, 295; and two-witness rule, 162, 381–82; and U.S. Constitution, 381–82; and women, 276

Treason Clause, 162, 381–82

treaties, 213; ratification of, 357, 449; reservations to, 449; as "supreme Law of the Land," 213. *See also specific treaties*

Treatise of Human Nature, A, 32

Treatise of Judicial Proof, 335

Treatise of the Pleas of the Crown, A, 269

Treatise on Courts Martial, A, 368

Treatise on Executive Clemency in Pennsylvania, 243, 317

Treatise on Man, His Intellectual Faculties and His Education, A, 149

Treatise on Political Economy, A, 551

Treatise on Poverty, Its Consequences, and the Remedy, A, 368

Treatise on the Breeding and Management of Livestock, A, 368

Treatise on the Law of Evidence, A, 368

Treatise on the Law of Prerogatives of the Crown, A, 399

Treatise on the Police of the Metropolis, A, 4

Treatise on Tolerance, 146

Treatise on Virtues and Rewards, A, 79, 279, 368–69

Treaty of Paris, 12, 229, 255, 299, 435

Trenchard, John, 194, 390

Trenton, New Jersey, 171

trial by battle, 406

trial by jury. *See* jury trial

trinity: speaking "impiously or maliciously" against, 189

Trinity College, 78

"Triple Tree," 278. *See also* Tyburn

Tripoli, 254

"Tristram Shandy," 77

Tron, Andrea, 35

Trop v. Dulles, 294

Trotter, George, 558

Trudaine, Madame, 60

True American, 171, 262

Trumbull, John (lawyer-poet), xiii, 100, 102, 130

Trumbull, John (painter), xiii, 41, 100, 102–3, 105, 130, 313

Trumbull, Jonathan (governor), 101, 103, 109

Trumbull, William, 482

truth(s), 39, 45, 259, 365, 441; as "basis of civil policy and jurisprudence," 174; "evangelical," 251; "Invincible," 175; "self-evident," 16, 70

Tucker, St. George, 145, 261, 271, 369–70, 384–86; as Annapolis delegate, 255; and annotation of William Blackstone's treatise, 223–24; and Cesare Beccaria's treatise, 384

Tucker's Blackstone, 369

Tudor dynasty, 222, 366, 405

Tufts University, 95

Tuileries Gardens, 104

Turgot, Anne-Robert-Jacques, 58, 60, 503

Turin, Italy, 72, 108, 114, 116–17, 252, 470, 480; citadel of, 36; court of, 423

Turnbull, Andrew, 32

Turnbull, Robert, 192–93, 211–12

Turpin, Philip, 184

Turra, Antonio, 257

Turra, Elisabetta Caminer, 256–57, 521–22

Tuscan(y), 27, 118, 161, 196–98, 322, 466; and Cesare Beccaria's treatise, 3, 26, 336; commissioner to, 252; death penalty's abolition in, 4, 66, 74, 104, 136–37, 199, 209, 212, 228, 243; dialect, 30; executions in, 26; "language," 177, 196; laws/penal code of, 51, 66, 161–62, 199, 335; minister from, 253; punishments in, 161–62; and Tagliaferro family, 231; torture abolished in, 389

'Twas the Night Before Christmas, 119

Twelve Tables, 26, 189, 222

Twelve Years a Slave, 112

Two Treatises of Government, 41

two-witness rule, 46, 365–66

Tyburn, 49, 145, 273, 277–78, 314

Tyler, Alice F., 293

Tyler, Royall, 552

tyranny, 26, 36, 54, 70, 73, 75, 132–33, 140, 197, 200, 253, 273–74, 289, 307, 331–32, 354, 357–60, 401, 432, 440, 442; "absolute," 143; British, 308, 342, 392, 433, 436; Cesare Beccaria's views on, 14, 38, 51, 353; "civil," 363; "Civil & Religious," 195; constraint of, 355; "ecclesiastical," 234, 363; English, 20; "feudal," 234; founders' views on, xv, 152; "hand of," 152; James Wilson's views on, 164; of majority, 409; Montesquieu's views on, 343; "over the people," 10; "taxation without representation" as, 142; and "unbridled majorities," 100; and unnecessary punishments, 16, 172, 343; versus judicial independence, 363; "Victim of," 175

tyrant(s), 71, 119, 159, 170–71, 234, 273, 330, 364, 391; criminals as, 179; men as, 311; petty, 378; "sanguinary" behavior of, 316

Tyson, Job, 298

Tytler, Alexander Fraser, 388

Ullmann v. United States, 393, 437

Ulm, Germany, 27

unalienable rights, 7, 41, 70, 143, 212, 236, 300, 362, 428, 438; as "essential Limitations in all Governments," 41. *See also* inalienable rights

Union Library, 145

United Kingdom, 449. *See also* England; Great Britain

United Nations, 449; Convention Against Torture and Other Cruel, Inhuman or Degrading Treatment or Punishment, 389, 427, 449; General Assembly resolutions, 427; International Covenant on Civil and Political Rights, 427; Standard Minimum Rules for the Treatment of Prisoners, 427; Universal Declaration of Human Rights, 427

United States: Army, 204, 351; as "asylum for the oppressed," 359–60; Attorney General, 6, 20, 169–70, 173, 225, 262, 330, 412–14, 433, 437, 440, 500, 558; Capitol, 16, 102, 312–14, 326, 362, 444, 453; Circuit Court for the District of Columbia, 284; Circuit Court for the Fourth Circuit, 175; Code, 22, 417; as "common law" country, 411; Comptroller of the Treasury, 173; as "conceived in Liberty," 16; as country of immigrants, 358–59, 432; Court of Appeals for the Eighth Circuit, 342; as "dedicated to the proposition that all men are created equal," 16; "early in-

fluenced by the views of Beccaria," 216; emigration to, 8, 201, 277, 313, 358–59, 363, 410; First Bank of the, 173; formation of, 19, 148, 218, 441; House of Representatives, 9, 140, 186, 202, 210, 333, 357–58, 374, 379, 383, 386–87, 418, 420–21; as "land of liberty, independence, and equality," 278; as "land of promise," 376; Minister to France, 140, 157, 341; Mint, 109; penitentiaries, 314, 316, 325, 330–31, 346–47; as perpetual Union, 359; Secretary of Navy, 20; Secretary of State, 170–71, 173, 182, 334, 383; Secretary of Treasury, 88, 230, 266–67, 371, 416; Secretary of War, 13, 156, 158, 267, 292, 309; Senate/Senator, 9, 102–3, 140, 143, 186, 202, 230, 239, 252, 262, 266–67, 357–60, 371, 379, 409, 417–18, 420, 425, 444, 453; State Department, 94; territories, 9; Vice President(s), 204, 224, 266–68, 284, 396. *See also* Bill of Rights; Confederation Congress; Congress; Constitution; Continental Congress; military; President(s); Supreme Court; *specific jurisdictions*

United States-Dakota War, 350–51

United States v. Coolidge, 417

United States v. Cornell, 293

United States v. Hudson, 417

Universal Declaration of Human Rights, 427

Universal Magazine, 320

universal suffrage, 353

University of Bologna, 355

University of Chicago, 33, 454

University of Connecticut, 239

University of Edinburgh, 79, 116, 239, 423

University of Glasgow, 41, 78

University of Heidelberg, 135

University of Lieden, 83

University of Maryland, 140, 413

University of Minnesota, 4, 152

University of Naples, 39, 117

University of North Carolina, 92

University of Oxford, 128
University of Pavia, 28, 35, 129, 267
University of Pennsylvania, 163, 227
University of Pittsburgh, 223
University of Prince Edward Island, 397
University of Southern California, 435
University of Tennessee, 29
University of Texas, 397
University of Turin, 117
University of Valencia, 437
University of Vienna, 62
University of Virginia, 94, 387
"unusual": meaning of, 406. *See also* "cruel
    and unusual punishments"
unwholesome food/drink: punishment for
    distributing, 282–83
unwritten laws/rights, 339, 408, 410. *See*
    also Ninth Amendment; Tenth
    Amendment
Upham, Thomas, 94, 242
Urgent Necessity of an Immediate Repeal of
    the Whole Penal Code against the
    Roman Catholics, The, 88
Urie, Robert, 78–79
Urofsky, Melvin, 399, 427
Utica, New York, 341
utilitarian(ism), 6, 14–15, 19, 37, 149, 202,
    204, 277, 280; philosophy of, 99
utility, 4, 98, 297, 337, 347, 416; common,
    54; principle of, 143; public, 185, 203,
    275
utopias, 21

vagrancy: whipping for, 373
Valaze, Dufriche de, 212
"Valentine," 246
Valley Forge, 112, 356
Valois, Jeanne de Saint-Rémy de, 198–99
Van Buren, Martin, 264, 401, 403
Van Rensselaer, J. S., 380
Van Schaack, Peter, 148, 290, 496
Vance, Joseph, 242
Varnum, James Mitchell, 9
Vasa, Gustavas, 359
Vasco, Francesco Dalmazzo, 133
Vatican, 36, 115, 328

Vattel, Emmerich de, 39, 41, 125, 186, 247,
    431, 448
Vaughan, Benjamin, 45, 130, 217–18, 220
Vaughan, Charles, 435
Vaughan, John, 130, 489
Vaughan, Samuel, 277
Vaughan, Jr., Samuel, 435
Vaughn, Mr., 129
Vaux, Richard, 226–27, 329
Vaux, Roberts, 244, 255, 340–41, 540
Veneroni, Giovanni, 502
Venetian Inquisition, 63
Venetian Republic, 521
vengeance, 159, 180, 211, 223, 233, 244,
    249, 264, 267, 280–81, 305, 346, 351,
    388, 420; "belongs not to man," 419. *See*
    also revenge
Venice, Italy, 4, 27, 35, 64, 115–16, 119,
    178, 201, 253, 257, 313–14
Vercelli, Italy, 108
Verme, Francis (Francesco) dal, 108–9,
    113–15
Vermont, 129, 158, 258–59; abolition of
    slavery in, 256; admission to Union,
    345; constitution, 256, 296–97, 370,
    375; corporal punishments in, 296–98;
    Declaration of Rights, 390; General
    Assembly, 297; and hard labor, 297;
    invocation of Cesare Beccaria in, 389;
    governor, 296; legislature, 315; and
    "sanguinary" punishments, 256, 296;
    state prison/penitentiary, 297–98, 325;
    Supreme Court, 375; Supreme Court
    of Judicature, 389–90, 552
Vernet, Jacob, 29
Verona, Italy, 108, 116
Verri, Alessandro, 30–31, 34, 60, 63–64,
    71, 108, 114, 117, 473; and Academy
    of Fists, 33–35; and Benjamin
    Franklin, 117; and Cesare Beccaria,
    31, 33–34, 60, 63–64, 71, 130; and
    Luigi Castiglioni, 128; as "protector of
    prisons," 30, 33; in Rome, 61
Verri, Carlo, 31
Verri, Gabriele, 30
Verri, Giovanni, 71

Verri, Pietro, 12, 30–32, 34, 60, 63–64, 71, 73–74, 79, 108, 114, 117, 355, 473, 521; and Academy of Fists, 33–35; and Adam Smith, 290; and Cesare Beccaria, 31–35, 60, 63–64, 71, 130, 290, 364; on "greatest equality possible," 355; and Luigi Castiglioni, 128; on "social pact," 355; on torture, 71, 364; on "well-being of each individual," 355

Versailles: court of, 109; garden of, 119

Vertot, René Aubert de, 356

Vespucci, Amerigo, 453

vestal virgins, execution of, 26

Viaggio, 12–13, 34, 109–12, 128, 130, 270, 373, 442, 447

Vicenza, Italy, 115–16

Vickers, Jesse, 215

Vickers, Solomon, 215

Vico, Giambattista, 31, 521

victim impact evidence, 15, 437

victim(s) of murder. *See* homicide(s)

Vienna, Austria, 29, 58, 62, 118–19

View of the Constitution of the United States, A, 142

View of the Customs, Manners, Drama, etc. of Italy, A, 137

View of the Hard-Labour Bill, A, 95, 98–99

View of the New-York State Prison, A, 192

Vigo, Giuseppe Maria Francesco, 230

Villareggio, Italy, 33

Vindication of the British Colonies, A, 138

Vindication of the Rights of Men, A, 278

Vindication of the Rights of Women, A, 278

Vindiciæ Gallicæ, 48

violence, 6, 69, 104, 107, 259. *See also specific forms of violence*

violent crimes, 42, 47, 50–51. *See also specific crimes*

Virgil, 93, 125, 178

Virginia, 11, 106–8, 112–14, 118, 130, 146, 177, 195–96, 198, 200–1, 255, 261, 288, 307, 384, 395, 399, 405, 413, 428, 441; act of 1796, 175; anti-death penalty efforts in, 6, 240; attorney general, 170; bar, 94, 369; benefit of clergy abolished in, 400; capital cases/crimes in, 183, 187, 189–91; capitol, 190, 326; Cesare Beccaria's treatise in, 94–95; colony of, 184; Committee of Revisors, 193, 195, 209, 370; circuit court, 94; Commissioner for Prisoners, 325; Commonwealth of, 9, 47, 184, 188, 190, 196–97, 207, 231, 326, 386; concealing property in, 190; constitution, 197, 245; convention, 112, 199, 245, 369; corporal punishments in, 269, 283; Council, 197; courts in, 309; "cruel and unusual punishments" clause, 382, 390; Declaration of Rights, 17, 75, 151, 199–200, 245–46, 370, 382, 390–91, 395; draft constitution, 9, 47, 188, 391; dueling in, 396; ear cropping in, 269; emigration to, 40, 112, 201; executions in, 11, 185, 156, 450; General Assembly, 47, 190, 209, 370; General Court, 94, 185; governor, 156, 170, 190, 196–98, 276, 325, 400, 443; grand jury charges, 164, 285–86; hard labor/incarceration in, 540; Historical Society, 94; horse-stealing in, 262, 344; House of Burgesses, 112, 250; House of Delegates, 94, 190, 261; legislature, 6, 9, 94, 187–88, 190–91, 206–7, 251, 282, 331, 357, 364; militia, 231; pardon(s) in, 185, 191, 443; penal code/reform in, 3, 19, 175, 190–1, 193–95, 197, 232, 240, 254, 261–62, 326–27, 345, 372, 381, 384–85; prison(s)/penitentiary in, 184, 190, 313, 325–26, 329–32, 341, 385–86; ratifying convention, 10, 390; receiving stolen horse in, 190; Regiment, 155, 231, 276; religious freedom in, 251, 364; slave codes in, 383; slave rebellion(s)/revolt(s) in, 11, 373, 443; slavery in, 11, 189, 400, 443; Special Court of Appeals, 94; stealing hogs in, 190; study of law in, 184–85; Supreme Court, 382; Talliaferro family in, 230–31; and testimony of blacks/slaves in, 47, 189, 191; and tobacco-related offenses, 190;

and torture, 369; transportation to, 52; treatment of slaves in, 112, 373; whipping in, 112, 373

Virginia Evangelical and Literary Magazine, The, 190

Virginia Gazette, 395–96

"Virginia Play," 376

virtue, 165, 216–17, 247, 320, 356, 358–59, 401, 445; "example of," 111; men of, 285, 323; of representatives, 199; as "soul of a republic," 216

Visconti, Matteo, 471

Visconti dominions, 471

Visit to the Philadelphia Prison, A, 192

Vitalli, Anthony, 113

Voltaire, 3–4, 94, 116, 252; and André Morellet, 33; and Benjamin Franklin, 123, 146; and Benjamin Rush, 146; and Casanova, 198; and Cesare Beccaria, 4, 19, 33, 59, 62, 87, 95, 104, 108, 146, 186–87, 218, 433; commentary of, 27–28, 36, 59, 64, 75, 80, 94–95, 103, 119, 137, 146–47, 186, 271, 298, 470; commentary on, 92, 448; on corporal punishments, 103; and criticism of English law, 279; on death penalty, 58–59, 103, 146–47, 388; on desertion, 58; on disproportionate punishments, 147; on English law, 280; on executioners, 59; and Frederick II, 61; and Giuseppe Gorani, 79; on "half proofs," 59; on hanging, 59, 146; influence of, 3, 27–28, 124, 239, 241, 251, 349, 368, 389, 431, 498; on innocence, 45; and Jean Calas, 28, 59, 81, 123–24, 146; and John Locke, 16; and John Wilkes, 87; on judges "fond of spilling human blood," 147; on "labour for the public," 147; on "labour on some public works," 59; and penal reform, 104, 146; and Philip Mazzei, 197; on proportionality, 147; on Quakers, 128; and religious tolerance, 124; on "sanguinary" tribunals and laws, 147; and Thomas Jefferson, 182; on tolerance/freedom of religion,

124, 178, 364; on torture, 366–67; writings/views of, 41, 79, 108, 124–25, 144, 147, 156, 178, 192, 243, 256, 365, 440

voting, 52–53, 76; and denial of rights, 11; and African-Americans, 440; of representatives, 301; and women's rights, 440

Voting Rights Act of 1965, 440

Vouglans, Muyart de (Pierre-François Murat de), 59–60, 365

Wagoner, Jennings, 244

Waldseemüller, Martin, 453

Wales: Prince of, 105; prisons in, 19, 22, 311, 328

Walker, Robert J., 371

Walker's Hibernian Magazine, 291

Wall, Rachel, 102–3

Wall Street, 332

Wallace, Mike, 169

Walnut Street Jail/Prison, 89, 168, 172, 192, 299, 325, 327, 433, 450

war(s), 42, 178, 217, 422; between France and Great Britain, 50, 302; eighteenth-century, 44; and executions, 163; as impeding progress/human rights, 21; involving France, 50, 250, 302; involving Spain, 250; "necessary," 159; and "oceans of blood," 46; as slowing anti-death penalty momentum, 269–70; times of, 163; "unending state of," 54. *See also* Articles of War; *specific wars*

War of 1812, 21, 191, 341, 346, 390, 414, 416, 503

War of Independence. *See* Revolutionary War

War of the Austrian Succession, 28, 35, 44, 49

Warburton, William, 82

Ward, Harry, 293, 440

Ward, Henry, 207

Ward, Samuel, 80

Warren, James, 249

Warren, Joseph, 87, 327, 356, 432

Warren, Mercy Otis, 142

Washington, Bushrod, 312, 381

Washington, D.C., 16, 186, 251, 255, 312, 314, 342; and Congress's power to legislate, 10; creation of, 10, 104–5, 307, 540; emancipation of slaves in, 313; and fear of "sanctuary of the blackest crimes," 10; mayor of, 412; penitentiary for, 421; sentencing practices in, 284–85; U.S. Attorney for, 342; and U.S. Supreme Court building, 286

Washington, George, 9, 12, 19, 100, 102, 104–5, 109–10, 136, 171; address of, 359; and Alexander Hamilton, 400; as *American Museum* subscriber, 244; and Andrew Burnaby, 32; on "arbitrary proceedings," 299; birthday of, 359; and Bushrod Washington, 381; bust of, 313–14; and Cesare Beccaria's treatise, 5, 151–52, 431; and Charles Asgill, 157–58, 291–92; and Charles Carroll of Carrollton, 248; "Cloaths of," 276; as commander/general, 22, 101, 103, 111, 151–58, 252, 254, 303, 359, 365, 371; and Continental Congress, 151–52, 155–56, 444; on corporal punishments, 276, 292; and Count dal Verme, 109; court appointments of, 425; on death penalty, 151–52, 154–56, 276, 292; on desertion, 276; and Edmund Randolph, 170; and Elias Boudinot, 158; on factions, 359; farewell address of, 359–60; fighting for liberty, 360; on "frequency" of executions, 151, 155–56; and General Charles Lee, 161; and George Mason, 151; and George Wythe, 186; on "hand of tyranny," 152; and Henry Knox, 156, 292; and honorary French citizenship, 303; on "Inhuman Treatment," 157; on "intermediate" punishment between death and 100 lashes, 151; and James McHenry, 309; and James Wilson, 163; and Jean-Louis de Lolme, 106; and John Adams, 292; and John and Lucy Paradise, 106, 201; and John Banister, 112; and John Blair, 196; and John Jay, 167; and John Jebb, 195; on "Law of retaliation," 157; and Lewis Nicola, 230; and Luigi Castiglioni, 12, 110–11, 129; on Major John André, 153–54; at Mount Vernon, 110, 358; on "necessity of frequent pardons," 152; and Noah Webster, 234; oath of office of, 332; and Paolo Andreani, 119, 200–2; pardons/clemency decisions of, 152, 154–55, 400; and Philip Mazzei, 196–97; as President, 5, 103, 176, 319; on "preventing crimes," 152; on proportionality, 155; on punishment/ "punishing Delinquents," 152, 154; and resignation speech, 358; and Robert Coram, 141; and Robert Dinwiddie, 276; on "sanguinary" punishments, 254; as slaveowner, 11, 22; and Society for Constitutional Information, 354; and Society of the Cincinnati, 358; and Thomas Bird, 426; and Valley Forge, 356; and William Bradford Jr., 170, 245; and William Rawle, 142; and William Talliaferro (Taliaferro), 231; and Yale College's honorary degree, 319

Washington, Martha, 106, 151

Washington City Gazette, The, 362

Washington (State): penitentiary in, 347

waterboarding, 46, 200, 449

Watson, John, 287

Watterston, George, 362–63

Way, Andrew, 412

"We the People," 422, 446, 455. *See also* Constitution; people

wealth, 50–51, 76; and high-status punishments, 394. *See also* poor; poverty; rich

Wealth of Nations, The, 6, 290, 360, 391, 448, 551

Webster, Daniel, 280–81, 417–21; and Jeremiah Mason, 143; and Joseph Story, 417–18; and William Blackstone's *Commentaries*, 223

Webster, Noah, 66, 88, 129–30, 148, 234, 252, 263
Weehawken, New Jersey, 204
wehrgeld, 160
Weightman, Roger, 412
Weinman, Adolph, 445
Welsh, Molly, 307
West, Benjamin, 13, 103, 118
West Indies, 261, 292, 313, 376
West Jersey, colony of, 232
West Point, New York, 153, 284
West Virginia: attorney general's report, 428; constitution, 374
Western civilization, 453
Western lands. *See* Northwest Ordinance of 1787
Western Medical Gazette, 372
Western State Penitentiary, 327
Westfield, Massachusetts, 122
Westminster, 86
Wharfield, Priscilla, 122
Wharton, Francis, 240
Wharton, Thomas, 341
What Is True Civilization, or Means to Suppress the Practice of Duelling, to Prevent, or to Punish Crimes, and to Abolish the Punishment of Death, 266
"wheelbarrow" law, 211, 322–23
"wheelbarrow" men, 184, 211–12, 287
Wheeler, Ephraim, 315
Wheeler, Glazier, 377
Whig Almanac, The, 424–25
Whig(s), 30, 77, 81, 111, 214, 276–77, 353, 391; "Committees," 102
whipping, 6, 9, 96, 102, 123, 129, 233, 237, 247, 276, 282–84, 407, 451; abandonment/abolition of, 287, 297, 371, 407, 454; for adultery, 373; as "bad punishment," 348; in colonial America, 169, 275–76; of criminals/villains, 377–78, 420; as "cruel," 540; in England, 225, 321; in Europe, 199, 273–74, 321; as "ineffectual," 163; as "infamous" punishment, 394; as military discipline, 151, 163, 284–85, 447; "moderate infliction of," 407; "out of

the State," 162; post(s), 102, 269, 276, 287, 298, 301, 325, 373, 378, 446; public, 446; of Quakers, 276; in Russia, 281; of slaves/blacks, 11, 373, 376; for stealing, 88; of Titus Oates, 273
Whipping Act of 1530, 373
Whiskey Rebellion, 7
White, Phillip, 157
White, Welsh, 223
White, William, 322
White House. *See* Executive Mansion
Whitehall, London, 288, 361
whites: assaulting/self-defense, 112, 191, 443; and conflicts with Native Americans, 123, 350–51; and death sentences/executions, 121, 242, 272, 284, 452; exonerations of, 236; punishment of, 11, 382–83; versus treatment of blacks, 62, 382–83
Whitman, James Q., 293
Whittier, John Greenleaf, 241
Why Are There No Common Law Crimes in Ohio?, 425
Wicked Wits, 101
Wickersham, George, 440
Wickliffe, Charles, 419–20, 558
Wickliffe, Robert, 558
Wigglesworth, Edward, 181
Wilberforce, William, 15, 184, 303, 336, 354, 366, 382–83
Wilemon, Henry, 121
Wilf, Steven, 20
"wilful destruction of a vessel at sea," 414–15
Wilkerson v. Utah, 452
Wilkes, John (English printer), 477
Wilkes, John (MP), 55, 81–87, 161
Wilkes County, Georgia, 111
Wilkinson, James, 204
Wilkites, 84–86
William and Mary. *See* College of William and Mary
William of Orange, 223. *See also* William III
William the Conquerer, 367
Williams, Benjamin, 397

Williams, David, 104

Williams, John (Dr.), 8

Williams, John (printer), 83

Williams College, 125

Williamsburg, Virginia, 106, 169, 185, 196, 230, 396

Williamson, Hugh, xv, 205, 387

Wills, Garry, 431

Wilmington, Delaware, 141

Wilmington Library Company, 141

Wilson, Bird, 167

Wilson, James: and Benjamin Rush, 399; and Cesare Beccaria, 4, 19, 138, 163–67, 171; on cruelty, 285, 370; on death penalty, 164; in debt, 403; on education, 399; and grand jury charge(s), 285–86; on happiness, 164, 433; law lectures of, 138, 163–64; as law professor, 163; on necessity for punishment, 164; and penal reform, 163–64, 229; on prevention of crime, 164; on proportionality, 164, 286; on Rome, 286; on "sanguinary laws," 164, 286; on "sanguinary spirit of the laws," 285; on severity of punishments, 164, 285; as signer of Constitution and Declaration of Independence, 19, 413, 433; and Society for Promoting Political Enquiries, 434–35; on torture, 164; on tyrants, 164; as U.S. Supreme Court Justice, 163

Winchester County Gaol, 350

Windsor, Vermont, 297, 325

Wisconsin: death penalty's abolition in, 242–43, 266; as part of Northwest Territory, 380

Wish, Harvey, 369

Wishingrad, Jay, 246

Wistar, Richard, 226–27

witchcraft: as capital crime, xv, 12, 63, 275; punishment of, 12, 62, 283, 404; trials for, 303

Withens, Francis, 273

Witherspoon, John, 202–3, 333

witnesses: and compulsory process, 426; detention of, 336; one vs. two, 210, 365, 381–82; and torture, 45, 223

Wits of Connecticut, 101

Wolcott, Oliver, 88

Wollaston, William, 433, 560

Wolleb-Ryhiner, Emanuel, 228

Wollstonecraft, Mary, 278–79

women: and adultery, 373; buried alive, 26; burning of, 63, 276, 404, 406; in Congress, 440; and discrimination/denial of rights, 6, 11, 52–53; and domestic violence, 275; "drawn & burnt," 404; and ducking stool, 96, 225; duels between, 55; education of, 30; execution of, 102–3, 121, 171, 242, 290; and Fourteenth Amendment, 382; happiness of, 311; pregnant, 121, 169; punishment of, 96, 269, 287, 298; "Remember the Ladies" letter, 11, 311; rights of, 439; and scarlet letter, 373; and scolding, 269; and suffrage/voting, 11, 52–53; and treason, 276; and views on executions, 350; whipping of, 287, 298

women's suffrage, 52–53

Wood, Gordon, 21

Wood, James, 325–26

Wood, Yolandea, 311

wooden horse, 233

Woodhouse, William, 89–90, 396

Worchester Gazette, 144

Worchester Magazine, The, 88

Wordsworth, William, 249–50

workhouses, 10, 294, 346

Workingmen's Party, 403

Works of Sir William Temple, The, 407

World Coalition Against the Death Penalty, 454

World War I, 243

World War II, 243, 382, 449

Wright, Patience, 353

Wright, Richard (M.D.), 126

Wright, Richard (minister), 286

writ of capias, 85, 214

written constitutions/bills of rights, 20, 299, 354, 405, 409, 436, 446. *See also* Bill of Rights; Constitution; state constitutions

written law(s), 338, 354, 374, 407–8, 444

wrongful convictions. *See* errors; innocence

Würtemberg, 243

Wymondham, England, 321; penitentiary in, 325

Wythe, George, 186–87, 193, 413; and Cesare Beccaria, 185; as lawyer/jurist, 185; and penal reform, 206–7; and Philip Mazzei, 196; poisoning of, 189; as signer of the Declaration of Independence, 185–86; and Taliaferro family, 231–32; and Thomas Jefferson, 185, 189, 230–32, 369–70, 372

Wyvill, Christopher, 354

Yale College/University, xii–xiii, 12, 66, 88, 101–2, 125, 129, 154, 163, 200, 202, 216, 233–35, 239, 296, 303, 372, 374; Art Gallery, 153; awarding of honorary LL.D. degrees, 319

Yale Law School, xii, 5

Yates, Jr., Abraham, 422

Yates, Joseph, 86

Yates, Peter, W., 303

Yeates, Jasper, 113, 226

yellow fever epidemic, 90, 244, 314

York, Pennsylvania, 434

Yorke, Philip, 43

Yorktown, battle of, 7

Young, David, 35, 55

Young, John, 254

Young, Thomas, 87

Young, Thomas (Dr.), 227

Young, William, 146, 309

Yverdon, Switzerland, 35, 59

Zeresola, Fabio de, 55

Zouch, Henry, 148